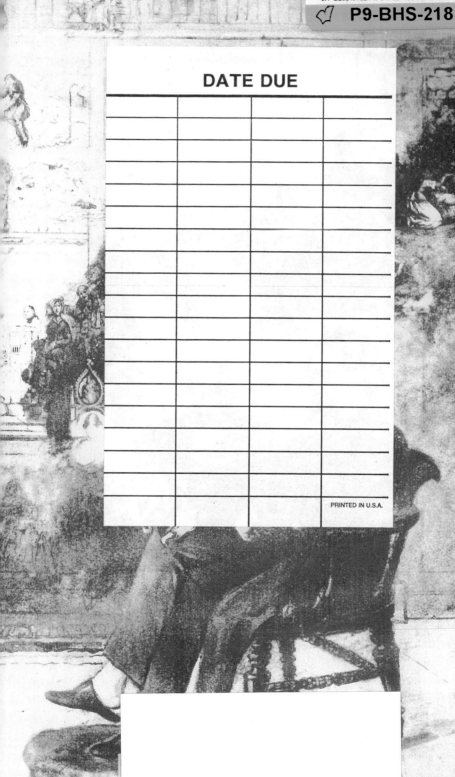

DATE DUE

PRINTED IN U.S.A.

EVERYONE IN DICKENS

Charles Dickens in 1849, at age thirty-seven.
Reproduced by permission of The Huntington Library, San Marino, California.

EVERYONE IN DICKENS

Volume I

*Plots, People and Publishing Particulars
in the Complete Works*

1833-1849

Compiled and Edited by

GEORGE NEWLIN

GREENWOOD PRESS
Westport, Connecticut • London

ublication Data

edited by George Newlin.

nd index.
Contents: v. 1. Plots, people and publishing particulars in the
complete works, 1833–1849—v. 2. Plots, people and publishing
particulars in the complete works, 1850–1870—v. 3. Characteristics
and commentaries, tables and tabulations: a taxonomy.
1. Dickens, Charles, 1812–1870—Characters. 2. Dickens, Charles,
1812–1870—Plots. I. Title.
PR4589.N48 1995
823′.8—dc20   95–2453
ISBN 0–313–29580–8 (set : alk. paper)
ISBN 0–313–29581–6 (v. 1 : alk. paper)
ISBN 0–313–29582–4 (v. 2 : alk. paper)
ISBN 0–313–29583–2 (v. 3 : alk. paper)

British Library Cataloguing in Publication Data is available.

Library of Congress Catalog Card Number: 95–2453

ISBN 0–313–29580–8 (set : alk. paper)
ISBN 0–313–29581–6 (v. 1 : alk. paper)
ISBN 0–313–29582–4 (v. 2 : alk. paper)
ISBN 0–313–29583–2 (v. 3 : alk. paper)

First published in 1995

Greenwood Press, 88 Post Road West, Westport, CT 06881
An imprint of Greenwood Publishing Group, Inc.

Printed in the United States of America

The paper used in this book complies with the Permanent Paper Standard issued by
the National Information Standards Organization (Z39.48–1984).

10 9 8 7 6 5 4 3 2

The endpapers are reproduced from the painting *Dickens's Dream* by Robert William
Buss, by permission of the Dickens House Museum, 48 Doughty Street, London WC1N
2LF.

Windows into ® Dickens

Everyone in Dickens, Volume I: Plots, People and Publishing Particulars
   in the Complete Works, 1833–1849
Everyone in Dickens, Volume II: Plots, People and Publishing Particulars
   in the Complete Works, 1850–1870
Everyone in Dickens, Volume III: Characteristics and Commentaries,
   Tables and Tabulations: A Taxonomy

This Work is dedicated to Toni Lawrence Putnam, my life companion, and to my other blessings: Colin, Ian, Colette, Jane and Elizabeth—not all children of my body, but all the precious offspring of my heart; to Toni's children Cate and Karl, Will and Eve, and Philip and Karon, and to Jane's Harry and Elizabeth's Jeff; to past blessings Pamela and Tim, and Jennifer; and to our Futures, represented so far by Whitney, Katie Lee, Brendan, Inigo, Jordan, Dylan, Rozele, Brittany, Calli, Camille, Clara (due September 1995) and a little stranger (due October 1995).

GCN

This Work is also dedicated to two remarkable institutions, valuable and highly important to literature and to Dickens studies in particular: the Dickens House in London, David Parker, Curator; and the Dickens Project at the University of California at Santa Cruz, Murray Baumgarten, founder, and John Jordan, Director. Both have been of immense importance in both tangible and intangible ways to the Editor's efforts, and it is a particular source of pleasure and pride that Windows into® Dickens (the series of which Everyone in Dickens constitutes the first three volumes) has the Project's official endorsement.

GCN

Contents

Classes of works are distinguished below as follows:

NOVELS	**Book-length nonfiction**
CHRISTMAS BOOKS	*Short independent works, plays*
CHRISTMAS STORIES	Miscellanies in collections
Collections named by the author	*wr:* not published at the time

Foreword

Like God, Dickens created a universe of plenitude. His genius materialized into fictional reality a body of novels and stories whose richness of character and categorization seem uncontainable, and sometimes inaccessible. How is one to look for a particular character or occupational type or . . . ? How is one to know how many orphans or lawyers or unworthy brothers or apothecaries appear in Dickens's universe? And how does one find them?

How is a poor scholar to make accurate statements about the literal facts that compose the material reality of Dickens's fictional worlds? And how is the eager but humanly limited reader expeditiously to find out how and exactly where Dickens has described and what he has had to say about revolution or factories or Valentine's Day or oysters or, as to his characters, Pecksniff as a signpost (pointing, but never going), or the charitable Cheerybles?

Now, like an expert surveyor of Dickens's universe, George Newlin has for the first time organized and charted almost its every feature. Where there were black holes and missing stars, there is now light. Almost every conceivable item of fact bearing on his people is contained within *Everyone in Dickens*. And Newlin's organizational schema provides access to this information.

Astoundingly, it includes all those mentioned in his nonfiction, and in the fiction of others as well: Newlin has given us access to every Shakespeare reference and every sourcing of the *Arabian Nights,* not to mention Dickens's debts to Burns and Byron, Campbell and Carlyle and all the others. He has also made it possible for a historian to find all references to Pitt the Younger, Melbourne and Russell, the murdering Mannings, and every other living (or previously living) soul Dickens talked about or even briefly alluded to. Newlin has even exhaustively indexed Dickens's outspoken and unreliable, but often very entertaining, *A Child's History of England.*

These are the two important features that great reference works possess: information and access. If you know, even in a general way, what you are looking for, they make it possible for you to get there. Dickens scholars have made previous efforts to provide information and access; some of them are estimable. But they have generally taken the form of either lists of characters or summaries of plots, and only a limited number of either or both. These efforts have been constrained by their available technology: the pen, the note-card, the typewriter.

Now, with his hand commanding the computer to use its powers to encode and arrange information, Newlin has created a reference work that supplants every other work that has attempted to be a *Dickens Encyclopedia* or *Dickens Dictionary* or *Guide to Dickens*. I don't need the previous ones any more. I will never need them again.

—Fred Kaplan, Distinguished Professor, City University of New York

Preface

Everyone knows computers are changing our lives in many ways. Not everyone contemplates this serenely. Some changes may be undesirable. Some, though desirable, call for old dogs to learn new tricks they have little inclination for. One thing is clear, though. The assembling, storage and retrieval of information is being transformed.

Windows into Dickens is an example of this transformation in the field of Dickens studies, but one which should inspire no alarm. Old dogs can rest easy. It is utterly user-friendly. If you can use a reference book, you can use *Windows into Dickens*. Big though it may be, physically it is in the book-form with which we are all familiar. Readers can forget computer technology.

They might choose to remember it, though, when they contemplate the completeness of the work. Only the computer can release compiler and compositor from the kinds of chores formerly prohibiting such a project. George Newlin, I know, will rejoice when a reader first draws his attention to an error or omission. Less even than the traditional scholar, the computer scholar is unable to regard a project as complete. You never finish. You stop. Except trivially, however, I find it hard to foresee *Windows into Dickens* being faulted as a Dickens reference work.

There have been many such. The earliest remains one of the most valuable. The chapter-by-chapter summaries found in *The Dickens Dictionary* by Gilbert A. Pierce (1872), augmented by William A. Wheeler (1878), have been unsurpassed as route maps for Dickens students. John Greaves's *Who's Who in Dickens* (1972) is still a faithful friend to Dickensians with imperfect memories. Norman Page's *Dickens Companion* (1984) offers the shortest of cuts to intricate and forgettable details of composition and publication. *The Dickens Index* by Nicolas Bentley, Michael Slater and Nina Burgis (1988), is the best vade-mecum for anyone likely to be puzzled by textual details of Dickens's fiction.

None, however, offers the complete coverage of characters that *Windows into Dickens* does. With delicious hubris, George Newlin entitles his volumes on this topic *Everyone in Dickens*. My guess is that hubris, for once, will be unmet by nemesis. The archives of the Dickens House include an immense card index of characters that the publishing technology of the day prevented John Greaves from including in *Who's Who in Dickens*. *Everyone in Dickens* covers characters unmentioned even in that, and covers much more adequately many of those mentioned. John Greaves's index card on John Scott, puzzlingly alluded to in *The Lazy Tour of Two Idle Apprentices,* simply reads, "the sole topic of conversation in Doncaster." Look up John Scott in Newlin's work, and see how much more you are offered.

Everyone in Dickens, I feel sure, is destined to become an essential reference book.

—*David Parker, Curator of the Dickens House, London*

Editor's Foreword
and a Word about the Computer

Dickens was great, to begin with. There is no doubt whatever about that. The register of his immortality was signed by Thackeray, Chesterton, Shaw, Santayana, Orwell, Edmund Wilson and many, many more. Tolstoy signed it. And Tolstoy's name was good for anything he chose to put his hand to.

Dickens was greater than he knew—than we know—and in many spheres. He was and is seen whole by no one (even his best biographers not excepted, if we are to judge by what came to print). Still held to be the greatest writer of English prose fiction, he excelled in reporting, journalism, periodical editing, acting, theatrical producing and directing, and dramatic reading. He was a dominant mover and shaker in education, public health, and private philanthropy, and he made heroic, not wholly unsuccessful efforts to rescue a goodly number of its practitioners from the oldest profession.

Dickens would drop almost anything when his vulnerable heart was touched. Despite (or because of) a severe poverty consciousness which kept him working frantically and living with suppressed fear all his life, he devoted countless hours to helping the less fortunate and rallying friends to assist colleagues in trouble. He did not forget the poor, the confused, the sick, the miserable: especially women and children unjustly abused and exploited, crushed and lost in the cracks and chasms of a tectonically changing world.

He knew more what it was to be Homeless ('Houseless') than those wretched wanderers themselves, for he saw accurately (there was never a more acute observer) and looked courageously, and he had the clear, unflinching, empathetic humanity to apprehend what he saw. He had the facility to describe this and other terrible things forcefully, with the seductive power of a great enchanter. He wanted to make a difference: he did.

Charles Dickens has much to give us today. He can make us laugh, for a start: he was and is the supreme humourist in fiction. He can make the hardest-hearted cry. And, once moved, we find it easier to see with our own eyes some dreadful things in our own world.

Perhaps we may even begin to do something about that eternal Soul Jacob Marley reminds us we have and had better tend to.

A Word about the Computer

When I saw what Fred Kaplan and David Parker had written, I realized that my use of the computer in this project had to be talked about.

First of all, and obvious enough, *Everyone in Dickens* and the volumes which will follow could not have been attempted without electronic word-processing. That said, it might be important to explain, particularly for those who might want to try this themselves, what my computer did *not* do.

When I began this work in 1989, technology, while amazingly advanced already, had not achieved certain innovations which might have helped me greatly, principally the scanner. Every word, every punctuation mark, every margin, tab and space instruction in the early years was created by me "by hand," that is, by finger, punching a key. I had been a competent typist, and a serious concert pianist. My fingers became so fast that I outran the basic program I was working with and often had to wait for my screen to show me what I had already written. Had I known what was coming I might have been paralyzed by an insidious rationalization: "Wait a few years, and then you can do this much quicker." I felt something like John Henry, the man who outraced new technology for a moment, only to fall dead on his own hammer.

Also, from the outset, using the relatively elementary Macintosh SE and an ink-jet printer with a basic system and program, I found myself having to upgrade every year or so as systems and programs improved, often first undoing manually what I had earlier created that way, before I could exploit new possibilities. Only when I invested last year in a laser printer and installed a doubled memory and the top of the line (at the moment) System 7.1 and Microsoft 5.0 for the Mac, did I really get to the threshold of effective computer work. But I had no customized program, and I am no computer maven: I'm a reader who types. Everything, tables and indexes included, in every volume was personally typed out by me, then perhaps moved or replicated elsewhere. In the words of my computer consultant, I "hand-carved" every page.

Probably I will use a scanner next time (I still do not own one), thereby sparing a lot of dogsbody time. (A scanner takes an electronic picture of a page placed on it and makes it instantly manipulable on a computer screen just as though input manually by keyboard.) But there has been a major benefit in typing everything myself: I have truly lived with what Dickens created, right down to the last detail, and I have edited—been forced to edit—discriminatingly as I went along. When it has seemed unbearably tedious and virtually endless, I have remembered that the Man Himself had only his pen, and he wrote on the order of eight million words with it (the first two volumes of EID contain about 840,000, Volume III about 332,000).

There is reason to hope that someday the material I have arranged in a multiplicity of documents on my hard disk will find its way onto a CD-ROM, or its successor, and users will be able to do what I can do with the box on my desk, and much more. The cost of bringing that about at the moment runs healthily up in six figures. What I myself do have now is the ability to move around quickly, find anything in a document in seconds, transfer material in moments and generally luxuriate in the results of six years of base-building.

It has been my responsibility to give the publisher camera-ready copy, and all its flaws are mine. That said, I will affirm that what is printed in these volumes has been arranged with all the thought and skill I have in me to be accessible and useful for all us old-fashioned people who like and use books.

Acknowledgments

A fundamental point needs to be made at the outset. Although considerable, including primary, research has been involved, particularly bearing on what Dickens actually wrote (for "everyone" has to be based on "every thing") this work has not been made by a professional scholar, nor does it grow from any new scholarly premise. It is, rather, a devoted amateur's contribution to aid the work of the scholars he greatly admires. My occasional interpolations, though sincere, may look naive to those who have lived with the Inimitable much longer than I, but, as is inevitable when dealing with a personality like Dickens's, one develops a point of view. Thanks to the editors at Greenwood Publishing Group, I have had a signal chance to express mine. In a few places I have done so. I am deeply and especially grateful to Robert Hagelstein, President, and Lynn Taylor, Executive Editor, at Greenwood; and my creative, acute and considerate production editor, Jane Lerner, has been indispensable.

Imperfect as it is, this work has benefited from generous help from four people whose credentials in the world of scholarship are undeniable. Fred Kaplan, America's outstanding Dickens biographer, has given generously at every turn and upon any seeking for advice, regardless of the hour of the day. Two great Dickensians of the United Kingdom, Professor Michael Slater (on the early journalism), and Dickens House Curator David Parker, have reviewed and consulted (David has been indefatigable, endlessly resourceful and a true friend, and Michael selflessly carved time out of a pressing schedule to spare me major and minor gaffes) as has Professor Patrick McCarthy of the University of California's Dickens Project. (The courteous helpfulness of the last-mentioned, and his conscientious promptness responding to a neophyte's queries, have been a model.) Nevertheless, the choices made and the manifold errors and omissions which doubt-less have been perpetrated are my responsibility alone.

Thanks are due to the invariably courteous and patient staffs of the Dickens House in London (an international treasure which should be better known); the Theatre Museum in London; the Henry W. and Albert A. Berg Collection at the New York Public Library; and the Sterling Library microform archive at Yale University. Linda Hooper, factotum and pillar of the Dickens Project at Santa Cruz, California, has been a source of friendship and support. Andrew Bean, Deputy Curator of the Dickens House, had arcane knowledge readily available. And I have had the stimulation of contact with England's extraordinary Kathleen Tillotson, who kept me off a tricky shore.

On the technical side, there have been the warmly supportive Merrell M. Clark, computer consultant and Tom Pinch of Scarsdale organists; and my brilliant high school classmate, Richard Walters, chair of the Computer Department at the University of California at Davis. Both did their best with a very hard case. And I have the good fortune to have a professional archivist for a brother. Carl Newlin's willingness to help at a critical moment made an important difference.

Over the years since the *Everyone* idea germinated, several people have made contributions, usually intangible and sometimes not highly specific but very important nevertheless. I wish to acknowledge them, for reasons each (I hope) remembers. They are Murray Baumgarten, Barbara Welter Blewer, Robert Brawer, Gilman Burke, Philip Collins, Kate Delano Condax, Jill Cowen, James W. Ellison, Judith Firth, Edward Guiliano, Ada Louise Huxtable, John O. Jordan, J. Robert Maguire, Michael Meller, Donald Oresman, Clarkson and Helga Potter, Gordon Philo (Charles Forsyte), Mordecai Pomerantz, Sirgay Sanger, Ralph Townley, Aileen Ward, Rhoda Weyr and Beverley Zabriskie.

There is no way to measure my personal debt to Charles Dickens, my mentor, inspiration and friend for the last six intense and joyful years.

Introduction

When I was being trained to be a lawyer, I heard a lot about the Law: about its theory and its rhetoric; but the essential insight of the case method, not always shared with me by my teachers, was that the accurate marshalling of all the relevant facts was the fundamental prerequisite to any useful work (there is an idealism implicit in this statement, now that I think of it, which might explain why I am no longer a lawyer). I learned, if I had not already known, that in life the facts are always surprising and fascinating, if not absolutely bizarre. They are far more interesting in their raw state than when interpreted, no matter how scrupulous and dispassionate the interpreter.

The facts of fiction are the same. *Everyone in Dickens* (EID) retrieves many, and it organizes them for accessibility, utility to scholarship and pleasure to the amateur as well as the professional Dickensian. It exists for the people, scholars and just readers, who would like to be able to find beloved Dickens characters quickly, discover new ones, and have a trove of accessible data on the man and his creations from which to choose works to read or re-read, or to embark on their own explorations and develop their own conclusions.

There has never before been a work of reference on Dickens which attempted to address *every* work attributed to him. (Where doubt exists, we have erred on the side of inclusion but we mention the doubts.) And never before has his *oeuvre* (speeches excepted) been arranged in the strictest practicable chronological order. It's no surprise that the story of Dickens's literary life is told when his people are assembled in the order of their appearance.

Charles John Huffam Dickens (1812-1870) wrote fourteen complete novels and half of another. We know so far (scholars will go on discovering) and reflect below that he created five Christmas Books and twenty Christmas Stories, some in collaboration, plus nine independent interpolations, twelve frameworks and much transitional material, set forth below *in haec verba,* for his beloved Christmas Numbers; 56 *Sketches by Boz* ranging from pure reporting to incandescently imagining to sheer fun-making; twelve drama reviews and 25 reports, mostly political, on assignment from *The Morning Chronicle;* a three-part pamphlet opposing restrictions on Sunday pleasures for the working class; 23 facetious sketches and a "remonstrance" on the foibles of young gentlemen and young couples; and 47 pieces (three in collaboration) for the *Examiner,* his friend Forster's journal. There were four plays, a musical farce (fragments remain), a comedietta (lost) and three joint efforts, one adapting his own work. (Other adaptations are disregarded here.)

He led and wrote for four periodicals (he *wrote* for several more): *Bentley's Miscellany:* six pieces, four fragments and a collaboration; *Master Humphrey's Clock:* ten fictional segments plus scaffolding, organized in six parts; *Household Words,* his preoccupation for ten years (1850-59, hereafter HW: 27 *Reprinted Pieces,* 87 pieces not otherwise collected, 49 collaborations, and the serialized book *A Child's History of England*); and, during his last decade, *All the Year Round* (hereafter AYR: 37 works collected as *The Uncommercial Traveller,* 17 other pieces and two collaborations) and a few fragments. There were 34 miscellaneous items, including letters to the press, three verse parodies and a pamphlet collaboration on reforming the Royal Literary Fund.

Dickens wrote six short works, primarily fictional: *The Lamplighter, To Be Read at Dusk, A Lazy Tour of Two Idle Apprentices* (a collaboration with Wilkie Collins), *Hunted Down, George Silverman's Explanation,* and *A Holiday Romance;* and two book-length travel works: *American Notes* and *Pictures from Italy.* There were the unpublished *Mrs Gamp and the Strollers, Autobiographical Fragments,* and "The Life of Our Lord," named by his son.

There were 116 speeches (4 were not reported), a beautiful child's prayer, and *Lines Addressed to Mark Lemon* (all minimally in evidence in EID but reflected in a later volume). Pro forma prefaces, verse prologues to others' works and some other little pieces drop through our screen.

The total of 646 works, big, medium, small and smaller, is tabulated:

Novels	15
Christmas Books	5
Christmas Stories (one a collaboration)	20
Christmas Story interpolations	9
Christmas Story frameworks	12
Sketches by Boz	56
The Morning Chronicle pieces so far identified	37
Sunday under Three Heads	3
Sketches of Young Gentleman, Young Couples	24
The Examiner	47
Plays (with collaborations; lost work included)	9
Bentley's Miscellany	11
Master Humphrey's Clock	10
Reprinted Pieces	27
Household Words not otherwise collected	87
Household Words collaborations	49
The Uncommercial Traveller	37
All the Year Round not otherwise collected	19
Miscellaneous articles, papers and pieces	34
Stand-alone short works, primarily fictional	6
Verse: three parodies, lines to Lemon	4
Travel volumes	2
Speeches (5 not reported; 19 brief acknowledgments)	116
A Child's History of England	1
Reformation of the Literary Fund	2
Mrs Gamp and the Strollers	1
Autobiographical Fragments	1
"The Life of Our Lord" and a child's prayer	2
	646

The first two volumes of *Everyone in Dickens* (EID) deal with all the above except the speeches and some fragments. Each work is given a frame containing publication data and relevant historical connective material, a plot or contents *précis* and in most instances a sub-index of all figures mentioned.

EID presents these figures in CD's words, organized hierarchically to give the most space to the most important, but neglecting no one, no matter how peripheral and whether or not given a name. Dickens was exuberantly stage-oriented (*"Every writer of fiction, although he may not adopt the dramatic form, writes in effect for the stage."* —1858 speech for the General Theatrical Fund), and the Characters are organized in stage terms: Principals, Supporting Roles, Others, Walk-ons, and the lowly Spear-carriers, given chapter cross-reference. Allocations are the editor's and arbitrary, of course: they are not *ex cathedra*.

Scholars may be interested in the rarely seen extracts from *Household Words'* Christmas Numbers, each exactly 48 fully-packed pages long, transferred complete from the original one-volume edition Dickens himself published under the HW rubric which I have the good fortune to own. The suppressed "necessary to be read" introduction to *American Notes* is exhumed here, as are other bits, like the "Advertisement" for *Pickwick*, not to be seen outside of rare book rooms.

EID's third volume, *A Taxonomy,* contains a series of twelve Indexes, supported by a set of tabular Notes and some statistical Essays on aspects of naming, orphanhood and other matters. Much of this work amounts in fact to a laboratory on Names and Naming, a Dickens specialty, but there is grist as well for the social historian in the material on the sexes, race and religion, relationships and vocations.

The break between Volumes I and II occurs at a significant inflection point in the Victorian era: its high noon of 1850, which coincided with what many regard as the zenith of Dickens's genius. Volume I ends with the *Autobiographical Fragments,* which marked a crucial development for Dickens as he strove to come to terms with bitterly painful aspects of his early life.

The effort to write down this material and deal with it "sobered him up." It is a commonplace of literary criticism, first, that *David Copperfield* (which begins Volume II), pervasively informed by the memories he had awakened, consummately blended the exuberance of his early, seemingly effortless flow with his sad and serious side, the path of his future: disciplined, ordered, regulated by thoughtful and conscious craft; and, second, that thereafter his work grew gradually more somber, less optimistic and spontaneous, even as it became more "professional" in focus and polish and in deliberate deployment of his immense skills.

Dickens will never die, for he has profoundly "made" the world we live in by colouring and informing that mind we use to perceive it. Despite the growing gravity and apprehension which coloured his view of that world, his manic, intoxicating humour remained vital in his darkest, least effervescent moments of creation and, fused with that grave and serious side, carries him and all of us out of any Slough of Despond and on to the realm of Sober Delight.

On the illustrations: With the rarest exceptions, no illustration is included in EID which CD did not approve (or have the chance to approve), and all are associated with the earliest issuances of the works. We have included as many as possible of those which depict the Characters, for they give us the pictorial dimension of CD's creation. (He cared very much about it: he considered close to twenty different renderings of Mr Dombey before choosing the one which most nearly conformed to his concept.) Thomas Hatton, in the *Nonesuch Dickensiana,* a 1937 prospectus for the Nonesuch edition, is our authority for illustrator attributions and most of the caption listings in the indexes. We have occasionally interpolated our own additional captions below the pictures.

On the text: We have tried to avoid arcane though sometimes interesting questions concerning which texts ought to be considered the last word. Even in his journalism, when CD collected the *Sketches by Boz,* the *Reprinted Pieces* and *The Uncommercial Traveller* he made some textual changes and elisions and altered titles. Matters of this sort we have largely left to specialists. (We acknowledge that we have been a little inconsistent, in that we provide some things—the Christmas Story links—which CD did not collect, while we follow his lead in others, like some fragments of the *Sketches,* which he chose to omit. The difference might be explained by our fondness for Christmas.) We have used the Charles Dickens edition (1868-1870) in several reincarnations: the 1894 Houghton Mifflin (New York), the 1895 Estes and Lauriat (Boston), the 1897 Gadshill (Chapman & Hall in London), the Oxford Illustrated (1957) and the Folio Society (the 1980's; London). We have delved into the Norton Critical and Clarendon (Oxford University Press) editions, but not to make text comparisons. Other sources are identified in particular cases.

On spelling and punctuation: English, as opposed to American, spellings are generally used, though we have not achieved complete consistency. Not all the texts were themselves consistent in such matters (certainly not with each other), and purity did not seem worth the nit-picking it would have required. Some archaisms, like ",—" have been modernized.

In addition to its obvious reference uses, this assemblage has a prime three-part purpose: to remind Dickensians and those who might become such that CD wrote more than just novels and *A Christmas Carol;* to highlight the fact that many of his smaller works are as diverting and satisfying to a general reader as anyone could wish; and to show that in his fiction and journalism alike this extraordinary author is still seminal and relevant today. (There are ways of using the material in EID in schools and colleges to make these points effectively.) Lastly, we hope EID may be a beguiling introduction to Charles Dickens for those who escaped being stuffed with him by the Doctor Blimbers of the world. In education today the opposite problem seems the greater.

And the Editor? I should like to be remembered as the Tommy Traddles of modern Dickensland, pertinacious in compilation, pithy in comment, and, hopefully, disinterested and dedicated in my representation of this the most satisfying of all imaginable clients.

Garrison, N.Y. June 9, 1995 (the 125th anniversary of CD's death)   GCN

P.S. We have identified 2,640 fictional "serious" surname usages, 401 named characters without surname (plus 65 pet and animal names) and 565 figures who bear sobriquets or names of parody, of which a few overlap one of the other categories. These make a total of 3,671 name usages, and nearly that many named characters, in CD's fiction. We count 6,336 listings (many are plural, but there is some overlap) in the generic characters index, 2,687 historical names, 254 composers and authors, and 396 figures of myth, the Bible and others' works. The total is 13,344 listings plus 95 documented, unused coinages. That is our "everyone."

How to Use *Everyone in Dickens*

If you know a character name but not the work, see the Index at the back of this volume or Volume II for page location of entry and any illustration, or check the appropriate Index in Volume III. If you know a title but not where to find it, look at *Titles Alphabetized,* page xxxv.

The abbreviation scheme is key. If you see an abbreviation you do not recognize, check *Abbreviations and Dates,* immediately following. We have tried our best to assure that all Dickens's works, whether or not extracted in EID, are included here and (except the speeches) in *Titles Alphabetized.*

Quotations from authors other than Dickens also are cited in abbreviation. The key is in *Bibliographic References,* page xlvii.

A Glossary with Annotations and references to the works is in Volume III.

At the top of the first page for each work appear the prefix of the work's abbreviation in EID, in bold if used in citation (novels and Christmas Books omit it) and its number, if any, in the sequence in its group; first publication and publisher; first publication in book form, if relevant; and the abbreviation suffix in bold. Here, as an example, is the slug for Pickwick Papers:

N 1 March 1836-Nov 1837 monthly by Chapman & Hall   1 vol 1837 **PP**

Nearly all works in EID have subindexes of figures given entries, usually organized as P (Principals), SR (Supporting Roles), O (Others) W (Walk-ons) and SC (Spear-carriers). SC figures are not extracted in EID and, unless mentioned in an entry, are simply listed, with chapter references where applicable. In the body of the EID entries, there are occasional cross-references to characters. These are cited by category (P, SR, etc.) if it is different from that in which the cross-reference occurs.

Arabic numbers at the ends of entries cite chapter or equivalent. Small roman is used for major book sections.

¶ means that the editor has broken paragraphing for readability.

[H] denotes a person who actually lived. Entries for such in this Volume are noted in the *Index of Historical Figures,* page 824, and all such names in the CD *œuvre* are collected in Volume III, Index IX. A category breakdown of these figures is in Volume III, Index X.

Abbreviations and Dates

Every novel, play, story, article, speech, preface, etc., is given an abbreviation, used in cross-reference throughout. In this list, novels and Christmas Books are in chronological order. All other works are given in alphabetical order of abbreviation. If a page number is not provided, there is no entry for the item in either Volume I or II: figures mentioned in it are covered elsewhere, and quotations from it may be cited in a later volume. Having reviewed the list, the invaluable David Parker suggested useful emendations and corrections.

HW/BV	Mr Booley's View of the Last Lord Mayor's Show	November 30	1850	953
HW/C	Chips (introductory)	July 6, 1850 through February 4	1854	940
HW/CB	A Crisis in the Affairs of Mr John Bull	November 23	1850	952
HW/CM	A Curious Misprint in the 'Edinburgh Review'	August 1	1857	1309
HW/CP	Cheap Patriotism	June 9	1855	1184
HW/DM	The Demeanour of Murderers	June 14	1856	1284
HW/DV	A December Vision	December 14	1850	953
HW/ES	A Narrative of Extraordinary Suffering	July 12	1851	987
HW/ET	Some Account of an Extraordinary Traveller	April 20	1850	928
HW/FC	A Few Conventionalities	June 28	1851	986
HW/FE	Chip: A Free (and Easy) School	December 6	1851	—
HW/FF	Frauds on the Fairies	October 1	1853	1040
HW/FL	Fast and Loose	March 24	1855	1282
HW/FS	The Finishing Schoolmaster	May 17	1851	979
HW/F&S	Fire and Snow	January 21	1854	1131
HW/GA	Gone Astray	August 13	1853	1039
HW/GB	The Great Baby	August 4	1855	1188
HW/GD	Gone to the Dogs	March 10	1855	1180
HW/GF	Gaslight Fairies	February 10	1855	1177
HW/GG	The Ghost of the Cock Lane Ghost Wrong Again (chip)	January 15	1853	—
HW/GH	The 'Good' Hippopotamus	October 12	1850	949
HW/GK	It is Not Generally Known	September 2	1854	1134
HW/GL	The Guild of Literature and Art	May 10	1851	977
HW/H	Homœopathy (chip)	November 15	1851	—
HW/HH	A Haunted House	July 23	1853	1038
HW/HN	The Household Narrative	April 13	1850	—
HW/HW	A Home for Homeless Women	April 23	1853	1033
HW/I	Insularities	January 19	1856	1278
HW/IL	The Individuality of Locomotives (chip)	September 21	1850	—
HW/IM	An Idea of Mine	March 13	1858	1319
HW/JB	Proposals for a National Jest-Book	May 3	1856	1282
HW/JT	The Late Mr Justice Talfourd	March 25	1854	1134
HW/L	The Friend of the Lions	February 2	1856	1280
HW/LE	Legal and Equitable Jokes	September 23	1854	1135
HW/LH	Address in Household Words: a Last Household Word	May 28	1859	1323
HW/LM	Reflections of a Lord Mayor	November 18	1854	1140
HW/LT	Lively Turtle	October 26	1850	951
HW/LW	The Last Words of the Old Year	January 4	1851	956
HW/MB	Mr Bull's Somnambulist	November 25	1854	1140
HW/ME	Murderous Extremes	January 3	1857	1303
HW/MP	The Murdered Person	October 11	1856	1287
HW/NE	Nobody, Somebody, and Everybody	August 30	1856	1286
HW/NY	New Year's Day	January 1	1859	1322
HW/OC	Our Commission	August 11	1855	1189
HW/OL	Old Lamps for New Ones	June 15	1850	937
HW/OP	That Other Public	February 3	1855	1177
HW/OS	On Strike	February 11	1854	1132
HW/P	Personal	June 12	1858	—
HW/PA	Proposals for Amusing Posterity	February 12	1853	1030
HW/PF	Perfect Felicity: in a Bird's Eye View	April 6	1850	928
HW/PP	Pet Prisoners	April 27	1850	929
HW/PW	A Preliminary Word: Address in the First Number of *Household Words*	March 30	1850	924
HW/R	From the Raven in the Happy Family	May 11, June 8, August 24	1850	931
HW/RD	Railway Dreaming	May 10	1856	1283
HW/RS	Railway Strikes	January 11	1851	967
HW/RT	Red Tape	February 15	1851	969
HW/RW	Ready Wit (chip)	February 4	1854	—
HW/S	Supposing (five parts)	April 20, 1850 through February 10	1855	929
HW/SA	Stores for the First of April	March 7	1857	1303
HW/SB	The Spirit Business	May 7	1853	1034
HW/SD	A Slight Depreciation of the Currency	November 3	1855	1190
HW/SG	Where We Stopped Growing	January 1	1853	1028
HW/SI	Chips: The Samaritan Institution	May 16	1857	1304

RP/FF	A Monument of French Folly	March 8 1851	971
RP/FW	Our French Watering-Place	November 4 1854	1136
RP/GA	The Ghost of Art	July 20 1850	940
RP/HF	Our Honourable Friend	July 31 1852	1013
RP/LA	Lying Awake	October 30 1852	1018
RP/LV	The Long Voyage	December 31 1853	1042
RP/NS	The Noble Savage	June 11 1853	1037
RP/OS	Out of Season [Out of the Season]	June 28 1856	1285
RP/OT	Out of Town	September 29 1855	1189
RP/PB	Prince Bull. A Fairy Tale	February 17 1855	1179
RP/PG	The Pair of Gloves	September 14 1850	943
RP/S	Our School	October 11 1851	993
RP/TP	Poor Man's Tale of a Patent	October 19 1850	949
RP/TS	The Sofa	September 14 1850	944
RP/V	Our Vestry	August 28 1852	1014
RP/WW	A Walk in a Workhouse	May 25 1850	935

			seqnce
	SPEECHES (as collected and dated, and mostly as captioned, in KFS in 1960)		
S/A1	Artists' Benevolent Fund: London [brief acknowledgment]	May 12 1838	2
S/A2	Artists' Benevolent Society [not reported]	May 11 1844	21
S/A3	Artists' Benevolent Fund	May 8 1858	75
S/A4	Artists' General Benevolent Fund	March 29 1862	87
S/AR	Administrative Reform Association: London	June 27 1855	55
S/B	At a Reading of *A Christmas Carol:* Bradford	December 28 1854	49
S/B1	Young Men of Boston: Banquet in His Honour	February 1 1842	8
S/B2	Farewell Reading in Boston	April 8 1868	107
S/BA	At a Reading for the Bristol Athenaeum [brief ackn]	January 19 1858	68
S/BM1	At a Reading of the *Carol:* Birmingham and Midland Institute	December 30 1853	48
S/BM2	Birmingham and Midland Institute: Annual Inaugural Meeting	September 27 1869	112
S/BM3	Birmingham and Midland Institute Prize-Giving	January 6 1870	113
S/BP	Conversazione: Birmingham Polytechnic Institution	February 28 1844	19
S/BS	Presentation to Dickens and Banquet to Literature and Art: Birmingham Society of Artists	January 6 1853	44
S/C	Presentation and Banquet in His Honour at Coventry	December 4 1858	80
S/CH	Presentation to Captain Hewett [of the *Britannia*]	January 29 1842	7
S/CL	Meeting for the Removal of Trade Restrictions on the Commerce of Literature [brief ackn]	May 4 1852	40
S/CM1	Lecture by A. H. Layard for the Chatham Mechanics' Institute [brief ackn]	April 17 1860	83
S/CM2	Reading: Chatham Mechanics' Institute [brief ackn]	December 18 1860	84
S/CM3	Reading: Chatham Mechanics' Institute [brief ackn]	January 16 1862	86
S/CT1	Commercial Travellers' Schools	December 30 1854	50
S/CT2	Commercial Travellers' Schools	December 22 1859	81
S/DC	Meeting for the Foundation of the Royal Dramatic College	July 21 1858	77
S/DD	Charitable Society for the Deaf and Dumb [brief ackn]	May 23 1843	15
S/DH	Dinner at Hartford in His Honour	February 7 1842	9
S/DM	Dramatic, Equestrian and Musical Sick Fund	February 14 1866	99
S/DP	Meeting of the Dramatic Profession on Dulwich College	March 13 1856	58
S/E	Public Dinner in Edinburgh in His Honour	June 25 1841	6
S/EP	At a Reading of the *Carol* for the Edinburgh Philosophical Institution [brief ackn]	March 26 1858	71
S/FB	Farewell Banquet Before Visit to the United States	November 2 1867	104
S/FD	After a Performance of *The Frozen Deep* [brief ackn]	August 24 1857	66
S/FR	The Farewell Reading	March 15 1870	114
S/GA	First Annual *Soirée* of the Glasgow Athenæum	December 28 1847	26
S/GB	Governesses' Benevolent Institution	April 20 1844	20
S/GI1	Gardeners' Benevolent Institution: London	June 9 1851	37
S/GI2	Gardeners' Benevolent Institution	June 14 1852	41
S/GL1	Banquet to Guild of Literature and Art: Manchester	August 31 1852	42
S/GL2	After the Opening of the Houses for the Guild of Literature and Art: Knebworth	July 21 1865	97
S/GS	Royal Geographical Society [brief ackn]	May 25 1857	64

S/H	Royal Free Hospital	May 6	1863	91
S/HC	Hospital for Consumption and Diseases of the Chest	May 6	1843	14
S/HI1	Royal Hospital for Incurables	June 5	1856	60
S/HI2	Royal Hospital for Incurables	May 21	1857	63
S/J	After Reading the *Carol*: Manchester [brief ackn]	July 31	1857	65
S/L	*Soirée* of the Liverpool Mechanics' Institution	February 26	1844	18
S/LB	Banquet in His Honour at St George's Hall, Liverpool	April 10	1869	110
S/LC	Prize-giving of the Institutional Association of Lancashire and Cheshire: Manchester	December 3	1858	79
S/LF1	Literary Fund: Anniversary Festival	May 8	1837	1
S/LF2	Literary Fund: Anniversary Festival [not reported]	May 12	1841	5
S/LF3	Royal Literary Fund: Annual General Meeting	March 14	1855	51
S/LF4	Royal Literary Fund: Special General Meeting	June 16	1855	54
S/LF5	Royal Literary Fund: Annual General Meeting	Marh 12	1856	57
S/LF6	Royal Literary Fund: Annual General Meeting	March 11	1857	61
S/LF7	Royal Literary Fund: Annual General Meeting	March 10	1858	70
S/LM	*Soirée* of the Leeds Mechanics' Institution	December 1	1847	25
S/LS	Southwark Literary and Scientific Institution	December 2	1840	4
S/M	Royal Society of Musicians	March 8	1860	82
S/M1	Banquet in Honour of W. C. Macready [not reported]	July 20	1839	3
S/M2	Banquet in Honour of W. C. Macready	March 1	1851	34
S/MA	First Annual *Soirée* of the Manchester Athenæum	October 5	1843	17
S/MF	Opening of the Manchester Free Library	September 2	1852	43
S/MH1	Banquet at the Mansion House: London [brief ackn]	July 7	1849	30
S/MH2	Banquet at the Mansion House [brief ackn]	May 2	1853	47
S/MH3	Banquet at the Mansion House	April 1	1861	85
S/MH4	Banquet at the Mansion House [unreported]	January 16	1866	98
S/N1	Newsvendors' Benevolent Institution: London	November 21	1849	31
S/N2	Newsvendors' Benevolent Institution	January 27	1852	38
S/N3	Newsvendors' Benevolent Institution	May 21	1855	53
S/N4	Newsvendors' Benevolent Institution	May 20	1862	88
S/N5	Newsvendors' Benevolent Institution	May 9	1865	95
S/N6	Newsvendors' Benevolent Institution	April 5	1870	115
S/NP	Newspaper Press Fund	May 20	1865	96
S/NY1	Banquet in His Honour: New York	February 18	1842	10
S/NY2	New York Farewell Dinner	April 18	1868	108
S/NY3	Farewell Reading in New York	April 20	1868	109
S/OH	Oxford and Harvard Boat Race Dinner: Sydenham	August 30	1869	111
S/P	Before a Reading in Providence, R. I. [brief ackn]	February 20	1868	106
S/PP1	Printers' Pension Society: London	April 4	1843	13
S/PP2	Printers' Pension Society	April 6	1864	92
S/PR	Playground and General Recreation Society:London	June 1	1858	76
S/PRA	Printers' Readers' Association: London	September 17	1867	103
S/R	Railway Benevolent Society	June 5	1867	102
S/RA1	Royal Academy Banquet [brief ackn]	April 30	1853	46
S/RA2	Royal Academy Banquet [brief ackn]	May 1	1858	74
S/RA3	Royal Academy Banquet (collected in 1988 reissue of KFS)	May 3	1862	88
S/RA4	Royal Academy Banquet [CD's last speech]	April 30	1870	116
S/RC	Metropolitan Rowing Clubs: London	May 7	1866	101
S/RE	At Two Readings at Edinburgh [brief ackn]	September 27and 28	1858	78
S/RP	At the First Reading for His Own Profit: London	April 29	1858	73
S/RS	'Social Supper' in His Honour: Richmond	March 18	1842	12
S/S1	The Sanatorium: London [brief ackn]	June 29	1843	16
S/S2	The Sanatorium	June 4	1844	22
S/SA1	Metropolitan Sanitary Association: London	February 6	1850	32
S/SA2	Metropolitan Sanitary Association	May 10	1851	36
S/SC	Hospital for Sick Children	February 9	1858	69
S/SM	After a Reading of the *Carol:* Sheffield Mechanics' Institute [brief ackn]	December 22	1855	56
S/SS	Meeting for the Establishment of the Shakespeare Foundation Schools	May 11	1864	94
S/TF1	General Theatrical Fund: London	April 6	1846	23
S/TF2	General Theatrical Fund	March 29	1847	24
S/TF3	General Theatrical Fund	April 17	1848	27

Titles Alphabetized

Speeches are not included, but the story-interludes in PP, NN and the Christmas Stories are here. If no page reference appears, there is no entry for the work in the body of either Volume I or II.

Bibliographic References

The following are the principal works we consulted in preparing EID, and they are occasionally cited. As with CD's works, we have used a shorthand abbrevation scheme.

ADFN   Dunkling, Leslie and Gosling, William; eds. *New American Dictionary of First Names*. New York: Signet paperback [1983]

AYR/O   Oppenlander, Ella Anne, ed. *Dickens' All the Year Round: Descriptive Index and Contributor List*. Troy, N.Y.: Whitston Publishing Co., 1984

BSB   Bentley, Nicolas; Slater, Michael; and Burgis, Nina. *The Dickens Digest*. Oxford and New York: Oxford University Press, 1988

CN/AYR   *Christmas Numbers from "All the Year Round," conducted by Charles Dickens*. London: 26, Wellington Street, Strand, W. C. and Messrs. Chapman and Hall, 193, Piccadilly, W. (undated; about 1868)

D   *The Dickensian*, 1905-date; various editors, beginning with B. W. Matz, currently Malcolm Andrews; The Dickens Fellowships, Dickens House, London

DP   Paroissien, David, ed. *Selected Letters of Charles Dickens*. Boston: Twayne Publishers, 1985.

EJ   Johnson, Edgar. *Charles Dickens: His Tragedy and Triumph*. 2 vols. New York: Simon and Schuster, 1952

FGK   Kitton, F. G. *The Minor Writings of Charles Dickens*. London: E. Stock, 1900

FK   Kaplan, Fred. *Dickens: A Biography*. New York: William Morrow, 1988

FKM   —ed. Charles Dickens' Book of Memoranda. New York: The New York Public Library [c1981]

FS   Dickens, Charles. The complete novels and Christmas Books. London: The Folio Society, 1981-88 (introductions by Christopher Hibbert)

GC   Guiliano, Edward; and Collins, Philip; eds. *The Annotated Dickens*. 2 vols. New York: Clarkson N. Potter [c1986]

GCVA   Chesterton, Gilbert Keith. *The Victorian Age in Literature*. New York: Henry Holt & Co., 1913

GKC   —*Criticisms and Appreciations of the Works of Charles Dickens*. London: J. M. Dent & Sons Ltd., 1911

HMCD   *The Writings of Charles Dickens*. New York: Houghton Mifflin, 1894. Edwin Percy Whipple ("and others") provided critical and bibliographical introductions and notes; indexes by Gilbert A. Pierce and William A. Wheeler

HS   Stone, Harry, ed. *Charles Dickens' Uncollected Writings from Household Words 1850-1859*. 2 vols. Bloomington and London: Indiana University Press [c1968]

HSN   —ed. *Dickens' Working Notes for His Novels.* Chicago: University of Chicago
         [c1987]

HW/L   Lohrli, Anne, comp. *Household Words: Table of Contents, List of Contributors
         and their Contributions; based on the Household Words Office Book.*
         Toronto: University of Toronto Press, 1973

JC   Cook, James, ed. *Bibliography of the Writings of Charles Dickens, with many
         curious and interesting Particulars relating to His Works.* London: Frank
         Kerslake, 1879

JF   Forster, John. *The Life of Charles Dickens.* 3 vols. London: Chapman and
         Hall, 1872-4

KFS   Fielding, K. J., ed. *The Speeches of Charles Dickens.* Oxford: Clarendon Press,
         1960 [reissued with new frontmatter 1988]

MA   Andrews, Malcolm. *Dickens and the Grown-up Child.* Iowa City: University of
         Iowa Press [c1994]

MMH   Hardwick, Michael and Mollie. *The Charles Dickens Encyclopedia.* New York
         and London: Scribners [c1973]*

MS/DW   Slater, Michael. *Dickens and Women.* Stanford, CA: Stanford University
         Press [c1983]

MP   Charles Dickens. *Miscellaneous Papers from 'The Morning Chronicle', 'The
         Daily News', 'The Examiner', 'Household Words', 'All the Year Round', etc.,*
         as collected by B. M. Matz; 2 vols. Millwood, N.Y.: Kraus Reprint, 1983

ND   Waugh, Arthur; Walpole, Hugh; Dexter, Walter; and Hatton, Thomas; eds.
         The Nonesuch Edition of the complete works of Charles Dickens.
         Bloomsbury. 16 vols, 1937-38

OID   *The Oxford Illustrated Dickens.* Oxford and New York: Oxford University
         Press, first printing, 1936

PA   Ackroyd, Peter. *Dickens.* New York: HarperCollins, 1990

PE   House, Madeline; Storey, Graham; Tillotson, Kathleen; Fielding, K.J.; Burgis,
         Nina and Easson, Angus; eds (to date). *The Pilgrim Edition of The Letters
         of Charles Dickens (1820-1855)* 7 vols (to date). Oxford: Clarendon Press,
         1965-93

PF   Fitzgerald, Percy. *Memories of Charles Dickens: with an account of "Household
         Words," and "All the Year Round" and of the Contributors Thereto.* Bristol:
         Arrowsmith, 1913

QC   Quiller-Couch, Sir Arthur. *Charles Dickens and Other Victorians.* New York:
         G. P. Putnam's Sons, 1925

---

*The original edition (there was a partial paperback reissue in 1993 by the Carol
Publishing Group, New York) contains in 530 pages an amazing amount of useful
information, including a collection of quotations and an index to them, and rosters of Places
in and out of London important in the *oeuvre,* and of the Dickens circle of friends and
important influences. *Pace* my friend Fred Kaplan, this stands high among EID's
predecessors. The remarkable Time Chart from this work was, with Mollie Hardwick's kind
permission, made the starting-point in our preparation of the Time Chart beginning at page
599 of Volume III. Much of the publication information in EID is based on the Hardwicks'
work.

"As a general rule Dickens can be read in any order; not only in any order of books, but even in any order of chapters. In an average Dickens book every part is so amusing and alive that you can read the parts backwards; you can read the quarrel first and then the cause of the quarrel; you can fall in love with a woman in the tenth chapter and then turn back to the first chapter to find out who she is. This is not chaos; it is eternity. It means merely that Dickens instinctively felt all his figures to be immortal souls who existed whether he wrote of them or not, and whether the reader read of them or not. There is a peculiar quality as of celestial pre-existence about the Dickens characters. Not only did they exist before we heard of them, they existed also before Dickens heard of them." GKC p3

"He had the power of creating people, both possible and impossible, who were simply precious and priceless people; and anything subtler added to that truth really only weakens it." GCVA p121

Gilbert Keith Chesterton (1874-1936) may have been Charles Dickens's greatest critic. He was certainly the most "Dickensian." He said many wise and delicious things—and some wrong-headed things as well—about the author and his works, and we have not been able to resist scattering a few of them through EID. We acknowledge that we have failed to give room to the many marvelous insights of others, but EID is not about criticism. We make an exception for Chesterton to give a slight but pungent leaven to our huge loaf of "facts."

For the short-hand EID uses in citing works not by Dickens, see Bibliographic References, page xlvii.

SKETCHES BY BOZ

George Cruikshank

Sketches by Boz

Illustrative of Every-day Life and Every-day People

These fifty-six sketches were published over a five-year period beginning in 1833 when CD was twenty-one. Uncertain at that time whether his profession was not perhaps the Stage, but having tried his hand at a written work of the imagination, which he called "A Sunday Out of Town," he "*dropped [it] stealthily one evening at twilight, with fear and trembling, into a dark letter-box, in a dark office up a dark court in Fleet Street.*" A few days later, he purchased from a bookseller named William Hall a copy of the new issue of *Monthly Magazine,* and it was there, "*in all the glory of print,*" as "A Dinner in Poplar Walk." "*I walked down to Westminster Hall, and turned into it for half an hour, because my eyes were so dimmed with joy and pride that they could not bear the street, and were not fit to be seen there.*" [from Preface to Cheap (1847) Edition of PP]

Not all the sketches in the series have come down to us in the form in which they first appeared. Some were revised or retitled. A few in fact were not written for periodical publication at all, but for the volumes published by John Macrone in 1836 as the First (February) and Second (December) Series. The 1839 volume organized the sketches in the four-part form reflected in what follows, but revisions only ended with the 1850 collected edition of CD's works.

The sketch that began it all is now *Mr Minns and His Cousin.* It is 46th in the sequence.

We can be grateful to the soldier of fortune Captain Holland, recently returned from fighting for Simon Bolivar in South America, who had purchased *The Monthly Magazine* and was encouraging emerging writers by giving them exposure. He did not pay them, but what he did was enough for Dickens. The bookseller who sold him the magazine which told him he was a writer came to him several sketches later with a new idea—and *Pickwick Papers* resulted.

References do not always agree on initial publication dates. The editor has relied on MS as the most current and authoritative source. Its Introduction clearly outlines the genesis of the *Sketches* and their published sequence, and the headnotes contain useful information on such matters as names considered by CD and not used, identities of parliamentary figures depicted, and the real people on whom CD sometimes modeled his characters.

From the preface to the first Cheap Edition, October 1850

"The whole of these Sketches were written and published, one by one, when I was a very young man. They were collected and republished while I was still a very young man; and sent into the world with all their imperfections (a good many) on their heads.

"They comprise my first attempts at authorship—with the exception of certain tragedies achieved at the mature age of eight or ten, and represented with great applause to overflowing nurseries. I am conscious of their often being extremely crude and ill-considered, and bearing obvious marks of haste and inexperience; particularly in that section of the present volume which is comprised under the general head of Tales.

"But as this collection is not originated now, and was very leniently and favorably received when it was first made, I have not felt it right either to remodel or expunge, beyond a few words and phrases here and there."

" . . . there is something in these stories which there is not in the ordinary stock comedies of that day: an indefinable flavour of emphasis and richness, a hint as of infinity of fun." GKC p8

"His subjects are indeed stock subjects; like the skylark of Shelley, or the autumn of Keats. But all the more because they are stock subjects the reader realises what a magician is at work." GKC p11

Illustrations: by (with exceptions noted) *George Cruikshank*

There follows the sequence of Sketches as now organized in the canon, with publishing information and their location in this Volume. For help in locating a Sketch by abbreviation, see Abbreviations and Dates at p xxiii. If you remember a Sketch's title but cannot spot it here, try Titles Alphabetized at p xxxv.

CONTENTS

Characters

Tales

*Publication abbreviations

BL	*Bell's Life in London and Sporting Chronicle,* a weekly newspaper
BW	*Bell's Weekly Magazine*
CC	*The Carlton Chronicle,* a short-lived weekly newspaper (started June 11, 1836 and expired May 13, 1837)
EC	*The Evening Chronicle,* an evening newspaper
LF	*Library of Fiction; or Family Story-teller; Consisting of Original Tales, Essays and Sketches of Character,* a monthly published by Chapman and Hall (C&H)
MC	*The Morning Chronicle,* a daily newspaper
MM	*The Monthly Magazine*
1st SB	First collected series: 1836
2d SB	Second collected series: 1837

CHARACTERS IN 'OUR PARISH'

Boy, drops a penny in church	B	7
-two, reporting a fire	B	7
Browns, three Miss: who lay in wait for the Curate; teachers	C	8
	LS	14
Bung: five children, so qualified to be beadle; a broker's man	EB	11
	BM	13
Children, of the parish; beneficiaries of the Child's Examination Society	LS	14
Churchwardens, and overseers: testifying in gilt letters	B	7
Clergyman, cadaverous and fascinating	C	8
-dozing and deceased without notice	C	8
Cook, wearing a large white bow and a smart head-dress	FS	10
CURATE, who rose and fell; preached a charity sermon	C	8
	LS	14
Daughter of a stoical lady, with a boy in her lap	BM	13
Dawson, Mr: local surgeon	FS	10
Fixem, a broker [who values goods attached for payment of debt]	BM	13
Friends, musical; of a good-humoured tenant	NN	15
Gentleman, red-faced, in a white hat: knocked up an old gentleman	NN	15
-serious and military; stole shirt, bed-clothes and teaspoon	NN	15
-stout and good-humoured, but a noisy tenant	NN	16
Gubbins, an ex-churchwarden; presented an inkstand	C	9
	EB	11
HALF-PAY CAPTAIN Purday, with too much time on his hands	C	9
	FS	10
	EB	12
Husband, under an execution; helpless and dependent on his wife	BM	13
Lady, his wife; with death in her face	BM	13
Master, of the workhouse	B	7
-a debtor with broker's men in possession; presence of mind	BM	13
Midwife, at Mrs Robinson's door at 2:30 in the morning	FS	10
Missionary: repeated a dialogue to great applause	LS	15
Mother: misery had changed her to a devil; died of a stroke	BM	14
NEIGHBOUR, hard-put to find a satisfactory tenant	NN	16
Old gentleman, powderheaded; discomforted living above the noisy tenant	NN	16
OLD LADY: a pillar parishioner and sad but loyal mother	C	9
Old woman: the ugliest and dirtiest the broker's man had ever seen	BM	14
Orator, an Irishman: quoted Latin to a ladies' charitable society	LS	15
Parker, Mrs Johnson: outraged at churchgoers without bibles	LS	15
-the seven Misses: officers of the distribution society	LS	15
Party-leader: of narrow principle, interrogative nose	EB	12
Purday, Captain: on half-pay, and inclined to stir things up	C	9
	FS	10
	EB	12
Robinson, Mr: which was he going to marry?	FS	10
Mrs: unidentified—for a while	FS	10
SCHOOLMASTER, a pauper and a widower	B	7
Simmons, a beadle who succumbed to the fire engine	B	7
	EB	12
Son, of the Old Lady: in India, and not to be spoken of	C	9
Spruggins, Thomas: ten small children, so qualified to be beadle	EB	12
Mrs: likely to add to the total	EB	12
Vestry-clerk, a short pudgy attorney; fond of muffins	B	8
	EB	12
Widow, with six small children, appealing for aid to the Board	B	8
-poor, with dying son William; tenants of a neighbour	NN	16
William, a lad of eighteen or so: an invalid dying of TB	NN	16
Willis, the four Misses: formal, stiff and cold	FS	11

SB 1 February 28, 1835   EC **B**

The Beadle. The Parish Engine. The Schoolmaster

A grandiose parish beadle; an ineffectual fire engine and the larger "engine" of officialdom; the sad history and vague present of a pauper schoolmaster.

Boy, in church. " . . . a penny is heard to ring on the stone floor of the aisle with astounding clearness . . . the victim who dropped the money ventures to make one or two distinct dives after it; and the beadle [**Simmons**], gliding softly round, salutes his little round head, when it again appears above the seat, with divers double knocks . . . . "

Two **boys.** "Two little boys run to the beadle as fast as their legs will carry them, and report from their own personal observation that some neighbouring chimney is on fire . . . . "

Churchwardens and **overseers.** " . . . respectable tradesmen, who wear hats with brims inclined to flatness, and who occasionally testify in gilt letters on a blue ground, in some conspicuous part of the church, to the important fact of a gallery having been enlarged and beautified, or an organ rebuilt."

Master, of the workhouse. " . . . whatever he was, it is clear his present position is a change for the better. His income is small certainly, as the rusty black coat and threadbare velvet collar demonstrate: but then he lives free of house-rent, has a limited allowance of coals and candles, and an almost unlimited allowance of authority in his petty kingdom. He is a tall, thin, bony man; always wears shoes and black cotton stockings with his surtout; and eyes you, as you pass his parlour-window, as if he wished you were a pauper, just to give you a specimen of his power. He is an admirable specimen of a small tyrant: morose, brutish, and ill-tempered; bullying to his inferiors, cringing to his superiors, and jealous of the influence and authority of the beadle."

Schoolmaster. " . . . nothing he ever did, or was concerned in, appears to have prospered . . . . His talents were great; his disposition easy, generous and liberal. His friends profited by the one, and abused the other . . . . He had children whom he loved, and a wife on whom he doted . . . .

"He is an old man now. Of the many who once crowded round him in all the hollow friendship of boon-companionship, some have died, some have fallen like himself, some have prospered—all have forgotten him. Time and misfortune have mercifully been permitted to impair his memory, and use has habituated him to his present condition. Meek, uncomplaining, and zealous in the discharge of his duties, he has been allowed to hold his situation long beyond the usual period; and he will no doubt continue to hold it, until infirmity renders him incapable, or death releases him."

Simmons. "The beadle of our parish is a splendid fellow. It is quite delightful to hear him, as he explains the state of the existing poor laws to the deaf old women in the board-room passage on business nights; and to hear . . . what 'we' . . . came to the determination of doing."

—*on duty:* "See him again on Sunday in his state coat and cocked-hat, with a large-headed staff for show in his left hand, and a small cane for use in his right. How pompously he marshals the children into their places! and how demurely the little urchins look at him askance as he surveys them when they are all seated, with a glare of the eye peculiar to beadles!"

Vestry-clerk. " . . . a short, pudgy little man, in black, with a thick gold watch-chain of considerable length, terminating in two large seals and a key. He is an attorney, and generally in a bustle; at no time more so, than when he is hurrying to some parochial meeting, with his gloves crumpled up in one hand, and a large red book under the other arm."

Widow. "A miserable-looking woman is called into the board-room, and represents a case of extreme destitution, affecting herself—a widow, with six small children."

> **Brown**, Mrs; landlady at No. 3, Little King William's Alley
> Footman, Head: of the Lord Mayor, reporting a beadle's joke
> Francis Hobler[H]; the beadle made a joke up to his standard
> Overseer, on the Parish Board
> Senior churchwarden
> Young men, amused when a boy is knocked on the head by a beadle

SB 2 May 19, 1835   EC C

The Curate. The Old Lady. The Half-pay Captain

A bachelor Curate interesting to the parish ladies until suddenly eclipsed by a new, unkempt chapel clergyman; an old lady who is Charity in action; a half-pay captain with too much time on his hands.

Three **Miss Browns**, "[who] had an obscure family pew just behind the churchwardens', were detected, one Sunday, in the free seats by the communion-table, actually lying in wait for the **curate** as he passed to the vestry!"

Clergyman, late. "A very quiet, respectable, dozing old gentleman, who had officiated in our chapel-of-ease for twelve years previously, died one fine morning, without having given any notice whatever of his intention."

Clergyman. "He was a pale, thin, cadaverous man, with large black eyes, and long straggling black hair: his dress was slovenly in the extreme, his manner ungainly, his doctrines startling; in short, he was in every respect the antipodes of the **curate**. Crowds of our female parishioners flocked to hear him; at first, because he was *so* odd-looking, then because his face was *so* expressive, then because he preached *so* well; and at last, because they really thought that, after all, there was something about him which it was quite impossible to describe . . . the chapel-of-ease is going to be enlarged, as it is crowded to suffocation every Sunday!"

Curate. "[He was] a young gentleman of such prepossessing appearance, and fascinating manners, that within one month after his first appearance . . . half the young-lady inhabitants were melancholy with religion, and the other half desponding with love. . . . He parted his hair on the centre of his forehead in the form of a Norman arch, wore a brilliant of the first water on the fourth finger of his left hand (which he always applied to his left cheek when he read prayers), and had a deep sepulchral voice of unusual solemnity. Innumerable were the calls made by prudent mammas on our new curate, and innumerable the invitations with which he was assailed, and which, to do him justice, he readily accepted."

—*apogee:* "The curate began to cough . . . . Here was a discovery—the curate was consumptive. How interestingly melancholy! If the young ladies were energetic before, their sympathy and solicitude now knew no bounds. Such a man as the curate—such a dear—such a perfect love—to be consumptive! It was too much. Anonymous presents of black-currant jam, and lozenges, elastic waistcoats, bosom friends, and warm stockings, poured in upon the curate until he was as completely fitted out, with winter clothing, as if he were on the verge of an expedition to the North Pole . . . ."

—*decline:* " . . . in short, the curate wasn't a novelty, and the other **clergyman** was. The inconstancy of public opinion is proverbial: the congregation migrated one by one. The curate coughed till he was black in the face—it was in vain. He respired with difficulty—it was equally ineffectual in awakening sympathy. Seats are once again to be had in any part of our parish church . . . ."

Gubbins. " . . . the inkstand was presented [to the **curate**] in a neat speech by Mr Gubbins, the ex-churchwarden . . . . "

Half-pay captain. "He is an old naval officer on half-pay, and his bluff and unceremonious behaviour disturbs the **old lady**'s domestic economy, not a little . . . he took to breeding silk-worms, which he would bring in two or three times a day, in little paper boxes, to show the old lady, generally dropping a worm or two at every visit . . . one morning a very stout silk-worm was discovered in the act of walking upstairs—probably with the view of inquiring after his friends, for, on further inspection, it appeared that some of his companions had already found their way to every room in the house. "

—*a public role:* "He attends every vestry meeting that is held; always opposes the constituted authorities of the parish, denounces the profligacy of the **churchwardens**, contests legal points against the **vestry-clerk**, *will* make the **tax-gatherer** call for his money till he won't call any longer, and then he sends it: finds fault with the sermon every Sunday, says that the organist ought to be ashamed of himself, offers to back himself for any amount to sing the psalms better than all the children put together, male and female; and, in short, conducts himself in the most turbulent and uproarious manner."

Old Lady. "The best known and most respected among our parishioners, is an old lady, who resided in our parish long before our name was registered in the list of baptisms. Our parish is a suburban one, and the old lady lives in a neat row of houses in the most airy and pleasant part of it. The house is her own; and it, and everything about it, except the old lady herself, who looks a little older than she did ten years ago, is in just the same state as when the old gentleman was living. The little front parlour, which is the old lady's ordinary sitting-room, is a perfect picture of quiet neatness; the carpet is covered with brown Holland, the glass and picture-frames are carefully enveloped in yellow muslin; the table-covers are never taken off, except when the leaves are turpentined and bees'-waxed, an operation which is regularly commenced every other morning at half-past nine o'clock—and the little nicknacks are always arranged in precisely the same manner."

"Thus, with the annual variation of a trip to some quiet place on the seacoast, passes the old lady's life. It has rolled on in the same unvarying and benevolent course for many years now, and must at no distant period be brought to its final close. She looks forward to its termination, with calmness and without apprehension. She has everything to hope and nothing to fear."

Son. "[The **old lady**] has a son in India, whom she always describes to you as a fine, handsome fellow—so like the profile of his poor dear father over the sideboard, but the old lady adds, with a mournful shake of the head, that he has always been one of her greatest trials; and that indeed he once almost broke her heart; but it pleased God to enable her to get the better of it, and she would prefer your never mentioning the subject to her again."

> Charlotte, Princess[H]; the Old Lady had her portrait
> Girls, little: neighbours and admirers of the Old Lady
> Leopold, Prince[H]; the Old Lady has his portrait with Charlotte
> Pensioners; old men and old women regularly aided by the Old Lady
> Pew-opener; she assisted the Old Lady when the organ played
> **Sarah**: the Old Lady called her maid by that name
> **Tomkins**, with a monument in the side aisle
> Woman, poor; with quadruplets

SB 3 June 18, 1835   EC **FS**

The Four Sisters

The four **Willis** sisters, parish residents for thirteen years and no longer young, are called upon by Mr **Robinson**, who takes them all to church for a wedding. He moves in. The neighbours wonder which is Mrs Robinson until a blessed event (with a **midwife** foreshadowing **Mrs Gamp**) gives the answer.

> **Cook**, "who wore a large white bow of unusual dimensions, in a much smarter head-dress than the regulation cap to which the **Miss Willises** invariably restricted the somewhat excursive tastes of female servants in general."
>
> **Dawson**. ". . . we fancied that Mr Dawson, the surgeon, &c., who displays a large lamp with a different colour in every pane of glass, at the corner of the row, began to be knocked up at night oftener than he used to be . . . . "
>
> **Half-pay captain**. "The old gentleman of silk-worm notoriety did not hesitate to express his decided opinion that Mr **Robinson** was of Eastern descent, and contemplated marrying the whole family at once . . . . "
>
> **Midwife**. " . . . we were very much alarmed by hearing a hackney-coach stop at **Mrs Robinson**'s door, at half-past two o'clock in the morning, out of which there emerged a fat old woman, in a cloak and nightcap, with a bundle in one hand, and pair of pattens in the other, who looked as if she had been suddenly knocked up out of bed for some very special purpose."
>
> **Robinson**. " . . . a gentleman in a public office, with a good salary and a little property of his own . . . the announcement of the eldest **Miss Willis**—'*We* are going to marry Mr Robinson.'"
>
> —*on the day:* " . . . [he] had arrived in a cab . . . dressed in a light-blue coat and double-milled kersey pantaloons, white neckerchief, pumps, and dress-gloves, his manner denoting . . . a considerable degree of nervous excitement."
>
> **Mrs Robinson**. "As the four sisters and Mr Robinson continued to occupy the same house . . . and as the married sister, whoever she was, never appeared in public without the other three, we are not quite clear that the neighbours ever would have discovered the real Mrs Robinson, but for a circumstance of the most gratifying description, which *will* happen occasionally in the best-regulated families."

The four **Miss Willises**. "It is a melancholy reflection that the old adage, 'time and tide wait for no man,' applies with equal force to the fairer portion of the creation; and willingly would we conceal the fact, that even thirteen years ago the Miss Willises were far from juvenile. Our duty as faithful parochial chroniclers, however, is paramount . . . and we are bound to state, that thirteen years since, the authorities in matrimonial cases, considered the youngest Miss Willis in a very precarious state, while the eldest sister was positively given over, as being far beyond all human hope."

—*at home:* "The house was the perfection of neatness—so were the four Miss Willises. Everything was formal, stiff and cold—so were the four Miss Willises . . . . There they always sat, in the same places, doing precisely the same things at the same hour. The eldest Miss Willis used to knit, the second to draw, the two others to play duets on the piano. They seemed to have no separate existence, but to have made up their minds just to winter through life together. They were three long graces in drapery, with the addition, like a school-dinner, of another long grace afterwards . . . and thus they vegetated— living in Polar harmony among themselves, and, as they sometimes went out, or saw company 'in a quiet way' at home, occasionally iceing the neighbours."

> Two gentlemen, "and a pair of ladies to correspond"
> Housemaid, at No. 23
> Lady, at No. 19
> Spinster, at No. 16
> Young ladies, at No. 17 and No. 18

SB 4 July 14, 1835 EC **EB**

The Election for Beadle

The **Party-leader** and Captain **Purday** oppose each other on all parish matters. When beadle **Simmons** suddenly dies, the establishment favors **Spruggins**, fifty, as having the most offspring. Purday sides with **Bung**, thirty-five. Eloquent speeches, with the insurgency effective getting out the vote; public indignation at a muffin procurement scandal: a Bung victory.

Bung. "'Bung for Beadle. Five small children!' . . . . [He] appeared in a cast-off coat of the **captain**'s—a blue coat with bright buttons: white trousers . . . . There was a serenity in the open countenance of Bung—a kind of moral dignity in his confident air—an 'I wish you may get it' sort of expression in his eye—which infused animation into his supporters, and evidently dispirited his opponents."

Gubbins. "He would not allude to individuals . . . . He would not advert to a gentleman who had once held a high rank in the service of his majesty; he would not say, that that gentleman was no gentleman . . . that he was a turbulent parishioner . . . that he had grossly misbehaved himself . . . that he was one of those discontented and treasonable spirits, who carried confusion and disorder wherever they went . . . that he harboured in his heart envy, and hatred, and malice, and all uncharitableness. No! He wished to have everything comfortable and pleasant, and therefore, he would say—nothing about him (cheers)."

Party-leader. "He is a tall, thin, bony man, with an interrogative nose, and little restless perking eyes, which appear to have been given him for the sole purpose of peeping into other people's affairs . . . [he] is deeply impressed with the importance of our parish business, and prides himself, not a little, on his style of addressing the parishioners in vestry assembled. His views are rather confined than extensive; his principles more narrow than liberal."

Captain Purday. "He immediately sided with **Bung**, canvassed for him personally in all directions, wrote squibs on **Spruggins**, and got his **butcher** to skewer them up on conspicuous joints in his shop-front; frightened his neighbour, the **old lady**, into a palpitation of the heart, by his awful denunciations of Spruggins's party; and bounced in and out, and up and down, and backwards and forwards, until all the sober inhabitants of the parish thought it inevitable that he must die of a brain fever, long before the election began."

—*orating:* "He would not say, he was astonished at the speech they had just heard; he would not say, he was disgusted (cheers) . . . he would not allude to men once in office, but now happily out of it, who had mismanaged the workhouse, ground the paupers, diluted the beer, slack-baked the bread, boned the meat, heightened the work, and lowered the soup (tremendous cheers)."

Simmons. "The lamented deceased had over-exerted himself, a day or two previously, in conveying an **aged female**, highly intoxicated, to the strong room of the workhouse. The excitement thus occasioned, added to a severe cold, which this indefatigable officer had caught in his capacity of director of the parish engine, by inadvertently playing over himself instead of a fire, proved too much for a constitution already enfeebled by age . . . ."

Thomas Spruggins. "'Spruggins for Beadle. Ten small children (two of them twins), and a wife! ! ! . . . . The majority of the lady inhabitants of the parish declared at once for Spruggins; and the *quondam* overseer [the **party-leader**] took the same side, on the ground that men with large families always had been elected to the office . . . although he must admit that, in other respects, Spruggins was the least qualified candidate of the two . . . ."

"Spruggins was a thin little man, in rusty black, with a long pale face, and a countenance expressive of care and fatigue, which might either be attributed to the extent of his family or the anxiety of his feelings."

Mrs Spruggins. " . . . the appearance of his lady, as she went about to solicit votes (which encouraged confident hopes of a still further addition to the house of Spruggins at no remote period) increased the general prepossession in his favour."

Vestry-clerk. "A threat of exclusive dealing was clearly established against the vestry-clerk—a case of heartless and profligate atrocity. It appeared that the delinquent had been in the habit of purchasing six penn'orth of muffins, weekly, from an **old woman** who rents a small house in the parish . . . a message was conveyed to her through the medium of the **cook**, couched in mysterious terms . . . that the vestry-clerk's appetite for muffins, in future, depended entirely on her vote on the beadleship."

Hopkins "for Beadle. Seven small children!"
Timkins "for Beadle. Nine small children!!!"

SB 5 July 28, 1835   EC **BM**

The Broker's Man

The diverse experiences of a broker's man. (He sequesters and values debtors' personal property pending repayment or execution.) In one case, **Bung** poses as a servant and guards the plate and silver while using them to serve dinner. He encounters abject poverty, and also a heroic wife who exhausts herself to death battling for her family.

Bung. " . . . his fluctuations have been between poverty in the extreme, and poverty modified, or . . . 'between nothing to eat and just half enough.' . . . He is just one of the careless, good-for-nothing, happy fellows, who float, cork-like on the surface, for the world to play at hockey with: knocked here, and there, and everywhere . . . but always reappearing and bounding with the stream buoyantly and merrily along."

" . . . prepossessing impudence at the election . . . a shrewd knowing fellow, with no inconsiderable power of observation . . . [a] power . . . not only of sympathising with, but to all appearance of understanding feelings to which . . . [he is an] entire stranger . . . ."

Daughter. " . . . of about nineteen or twenty, who, I suppose, had been a-listening at the door, and who had got a little **boy** in her arms: she sat him down in the [stoical] **lady**'s lap, without speaking . . . . "

Fixem, a broker. "'My name,' says Fixem, winking to the **master** to send the servant away, and putting the warrant into his hands folded up like a note, 'My name's Smith,' says he . . . . "

"' . . . [the **lady**] hugged the poor little fellow to her bosom, and cried over him, till even old Fixem put on his blue spectacles to hide the two tears, that was a-trickling down, one on each side of his dirty face.'"

Husband, of a **lady**. "' . . . . his wife was wasting away, beneath cares of which she never complained, and griefs she never told. I saw that she was dying before his eyes; I knew that one exertion from him might have saved her, but he never made it. I don't blame him: I don't think he could rouse himself . . . he was a lost man when left to himself.'"

Lady. "' . . . in come a lady, as white as ever I see any one in my days, except about the eyes, which were red with crying. She walked in, as firm as I could have done; shut the door carefully after her, and sat herself down with a face as composed as if it was made of stone. "What is the matter, gentlemen?" says she, in a surprisin' steady voice. "*Is* this an execution?"'"

"Bitter cold and damp weather it was, yet, though her dress was thin, and her shoes none of the best, during the whole three days, from morning to night, she was out of doors running about to try and raise the money. The money *was* raised and the execution was paid out . . . . But if ever I saw death in a woman's face, I saw it in hers that night."

Master. "'Who the devil are you, and how dare you walk into a gentleman's house without leave?' says the master, as fierce as a bull in fits."

—*presence of mind:* "'Anybody else, my dear fellow' . . . pushing me down the passage to get out of the way . . . 'I have put this man in possession of all the plate and valuables, and I cannot allow him, on any consideration whatever, to leave the house. **Bung**, you scoundrel, go and count those forks in the breakfast-parlour instantly.'"

Mother. " . . . misery had changed her to a devil. If you had heard how she cursed the little naked children as was rolling on the floor, and seen how savagely she struck the infant when it cried with hunger, you'd have shuddered as much as I did."

Old woman. "' . . . the ugliest and dirtiest I ever see—who sat rocking herself backwards and forwards, backwards and forwards, without once stopping except for an instant now and then, to clasp together the withered hands which, with these exceptions, she kept constantly rubbing upon her knees, just raising and depressing her fingers convulsively, in time to the rocking of the chair."

> Boy, little, in the arms of the stoical lady's daughter
> Children, of the mother deranged by misery
> -three or four, fine-looking; of a stoical mother
> Gentleman, guest of the master under attachment; needed a cab
> Husband, had been transported a few weeks before
> Infant, struck by the mother deranged by misery
> **John**, a servant in livery; receives the broker and his man
> **Johnson's**: a fictitious enterprise cited by Fixem
> Lodgers: they blew up when their possessions were attached
> Servant girl, very small: opened the door to the broker's man
> **Smith**, a name assumed by Fixem as a blind to protect a debtor
> **Thompson**: fictitious person cited by Fixem, speaking to a debtor

SB 6 August 20, 1835   EC **LS**

The Ladies' Societies

Ladies' charitable societies vie for parish popularity: one, led by **Mrs Johnson Parker**, distributes bibles and prayer-books; another examines charity schoolchildren (the three **Miss Browns**, leaders); and a third lends childbed linen. The examining society briefly gains ascendancy, but an Irish orator wins the day for the distributionists.

Three **Miss Browns**. They "taught, and exercised, and examined, and re-examined the unfortunate children, until the boys grew pale, and the girls consumptive with study and fatigue. The three Miss Browns stood it out very well, because they relieved each other; but the **children** . . . exhibited decided symptoms of weariness and care."

Children. " . . . [they] were yellow-soaped and flannelled, and towelled, till their faces shone again; every pupil's hair was carefully combed into his or her eyes . . . the girls were adorned with snow-white tippets, and caps bound round the head by a single purple ribbon: the necks of the elder boys were fixed into collars of startling dimensions."

Curate. "The curate preached a charity sermon on behalf of the charity school, and . . . expatiated in glowing terms on the praiseworthy and indefatigable exertions of certain estimable individuals."

Missionary. "He repeated a dialogue he had heard between two negroes, behind a hedge, on the subject of distribution societies; the approbation was tumultuous."

Orator. "He talked of green isles—other shores—vast Atlantic—bosom of the deep—Christian charity—blood and extermination—mercy in hearts—arms in hands—altars and homes—household gods. He wiped his eyes, he blew his nose, and he quoted Latin . . . even the orator was overcome."

Mrs Johnson Parker. " . . . the mother of seven extremely fine girls—all unmarried—hastily reported . . . that five **old men**, six **old women**, and children innumerable, in the free seats near her pew were in the habit of coming to church every Sunday, without either bible or prayer-book. Was this to be borne in a civilised country? Could such things be tolerated in a Christian land? Never!"

—daughters: "A ladies' bible and prayer-book distribution society was instantly formed . . . treasurers, auditors, and secretary, the Misses Johnson Parker . . . . "

> Boy, eldest; delivered Henry Browns' address from behind his collar
> **Henry Brown**: wrote an address giving child examiners victory
> Ladies, married: members of the childbed linen loan society
> Ladies, unmarried: honorary members of the loan society
> Pew-openers, three: assisting the three Miss Browns
> Very old lady: heard to mumble "Exeter Hall"

SB 7 March 18, 1836   MC **NN**

Our Next-door Neighbour

The neighbour seeks a satisfactory tenant. The first is noisy with his friends in the night; the second steals everything; the third is a pair: a widow and son **William**, who dies while desperately struggling to support his mother.

Friends of a good-humoured tenant, "who used to come at ten o'clock, and begin to get happy about the small hours, when they evinced their perfect contentment by singing songs with half-a-dozen verses of two lines each, and a chorus of ten, which chorus used to be shouted forth by the whole strength of the company, in the most enthusiastic and vociferous manner . . . . "

Red-faced **gentleman**. " . . . the red-faced man in the white hat said he hoped he'd excuse his giving him so much trouble, but he'd feel obliged if he'd favour him with a glass of cold spring water, and the loan of a shilling for a cab to take him home . . . . "

Serious **gentleman**. " . . . tall, thin . . . with a profusion of brown hair, reddish whiskers, and very slightly developed moustaches. He wore a braided surtout, with frogs behind, light grey trousers, and wash-leather gloves, and had altogether rather a military appearance. So unlike the roystering single gentleman. Such insinuating manners, and such a delightful address!"

" . . . . The serious man had left the house mysteriously; carrying with him the shirt, the prayer-book, a tea-spoon, and the bedclothes."

Stout **gentleman**. " . . . good-humoured looking . . . of about five-and-thirty, [he] appeared as a candidate. . . [and] displayed a most extraordinary partiality for sitting up till three or four o'clock in the morning, drinking whiskey-and-water, and smoking cigars; then he invited friends home, who used to come at ten o'clock, and begin to get happy about the small hours . . . . "

Old gentleman. " . . . the powdered-headed old gentleman . . . slammed the door and went upstairs, and threw the contents of his water jug out of window—very straight, only it went over the wrong man . . . . "

Neighbour. " . . . our next-door neighbour was obliged to tell the single gentleman, that unless he gave up entertaining his friends at home, he really must be compelled to part with him."

"Our next-door neighbour was now perfectly happy. He had got a lodger at last, of just his own way of thinking—a serious, well-disposed man, who abhorred gaiety, and loved retirement. He took down the bill with a light heart, and pictured in imagination a long series of quiet Sundays, on which he and his lodger would exchange mutual civilities and Sunday papers."

Widow. " . . . a lady of about fifty, or it might be less. The mother wore a widow's weeds . . . . "

"' . . . [William] is not very strong, and has exerted himself too much lately.' Poor thing! The tears that streamed through her fingers, as she turned aside, as if to adjust her close widow's cap, too plainly showed how fruitless was the attempt to deceive herself."

William. "The new lodgers . . . a young lad of eighteen or nineteen and his mother . . . clothed in deep mourning. They were poor—very poor; for their only means of support arose from the pittance the boy earned, by copying writings, and translating for booksellers."

" . . . day after day, could we see more plainly that nature had set that unearthly light in his plaintive face, which is the beacon of her worst disease."

—*death:* "The boy raised himself by a violent effort, and . . . fell back, and a strange expression stole upon his features; not of pain or suffering, but an indescribable fixing of every line and muscle."

CHARACTERS IN 'SCENES'

SB 8 July 21, 1835   EC **SM**

The Streets—Morning

London streets and their denizens: the scene from early morning until noon.
Middle-aged men embody the Commuter in all ages, times and places.

George Cruikshank

Apprentices. " . . . the sun . . . shines with sufficient force to rouse the
dismal laziness of the apprentice, who pauses every other minute from his task
of sweeping out the shop and watering the pavement in front of it, to tell another apprentice similarly employed, how hot it will be today . . . . "

Cab-drivers. " . . . the cab-drivers and **hackney-coachmen** who are on
the stand polish up the ornamental part of their dingy vehicles—the former
wondering how people can prefer 'them wild beast cariwans of homnibuses, to a
riglar cab with a fast trotter,' . . . "

Clerks. " . . . the early clerk population of Somers and Camden Towns, Islington, and Pentonville, are fast pouring into the city, or directing their steps towards Chancery Lane and the Inns of Court."

Drunken man. "The last drunken man, who shall find his way home before sunlight, has just staggered heavily along, roaring out the burden of the drinking song of the previous night . . . . "

Hackney-coachmen. " . . . admiring how people can trust their necks into one of 'them crazy cabs, when they can have a 'spectable 'ackney cotche with a pair of 'orses as von't run away with no vun;' a consolation unquestionably founded on fact, seeing that a hackney-coach horse never was known to run at all, 'except,' as the smart cabman in front of the rank observes, 'except one, and *he* run back'ards.'"

Jews. " . . . the coaches which are just going out are surrounded by the usual crowd of Jews and nondescripts, who seem to consider, Heaven knows why, that it is quite impossible any man can mount a coach without requiring at least sixpennyworth of oranges, a penknife, a pocket-book, a last year's annual, a pencil-case, a piece of sponge, and a small series of caricatures."

Men, middle-aged, "whose salaries have by no means increased in the same proportion as their families, plod steadily along, apparently with no object in view but the counting-house; knowing by sight almost everybody they meet or overtake, for they have seen them every morning (Sundays excepted) during the last twenty years, but speaking to no one. If they do happen to overtake a personal acquaintance, they just exchange a hurried salutation, and keep walking on, either by his side or in front of him, as his rate of walking may chance to be. As to stopping to shake hands, or to take the friend's arm, they seem to think that as it is not included in their salary they have no right to do it."

Office lads. "Small office lads in large hats, who are made men before they are boys, hurry along in pairs, with their first coat carefully brushed, and the white trousers of last Sunday plentifully besmeared with dust and ink. It evidently requires a considerable mental struggle to avoid investing part of the day's dinner-money in the purchase of the stale tarts so temptingly exposed in dusty tins at the pasty-cooks' doors; but a consciousness of their own importance and the receipt of seven shillings a week, with the prospect of an early rise to eight, comes to their aid, and they accordingly put their hats a little more on one side . . . . "

Public-house workers. "Rough, sleepy-looking animals of strange appearance, something between ostlers and hackney-coachmen, begin to take down the shutters of early public-houses . . . . "

Servant. "The servant of all work, who, under the plea of sleeping very soundly . . . awakes all of a sudden, with well-feigned astonishment, and goes down-stairs very sulkily, wishing, while she strikes a light, that the principle of spontaneous combustion would extend itself to coals and kitchen range."

Sweep, "who, having knocked and rung till his arm aches, and being interdicted by a merciful legislature from endangering his lungs by calling out, sits patiently down on the door-step . . . . "

Waggoner. " . . . the sleepy waggoner impatiently urging on his tired horses, or vainly endeavouring to awaken the **boy**, who, luxuriously stretched on the top of the fruit-baskets, forgets, in happy oblivion, his long-cherished curiosity to behold the wonders of London."

Young man, employed by **Mr Todd**. He "is almost as good-looking and fascinating as the baker himself . . . being fond of mails, but more of females,

takes a short look at the mails, and a long look at the girls, much to the satisfaction of all parties concerned."

> Apprentices, milliners'; hardest worked, worst paid and worst used
> -staymakers'; the same
> Bakers, their shops filled with servants and children waiting for rolls
> Basket-women, carrying heavy baskets of fruit
> Bricklayer's labourer, the day's dinner tied up in a handkerchief
> **Betsy Clark**; next door has just taken in her milk too
> Costermonger, jingling cart with consumptive donkey
> Master, whom the missis has sent up in his drapery
> Mistress, of Betsy Clark; tapping angrily at her window
> -ringing for half an hour previously
> Passengers, going in and out by the early coach: blue and dismal
> Piemen, expatiating on the excellence of their pastry
> Policeman, occasionally seen, listlessly gazing on the prospect
> Schoolboys, on a stolen bathing expedition in boisterous mirth
> Shopmen, engaged in cleaning and decking windows for the day
> **Todd**, a baker; his boy a favourite
> Vagrant, houseless: penury and police have left him in the streets

SB 9 January 17, 1836   BL **SN**

The Streets—Night

London activity as night falls: Mmes **Macklin**, **Walker** and **Peplow** share an
interest in muffins and tea; street vendors, shops closing, beggars, and the
worlds of theatre and harmonic conviviality.

> " . . . *the streets of London, to be beheld in the very height of their glory,
> should be seen on a dark, dull, murky winter's night, when there is just
> enough damp gently stealing down to make the pavement greasy, without
> cleansing it . . . .* "

Beer boy. " . . . the nine o'clock 'beer,' who comes round with a lantern in
front of his tray, and says, as he lends **Mrs Walker** 'Yesterday's 'Tiser,' that
he's blessed if he can hardly hold the pot, much less feel the paper, for it's one of
the bitterest nights he ever felt . . . . "

Chandler. "The little chandler's shop with the cracked bell behind the
door, whose melancholy tinkling has been regulated by the demand for quar-
terns of sugar and half-ounces of coffee, is shutting up."

Cheesemonger's. " . . . where great flaring gas-lights, unshaded by any
glass, display huge piles of bright red and pale yellow cheeses, mingled with little fivepenny dabs of dingy bacon, various tubs of weekly Dorset, and cloudy
rolls of 'best fresh.'"

Kidney-pie merchant. "The candle in the transparent lamp, manufactured of oil-paper, embellished with 'characters,' has been blown out fifty times,
so the kidney-pie merchant, tired with running backwards and forwards to the
next wine-vaults, to get a light, has given up the idea of illumination in despair,
and the only signs of his 'whereabout,' are the bright sparks, of which a long irregular train is whirled down the street every time he opens his portable oven
to hand a hot kidney-pie to a customer."

Master Peplow. "[He] darts down the street, with a velocity which nothing but buttered muffins in perspective could possibly inspire, and drags the [**muffin**] **boy** back by main force . . . . "

Policeman. " . . . a little prophetic conversation with the policeman at the street-corner, touching a probable change in the weather, and the setting-in of a hard frost . . . the policeman, with his oilskin cape buttoned closely round him, seems as he holds his hat on his head, and turns round to avoid the gust of wind and rain which drives against him at the street-corner, to be very far from congratulating himself on the prospect before him."

Potato merchant. "Even the little block-tin temple sacred to baked potatoes, surmounted by a splendid design in variegated lamps, looks less gay than usual . . . . "

Three **professional gentlemen**. " . . . at the top of the centre table, one of whom is in the chair—the little pompous man with the bald head just emerging from the collar of his green coat. The others are seated on either side of him— the stout man with the small voice, and the thin-faced dark man in black. The little man in the chair is a most amusing personage—*such* condescending grandeur, and *such* a voice!"

" . . . the little pompous man gives another knock, and says 'Gen'l'men, we will attempt a glee, if you please.' This announcement calls forth tumultuous applause . . . . "

Smuggins. "That little round-faced man, with the small brown surtout, white stockings and shoes, is in the comic line; the mixed air of self-denial, and mental consciousness of his own powers, with which he acknowledges the call of the chair, is particularly gratifying . . . after a considerable quantity of coughing by way of symphony, and a most facetious sniff or two, which afford general delight, [he] sings a comic song, with a fal-de-ral—tol-de-ral chorus at the end of every verse, much longer than the verse itself. It is received with unbounded applause . . . . "

Theatre-goers. " . . . the half-price pit and box frequenters of the theatres throng to the different houses of refreshment; and chops, kidneys, rabbits, oysters, stout, cigars, and 'goes' innumerable, are served up amidst a noise and confusion of smoking, running, knife-clattering, and water-chattering, perfectly indescribable."

Bill Thompson. " . . . [one admires] the inimitable manner in which Bill Thompson can 'come the double monkey,' or go through the mysterious involutions of a sailor's hornpipe."

Waiter. "'Pray give your orders, gen'l'm'n—pray give your orders,'—says the pale-faced man with the red head; and demands for 'goes' of gin and 'goes' of brandy, and pints of stout, and cigars of peculiar mildness, are vociferously made from all parts of the room."

Mrs Walker, "who sees her husband coming down the street; and as he must want his tea, poor man, after his dirty walk from the Docks, she instantly runs across, muffins in hand . . . . "

Watermen. " . . . with dim dirty lanterns in their hands, and large brass plates upon their breasts, who have been shouting and rushing about for the last two hours, retire to their watering-houses to solace themselves with the creature comforts of pipes and purl . . . . "

Woman. "That wretched woman with the **infant** in her arms, round whose meagre form the remnant of her own scanty shawl is carefully wrapped, has been attempting to sing some popular ballad, in the hope of wringing a few pence from the compassionate passerby. A brutal laugh at her weak voice is all she has gained."

> Boys, who usually play in the streets, crouched in little knots
> Flat-fish vendors
> Fruit vendors, lingering hopelessly in their kennels for customers
> **Mrs Macklin**, who opened her street-door and screamed "Muffins!"
> Oyster vendors
> **Mrs Peplow**, over the way; lets loose Master Peplow
> **Walker**, who has walked from the Docks
> Young gentleman, nearby with a blue stock

SB 10 October 10, 1834   MC **ST**

Shops and their Tenants

The vicissitudes of shopkeepers and their families and landlords. The slow, sad decline of one location, a fine home converted to a succession of commercial efforts. It ends as a "dairy" with perambulant chickens, selling fresh-laid eggs.

Haberdasher, and linen-draper. " . . . he did nothing but walk up and down the shop, and hand seats to the ladies, and hold important conversations with the handsomest of the young men . . . . "

Loungers. " . . . we have not the slightest commiseration for the man who can take up his hat and stick, and walk from Covent Garden to St Paul's Churchyard . . . without deriving some amusement . . . from his perambulation . . . . Large black stocks and light waistcoats, jet canes and discontented countenances, are the characteristics of the race; other people brush quickly by you, steadily plodding on to business, or cheerfully running after pleasure. These men linger listlessly past, looking as happy and animated as a policeman on duty. Nothing seems to make an impression on their minds: nothing short of being knocked down by a porter, or run over by a cab, will disturb their equanimity."

Stationer. " . . . we trembled for his success. He was a widower evidently, and had employment elsewhere, for he passed us every morning on his road to the city."

"The business was carried on by his eldest **daughter**. Poor girl! she needed no assistance . . . we never passed at night without seeing the eldest girl at work . . . . "

Tobacconist. "The tobacconist remained in possession longer than any tenant within our recollection. He was a red-faced, impudent, good-for-nothing dog, evidently accustomed to take things as they came, and to make the best of a bad job. He sold as many cigars as he could, and smoked the rest. He occupied the shop as long as he could make peace with the landlord, and when he could no longer live in quiet, he very coolly locked the door, and bolted himself."

Young lady. " . . . in amber, with the large ear-rings, who, as she sits behind the counter in a blaze of adoration and gas-light, is the admiration of all the female servants in the neighbourhood, and the envy of every milliner's apprentice within two miles round."

Two **young men**. "Such ribbons and shawls! and two such elegant young men behind the counter, each in a clean collar and white neckcloth, like the lover in a farce."

> Bonnet-shape maker
> Green-grocer
> Marine-store dealer
> Tailor, a tenant
> Theatrical hair-dresser, who ornamented his window

SB 11 October 4, 1836   MC **SY**

Scotland Yard

The new London Bridge transforms a grimy coalheaver-dominated district. CD predicts that Scotland Yard will soon be completely forgotten.

Boot-maker. " . . . he exposes for sale, boots—real Wellington boots—an article which a few years ago, none of the original inhabitants had ever seen or heard of."

Coalheaver. "The oldest heaver present proved to demonstration, that the moment the piers [of London bridge] were removed, all the water in the Thames would run clean off, and leave a dry gully in its place."

Eating-house keepers.—*before:* "[They] exhibited joints of a magnitude, and puddings of a solidity, which coalheavers alone could appreciate . . . . "

—*after:* "One of the eating-house keepers began to court public opinion, and to look for customers among a new class of people. He covered the little dining-tables with white cloths, and got a painter's apprentice to inscribe something about hot joints from twelve to two, in one of the little panes of his shop-window."

"The eating-house keeper who manfully resisted the innovation of table-cloths, was losing ground every day . . . . "

Fruit-pie maker.—*before:* "[He] displayed on his well-scrubbed window-board large white compositions of flour and dripping, ornamented with pink stains, giving rich promise of the fruit within, which made [the coalheavers'] huge mouths water, as they lingered past."

—*after:* "The fruit-pie maker . . . took to smoking cigars, and began to call himself a pastrycook, and to read the papers."

Old man. " . . . there remains but one old man, who seems to mourn the downfall of this ancient place. He holds no converse with human kind, but, seated on a wooden bench . . . watches in silence the gambols of his sleek and well-fed dogs. He is the presiding genius of Scotland Yard . . . . Misery and want are depicted in his countenance; his form is bent by age, his head is grey with length of trial . . . . "

Tailor.—*before:* "The tailor displayed in his window a Lilliputian pair of leather gaiters, and a diminutive round frock, while each doorpost was appropriately garnished with a model of a coal-sack."

—*after:* "The tailor exhibits in his window the pattern of a foreign-looking brown surtout, with silk buttons, a fur collar, and fur cuffs. He wears a stripe down the outside of each leg of his trousers: and we have detected his **assistants** (for he has assistants now) in the act of sitting on the shop-board in the same uniform . . . [he] informs the public that gentlemen may have their own materials made up."

Waggoners. " . . . a race of strong and bulky men, who repaired to the wharfs in Scotland Yard regularly every morning, about five or six o'clock, to fill heavy waggons with coal, with which they proceeded to distant places up the country, and supplied the inhabitants with fuel. When they had emptied their waggons, they again returned for a fresh supply . . . . "

Dressmaker, who employs a young lady with pockets in her apron
-employee with the pockets
Duke, the King's brother; laid the first stone of new London Bridge
Jeweller: "ladies' ears may be pierced within"
Lord Mayor of London, not assassinated for tearing down a bridge
Tailor's wife, come to fetch him home from the public-house

SB 12 September 27, 1835   BL **SD**

Seven Dials

"The Dials" and its tatterdemalion inhabitants and shops. Colourful pugnacity, drink, wife-beating, police interventions. MS: "Seven streets converged on a central space in the middle of which was a Doric column surmounted by a hexagonal stone, each face of which bore a sundial facing the opening of one of the streets (or, in one case, two streets which opened into the same angle of this central area)." p70. [*But then, weren't there only Six Dials?*]

"Seven Dials! the region of song and poetry . . . . "

Shabby-genteel man. "The shabby-genteel man is an object of some mystery, but as he leads a life of seclusion, and never was known to buy anything beyond an occasional pen, except half-pints of coffee, penny loaves, and ha'porths of ink, his fellow-lodgers very naturally suppose him to be an author; and rumours are current in the Dials, that he writes poems for Mr **Warren**."

Shopman, "in the baked 'jemmy' line, or the fire-wood and hearth-stone line, or any other line which requires a floating capital of eighteen-pence or thereabouts: and he and his family live in the shop, and the small back parlour behind it . . . [he] ill-treats his family . . . . "

Sarah Sullivan. "On one side, a little crowd has collected round a couple of ladies, who having imbibed the contents of various 'three-outs' of gin and bitters in the course of the morning, have at length differed on some point of domestic arrangement, and are on the eve of settling the quarrel satisfactorily, by an appeal to blows, greatly to the interest of other ladies who live in the same house, and tenements adjoining, and who are all partisans on one side or other."

"'Vy don't you pitch into her, Sarah?' exclaims one half-dressed **matron** by way of encouragement. 'Vy don't you? if *my* 'usband had treated her with a drain last night, unbeknown to me, I'd tear her precious eyes out—a wixen!'"

'"Here's poor dear Mrs Sulliwin, as has five blessed children of her own, can't go out a-charing for one arternoon, but what hussies must be a-comin', and 'ticing avay her oun' 'usband, as she's been married to twelve year come next Easter Monday, for I see the certificate ven I vas a-drinkin' a cup o' tea vith her, only the werry last blessed Ven'sday as ever vas sent. I 'appen'd to say promiscuously, 'Mrs Sulliwin,' says I—'

'"What do you mean by hussies?' interrupts [**Mary**] a champion of the other party, who has evinced a strong inclination throughout to get up a branch fight on her own account . . . 'What do you mean by hussies?' . . .

'"Niver mind,' replies the opposition expressively, 'niver mind; *you* go home, and, ven you're quite sober, mend your stockings.'

George Cruikshank

"This somewhat personal allusion, not only to the lady's habits of intemperance, but also to the state of her wardrobe, rouses her utmost ire, and she accordingly complies with the urgent request of the bystanders to 'pitch in,' with considerable alacrity. The scuffle became general, and terminates . . . with 'arrival of the **policeman**, interior of the station-house, and impressive *dénouement.*'"

> Boys: their only recreation (fighting excepted) is leaning against posts
> Catnach[H]: published a street-flyer in Seven Dials
> Chandler, with a dark shop and a cracked bell behind the door
> Irishman, comes home every other night: attacks everybody
> Jobbing man, carpet-beater: extends professional pursuits to his wife
> Tom King[H], who kept a coffee-house in Covent Garden
> Ladies, ready to observe a female encounter
> Man, with a wife, in a front room
> Old woman, interested in a battle between Mary and Sarah
> Pitts[H]: published a street-flyer in Seven Dials
> Pot-boy, who encourages Mary
> Young gentlemen, with a passion for shop tills developed at an early age
> Young lady, who takes in tambour-work and can't bear "anything low"

SB 13 October 11, 1836   MC **MS**

Meditations in Monmouth Street

A walker pauses to visualize the former users of clothes and shoes seen in second-hand shops. In a *tour de force* of imagination, he gets a man's whole life from the hangings in one store. He sees a ballet in another.

People Imagined

Man. "There was the man's whole life written as legibly on those clothes, as if we had his autobiography engrossed on parchment before us.

"The first was a patched and much-soiled skeleton suit; one of those straight blue cloth cases in which small boys used to be confined, before belts and tunics had come in, and old notions had gone out: an ingenious contrivance for displaying the full symmetry of a boy's figure, by fastening him into a very tight jacket, with an ornamental row of buttons over each shoulder, and then buttoning his trousers over it, so as to give his legs the appearance of being hooked on, just under the armpits."

"They were decent people, but not overburdened with riches, or he would not have so far outgrown the suit when he passed into those corduroys with the round jacket; in which he went to a boys' school, however, and learnt to write—and in ink of pretty tolerable blackness, too, if the place where he used to wipe his pen might be taken as evidence.

"A black suit and the jacket changed into a diminutive coat. His father had died, and the mother had got the boy a message-lad's place in some office. A long-worn suit that one; rusty and threadbare before it was laid aside, but clean and free from soil to the last."

" . . . we felt as much sorrow when we saw . . . the change that began to take place now . . . . The next suit, smart but slovenly; meant to be gay, and yet not half so decent as the threadbare apparel; redolent of the idle lounge, and the blackguard companions, told us, we thought, that the widow's comfort had rapidly faded away."

"A long period had elapsed, and a greater change had taken place, by the time of casting off the suit that hung above. It was that of a stout, broad-shouldered, sturdy-chested man; and we knew at once, as anybody would, who glanced at that broad-skirted green coat, with the large metal buttons, that its wearer seldom walked forth without a dog at his heels, and some idle ruffian, the very counterpart of himself, at his side. The vices of the boy had grown with the man . . . ."

"A coarse round frock, with a worn cotton neckerchief, and other articles of clothing of the commonest description, completed the history. A prison, and the sentence—banishment or the gallows."

George Cruikshank

Market-gardener. "There was one pair of boots in particular—a jolly, good-tempered, hearty-looking, pair of tops, that excited our warmest regard; and we had got a fine, red-faced, jovial fellow of a market-gardener into them, before we had made their acquaintance half a minute. They were just the very thing for him. There were his huge fat legs bulging over the tops, and fitting them too tight to admit of his tucking in the loops he had pulled them on by; and his knee-cords with an interval of stocking; and his blue apron tucked up round his waist; and his red necker-chief and blue coat, and a white hat stuck on one side of his head; and there he stood with a broad grin on his great red face, whistling away, as if any other idea but that of being happy and comfortable had never entered his brain."

Old gentleman. " . . . excessive gallantry of a very old gentleman with a silver-headed stick, who tottered into a pair of large list shoes, that were standing in one corner of the board, and indulged in a variety of gestures expressive of his admiration of the lady in the cloth boots . . . . "

Smart female. " . . . in a showy bonnet, [she] stepped into a pair of grey cloth boots, with black fringe and binding, that were studiously pointing out their toes on the other side of the top-boots, and seemed very anxious to engage his attention . . . . "

The Others

Lady. " . . . we heard a shrill, and by no means musical voice, exclaim, 'Hope you'll know me agin, imperence!' and on looking intently . . . we found that it proceeded. . . from a bulky lady of elderly appearance who was seated in a chair at the head of the cellar-steps . . . we were conscious that in the depth of our meditations we might have been rudely staring at the old lady for half an hour without knowing it . . . . "

Inhabitants. "[They]are a distinct class; a peaceable and retiring race, who immure themselves for the most part in deep cellars, or small back parlours, and who seldom come forth into the world, except in the dusk and coolness of the evening, when they may be seen seated, in chairs on the pavement, smoking their pipes, or watching the gambols of their engaging children as they revel in the gutter, a happy troop of infantine scavengers.

"Their countenances bear a thoughtful and a dirty cast, certain indications of their love of traffic; and their habitations are distinguished by that disregard of outward appearance and neglect of personal comfort, so common among people who are constantly immersed in profound speculations, and deeply engaged in sedentary pursuits." ¶

> Clipe, tailor (in illustration, only)
> Jews, red-headed, red-whiskered; thrusting into a suit of clothes
> Moses Levy, slopseller (illustration only)
> P. Patch, slopseller (illustration only)
> Servant-maid, imagined in a pair of Denmark satin shoes
> Young fellow, imagined in a pair of long-quartered pumps

SB 14 January 31, 1835   EC **HC**

Hackney-Coach Stands

The nature and uses of the London hackney-coach. Its varying clientele, its past gentility, its present disreputableness.

"We readily concede to [other cities] the possession of certain vehicles, which may look almost as dirty, and even go almost as slowly, as London hackney-coaches . . . . "

Bridesmaid. " . . . a little, dumpy, good-humoured young woman . . . . The moment they were in, the bridesmaid threw a red shawl, which she had, no doubt, brought on purpose, negligently over the number on the door, evidently to delude pedestrians into the belief that the hackney-coach was a private carriage; and away they went, perfectly satisfied that the imposition was successful, and quite unconscious that there was a great staring number stuck up behind, on a plate as large as a schoolboy's slate. A shilling a mile!—the ride was worth five, at least, to them."

Four **children**. " . . . four small children forthwith rush out, and scream 'Coach!' with all their might and main . . . .The children get into everybody's way, and the youngest, who has upset himself in his attempts to carry an umbrella, is borne off wounded and kicking."

Old lady. "The old lady, who has been stopping there for the last month, is going back to the country. Out comes box after box, and one side of the vehicle is filled with luggage in no time . . . . A cloak is handed in, and a little basket, which we could almost swear contains a small black bottle, and a paper of sandwiches."

Servant-girl. " . . . with the pink ribbons . . . one little villain . . . runs up the street at the top of his speed, pursued by the servant; not ill-pleased to have such an opportunity of displaying her attractions. She brings him back, and, after casting two or three gracious glances across the way, which are either intended for us or the **pot-boy** (we are not quite certain which), shuts the door . . . . "

Tom, a coachman. "The coachman himself is in the watering-house . . . . "

—*summoned*: "A response is heard from the tap-room; the coachman, in his wooden-soled shoes, makes the street echo again as he runs across it; and then there is such a struggling, and backing, and grating of the kennel, to get the coach-door opposite the house-door, that the **children** are in perfect ecstasies of delight. What a commotion!"

Waterman. " . . . his hands forced into his pockets as far as they can possibly go, is dancing the 'double shuffle,' in front of the pump, to keep his feet warm."

—*summoned:* "The waterman darts from the pump, seizes the horses by their respective bridles, and drags them, and the coach too, round to the house, shouting all the time for the coachman at the very top, or rather very bottom of his voice, for it is a deep bass growl."

Bride, with a thin white dress and a great red face
Bridegroom, in blue coat, yellow waistcoat, white trousers, gloves
Daughter, of old lady; married
Friend, of the bridegroom, dressed the same
Richard Martin[H]: a founder of society for prevention of cruelty to animals
Servants, handing the old lady into the coach

SB 15 October 11, 1836   MC **DC**

Doctors' Commons

This lawyers' college housed a curious congeries of courts, which registered Wills, issued marriage licenses, granted divorces, heard cases in Admiralty and excommunicated for improprieties. A visitor describes two principal parts and their personnel and clients.

Arches Court

Apparitor. " . . . a fat-faced, smirking, civil-looking body, in a black gown, black kid gloves, knee shorts, and silks, with a shirt-frill in his bosom, curls on his head, and a silver staff in his hand, whom we had no difficulty in recognising as the officer of the Court."

Bellman. " . . . a little thin old man, with long grizzly hair, crouched in a remote corner, whose duty . . . was to ring a large hand-bell when the Court opened in the morning, and who, for aught his appearance betokened to the contrary, might have been similarly employed for the last two centuries at least."

Michael Bumple, plaintiff. *See* **Thomas Sludberry**.

Doctor. " . . . one of the bewigged gentlemen in the red robes, who was straddling before the fire in the centre of the Court, in the attitude of the brazen Colossus, to the complete exclusion of everybody else. He had gathered up his robe behind, in much the same manner as a slovenly woman would her petticoats on a very dirty day, in order that he might feel the full warmth of the fire.

"His wig was put on all awry, with the tail straggling about his neck; his scanty grey trousers and short black gaiters, made in the worst possible style, imparted an additional inelegant appearance to his uncouth person; and his limp, badly-starched shirt-collar almost obscured his eyes. We shall never be able to claim any credit as a physiognomist again, for, after a careful scrutiny of this gentleman's countenance, we had come to the conclusion that it bespoke nothing but conceit and silliness, when our friend with the silver staff [the **Apparitor**] whispered in our ear that he was no other than a doctor of civil law . . . . "

Judge. " . . . a very fat and red-faced gentleman, in tortoise-shell spectacles, whose dignified appearance announced the judge . . . he spoke very fast, but that was habit; and rather thick, but that was good living."

Proctors. " . . . a number of very self-important-looking personages, in stiff neckcloths, and black gowns with white fur collars . . . . "

Thomas Sludberry. ". . . it appeared, by some eight-and-twenty affidavits . . . that on a certain night, at a certain vestry-meeting, in a certain parish particularly set forth, Thomas Sludberry, the party appeared against in that suit, had made use of, and applied to **Michael Bumple**, the promoter, the words 'You be blowed;' and that, on said Michael Bumple and others remonstrating with the said Thomas Sludberry, on the impropriety of his conduct, the said Thomas Sludberry repeated the aforesaid expression 'You be blowed' and furthermore desired and requested to know, whether the said Michael Bumple 'wanted anything for himself;' adding, 'that if the said Michael Bumple did want something for himself, he, the said Thomas Sludberry, was the man to give it him . . . . "

"[The **judge**] pronounced upon Sludberry the awful sentence of excommunication for a fortnight, and payment of the costs of the suit. Upon this, Sludberry, who was a little, red-faced, sly-looking, ginger-beer seller, addressed the Court, and said, if they'd be good enough to take off the costs, and excommunicate him for the term of his natural life instead, it would be much more convenient to him, for he never went to church at all."

Prerogative Office

Clerks. "It was curious to contrast the lazy indifference of the attorneys' clerks who were making a search for some legal purpose, with the air of earnestness and interest which distinguished the strangers [**searchers**] . . . the former pausing every now and then with an impatient yawn, or raising their heads to look at the people who passed up and down the room; the latter stooping over the book, and running down column after column of names in the deepest abstraction."

Miser. " . . . a hard-featured old man with a deeply-wrinkled face, was intently perusing a lengthy will with the aid of a pair of horn spectacles: occasionally pausing from his task, and slily noting down some brief memorandum of the bequests contained in it. Every wrinkle about his toothless mouth, and sharp keen eyes, told of avarice and cunning. His clothes were nearly threadbare, but it was easy to see that he wore them from choice and not from necessity; all his looks and gestures down to the very small pinches of snuff which he every now and then took from a little tin canister, told of wealth, and penury, and avarice.

"As he leisurely closed the register, put up his spectacles, and folded his scraps of paper in a large leathern pocket-book, we thought what a nice hard bargain he was driving with some poverty-stricken legatee . . . . The old man stowed his pocket-book carefully in the breast of his great-coat, and hobbled away with a leer of triumph. That will had made him ten years younger at the lowest computation."

Searcher. " . . . a little dirty-faced man in a blue apron, who after a whole morning's search, extending some fifty years back, had just found the will to which he wished to refer, which one of the officials was reading to him in a low hurried voice from a thick vellum book with large clasps. It was perfectly evident that the more the **clerk** read, the less the man with the blue apron understood about the matter."

> Court-keeper, in black; of about twenty-stone weight
> Doctors, solemn in crimson gowns and wigs
> Official, in the Prerogative Court: reading rapidly to a searcher
> Registrar, in the Arches' Court: in an armchair and a wig

SB 16 March 17, 1835   EC **LR**

London Recreations

The varieties of recreation possible in and around London; emphasizing gardening (sincere and insincere) and tea-gardening. CD's nicest description of the suburban joy of digging, with one's mate, in one's dirt and making things grow.

Gardeners

City man. "If the regular City man who . . . drives home to Hackney, Clapton, Stamford Hill, or elsewhere, can be said to have any daily recreation beyond his dinner, it is his garden. He never does anything to it with his own hands; but he takes great pride in it notwithstanding . . . .

" . . . when the cloth is removed, and he has drunk three or four glasses of his favourite port, he orders the French windows of his dining-room (which of course look into the garden) to be opened, and throwing a silk handkerchief over his head, and leaning back in his armchair, descants at considerable length upon its beauty, and the cost of maintaining it . . . when he has exhausted the subject, he goes to sleep."

Old gentleman, "who resides some short distance from town—say in the Hampstead Road, or the Kilburn Road, or any other road where the houses are small and neat, and have little slips of back garden. He and his **wife**—who is as clean and compact a little body as himself—have occupied the same house ever since he retired from business twenty years ago . . . .

"In fine weather the old gentleman is almost constantly in the garden; and when it is too wet to go into it, he will look out of the window at it, by the hour together. He has always something to do there, and you will see him digging, and sweeping, and cutting, and planting, with manifest delight. In the spring-time, there is no end to the sowing of seeds, and sticking little bits of wood over them, with labels, which look like epitaphs to their memory; and in the evening, when the sun has gone down, the perseverance with which he lugs a great watering-pot about is perfectly astonishing. The only other recreation he has is the newspaper, which he peruses every day, from beginning to end . . . . "

Wife. "The old lady is very fond of flowers, as the hyacinth-glasses in the parlour-window, and geranium-pots in the little front court, testify. She takes great pride in the garden too: and when one of the four fruit-trees produces rather a larger gooseberry than usual, it is carefully preserved under a wine-glass on the sideboard, for the edification of visitors . . . . "

Tea-gardeners

Gentlemen. " . . . in alarming waistcoats, and steel watch-guards, promenading about, three abreast, with surprising dignity (or as the gentleman in the next box facetiously observes, 'cutting it uncommon fat!') . . . . "

Grandmother. " . . . she is in perfect ecstasies, and does nothing but laugh herself into fits of coughing, until they have finished the 'gin-and-water warm with', of which **Uncle Bill** ordered 'glasses round' after tea, 'just to keep the night air out, and do it up comfortable and riglar arter sich an as-tonishing hot day!'"

Husbands. " . . . in perspective ordering bottles of ginger-beer for the objects of their affections, with a lavish disregard of expense . . . . "

Ladies. " . . . with great, long, white pocket-handkerchiefs like small table-cloths in their hands, chasing one another on the grass in the most playful and interesting manner, with the view of attracting the attention of the aforesaid **gentlemen** . . . . "

Sally. " . . . **Uncle Bill**'s hints—such as . . . 'I shall look out for the cake, Sally, I'll be godfather to your first—wager it's a boy,' and so forth, are equally embarrassing to the young people, and delightful to the elder ones."

Waiters. " . . . who have been running about incessantly for the last six hours, think they feel a little tired, as they count their glasses and their gains."

Wives. " . . . washing down huge quantities of 'shrimps' and 'winkles,' with an equal disregard of their own bodily health and subsequent comfort . . . . "

Women. "Those two motherly-looking women in the smart pelisses, who are chatting so confidentially, inserting a 'ma'am' at every fourth word, scraped an acquaintance about a quarter of an hour ago . . . . "

> Boy, little; in a three-cornered pink satin hat with black feathers
> -*pl* taking Sunday pleasure; in great silk hats, smoking cigars
> Father, in a tea-garden
> Gentleman, in a tea-garden; commenting on promenaders
> -*pl* in pink shirts and blue waistcoats; mishandling canes
> Johnson[H], for whom a nursery-ground is named
> Men in blue coats and drab trousers, walking and smoking pipes
> Mistress, in a tea-garden box
> Thomson, after whom a great room in a tea-garden is named
> Young man, evidently keeping company with Uncle Bill's niece Sally

SB 17 June 6, 1835   EC **R**

The River

Water-partying on the Thames; a rowing-match; and the London Bridge steam-wharf where boaters to Gravesend and Margate board.

"Who ever heard of a successful water-party?"

Alick, "a damp earthy child in red worsted socks, takes certain small jumps upon the deck, to the unspeakable satisfaction of his family circle."

Bashful men, "who have been looking down the hatchway at the engine, find, to their great relief, a subject on which they can converse with one another—and a copious one too—Steam."

Dando. " . . . the head man, with the legs of his trousers carefully tucked up at the bottom, to admit the water, we presume—for it is an element in which he is infinitely more at home than on land—is quite a character . . . . Watch him, as taking a few minutes' respite from his toils, he negligently seats himself on the edge of a boat, and fans his broad bushy chest with a cap scarcely half so furry. Look at his magnificent, though reddish whiskers, and mark the somewhat native humour with which he 'chaffs' the boys and 'prentices, or cunningly gammons the gen'lm'n into the gift of a glass of gin, of which we verily believe he swallows in one day as much as any six ordinary men, without ever being one atom the worse for it."

Father. " . . . a little thin man—who entirely concurs . . . that it's high time something was done with these steam companies, and that as the Corporation Bill failed to do it, something else must . . . . "

Officer, "who replies, that that company, ever since it has been St Kat'rine's Dock Company, has protected life and property;' that if it had been the London Bridge Wharf Company, indeed, he shouldn't have wondered, seeing that the morality of that company (they being the opposition) can't be answered for, by no one . . . . "

Old women, "who have brought large wicker hand-baskets with them, set seriously to work at the demolition of heavy sandwiches, and pass round a wine-glass, which is frequently replenished from a flat bottle like a stomach-warmer, with considerable glee . . . . "

Porters. " . . . the 'fares' resign themselves and their luggage into the hands of the porters, who seize all the packages at once as a matter of course, and run away with them, heaven knows where . . . . "

Tom. "'Pull round, Tom, can't you?' re-echoes one of the party . . . and the unfortunate young man, at the imminent risk of breaking a blood-vessel, pulls and pulls, until the head of the boat fairly lies in the direction of Vauxhall Bridge."

Water partygoers. "They approach in full aquatic costume, with round blue jackets, striped shirts, and caps of all sizes and patterns, from the velvet skull-cap of French manufacture, to the easy head-dress familiar to the students of the old spelling-books . . . . "

" . . . the sight of the water rapidly cools their courage, and the air of self-denial with which each of them insists on somebody else's taking an oar, is perfectly delightful."

Young ladies. "[They] become extremely plaintive, and expatiate to Mr **Brown**, or young Mr **O'Brien**, who has been looking over them, on the blueness of the sky, and brightness of the water; on which Mr Brown or Mr O'Brien, as the case may be, remarks in a low voice that he has been quite insensible of late to the beauties of nature—that his whole thoughts and wishes have centred in one object alone—whereupon the young lady looks up, and failing in her attempt to appear unconscious, looks down again; and turns over the next leaf with great difficulty, in order to afford opportunity for a lengthened pressure of the hand."

> Attendant: "other boat, sir"
> Children, stout; with stout parents looking for the right boat
> Coxswain: looks as easy as if he were steering in the Bay of Biscay
> John Dando[H], who swallowed oysters hugely and did not pay
> Rev Thomas Dilworth[H]: portrait has him in curious cap
> Father, stout, looking for the boat to Gravesend
> Fellows, in great rough trousers and Guernsey shirts
> Gentleman in a foraging-cap, who plays the harp
> George, cheered in a Thames rowing-match
> 'Jack' (odd-job man) on the river: can do nothing but lounge about
> Mother, stout; distracted by maternal anxiety on the river
> "Sulliwin" cheered in a Thames rowing-match
> Watermen, assembled at different river stairs to discuss candidates

SB 18 May 9, 1835   EC **A**

Astley's

A visitor recalls childhood days at the equitation theatre and circus. He now finds the audience more diverting than the performances. The piece includes a rare CD portrait of a normal adolescent, the moody **George**.

Actors, off-duty. " . . . an indescribable public-house-parlour swagger, and a kind of conscious air . . .

—the heavy: " . . . a thin pale man, with a very long face, in a suit of shining black, thoughtfully knocking that part of his boot which once had a heel, with an ash stick. He is the man who does the heavy business, such as prosy fathers, virtuous servants, curates, landlords, and so forth."

—leading man: "That young fellow in the faded brown coat, and very full light green trousers, pulls down the wristbands of his check shirt, as ostentatiously as if it were of the finest linen, and cocks the white hat of the summer-before-last as knowingly over his right eye, as if it were a purchase of yesterday. Look at the dirty white Berlin gloves, and the cheap silk handkerchief stuck in the bosom of his threadbare coat."

Child, " . . . in a braided frock, and high state of astonishment, with very large round eyes, opened to their utmost width, was lifted over the seats—a process which occasioned a considerable display of little pink legs . . . . "

Clown. " . . . the clown throws himself on the ground, and goes through a variety of gymnastic convulsions, doubling himself up, and untying himself again, and making himself look very like a man in the most hopeless extreme of human agony, to the vociferous delight of the gallery . . . . "

[Andrew] Ducrow, manager. " . . . arisen to shed the light of classic taste and portable gas over the sawdust of the circus . . . . "

George. " . . . the eldest son, a boy of fourteen years old, who was evidently trying to look as if he did not belong to the family . . . waxed indignant, and remonstrated in no very gentle terms on the gross impropriety of having his name repeated in so loud a voice at a public place, on which all the children laughed very heartily, and one of the little boys wound up by expressing his opinion, that 'George began to think himself quite a man now,' whereupon both pa and ma laughed too; and George . . . assumed a look of profound contempt, which lasted the whole evening."

" . . . the whole party seemed quite happy, except the exquisite in the back of the box, who, being too grand to take any interest in the children, and too insignificant to be taken notice of by anybody else, occupied himself, from time to time, in rubbing the place where the whiskers ought to be, and was completely alone in his glory."

Girl. " . . . a small coquette of twelve years old, who looked like a model of her mamma on a reduced scale; and who, in common with the other little girls (who, generally speaking, have even more coquettishness about them than much older ones), looked very properly shocked, when the knight's squire kissed the princess's confidential chambermaid."

Governess. " . . . peeped out from behind the pillar, and timidly tried to catch ma's eye, with a look expressive of her high admiration of the whole family . . . whenever she could catch ma's eye, put her handkerchief to her mouth, and appeared, as in duty bound, to be in convulsions of laughter also."

Mother. " . . . she was perfectly overcome by the drollery of the principal comedian, and laughed till every one of the immense bows on her ample cap trembled . . . . "

Riding-master, "follows the **clown** with a long whip in his hand, and bows to the audience with graceful dignity. He is none of your second-rate riding-masters in nankeen dressing-gowns, with brown frogs, but the regular gentleman-attendant on the principal riders, who always wears a military uniform

with a table-cloth inside the breast of the coat, in which costume he forcibly reminds one of a fowl trussed for roasting ... everybody remembers his polished
boots, his graceful demeanour, stiff, as some misjudging persons have in their
jealousy considered it, and the splendid head of black hair, parted high on the
forehead, to impart to the countenance an appearance of deep thought and
poetic melancholy. His soft and pleasing voice, too, is in perfect unison with his
noble bearing, as he humours the clown by indulging in a little badinage . . . ."

Schoolmistress. " . . . [we] wince momentarily, as we remember the hard
knuckles with which the reverend old lady who instilled into our mind the first
principles of education for ninepence per week, or ten and sixpence per quarter,
was wont to poke our juvenile head occasionally, by way of adjusting the confusion of ideas in which we were generally involved."

Miss Woolford. "The graceful air, too, with which [the **riding-master**] introduces Miss Woolford into the arena, and, after assisting her to the saddle,
follows her fairy courser round the circle . . . . "

"On the lady's announcing with a sweet smile that she wants the two flags,
they are, with sundry grimaces, procured and handed up . . . and round goes
Miss Woolford again on her graceful performance . . . . "

> Actors, in splendid armour, who vowed to rescue the lady or perish
> Philip ASTLEY[H], former cavalry sergeant-major: started a riding exhibition
> Boys, in blue jackets and trousers, lay-down shirt collars
> Father, giving very audible directions from the box-door
> Girls ushered into the box by a governess
> *Lucretia*, legendary subject of a famous literary rape
> Performers: a groom or two; some shabby-genteel men

SB 19 April 16, 1835   EC **GF**

Greenwich Fair

Atmosphere, facilities, professionals and amateurs at London's great annual
"country fair." A temporary ballroom, with ladies in their escorts' hats, and the
men in their ladies' bonnets, or false noses and "tinder box looking hats."

> *"If Parks be 'the lungs of London,' we wonder what Greenwich Fair
> is—a periodical breaking out, we suppose, a sort of spring-rash: a three
> days' fever, which cools the blood for six months afterwards . . . . "*

Announcer, for the menagerie. ". . . is generally a very tall, hoarse man, in
a scarlet coat, with a cane in his hand, with which he occasionally raps the pictures . . . 'The fe-ro-cious lion (tap, tap) who bit off the gentleman's head last
Cambervel vos a twelvemonth, and has killed on the awerage three keepers a
year ever since he arrived at matoority. No extra charge on this account recollect; the price of admission is only sixpence.'"

Decoy, a gentleman in top-boots, "who is standing by, and who, in a low
tone, regrets his own inability to bet, in consequence of having unfortunately
left his purse at home, but strongly urges the **stranger** not to neglect such a
golden opportunity. The 'plant' is successful, the bet is made, the stranger of
course loses . . . . "

Dwarf. " . . . he has always a little box, about two feet six inches high, into which, by long practice, he can just manage to get, by doubling himself up like a boot-jack; this box is painted outside like a six-roomed house, and as the crowd see him ring a bell, or fire a pistol out of the first-floor window, they verily believe that it is his ordinary town residence, divided like other mansions into drawing-rooms, dining-parlour, and bedchambers."

Giant. "As a giant is not so easily moved, a pair of indescribables of most capacious dimensions, and a huge shoe, are usually brought out, into which two or three stout men get all at once, to the enthusiastic delight of the crowd, who are quite satisfied with the solemn assurance that these habiliments form part of the giant's everyday costume."

Gipsy. " . . . a sun-burnt woman in a red cloak 'telling fortunes' and prophesying husbands, which it requires no extraordinary observation to describe, for the originals are before her. Thereupon, the lady concerned laughs and blushes . . . and the gentleman described looks extremely foolish, and squeezes her hand, and fees the gipsy liberally; and the gipsy goes away, perfectly satisfied herself, and leaving those behind her perfectly satisfied also: and the prophecy, like many other prophecies of greater importance, fulfils itself in time."

Ladies, "in 'carawans' scream with fright at every fresh concussion, and their **admirers** find it necessary to sit remarkably close to them, by way of encouragement . . . . "

Manager. "'All in to begin,' shouts the manager, when no more people can be induced to 'come for'erd,' and away rush the leading members of the company to do the dreadful in the first piece."

Little old men and **women**. " . . . with a small basket under one arm, and a wine-glass, without a foot, in the other hand, tender 'a drop o' the right sort' to the different groups . . . . "

Pensioners. " . . . for the moderate charge of a penny, [they] exhibit the mast-house, the Thames and shipping, the place where the men used to hang in chains, and other interesting sights, through a telescope . . . . "

Performers. "The company are now promenading outside in all the dignity of wigs, spangles, red-ochre, and whitening. See with what a ferocious air the gentleman who personates the Mexican chief, paces up and down, and with what an eye of calm dignity the principal **tragedian** gazes on the crowd below, or converses confidentially with the **harlequin**! . . . .They look so noble in those Roman dresses, with their yellow legs and arms, long black curly heads, bushy eyebrows, and scowl expressive of assassination, and vengeance, and everything else that is grand and solemn.

"Then, the ladies . . . such innocent and awful-looking beings; as they walk up and down the platform in twos and threes, with their arms round each other's waists, or leaning for support on one of those majestic men! Their spangled muslin dresses and blue satin shoes and sandals (a *leetle* the worse for wear) are the admiration of all beholders . . . ." ¶

John Richardson. "This immense booth, with the large stage in front, so brightly illuminated with variegated lamps, and pots of burning fat, is 'Richardson's,' where you have a melo-drama (with three murders and a ghost), a pantomime, a comic song, an overture, and some incidental music, all done in five-and-twenty minutes."

Servants. "Servants-of-all work, who are not allowed to have followers, and have got a holiday for the day, make the most of their time with the faithful **admirer** who waits for a stolen interview at the corner of the street every night, when they go to fetch the beer . . . . "

Young ladies. " . . . the fair objects of their [swains'] regard enhance the value of stolen kisses, by a vast deal of struggling, and holding down of heads, and cries of 'Oh! Ha'done, then, **George**—Oh, do tickle him for me, **Mary**—Well, I never!' and similar Lucretian ejaculations . . . . "

Young ladies. " . . . unbonneted young ladies, in their zeal for the interest of their employers, seize you by the coat, and use all the blandishments . . . to induce you to purchase half a pound of the real spice nuts . . . . "

Actor, enacting the "swell" in the pantomime
Actress, leading tragic: foots it to perfection with the "swell"
Albino: a beautiful young lady with white hair and pink eyes
Apprentices, grown sentimental
Clowns, four, engaged in a mock broadsword combat
Columbine, in performance
Thomas Horner[H as Hornor]: commissioned a large mural
Man, in countryman's dress: "Come for'erd, come for'erd"
-with three thimbles and a pea on a little round board
Mechanic, lingering on the grass and proud of England

Proprietress, of the "jack-in-the-box" entertainment at a fair
Straw-bonnet makers, who grow kind
Swains, love-sick and violently affectionate due to gin-and-water
Turnpike-men, in despair
Vendors, of gingerbread and toys

SB 20 August 11, 1835 EC **PT**

Private Theatres

The activities and working conditions of vanity amateur actors, who choose stage names and roles with conscious care.

" . . . *donkeys who are prevailed upon to pay for permission to exhibit their lamentable ignorance and boobyism.* "

Audience. "The principal patrons . . . are dirty **boys**, low copying-**clerks** in attorneys' offices, capacious-headed **youths** from city counting-houses, **Jews** whose business, as lenders of fancy dresses, is a sure passport to the amateur stage, **shop-boys** who now and then mistake their masters' money for their own; and a choice miscellany of idle vagabonds . . . . "

—*the younger crowd:* " . . . **boys** of from fifteen to twenty-one years of age, who throw back their coat and turn up their wristbands, after the portraits of **Count D'Orsay**, hum tunes and whistle when the curtain is down, by way of persuading the people near them, that they are not at all anxious to have it up again, and speak familiarly of the inferior performers as Bill Such-a-one, and Ned So-and-so . . . . "

Belville, etc. "With the double view of guarding against the discovery of friends or employers, and enhancing the interest of an assumed character, by attaching a high-sounding name to its representative, these geniuses assume fictitious names . . . . Belville, **Melville**, **Treville**, **Berkeley**, **Randolph**, **Byron**, **St Clair**, and so forth, are among the humblest; and the less imposing titles of **Jenkins**, **Walker**, **Thomson**, **Barker**, **Solomons** &c., are completely laid aside."

Comedian. "The short thin man . . . whose white face is so deeply seared with the small-pox, and whose dirty shirt-front is inlaid with open-work, and embossed with coral studs like ladybirds, is the low comedian and comic singer of the establishment."

Country managers, opulent. " . . . in the centre box, with an opera-glass ostentatiously placed before them, are friends of the **proprietor** . . . as he confidentially informs every individual among the crew . . . . "

Female. "The black-eyed female with whom [the **milksop**] is talking so earnestly, is dressed for the 'gentlewoman.' It is *her* first appearance, too—in that character."

Lady performers. " . . . they are quite above any formal absurdities; the mere circumstance of your being behind the scenes is a sufficient introduction to their society—for of course they know that none but strictly respectable persons would be admitted into that close fellowship with them, which acting engenders."

Jem Larkins. "That gentleman in the white hat and checked shirt, brown coat and brass buttons, lounging behind the stage-box on the O.P. [Opposite Prompt—stage left] side, is Mr **Horatio St Julien**, alias Jem Larkins. His line is genteel comedy—his father's, coal and potato."

Milksop. "That stupid-looking milksop, with light hair and bow legs—a kind of man whom you can warrant town-made—is fresh caught; he plays *Malcolm* tonight, just to accustom himself to an audience. He will get on better by degrees; he will play *Othello* in a month, and in a month more, will very probably be apprehended on a charge of embezzlement."

George Cruikshank

Nathan. "'Look sharp below there, gents,' exclaims the dresser, a red-headed and red-whiskered Jew, calling through the trap . . . . "

Orchestra. " . . . two **fiddles** and a **flute** in the orchestra, who have got through five overtures since seven o'clock (the hour fixed for the commencement of the performances), and have just begun the sixth . . . . 'The flute says he'll be blowed if he plays any more . . . . '"

Proprietor. "The proprietor of a private theatre may be an ex-scene-painter, a low coffee-house-keeper, a disappointed eighth-rate actor, a retired smuggler, or uncertificated bankrupt."

Charley Scarton "is to take the part of an English sailor, and fight a broadsword combat with six unknown bandits, at one and the same time (one theatrical sailor is always equal to half a dozen men at least) . . . . "

Supernumerary. " . . . some mouldy-looking man in a fancy neckerchief, whose partially corked eyebrows, and half-rouged face, testify to the fact of his having just left the stage or the circle . . . ."

Woman. "The large woman . . . is the *Lady Macbeth* of the night; she is always selected to play the part, because she is tall and stout, and *looks* a little like **Mrs Siddons**—at a considerable distance."

Young lady. " . . . the young lady with the liberal display of legs, who is kindly painting [*Banquo*'s] face with a hare's foot, is dressed for *Fleance*."

> **Beverley**: stage name of Loggins
> Boy, of fourteen, having his eyebrows made up to play Duncan
> Girl, coming out, in a hornpipe after the tragedy
> Jewess, stout; the mother of a pale bony little girl
> Jones, on the stage crew
> **Loggins**, actor
> Manager, all affability: he has taken your money and will again
> Men, with corked countenances, in very old green tunics: the army
> **Palmer**: to play *The Unknown Bandit*
> Snuff-shop-looking figure, who plays Banquo
> **Horatio St Julien**: stage name of Jem Larkins
> White, on the stage crew

SB 21 October 26, 1835   MC **VG**

Vauxhall Gardens by Day

A tour of London's principal amusement park, normally active only at night, to see how it fares in the sun. A balloonist goes up with his family and a Lord.

> "*Vauxhall by daylight! A porter-pot without porter, the House of Commons without the Speaker, a gas-lamp without the gas—pooh, nonsense, the thing was not to be thought of.*"

Blackmore. " . . . we had beheld the undaunted Mr Blackmore make his terrific ascent, surrounded by flames of fire, and peals of artillery . . . . "

Comic singer. " . . . was the especial favourite . . . . A marvellously facetious gentleman that comic singer is; his distinguishing characteristics are, a wig approaching to the flaxen, and an aged countenance, and he bears the name of one of the English counties, if we recollect right.* He sang a very good song about the seven ages, the first half-hour of which afforded the assembly the purest delight; of the rest we can make no report, as we did not stay to hear any more." [*MS says this was Paul Bedford.]

Gentleman, with a family. " . . . with his wife, and children, and mother, and wife's sister, and a host of female friends, in all the gentility of white pocket-handkerchiefs, frills, and spencers, 'Mr **Green** is a steady hand, sir, and there's no fear about him.'"

Charles Green. "'He's a rum 'un is Green [said the little **man**]; think o' this here being up'ards of his two hundredth ascent; ecod, the man as is ekal to Green never had the toothache yet, nor won't have within this hundred year, and that's all about it. When you meets with real talent, and native, too, encourage it, that's what I say' . . . . "

Little man. "There was one little man in faded black, with a dirty face and a rusty black neckerchief with a red border, tied in a narrow wisp round his neck, who entered into conversation with everybody, and had something to say upon every remark that was made within his hearing."

Rope-dancers. "The sun shone upon the spangled dresses of the performers, and their evolutions were about as inspiriting and appropriate as a country-dance in a family vault."

Singer. " . . . in a dress coat . . . . We knew the small gentleman well; we had seen a lithographed semblance of him, on many a piece of music, with his mouth wide open as if in the act of singing; a wine-glass in his hand; and a table with two decanters and four pine-apples on it in the background."

Singer. A tall lady, "in a blue sarcenet pelisse and bonnet of the same, ornamented with large white feathers . . . commenced a plaintive duet."

Madame Somebody, " . . . where the white garments of Madame Somebody (we forget even her name now), who nobly devoted her life to the manufacture of fireworks, had so often been seen fluttering in the wind, as she called up a red, blue, or parti-coloured light to illumine her temple!"

> Females in spencers, watching the balloon ascent
> Gentleman, dinner in a pocket handkerchief, fainting with joy
> -watching a balloon ascension
> Green, son of Charles[H]; and his wife: up for the first time—"My eye!"
> Lord, a balloon ascent: tried to wave flags as if not nervous
> Man, in a boat: heard young Green exclaim "My eye!" from a balloon
> Mary, a sister concerned about a noble balloonist
> Orchestra: small party of dismal men in cocked hats
> C. H. Simpson[H]: famed Master of Ceremonies at Vauxhall Gardens

SB 22 February 19, 1835   EC **EC**

Early Coaches

Reminiscing: the grim preliminaries to a cold journey by stage-coach.

> *"Breaking a man alive upon the wheel, would be nothing to breaking his rest, his peace, his heart—everything but his fast—upon four . . . . "*

Clerks. "Some half-dozen people are 'booking' brown-paper parcels, which one of the clerks flings . . . with an air of recklessness which you, remembering the new carpet-bag you bought in the morning, feel considerably annoyed at . . . .

" . . . one . . . with his pen behind his ear, and his hands behind him, is standing in front of the fire, like a full-length portrait of Napoleon . . . .

" . . . the other with his hat half off his head, enters the passengers' names in the books with a coolness which is inexpressibly provoking; and the villain whistles—actually whistles—while a man asks him what the fare is outside, all the way to Holyhead!—in frosty weather, too!"

"They are clearly an isolated race, evidently possessing no sympathies or feelings in common with the rest of mankind."

Coachman. " . . . in a rough blue great-coat, of which the buttons behind are so far apart, that you can't see them both at the same time."

Outsides. " . . . pacing up and down the pavement to keep themselves warm; they consist of two **young men** with very long hair, to which the sleet has communicated the appearance of crystallised rats' tails; one thin **young woman** cold and peevish, one **old gentleman** ditto ditto, and something in a cloak and cap, intended to represent a **military officer**; every member of the party, with a large stiff shawl over his chin, looking exactly as if he were playing a set of Pan's pipes."

Porters, "looking like so many Atlases, keep rushing in and out, with large packages on their shoulders . . . . "

Servant. " . . . your shivering servant, who has been vainly endeavouring to wake you for the last quarter of an hour, at the imminent risk of breaking either his own knuckles or the panels of the door."

Tap-waiter. "The first stroke of six peals . . . just as you take the first sip . . . . You find yourself at the booking-office in two seconds, and the tap-waiter finds himself much comforted by your brandy-and-water in about the same period."

> **Bob**, a coach guard: "Five minutes behind time already!"
> Boys, shop: who can't wake their masters and cry with the cold
> **Harry**, an ostler: "Let 'em go! Give 'em their heads."
> *Ixion*, mythical figure who discovered a perpetual motion machine
> Milk-woman, trudging slowly; list around each foot
> Policemen, on a cold early morning: sprinkled with powdered glass

SB 23 September 26, 1834   MC **O**

Omnibuses

The omnibus, an 1829 innovation, had given rise to the "cad," a conductor typically aggressive, imaginative and unscrupulous, and passenger recrimination. Omnibus companies often competed for customers on the same routes.

Cad. "This young gentleman is a singular instance of self-devotion; his somewhat intemperate zeal on behalf of his employers is constantly getting him into trouble, and occasionally into the house of correction. He is no sooner emancipated, however, than he resumes the duties of his profession with unabated ardour. His principal distinction is his activity."

—*packing them in:* "The impression on the cad's mind evidently is, that [the omnibus] is amply sufficient for the accommodation of any number of persons that can be enticed into it. 'Any room?' cries a very hot **pedestrian**. 'Plenty o'room, sir,' replies the conductor, gradually opening the door, and not disclosing the real state of the case until the wretched man is on the steps. 'Where?' inquires the entrapped individual, with an attempt to back out again. 'Either side, sir,' rejoins the cad, shoving him in, and slamming the door. 'All right, **Bill**.' Retreat is impossible; the newcomer rolls about, till he falls down somewhere, and there he stops."

Driver. " . . . the driver of the opposition taunts our people with his having 'regularly done 'em out of that old swell,' and the voice of the 'old swell' is heard, vainly protesting against this unlawful detention."

Old gentleman. "A second omnibus now comes up, and stops immediately behind us. [He] elevates his cane in the air, and runs with all his might towards our omnibus; we watch his progress with great interest; the door is opened to receive him, he suddenly disappears—he has been spirited away by the opposition."

Passenger. "There is a little testy old man, with a powdered head, who always sits on the right-hand side of the door as you enter, with his hands folded on the top of his umbrella. He is extremely impatient, and sits there for the purpose of keeping a sharp eye on the **cad**, with whom he generally holds a running dialogue. He is very officious in helping people in and out, and always volunteers to give the cad a poke with his umbrella, when any one wants to alight. He usually recommends ladies to have six-pence ready, to prevent delay; and if anybody puts a window down, that he can reach, he immediately puts it up again."

Passenger, stout. " . . . in the white neckcloth, at the other end of the vehicle, looks very prophetic, and says that something must shortly be done with these fellows, or there's no saying where all this will end . . . ."

Bill, omnibus driver
Boy, on a stage coach with no perceptible neck, to be left till called for
Driver, of an omnibus; a dashing whip
Guard, on a stage coach
Paupers, propitiatory to the beadle in the court-room
Passenger, stage coach: a glass of warm rum-and-water at each change
Shabby-genteel passenger: something must be done about the cads

SB 24 December 1836   CC and BL; consolidated in 2d SB **LC**

The Last Cab-driver, and the First Omnibus Cad

Two memorable portraits: the intransigent, combative driver of a cabriolet painted red; and "Aggerawatin" **William Barker**, an omnibus conductor.

William Barker. " . . . touching his hat, [he] asked, as a matter of course, for 'a copper for the waterman.' Now, the **fare** was by no means a handsome man; and, waxing very indignant at the demand, he replied—'Money! What for? Coming up and looking at me, I suppose!'—'Vell, sir,' rejoined the waterman, with a smile of immovable complacency, *'that's* worth two-pence.'"

" . . . the flattering designation of 'Aggerawatin Bill' . . . a playful and expressive *sobriquet,* illustrative of Mr Barker's great talent in 'aggerawatin' and rendering wild such subjects of her Majesty as are conveyed from place to place, through the instrumentality of omnibuses."

—*early life:* " . . . little is known . . . . A want of application, a restlessness of purpose, a thirsting after porter, a love of all that is roving and cadger-like in nature, shared in common with many other great geniuses, appear to have been his leading characteristics. The busy hum of a parochial free-school, and the shady repose of a county gaol, were alike inefficacious in producing the slightest alteration in Mr Barker's disposition. His feverish attachment to change and variety nothing could repress; his native daring no punishment could subdue."

—*his love, and its consequence:* "If Mr Barker can be fairly said to have had any weakness in his earlier years, it was an amiable one—love; love in its most comprehensive form—a love of ladies, liquids, and pocket-handkerchiefs. It was no selfish feeling; it was not confined to his own possessions, which but too many men regard with exclusive complacency. No; it was a nobler love—a general principle. It extended itself with equal force to the property of other people.

"There is something very affecting in this. It is still more affecting to know, that such philanthropy is but imperfectly rewarded. Bow Street, Newgate, and Millbank, are a poor return for general benevolence, evincing itself in an irrepressible love for all created objects. Mr Barker felt it so. After a lengthened interview with the highest legal authorities, he quitted his ungrateful country, with the consent, and at the expense, of its Government; proceeded to a distant shore; and there employed himself, like another Cincinnatus, in clearing and cultivating the soil—a peaceful pursuit, in which a term of seven years glided almost imperceptibly away."

—*a new technology*: " . . . his active mind at once perceived how much might be done in the way of enticing the youthful and unwary, and shoving the old and helpless, into the wrong bus, and carrying them off, until, reduced to despair, they ransomed themselves by the payment of sixpence a head, or, to adopt his own figurative expression in all its native beauty, 'till they was rig'larly done over, and forked out the stumpy.'"

—*professional qualifications:* "He could tell at a glance where a passenger wanted to go to, and would shout the name of the place accordingly, without the slightest reference to the real destination of the vehicle. He knew exactly the kind of old lady that would be too much flurried by the process of pushing in and pulling out of the caravan, to discover where she had been put down, until too late; had an intuitive perception of what was passing in a passenger's mind when he inwardly resolved to 'pull that cad up to-morrow morning;' and never failed to make himself agreeable to female servants, whom he would place next the door, and talk to all the way."

—*humanity:* "Human judgment is never infallible, and it would occasionally happen that Mr Barker experimentalised with the timidity or forbearance of the wrong person, in which case a summons to a Police-office was, on more than one occasion, followed by a committal to prison."

Cab-driver. "He was a man of most simple and prepossessing appearance. He was a brown-whiskered, white-hatted, no-coated cabman; his nose was generally red, and his bright blue eye not unfrequently stood out in bold relief against a black border of artificial workmanship; his boots were of the Wellington form, pulled up to meet his corduroy knee-smalls, or at least to approach as near them as their dimensions would admit of; and his neck was usually garnished with a bright yellow handkerchief. In summer he carried in his mouth a flower; in winter, a straw—slight, but to a contemplative mind, certain indications of a love of nature, and a taste for botany."

—*omnipresence*: "You had hardly turned into the street, when you saw a trunk or two, lying on the ground: an uprooted post, a hat-box, a portmanteau, and a carpet-bag, strewed about in a very picturesque manner: a horse in a cab standing by, looking about him with great unconcern . . . 'Anybody hurt, do you know?'—'O'ny the fare, sir.'"

—*bellicose:* "The driver . . . was wont to set the feelings and opinions of society at complete defiance. Generally speaking, perhaps, he would as soon carry a fare safely to his destination, as he would upset him—sooner, perhaps, because in that case he not only got the money, but had the additional amusement of running a longer heat against some smart rival. But society made war upon him in the shape of penalties, and he must make war upon society . . . . So he bestowed a searching look upon the fare, as he put his hand in his waistcoat pocket, when he had gone half the mile, to get the money ready; and if he brought forth eightpence, out he went."

Complainant. "A tall, weazen-faced man, with an impediment in his speech, would be endeavouring to state a case of imposition against the red cab's **driver** . . . . "

Governor, of the House of Correction. "'[**Barker**] positively refused to work on the wheel; so, after many trials, I was compelled to order him into solitary confinement. He says he likes it very much though, and I am afraid he does, for he lies on his back on the floor, and sings comic songs all day!'"

[**Francis**] **Hobler**. " . . . every vein in [his] countenance was swollen with laughter, partly at the **Lord Mayor**'s facetiousness, but more at his own . . . . "

Landlord. "Mr **Barker** it *ought* to have been, who honestly indignant at being ignominiously ejected from a house of public entertainment, kicked the landlord in the knee, and thereby caused his death."

Lord Mayor. "The ubiquity of this red cab, and the influence it exercised over the risible muscles of justice itself, was perfectly astonishing . . . the whole court resounded with merriment. The Lord Mayor threw himself back in his chair, in a state of frantic delight at his own joke . . . . "

Omnibus driver. "An enterprising young cabman, of established reputation as a dashing whip—for he had compromised with the parents of three scrunched children, and just 'worked out' his fine, for knocking down an old lady—was the driver . . . . "

Former **passenger**. " . . . the loquacious little gentleman, making a mental calculation of the distance, and finding that he had already paid more than he ought, avowed his unalterable determination to 'pull up' the cabman in the morning . . . .

"There was a steadiness of purpose, and indignation of speech, about the little gentleman, as he took an angry pinch of snuff . . . which made a visible impression on the mind of the red-**cab-driver**."

Beadle, in Mansion-House court
Cincinnatus[H]: emperor for sixteen days, then back to the farm
Lucina, Roman goddess of light and patroness of childbirth
Proprietor, of an omnibus: knowing Barker's qualifications hired him

SB 25 March 7/April 11, 1835   EC; consolidated in 2d SB **P**

A Parliamentary Sketch

House of Commons entry halls on the night of an important debate; Members
(identified by MS) and the public in several variety; Bellamy's and its denizens.

> " . . . *we have made some few calls at the aforesaid house in our time* . . .
> *a great deal too often for our personal peace and comfort.* . . . "

"The Captain." " . . . the spare, squeaking old man . . . who, elevating a little cracked bantam sort of voice to its highest pitch, invokes damnation upon
his own eyes or somebody else's at the commencement of every sentence he
utters . . . a complete walking reservoir of spirits and water."

Head usher. " . . . that stout man with the hoarse voice, in the blue coat,
queer-crowned, broad-brimmed hat, white corduroy breeches, and great boots,
who has been talking incessantly for half an hour past . . . . That is the great
conservator of the peace of Westminster. You . . . remarked the grace with
which he saluted the noble Lord who passed just now, [and] the excessive dignity of his air, as he expostulates with the crowd."

Intruder. " . . . some unfortunate individual appears, with a very smirking
air, at the bottom of the long passage . . . down goes the unfortunate man five
stairs at a time, turning round at every stoppage, to come back again, and de-
nouncing bitter vengeance against the commander-in-chief, and all his supernumeraries."

Jane. " . . . the **Hebe** of Bellamy's . . . as great a character as **Nicholas**, in
her way. Her leading features are a thorough contempt for the great majority
of her visitors; her predominant quality, love of admiration, as you cannot fail
to observe, if you mark the glee with which she listens to something the **young
Member** near her mutters somewhat unintelligibly in her ear (for his speech is
rather thick from some cause or other), and how playfully she digs the handle of
a fork into the arm with which he detains her, by way of reply."

Members. "That smart-looking fellow in the black coat with velvet fac-
ings and cuffs, who wears his D'Orsay hat so rakishly, is '**Honest Tom**,' a
metropolitan representative* . . . . " [*Thomas Slingsbury Duncombe, Radical
M.P. for Finsbury]

"The quiet gentlemanly-looking man* in the blue surtout, grey trousers,
white neckerchief, and gloves, whose closely-buttoned coat displays his manly
figure and broad chest to great advantage, is a very well-known character. He
has fought a great many battles in his time, and conquered like the heroes of
old, with no other arms than those the gods gave him." [*John Gully, former
prizefighter, M.P. for Pontefract]

"The old hard-featured man* . . . is a really good specimen of a class of men
now nearly extinct. He is a **county Member**, and has been from time whereof
the memory of man is not to the contrary. Look at his loose, wide, brown coat,

with capacious pockets on each side; the knee-breeches and boots, the immensely long waistcoat, and silver watch-chain dangling below it, the wide-brimmed brown hat, and the white handkerchief tied in a great bow, with straggling ends sticking out beyond his shirt-frill. It is a costume one seldom sees nowadays, and when the few who wear it have died off, it will be quite extinct. He . . . thinks it quite impossible that a man can say anything worth hearing, unless he has sat in the House for fifteen years at least, without saying anything at all." [*George Byng, Liberal M.P. for Middlesex]

"That singularly awkward and **ungainly-looking man**, in the brownish-white hat, with the straggling black trousers which reach about half-way down the legs of his boots, who is leaning against the meat-screen, apparently deluding himself into the belief that he is thinking about something, is a splendid sample of a Member of the House of Commons concentrating in his own person the wisdom of a constituency . . . did you ever see a countenance so expressive of the most hopeless extreme of heavy dulness, or behold a form so strangely put together?"

"The small gentleman with the sharp nose . . . an ex-Alderman, and a sort of **amateur fireman**. He, and the celebrated fireman's dog, were observed to be remarkably active at the conflagration of the two Houses of Parliament—they both ran up and down, and in and out, getting under people's feet, and into everybody's way, fully impressed with the belief that they were doing a great deal of good, and barking tremendously. The dog went quietly back to his kennel with the engine, but the gentleman kept up such an incessant noise for some weeks after the occurrence, that he became a positive nuisance."

". . . [a] ferocious-looking gentleman,* with a complexion almost as sallow as his linen, and whose large black moustache would give him the appearance of a figure in a hairdresser's window, if his countenance possessed the thought which is communicated to those waxen caricatures of the human face divine. He is a **militia-officer**, and the most amusing person. Can anything be more exquisitely absurd than the burlesque grandeur of his air, as he strides up to the lobby, his eyes rolling like those of a Turk's head in a cheap Dutch clock?" [*Colonel Sibthorp, eccentric High Tory M.P. for Lincoln]

"Take one look around you and retire! The body of the House and the side galleries are full of Members; some, with their legs on the back of the opposite seat; some, with theirs stretched out to their utmost length on the floor; some going out, others coming in; all talking, laughing, lounging, coughing, oh-ing, questioning, or groaning; presenting a conglomeration of noise and confusion, to be met with in no other place in existence, not even excepting Smithfield on a market-day, or a cock-pit in its glory."

Nicholas. " . . . the steady honest-looking old fellow in black . . . is the butler of **Bellamy**'s, and has held the same place, dressed exactly in the same manner, and said precisely the same things, ever since the oldest of its present visitors can remember. An excellent servant Nicholas is—an unrivalled compounder of salad-dressing—an admirable preparer of soda-water and lemon—a special mixer of cold grog and punch—and, above all, an unequalled judge of cheese. If the old man have such a thing as vanity in his composition, this is certainly his pride; and if it be possible to imagine that anything in this world could disturb his impenetrable calmness, we should say it would be the doubting his judgment on this important point.

" . . . sleek, knowing-looking head and face—his prim white neckerchief, with the wooden tie into which it has been regularly folded for twenty years past,

merging by imperceptible degrees into a small-plaited shirt-frill—and his comfortable-looking form encased in a well-brushed suit of black . . . ."

Peer. "Mark the air with which he gloats over that Stilton, as he removed
the napkin which has been placed beneath his chin to catch the superfluous
gravy of the steak, and with what gusto he imbibes the porter which has been
fetched, expressly for him, in the pewter pot. Listen to the hoarse sound of that
voice, kept down as it is by layers of solids, and deep draughts of rich wine, and
tell us if you ever saw such a perfect picture of a regular *gourmand* . . . . "

Smith. "(. . . our new member) . . . . [he] turns round with an air of enchanting urbanity . . . seizes both the hands of his gratified constituent, and, after
greeting him with the most enthusiastic warmth, darts into the lobby with an
extraordinary display of ardour in the public cause, leaving an immense impression in his favour on the mind of his 'fellow-townsman.'"

Sir John Thomson. "Every now and then you hear earnest whispers of
'That's Sir John Thomson.' 'Which? him with the gilt order round his neck?' 'No,
no; that's one of the **messengers**—that other with the yellow gloves, is Sir
John Thomson.'"

> Baronet, Lord's-Day-Bill [Andrew Agnew]: proponent of sabbath restrictions
> Lord Castlereagh[H], former Foreign Secretary
> Collins, a constable on duty at the House of Commons
> Constable, special: on duty at the House of Commons
> Door-keeper, tall, stout and in black: "not an inch" of room
> Honest Tom, M.P.
> Thomas Babington Macaulay[H], sometime M.P.
> Man, timid, thin: in the crowd; "Will they divide tonight?"
> Member of Parliament, large; in a cloak with white lining
> -unimportant: speaking amidst a hum of voices
> -well-known character; has conquered by his own arms
> Reporter, correspondent of an Irish newspaper, in a rough great-coat
> Spencer Perceval[H], murdered Prime Minister
> Servants, liveried, at the House of Commons: form lines in the passage
> Richard Brinsley Sheridan[H], playwright and M.P.
> Lord Edward Stanley[H], three times Prime Minister
> Wilson, a constable at the House of Commons

SB 26 April 7, 1835   EC **PD**

Public Dinners

Those who raise money for charity at public dinners are gently spoofed. So are
the waiters, the stewards, the musicians, and even the orphan beneficiaries.

Driver, "[who] turns a deaf ear to your earnest entreaties . . . and persists
in carrying you to the very door of the Freemasons', round which a crowd of
people are assembled to witness the entrance of the indigent orphans' friends."

Lord Fitz Binkle. "The chairman rises, and after stating that he feels it
quite unnecessary to preface the toast he is about to propose, with any observations whatever, wanders into a maze of sentences, and flounders about in
the most extraordinary manner, presenting a lamentable spectacle of mysti-

fied humanity, until he arrives at the words, 'constitutional sovereign of these realms,' at which elderly **gentlemen** exclaim 'Bravo!' and hammer the table tremendously with their knife-handles.

George Cruikshanks

"'Under any circumstances, it would give him the greatest pride, it would give him the greatest pleasure—he might almost say, it would afford him satisfaction [cheers] to propose that toast. What must be his feelings, then, when he has the gratification of announcing, that he has received her Majesty's commands to apply to the Treasurer of her Majesty's Household, for her Majesty's annual donation of £25 in aid of the funds of this charity!'

"This announcement (which has been regularly made by every chairman, since the first foundation of the charity, forty-two years ago) calls forth the most vociferous applause . . . . " ¶

—*subscriber:* "'Lord Fitz Binkle, the chairman of the day, in addition to an annual donation of fifteen pounds—thirty guineas [prolonged knocking: several gentlemen knock the stems off their wine-glasses, in the vehemence of their approbation].'"

Guests. " . . . several gentlemen are gliding along the sides of the tables, looking into plate after plate with frantic eagerness, the expression of their countenances growing more and more dismal as they meet with everybody's card but their own."

Musicians. "The musicians are scraping and grating and screwing tremendously—playing no notes but notes of preparation . . . . "

Orphans. " . . . the **stewards** (looking more important than ever) leave the room, and presently return, heading a procession of indigent orphans, boys and girls, who walk round the room, curtseying, and bowing, and treading on each other's heels, and looking very much as if they would like a glass of wine apiece, to the high gratification of the company generally, and especially of the lady **patronesses** in the gallery."

Singers. "There is something peculiar in their air and manner, though you could hardly describe what it is; you cannot divest yourself of the idea that they have come for some other purpose than mere eating and drinking."

—**"Fitz."** " . . . a little man, with a long and rather inflamed face, and grey hair brushed bolt upright in front; he wears a wisp of black silk round his neck, without any stiffener, as an apology for a neckerchief, and is addressed by his companions by the familiar appellation of 'Fitz,' or some such monosyllable."

—Large-headed **man**. " . . . with black hair and bushy whiskers . . . . "

—Stout **man**. " . . . in a white neckerchief and buff waistcoat, with shining dark hair, cut very short in front, and a great round healthy-looking face, on which he studiously preserves a half sentimental simper."

—Round-faced **person**. " . . . in a dress-stock and blue under-waistcoat."

"The singers, whom you discover to be no other than the very party that excited your curiosity at first, after 'pitching' their voices immediately begin *too-too*-ing most dismally, on which the regular old stagers burst into occasional cries of—'Sh—sh—**waiters**!—Silence, waiters . . . and other exorcisms, delivered in a tone of indignant remonstrance. The grace is soon concluded . . . . "

Stewards. " . . . out burst the orchestra, up rise the visitors, in march fourteen stewards, each with a long wand in his hand, like the evil genius in a pantomime . . . . "

Toast-master. "'Pray, silence, gentlemen, if you please, for *Non nobis!*' shouts the toast-master with stentorian lungs—a toast-master's shirt-front, waistcoat, and neckerchief, by-the-bye, always exhibit three distinct shades of cloudy-white . . . . "

Waiters. "Tureens of soup are emptied with awful rapidity—waiters take plates of turbot away, to get lobster-sauce, and bring back plates of lobster-sauce without turbot . . . . "

> Lady Fitz Binkle: she subscribed an extra twenty pounds!
> Gentlemen, elderly, stout, red-faced; running with unbecoming speed
> Hickson, Smith, Tompkins and Wilson, subscribers
> Men, priggish; kissing hands to the lady patronesses present
> Music director, in blue coat and bright buttons: calls out "Band!"
> Nixon family, prominent subscribers: Charles, James, Thomas, father
> Secretary, reading the list of subscriptions at a charity dinner
> Senior officer, of a charity; toasting the secretary and Mr Walker
> Walker, auditor of the charity

The First of May
(first called 'A Little Talk about Spring and the Sweeps')

Traditional dancing in the spring became the special preserve of London's chimney-sweeps: a parade and a dinner. The state of the profession.

George Cruikshank

Chimney-sweep. "Stories were related of a young boy who, having been stolen from his parents in his infancy, and devoted to the occupation of chimney-sweeping, was sent, in the course of his professional career, to sweep the chimney of his mother's bedroom; and how, being hot and tired when he came out of the chimney, he got into the bed he had so often slept in as an infant, and was discovered and recognised therein by his mother, who once every year of her life, thereafter, requested the pleasure of the company of every London sweep, at half-past one o'clock, to roast beef, plum-pudding, porter, and six-pence."

Master sweep. "We remember, in our young days, a little sweep about our own age, with curly hair and white teeth, whom we devoutly and sincerely believed to be the lost son and heir of some illustrious personage—an impression which was resolved into an unchangeable conviction on our infant mind, by the subject of our speculations informing us, one day, in reply to our question . . . 'that he believed he'd been born in the vurkis, but he'd never know'd his father' . . . at the present moment . . . [he] is settled down as a master-sweep . . . his distinguishing characteristics being a decided antipathy to wash-ing himself, and the possession of a pair of legs very inadequate to the support of his unwieldy and corpulent body."

Master sweeps, "influenced by a restless spirit of innovation, actually in-terposed their authority, in opposition to the dancing, and substituted a dinner—an anniversary dinner at White Conduit House—where clean faces appeared in lieu of black ones smeared with rose pink; and knee cords and tops superseded nankeen drawers and rosetted shoes."

Paraders. " . . . two **clowns** who walked upon their hands in the mud, to the immeasurable delight of all the spectators . . . . "

—" . . . and last, though not least, the '**green**,' ["Jack-in-the-green"] animated by no less a personage than our identical friend in the tarpaulin suit . . . rolled about, pitching first on one side and then on the other . . . . "

—'**Her ladyship** was attired in pink crape over bed-furniture, with a low body and short sleeves. The symmetry of her ankles was partially concealed by a very perceptible pair of frilled trousers; and the inconvenience which might have resulted from the circumstance of her white satin shoes being a few sizes too large, was obviated by their being firmly attached to her legs with strong tape sandals.

"Her head was ornamented with a profusion of artificial flowers; and in her hand she bore a large brass ladle, wherein to receive what she figuratively de-nominated 'the tin.'"

—" . . . '**my lord**,' habited in a blue coat and bright buttons, with gilt paper tacked over the seams, yellow knee-breeches, pink cotton stockings, and shoes; a cocked hat, ornamented with shreds of various-coloured paper, on his head, a *bouquet* the size of a prize cauliflower in his button-hole, a long Belcher hand-kerchief . . . and a thin cane . . . . "

Sluffen. " . . . the celebrated Mr Sluffen . . . ' . . . he 'ad been a chummy—he begged the cheerman's parding for usin' such a wulgar hexpression—more nor thirty year—he might say he'd been born in a chimbley—and he know'd uncom-mon vell as 'sheenery vos vus nor o' no use; and as to kerhewelty to the boys, everybody in the chimbley line know'd as vell as he did, that they liked the climbin' better nor nuffin as vos.'"

> Musician, with a drum
> -with a flageolet
> Parader, in costume: a gentleman in a suit of tarpaulin
> *Paul Pry,* compared with Caleb Williams
> Alderman Waithman[H]: Member of Parliament; Lord Mayor
> Woman, in a large shawl, with a box under her arm for money
> *Caleb Williams,* compared with Paul Pry
> Young gentleman, in girl's clothes and a widow's cap
> Frederick, Duke of York: second son of George III

SB 28 December 15, 1834   MC **BS**

Brokers' and Marine-store Shops

Detailed observations of the contents and atmosphere of these shops, handling second-hand items in the theatrical regions of Drury Lane and Covent Garden, in the Ratcliff Highway slum, and in the "Rules"—a district near King's Bench Prison in which certain debtors could live (but not leave) out of prison.

Debtor. "Light articles of clothing, first of the ruined man, then of his wife, at last of their children, even of the youngest, have been parted with, piece-meal."

Errand-boys, in a theatrical neighbourhood. "The errand-boys and **chand-ler**'s-shop-keepers' **sons** are all stage-struck: they 'gets up' plays in back kitchens hired for the purpose . . . . "

Pot-boy, in Drury Lane. "There is not a potboy in the vicinity who is not, to a greater or less extent, a dramatic character."

Sailor. "A sailor generally pawns or sells all he has before he has been long ashore, and if he does not, some favoured companion kindly saves him the trouble."

Wives. " . . . a strange animal . . . with a mass of worsted-work in his mouth, which conjecture has likened to a basket of flowers . . . is a tempting article to young wives in the humbler ranks of life, who have a first-floor front to furnish . . . . "

Young ladies. "[T]here are large bunches of cotton pocket-handkerchiefs, in colour and pattern unlike any one ever saw before, with the exception of those on the backs of the three young ladies without bonnets who passed just now."

SB 29 February 7, 1835   EC **GS**

Gin-shops

Sudden manias in decor, advertising and marketing among linen-drapers, chemists, and publicans; the bar of a Drury Lane gin-shop; an Irish dispute.

"Gin-drinking is a great vice in England, but wretchedness and dirt are a greater . . . . "

Barmaids. " . . . two showily-dressed damsels with large necklaces, dis-pensing the spirits and 'compounds.'"

Female. " . . . in the faded feathers who has just entered . . . after stating explicitly, to prevent any subsequent misunderstanding, that 'this gentleman pays,' calls for 'a glass of port wine and a bit of sugar.'"

Irish labourers. ". . . who have been alternately shaking hands with, and threatening the life of each other, for the last hour, become furious in their dis-putes, and finding it impossible to silence one **man**, who is particularly anxious to adjust the difference, they resort to the expedient of knocking him down and jumping on him afterwards . . . a scene of riot and confusion ensues; half the Irishmen get shut out, and the other half get shut in; the **potboy** is knocked among the tubs in no time . . . the **police** come in; the rest is a confused mixture of arms, legs, staves, torn coats, shouting, and struggling. Some of the party are borne off to the station-house, and the remainder slink home to beat their wives for complaining, and kick the children for daring to be hungry."

Proprietor. " . . . a stout coarse fellow in a fur cap, put on very much on one side to give him a knowing air, and to display his sandy whiskers to the best advantage."

Washerwomen. "The two old washerwomen, who are seated on the little bench to the left of the bar, are rather overcome by the headdresses and haughty demeanour of the young ladies who officiate."

Young fellow, "in a brown coat and bright buttons, who, ushering in his two companions, and walking up to the bar in as careless a manner as if he had been used to green and gold ornaments all his life, winks at one of the young ladies with singular coolness, and calls for a 'kervorten and a three-out-glass,' just as if the place were his own."

> Old men, who came in "just to have a drain" have become drunk
> Stragglers, cold and wretched; last stage of emaciation and disease
> Women, elderly, fat and comfortable: a glass of "rum-srub" each

SB 30 June 30, 1835   EC **PS**

The Pawnbroker's Shop

Classes of pawnbroker's shops: their contents, their custom and the degradation they witness.

> *"Of the numerous receptacles for misery and distress with which the streets of London unhappily abound, there are, perhaps, none which present such striking scenes as the pawnbrokers' shops . . . . "*

Employee, "whose allusions to 'that last bottle of soda-water last night,' and 'how regularly round my hat he felt himself when the young 'ooman gave 'em in charge,' would appear to refer to the consequences of some stolen joviality of the preceding evening."

Henry. " . . . the jewelled shopman . . . behind the counter, with the curly black hair, diamond ring, and double silver watch-guard . . . . "

Jinkins. " . . . an unshaven, dirty, sottish-looking fellow, whose tarnished paper-cap, stuck negligently over one eye, communicates an additionally repulsive expression to his very uninviting countenance. He was enjoying a little relaxation from his sedentary pursuits a quarter of an hour ago, in kicking his wife up the court."

Jinkins child. " . . . knocking the little scanty blue bonnet of the unfortunate child over its still more scanty and faded-looking face."

Mrs Jinkins. " . . . a wretched worn-out woman, apparently in the last stage of consumption, whose face bears evident marks of recent ill-usage, and whose strength seems hardly equal to the burden—light enough, God knows!— of the thin, sickly **child** she carries in her arms . . . . "

"'He's got a wife, ma'am, as takes in mangling, and is as 'dustrious and hard-working a young 'ooman as can be . . . and we hears him a beaten' on her sometimes when he comes home drunk, the whole night through . . . and she, poor creater, won't swear the peace agin him, nor do nothin', because she likes the wretch arter all—worse luck!'"

Mrs Mackin. "'What do you strike the boy for, you brute?' exclaims a slip-shod woman, with two flat irons in a little basket. 'Do you think he's your wife, you willin? . . . I wish I had the cutting of you up, you wagabond! (loud.) Oh! you precious wagabond! (rather louder.) Where's your wife, you willin? (louder still; women of this class are always sympathetic and work themselves into a tremendous passion on the shortest notice.) Your poor dear wife as you uses worser nor a dog—strike a woman—you a man! (very shrill;) I wish I had you—I'd murder you, I would, if I died for it!'"

Pawnbroker, "in a gay dressing-gown . . . ."

Prostitute. "In the next box is a young female, whose attire, miserably poor but extremely gaudy, wretchedly cold but extravagantly fine, too plainly bespeaks her station. The rich satin gown with its faded trimmings, the worn-out thin shoes, and pink silk stockings, the summer bonnet in winter, and the sunken face, where a daub of rouge only serves as an index to the ravages of squandered health never to be regained, and lost happiness never to be restored, and where the practised smile is a wretched mockery of the misery of the heart, cannot be mistaken."

Prostitute. " . . . the lowest of the low; dirty, unbonneted, flaunting, and slovenly . . . [a] half-intoxicated leer . . . [she] has but two more stages—the hospital and the grave."

Urchin. " . . . a ragged urchin, who, being unable to bring his face on a level with the counter by any other process, has employed himself in climbing up, and then hooking himself on with his elbows—an uneasy perch, from which he has fallen at intervals, generally alighting on the toes of the person in his immediate vicinity."

Young girl. " . . . a young delicate girl of about twenty, and an elderly female, evidently her **mother** . . . the articles they have brought to raise a present supply upon . . . are a small gold chain and a 'Forget-me-not' ring: the girl's property, for they are both too small for the mother . . . want has hardened the mother, and her example has hardened the girl, and the prospect of receiving money . . . appears to have obliterated the consciousness of self-humiliation, which the idea of their present situation would once have aroused."

James Ferguson[H]: astronomer
Old woman, pawnshop customer, thinking herself safe fomenting argument
Mrs Tatham, sallow-looking pawnshop customer with a bundle

SB 31 October 23, 1834   MC **CC**

Criminal Courts
(first called 'The Old Bailey')

Reminiscence and observation: Newgate Prison; trials in the Old and New Courts of the Old Bailey; a prefiguring of the **Artful Dodger**.

" . . . *every trial seems a mere matter of business. There is a great deal of form, but no compassion; considerable interest, but no sympathy.*"

Beadle. "Here a stout beadle runs out, and vociferates for the [**pickpocket**'s] witnesses at the very top of his voice; for you hear his cry grow fainter and fainter as he descends the steps into the court-yard below. After an absence of five minutes, he returns, very warm and hoarse, and informs the Court of what it knew perfectly well before—namely, that there are no such witnesses in attendance."

Boy, "of about fourteen or fifteen . . . . He had formed dissolute connexions; idleness had led to crime . . . he descended the steps with a dogged look, shaking his head with an air of bravado and obstinate determination . . . . The woman put her hand upon his shoulder in an agony of entreaty, and the boy sullenly raised his head as if in refusal . . . . Perhaps the wretchedness of his **mother** made some impression on the boy's heart; perhaps some undefined recollection of the time when he was a happy child, and she his only friend and best companion, crowded on him—he burst into tears; and covering his face with one hand, and hurriedly placing the other in his mother's, walked away with her."

Hackney-coachmen. "We were never tired of wondering how the hackney-coachmen on the opposite stand could cut jokes in the presence of such horrors, and drink pots of half-and-half so near the last drop."

Mother, "of decent appearance, though evidently poor . . . . The woman was crying bitterly; she carried a small bundle in her hand . . . . [Her **boy**] had been long in prison, and, after receiving some trifling additional punishment, had been ordered to be discharged that morning. It was first offence, and his poor old mother, still hoping to reclaim him, had been waiting at the gate to implore him to return home."

Pickpocket. "A boy of thirteen is tried . . . . He is called upon for his defence, and contents himself with a little declamation about the jurymen and his country—asserts that the police force generally have entered into a conspiracy 'again' him. However probable this statement may be, it fails to convince the Court . . . . 'S'elp me, gen'lm'n, I never vos in trouble afore—indeed, my Lord, I never vos. It's all a howen to my having a twin brother, vich has wrongfully got into trouble, and vich is so exactly like me, that no vun ever knows the difference atween us.'

—sentenced: "Finding it impossible to excite compassion, he gives vent to his feelings in an imprecation bearing reference to the eyes of 'old big vig!' and as he declines to take the trouble of walking from the dock, is forthwith carried out, congratulating himself on having succeeded in giving everybody as much trouble as possible."

Prisoner. "Mark how restlessly he has been engaged . . . in forming all sorts of fantastic figures with the herbs which are strewed upon the ledge before him; observe the ashy paleness of his face when a particular witness appears, and how he changes his position and wipes his clammy forehead and feverish hands, when the case for the prosecution is closed, as if it were a relief to him to feel that the jury knew the worst."

Turnkeys. " . . . an ill-looking fellow in a broad-brimmed hat, Belcher handkerchief and top-boots: with a brown coat, something between a greatcoat and a 'sporting' jacket, on his back, and an immense key in his left hand . . . and two or three more turnkeys, who look like multiplications of the first one, seated round a fire . . . . "

Barristers, who are quite dignified enough in their own opinion
Female, at Old Bailey: a shriek at the verdict of Guilty
Foreman, of a jury in the Old Court at Old Bailey: "Guilty"
Governor, of the gaol reporting to the judge on a pickpocket
Jack Ketch[H], the quintessential hangman
Judges, with whose great dignity everybody is acquainted
Lord Mayor, cool and splendid; with a *bouquet* in front of him
Sheriffs, at Old Bailey; almost as dignified as the Lord Mayor

A Visit to Newgate

An extended essay: physical layout, the staff, the cells and their inhabitants; those marked for death. Here is the reality of **Fagin**'s boys.

> " . . . *men in full health and vigour, in the flower of youth or the prime of life, with all their faculties and perceptions as acute and perfect as your own; but dying, nevertheless . . . .*"

John Bishop. " . . . a style of head and set of features, which might have afforded sufficient moral grounds for his instant execution at any time, even had there been no other evidence against him."

Daughter. "The girl was thinly clad, and shaking with the cold. Some ordinary word of recognition passed between her and her **mother** when she appeared at the grating, but neither hope, condolence, regret, nor affection was expressed. . . . The mother whispered her instructions, and the girl received them with her pinched-up half-starved features twisted into an expression of careful cunning. "

Mother, of a prisoner. " . . . a yellow, haggard, decrepit old woman, in a tattered gown that had once been black, and the remains of an old straw bonnet, with faded ribbon of the same hue . . . . It is impossible to imagine a more poverty-stricken object, or a creature so borne down in soul and body, by excess of misery and destitution, as the old woman . . . [she] was talking in that low, stifled tone of voice which tells so forcibly of mental anguish; and every now and then burst into an irrepressible sharp, abrupt cry of grief, the most distressing sound that ears can hear."

Mother, a prisoner. "A squalid-looking woman in a slovenly, thick-bordered cap, with her arms muffled in a large red shawl, the fringed ends of which straggled nearly to the bottom of a dirty white apron . . . . "

Pickpockets, boy prisoners. " . . . some with shoes, some without; some in pinafores without jackets, others in jackets without pinafores, and one in scarce anything at all. The whole number, without an exception we believe, had been committed for trial on charges of pocket-picking; and fourteen such terrible little faces we never beheld.—There was not one redeeming feature among them—not a glance of honesty—not a wink expressive of anything but the gallows and the hulks, in the whole collection. As to anything like shame or contrition, that was entirely out of the question."

Men **prisoners**. "Huddled together on two opposite forms, by the fireside, sit twenty men perhaps; here, a boy in livery; there, a man in a rough greatcoat and top-boots; farther on, a desperate-looking fellow in his shirt-sleeves, with an old Scotch cap upon his shaggy head; near him again, a tall ruffian, in a smock-frock: next to him, a miserable being of distressed appearance, with his head resting on his hand;—all alike in one respect, all idle and listless. When they do leave the fire, sauntering moodily about, lounging in the window, or leaning against the wall, vacantly swinging their bodies to and fro."

Prisoners, sentenced to death. " . . . men of all ages and appearances, from a hardened **old offender** with a swarthy face and grizzly beard of three days' growth, to a **handsome boy**, not fourteen years old, and of singularly youthful appearance even for that age, who had been condemned for burglary. There was nothing remarkable in the appearance of these prisoners. One or two decently-dressed **men** were brooding with a dejected air over the fire; several little groups of two or three had been engaged in conversation . . . and the remainder were crowded round a **young man** seated at a table, who appeared to be engaged in teaching the younger ones to write . . . we question whether there was a man among them . . . who did not know that although he had undergone the [sentencing] ceremony, it never was intended that his life should be sacrificed."

—*particular cases:* "The man . . . entertaining some hopes of escape,* was lounging at the greatest distance he could place between himself and his companions, in the window nearest to the door. He was probably aware of our approach, and had assumed an air of courageous indifference . . . . " [*MS: Robert Swan, a guardsman convicted of robbery with menaces: reprieved]

"One* . . . imperfectly seen in the dim light, had his back towards us, and was stooping over the fire, with his right arm on the mantelpiece, and his head sunk upon it." [*MS: John Smith, convicted of a homosexual offence; no reprieve for such as he—hanged]

"The other* was leaning on the sill of the farthest window. The light fell full upon him, and communicated to his pale, haggard face, and disordered hair, an appearance which, at that distance, was ghastly. His cheek rested upon his hand; and, with his face a little raised, and his eyes wildly staring before him, he seemed to be unconsciously intent on counting the chinks in the opposite wall." [*MS: John Pratt, convicted of a homosexual offence; hanged]

Prisoner, a young girl. " . . . about two-and-twenty . . . . The girl was a good-looking robust female, with a profusion of hair streaming about in the wind—for she had no bonnet on—and a man's silk pocket-handkerchief loosely thrown over a most ample pair of shoulders . . . . Hardened beyond all hope of redemption, she listened doggedly to her mother's entreaties, whatever they were: and, beyond inquiring after '**Jem**,' and eagerly catching at the few halfpence her miserable parent had brought her, took no more apparent interest in the conversation than the most unconcerned spectators."

Women **prisoners**. "The women rose hastily, on our entrance, and retired in a hurried manner to either side of the fireplace. They were all cleanly—many of them decently—attired, and there was nothing peculiar, either in their appearance or demeanour. One or two resumed the needlework which they had probably laid aside at the commencement of their meal; others gazed at the visitors with listless curiosity; and a few retired behind their companions to the very end of the room, as if desirous to avoid even the casual observation of the strangers."

Turnkey. " . . . a respectable-looking man of about two or three and fifty, in a broad-brimmed hat, and full suit of black, who, but for his keys, would have looked quite as much like a clergyman as a turnkey. We were disappointed; he had not even top boots on."

> John Bishop[H], body-snatcher
> Clerks, at Old Bailey
> Thomas Head[H] (alias Williams), notorious murderer
> Prisoners, Irish women, at Newgate; indifferent to visitors
> Schoolmaster, teaching prisoners in Newgate
> Servant, at the Governor's house at Newgate Prison
> Jack Sheppard[H], the only twice-escaped prisoner at Newgate
> Turnkey, at the gate to the condemned yard
> Dick Turpin[H], highwayman
> Wardsmen and wardswomen, at Newgate Prison; prisoners chosen for good conduct

CHARACTERS IN 'CHARACTERS'

SB 33 April 23, 1835   EC **TP**

Thoughts About People

Portraits of two men alone in London: **Mr Smith**, a timid bachelor of humdrum routine; and a testy Old Boy, self-indulgent and solitary by choice. In contrast, innocently pretentious apprentices doing no harm.

Apprentices. " . . . harmless efforts at the grand and magnificent . . . . There were four of them, all arm-in-arm, with white kid gloves like so many bridegrooms, light trousers of unprecedented patterns, and coats for which the English language has yet no name—a kind of cross between a great-coat and a surtout, with the collar of the one, the skirts of the other, and pockets peculiar to themselves.

"Each of the gentlemen carried a thick stick, with a large tassel at the top, which he occasionally twirled gracefully round; and the whole four, by way of looking easy and unconcerned, were walking with a paralytic swagger irresistibly ludicrous. One of the party had a watch about the size and shape of a reasonable Ribstone [*sic*.] pippin, jammed into his waistcoat-pocket, which he carefully compared with the clocks at St Clement's and the New Church, the illuminated clock at Exeter 'Change, the clock of St Martin's Church, and the clock of the Horse Guards."

Old Boy, a type. " . . . with white heads and red faces, addicted to port wine and Hessian boots, who from some cause, real or imaginary—generally the former, the excellent reason being that they are rich, and their relations poor— grow suspicious of everybody, and do the misanthropical in chambers, taking great delight in thinking themselves unhappy, and making everybody they come near, miserable."

—*recreation:* " . . . you will know them at coffee-houses by their discontented exclamations and the luxury of their dinners; at theatres, by their always sitting in the same place and looking with a jaundiced eye on all the young people near them; at church, by the pomposity with which they enter, and the loud tone in which they repeat the responses; at parties, by their getting cross at whist and hating music."

—*at home:* " . . . [he] will have his chambers splendidly furnished, and collect books, plate, and pictures about him in profusion; not so much for his own gratification, as to be superior to those who have the desire, but not the means, to compete with him."

—*family:* "Sometimes he will be appealed to by a **poor relation**—a married nephew perhaps—for some little assistance: and then he will declaim with honest indignation on the improvidence of young married people, the worthlessness of a wife, the insolence of having a family, the atrocity of getting into debt with a hundred and twenty-five pounds a year, and other unpardonable crimes; winding up his exhortations with a complacent review of his own conduct, and a delicate allusion to parochial relief."

—*departure:*   "He dies, some day after dinner, of apoplexy, having bequeathed his property to a Public Society, and the Institution erects a tablet to his memory, expressive of their admiration of his Christian conduct in this world, and their comfortable conviction of his happiness in the next."

George Cruikshank.

Smith. "He was a tall, thin, pale person, in a black coat, scanty grey trousers, little pinched-up gaiters, and brown beaver gloves. He had an umbrella in his hand—not for use, for the day was fine—but, evidently, because he always carried one to the office in the morning. He walked up and down before the little patch of grass on which the chairs are placed for hire, not as if he were doing it for pleasure or recreation, but as if it were a matter of compulsion, just as he would walk to the office every morning from the back settlements of Islington.

" . . . [he] was walking here for exercise and amusement—perhaps for the first time in his life. We were inclined to think he had never had a holiday before, and that he did not know what to do with himself. Children were playing on the grass; groups of people were loitering about, chatting and laughing; but the man walked steadily up and down, unheeding and unheeded, his spare pale face looking as if it were incapable of bearing the expression of curiosity or interest." ¶

—*employer:* "Sometimes, there is a letter or two to take up to his employer's, in Russell Square; and then, the wealthy **man of business**, hearing his voice, calls out from the dining-parlour—'Come in, Mr Smith:' and Mr Smith, putting his hat at the feet of one of the hall chairs, walks timidly in, and being condescendingly desired to sit down, carefully tucks his legs under his chair, and sits at a considerable distance from the table while he drinks the glass of sherry which is poured out for him by the **eldest boy**, and after drinking which, he backs and slides out of the room, in a state of nervous agitation from which he does not perfectly recover, until he finds himself once more in the Islington Road."

—*in sum:* "Poor, harmless creatures such men are; contented but not happy; broken-spirited and humbled, they may feel no pain, but they never know pleasure."

> Boy, son of Mr Smith's landlady; does addition problems
> Cabmen, cads and hackney-coachmen: admired for impudence and self-possession
> Waiter, recites the bill of fare in a rather confidential manner

SB 34 December 27, 1835   BL **CD**

A Christmas Dinner

A multi-generation family dinner at **Uncle George**'s. The genial influence of the Christmas spirit melts grudges and rekindles loving relationships.

Cousin. " . . . a young scape-grace . . . in some disgrace with the old people, for certain heinous sins of omission and commission—neglecting to call, and persisting in drinking Burton Ale—astonishes everybody into convulsions of laughter by volunteering the most extraordinary comic songs that ever were heard."

Uncle George. " . . . **grandpapa** getting old, and **grandmamma** getting old too, and rather infirm, they have given up house-keeping, and domesticated themselves with uncle George . . . [who] tells stories, and carves poultry, and takes wine, and jokes with the children at the side-table, and winks at the **cousins** that are making love, or being made love to, and exhilarates everybody with his good humour and hospitality . . . . "

Grandmamma. " . . . sends in most of the good things . . . very secret and mysterious for two or three days beforehand, but not sufficiently so to prevent rumours getting afloat that she has purchased a beautiful new cap with pink ribbons for each of the servants, together with sundry books, and pen-knives, and pencil-cases, for the younger branches; to say nothing of divers secret additions to the order originally given by **aunt George** at the pastry-cook's, such as another dozen of mince-pies for the dinner, and a large plum-cake for the children." *See also* **Aunt Margaret**.

Grandpapa. "[He] always *will* toddle down all the way to Newgate Market, to buy the turkey, which he engages a **porter** to bring home behind him in triumph, always insisting on the man's being rewarded with a glass of spirits, over and above his hire, to drink 'a merry Christmas and a happy new year' to **aunt George**."

Aunt Margaret. " . . . **grandmamma** draws herself up, rather stiff and stately; for Margaret married a poor man without her consent, and poverty not being a sufficiently weighty punishment for her offence, has been discarded by her friends, and debarred the society of her dearest relatives . . . . The air of conscious rectitude, and cold forgiveness, which the old lady has assumed, sits ill upon her; and when the poor girl is led in by her sister, pale in looks and broken in hope—not from poverty, for that she could bear, but from the consciousness of undeserved neglect, and unmerited unkindness—it is easy to see how much of it is assumed."

> Baby, ushered upstairs by the Nurse
> Cousins, flirting with each other
> **Aunt Jane**, married to Uncle Robert
> Husband of Aunt Margaret, poor but nice; attentive to grandmamma
> Porter, who brings back the turkey
> **Uncle Robert**: ushered upstairs with Aunt Jane and the baby
> Servant, stout: staggers in with a gigantic pudding, holly on top

SB 35 January 3, 1836   BL **NY**

The New Year

Quadrilles at the **Dobbles**': junior clerk **Tupple** is the star guest orator.

Dobble. "The master of the house with the green blinds is in a public office; we know the fact by the cut of his coat, the tie of his neckcloth, and the self-satisfaction of his gait . . . . "

—*toasted:* "They have seen him to-night in the peaceful bosom of his family; they should see him in the morning, in the trying duties of his office. Calm in the perusal of the morning papers, uncompromising in the signature of his name, dignified in his replies to the inquiries of stranger applicants, deferential in his behaviour to his superiors, majestic in his deportment to the messengers. (Cheers.)"

Dobble girls. " . . . we just now saw one of the young ladies 'doing' another of the young ladies' hair, near one of the bedroom windows, in an unusual style of splendour, which nothing else but a quadrille party could possibly justify."

Master Dobble. "Here Mr Dobble, junior, who has been previously distending his mouth to a considerable width, by thrusting a particularly fine orange into that feature, suspends operations, and assumes a proper appearance of intense melancholy."

Guest, "in a pink under-waistcoat, sitting towards the bottom of the table, is observed to grow very restless and fidgety, and to evince strong indications of some latent desire to give vent to his feelings in a speech . . ."

Musicians. " . . . exhibit unequivocal symptoms of having drunk the new year in, while the company were out . . . . "

Tupple. " . . . a tidy sort of young man, with a tendency to cold and corns, who comes in a pair of boots with black cloth fronts, and brings his shoes in his coat-pocket, which shoes he is at this very moment putting on in the hall."

—*introduced:* "Tupple rubs his hands very hard, and smiles as if it were all capital fun, and keeps constantly bowing and turning himself round, till the whole family have been introduced, when he glides into a chair at the corner of the sofa, and opens a miscellaneous conversation with the young ladies upon the weather, and the theatres, and the old year, and the last new murder, and the balloon, and the ladies' sleeves, and the festivities of the season, and a great many other topics of small talk."

—*in his glory:* "Charming person Mr Tupple—perfect ladies' man—such a delightful companion, too! Laugh!—nobody ever understood papa's jokes half so well as Mr Tupple, who laughs himself into convulsions at every fresh burst of facetiousness. Most delightful partner! talks through the whole set! and although he docs seem at first rather gay and frivolous, so romantic and with so *much* feeling! Quite a love . . . . Ma says he shall be asked to every future din-ner-party, if it's only to talk to people between the courses, and distract their attention when there's any unexpected delay in the kitchen."

> **Julia Dobble**, the eldest daughter
> **Mrs Dobble**: a courteous salute for the visitor
> Footman, in blue coat: a messenger from the office in disguise
> Men, taking up the front drawing-room carpet for quadrilles
> Pastry-cook's men, with green boxes on their heads

SB 36 October 4, 1835   BL **EE**

Miss Evans and the Eagle

Jemima Evans, keeping company with **Samuel Wilkins**, double dates for an evening of shrub, sherry and vaudeville. The ladies flirt, but not with their es-corts. Remonstrances and blows; the admiring strangers decamp.

Jemima Evans. " . . . a Being for whom, from that time forth, he felt fate had destined him. He came, and conquered—proposed, and was accepted—loved, and was beloved. Mr **Wilkins** 'kept company' with Jemima Evans."

—*dressed for a date:* " . . . in a white muslin gown carefully hooked and eyed, a little red shawl, plentifully pinned, a white straw bonnet trimmed with red ribbons, a small necklace, a large pair of bracelets, Denmark satin shoes, and open-worked stockings; white cotton gloves on her fingers, and a cambric pocket-handkerchief, carefully folded up, in her hand—all quite genteel and ladylike."

Friend. " . . . who should Miss **J'mima Ivins** stumble upon, by the most fortunate accident in the world, but a young lady as she knew, with her **young man**!"

Waiters. " . . . rushing to and fro with glasses of negus, and . . . brandy-and-water, and bottles of ale, and bottles of stout; and ginger-beer was going off in one place, and practical jokes were going on in another . . . . "

Whiskers and **Waistcoat**. " . . . a strange gentleman with large whiskers *would* stare at Miss **J'mima Ivins**, and another gentleman in a plaid waistcoat *would* wink at Miss J'mima Ivins's **friend** . . . waistcoat and whiskers . . . made divers remarks complimentary to the ankles of Miss J'mima Ivins and friend, in an audible tone."

Samuel Wilkins. " . . . a journeyman carpenter of small dimensions, decidedly below the middle size—bordering, perhaps, upon the dwarfish. His face was round and shining, and his hair carefully twisted into the outer corner of each eye, till it formed a variety of that description of semi-curls, usually known as 'aggerawators.' His earnings were all-sufficient for his wants . . . his manner undeniable—his sabbath waistcoats dazzling . . . many women have been captivated by far less substantial qualifications."

—*altercation:* "'What do you mean by that, scoundrel!' exclaimed Mr Samuel Wilkins, grasping the gilt-knobbed dress-cane firmly in his right hand . . . . 'Take that,' exclaimed Mr Samuel Wilkins . . . 'Give it him,' said the waistcoat. 'Horficer!' screamed the ladies. Miss **J'mima Ivins**'s beau, and the friend's **young man**, lay gasping on the gravel, and the waistcoat and whiskers were seen no more."

Young man. " . . . exhibited symptoms of boiling over, and began to mutter about 'people's imperence,' and 'swells out o' luck;' and to intimate, in oblique terms, a vague intention of knocking somebody's head off . . . . "

> **Misses Evans**: the two youngest
> **Mrs Evans**: tell J'mima to put on her white muslin!
> **Tilly**, a maid at the Evans's

SB 37 December 13, 1835 BL **PO**

The Parlour Orator

The red-faced **Rogers** holds forth on Reform, politics, freedom, slavery and the need for Proof in place of assertions.

> "*A numerous race are these red-faced men . . . . Weak-pated dolts they are, and a great deal of mischief they do to their cause, however good.*"

Ellis. " . . . a sharp-nosed, light-haired man in a brown surtout reaching nearly to his heels, who took a whiff at his pipe, and an admiring glance at the red-faced man, alternately."

Landlord. " . . . a modest public-house of the old school, with a little old bar, and a little old landlord, who, with a **wife** and **daughter** of the same pattern, was comfortably seated in the bar . . . . "

Rogers. " . . . a stoutish man of about forty, whose short, stiff, black hair curled closely round a broad high forehead, and a face to which something besides water and exercise had communicated a rather inflamed appearance. He was smoking a cigar, with his eyes fixed on the ceiling, and had that confident oracular air which marked him as the leading politician, general authority, and universal anecdote-relater, of the place."

—*in form:* "'Prove it!' sneered the man with the red face. What! bending beneath the yoke of an insolent and factious oligarchy; bowed down by the domination of cruel laws; groaning beneath tyranny and oppression on every hand, at every side, and in every corner. Prove it!—' The red-faced man abruptly broke off, sneered melo-dramatically, and buried his countenance and his indignation together, in a quart pot."

Snobee. ""'Mr Snobee . . .is a fit and proper person to represent the borough in Parliament . . . He is a friend to Reform . . . . The abolitionist of the national debt, the unflinching opponent of pensions, the uncompromising advocate of the negro, the reducer of sinecures and the duration of Parliaments; the extender of nothing but the suffrages of the people" . . . . '"

> Broker, stout, in a large waistcoat
> Daughter of a landlord: Won't you walk into the parlour?
> Friend, elderly; white head and broad-brimmed brown hat
> **Tommy**, a little greengrocer with a chubby face
> Wife of a landlord: You had much better step into the parlour, sir.
> **Wilson**, association member

SB 38 August 6, 1836   CC **HP**

The Hospital Patient

A man arrested for assault is brought to face the young woman in the hospital. She refuses to testify against him. Undone, he sobs. She dies.

Jack. "There was a powerful, ill-looking young fellow at the bar . . . on the very common charge of having, on the previous night, ill-treated a woman, with whom he lived in some court hard by. Several witnesses bore testimony to acts of the grossest brutality; and a certificate was read from the **house-surgeon** . . . intimating that her recovery was extremely doubtful."

—*at the hospital:* "It was easy to see . . . by the whiteness of his countenance, and the constant twitching of the muscles of his face, that he dreaded what was to come . . . . Brute as the man was, he was not prepared for [her absolution]. He turned his face from the bed, and sobbed."

Magistrates. " . . . after one magistrate had complained bitterly of the cold, and the other of the absence of any news in the evening paper, it was announced that the patient was prepared . . . . "

Patients. "Two or three of the beds were empty, and their recent occupants were sitting beside them, but with faces so wan, and eyes so bright and glassy, that it was fearful to meet their gaze."

Pickpocket. " . . . the very prepossessing appearance of a pickpocket, who having declined to take the trouble of walking to the Police Office, on the ground that he hadn't the slightest wish to go there at all, was being conveyed thither in a wheelbarrow, to the huge delight of a crowd."

Victim. "She was a fine young woman of about two or three and twenty. Her long black hair, which had been hastily cut from near the wounds on her head, streamed over the pillow in jagged and matted locks. Her face bore deep marks of the ill-usage she had received; her hand was pressed upon her side, as if her chief pain were there; her breathing was short and heavy; and it was plain to see that she was dying fast."

—*seeing the prisoner:* "The girl started up, with an energy quite preternatural; the fire gleamed in her heavy eyes, and the blood rushed to her pale and sunken cheeks. It was a convulsive effort. She fell back upon her pillow, and covering her scarred and bruised face with her hands, burst into tears."

"'**Jack**,' murmured the girl, laying her hand upon his arm, 'they shall not persuade me to swear your life away. He didn't do it, gentlemen. He never hurt me.'"

Young girl. " . . . on a third [bed], there lay stretched a young girl, apparently in the heavy stupor often the immediate precursor of death: her face was stained with blood, and her breast and arms were bound up in folds of linen."

> Child, enveloped in bandages, half-consumed by fire
> Clerk, court: accompanying a prisoner
> Patient, a female rendered hideous by a dreadful accident; in pain
> Police guards introduced as "Dressers," smelling strongly of tobacco smoke
> Police officer, keeping custody of a prisoner on a visit
> Policemen, bringing in a pickpocket

SB 39 November 25,1835   BL **JD**

The Misplaced Attachment of Mr John Dounce
(first called 'Love and Oysters')

Cautionary tale for vulnerable Old Boys: John Dounce, previously steady, sees and loves an oyster-shop girl. He evicts his daughters, cuts his friends. His suit is summarily rejected. Demoralized, he marries (sixth try) his cook.

John Dounce. " . . . a retired glove and braces maker, a widower, resident with three daughters—all grown up, and all unmarried . . . He was a short, round, large-faced, tubbish sort of man, with a broad-brimmed hat, and a square coat; and had that grave, but confident, kind of roll, peculiar to old boys in general. Regular as clockwork—breakfast at nine—dress and tittivate a little—down to the Sir Somebody's Head—a glass of ale and the paper—come back again, and take daughters out for a walk—dinner at three—glass of grog and pipe—nap—tea—little walk—Sir Somebody's Head again—capital house—delightful evenings."

—*in love:* "If the **young lady** had appeared beautiful by night, she was perfectly irresistible by day; and from this time forward, a change came over the spirit of John Dounce's dream. He bought shirt-pins; wore a ring on his third finger; read poetry . . . 'went on' altogether in such an uproarious manner, that the three **Miss Dounces** went off on small pensions, he having made the tenement in Cursitor Street too warm to contain them; and in short, comported and demeaned himself in every respect like an unmitigated old Saracen . . . ."

—*undone:* "The . . . **young lady**, having derived sufficient profit and emolument from John Dounce's attachment, not only refused, when matters came to a crisis, to take him for better for worse, but expressly declared, to use her own forcible words, that she 'wouldn't have him at no price;' and John Dounce, having lost his old friends, alienated his relations, and rendered himself ridiculous to everybody, made offers successively to a **school-mistress**, a **landlady**, a **feminine tobacconist**, and a **house-keeper**; and, being directly rejected by each and every of them, was accepted by his **cook**, with whom he now lives, a henpecked husband, a melancholy monument of antiquated misery, and living warning to all uxorious old boys."

Harris, "the law-stationer, and Mr **Jennings**, the robe-maker (two jolly young fellows like himself [**Dounce**]) . . . and there they sat every night till just ten minutes before twelve, drinking their brandy-and-water, and smoking their pipes, and telling stories, and enjoying themselves with a kind of solemn joviality particularly edifying."

Jones, "the barrister's clerk—rum fellow that Jones—capital company . . . hoaxing scamp . . . [he] used to recount how he had observed a lady in white feathers, in one of the pit boxes, gazing intently on Mr **Dounce** all the evening, and how he had caught Mr Dounce, whenever he thought no one was looking at him, bestowing ardent looks of intense devotion on the lady in return . . . ."

Young lady. " . . . a newly-opened oyster-shop, on a magnificent scale, with natives laid, one deep, in circular marble basins in the windows . . . .

"Behind the natives were the barrels, and behind the barrels was a young lady of about five-and-twenty, all in blue, and all alone—splendid creature, charming face and lovely figure! It is difficult to say whether Mr John Dounce's red countenance . . . excited the lady's risibility, or whether a natural exuberance of animal spirits proved too much for that staidness of demeanour which the forms of society rather dictatorially prescribe. But certain it is, that the lady smiled; then put her finger upon her lip, with a striking recollection of what was due to herself; and finally retired, in oyster-like bashfulness, to the very back of the counter."

—*on an errand:* " . . . she ran out of the shop, and down the street, her long auburn ringlets shaking in the wind in the most enchanting manner; and back she came again, tripping over the coal-cellar lids like a whipping-top, with a tumbler of brandy-and-water, which Mr **John Dounce** insisted on her taking a share of, as it was regular ladies' grog—hot, strong, sweet, and plenty of it."

> Master Betty[H]: child prodigy actor
> Lady in white feathers, allegedly gazing at John Dounce
> Servant, black, and six foot high; in blue and silver—allegedly
> Five women, the finest of that day, sir: they succoured John Dounce

SB 40 November 22, 1835   BL **MM**

The Mistaken Milliner: A Tale of Ambition
(first called 'The Vocal Dressmaker')

Amelia Martin, vain milliner, allows adventurers **Jennings Rodolph** and wife to persuade her to undertake a singing career. She makes dresses for Mrs Rodolph, who loves clothes, and gets free occasional lessons in exchange. The milliner neglects her business. At her debut she is inaudible and discomfited. Mrs Rodolph keeps the dresses.

> *"Now 'coming out,' either in acting, or singing, or society, or facetiousness . . . is all very well . . . if he or she can but manage to come out with a burst, and being out to keep out, and not go in again . . . . "*

Customer. " . . . **Miss Martin**, after contemplating the figure and general appearance of the young lady in service with great apparent admiration, would say how well she would look, to be sure, in a low dress with short sleeves; made very full in the skirts, with four tucks in the bottom . . . . "

Father, of the **journeyman**. " . . . even the funny old gentleman began singing. His song had properly seven verses, but as he couldn't recollect more than the first one, he sung that over seven times, apparently very much to his own personal gratification."

Journeyman. "A **friend** of **Miss Martin**'s who had long been keeping company with an ornamental painter and decorator's journeyman, at last consented (on being at last asked to do so) to name the day which would make the aforesaid journeyman a happy husband."

Amelia Martin, "was pale, tallish, thin, and two-and-thirty—what ill-natured people would call plain, and police reports interesting. She was a milliner and dressmaker, living on her business and not above it . . . . you'd just have knocked . . . and down would have come Miss Martin herself, in a merino gown of the newest fashion, black velvet bracelets on the genteelest principle, and other little elegancies of the most approved description. . . . Miss Amelia Martin's principal foible was vanity . . . . "

—*called upon:* " . . . after sundry hesitatings and coughings, with a preparatory choke or two, and an introductory declaration that she was frightened to death to attempt it before such great judges of the art, [she] commenced a species of treble chirruping containing frequent allusions to some young gentleman of the name of Hen-e-ry, with an occasional reference to madness and broken hearts."

—*a debut:* "The symphony began, and was soon afterwards followed by a faint kind of ventriloquial chirping, proceeding apparently from the deepest recesses of the interior of Miss Amelia Martin. 'Sing out'—shouted one **gentleman** in a white great-coat. 'Don't be afraid to put the steam on, old gal,' exclaimed another . . . .

" . . . Miss Amelia Martin left the orchestra, with much less ceremony than she had entered it; and, as she couldn't sing out, never came out."

The **Jennings Rodolphs**, "with whom the ornamental painter's **journeyman** had been fortunate enough to contract an intimacy . . . the leading characteristic of Mrs Jennings Rodolph [was] an attachment to dress."

—*the mark admired:* "Mr Jennings Rodolph frequently interrupted the progress of the song, by ejaculating 'Beautiful!'—'Charming!'—'Brilliant!'—'Oh!! splendid,' &c.; and at its close the admiration of himself, and his lady, knew no bounds."

—*an exchange:* "Miss Martin studied incessantly—the practising was the consequence. Mrs Jennings Rodolph taught gratuitously now and then—the dresses were the result."

Harry Taplin. "The comic gentleman was all smiles and blandness—he had composed a duet expressly for the occasion, and **Miss Martin** should sing it with him."

> **Signora Marra Boni**, a model of singing (a play on "marrowbones")
> Clerk, engaged to be married
> Journeyman, brother, with such an eye!
>> mother, such a dear old lady
>> sister, such a charming girl
> **Julia Montague**, soloist (on this occasion only): "I am a Friar"

SB 41 October 11, 1835   BL **DA**

The Dancing Academy

Over-mothered **Augustus Cooper** seeks the wider world through dancing lessons. **Miss Billsmethi**, academician's daughter, smitten with him, takes highly vocal umbrage at his flirting with another. **Mrs Cooper** averts an action in the breach by paying twenty pounds. Augustus still lives with her.

" . . . *as he has lost his ambition for society, and never goes into the world, he will never see this account of himself, and will never be any the wiser.*"

Master Billsmethi, "when everybody else was breathless, danced a hornpipe, with a cane in his hand, and a cheese-plate on his head, to the unqualified admiration of the whole company."

Miss Billsmethi. " . . . with her hair curled in a crop all over her head, and her shoes tied in sandals all over her ankles."

—*jilted:* " . . . [she] began screaming in the loudest key of her voice, at the rate of fourteen screams a minute; and being unsuccessful, in an onslaught on the eyes and face, first of the lady in gauze and then of Mr **Augustus Cooper**, called distractedly on the other three-and-seventy **pupils** to furnish her with oxalic acid for her own private drinking; and, the call not being honoured, made another rush at Mr Cooper, and then had her stay-lace cut, and was carried off to bed."

Signor Billsmethi. "Of all the dancing academies that ever were established, there never was one more popular in its immediate vicinity than Signor Billsmethi's . . . . There was public tuition and private tuition—an assembly-room and a parlour. Signor Billsmethi's family were always thrown in with the parlour, and included in parlour price; that is to say, a private pupil had Signor Billsmethi's parlour to dance *in,* and Signor Billsmethi's family to dance *with;* and when he had been sufficiently broken in in the parlour, he began to run in couples in the assembly-room."

—*tact with the public:* "The Signor was at home, and, what was still more gratifying, he was an Englishman! Such a nice man—and so polite! The list . . . would have been filled up, that very morning, only Signor Billsmethi was dissatisfied with the reference . . . .

"'And very much delighted I am, Mr **Cooper**,' said Signor Billsmethi, 'that I did *not* take her. I assure you, Mr Cooper—I don't say it to flatter you, for I know you're above it—that I consider myself extremely fortunate in having a gentleman of your manners and appearance, sir."

—*teaching:* " . . . [they] danced a quadrille—none of your slipping and sliding about, but regular warm work, flying into corners, and diving among chairs, and shooting out at the door—something like dancing! Signor Billsmethi in particular, notwithstanding his having a little fiddle to play all the time, was out on the landing every figure . . . . "

Augustus Cooper. " . . . was in the oil and colour line—just the age, with a little money, a little business, and a little **mother**, who, having managed her husband and his business in his lifetime, took to managing her son and *his* business after his decease . . . he had been cooped up in the little back parlour . . . on week-days, and in a little deal box without a lid . . . at Beth-el Chapel, on Sundays, and had seen no more of the world than if he had been an infant all his days . . . . "

— *a meeting:* " . . . **Signor Billsmethi** said they were as handsome a pair as ever he'd wish to see; upon which the young lady exclaimed, 'Lor, pa!' and blushed as red as Mr Cooper himself—you might have thought they were both standing under a red lamp at a chemist's shop . . . . "

—*a setback:* " . . . not being remarkable for quickness of apprehension, [he] was at a loss to understand what [the hysterics] meant . . . he deemed it prudent to make a precipitate retreat . . . a lawyer's letter came next day . . . after walking twice to the Serpentine for the purpose of drowning himself, and coming twice back without doing it, [he] made a confidante of his mother . . . . "

Young lady, in gauze. " . . . whether it was the strength of the compounds, or the beauty of the ladies . . . Mr **Augustus Cooper** encouraged, rather than repelled, the very flattering attentions of a young lady in brown gauze over white calico who had appeared particularly struck with him from the first . . . . "

Young White, "at the gas-fitter's over the way, three years younger than [**Augustus**], had been flaring away like winkin'—going to the theatre—supping at harmonic meetings—eating oysters by the barrel—drinking stout by the gallon—even stopping out all night, and coming home as cool in the morning as if nothing had happened."

Apprentice, in the oil and colour line: put Augustus to bed by force
Boy, an animated sandwich; advertisement on two boards
Gentlemen, two dancing pupils; such nice people, not a bit of pride
Lady, a potential Columbine; inspired Augustus to learn his steps
Potboy, extra; laid on for the occasion of a special dance
Pupils, three-and-seventy in number
Young lady, a quadrille partner of Master Billsmethi
Young ladies, fourteen; in a grand Sicilian shawl dance

SB 42 November 5, 1834   MC **SG**

Shabby-genteel People

Describes and defines a certain type of male, who feels his poverty and vainly tries to conceal it, found only in the city.

Lounger. "If you meet a man . . . with his hands in the pockets of a pair of drab trousers plentifully besprinkled with grease-spots: the trousers made very full over the boots, and ornamented with two cords down the outside of each leg—wearing, also, what has been a brown coat with bright buttons, and hat very much pinched up at the side, cocked over his right eye—don't pity him. He is not shabby-genteel. The 'harmonic meetings' at some fourth-rate public-house, or the purlieus of a private theatre, are his chosen haunts; he entertains a rooted antipathy to any kind of work, and is on familiar terms with several pantomime men at the large houses."

Shabby-genteel [theoretical]. " . . . if you see hurrying along a by-street, keeping as close as he can to the area-railings, a man of about forty or fifty, clad in an old rusty suit of threadbare black cloth which shines with constant wear as if it had been beeswaxed—the trousers tightly strapped down, partly for the look of the thing and partly to keep his old shoes from slipping off at the heels—if you observe, too, that his yellowish-white neckerchief is carefully pinned up, to conceal the tattered garment underneath, and that his hands are encased in the remains of an old pair of beaver gloves, you may set him down as a shabby-genteel man . . . [a] depressed face, and timorous air of conscious poverty . . . . "

—*occupation:* "[He] may have no occupation, or he may be a corn agent, or a coal agent, or a wine merchant, or a collector of debts, or a broker's assistant, or a broken-down attorney. He may be a clerk of the lowest description, or a contributor to the press in the same grade."

Shabby-genteel [actual]. "He first attracted our notice, by sitting opposite to us in the reading-room at the British Museum; and what made the man more remarkable was, that he always had before him a couple of shabby-genteel books—two old dog's-eared folios, in mouldy worm-eaten covers, which had once been smart. He was in his chair every morning, just as the clock struck ten; he was always the last to leave the room in the afternoon; and when he did, he quitted it with the air of a man who knew not where else to go for warmth and quiet. There he used to sit all day, as close to the table as possible, in order to conceal the lack of buttons on his coat: with his old hat carefully deposited at his feet, where he evidently flattered himself it escaped observation."

"He looked somewhat better at the beginning of the week than at the conclusion, because the neckerchief, though yellow, was not quite so dingy; and in the midst of all this wretchedness, he never appeared without gloves and straps."

—*after an absence:* "He had undergone some strange metamorphosis . . . . His clothes were a fine, deep, glossy black; and yet they looked like the same suit; nay, there were the very darns with which old acquaintance had made us familiar. The hat, too—nobody could mistake the shape of that hat, with its high crown gradually increasing in circumference towards the top. Long service had imparted to it a reddish-brown tint; but now it was as black as the coat.

The truth flashed suddenly upon us—they had been 'revived.' It is a deceitful liquid that black and blue reviver . . . . It betrays its victims into a temporary assumption of importance . . . . It elevates their spirits for a week, only to depress them, if possible, below their original level. It was so in this case . . . . "

Engraver, a drunken shabby-genteel man in a damp back-parlour

SB 43 October 18, 1835   BL **MN**

Making a Night of It

Potter and **Smithers**, both clerks in the city and thick-and-thin pals, spend the evening and make a night of it on pay-day.

" . . . *the rest of the entertainment was a confused mixture of heads and heels, black eyes and blue uniforms, mud and gas-lights, thick doors, and stone paving.*"

Magistrate. " . . . the magistrate, after an appropriate reprimand, fined [them] five shillings each, for being what the law vulgarly terms drunk; and thirty-four pounds for seventeen assaults at forty shillings a-head, with liberty to speak to the prosecutors."

Thomas Potter. " . . . off-hand, dashing, amateur-pickpocket-sort-of-manner . . . a rough blue coat with wooden buttons, made upon the fireman's principle, in which, with the addition of a low-crowned, flower-pot-saucer-shaped hat, he had created no inconsiderable sensation . . . [his] great aim it was to be considered as a 'knowing card,' a 'fast goer' . . . . "

—*his night out:* " . . . he would keep laughing out loud, and volunteering inarticulate declarations that he was 'all right;' in proof of which he feebly bespoke the evening paper after the next gentleman, but finding it a matter of some difficulty to discover any news in its columns, or to ascertain distinctly whether it had any columns at all, walked slowly out to look for the moon, and, after coming back quite pale with looking up at the sky so long . . . laid his head on his arm, and went to sleep also."

—*after ejection:* "Mr Thomas Potter . . . was valorous and peremptory. They had come out to make a night of it: and a night must be made."

Robert Smithers. "There was a spice of romance in Mr Smithers's disposition, a ray of poetry, a gleam of misery, a sort of consciousness of he didn't exactly know what, coming across him he didn't precisely know why . . . a surtout and shoes, with a narrow black neckerchief and a brown hat, very much turned up at the sides . . . . "

—*his night out:* " . . . what with the drinking, and lighting, and puffing, and the stale ashes on the table, and the tallow-grease on the cigars, [he] began to doubt the mildness of the Havannahs, and to feel very much as if he had been sitting in a hackney-coach with his back to the horses."

—*after ejection:* " . . . being constitutionally one of the slow-goers, and having had quite enough of fast-going, in the course of his recent expulsion . . . proceeded to indulge in circuitous references to the beauties of sleep . . . [he] was three parts dull, and the other dismal . . . . "

Theatre-goers. "'Give that dog a bone!' cried one gentleman . . . .

"'Where have you been a-having half a pint of intermediate beer?' cried a second.

"'Tailor!' screamed a third."

"'Barber's clerk!' shouted a fourth."

"'Throw him O—VER!' roared a fifth; while numerous voices concurred in desiring Mr **Thomas Potter** to 'go home to his mother!'"

> *Damon*, mythical figure extremely ready to put in special bail for a friend
> *Pythias*, a certain trumplike, mythological punctuality in turning up

SB 44 November 29, 1835   BL **PV**

The Prisoners' Van

A passer-by observes Her Majesty's carriage, conveying two prostitutes and others to prison.

> " . . . *an impression on our mind we would gladly have avoided, and would willingly have effaced.*"

Bella. " . . . had certainly not attained her fourteenth year . . . gaudily dressed . . . .[and] weeping bitterly—not for display, or in the hope of producing effect, but for very shame; her face was buried in her handkerchief: and her whole manner was but too expressive of bitter and unavailing sorrow."

Cobbler. " . . . we turned round to an unshorn, sallow-looking cobbler, who was standing next us with his hands under the bib of his apron, and put the usual question of 'What's the matter?' The cobbler eyed us from head to foot, with superlative contempt, and laconically replied 'Nuffin.'"

Emily. " . . . two additional years of depravity had fixed their brand upon the elder girl's features, as legibly as if a red-hot iron had seared them."

"'Hold up your head, you chicken' . . . boisterously tearing the other girl's handkerchief away; 'Hold up your head, and show 'em your face. I an't jealous, but I'm blessed if I an't game!'"

Prisoners. "There were other prisoners—**boys** of ten, as hardened in vice as men of fifty—a houseless **vagrant**, going joyfully to prison as a place of food and shelter, handcuffed to a **man** whose prospects were ruined, character lost, and family rendered destitute, by his first offence."

> Boys, in the crowd: "Here's the wan!"
> Driver, of the prisoners' van
> Man, colleague of the prisoners' van driver
> -in the crowd: inexpressibly delighted with the ladies in the van
> Mother, of Emily and Bella: sordid and rapacious
> Woman in the crowd: red-faced: "How long are you for, Emily?"

CHARACTERS IN 'TALES'

SB 45 May and August 1834 MM **BH**

The Boarding-House

Précis

Mrs Tibbs uses an inheritance to buy a house and convert it for boarders. Softspoken little **Tibbs**, with a small annuity, sits at the foot of the table. The widow **Maplesone** and daughters **Matilda** and **Julia** join the boarding group, which includes the Byronic **Hicks**, empty-headed **Simpson** and vain old bachelor **Calton**, on the lookout.

Over six months, marital ideas flourish secretly. Mrs Tibbs is kept unaware. Calton and Hicks discover they are to marry the mother and the elder daughter. They both ask Tibbs to stand as father, but he thinks they refer to his plan to give Julia away to Simpson. In the event, Calton does not go to the altar. He is taken to Court, for breach. Hicks marries, but wanders off afterward, and Julia runs off with Another after Simpson is taken up for her dressmakers' bill. For having connived at or participated in the departure of every boarder, Tibbs is banished to the kitchen. 1

Advertising works, and the carnivorous widow **Bloss** and maid **Agnes** complete the house, whose other new boarders are hypochondriac **Gobler**, morose **John Evenson**, Tory snob **Wisbottle**; artistic **Tomkins** and the uncouth **O'Bleary**. **Dr Wosky** looks in on Mrs Bloss, too idle not to be ill.

Evenson tells Mrs Tibbs of nocturnal noises, and they plan surveillance. They overhear and misunderstand, and are in turn misunderstood. A desperate Tibbs is heard begging a kiss from Agnes, and Mrs Bloss rouses the house, fearing fire. O'Bleary has had eyes on her, but Gobler got there first, and Mrs Bloss and he retire in wedded bliss to eat meat in a suburb. Tibbs departs, leaving half his annuity behind. Mrs Tibbs will sell out. 2

The Proprietors

Tibbs. " . . . by no means a large man. He had, moreover, very short legs, but, by way of indemnification, his face was peculiarly long. He was to his wife what the 0 is in 90—he was of some importance *with* her—he was nothing without her. Mrs Tibbs was always talking. Mr Tibbs rarely spoke; but, if it were at any time possible to put in a word, when he should have said nothing at all, he had that talent." 1

—*raconteur*: "Mrs Tibbs detested long stories, and Mr Tibbs had one, the conclusion of which had never been heard by his most intimate friends. It always began, 'I recollect when I was in the volunteer corps, in eighteen hundred and six'—but, as he spoke very slowly and softly, and his better half very quickly and loudly, he rarely got beyond the introductory sentence. He was a melancholy specimen of the story-teller. He was the wandering Jew of Joe Millerism." 1

—*getting dinner*: "He was busy eating the fish with his eyes . . . . "

"'My dear,' said Mrs Tibbs to her spouse after every one else had been helped, 'what do you take?' The inquiry was accompanied with a look intimating that he mustn't say fish, because there was not much left. Tibbs . . . coolly replied, 'Why—I'll take a little—fish, I think.'

"'Did you say fish, my dear?' (another frown).

"'Yes dear,' replied the villain, with an expression of acute hunger depicted in his countenance. The tears almost started to Mrs Tibbs's eyes, as she helped her 'wretch of a husband,' as she inwardly called him, to the last eatable bit of salmon on the dish.

"'**James**, take this to your master, and take away your master's knife.' This was deliberate revenge, as Tibbs never could eat fish without one." 1

—*disaster:* "That wretched little man returned home, on the day of the wedding[s], in a state of partial intoxication; and, under the influence of wine, excitement, and despair, actually dared to brave the anger of his wife. Since that ill-fated hour he has constantly taken his meals in the kitchen, to which apartment, it is understood, his witticisms will be in future confined: a turn-up bedstead having been conveyed there by Mrs Tibbs's order . . . ." 1

—*and in compensation:* "'He wanted to kiss me as I came up the kitchen-stairs, just now,' said **Agnes**, indignantly; 'but I gave it him—a little wretch!'

" . . . . A long course of snubbing and neglect; his days spent in the kitchen, and his nights in the turn-up bed-stead, had completely broken the little spirit that the unfortunate volunteer had ever possessed . . . . He was actually a sort of journey-man [Don] Giovanni of the basement story." 2

Mrs Tibbs ". . . somewhat short of stature . . . [she] was, beyond all dispute, the most tidy, fidgety, thrifty little personage that ever inhaled the smoke of London; and the house of Mrs Tibbs was, decidedly, the neatest in all Great Coram Street " 1

—*housekeeping:* "The area and the area-steps, and the street-door and the street-door steps, and the brass handle, and the door-plate, and the knocker, and the fan-light, were all as clean and bright, as indefatigable white-washing, and hearth-stoning, and scrubbing and rubbing, could make them. The wonder was, that the brass door-plate, with the interesting inscription 'MRS TIBBS,' had never caught fire from constant friction, so perseveringly was it polished. There were meat-safe-looking blinds in the parlour-windows, blue and gold curtains in the drawing-room, and spring-roller blinds, as Mrs Tibbs was wont in the pride of her heart to boast, 'all the way up.' The bell-lamp in the passage looked as clear as a soap-bubble; you could see yourself in all the tables, and French-polish yourself on any one of the chairs. The banisters were beeswaxed; and the very stair-wires made your eyes wink, they were so glittering." 1

—*upset:* "' . . . I saw Mr Tibbs, who, it seems had been disturbed also.— Bless me, Mrs Tibbs, you change colour!'

"'No, no—it's nothing,' returned Mrs T. in a hurried manner; 'it's only the heat of the room. . . .

"'Oh,' said **Evenson**, in a most soothing tone—he liked to make mischief—'I should hope Mr Tibbs was not in any way implicated. He always appeared to me very harmless.'

"'I have generally found him so,' sobbed poor little Mrs Tibbs; crying like a watering-pot . . . her curiosity was excited, her jealousy was roused . . . ." 2

The Boarders

Mrs Bloss. " . . . there arrived a single lady with a double knock, in a pelisse the colour of the interior of a damson pie; a bonnet of the same, with a regular conservatory of artificial flowers; a white veil, and a green parasol, with a cobweb border.

"The visitor (who was very fat and red-faced) was shown into the drawing-room . . . .

"'I called in consequence of an advertisement,' said the stranger, in a voice as if she had been playing a set of Pan's pipes for a fortnight without leaving off." 2

"'Money isn't no object whatever to me,' said the lady, 'so much as living in a state of retirement and obtrusion.'" 2

—*her delicate health:* "'I am constantly attended by a medical man . . . . I have been a shocking unitarian for some time—I, indeed, have had very little peace since the death of Mr Bloss . . . . I am going through a course of treatment which renders attention necessary. I have one mutton-chop in bed at half-past eight, and another at ten, every morning.'" 2

" . . . [she] was exceedingly vulgar, ignorant, and selfish . . . an odd mixture of shrewdness and simplicity, liberality and meanness. Bred up as she had been, she knew no mode of living so agreeable as a boarding-house; and having nothing to do, and nothing to wish for, she naturally imagined she must be very ill—an impression which was most assiduously promoted by her medical attendant, **Dr Wosky**, and her handmaid **Agnes**: both of whom, doubtless for good reasons, encouraged all her extravagant notions." 2

—*envoi:* "**Mrs Gobler** exists: Mrs Bloss has left us for ever. In a secluded retreat . . . far, far removed from the noisy strife of that great boarding-house, the world, the enviable **Gobler** and his pleasing wife revel in retirement: happy in their complaints, their table, and their medicine; wafted through life by the grateful prayers of all the purveyors of animal food within three miles round." 2

Calton. " . . . a superannuated beau—an old boy. He used to say of himself that although his features were not regularly handsome, they were striking. They certainly were. It was impossible to look at his face without being reminded of a chubby street-door knocker, half-lion half-monkey; and the comparison might be extended to his whole character and conversation.

"He had stood still, while everything else had been moving. He never originated a conversation, or started an idea; but if any commonplace topic were broached, or, to pursue the comparison, if anybody *lifted him up,* he would hammer away with surprising rapidity. He had the tic-douloureux occasionally, and then he might be said to be muffled, because he did not make quite as much noise as at other times, when he would go on prosing, rat-tat-tat the same thing over and over again.

"He had never been married; but he was still on the look-out for a wife with money. He had a life interest worth about £300 a year—he was exceedingly vain, and inordinately selfish. He had acquired the reputation of being the very pink of politeness, and he walked round the park, and up Regent Street, every day." ¶1

—*marital:* " . . . as he had found some difficulty in getting any one to give the lady away, it occurred to him that the best mode of obviating the inconvenience would be not to take her at all. The lady, however, 'appealed,' as her counsel said on the trial of the cause, *Maplesone v Calton,* for a breach of promise, 'with a broken heart, to the outraged laws of her country.' She recovered damages to the amount of £1,000 which the unfortunate knocker was compelled to pay." 1

John Evenson. " . . . a stern-looking man, of about fifty, with very little hair on his head . . . . He was very morose and discontented. He was a thorough radical, and used to attend a great variety of public meetings, for the express purpose of finding fault with everything that was proposed." 2

" . . . [he] extended his dislike to almost every created object, masculine, feminine, or neuter." 2

Gobler. "' . . . we have a gentleman now with us, who is in a very delicate state of health—a Mr Gobler . . . .

"'Why the fact is,' replied **Mrs Tibbs**, with a most communicative air, 'he has no stomach whatever.'" 2

" . . . the mysterious tenant of the back drawing-room was a lazy, selfish hypochondriac; always complaining and never ill. As his character in many re-spects closely assimilated to that of **Mrs Bloss**, a very warm friendship soon sprung up between them. He was tall, thin, and pale; he always fancied he had a severe pain somewhere or other, and his face invariably wore a pinched, screwed-up expression; he looked, indeed, like a man who had got his feet in a tub of exceedingly hot water, against his will." 2

Messrs Simpson, Hicks and Calton

Septimus Hicks, "who was a tallish, white-faced young man, with spec-tacles, and a black ribbon round his neck instead of a neckerchief—a most in-teresting person; a poetical walker of the hospitals, and a 'very talented young man.' He was fond of 'lugging into conversation all sorts of quotations from Don Juan, without fettering himself by the propriety of their application; in which particular he was remarkably independent . . . . He was quite sure of his author, because he had never read any other." 1

—*marital:* "Mr Septimus Hicks having walked the hospitals, took it into his head to walk off altogether. His injured wife [*née* **Matilda Maplesone**] is at present residing with her mother at Boulogne." 1

The **Maplesones**. **Mrs** Maplesone was an enterprising widow of about fifty: shrewd, scheming, and good-looking. She was amiably anxious on behalf of her daughters; in proof whereof she used to remark, that she would have no objection to marry again, if it would benefit her dear girls—she could have no other motive." 1

—**Julia**. "'Yes, Ma.'

"'Don't stoop.'—This was said for the purpose of directing general attention to Miss Julia's figure, which was undeniable." 1

—**Matilda**. "They had been at different watering-places, for four seasons; they had gambled at libraries, read books in balconies, sold at fancy fairs, danced at assemblies, talked sentiment—in short, they had done all that industrious girls could do—but, as yet, to no purpose." 1

Frederick O'Bleary "was an Irishman, recently imported; he was in a perfectly wild state; and had come over to England to be an apothecary, a clerk in a government office, an actor, a reporter, or anything else that turned up— he was not particular. . . . He felt convinced that his intrinsic merits must procure him a high destiny. He wore shepherd's-plaid inexpressibles, and used to look under all the ladies' bonnets as he walked along the streets." 2

Simpson. "[He] was one of those young men, who are in society what walking gentlemen are on the stage, only infinitely worse skilled in his vocation . . . . He was as empty-headed as the great bell of St Paul's; always dressed according to the caricatures published in the monthly fashions; and spelt Character with a K." 1

—*killing attire:* "[He] wore a maroon-coloured dress-coat, with a velvet collar and cuffs of the same tint—very like that which usually invests the form of the distinguished unknown who condescends to play the 'swell in the pantomime . . . . '" 1

"His hair was like a wig, and distinguished by that insinuating wave which graces the shining locks of those *chef-d'oeuvres* of art surmounting the waxen images in **Bartellot**'s window in Regent Street; his whiskers meeting beneath his chin, seemed strings wherewith to tie it on, ere science had rendered them unnecessary by her patent invisible springs." 1

—*conversation:* " . . . as Mr Simpson sat with a smile upon his face and said 'Yes,' or 'Certainly,' at intervals of about four minutes each, he received full credit for understanding what was going forward." 1

—*marital:* "Mr Simpson, having the misfortune to lose his wife six weeks after marriage (by her eloping with an officer during his temporary sojourn in the Fleet Prison, in consequence of his inability to discharge her little mantuamaker's bill), and being disinherited by his father, who died soon afterwards, was fortunate enough to obtain a permanent engagement at a fashionable haircutter's; hairdressing being a science to which he had frequently directed his attention." 1

Alfred Tomkins, "was a clerk in a wine-house; he was a connoisseur in paintings, and had a wonderful eye for the picturesque . . . [he] had a great character for finding out beauties which no one else could discover—he certainly deserved it." 2

Wisbottle, "was a high Tory. He was a clerk in the Woods and Forests Office, which he considered rather an aristocratic employment; he knew the peerage by heart, and could tell you, off-hand, where any illustrious personage lived. He had a good set of teeth, and a capital tailor." 2

"It should be added, that, in addition to his partiality for whistling, Mr Wisbottle had a great idea of his singing powers." 2

—*snob:* "' . . . the Dowager **Marchioness of Publiccash** was most magnificently dressed, and so was the **Baron Slappenbachenhausen**.'

"'What was he presented on?' inquired **Evenson**.

"'On his arrival in England.'" 2

"'I saw the **Count de Canky** and **Captain Fitzthompson** in the Gardens,' said Wisbottle; 'they appeared much delighted.'" 2

Others

Agnes. " . . . in a cherry-coloured merino dress, open-work stockings, and shoes with sandals: like a disguised Columbine." 2 *And see* **Mrs Bloss**—*her delicate health.*

Bloss. "**Mrs Tibbs** looked at the relict of the departed Bloss, and thought he must have had very little peace in his time." 2

"Her deceased better-half had been an eminent cork-cutter, in which capacity he had amassed a decent fortune. He had no relative but his **nephew**, and no friend but his cook. The former had the insolence one morning to ask for the loan of fifteen pounds; and, by way of retaliation, he married the latter next day; he made a will immediately afterwards, containing a burst of honest indignation against his nephew . . . and a bequest of his whole property to his wife. He felt ill after breakfast, and died after dinner . . . . He never dishonoured a bill, or gave away a halfpenny."

Robinson. "**Mrs Tibbs** went through an admirable bit of serious pantomime with a servant who had come up to ask some question about the fish-sauce . . . the servant again appeared at the door, and commenced telegraphing most earnestly to her 'Missis' . . . .

"'Robinson, what *do* you want?' said Mrs Tibbs to the servant, who, by way of making her presence known to her mistress, had been giving sundry hems and sniffs outside the door during the preceding five minutes." 1

Dr Wosky. "He was a little man with a red face—dressed of course in black, with a stiff white neckerchief. He had a very good practice, and plenty of money, which he had amassed by invariably humouring the worst fancies of all the females of all the families he had ever been introduced into." ii

"'We must take stimulants,' said the cunning Wosky—'plenty of nourishment, and above all, we must keep our nerves quiet; we positively must not give way to our sensibilities. We must take all we can get,' concluded the doctor, as he pocketed his fee, 'and we must keep quiet.'" 2

Clerk for a lawyer; on his way home
Lindley Murray[H], grammarian

Officer, who runs away with Julia Simpson
Orson, legendary Valentine's uncouth brother
Postman, hammering his way down the street at a penny a knock
Sir Charles Rampart: commanded a regiment of volunteers
George Henry Robins[H], auctioneer
Captain Sir John Ross[H]: polar explorer
Servant, female; engaged by Mrs Tibbs
Duke of Wellington[H], installed as Chancellor at Oxford

SB 46 December 1833   MM **MC**

Mr Minns and His Cousin
(the beginning of it all, as 'A Dinner at Poplar Walk')

Augustus Minns, bachelor, who abominates children and dogs, is pressed to come to dinner by his vulgar cousin **Budden**, who calls with dog but without warning. Minns shares a coach inside with an irrepressible boy, is late for dinner, finds his godson insufferable, and has interminable toasts inflicted on him. He leaves at first opportunity but misses his coach and walks home in the rain. He makes a new will in the morning.

Principals

Octavius Budden, "having realised a moderate fortune by exercising the trade or calling of a corn-chandler, and having a great predilection for the country, had purchased a cottage in the vicinity of Stamford Hill, whither he retired with the wife of his bosom, and his only son . . . . "

—*manners:* "'Have you breakfasted?' inquired **Minns**.

"'Oh, no!—came to breakfast with you; so ring the bell, my dear fellow, will you? and let's have another cup and saucer, and the cold ham.—Make myself at home, you see!' continued Budden, dusting his boots with a table-napkin . . . .

"'Don't you think you'd like the ham better,' interrupted Minns, 'if you cut it the other way?' He saw, with feelings which it is impossible to describe, that his visitor was cutting, or rather maiming, the ham, in utter violation of all established rules.

"'No, thank ye,' returned Budden, with the most barbarous indifference to crime, 'I prefer it this way, it eats short.'"

—*abode:* " . . . a yellow brick house with a green door, brass knocker, and door-plate, green window-frames and ditto railings, with 'a garden' in front, that is to say, a small loose bit of gravelled ground, with one round and two scalene triangular beds, containing a fir-tree, twenty or thirty bulbs, and an unlimited number of marigolds. The taste of Mr and Mrs Budden was further displayed by the appearance of a Cupid on each side of the door, perched upon a heap of large chalk flints, variegated with pink conch-shells."

Augustus Minns "was a bachelor, of about forty as he said—of about eight-and-forty as his friends said. He was always exceedingly clean, precise, and tidy; perhaps somewhat priggish, and the most retiring man in the world. He usually wore a brown frock-coat without a wrinkle, light inexplicables without a spot, a neat neckerchief with a remarkably neat tie, and boots without a fault; moreoever, he always carried a brown silk umbrella with an ivory handle. He was a clerk in Somerset House, or, as he said himself, he held 'a responsible situation under Government.'"

—*pet hates:* "There were two classes of created objects which he held in the deepest and most unmingled horror; these were dogs, and children. He was not unamiable, but he could, at any time, have viewed the execution of a dog, or the assassination of an infant, with the liveliest satisfaction. Their habits were at variance with his love of order; and his love of order was as powerful as his love of life."

—*invited for dinner:* " . . . **Budden** departed, leaving his cousin looking forward to his visit on the following Sunday, with the feelings of a penniless poet to the weekly visit of his Scotch landlady."

—*responding:* "After as long a pause as decency would admit, he rose . . . . The words 'present company—honour—present occasion,' and 'great happiness'—heard occasionally, and repeated at intervals, with a countenance expressive of the utmost confusion and misery, convinced that the company that he was making an excellent speech . . . . "

—*afterward:* " . . . as it was a very wet night, the nine o'clock stage had come round to know whether there was anybody going to town, as, in that case, he (the nine o'clock) had room for one inside.

" . . . as he was by no means remarkable for speed, it is no matter of surprise that when he accomplished the feat of 'running round' to the Swan, the coach—the last coach—had gone without him.

"It was somewhere about three o'clock in the morning, when Mr Augustus Minns knocked feebly at the street-door of his lodgings in Tavistock Street, cold, wet, cross, and miserable. He made his will next morning, and his professional man informs us, in that strict confidence in which we inform the public, that neither the name of Mr **Octavius Budden**, nor of **Mrs Amelia Budden**, nor of **Master Alexander Augustus Budden**, appears therein."

Supporting Roles

Alexander ("Alick") Augustus Budden, "habited in a sky-blue suit with silver buttons . . . hair of nearly the same colour as the metal."

with his godfather: "'Woll, my little follow you are a fine boy, ain't you?' said Mr **Minns**, as happy as a tomtit on birdlime.

"'Yes.'

"'How old are you?'

"'Eight, next We'nsday. How old are *you?*'

"'Alexander,' interrupted his mother, 'how dare you ask Mr Minns how old he is!'

"'He asked me how old *I* was,' said the precocious child, to whom Minns had from that moment internally resolved that he never would bequeath one shilling."

Mrs Amelia Budden. " . . . the lady pressed so strongly upon her husband the propriety of cultivating the friendship of Mr **Minns** in behalf of their son, that Mr **Budden** at last made up his mind . . . ."

—*presiding:* " . . . a great deal of by-play took place between Mrs B. and the servants, respecting the removal of the dishes, during which her countenance assumed all the variations of a weather-glass, from 'stormy' to 'set fair.'"

Jones. " . . . a little smirking man with red whiskers, sitting at the bottom of the table, who during the whole of dinner had been endeavouring to obtain a listener to some stories about **Sheridan**, called out, with a very patronising air, '**Alick**, what part of speech is *be?*'"

—*making a toast:* "'It has on several occasions, in various instances, under many circumstances, and in different companies, fallen to my lot to propose a toast to those by whom, at the time, I have had the honour to be surrounded. I have sometimes, I will cheerfully own—for why should I deny it?—felt the overwhelming nature of the task I have undertaken, and my own utter incapability to do justice to the subject. If such have been my feelings, however, on former occasions, what must they be now—now—under the extraordinary circumstances in which I am placed. (Hear! hear!) To describe my feelings accurately, would be impossible . . . . '"

Others

Brogson. " . . . an elderly gentleman in a black coat, drab knee-breeches, and long gaiters, who, under pretence of inspecting the prints in an Annual, had been engaged in satisfying himself on the subject of Mr **Minns**'s general appearance, by looking at him over the tops of the leaves . . . . "

Child, on a coach. "The child was an affectionate and an amiable infant; the little dear mistook **Minns** for his other parent, and screamed to embrace him . . . .

"Playfulness was agreeably mingled with affection in the disposition of the boy. When satisfied that Mr Minns was not his parent, he endeavoured to attract his notice by scraping his drab trousers with his dirty shoes, poking his chest with his mamma's parasol, and other nameless endearments peculiar to infancy, with which he beguiled the tediousness of the ride, apparently very much to his own satisfaction."

Dog. " . . . a large white dog, dressed in a suit of fleecy hosiery, with pink eyes, large ears, and no perceptible tail . . . **Minns**, casting a diabolical look at the dog, who, with his hind legs on the floor, and his fore paws resting on the table, was dragging a bit of bread and butter out of a plate, preparatory to devouring it, with the buttered side next the carpet."

> **Bill**, an ostler
> Boy, stumpy; in drab livery, cotton stockings and Budden employ
> Coachman, looking as much unlike a man in a hurry as possible
> **Grogus**, the great ironmonger: neighbour of the Buddens
> Landlord, for twenty years quarrelling with tenant Minns
> Mother, of a child on a coach
> Servant, male, of Mr Minns, who brought him a most unwelcome card

SB 47 June 7, 1834   BW **S**

Sentiment

To break off a romance, **Cornelius Brook Dingwall**, M.P., sends daughter **Lavinia** to Minerva House, the **Misses Crumpton**'s finishing school. Her suitor, under his true name **Theodosius Butler**, meets her at a ball, explains his pen name pseudonym of **M'Neville Walter** and gains her renewed commitment. They elope. Maria Crumpton carries the news to the furious Member, Lavinia repents her hasty marriage in penury. The school continues.

Principals

Cornelius Brook Dingwall, Esq. M. P. "was very haughty, solemn, and portentous. He had, naturally, a somewhat spasmodic expression of countenance, which was not rendered the less remarkable by his wearing an extremely stiff cravat. He was wonderfully proud of the M. P. attached to his name, and never lost an opportunity of reminding people of his dignity. He had a great idea of his own abilities, which must have been a great comfort to him, as no one else had; and in diplomacy, on a small scale, in his own family arrangements, he considered himself unrivalled."

—*surprising us all:* "On cool reflection, [he] was reluctantly compelled to admit that the untoward result of his admirable arrangements was attributable, not to the **Miss Crumptons**, but his own diplomacy. He however consoles himself, like some other small diplomatists, by satisfactorily proving that if his plans did not succeed, they ought to have done so."

Lavinia Brook Dingwall. " . . . in full ball costume, with an immense gold chain round her neck, and her dress looped up with a single rose; an ivory fan in her hand, and a most interesting expression of despair in her face."

George Cruikshank

—*introduced:* " . . . [she] languidly raised her head.

"'**Edward**!' she exclaimed, with a half-shriek, on seeing the well-known nankeen legs [of "Edward **M'Neville Walter**"] . . . .

"'Oh, Edward!' exclaimed that most romantic of all romantic young ladies, as the light of science seated himself beside her, 'Oh Edward, is it you?'"

—*envoi:* "[The] young wife begins to think that ideal misery is preferable to real unhappiness; and that a marriage contracted in haste, and repented at leisure, is the cause of more substantial wretchedness than she ever anticipated."

Theodosius Butler "was one of those immortal geniuses who are to be met with in almost every circle. They have, usually, very deep, monotonous voices. They always persuade themselves that they are wonderful persons, and that they ought to be very miserable, though they don't precisely know why. They are very conceited, and usually possess half an idea; but, with enthusiastic young ladies, and silly young gentlemen, they are very wonderful persons."

—*explaining:* "'**Lavinia**, hear me,' replied the hero, in his most poetic strain. 'Do not condemn me unheard. If anything that emanates from the soul of such a wretch as I, can occupy a place in your recollection—if any being, so vile, deserve your notice . . . . "

—*rewarded:* "Mr and Mrs Butler are at present rusticating in a small cottage . . . . They have no family. Mr Theodosius looks very important, and writes incessantly; but, in consequence of a gross combination on the part of publishers, none of his productions appear in print."

Amelia Crumpton. "'The Misses Crumpton,' were two unusually tall, particularly thin, and exceedingly skinny personages; very upright, and very yellow. Miss Amelia Crumpton owned to thirty-eight . . . . They dressed in the most interesting manner—like twins! and looked as happy and comfortable as a couple of marigolds run to seed. They were very precise, had the strictest possible ideas of propriety, wore false hair, and always smelt very strongly of lavender."

Maria Crumpton "admitted she was forty; an admission which was rendered perfectly unnecessary by the self-evident fact of her being at least fifty."

—*missing a point:* "Fortunately as [she] possessed no remarkable share of penetration, and as it was one of the diplomatic arrangements that no attention was to be paid to Miss **Lavinia**'s incoherent exclamations [seeing **Butler**], she was perfectly unconscious of the mutual agitation of the parties . . . . "

Others

Master Frederick Brook Dingwall. "One of those public nuisances, a spoilt child, was playing about the room, dressed after the most approved fashion—in a blue tunic with a black belt a quarter of a yard wide, fastened with an immense buckle—looking like a robber in a melodrama, seen through a diminishing glass . . . . "

Mrs Brook Dingwall. "'Mr Brook Dingwall would like Miss Brook Dingwall to learn everything,' said Mrs Brook Dingwall, who hardly ever said anything at all."

Dadson, "the writing-master . . . in a white waistcoat, black knee-shorts, and ditto silk stockings, displaying a leg large enough for two writing-masters. . . . The writing-master danced every set, springing about with the most fearful agility . . . . "

Mrs Dadson, "in green silk, with shoes and cap-trimmings to correspond. . . . Setting her down to whist was a half-yearly piece of generalship on the part of the **Miss Crumptons**; it was necessary to hide her somewhere, on account of her being a fright."

Hilton. "The popular Mr Hilton was the next arrival; and he having, at the request of the **Miss Crumptons**, undertaken the office of Master of the Ceremonies, the quadrilles commenced with considerable spirit."

Emily Smithers, "the belle of the house . . . . "

Caroline Wilson, "who was [**Emily**'s] bosom friend, because she was the ugliest girl in Hammersmith, or out of it."

Young ladies, at Minerva House, "where some twenty girls of the ages of from thirteen to nineteen inclusive, acquired a smattering of everything, and a knowledge of nothing; instruction in French and Italian, dancing lessons twice a week; and other necessaries of life."

Young men. " . . . some twenty young men, who stood near the door, and talked to one another, occasionally bursting into a giggle."

> **Lavinia Butler** (*née* Brook Dingwall)
> Footman, employed by Brook Dingwall
> Harp player, in a state of intoxication
> **James**, a red-hot looking footman in bright livery
> **Signor Lobskini**, singing master in a black wig
> Ignaz Moscheles[H]: pianist/composer (taught Fanny Dickens)
> Mothers, who looked like the stout people knocked down in pantomimes
> **Sir Alfred Muggs**: recommended Minerva House to Brook Dingwall
> Musicians: pianoforte and violins
> Old gentleman, lame; annoyed at the ladies' incessant practicing
> **Laetitia Parsons**, pianist who played "Recollections of Ireland"
> Pastrycook, of Hammersmith; correspondence with Crumptons

SB 48 March 31, 1836   LF **TR**

The Tuggses at Ramsgate

Grocer **Tuggs** receives a great inheritance. The family chooses Ramsgate for recreation. They are quickly marked. The son **Simon** (now **Cymon**) is entrapped by **Belinda Waters**, her husband **Walter** and one Lieutenant **Slaughter**. The Sting is £1,500.

Title Roles

Charlotte. " . . . the form of [the] only daughter, the accomplished Miss Charlotte Tuggs, was fast ripening into that state of luxuriant plumpness which had enchanted the eyes, and captivated the heart, of Mr Joseph Tuggs in his earlier days."

—*translated:* "And I shall call myself **Charlotta**,' said Miss Tuggs."

Joseph, "a little dark-faced man, with shiny hair, twinkling eyes, short legs, and a body of very considerable thickness, measuring from the centre button of his waistcoat in front, to the ornamental buttons of his coat behind."

—*occupation:* "Mr Joseph Tuggs was a grocer. It might be supposed that a grocer was beyond the breath of calumny; but no—the neighbours stigmatised him as a chandler; and the poisonous voice of envy distinctly asserted that he dispensed tea and coffee by the quartern, retailed sugar by the ounce, cheese by the slice, tobacco by the screw, and butter by the pat."

—*translated:* " . . . in a bottle-green great-coat, with a velvet collar of the same; and a blue travelling-cap with a gold band."

Mrs. "The figure of the amiable Mrs Tuggs, if not perfectly symmetrical, was decidedly comfortable . . . . "

Simon " . . . was as differently formed in body, as he was differently constituted in mind, from the remainder of his family. There was that elongation in his thoughtful face, and that tendency to weakness in his interesting legs, which tell so forcibly of a great mind and romantic disposition. The slightest traits of character in such a being, possess no mean interest to speculative minds. He usually appeared in public, in capacious shoes with black cotton stockings; and was observed to be particularly attached to a black glazed stock, without tie or ornament of any description . . . . Mr Simon Tuggs kept his father's books, and his own counsel."

—*translated:* "'I shall always sign myself '**Cymon**' in future,' . . . . "

—*stricken:* "A pair of puce-coloured boots were seen ascending the steps, a white handkerchief fluttered, a black eye gleamed. The **Waters**es were gone, and Mr Cymon Tuggs was alone in a heartless world."

—*stung:* " . . . . Lieutenant **Slaughter** brought a message—the captain brought an action . . . . When Mr Cymon Tuggs recovered from the nervous disorder into which misplaced affection, and exciting circumstances, had plunged him, he found that his family had lost their pleasant acquaintance; [and] that his father was minus fifteen hundred pounds . . . . "

The Conspirators

Lieutenant **Slaughter**. "Two iron-shod boots and one gruff voice was heard by Mr **Cymon** to advance, and acknowledge the honour of the introduction. The sabre of the lieutenant rattled heavily upon the floor, as he seated himself at the table. Mr Cymon's fears almost overcame his reason."

Belinda Waters. " . . . a young lady in a puce-coloured silk cloak, and boots of the same; with long black ringlets, large black eyes, brief petticoats, and un-exceptionable ankles."

—*the hook:* "'Mr **Cymon**,' said the lady suddenly, in a low tone, 'Mr Cymon—I am another's.'

"Mr Cymon expressed his perfect concurrence in a statement which it was impossible to controvert.

"'If I had not been——' resumed Belinda; and there she stopped.

"'What—what?' said Mr Cymon earnestly. 'Do not torture me. What would you say?'

"'If I had not been'—continued Mrs Captain Waters—'if, in earlier life, it had been my fate to have known, and been beloved by, a noble youth—a kindred soul—a congenial spirit—one capable of feeling and appreciating the sentiments which—"

Captain **Walter Waters**. "'Delightful morning, sir!' said a stoutish, military-looking gentleman in a blue surtout buttoned up to his chin, and white trousers chained down to the soles of his boots."

—*the trap:* "'My husband!' exclaimed **Belinda**. 'You little know him. Jealous and revengeful; ferocious in his revenge—a maniac in his jealousy! Would you be assassinated before my eyes?'"

Others

Amelia. "'Amelia, my dear, throw for your sister,' said the **stout lady** . . . . 'Nice figure, Amelia,' whispered the stout lady to a **thin youth** beside her."

Fly-man. " . . . Mr **Joseph Tuggs** beckoned to the proprietor of a dingy conveyance of a greenish hue, lined with faded striped calico; and, the luggage and the family having been deposited therein, the animal in the shafts, after describing circles in the road for a quarter of an hour, at last consented to depart in quest of lodgings."

Flymen. "'Here's the gen'lm'n at last!' said one, touching his hat with mock politeness. 'Werry glad to see you, sir,—been a-waitin' for you these six weeks. Jump in, if you please, sir!'"

"'Nice light fly and a fast trotter, sir,' said another: 'fourteen mile a hour, and surroundin' objects rendered inwisible by extreme welocity!'"

"'Large fly for your luggage, sir,' cried a third. 'Werry large fly here, sir—reg'lar bluebottle!'"

"'Here's your fly, sir!' shouted another aspiring charioteer, mounting the box, and inducing an old grey horse to indulge in some imperfect reminiscences of a canter. 'Look at him, sir!—temper of a lamb and haction of a steam-ingein!'"

Mary Golding. " . . . who, in her bathing costume, looked as if she was enveloped in a patent Mackintosh, of scanty dimensions."

Jane. "'Throw, Jane, my dear,' said the **stout lady**. An interesting display of bashfulness—a little blushing in a cambric handkerchief—a whispering to a younger sister."

Ladies, in the library. "There were young ladies, in maroon-coloured gowns and black velvet bracelets, dispensing fancy articles in the shop, and presiding over games of chance in the concert-room. There were marriageable daughters, and marriage-making mammas, gaming and promenading, and turning over music, and flirting."

Landlady. "'Five guineas a week, ma'am, *with* attendance,' replied the lodging-house keeper. (Attendance means the privilege of ringing the bell as often as you like, for your own amusement.)

"'Rather dear,' said **Mrs Tuggs**.

"'Oh dear, no, ma'am!' replied the mistress of the house, with a benign smile of pity at the ignorance of manners and customs which the observation betrayed. 'Very cheap!'

"Such an authority was indisputable."

Mother, stout, with four daughters. " . . . she turned to a walking [**male**] advertisement of Rowlands' Macassar Oil, who stood next her, and said, '**Jane** is so *very* modest and retiring' but I can't be angry with her for it. An artless and unsophisticated girl is *so* truly amiable, that I often wish **Amelia** was more like her sister!'"

The **Tippinses**. " . . . a short female, in a blue velvet hat and feathers, was led into the orchestra, by a fat man in black tights and cloudy Berlins."

"The talented Tippin having condescendingly acknowledged the clapping of hands and shouts of 'bravo!' which greeted her appearance, proceeded to sing the popular cavatina of 'Bid me discourse,' accompanied on the piano by Mr Tippin; after which, Mr Tippin sang a comic song, accompanied on the piano by Mrs Tippin: the applause consequent upon which, was only to be exceeded by the enthusiastic approbation bestowed upon an air with variations on the guitar, by Miss Tippin . . . . "

Young gentlemen, "making objects of themselves in open shirt-collars . . . . Three machines—three horses—three flounderings—three turnings round— three splashes—three gentlemen, disporting themselves in the water like so many dolphins."

Young ladies, "tittered . . . . " "And, sure enough, four young ladies, each furnished with a towel, tripped up the steps of a bathing-machine. In went the horse, floundering about in the water; round turned the machine; down sat the **driver**; and presently out burst the young ladies aforesaid, with four distinct splashes."

Marquis Carriwini: probably fictional acquaintance of Belinda
Children at Ramsgate
Cower, solicitor in the Temple; source of good news for Tuggs
Duchess of Dobbleton: alleged to resemble Mrs Tuggs
Donkey boys, at Ramsgate: "Kim up!" shouted to propel the donkeys
Donkey proprietor: his charges are three parts blood, one corn
Driver, of a horse for a bathing machine
Family, at Ramsgate: five children milk-and-watering
Gentleman, whiskered; walking advertisement for Macassar Oil
Goddess, presiding at the gaming table at Ramsgate
Ladies, at Ramsgate: carrying about portable chairs
Mary Ann: gambling in the library at Ramsgate
Nursemaids at Ramsgate, displaying their charms to advantage
Old gentlemen at Ramsgate, peering through long telescopes
Old ladies, talking at Ramsgate
Porters, at Ramsgate; a dozen men in smock-frocks
Servant, female at Ramsgate, with the fatal invitation to Cymon Tuggs
Solicitor, from the Temple, in black; green umbrella and blue bag
Harry Thompson, allegedly descried on a beach
Ticket taker: on the paddle-box at Ramsgate
Master Tippin; expert in chin-music
Waiters at the Pegwell Bay Hotel at Ramsgate
Youth, thin; cordially acquiesced in the sentiment of the stout lady

SB 49 February 1834   **MM HS**

Horatio Sparkins

The parvenu **Maldertons**, determined to rise, want to marry off **Teresa**, and the handsome, talkative but mysterious **Horatio Sparkins** makes a great impression at the assembly. They invite him for dinner, and family friend **Flamwell** looks him over. His grandiloquent address sweeps all before him. But the next day, shopping for bargains in an inferior shop, the Malderton ladies are stunned to recognize Teresa's beau in the assistant shopman, **Samuel Smith**. Teresa is still unmarried.

Principals

Malderton, "was a man whose whole scope of ideas was limited to Lloyd's, the Exchange, the India House, and the Bank. A few successful speculations had raised him from a situation of obscurity and comparative poverty, to a state of affluence. As frequently happens in such cases, the ideas of himself and his family became elevated to an extraordinary pitch as their means increased; they affected fashion, taste, and many other fooleries, in imitation of their betters, and had a very decided and becoming horror of anything which could, by possibility, be considered *low*.

"He was hospitable from ostentation, illiberal from ignorance, and prejudiced from conceit. Egotism and the love of display induced him to keep an excellent table: convenience, and a love of good things of this life, ensured him plenty of guests. He liked to have clever men, or what he considered such, at his table, because it was a great thing to talk about; but he never could endure what he called 'sharp fellows.' Probably he cherished this feeling out of compliment to his two sons, who gave their respected parent no uneasiness in that particular." ¶

Teresa Malderton "'You should recollect, my dear . . . that Teresa is now eight-and-twenty; and that it really is very important that something should be done.'"

"[She] was a very little girl, rather fat, with vermilion cheeks, but good-humoured, and still disengaged, although, to do her justice, the misfortune arose from no lack of perseverance on her part."

Horatio Sparkins, "the young man with the black whiskers and the white cravat . . . . "

—*his mystery:* "Who could he be? He was evidently reserved, and apparently melancholy. Was he a clergyman?—He danced too well. A barrister? —He said he was not called. He used very fine words, and talked a great deal. Could he be a distinguished foreigner, come to England . . . with the view of becoming acquainted with high life, polished etiquette, and English refinement? —No, he had not a foreign accent. Was he a surgeon, a contributor to the magazines, a writer of fashionable novels, or an artist?—No; to each and all of these surmises, there existed some valid objection.—'Then,' said everybody, 'he must be somebody . . . because he perceives our superiority, and pays us so much attention.'"

"' . . . you have been much among the silk gowns, or I mistake?' inquired **Flamwell**, deferentially.

"'Nearly all my life,' returned Sparkins.

"The question was thus pretty well settled .... He was a young gentleman 'about to be called.'"

"'Mr Sparkins,' said Flamwell, returning to the charge, 'do you happen to know Mr **Delafontaine**, of Bedford Square?'

"'I have exchanged cards with him; since which, indeed, I have had an opportunity of serving him considerably,' replied Horatio, slightly colouring; no doubt, at having been betrayed into making the acknowledgment."

—*at the Assembly:* "The elegant Sparkins attitudinised with admirable effect, until the family had crossed the room. He then started up, with the most natural appearance of surprise and delight; accosted **Mrs Malderton** with the utmost cordiality; saluted the young ladies in the most enchanting manner; bowed to, and shook hands with, Mr **Malderton**, with a degree of respect amounting almost to veneration; and returned the greetings of the two young men in a half-gratified, half-patronising manner, which fully convinced them that he must be an important, and, at the same time, condescending personage."

—*wooing:* "'How delightful!' said the interesting Horatio to his partner, as they promenaded the room at the conclusion of the set—'how delightful, how refreshing it is, to retire from the cloudy storms, the vicissitudes, and the troubles of life, even if it be but for a few short fleeting moments: and to spend those moments, fading and evanescent though they be, in the delightful, the blessed society of one individual—whose frowns would be death, whose coldness would be madness, whose falsehood would be ruin, whose constancy would be bliss; the possession of whose affection would be the brightest and best reward that Heaven could bestow on man!'"

—*on duty:* "'I want to see some silks,' answered **Mrs Malderton**.

"'Directly, ma'am.—Mr [**Samuel**] **Smith**! Where *is* Mr Smith?'

"'Here, sir,' cried a voice at the back of the shop.

"'Pray make haste, Mr Smith . . . . You never are to be found when you're wanted, sir.'

"Mr Smith, thus enjoined to use all possible dispatch, leaped over the counter with great agility, and placed himself before the newly-arrived customers. Mrs Malderton uttered a faint scream; **Miss Teresa**, who had been stooping down to talk to her sister, raised her head, and beheld—Horatio Sparkins!"

Supporting Roles

Jacob Barton, "was a large grocer; so vulgar, and so lost to all sense of feeling, that he actually never scrupled to avow that he wasn't above his business: 'he'd made his money by it, and he didn't care who know'd it.'"

Flamwell, "a little spoffish man, with green spectacles . . . was one of those gentlemen of remarkably extensive information whom one occasionally meets in society, who pretend to know everybody but in reality know nobody. At **Malderton**'s, where any stories about great people were received with a greedy ear, he was an especial favourite; and, knowing the kind of people he had to deal with, he carried his passion of claiming acquaintance with everybody, to the most immoderate length. He had rather a singular way of telling his greatest lies in a parenthesis, and with an air of self-denial, as if he feared being thought egotistical."

—*his diagnosis:* "'I don't know who he is,' he whispered to Mr **Malderton**, confidentially, as they followed **Horatio** up to the drawing-room. 'It's quite clear, however, that he belongs to the law, and that he is somebody of great importance, and very highly connected.'"

The other **Maldertons**

—**Frederick**, "the eldest son, in full-dress costume, was the very *beau ideal* of a smart waiter . . . . "

"[He was] the family authority on all points of taste, dress, and fashionable arrangement; who had lodgings of his own in town; who had a free admission to Covent Garden theatre; who always dressed according to the fashions of the months; who went up the water twice a week in the season; and who actually had an intimate friend who once knew a gentleman who formerly lived in the Albany . . . . "

—**Marianne**, "engaged in netting a purse, and looking sentimental."

—**Mrs**, "who was a little fat woman . . . looked like her eldest daughter multiplied by two."

—Thomas, "the youngest, with his white dress-stock, blue coat, bright buttons, and red watch-ribbon, strongly resembled the portrait of that interesting but rash young gentleman, **George Barnwell**."

—*impressed:* "'Yes, [**Sparkins**] is a prime fellow,' interposed Tom, who always managed to put his foot in it—'he talks just like an auctioneer.'

"'Tom!' said his father solemnly, 'I think I desired you, before, not to be a fool.' Tom looked as happy as a cock on a drizzly morning."

"'He talks very loud and nicely,' timidly observed Tom, 'but I don't exactly understand what he means.'"

Others

Hon. **Augustus Fitz-Edward Fitz-John Fitz-Osborne**. "' . . . from your description . . . he bears a strong resemblance . . . . He is a very talented young man, and rather eccentric [said **Flamwell**]. It's extremely probable he may have changed his name for some temporary purpose.'"

John. ". . . a man who, on ordinary occasions, acted as half-groom, half-gardener; but who, as it was important to make an impression on Mr **Sparkins**, had been forced into a white neckerchief and shoes, and touched up, and brushed, to look like a second footman."

Proprietor, of "a dirty-looking ticketed linen-draper's shop, with goods of all kinds, and labels of all sorts and sizes, in the window . . . .

"'Pray be seated, ladies. What is the first article?' inquired the obsequious master of the ceremonies of the establishment, who, in his large white neck-cloth and formal tie, looked like a bad 'portrait of a gentleman' in the Somerset House exhibition."

> *George Barnwell:* character in a George Lillo play: hanged for murder
> Groom, serving Malderton: takes Sparkins' great black horse
> **Lord Gubbleton**, a Flamwell friend; his health concerns Malderton
> **John**, a manservant
> **Jones, Spruggins and Smith**, drapers
> Prince Leopold[H]: handsome husband of Princess Charlotte
> **Sir Thomas Noland**: his name dropped
> Captain Sir John Ross[H]: polar explorer
> **Samuel Smith**, linen-draper

SB 50 1836   1st SB **BV**

The Black Veil

A doctor newly in practice has a first client: a distraught woman who persuades him to meet her in a wretched and dangerous quarter of London. He goes, with trepidation, and sees on a bed—a corpse. The man had been hanged that morning. The woman faints as she acknowledges her son.

Professional and Client

Surgeon. " . . . a young medical practitioner, recently established in business . . . had not yet witnessed enough of the miseries which are daily presented before the eyes of its members, to have grown comparatively callous to human suffering."

—*in a dangerous neighbourhood:* " . . . whatever reflection made him hesitate, he *did* hesitate: but, being a young man of strong mind and great personal courage, it was only for an instant . . . . "

—*afterward:* "For many years after . . . the young surgeon was a daily visitor at the side of the harmless mad woman; not only soothing her by his presence and kindness, but alleviating the rigour of her condition by pecuniary donations for her comfort and support, bestowed with no sparing hand . . . amid all the honours of rank and station which have since been heaped upon him, and which he has so well earned, he can have no reminiscence more gratifying to his heart than that connected with The Black Veil."

Woman. "It was a singularly tall woman, dressed in deep mourning . . . . The upper part of her figure was carefully muffled in a black shawl, as if for the purpose of concealment; and her face was shrouded by a thick black veil. She stood perfectly erect, her figure was drawn up to its full height, and though the **surgeon** felt that the eyes beneath the veil were fixed on him, she stood perfectly motionless, and evinced, by no gesture whatever, the slightest consciousness of his having turned towards her."

"There was a desperate earnestness in this woman's manner, that went to the young man's heart."

—*revealed:* "Her features were those of a woman about fifty, who had once been handsome. Sorrow and weeping had left traces upon them which not time itself would ever have produced without their aid; her face was deadly pale; and there was a nervous contortion of the lip, and an unnatural fire in her eye, which showed too plainly that her bodily and mental powers had nearly sunk beneath an accumulation of misery."

"The mother was a widow without friends or money, and had denied herself necessaries to bestow them on her orphan boy."

Others

Rose. " . . . he thought . . . how happy it would make Rose if he could only tell her that he had found a patient at last, and hoped to have more, and to come down again, in a few months' time, and marry her, and take her home to gladden his lonely fireside, and stimulate him to fresh exertions."

Tall man. "The door-chain was softly unfastened; the door opened; and a tall, ill-favoured man, with black hair, and a face, as the **surgeon** often declared afterwards, as pale and haggard as the countenance of any dead man he ever saw, presented himself."

Tom. " . . . a corpulent round-headed boy, who, in consideration of the sum of one shilling per week and his food, was let out by the parish to carry medicine and messages. As there was no demand for the medicine, however, and no necessity for the messages, he usually occupied his unemployed hours— averaging fourteen a day—in abstracting peppermint drops, taking animal nourishment, and going to sleep."

Filthy **woman**, in Walworth. "Occasionally, a filthy-looking woman would make her appearance from the door of a dirty house, to empty the contents of some cooking utensil into the gutter in front, or to scream after a little slip-shod **girl** . . . . "

The First Patient

A son. "That boy, unmindful of her prayers, and forgetful of the sufferings she had endured for him—incessant anxiety of mind, and voluntary starvation of body—had plunged into a career of dissipation and crime."

"Stretched upon the bed, closely enveloped in a linen wrapper, and covered with blankets, lay a human form, stiff and motionless. The head and face, which were those of a man, were uncovered, save by a bandage which passed over the head and under the chin. The eyes were closed. The left arm lay heavily across the bed . . . . "

"The **surgeon** turned his face towards the bed, and bent over the body which now lay full in the light of the window. The throat was swollen, and a livid mark encircled it. The truth flashed suddenly upon him.

"'This is one of the men who were hanged this morning!' he exclaimed, turning away with a shudder.

"It is,' replied the **woman**, with a cold, unmeaning stare.

"'Who was he?' inquired the surgeon.

"'*My son,*' rejoined the woman; and fell senseless at his feet."

> Baby, carried by a young girl
> John Bishop[H], body-snatcher
> William Burke[H], murderer who sold bodies to an anatomist
> Criminal, equally guilty with the son, had gotten off
> Girl, in wretched London district, with baby nearly as big as she

SB 51 October 1834   MM **SE**

The Steam Excursion

Percy Noakes agrees to arrange a steamboat party. After a deadlock, the final guest list includes both the **Tauntons** and the **Briggses**, bitter enemies. An early morning London street scene; embarkation of food, musicians and many people.   The Tauntons bring dashing Captain **Helves**, who attaches himself to **Julia** Briggs and tells tall stories. A squall blows away the fun, and even jokester **Hardy** has to lean on the rail.

Leadership

Hardy. "' . . . a stout gentleman of about forty, pausing at the door in the attitude of an awkward harlequin . . . . He was an Astley-Cooperish Joe Miller— a practical joker, immensely popular with married ladies, and a general favourite with young men. He was always engaged in some pleasure excursion or other, and delighted in getting somebody into a scrape on such occasions. He could sing comic songs, imitate hackney-coachmen and fowls, play airs on his chin, and execute concertos on the Jews'-harp. He always eat [*sic*.] and drank most immoderately, and was the bosom friend of Mr **Percy Noakes**. He had a red face, a somewhat husky voice, and a tremendous laugh."

—on board: "There was Mr Hardy, in a blue jacket and waistcoat, white trousers, silk stockings, and pumps—in full aquatic costume, with a straw hat on his head, and an immense telescope under his arm . . . . "

—in full spate: " . . . having played one or two very brilliant fantasias on the Jews'-harp, and having frequently repeated the exquisitely amusing joke of slily chalking a large cross on the back of some member of the committee . . . . "

—stirrings: "'Don't it blow?' inquired some one . . . .

"'No, I don't think it does,' responded Hardy, sincerely wishing that he could persuade himself that it did not; for he sat near the door, and was almost blown off his seat."

—in heavy weather: "'Will you go on deck?'

"'No, I will *not.*' This was said with a most determined air, and in a voice which might have been taken for an imitation of anything; it was quite as much like a guinea-pig as a bassoon."

"Mr Hardy was observed, some hours afterwards, in an attitude which induced his friends to suppose that he was busily engaged in contemplating the beauties of the deep; they only regretted that his taste for the picturesque should lead him to remain so long in a position, very injurious at all times, but especially so to an individual labouring under a tendency of blood to the head."

Percy Noakes "was a law student . . . 'a devilish good fellow.' He had a large circle of acquaintance, and seldom dined at his own expense. He used to talk politics to papas, flatter the vanity of mammas, do the amiable to their daughters, make pleasure engagements with their sons, and romp with the younger branches. Like those paragons of perfection, advertising footmen out of place, he was always 'willing to make himself generally useful.' . . . He was always making something for somebody, or planning some party of pleasure, which was his great *forte.* He invariably spoke with astonishing rapidity; was smart, spoffish, and eight-and-twenty."

—on a project: "Mr Percy Noakes brushed his hat, whisked the crumbs off his inexplicables with a silk handkerchief, gave the ends of his hair a persuasive roll round his forefinger, and sallied forth . . . . "

—on board: " . . . [he] took off his coat and rushed backwards and forwards, doing nothing, but quite convinced he was assisting everybody . . . and Mr Percy Noakes panted with the violence of his exertions."

—attention to detail: " . . . [he] having considered it as important that the number of young men should exactly tally with that of the young ladies, as that the quantity of knives on board should be in precise proportion to the forks."

The Led

The **Briggses**.

*—***Alexander**, "the youngest, was under articles to his brother [**Samuel**] . . . [he] was deservedly celebrated for possessing all the pertinacity of a bankruptcy-court attorney, combined with the obstinacy of that useful animal which browses on the thistle . . . . "

*—***Julia**. "Captain **Helves** danced one set with Miss **Emily Taunton**, and another set with Miss **Sophia Taunton**. **Mrs Taunton** was in ecstasies. The victory appeared to be complete; but alas! the inconstancy of man! Having performed this necessary duty, he attached himself solely to Miss Julia Briggs,

with whom he danced no less than three sets consecutively, and from whose
side he evinced no intention of stirring for the remainder of the day."

—**Kate**. "'Where could they have picked up that military man?' inquired
Mrs Briggs . . . .

"'I can't imagine,' replied Miss Kate, bursting with vexation; for the very
fierce air with which the gallant captain [**Helves**] regarded the company, had
impressed her with a high sense of his importance."

—The **Misses**. "' . . . if the Misses Briggs will oblige us with something
before dinner, I am sure we shall be very much delighted.'

"One of those hums of admiration followed the suggestion, which one frequently hears in society, when nobody has the most distant notion what he is
expressing his approval of. The three Misses Briggs looked modestly at their
mamma, and the mamma looked approvingly at her daughters, and Mrs
Taunton looked scornfully at all of them."

—**Mrs**. "Between the Briggses and the **Tauntons** there existed a degree of
implacable hatred, quite unprecedented. The animosity between the
Montagues and Capulets, was nothing to that which prevailed between these
two illustrious houses . . . . If the Miss Briggses appeared in smart bonnets, the

Miss Tauntons eclipsed them with smarter. If Mrs Taunton appeared in a cap of all the hues of the rainbow, Mrs Briggs forthwith mounted a toque, with all the patterns of the kaleidoscope."

—*attuned:* " . . . there was . . . a vast deal of screwing and tightening, and winding and turning, during which Mrs Briggs expatiated to those near her on the immense difficulty of playing a guitar, and hinted at the wondrous proficiency of her daughters in that mystic art."

—**Samuel**, solicitor. " . . . a mere machine, a sort of self-acting legal walking-stick . . . . "

Edkins. " . . . in a green stock and spectacles of the same, a member of the honourable society of the Inner Temple . . . . "

—*in a squall:* "The young gentleman with the spectacles, who had been in a fluctuating state for some time—at one moment bright, and at another dismal, like a revolving light on the sea-coast—rashly announced his wish to propose a toast.   After several ineffectual attempts to preserve his perpendicular, the young gentleman, having managed to hook himself to the centre leg of the table with his left hand, proceeded . . . ."

Master **Fleetwood**. " . . . the boy about four . . . attired for the occasion in a nankeen frock, between the bottom of which, and the top of his plaid socks, a considerable portion of two small mottled legs was discernible. He had a light blue cap with a gold band and tassel on his head, and a damp piece of gingerbread in his hand, with which he had slightly embossed his countenance."

Captain Helves. " . . . a lion—a gentleman with a bass voice and an incipient red moustache."

—*a duet:* " . . . [it] was loudly applauded, and, certainly, the perfect independence of the parties deserved great commendation. Miss **Emily** sang her part, without the slightest reference to the captain; and the captain sang so loud, that he had not the slightest idea what was being done by his partner. After having gone through the last few eighteen or nineteen bars by himself, therefore, he acknowledged the plaudits of the circle with that air of self-denial which men usually assume when they think they have done something to astonish the company."

—*a tall story:* "Helves was the sole lion for the remainder of the day—impudence and the marvellous are pretty sure passports to any society."

—*after landing:* " . . . Mr **Samuel** arrested him, in the way of business, pursuant to instructions received from Messrs. **Scroggins** and **Payne**, whose town-debts the gallant captain had condescended to collect, but whose accounts, with the indiscretion sometimes peculiar to military minds, he had omitted to keep with that dull accuracy which custom has rendered necessary."

The **Tauntons**

—**Emily**. "was making a watch-guard . . . . " *See* Captain **Helves**—*a duet*

—**Mrs**. "She was a good-looking widow of fifty, with the form of a giantess and the mind of a child. The pursuit of pleasure, and some means of killing time, were the sole end of her existence. She doted on her daughters, who were as frivolous as herself."

—*her lion:* "Mrs Taunton complains that she has been much deceived in [Captain **Helves**]. He introduced himself to the family on board a Gravesend steam-packet, and certainly, therefore, ought to have proved respectable."

—**Sophia** "was at the piano, practising a new song—poetry by the young officer, or the police-officer, or the custom-house officer, or some other interesting amateur."

Miss **Wakefield** "The girl was about six years old . . . [and] was dressed in a white frock with a pink sash and dog's-eared-looking little spencer: a straw bonnet and green veil, six inches by three and a half . . . . "

Professional Support

Three **watermen**. "'Boat, sir?' cried one of the three watermen who were mopping out their boats, and all whistling. 'Boat, sir?'"

"'Would you prefer a wessel, sir?' inquired another, to the infinite delight of the 'Jack-n-the-water.'"

"'Did you want to be put on board a steamer, sir?' inquired an old fireman-waterman, very confidentially. He was dressed in a faded red suit, just the colour of the cover of a very old Court-guide."

> **Al Bowlar, Ram Chowdar Doss Azuph**; a devilish pleasant fellow
> Apprentice, with quenched-looking sleepy eyes, taking down shutters
> Ballast-heavers, shocking to young ladies
> Boy, stationed at the hatchway to pass instructions to the engineer
> Children, town-made, with parenthetical legs
> Coal-whippers, horrifying to young ladies
> Engineer, on a steam excursion
> Flageolet: been werry ill, and is in a dreadful prusperation
> **Fleetwood**, and his wife; unfit for duty
> Ladies of the street, in forced merriment
> **Loggins**, solicitor of Boswell Court, who sent an excuse
> Master, of the boat
> Milkwoman, occasionally seen pacing slowly along
> Nurserymaids, flaunting: a feature of London gardens
> Old gentleman, bald; trying to look through a doctored telescope
> *-pl* gravely, perseveringly walking the deck in pairs
> Old lady, who wondered what a gum-gum really is
> Pastrycook's men, laying out the dinner on the vessel
> Policeman, observant on the street
> Porters, for the steam excursion, running with crushing luggage
> Proprietor, of a street-breakfast, with coffee boiling, slices of bread & butter
> **Scroggins & Payne**: they first hired, then arrested Captain Helves
> **Simson**, guest proposed for a steam excursion
> Steward: as fast as he put the fire-irons up, they fell down again
>   wife, who laughed till she cried at Percy's feckless efforts
> **Mrs Stubbs**, a dirty laundress with a barrel of dirt and cinders
> Sweep, little and longing as he views tempting delicacies
> Violinist, a young man; without brandy, can't answer for consequences
> Wakefield, and his wife: not a factor
> **Wizzle,** guest proposed for a steam excursion
> Young ladies, on excursion; shocked by coal-whippers, ballast heavers
> Young men on the street, in mirth and disorder, not having been to bed

SB 52 1836   lst SB **WD**

The Great Winglebury Duel

A farce (CD later made it the play *The Strange Gentleman*) of mistaken identity and misunderstanding in a hotel at Great Winglebury on the way to Gretna Green, traditional destination of eloping couples. A duel does not take place.

Principals

Miss Julia Manners, "a buxom richly-dressed female of about forty . . . . "

"'But to run away—actually run away—with a young man!' remonstrated the mayor.

"'You wouldn't have me actually run away with an old one, I presume?' was the cool rejoinder.

—*forthright:* "' . . . the property had the encumbrance of your management; and all I will say of that, is, that I only wonder it didn't die of consumption instead of its master. You helped yourself then:—help me now.'"

—*adaptable:* " . . . she wanted a young husband, and the only course open to Mr **Trott** to retrieve his disgrace was a rich wife. So they came to the conclusion that it would be a pity to have all this trouble and expense for nothing; and that as they were so far on the road already, they had better go to Gretna Green, and marry each other; and they did so."

Joseph Overton. "' . . a sleek man, about ten years older [than forty], in drab shorts and continuations, black coat, neckcloth, and gloves."

—*realistic:* "Mr Joseph Overton was a man of the world, and an attorney; and as certain indistinct recollections of an odd thousand pounds or two, appropriated by mistake, passed across his mind, he hemmed deprecatingly, smiled blandly, remained silent for a few seconds; and finally inquired, 'What do you wish me to do?'"

Top-boots. "A man thrust in a red head with one eye in it, and being again desired to 'come in,' brought in the body and the legs to which the head belonged, and a fur cap which belonged to the head.

"'You are the upper-boots, I think?' inquired Mr **Trott**.

"'Yes, I am the upper-boots,' replied a voice from inside a velveteen case, with mother-of-pearl buttons—'that is, I'm the boots as b'longs to the house; the other man's my man, as goes errands and does odd jobs. Top-boots and half-boots, I calls us.'"

—*on duty:* " . . . the one-eyed boots was immediately instructed to repair to number nineteen, to act as custodian of the person of the supposed lunatic until half-past twelve o'clock. In pursuance of this direction, that somewhat eccentric gentleman armed himself with a walking-stick of gigantic dimensions, and repaired, with his usual equanimity of manner, to Mr **Trott's** apartment, which he entered without any ceremony, and mounted guard in, by quietly depositing himself on a chair near the door, where he proceeded to beguile the time by whistling a popular air with great apparent satisfaction."

" . . . as he remembered to have heard, somewhere or other, that the human eye had an unfailing effect in controlling mad people, he kept his solitary organ of vision constantly fixed on Mr Alexander Trott."

Alexander Trott. "Mr Trott was a young man, had highly promising whiskers, an undeniable tailor, and an insinuating address—he wanted nothing but valour, and who wants that with three thousand a year?"

—*challenged:* "Long and weary were his reflections, as, burying his face in his hand, he sat, ruminating on the best course to be pursued. His mental direction-post pointed to London. He thought of the 'governor's' anger, and the loss of the fortune which the paternal **Brown** had promised the paternal Trott his daughter [**Emily**] should contribute to the coffers of his son. Then the words 'To Brown's' were legibly inscribed on the said direction-post, but **Horace Hunter**'s denunciation rung in his ears;—last of all it bore, in red letters, the words, 'To Stiffun's Acre' . . . . "

—*alarmed:* "'Bless me!' exclaimed Trott, in an agony of apprehension, 'can such things happen in a country like this? Such unrelenting and cold-blooded hostility!' He wiped off the concentrated essence of cowardice that was oozing fast down his forehead, and looked aghast . . . . "

Supporting Roles

Horace Hunter, epistolarian. "'SIR. From Great Winglebury church, a footpath leads through four meadows to a retired spot known to the townspeople as Stiffun's Acre.' (**Mr Trott** shuddered.) 'I shall be waiting there alone, at twenty minutes before six o'clock to-morrow morning. Should I be disappointed in seeing you there, I will do myself the pleasure of calling with a horsewhip.'

"'P.S. There is a gunsmith's in the High Street; and they won't sell gunpowder after dark—you understand me.

"'P.P.S. You had better not order your breakfast in the morning until you have met me. It may be an unnecessary expense.'"

Lord Peter. "'Dear Lord Peter is considerably afraid of the resentment of his family [said **Julia Manners**] . . . not being considered very prudent or sagacious by his friends . . . .'"

—*jilted:* " . . . [having] been detained beyond his time by drinking champagne and riding a steeple-chase, [he] went back to the Honourable **Augustus Flair**'s, and drank more champagne, and rode another steeple-chase, and was thrown and killed."

Others

Ostlers. "Suddenly, the loud notes of a key-bugle broke the monotonous stillness of the street . . . up started the ostlers . . . as if they were electrified—unstrapping, and unchaining, and unbuckling, and dragging willing horses out, and forcing reluctant horses in, and making a most exhilarating bustle."

Thomas. " . . . [the waiter] pulled down the window-blind, and then pulled it up again . . . adjusted the glasses on the sideboard, brushed a place that was *not* dusty, rubbed his hands very hard, walked stealthily to the door, and evaporated."

> Boots, a subordinate "Half-boots"; does errands for "Top-boots"
> Boys, ragged; standing a little apart as the coach arrives
> Chambermaid, at the Winglebury Arms
> Coachman, delivering a lady at the Winglebury Arms
> **Cornberry**: he wooed and died, leaving his property unencumbered
> Hon. **Augustus Flair**, M. P.
> Guard: "Lady inside here!" on arriving at the Winglebury Arms
> Loungers, around the horse-trough waiting for the coach
> Post-boys: listless in shiny hats and smock-frocks: talk of cattle
> **Tom**, driver of a chaise
> Waiters, four: at the Winglebury Arms: hold and escort Trott
> Mrs Williamson, stout landlady of the Winglebury Arms

SB 53 January 1834   MM **JP**

Mrs Joseph Porter
(first called 'Mrs Joseph Porter "Over the Way"')

The star is the amateur theatre. Every imaginable disaster occurs in a **Gattleton** family production of *Othello,* much to the delight of excluded and sarcastic neighbour **Mrs Porter**.

The Players

Evans "was pronounced by all his lady friends to be 'quite a dear.' He looked so interesting, and had such lovely whiskers: to say nothing of his talent for writing verses in albums and playing the flute! *Roderigo* simpered and bowed."

—*on the night:* "Mr Evans, naturally too tall for the scenery, wore a black velvet hat with immense white plumes, the glory of which was lost in 'the flies;' and the only other inconvenience of which was, that when it was off his head he could not put it on, and when it was on he could not take it off. Notwithstanding all his practice, too, he fell with his head and shoulders as neatly through one of the side scenes, as a harlequin would jump through a panel in a Christmas pantomime."

The **Gattletons**.

—**Caroline**. "'. . . young What's-his-name saying he wondered how Miss Caroline, with such a foot and ankle, could have the vanity to play *Fenella* [said **Mrs Joseph Porter**].'"

—**Lucina**. " . . . every sofa in the house was more or less damaged by the perseverance and spirit with which Mr Sempronius Gattleton, and Miss Lucina, rehearsed the smothering scene in 'Othello' . . . ."

—**Mr**, the elder, "who had been appointed prompter, and took as much interest in the play as the youngest of the company."

—*on the night:* "'*(Aside)* Why don't you prompt, father?'

"'Because I've mislaid my spectacles,' said poor Mr Gattleton, almost dead with the heat and bustle."

—**Mrs**. " . . . . [she] was a kind, good-tempered, vulgar soul, exceedingly fond of her husband and children, and entertaining only three dislikes. In the first place, she had a natural antipathy to anybody else's unmarried daughters; in the second, she was in bodily fear of anything in the shape of ridicule; lastly—almost a necessary consequence of this feeling—she regarded, with feelings of the utmost horror, one **Mrs Joseph Porter**, over the way."

—**Sempronius**, "a stock-broker in especially comfortable circumstances . . . . In consideration of his sustaining the trifling inconvenience of bearing all the expenses of the play . . . unanimously elected stage-manager . . . ."

Harleigh, "smiled, and looked foolish—not an unusual thing with him—hummed 'Behold how brightly breaks the morning,' and blushed as red as the fisherman's nightcap he was trying on."

—*on the night:* " . . . [he] was hoarse, and rather unwell, in consequence of the great quantity of lemon and sugar-candy he had eaten to improve his voice . . . . The orchestra complained that Mr Harleigh put them out, and Mr Harleigh declared that the orchestra prevented his singing a note."

Wilson. "' . . . Mr Wilson, who was to have played *Iago,* is—that is, has been—or, in other words, Ladies and Gentlemen, the fact is . . . unavoidably detained at the Post Office this evening.'"

" . . . the original *Iago* unexpectedly arrived . . . as *Iago* could not get on any of the stage boots, in consequence of his feet being violently swelled with the heat and excitement, he was under the necessity of playing the part in a pair of Wellingtons, which contrasted rather oddly with his richly embroidered pantaloons."

The Audience

Thomas Balderstone, "**Mrs Gattleton**'s brother, familiarly called in the family 'Uncle Tom' . . . was very rich, and exceedingly fond of his nephews and nieces . . . one of the best-hearted men in existence: always in a good temper, and always talking. It was his boast that he wore top-boots on all occasions, and had never worn a black silk neckerchief; and it was his pride that he remembered all the principal plays of Shakespeare from beginning to end—and so he did. The result of this parrot-like accomplishment was, that he was not only perpetually quoting himself, but that he could never sit by, and hear a misquotation from the 'Swan of Avon' without setting the unfortunate delinquent right."

—*on the night:* " . . . having mounted his hobby, nothing could induce him to dismount; so, during the whole remainder of the play, he performed a kind of running accompaniment, by muttering everybody's part as it was being delivered, in an under-tone. The audience were highly amused, **Mrs Porter** delighted, the performers embarrassed; Uncle Tom never was better pleased in all his life; and Uncle Tom's nephews and nieces had never, although the declared heirs to his large property, so heartily wished him gathered to his fathers as on that memorable occasion."

Emma Porter. "'Never mind, ma,' said Miss Emma Porter . . . trying to look unconcerned; 'if they had invited me, you know that neither you nor pa would have allowed me to take part in such an exhibition.'"

Mrs Joseph Porter. " . . . the good folks of Clapham and its vicinity stood very much in awe of scandal and sarcasm; and thus Mrs Joseph Porter was courted, and flattered, and caressed, and invited, for much the same reason that induces a poor author, without a farthing in his pocket, to behave with extraordinary civility to a two-penny postman."

—*delighted:* "In short, the whole affair was, as Mrs Joseph Porter triumphantly told everybody, 'a complete failure.' The audience went home at four o'clock in the morning, exhausted with laughter, suffering from severe headaches, and smelling terribly of brimstone and gunpowder."

Other Roles

Fishermen. "The fishermen, who were hired for the occasion, revolted to the very life, positively refusing to play without an increased allowance of spirits; and, their demand being complied with, getting drunk in the eruption-scene as naturally as possible."

First **Flute**. "The unfortunate individual, however, who had undertaken to play the flute accompaniment 'at sight,' found, from fatal experience, the perfect truth of the old adage, 'out of sight, out of mind;' for being very near-sighted, and being placed at a considerable distance from his music-book, all he had an opportunity of doing was to play a bar now and then in the wrong place, and put the other performers out."

Second **flute**. "A self-taught deaf gentleman, who had kindly offered to bring his flute, would be a most valuable addition to the orchestra . . . [he] *too-too'd* away, quite unconscious that he was at all wrong, until apprised, by the applause of the audience, that the overture was concluded."

Miss Jenkins. "[Her] talent for the piano was too well known to be doubted for an instant . . . . "

—*on the night:* "The pianoforte player hammered away with laudable perseverance . . . [and] overpowered by the extreme heat of the room, fainted away at the commencement of the entertainment . . . ."

Aldermen, two: in the audience
Bob: lent his checked shirt to Tom so he could make a fisherman
Brown: the violoncello sounded very well in Othello, considering
Cape: he had practised the violin accompaniment to Othello
Sir Thomas Glumper, mysteriously knighted in the last reign
Gubbins family, in the audience
Hickson family, in the audience
Nixon family, in the audience
Porter father, invisible but invoked
Sheriff, in perspective: in the audience
Smith family, in the audience
Thomas, the pastrycook, said twelve dozen tarts were ordered
Tom, the Gattletons' man, recruited for another fisherman in *Othello*

A Passage in the Life of Mr Watkins Tottle

Watkins Tottle, living exiguously, owes money to **Gabriel Parsons**, of gallant background, who finds an eligible marital prospect for him. Tottle is taken up for debt (CD's most complete picture of a spunging-house, based on recent experience), and Parsons buys him out, but the project falls short when **Miss Lillerton**'s troth to the Rev **Timson** is revealed. Tottle has misunderstood and been misunderstood, and the shock, to our shock, is mortal.

Principals

Miss Lillerton. "'I know a lady . . . who's just the thing for you [said **Parsons**]. Well educated; talks French; plays the piano; knows a good deal about flowers, and shells, and all that sort of thing; and has five hundred a year, with an uncontrolled power of disposing of it, by her last will and testament.'"

"'What coloured hair has the lady?' inquired Mr **Watkins Tottle**.

"'Egad, I hardly recollect,' replied Gabriel, with coolness. 'Perhaps I ought to have observed at first, she wears a front.'

"'A what?' ejaculated Tottle.

"'One of those things with curls, along here,' said Parsons, drawing a straight line across his forehead, just over his eyes, in illustration of his meaning. 'I know the front's black; I can't speak quite positively about her own hair; because, unless one walks behind her, and catches a glimpse of it under her bonnet, one seldom sees it; but I should say that it was rather lighter than the front—a shade of a greyish tinge, perhaps.'" 1

—*delicacy:* "' . . . there was an old portrait of some man . . . with two large black staring eyes, hanging up in her bedroom; she positively refused to go to bed there, till it was taken down, considering it decidedly wrong.'" 1

—*introduced:* " . . . a lady of very prim appearance, and remarkably inanimate. She was one of those persons at whose age it is impossible to make any reasonable guess; her features might have been remarkably pretty when she was younger, and they might always have presented the same appearance. Her complexion—with a slight trace of powder here and there—was as clear as that of a well-made wax doll, and her face as expressive. She was handsomely dressed, and was winding up a gold watch." 1

—*meeting again:* "'Here's Mr **Tottle**, my dear,' said **Mrs Parsons**, addressing Miss Lillerton. The lady turned quickly round, and acknowledged his courteous salute with the same sort of confusion that Watkins had noticed on their first interview, but with something like a slight expression of disappointment or carelessness." 2

Gabriel Parsons. " . . . a short elderly gentleman with a gruffish voice . . . delicately insinuated that, in the absence of whiskey, he would not be averse to brandy . . . . He was a rich sugar-baker, who mistook rudeness for honesty, and abrupt bluntness for an open and candid manner; many besides Gabriel mistake bluntness for sincerity." 1

—*home:* " . . . a cardboard-looking house with disguised chimneys, and a lawn like a large sheet of green letter-paper . . . . " 1

—wooing: "' . . . I used to like nothing so well as sitting by her side—we didn't talk so much then, but I remember I used to have a great notion of looking at her out of the extreme corner of my left eye—and then I got very miserable and sentimental, and began to write verses, and use Macassar oil.'" 1

Charles Timson. "'Timson, that's **Tottle**—Tottle, that's Timson; bred for the church, which I fear will never be bread for him;' and [**Parsons**] chuckled at the old joke." 2

"'He's waiting for a living, and has been assisting his uncle . . . .'" 2

—greeting Mr **Tottle**: "'How do *you* do, sir?' replied Timson, with as much coldness as if it were a matter of perfect indifference to him how he did, as it very likely was." 2

—a misunderstanding: "'Then, sir,' said Timson, seizing both **Tottle**'s hands, 'allow me in his presence to thank you most unfeignedly and cordially, for the noble part you have acted in this affair.'

"'He thinks I recommended him' thought Tottle. 'Confound these fellows! they never think of anything but their fees.'" 2

Watkins Tottle "was a rather uncommon compound of strong uxorious inclinations, and an unparalleled degree of anti-connubial timidity. He was about fifty years of age; stood four feet six inches and three quarters in his socks—for he never stood in stockings at all—plump, clean, and rosy. He looked something like a vignette to one of Richardson's novels, and had a clean-cravatish formality of manner, and kitchen-pokerness of carriage, which Sir Charles Grandison himself might have envied. He lived on an annuity, which was well adapted to the individual who received it, in one respect—it was rather small. He received it in periodical payments on every alternate Monday; but he ran himself out, about a day after the expiration of the first week, as regularly as an eight-day clock; and then, to make the comparison complete, his landlady wound him up, and he went on with a regular tick." 1

—his imagination: " . . . the idea of matrimony had never ceased to haunt him . . . fancy transformed his small parlour . . . into a neat house in the suburbs; the half-hundredweight of coals under the kitchen-stairs suddenly sprang up into three tons of the best Walls-end; his small French bed-stead was converted into a regular matrimonial four-poster; and in the empty chair on the opposite side of the fireplace, imagination seated a beautiful young lady, with a very little independence or will of her own, and a very large independence under a will of her father's." 1

—abashed: "'Now, were you ever in love, Tottle?' [**Parsons**] inquired.

"Mr Watkins Tottle blushed up to the eyes, and down to the chin, and exhibited a most extensive combination of colours as he confessed the soft impeachment."

—wooing: "'I can only impute [the slow passing of the morning] to my unavoidable absence from your society, madam,' said Watkins, 'and that of **Mrs Parsons**.'

"During this short dialogue the ladies had been leading the way to the house.

"'What the deuce did you stick Fanny into that last compliment for?' inquired **Parsons**, as they followed together; 'it quite spoilt the effect.'

"'Oh! it really would have been too broad without,' replied Watkins Tottle, 'much too broad!'"

"'He's mad!' Parsons whispered his wife, as they entered the drawing-room, 'mad from modesty.'" 2

—*an unintentionally ambiguous proposal:* "'How can I promote your happiness, Mr Tottle?'

"Here was the time for a flourish—'By allowing me,' replied Watkins, falling bump on his knees, and breaking two brace-buttons and a waistcoat-string, in the act—'By allowing me to be your slave, your servant—in short, by unreservedly making me the confidant of your heart's feelings—may I say for the promotion of your own happiness—may I say, in order that you may become the wife of a kind and affectionate husband?'

"'Disinterested creature!' exclaimed **Miss Lillerton**, hiding her face in a white pocket-handkerchief with an eyelet-hole border." 2

—*ambiguity revealed:* "'I say that so long as we see you to breakfast,' replied **Timson**, 'we will excuse your being absent from the ceremony, though of course your presence at it would give us the utmost pleasure.'

"Mr Watkins Tottle staggered against the wall, and fixed his eyes on Timson with appalling perseverance." 2

—*returned home:* " . . . he went through the formalities of eating and drinking as usual, but a week afterwards he was seized with a relapse, while perusing the list of marriages in a morning paper, from which he never perfectly recovered.

"A few weeks after the last-named occurrence, the body of a gentleman unknown was found in the Regent's canal." 2

Parsons Ménage

Martha. "**She** went into **Fanny**'s service when we were first married, and has been with us ever since; but I don't think she has felt one atom of respect for me since the morning she saw me released, when she went into violent hysterics, to which she has been subject ever since.'" 1

Fanny Parsons. "Mrs Gabriel Parsons drank four glasses of port on the plea of being a nurse just then . . . ." 1

—*at table:* "**Watkins** . . . broke a tumbler. The countenance of the lady of the house, which had been all smiles previously, underwent an awful change....

"'Not the least consequence,' replied Mrs Parsons, in a tone which implied that it was of the greatest consequence possible . . . ." 2

—*on marriage:* "Mrs Parsons talked *to* **Miss Lillerton** and *at* her better half; expatiated on the impatience of men generally; hinted that her husband was peculiarly vicious in this respect, and wound up by insinuating that she must be one of the best tempers that ever existed, or she never could put up with it." 2

The Spunging House

Harry. " . . . a genteel-looking young man was talking earnestly, and in a low tone, to a young female, whose face was concealed by a thick veil . . . ." 2

Ikey, a bailiff. " . . . in a coarse Petersham great coat, whity-brown neckerchief, faded black suit, gamboge-coloured top-boots, and one of those large-crowned hats, formerly seldom met with, but now very generally patronised by gentlemen and costermongers." 2

Solomon Jacobs, proprietor of a spunging house. "'Our governor's wide awake, he is. I'll never say nothin' agin him, nor no man; but he knows what's o'clock, he does uncommon.'" 2

Jem. " . . . a sallow-faced, red-haired, sulky boy, who, after surveying Mr **Gabriel Parsons** through the glass, applied a large key to an immense wooden excrescence, which was in reality a lock . . . ." 2

Kate. "She had been weeping bitterly, and the noxious atmosphere of the room acting upon her excited feelings and delicate frame, rendered the support of her companion [**Harry**] necessary as they quitted it together.

"There was an air of superiority about them both, and something in their appearance so unusual in such a place, that a respectful silence was observed until the whirr—r—bang of the spring door announced that they were out of hearing." 2

Willis, "of vulgar manners, dressed in the very extreme of the prevailing fashion, was pacing up and down the room, with a lighted cigar in his mouth and his hands in his pockets, ever and anon puffing forth volumes of smoke, and occasionally applying, with much apparent relish, to a pint pot, the contents of which were 'chilling' on the hob." 2

Boy, Parsons servant; groping under the table for broken glass
Boys, hoping for a chance to hold a horse
Bridesmaids, two friends of Fanny Parsons
Carpenter, the housemaid's sweetheart, who extricated Parsons
Children playing in the road, contributing to a traffic jam
Coal-dealer, in a spunging house: stout and hearty-looking
     wife: an equally comfortable-looking personage
Debtors, two: playing cribbage in a spunging house
Father and mother of Mrs Parsons: objected to the match for lack of money
Sir Charles Grandison, eponymous hero of Richardson novel
John, a footman
Man, acting as father at a wedding for five shillings and porter
-maniac, who had escaped from a neighbouring mad-house
Policemen, backing horses into shop-windows to clear traffic
Samuel Richardson[H]: novelist
Frank Ross: referred to a flannel petticoat in the presence of a lady
Tom, a gardener in a blue apron: let himself out to do the ornamental
Tom, Charles Timson's uncle's servant
Walker, a debtor playing cribbage in a spunging house
Woman, dirty; employee in the spunging house visited by Parsons
Women, with basket and door-key, contributing to traffic jam

SB 55 April 1834   MM **BC**

The Bloomsbury Christening

Sour **Nicodemus Dumps** (shadowy prefigure of **Scrooge**) unwarily promises his nephew to be godfather to a new arrival. He is obliged to go by omnibus (a supreme vignette on the perils of public transportation in the days of omnibuses competing on the same routes) to the **Kitterbell** christening. Artful dodgers get the silver mug. Dumps gives a toast to end toasts. *See* HW/RW and MC/BF

The Misanthrope

Nicodemus Dumps "was a bachelor, six feet high, and fifty years old: cross, cadaverous, odd, and ill-natured. He was never happy but when he was miserable; and always miserable when he had the best reason to be happy. The only real comfort of his existence was to make everybody about him wretched—then he might be truly said to enjoy life."

—*likes and dislikes:* "He was familiar with the face of every tombstone, and the burial service seemed to excite his strongest sympathy . . . . Cold as he was, and wretched as he declared himself to be, he was not wholly unsusceptible of attachments. He revered the memory of **Hoyle**, as he was himself an admirable and imperturbable whist-player, and he chuckled with delight at a fretful and impatient adversary. He adored King **Herod** for his massacre of the innocents; and if he hated one thing more than another, it was a child . . . perhaps his greatest antipathies were cabs, old women, doors that would not shut, musical amateurs, and omnibus cads. He subscribed to the 'Society for the Suppression of Vice' for the pleasure of putting a stop to any harmless amusements; and he contributed largely towards the support of two itinerant methodist **parsons**, in the amiable hope that if circumstances rendered any people happy in this world, they might perchance be rendered miserable by fears for the next."

—*committing himself:* "'Not born yet!' echoed Dumps, with a gleam of hope lighting up his lugubrious visage. 'Oh, well, it *may* be a girl, and then you won't want me; or if it is a boy, it may die before it is christened' . . . .

"' . . . distressing cases frequently occur during the first two or three days of a child's life; fits, I am told, are exceedingly common, and alarming convulsions are almost matter of course' . . . [telling a horror story]

"'The child died, of course. However, your child *may* not die; and if it should be a boy, and should *live* to be christened, why I suppose I must be one of the sponsors.' Dumps was evidently good-natured on the faith of his anticipations."

—going to a party: "'It's a large party,' sighed the unhappy godfather, wiping the perspiration from his forehead, and leaning against the area-railings. It was some time before the miserable man could muster up courage to knock at the door . . . .

"'Mr Dumps!' shouted the **greengrocer** in a stentorian voice . . . everybody looked at the door, and in came Dumps, feeling about as much out of place as a salmon might be supposed to be on a gravel-walk."

—the speech: "' . . . I, as one of the godfathers . . . venture to rise to propose a toast. I need hardly say that it is the health and prosperity of that young gentleman, the particular event of whose early life we are here met to celebrate —(applause).

"'Ladies and gentlemen, it is impossible to suppose that our friends here, whose sincere well-wishers we all are, can pass through life without some trials, considerable suffering, severe affliction, and heavy losses!'—Here the arch-traitor paused, and slowly drew forth a long, white pocket-handkerchief—his example was followed by several ladies. 'That these trials may be long spared them is my most earnest prayer, my most fervent wish (a distinct sob from the grandmother).

"'I hope and trust, ladies and gentlemen, that the infant whose christening we have this evening met to celebrate, may not be removed from the arms of his parents by premature decay (several cambrics were in requisition): that his young and now *apparently* healthy form may not be wasted by lingering disease. (. . . a great sensation was manifest among the married ladies.)

"'You, I am sure, will concur with me in wishing that he may live to be a comfort and a blessing to his parents. ('Hear, hear!' and an audible sob from Mr **Kitterbell**.) But should he not be what we could wish—should he forget in after times the duty which he owes to them—should they unhappily experience that distracting truth, "how sharper than a serpent's tooth it is to have a thankless child"'—Here **Mrs Kitterbell**, with her handkerchief to her eyes, and accompanied by several ladies, rushed from the room, and went into violent hysterics in the passage . . . ." ¶

—aftermath: " . . . this occurrence quite put a stop to the harmony of the evening . . . the company slowly departed. Dumps left the house . . . and walked home with a light step, and (for him) a cheerful heart."

Others

The **Kitterbells**

*—***Charles*** "was a small, sharp, spare man, with a very large head, and a broad, good-humoured countenance. He looked like a faded giant, with the head and face partially restored; and he had a cast in his eye which rendered it quite impossible for any one with whom he conversed to know where he was looking . . . [he] was one of the most credulous and matter-of-fact little personages that ever took *to* himself a wife, and *for* himself a house in Great Russell Street, Bedford Square."

*—***Frederick Charles William***. "'He cries a good deal, and is a very singular colour. . . . We think he will be a sharp child; and **nurse** says she's sure he will, because he never goes to sleep . . . . He has been vaccinated, but in consequence of the operation being rather awkwardly performed, some small particles of glass were introduced into the arm with the matter. Perhaps this may in some degree account for his being rather fractious; at least, so nurse says.'"

" . . . in came the nurse, with a remarkably small parcel in her arms, packed up in a blue mantle trimmed with white fur."

"'Oh! what dear little arms!' . . . holding up an arm and fist about the size and shape of the leg of a fowl cleanly picked . . . .

"'Can it open its eyes, nurse?' . . . the single ladies unanimously voted him an angel . . . the married ones, *nem. con.*, agreed that he was decidedly the finest baby they had ever beheld—except their own."

—**Jemima**. "'I'm sure,' said Mrs Kitterbell, with a languid smile, and a slight cough. "'I'm sure—hem—any friend—of Charles's— hem—much less a relation, is —'

"' . . . a tall, thin young lady, with very light hair, and a particularly white face—one of those young women who almost invariably, though one hardly knows why, recall to one's mind the idea of a cold fillet of veal."

—*her parents:* "**Dumps** . . . took no notice whatever of the **father**, who had been bowing incessantly for three minutes and a quarter [and] seized the hand of the **mother** as warmly as if she was his own parent . . . . "

The 'Admiral Napier'

Cad. "'Now, sir!' cried the young gentleman who officiated as 'cad' to the 'Lads of the Village' . . . .

"'This vay, sir!' shouted the **driver** of the 'Hark-away,' pulling up his vehicle immediately across the door of the opposition—'This vay, sir—he's full.' **Dumps** hesitated, whereupon the 'Lads of the Village' commenced pouring out a torrent of abuse against the 'Hark-away' . . . . "

Clerk. "'Perhaps the *box* would suit the gentleman better,' suggested a very damp lawyer's clerk, in a pink shirt, and a smirking countenance."

Old gentleman. "'For Heaven's sake, where am I to sit?' inquired the miserable man of an old gentleman, into whose stomach he had just fallen for the fourth time.

"'Anywhere but on my *chest,* sir,' replied the old gentleman in a surly tone."

Second **old gentleman**. "'I beg your pardon, sir,' said a little prim, wheezing old gentleman, sitting opposite **Dumps**, 'I beg your pardon; but have you ever observed, when you have been in an omnibus on a wet day, that four people out of five always come in with large cotton umbrellas, without a handle at the top, or the brass spike at the bottom?'

"'Why, sir,' returned Dumps, as he heard the clock strike twelve, 'it never struck me before; but now you mention it, I—-Hollo! hollo!' shouted the persecuted individual, as the omnibus dashed past Drury Lane, where he had directed to be set down . . . . "

Passenger, "After a great deal of struggling and falling about, **Dumps** at last managed to squeeze himself into a seat, which, in addition to the slight disadvantage of being between a window that would not shut, and door that must be open, placed him in close contact with a passenger, who had been walking about all the morning without an umbrella, and who looked as if he had spent the day in a full water-butt—only wetter."

Tom, a conductor—*decisive:*   "[He] settled the contest . . . by seizing **Dumps** round the waist, and thrusting him into the middle of his vehicle, which had just come up and only wanted the sixteenth inside."

"'All right,' said the 'Admiral,' and off the thing thundered, like a fire-engine at full gallop, with the kidnapped customer inside, standing in the position of a half doubled-up bootjack, and falling about with every jerk of the machine, first on the one side, and then on the other, like a 'Jack-in-the-green,' on May-day...."

"'Don't bang the door so,' said Dumps to the conductor, as he shut it after letting out four of the passengers; 'I am very nervous—it destroys me.'

"'Did any gen'lm'n say anythink?' replied the cad, thrusting in his head, and trying to look as if he didn't understand the request.

"'I told you not to bang the door so!' repeated Dumps, with an expression of countenance like the knave of clubs, in convulsions.

"'Oh! vy, it's rather a sing'ler circumstance about this here door, sir, that it von't shut without banging,' replied the conductor; and he opened the door very wide, and shut it again with a terrific bang, in proof of the assertion."

--duplicitous: "'Hold hard!' said the conductor; 'I'm blowed if we he'n't forgot the gen'lm'n as vas to be set down at Doory Lane.—Now, sir, make haste, if you please,' he added, opening the door, and assisting **Dumps** out with as much coolness as if it was 'all right.' Dumps's indignation was for once getting the better of his cynical equanimity. 'Drury Lane!' he gasped, with the voice of a boy in a cold bath for the first time.

"Doory Lane, sir?—yes, sir,—third turning on the right-hand side, sir.'

"Dumps's passion was paramount: he clutched his umbrella, and was striding off with the firm determination of not paying the fare. The cad, by a remarkable coincidence, happened to entertain a directly contrary opinion, and Heaven knows how far the altercation would have proceeded, if it had not been most ably and satisfactorily brought to a close by the **driver**.

"' .... 'Hollo, Tom! tell the gentleman if so be as he feels aggrieved, we will take him up to the Edge-er (Edgeware) Road for nothing, and set him down at Doory Lane when we comes back. He can't reject that, anyhow.'

"The argument was irresistible: Dumps paid the disputed sixpence, and in a quarter of an hour was on the staircase of No. 14, Great Russell Street."

The Main Event

Clergyman. " . . . [he] had to dine some distance from town, and had two churchings, three christenings, and a funeral to perform in something less than an hour . . . with the exception of **Dumps** nearly letting the child fall into the font when he handed it to the clergyman, the whole affair went off in the usual business-like and matter-of-course manner . . . . "

Danton "was a young man of about five-and-twenty, with a considerable stock of impudence, and a very small share of ideas: he was a great favourite, especially with young ladies of from sixteen to twenty-six years of age, both inclusive. He could imitate the French-horn to admiration, sang comic songs most inimitably, and had the most insinuating way of saying impertinent nothings to his doting female admirers. He had acquired, somehow or other, the reputation of being a great wit, and, accordingly, whenever he opened his mouth, everybody who knew him laughed very heartily."

Greengrocer, "who had been hired to wait for seven and sixpence, and whose calves alone were worth double the money . . . . "

Musicians. " . . . [they] did not play with quite as much spirit as could have been wished . . . they had been engaged on board a steamer all day, and had played almost without cessation all the way to Gravesend, and all the way back again."

Nurse. "'... we have just discovered the cause of little **Frederick**'s restlessness. It is not fever, as I apprehended, but a small pin, which nurse accidentally stuck in his leg yesterday evening. We have taken it out, and he appears more composed, though he still sobs a good deal.'"

Young ladies. "An universal rush of the young ladies immediately took place. (Girls are always *so* fond of babies in company.)

"'Oh, you dear!' said one.

"'How sweet!' cried another, in a low tone of the most enthusiastic admiration.

"'Heavenly!' added a third."

Young man. "The shock [of collision] so disarranged **Dumps**'s nerves, as well as his dress, that he could hardly stand. The gentleman took his arm, and in the kindest manner walked with him as far as Furnival's Inn. Dumps, for about the first time in his life, felt grateful and polite; and he and the gentlemanly-looking young man parted with mutual expressions of good-will.

"'There are at least some well-disposed men in the world' ....

—*but then again:* "'What have you lost? Your pocket-book?'

"'No,' returned Dumps, diving first into one pocket and then into the other, and speaking in a voice like **Desdemona** with the pillow over her mouth ....

"'Not—not—the *mug* you spoke of this morning?'

"'Yes, the *mug!*' replied Dumps, sinking into a chair.

"'How *could* you have done it?' inquired **Kitterbell**. 'Are you sure you brought it out?'

"'Yes! yes! I see it all!' said Dumps, starting up as the idea flashed across his mind; 'miserable dog that I am—I was born to suffer. I see it all: it was the gentlemanly-looking young man!'"

Boy, messenger with Dumps's pumps, stockings and cravat
Child in a Dumps story: suddenly black in the face, spasmodic and dead
Clerks, from Islington in fine weather, white stockings, clean boots
Coquette, with a large bustle, who looked like a French lithograph
Females: three guests at a christening in pink dresses and shoes
Gentleman, in three waistcoats, admiring a coquette
Hackney-coachman, knocking at Kitterbell's door
King Herod[H]: admired by a misanthrope
Edmund Hoyle[H]: authority on whist
Jane, female servant, warm and bustling: ushered Dumps
Landlady, of Nicodemus Dumps: she swore she heard him laugh
Man, artfully drunk in the street, collided with Dumps
Married ladies, eating as much as possible: fear won't have enough
Mrs Maxwell, a christening guest
Old gentleman, in a blue coat, a guest at a christening
Old lady, in a large toque; with three daughters in pink
Old woman: the fine season unprecedented to the oldest inhabitant
Sisters, of Mrs Kitterbell at a christening
Waiters, in a chophouse, astonished by Dumps
Mr and Mrs **Wilson**, over the way: the other godparents

The Drunkard's Death

The damage a drunken man does to his family; his succumbing to renewed temptation and inadvertent betrayal of his criminal son to justice; his degradation and debased suicide.

The **Wardens**

—**Henry**. "'He died in my arms—shot like a dog, by a gamekeeper. He staggered back, I caught him, and his blood trickled down my hands. It poured out from his side like water. He was weak, and it blinded him, but he threw himself down on his knees, on the grass, and prayed to God, that if his mother was in heaven, He would hear her prayers for pardon for her youngest son.'"

—**John**. "'John's gone to America . . . .'"

—**Mary**. " . . . a girl, whose miserable and emaciated appearance was only to be equalled by that of the candle which she shaded with her hand, peeped anxiously out."

—**Mrs**. " . . . it was not towards her [mother] that the wan face turned; it was not her hand that the cold and trembling fingers clasped; they pressed the husband's arm; the eyes so soon to be closed in death rested on his face, and the man shook beneath their gaze."

—**William**. " . . . a young man of about two-and-twenty, miserably clad in an old coarse jacket and trousers."

"'If I am taken,' said the young man, 'I shall be carried back into the country, and hung for that man's murder. They cannot trace me here, without your assistance, father.'"

—*his curse:* "'Listen to me, father,' he said, in a tone that made the drunkard's flesh creep. 'My brother's blood, and mine, is on your head: I never had kind look, or word, or care, from you, and alive or dead, I never will forgive you. Die when you will, or how, I will be with you. I speak as a dead man now, and I warn you, father, that as surely as you must one day stand before your Maker, so surely shall your children be there, hand in hand, to cry for judgment against you.'"

—**Warden**—*at his wife's bedside:* "His dress was slovenly and disordered, his face inflamed, his eyes blood-shot and heavy. He had been summoned from some wild debauch to the bed of sorrow and death."

—*a mission failed:* "He got some medicine for the girl, and a trifle in the way of pecuniary assistance. On his way back, he earned sixpence by holding a horse; and he turned homewards with enough money to supply their most pressing wants for two or three days to come. He had to pass the public-house. He lingered for an instant, walked past it, turned back again, lingered once more, and finally slunk in . . . ."

"The man thought of his hungry children, and his son's danger. But they were nothing to the drunkard. He *did* drink; and his reason left him."

—*a mission accomplished:* "Strange and fantastic forms rose to the surface, and beckoned him to approach; dark gleaming eyes peered from the water, and seemed to mock his hesitation, while hollow murmurs from behind urged him onwards. He retreated a few paces, took a short run, desperate leap, and plunged into the river.

"Not five seconds had passed when he rose to the water's surface—but what a change had taken place in that short time, in all his thoughts and feelings! Life—life in any form, poverty, misery, starvation—anything but death. He fought and struggled with the water that closed over his head, and screamed in agonies of terror . . . the tide bore him onward, under the dark arches of the bridge, and he sank to the bottom.

"Again he rose, and struggled for life . . . . Bright flames of fire shot up from earth to heaven, and reeled before his eyes, while the water thundered in his ears, and stunned him with its furious roar.

"A week afterwards the body was washed ashore, some miles down the river, a swollen and disfigured mass. Unrecognised and unpitied, it was borne to the grave . . . . "

Children, of a dying mother; their father becomes a drunkard
Detectives: they take William Warden thanks to his father
Mother, of a dying woman; bathed in tears, supporting her daughter's head
Passer-by: the drunkard begged a few halfpence
Tom, a detective
Watch: passed Warden but did not see him

Contributions as a Staff Member to
The Morning Chronicle

After a stint shorthand-reporting Parliamentary debates for the *Mirror of Parliament,* CD was introduced by his friend Thomas Beard, a staff reporter, to the highly partisan, pro-Reform *Chronicle* in August 1834. It was a stirring, indeed a thrilling, time politically: William IV would shortly dismiss Melbourne's Whig Government, the Duke of Wellington would decline to lead, and Sir Robert Peel was to come to power—for five months. The Reform Bill of 1832 would meet the test: henceforth the majority party in the House of Commons would govern, the monarch's wishes to the contrary notwithstanding. CD left the *Chronicle* in late 1836, having signed on to start *Bentley's Miscellany.*

Periodicals in CD's day did not "byline" their correspondents, so his political reporting and drama reviewing for the *Chronicle* will probably never be fully known. But mentions in his letters, scrupulously researched by PE's editors, let us pinpoint many contributions. William N. Carlton and Patrick McCarthy have ferreted out attributable pieces, their publication venue the *Dickensian* (abbrev D). Citations to the scholarship justifying including each piece here follow its date.

Though routine in comparison with later things, these pieces give insight into the kinds of experience CD was gaining; the observations he was making, of people and of processes; and the intellective digestive process he was going through, with results to be reflected through the rest of his literary life.

He remembered the time vividly (as he remembered everything, apparently) and told of it years later in a speech to the guild of printers: "*I have often transcribed for the printer, from my shorthand notes, important public speeches in which the strictest accuracy was required, and a mistake in which would have been to a young man severely compromising, writing on the palm of my hand, by the light of a dark lantern, in a post-chase and four, galloping through a wild country, and through the dead of night, at the then surprising rate of fifteen miles an hour.*"

Michael Slater brought to our attention two political reports which we otherwise could easily have missed: September 17, 1834 from Edinburgh MC/EG1 and December 17, 1835 from Northamptonshire MC/NE2.

CONTENTS

PERSONS MENTIONED

MC September 17 (Walter Dexter D 30 p5) and 18 (PE I 41n), 1834   **EG1, 2**

Reception of Earl Grey

Soon after joining the *Chronicle,* CD went to Edinburgh with Beard to report on a banquet honouring an eminent Whig politician. He wrote a preliminary report on a charity fund-raiser. The next day a longer piece appeared on the Grey dinner, the first part of which "seems clearly CD's," say the PE editors. The remarks of the principal speaker are quoted *in extenso* (this seems invariably to have been the case: CD had the shorthand for it). In these debut pieces the neophyte signals his view that the common man is better copy than the "nob."

Charity pupils, from the Blind Asylum, "who occupied the warmest seats in the enclosure, were very hot and uncomfortable, and appeared very glad to be filed off from a scene in which they could take little interest, and with which their pensive careworn faces painfully contrasted." 1

Gentleman, impatient. "It had been announced that the dinner would take place at five o'clock precisely; but **Earl Grey**, and the other principal visitors . . . did not arrive until shortly after six. Previous to their arrival, some slight confusion, and much merriment, was excited by the following circumstance:—A gentleman who . . . having sat with exemplary patience for some time in the immediate vicinity of cold fowls, roast beef, lobsters, and other tempting delicacies (for the dinner was a cold one), appeared to think that the best thing he could possibly do, would be to eat his dinner, while there was any thing to eat. He accordingly laid about him with right good will; the example was contagious, and the clatter of knives and forks became general.

"Hereupon, several **gentlemen**, who were not hungry, cried out 'Shame!' and looked very indignant; and several gentlemen who were hungry, cried 'Shame!' too, eating, nevertheless, all the while, as fast as they possibly could. In this dilemma, one of the **steward**s mounted a bench, and feelingly represented to the delinquents the enormity of their conduct, imploring them, for decency's sake, to defer the process of mastication until the arrival of Earl Grey. This address was loudly cheered, but totally unheeded; and this is, perhaps, one of the few instances on record of a dinner having been virtually concluded before it began." ¶ 2

Sir John Dalrymple, at whose seat at Oxenford Earl Grey had rested 2
John Gracie, who had the arduous task of supervising the preparations 2
Gray, deputed to welcome the Earl on behalf of people of Edinburgh and Dalkeith 2
Grey friends: Sir J. S. Craig, Ellice, Duke and Duchess of Hamilton, Sir T. Lauder 2
Countess Grey, wife of the Earl, and her daughter Lady Georgiana 2
Rev Henry Grey, who said grace 2
Lord Advocate, who was appointed croupier (assistant chairman) of the dinner) 2
Piper, playing by way of variation from the military band 1
Lord Provost, presiding 2
At a principal table: 2

Attorney General	Lord Dinorben	General Count Flahault
James Abercrombie, M.P.	Earl of Dunham	Sir John Hobhouse
Professor Arago	Lord Elphinstone	Lord Lynedock
Attorney General	Baron d'Ende	Earl of Stair
Lord Belhaven	Earl of Errol	Earl of Strathearne
Marquess of Breadalbane	Cutlar Fergusson, M.P.	

Earl Rosebery, who took the chair at the dinner 2
George Smart, who presented an address from the inhabitants of Musselburgh 2

MC October 14, 1834 (PE I 42n) **BF**

Buckstone Farce

Review of *The Christening* (CD strikingly does not mention its name), a farce at the Adelphi with obvious debts to SB/BC. In his first recorded professional theatre criticism, CD must have felt quite at home:

"We hailed one or two of the characters with great satisfaction—they are old and very particular friends of ours. We met with them, and several of the jokes we heard last night, at a certain 'Bloomsbury Christening' described in 'The Monthly Magazine' some little time since. We make the remark in no spirit of ill-nature . . . . "

[**John Baldwin**] **Buckstone**. "[He] has added excellent materials of his own, and produced a very sprightly and amusing interlude, which we hope and believe will have a long run."

Grum, played by **Wilkinson**. " . . . a surly misanthrope, who is entrapped into becoming sponsor for the first child of *Mr Hopkins Twiddie* (Mr **Buckstone**), and the confusion arising from certain mistakes occasioned by a changing of children, and confounding of people, which frequently take place on the stage, and never occur elsewhere."

Mrs Keeley, who played a busy, meddling godmother; her acting extremely good

MC   December 1, 1834 (PE I 46n*)   **BL**

Meeting of Birmingham Liberals

The King dismissed the Melbourne government on November 14.   National reaction betrayed widespread fear that the monarch might seek to frustrate much of what had just been achieved with passage of the Reform Bill.   The *Chronicle* was in the thick of it and eager to fan agitation for the Liberal cause. CD's report exemplifies his shorthand skills, for it includes, apparently *verbatim,* three long Reformist speeches critical of the Duke of Wellington.

Edmonds, whose reference to **Lord Durham**, "as the fittest person to be called to his Majesty's councils, was hailed with the most enthusiastic cheering we ever heard."

Liberals. " . . . perfect order was preserved throughout, and the appearance of a vast body of persons, who were all respectably and cleanly dressed, was most imposing . . . . "

H. Smith. "'Gentlemen it has pleased his Majesty, by the exercise of his royal prerogative—with the exercise of which I am persuaded no Englishman will ever wish or dare to interfere; and it has pleased him also in the depth of a wisdom, the profundity of which no Englishman is, or ever will be, able to fathom, to summon to his councils—I will not say an Administration, but an individual [the **Duke of Wellington**], combining in his own person the character of both, who has ever shown himself most obstinately, and determinately [*sic.;* CD probably meant to write "determinedly"], and pugnaciously opposed to the interests of his country, except when he had to defend them from enemies abroad.'"

Speakers: William Beale, James James, M. Muntz, Rev Mr O'Donnell, William Phipson

*The normally impeccable PE editors say they quote from the "2nd edtn" of the *Chronicle* of Saturday, November 29, 1834, but there was none, because the full report apparently did not arrive in time. It was printed the following Monday, December 1.

MC　December 5, 1834 (PE I 49 & n)　　　**SS**

St Saviour's, Southwark

Report of a debate on proposed reforms affecting the established church and other matters. "The Parish" in action. Resolutions moved to demand a reform administration and to go on record as distrustful of the Duke of Wellington. The flavour of the genuine English parochial surname.

> Ellis, parish auditor; objected to the expense of public meetings held in the church
> Lock, parishioner: spoke at length defending using the church for political discussion
> Partridge, senior churchwarden
> Speakers: Crosby, Davis, Shears and Wild

MC　December 18, 1834 (Wm J. Carlton D Spring 1951)　　　**SW**

The Story without a Beginning
[translated from the German by Boz]

A remarkable first foray into the art of allegory in political satire, telling the story of **William IV's** self-inflicted cabinet crisis. The **Whigs** are the bees, the **Tories** are the insects, and the flowers represent the People.

Child. "And the child [King **William IV**] was happy, and he trod on soft carpets, and feasted on rich delicacies, and listened to the sound of music, and his mind was easy, and the child was quite at home, for it was not his first childhood, but his second childhood."

Ireland. "There was one bed of flowers which had been beautiful; they blossomed still a bright, bright green, but they hung their heads, and were fast fading away. They had been forced in their youth, and cut down, and grafted on an old stem; their natural juices were dried up, and they withered fast."

Tories. "And the insects and reptiles that bask in sunshine, and retreat to small dark corners when the air is cold, hated the flowers, and stung them, and tried to spoil their growth."

Whigs. "Now, the **child** had gardeners who ministered to the flowers. They were bees—active, hard-working bees; they found the roots choaked [*sic.*] up by weeds; and their growth impeded by the remains of some burrows [boroughs] that had become close and rotten. They were very small, but they harboured rats in myriads, and some of them had the magical property, when one body was dissolved, of disgorging two carcasses on the neighbouring commons [House of]; and at last the corruption became quite insupportable. So the bees went actively to work, and let streams of running water into the burrows, and pulled up the weeds by the roots; but the **insects** had always lived in the weeds and the burrows; and as they were now turned out of their retreats, and had no means of getting to the commons, they crawled to the child, and cried bitterly."

MC January 10, 1835 (PE I 52n)   **EC**

GENERAL ELECTIONS IN THE METROPOLIS
COLCHESTER

Report on the chairing of the successful (Tory) candidates.

Boys. "A few boys who were stationed in the principal street, attempted to hiss **Sir Henry Smyth**, but the formidable disturbance was gallantly quelled by several gentlemen on horseback, who forthwith rode up to the spot, and put as many of the unfortunate offenders into the cage as they happened to catch."

Sir Henry Smyth. "It will be recollected that Sir Henry Smyth quitted the House of Commons in disgust on the passage of the Catholic Relief Bill. Time, however, has, happily for the Legislature of the country, softened down his recollection of that dreadful measure, and he has fortunately been induced again to solicit a return to Parliament, even after the additional enormity of the Reform Bill."

MC January 12, 1835 (PE I 52n)   **EE**

GENERAL ELECTIONS IN THE METROPOLIS
ESSEX—NOMINATION

Datelined Braintree (Northern Division), a report on the special county court to nominate two Members of Parliament, held in a field. A gay sight reminiscent of PP's Eatanswill. On a show of hands, the Tories were elected.

The **Blues**. "As the intermediate space [between the waggon-hustings] was entirely filled by a closely packed crowd, the greater part of whom wore favours, and as the day, though cold, was a remarkably bright one, the general effect was exceedingly lively and animated; an effect to which the blue bonnets, blue ribands, and blue dresses of the ladies in the carriages contributed, much more than the blue countenances of the cold gentlemen on the hustings."

> Alexander Baring, a Tory candidate: he shared a waggon
> J. P. Elwes seconded Baring's nomination
> Harvey, M.P. (Whig) for Southwark: a speech of great ability, sarcasm and eloquence
> High Sheriff, who had a waggon and judged the hand vote
> Hublin seconded Tyrell's nomination amidst great confusion, frequent interruptions
> William Kudley, nominated Henry Tuffnel
> Sir Henry Smyth, M.P. (Tory) for Colchester, who nominated Tyrell
> Tuffnel (mistake?) spoke for Tyrell and nominated Baring for the blues
> Henry Tuffnel, Whig candidate
> Sir John Tysson Tyrell, Bart., a Tory candidate: he shared a waggon
> Unwin, a Dissenter, who seconded Tuffnel's nomination

MC January 13, 1835 (PE I 52n) **E**

GENERAL ELECTIONS IN THE METROPOLIS
ESSEX (SOUTH)—NOMINATION

Chelmsford is the central locality in this district. **Podsnap** OMF is prefigured in the words of a Tory candidate. The Tories were elected by show of hands.

Cotton, nominating **Thomas William Bramston** in "a long rambling speech, the greater part of which appeared quite unintelligible to every person present. He was an advocate of reform [oh!], but he would not reform institutions by pulling them down. His object was improvement, not annihilation."

Robert Westley Hall Dare. "He assured them that, highly as he esteemed the honour of being one of their representatives on the last occasion—doubly grateful as he was for the reception he had met with that day, by the great concourse of friends who had escorted him into the town, nothing but the consciousness that the constitution was in great danger, and that every man was called upon to use his best exertions for his country's benefit, could have again induced him to come forward.

"They had arrived at a most important crisis. They had been asked who created it? He replied—that wretched remnant of a Whig Ministry, who, deserted by all that was valuable in its original composition, was obliged at last, in its miserable struggles for existence, to cast itself into the arms of the Destructives [loud cheers from the **Blues**. The epithet 'wretched remnant' appeared to give inexpressible satisfaction to one **individual** in the vicinity of the speaker, who from this moment to the conclusion of the proceedings, soliloquized audibly at every pause, 'Wretched remnant! Ha, ha, ha! Oh Lord! I shall never forget it!]

"Under their auspices, that constitution which Englishmen had been brought up to revere as their first birth-right—that constitution which had earned for England the first place among the nations of the earth—that constitution which, in the beautiful language of Mr **Canning**, had been the envy and admiration of surrounding nations, but the peculiar boast and privilege of our own—had been gradually frittered away; it now stood trembling in the balance; and would infallibly kick the beam, if demagogues, assisted by that wretched remnant, were to succeed in trampling under foot the King's prerogative, and dictating to him who should be his Ministers [loud cheers].

"If they elected him (Mr H. Dare) it was his object to give full, fair, but at the same time independent support to his Majesty's Government, in maintaining which he sought to maintain the King's prerogative. It was essential for their liberties that the King's prerogative should be maintained, because they might rest assured that if the balance of their blessed constitution were once destroyed, their liberties, freedom, and franchises, would very soon follow in its wake." ¶

Abdy, who seconded Bramston's nomination
Blues: they displayed some very tasty and well-designed flags
Bramston, who spoke in favor of Hall Dare and the Church of England
Champion Edward Branfill, the Whig candidate: he favoured malt-tax repeal
Davis, who nominated Hall Dare in a short and pithy speech
John Disney, advocated malt-tax repeal; nominated Branfill, second Joseph Pattison

MC January 14, 1835 (PE I 52n)   ES

GENERAL ELECTIONS IN THE METROPOLIS
SUDBURY

Messrs. **Benjamin** and **Adams Smith** "deserved great credit for the exertions they had used in rescuing this borough from the trammels of Toryism." CD quotes a speech by Adams Smith summarizing the achievements of the Whig administration which had put through the Reform Bill.

MC January 17, 1835 (PE I 52n)   S

GENERAL ELECTIONS IN THE METROPOLIS
SUFFOLK—NOMINATION

Bury St Edmunds is the seat of Suffolk's Western Division. CD's description is characteristic in its freshness of observation and delight in spectacle, doubtless less delightful to older hands. Flirting with women's suffrage. **Rushbrook** (whose address, unusually, is crisp enough to quote) and **Wilson** were elected.

Candidates. " . . . the hustings in front of the abbey, the windows and roofs of the opposite houses, and every spot of ground from which it was possible to obtain a glimpse of the candidates, were densely crowded. A great number of men wearing the colours and bearing the banners of the candidates, were arranged in front of the hustings. The colours of the Conservative candidates were, of course, blue; those of Mr **Wilson** orange and green; and those of Mr **Hales** green and white. They were all of silk, and very elegantly worked. There could not have been less than five hundred horsemen present; and the effect of the whole was really brilliant. We never saw arrangements, on any similar occasion, which were so well 'got up' or made with such an apparent disregard of expense. They reflected great credit, not only upon the taste, but upon the liberality of all the parties concerned."

Colonel Rushbrook "then presented himself, and met with a very cordial reception. He said, that during his canvas he had received from his friends, and from the inhabitants of that town generally, proofs of attachment and affectionate remembrance which would never be effaced from his mind while memory held her place [cheers] . . . . ["*While memory holds a seat in this distracted globe . . .*" *Hamlet I v*]

"He (Colonel Rushbrook) was painfully conscious of the scantiness of his pretensions to, and want of experience in, a public oration. Zeal and integrity founded the only counterpoise to these disadvantages he had to offer [cheers]. They might depend upon it that his best exertions should be used to support the manly, straightforward, and noble declaration of their Gracious Sovereign. He trusted he should best do so by supporting the Administration that Sovereign had chosen, convinced as he (Colonel Rushbrook) was that they would not deceive the people, and that they would do their utmost to correct abuses and improve the condition of the country.

"He should be proud to render his support to an Administration, the members of which had so long bestowed their best attention on the primitive, the vital, interest of this country—he meant that of agriculture [cheers]. He trusted they had it in contemplation to repeal the malt-tax; it was an impost which he wished to see abolished, both on moral and political grounds; morally, because he wished the cottager to have the power of indulging in his favourite beverage under his own roof, where his wife and children might be sharers in the enjoyment he derived from his wholesome home-brewed, in which case he would not be driven to the selfish indulgence and demoralizing company of a beer-shop; and politically, because he was desirous to remove a burden which rested exclusively on the shoulders of one portion of the community, instead of being borne, as it ought, by the whole [cheers].

"He should be most happy to support any measure for the improvement of our institutions, both ecclesiastical and civil; but his principle was to improve, not to destroy—to ameliorate, not to annihilate, the constitution of Church and State. Far be it from him to indulge in any invective against a fallen foe, but one party having been tried and found wanting [cheers and 'No!']—if they deserted the one now in power, what had they to hope or expect but that dreadful reflection, which was to the mind as mortification to the body—that the disease was beyond a cure? He conjured them to return such men to Parliament as would stand or fall by the constitution and by their country. He conjured them, as they revered their altars and homes, to discharge their duty faithfully, zealously, and fearlessly; and to bear in mind the words of England's immortal bard—

—————'Nought shall make us rue
If Britain to herself do prove but true.' [cheers]" ¶

Sheriff, asking for a show of hands. "An immense number (including those of the ladies, of whom there were a great number at the opposite windows) was immediately raised. The Sheriff observed that he had not been able to form a decided opinion from the first show of hands, and he must therefore beg them to repeat it; suggesting, at the same time, that as the House of Commons had not yet had the gallantry to extend the right of voting for counties to the fairer portion of the community, it would perhaps be desirable for them not to hold up their hands again [laughter and cheers]."

Philip Bennett seconded Rushbrook's nomination in a long speech
Colonel Cormack, who seconded the Hales nomination
Sir Henry Bunbury, who nominated Hales
Sir Thomas Gooch, whose words were inaudible because of the uproar
John Turner Hales, who quoted, "a bold peasantry, a country's pride/
    When once destroyed can never be supplied"
Hart Logan, who resented accusation that he favoured foreign corn
Mapletoft proposed Hart Logan
Pooley, who seconded Logan nomination
Powell, who seconded Wilson nomination
Sir Thomas Middleton, whose words were inaudible because of the uproar
Tyrell, late M.P., who proposed Henry Wilson
Waddington, who nominated Colonel Rushbrook
Henry Wilson, a victorious nominee; a long speech

MC January 22 (?), 1835 (Carlton D January 1960)   **MC**

The Maid of Castile

Reviews of *The Station House* by Charles Dance, *The Farmer's Son, The Maid of Castile* and *Is He Jealous?* presented at the Adelphi on January 21, 1835.

Anderson's singing "does not much mend the matter. This gentleman's vocal powers we have yet to discover."

Mrs Nisbett, whose "impersonation of *The Maid of Castile* . . . possesses an excellence which quite suffices to render the piece a favourite one . . . . "

> Mrs Brindal is an actress of very great capacity
> Barnett's performance affords much promise
> Mrs Nisbett's sister appears to us little inferior

MC May 2, 1835 (PE I 58 & n, 59 & n)   **JR**

EXPRESS FROM EXETER
Morning Chronicle Office Saturday Morning, Six O'Clock
SOUTH DEVON ELECTION
[from our own Reporters]

Speed, speed, speed. The headline gives the feeling. CD rode a stage through the night, writing and balancing his despatch on his knee, his light held by his fellow reporter. Imagine the rough road, the rain, the rocking carriage, the pressure to get there first, the exhilaration of totally absorbed focus on accomplishing the task, bringing the good news and serving the Cause. Ah, youth.

Lord John Russell (1792-1878; leading Whig politician, later Prime Minister; Home Secretary from April 1835): his reception and his speech in the by-election necessitated by his accepting national office. Noise, tumult, victory.

Lord John Russell. "His self possession appeared to arouse the utmost indignation of the Blues, for the noise, if possible, increased."

> Sir Thomas Acland, who got silence: pleaded for a hearing for Russell
> Baldwin Fulford, who proposed Mr Parker and discussed Irish Church question
> High Sheriff (Samuel Trehawke Kekewich) arrived to get things started
> Henry Northcote, who seconded the Parker nomination in heavy rain
> Observed on the hustings:
>
> | Dr Bowring, M.P. | Edward Divett | Sir T. Lethbridge |
> | C. Buller, M.P. | Lord Ebrington | J. Sillifant, Esq, Jun. |
> | Sir I. B. Y. Buller, Bart., M.P. | Hon. Newton Fellowes | W. Newman |
> | I. C. Bulteel | Captain Hamlin | |
>
> Parker, Russell's opponent: greeted with cheers, hisses; the latter predominating
> Ralph Sanders, under-Sheriff, who was thanked for his arrangements
> Colonel Seale, who protested uproar and demanded a hearing for Lord Russell

MC　July 8, 1835 (Patrick McCarthy D Autumn 1983)　　　　　**C**

Colosseum

CD visited the theatre/exhibition to view the Hall of Mirrors, which he praises. New proprietors **John Braham** and **Frederick Yates** were beginning well.

　　Frederick Yates. " . . . another very prominent feature of the evening was that Colossus of stage management and theatrical contrivance—Yates, who was quite as much at home, and even more energetic, bustling, and vehement, than he used to appear in his old sphere of action—the Adelphi Theatre."

MC　July 10, 1835 (McCarthy D Autumn 1983)　　　　　**CF**

Grand Colosseum Fete

The party occurred on July 9, and "everybody was there." To the convivial dandy CD, a "rational" person spends time, thought and money on his costume, whether or not he can afford it. His sneer is surprising and uncharacteristic.

　　Party-goers. " . . . the ball, as far as the company was concerned, was like all other public balls—that there were match-making mammas in abundance —sleepy papas in proportion—unmarried daughters in scores—marriageable men in rather smaller numbers—greedy dowagers in the refreshment room— flirting daughters in the corners—and envious old maids everywhere—we have said all we need . . . .

　　"**The great** majority of the company were in their customary full-dress costume; but there was a plentiful sprinkling of fancy dresses, in the manufacture of which, however, we would be disposed to say but little fancy or money had been expended. Their awkward and melancholy-looking wearers contrasted very disadvantageously with the rational portion of the company."

MC　September 8, 1835(?) (Carlton D January 1960)　　　　　**Z**

Zarah

A review of a new play at the Adelphi, as quoted by Carlton.

　　Mrs Nisbett. "Her whole performance, indeed, was admirable. Her attire was picturesque in the extreme, composed of bright colours and glittering ornaments after the gipsy fashion, but full of barbaric grace, and calculated to set off to advantage the fine form and features of the wearer."

MC October 9, 1835 (Carlton D January 1960)   **RP**

The Rival Pages

Unfavourable drama review of a piece at the Queen's Theatre.

Mrs Honey "also strove to rescue the piece from its inevitable fate, but even her efforts and her attractions could not accomplish so difficult an object."

Williams, as the *Count de Cornichon.* ". . . his endeavours, though praiseworthy, were unsuccessful."

> T. Green, who played *Francis the First*
> Miss Murray, who played a page
> Selby, who played the *Marquis de Reville*

MC October 13, 1835 (PE I 76n)   **RC**

The Reopening of the Colosseum

Review of a pageant, *The Dream of Raphael,* at the Colosseum Theatre, starring **Ducrow**, and "two novelty diversions": "the courses of the Enchanted Chariot, and round flights of the Mechanical Peacock."

[**Andrew**] **Ducrow** "displayed all that wonderful skill and taste for which he is eminently remarkable in a department of his art peculiarly his own; but it was too long: *Raphael* is decidedly the most prosy individual that ever presented himself on any stage, and his introductory descriptions were melancholy in the extreme."

MC October 20, 1835 (PE I 77&n)   **YK**

The Yellow Kids

Review of a farce performed at the Adelphi. "Less dancing in the wrong places would have been desirable."

Benjamin Webster, playing *Anatole Perrot Tims,* a lodger. "[His] is by many degrees the most prominent part, and he played it respectably; he should avoid palpable imitations of **Buckstone**, however . . . . "

> Miss Ayres played the landlady's niece
> Miss Daly played *Mrs Rocket,* who dislikes her husband and is drawn to *Davenant*
> Mrs Daly played *Mrs Sniggs,* the landlady
> Hemming plays *Captain Davenant,* who owns a pair of yellow kid gloves
> O. Smith plays the jealous husband, *Ex-Captain Rocket*

MC October 27, 1835 (? Carlton D January 1960) **KC**

The King's Command

Carlton is not sure that CD is the critic who panned the piece.

Mrs Keeley. "Bare as it was of incident, the dry humour of WILKINSON, and the excellent acting of MRS KEELEY [as *Lucy Prate-apace*], saved it from the fate which, without their efforts, it would inevitably have experienced."

Wilkinson. As *Simon Knockernose*, "he looked more like a waterman of one of the Lord Mayor's state-barges than a gardener."

> Miss E. Clifford played the *Countess Dowager of Pembroke*
> Hemming was *Lord Berkeley*
> Vining, who played Edward IV

MC November 4, 1835 (Carlton D January 1960) **CN**

The Castilian Noble and the Contrabandista

Carlton's article says that CD reported **Mrs Keeley** as having sung "two pretty songs in her best manner" and **O. Smith** as having "elicited much applause."

MC November 11 and 12, 1835 (PE I 86n, 91n) **EB1, 2**

EXPRESS FROM BRISTOL
Morning Chronicle Office
Wednesday Morning, Seven O'Clock
GRAND DINNER TO LORD JOHN RUSSELL

The first report, a long three and a half columns, contains the full speech of the honoree, ending to "loud and prolonged cheering." It is hard to imagine how CD dealt with his shorthand draft, for he stayed on to do the follow-up.

> *"Our Express left Bristol the moment the Noble Lord had ceased speaking. We shall give a full report of the remainder of the proceedings tomorrow."*

If he was taking it all down in shorthand, when did he have time to transcribe it for the coach? Could anyone else have taken his copy and done the transcription on the way to London? Or did he take it, and another remain to follow up?

The second report details the toasts, Lord Russell's reply (which included an attack on **Sir William Follett**, a member of the bar and later prominent in a losing cause against his mentor: see MC/MN), and other remarks, including some by the poet **Thomas Moore**, who was toasted as "The Historian of Ireland, the Bard of Freedom."

> Lord Andover, at the head table
> Bligh, of the Plate Committee, presenting an épergne to Russell
> Dr Carpenter, who represented the clergy in thanking for a toast
> Lord Ebrington, who accompanied Lord Russell
> Charles James Fox, cited by Lord Russell as for reform but lacking the means
> Lord Grey, cited and praised by Lord Russell
> Earl of Kerry, at the head table
> Marquess of Lansdowne, who had been Lord Russell's host
> Daniel O'Connell, cited in Russell's speech
> Lord Seagrave, at the head table
> J. G. Smith, who presided

MC November 13, 1835 (PE I 92n)   **DB**

GREAT POLITICAL DINNER AT BATH
[from our own reporter]

A dinner for the Liberal M.P.'s **General Palmer** and **J. A. Roebuck**, attended by 700 "electors" and at least 500 ladies. The decor is described in detail. Palmer was brief, Roebuck longer. A good many toasts, "and the hilarity of the evening was continued until a late hour."

> Hume toasted
> Colonel Napier returned thanks for a toast to the Army and the Navy
> Princess Victoria toasted

MC November 17, 1835 (Carlton D January, 1960)   **ZR**

Zarah Revisited

Report on developments at the Adelphi, where *Zarah, The Station-House, The Castilian Noble and the Contrabandista,* and *The Rival Pages* were on the bill; observations on petticoat rule in the theatre, for **Mrs Nisbett** was managing.

Mrs Nisbett. "Admirable managers [the ladies] are, and the influence they possess is really extraordinary. Here we have **Buckstone, O. Smith, Hemming, Wrench, Vining, Mitchell, Green, Wilkinson, Williams, W. Bennett, Attwood**, and a host of others under petticoat government; not ashamed of the fact either, but apparently glorying in it; and **Mrs Keeley, Mrs Honey, Mrs Clifford**, the **Miss**[es] **Mordaunt, Miss Daly, Miss Ayres**, and the treasurer only knows who besides, lent their powerful aid to the captivation of other victims! There must be a Salique law in theatricals, or there is really no telling where all this will end."

> Brown, King and Gibson, on the bill and encored

MC November 24 1835 (PE I 97n)   **DS**

Dream of the Sea

Review of a new burletta by **Buckstone**.

Buckstone, "as the Muffin Boy . . . tinkled his bell as merrily as if there were no such wiseacres as Mr **Laing** in existence, and no Hatton-garden law on record." [*Magistrate Laing, notoriously irascible and peremptory judge, was the model for* ***Fang*** *in OT*]

"Mr Buckstone's dramas have attracted full audiences to this house, and afforded general delight to the play-going public. We are happy to see such a return to the old system as the production of any piece by him; but we should be more happy to see one in his old pleasant domestic style, where the situations are not wholly improbable, nor the incidents palpably absurd."

Participants: Miss Daly, Hemming and Vining

MC December 2, 3, and 4 1835 (PE I 101n)   **HH**

Calamitous Event at Hatfield House

The Dowager **Marchioness of Salisbury**, over 80, was killed in this fire. The first report was CD's, and the two follow-ups, which discussed issues of safety in searching the ruins for the body (not then recovered), probably were. The physical descriptions of the fire's consequences are detailed and vivid.

Marchioness. "There appears every reason to suppose that the ill-fated lady suffered little from burning, and that she was most probably suffocated by the dense smoke at a very early period of the fire. She made no reply when the door was opened and her name pronounced, at which time the smoke would have rendered any attempt to enter the room certain destruction." [1]

Marquess. "The grief and horror of the Marquess of Salisbury on ascertaining the danger of his mother's situation were extreme. He rushed up the staircase calling frantically on her name, burst open the door of her chamber, and would have infallibly perished in the act of exploring it, had he not been forcibly seized by two members of the household, both strong men, who removed him from the door by main force . . . . But, however regardless of his own personal safety, the presence of mind and energy of the Noble Marquess were of material assistance in checking the progress of the devastation. He was on the spot for many hours superintending the operations of the firemen, and in one instance even directing the engine with his own hand." [1]

W. C. Talbot. "Too much praise cannot be bestowed upon the bravery and exertions of the different gentlemen who have been detained by . . . their personal esteem and affection for the Noble **Marquess** and his family. Among the latter the Hon. W. C. Talbot is nobly conspicuous. His unremitting zeal, perfect self-command, and utter disregard of personal danger, can only be imagined by those who have had an opportunity of witnessing his exertions." [1]

MC December 16 (PE I 106 & n) and 17 (probably), 1835   **NE1, 2**

NORTHAMPTONSHIRE ELECTION
(BY EXPRESS)

A special by-election was called on the death of the incumbent. The tumult exceeds anything in CD's fiction. In a letter to Catherine Hogarth, he says of the **Tories,** "Such a ruthless set of bloody-minded villains, I never set eyes on, in my life. In their convivial moments yesterday after the business of the day was over, they were perfect savages." The reporter December 17 (it seems proper to assume CD) mentioned the Tories' "disgraceful conduct yesterday."

Crowd, collected early. "These people were principally the friends and supporters of Mr **Hanbury** [the Liberal], and were all on foot. Perfect order and good humour existed among them, and would no doubt have continued to prevail, but for an outrage of the most disgraceful nature I ever witnessed." 1

John George. "The body [of **horsemen**] was headed by a person by the name of John George, of Bythorn, who dashed his horse among the defenceless people, with a reckless disregard of lives and limbs, and laid about him in all directions with a thick ash stick . . . before a single missile had been thrown by the Buff party, this man George produced from his pocket a pistol, and levelled it at a person in the crowd . . . some person threw, I think, a piece of stick, which struck him on the nose and fetched a little blood. The man, foaming with passion, again produced the pistol, levelled it, cocked it, and in another instant would, in all probability, have committed murder . . . . " 1

Horsemen. "Before the arrival of the **Sheriff** . . . a large body of horsemen in Mr **Maunsell's** [the Conservative] interest arrived, with bludgeons and loaded riding or hunting whips, galloped up to the spot, and actually charged the mob . . . bearing down all before them with a degree of ruffianly barbarity, and brutal violence, of which no description could convey an adequate idea. The whole of this cowardly and unmanly proceeding was preconceived." 1

Lucas. "A very eccentric person, of the name of Lucas . . . commenced singing 'The Death of Nelson', and complaining that some gentleman present had stolen his wife, also ineffectually attempted to address the electors. After performing an inaudible duet with Mr **Tryon**, which lasted about ten minutes, they both gave up the attempt." 1

Lord Milton, the late; eulogized by the **Sheriff**. "A young Nobleman of great promise, possessing a disposition, talent and attainments of the first order, a mind liberal, enlightened, and highly cultivated, with clear, enlightened and comprehensive views of all the great questions of public policy that now engross public attention—a young Nobleman, in short, every way qualified to promote and advance the best interests of our beloved country, is by the will of Heaven removed suddenly from us in the prime of his life . . . . " 1

Sheriff (Lewis Lloyd, Esq). "Gentlemen on horseback, continued the Sheriff, must retire to the rear, and not intercept the passage to the hustings [cheers]." 1

" . . . after he had given [his pistol] up, [**George**] made his way to the back of the Sheriff, and assured him that it was his practice to carry fire-arms. The Sheriff replied that it was a very improper one, and a **gentleman** standing by inquired whether it was loaded. 'Loaded!' was the rejoinder, 'To be sure it was!'

There being no signs of a cessation of the confusion, the High Sheriff again entreated the horsemen to retire, when they not only refused to do so, but accused him of partiality, for making a request which nothing but brutality and violence would have rendered necessary for a moment." 1

"There being no other candidate to be proposed, the Sheriff called for a show of hands. As the number appeared to be nearly equal, the Sheriff refused a second show, and declared it to be in favour of Mr **Hanbury**. This announcement was received with tremendous cheering." 1 [*A poll was demanded, and the result was nearly two to one for* **Maunsell,** *as reported in NE3*]

> Henry Fitzroy tried to address crowd: incessant noise and confusion prevented 1
> Markham, Under-Sheriff: requested horsemen to move to rear, but was ignored 1
> O'Brien, to nominate Hanbury; began by demanding that George be disarmed 1
> George Payne, who nominated Maunsell 1
> George Robinson, prevented by noise the first day 1; delivered a fighting speech 2
> Tryon seconded the Maunsell nomination
> Vernon Smith, seconding Hanbury 1; fighting rebuttal of Robinson 2

MC December 19, 1835 (PE I 108&n)   **NE3**

NORTHAMPTONSHIRE ELECTION
(BY EXPRESS)

Third report: the results of the poll. One might suspect that such intemperate language had to have come from editors at home base, but CD felt this way, as his letters show. In one, he calls the Conservatives "beastly swine who wallow in the Public Houses down here," suggesting that Kettering was the model for the greatly softened PP's "Eatanswill" (say the name aloud as three words).

Maunsell. "The speaker concluded a few desultory observations, which were nearly drowned by the vociferous howlings of his own party, and the hooting of the other, by expressing his conviction that the day of his return would be a very proud one . . . . "

Tories. "No artifice has been left untried, no influence has been withheld, no chicanery neglected by the Tory party; and the glorious result is, that Mr **Maunsell** is placed at the head of the poll, by the most ignorant, drunken, and brutal electors in these kingdoms, who have been treated and fed, and driven up to the poll the whole day, like herds of swine."

MC January 12, 1836 (PE I 117n)   **OH**

One Hour; or, a Carnival Ball

Favourable review of a comedy at the Olympic Theatre by **T. Haynes Bayley** [*sic.*] A rare word from CD on the Dance.

Charles Mathews. "We are very happy that young MATHEWS has had so early an opportunity of appearing in this piece, as his performance cannot fail to increase very materially the fame he is so rapidly acquiring. His acting throughout was easy, gentlemanly, and humorous, without being in the slightest degree overstrained. In the ball scene, dressed in the costume of a Neapolitan peasant, he danced, with Miss FITZWALTER, the national dance of *The Tarantella,* in a style which fairly took the audience by surprise. It was not the cold artificial dancing of an actor going through a figure, because it was in his part, or the burlesque posturing of a low comedian, determined to raise a laugh at all hazards: it was the sparkling joyousness of an Italian peasant, revelling in the beauty of everything around him, and dancing for very lightness of heart and gaiety. Anything more elegant or delightful we never saw, within the walls of a theatre or without; the audience were unanimously of the same opinion, for the house resounded with a thunder of applause."

Madame Vestris. "We never saw VESTRIS to greater advantage than in the *tête-à-tête* with Mr **Swiftly**; distinguished as her performance is for ease, vivacity, and nature, on all occasions, she never acted better."

MC   January 15, 1836 (PE I 118n)   W

The Waterman

Review of this musical by **Charles Dibdin**, whose name is unmentioned, and **John Braham**'s performance as *Tom Tig* at the St James's. *The Spoiled Child, Monsieur Jacques,* and *Rasselas* were on the bill.

John Braham. "An admirer of Braham—and who is not?—should embrace the opportunity of seeing his performance as *Tom Tig* . . . . It is perfectly delightful to witness. With all his energies unimpaired, with his splendid voice as fine as ever, and a spirit which nobody but himself could infuse into the character, he at once delights his audience and appears to revel in the fine English melodies, in the execution of which he has always stood, and, judging from present appearances, will continue to stand, unrivalled."

MC   January 19, 1836 (Carlton D January 1960)   MC **BH**

Brown's Horse

CD hated this burlesque of *The Bronze Horse,* but **Braham** "put us in good humour with ourselves and every one about us, and we are therefore disinclined to say more."

MC   January 22, 1836 (PE 119n)   MC **LV**

LICENSED VICTUALLERS' CHARITY SCHOOL
THE NEW BUILDING

Report on the laying of the cornerstone for a new charity school at Kennington Lane, by **Lord Melbourne**. The truth overwhelms the SB/PD (April 1835)

parody in the description of the Procession: "Shortly after three o'clock the procession arrived in the following order:—

Policemen to clear the way.

Beadles of Lambeth parish.

Eight past Committee-men, four abreast, each carrying a gold-headed wand, with a white favour at the top of it.

Full military band, four abreast.

Past Committee-men, four abreast, with wands and favours, as above.

Past Trustees, four abreast, with wands and favours.

Past Chairmen, four abreast, with wands and favours.

Stewards of the day, four abreast, with wands and favours.

Gentlemen of *The Morning Advertiser.*

The Chairman, Trustees, and Governors of the Licensed Victuallers' Asylum, four abreast.

School Banner.

Mrs Grady, Schoolmistress.—Mrs Dallanore, Matron.

Girls, two abreast, the smallest walking first.

The Ministers of St. Mark's Church, Kennington.

The Audit Committee of the Friendly Society of Licensed Victuallers, three abreast.

Sixteen present Committee-men, four abreast, wearing sky-blue rosettes on the left breast.

Six present Trustees, three abreast, with rosettes, as above.

Messrs. Webb and Co., builders, carrying the silver trowel, the level, &c.

Mr. Rose, jun., carrying plans; Mr. Wire, solicitor.

Mr. Rose, architect, carrying plans.

Mr. Anderson, editor; Mr Francis Ward, Chairman, wearing a sky blue rosette.

Mr. Blake, Secretary.

B. Hawes, Esq., M.P. for Lambeth.

The Right Hon. Lord Viscount Melbourne.

Right Hon. C. T. D'Eyncourt, M.P. for Lambeth.

Members of Parliament and other visitors, four abreast.

Beadles of Lambeth parish.

Policemen, to close the procession.

Charity scholars. "There is no degrading dress—no charity livery to remind the children of their destitution . . . . "

Lord Melbourne, "in acknowledging the compliment, observed that he had to offer a most sincere apology to the meeting, if his recent indisposition and the avocations in which he had been lately engaged, had occasioned any delay, or thrown any obstacle in the way of the celebration of that ceremony which they had assembled to witness. He regretted that the same causes would prevent his having the pleasure of participating in the subsequent festivities of the day."

MC February 4, 1836 (PE I 123n)   MC **R**

Rienzi, the last of the Tribunes

Review of **Buckstone**'s adaptation of a **Bulwer-Lytton** novel at the Adelphi.

Elton "was the hero of the piece, and delivered what was set down for him exceedingly well. He would look the character much better were his figure taller and more commanding."

> Participants: Miss Daly, Mrs Honey, Messrs Buckstone, Hemming, O. Smith, Vining, Webster, and Wilkinson.

MC May 28, 1836 (PE I 151-2nn)   MC **RD**

GREAT REFORM DINNER AT IPSWICH
(BY EXPRESS)
Morning Chronicle office, Saturday morning, half-past 7

CD's opening words suggest that at times he himself could be infected beyond parody by his subject-matter (unless it is a conscious, straight-faced spoof of what he has been doing for nearly two years and is about to stop). Compare the dispatches of "**Boz**" in B/M1 and /M2. The occasion was an appearance of **Daniel O'Connell**, M. P., at the center of the Irish Church Question. There are five full columns of proceedings and speeches, O'Connell's two the longest.

"IPSWICH, Friday

"The anxiety felt by all classes of **Reformers** in Ipswich for the arrival of the time which should again bring the Liberal Representatives of the Borough, Messrs. **Morrison** and **Wason**, among them, has never been equalled in the anticipation of any previous event, which, however joyful and satisfactory, may have hitherto animated the minds of our fellow-townsmen."

Morrison. " . . . amidst great uproar, proceeded to introduce Mr **O'Connell** to the meeting. It was with the greatest difficulty he could obtain an audience, and the conduct of the **Tories** was most outrageous and disgraceful."

Daniel O'Connell (1775-1847), "the Liberator." " . . . the gold-banded cap, which decorated the Liberator's brow, was wrested from it by some ruffianly hand . . . . "

> Colonel Addison, with the Mayors of Yarmouth, Ipswich and Bury St Edmunds
> Rev Mr Eyres said grace
> J.P. Reade recommended expelling the Bishops from the Lords; toasted O'Connell

MC   June 23, 1836 (PE I 153n)   **MN**

COURT OF COMMON PLEAS
Melbourne v. Norton

Report on an action brought against **William Lamb, Viscount Melbourne** by **George Chappell Norton**, accusing him of criminal conversation with Mrs (**Caroline**) Norton. On the bench were the **Lord Chief Justice** and Lords **Lichfield, Lucan** and **Grantley**. For the Plaintiff: **Sir William Follett**, and Messrs **Crowder** and **Bayley**; for the Defendant: the **Attorney-General**, Mr Sergeant **Talfourd** and Mr **Thesiger**.

CD gives a transcript of the entire one-day trial, which ended at 11:30 pm, including all summations (which are amazing when one considers that they had to be substantially *extempore*) and the judge's summary and charge. Will we ever again see such a thing *in one day?* The names of the barristers, jurymen and witnesses, colourfully and uncannily apt as to class, might have given the great fictionist in the room food for thought (some of the most characteristic are in **bold** below). CD's resentment of puffed-up junior lawyers finds a vent. The prosecution introduced several suspiciously salutationless notes from the defendant to Mrs Norton. CD may well have remembered their innocuous contents when he wrote *Bardell v Pickwick* a few months later.

Reading the trial today, it seems obvious that the plaintiff was doomed to lose: it was not "the thing" to bring such an action against one of England's' most respected and distinguished citizens, despite the fact that his conduct was, to put it mildly, indiscreet. The evidence had cumulative weight, but the witnesses were impeachable on extraneous grounds (unsought pregnancies, for instance) and they were all (theoretically bribable) servants, a few with drinking problems. The prosecuting barrister was a prominent Tory. Does one detect the smell of a political vendetta? The jury's verdict came "in seconds."

Barristers. " . . . difficulties of ingress and egress were . . . very great.
"These difficulties were wholly occasioned by the very indecent behaviour of a large concourse of barristers of small standing—young gentlemen who being never called into court by any higher motive than curiosity would appear to have acquired but a very imperfect understanding of the behaviour of gentlemen when they get there. From professional gentlemen of long standing and extensive practice the **Reporters** received every accommodation that could be furnished in such a place; but from these youths from the very first moment of their preventing the progress of business, by their self-important cries of 'Room for the bar,' down to the last moment of the trial, they experienced nothing but a series of gratuitous annoyances and ungentlemanly interruptions during their progress to and from the crowded court."

Special jury

Sir R. Peel, Bart., M.P.	John Donne, Esq.
P. B. Thompson, Esq., M.P.	Henry M'Kenzie, Esq.
R. Stafford, Esq.	William Brownson, Esq.
W. Rowlandson, Esq.	William Hopkinson, Esq.
Aug. Ruff, Esq.	Val. Collard, Esq.
Anthony Hammond, Esq.	Francis Baring, Esq.
George Robert Smith, Esq.	William Barton, Esq.
John Esdaile, Esq.	Joseph Pulley, Esq.
Charles Wilkinson, Esq.	John Simpson, Esq.

The twelve separately sworn to try the case:
   Messrs Stafford, Rowlandson and Ruff, merchants
   Mr Hammond, Esq.
   Messrs Smith, Wilkinson, Donne, Hopkinson, merchants
   Mr Collard, Esq.
   William Barker, Esq.
   Robert Smith and John Simpson, merchants

Witnesses
   Joseph Compton **Pott**, ecclesiastical clerk
   William Fletcher Norton, "connected with the plaintiff"
   George Darby, a friend of Norton's
   Georgiana Veitch, lady's maid for Miss Norton, Norton's sister
   Trinette Elliott, maid for Mrs Norton; let go when in a family way
   Ellen Monk, nurse for Mrs Norton's children
   Eliza Gibson, sometime lady's maid for Mrs Norton
   Thomas Bulliman, footman for Norton for one month
   Thomas Tucker, footman for Norton
   William Clarke, clerk
   William Lawley, job coachman for Colonel Armstrong (Norton friend)
   John Fluke, coachman for Norton; tended to drink
   Ann Cumming, nurse for the Nortons (acknowledged getting into
      trouble with one **Owen**: "He kept me out one Saturday night; he
      promised to marry me, and obtained an advantage over me.")
   Martha Morris, a servant
   James Benboe (or Benbow), footman
   Maria Foggis, cook

Persons referred to by the witnesses

Lady Seymour, Mrs Norton's sister	Currie, occupation unclear
Captain Blackwood, eldest son of	Lord Grantley
Lord Dufferin (married to another sister)	Norrington, a saddler
William Mansell, Miss Norton's footman	Lord Wynford
Mrs Cummins, of the serving class	**John Sly**, a hempseller
John Cumbers, a landlord at the Robin	Mrs Garrett
Hood tavern	**Mrs Lilly**, a nurse
Vizard: carried a message from Mrs Norton	General Fife, an employer
Head, Lord Grantley's steward	Mrs Moore, former nurse for
Mrs (Doctor) Herbert, who employed	Mrs Norton
Cumming	

Jury. "The jury having turned round in the box, and conferred during a few seconds,
   "THE FOREMAN [unidentified] said—My Lord, we are agreed. It is my duty to say that our verdict is for THE DEFENDANT."

SUNDAY

UNDER THREE HEADS.

AS IT IS;

AS SABBATH BILLS WOULD MAKE IT;

AS IT MIGHT BE MADE.

With Illustrations.

LONDON: CHAPMAN AND HALL,—186, STRAND.

PRICE TWO SHILLINGS.

Sunday under Three Heads

A monograph in three linked sections opposing a Sunday Observance Bill, introduced in Parliament by **Sir Andrew Agnew**. The bill proposed to eliminate recreational opportunity for working people in the name of spiritual uplift. Though primarily a special-purpose tract, the work pictures interesting people, congenial and otherwise. MS reports that Agnew's third try was defeated "by only a mere thirty-two votes . . . . Unabashed by Dickens's polemics, Agnew introduced his bill again in 1837 and this time it passed its second reading but was lost when Parliament was dissolved on the death of William IV. Agnew was not re-elected, and no one else took up the cause."

> " . . . *[the Bill] is, from beginning to end, a piece of deliberate cruelty, and crafty injustice . . . . It is directly, exclusively, and without the exception of a solitary instance, against the amusement and recreations of the poor.*"

> " . . . *three remarkable pamphlets upon the English Sunday, called Sunday under Three Heads. Here, at least, we find the eternal Dickens, though not the eternal Dickens of fiction . . . on the subject of the English Sunday he does stand for his own philosophy. He stands for a particular view, remote at present both from Liberals and Conservatives. He was, in a conscious sense, the first of its spokesmen. He was in every sense the last.*
>
> "*In his appeal for the pleasures of the people, Dickens has remained alone. The pleasures of the people have now no defender, Radical or Tory. The Tories despise the people. The Radicals despise the pleasures.*" *GKC p243*

CONTENTS

PERSONS MENTIONED

I AS IT IS

Beadle. "Long rows of cleanly-dressed charity children, preceded by a portly beadle and a withered **schoolmaster**, are returning to their welcome [Sunday] dinner . . . . "

Beer-men. " . . . it is evident, from the number of men with beer-trays who are running from house to house, that no inconsiderable portion of the population are about to take theirs [dinner] at this early hour."

First **clergyman**. "The clergyman enters the reading-desk—a young man of noble family and elegant demeanour, notorious at Cambridge for his knowledge of horse-flesh and dancers, and celebrated at Eton for his hopeless stupidity. The service commences. Mark the soft voice in which he reads, and the impressive manner in which he applies his white hand, studded with brilliants, to his perfumed hair. Observe the graceful emphasis with which he offers up the prayers for the King, the Royal Family, and all the Nobility; and the nonchalance with which he hurries over the more uncomfortable portions of the service, the seventh commandment for instance [against adultery], with a studied regard for the taste and feeling of his auditors only to be equalled by that displayed by . . . . "

Second **clergyman**. " . . . the sleek divine who succeeds [the first **clergyman**], who murmurs, in a voice kept down by rich feeding, most comfortable doctrines for exactly twelve minutes, and then arrives at the anxiously expected 'Now to God,' which is the signal for the dismissal of the congregation."

Clerk. "There is a dapper smartness, struggling through very limited means, about the young man [on the road], which induces one to set him down at once as a junior clerk to a tradesman or attorney."

Mary. " . . . the smart servant of all work, who has been loitering at the corner of the square for the last ten minutes . . . is evidently waiting for somebody, and though she may have made up her mind to go to church with him one of these mornings, I don't think they have any such intention on this particular afternoon."

—*her* "**young man:**" "Here he is at last. The white trousers, blue coat, and yellow waistcoat—and more especially that cock of the hat—indicate, as surely as inanimate objects can, that Chalk Farm and not the parish church is their destination. The girl colours up, and puts out her hand with a very awkward affectation of indifference. He gives it a gallant squeeze, and away they walk, arm in arm, the girl just looking back towards her 'place' with an air of conscious self-importance, and nodding to her fellow-**servant** who has gone up to the two-pair-of-stairs window, to take a full view . . . . "

Milliner's assistant. "You may tell a young woman in the employment of a large dress-maker, at any time, by a certain neatness of cheap finery and humble following of fashion which pervade her whole attire; but unfortunately there are other tokens not to be misunderstood—the pale face with its hectic bloom, the slight distortion of form which no artifice of dress can wholly conceal, the unhealthy stoop, and the short cough—the effects of hard work and close application to a sedentary employment, upon a tender frame."

The Poor. "**Women** with scarcely the articles of apparel which common decency requires, with forms bloated by disease, and faces rendered hideous by habitual drunkenness—**men** reeling and staggering along—**children** in rags and filth—whole streets of squalid and miserable appearance, whose inhabitants are lounging in the public road, fighting, screaming, and swearing . . . . "

Preacher. "The preacher enters the pulpit. He is a coarse, hard-faced man of forbidding aspect, clad in rusty black, and bearing in his hand a small plain Bible from which he selects some passage for his text, while the hymn is concluding . . . he calls upon the Sacred Founder of the Christian faith to bless his ministry, in terms of disgusting and impious familiarity not to be described. He begins his oration in a drawling tone, and his hearers listen with silent attention. He grows warmer as he proceeds with his subject, and his gesticulation becomes proportionately violent. He clenches his fists, beats the book upon the desk before him, and swings his arms wildly about his head."

" . . . working himself up to a pitch of enthusiasm amounting almost to frenzy, he denounces sabbath-breakers with the direst vengeance of offended Heaven. He stretches his body half out of the pulpit, thrusts forth his arms with frantic gestures, and blasphemously calls upon the Deity to visit with eternal torments those who turn aside from the word, as interpreted and preached by—himself."

Timothy Sparks, *nom-de-plume*. "That your Lordship [**Agnew**] would ever have contemplated Sunday recreations with so much horror, if you had been at all acquainted with the wants and necessities of the people who indulged in them, I cannot imagine possible."

William. "Here he is, at last. The white trousers, blue coat, and yellow waistcoat—and more especially that cock of the hat—indicate, as surely as inanimate objects can, that Chalk Farm and not the parish church are their destination."

Working man. "Look at the group of **children** who surround that working man who has just emerged from the baker's shop at the corner of the street, with the reeking dish, in which a diminutive joint of mutton simmers above a vast heap of half-browned potatoes. How the young rogues clap their hands, and dance round their father, for very joy at the prospect of the feast: and how anxiously the youngest and chubbiest of the lot lingers on tiptoe by his side, trying to get a peep into the interior of the dish. They turn up the street, and the chubby-faced **boy** trots on as fast as his little legs will carry him, to herald the approach of the dinner to '**Mother**' who is standing with a baby in her arms on the doorstep, and who seems almost as pleased with the whole scene as the children themselves . . . . "

Sir Andrew Agnew[H]: introducer of the Sabbath Observance Bill
Charity children in long rows, cleanly dressed
Clerk, in a dissenting chapel
-pl employed in counting-houses, procuring early breakfast
Miss Emily: mistress for whom Mary works
Footmen, powdered: glide along the aisle, placing richly-bound prayer books
Man, very poor, purchasing scanty quantity of necessaries
    Woman by his side, thin and sickly
Schoolmaster, withered: leading the file of charity children
Servant, who has gone upstairs to take a full view of Mary's young man
-pl liveried: all bustle and commotion
Young girl, screams and falls senseless in the chapel
Young man and woman, in their best attire with a scheme of pleasure

II AS SABBATH BILLS WOULD MAKE IT

Sir Andrew Agnew. "The provisions of the bill introduced into the House of Commons by Sir Andrew Agnew, and thrown out by that House on the motion for the second reading, on the 18th of May in the present year, by a majority of 32, may very fairly be taken as a test of the length to which the fanatics, of which the honourable Baronet is the distinguished leader, are prepared to go."

"The idea of making a man truly moral through the ministry of constables, and sincerely religious under the influence of penalties, is worthy of the mind which could form such a mass of monstrous absurdity as this bill is composed of."

"It may be asked, what motives can actuate a man who has so little regard for the comfort of his fellow-beings, so little respect for their wants and necessities, and so distorted a notion of the beneficence of his Creator. I reply, an envious, heartless, ill-conditioned dislike to seeing those whom fortune has placed below him, cheerful and happy—an intolerant confidence in his own high worthiness before God, and a lofty impression of the demerits of others—pride, selfish pride, as inconsistent with the spirit of Christianity itself, as opposed to the example of its Founder upon earth."

Enthusiasts. " . . . who would make earth a hell, and religion a torment: men who, having wasted the earlier part of their lives in dissipation and depravity, find themselves when scarcely past its meridian, steeped to the neck in vice, and shunned like a loathsome disease. Abandoned by the world, having nothing to fall back upon, nothing to remember but time mis-spent, and energies misdirected, they turn their eyes and not their thoughts to Heaven...."

Informer, with his notebook
Landlord, fined and a window-duty imposed
Tea-gardeners: man, and his wife and children; ordering ale and a biscuit
Waiter, responding to orders on the Sabbath

III AS IT MIGHT BE MADE

Minister. "The impressive service of the Church of England was spoken—not merely *read*—by a grey-headed minister . . . . He seemed intimately acquainted with the circumstances of all his parishioners; for I heard him inquire after one man's youngest child, another man's wife, and so forth; and . . . he was fond of his joke."

"What was my agreeable surprise to see the old gentleman standing at the stile, with his hands in his pockets, surveying the whole [cricket] scene with evident satisfaction! . . . it was his field they played in; and . . . it was he who had purchased stumps, bats, ball, and all!

" . . . . It is such men as this who would do more in one year to make people properly religious, cheerful, and contented, than all the legislation of a century could ever accomplish."

Old man. "I could not but take notice of one old man in particular, with a bright-eyed **grand-daughter** by his side, who was giving a sunburnt **young fellow** some instructions in the game, which he received with an air of profound deference, but with an occasional glance at the girl, which induced me to think that his attention was rather distracted . . . . "

> Clerk, in a country church: voices led by him, proud and gratified
> Girl, bashful-looking; on the arm of a young fellow

HKB   ORRIN SMITH, S P

N 1 March 1836-Nov 1837 monthly by Chapman & Hall   1 vol 1837 **PP**
U.S. publication 1836-37 by Carey, Lea & Blanchard, Philadelphia (5 vols.)
Extensive stylistic revisions made for the 1847 edition, minor ones in 1867

The Posthumous Papers of the Pickwick Club,

containing a Faithful Record of the Perambulations, Perils, Travels, Adventures and Sporting Transactions of the Corresponding Members, edited by Boz

"Pickwick will always be remembered as the great example of everything that made Dickens great; of the solemn conviviality of great friendships, of the erratic adventures of old English roads, of the hospitality of old English inns, of the great fundamental kindliness and honour of old English manners. First of all, however, it will always be remembered for its laughter, or, if you will, for its folly. A good joke is the one ultimate and sacred thing which cannot be criticised. Our relations with a good joke are direct and even divine relations. We speak of 'seeing' a joke just as we speak of 'seeing' a ghost or a vision. If we have seen it, it is futile to argue with us; and we have seen the vision of Pickwick." GKC pp24-5

"The quality which makes the Pickwick Papers one of the greatest of human fairy tales is a quality which all the great fairy tales possess, and which marks them out from most modern writing. A modern novelist generally endeavours to make his story interesting, by making his hero odd . . . . But in a fairy tale the boy sees all the wonders of fairyland because he is an ordinary boy. In the same way Mr Samuel Pickwick sees an extraordinary England because he is an ordinary old gentleman. He does not see things through the rosy spectacles of the modern optimist or the green-smoked spectacles of the pessimist; he sees it through the crystal glasses of his own innocence. One must see the world clearly even in order to see its wildest poetry. One must see it sanely even in order to see that it is insane." GKC p236

ADVERTISEMENT

"THE PICKWICK CLUB, so renowned in the annals of Huggin-lane, and so closely entwined with the thousand interesting associations connected with Lothbury and Cateaton-street, was founded in the year One Thousand Eight Hundred and Twenty-two, by **Mr Samuel Pickwick**—the great traveller, whose fondness for the useful arts prompted his celebrated journey to Birmingham in the depth of winter; and whose taste for the Beauties of Nature, even led him to penetrate to the very borders of Wales in the height of summer.

"This remarkable man would appear to have infused a considerable portion of his restless and inquiring spirit into the breasts of other Members of the Club, and to have awakened in their minds the same insatiable thirst for Travel, which so eminently characterised his own. The whole surface of Middlesex, a part of Surrey, a portion of Essex, and several square miles of Kent, were in their turns examined, and reported on.

"In a rapid Steamer, they smoothly navigated the placid Thames; and in an open boat, they fearlessly crossed the turbid Medway. High-roads and bye-roads, towns and villages, public conveyances and their passengers, first-rate inns, and road-side public houses, races, fairs, regattas, elections, meetings, market-days— all the scenes that can possibly occur to enliven a country place, and at which different traits of character may be observed and recognised, was alike visited and beheld, by the ardent Pickwick, and his enthusiastic followers.

"The Pickwick Travels, the Pickwick Diary, the Pickwick Correspondence—in short the whole of the Pickwick Papers, were carefully preserved and duly registered by the Secretary, from time to time, in the voluminous Transactions of the Pickwick Club. These Transactions have been purchased from the patriotic Secretary, at an immense expense, and placed in the hands of 'Boz,' the author of Sketches Illustrative of Every Day Life, and Every Day People—a gentleman whom the publishers consider highly qualified for the task of arranging these important documents, and placing them before the public in an attractive form. He is at present deeply immersed in his arduous labors, the first fruits of which appeared on the 31st of March [1836].

"Seymour has devoted himself, heart and graver, to the task of illustrating the beauties of Pickwick. It was reserved to Gibbon to paint, in colours that will never fade, the Decline and Fall of the Roman Empire—to Hume to chronicle the strife and turmoil of the two proud Houses that divided England against herself—to Napier to pen, in burning words, the History of the War in the Peninsula;—the deeds and actions of the gifted Pickwick, yet remain for 'Boz' and SEYMOUR to hand down to posterity.

"From the present appearance of these important documents, and the probable extent of the selections from them, it is presumed that the series will be completed in about twenty numbers."

—advertisement on back cover and back inside of The Library of Fiction, No.1 (it contained SB/TR*).* In the Berg Collection. James Kinsley, editor of Oxford's Clarendon Edition of PP, assures us that the above is by CD. Much of what he intended to depict, in places visited and exploits undertaken, never came to pass, but one is not particularly inclined to bemoan Huggin Lane and Cateaton Street (the latter is **Tom Smart**'s home base). The "turbid Medway" and the Thames steamer, however . . . . (sigh)

PRÉCIS

The Pickwick Club in London establishes a Corresponding Society of four members, charged with the duty of travel and observation, and subsequent reporting to the Club. The four are Club founder **Samuel Pickwick**, the amorous **Tracy Tupman**, the poetical **Augustus Snodgrass**, and **Nathaniel Winkle**, reputed sportsman. The year is 1827. 1

On the group's way to Rochester, **Alfred Jingle**, shabby adventurer, attaches himself and persuades Tupman to go to a ball. Tupman takes Winkle's coat to lend to Jingle, who mischievously cuts out local Doctor **Slammer** with the wealthy widow **Mrs Budger**. A challenge follows the next morning, but it is delivered to an astonished Winkle, who recruits Snodgrass as his second but is spared on the ground as Slammer realizes he is not the man. 2

Pickwick and friends entangle themselves at a military review but are rescued by **Wardle**, who is with his sister **Rachael** and daughters **Isabella** and **Emily**, and the **Fat Boy** (**Joe Lambert**), a virtuosic sleeper and eater. The Pickwickians are invited to the Wardle home, Manor Farm at Dingley Dell, and are provided with horses for the excursion. Winkle *et al* manage the horses poorly and end by walking to the Farm. 4-5

After an evening of whist and stories, Wardle takes the party out bird-hunting, but Winkle disgraces himself again, wounding Tupman. The latter woos Rachael while the rest go to Muggleton to watch cricket. They again encounter Jingle, who cadges an invitation to the Farm. Once there, he cuts out Tupman and elopes with Rachael. 6-9

Pickwick and friends pursue the couple to the White Hart Inn, where the boots, **Sam Weller**, shows the party where to find them. Jingle accepts cash, and the party returns to the Farm. Tupman has fled in embarrassment, but they follow him to Kent, where a Pickwickian antiquity is uncovered. 10-11

Pickwick decides to take Weller as his man but bungles the announcement to his landlady, **Mrs Bardell**, who faints in his arms, believing he has proposed marriage. Sam Weller is engaged and enrobed. 12

The party goes to Eatanswill to observe a parliamentary election. A bagman tells a story. They attend **Mrs Leo Hunter**'s masquerade breakfast, where they find Jingle under an alias. He flees and they pursue. 13-15

Catching up with Jingle and his man, **Job Trotter**, Mr Pickwick is tricked and embarrassed at a young ladies' school. His companions rejoin him just as he receives a letter from Messrs **Dodson** and **Fogg**, counsel to Mrs Bardell, who is suing him for breach of promise. 16-18

Off on a shoot, as Winkle again disgraces himself while Tupman undeservedly gains praise, Mr Pickwick falls asleep in a wheelbarrow and is sent to the pound by the irate landowner, Captain **Boldwig**. 19

Pickwick visits Dodson and Fogg and is insulted. On the way to his lawyer, **Perker**, stage-coachman **Tony Weller**, Sam's father, enters the story. At a hotel at Ipswich, after dining with new acquaintance **Peter Magnus**, Mr Pickwick gets lost and encounters **Miss Witherfield** (admired by Magnus), from whose bedroom he precipitately retreats. 20-22

Magnus challenges Pickwick to a duel, and to prevent bloodshed, the lady arranges for Pickwick and Tupman, his second, to be arrested and haled before **George Nupkins**, the mayor. They find Jingle adventuring again and by exposing him gain release. **Mary**, the Nupkins housemaid, is kissed by Sam Weller for the first, but not the last, time. 23-25

Mr Pickwick goes to London, and Sam interviews Mrs Bardell. Sam visits his newly-married father, whose wife admires preacher **Stiggins**. Mr Pickwick returns to Dingley Dell for Christmas. 26-28

Christmas at Dingley Dell brings two medical students, **Benjamin Allen** and **Bob Sawyer**. Allen's sister, **Arabella**, has impressed both Winkle and Sawyer. Mr Pickwick distinguishes himself on skates but Winkle does not. Mr Wardle's mistletoe is a great success. 29-30

Mr Serjeant **Snubbin** takes the Pickwick case (Serjeant **Buzfuz** for the plaintiff) and Bob Sawyer entertains. Sam writes Mary a letter. 31-33

Bardell v Pickwick ends in money judgment for the plaintiff, which Mr Pickwick refuses to pay. He heads off to Bath for entertainment, but Winkle has to leave town, having been misunderstood by an impetuous husband, **Dowler**, and Sam is sent to collect him. 34-37

Winkle bumps into Sawyer and learns he may be lucky in love. Sam finds him and sticks to him until Mr Pickwick arrives. The search for Arabella turns up Mary. Mr Pickwick aids Winkle's love. 38-39

Mr Pickwick goes to debtor's prison, where he meets many inmates, including Jingle and Trotter. He refuses to pay any fine. Sam loyally gets himself committed to prison. An inmate dies, and the plight of the debtors wrings the Pickwick heart. Mr Pickwick discovers that Mrs Bardell has been jailed for costs. His gallantry impels him to make a payment, releasing her and himself, with Sam. 40-48

The Winkle love has ended in elopement, and Pickwick tact assuages Allen's and Sawyer's hard feelings, before he goes on to tackle Winkle, Sr. Mr Pickwick sojourns on the road and reencounters two rival Eatanswill editors, **Pott** and **Slurk**. A letter arrives revealing that Tony Weller is a widower, sincerely saddened at the loss of a softened Susan. Sam goes to his father, who enthusiastically kicks Stiggins into the world. 49-53

Mr Pickwick aids Jingle, to whom Trotter loyally adheres, and Dodson and Fogg receive the rough side of the Pickwick tongue. 54

Snodgrass and Emily Wardle are a pair. Tony Weller is an heir and learns a little of the law. He entrusts his funds to Pickwick management, and Winkle, Sr, succumbs to Arabella. After a two-year wait, Sam and Mary marry and together attend Mr Pickwick, who states that the happiness of young folk is his first priority in life. All ends joyfully. 55-58

CONTENTS

Illustrations by (with exceptions noted) *Hablôt K. Browne* ("Phiz")

CHARACTERS

("Int" means an Interlude: an interpolated story almost compulsively told, in the mode of CD's childhood favourite, the *Arabian Nights,* by a person encountered by a Protagonist.)

Allen, Arabella; later Winkle; charming fur-topped boots	SR	190
Benjamin: her brother, rather dirty would-be physician	SR	190
Apprentice, bony; to Old Lobbs	Int	222
Attorney, from London, of no great nicety	Int	223
Aunt of Arabella, who breaks bad news	O	200
Authors: half a dozen lions from London	W	218
Ayresleigh: a debtor	O	200
Bagman: flirtatious one-eyed teller of tales	O	200
Baillie: Scottish local magistrate with a large family	Int	225
Bailmen, slim and lame; stout and burly; weazen and drunken-looking	O	200
Bamber, Jack: law clerk and story-teller	O	200
Bantam, Angelo Cyrus: ornamenting Bath	O	200
Bardell: deceased and mourned in Court	O	200
Mrs Martha: landlady misunderstands and sues for breach	P	179
Master **Thomas**; her son, who gets loyally upset	SR	191
Barmaid, wounded in line of duty	W	218
Beller, Henry: temperance convert	O	201
Benjamin, Pell's boy with a blue bag	O	201
Betsy, dirty little girl	W	218
Bladud, Prince: son of Hudibras	Int	224
Blotton: Pyrrhic debunker of antiquarian claims; haberdasher	O	201
Boldwig, Captain: choleric landholder	O	201
Bolo, Miss: whist player with strong views on correct bidding	O	201
Boy, in debtor's prison	O	201
-in a hairy cap with a drover's whistle	W	218
Brothers, proud and humble, of a madman's wife	Int	222
Budger, Mrs: a widow of means	O	202
Bulder family	O	202
Burton, Thomas: temperance convert	O	202
Buzfuz, Mr Serjeant: legal counsel to Mrs Bardell	SR	191
Chair/Man, who comes to life and helps Tom Smart	Int	222
Chambermaid: colleague of Sam Weller	W	219

Spear-carriers   chapter

*"It has been observed of **Mr. Pickwick**, that there is a decided change in his character, as these pages proceed, and that he becomes more good and more sensible. I do not think this change will appear forced or unnatural to my readers, if they will reflect that in real life the peculiarities and oddities of a man who has anything whimsical about him, generally impress us* [perhaps this includes the author himself] *first, and that it is not until we are better acquainted with him that we usually begin to look below these superficial traits, and to know the better part of him." —preface*

Prelude—an inspiration revealed

"'Well, **Sam**,' said Mr **Pickwick**, 'what's the matter now?'

"'Here's rayther a rum go, sir,' replied Sam . . . . 'I'm wery much afeerd, sir, that the proprieator o' this here coach [the Bath stage] is a playin' some imperence vith us.'

"'How is that, Sam?' said Mr Pickwick; 'aren't the names down on the way-bill?'

"'The names is not only down on the vay-bill, sir,' replied Sam, 'but they've painted vun on 'em up, on the door o' the coach.' As Sam spoke, he pointed to that part of the coach door on which the proprietor's name usually appears; and there, sure enough, in gilt letters of a goodly size, was the magic name of PICKWICK!*

"'Dear me!' exclaimed Mr Pickwick, quite staggered by the coincidence, 'what a very extraordinary thing!'

"'Yes, but that ain't all,' said Sam, again directing his master's attention to the coach door, 'not content vith writin' up Pickwick, they puts "Moses" afore it, vich I call addin' insult to injury, as the parrot said ven they not only took him from his native land, but made him talk the English langwidge arterwards.'" 35 [For more "Wellerisms" *see* 185ff]

*"The veritable family of this name, living at Bath, changed their name, after it had become too intimately associated with the novel, to Sainsbery."—HMCD XXXII p 52 *See also* "I Thought of Mr Pickwick" in *Threads to Pull On,* vol. III.

Our Eponymous Hero

Samuel Pickwick. "A casual observer . . . might possibly have remarked nothing extraordinary in the bald head, and circular spectacles . . . to those who knew that the gigantic brain of Pickwick was working beneath that forehead, and that the beaming eyes of Pickwick were twinkling behind those glasses, the sight was indeed an interesting one. There sat the man who had traced to their source the mighty ponds of Hampstead, and agitated the scientific world with his Theory of Tittlebats, as calm and unmoved as the deep waters of the one on a frosty day, or as a solitary specimen of the other in the inmost recesses of an earthen jar.

"And how much more interesting did the spectacle become, when starting into full life and animation, as a simultaneous call for 'Pickwick' burst from his followers, that illustrious man slowly mounted into the Windsor chair, on which he had been previously seated, and addressed the club he himself had founded. What a study for an artist did that exciting scene present! The eloquent Pickwick, with one hand gracefully concealed behind his coat tails, and the other waving in the air, to assist his glowing declamation; his elevated position revealing those tights and gaiters, which, had they clothed an ordinary man, might have passed without observation, but which, when Pickwick clothed them—if we may use the expression—inspired voluntary awe and respect; surrounded by the men who had volunteered to share the perils of his travels, and who were destined to participate in the glories of his discoveries." ¶1

—*at home:* "Mr Pickwick's apartments in Goswell Street, although on a limited scale, were not only of a very neat and comfortable description, but peculiarly adapted for the residence of a man of his genius and observation . . . . There were no children, no servants, no fowls. The only other inmates of the house were a large man and a small boy; the first a lodger, the second a production of **Mrs Bardell**'s . . . . Cleanliness and quiet reigned throughout the house; and in it Mr Pickwick's will was law." 12

—*indignant:* "If any dispassionate spectator could have beheld the countenance of the illustrious man . . . he would have been almost induced to wonder that the indignant fire which flashed from his eyes, did not melt the glasses of his spectacles—so majestic was his wrath. His nostrils dilated, and his fists clenched involuntarily, as he heard himself addressed by the villain [**Jingle**]. But he restrained himself again—he did *not* pulverise him.

"'Here,' continued the hardened traitor, tossing the [marriage] licence at Mr Pickwick's feet; 'get the name altered—take home the lady—do for Tuppy.'

"Mr Pickwick was a philosopher, but philosophers are only men in armour, after all. The shaft had reached him, penetrated through his philosophical harness, to his very heart. In the frenzy of his rage he hurled the inkstand madly forward, and followed it up himself. "10

—*antiquarian:* "'I can discern a cross, and a B, and then a T. This is important,' continued Mr Pickwick, starting up. 'This is some very old inscription, existing perhaps long before the ancient alms-houses in this place. It must not be lost.'

"He tapped at the cottage door. A **labouring man** opened it.

"'Do you know how this stone came here, my friend?' inquired the benevolent Mr Pickwick.

"'No, I doan't sir,' replied the man civilly. 'It was here long afore I war born, or any on us.'

"Mr Pickwick glanced triumphantly at his companion.

"'You—you—are not particularly attached to it, I dare say,' said Mr Pickwick, trembling with anxiety. 'You wouldn't mind selling it, now?'

"'Ah! but who'd buy it?' inquired the man, with an expression of face which he probably meant to be very cunning.

"'I'll give you ten shillings for it, at once,' said Mr Pickwick, 'if you would take it up for me.'

"The astonishment of the village may be easily imagined, when (the little stone having been raised with one wrench of a spade), Mr Pickwick, by dint of great personal exertion, bore it with his own hands to the inn, and after having carefully washed it, deposited it on the table.

"The exultation and joy of the Pickwickians knew no bounds, when their patience and assiduity, their washing and scraping, were crowned with success. The stone was uneven and broken, and the letters were straggling and irregular, but the following fragment of an inscription was clearly to be deciphered:

```
            +
    B  I  L  S  T
    U  M
    P  S  H  I
    S  M
    A  R  K
```

"Mr Pickwick's eyes sparkled with delight, as he sat and gloated over the treasure he had discovered. He had attained one of the greatest objects of his ambition. In a county known to abound in remains of the early ages; in a village in which there still existed some memorials of the olden time, he—he, the Chairman of the Pickwick Club—had discovered a strange and curious inscription of unquestionable antiquity, which had wholly escaped the observation of the many learned men who had preceded him. He could hardly trust the evidence of his senses." 11 *But see* **Blotton** O

—*convivial imbibition:* "His countenance beamed with the most sunny smiles, laughter played around his lips, and good-humoured merriment twinkled in his eye. Yielding by degrees to the influence of the exciting liquid, rendered more so by the heat, Mr Pickwick expressed a strong desire to recollect a song which he had heard in his infancy, and the attempt proving abortive, sought to stimulate his memory with more glasses of punch, which appeared to have quite a contrary effect; for, from forgetting the words of the song, he began to forget how to articulate any words at all; and finally, after rising to his legs to address the company in an eloquent speech, he fell into the barrow, and fast asleep, simultaneously." 19

—*at play:* "It was the most intensely interesting thing, to observe the manner in which Mr Pickwick performed his share in the ceremony [sliding on the skating-slide]; to watch the torture of anxiety with which he viewed the person behind, gaining upon him at the imminent hazard of tripping him up; to see him gradually expend the painful force he had put on at first, and turn slowly round on the slide, with his face towards the point from which he had started; to contemplate the playful smile which mantled on his face when he had accomplished the distance, and the eagerness with which he turned round when he had done so, and ran after his predecessor: his black gaiters tripping pleasantly through the snow, and his eyes beaming cheerfulness and gladness through his spectacles. And when he was knocked down (which happened upon the average every third round), it was the most invigorating sight that can possibly be imagined, to behold him gather up his hat, gloves, and handkerchief, with a glowing countenance, and resume his station in the rank, with an ardour and enthusiasm that nothing could abate." 30

—*to his valet:* "'Bless his old gaiters,' rejoined **Sam** . . . .'He's a keepin' guard in the lane vith that 'ere dark lantern, like a amiable Guy Fawkes ! I never see such a fine creetur in my days. Blessed if I don't think his heart must ha' been born five-and-twenty year arter his body, at least!'" 39

"'I never heered, mind you, nor read of in story-books, nor see in picters, any angel in tights and gaiters—not even in spectacles, as I remember, though that may ha' been done for anythin' I know to the contrairey—but mark my vords . . . he's a reg'lar thoroughbred angel for all that; and let me see the man as wenturs to tell me he knows a better vun.'" 45

—*his chief pleasure:* "'The happiness of young people,' said Mr Pickwick, a little moved, 'has ever been the chief pleasure of my life.'" 57

Other Principals

Mrs Martha Bardell, "the relict and sole executrix of a deceased custom-house officer—was a comely woman of bustling manners and agreeable appearance, with a natural genius for cooking, improved by study and long practice, into an exquisite talent." 12

—misunderstanding: "'Mrs Bardell,' said Mr **Pickwick**, at last, as that amiable female approached the termination of a prolonged dusting of the apartment . . . .

"'Do you think it a much greater expense to keep two people, than to keep one?'

"'La, Mr Pickwick,' said Mrs Bardell colouring up to the very border of her cap, as she fancied she observed a species of matrimonial twinkle in the eyes of her lodger; 'La, Mr Pickwick, what a question!' . . .

"Mrs Bardell . . . had long worshipped Mr Pickwick at a distance, but here she was, all at once, raised to a pinnacle to which her wildest and most extravagant hopes had never dared to aspire. Mr Pickwick was going to propose—a deliberate plan, too—sent her little boy to the Borough, to get him out of the way—how thoughtful —how considerate!

"'Well,' said Mr Pickwick, 'what do you think?'

"'Oh, Mr Pickwick,' said Mrs Bardell, trembling with agitation, 'you're very kind, sir' . . . .

"'Oh you dear—' said Mrs Bardell.

"Mr Pickwick started.

"'Oh you kind, good, playful dear,' said Mrs Bardell; and without more ado, she rose from her chair, and flung her arms round Mr Pickwick's neck, with a cataract of tears and a chorus of sobs." 12

Alfred Jingle. "He was about the middle height, but the thinness of his body, and the length of his legs, gave him the appearance of being much taller. The green coat had been a smart dress garment in the days of swallow-tails, but had evidently in those times adorned a much shorter man than the stranger, for the soiled and faded sleeves scarcely reached to his wrists. It was buttoned closely up to his chin, at the imminent hazard of splitting the back; and an old stock, without a vestige of shirt collar, ornamented his neck.

"His scanty black trousers displayed here and there those shiny patches which bespeak long service, and were strapped very tightly over a pair of patched and mended shoes, as if to conceal the dirty white stockings, which were nevertheless distinctly visible. His long black hair escaped in negligent waves from beneath each side of his old pinched up hat; and glimpses of his bare wrists might be observed between the tops of his gloves, and the cuffs of his coat sleeves. His face was thin and haggard; but an indescribable air of jaunty impudence and perfect self-possession pervaded the whole man." ¶2

—*his rapid-fire:* "'Ah! you should keep dogs—fine animals—sagacious creatures—dog of my own once—Pointer—surprising instinct—out shooting one day—entering enclosure—whistled—dog stopped—whistled again—**Ponto**—no go; stock still—called him—Ponto, Ponto—wouldn't move—dog transfixed—staring at a board—looked up, saw an inscription—"Game-keeper has orders to shoot all dogs found in this enclosure"—wouldn't pass it—wonderful dog—valuable dog that—very.'" 2

—*at cricket:* "'Well, and how came you here?' said Mr **Pickwick**, with a smile in which benevolence struggled with surprise.

"'Come,' replied the stranger—'stopping at Crown—Crown at Muggleton —met a party—flannel jackets—white trousers—anchovy sandwiches—devilled kidneys—splendid fellows—glorious.'

"Mr Pickwick was sufficiently versed in the stranger's system of stenography to infer from this rapid and disjointed communication that he had, somehow or other, contracted an acquaintance with the All-Muggletons, which he had converted, by a process peculiar to himself, into that extent of good fellowship on which a general invitation may be easily founded." 7

—*wooing:* "Mr Jingle within five minutes after his arrival at Manor Farm . . . had inwardly resolved to lay siege to the heart of [**Rachael**] the spinster aunt, without delay. He had observation enough to see that his off-hand manner was by no means disagreeable to the fair object of his attack; and he had more than a strong suspicion that she possessed that most desirable of all requisites, a small independence. . . . She blushed slightly, and cast a grateful look on Mr Jingle.

"That insinuating gentleman sighed deeply, fixed his eyes on the spinster aunt's face for a couple of minutes, started melodramatically, and suddenly withdrew them.

"'You seem unhappy, Mr Jingle,' said the lady, in a plaintive voice. 'May I show my gratitude for your kind interference, by inquiring into the cause, with a view, if possible, to its removal?'

"'Ha!' exclaimed Mr Jingle, with another start—'removal! remove *my* unhappiness and your love bestowed upon a man who is insensible to the blessing—who even now contemplates a design upon the affections of the niece of the creature who—but no; he is my friend; I will not expose his vices. Miss Wardle—farewell!' At the conclusion of this address, the most consecutive he was ever known to utter, Mr Jingle applied to his eyes the remnant of a handkerchief . . . and turned towards the door.

"'Stay, Mr Jingle!' said the spinster aunt emphatically. 'You have made an allusion to Mr **Tupman**—explain it.'

"'Never!' exclaimed Jingle, with a professional (i.e. theatrical) air. 'Never!' and, by way of showing that he had no desire to be questioned further, he drew a chair close to that of the spinster aunt and sat down.

"'Mr Jingle,' said the aunt, 'I entreat—I implore you, if there is any dreadful mystery connected with Mr Tupman, reveal it.'

"'Can I,' said Mr Jingle, fixing his eyes on the aunt's face—'can I see—lovely creature—sacrificed at the shrine—heartless avarice!' He appeared to be struggling with various conflicting emotions for a few seconds, and then said in a low deep voice—

"'Tupman only wants your money.'

"'The wretch!' exclaimed the spinster, with energetic indignation. (Mr Jingle's doubts were resolved. She *had* money.)" 8

—*in debtor's prison:* "Yes; in tattered garments, and without a coat; his common calico shirt, yellow and in rags; his hair hanging over his face; his features changed with suffering, and pinched with famine; there sat Mr Alfred Jingle: his head resting on his hand, his eyes fixed upon the fire, and his whole appearance denoting misery and dejection!. . . .

"'Oh, said Mr **Pickwick** . . . . 'You have pawned your wardrobe.'

"'Everything—Job's too—all shirts gone—never mind—saves washing. Nothing soon—lie in bed—starve—die—Inquest—little bone-house—poor prisoner—common necessaries—hush it up—gentlemen of the jury—warden's tradesmen—keep it snug—natural death—coroner's order—work-house funeral—serve him right—all over—drop the curtain.'" 43

Tracy Tupman. ". . . the too susceptible Tupman, who to the wisdom and experience of maturer years superadded the enthusiasm and ardour of a boy, in the most interesting and pardonable of human weaknesses—love. Time and feeding had expanded that once romantic form; the black silk waistcoat had become more and more developed; inch by inch had the gold watch-chain beneath it disappeared from within the range of Tupman's vision; and gradually had the capacious chin encroached upon the borders of the white cravat: but the soul of Tupman had known no change —admiration of the fair sex was still its ruling passion." 1

—*wooing:* "'Miss **Wardle**!' said he.

"The spinster aunt trembled; till some pebbles which had accidentally found their way into the large watering-pot shook like an infant's rattle.

"'Miss Wardle,' said Mr Tupman, 'you are an angel.'

"'Mr Tupman!' exclaimed **Rachael**, blushing as red as the watering-pot itself.

"'Nay,' said the eloquent Pickwickian—'I know it but too well.'

"'All women are angels, they say,' murmured the lady, playfully.

"'Then what can *you* be; or to what, without presumption, can I compare you?' replied Mr Tupman. 'Where was the woman ever seen who resembled you? Where else could I hope to find so rare a combination of excellence and beauty? Where else could I seek to——Oh!' Here Mr Tupman paused, and pressed the hand which clasped the handle of the happy watering-pot.

"The lady turned aside her head. 'Men are such deceivers,' she softly whispered.

"'They are, they are,' ejaculated Mr Tupman; 'but not all men. There lives at least one being who can never change—one being who would be content to devote his whole existence to your happiness—who lives but in your eyes—who breathes but in your smiles—who bears the heavy burden of life itself only for you.'

"'Could such an individual be found,' said the lady——

"'But he *can* be found,' said the ardent Mr Tupman, interposing. 'He *is* found. He is here, Miss Wardle.' And ere the lady was aware of his intention, Mr Tupman had sunk upon his knees at her feet." 8

—*insulted:* "'I shall go as a Bandit,' interrupted Mr Tupman . . . .

"'You don't mean to say,' said **Mr Pickwick**, gazing with solemn sternness at his friend. 'You don't mean to say, Mr Tupman, that it is your intention to put yourself into a green velvet jacket, with a two-inch tail?'

"'Such *is* my intention, sir,' replied Mr Tupman warmly. 'And why not, sir?'

"'Because, sir,' said Mr Pickwick, considerably excited, 'Because you are too old, sir.'

"'Too old!' exclaimed Mr Tupman.

"'And if any further ground of objection be wanting,' continued Mr Pickwick, 'you are too fat, sir.'

"'Sir,' said Mr Tupman, his face suffused with a crimson glow. 'This is an insult.'

"'Sir,' replied Mr Pickwick in the same tone, 'It is not half the insult to you, that your appearance in my presence in a green velvet jacket, with a two-inch tail, would be to me.'

"'Sir,' said Mr Tupman, 'you're a fellow.'

"'Sir,' said Mr Pickwick, 'you're another.'" 15

—*envoi:* "Mr Tupman . . . took lodgings at Richmond, where he has ever since resided. He walks constantly on the Terrace during the summer months, with a youthful and jaunty air which has rendered him the admiration of the numerous elderly ladies of single condition, who reside in the vicinity. He has never proposed again." 57

Sam Weller. "' . . . a man was busily employed in brushing the dirt off a pair of boots . . . . He was habited in a coarse-striped waistcoat, with black calico sleeves, and blue glass buttons; drab breeches and leggings. A bright red handkerchief was wound in a very loose and unstudied style round his neck, and an old white hat was carelessly thrown on one side of his head. There were two rows of boots before him, one cleaned and the other dirty, and at every addition he made to the clean row, he paused from his work, and contemplated its results with evident satisfaction. . . ." 10

—*hat:* "' . . . down he sat without further bidding, having previously deposited his white hat on the landing outside the door. 'Ta'nt a werry good 'un to look at,' said Sam, 'but it's an astonishin' 'un to wear; and afore the brim went, it was a werry handsome tile. Hows'ever it's lighter without it, that's one thing, and every hole lets in some air, that's another—wentilation gossamer, I calls it.'" 12

—*uniform:* ". . . before night had closed in, Mr Weller was furnished with a grey coat with the P. C. button, a black hat with a cockade to it, a pink striped waistcoat, light breeches and gaiters, and a variety of other necessaries, too numerous to recapitulate." 12

—*life story:* "'When I wos first pitched neck and crop into the world, to play at leap-frog with its troubles,' replied Sam, 'I wos a carrier's boy at startin': then a vagginer's, then a helper, then a boots. Now I'm a gen'l'm'n's servant. I shall be a gen'l'm'n myself one of these days, perhaps, with a pipe in my mouth, and a summer-house in the back garden. Who knows? *I* shouldn't be surprised, for one.'" 16

—on filial piety: "' . . . if ever I wanted anythin' o' my father, I alvays asked for it in a wery 'spectful and obligin' manner. If he didn't give it me, I took it, for fear I should be led to do anythin' wrong, through not havin' it. I saved him a world o' trouble in this vay, sir.'" 27

Wellerisms

"No, no; reg'lar rotation, as Jack Ketch said, wen he tied the men up." 10

"Then the next question is, what the devil do you want with me, as the man said wen he see the ghost?" 10

"That's the pint, sir; out vith it, as the father said to the child, wen he swallowed a farden." 12

"He wants you particklar; and no one else'll do, as the Devil's private secretary said ven he fetched avay Doctor Faustus." 15

"Here's your servant, sir. Proud o' the title, as the Living Skellinton said, ven they show'd him." 15

"There's nothin' so refreshin' as sleep, sir, as the servant-girl said afore she drank the egg-cupful o' laudanum." 16

"If you walley my precious life don't upset me, as the gen'l'm'n said to the driver when they was a carryin' him to Tyburn." 19

"And a wery good notion of a lunch it is, take it altogether . . . . Now, gen'l'm'n, 'fall on,' as the English said to the French when they fixed bagginets." 19

"I think [my father]'s a wictim o' connubiality, as Blue Beard's domestic chaplain said, with a tear of pity, ven he buried him." 20

"That's what I call a self-evident proposition, as the dog's-meat man said, when the housemaid told him he warn't a gentleman." 22

"It's over, and can't be helped, and that's one consolation, as they always says in Turkey, ven they cuts the wrong man's head off." 23

"Business first, pleasure arterwards, as King Richard the Third said wen he stabbed the t'other king in the Tower, afore he smothered the babbies." 25

"Werry glad to see you, indeed, and hope our acquaintance may be a long 'un, as the gen'l'm'n said to the fi' pun' note." 25

"Werry sorry to 'casion any personal inconwenience, ma'am, as the housebreaker said to the old lady when he put her on the fire . . . . " 26

"All good feelin', sir—the wery best intentions, as the gen'l'm'n said ven he run avay from his wife 'cos she seemed unhappy with him." 27

"There; now we look compact and comfortable, as the father said ven he cut his little boy's head off, to cure him squintin'." 28

"Fine time for them as is well wropped up, as the Polar Bear said to himself, ven he was practising his skating." 30

"So I take the privilidge of the day . . . as the gen'l'm'n in difficulties did, ven he valked out of a Sunday . . . . " 33

"Oh, quite enough to get, sir, as the soldier said ven they ordered him three hundred and fifty lashes." 34

"Hooroar for the principle, as the money-lender said ven he wouldn't renew the bill." 35

" . . . vich I call addin' insult to injury, as the parrot said ven they not only took him from his native land, but made him talk the English langwidge arterwards." 35

" . . . this is rayther too rich, as the young lady said, wen she remonstrated with the pastry-cook, arter he'd sold her a pork-pie as had got nothin' but fat inside." 38

" . . . allow me to express a hope as you won't reduce me to extremities; in saying wich, I merely quote wot the nobleman said to the fractious pennywinkle, ven he vouldn't come out of his shell by means of a pin, and he conseqvently began to be afeered that he should be obliged to crack him in the parlour-door." 38

" . . . if this don't beat cock-fightin', nothin' never vill, as the Lord Mayor said, ven the chief secretary o' state proposed his missis's health arter dinner." 39

"P'raps if vun of us wos to brush, without troubling the man, it 'ud be more agreeable for all parties, as the schoolmaster said wen the young gentleman objected to being flogged by the butler." 42

". . . it's my 'pinion that you're a comin' it a great deal too strong, as the mail-coachman said to the snow-storm, ven it overtook him." 42

" . . . anythin' for a quiet life, as the man said wen he took the sitivation at the lighthouse." 43

"He's a malicious, bad-disposed, vorldly-minded, spiteful, windictive creetur, with a hard heart as there ain't no soft'nin'. As the wirtuous clergyman remarked of the old gen'l'm'n with the dropsy, ven he said, that upon the whole he thought he'd rayther leave his property to his vife than build a chapel vith it." 44

"Avay with melincholly, as the little boy said ven his school-missis died." 44

"Set down, sir; ve make no extra charge for the settin' down, as the king remarked wen he blowed up his ministers." 45

"This is rayther a change for the worse . . . as the gen'l'm'n said, wen he got two doubtful shillin's and sixpenn'orth o' pocket pieces for a good half-crown." 45

"If you know'd who was near, sir, I rayther think you'd change your note. As the hawk remarked to himself with a cheerful laugh, ven he heerd the robin redbreast a singin' round the corner." 47

"I only assisted natur', ma'am; as the doctor said to the boy's mother, arter he'd bled him to death." 47

"Sorry to do anythin' as may cause an interruption to such wery pleasant proceedin's, as the king said wen he dissolved the parliament." 48

"Wotever is, is right, as the young nobleman sveetly remarked wen they put him down in the pension list 'cos his mother's uncle's vife's grandfather vunce lit the king's pipe vit a portable tinder-box." 51

" . . . it wos to be—and wos, as the old lady said arter she'd married the footman." 52

Tony Weller, fifty-eight.—*recognizing an offspring:* " . . . one stout, red-faced, elderly man . . . [who] was smoking with great vehemence, but between every half-dozen puffs, he took his pipe from his mouth, and looked first at Mr [**Sam**] Weller and then at Mr **Pickwick**. Then, he would bury in a quart pot, as much of his countenance as the dimensions of the quart pot admitted of its receiving, and take another look at Sam and Mr Pickwick. Then he would take another half-dozen puffs with an air of profound meditation and look at them again. At last the stout man, putting up his legs on the seat, and leaning his back against the wall, began to puff at his pipe without leaving off at all, and to stare through the smoke at the newcomers, as if he had made up his mind to see the most he could of them.

"At first the evolutions of the stout man had escaped Mr Weller's observation, but by degrees, as he saw Mr Pickwick's eyes every now and then turning towards him, he began to gaze in the same direction, at the same time shading his eyes with his hand, as if he partially recognised the object before him, and wished to make quite sure of its identity. His doubts were speedily dispelled, however; for the stout man having blown a thick cloud from his pipe, a hoarse voice, like some strange effort of ventriloquism, emerged from beneath the capacious shawls which muffled his throat and chest, and slowly uttered these sounds—'Wy, Sammy!'" 20

—*his plenitude:* "It is very possible that at some earlier period of his career, Mr Weller's profile might have presented a bold and determined outline. His face, however, had expanded under the influence of good living, and a disposition remarkable for resignation; and its bold fleshy curves had so far extended beyond the limits originally assigned them, that unless you took a full view of his countenance in front, it was difficult to distinguish more than the extreme tip of a very rubicund nose.

"His chin, from the same cause, had acquired the grave and imposing form which is generally described by prefixing the word 'double' to that expressive feature; and his complexion exhibited that peculiarly mottled combination of colours which is only to be seen in gentlemen of his profession, and in underdone roast beef.

"Round his neck he wore a crimson travelling shawl, which merged into his chin by such imperceptible gradations, that it was difficult to distinguish the folds of the one, from the folds of the other. Over this, he mounted a long waist-coat of a broad pink-striped pattern, and over that again, a wide-skirted green coat, ornamented with large brass buttons, whereof the two which garnished the waist, were so far apart, that no man had ever beheld them both, at the same time. His hair, which was short, sleek, and black, was just visible beneath the capacious brim of a low-crowned brown hat. His legs were encased in knee-cord breeches, and painted top-boots: and a copper watch-chain, terminating in one seal, and a key of the same material, dangled loosely from his capacious waistband." ¶23

—*professional joke:* "'. . . coaches, Sammy, is like guns—they requires to be loaded with wery great care, afore they go off.'" 23

—*Tony Wellerisms:* "'Wen you're a married man, Samivel, you'll understand a good many things as you don't understand now; but vether it's worth while goin' through so much, to learn so little, as the charity-boy said ven he got to the end of the alphabet, is a matter o' taste. *I* rayther think it isn't.'" 27

"' . . . [**Sam**'s romance]'ll be a wery agonizin' trial to me at my time of life, but I'm pretty tough, that's vun consolation, as the wery old turkey remarked wen the farmer said he wos afeered he should be obliged to kill him for the London market.'" 33

—*laughing:* "Here the old gentleman shook his head from side to side, and was seized with a hoarse internal rumbling, accompanied with a violent swelling of the countenance, and a sudden increase in the breadth of all his features; symptoms which alarmed his son not a little.

"'Don't be frightened, Sammy, don't be frightened,' said the old gentleman, when, by dint of much struggling, and various convulsive stamps upon the ground, he had recovered his voice. 'It's only a kind o' quiet laugh as I'm a tryin' to come, Sammy.'

"'Well, if that's wot it is,' said **Sam**, 'you'd better not try to come it agin. You'll find it rayther a dangerous inwention.'

"'Don't you like it, Sammy?' inquired the old gentleman.

"'Not at all,' replied Sam.

"'Well,' said Mr Weller, with the tears still running down his cheeks, 'it 'ud ha' been a wery great accommodation to me if I could ha' done it, and 'ud ha' saved a good many vords atween your mother-in-law and me, sometimes; but I am afeered you're right, Sammy: it's too much in the appleplexy line—a deal too much, Samivel.'" 45

—*on corpulence:* "'Vait a minit, Sammy; ven you grow as old as your father, you von't get into your veskit quite as easy as you do now, my boy . . . you'll find that as you get vider, you'll get viser. Vidth and visdom, Sammy, alvays grows together.'

" . . . Mr Weller . . . contrived, by a dexterous twist of his body, to get the bottom button of his coat to perform its office." 55

Nathaniel Winkle. ". . . the sporting Winkle . . . communicating additional lustre to a new green shooting coat, plaid neckerchief, and closely-fitted drabs." 1 "He had always been looked up to as a high authority on all matters of amusement and dexterity, whether offensive, defensive, or inoffensive . . . ." 2

—*marksman:* "'Come along,' shouted [**Wardle**], addressing Mr Winkle; 'a keen hand like you ought to have been up long ago, even to such poor work as this.'

"Mr Winkle responded with a forced smile, and took up the spare gun with an expression of countenance which a metaphysical rook, impressed with a foreboding of his approaching death by violence, may be supposed to assume. It might have been keenness, but it looked remarkably like misery . . . .

"'Now, Mr Winkle,' said the host, reloading his own gun. 'Fire away.'

"Mr. Winkle advanced, and levelled his gun. Mr. **Pickwick** and his friends cowered involuntarily to escape damage from the heavy fall of rooks, which they felt quite certain would be occasioned by the devastating barrel of their friend. There was a solemn pause—a shout—a flapping of wings—a faint click. . . .

"'Odd,' said the old gentleman, taking the gun. 'Never knew one of them miss fire before. Why, I don't see anything of the cap.'

"'Bless my soul,' said Mr Winkle. "I declare I forgot the cap!'

"The slight omission was rectified. Mr Pickwick crouched again. Mr Winkle stepped forward with an air of determination and resolution; and Mr **Tupman** looked out from behind a tree. The boy shouted; four birds flew out. Mr Winkle fired. There was a scream as of an individual—not a rook—in corporeal anguish. Mr Tupman had saved the lives of innumerable unoffending birds by receiving a portion of the charge in his left arm." 7

—*a second hunt:* "Mr Winkle flashed, and blazed, and smoked away, without producing any material results worthy of being noted down; sometimes expending his charge in mid-air, and at others sending it skimming along so near the surface of the ground as to place the lives of the two dogs on a rather uncertain and precarious tenure. As a display of fancy shooting, it was extremely varied and curious; as an exhibition of firing with any precise object, it was, upon the whole, perhaps a failure. It is an established axiom, that 'every bullet has its billet.' If it apply in an equal degree to shot, those of Mr Winkle were unfortunate foundlings, deprived of their natural rights, cast loose upon the world, and billeted nowhere." 19

Supporting Roles

Arabella Allen. ". . . a young lady with black eyes, an arch smile, and a pair of remarkably nice boots with fur round the tops." 28

" . . . who, now a very pleasing compound of blushes and confusion and lilac silk and a smart bonnet and a rich lace veil, looked prettier than ever.

"'Miss Arabella Allen!' exclaimed Mr **Pickwick**, rising from his chair.

"'No,' replied Mr **Winkle**, dropping on his knees, 'Mrs Winkle.'" 47

—*meeting a new relative:* " . . . . 'You have been recently married, ma'am?'

"'I have' replied **Arabella**, in a scarcely audible tone . . . .

"'Without having represented to your husband the propriety of first consulting his father, on whom he is dependent, I think?' said the stranger.

"Arabella applied her handkerchief to her eyes . . . .

"'And without having sufficient property of your own to afford your husband any permanent assistance in exchange for the worldly advantages which you knew he would have gained if he had married agreeably to his father's wishes?' said the old gentleman. 'This is what boys and girls call disinterested affection, till they have boys and girls of their own, and then they see it in a rougher and very different light!' . . .

"'It was my fault: all my fault, sir,' replied poor Arabella, weeping.

"'Nonsense,' said the old gentleman; 'it was not your fault that he fell in love with you, I suppose? Yes, it was, though' said [he], looking rather slyly at Arabella. 'It was your fault. He couldn't help it.'" 56

Benjamin Allen. "[He] was a coarse, stout, thick-set young man, with black hair cut rather short, and a white face cut rather long. He was embellished with spectacles, and wore a white neckerchief. Below his single-breasted surtout, which was buttoned up to his chin, appeared the usual number of pepper-and-salt coloured legs, terminating in a pair of imperfectly polished boots. Although his coat was short in the sleeves, it disclosed no vestige of a linen wristband; and although there was quite enough of his face to admit of the encroachment of a shirt collar, it was not graced by the smallest approach to that appendage. He presented, altogether, rather a mildewy appearance, and emitted a fragrant odour of full-flavoured Cubas." 30

Master **Thomas Bardell**. "Clad in a tight suit of corduroy, spangled with brass buttons of a very considerable size, he at first stood at the door astounded and uncertain; but by degrees, the impression that his mother must have suffered some personal damage, pervaded his partially developed mind, and considering Mr **Pickwick** as the aggressor, he set up an appalling and semi-earthly kind of howling, and butting forward with his head, commenced assailing that immortal gentleman about the back and legs, with such blows and pinches as the strength of his arm, and the violence of his excitement, allowed." 13

Mr Serjeant Buzfuz. ". . . with a fat body and a red face . . . nodded in a friendly manner . . . and said it was a fine morning." 34

Bardell against Pickwick

—opening statement: "'I intreat the attention of the jury to the wording of this document. "Apartments furnished for a single gentleman"'! **Mrs Bardell's** opinions of the opposite sex, gentlemen, were derived from a long contemplation of the inestimable qualities of her lost husband. She had no fear, she had no distrust, she had no suspicion, all was confidence and reliance. "Mr **Bardell**," said the widow; "Mr Bardell was a man of honour, Mr Bardell was a man of his word, Mr Bardell was no deceiver, Mr Bardell was a single gentleman himself; *to* single gentlemen I look for protection, for assistance, for comfort, and for consolation; *in* single gentlemen I shall perpetually see something to remind me of what Mr Bardell was, when he first won my young and untried affections; to a single gentleman, then, shall my lodgings be let."

"'Actuated by this beautiful and touching impulse (among the best impulses of our imperfect nature, gentlemen,) the lonely and desolate widow dried her tears, furnished her first floor, caught the innocent boy to her maternal bosom, and put the bill up in her parlour-window. Did it remain there long? No. The serpent was on the watch, the train was laid, the mine was preparing, the sapper and miner was at work. Before the bill had been in the parlour-window three days— three days—gentlemen—a Being, erect upon two legs, and bearing all the outward semblance of a man, and not of a monster, knocked at the door of Mrs Bardell's house. He inquired within; he took the lodgings; and on the very next day he entered into possession of them. This man was **Pickwick**—Pickwick, the defendant.'

"Serjeant Buzfuz, who had proceeded with such volubility that his face was perfectly crimson, here paused for breath." ¶34

Fat Boy (Joe Lambert). "Fastened up behind [**Wardle's**] barouche was a hamper of spacious dimensions—one of those hampers which always awakens in a contemplative mind associations connected with cold fowls, tongues, and bottles of wine—and on the box sat a fat and red-faced boy, in a state of somnolency, whom no speculative observer could have regarded for an instant without setting down as the official dispenser of the contents of the before-mentioned hamper, when the proper time for their consumption should arrive." 4

—contemplating food: "'Now, Joe, the fowls. Damn that boy; he's gone to sleep again . Joe! Joe!' (Sundry taps on the head with a stick, and the fat boy, with some difficulty, roused from his lethargy.) 'Come, hand in the eatables.'

"There was something in the sound of the last word which roused the unctuous boy. He jumped up: and the leaden eyes, which twinkled behind his mountainous cheeks, leered horribly upon the food as he unpacked it from the basket . . . ." 4

—flirting: "'I say! How nice you look!'

"This was said in an admiring manner, and was, so far, gratifying; but still there was enough of the cannibal in the young gentleman's eyes to render the compliment a double one.

"'Dear me, Joseph,' said **Mary**, affecting to blush, 'what do you mean?'

"The fat boy gradually recovering his former position, replied with a heavy sigh, and remaining thoughtful for a few moments, drank a long draught of the porter. Having achieved this feat he sighed again, and applied himself assiduously to the pie.

"'What a nice young lady Miss **Emily** is!' said Mary, after a long silence.

"The fat boy had by this time finished the pie. He fixed his eyes on Mary, and replied:

"'I knows a nicerer.'

"'Indeed!' said Mary.

"'Yes, indeed!' replied the fat boy, with unwonted vivacity.

"'What's her name?' inquired Mary.

"'What's yours?'

"'Mary.'

"'So's hers,' said the fat boy. 'You're her.' The boy grinned to add point to the compliment, and put his eyes into something between a squint and a cast, which there is reason to believe he intended for an ogle." 54

Jackson. "'Mr **Dodson** ain't at home, and Mr **Fogg**'s particularly engaged,' replied the [clerk's] voice; and at the same time the head to which the voice belonged, with a pen behind its ear, looked over the partition, and at Mr **Pickwick.**

"It was a ragged head, the sandy hair of which, scrupulously parted on one side, and flattened down with pomatum, was twisted into little semi-circular tails round a flat face ornamented with a pair of small eyes, and garnished with a very dirty shirt collar, and a rusty black stock." 20

—on duty: " . . . there hurried into [the court clerk's office] an individual in a brown coat and brass buttons, whose long hair was scrupulously twisted round the rim of his napless hat, and whose soiled drab trousers were so tightly strapped over his Blucher boots, that his knees threatened every moment to start from their concealment. He produced from his coat pockets a long and narrow strip of parchment, on which the presiding functionary impressed an illegible black stamp. He then drew forth four scraps of paper, of similar dimensions, each containing a printed copy of the strip of parchment, with blanks for a name; and having filled up the blanks, put all the five documents in his pocket, and hurried away . . . .

"'Beg your pardon, Mr **Pickwick**,' said Jackson, deliberately depositing his hat on the floor, and drawing from his pocket the strip of parchment. 'But personal service, by clerk or agent, in these cases, you know, Mr Pickwick—nothing like caution, sir, in all legal forms?'

"Here Mr Jackson cast his eye on the parchment; and, resting his hands on the table, and looking round with a winning and persuasive smile, said: 'Now, come; don't let's have no words about such a little matter as this. Which of you gentlemen's name's **Snodgrass**?'" 31

Peter Magnus. "[He] was an important-looking, sharp-nosed, mysterious-spoken personage, with a bird-like habit of giving his head a jerk every time he said anything . . . 'That's my card, sir, Magnus, you will perceive, sir—Magnus is my name. It's rather a good name, I think, sir?'

"'A very good name, indeed,' said Mr **Pickwick**, wholly unable to repress a smile.

"'Yes, I think it is,' resumed Mr Magnus. 'There's a good name before it, too, you will observe. Permit me, sir—if you hold the card a little slanting, this way, you catch the light upon the up-stroke. There—Peter Magnus—sounds well, I think, sir.'

"'Very,' said Mr Pickwick.

"'Curious circumstance about those initials, sir,' said Mr Magnus. 'You will observe—P.M.—post meridian. In hasty notes to intimate acquaintance I sometimes sign myself "Afternoon." It amuses my friends very much, Mr Pickwick.'

"'It is calculated to afford them the highest gratification, I should conceive,' said Mr Pickwick, rather envying the ease with which Mr Magnus's friends were entertained." 22

—coached: " . . . 'I should commence, sir, with a tribute to the lady's beauty and excellent qualities; from them, sir, I should diverge to my own unworthiness.'

"'Very good,' said Mr Magnus.

"'Unworthiness for *her* only, mind sir,' resumed Mr **Pickwick**; for to shew that I was not wholly unworthy, sir, I should take a brief review of my past life, and present condition. I should argue, by analogy, that to anybody else, I must be a very desirable object. I should then expatiate on the warmth of my love, and the depth of my devotion. Perhaps I might then be tempted to seize her hand.'

"'Yes, I see,' said Mr Magnus; 'that would be a very great point.'

"'I should then, sir,' continued Mr Pickwick, growing warmer as the subject presented itself in more glowing colours before him: 'I should then, sir, come to the plain and simple question, "Will you have me?" I think I am justified in assuming that upon this, she would turn away her head.'

"'You think that may be taken for granted?' said Mr Magnus; 'because if she did not do that at the right place, it would be embarrassing.'

"'I think she would,' said Mr Pickwick. 'Upon this, sir, I should squeeze her hand, and I think—I *think*, Mr Magnus—that after I had done that, supposing there was no refusal, I should gently draw away the handkerchief, which my slight knowledge of human nature leads me to suppose the lady would be applying to her eyes at the moment, and steal a respectful kiss. I think I should kiss her, Mr Magnus; and at this particular point, I am decidedly of opinion that if the lady were going to take me at all, she would murmur into my ears a bashful acceptance.'

"Mr Magnus started; gazed on Mr Pickwick's intelligent face, for a short time in silence; and then . . . shook him warmly by the hand, and rushed desperately from the room." 24

Mary. "'Mary,' said Mr **Muzzle** to the pretty servant-girl, 'this is Mr [**Sam**] **Weller** . . . .

"'And your master's a knowin' hand, and has just sent me to the right place,' said Mr Weller, with a glance of admiration at Mary. 'If I wos master o' this here house, I should alvays find the materials for comfort vere Mary wos.'

"'Lor, Mr Weller,' said Mary, blushing." 25

—*better acquainted:* "'Get your hat, **Sam**,' said Mr **Pickwick**.

"'It's below stairs, sir,' said Sam, and he ran down after it.

"Now, there was nobody in the kitchen, but the pretty housemaid; and as Sam's hat was mislaid, he had to look for it; and the pretty housemaid lighted him. They had to look all over the place for the hat. The pretty housemaid, in her anxiety to find it, went down on her knees, and turned over all the things that were heaped together in a little corner by the door. It was an awkward corner. You couldn't get at it without shutting the door first.

"'Here it is,' said the pretty housemaid. 'This is it, ain't it?'

"'Let me look,' said Sam.

"The pretty housemaid had stood the candle on the floor; as it gave a very dim light, Sam was obliged to go down on *his* knees before he could see whether it really was his own hat or not. It was a remarkably small corner, and so—it was nobody's fault but the man's who built the house—Sam and the pretty housemaid were necessarily very close together.

"'Yes, this is it,' said Sam. 'Good bye!'

"'Good bye!' said the pretty housemaid.

"'Good bye!' said Sam; and as he said it, he dropped the hat that had cost so much trouble in looking for.

"'How awkward you are,' said the pretty housemaid. 'You'll lose it again, if you don't take care.'

"So, just to prevent his losing it again, she put it on for him.

"Whether it was that the pretty housemaid's face looked prettier still, when it was raised towards Sam's, or whether it was the accidental consequence of their being so near to each other, is matter of uncertainty to this day; but Sam kissed her.

"'You don't mean to say you did that on purpose,' said the pretty house-maid, blushing.

"'No, I didn't then,' said Sam; 'but I will now.'

"So he kissed her again.

"'Sam!' said Mr Pickwick, calling over the banisters.

"'Coming, sir,' replied Sam, rushing up stairs.

"'How long you have been!' said Mr Pickwick.

"'There was something behind the door, sir, which perwented our getting it open, for ever so long, sir,' replied Sam.

"And this was the first passage of Mr Weller's first love." 25 *And see* **Fat Boy**—*flirting*

Perker. "He was a little high-dried man, with a dark squeezed-up face, and small restless black eyes, that kept winking and twinkling on each side of his little inquisitive nose, as if they were playing a perpetual game of peep-bo with that feature. He was dressed all in black, with boots as shiny as his eyes, a low white neckcloth, and a clean shirt with a frill to it. A gold watch-chain, and seals, depended from his fob. He carried his black kid gloves *in* his hands, not *on* them; and as he spoke, thrust his wrists beneath his coat-tails, with the air of a man who was in the habit of propounding some regular posers." 10

Bob Sawyer entertaining

Bob Sawyer, "who was habited in a coarse blue coat, which, without being either a great-coat or a surtout, partook of the nature and qualities of both, had about him that sort of slovenly smartness, and swaggering gait, which is peculiar to young gentlemen who smoke in the streets by day, shout and scream in the same by night, call waiters by their Christian names and do various other acts and deeds of an equally facetious description. He wore a pair of plaid trousers, and a large rough double-breasted waistcoat; out of doors, he carried a thick stick with a big top. He eschewed gloves, and looked, upon the whole, something like a dissipated Robinson Crusoe." 30

—*entertaining:* "Another knock at the door, announced a large-headed young man in a black wig, who brought with him a scorbutic youth [**Noddy**] in a long stock. The next comer was a gentleman [**Gunter**] in a shirt emblazoned with pink anchors, who was closely followed by a pale youth with a plated watchguard. The arrival of a prim personage in clean linen and cloth boots rendered the party complete." 32

Augustus Snodgrass. ". . . the poetic Snodgrass . . . poetically enveloped in a mysterious blue coat with a canine-skin collar . . . ." 1

—*observing a peacetime military maneuver:* "'It is indeed a noble and a brilliant sight,' said Mr. Snodgrass, in whose bosom a blaze of poetry was rapidly bursting forth, 'to see the gallant defenders of their country drawn up in brilliant array before its peaceful citizens; their faces beaming—not with warlike ferocity, but with civilised gentleness; their eyes flashing—not with the rude fire of rapine or revenge, but with the soft light of humanity and intelligence.'" 4

—*evidently an allergy:* "'Is anything the matter with Mr Snodgrass, sir?' inquired **Emily**, with great anxiety.

"'Nothing the matter, ma'am,' replied the stranger. 'Cricket dinner— glorious party—capital songs—old port—claret—good—very good—wine, ma'am— wine.'

"'It wasn't the wine,' murmured Mr Snodgrass, in a broken voice. 'It was the salmon.' (Somehow or other, it never *is* the wine, in these cases.)" 8

Mr Serjeant Snubbin. " . . . a lantern-faced, sallow-complexioned man, of about five-and-forty, or—as the novels say—he might be fifty. He had that dull-looking boiled eye which is often to be seen in the heads of people who have applied themselves during many years to a weary and laborious course of study; and which would have been sufficient, without the additional eye-glass which dangled from a broad black riband round his neck, to warn a stranger that he was very near-sighted.

"His hair was thin and weak, which was partly attributable to his having never devoted much time to its arrangement, and partly to his having worn for five-and-twenty years the forensic wig which hung on a block beside him. The marks of hair-powder on his coat collar, and the ill-washed and worse tied white neckerchief round his throat, showed that he had not found leisure since he left the court to make any alteration in his dress: while the slovenly style of the remainder of his costume warranted the inference that his personal appearance would not have been very much improved if he had.

"Books of practice, heaps of papers, and opened letters, were scattered over the table, without any attempt at order or arrangement; the furniture of the room was old and ricketty; the doors of the book-case were rotting on their hinges; the dust flew out from the carpet in little clouds at every step; the blinds were yellow with age and dirt; the state of everything in the room showed, with a clearness not to be mistaken, that Mr Serjeant Snubbin was far too much occupied with his professional pursuits to take any great heed or regard of his personal comforts." 31

Mr Justice Stareleigh "was a most particularly short man, and so fat, that he seemed all face and waistcoat. He rolled in, upon two little turned legs, and having bobbed gravely to the bar, who bobbed gravely to him, put his little legs underneath his table, and his little three-cornered hat upon it; and when Mr Justice Stareleigh had done this, all you could see of him was two queer little eyes, one broad pink face, and somewhere about half of a big and very comical-looking wig. . . Mr Justice Stareleigh's temper bordered on the irritable, and brooked not contradiction" 34

Job Trotter. " . . . a young fellow in mulberry-coloured livery, who was sitting on a bench in the yard, reading what appeared to be a hymn-book, with an air of deep abstraction . . . who had a large, sallow, ugly face, very sunken eyes, and a gigantic head, from which depended a quantity of lank black hair." 16

Wardle. "In an open barouche . . . stood a stout old gentleman, in a blue coat and bright buttons, corduroy breeches and top-boots. . . ." 4

—*skating:* "'It looks a nice warm exercise that, doesn't it?' [Mr **Pickwick**] inquired of Wardle, when that gentleman was thoroughly out of breath, by reason of the indefatigable manner in which he had converted his legs into a pair of compasses, and drawn complicated problems on the ice.

"'Ah, it does indeed,' replied Wardle. 'Do you slide?' . . . dragging off his skates with the impetuosity which characterised all his proceedings. 'Here; I'll keep you company; come along!' And away went the good tempered old fellow down the [skating] slide, with a rapidity which came very close upon Mr [**Sam**] **Weller**, and beat the **fat boy** all to nothing." 30

" . . . the good old gentleman was overflowing with hilarity and kindness . . . ." 57

Mrs Wardle, sr, seventy-two. "A very old lady, in a lofty cap and faded silk gown—no less a personage than Mr **Wardle's** mother—occupied the post of honour on the right-hand corner of the chimney-piece; and various certificates of her having been brought up in the way she should go when young, and of her not having departed from it when old, ornamented the walls, in the form of samplers of ancient date, worsted landscapes of equal antiquity, and crimson silk tea-kettle holders of a more modern period." 6

—*out of sorts:* "The old lady was seated in customary state in the front parlour, but she was rather cross, and, by consequence, most particularly deaf. She never went out herself, and like a great many other old ladies of the same stamp, she was apt to consider it an act of domestic treason, if anybody else took the liberty of doing what she couldn't. So, bless her old soul, she sat as upright as she could, in her great chair, and looked as fierce as might be—and that was benevolent after all." 28

Rachael Wardle. "' . . . that's my sister, Miss Rachael Wardle. She's a Miss, she is; and yet she an't a Miss—eh, sir, eh?' And the stout gentleman playfully inserted his elbow between the ribs of **Mr Pickwick**, and laughed very heartily." 4

"'Elderly lady—thin face—rather skinny—eh?'" 9

"' . . . lady's free to act as she pleases—more than one-and-twenty.'

"'More than one-and-twenty!' ejaculated Wardle, contemptuously. 'More than one-and-forty!'

"'I an't,' said the spinster aunt, her indignation getting the better of her determination to faint.

"'You are,' replied Wardle, 'you're fifty if you're an hour.'

"Here the spinster uttered a loud shriek, and became senseless." 10 *And see* **Jingle** P—*wooing and* **Tupman** P—*wooing*

Under the Mistletoe at Dingley Dell

Others

Aunt. "'My dear **Benjamin** [**Allen**],' said the old lady, struggling with a great shortness of breath, and trembling from head to foot: 'don't be alarmed, my dear, but I think I had better speak to Mr **Sawyer**, alone, for a moment'" 48

Ayresleigh, imprisoned for debt. " . . . a middle-aged man in a very old suit of black, who looked pale and haggard, and paced up and down the room incessantly; stopping, now and then, to look with great anxiety out of the window as if he expected somebody, and then resuming his walk." 40

Bagman. "'Well, gents,' said a stout, hale personage of about forty, with only one eye — a very bright black eye, which twinkled with a roguish expression of fun and good humour, 'our noble selves, gents. I always propose that toast to the company, and drink **Mary** to myself. Eh, Mary! . . . .

"' . . . he went through the not very difficult process of winking upon the company with his solitary eye . . . ." 14

Three **bailmen**. " . . . three or four men of shabby-genteel appearance . . . were curious-looking fellows. One, was a slim and rather lame man in rusty black, and a white neckerchief; another was a stout burly person, dressed in the same apparel, with a great reddish-black cloth round his neck; a third, was a little weazen drunken-looking body, with a pimply face. They were loitering about, with their hands behind them, and now and then with an anxious countenance whispered something in the ear of some of the gentlemen with papers, as they hurried by." 40

Jack Bamber. " . . . a little yellow high-shouldered man . . .raised his shrivelled face, and bent his grey eye . . . with a keen inquiring look . . . . There was a fixed grim smile perpetually on his countenance; he leant his chin on a long skinny hand, with nails of extraordinary length; and as he inclined his head to one side, and looked keenly out from beneath his ragged grey eyebrows, there was a strange, wild slyness in his leer, quite repulsive to behold." 20

Angelo Cyrus Bantam. " . . . a charming young man of not much more than fifty, dressed in a very bright blue coat with resplendent buttons, black trousers, and the thinnest possible pair of highly-polished boots. A gold eyeglass was suspended from his neck by a short broad black ribbon; a gold snuffbox was lightly clasped in his left hand; gold rings innumerable glittered on his fingers; and a large diamond pin set in gold glistened in his shirt frill. He had a gold watch, and a gold curb chain with large gold seals; and he carried a pliant ebony cane with a heavy gold top. His linen was of the very whitest, finest, and stiffest; his wig of the glossiest, blackest and curliest. His snuff was princes' mixture; his scent *bouquet du roi*. His features were contracted into a perpetual smile; and his teeth were in such perfect order that it was difficult at a small distance to tell the real from the false." 35

—*on duty:* " . . . [he] emerged from his chariot at the door of the Assembly Rooms in the same wig, the same teeth, the same eye-glass, the same watch and seals, the same rings, the same shirt-pin, and the same cane. The only observable alterations in his appearance were, that he wore a brighter blue coat, with a white silk lining: black tights, black silk stockings, and pumps, and a white waistcoat, and was, if possible, just a thought more scented." 35

Bardell, deceased. "'The late Mr Bardell [continued Serjeant **Buzfuz**, in a soft and melancholy voice], after enjoying, for many years, the esteem and confidence of his sovereign, as one of the guardians of his royal revenues, glided almost imperceptibly from the world, to seek elsewhere for that repose and peace which a custom-house can never afford.'

"At this pathetic description of the decease of Mr Bardell, who had been knocked on the head with a quart-pot in a public-house cellar, the learned serjeant's voice faltered . . . ." 34

Henry Beller, a convert to Temperance, "was for many years toast-master at various corporation dinners, during which time he drank a great deal of foreign wine . . . . Is out of employ now: and never touches a drop of foreign wine by any chance' (tremendous plaudits)." 33

Benjamin, a boy; and blue bag. The "professional establishment of the more opulent of these [debtors' attorneys] . . . . " 43

—*business done:* " . . . and there were treaties entered into . . . and ratifications of the same, and inventories to be made out, and lunches to be taken, and dinners to be eaten, and so many profitable things to be done, and such a mass of papers accumulated, that Mr **Solomon Pell**, and the boy, and the blue bag to boot, all got so stout that scarcely anybody would have known them for the same man, boy, and bag, that had loitered about Portugal Street, a few days before." 55

Blotton. "Mr Blotton, with a mean desire to tarnish the lustre of the immortal name of **Pickwick**, actually undertook a journey to Cobham in person, and on his return sarcastically observed in an oration at the club, that he had seen the man from whom the stone was purchased; that the man presumed the stone to be ancient, but solemnly denied the antiquity of the inscription—inasmuch as he represented it to have been rudely carved by himself in an idle mood, and to display letters intended to bear neither more nor less than the simple construction of—'B I L L S T U M P S, H I S M A R K;' and that Mr Stumps, being little in the habit of original composition, and more accustomed to be guided by the sound of words than by the strict rules of orthography, had omitted the concluding 'L' of his christian name." 11 *See* **Samuel Pickwick—** *antiquarian*

Captain Boldwig. "[He] was a little fierce man in a stiff black neckerchief and blue surtout, who, when he did condescend to walk about his property, did it in company with a thick rattan stick with a brass ferrule, and a gardener [**Hunt**] and sub-gardener [**Wilkins**] with meek faces, to whom (the gardeners, not the stick) Captain Boldwig gave his orders with all due grandeur and ferocity . . . ." 19

Miss Bolo. A lady "of an ancient and whist-like appearance . . . .If [**Mr Pickwick**] played a wrong, card, Miss Bolo looked a small armoury of daggers . . . at the end of every hand, Miss Bolo would inquire with a dismal countenance and reproachful sigh, why Mr Pickwick had not returned that diamond, or led the club, or roughed the spade, or finessed the heart, or led through the honour, or brought out the ace, or played up to the king, or some such thing . . . and when they left off at ten minutes past eleven, Miss Bolo rose from the table considerably agitated, and went straight home, in a flood of tears, and a sedan-chair." 35

Boy, in debtor's prison. " . . . a mere boy of nineteen or twenty, who, though it was yet barely ten o-clock, was drinking gin and water, and smoking a cigar: amusements to which, judging from his inflamed countenance, he had devoted himself pretty constantly for the last year or two of his life. . . . " 40

Mrs Budger. " . . . a little old widow, whose rich dress and profusion of ornament bespoke her a most desirable addition to a limited income." 2 *See* Doctor **Slammer**

The **Bulders**. "Miss Bulder was warmly welcomed by the Miss **Clubbers**; the greeting between Mrs Colonel Bulder and Lady Clubber was of the most affectionate description; Colonel Bulder and Sir Thomas Clubber exchanged snuff-boxes, and looked very much like a pair of **Alexander Selkirk**s—'Monarchs of all they surveyed.'" 2

Thomas Burton. "Has a wooden leg; finds a wooden leg expensive, going over the stones; used to wear second-hand wooden legs, and drink a glass of hot gin and water regularly every night—sometimes two . . . . Buys new wooden legs now, and drinks nothing but water and weak tea. The new legs last twice as long as the others used to do, and he attributes this solely to his temperate habits (triumphant cheers).'" 33

Chancery prisoner. He "had been [in the Fleet] long enough to have lost friends, fortune, home, and happiness, and to have acquired the right of having a room to himself . . . . He was a tall, gaunt, cadaverous man, in an old greatcoat and slippers: with sunken cheeks, and a restless, eager eye. His lips were bloodless, and his bones sharp and thin. God help him! the iron teeth of confinement and privation had been slowly filing him down for twenty years." 42

Chaplain, imprisoned for debt. " . . . [a] gentleman in very shabby black, and a seal-skin cap . . . who fastened his coat all the way up to his chin by means of a pin and a button alternately, had a very coarse red face, and looked like a drunken chaplain; which, indeed, he was." 42

Clergyman. " . . . a bald-headed old gentleman, with a good-humoured benevolent face—the clergyman of Dingley Dell . . . . " 6

The **Clubbers**. "'Sir Thomas Clubber, Lady Clubber, and the Miss Clubbers!' shouted the man at the door in a stentorian voice. A great sensation was created throughout the room by the entrance of a tall gentleman in a blue coat and bright buttons, a large lady in blue satin, and two young ladies, on a similar scale, in fashionably-made dresses of the same hue.

" . . . distinguished gentlemen crowded to render homage to the Miss Clubbers; and Sir Thomas Clubber stood bolt upright, and looked majestically over his black neckerchief at the assembled company." 2

Elizabeth (Betsey) Cluppins. "[She was] a little brisk, busy-looking woman . . ." 26

—*on the witness-stand:* "'I was [in the back room] unbeknown to **Mrs Bardell**; I had been out with a little basket, gentlemen, to buy three pound of red kidney purtaties . . . when I see Mrs Bardell's street door on the jar.'

"'On the what?' exclaimed the little judge.

"'Partly open, my Lord,' said Serjeant **Snubbin**.

"'She said on the jar,' said the little judge, with a cunning look.

"'It's all the same, my Lord,' said Serjeant Snubbin. The little judge looked doubtful, and said he'd make a note of it. Mrs. Cluppins then resumed:

"'I walked in, gentlemen, just to say good mornin', and went, in a permiscuous manner, up stairs, and into the back room. Gentlemen, there was the sound of voices in the front room, and—'

"'And you listened, I believe, Mrs Cluppins?' said Serjeant **Buzfuz**.

"'Beggin' your pardon, sir,' replied Mrs Cluppins, in a majestic manner, 'I would scorn the haction. The voices was very loud, sir, and forced themselves upon my ear.'" 34

Convivial **coachman**. "After a short silence, a gentleman in an embroidered coat reaching down to his heels, and a waistcoat of the same which kept one half of his legs warm, stirred his gin and water with great energy, and putting himself upon his feet, all at once, by a violent effort, said he was desirous of offering a few remarks to the company . . . . " 37

Hoarse **coachman**. ". . . the porter, cold beef, and oysters being promptly produced, the lunch was done ample justice to . . . but if one individual evinced greater powers than another, it was the coachman with the hoarse voice, who took an imperial pint of vinegar with his oysters, without betraying the least emotion." 55

Cobbler. "His face was a queer, good-tempered, crooked-featured piece of workmanship, ornamented with a couple of eyes that must have worn a very joyous expression at one time, for they sparkled yet. The man was sixty, by years, and Heaven knows how old by imprisonment, so that his having any look approaching to mirth or contentment was singular enough. He was a little man, and, being half doubled up as he lay in bed, looked about as long as he ought to have been without his legs. He had a great red pipe in his mouth, and was smoking, and staring at the rush-light, in a state of enviable placidity." 45

Cook. " . . . she uttered a loud and piercing shriek, and rushing on Mr **Job Trotter**, who rose from his chair on the instant, tore and buffeted his large flat face, with an energy peculiar to excited females, and twining her hands in his long black hair, tore therefrom about enough to make five or six dozen of the very largest-sized mourning-rings. Having accomplished this feat with all the ardour which her devoted love for Mr **Muzzle** inspired, she staggered back; and being a lady of very excitable and delicate feelings, she instantly fell under the dresser, and fainted away." 25

Countryman. "Horses, dogs, and drink, had brought him there [the Fleet], pell-mell. There was a rusty spur on the solitary boot, which he occasionally jerked into the empty air, at the same time giving the boot a smart blow, and muttering some of the sounds by which a sportsman encourages his horse. He was riding, in imagination, some desperate steeple-chase at that moment. Poor wretch! He never rode a match on the swiftest animal in his costly stud, with half the speed at which he had torn along the course that ended in the Fleet." 42

Dodson, counsel to **Mrs Bardell**. " . . . a plump, portly, stern-looking man, with a loud voice . . . . " 20

Dowler. " . . . a stern-eyed man of about five-and-forty, who had a bald and glossy forehead, with a good deal of black hair at the sides and back of his head, and large black whiskers. He was buttoned up to the chin in a brown coat; and had a large seal-skin travelling cap, and a great-coat and cloak, lying on the seat beside him. He looked up from his breakfast . . . with a fierce and peremptory air, which was very dignified . . . . " 35

Mrs Dowler. "'She's a fine woman,' said Mr Dowler. 'I am proud of her . . . . She shall know you. She shall esteem you. I courted her under singular circumstances. I won her through a rash vow. Thus. I saw her; I loved her; I proposed; she refused me,—"you love another?"—"Spare my blushes."—"I know him."—"You do."—"Very good; if he remains here, I'll skin him." . . . .

" ' . . . . He fled. I married her. Here's the coach. That's her head.'

"As Mr Dowler concluded, he pointed to a stage which had just driven up, from the open window of which a rather pretty face in a bright blue bonnet was looking among the crowd on the pavement: most probably for the rash man himself." 35

Dubbley, a special constable. "At the word of command, a dirty-faced man, something over six feet high, and stout in proportion, squeezed himself through the half-open door (making his face very red in the process), and entered the room." 24

Captain **Charles Fitz-Marshall**. " . . . a young man dressed as a naval officer . . . presented to the astonished Pickwickians, the identical form and features of Mr **Alfred Jingle**."15

Wilkins Flasher. "The office of Wilkins Flasher, Esquire, of the Stock Exchange, was in a first floor up a court behind the Bank of England; the house of Wilkins Flasher, Esquire, was at Brixton, Surrey; the horse and stanhope of Wilkins Flasher, Esquire, were at an adjacent livery stable; the groom of Wilkins Flasher, Esquire, was on his way to the West End to deliver some game; the clerk of Wilkins Flasher, Esquire, had gone to his dinner; and so Wilkins Flasher, Esquire, himself, cried, 'Come in' . . . . Both gentlemen [Flasher and **Simmery**] had very open waistcoats and very rolling collars, and very small boots, and very big rings, and very little watches, and very large guard-chains, and symmetrical inexpressibles, and scented pocket-handkerchiefs." 55

Fogg, counsel to **Mrs Bardell**. " . . . [he] was an elderly, pimply-faced, vegetable-diet sort of man, in a black coat, dark mixture trousers, and small black gaiters; a kind of being who seemed to be an essential part of the desk at which he was writing, and to have as much thought or sentiment." 20

Footman, in blue. " . . . a light-haired, stiff-necked, free and easy sort of footman, with a swaggering air and pert face, [he] had attracted Mr **Weller**'s especial attention . . . 'Your health, sir,' said **Sam**. 'I like your conwersation. I think it's wery pretty.'" 37

George, an insolvent coachman, "had contracted a speculative but imprudent passion for horsing long stages, which had led to his present embarrassments, looked extremely well, and was soothing the excitement of his feelings with shrimps and porter." 43

Goodwin. " . . . a young lady whose ostensible employment was to preside over [**Mrs Pott**'s] toilet, but who rendered herself useful in a variety of ways, and in none more so than in the particular department of constantly aiding and abetting her mistress in every wish and inclination opposed to the desires of the unhappy **Pott**." 18

Thomas Groffin. "'I beg this court's pardon,' said the chemist, who was a tall, thin, yellow-visaged man, 'but I hope this court will excuse my attendance . . . there'll be murder before this trial's over . . . I've left nobody but an errand-boy in my shop. He is a very nice boy, my Lord, but he is not acquainted with drugs; and I know that the prevailing impression on his mind is, that Epsom salts means oxalic acid; and syrup of senna, laudanum. That's all, my Lord.' With this, the tall chemist composed himself into a comfortable attitude, and, assuming a pleasant expression of countenance, appeared to have prepared himself for the worst." 34

Daniel Grummer, a constable. An "elderly gentleman in . . . top-boots, who was chiefly remarkable for a bottle-nose, a hoarse voice, a snuff-coloured surtout, and a wandering eye." 24

"Mr Grummer's mode of proceeding was professional, but peculiar. His first act was to bolt the door on the inside; his second, to polish his head and countenance very carefully with a cotton handkerchief; his third, to place his hat, with the cotton handkerchief in it, on the nearest chair; and his fourth, to produce from the breast-pocket of his coat a short truncheon, surmounted by a brazen crown, with which he beckoned to **Mr Pickwick** with a grave and ghost-like air." 24

Jack Hopkins, teller of tall medical tales. "He wore a black velvet waistcoat, with thunder-and-lightning buttons; and a blue striped shirt, with a white false collar." 32

Anthony Humm. "The president [of the United Grand Junction Ebenezer Temperance Association] was the straight-walking Mr Anthony Humm, a converted fireman, now a schoolmaster, and occasionally an itinerant preacher . . . [he was] a sleek, white-faced man, in a perpetual perspiration . . . ." 33

Mrs Leo Hunter greets her guests

Leo Hunter. " . . . a grave man, who started up on his entrance, and said, with an air of profound respect:

"'**Mr Pickwick**, I presume?'

"'The same.'

"'Allow me, sir, the honour of grasping your hand. Permit me, sir to shake it,' said the grave man. . . . 'We have heard of your fame, sir. The noise of your antiquarian discussion has reached the ears of Mrs Leo Hunter—my wife, sir; *I* am *Mr* Leo Hunter' — the stranger paused, as if he expected that Mr Pickwick would be overcome by the disclosure. . . ." 15

Minerva (Mrs Leo) Hunter. "'Mrs Leo Hunter has many . . . breakfasts, sir . . . "feasts of reason, sir and flows of soul," as somebody who wrote a sonnet to Mrs Leo Hunter on her breakfasts, feelingly and originally observed.'

"'Was *he* celebrated for his works and talents?' inquired **Mr Pickwick**.

"'He was, sir,' replied the grave man, 'all Mrs Leo Hunter's acquaintance are; it is her ambition, sir, to have no other acquaintance.'" 15

—*greeting a guest:* "'**Mr Pickwick**, ma'am, said a servant, as that gentleman approached the presiding goddess, with his hat in his hand, and the Brigand [**Tupman**] and Troubadour [**Snodgrass**] on either arm.

"'What! Where?' exclaimed Mrs Leo Hunter, starting up, in an affected rapture of surprise.

"'Here,' said Mr Pickwick.

"'Is it possible that I have really the gratification of beholding Mr Pickwick himself!' ejaculated Mrs Leo Hunter.

"'No other, ma'am,' replied Mr Pickwick, bowing very low." 15

Hunter daughters. " '. . . here are my little girls; I had almost forgotten them,' said **Minerva**, carelessly pointing towards a couple of full-grown young ladies, of whom one might be about twenty, and the other a year or two older, and who were dressed in very juvenile costumes—whether to make them look young, or their mamma younger . . . ." 15

Dismal Jemmy (James Hutley). " . . . a care-worn looking man, whose sallow face, and deeply sunken eyes, were rendered still more striking than nature had made them, by the straight black hair which hung in matted disorder half way down his face. His eyes were almost unnaturally bright and piercing; his cheek-bones were high and prominent; and his jaws were so long and lank, that an observer would have supposed that he was drawing the flesh of his face in, for a moment, by some contraction of the muscles, if his half-opened mouth and immovable expression had not announced that it was his ordinary appearance. Round his neck he wore a green shawl, with the large ends straggling over his chest, and making their appearance occasionally beneath the worn button-holes of his old waistcoat. His upper garment was a long black surtout; and below it he wore wide drab trousers, and large boots, running rapidly to seed." 3

Landlady. "'Ugh, you brute!' ejaculated the kind-hearted landlady. 'Poor dear.' And with sundry ejaculations, of 'Come now, there's a dear—drink a little of this—it'll do you good—don't give way so—there's a love,' &c, &c, the landlady, assisted by a chambermaid, proceeded to vinegar the forehead, beat the hands, titillate the nose, and unlace the stays of the spinster aunt [**Rachael**], and to administer such other restoratives as are usually applied by compassionate females to ladies who are endeavouring to ferment themselves into hysterics."10

Laundress. " . . . a thin, miserable-looking old woman. . . whose appearance, as well as the condition of [**Perker**'s] office . . . indicated a rooted antipathy to the application of soap and water. . . ." 20

Lowten, lawyer's clerk. " . . . a puffy-faced young man, who filled the chair at the head of the table. . . ." 20

—*on friendship:* "'Friendship's a very good thing in its way: we are all very friendly and comfortable at the Stump, for instance, over our grog, where every man pays for himself; but damn hurting yourself for anybody else, you know! No man should have more than two attachments—the first, to number one, and the second to the ladies; that's what I say—ha! ha!'" 53

Solomon Lucas, costumer. "His wardrobe was extensive—very extensive —not strictly classical perhaps, nor quite new, nor did it contain any one garment made precisely after the fashion of any age or time, but everything was more or less spangled; and what can be prettier than spangles!" 15

Mallard. " . . . an elderly clerk, whose sleek appearance, and heavy gold watch-chain, presented imposing indications of the extensive and lucrative practice of [his employer] Mr Serjeant **Snubbin**." 31

Martin, a driver. " . . . a surly-looking man with his legs dressed like the legs of a groom, and his body attired in the coat of a coachman." 48

—*under assault:* " . . . [**Benjamin Allen**] made a precipitate rush at Mr Martin, and, twisting his hand in the neckcloth of that taciturn servitor, expressed an intention of choking him where he stood. This intention, with a promptitude often the effect of desperation, he at once commenced carrying into execution, with much vigour and surgical skill.

"Mr Martin, who was a man of few words and possessed but little power of eloquence or persuasion, submitted to this operation with a very calm and agreeable expression of countenance, for some seconds; finding, however, that it threatened speedily to lead to a result which would place it beyond his power to claim any wages, board or otherwise, in all time to come, he muttered an inarticulate remonstrance and felled Mr Benjamin Allen to the ground." 48

Martin. " . . . a tall, raw-boned gamekeeper . . . bearing a bag of capacious dimensions, and accompanied by a brace of pointers. . . . [He] looked with some surprise from Mr **Winkle**, who was holding his gun as if he wished his coat pocket to save him the trouble of pulling the trigger, to Mr **Tupman**, who was holding his as if he were afraid of it—as there is no earthly reason to doubt he really was . . . .

"'You mustn't handle your piece in that ere way, when you come to have the charge in it, sir,' said the tall gamekeeper, gruffly, 'or I'm damned if you won't make cold meat of some on us.'" 19

Betsy Martin, Temperance convert. "' . . . widow, one child, and one eye. Goes out charing and washing, by the day; never had more than one eye, but knows her mother drank bottled stout, and shouldn't wonder if that caused it (immense cheering). Thinks it not impossible that if she had always abstained from spirits, she might have had two eyes by this time (tremendous applause).'" 33

Two **Miss Matinters**, "being single and singular, paid great court to the Master of Ceremonies, in the hope of getting a stray partner now and then." 35

Mivins, debtor, also known as "the **Zephyr**." " . . . a man in a broad-skirted green coat, with corduroy knee smalls and grey cotton stockings, was performing the most popular steps of a hornpipe, with a slang and burlesque caricature of grace and lightness, which, combined with the very appropriate character of his costume, was inexpressibly absurd." 41

Brother **Mordlin**, a Temperance singer. "The neatness of the young man's attire, the dexterity of his feathering, the enviable state of mind which enabled him in the beautiful words of the poet, to

'Row along, thinking of nothing at all,'

all combined to prove that he must have been a water-drinker (cheers). Oh, what a state of virtuous jollity! (rapturous cheering.)" 33

Mottle-faced gentleman, "who reviewed the company, and slowly lifted his hand, upon which every man (including him of the mottled countenance) drew a long breath, and lifted his tumbler to his lips. In one instant the mottled-faced gentleman depressed his hand again, and every glass was set down empty. It is impossible to describe the thrilling effect produced by this striking ceremony. At once dignified, solemn, and impressive, it combined every element of grandeur." 55

Jonas Mudge. " . . . a large wooden money-box was conspicuously placed upon the green baize cloth of the business table, behind which the secretary stood, and acknowledged, with a gracious smile, every addition to the rich vein of copper which lay concealed within." 33

Lord **Mutanhed**. "'You see the splendidly dressed young man coming this way?'

"'The one with the long hair, and the particularly small forehead?' inquired Mr **Pickwick**.

" . . . 'Gwacious heavens!' said his lordship. 'I thought evewebody had seen the new mail cart; it's the neatest pwettiest, gwacefullest thing that ever wan upon wheels. Painted wed, with a cweam piebald.' . . And a little seat in fwont with an iwon wail, for the dwiver,' added his lordship. 'I dwove it over to Bwistol the other morning, in a cwimson coat, with two servants widing a quarter of a mile behind; and confound me if the people didn't wush out of their cottages, and awest my pwogwess, to know if I wasn't the post. Glorwious, glorwious!'" 35

Muzzle, "an undersized footman, with a long body and short legs." 26

Namby, sheriff's officer. " . . . a man of about forty, with black hair, and carefully combed whiskers. He was dressed in a particularly gorgeous manner, with plenty of articles of jewellery about him—all about three sizes larger than those which are usually worn by gentlemen—and a rough great-coat to crown the whole. Into one pocket of this great-coat, he thrust his left hand the moment he dismounted, while from the other he drew forth, with his right, a very bright and glaring silk handkerchief, with which he whisked a speck or two of dust from his boots, and then, crumbling it in his hand, swaggered up the court." 40

George Nupkins, Esquire. " . . . the principal magistrate was as grand a person as the fastest walker would find out, between sunrise and sunset, on the twenty-first of June . . . ." 24

—*on duty:* "Mr Nupkins threw himself back, with thrilling solemnity, and scrutinised the faces of his unwilling visitors." 25

—*laughter in his court:* "'**Grummer**,' said Mr Nupkins, reddening with passion, 'how dare you select such an inefficient and disreputable person for a special constable, as that man? How dare you do it, sir? . . . You shall repent of this neglect of duty, Mr Grummer; you shall be made an example of. Take that fellow's staff away. He's drunk. You're drunk, fellow.'

"'I am not drunk, your worship,' said the man.

"'You *are* drunk,' returned the magistrate. 'How dare you say you are not drunk, sir, when I say you are?'" 25

Old man, debtor. " . . . [he] was seated on a small wooden box, with his eyes rivetted on the floor, and his face settled into an expression of the deepest and most hopeless despair . . . . The [**grand-daughter**'s] voice that had been music to him, and the eyes that had been light, fell coldly on his senses. His limbs were shaking with disease, and the palsy had fastened on his mind." 42

Solomon Pell, debtor's attorney. "[He] was a fat flabby pale man, in a surtout which looked green one minute and brown the next: with a velvet collar of the same cameleon [*sic.*] tints. His forehead was narrow, his face wide, his head large, and his nose all on one side, as if Nature, indignant with the propensities she observed in him in his birth, had given it an angry tweak [from] which it had never recovered. Being short-necked and asthmatic, how-

ever, he respired principally through this feature; so, perhaps, what it wanted
in ornament, it made up in usefulness." 43

"' . . . a limb o' the law, Sammy, as has got brains like the frogs, dispersed
all over his body, and reachin' to the wery tips of his fingers . . . . '" 43

Phunky. " . . . . Although an infant barrister, he was a full-grown man. He
had a very nervous manner, and a painful hesitation in his speech; it did not
appear to be a natural defect, but seemed rather the result of timidity, arising
from the consciousness of being 'kept down' by want of means, or interest, or
connexion, or impudence, as the case might be. He was overawed by the
Serjeant, and profoundly courteous to the attorney." 31

Pott. "[He was] a tall, thin man, with a sandy-coloured head inclined to
baldness, and a face in which solemn importance was blended with a look of unfathomable profundity. He was dressed in a long brown surtout, with a black
cloth waistcoat, and drab trousers. A double eye-glass dangled at his waistcoat: and on his head he wore a very low-crowned hat with a broad brim. The
new-comer was introduced . . . as Mr Pott, the editor of the Eatanswill Gazette." 13

Mrs Pott. "If Mr **Pott** had a weakness, it was, perhaps, that he was *rather*
too submissive to the somewhat contemptuous control and sway of his wife. . . .
'It is a high treat to me, I assure you [said she], to see any new faces; living as
I do, from day to day, and week to week, in this dull place, and seeing nobody.'

"'Nobody, my dear!' exclaimed Mr Pott, archly.

"'Nobody but *you*,' retorted Mrs Pott, with asperity." 13

Price, debtor. "[He was] engaged in stirring the fire with the toe of his right
boot . . . a coarse vulgar young man of about thirty, with a sallow face and
harsh voice: evidently possessed of that knowledge of the world, and captivating freedom of manner, which is to be acquired in public-house parlours, and at
low billiard-tables." 40

Prisoner, singing. " . . . evidently very drunk . . . sitting up between the
sheets, warbling as much as he could recollect of a comic song, with the most
intensely sentimental feeling and expression . . . . " 41

Pruffle. "'There is something very extraordinary in the air tonight. Did
you see that?' said the scientific gentleman, pointing out of the window . . . .
What should you say was the cause of those lights, now?'

"The scientific gentleman smilingly anticipated Pruffle's reply that he could
assign no cause for them at all. Pruffle meditated.

"'I should say it was thieves, sir,' said Pruffle at length.

"'You're a fool, and may go down-stairs,' said the scientific gentleman.

"'Thank you, sir,' said Pruffle. And down he went." 39

Mary Ann Raddle. " . . . a little fierce woman bounced into the room, all in
a tremble with passion, and pale with rage. . . . She had bustled up to the
apartment of the unlucky **Bob Sawyer**, so bent upon going into a passion, that
in all probability, payment [of the rent] would have rather disappointed her
than otherwise. She was in excellent order for a little relaxation of the kind:
having just exchanged a few introductory compliments with **Mr R**. in the front
kitchen." 32

Tom Roker, a tipstaff. "'This here is the hall flight . . . .

"'Live down there! yes, and die down there, too, wery often! . . . and what of that? Who's got to say anything agin it? Live down there! Yes, and a wery good place it is to live in, ain't it?'" 41

Red-headed man. " . . . to him Mr **Pickwick** called lustily—'Hallo there!'

"The red-headed man raised his body, shaded his eyes with his hand, and stared, long and coolly, at Mr Pickwick and his companions . . . .

"'How far is it to Dingley Dell?'

"'Better er seven mile.'

"'Is it a good road?'

"'No t'ant.' Having uttered this brief reply, and apparently satisfied himself with another scrutiny, the red-headed man resumed his work." 5

Sam, and his horse. "'How old is that horse, my friend?' inquired Mr. **Pickwick**, rubbing his nose with the shilling he had reserved for the fare.

"'Forty-two,' replied the driver, eyeing him askant.

"'What!' ejaculated Mr. Pickwick, laying his hand upon his notebook. The driver reiterated his former statement. Mr. Pickwick looked very hard at the man's face, but his features were immovable, so he noted down the fact forthwith." 2

—*actively aggrieved:* "'Here's your fare,' said Mr **Pickwick**, holding out the shilling to the driver.

"What was the learned man's astonishment, when that unaccountable person flung the money on the pavement, and requested in figurative terms to be allowed the pleasure of fighting him (Mr Pickwick) for the amount! . . .

"'Come on!' said the cab-driver, sparring away like clock-work. 'Come on—all four on you . . . .

"'Would any body believe,' continued the cab-driver, appealing to the crowd, 'would any body believe as an informer 'ud go about in a man's cab, not only takin' down his number, but ev'ry word he says into the bargain . . . . But I'll give it him, if I've six months for it. Come on!' and the cabman dashed his hat upon the ground, with a reckless disregard of his own private property and knocked Mr Pickwick's spectacles off, and followed up the attack with a blow on Mr Pickwick's nose, and another on Mr Pickwick's chest, and a third in Mr **Snodgrass**'s eye, and a fourth, by way of variety, in Mr **Tupman**'s waistcoat, and then danced into the road, and then back again to the pavement, and finally dashed the whole temporary supply of breath out of Mr **Winkle**'s body; and all in half-a-dozen seconds." 2

Susannah Sanders. "[She] was a big, fat, heavy-faced personage," a friend of **Mrs Bardell**. 26

—*during testimony:* "Mrs Sanders, whose eyes were intently fixed on the judge's face, planted herself close by [Mrs **Cluppins**, on the stand], with the large umbrella: keeping her right thumb pressed on the spring with an earnest countenance, as if she were fully prepared to put it up at a moment's notice." 34

Scientific gentleman. " . . . an elderly gentleman of scientific attainments was seated in his library . . . writing a philosophical treatise, and ever and anon moistening his clay and his labours with a glass of claret from a venerable-looking bottle which stood by his side . . . when he was very much surprised by observing a most brilliant light glide through the air, at a short distance above the ground, and almost instantaneously vanish. . . . He had no wife to call in and astonish, so he rang the bell for his servant." 39 *And see* **Pruffle**

Shepherd. "'. . . in comes a fat chap in black, vith a great white face, a smilin' avay like clockwork. Such goin's on, Sammy! "The kiss of peace," says the shepherd; and then he kissed the women all round . . . . such eatin' and drinkin'! I wish you could ha' seen the shepherd walkin' into the ham and muffins. I never see such a chap to eat and drink; never.'" 22

Tupman, Jingle and Doctor Slammer

Doctor **Slammer**. " . . . a little fat man, with a ring of upright black hair round his head, and an extensive bald plain on the top of it . . . . The Doctor took snuff with everybody, chatted with everybody, laughed, danced, made jokes, played whist, did everything, and was everywhere. To these pursuits, multifarious as they were, the little Doctor added a more important one than any—he was indefatigable in paying the most unremitting and devoted attention to [Mrs. **Budger**]." 2

—*on being cut out:* "'Sir!' said the Doctor, in an awful voice, producing a card, and retiring into an angle of the passage, 'my name is Slammer, Doctor

Slammer, sir—97th Regiment— Chatham Barracks —my card, sir, my card.' He would have added more, but his indignation choked him.

"'Ah! replied [**Jingle**], coolly, 'Slammer—much obliged—polite attention— not ill now, Slammer—but when I am—knock you up.'" 2

Samuel Slumkey. " . . . the Blue candidate . . . in topboots, and a blue neckerchief, advanced and seized the hand of [**Pott**], and melodramatically testified by gestures to the crowd, his ineffaceable obligations to the Eatanswill Gazette." 13

Slurk, editor. " . . . a stern stranger . . . who seemed habitually suspicious in look and manner . . . a shortish gentleman, with very stiff black hair cut in the porcupine or blacking-brush style, and standing stiff and straight all over his head; his aspect was pompous and threatening; his manner was peremptory; his eyes were sharp and restless; and his whole bearing bespoke a feeling of great confidence in himself, and a consciousness of immeasurable superiority over all other people." 51

Smangle. " . . . [he] was an admirable specimen of a class of gentry which never can be seen in full perfection but in such places [as debtor's prisons];— they may be met with, in an imperfect state, occasionally about stable-yards and public-houses; but they never attain their full bloom except in these hot-beds, which would almost seem to be considerately provided by the Legislature for the sole purpose of rearing them.

"He was a tall fellow, with an olive complexion, long dark hair, and very thick bushy whiskers meeting under his chin. He wore no neckerchief, as he had been playing rackets all day, and his open shirt collar displayed their full luxuriance. On his head he wore one of the common eighteen penny French skull-caps, with a gawdy tassel dangling therefrom, very happily in keeping with a common fustian coat. His legs—which, being long, were afflicted with weakness—graced a pair of Oxford-mixture trousers, made to show the full symmetry of those limbs. Being somewhat negligently braced, however, and, moreover, but imperfectly buttoned, they fell in a series of not the most graceful folds over a pair of shoes sufficiently down at heel to display a pair of very soiled white stockings. There was a rakish, vagabond smartness, and a kind of boastful rascality, about the whole man, that was worth a mine of gold." 41

Joseph Smiggers, "Esq. P. V. P. M. P. C.*" [*Perpetual Vice-President— Member Pickwick Club] 1

Miss Smithers. " . . . an inquisitive boarder, who had been peeping between the hinges [of the garden door], set up a fearful screaming [and] proceeded to go into hysterics of four young lady power." 16

The **Smithies**. "'Mr Smithie, Mrs Smithie, and the Misses Smithie,' was the next announcement . . . .

" . . . . Mr. Smithie bowed deferentially to Sir **Thomas Clubber**; and Sir Thomas Clubber acknowledged the salute with conscious condescension. Lady Clubber took a telescopic view of Mrs. Smithie and family through her eye-glass, and Mrs Smithie stared in her turn at Mrs Somebody else, whose husband was not in the Dock-yard at all." 2

Count **Smorltork**. "'Count, Count,' screamed **Mrs Leo Hunter** to a well-whiskered individual in a foreign uniform . . .'the famous foreigner—gathering materials for his great work on England—hem!—Count Smorltork, Mr **Pickwick**' . . . .

"'The word politics, sir,' said Mr Pickwick, 'comprises, in itself, a difficult study of no inconsiderable magnitude.'

"'Ah!' said the Count, drawing out the tablets again, 'ver good—fine words to begin a chapter. Chapter forty-seven. Poltics. The word poltic surprises by himself—' And down went Mr Pickwick's remark, in Count Smorltork's tablets, with such variations and additions as the Count's exuberant fancy suggested, or his imperfect knowledge of the language, occasioned." 15

Honourable **Wilmot Snipe**. "'Who's that little boy with the light hair and pink eyes, in a fancy dress?' . . . 'Hush, pray— pink eyes—fancy dress—little boy—nonsense—Ensign 97th—Honourable Wilmot Snipe—great family— Snipes—very.'" 2

Lady **Snuphanuph**. "' . . . do you see the lady in the gauze turban?'

"'The fat old lady?' inquired Mr **Pickwick**, innocently.

"'Hush, my dear sir—nobody's fat or old in Ba—ath. That's the Dowager Lady Snuphanuph.'" 35

Staple. " . . . a little man with a puffy Say-nothing-to-me-or-I'll-contra-dict-you sort of countenance, who remained very quiet; occasionally looking round him when the conversation slackened, as if he contemplated putting in something very weighty; and now and then bursting into a short cough of inex-pressible grandeur." 7

Mr Stiggins holding forth

Stiggins." . . . in threadbare black clothes, with a back almost as long and stiff as that of the chair itself . . . . He was a prim-faced, red-nosed man, with a long, thin countenance, and semi-rattlesnake sort of eye—rather sharp, but decidedly bad. He wore very short trousers, and black-cotton stockings, which, like the rest of his apparel, were particularly rusty. His looks were starched, but his white neckerchief was not, and its long limp ends straggled over his closely-buttoned waistcoat in a very uncouth and unpicturesque fashion. A pair of old, worn beaver gloves, a broad-brimmed hat, and a faded green umbrella, with plenty of whalebone sticking through the bottom, as if to counterbalance the want of a handle at the top, lay on a chair beside him, and, being disposed in a very tidy and careful manner, seemed to imply that the red-nosed man . . . had no intention of going away in a hurry." 27

Brother Tadger. " . . . a little emphatic man, with a bald head, and drab shorts . . . suddenly rushed up the ladder, at the imminent peril of snapping the two little legs . . . . " 33

—*unfairly handled:* "'Brother Tadger, sir!' said Mr **Stiggins**, suddenly increasing in ferocity, and turning sharp round on the little man in the drab shorts, '*you* are drunk, sir!' With this, Mr Stiggins, entertaining a praiseworthy desire to promote the sobriety of the meeting, and to exclude therefrom all improper characters, hit brother Tadger on the summit of the nose with such unerring aim, that the drab shorts disappeared like a flash of lightning. Brother Tadger had been knocked, head first, down the ladder." 33

Tipstaff. "There is not a messenger or process-server attached to [the Insolvent Court], who wears a coat that was made for him; not a tolerably fresh, or wholesome-looking man in the whole establishment, except a little white-headed apple-faced tipstaff, and even he, like an ill-conditioned cherry preserved in brandy, seems to have artificially dried and withered up into a state of preservation to which he can lay no natural claim." 43

Tom, Mrs **Cripps**'s son, in grey livery. " . . . marvelling at the unwonted prolongation of the [**Sawyer/Allen**] dinner, cast an anxious look . . . towards the glass door, distracted by inward misgivings regarding the amount of minced veal which would be ultimately reserved for his individual cravings. . . . " 48

Miss Tomkins. "'Oh, the man—the man—behind the door!' . . .

"The lady abbess no sooner heard this appalling cry, than she retreated to her own bed-room, double-locked the door, and fainted away comfortably." 16

Trundle. " . . . a young gentleman apparently enamoured of one of the young ladies in scarfs and feathers. . . . " 4 *See* **Isabella Wardle**

Tuckle. " . . . a stoutish gentleman in a bright crimson coat with long tails, vividly red breeches and a cocked hat, who was standing with his back to the fire, and had apparently just entered, for besides retaining his cocked hat on his head, he carried in his hand a high stick, such as gentlemen of his profession usually elevate in a sloping position over the roofs of carriages." 37

Turnkeys. "The stout turnkey . . . sat down, and looked at [Mr **Pickwick**] carelessly, from time to time, while a long thin man who had relieved him, thrust his hands beneath his coat-tails, and planting himself opposite, took a good long view of him. A third rather surly-looking gentleman: who had apparently been disturbed at his tea . . . stationed himself close to Mr Pickwick; and resting his hands on his hips, inspected him narrowly; while two others mixed with the group, and studied his features with most intent and thoughtful faces. . . . At length the likeness was completed, and Mr Pickwick was informed, that he might now proceed into the prison." 40

Waiter, at The Great White Horse. "A corpulent man, with a fortnight's napkin under his arm, and coeval stockings on his legs, slowly desisted from his occupation of staring down the street . . . and, after minutely inspecting [Mr **Pickwick**'s] appearance, from the crown of his hat to the lowest button of his gaiters replied . . . ." 22

Waiter, at The Old Royal Hotel. "With his mind apparently relieved from an overwhelming weight, by having at last got an order for something, the waiter imperceptibly melted away." 50

H. Walker, convert to Temperance. "' . . . tailor, wife, and two children . . . . Is now out of work and penniless; thinks it must be the porter (cheers) or the loss of the use of his right hand; is not certain which . . . . " 33

Emily Wardle, "one of "two young ladies in scarfs and feathers . . . ." 4

"'Short girl—black eyes—niece Emily' . . . if there were one individual in the whole world, of whom the spinster aunt entertained a mortal and deeply-rooted jealousy, it was this identical niece." 8

Isabella (Bella) Wardle. "'. . . [**Trundle**'s] wife I know to be a very amiable and lovely girl, well qualified to transfer to another sphere of action the happiness which for twenty years she has diffused around her, in her father's house [toasted Mr **Pickwick**].'" 28

Watty, "a rustily-clad, miserable-looking man, in boots without toes and gloves without fingers. There were traces of privation and suffering—almost of despair—in his lank and care-worn countenance; he felt his poverty, for he shrunk to the dark side of the staircase . . ." 31

Mrs Weller, formerly **Susan Clarke**. " . . . a rather stout lady of comfortable appearance . . . the quondam relict and sole executrix of the dead-and-gone Mr **Clarke**. . . ." 27

—*her demise,* reported by her widower (written by another):

> "'Markis Gran
> By dorken
> Wensdy

"'My dear Sammle,

"'I am wery sorry to have the pleasure of bein a Bear of ill news your Mother in law cort cold consekens of imprudently settin too long on the damp grass in the rain a hearin of a shepherd who warnt able to leave off till late at night owen to his havin vound his-self up vith brandy and vater and not being able to stop his-self till he got a little sober which took a many hours to do the doctor says that if she'd svallo'd varm brandy and vater artervards insted of afore she mightn't have been no vus her veels wos immedetly greased and everythink done to set her agoin as could be inwented your farther had hopes as she vould have vorked round as usual but just as she wos a turnen the corner my boy she took the wrong road and vent down hill vith a welocity you never see and notvithstanding that the drag wos put on drectly by the medikel man it wornt of no use at all for she paid the last pike at twenty minutes afore six o'clock yesterday evenin havin done the journey wery much under the reglar time vich praps was partly owen to her haven taken in wery little luggage . . . so he sends his dooty in which I join and am Samivel infernally yours

"'**TONY VELLER**'" 52

Whiffers. "[He] could have wished to have spared that company [of footmen] the painful and disgusting detail on which he was about to enter, but as the explanation [for his resignation] had been demanded of him, he had no alternative but to state, boldly and distinctly, that he had been required to eat cold meat. . . ." 37

Widow. ". . . a very buxom-looking cook, dressed in mourning . . . silently stationed herself at the back of [**Sam**'s] father's chair, and announced her presence by a slight cough . . . .The buxom female shook her head with a compassionate and sympathising air . . . .'You see . . . as I was telling him yesterday, he will feel lonely, he can't expect but what he should, sir, but he should keep up a good heart, because, dear me, I'm sure we all pity his loss, and are ready to do anything for him; and there's no situation in life, so bad, Mr Samuel, that it can't be mended. Which is what a very worthy person said to me when my husband died.' Here the speaker, putting her hand before her mouth, coughed again, and looked affectionately at the elder Mr **Weller**." 52

Wife, of **clergyman**. " . . . next him sat his wife, a stout blooming old lady, who looked as if she were well skilled, not only in the art and mystery of manufacturing home-made cordials greatly to other people's satisfaction, but of tasting them occasionally very much to her own." 6

Wife, of **debtor**. "A young woman, with a child in her arms, who seemed scarcely able to crawl, from emaciation and misery, was walking up and down the passage in conversation with her husband, who had no other place to see her in. As they passed Mr **Pickwick**, he could hear the female sob; and once she burst into such a passion of grief, that she was compelled to lean against the wall for support . . . . " 41

Wife, of red-headed **man**. "A tall bony woman—straight all the way down—in a coarse blue pelisse, with the waist an inch or two below her armpits . . . . " 5

Winkle, Sr. " . . . a little old gentleman in a snuff-coloured suit, with a head and face the precise counterpart of those belonging to Mr. **Winkle** junior, excepting that he was rather bald, trotted into the room . . . . " 50 *See* **Arabella Allen** SR

Miss Witherfield. "Mr **Pickwick** [in the wrong bedroom] almost fainted with horror and dismay. Standing before the dressing glass was a middle-aged lady, in yellow curlpapers, busily engaged in brushing what ladies call their 'back-hair.'" 22 *See* **Peter Magnus**—*coached* SR

Jane Wugsby. "'I came to ask, ma, whether I might dance with the youngest Mr **Crawley**,' whispered the prettier and younger of the two . . . .

"'Good God, Jane, how can you think of such things? ' replied the mamma, indignantly. 'Haven't you repeatedly heard that his father has eight hundred a-year, which dies with him? I am ashamed of you. Not on any account.'" 35

Miss Wugsby. "'Ma,' whispered the other, who was much older than her sister, and very insipid and artificial, 'Lord **Mutanhed** has been introduced to me. I said I thought I wasn't engaged, ma.'

"'You're a sweet pet, my love,' replied Mrs Colonel **Wugsby**, tapping her daughter's cheek with her fan, 'and are always to be trusted. He's immensely rich, my dear. Bless you!'" 35

Mrs Colonel **Wugsby**. A lady "of ancient and whist-like appearance . . ." 35

Walk-ons

Authors. " . . . there were [at **Mrs Hunter'**s breakfast] half a dozen lions from London—authors, real authors, who had written whole books, and printed them afterwards—and here you might see 'em, walking about, like ordinary men, smiling, and talking—aye, and talking pretty considerable nonsense too, no doubt with the benign intention of rendering themselves intelligible to the common people about them." 15

Barmaid, wounded. She "had positively refused to draw [a customer] any more liquor; in return for which he had (merely in playfulness) drawn his bayonet, and wounded the girl in the shoulder." 2

Betsy. " . . . a dirty slipshod girl in black cotton stockings, who might have passed for the neglected daughter of a superannuated dustman in very reduced circumstances, thrust in her head . . . . " 32

Boy, in cap. " . . . a young boy of about three feet high, or thereabouts, in a hairy cap and fustian over-alls, whose garb bespoke a laudable ambition to attain in time the elevation of an hostler . . . the young gentleman walked away, awakening all the echoes in George Yard as he did so, with several chaste and extremely correct imitations of a drover's whistle, delivered in a tone of peculiar richness and volume." 33

extremely correct imitations of a drover's whistle, delivered in a tone of peculiar richness and volume." 33

Chambermaid. "A loud ringing of one of the bells, was followed by the appearance of a smart chambermaid in the upper sleeping gallery . . . . " 10

Coach guard. " . . . Mr **Weller** and the guard try to squeeze the cod-fish into the boot, first head first, and then tail first, and then top upward, and then bottom upward, and then side-ways, and then long-ways, all of which artifices the implacable cod-fish sturdily resists, until the guard accidentally hits him in the very middle of the basket, whereupon he suddenly disappears into the boot, and with him, the head and shoulders of the guard himself, who, not calculating upon so sudden a cessation of the passive resistance of the cod-fish, experiences a very unexpected shock, to the unsmotherable delight of all the porters and bystanders." 28

Crookey, "who in dress and general appearance looked something between a bankrupt grazier, and a drover in a state of insolvency. . . . " 40

Crushton. " 'The other gentleman . . . in the red under waistcoat and dark moustache, is the Honourable . . . ' . . . the obsequious Mr Crushton." 35

Debtor. " . . . the man took the child in his arms, and tried to soothe [his **wife**]." 41

Emma, buxom servant to **Wardle**. " . . . Mr **Tupman** . . . had lingered behind to snatch a kiss from Emma, for which he had been duly rewarded with sundry pushings and scratchings . . . . " 5

" . . . Emma bestowed a half-demure, half-impudent, and all pretty, look of recognition, on Mr Tupman, which was enough to make the statue of Bonaparte in the passage, unfold his arms, and clasp her within them." 28

Horatio Fizkin, candidate. "[He] had been prevailed upon by his friends to stand forward in the Buff interest." 13

Gentlemen, two very stout: One " . . . whose body and legs looked like half a gigantic roll of flannel, elevated on a couple of inflated pillow-cases." Another, "who strongly resembled the other half of the roll of flannel aforesaid." 7

Ghost. "" . . . it does appear to me somewhat inconsistent, that when you have an opportunity of visiting the fairest spots of earth . . . you should always return exactly to the very places where you have been most miserable." "Egad, that's very true; I never thought of that before," said the ghost.'" 20

Grand-daughter, of a prisoner. "A young girl—his little grand-daughter— was hanging about him: endeavouring, with a thousand childish devices, to engage his attention; but the old man neither saw nor heard her." 42

Grundy, law clerk. "'Mr Grundy's going to oblige the company with a song,' said the chairman.

"'No he ain't,' said Mr Grundy." 20

Miss Gwynn. "'It's my opinion, **Miss Tomkins**,' said the writing and ciphering governess, 'that his [Mr **Pickwick**'s] man-servant keeps him. I think he's a madman, Miss Tomkins, and the other's his keeper.'" 16

Harris, a greengrocer, "put on a pair of wash-leather gloves to hand the plates with, and stationed himself behind Mr **Tuckle**'s chair." 37

Isaac. " . . . a shabby man in black leggings . . . with a thick ash stick in his hand . . . was seated on the box, smoking a cigar." 46

Labouring man. *See* **Samuel Pickwick** OEH—*antiquarian*

Lanky man. "'By and bye . . . a lanky chap with a red nose and a white neckcloth rushes up, and sings, out, "Here's the shepherd a coming to wisit his faithful flock"'" 22

Stupefied man. " . . . a little timid-looking nervous man, whose appearance bespoke great poverty, and who had been crouching on his bedstead . . . apparently stupefied by the novelty of his situation." 42

Martin, a butcher. " . . . a gentleman, prematurely broad for his years: clothed in a professional blue frock, and top-boots with circular toes: entered the room nearly out of breath . . . ." 42

Miller. "A little hard-headed, Ribston-pippin-faced man . . ." 6

Neddy, turnkey, "was paring the mud off his shoes with a five-and-twenty bladed pocket knife . . . [he] appeared of a taciturn and thoughtful cast . . . ." 42

Henrietta Nupkins, "who possessed all her mamma's haughtiness without the turban, and all her ill-nature without the wig . . . ." 25

Mrs Nupkins. "[She] was a majestic female in a pink gauze turban and a light brown wig." 25

Dr. Payne. " . . . a portly personage in a braided surtout . . . was sitting with perfect equanimity on a camp-stool." 2

Poor relations. "How [they] ever reached London—whether they walked, or got behind coaches, or procured lifts in wagons, or carried each other by turns—is uncertain; but there they were . . .the very first people that knocked at the door of Mr **Pickwick**'s house, on the [**Snodgrass**] bridal morning, were the two poor relations, all smiles and shirt collar." 56

The **Porkenhams**. "Mrs **Nupkins** and Miss **Nupkins** had . . . hurled Captain **Fitz-Marshall** at the devoted heads of their select circle of acquaintance, until their bosom friends, **Mrs** Porkenham and the **Miss** Porkenham, and Mr **Sidney** Porkenham, were ready to burst with jealousy and despair." 25

Postilions. "The postilions, each with a broad grin convulsing his countenance, were viewing the adverse [**Pickwick/Wardle**] party from their saddles. . . ." 9

Raddle. " . . . compressed into a very small compass . . . a gentleman of heavy and subdued demeanour, who, whenever he ventured to make an observation, was snapped up short. . . . " 46 *And see* **Mary Anne Raddle** O

Reader, in the law. " . . . a small-eyed peremptory young gentleman . . . who had written a lively book about the law of demises, with a vast quantity of marginal notes and references . . . . " 47

Mrs Rogers. "[She] was the lodger, and her servant was in waiting, so she was more gracious than intimate, in right of her position." 46

Two **servants**. " . . . a couple of large-headed, circular-visaged males rose from their seats in the [**Wardle**] chimney-corner (for although it was a May evening, their attachment to the wood fire appeared as cordial as if it were Christmas) . . . . " 5

Shiny William. " . . . so called, probably, from his sleek hair and oily countenance . . ." 5

Frank Simmery. He was "a very smart young gentleman who wore his hat on his right whisker, and was lounging over the desk, killing flies with a ruler." 55 *And see* **Wilkins Flasher** O

Simpson. " . . . he was leaning out of the window as far as he could without over-balancing himself, endeavouring, with great perseverance, to spit upon the crown of the hat of a personal friend on the parade below . . ." 42

Skimpin, junior to Mr Serjeant **Buzfuz**. " . . . being a promising young man of two or three and forty, was of course anxious to confuse a witness who was notoriously predisposed in favour of the other side . . . . " 34

Slasher. "'Best [operator] alive . . . . Took a boy's leg out of the socket last week—boy ate five apples and a ginger bread cake—exactly two minutes after it was all over . . . . '" 32

John Smauker. " . . . a powdered-headed footman in gorgeous livery, and of symmetrical stature." 35

Smouch. " . . . a shabby-looking man in a brown great-coat shorn of divers buttons . . . ." 40

Lieutenant **Tappleton**. "An officer in undress uniform . . . turned round as Mr. **Winkle** entered, and made a stiff inclination of the head." 2

Mrs Tomlinson. " . . . the post-office keeper, seemed by mutual consent to have been chosen the leader of the trade party [at the Rochester ball]." 2

Tommy, a waterman. "A strange specimen of the human race, in a sack-cloth coat, and apron of the same, who with a brass label and number round his neck, looked as if he were catalogued in some collection of rarities." 2

Figures in Interludes

The Stroller's Tale 3

John, an Actor. " . . . a low pantomime actor; and . . . an habitual drunkard. In his better days, before he had become enfeebled by dissipation and emaciated by disease, he had been in the receipt of a good salary . . . . His besetting sin gained so fast upon him, however, that it was found impossible to employ him . . . . "

—his **wife**. "A wretched-looking woman . . . [with a] pale face and wasted form . . . . "

The Convict's Return 6

Edmunds. "He was a morose, savage-hearted, bad man: idle and dissolute in his habits; cruel and ferocious in his disposition. Beyond the few lazy and reckless vagabonds with whom he sauntered away his time in the fields, or sotted in the alehouse, he had not a single friend or acquaintance; no one cared to speak to the man whom many feared, and every one detested—and Edmunds was shunned by all."

Mrs Edmunds. "Of the acuteness of that woman's sufferings, of the gentle and enduring manner in which she bore them, of the agony of solicitude with which she reared [her son], no one can form an adequate conception."

John Edmunds. " . . . the boy had become a robust and well-grown youth . . . [but] . . . had linked himself with depraved and abandoned men, and was madly pursuing a headlong career . . . . "

A Madman's Manuscript 11

Three Brothers. "'How those three proud, overbearing brothers humbled themselves before me!'"

Father. "'The old white-headed father, too—such deference—such respect—such devoted friendship—he worshipped me!'"

Madman. "'Ho! ho! It's a grand thing to be mad! to be peeped at like a wild lion through the iron bars—to gnash one's teeth and howl, through the long still night, to the merry ring of a heavy chain . . . . Hurrah for the madhouse! Oh, it's a rare place!'"

Wife. "'I don't remember forms or faces now, but . . . I see, standing still and motionless in one corner of this cell, a slight and wasted figure with long black hair, which streaming down her back, stirs with no earthly wind, and eyes that fix their gaze on me, and never wink or close . . . the face is very pale, and the eyes are glassy bright . . . .'"

The Bagman's Story 14

Chair/Man. " . . . a strange, grim-looking high-backed chair, carved in the most fantastic manner, with a flowered damask cushion, and the round knobs at the bottom of the legs carefully tied up in red cloth, as if it had got the gout in its toes. . . . **Tom [Smart]** gazed at the chair . . . a most extraordinary change seemed to come over it. The carving of the back gradually assumed the lineaments and expression of an old shrivelled human face; the damask cushion became an antique, flapped waistcoat; the round knobs grew into a couple of feet, encased in red cloth slippers; and the old chair looked like a very ugly old man, of the previous century, with his arms a-kimbo. . . . The chair was an ugly old gentleman; and what was more, he was winking at Tom Smart."

Jinkins. " . . . a very tall man—in a brown coat and bright basket buttons, and black whiskers, and wavy black hair, who was seated at tea with the **widow** . . . . "

Tom Smart and conveyance. "If any bagman of that day could have caught sight of the little neck-or-nothing sort of gig, with a clay-coloured body and red wheels, and the vixenish, ill-tempered, fast-going bay mare, that looked like a cross between a butcher's horse and a two-penny post-office pony, he would have known at once, that this traveller could have been no other than Tom Smart, of the great house of Bilson and Slum, Cateaton Street, City."

Waitress. " . . . smartly-dressed . . . bright eye and a neat ankle . . . . "

Widow. " . . . of somewhere about eight and forty or thereabouts, with a face as comfortable as the bar, who was evidently the landlady of the house, and the supreme ruler over all these agreeable possessions."

The Parish Clerk: A Tale of True Love 17

Apprentice. " . . . with the thin legs . . . . "

Henry. "The only eye-sore in the whole place, was another cousin . . . whom **Maria Lobbs** called 'Henry,' and who seemed to keep Maria Lobbs all to himself, up in one corner of the table."

Kate. " . . . an arch, impudent-looking, bewitching . . . wicked little cousin, who, half afraid for her brother, and half laughing at **Nathaniel Pipkin**, presented as bewitching an expression of countenance, with a touch of shyness in it too, as any man, old or young, need look upon."

Maria Lobbs. " . . . blooming countenance . . . the only daughter . . . pretty face. . . but the eyes of Maria Lobbs had never looked so bright, the cheeks of Maria Lobbs had never looked so ruddy . . . . "

Old Lobbs. "Now, if old Lobbs had entertained the most remote or distant idea of the state of the affections of **Nathaniel Pipkin**, he would have just razed the school-room to the ground, or exterminated its master from the surface of the earth, or committed some other outrage and atrocity of an equally ferocious and violent description; for he was a terrible old fellow, was Lobbs, when his pride was injured, or his blood was up."

Nathaniel Pipkin, a schoolmaster, "was a harmless, inoffensive, good-natured being, with a turned-up nose and rather turned-in legs: a cast in his eye, and a halt in his gait . . . . "

The Old Man's Tale about the Queer Client 21

Attorney. " . . . a London attorney, then well known as a man of no great nicety in his professional dealings . . . ."

George Heyling. "The healthy, strong-made man, who could have borne almost any fatigue of active exertion, was wasting beneath the close confinement and unhealthy atmosphere of a crowded prison."

Mary Heyling. "The slight and delicate woman was sinking beneath the combined effects of bodily and mental illness."

Heyling son. " . . . no expression of interest or amusement lighted up his thin and sickly face . . . . The hard realities of the world, with many of its worst privations—hunger and thirst, and cold and want—had all come home to him, from the first dawnings of reason: and though the form of childhood was there, its light heart, its merry laugh, and sparkling eyes, were wanting . . . .The child's young heart was breaking."

Old Man. " . . . an old man, wringing his hands in agony, was running to and fro, shrieking for assistance . . . "

The Story of the Goblins who stole a Sexton 29

Goblin. "His long fantastic legs which might have reached the ground, were cocked up, and crossed after a quaint, fantastic fashion; his sinewy arms were bare; and his hands rested on his knees. On his short round body, he wore a close covering, ornamented with small slashes; a short cloak dangled at his back; the collar was cut into curious peaks, which served the goblin in lieu of ruff or neckerchief; and his shoes curled up at his toes into long points. On his head, he wore a broad-brimmed sugar-loaf hat, garnished with a single feather. The hat was covered with the white frost; and the goblin looked as if he had sat on the same tombstone very comfortably, for two or three hundred years. He was sitting perfectly still; his tongue was put out, as if in derision; and he was grinning at **Gabriel Grub** with such a grin as only a goblin could call up."

Gabriel Grub, a sexton, "was an ill-conditioned, cross-grained, surly fellow . . . who consorted with nobody but himself, and an old wicker bottle which fitted into his large deep waistcoat pocket—and who eyed each merry face . . . with such a deep scowl of malice and ill-humour, as it was difficult to meet, without feeling something the worse for."

Gabriel Grub turns to his old wicker bottle

The True Legend of Prince Bladud 36

Prince **Bladud**. " . . . King **Lud** saw the Prince his son, and found he had grown up such a fine young man . . . . "

Lud Hudibras, king of Britain. "He was a mighty monarch. The earth shook when he walked; he was so very stout. His people basked in the light of his countenance: it was so red and glowing. He was, indeed, every inch a king. And there were a good many inches of him too, for although he was not very tall, he was a remarkable size round, and the inches that he wanted in height, he made up in circumference."

Continuing the Story of the Bagman's Uncle 49

Baillie and family. " . . . a Baillie Mac something and four syllables after it . . . the baillie's wife, and the baillie's three daughters, and the baillie's grown-up son, and three or four stout, bushy eye-browed, canny old Scotch fellows . . . . The lassies were pretty and agreeable; the baillie's wife was one of the best creatures that ever lived . . . . "

Ill-looking **fellow**, "in a close brown wig and a plum-coloured suit, wearing a very large sword, and boots up to his hips. . . . "

Jack Martin " . . . was a trifle shorter than the middle size; he was a thought stouter too, than the ordinary run of people, and perhaps his face might be a shade redder. He had the jolliest face you ever saw, gentlemen: something like Punch, with a handsomer nose and chin; his eyes were always twinkling and sparkling with good humour; and a smile—not one of your un-meaning wooden grins, but a real, merry, hearty, good-tempered smile—was perpetually on his countenance."

Young gentleman. " . . . in a powdered wig, and a sky-blue coat trimmed with silver, made very full and broad in the skirts, which were lined with buck-ram. . . . He wore knee breeches, and a kind of leggings rolled up over his silk stockings, and shoes with buckles; he had ruffles at his wrists, a three-cornered hat on his head, and a long taper sword by his side."

Young lady. " . . . attired in an old-fashioned green velvet dress with a long waist and stomacher. She had no bonnet on her head . . . which was muffled in a black silk hood, but she looked round for an instant . . . and such a beautiful face as she disclosed, my uncle had never seen—not even in a picture. She got into the coach, holding up her dress . . . he wouldn't have believed it possible that legs and feet could have been brought to such a state of perfection . . . . "

"All who love Dickens have a strange sense that he is really inexhaustible. It is this fantastic infinity that divides him even from the strongest and healthiest romantic artists of a later day—from Stevenson, for example. I have read Treasure Island twenty times; nevertheless I know it. But I do not really feel as if I knew all Pickwick; I have not so much read it twenty times as read in it a million times; and it almost seemed as if I always read something new. We of the true faith look at each other and understand; yes, our master was a magician. I believe the books are alive; I believe that leaves still grow in them, as leaves grow on trees. I believe that this fairy library flourishes and increases like a fairy forest . . . . " GKC pp xx-xxi

Plays

The Plays are of slight importance, though CD's name coinages have interest. These three are the only plays acted in his time of which CD was sole author, leaving aside *O'Thello,* a family farce acted in 1833 but never published (only doggerel scraps remain) and a "Venetian comedietta," *The Stratagems of Rozanza,* which he wrote at age sixteen, and which his mother copied out by hand in 131 pages (!), now lost. His 1838 farce *The Lamplighter* was withdrawn and reappeared as a story in 1841 (L, page 466). CD tried his hand at at least two stage adaptations of Boz sketches besides P/SG, not reflected here.

DRAMATIS PERSONÆ

Benson, Lucy: a coquette whose mother is dead	VC	228
Old (father)	VC	228
Brown, Emily; designated by her parents as a future wife	SG	227
Dobbs, Julia; looking for a husband	SG	227
Johnson, John; detained at the inn	SG	227
Limbury, Mrs Peter; and husband	W?	229
Lovetown, Alfred, Esq.	W?	229
Mrs Lovetown	W?	229
Noakes, Mrs; landlady	SG	227
Overton, Owen; Mayor of the town	SG	227
Peter, Lord; young and too late	SG	227
Rose, Lucy Benson's cousin	VC	229
Sparks, Tom; the boots	SG	227
Stokes, Martin; very small farmer	VC	229
Tapkins, Felix, Esq.	W?	229
Tinkles, Horatio; the epistolary challenger	SG	227
Tomkins, Charles; incognito at the inn	SG	228
Trott, Walker [say it aloud]; the Strange Gentleman: receives a challenge	SG	227
Waiters three: John, Tom and Will at the St James's Arms	SG	228
Wilson, Mary; awkwardly situated at the inn	SG	228

P 1 opened September 29, 1836   published 1837 **SG**

The Strange Gentleman

The plot appears in SB/WD with different character names. The play opened
at the St James Theatre, and ran at least seventy performances overall.

   Emily Brown, "'whom my respected but swine-headed parents have
picked out for my future wife' [says **Trott**]."

   Julia Dobbs, "looking for a husband at the St James's Arms."

   —*costume:* "A handsome white travelling-dress, cashmere shawl, white
silk stockings; shoes and gloves. A bonnet to correspond."

   John Johnson, "detained at the St James's Arms."

   —*costume:* "White fashionable trousers, boots, light vest, frock coat, black
hat, gloves, etc."

   "'My harebrained, madcap swain . . . implores me to leave my guardian's
house [says **Mary**], and accompany him on an expedition to Gretna Green . . . .
He bears me off, and, when we get exactly half-way, discovers that his money
is all gone . . . . '"

   Mrs Noakes, "the Landlady at the St James's Arms."

   —*costume:* "A chintz gown, rather of a dark pattern, French apron, and
handsome cap."

   Owen Overton, Mayor. —*costume:* "Black smalls, and high black boots.
A blue body coat, rather long in the waist, with yellow buttons, buttoned close
up to the chin. A white stock; ditto gloves. A broad-brimmed low-crowned
white hat."

   Lord Peter. "'That's the young nobleman who's going to run away with
me, Mr **Overton** [says **Julia**] . . . [he] is young and wild, and the fact is his
friends do not consider him very sagacious or strongminded.'"

   Tom Sparks, "a one-eyed 'Boots' at the St James's Arms."

   —*costume:* "Leather smalls, striped stockings, and lace-up half boots, red
vest, and a Holland stable jacket; coloured kerchief, and red wig."

   "' . . . are you the Boots?

   "'I'm the head o' that branch o' the establishment. There's another man
under me, as brushes the dirt off, and puts the blacking on. The fancy work's
my department; I do the polishing, nothing else.'"

   Horatio Tinkles, challenger, "'presents his compliments to his enemy,
and requests the pleasure of his company tomorrow morning, under the clump
of trees, on Corpse Common, to which any of the town's people will direct him,
and where he hopes to have the satisfaction of giving him his gruel. His punc-
tuality will be esteemed a personal favour, as it will save Mr Tinkles the trouble and inconvenience of calling with a horsewhip in his pocket. Mr Tinkles has
ordered breakfast at the Royal for *one*. It is paid for. The individual who returns alive can eat it.'"

   The **Strange Gentleman [Walker Trott]**, "just arrived at the St James's
Arms."

—*costume:* "A light blue plaid French-cut trousers and vest. A brown cloth frock coat, with full skirts, scarcely covering the hips. A light blue kerchief, and eccentric low-crowned broad-brimmed white hat. Boots."

"'He's a wonderful man to talk, ma'am [says **Will**]—keeps on like a steam engine.'"

Charles Tomkins, "incognito at the St James's Arms."

—*costume:* "Shepherd's plaid French-cut trousers; boots; mohair fashionable frock coat, buttoned up; black hat, gloves, etc."

Three **waiters**: **John**, **Tom**, **Will**, "at the St James's Arms."

—*costume:* "All in black trousers, black stockings and shoes, white vests, striped jackets, and white kerchiefs."

Mary Wilson, "[Fanny's] sister, awkwardly situated at the St James's Arms."

—*costume:* "Fashionable walking-dress, white silk stockings; shoes and gloves."

> Chambermaid, at the St James's Arms
> George Edmunds, betrothed to Lucy Benson
> John Ellis, solicitor
> Fanny Wilson, with an appointment at the inn
> Woolley, mourned by Julia: he would have married her

P 2   opened December 6, 1836   published by Bentley 1836, C&H 1837 **VC**

The Village Coquettes

The book for a farce/musical (music by John Hullah) whose premise is that young ladies of a silly, superficial inclination can respond to truth and sincerity. It contains a sympathetic, competent father, rare in CD.   It ran nineteen times at the St James, and CD remarked much later when asked if he had a copy, "*. . . if I knew it was in my house and if I could not get rid of it in any other way, I would burn the wing of the house where it was.*"

"'*Either the Honourable Gentleman is in the right, or he is not,*' is a phrase in *very common use within the walls of Parliament. This drama may have a plot, or it may not; and the songs may be poetry, or they may not; and the whole affair, from beginning to end, may be great nonsense, or it may not, just as the honourable gentleman or lady who reads it may happen to think.*"

Lucy Benson. "Oh, sir [addressing **Squire Norton**]! call me coquette, faithless, treacherous, deceitful, what you will; I deserve it all . . . A weak, despicable vanity induced me to listen with a ready ear to your honour's addresses, and to cast away the best and noblest heart that ever woman won."

Old Benson. "'Do you know that from infancy I have almost worshipped her, fancying that I saw in her young mind the virtues of a mother, to whom the anguish of this one hour would have been worse than death! Calm!—Do you know that I have a heart and soul within me; or do you believe that because I am of lower station I am a being of a different order from yourself, and that Nature has denied me thought and feeling! Calm! Man, do you know that I am this girl's father?'"

Rose, [**Lucy**'s] cousin. "'I believe her to have an excellent disposition, though it is a little disguised by girlish levity sometimes . . . . "

Martin Stokes, "a very small farmer with a very large circle of particular friends. . . . 'You're a remarkably pleasant fellow, Stokes [says **Flam**], in general conversation—very—but when you descend into particularities, you become excessively prosy. On some points—money matters, for instance—you have a very grasping imagination, and seem disposed to dilate upon them at too great a length. You must cure yourself of this habit—you must, indeed."

> Young Benson, brother of Lucy
> Augustus Frederick Charles Thomson Camharado: married to another
> Cary, a village girl
> Hon Sparkins Flam, friend of Squire Norton's
> Hyfenstyfenlooberhausen, married to someone else
> John Maddox, attached to Rose, Lucy Benson's cousin
> Edward Montague, father
> Susan, a villager

P 3 opened March 3, 1837   not publ; U.S. reprint by J. R. Osgood 1877 **W?**

Is She his Wife? Or, Something Singular!

This one-act comic burletta had a short run at the St James. **Mrs Lovetown** feels neglected by her husband, so she stimulates his interest by making up to bachelor **Tapkins**. Overhearing (by her intent) her soliloquy of love for him, Tapkins misunderstands and concludes that she is not married to **Alfred**, who sees them together and decides to make up to **Mrs Limbury** . . .

Mrs Peter Limbury. "'This Mrs Limbury [says **Alfred**] is a vain, conceited woman, ready to receive the attentions of anybody who feigns admiration for her, partly to gratify herself, and partly to annoy the jealous little husband whom she keeps under such strict control.'"

Alfred Lovetown, Esq. "' . . . I'm tired of the country; green fields, and blooming hedges, and feathered songsters are fine things to talk about and read about and write about; but I candidly confess that I prefer paved streets, area railings, and dustman's bells, after all.'"

Mrs Lovetown. "'If I did not know you to be one of the sweetest creatures in existence, my dear, I should be strongly disposed to say that you were a very close imitation of an aggravating female' [says **Alfred**]."

"' . . . if I hadn't know *you* to be such an exquisite, good-tempered, attentive husband, I should have mistaken you for a very great brute.'"

Felix Tapkins, Esq., "formerly of the India House, Leadenhall Street, and Prospect Place, Poplar; but now of the Rustic Lodge, near Reading."

"'Felix by name, Felix by nature—what the deuce should I be unhappy for, or anybody be unhappy for?'"

> Horse: pace like a rocking-horse, carries its tail like a hat-peg
> Jim, ostler to Tapkins
> John, servant to Lovetown
> Peter Limbury, detested by Mrs Lovetown

N 2 Feb 1837-April 1839 monthly in BM   Bentley 3 vols Nov 1838 **OT**
Bradbury & Evans 1 vol 1846 *

The Adventures of

Oliver Twist

or

𝕿𝖍𝖊 𝕻𝖆𝖗𝖎𝖘𝖍 𝕭𝖔𝖞'𝖘 𝕻𝖗𝖔𝖌𝖗𝖊𝖘𝖘

"I had read of thieves by scores; seductive fellows (amiable for the most part), faultless in dress, plump in pocket, choice in horse-flesh, bold in bearing, fortunate in gallantry, great at a song, a bottle, pack of cards or dice-box, and fit companions for the bravest. But I had never met (except in HOGARTH) with the miserable reality. It appeared to me that to draw a knot of such associates in crime as really did exist; to paint them in all their deformity, in all their wretchedness, in all the squalid misery of their lives; to show them as they really were, for ever skulking uneasily through the dirtiest paths of life, with the great black ghastly gallows closing up their prospect, turn them where they might; it appeared to me that to do this, would be to attempt a something which was needed, and which would be a service to society. And I did it as I best could."

—Preface

"With the exception of some gorgeous passages, both of humour and horror, the interest of the book lies not so much in its revelation of Dickens's literary genius as in its revelation of those moral, personal, and political instincts which were the make-up of his character and the permanent support of that literary genius. It is by far the most depressing of all his books; it is in some ways the most irritating; yet its ugliness gives the last touch of honesty to all that spontaneous and splendid output. Without this one discordant note all his merriment might have seemed like levity."
GKC p39

*The publishing history of OT is too complex to be given properly in a few lines. Kathleen Tillotson's Introduction to Oxford University Press's Clarendon edition (1966) summarizes it.

PRÉCIS

A boy child is born in a workhouse, his mother dying unidentified. The beadle, **Bumble**, names him **Oliver Twist**, and he survives. Representing his starving peers, he asks for "more." It is predicted he will be hung. 1-2

At nine, he takes service with **Sowerberry**, undertaker, having escaped chimney-sweeping for the harsh **Gamfield**. He meets charity boy **Noah Claypole**, and **Charlotte**, maid-servant. He observes privation, attends an abject funeral and mourns professionally as a juvenile mute. 3-5

Goaded into thrashing Noah, Oliver is thrashed in turn and runs away to London, encountering **Jack Dawkins**, the **Artful Dodger**, en route. 6-8

The Dodger brings Oliver to **Fagin**, teacher and mentor of pickpockets, who sends him out to learn the trade. He is chased when Mr **Brownlow**'s handkerchief is lifted by the Dodger and taken to Mr **Fang**'s court. A bookstall keeper exonerates him. Brownlow takes him home. Oliver's resemblance to a lady's portrait is remarked. 9-11

Fearing exposure, Fagin intrigues with **Bill Sikes** and **Nancy**, his girl, to locate and recapture Oliver. Oliver goes on an errand for Brownlow, whose friend **Grimwig** predicts he will not return. Nancy waylays him, returns him to Fagin, then protects him from ill-treatment. 12-16

Brownlow advertises for Oliver and gets Bumble instead. Fagin and Sikes plan to involve Oliver in a robbery, and Bill takes him to the site. Oliver, the smallest of the burglars, is inserted in the house and is shot. 17-22

Bumble prepares to woo Mrs **Carney**, matron of the workhouse. She is summoned to the bedside of the dying **Sally**, who had tended Oliver's mother. A secret is almost revealed. Two old paupers overhear. 23-24

Searching for Oliver, Fagin meets with **Monks**, who saw Oliver caught in the pickpocket episode and is mysteriously interested in him. Bumble completes his wooing and denounces Noah and Charlotte for their own. 25-27

Sikes has abandoned wounded Oliver, who crawls back to the burgled house and is put to bed under care of **Rose Maylie**. Mr **Losberne**, local surgeon, convinces the butler **Giles** and the police of Oliver's innocence. 28-31

Losberne tries ineptly to help Oliver confirm his story of Fagin. Brownlow has left for the West Indies. Rose becomes ill, and on an errand for her, Oliver bumps into Monks. Rose survives and recovers. She declines a suitor, **Harry Maylie**, because her birth is clouded. 32-36

Bumble, humbled by his new wife, seeks pub solace and encounters Monks. The Bumbles and Monks conspire to conceal Oliver's identity. 37-38

Monks and Fagin, overheard by Nancy, plot against Oliver. Nancy warns Rose, and Monks is revealed as Oliver's half-brother, seeking to steal his inheritance. Oliver finds that Brownlow has returned, and Rose reunites them. They plan to frustrate Monks. 39-41

Noah and Charlotte turn up and connect with Fagin. The Dodger has been arrested, and Noah observes his trial, then follows Nancy at Fagin's behest. Noah overhears her with Brownlow and Rose. He reports to Fagin, who tells Sikes. Sure she has betrayed him, Sikes awakens Nancy, murders her, then flees with his dog. 42-48

Brownlow has had Monks seized. He confronts him and clarifies the rights of Oliver. Sikes is pursued and cornered. The Dodger's colleague **Charley Bates** calls for help. Sikes hangs himself trying to escape. His dog dies. 49-50

The Bumbles exposed, Oliver's origin is fully explained. Rose is his aunt, her birth legitimate. Fagin, taken, tried and condemned to death, surrenders relevant papers. Rose and Harry marry. Brownlow adopts Oliver. The Bumbles lose their livelihoods. Monks is exiled and dies. 51-53

CONTENTS

CHARACTERS

Apothecary's apprentice, somewhat pessimistic	W	259
Artful Dodger (Jack Dawkins), a superlative stalker	P	243
Barker, Phil; a mark for fleecing	W	259
Barney, adenoidal thief	O	253
Bates, Charley; one of Fagin's dodgers	SR	249
The Baytons, abjectly poor and bereaved	O	253
Bedwin, Mrs; a refuge for Oliver	O	253
Ben, a postoffice guard	W	259
Bet (Betsy), Nancy's friend; professional of the streets	O	253
Bill, a gravedigger: "Fill up!"	W	259
Blathers, a Bow Street police officer, at ease in good society	O	254
Bolter, Morris; alias for Noah Claypole	SR	243
Book-stall keeper: insists on exonerating Oliver	O	254
Boy, in the workhouse	O	254
Boys, learning a trade with Fagin	W	259
Brittles, a manservant; still a youth	O	254
Brownlow, Oliver's benefactor with a hydraulic heart	P	237
Bull's-eye, cautiously loyal, ultimately devoted dog: *see* Sikes	(P)	248
Bumble, a beadle and a bully	P	238
Bystander, helpfully stopping Oliver	O	254
Charlotte, maidservant allied with Noah	SR	249
Chickweed, Conkey; publican and cockfighter	W	259
Chitling, Tom; one of Fagin's dodgers	O	254
Claypole, Noah; workhouse product and emptier of tills	P	241
Clergyman, a fast reader	W	259
Clerk, at a cemetery	W	259
Constable, large in all categories	O	254
Cook at an inn; good-tempered man, critical to the plot	W	259
Corney, Mrs; later Bumble, and a superior bully	SR	249

Spear-carriers chapter

The Title Role

Oliver Twist. " . . .a pale thin child, somewhat diminutive in stature, and decidedly small in circumference. But nature or inheritance had implanted a good sturdy spirit in Oliver's breast. It had had plenty of room to expand, thanks to the spare diet of the establishment; and perhaps to this circumstance may be attributed his having any ninth birth-day at all." 2

—*his mission:* "The room in which the boys were fed, was a large stone hall, with a copper at one end: out of which the master, dressed in an apron for the purpose, and assisted by one or two women, ladled the gruel at meal-times. Of this festive composition each boy had one porringer, and no more—except on occasions of great public rejoicing, when he had two ounces and a quarter of bread besides.

"The bowls never wanted washing. The boys polished them with their spoons till they shone again; and when they had performed this operation (which never took very long, the spoons being nearly as large as the bowls), they would sit staring at the copper, with such eager eyes, as if they could have devoured the very bricks of which it was composed; employing themselves, meanwhile, in sucking their fingers most assiduously, with the view of catching up any stray splashes of gruel that might have been cast thereon.

"Boys have generally excellent appetites. Oliver Twist and his companions suffered the tortures of slow starvation for three months: at last they got so voracious and wild with hunger . . . . A council was held; lots were cast who should walk up to the master after supper that evening, and ask for more; and it fell to Oliver Twist.

"The evening arrived; the boys took their places. The master, in his cook's uniform, stationed himself at the copper; his pauper assistants ranged themselves behind him; the gruel was served out; and a long grace was said over the short commons. The gruel disappeared; the boys whispered each other, and winked at Oliver; while his next neighbours nudged him. Child as he was, he was desperate with hunger, and reckless with misery. He rose from the table; and advancing to the master, basin and spoon in hand, said, somewhat alarmed at his own temerity:

"'Please, sir, I want some more.'

"The master . . . turned very pale. He gazed in stupefied astonishment on the small rebel for some seconds, and then clung for support to the copper. The assistants were paralysed with wonder; the boys with fear.

"The master aimed a blow at Oliver's head with the ladle, pinioned him in his arms; and shrieked aloud for the beadle." ¶2

CD alludes in BH 11 to a popular ballad about such a workhouse boy. He vanished after making this request and his bones were later found in the soup-copper: 'And ve all of us say, and ve say it sincere, That he was pushed in there by the overseer.' BSB p 16

—*his first meal out:* "I wish some well-fed philosopher . . . could have seen Oliver Twist clutching at the dainty viands that the dog had neglected. I wish he could have witnessed the horrible avidity with which Oliver tore the bits asunder with all the ferocity of famine. There is only one thing I should like better; and that would be to see the philosopher making the same sort of meal himself, with the same relish." 4

Other Principals

Brownlow. " . . . a very respectable-looking personage, with a powdered head and gold spectacles . . . in a bottle-green coat with a black velvet collar; wore white trousers; and carried a smart bamboo cane under his arm. He had taken up a book from the stall, and there he stood, reading away, as hard as if he were in his elbow-chair, in his own study." 10

—*dignified and plucky: see* **Fang** SR

—*his heart,* "being large enough for any six ordinary old gentlemen of humane disposition, forced a supply of tears into his eyes, by some hydraulic process which we are not sufficiently philosophical to be in a condition to explain." 12

"'My dear child,' said the old gentleman . . . 'you need not be afraid of my deserting you, unless you give me cause . . . I am more interested in your behalf than I can well account for, even to myself. The persons on whom I have bestowed my dearest love, lie deep in their graves; but, although the happiness and delight of my life lie buried there too, I have not made a coffin of my heart, and sealed it up, for ever, on my best affections. Deep affliction has but strengthened and refined them.'" 14

—*decisive:* "'You will decide quickly,' said Mr Brownlow, with perfect firmness and composure . . . [if] you appeal to my forbearance, and the mercy of those you have deeply injured, seat yourself, without a word, in that chair. It has waited for you two whole days.'

"**Monks** muttered some unintelligible words, but wavered still.

"'You will be prompt,' said Mr Brownlow. 'A word from me, and the alternative has gone forever.'

"Still the man hesitated.

"'I have not the inclination to parley,' said Mr Brownlow, 'and, as I advocate the dearest interests of others, I have not the right.'

"'Is there—' demanded Monks with a faltering tongue—'is there—no middle course?'

"'None.'

"Monks looked at the old gentleman, with an anxious eye; but, reading in his countenance nothing but severity and determination, walked into the room, and, shrugging his shoulders, sat down." 49

Bumble. "[He] was a fat man, and a choleric; so . . . he gave the little wicket a tremendous shake, and then bestowed upon it a kick which could have emanated from no leg but a beadle's. . . Mr. Bumble had a great idea of his oratorical powers and his importance." 2

—*literary turn:* "'We name our foundlings in alphabetical order. The last was a S–Swubble, I named him. This was a T—**Twist**, I named *him*. The next one as comes will be Unwin, and the next Vilkins. I have got names ready made to the end of the alphabet, and all the way through it again, when we come to Z.'

"'Why, you're quite a literary character, sir!' said **Mrs Mann**." 2 *And see* Volume III Essay, *The Bumble Principle*

—*qualifications:* "He had a decided propensity for bullying: derived no inconsiderable pleasure from the exercise of petty cruelty; and, consequently, was (it is needless to say) a coward. This is by no means a disparagement to his character; for many official personages, who are held in high respect and admiration, are the victims of similar infirmities. The remark is made, indeed, rather in his favour than otherwise, and with a view of impressing the reader with a just sense of his qualifications for office." 37

—*the practical philosopher:* "'Ain't you a-trembling while I speak, sir?' said Mr. Bumble.

"'No!' replied **Oliver**, boldly . . . .

"'Oh, you know, Mr. Bumble, he must be mad,' said **Mrs Sowerberry**. 'No boy in half his sense could venture to speak so to you.'

"'It's not Madness, ma'am,' replied Mr. Bumble, after a few moments of deep meditation. It's Meat.'

"'What?' exclaimed Mrs. Sowerberry.

"'Meat, ma'am, meat,' replied Mr. Bumble, with stern emphasis. 'You've over-fed him, ma'am. You've raised a artificial soul and spirit in him, ma'am, unbecoming a person of his condition: as the board, Mrs. Sowerberry, who are practical philosophers, will tell you. What have paupers to do with soul or spirit? It's quite enough that we let 'em have live bodies. If you had kept the boy on gruel, ma'am, this would never have happened."' 7

—*wooing:* "'**Mrs Corney**, ma'am,' said Mr Bumble, slowly, and marking the time with his teaspoon, 'I mean to say this, ma'am' that any cat or kitten, that could live with you, ma'am, and not be fond of its home, must be a ass, ma'am.'

"'Oh, Mr Bumble!' remonstrated Mrs Corney.

"'It's of no use disguising facts, ma'am,' said Mr Bumble, slowly flourishing the teaspoon with a kind of amorous dignity which made him doubly impressive; 'I would drown it myself, with pleasure.'

"'Then you're a cruel man,' said the matron vivaciously, as she held out her hand for the beadle's cup; 'and a very hard-hearted man besides.'

"'Hard-hearted, ma'am?' said Mr Bumble. 'Hard?' Mr Bumble resigned his cup without another word; squeezed Mrs Corney's little finger as she took it; and inflicting two open handed slaps upon his laced waistcoat, gave a mighty sigh, and hitched his chair a very little morsel farther from the fire.

"It was a round table; and as Mrs Corney and Mr Bumble had been sitting opposite each other, with no great space between them, and fronting the fire, it will be seen that Mr Bumble, in receding from the fire, and still keeping at the table, increased the distance between himself and Mrs Corney; which proceeding, some prudent readers will doubtless be disposed to admire, and to consider an act of great heroism on Mr Bumble's part: he being in some sort tempted by time, place, and opportunity, to give utterance to certain soft nothings, which however well they may become the lips of the light and thoughtless, do seem immeasurably beneath the dignity of judges of the land, members of parliament, ministers of state, lord mayors, and other great public functionaries, but more particularly beneath the stateliness and gravity of a beadle: who (as is well known) should be the sternest and most inflexible among them all.

"Whatever were Mr Bumble's intentions, however (and no doubt they were of the best): it unfortunately happened, as has been twice before remarked, that the table was a round one; consequently Mr Bumble, moving his chair by little and little, soon began to diminish the distance between himself and the matron; and, continuing to travel round the outer edge of the circle, brought his chair, in time, close to that in which the matron was seated. Indeed, the two chairs touched; and when they did so, Mr Bumble stopped.

"Now, if the matron had moved her chair to the right, she would have been scorched by the fire; and if to the left, she must have fallen into Mr Bumble's arms; so (being a discreet matron, and no doubt foreseeing these consequences at a glance) she remained where she was, and handed Mr Bumble another cup of tea . . . .

"The beadle drank his tea to the last drop; finished a piece of toast; whisked the crumbs off his knees; wiped his lips; and deliberately kissed the matron.

"'Mr Bumble!' cried that discreet lady in a whisper; for the fright was so great, that she had quite lost her voice, 'Mr Bumble, I shall scream!' Mr Bumble made no reply; but in a slow and dignified manner, put his arm round the matron's waist." 23

—*defeated:* "'The prerogative of a man is to command.'

"'And what's the prerogative of a woman, in the name of Goodness?' cried the relict of Mr. Corney deceased.

"'To obey, ma'am,' thundered Mr. Bumble. 'Your late unfortunate husband should have taught it you; and then, perhaps he might have been alive now. I wish he was, poor man!'

"Mrs Bumble, seeing at a glance, that the decisive moment had now arrived, and that a blow struck for the mastership on one side or other, must necessarily be final and conclusive, no sooner heard this allusion to the dead and gone, than she dropped into a chair, and with a loud scream that Mr. Bumble was a hard-hearted brute, fell into a paroxysm of tears.

"But, tears were not the things to find their way to Mr. Bumble's soul; his heart was waterproof. Like washable beaver hats that improve with rain, his nerves were rendered stouter and more vigorous, by showers of tears, which, being tokens of weakness and so far tacit admissions of his own power, pleased and exalted him. He eyed his good lady with looks of great satisfaction, and begged, in an encouraging manner, that she should cry her hardest: the exercise being looked upon, by the faculty, as strongly conducive to health.

"'It opens the lungs, washes the countenance, exercises the eyes, and softens down the temper,' said Mr. Bumble. 'So cry away.'

"As he discharged himself of this pleasantry, Mr. Bumble took his hat from a peg, and putting it on, rather rakishly, on one side, as a man might, who felt he had asserted his superiority in a becoming manner, thrust his hands into his pockets, and sauntered towards the door, with much ease and waggishness depicted in his whole appearance.

"Now, Mrs. Corney that was, had tried the tears, because they were less troublesome than a manual assault; but, she was quite prepared to make trial of the latter mode of proceeding, as Mr. Bumble was not long in discovering.

"The first proof he experienced of the fact, was conveyed in a hollow sound, immediately succeeded by the sudden flying off of his hat to the opposite end of the room. This preliminary proceeding laying bare his head, the expert lady, clasping him tightly round the throat with one hand, inflicted a shower of blows (dealt with singular vigour and dexterity) upon it with the other. This done, she created a little variety by scratching his face, and tearing his hair; and, having, by this time, inflicted as much punishment as she deemed necessary for the offence, she pushed him over a chair, which was luckily well situated for the purpose: and defied him to talk about his prerogative again, if he dared." 37

—*and the Law:* "'It was all Mrs. Bumble. She *would* do it,' urged Mr. Bumble; first looking round to ascertain that his partner had left the room.

"'That is no excuse,' replied Mr. **Brownlow.** '. . . the law supposes that your wife acts under your direction.'

"'If the law supposes that,' said Mr. Bumble, squeezing his hat emphatically in both hands, 'the law is a ass—a idiot. If that's the eye of the law, the law is a bachelor; and the worst I wish the law is, that his eye may be opened by experience—by experience.'" 51

Noah Claypole "entered the shop with a dignified air, which did him great credit. It is difficult for a large-headed, small-eyed youth, of lumbering make and heavy countenance, to look dignified under any circumstances, but it is more especially so, when superadded to these personal attractions are a red nose and yellow smalls." 5

" . . . [he] was one of those long-limbed, knock-kneed, shambling, bony people, to whom it is difficult to assign any precise age—looking as they do, when they are yet boys, like undergrown men, and when they are almost men, like overgrown boys." 42

—*gallantry:* "'Come here, **Charlotte**, and I'll kiss yer.'

"'What!' said Mr **Bumble**, bursting into the room. 'Say that again, sir.'

"Charlotte uttered a scream, and hid her face in her apron. Mr Claypole, without making any further change in his position than suffering his legs to reach the ground, gazed at the beadle in drunken terror.

"'Say it again, you wile, owdacious fellow!' said Mr Bumble. 'How dare you mention such a thing, sir? And how dare you encourage him, you insolent minx? Kiss her!' exclaimed Mr Bumble, in strong indignation. 'Faugh!'

"'I didn't mean to do it!' said Noah, blubbering. 'She's always a-kissing of me, whether I like it, or not.'

"'Oh, Noah,' cried Charlotte, reproachfully.

"'Yer are; yer know yer are!' retorted Noah. 'She's always a-doin' of it. Mr Bumble, sir; she chucks me under the chin, please, sir; and makes all manner of love!'" 27

George Cruikshank

—*ambitions:* "'I mean to be a gentleman,' said Mr Claypole . . . . 'No more jolly old coffins, **Charlotte**, but a gentleman's life for me: and, if yer like yer shall be a lady.'

"'I should like that well enough, dear,' replied Charlotte; 'but tills ain't to be emptied every day, and people to get clear off after it.'

"'Tills be blowed!' said Mr Claypole; 'there's more things besides tills to be emptied.'

"'What do you mean?' asked his companion.

"'Pockets, women's ridicules, houses, mail-coaches, banks!' said Mr Claypole, rising with the porter.

"'But you can't do all that, dear,' said Charlotte.

"'I shall look out to get into company with them as can,' replied Noah. 'They'll be able to make us useful some way or another. Why, you yourself are worth fifty women; I never see such a precious sly and deceitful creetur as yer can be when I let yer.'

"'Lor, how nice it is to hear you say so!' exclaimed Charlotte, imprinting a kiss upon his ugly face." 42

—undercover: "'What name shall I tell my good friend?'

"'Mr Bolter,' replied Noah, who had prepared himself for such an emergency. 'Mr **Morris Bolter**. This is Mrs Bolter.'

"'Mrs Bolter's humble servant,' said **Fagin**, bowing with grotesque politeness. 'I hope I shall know her better very shortly.'

"'Do you hear the gentleman, **Charlotte**?' thundered Mr Claypole.

"'Yes, Noah, dear!' replied Mrs Bolter, extending her hand.

"'She calls me Noah, as a sort of fond way of talking,' said Mr Morris Bolter, late Claypole, turning to Fagin. 'You understand?'

"'Oh, yes, I understand—perfectly,' replied Fagin, telling the truth for once." 52

—envoi: "After some consideration, he went into a business as an Informer, in which calling he realises a genteel subsistence. His plan is, to walk out once a week during church time attended by **Charlotte** in respectable attire. The lady faints away at the doors of charitable publicans, and the gentleman being accommodated with three-pennyworth of brandy to restore her, lays an information next day, and pockets half the penalty. Sometimes Mr Claypole faints himself, but the result is the same." 53

Artful Dodger (Jack/John Dawkins). " . . . one of the queerest looking boys that **Oliver** had ever seen. He was a snub-nosed, flat-browed, common-faced boy enough; and as dirty a juvenile as one would wish to see; but he had about him all the airs and manners of a man. He was short of his age [about ten or eleven]: with rather bow-legs, and little, sharp, ugly eyes. His hat was stuck on the top of his head so lightly, that it threatened to fall off every moment—and would have done so, very often, if the wearer had not had a knack of every now and then giving his head a sudden twitch, which brought it back to its old place again. He wore a man's coat, which reached nearly to his heels. He had turned the cuffs back, half-way up his arm, to get his hands out of the sleeves: apparently with the ultimate view of thrusting them into the pockets of his corduroy trousers; for there he kept them. He was, altogether, as roystering and swaggering a young gentleman as ever stood four feet six, or something less, in his bluchers." 8

—in the dock: "It was indeed Mr Dawkins, who, shuffling into the office with the big coat sleeves tucked up as usual, his left hand in his pocket, and his hat in his right hand, preceded the jailer, with a rolling gait altogether indescribable, and, taking his place in the dock, requested in an audible voice to know what he was placed in that 'ere disgraceful sitivation for. . . . 'I'm an Englishman, ain't I? . . . Where are my priwileges?'

"'You'll get your privileges soon enough,' retorted the jailer, 'and pepper with 'em.'

"'We'll see wot the Secretary of State for the Home Affairs has got to say to the beaks, if I don't,' replied Mr Dawkins. 'Now then! Wot is this here business? I shall thank the madg'strates to dispose of this here little affair, and not to keep me while they read the paper, for I've got an appointment with a genelman in the City, and as I'm a man of my word, and wery punctual in business matters, he'll go away if I ain't there to my time, and then pr'aps there won't be an action for damage against them as kep me away. Oh no, certainly not!' . . . .

"'I never see such an out-and-out young wagabond, your worship,' observed the officer with a grin. 'Do you mean to say anything, you young shaver?'

"'No,' replied the Dodger,' not here, for this ain't the shop for justice; besides which, my attorney is a-breakfasting this morning with the Wice President of the House of Commons; but I shall have something to say elsewhere, and so will he, and so will a wery numerous and 'spectable circle of acquaintance as'll make them beaks wish they'd never been born, or that they'd got their footmen to hang 'em up to their own hat-pegs, 'afore they let 'em come out this morning to try it on upon me. I'll . . . .

" . . . the Dodger suffered himself to be led off by the collar; threatening, till he got into the yard, to make a parliamentary business of it; and then grinning in the officer's face, with great glee and self-approval." 43 *And see* SB/CC

Fagin. " . . . a very old shrivelled Jew, whose villainous-looking and repulsive face was obscured by a quantity of matted red hair. He was dressed in a greasy flannel gown, with his throat bare . . . ." 8

—*as pedagogue:* " . . . the merry old gentleman and the two boys played at a very curious and uncommon game, which was performed in this way. The merry old gentleman, placing a snuff-box in one pocket of his trousers, a note-case in the other, and a watch in his waistcoat pocket, with a guard-chain round his neck, and sticking a mock diamond pin in his shirt: buttoned his coat tight round him, and putting his spectacle-case and handkerchief in his pockets, trotted up and down the room with a stick, in imitation of the manner in which old gentlemen walk about the streets . . . .

"Sometimes he stopped at the fire-place, and sometimes at the door, making believe that he was staring with all his might into shop-windows. At such times he would look constantly round him, for fear of thieves, and would keep slapping all his pockets in turn, to see that he hadn't lost anything, in such a very funny and natural manner, that **Oliver** laughed till the tears ran down his face.

"All this time, the two boys followed him closely about: getting out of his sight, so nimbly, every time he turned round, that it was impossible to follow their motions. At last, the **Dodger** trod upon his toes, or ran upon his boot accidentally, while **Charley Bates** stumbled up against him behind; and in that one moment they took from him, with the most extraordinary rapidity, snuff-box, note-case, watch-guard, chain, shirt-pin, pocket-handkerchief, even the spectacle-case. If the old gentleman felt a hand in any one of his pockets, he cried out where it was; and then the game began all over again." ¶9

—*his moral standards:* "Whenever the **Dodger** or **Charley Bates** came home at night, empty-handed, he would expatiate with great vehemence on the misery of idle and lazy habits; and would enforce upon them the necessity of an active life, by sending them supperless to bed. On one occasion, indeed, he even went so far as to knock them both down a flight of stairs; but this was carrying out his virtuous precepts to an unusual extent." 10

—*taking a stroll:* "As he glided stealthily along, creeping beneath the shelter of the walls and doorways, the hideous old man seemed like some loathsome reptile, engendered in the slime and darkness through which he moved: crawling forth, by night, in search of some rich offal for a meal."19

—*contemplating death:* "It was not until the night of this last awful day, that a withering sense of his helpless, desperate state came in its full intensity upon his blighted soul; not that he had ever held any defined or positive hope of mercy, but that he had never been able to consider more than the dim probability of dying so soon . . . . He had sat there, awake, but dreaming. Now, he started up, every minute, and with gasping mouth and burning skin, hurried to and fro, in such a paroxysm of fear and wrath that even [the guards]—used to such sights—recoiled from him with horror. He grew so terrible, at last, in all the tortures of his evil conscience, that one man could not bear to sit there, eyeing him alone; and so the two kept watch together.

" . . . his head was bandaged with a linen cloth. His red hair hung down upon his bloodless face; his beard was torn, and twisted into knots; his eyes shone with a terrible light; his unwashed flesh crackled with the fever that burnt him up. " 52

Rose Maylie (actually **Fleming**). "[She] was in the lovely bloom and springtime of womanhood; at that age, when, if ever angels be for God's good purposes enthroned in mortal forms, they may be, without impiety, supposed to abide in such as hers.

"She was not past seventeen. Cast in so slight and exquisite a mould; so mild and gentle; so pure and beautiful; that earth seemed not her element, nor its rough creatures her fit companions. The very intelligence that shone in her deep blue eye, and was stamped upon her noble head, seemed scarcely of her

age, or of the world; and yet the changing expression of sweetness and good
humour, the thousand lights that played about the face, and left no shadow
there; above all, the smile, the cheerful, happy smile, were made for Home, and
fireside peace and happiness." 29

—*ill:* " . . . the hue of her countenance had changed to a marble whiteness.
Its expression had lost nothing of its beauty; but it was changed; and there
was an anxious, haggard look about the gentle face, which it had never worn
before. Another minute, and it was suffused with a crimson flush: and a heavy
wildness came over the soft blue eye. Again this disappeared, like the shadow
thrown by a passing cloud; and she was once more deadly pale." 33

Nancy. "[She and **Bet**] wore a good deal of hair, not very neatly turned up
behind, and were rather untidy about the shoes and stockings. They were not
exactly pretty, perhaps; but they had a great deal of colour in their faces, and
looked quite stout and hearty. Being remarkably free and agreeable in their
manners, **Oliver** thought them very nice girls indeed." 9

—*humanity:* "The Jew inflicted a smart blow on Oliver's shoulders with the club; and was raising it for a second, when the girl, rushing forward, wrested it from his hand. She flung it into the fire, with a force that brought some of the glowing coals whirling out into the room.

"'I won't stand by and see it done, **Fagin**,' cried the girl. 'You've got the boy, and what more would you have?—Let him be—let him be—or I shall put that mark on some of you, that will bring me to the gallows before my time.'

"The girl stamped her foot violently on the floor as she vented this threat; and with her lips compressed, and her hands clenched, looked alternately at the Jew and the other robber: her face quite colourless from the passion of rage into which she had gradually worked herself." 16

—*shame:* "The girl's life had been squandered in the streets, and among the most noisome of the stews and dens of London, but there was something of the woman's original nature left in her still; and when she heard a light step approaching . . . and thought of the wide contrast which the small room would in another moment contain, she felt burdened with the sense of her own deep shame, and shrunk as though she could scarcely bear the presence of [**Rose Maylie**] with whom she had sought this interview." 40

—*scruples:* "She remembered that both the crafty Jew and the brutal **Sikes** had confided to her schemes, which had been hidden from all others: in the full confidence that she was trustworthy and beyond the reach of their suspicion. Vile as those schemes were, desperate as were their originators, and bitter as were her feelings towards **Fagin** . . . still, there were times when, even towards him, she felt some relenting, lest her disclosure should bring him within the iron grasp he had so long eluded, and he should fall at last—richly as he merited such a fate—by her hand." 44

Bill Sikes and **Bull's-eye**. "'Come in, you sneaking warmint; wot are you stopping outside for, as if you was ashamed of your master! Come in!'

"The man who growled out these words, was a stoutly-built fellow of about five-and-thirty, in a black velveteen coat, very soiled drab breeches, lace-up half boots, and grey cotton stockings, which inclosed a bulky pair of legs, with large swelling calves—the kind of legs, which in such costume, always look in an unfinished and incomplete state without a set of fetters to garnish them. He had a brown hat on his head, and a dirty belcher handkerchief round his neck: with the long frayed ends of which he smeared the beer from his face as he spoke. He disclosed, when he had done so, a broad heavy countenance with a beard of three days' growth, and two scowling eyes; one of which displayed various parti-coloured symptoms of having been recently damaged by a blow.

"'Come in, d'ye hear?' growled this engaging ruffian.

"A white shaggy dog [**Bull's-eye**] with his face scratched and torn in twenty different places, skulked into the room." 13

—*their end nears:* "The dog, though—if any descriptions of him were out, it would not be forgotten that the dog was missing, and had probably gone with him. This might lead to his apprehension as he passed along the streets. He resolved to drown him, and walked on, looking about for a pond: picking up a heavy stone and tying it to his handkerchief as he went.

"The animal looked up into his master's face while these preparations were making; and, whether his instinct apprehended something of their purpose, or the robber's sidelong look at him was sterner than ordinary, skulked a little farther in the rear than usual, and cowered as he came more slowly along." 48

—*it arrives:* " . . . the murderer, looking behind him on the roof, threw his arms above his head, and uttered a yell of terror.

"'The eyes again!' he cried in an unearthly screech.

"Staggering as if struck by lightning, [Sikes] lost his balance and tumbled over the parapet. The noose was at his neck. It ran up with his weight, tight as a bow-string, and swift as the arrow it speeds. He fell for five and thirty feet. There was a sudden jerk, a terrific convulsion of the limbs; and there he hung, with the open knife clenched in his stiffening hand . . . .

"A dog, which had lain concealed till now, ran backwards and forwards on the parapet with a dismal howl, and, collecting himself for a spring, jumped for the dead man's shoulders. Missing his aim, he fell into the ditch, turning completely over as he went; and striking his head against a stone, dashed out his brains." 50

Supporting Roles

Charley Bates. "'You'd like to be able to make pocket-handkerchiefs as easy as Charley Bates, wouldn't you, my dear?' said the Jew.

"'Very much, indeed, if you'll teach me, sir,' replied **Oliver**.

"Master Bates saw something so exquisitely ludicrous in this reply that he burst into another laugh; which laugh, meeting the coffee he was drinking, and carrying it down some wrong channel, very nearly terminated in his premature suffocation." 9

George Cruikshank

Charlotte. " . . . a slatternly girl, in shoes down at heel, and blue worsted stockings very much out of repair." 4

She "was young, but of a robust and hardy make, as she need have been to bear the weight of the heavy bundle which was strapped to her back." 42 *And see* **Noah Claypole** P

Mrs Corney. "[She] sat her herself down before a cheerful fire in her own little room, and glanced, with no small degree of complacency, at a small round table: on which stood a tray of corresponding size, furnished with all necessary materials for the most grateful meal that matrons enjoy . . . . The small teapot, and the single cup, had awakened in her mind sad recollections of **Mr Corney**

(who had not been dead more than five-and-twenty years); and she was over-powered.

"'I shall never get another!' said Mrs. Corney, pettishly. 'I shall never get another—like him'" 23 *But see* **Bumble** P—*wooing*

Fang, "who was a lean, long-backed, stiff-necked, middle-sized man, with no great quantity of hair, and what he had, growing on the back and sides of his head. His face was stern, and much flushed. If he were really not in the habit of drinking rather more than was exactly good for him, he might have brought an action against his countenance for libel, and have recovered heavy damages.

"[He] was . . . perusing a leading article in a newspaper of the morning, adverting to some recent decision of his, and commending him, for the three hundred and fiftieth time, to the special and particular notice of the Secretary of State for the Home Department. He was out of temper; and he looked up with an angry scowl . . . .

"'Officer!' said Mr Fang, tossing the card contemptuously away with the newspaper. 'Who is this fellow?'

"'My name, sir,' said the old gentleman, speaking *like* a gentleman, 'my name, sir, is **Brownlow**. Permit me to inquire the name of the magistrate who offers a gratuitous and unprovoked insult to a respectable person, under the protection of the bench.'" 11

Grimwig. " . . . a stout old gentleman, rather lame in one leg . . . in a blue coat, striped waistcoat, nankeen breeches and gaiters, and a broad-brimmed white hat, with the sides turned up with green. A very small-plaited shirt frill stuck out from his waistcoat; and a very long steel watch-chain, with nothing but a key at the end, dangled loosely below it. The ends of his white neckerchief were twisted into a ball about the size of an orange; the variety of shapes into which his countenance was twisted, defy description. He had a manner of screwing his head on one side when he spoke; and of looking out of the corners of his eyes at the same time: which irresistibly reminded the beholder of a parrot." 14

—*envoi:* " . . . Mr Grimwig plants, fishes, and carpenters, with great ardour; doing everything in a very singular and unprecedented manner, but always maintaining with his favourite asseveration, that his mode is the right one. On Sundays, he never fails to criticise the sermon to the young clergyman's face: always informing Mr **Losberne**, in strict confidence afterwards, that he considers it an excellent performance, but deems it as well not to say so." 53

Mr Losberne. " . . . a surgeon in the neighbourhood, known through a circuit of ten miles round as 'the doctor,' had grown fat, more from good humour than from good living: and was as kind and hearty, and withal as eccentric an old bachelor, as will be found in five times that space, by any explorer alive." 29

—*practicality:* "'Dear, dear! So unexpected! In the silence of night, too!'

"The doctor seemed especially troubled by the fact of the robbery having been unexpected, and attempted in the night-time; as if it were the established custom of gentlemen in the house-breaking way to transact business at noon, and to make an appointment, by post, a day or two previous." 29

—*his instincts:* " . . . the excellent doctor had never acted upon anything but impulse all through his life, and it was no bad compliment to the nature of the impulses which governed him, that so far from being involved in any peculiar troubles or misfortunes, he had the warmest respect and esteem of all who knew him." 32

—envoi: "Soon after the marriage of the young people [**Rose** and **Harry Maylie**], the worthy doctor returned to Chertsey, where, bereft of the presence of his old friends, he would have been discontented if his temperament had admitted of such a feeling; and would have turned quite peevish if he had known how. For two or three months, he contented himself with hinting that he feared the air began to disagree with him; then, finding that the place really no longer was, to him, what it had been, he settled his business on his assistant, took a bachelor's cottage outside the village of which his young friend was pastor, and instantaneously recovered. Here, he took to gardening, planting, fishing, carpentering, and various other pursuits of a similar kind: all undertaken with his characteristic impetuosity. In each and all, he has since become famous throughout the neighborhood, as a most profound authority." 53

Harry Maylie. "[He] seemed about five-and-twenty years of age, and was of the middle height; his countenance was frank and handsome; and his demeanour easy and prepossessing." 34

—eloquent: "'I was brought here, by the most dreadful and agonising of all apprehensions,' said the young man; 'the fear of losing the one dear being on whom my every wish and hope are fixed. You had been dying: trembling between earth and heaven. . . .

"'A creature,' continued the young man, passionately, 'a creature as fair and innocent of guile as one of God's own angels, fluttered between life and death. Oh! who could hope, when the distant world to which she was akin, half opened to her view, that she would return to the sorrow and calamity of this!

"**Rose**, Rose, to know that you were passing away like some soft shadow, which a light from above, casts upon the earth; to have no hope that you would be spared to those who linger here; hardly to know a reason why you should be; to feel that you belonged to that bright sphere whither so many of the fairest and the best have winged their early flight; and yet to pray, amid all these consolations, that you might be restored to those who loved you—these were distractions almost too great to bear.

"They were mine, by day and night; and with them, came such a rushing torrent of fears, and apprehensions, and selfish regrets, lest you should die, and never know how devotedly I loved you, as almost bore down sense and reason in its course. You recovered. Day by day, and almost hour by hour, some drop of health came back, and mingling with the spent and feeble stream of life which circulated languidly within you, swelled it again to a high and rushing tide. I have watched you change almost from death, to life, with eyes that turned blind with their eagerness and deep affection. Do not tell me that you wish I had lost this; for it has softened my heart to all mankind.'" 35

Mrs Maylie. "[She] was well advanced in years, but the high-backed oaken chair in which she sat, was not more upright than she. Dressed with the utmost nicety and precision, in a quaint mixture of by-gone costume, with some slight concessions to the prevailing taste, which rather served to point the old style pleasantly than to impair its effect, she sat, in a stately manner, with her hands folded on the table before her. Her eyes (and age had dimmed but little of their brightness) were attentively fixed upon her young companion." 29

—her courage: " . . . she checked her lamentations [over **Rose**'s illness] as though by one effort; and drawing herself up as she spoke, became composed and firm. [**Oliver**] was still more astonished to find that this firmness lasted;

and that, under all the care and watching which ensued, Mrs Maylie was ever ready and collected: performing all the duties which devolved upon her, steadily, and, to all external appearance, even cheerfully. But he was young, and did not know what strong minds are capable of, under trying circumstances. How should he, when their possessors so seldom know themselves?" 33

Monks. " . . . . Death!' muttered the man to himself, glaring at [**Oliver**] with his large dark eyes. 'Who would have thought it! Grind him to ashes! He'd start up from a stone coffin, to come in my way! . . . . Rot you!' murmured the man, in a horrible passion; between his clenched teeth . . . .

"The man shook his fist, as he uttered these words incoherently. He advanced towards Oliver, as if with the intention of aiming a blow at him, but fell violently on the ground: writhing and foaming, in a fit." 33

—*described:* "'He is tall . . . and a strongly made man, but not stout; he has a lurking walk; and as he walks, constantly looks over his shoulder, first on one side, and then on the other. Don't forget that, for his eyes are sunk in his head so much deeper than any other man's, that you might almost tell him by that alone. His face is dark, like his hair and eyes; and, although he can't be more than six or eight and twenty, withered and haggard. His lips are often discoloured and disfigured with the marks of teeth; for he has desperate fits, and sometimes even bites his hands and covers them with wounds . . . . " 46

Sowerberry, undertaker. " . . . a tall, gaunt, large-jointed man . . . in a suit of threadbare black, with darned cotton stockings of the same colour, and shoes to answer. His features were not naturally intended to wear a smiling aspect, but he was in general rather given to professional jocosity. His step was elastic, and his face betokened inward pleasantry . . . ." 4

Mrs Sowerberry."[She] presented the form of a short, thin, squeezed-up woman, with a vixenish countenance." 4

—*matrimonial diplomacy:* "'Oh, don't tell me what you were going to say,' interposed Mrs. Sowerberry. 'I am nobody; don't consult me, pray. *I* don't want to intrude upon your secrets.' As Mrs. Sowerberry said this, she gave an hysterical laugh, which threatened violent consequences.

"'But my dear,' said Sowerberry, 'I want to ask your advice.'

"'No, no, don't ask mine,' replied Mrs. Sowerberry, in an affecting manner: 'ask somebody else's.' Here, there was another hysterical laugh, which frightened Mr. Sowerberry very much. This is a very common and much-approved matrimonial course of treatment, which is often very effective. It at once reduced Mr. Sowerberry to begging, as a special favour, to be allowed to say what Mrs. Sowerberry was most curious to hear. After a short altercation of less than three quarters of an hour's duration, the permission was most graciously conceded." 5

Others

Barney, afflicted with adenoids. " . . . another Jew: younger than **Fagin**, but nearly as vile and repulsive in appearance . . . . 'Is anybody here, Barney?' inquired Fagin . . . .

"'Dot a shoul,' replied Barney; whose words: whether they came from the heart or not: made their way through the nose. . . . 'Dobody but Biss Dadsy . . . She's bid havid a plate of boiled beef id the bar. . . .'" 15

The **Baytons**. "There was no fire in the room; but a **man** was crouching, mechanically, over the empty stove. An **old woman**, too, had drawn a low stool to the cold hearth, and was sitting beside him. There were some ragged **children** in another corner; and in a small recess, opposite the door, there lay upon the ground, something covered with an old blanket . . . [**Oliver**] felt that it was a corpse. The man's face was thin and very pale; his hair and beard were grizzly; his eyes were bloodshot." 5

"The old woman's face was wrinkled; her two remaining teeth protruded over her under lip; and her eyes were bright and piercing. **Oliver** was afraid to look at either her or the man. They seemed so like the rats he had seen outside." 5

Mrs Bedwin. " . . . a motherly old lady, very neatly and precisely dressed . . . very gently placed **Oliver**'s head upon the pillow; and, smoothing back his hair from his forehead, looked so kindly and lovingly in his face, that he could not help placing his little withered hand in hers, and drawing it round his neck." 12

Bet (or **Betsy**). "[She] merely expressed an emphatic and earnest desire to be 'blessed' if she would; a polite and delicate evasion of the request [to reconnoiter], which shows the young lady to have been possessed of that natural good breeding which cannot bear to inflict upon a fellow-creature the pain of a direct and pointed refusal . . . [she] was gaily, not to say gorgeously attired, in a red gown, green boots, and yellow curl-papers . . . ." 13

—*distraught*: "'Poor Bet! She went to see [**Nancy**'s] Body, to speak to who it was . . . and went off mad, screaming and raving, and beating her head against the boards; so they put a strait-weskut on her and took her to the hospital—and there she is.'" 50

Blathers, a Bow Street officer, "who was a stout personage of middle height, aged about fifty: with shiny black hair, cropped pretty close; half-whiskers, a round face, and sharp eyes." 31

Book-stall keeper. " . . . a couple of men were preparing to carry the insensible boy to his cell; when an elderly man of decent but poor appearance, clad in an old suit of black, rushed hastily into the office . . . . 'I *will* speak,' cried the man; 'I will not be turned out. I saw it all. I keep the book-stall. I demand to be sworn. I will not be put down. Mr **Fang**, you must hear me. You must not refuse, sir.'

"The man was right. His manner was determined; and the matter was growing rather too serious to be hushed up." 11

Boy, in the workhouse. " . . . one boy, who was tall for his age . . . hinted darkly to his companions, that unless he had another basin of gruel *per diem*, he was afraid he might some night happen to eat the boy who slept next him, who happened to be a weakly youth of tender age. He had a wild, hungry eye; and they implicitly believed him." 2

Brittles. "'I am agreeable to anything which is agreeable to Mr **Giles**,' said a shorter man; who was by no means of a slim figure, and who was very pale in the face, and very polite: as frightened men frequently are . . . a lad of all-work: who, having entered [his mistress'] service a mere child, was treated as a promising young boy still, though he was something past thirty." 28

Bystander. "'Poor fellow!' said [**Brownlow**], 'he has hurt himself.'

"'I did that, sir,' said a great lubberly fellow, stepping forward; 'and preciously I cut my knuckle agin' his mouth. I stopped him, sir.'

"The fellow touched his hat with a grin, expecting something for his pains; but, the old gentleman, eyeing him with an expression of dislike, looked anxiously round, as if he contemplated running away . . . . " 10

Tom Chitling "was older in years than the **Dodger**: having perhaps numbered eighteen winters; but there was a degree of deference in his deportment towards that young gentleman which seemed to indicate that he felt himself conscious of a slight inferiority in point of genius and professional acquirements. He had small twinkling eyes, and a pockmarked face; wore a fur cap, a dark corduroy jacket, greasy fustian trousers, and an apron. His wardrobe was, in truth, rather out of repair . . . in consequence of having worn the regimentals for six weeks past, he had not been able to bestow any attention on his private clothes." 18

Constable. "[He] had a large staff, a large head, large features, and large half-boots; and he looked as if he had been taking a proportionate allowance of ale—as indeed he had." 4

Toby Crackit, "who was dressed in a smartly-cut snuff-coloured coat, with large brass buttons; an orange neckerchief; a coarse, staring, shawl-pattern waistcoat, and drab breeches. [He] had no very great quantity of hair, either upon his head or face; but what he had, was of a reddish dye, and tortured into long corkscrew curls, through which he occasionally thrust some very dirty fingers, ornamented with large common rings. He was a trifle above the middle size, and apparently rather weak in the legs; but this circumstance by no means detracted from his own admiration of his top-boots, which he contemplated, in their elevated situation, with lively satisfaction." 22

Dick . "The child was pale and thin; his cheeks were sunken; and his eyes large and bright. The scanty parish dress, the livery of his misery, hung loosely on his feeble body; and his young limbs had wasted away, like those of an old man . . . .

"'I should like,' faltered the child, 'if somebody that can write, would put a few words down for me on a piece of paper, and fold it up and seal it, and keep it for me, after I am laid in the ground.'

"'Why, what does the boy mean?' exclaimed Mr **Bumble**, on whom the earnest manner and wan aspect of the child had made some impression . . . .

"'I should like,' said the child, 'to leave my dear love to poor **Oliver Twist**; and to let him know how often I have sat by myself and cried to think of his wandering about in the dark nights with nobody to help him. And I should like to tell him,' said the child, pressing his small hands together, and speaking with great fervour, 'that I was glad to die when I was very young; for, perhaps, if I had lived to be a man, and had grown old, my little sister who is in Heaven, might forget me, or be unlike me; and it would be so much happier if we were both children there together.'

"Mr Bumble surveyed the little speaker, from head to foot, with indescribable astonishment; and, turning to his companion, said, 'They're all in one story, **Mrs Mann**. That out-dacious Oliver has demogalized them all!'" 17

Doctor. " . . . with a very large and loud-ticking gold watch in his hand, [he] felt [**Oliver**'s] pulse and said he was a great deal better.

"'You are a great deal better, are you not, my dear? said the gentleman.

"'Yes, thank you, sir,' replied Oliver.

"'Yes, I know you are,' said the gentleman. 'You're hungry too, an't you?'

"'No, sir,' answered Oliver.

"'Hem!' said the gentleman. 'No, I know you're not. He is not hungry, Mrs **Bedwin**,' said the gentleman: looking very wise.

"The old lady made a respectful inclination of the head, which seemed to say that she thought the doctor was a very clever man. The doctor appeared much of the same opinion himself. . . [he] hurried away: his boots creaking in a very important and wealthy manner as he went down-stairs." 12

Duff, an officer from Bow Street, "was a red-headed, bony man, in top-boots; with a rather ill-favoured countenance, and a turned-up sinister-looking nose . . . who did not appear quite so much accustomed to good society, or quite so much at his ease in it [as **Blathers**] . . . seated himself, after undergoing several muscular affections of the limbs, and forced the head of his stick into his mouth, with some embarrassment." 31

Agnes Fleming. "The patient . . . stretched out her hand towards the child . . . . She imprinted her cold white lips passionately on its forehead; passed her hands over her face; gazed wildly round; shuddered; fell back—and died. They chafed her breast, hands, and temples; but the blood had stopped for ever. They talked of hope and comfort. They had been strangers too long." 1

"'Both the nurse and doctor said, that that mother of his made her way here, against difficulties and pain that would have killed any well-disposed woman weeks before.'" 7

Gamfield. "[He] did happen to labour under the slight imputation of having bruised three or four boys to death already . . . [his] villainous countenance was a regular stamped receipt for cruelty." 3

—*on proper working conditions:* "'It's a nasty trade,' said Mr **Limbkins**, when Gamfield had again stated his wish [to apprentice **Oliver**].

"'Young boys have been smothered in chimneys before now,' said another gentleman.

"'That's acause they damped the straw afore they lit it in the chimbley to make 'em come down agin,' said Gamfield; 'that's all smoke, and no blaze; vereas smoke ain't o' no use at all in making a boy come down, for it only sinds him to sleep, and that's wot he likes. Boys is wery obstinit, and wery lazy gen'lmen, and there's nothink like a good hot blaze to make 'em come down vith a run. It's humane too, gen'lmen, acause, even if they've stuck in the chimbley, roasting their feet makes 'em struggle to hextricate theirselves.'" 3

Gentleman, in the white waistcoat. "'Compose yourself, **Bumble**, and answer me distinctly. Do I understand that he asked for more, after he had eaten the supper allotted by the dietary?'

"'He did, sir,' replied Bumble.

"'That boy will be hung,' said the gentleman in the white waistcoat. 'I know that boy will be hung.'" 2

Giles. " . . . dressed with scrupulous care in a full suit of black, [he] was in attendance upon [the **Maylies**]. He had taken his station some halfway between the sideboard and the breakfast-table; and, with his body drawn up to its full height, his head thrown back, and inclined the merest trifle on one side, his left leg advanced, and his right hand thrust into his waistcoat, while his left hung down by his side, grasping a waiter, looked like one who laboured under a very agreeable sense of his own merits and importance." 29

—-*rewarded:* " . . . having called for a mug of ale, [Mr **Giles**] announced, with an air of majesty, which was highly effective, that it had pleased his mistress, in consideration of his gallant behaviour in the occasion of that attempted robbery, to deposit, in the local savings-bank, the sum of five and twenty pounds, for his sole use and benefit. At this, the two women-servants lifted up their hands and eyes, and supposed that Mr Giles would begin to be quite proud now; whereunto Mr Giles, pulling out his shirt-frill, replied, 'No, no;' and that if they observed that he was at all haughty to his inferiors, he would thank them to tell him so. And then he made a great many other remarks, no less illustrative of his humility, which were received with equal favour and applause, and were, withal, as original and as much to the purpose, as the remarks of great men commonly are." 34

Harry. " . . . an antic fellow, half pedlar and half mountebank, who travelled about the country on foot to vend hones, strops, razors, wash-balls, harness-paste, medicine for dogs and horses, cheap perfumery, cosmetics, and such-like wares, which he carried in a case slung on his back. . . ." 48

Four **housemaids**. "**Nancy** remained, pale and almost breathless, listening with quivering lip to the very audible expressions of scorn, of which the chaste housemaids were very prolific; and of which they became still more so, when the man returned, and said the young woman was to walk up-stairs.

"'It's no good being proper in this world,' said the first housemaid.

"'Brass can do better than the gold what has stood the fire,' said the second.

"The third contented herself with wondering 'what ladies was made of;' and the fourth took the first in a quartette of 'Shameful!' with which the Dianas concluded." 39

Hunchback. " . . .a little ugly hump-backed man. . . set up a yell, and danced upon the ground, as if wild with rage . . . [and] looked into the carriage, and eyed **Oliver** for an instant with a glance so sharp and fierce and at the same time so furious and vindictive, that, waking or sleeping, he could not forget it for months afterwards . . . they could see him some distance behind: beating his feet upon the ground, and tearing his hair, in transports of real or pretended rage." 32

Kags. " . . . a robber of fifty years, whose nose had been almost beaten in, in some old scuffle, and whose face bore a frightful scar which might probably be traced to the same occasion." 50

Edward Leeford. *See* **Monks** P *and* **Mrs Leeford**

Mrs Leeford. "[Her son **Edward**] had left her, when only eighteen; robbed her of jewels and money; gambled, squandered, forged, and fled to London: where for two years he had associated with the lowest outcasts. She was sinking under a painful and incurable disease, and wished to recover him before she died.'" 51

Limbkins, chairman of the workhouse board. " . . . a particularly fat gentleman with a very round, red face." 2

Two **magistrates**. " . . . old gentlemen with powdered heads: one of whom was reading the newspaper; while the other was perusing, with the aid of a pair of tortoise-shell spectacles, a small piece of parchment which lay before him. . . [he] was half blind and half childish, so he couldn't reasonably be expected to discern what other people did . . . . " 3

Mrs Mann, supervisor of a branch-workhouse. " . . . an elderly female, who received the culprits at and for the consideration of sevenpence-halfpenny per small head per week . . . a good round diet for a child; a great deal may be got for sevenpence-halfpenny, quite enough to overload its stomach, and make it uncomfortable. The elderly female was a woman of wisdom and experience; she knew what was good for herself. So, she appropriated the greater part of the weekly stipend to her own use, and consigned the rising parochial generation to even a shorter allowance than was originally provided for them. Thereby finding in the lowest depth a deeper still; and proving herself a very great experimental philosopher." 2

Martha. " . . . a withered old female pauper, hideously ugly . . . . Her body was bent by age; her limbs trembled with palsy; her face, distorted into a mumbling leer, resembled more the grotesque shaping of some wild pencil, than the work of Nature's hand." 23

Nurse. " . . . a fat old woman who had just come: bringing with her, in a little bundle, a small Prayer Book and a large nightcap. Putting the latter on her head and the former on the table, the old woman, after telling **Oliver** that she had come to sit up with him, drew her chair close to the fire and went off into a series of short naps, chequered at frequent intervals with sundry tumblings forward, and divers moans and chokings. These, however, had no worse effect than causing her to rub her nose very hard, and then fall asleep again." 12

Old lady. " . . . the old lady, who had a ship-wrecked grandson wandering barefoot in some distant part of the earth, took pity upon the poor orphan, and gave him what little she could afford—and more—with such kind and gentle words, and such tears of sympathy and compassion, that they sank deeper into Oliver's soul, than all the sufferings he had ever undergone." 8

Sally, an ancient pauper, now dying. "'Did she drink the hot wine the doctor said she was to have?' . . . 'I tried to get it down . . . but her teeth were tight set, and she clenched the mug so hard that it was as much as I could do to get it back again. So *I* drank it; and it did me good!' 'I mind the time,' said the first speaker, 'when she would have done the same, and made rare fun of it afterwards.' 'Ay, that she would,' rejoined the other; 'she had a merry heart. A many, many, beautiful corpses she laid out, as nice and neat as wax-work.'" 24

Slout, master of the workhouse. " . . . a fat healthy man . . ." 2

Mrs Thingummy, a nurse. " . . . a pauper old woman, who was rendered rather misty by an unwonted allowance of beer . . . . 'Lor bless her heart, no [talk of death yet]! interposed the nurse, hastily depositing in her pocket a green glass bottle, the contents of which she had been tasting in a corner with evident satisfaction." 1

Tinker, assisting **Giles** and **Brittles** in the pursuit of burglars. "'I'll tell what it is, gentlemen,' said he, 'we're all afraid.'" 28

Turnpike-man. " . . . if it had not been for a good-hearted turnpike-man, and a benevolent old lady, Oliver's troubles would have been shortened by the very same process which had put an end to his mother's; in other words, he would most assuredly have fallen dead upon the king's highway. But the turnpike-man gave him a meal of bread and cheese . . . . " 8

Walk-ons

Apothecary's apprentice, watching old **Sally**. "'Oh!' said the young man, turning his face towards the bed, as if he had previously forgotten the patient, 'it's all U. P. there, **Mrs Corney**.'" 24

Phil Barker, a mark. "'I say . . . what a time this would be for a sell! I've got Phil Barker here: so drunk, that a boy might take him.'

"'Aha! But it's not Phil Barker's time,' said [**Fagin**], looking up. 'Phil has something more to do, before we can afford to part with him. . . .'" 26

Ben, a postoffice guard. "'I heered talk of a murder. . . down Spitalfields way, but I don't reckon much upon it.'" 48

Bill. "'Now, Bill!' said **Sowerberry** to the grave-digger. 'Fill up!'" 5

Boys at **Fagin**'s. "Seated around the table were four or five boys, none older than the **Dodger**, smoking long clay pipes, and drinking spirits with the air of middle-aged men." 8

Conkey Chickweed "kept a public house over Battlebridge way, and he had a cellar, where a good many young lords went to see cock-fighting, and badger-drawing, and that; and a wery intellectual manner the sports was conducted in, for I've seen 'em off'en.'" 31 *And see* **Jem Spyers**

Clergyman. " . . . the reverend gentleman, having read as much of the burial service [for **Mrs Bayton**] as could be compressed into four minutes, gave his surplice to the clerk, and walked away again." 5

Clerk at a cemetery, "who was sitting by the vestry-room fire, seemed to think it by no means improbable that it might be an hour or so, before [the **clergyman**] came." 6

Cook. "[**Nancy**'s] appeal produced an effect on a good-tempered-faced man-cook, who with some other of the servants was looking on, and who stepped forward to interfere." 39

Employee, in a hotel. "'Now, young woman!' said a smartly-dressed female, looking out from a door behind [**Nancy**], 'who do you want here?'" 39

Flutist. " . . . a miserable shoeless criminal,who had been taken up for playing the flute, and who, the offence against society having been clearly proved, had been very properly committed by Mr **Fang** to the House of Correction for one month . . . . " 13

Guard, at a post-office. "'Damn that'ere bag,' said the guard; 'are you gone to sleep in there?' 'Coming!' called the office keeper, running out. 'Coming,' growled the guard. 'Ah, and so's the young 'ooman of property that's going to take a fancy to me, but I don't know when.'" 48

Guards at Newgate Prison. " . . . two men appeared: one bearing a candle, which he thrust into an iron candlestick fixed against the wall: the other dragging in a mattress on which to pass the night; for the prisoner was to be left alone no more." 52 *See* **Fagin** P—*contemplating death*

Guards privately hired. "The door being opened, a sturdy man got out of the coach and stationed himself on one side of the steps, while another man, who had been seated on the box, dismounted too, and stood upon the other side. At a sign from Mr **Brownlow**, they helped out a third man, and taking him between them, hurried him into the house. This man was **Monks**." 49

Jailer at Newgate Prison. "[He] took the disengaged hand of **Oliver**; and, whispering him not to be alarmed, looked on without speaking." 52

Jews. "Venerable men of [**Fagin**'s] own persuasion had come to pray beside him, but he had driven them away with curses. They renewed their charitable efforts, and he beat them off." 52

Joe, hotel waiter. "To him, **Nancy** repeated her request. 'What name am I to say?' . . . .It's of no use saying any,' replied Nancy. 'Nor business?' said the man. 'No, nor that neither,' rejoined the girl. 'I must see the lady.' 'Come!' said the man, pushing her towards the door. 'None of this. Take yourself off.'" 39

Landlord of The George. " . . . a tall gentleman in a blue neckcloth, a white hat, drab breeches, and boots with tops to match, leaning against a pump by the stable-door, picking his teeth with a silver tooth-pick." 33

Landlord of The Three Cripples. " . . . a coarse, rough, heavy built fellow, who, while the songs were proceeding, rolled his eyes hither and thither, and, seeming to give himself up to joviality, had an eye for everything that was done, and an ear for everything that was said—and sharp ones, too." 26

Lively, dealer in stolen goods. " . . . a salesman of small stature, who had squeezed as much of his person into a child's chair as the chair would hold, and was smoking a pipe at his warehouse door." 26

Policeman. " . . . a police officer (who is generally the last person to arrive in such cases) at that moment made his way through the crowd, and seized **Oliver** by the collar." 10

Prisoner. "[in] prison for hawking tin saucepans without a licence; thereby doing something for his living, in defiance of the Stamp-office." 13

Jem Spyers. "' . . . one morning, he walked into the bar, and taking out his snuff-box, says, "**Chickweed**, I've found out who done this here robbery." "Have you?" said Chickweed. "Oh, my dear Spyers, only let me have wengeance, and I shall die contented! . . ." "Come, said Spyers, offering him a pinch of snuff, "none of that gammon! You did it yourself." So he had; and a good bit of money he had made by it, too. . . . '" 31

Surgeon, for the parish. "As [**Agnes Fleming**] spoke, he rose, and advancing to the bed's head, said, with more kindness than might have been expected of him:

"'Oh, you must not talk about dying yet.'" 1

Contributions to
Bentley's Miscellany

In 1837, Dickens undertook to edit for publisher Richard Bentley a new magazine, *Bentley's Miscellany*. It was a turbulent project for him. Bentley had a
strong mind of his own, and CD was pressed by hastily made overcommit-
ments. He left in early 1839, having contributed six pieces (including his
farewell); some fragments and a collaboration; and the serialized *Oliver Twist*.
"Mudfog" is Chatham, CD's home town. The correspondent reporting on The
Mudfog Association is "Boz," here given independent life.

CONTENTS

CHARACTERS

B January 1837   BM **T**

Public Life of Mr Tulrumble,
Once Mayor of Mudfog

Tulrumble succeeds the late **Sniggs** as Lord Mayor of Mudfog. The investiture procession is a catastrophe: its principal ornament, the town drunk in a suit of armour, engenders ridicule, not awe. As Mayor, Tulrumble takes it into his head to improve local morals and causes the pub to lose its music licence. Reaction is bitter: the ostracism is too much; he reverses course.

Principals

Nicholas Tulrumble. " . . . no one was so eminently distinguished, during many years, for the quiet modesty of his appearance and demeanour, as Nicholas Tulrumble, the well-known coal-dealer. However exciting the subject of discussion, however animated the tone of the debate, or however warm the personalities exchanged . . . Nicholas Tulrumble was always the same. To say truth, Nicholas, being an industrious man, and always up betimes, was apt to fall asleep when a debate began, and to remain asleep till it was over, when he would wake up very much refreshed, and give his vote with the greatest complacency."

—*as Mayor:* "He descanted in glowing terms upon the increasing depravity of his native town of Mudfog, and the excesses committed by its population . . . he went on to state, how the number of people who came out [of the Jolly Boatmen] with beer-jugs averaged twenty-one in five minutes, which, being multiplied by twelve . . . and multiplied again by fifteen . . . yielded three thousand seven hundred and eighty people with beer-jugs per day, or twenty-six thousand four hundred and sixty people with beer-jugs, per week.

"Then he proceeded to show that a tambourine and moral degradation were synonymous terms, and a fiddle and vicious propensities wholly inseparable. . . in the end, the corporation, who were posed with the figures, and sleepy with the speech, and sadly in want of dinner into the bargain, yielded the palm to Nicholas Tulrumble, and refused the music licence to the Jolly Boatmen." ¶

—a turnabout: "'Are you going to put down pipes, Mr Tulrumble?' said one.

"'Or trace the progress of crime to 'bacca?' growled another.

"'Neither,' replied Nicholas Tulrumble, shaking hands with them both, whether they would or not. 'I've come down to say that I'm very sorry for having made a fool of myself, and that I hope you'll give me up the old chair again.'"

Edward Twigger, known as **Bottle-nosed Ned**. " . . . a merry-tempered, pleasant-faced, good-for-nothing sort of vagabond, with an invincible dislike to manual labour, and an unconquerable attachment to strong beer and spirits, whom everybody knew, and nobody, except his wife, took the trouble to quarrel with . . . . He was drunk upon the average once a day, and penitent upon an equally fair calculation once a month; and when he was penitent he was invariably in the very last stage of maudlin intoxication.

George Cruikshank

"He was a ragged, roving, roaring kind of fellow, with a burly form, a sharp wit, and ready head, and could turn his hand to anything when he chose to do it. He was by no means opposed to hard labour on principle, for he would work away at a cricket-match by the day together—running, and catching, and batting, and bowling, and revelling in toil which would exhaust a galley-slave. He would have been invaluable to a fire-office; never was a man with such a natural taste for pumping engines, running up ladders, and throwing furniture out of two-pair-of-stairs' windows: nor was this the only element in which he was at home; he was a humane society in himself, a portable drag, an animated life-preserver, and had saved more people in his time from drowning than the Plymouth life-boat, or **Captain Manby**'s apparatus.

"With all these qualifications, notwithstanding his dissipation, Bottle-nosed Ned was a general favourite; and the authorities of Mudfog, remembering his numerous services to the population, allowed him in return to get drunk in his own way, without the fear of stocks, fine, or imprisonment. He had a general licence, and he showed his sense of the compliment by making the most of it."

—*common sense:* "'I want you to wear this [suit of brass armour of gigantic dimensions] next Monday, Twigger,' said the Mayor . . . .

"'I couldn't stand under it, sir,' said Twigger; 'it would make mashed potatoes of me if I attempted it . . . . I should as soon have thought of a man's wearing the case of an eight-day clock to save his linen,' said Twigger, casting a look of apprehension at the brass suit . . . ."

—*inspirited:* " . . . down Ned Twigger sat himself in his brass livery on the top of the kitchen-table; and in a mug of something strong, paid for by the unconscious **Nicholas Tulrumble**, and provided by the companionable **footman**, drank success to the Mayor and his procession . . . .

"It is a melancholy fact that Mr Twigger having full licence to demand a single glass of rum on the putting on of every piece of the armour, got, by some means or other, rather out and drank about four glasses to a piece instead of one, not to mention the something strong which went on the top of it . . . [he] no sooner found himself outside the gate of Mudfog Hall, than he also found himself in a very considerable state of intoxication; and hence his extraordinary style of progressing . . . .

"Mr Twigger, not having been penitent for a good calendar month, took it into his head to be most especially and particularly sentimental, just when his repentance could have been most conveniently dispensed with. Immense tears were rolling down his cheeks, and he was vainly endeavouring to conceal his grief by applying to his eyes a blue cotton pocket-handkerchief with white spots—an article not strictly in keeping with a suit of armour some three hundred years old, or thereabouts.

"'Twigger, you villain!' said Nicholas Tulrumble, quite forgetting his dignity, 'go back.'

"'Never,' said Ned. 'I'm a miserable wretch. I'll never leave you.'

"The by-standers of course received this declaration with acclamations of 'That's right, Ned; don't!'

"'I don't intend it,' said Ned, with all the obstinacy of a very tipsy man. 'I'm very unhappy. I'm the wretched father of an unfortunate family; but I am very faithful, sir. I'll never leave you.' Having reiterated this obliging promise, Ned proceeded in broken words to harangue the crowd upon the number of years he had lived in Mudfog, the excessive respectability of his character, and other topics of the like nature." ¶

Others

Circus rider. " . . . the gate flew open, and out came a gentleman, on a moist-sugar coloured charger, intended to represent a herald, but bearing a much stronger resemblance to a court-card on horseback."

—*a failure:* "[The Mudfog crowd] no sooner recognized the herald, than they began to growl forth the most unqualified disapprobation . . . for a professional gentleman to sit astride in the saddle, with his feet in the stirrups, was rather too good a joke. So the herald was a decided failure, and the crowd hooted with great energy, as he pranced ingloriously away."

Corporation. " . . . the sage men of Mudfog spend hour after hour in grave deliberation. Here they settle at what hour of the night the public-houses shall be closed, at what hour of the morning they shall be permitted to open, how soon it shall be lawful for people to eat their dinner on church-days, and other great political questions . . . ."

Crowd member. " . . . in a hairy waistcoat like the top of a trunk, [he] had previously expressed his opinion that if **Ned** hadn't been a poor man, [the Mayor] wouldn't have dared do it, hinted at the propriety of breaking the four-wheel chaise, or **Nicholas**'s head, or both, which last compound proposition the crowd seemed to consider a very good notion."

Landlord. "The licensing day came, and the red-faced landlord of the Jolly Boatmen walked into the town-hall, looking as jolly as need be, having actually put on an extra fiddle for that night, to commemorate the anniversary of the Jolly Boatmen's music licence."

Supernumeraries in the procession. " . . . in striped shirts and black velvet caps, to imitate the London watermen . . . many base imitations of running-footmen . . . the men who played the wind instruments, looking up into the sky (we mean the fog) with musical fervour, walked through pools of water and hillocks of mud, till they covered the powdered heads of the running-footmen aforesaid with splashes, that looked curious, but not ornamental . . . the **barrel-organ performer** put on the wrong stop, and played one tune while the band played another . . . . "

Tulrumble, junior, "took to smoking cigars, and calling the footman a 'feller' . . . . [He] couldn't make up his mind to be anything but magnificent, so he went up to London and drew bills on his father; and when he had overdrawn, and got into debt, he grew penitent and came home again."

Mrs Twigger. " . . . **Ned** no sooner caught a glimpse of her face and form, than from the mere force of habit he set off towards his home just as fast as his legs could carry him . . . . So Mrs Twigger had plenty of time to denounce **Nicholas Tulrumble** to his face: to express her opinion that he was a decided monster; and to intimate that, if her ill-used husband sustained any personal damage from the brass armour, she would have the law of Nicholas Tulrumble for manslaughter. When she had said all this with due vehemence, she posted after Ned . . . . "

Footman, servant to Tulrumble
Captain Manby[H], inventor of life-saving apparatus
Sniggs, late mayor of Mudfog

B October 1837 BM **M1**

Full Report of the First Meeting of
The Mudfog Association for the Advancement of Everything

Boz breathlessly describes on the spot the proceedings of this local echo of the Royal Society. CD's name coinages are dense with sometimes heavy wit, but it is apparent that these Reports were to him a revelation of the joys of comic nomenclature. There is perfunctory naming in the early SB, but after BM1/2 CD never again named a significant character without conscious craft.

Gown

Knight Bell (M.R.C.S.). He "'exhibited a wax preparation of the interior of a gentleman who in early life had inadvertently swallowed a door-key . . . a **medical student** of dissipated habits, being present at the *post mortem* examination, found means to escape . . . with that portion of the coats of the stomach upon which an exact model of the instrument was distinctly impressed, with which he hastened to a **locksmith** of doubtful character, who made a new key . . . the medical student entered the house of the deceased gentleman, and committed a burglary to a large amount, for which he was subsequently tried and executed.'"

"' . . . for some years [before the key dissolved] the gentleman was troubled with a night-mare . . . he always imagined himself a wine-cellar door.'"

Jobba. He "'produced a forcing-machine on a novel plan, for bringing joint-stock railway shares prematurely to a premium. The instrument was in the form of an elegant gilt weather-glass, of most dazzling appearance, and was worked behind, by strings, after the manner of a pantomime trick, the strings being always pulled by the directors of the company to which the machine belonged.'"

Dr. Kutankumagen, of Moscow. He "'read to the section a report . . . strikingly illustrative of the power of medicine, as exemplified in his successful treatment of a virulent disorder.'" *See* **Patient**.

Members, of the Association. "' . . . the noble visages of the professors and scientific gentlemen, who, some with bald heads, some with red heads, some with brown heads, some with grey heads, some with black heads, some with block heads, presented a *coup d'oeil* which no eye-witness will readily forget.'"

Professor Muff "'and **Nogo** have just driven up to the hotel door; they at once ordered dinner with great condescension. We are all very much delighted with the urbanity of their manners, and the ease with which they adapt themselves to the forms and ceremonies of ordinary life. Immediately on their arrival they sent for the **head waiter**, and privately requested him to purchase a live dog—as cheap a one as he could meet with—and to send him up after dinner, with a pie-board, a knife and fork, and a clean plate.'"

—*in session:* "'[He] related a very extraordinary and convincing proof of the wonderful efficacy of the system of infinitesimal doses, which the section were doubtless aware was based upon the theory that the very minutest amount of any given drug, properly dispersed through the human frame, would be productive of precisely the same result as a very large dose administered in the usual manner.'" *See* **Publican**.

Patient. "'He was then labouring under symptoms peculiarly alarming to any medical man. His frame was stout and muscular, his step firm and elastic, his cheeks plump and red, his voice loud, his appetite good, his pulse full and round. He was in the constant habit of eating three meals *per diem,* and of drinking at least one bottle of wine, and one glass of spirituous liquors diluted with water, in the course of the four-and-twenty hours. He laughed constantly, and in so hearty a manner that it was terrible to hear him.

"By dint of powerful medicine, low diet, and bleeding, the symptoms in the course of three days perceptibly decreased. A rigid perseverance in the same course of treatment for only one week, accompanied with small doses of water-gruel, weak broth, and barley-water, led to their entire disappearance. In the course of a month he was sufficiently recovered to be carried down-stairs by two **nurses**, and to enjoy an airing in a close carriage, supported by soft pillows. At the present moment he was restored so far as to walk about, with the slight assistance of a crutch and a **boy** . . . he ate little, drank little, slept little, and was never heard to laugh by any accident whatever.'"

Publican. "'[Professor **Muff**] had tried the experiment in a curious manner upon a publican who had been brought into the hospital with a broken head, and was cured upon the infinitesimal system in the incredibly short space of three months. This man was a hard drinker. He . . . had dispersed three drops of rum through a bucket of water, and requested the man to drink the whole. What was the result? Before he had drunk a quart, he was in a state of beastly intoxication; and five other men were made dead drunk with the remainder.'"

Slug. "'His complexion is a dark purple, and he has a habit of sighing constantly. He looked extremely well, and appeared in high health and spirits.'"

"'. . . [it was] suggested that Jack and Jill might perhaps be exempted from the general censure, inasmuch as the hero and heroine, in the very outset of the tale, were depicted as going *up* a hill to fetch a pail of water, which was a laborious and useful occupation—supposing the family linen was being washed, for instance.

"'[He] feared that the moral effect of this passage was more than counter-balanced by another in a subsequent part of the poem, in which very gross allusion was made to the mode in which the heroine was personally chastised by her mother

"'"*For laughing at Jack's disaster;*"

besides, the whole work had this one great fault, *it was not true.* '"

Professor Snore. "'The three professors arrived at ten minutes after two o'clock, and . . . drove straight to the Pig and Tinder-box, where they threw off the mask at once, and openly announced their intention of remaining . . . . How such a man as Professor Snore, or, which is still more extraordinary, such an individual as Professor **Doze**, can quietly allow himself to be mixed up with such proceedings as these . . . .'"

Professor Wheezy. "'Why [he], of all people in the world, should repair to the Original Pig in preference to the Pig and Tinder-box, it is not easy to conceive. The professor is a man who should be above all such petty feelings . . . it gives me great pain to speak in terms of censure or disapprobation of a man of such transcendent genius and acquirements. . . . '"

Wigsby, "'who produced a cauliflower somewhat larger than a chaise-umbrella, which had been raised by no other artificial means than the simple application of highly carbonated soda-water as manure. He explained that by scooping out the head, which would afford a new and delicious species of nourishment for the poor, a parachute, in principle something similar to that constructed by **M. Garnerin**, was at once obtained; the stalk of course being kept downwards.'"

Woodensconce. "'The distinguished gentleman was fast asleep on his arrival, and I am informed by the **guard** that he had been so the whole way. He was, no doubt, preparing for his approaching fatigues; but what gigantic visions must those be that flit through the brain of such a man when his body is in a state of torpidity!'"

Town

Augustus. "He is a pug-dog, of rather intelligent appearance, in good condition, and with very short legs. He has been tied to a curtain-peg in a dark room, and is howling dreadfully.'"

"'The dog has just been rung for. With an instinct which would appear almost the result of reason, the sagacious animal seized the waiter by the calf of the leg when he approached to take him, and made a desperate, though ineffectual resistance."

"'The dog's tail and ears have been sent down-stairs to be washed; from which circumstance we infer that the animal is no more. His forelegs have been delivered to the boots to be brushed, which strengthens the supposition.'"

—*provenance*: "' . . . [he] was surreptitiously obtained—stolen, in fact—by some person attached to the stable department, from an **unmarried lady** resident in this town. Frantic on discovering the loss of her favourite, the lady rushed distractedly into the street, calling in the most heart-rending and pathetic manner upon the passengers to restore her, her Augustus—for so the deceased was named, in affectionate remembrance of a former lover of his mistress, to whom he bore a striking personal resemblance. . . . '"

Elderly female. "' . . . an elderly female, in a state of inebriety, has declared in the open street her intention to "do" for Mr **Slug**. Some statistical returns compiled by that gentleman, relative to the consumption of raw spirituous liquors in this place, are supposed to be the cause of the wretch's animosity.'"

"'The disturbance, I am happy to inform you, has been completely quelled, and the ringleader taken into custody. She had a pail of cold water thrown over her, previous to being locked up, and expresses great contrition and uneasiness.'"

Lady, unmarried. " ' . . . she arrived, at the very instant when [**Augustus's**] detached members were passing through the passage on a small tray. Her shrieks still reverberate in my ears! I grieve to say that the expressive features of Professor **Muff** were much scratched and lacerated by the injured lady; and that Professor **Nogo**, besides sustaining several severe bites, has lost some handfuls of hair from the same cause . . . . The unfortunate lady remains at the Pig and Tinder-box, and up to this time is reported in a very precarious state."

Recruiting sergeant. "' . . . the civil authorities, apprehensive of some outbreak of popular feeling, had commanded a recruiting sergeant and two

corporals to be under arms; and that, with the view of not irritating the people unnecessarily by their presence, they had been requested to take up their position before daybreak in a turnpike, distant about a quarter of a mile from the town.'"

Women. "'. . . a brilliant concourse of those lovely and elegant women for which Mudfog is justly acknowledged to be without a rival in the whole world. The contrast between their fair faces and the dark coats and trousers of the scientific gentlemen I shall never cease to remember while Memory holds her seat.'"

Blunderum, on the learned pig
Doctor **W. R. Fee**, Association member
X. Ledbrain, Association member
Dr **Neeshawts**, Association member

Professor **Queerspeck**, a railway model
Sergeant, recruiting: to keep the peace
Solomon (not Toby): the pig in question

B September 1838   BM **M2**

Full Report of the Second Meeting of
The Mudfog Association for the Advancement of Everything

The Correspondent

Boz. "We announced . . . that when the Second Meeting of the Society should take place, we should be found again at our post, renewing our gigantic and spirited endeavours, and once more making the world ring with the accuracy, authenticity, immeasurable superiority, and intense remarkability of our account of its proceedings. In redemption of this pledge, we caused to be dispatched per steam to Oldcastle (at which place this second meeting of the Society was held on the 20th instant), the same superhumanly-endowed gentleman who furnished the former report, and who—gifted by nature with transcendent abilities, and furnished by us with a body of assistants scarcely inferior to himself—has forwarded a series of letters which, for faithfulness of description, power of language, fervour of thought, happiness of expression, and importance of subject-matter, have no equal in the epistolary literature of any age or country."

Gown

Blank, "who exhibited a model of a fashionable annual, composed of copperplates, gold leaf, and silk boards, and worked entirely by milk and water.

"'**MR PROSEE**, after examining the machine, declared it to be so ingeniously composed, that he was wholly unable to discover how it went on at all.

"'MR BLANK.—Nobody can, and that is the beauty of it.'"

Blubb, "'who delivered a lecture upon the cranium before him, clearly showing that Mr **Greenacre** possessed the organ of destructiveness to a most unusual extent, with a most remarkable development of the organ of carveativeness.'"

Coppernose "'called the attention of the section to a proposition of great magnitude and interest, illustrated by a vast number of models, and stated with much clearness and perspicuity in a treatise entitled "Practical

Suggestions on the necessity of providing some harmless and wholesome relaxation for the young noblemen of England.'""

Sir William Courtenay (otherwise **Thom**). "'... the deceased Thom employed a woman to follow him about all day with a pail of water, assuring her that one drop ... placed upon his tongue, after death, would restore him. What was the obvious inference? That Thom, who was marching and countermarching in osier beds, and other swampy places, was impressed with a presentiment that he should be drowned; in which case, had his instructions been complied with, he could not fail to have been brought to life again instantly by his own prescription.'"

Crinkles, "'who exhibited a most beautiful and delicate machine, of little larger size than an ordinary snuff-box, manufactured entirely by himself, and composed exclusively of steel, by the aid of which more pockets could be picked in one hour than by the present slow and tedious process in four-and-twenty ... he had succeeded in putting himself in communication with Mr **Fogle Hunter**, and other gentlemen connected with the swell mob, who had awarded the invention the very highest and most unqualified approbation.'"

Signor Gagliardi. "'... automaton figures, which, with the assistance of the ingenious Signor Gagliardi, of Windmill Street, in the Haymarket, [**Coppernose**] had succeeded in making with such nicety, that a policeman, cab-driver, or old woman, made upon the principle of the models exhibited, would walk about until knocked down like any real man ....'"

Gimlet-eyed Tommy. "'[He] and other members of a secondary grade of the [pickpocket] profession whom he was understood to represent, entertained an insuperable objection to [**Crinkles**'s invention] being brought into general use, on the ground that it would have the inevitable effect of almost entirely superseding manual labour, and throwing a great number of highly-deserving persons out of employment.'"

Professor Grime, "'having lost several teeth, is unable, I observe, to eat his crusts without previously soaking them in his bottled porter. How interesting are these peculiarities! ... Professors **Woodensconce** and Grime, with a degree of good humour that delights us all, have just arranged to toss for a bottle of mulled port ... Professor Grime has won .... There is an exultation about Professor Grime incompatible, I fear, with true greatness.'"

Sir William Joltered, President of the Section on *Zoology and Botany*. "'[He] highly complimented the learned gentleman [Professor **Pumpkinskull**] ... and remarked that only a week previous he had seen some young gentlemen at a theatre eyeing a box of ladies with a fierce intensity, which nothing but the influence of some brutish appetite could possibly explain.'"

Professor John Ketch, "'who was then called upon to exhibit the skull of the late Mr **Greenacre**, which he produced from a blue bag, remarking, on being invited to make any observations that occurred to him, "that he'd pound it as that 'ere 'spectable section had never seed a more gamerer cove nor he vos.'""

Kwakley. "'... stopping in the market-place to observe the spot where Mr Kwakley's hat was blown off yesterday. It is an uneven piece of paving, but has certainly no appearance which would lead one to suppose that any such event had recently occurred there.'"

"'[He] stated the result of some most ingenious statistical inquiries relative to the difference between the value of the qualification of several members of Parliament as published to the world, and its real nature and amount.'"

Lady patient. "The patient was a married lady in the middle rank of life, who, having seen another lady at an evening party in a full suit of pearls, was suddenly seized with a desire to possess a similar equipment, although her husband's finances were by no means equal to the necessary outlay. Finding her wish ungratified, she fell sick . . . the prominent tokens of the disorder were sullenness, a total indisposition to perform domestic duties, great peevishness, and extreme languor, except when pearls were mentioned, at which times the pulse quickened, the eyes grew brighter, the pupils dilated, and the patient, after various incoherent exclamations, burst into a passion of tears, and exclaimed that nobody cared for her, and that she wished herself dead.

"' . . . [**Dr Grummidge**] began by ordering a total abstinence from all stimulants, and forbidding any sustenance but weak gruel; he then took twenty ounces of blood, applied a blister under each ear, one upon the chest, and another on the back; having done which, and administered five grains of calomel, he left the patient to her repose. The next day she was somewhat low, but decidedly better, and all appearances of irritation were removed. The next day she improved still further, and on the next again. On the fourth there was some appearance of a return of the old symptoms, which no sooner developed themselves, than he administered another dose of calomel, and left strict orders that, unless a decidedly favourable change occurred within two hours, the patient's head should be immediately shaved to the very last curl.

"'From that moment she began to mend, and, in less than four-and-twenty hours was perfectly restored.'" ¶

Member. "'THE PRESIDENT wished to know whether any gentleman could inform the section what had become of the dancing-dogs?

"'A MEMBER replied, after some hesitation, that . . . the dogs had abandoned their professional duties, and dispersed themselves in different quarters of the town to gain a livelihood by less dangerous means. He was given to understand that. . . they had supported themselves by lying in wait for and robbing blind men's poodles.'"

Professor Muff. "'Will you allow me to ask you, sir, of what materials it is intended that the magistrates' heads shall be composed?

"' . . . The magistrates will have wooden heads, of course, and they will be made of the toughest and thickest materials that can possibly be obtained.

"'PROFESSOR MUFF.—I am quite satisfied. This is a great invention'"

Professor Mull, "'who spoke from personal observation and personal experience, when he said that many children of great abilities had been induced to believe, from what they had observed in the streets . . . that all monkeys were born in red coats and spangles, and that their hats and feathers also came by nature.'"

Professor Nogo "'has this moment arrived with his nightcap on under his hat. He has ordered a glass of cold brandy and water, with a hard biscuit and a bason, and has gone straight to bed. What can this mean?'"

Professor Pumpkinskull, "'who is an influential member of the council . . . [and] behaved with the utmost politeness . . . .

"'He wished to know whether it were possible that a constant outward application of bears'-grease by the young gentlemen about town had imperceptibly infused into those unhappy persons something of the nature and quality of the bear. He shuddered as he threw out the remark; but if this theory, on inquiry, should prove to be well founded, it would at once explain a great deal of unpleasant eccentricity of behaviour, which, without some such discovery, was wholly unaccountable.'"

Secretary, of the Association. "'A paper was read by the secretary descriptive of a bay pony . . . . The pony had one distinct eye, and it had been pointed out to him by his friend **Captain Blunderbore**, of the Horse Marines . . . that whenever he winked this eye he whisked his tail (possibly to drive the flies off), but that he always winked and whisked at the same time. The animal was lean, spavined, and tottering; and the author proposed to constitute it of the family of *Fitfordogsmeataurious.*'"

Q. J. Snuffletoffle. "'[He] had heard of a pony winking his eye, and likewise of a pony whisking his tail, but whether they were two ponies or the same pony he could not undertake positively to say. At all events, he was acquainted with no authenticated instance of a simultaneous winking and whisking, and he really could not but doubt the existence of such a marvellous pony in opposition to all those natural laws by which ponies were governed.'"

Tickle, "'who displayed his newly-invented spectacles, which enabled the wearer to discern, in very bright colours, objects at a great distance, and rendered him wholly blind to those immediately before him. It was, he said, a most valuable and useful invention . . . a large number of most excellent persons and great statesmen could see, with the naked eye, most marvellous horrors on West India plantations, while they could discern nothing whatever in the interior of Manchester cotton mills. He must know, too, with what quickness of perception most people could discover their neighbour's faults, and how very blind they were to their own.'"

Town

The Tyrant Sowster.

Beadle Sowster. " . . . the active and intelligent beadle of this place . . . is a fat man, with a more enlarged development of that peculiar conformation of countenance which is vulgarly termed a double chin than I remember to have ever seen before. He has also a very red nose, which he attributes to a habit of early rising—so red, indeed, that but for this explanation I should have supposed it to proceed from occasional inebriety . . . .'"

"'Even if I had been totally ignorant of the man's real character, and [his picture] had been placed before me without remark, I should have shuddered involuntarily. There is an intense malignity of expression in the features, and a baleful ferocity of purpose in the ruffian's eye, which appals and sickens. His whole air is rampant with cruelty, nor is the stomach less characteristic of his demoniac propensities.'"

Old gentleman. "'An interesting old gentleman, who came to the wharf in an omnibus, has just quarrelled violently with the **porters**, and is staggering towards the vessel with a large trunk in his arms. I trust and hope that he may reach it in safety; but the board he has to cross is narrow and slippery. Was that a splash? Gracious powers!

"'I have just returned from the deck. The trunk is standing upon the extreme brink of the wharf, but the old gentleman is nowhere to be seen. The **watchman** is not sure whether he went down or not, but promises to drag for him the first thing to-morrow morning . . . . '"

Brown (of Edinburgh), of the Mudfog
Doctor **Buffer**, of the Mudfog
Drawley, of the Association
Dull of the Mudfog; section on umbogology
Dummy, umbogologist
Hon and Rev **Long Eers**, of the Mudfog
Flummery, botanist
Dr **Foxey**, expert on the steam-engine
Grub, of the section on umbogology
X. Misty, of the Mudfog

X. X. Misty: dancing bears and monkeys
Muddlebranes, Association member
Noakes, statistician
Purblind, of the Mudfog
Professor **Rummun**, of the Mudfog
Smith, of London; of the Mudfog
Sir Hookham Snivey, of the Mudfog
Dr **Soemup**, President; Mudfog Anatomy
Steward, casually serving out cheese
Styles, statistician

B February 1837 (G. Seawin, D 54 p48)   **TA**

Theatrical Advertisement: Extraordinary

This one-page fragment marked "ed B.M. Dickens" was probably written as filler, spoofing the "off-Broadway" of the day: the scroungy theatres on the Surrey-side, whose managers developed some of their material plagiaristically.

Managers. "F.T. and O. also recommend their celebrated elastic, self-acting, portable, Anglo-Parisian pen, skilfully contrived to fit all hands, and which enables the writer, after six lessons upon the Hamiltonian system, to translate any French piece into *Surrey-side English;* thereby superseding the necessity of employing and paying any author or adaptor who thinks it worth his while to embarrasss himself with the study of reading, writing, or any other abstruse or outlandish knowledge whatsoever." [F. may be Edward Fitzball[H] and O. may be David Osbaldiston[H]: Malcolm Morley "Messrs Four, Two and One" D 57 p.78 (1961), to which our attention was directed by Michael Slater.]

Messenger, who dropped a flyer in the editor's box. " . . . an unknown gentleman, who slipped unseen into our *sanctum,* clothed in a whity-brown suit, half-boots, and blue cotton stockings."

B March 1837   **BM P**

The Pantomime of Life

Analogizing political and other citizenry to the stock characters of the Pantomime. The piece contains a supremely Dickensian name coinage.

Elderly gentleman. " . . . with a large face and strongly marked features. . . . His countenance beams with a sunny smile, and a perpetual dimple is on his broad, red cheek. He is evidently an opulent elderly gentleman, comfortable in circumstances, and well-to-do in the world. He is not unmindful of the adornment of his person, for he is richly, not to say gaudily dressed; and that he indulges to a reasonable extent in the pleasures of the table may be inferred from the joyous and oily manner in which he rubs his stomach, by way of informing the audience that he is going home to dinner."

The Honourable Captain Fitz-Whisker Fiercy. " . . . the captain is a good-natured, kind-hearted, easy man, and, to avoid being the cause of disappointment to any, he most handsomely gives orders to all. Hampers of wine, baskets of provisions, cart-loads of furniture, boxes of jewellery, supplies of luxuries of the costliest description, flock to the house . . . where they are received with the utmost readiness by the highly respectable **Do'em**; while the captain himself struts and swaggers about with that compound air of conscious superiority and general blood-thirstiness which a military captain should always, and does most times, wear, to the admiration and terror of plebeian men."

Old gentleman. "Take that old gentleman who has just emerged from the *Café de l'Europe* in the Haymarket, where he has been dining at the expense of the young man upon town with whom he shakes hands as they part at the door of the tavern. The affected warmth of that shake of the hand, the courteous nod, the obvious recollection of the dinner, the savoury flavour of which still hangs upon his lips, are all characteristics of his great prototype [Pantaloon].

"He hobbles away humming an opera tune, and twirling his cane to and fro, with affected carelessness. Suddenly he stops—'tis at the milliner's window. He peeps through one of the large panes of glass; and, his view of the ladies within being obstructed by the India shawls, directs his attentions to the **young girl** with the band-box in her hand, who is gazing in at the window also. See! he draws beside her. He coughs; she turns away from him. He draws near her again; she disregards him. He gleefully chucks her under the chin, and, retreating a few steps, nods and beckons with fantastic grimaces, while the girl bestows a contemptuous and supercilious look upon his wrinkled visage. She turns away with a flounce, and the old gentleman trots after her with a toothless chuckle. The pantaloon to the life!"

Supernumerary. " . . . we had never been able to understand for what possible purpose a great number of odd, lazy, large-headed men, whom one is in the habit of meeting here, and there, and everywhere, could ever have been created. We see it all, now. They are the supernumeraries in the pantomime of life; the men who have been thrust into it, with no other view than to be constantly tumbling over each other, and running their heads against all sorts of strange things.

"We sat opposite to one of these men at a supper-table, only last week. Now we think of it, he was exactly like the gentlemen with the pasteboard heads and faces, who do the corresponding business in the theatrical pantomimes; there was the same broad stolid simper—the same dull leaden eye—the same unmeaning, vacant stare; and whatever was said, or whatever was done, he always came in at precisely the wrong place, or jostled against something that he had not the slightest business with."

Young man. "At one time we were disposed to think that the harlequin was neither more nor less than a young man of family and independent property, who had run away with an opera-dancer, and was fooling his life and his means away in light and trivial amusements. On reflection, however, we re-

membered that harlequins are occasionally guilty of witty and even clever acts,
and we are rather disposed to acquit our young men of family and independent
property, generally speaking, of any such misdemeanours. On a more mature
consideration of the subject, we have arrived at the conclusion that the
harlequins of life are just ordinary men, to be found in no particular walk or degree, on whom a certain station, or particular conjunction of circumstances,
confers the magic wand."

> Brown, King and Gibson[H], famous music-hall and pantomime performers

B May 1837   BM **L**

Some Particulars Concerning a Lion

The Great Man

Lion. "The lion was a literary one . . . there were little private consultations in different corners, relative to the personal appearance and stature of
the lion; whether he was shorter than they had expected to see him, or taller, or
thinner, or fatter, or younger, or older; whether he was like his portrait, or unlike it; and whether the particular shade of his eyes was black, or blue, or hazel,
or green, or yellow, or mixture. At all these consultations the keeper assisted;
and, in short, the lion was the sole and single subject of discussion till they sat
him down to whist . . . . "

—*at table:* " . . . if you wish to see a tame lion under particularly favourable
circumstances, feeding-time is the period of all others to pitch upon."

—*cooperative:* "We have known bears of undoubted ability who, when the
expectations of a large audience have been wound up to the utmost pitch, have
peremptorily refused to dance; well-taught monkeys, who have unaccountably
objected to exhibit on the slack wire; and elephants of unquestioned genius, who
have suddenly declined to turn the barrel-organ; but we never once knew or
heard of a biped lion, literary or otherwise—and we state it as a fact which is
highly creditable to the whole species—who, occasion offering, did not seize with
avidity on any opportunity which was afforded him, of performing to his heart's
content on the first violin."

Others

Keeper. " . . . when the lion at last appeared, we overheard his keeper, who
was a little prim man, whisper to several gentlemen of his acquaintance, with
uplifted hands, and every expression of half-suppressed admiration, that——
(naming the lion again) was in such cue to-night!"

—*at table:* "Of course the keeper was there already. He had planted himself at precisely that distance from his charge which afforded him a decent pre-
text for raising his voice, when he addressed him, to so loud a key as could not
fail to attract the attention of the whole company, and immediately began to
apply himself seriously to the task of bringing the lion out, and putting him
through the whole of his manoeuvres."

Lady. " . . . a lady of our acquaintance called on us and resolutely declined
to accept our refusal of her invitation . . . 'for . . . I have got a lion coming.'"

Master of the house. " . . . after gliding out (unobserved as he flattered
himself) to peep over the banisters, came into the room, rubbing his hands to-

gether with great glee, and cried out in a very important voice, 'My dear, Mr —— (naming the lion) has this moment arrived.'"

Young gentlemen, who had been cutting great figures: they sank suddenly
Young ladies, previously gay: grew extremely quiet and sentimental
Young man, there to play the pianoforte: struck false notes in his excitement

BC August 1838 (W. J. Carlton, D 54 p178) **RB**

Mr Robert Bolton, the "Gentleman connected with the Press"

Carlton no doubt accurately impeaches early decisions to include this piece as by CD. George Bentley said it was (the scholarly HMCD has it, for example), but Carlton reports that one **John H. Leigh Hunt** (probably **Leigh Hunt**'s son) not only claimed authorship but was in fact paid £2 for the sketch. HS has taught us, however, to look for CD in the work of others which he chose to print, so we include the following. Carlton admits these bits suggest the master.

Admirer, of Mr **Bolton**. " . . . a large stomach surmounted by a man's head, and placed on the top of two particularly short legs."

Robert Bolton's fingers "peeped through the ends of his black kid gloves" and two toes on each foot "took a similar view of society through the extremities of his high-lows . . . ."

B February 1839 **BM FE**

Familiar Epistle from a Parent to a Child
Aged Two Years and Two Months

Farewell to *Bentley's*—and to the stage coach, given way to iron rails.

Post-Office Guard, "dejected and disconsolate . . . dismounted slowly from the little box in which he sits in ghastly mockery of his old condition with pistol and blunderbuss beside him, ready to shoot the first highway-man (or railwayman) who shall attempt to stop the horses, which now travel (when they travel at all) *inside* and in a portable stable invented for the purpose—he dismounted . . . slowly and sadly, from his post, and looking mournfully about him as if in dismal recollection of the old roadside public-house—the blazing fire—the glass of foaming ale—the buxom hand-maid and admiring hangers-on of tap-room and stable, all honoured by his notice; and, retiring a little apart, stood leaning against a signal-post, surveying the engine with a look of combined affliction and disgust which no words can describe.

"His scarlet coat and golden lace were tarnished with ignoble smoke; flakes of soot had fallen on his bright green shawl—his pride in days of yore—the steam condensed in the tunnel from which we had just emerged, shone upon his hat like rain . . . it was plain to see that he felt his office and himself had alike no business there . . . . "

Sketches of Young Gentlemen

Twelve sketches and Conclusion: pamphlet issued anonymously in purported
response to "Sketches of Young Ladies," by 'Quiz.' "YG" below is of course
"young gentleman" (singular or plural). CD gained part of his facetious effect
by frequent repetition of the phrase, but it is tedious today on the page (reading
aloud is another matter). Chapman and Hall is abbreviated C&H.

CONTENTS

CHARACTERS

YG 1 1838   C&H **B**

The Bashful Young Gentleman

"Bashful young gentlemen should be cured or avoided. They are never hopeless, and never will be, while female beauty and attractions retain their influence . . . . "

Bashful Young Gentleman: "This was a fresh coloured YG, with as good a promise of light whisker as one might wish to see, and possessed of a very velvet-like soft-looking countenance. We do not use the latter term invidiously, but merely to denote a pair of smooth, plump, highly-coloured cheeks of capacious dimensions, and a mouth rather remarkable for the fresh hue of the lips than for any marked or striking expression it presented. His whole face was suffused with a crimson blush, and bore that downcast, timid, retiring look, which betokens a man ill at ease with himself."

—*behaviour:* " . . . making his way towards us who were standing in a window, and wholly neglecting several persons who warmly accosted him, he seized our hand with visible emotion, and pressed it with a convulsive grasp for a good couple of minutes, after which he dived in a nervous manner across the room, oversetting in his way a fine **little girl** of six years and quarter old—and shrouding himself behind some hangings, was seen no more . . . in making a desperate effort to get through the ceremony of introduction, [he] had, in the bewilderment of his ideas, shaken hands with us at random."

—*at table:* " . . . . [he] overset his bread. . . in various semi-successful attempts to prevent its fall, played with it a little, as gentlemen in the streets may be seen to do with their hats on a windy day, and then giving the roll a smart rap in his anxiety to catch it, knocked it with great adroitness into a tureen of white soup at some distance, to the unspeakable terror and disturbance of a very amiable **bald gentleman**, who was dispensing the contents."

Carter. " . . . making a great number of bows in acknowledgment of several little messages to his sister, [**Hopkins**] walks backward a few paces, and comes with great violence against a lamp-post, knocking his hat off in the contact, which in his mental confusion and bodily pain he is going to walk away without, until a great roar from a carter attracts his attention, when he picks it up . . . . "

Hopkins. "The **young lady** who was most anxious to speak, here inquires, with an air of great commiseration, how his dear sister **Harriet** is to-day; to which the YG, without the slightest consideration, replies with many thanks, that she is remarkably well. 'Well, Mr Hopkins!' cries the young lady, 'why we heard she was bled yesterday evening, and have been perfectly miserable about her.' 'Oh, ah,' says the YG, 'so she was. Oh, she's very ill, very ill indeed.' The YG then shakes his head, and looks very desponding (he has been smiling perpetually up to this time) . . . . "

Miss Lambert. "'Miss Lambert, let me introduce Mr **Hopkins** for the next quadrille' . . . . The young lady more than half expects that the bashful YG will say something, and the bashful YG feeling this, seriously thinks whether he has got anything to say, which, upon mature reflection, he is rather disposed to conclude he has not, since nothing occurs to him . . . he gives the young lady his arm, and after inquiring where she will stand, and receiving a reply that she has no choice, conducts her to the remotest corner of the quadrille . . . . "

Single lady. " . . .[the bashful YG] was requested to pair off with a lively single lady of two or three and thirty . . . the talkative lady, who not noting the wildness of his eye, firmly believed she had secured a listener."

Hostess, eagle-eyed at spotting the Bashful YG
Mamma, whispered by her daughter, awaiting speech from Bashful YG

The Out-and-Out Young Gentleman

"Out-and-out* young gentlemen may be divided into two classes—those who have something to do, and those who have nothing. I shall commence with the former, because that species come more frequently under the notice of young ladies . . . . . " *thorough-going; complete; incorrigible

Dummins—*in society:* "As the out-and-out YG is by no means at his ease in ladies' society, he shrinks into a corner of the drawing-room when they reach the friend's, and unless one of his **sisters** is kind enough to take to him, remains there . . . . Having protracted their sitting until long after the host and the other guests have adjourned to the drawing-room, and finding that they have drained the decanters empty, they follow them thither with complexions rather heightened, and faces rather bloated with wine . . . . "

Out-and-Out Young Gentleman—*his dress:* "[He] is usually no great dresser, his instructions to his tailor being all comprehended in the one general direction to 'make that what's-a-name a regular bang-up sort of thing.' For some years past, the favourite costume of the out-and-out YG has been a rough pilot coat, with two gilt hooks and eyes to the velvet collar; buttons somewhat larger than crown-pieces; a black or fancy neckerchief, loosely tied; a wide-brimmed hat, with a low crown; tightish inexpressibles, and iron-shod boots. Out of doors he sometimes carries a large ash stick, but only on special occasions, for he prefers keeping his hands in his coat pockets. He smokes at all hours, of course, and swears considerably."

—*employment:* "The out-and-out YG is employed in a city counting-house or solicitor's office, in which he does as little as he possibly can . . . ."

—*taking the air:* "In the streets at evening time, out-and-out YG have a pleasant custom of walking six or eight abreast, thus driving females and other inoffensive persons into the road . . . . In all places of public resort, the out-and-outers are careful to select each a seat to himself, upon which he lies at full length, and (if the weather be very dirty, but not in any other case) he lies with his knees up, and the soles of his boots planted firmly on the cushion, so that if any low fellow should ask him to make room for a lady, he takes ample revenge upon her dress, without going at all out of his way to do it."

—*at the theatre:* "He always sits with his hat on, and flourishes his stick in the air while the play is proceeding, with a dignified contempt for the performance; if it be possible for one or two out-and-out YG to get up a little crowding in the passages, they are quite in their element, squeezing, pushing, whooping, and shouting in the most humorous manner possible."

Varmint Blake. " . . . long favourably known to his familiars as 'Mr Warmint Blake,' who upon divers occasions has distinguished himself in a manner that would not have disgraced the fighting man, and who—having been a pretty long time about town—had the honour of once shaking hands with the celebrated Mr **Thurtell** himself."

Hostess, agitated: thinks Blake and Dummins rather too wild
Mother, of the Out-and-Out YG; treated with becoming contempt
Sisters, of the Out-and-Out YG: no notion of life or gaiety; weak-spirited
Tom Smith, envied by the Out-and-Out YG, for his ring-side seat at a fight
John Thurtell[H], pugilist and gambler

YG 3 1838   C&H **VF**

The Very Friendly Young Gentleman

"The very friendly YG is very friendly to everybody, but he attaches himself particularly to two, or at most to three families: regulating his choice by their dinners, their circle of acquaintance, or some other criterion in which he has an immediate interest. He is of any age between twenty and forty, unmarried of course, must be fond of children, and is expected to make himself generally useful if possible."

Mincin. " . . . our friend motioned towards a gentleman who had been previously showing his teeth by the fireplace . . . . It required no great penetration on our part to discover at once that Mr Mincin was in every respect a very friendly YG.

"'I am delighted,' said Mincin, hastily advancing, and pressing our hand warmly between both of his, 'I am delighted, I am sure, to make your acquaintance—(here he smiled)—very much delighted indeed—(here he exhibited a little emotion)—I assure you that I have looked forward to it anxiously for a very long time:' here he released our hands, and rubbing his own, observed that the day was severe, but that he was delighted to perceive from our appearance that it agreed with us wonderfully . . . . "

—*caring for his hostess:* " . . . he exerted much strength and skill in wheeling a large easy-chair up to the fire, and the **lady** being seated in it, carefully closed the door, stirred the fire, and looked to the windows to see that they admitted no air; having satisfied himself upon all these points, he expressed himself quite easy in his mind, and begged to know how she found herself to-day. Upon the lady's replying very well, Mr Mincin (who it appeared was a medical gentleman) offered some general remarks upon the nature and treatment of colds in the head, which occupied us agreeably until dinner-time."

—*in conversation:* " . . . Mr Mincin's extreme friendliness became every moment more apparent; he was so amazingly friendly, indeed, that it was impossible to talk about anything in which he had not the chief concern. We happened to allude to some affairs in which our friend and we had been mutually engaged nearly fourteen years before, when Mr Mincin was all at once reminded of a joke which our friend had made on that day four years, which he positively must insist upon telling . . . . "

—*balancing act:* "Mr Mincin is invited to an evening party with his dear friends the **Martins**, where he meets his dear friends the **Cappers**, and his dear friends the **Watsons**, and a hundred other dear friends . . . . He is as much at home with the Martins as with the Cappers; but how exquisitely he balances his attentions, and divides them among his dear friends! If he flirts with one of the Miss Watsons, he has one little Martin on the sofa pulling his hair, and the other little Martin on the carpet riding on his foot. He carries Mrs Watson down to supper on one arm, and Miss Martin on the other, and takes wine so judiciously, and in such exact order, that it is impossible for the most punctilious old lady to consider herself neglected."

Wilkins, of Chichester: a pumpkin four feet high

YG 4 1838 C&H **M**

The Military Young Gentleman

"These YG may be divided into two classes—YG who are actually in the army, and YG who, having an intense and enthusiastic admiration for all things appertaining to a military life, are compelled by adverse fortune or adverse relations to wear out their existence in [a] counting-house."

Butcher. " . . . we find it is the custom of military YG to plant themselves opposite the sentries, and contemplate them at leisure, in periods varying from fifteen minutes to fifty, and averaging twenty-five. We were much struck a day or two since, by the behaviour of a very promising young butcher who (evincing an interest in the service, which cannot be too strongly commended or encouraged), after a prolonged inspection of the sentry, proceeded to handle his boots with great curiosity, and as much composure and indifference as if the man were wax-work."

Gentleman. " . . . the flaxen-headed **YG** . . . coughs to induce some ladies in the next box but one to look round, in order that their faces may undergo the same ordeal of criticism to which [the military YG] have subjected, in not a wholly inaudible tone, the majority of the female portion of the audience. Oh! a gentleman in the same box looks round as if he were disposed to resent this as an impertinence . . . . "

Mamma. " . . . the **Military YG**, stimulated by the mamma, introduces the two other[s] . . . who take their seats behind the **young ladies** and commence conversation; whereat the mamma bestows a triumphant bow upon a rival mamma, who has not succeeded in decoying any Military YG, and prepares to consider her visitors from that moment three of the most elegant and superior YG in the whole world."

Military YG, actual. "He wears his undress uniform, which somewhat mars the glory of his outward man; but still how great, how grand, he is! What a happy mixture of ease and ferocity in his gait and carriage, and how lightly he carries that dreadful sword under his arm, making no more ado about it than if it were a silk umbrella! The lion is sleeping: only think if an enemy were in sight, how soon he'd whip it out of the scabbard, and what a terrible fellow he would be!"

Military YG, in an office. "The whole heart and soul of the military YG are concentrated in his favourite topic. There is nothing that he is so learned upon as uniforms; he will tell you, without faltering for an instant, what the habiliments of any one regiment are turned up with, what regiment wear stripes down the outside and inside of the leg, and how ma-ny buttons the Tenth had on their coats; he knows to a fraction how many yards and odd inches of gold lace it takes to make an ensign in the guards; is deeply read in the comparative merits of different bands, and the apparelling of trumpeters; and is very luminous indeed in descanting upon 'crack regiments,' and the 'crack' gentlemen who compose them . . . ."

Three other **military YG**, "arm-in-arm . . . clanking their iron heels on the pavement, and clashing their swords with a noise, which should cause all peaceful men to quail at heart."

"See how the flaxen-haired YG with the weak legs—he who has his pocket-handkerchief thrust into the breast of his coat—glares upon the faint-hearted civilians who linger to look upon his glory . . . . "

"[See] how the next YG elevates his head in the air, and majestically places his arms a-kimbo . . . . "

" . . . the third stands with his legs very wide apart, and clasps his hands behind him."

Officers. " . . . grey-headed officers with tokens of many battles about them, who have nothing at all in common with the **military YG**, and who—but for an old-fashioned kind of manly dignity in their looks and bearing—might be common hard-working soldiers for anything they take the pains to announce to the contrary!"

Colonel Fitz-Sordust: commanded theatre performances
Young man, a brother of the young ladies at the theatre

YG 5 1838 C&H **P**

The Political Young Gentleman

"If the political YG be resident in a country town . . . he is wholly absorbed in his politics; as a pair of purple spectacles communicate the same uniform tint to all objects near and remote, so the political glasses, with which the YG assist his mental vision, give to everything the hue and tinge of party feeling. The political YG would as soon think of being struck with the beauty of a young lady in the opposite interest, as he would dream of marrying his sister to the opposite member."

Political YG, *Conservative.* " . . . he has usually some vague ideas about Ireland and the Pope which he cannot very clearly explain, but which he knows are the right sort of thing, and not to be very easily got over by the other side. He has also some choice sentences regarding church and state, culled from the banners in use at the last election, with which he intersperses his conversation at intervals with surprising effect. But his great topic is the constitution, upon which he will declaim, by the hour together, with much heat and fury; not that he has any particular information on the subject, but because he knows that the constitution is somehow church and state, and church and state somehow the constitution, and that the fellows on the other side say it isn't, which is quite a sufficient reason for him to say it is, and to stick to it."

Political YG, *Radical.* "If the political young gentleman be a Radical, he is usually a very profound person indeed, having great store of theoretical questions to put to you, with an infinite variety of possible cases and logical deductions therefrom. If he be of the utilitarian school, too, which is more than probable, he is particularly pleasant company, having many ingenious remarks to offer upon the voluntary principle and various cheerful disquisitions connected with the population of the country, the position of Great Britain in the scale of nations, and the balance of power.

"Then he is exceedingly well versed in all doctrines of political economy as laid down in the newspapers, and knows a great many parliamentary speeches by heart; nay, he has a small stock of aphorisms, none of them exceeding a couple of lines in length, which will settle the toughest question and leave you nothing to say. He gives all the young ladies to understand, that **Miss Martineau** is the greatest woman that ever lived; and when they praise the good looks of Mr **Hawkins** the new member, says he's very well for a representative, all things considered, but he wants a little calling to account, and he is more than half afraid it will be necessary to bring him down on his knees for that vote on the miscellaneous estimates." ¶

YG 6 1838 C&H **D**

The Domestic Young Gentleman

Felix Nixon. "Felix, then, is a YG who lives at home with his mother . . . . He wears India-rubber goloshes when the weather is at all damp, and always has a silk handkerchief neatly folded up in the right-hand pocket of his great-coat, to tie over his mouth when he goes home at night; moreover, being rather near-sighted, he carries spectacles for particular occasions, and has a weakish tremulous voice, of which he makes great use, for he talks as much as any old lady breathing."

—*his conversation:* "The two chief subjects of Felix's discourse, are himself and his mother, both of whom would appear to be very wonderful and interesting persons. As Felix and his mother are seldom apart in body, so Felix and his mother are scarcely ever separate in spirit. If you ask Felix how he finds himself to-day, he prefaces his reply with a long and minute bulletin of his mother's state of health . . . . "

—*and the opposite sex:* "Felix is rather prim in his appearance, and perhaps a little priggish about his books and flute, and so forth, which have all their peculiar corners of peculiar shelves in his bedroom: indeed all his female acquaintance (and they are good judges) have long ago set him down as a thorough old bachelor. He is a favourite with them however, in a certain way, as an honest, inoffensive, kind-hearted creature; and . . . his peculiarities harm nobody, not even himself . . . . "

—*passing through a danger:* ". . . a **hackney coachman** who wanted to overcharge him one night for bringing them home from a play, upon which Felix gave the aforesaid coachman a look which his mother thought would have crushed him to the earth, but which did not crush him quite, for he continued to demand another six-pence, notwithstanding that Felix took out his pocket-book, and, with the aid of a flat candle, pointed out the fare in print, which the coachman obstinately disregarding, he shut the street-door with a slam which his mother shudders to think of; and then, roused to the most appalling pitch of passion by the coachman knocking a double knock to show that he was by no means convinced, he broke with uncontrollable force from his parent and the

servant girl, and running into the street without his hat, actually shook his fist at the coachman . . . . "

Mrs Nixon, "a good-humoured, talkative, bustling little body . . . [she] edifies her acquaintance with a circumstantial and alarming account, how [**Felix**] sneezed four times and coughed once after being out in the rain the other night, but having his feet promptly put into hot water, and his head into a flannel-something . . . was happily brought round by the next morning, and enabled to go to business as usual."

> Doctor: dire warnings on reading French late at night
> **Amelia Grey** and **Miss Grey**, in the same row with the Domestic YG
> Miss **Julia Thompson**, resident in the same row with the Domestic YG

YG 7 1838   C&H **C**

The Censorious Young Gentleman

"The censorious YG has the reputation among his familiars of a remarkably clever person, which he maintains by receiving all intelligence and expressing all opinions with a dubious sneer, accompanied with a half smile, expressive of anything you please but good-humour. This sets people about thinking what on earth the censorious YG means, and they speedily arrive at the conclusion that he means something very deep indeed. . . . It is extraordinary how soon a censorious YG may make a reputation in his own small circle if he bear this in his mind, and regulate his proceedings accordingly."

Fairfax. "' . . . we were remarking what a very mysterious man you are.' 'Aye, aye!' observes Mr Fairfax, 'Indeed!' Now Mr Fairfax says this aye, aye, and indeed, which are slight words enough in themselves, with so very unfathomable an air, and accompanies them with such a very equivocal smile, that **ma** and the **young ladies** are more than ever convinced that he means an immensity, and so tell him he is a very dangerous man, and seems to be always thinking ill of somebody, which is precisely the sort of character the censorious YG is most desirous to establish; wherefore he says, 'Oh, dear, no,' in a tone, obviously intended to mean, 'You have me there,' and which gives them to understand that they have hit the right nail on the very centre of its head."

—*technique:* "'She is very lady-like, is she not?' 'Lady-like!' repeats the censorious YG (for he always repeats when he is at a loss for anything to say). 'Did you observe her manner? . . that's all I ask.' 'I thought I had done so,' rejoins the poor lady, much perplexed; 'I did not observe it very closely perhaps.' 'Oh, not very closely,' rejoins the censorious YG, triumphantly. 'Very good; then I did. Let us talk no more about her.'"

> **Mrs Barker**: is she ladylike? asks Mrs Thompson
> **Emily**, does not scruple to state that she considers Fairfax a horror
> **Miss Greenwood**, who wonders if Fairfax will ever be married
> **Miss Marshall**, who thinks Fairfax a very mysterious person
> **Mrs Thompson**, who thinks Fairfax not a horror but of very great ability
> Young gentleman, modest and a silent listener

YG 8 1838   C&H **F**

The Funny Young Gentleman

Griggins, "being announced, presented himself, amidst another shout of laughter and a loud clapping of hands from the younger branches. This welcome he acknowledged by sundry contortions of countenance, imitative of the clown in one of the new pantomimes, which were so extremely successful, that one stout **gentleman** rolled upon an ottoman in a paroxysm of delight, protesting, with many gasps, that if somebody didn't make that fellow Griggins leave off, he would be the death of him, he knew."

"To recount all the drollery of Mr Griggins at supper . . . . How he drank out of other people's glasses, and ate of other people's bread, how he frightened into screaming convulsions a **little boy** who was sitting up to supper in a high chair, by sinking below the table and suddenly reappearing with a mask on; how the hostess was really surprised that anybody could find a pleasure in tormenting children, and how the host frowned at the hostess, and felt convinced that Mr Griggins had done it with the very best intentions . . . would occupy more of our room and our readers' patience, than either they or we can conveniently spare. Therefore we change the subject, merely observing that we have offered no description of the funny young gentleman's personal appearance, believing that almost every society has a Griggins of its own, and leaving all readers to supply the deficiency . . . . "

—*a charming exploit:* "[Griggins] made one most excellent joke in snuffing a candle, which was neither more nor less than setting fire to the hair of a pale young gentleman who sat next him, and afterwards begging his pardon with considerable humour. As the young gentleman could not see the joke, however, possibly in consequence of its being on the top of his own head, it did not go off quite as well as it might have done . . . . "

    Brown, a host paralysed with wonder and laughter at droll dog Griggins
      Mrs: taken to task for allowing Griggins such license
    Young gentleman: didn't see the joke
    Young ladies, terrified by a postman's knock
    Young lady, turned the conversation from slaughterous direction

YG 9 1838   C&H **T**

The Theatrical Young Gentleman

"*The theatrical YG has early and important information on all theatrical topics.*"

"*The theatrical YG, from often frequenting the different theatrical establishments, has pet and familiar names for them all.*"

"*The theatrical YG has a great reverence for all that is connected with the stage department of the different theatres.*"

"*The theatrical YG is a great advocate for violence of emotion and redundancy of action.*"

Mr [Edward] Fitz Ball. "[The **YG**] looks upon Mr Fitz Ball as the principal dramatic genius and poet of the day; but holds that there are great writers extant besides him,—in proof whereof he refers you to various dramas and melo-dramas recently produced, of which he takes in all the sixpenny and threepenny editions as fast as they appear."

Mr [John] Liston. [The **YG**] is advised that Mr Liston always had a footman in gorgeous livery waiting at the side-scene with a brandy bottle and tumbler, to administer half a pint or so of spirit to him every time he came off, without which assistance he must infallibly have fainted."

Theatrical YG. "Well,' says he, abruptly when you meet him in the street, 'here's a pretty to-do. **Flinkins** has thrown up his part in the melodrama at the Surrey.'—'And what's to be done?' you inquire with as much gravity as you can counterfeit. 'Ah, that's the point,' replies the theatrical YG, looking very serious. '**Boozle** declines it; positively declines it. From all I am told, I should say it was decidedly in Boozle's line, and that he would be very likely to make a great hit in it; but he objects on the ground of Flinkins having been put up in the part first, and says no earthly power shall induce him to take the character.'"

"'Don't mention it, but I hear that the last scene, when he is first poisoned, and then stabbed, by **Mrs Flinkins** as Vengedora, will be the greatest thing that has been done these many years.' With this piece of news, and laying his finger on his lips as a caution for you not to excite the town with it, the theatrical YG hurries away."

> **T Baker**, lukewarm toast and water, to sustain favourite characters
> Paul Bedford[H], comedian and singer
> George Bennett[H], actor
> Jemmy (John Baldwin) Buckstone[H], actor, director, dramatist
> John Braham[H], singer and manager
> Helen Faucit[H], Shakespearean actress
> John Pritt Harley[H], actor
> Laura Honey[H], actress
> Priscilla Horton[H], actress
> Charley (Charles J.) Matthews[H; should be Mathews], actor
> Louisa Nisbett[H], comic actress
> Sheriff[H], American singer and a talented and lady-like actress
> Harriet Deborah Taylor[H], actress
> Fred (Frederick) Yates[H], actor and manager
> Charley (Charles) Young[H], actor

[CD reviewed the work of many of the above in the *Morning Chronicle*. *See* MC and Index IX in Volume III.]

YG 10 1838   C&H **V**

The Poetical Young Gentleman

"The poetical young gentleman is fond of quoting passages from his favourite authors, who are all of the gloomy and desponding school. He has a great deal to say, too, about the world, and is much given to opining, especially if he has taken anything strong to drink, that there is nothing in it worth living for."

John Milkwash. "The favourite attitude of the poetical YG is lounging on a sofa with his eyes fixed upon the ceiling, or sitting bolt upright in a high-backed chair, staring with very round eyes at the opposite wall. When he is in one of these positions, his **mother**, who is a worthy affectionate old soul, will give you a nudge to bespeak your attention without disturbing the abstracted one, and whisper with a shake of the head, that John's imagination is at some extraordinary work or other, you may take her word for it. Hereupon John looks more fiercely intent upon vacancy than before, and suddenly snatching a pencil from his pocket, puts down three words, and a cross on the back of a card, sighs deeply, paces once or twice across the room, inflicts a most unmerciful slap upon his head, and walks moodily up to his dormitory."

—insight: "The poetical YG is apt to acquire peculiar notions of things too, which plain ordinary people, unblessed with a poetical obliquity of vision, would suppose to be rather distorted. For instance, when the sickening murder and mangling of a wretched woman was affording delicious food wherewithal to gorge the insatiable curiosity of the public, our friend the poetical young gentleman was in ecstasies—not of disgust, but admiration . . . it came out, in a fine torrent of eloquence, that the murderer was a great spirit, a bold creature full of daring and nerve, a man of dauntless heart and determined courage, and withal a great casuist and able reasoner, as was fully demonstrated in his philosophical colloquies with the great and noble of the land."

Poetical YG. "We know a poetical YG—a very poetical YG. We do not mean to say that he is troubled with the gift of poesy in any remarkable degree, but his countenance is of a plaintive and melancholy cast, his manner is abstracted and bespeaks affliction of soul: he seldom has his hair cut, and often talks about being an outcast and wanting a kindred spirit; from which, as well as from many general observations in which he is wont to indulge, concerning mysterious impulses, and yearnings of the heart, and the supremacy of intellect gilding all earthly things with the glowing magic of immortal verse, it is clear ... that he has been stricken poetical."

" ... a singular epidemic raged among the young gentlemen, vast numbers of whom, under the influence of the malady, tore off their neckerchiefs, turned down their shirt collars, and exhibited themselves in the open streets with bare throats and dejected countenances, before the eyes of an astonished public."

> O. Smith (Richard John)[H], of the Adelphi theatre; actor
> Young lady, who opened her album to receive a verse

YG 11 1838   C&H **TO**

The "Throwing-Off" Young Gentleman

"Ladies, ladies, the throwing-off* YG are often swindlers, and always fools. So pray you avoid them." [*boasting, vaunting, name-dropping, faking]

Caveton. "Sometimes the throwing-off YG happens to look in upon a little family circle of young ladies who are quietly spending the evening together, and then indeed is he at the very height and summit of his glory; for it is to be observed that he by no means shines to equal advantage in the presence of men as in the society of over-credulous young ladies .... "

"'Did you ever see a more lovely blue than this flower, Mr Caveton?' asks [**Miss Lowfield**] who, truth to tell, is rather smitten with the throwing-off YG. 'Never,' he replies, bending over the object of admiration, 'never but in your eyes.'"

"'Think not so meanly of me, Miss Lowfield, I beseech, as to suppose that title, lands, riches, and beauty, can influence *my* choice. The heart, the heart, Miss Lowfield.'"

Throwing-Off YG—*family wealth:* "The throwing-off YG has so often a father possessed of vast property in some remote district of Ireland, that we look with some suspicion upon all YG who volunteer this description of themselves. The deceased grandfather of the throwing-off YG was a man of immense possessions, and untold wealth .... "

—*accomplished:* "The throwing-off YG is a universal genius; at walking, running, rowing, swimming, and skating, he is unrivalled; at all games of chance or skill, at hunting, shooting, fishing, riding, driving, or amateur theatricals, no one can touch him—that is *could* not, because he gives you carefully to understand, lest there should be any opportunity of testing his skill, that he is quite out of practice just now, and has been for some years."

—*circle:* " ... he 'happens to be acquainted' with a most extraordinary variety of people in all parts of the world. Thus in all disputed questions, when the throwing-off YG has no argument to bring forward, he invariably happens to be acquainted with some distant person, intimately connected with the subject, whose testimony decides the point against you .... "

—*music:* "We have seen a throwing-off YG who, to our certain knowledge, was innocent of a note of music, and scarcely able to recognise a tune by ear, volunteer a Spanish air upon the guitar when he had previously satisfied himself that there was not such an instrument within a mile of the house."

"We have heard another throwing-off YG, after striking a note or two upon the piano, and accompanying it correctly (by dint of laborious practice) with his voice, assure a circle of wondering listeners that so acute was his ear that he was wholly unable to sing out of tune, let him try as he would."

YG 12 1838   C&H **YL**

The Young Ladies' Young Gentleman

Balim. " . . . [he] hummed a fragment of an air, which induced a young lady to inquire whether he had danced to that the night before. 'By Heaven, then, I did,' replied the YG, 'and with a lovely **heiress**; a superb creature, with twenty thousand pounds.' 'You seem rather struck,' observed another young lady. 'Gad, she was a sweet creature,' returned the YG, arranging his hair."

—*prank in a coach:* "At length, a short silence occurring, the **young ladies** on either side of the YG fell suddenly fast asleep; and the YG, winking upon us to preserve silence, won a pair of gloves from each, thereby causing them to wake with equal suddenness and to scream very loud. The lively conversation to which this pleasantry gave rise, lasted for the remainder of the ride, and would have eked out a much longer one."

—*at a picnic:* " . . . he flourished wonderfully, being still surrounded by a little group of young ladies, who listened to him as an oracle, while he ate from their plates and drank from their glasses in a manner truly captivating from its excessive playfulness."

—*in his element:* "The young ladies' YG was seated upon the ground, at the feet of a few young ladies who were reclining on a bank; he was so profusely decked with scarfs, ribands, flowers, and other pretty spoils, that he looked like a lamb—or perhaps a calf would be a better simile—adorned for the sacrifice. One young lady supported a parasol over his interesting head, another held his hat, and a third his neckcloth, which in romantic fashion he had thrown off; the YG himself, with his hand upon his breast, and his face moulded into an expression of the most honeyed sweetness, was warbling forth some choice specimens of vocal music in praise of female loveliness, in a style so exquisitely perfect, that we burst into an involuntary shout of laughter, and made a hasty retreat."

—*expertise:* " . . . one **elderly lady** assured us, that in the course of a little lively *badinage* on the subject of ladies' dresses, he had evinced as much knowledge as if he had been born and bred a milliner."

—*milieu:* ". . . divers young ladies . . . looking anxiously over the breakfast-parlour blinds . . . one young lady, more adventurous than the rest, proposed that an express should be straightway sent to dear Mr Balim's lodgings."

" . . . one sprightly **little girl** of eight or ten years old, who . . . remarked that perhaps Mr Balim might have been married that morning—for which impertinent suggestion she was summarily ejected from the room by her eldest sister."

" . . . the **young lady** who had spoken first, and who sat on his right, struck him a severe blow on the arm with a rosebud, and said he was a vain man . . . . "

Young Ladies' YG, "who has usually a fresh colour and very white teeth, which latter articles, of course, he displays on every possible opportunity. He has brown or black hair, and whiskers of the same, if possible; but a slight tinge of red, or the hue which is vulgarly known as *sandy,* is not considered an objection. If his head and face be large, his nose prominent, and his figure square, he is an uncommonly fine young man, and worshipped accordingly. Should his whiskers meet beneath his chin, so much the better, though this is not absolutely insisted on; but he must wear an under-waistcoat, and smile constantly."

Coachmen, with hampers between legs large than wheelbarrows
Daughter, who hoped no accident had happened to Balim
Lady, married: aware of custom of packing closely at gipsy-parties
Little boy, running into the room
-*pl* sitting on the box
Mamma, talking
Papa (a bear): if Balim didn't choose to come, he might stop at home
Young gentlemen, looking anxiously over the blinds for Balim
Young ladies, drawn to their YG

Sketches of Young Couples

CD followed SYG with these responses to the announcement of Victoria's impending marriage to Albert. He concludes, "We have taken for the subjects of the foregoing moral essays, twelve samples of married couples, carefully selected from a large stock on hand, open to the inspection of all comers." But there are only eleven. He miscounts the doting couple's children too.

> *"This is in many respects a particularly bad-tempered selection of portraits of the marital state . . . . "* PA p 296 [But see the touching YC/Y and its sequel, YC/O, as well as the affectionate YC/N.]

CONTENTS

CHARACTERS

YC 1840   C&H **R**

An Urgent Remonstrance

Queen Victoria's announcement of her intention "to ally myself" with Albert inspires reflections on the dangers Leap Year presents to Society.

> **John**, a type of cousin taken violently into possession by a young lady
> **Smith**, of Stepney: chosen by a young lady
> Young lady, who chose her cousin John
> Young lady, who chose Smith of Stepney and so informed her father

YC 1 1840   C&H **Y**

The Young Couple

A wedding about to take place, the maids eagerly and delightedly observe.

Jane Adams. " . . . all fluttering in smart new dress and streaming ribands, [**Anne**'s] friend Jane Adams, who comes all out of breath to redeem a solemn promise of taking her in, under cover of the confusion, to see the breakfast table spread forth in state, and—sight of sights!—her young mistress ready dressed for church."

Anne. "Heaven alone can tell in what bright colours this marriage is painted upon the mind of the little housemaid at number six, who has hardly slept a wink all night with thinking of it, and now stands on the unswept door-steps leaning upon her broom, and looking wistfully towards the enchanted house."

Children, "who would cry more but that they are so finely dressed, and yet sob for fear sister **Emma** should be taken away . . . . "

"Of these, one is a little fellow of six or eight years old, brother to the bride—and the other a girl of the same age, or something younger, whom he calls 'his wife.' The real bride and bridegroom are not more devoted than they: he all love and attention, and she all blushes and fondness, toying with a little bouquet which he gave her this morning, and placing the scattered rose-leaves in her bosom with nature's own coquettishness. They have dreamt of each other in their quiet dreams, these children, and their little hearts have been nearly broken when the absent one has been dispraised in jest. When will there come in after-life a passion so earnest, generous, and true as theirs; what, even in its gentlest realities, can have the grace and charm that hover round such fairy lovers!"

Emma Fielding. "There is Miss Emma 'looking like the sweetest picter,' in a white chip bonnet and orange flower, and all other elegancies becoming a bride, (with the make, shape, and quality of every article of which [**Anne**] is perfectly familiar in one moment, and never forgets to her dying day) . . . . "

Harvey. "There are two points on which **Anne** expatiates over and over again, without the smallest appearance of fatigue or intending to leave off; one is, that she 'never see in all her life such a—oh such a angel of a gentleman as Mr Harvey' . . . . "

John. " . . . who should come in but Mr John! to whom **Jane** says that it's only **Anne** from number six; and John says *he* knows, for he's often winked his eye down the area, which causes Anne to blush and look confused . . . . At last Mr John, who has waxed bolder by degrees, pleads the usage at weddings, and claims the privilege of a kiss, which he obtains after a great scuffle . . . . "

> Aunt, an old maid but neither cross nor ugly; cheerful, tender-hearted
> Baker, in a vision
> Bridesmaid, all smiles and tears
> Butterman, smart and most insinuating
> Cook, caught up in preliminaries
> **Fielding**, comforting Mamma: how long she has been looking forward
>   Sister, with her arms round Emma's neck
> Women servants, clustered in the hall, whispering

YC 2 1840   C&H **F**

The Formal Couple

"The formal couple are the most prim, cold, immovable, and unsatisfactory people on the face of the earth. Their faces, voices, dress, house, furniture, walk, and manner, are all the essence of formality, unrelieved by one redeeming touch of frankness, heartiness, or nature."

Formal Children. "If the formal couple have a family (which they sometimes have), they are not children, but little, pale, sour, sharp-nosed men and women; and so exquisitely brought up, that they might be very old dwarfs for anything that appeareth to the contrary. Indeed, they are so acquainted with forms and conventionalities, and conduct themselves with such strict decorum, that to see the little girl break a looking-glass in some wild outbreak, or the little boy kick his parents, would be to any visitor an unspeakable relief and consolation."

Formal gentleman—*at a funeral:* "Here his deportment is of the most faultless description; he knows the exact pitch of voice it is proper to assume, the sombre look he ought to wear, the melancholy tread which should be his gait for the day. He is perfectly acquainted with all the dreary courtesies to be observed in a mourning-coach; knows when to sigh, and when to hide his nose in the white handkerchief; and looks into the grave and shakes his head when the ceremony is concluded, with the sad formality of a mute."

Formal lady. "'What kind of funeral was it?' says the formal lady . . . . 'Oh!' replies the formal gentleman, 'there never was such a gross and disgusting impropriety; there were no feathers.' 'No feathers!' cries the lady, as if on wings of black feathers dead people fly to Heaven, and, lacking them, they must of necessity go elsewhere . . . . 'You will recollect, my dear,' says the formal lady, in a voice of stately reproof, 'that when we first met this poor man who is now dead and gone, and he took that very strange course of addressing me at dinner without being previously introduced, I ventured to express my opinion that the family were quite ignorant of etiquette, and very imperfectly acquainted with the decencies of life. You have now had a good opportunity of judging for yourself, and all I have to say is, that I trust you will never go to a funeral *there* again.'"

Gentleman. " . . . when that baby's health was drunk, and allusions were made, by a grey-headed gentleman proposing it, to the time when he had dandled in his arms the young Christian's mother,—certain we are that then the formal lady took the alarm, and recoiled from the old gentleman as from a hoary profligate."

Godfather. " . . . one of the godfathers; a red-faced elderly gentleman, who, being highly popular with the rest of the company, had it all his own way, and was in great spirits."

" . . . the godfather . . . in the course of his observations darkly hinted at babies yet unborn, and even contemplated the possibility of the subject of that festival having brothers and sisters, the **formal lady** could endure no more, but, bowing slightly round, and sweeping haughtily past the offender, left the room in tears, under the protection of the **formal gentleman**."

William Etty[H]; painter of the female nude: Formal Couple thinks of prosecution
Firemen-watermen: lying by until someone was exhausted

YC 3 1840   C&H **L**

The Loving Couple

"There cannot be a better practical illustration of the wise saw and ancient instance, that there may be too much of a good thing, than is presented by a loving couple."

Mr Augustus and **Mrs Augusta Leaver**. "The loving couple . . . loving all the way to Twickenham, but when we arrived there (by which time the amateur crew looked very thirsty and vicious) they were more playful than ever, for Mrs Leaver threw stones at Mr Leaver, and Mr Leaver ran after Mrs Leaver on the grass, in a most innocent and enchanting manner.

"At dinner, too, Mr Leaver *would* steal Mrs Leaver's tongue, and Mrs Leaver *would* retaliate upon Mr Leaver's fowl; and when Mrs Leaver was going to take some lobster salad, Mr Leaver wouldn't let her have any, saying that it made her ill, and she was always sorry for it afterwards, which afforded Mrs Leaver an opportunity of pretending to be cross, and showing many other prettinesses.

"But this was merely the smiling surface of their loves . . . Mr Leaver took upon himself to propose the bachelors who had first originated the notion of that entertainment, in doing which, he affected to regret that he was no longer of their body himself, and pretended grievously to lament his fallen state. This Mrs Leaver's feelings could not brook, even in jest, and consequently, exclaiming aloud, 'He loves me not, he loves me not!' she fell in a very pitiable state into the arms of **Mrs Starling**, and, directly becoming insensible, was conveyed by that lady and her husband into another room."

"Presently Mr Leaver came running back to know if there was a medical gentleman in company, and as there was, (in what company is there not?) both Mr Leaver and the **medical gentleman** hurried away together.

"The medical gentleman was the first who returned, and among his intimate friends he was observed to laugh and wink, and look as unmedical as might be; but when Mr Leaver came back he was very solemn, and in answer to all inquiries, shook his head, and remarked that Augusta was far too sensitive to be trifled with . . . . "

"Very few of the party missed the loving couple; and the few who did, heartily congratulated each other on their disappearance." ¶

Coxswain, appointed for an excursion
Oarsmen: eight gentlemen threw themselves into strong paroxysms

YC 4 1840   C&H **C**

The Contradictory Couple

"One would suppose that two people who are to pass their whole lives together, and must necessarily be very often alone with each other, could find little pleasure in mutual contradiction; and yet what is more common than a contradictory couple?"

Charlotte and **Edward**. "'What a very extraordinary thing it is,' says he, 'that you will contradict, Charlotte!' 'I contradict!' cries the lady, 'but that's just like you.' 'What's like me?' says the gentleman sharply. 'Saying that I contradict you,' replies the lady. 'Do you mean to say that you do not contradict me?' retorts the gentleman; 'do you mean to say that you have not been contradicting me the whole of this day? Do you mean to tell me now, that you have not?' 'I mean to tell you nothing of the kind,' replies the lady quietly; 'when you are wrong, of course I shall contradict you.'"

"She now lets down her back hair, and proceeds to brush it; preserving at the same time an air of conscious rectitude and suffering virtue, which is intended to exasperate the gentleman—and does so."

> **Blackburn** family: a question of the number of their doors
> **Mrs Bluebottle**, who gave a party
> Daughter **Charlotte**
>   brother, master **James**, growing talkative
> **Jenkins**, appealed to be Charlotte
> **Morgan**: is he Jenkins? Charlotte so insists, Edward so denies
> **Mrs Parsons**, a very tall lady indeed; quite a giantess

YC 5 1840   **C&H D**

The Couple who Dote upon their Children

"The children are either the healthiest in all the world, or the most unfortunate in existence. In either case, they are equally the theme of their doting parents, and equally a source of mental anguish and irritation to their doting parents' friends."

" . . . we were once slightly acquainted with a lady and gentleman who carried their heads so high and became so proud after their youngest child fell out of a two-pair-of-stairs window without hurting himself much, that the greater part of their friends were obliged to forego their acquaintance."

*"**Doctor Johnson** used to tell a story of a man who had but one idea, which was a wrong one. The couple who dote upon their children are in the same predicament . . . . "*

Whiffler "must have to describe at his office such excruciating agonies constantly undergone by his eldest boy, as nobody else's eldest boy ever underwent; or he must be able to declare that there never was a child endowed with such amazing health, such an indomitable constitution, and such a cast-iron frame, as his child. His children must be, in some respect or other, above and beyond the children of all other people."

Mrs Whiffler "will never cease to recollect the last day of the old year as long as she lives, for it was on that day that the baby had the four red spots on its nose which they took for measles . . . . "

The Children

Dick " . . . a discussion ensues upon the different character of **Tom**'s wit and Dick's wit, from which it appears that Dick's humour is of a lively turn, while Tom's style is the dry and caustic."

Emily. " . . . **Whiffler** . . . begs [his friend] to take notice of . . . Emily's figure, or little **Bob**'s calves, or **Fanny**'s mouth, or **Carry**'s head . . . .

Georgiana. " . . . it was on a Good Friday that [**Mrs Whiffler**] was frightened by the donkey-cart when she was in the family way with Georgiana."

Ned. " . . . it was on the fifth of November that Ned asked whether wooden legs were made in heaven and cocked hats grew in gardens."

"Everything reminds Mr **Whiffler** of Ned, or **Mrs Whiffler** of **Mary Anne**, or of the time before Ned was born, or the time before Mary Anne was thought of."

—*miscounted:* "' . . . will you, **Saunders**,' says Mr Whiffler, in an impressive manner, 'will you cement and consolidate our friendship by coming into the family (so to speak) as a godfather?' 'I shall be proud and delighted,' replies Mr Saunders: 'which of the children is it? Really, I thought they were all christened; or—' 'Saunders,' Mr Whiffler interposes, 'they are all christened; you are right. The fact is, that Mrs Whiffler is—in short, we expect another.' 'Not a ninth!' cries the friend, all aghast at the idea. 'Yes, Saunders,' rejoins Mr Whiffler, solemnly, 'a ninth.'" [But there all *already* nine.]

Footman, who got severely scratched at the Whifflers'
Nurse, who got severely scratched at the same address

YC 6 1840   C&H **I**

The Cool Couple

"*The cool* couple are seldom alone together, and when they are, nothing can exceed their apathy and dulness: the gentleman being for the most part drowsy, and the lady silent. If they enter into conversation, it is usually of an ironical or recriminatory nature.*" [*indifferent, blasé, inert, unsympathetic]

Charles. " . . . when the gentleman has indulged in a very long yawn and settled himself more snugly in his easy-chair, the lady will perhaps remark, 'Well, I am sure, Charles! I hope you're comfortable.' To which the gentleman replies, 'Oh yes, he's quite comfortable—quite.'"

Louisa. " . . . she remembers that her poor papa used to say again and again, almost every day of his life, 'Oh, my dear Louisa, if you only marry a man who understands you, and takes the trouble to consider your happiness and accommodate himself a very little to your disposition, what a treasure he will find in you!'"

Mrs Mortimer, who has issued an invitation

YC 7 1840   C&H **P**

The Plausible Couple

"*The plausible couple have many titles. They are 'a delightful couple,' an 'affectionate couple,' 'a most agreeable couple,' 'a good-hearted couple,' and 'the best-natured couple in existence.' The truth is, that the plausible couple are people of the world . . . .*"

The **Clickits**. " . . . she is sure she has heard the Clickits speak of you—she must not tell you in what terms, or you will take her for a flatterer. You admit a knowledge of the Clickits; the plausible lady immediately launches out in their praise."

Fithers. "Their friend, Mr **Slummery**, say they, is unquestionably a clever painter, and would no doubt be very popular, and sell his pictures at a very high price, if that cruel Mr Fithers had not forestalled him in his department of art, and made it thoroughly and completely his own—Fithers, it is to be observed, being present and within hearing, and Slummery elsewhere."

Mrs Jackson. "'We never flatter, my dear Mrs Jackson,' say the plausible couple; 'we speak our minds. Neither you nor Mr Jackson have faults enough. It may sound strangely, but it is true. You have not faults enough. You know our way—we must speak out, and always do. Quarrel with us for saying so, if you will; but we repeat it—you have not faults enough!'"

Little girl. "The plausible lady . . . is sitting with a little girl upon her knee, enraptured by her artless replies, and protesting that there is nothing she delights in so much as conversing with these fairies . . . . "

Mrs Tabblewick. ". . . they once thought her the most beautiful woman ever seen; still, if you press them for an honest answer, they are bound to say that this was before they had ever seen our lovely friend on the sofa, (the sofa is hard by, and our lovely friend can't help hearing the whispers in which this is said;) since that time, perhaps they have been hardly fair judges; Mrs Tabblewick is no doubt extremely handsome—very like our friend, in fact, in the form of the features—but in point of expression, and soul, and figure, and air altogether—oh dear!"

Bobtail and **Lavinia Widger**. "The plausible couple are no less plausible to each other than to third parties. They are always loving and harmonious. The plausible gentleman calls his wife 'darling,' and the plausible lady addresses him as 'dearerst' . . . Mrs Widger is 'Lavinia, darling,' and Mr Widger is 'Bobtail, dearest.' Speaking of each other, they observe the same tender form."

"As the plausible couple never laud the merits of any absent person, without dexterously contriving that their praises shall reflect upon somebody who is present, so they never depreciate anything or anybody, without turning their depreciation to the same account."

> **Mrs Finching**: she has had a baby
> Lovely friend, on the couch within earshot
> Lady, who dotes on her children
> **Slummery**, a clevery painter, but . . .

YC 8 1840   C&H **N**

The Nice Little Couple

" As we find ourself in the predicament of not being able to describe (to our own satisfaction) nice little couples in the abstract, we purpose telling in this place a little story about a nice little couple of our acquaintance."

Chirrup "has the smartness, and something of the brisk, quick manner of a small bird . . . a warm-hearted little fellow; and if you catch his eye when he has been slyly glancing at **Mrs Chirrup** in company, there is a certain complacent twinkle in it, accompanied, perhaps, by a half-expressed toss of the head, which as clearly indicates what has been passing in his mind as if he had put it into words, and shouted it out through a speaking-trumpet."

"As they stand side by side, you find that Mr Chirrup is the least possible shadow of a shade taller than Mrs Chirrup, and that they are the neatest and best-matched little couple that can be, which the chances are ten to one against your observing with such effect at any other time, unless you see them in the street arm-in-arm, or meet them some rainy day trotting along under a very small umbrella."

Mrs Chirrup "is the prettiest of all little women, and has the prettiest little figure conceivable. She has the neatest little foot, and the softest little voice, and the pleasantest little smile, and the tidiest little curls, and the brightest little eyes, and the quietest little manner, and is, in short, altogether one of the most engaging of all little women, dead or alive. She is a condensation of all the domestic virtues—a pocket edition of the young man's best companion—a little woman at a very high pressure, with an amazing quantity of goodness and usefulness in an exceedingly small space. Little as she is, Mrs Chirrup might furnish forth matter for the moral equipment of a score of housewives, six feet high in their stockings . . . and of corresponding robustness."

Bachelor, thoroughly enjoying himself

YC 9 1840   C&H **E**

The Egotistical Couple

"The egotistical couple have undergone every calamity, and experienced every pleasurable and painful sensation of which our nature is susceptible. You cannot by possibility tell the egotistical couple anything they don't know, or describe to them anything they have not felt. They have been everything but dead. Sometimes we are tempted to wish they had been even that, but only in our uncharitable moments, which are few and far between."

Protagonists

Exemplars. " . . . entertaining . . . with a minute account of what weather and diet agreed with them, and what weather and diet disagreed with them, and at what time they usually got up, and at what time went to bed, with many other particulars of their domestic economy too numerous to mention; the egotistical couple at length took their leave . . . ."

Sliverstone. " . . . all the gentleman's [egotisim is] about his wife . . . [he] launches out into glowing praises of [her] conduct . . . in the production of eight young children, and the subsequent rearing and fostering of the same."

Mrs Sliverstone. " . . . all the lady's egotism is about her husband . . . [he] is a clerical gentleman, and occasionally writes sermons, as clerical gentlemen do. If you happen to obtain admission at the street-door while he is so engaged, Mrs Sliverstone appears on tip-toe, and speaking in a solemn whisper, as if there were at least three or four particular friends up-stairs, all upon the point of death, implores you to be very silent, for Mr Sliverstone is composing, and she need not say how very important it is that he should not be disturbed . . . and thus the husband magnifies the wife, and the wife the husband."

Eminences cited

Sir Chipkins Glogwog. " . . . who it was that had told that capital story about the mashed potatoes. 'Who, my dear?' returned the egotistical lady, 'why Sir Chipkins, of course; how can you ask!'"

[James] Greenacre. " . . . in the same omnibus with Mr Greenacre, when he carried his victim's head about town in a blue bag, [the couple] remarked a singular twitching in the muscles of his countenance . . . . "

[James] Hatfield. " . . . the egotistical gentleman's grandfather sat upon his right hand and was the first man who collared him . . . . "

Duke of Scuttlewig. " . . . after laying the story at the doors of a great many great people, [the egotistical gentleman] happily left it at last with the Duke of Scuttlewig . . . . "

Lord Slang. " . . . [the egotistical gentleman] presumed we had often met Lord Slang . . . . "

Dowager Lady Snorflerer. " . . . the egotistical gentleman . . . inquired if we happened to be acquainted with the Dowager Lady Snorflerer."

    Briggs: never let him complain of not being well
      Mrs: should be thankful to be in ignorance of real suffering
    Verger in Mr Sliverstone's church

The Couple who Coddle Themselves

" . . . *couples who coddle themselves are selfish and slothful . . . they charge upon every wind that blows, every rain that falls, and every vapour that hangs in the air, the evils which arise from their own imprudence or the gloom which is engendered in their own tempers . . . .* "

Mrs Chopper. " . . . a mysterious old lady who lurks behind a pair of spectacles, and is afflicted with a chronic disease, respecting which she has taken a vast deal of medical advice, and referred to a vast number of medical books, without meeting any definition of symptoms that at all suits her, or enables her to say, 'That's my complaint.' Indeed, the absence of authentic information upon the subject of this complaint would seem to be Mrs Chopper's greatest ill, as in all other respects she is an uncommonly hale and hearty gentlewoman."

Merrywinkle "is a rather lean and long-necked gentleman, middle-aged and middle-sized, and usually troubled with a cold in the head."

"Mr Merrywinkle's leaving home to go to business on a damp or wet morning is a very elaborate affair. He puts on wash-leather socks over his stockings, and India-rubber shoes above his boots, and wears under his waistcoat a cuirass of hare-skin. Besides these precautions, he winds a thick shawl round his throat, and blocks up his mouth with a large silk handkerchief. Thus accoutred, and furnished besides with a great-coat and umbrella, he braves the dangers of the streets; travelling in severe weather at a gentle trot, the better to preserve the circulation, and bringing his mouth to the surface to take breath, but very seldom, and with the utmost caution.

"His office-door opened, he shoots past his clerk at the same pace, and diving into his own private room, closes the door, examines the window-fastenings, and gradually unrobes himself: hanging his pocket-handkerchief on the fender to air, and determining to write to the newspapers about the fog, which, he says, 'has really got to that pitch that it is quite unbearable.'" ¶

—*mealtime:* " . . . Mr Merrywinkle, in his desire to gratify his appetite, is not unmindful of his health, for he has a bottle of carbonate of soda with which to qualify his porter, and a little pair of scales in which to weigh it out. Neither in his anxiety to take care of his body is he unmindful of the welfare of his immortal part, as he always prays that for what he is going to receive he may be made truly thankful; and in order that he may be as thankful as possible, eats and drinks to the utmost."

Mrs Merrywinkle's "maiden name was **Chopper** . . . . Her father died when she was . . . 'yet an infant' . . . . [she] is a delicate looking lady, with very light hair, and is exceedingly subject to the same unpleasant disorder [a cold in the head]."

—*mealtime:* "Now the dinner is always a good one, the appetites of the diners being delicate, and requiring a little of what Mrs Merrywinkle calls 'tittivation;' the secret of which is understood to lie in good cookery and tasteful spices, and which process is so successfully performed in the present instance, that both Mr and Mrs Merrywinkle eat a remarkably good dinner, and even the afflicted Mrs Chopper wields her knife and fork with much of the spirit and elasticity of youth."

YC 11 1840   C&H O

The Old Couple

Jane Adams. "There is an aged woman who once lived servant with the old lady's father, and is sheltered in an alms-house not far off. She is still attached to the family, and loves them all; she nursed the children in her lap, and tended in their sickness those who are no more."

—*at the celebration:* " . . . two great-grandchildren rush out at a given signal, and presently return, dragging in old Jane Adams leaning upon her crutched stick, and trembling with age and pleasure. Who so popular as poor old Jane, nurse and story-teller in ordinary to two generations; and who so happy as she, striving to bend her stiff limbs into a curtsey, while tears of pleasure steal down her withered cheks!"

Anne. "[**Jane**] recollects she took a friend of hers up-stairs to see Miss Emma dressed for church; her name was—ah! she forgets the name, but she remembers that she was a very pretty girl, and that she married not long afterwards, and lived—it has quite passed out of her mind where she lived, but she knows she had a bad husband who used her ill, and that she died in Lambeth workhouse."

Crofts. "'Eighty years old, Crofts, and never had a headache,' [**Harvey**] tells the barber who shaves him (the barber being a young fellow, and very subject to that complaint)."

The **Harveys**. [**Jane Adams**'s] old mistress has still something of youth in her eyes; the young ladies are like what she was but not quite so handsome, nor are the gentlemen as stately as Mr Harvey used to be."

"See them among their grandchildren and great-grandchildren; how garrulous they are, how they compare one with another, and insist on likenesses which no one else can see; how gently the old lady lectures the girls on points of breeding and decorum, and points the moral by anecdotes of herself in her young days—how the old gentleman chuckles over boyish feats and roguish tricks . . . . "

"The old couple sit side by side, and the old time seems like yesterday indeed. Looking back upon the path they have travelled, its dust and ashes disappear; the flowers that withered long ago, show brightly again upon its borders, and they grow young once more in the youth of those about them."

Lucy. "[The bachelor] recollects something of a favourite playmate; her name was Lucy—so they tell him. He is not sure whether she was married, or went abroad, or died." [*Lucy Stroughill lived next door to CD when he was eight or nine, and his childhood memories of her were vivid. Look at* **Children**, *page 296*]

> Bachelor, peevish, racked by rheumatic pains; quarrelling with the world
> **Harveys**: son, who died as a man: that was the worst; grief now softened
>   eldest son: his house is the site of celebration
>   girl, a slight young thing too delicate for earth
>   infant: they wept for him
> Little boy, grandson of the Harveys: little, chubby and triumphant
> Old Parr[H]: English farmer who may have lived 152 years

N 3   April 1838-Oct 1839 in monthly parts by C&H   3 vols 1839 **NN**
U.S. publication in monthly parts 1838-39 by Carey, Lea & Blanchard, Philadelphia,
succeeded by Lea & Blanchard; New York publication by James Turney

The Life and Adventures
of
Nicholas Nickleby

Containing a Faithful Account of the
Fortunes, Misfortunes, Uprisings, Downfallings and
Complete Career of the Nickleby Family, edited by Boz

"If . . . there is a supreme point of spring, Nicholas Nickleby is the supreme point of Dickens's spring . . . this book coincided with his resolution to be a great novelist and his final belief that he could be one." GKC p31

"It is his first definite attempt to write a young and chivalrous novel. In this sense the comic characters and the comic scenes are secondary; and indeed the comic characters and the comic scenes, admirable as they are, could never be considered as in themselves superior to such characters and such scenes in many of the other books. But in themselves how unforgettable they are." GKC pp35-6

PRÉCIS

Godfrey Nickleby had two sons: **Ralph**, who went to the city to make money; and **Nicholas**, the country mouse, who married and had son **Nicholas** (NN) and daughter **Kate**. His wife **Mrs Nickleby** (Mrs N) wanted more income, and he tried, but lost his principal instead and died. 1

Ralph, a thriving usurer, employs **Newman Noggs**, a failure. Ralph's muffin and crumpet company has a meeting. Informed that his brother's family is in London to see him, Ralph calls and encounters their landlady, kind **Miss La Creevy**. Ralph urges NN to Yorkshire employment in a boys' school, promising to provide for the ladies. He consigns him to **Wackford Squeers**, master of Dotheboys Hall ("Do (that is, cheat) the boys"). 2-4

NN, seen off by mother and sister, departs with Squeers and forlorn **Snawley** boys. The coach's breakdown occasions some story-telling. NN meets the unprepossessing **Mrs Squeers** and the pitiable **Smike. 5-7**

Morning exposes NN to the school's vicious system and Squeers's cruelty. His daughter **Fanny** invites NN to a gathering with her bosom friend **Matilda Price** and the latter's fiancé, **John Browdie**. Matilda flirts, NN is congenial, and Fanny is chagrined. 8-9

Ralph finds Kate a place at **Madame Mantalini's** millinery and a home in a dingy house he owns. Noggs escorts her and Mrs N. 10-11

NN is miserable, and Smike so much so that he runs away. He is pursued and brought back for condign punishment. NN intervenes to stop the whipping and turns it upon Squeers. 12-13

NN heads back to London, aided by Browdie, and connects with Noggs. He walks in on a **Kenwigs** party and meets Mr **Lillyvick**, water-rate collector, and **Henrietta Petowker**, actress. Noggs shows him Fanny's denunciation of him. 14-15

Needing work, NN goes to **Gregsbury**, an M.P., but declines his employ. He begins tutoring the Kenwigs children in French. Kate is at the Mantalini shop. **Miss Knag** is first enamoured and then incensed with her. 16-18

Ralph invites Kate to preside at dinner. She meets Sir **Mulberry Hawk**; his butt, Lord **Frederick Verisopht**; and other hangers-on. Hawk makes himself obnoxious, outraging Kate. 19

Kate and NN reunite, and NN tries vainly to educate the witless Mrs N. Smike has followed NN to London. The Mantalini firm goes under the hammer, and Kate becomes companion to vaporish **Mrs Wititterly**. 20-21

NN and Smike, headed for Portsmouth, fall in with the **Crummles** troupe. They are enlisted in the acting company. NN accompanies **Miss Snevellicci** on a town-wide canvas, and Miss Petowker appears, followed by Lillyvick, who weds her. 22-25

Kate is pursued by Hawk and Verisopht, who are aided by toadies **Pyke** and **Pluck** and by Mrs N's blindness and Mrs Wititterly's stupidity. Kate demands protection from Ralph. Noggs warns NN of her plight, and after an abortive duel with a jealous rival he leaves the troupe for London. 26-30

NN overhears Hawk discussing Kate in a bar. He demands his name. There is a struggle which ends in an accident disabling Hawk. NN collects Kate and his mother and expels Ralph from their lives. Squeers arrives and complains to Ralph about NN. They plan revenge through Smike. 31-34

Once more seeking employment, NN encounters the **Cheeryble** brothers and his tide turns. He appalls the Kenwigs, telling of the Lillyvick nuptials. He distinguishes himself as clerk, trained by **Tim Linkinwater**. A **lunatic** in small-clothes makes avowals to a receptive Mrs N. 35-37

Smike is recaptured by Squeers but freed by Browdie. NN sees and is smitten by **Madeline Bray**. He tries to find out who she is. The smallclothes are unmasked, but Mrs N is still impressed. NN encounters **Frank Cheeryble**, a nephew, whose interest in Kate is soon apparent. 38-43

Ralph is accosted by **Brooker**, a former acquaintance, but ignores him. He finds Madame Mantalini at last convinced her husband **Alfred** is unworthy. With Squeers and **Snawley**, who claims that Smike is his son, Ralph goes to NN and demands the boy. NN defies them. 44-45

The Cheerybles ask NN to take covert aid to Madeline, who lives with her selfish father. **Arthur Gride**, **Bray**'s creditor, admires her and enlists Ralph's aid in arranging their marriage. He knows (she does not) that she is an heiress. NN meets Crummles on the way to America. 46-48

Smike is failing, in love with Kate. Mrs N's lunatic admirer drops in and drops out. Hawk has recovered and seeks vengeance on NN, but Lord Verisopht opposes this. Hawk kills him in a duel and flees abroad. 49-50

Through Noggs, NN learns of Gride's marital intentions. Lillyvick has been deserted by his new wife and is reunited with the Kenwigses. NN visits Gride, hoping to dissuade him from the marriage, but fails. He reappears, to bear Madeline away when her father is stricken and dies. Kate nurses the bereaved Madeline, and Smike fades more seriously. 51-55

Gride has been robbed by his servant **Peg Sliderskew** of papers whose disclosure would mean his ruin. Ralph suffers large losses but is consumed more with dreams of vengeance on NN. He sets Squeers to spy on Peg. Noggs and Frank catch Squeers in his moment of success. He is incarcerated. 56-57

Smike dies. Ralph seeks and after opposition from **Mrs Snawley** at last finds Squeers. He goes to a meeting with the Cheerybles. Brooker tells him Smike was his son. 58-60

Ralph decides that his suicide will be the best revenge and hangs himself. NN and Madeline find each other, as do Frank and Kate, and (to Mrs N's chagrin) Linkinwater and Miss La Creevy . Alfred Mantalini is discovered in humiliating circumstances, Dotheboys Hall erupts in rebellion, and the Good triumphs. 61-65

CONTENTS

Illustrations by *Hablôt K. Browne* ("Phiz")

CHARACTERS

Adams, Captain; second to Verisopht	O	359
African Swallower	CTT	359
Alice, a sister of York	Int	374
Alphonse, a page (with the face of Bill)	O	359
Ancestor of Grogzwig	Int	374
Attendant, to Madeline Bray: black-leaded face	O	359
Bachelor admirer of Mrs Kenwigs's sister	O	359
Bank clerk, friend of the Cheerybles	O	359
Bar-maid, who does not object to being admired	O	360
Belling, sitting apprehensively on his trunk	BDH	339
Belvawney, Miss; seldom in speaking parts	CTT	358
Bevan, Mrs	HHR	330
Biffin, Sarah[H]; born without arms or legs	HHR	330
Blockson, Mrs, charwoman; a trial to Mortimer Knag	O	360
Bobster, Cecilia; wooed in error	O	360
an irasicible father	W	368
Bolder, terrified; warts on his hands	BDH	339
Bonney, Mr; muffin company promoter	MCC	373
Borum, Augustus; pinching young man	O	360
boys; pulling the Phenomenon apart	W	368
Charlotte; carries off a parasol	W	368
Emma; does stare	W	368
Mrs; mother of six theater fans	O	360
Box-keeper, assistant; abused by Pyke	W	369
Boy, hump-backed, invalid in bed	W	369
Boys, at Dotheboys Hall	SR	338
Bravassa, Miss; who had her picture made	CTT	358
Bray, Madeline; beloved of Nicholas Nickleby	DD	325
Mrs; deceased, loved by a Cheeryble	O	360
Walter; handsome, spoiled, selfish widower and father	O	360
Two bricklayers, observing Smike kidnapped	W	369
Brooker, old acquaintance fallen on evil days	O	360
Browdie, John; bluff Yorkshireman	SR	340
Matilda, formerly **Price**; flirt and confidante	SR	350
Browndock, Mrs	HHR	330
Bulph, pilot and landlord	O	361

Spear-carriers

The Hero

> *"If Nicholas be not always found to be blameless or agreeable, he is not always intended to appear so. He is a young man of an impetuous temper and of little or no experience; and I saw no reason why such a hero should be lifted out of nature." —Preface*

Nicholas Nickleby. " . . . the uncle and nephew looked at each other for some seconds without speaking. The face of the old man was stern, hardfeatured and forbidding; that of the young one, open, handsome, and ingenuous. The old man's eye was keen with the twinklings of avarice and cunning; the young man's, bright with the light of intelligence and spirit. His figure was somewhat slight, but manly and well-formed. . . . " 3

—*rousing himself:* " . . . being out of spirits, and not seeing any especial reason why he should make himself agreeable, [he] looked out of the window and sighed involuntarily . . . .

"'Well,' thought Nicholas, 'as I am here, and seem expected for some reason or other to be amiable, it's of no use looking like a goose. I may as well accommodate myself to the company.'

"We blush to tell it, but his youthful spirits and vivacity getting for a time the better of his sad thoughts, he no sooner formed this resolution than he saluted **Miss Squeers** and the friend with great gallantry, and drawing a chair to the tea-table, began to make himself more at home than in all probability an usher has ever done in his employer's house since ushers were first invented." 9

—*indignant and expressing it:* "**Squeers** caught [**Smike**] firmly in his grip; one desperate cut had fallen on his body—he was wincing from the lash and uttering a scream of pain—it was raised again, and again about to fall—when Nicholas Nickleby suddenly starting up, cried 'Stop!' in a voice that made the rafters ring . . . .

"'I have a long series of insults to avenge,' said Nicholas, flushed with passion; 'and my indignation is aggravated by the dastardly cruelties practised on helpless infancy in this foul den. Have a care; for if you do raise the devil within me, the consequences shall fall heavily upon your own head.'

"He had scarcely spoken when Squeers, in a violent outbreak of wrath and with a cry like a howl of a wild beast, spat upon him, and struck him a blow across the face with his instrument of torture, which raised up a bar of livid flesh as it was inflicted. Smarting with the agony of the blow, and concentrating into that one moment all his feelings of rage, scorn, and indignation,

Nicholas sprang upon him, wrested the weapon from his hand, and, pinning him by the throat, beat the ruffian till he roared for mercy." 13

—*his spirit:* " . . . Nicholas was not, in the ordinary sense of the word, a young man of high spirit. He would resent an affront to himself, or interpose to redress a wrong offered to another, as boldly and freely as any knight that ever set lance in rest; but he lacked that peculiar excess of coolness and great-minded selfishness, which invariably distinguish gentlemen of high spirit . . . .

"Nicholas, therefore, not being a high-spirited young man according to common parlance, and deeming it a greater degradation to borrow, for the supply of his necessities, from **Newman Noggs**, than to teach French to the little **Kenwigses** for five shillings a week, accepted the offer . . . and betook himself to the first floor with all convenient speed." 16

—*eloquent:* "You [**Ralph**] . . . sent me to a den where sordid cruelty, worthy of yourself, runs wanton, and youthful misery stalks precocious; where the lightness of childhood shrinks into the heaviness of age, and its every promise blights, and withers as it grows . . . ." 20

"'You are known to me now. There are no reproaches I could heap upon your head which would carry with them one thousandth part of the grovelling shame that this assurance will awaken even in your breast.

"'Your brother's widow and her orphan child spurn the shelter of your roof, and shun you with disgust and loathing. Your kindred renounce you, for they know no shame but the ties of blood which bind them in name with you.

"'You are an old man, and I leave you to the grave. May every recollection of your life cling to your false heart, and cast their darkness on your death-bed.'" 33

—*a brother's moment:* "'I tell you again, Miss Nickleby is my sister. Will you or will you not answer for your unmanly and brutal conduct?'

"'To a proper champion—yes. To you—no,' returned Sir **Mulberry**, taking the reins in his hand. "Stand out of the way, dog. **William**, let go her head . . . .'

"The man obeyed. The animal reared and plunged as though it would dash the carriage into a thousand pieces, but Nicholas, blind to all sense of danger, and conscious of nothing but his fury, still maintained his place and his hold upon the reins . . . .

" . . . Sir Mulberry shortening his whip, applied it furiously to the head and shoulders of Nicholas. It was broken in the struggle; Nicholas gained the heavy handle, and with it laid open one side of his antagonist's face from the eye to the lip. He saw the gash; knew that the mare had darted off at a wild mad gallop; a hundred lights danced in his eyes, and he felt himself flung violently upon the ground.

"He was giddy and sick, but staggered to his feet directly, roused by the loud shouts of the men who were tearing up the street, and screaming to those ahead to clear the way. He was conscious of a torrent of people rushing quickly by—looking up, could discern the cabriolet whirled along the foot pavement with frightful rapidity—then heard a loud cry, the smashing of some heavy body, and the breaking of glass—and then the crowd closed in in the distance, and he could see or hear no more." 32

—*the family resemblance:* As the brother and sister stood side by side with a gallant bearing which became them well, a close likeness between them was apparent, which many, had they only seen them apart, might have failed to remark. The air, carriage, and very look and expression of the brother were all reflected in the sister, but softened and refined to the nicest limit of feminine delicacy and attraction. More striking still was some indefinable resemblance in the face of **Ralph** to both. While they had never looked more handsome nor he more ugly, while they had never held themselves more proudly, nor he shrunk half so low, there never had been a time when this resemblance was so perceptible . . . . " 54

The Villain

Ralph Nickleby. He "deduced . . . that riches are the only true source of happiness and power, and that it is lawful and just to compass their acquisition by all means short of felony . . . .

"Not confining himself to theory, or permitting his faculties to rust even at that early age in mere abstract speculations, this promising lad commenced usurer on a limited scale at school, putting out at good interest a small capital of slate-pencil and marbles, and gradually extending his operations until they aspired to the copper coinage of this realm, in which he speculated to considerable advantage." 1

—*fraternal feeling:* "On the death of his father, [he] . . . applied himself passionately to his old pursuit of money-getting, in which he speedily became so buried and absorbed, that he quite forgot his brother for many years; and if at times a recollection of his old play-fellow broke upon him through the haze in which he lived . . . it brought along with it a companion thought, that if they were intimate he would want to borrow money of him: and Mr Ralph Nickleby shrugged his shoulders, and said things were better as they were." 1

"'When my brother was such as [**Nicholas**],' said Ralph, 'the first comparisons were drawn between us—always in my disfavour. *He* was open, liberal, gallant, gay; *I* a crafty hunks of cold and stagnant blood, with no passion but love of saving, and no spirit beyond a thirst for gain. I recollected it well when I first saw this whipster; but I remember it better now.'" 34

—*occupation:* "Mr Ralph Nickleby was not, strictly speaking, what you would call a merchant: neither was he a banker, nor an attorney, nor a special pleader, nor a notary. He was certainly not a tradesman, and still less could he lay any claim to the title of a professional gentleman; for it would have been impossible to mention any recognised profession to which he belonged. Nevertheless, as he lived in a spacious house in Golden Square, which, in addition to a brass plate upon the street-door, had another brass plate two sizes and a half smaller upon the left-hand doorpost, surmounting a brass model of an infant's fist grasping a fragment of a skewer, and displaying the word 'Office,' it was clear that Mr Ralph Nickleby did, or pretended to do, business of some kind . . . . He knew nobody round about and nobody knew him, although he enjoyed the reputation of being immensely rich. The tradesmen held that he was a sort of lawyer, and the other neighbours opined that he was a kind of general agent; both of which guesses were as correct and definite as guesses about other people's affairs usually are, or need to be." 2

—*first appearance:* "he wore a bottle-green spencer over a blue coat; a white waistcoat, grey mixture pantaloons, and Wellington boots drawn over them: the corner of a small-plaited shirt frill struggled out, as if insisting to show itself, from between his chin and the top button of his spencer, and the garment was not made low enough to conceal a long gold watch-chain, composed of a series of plain rings, which had its beginning at the handle of a gold repeater in Mr Nickleby's pocket, and its termination in two little keys, one belonging to the watch itself, and the other to some patent padlock. He wore a sprinkling of powder upon his head, as if to make himself look benevolent; but if that were his purpose, he would have perhaps have done better to powder his countenance also, for there was something in its very wrinkles, and in his cold restless eye, which seemed to tell of cunning that would announce itself in spite of him." 2

—*shaken:* " . . . a comb fell from **Kate**'s hair, close at her uncle's feet; and as he picked it up and returned it to her hand, the light from a neighbouring lamp shone upon her face. The lock of hair that had escaped and curled loosely over her brow, the traces of tears yet scarcely dry, the flushed cheek, the look of sorrow, all fired some dormant train of recollection in the old man's breast; and the face of his dead brother seemed present before him, with the very look it wore on some occasion of boyish grief, of which every minute circumstance flashed upon his mind, with the distinctness of a scene of yesterday.

"Ralph Nickleby, who was proof against all appeals of blood and kindred— who was steeled against every tale of sorrow and distress—staggered while he looked, and reeled back into his house, as a man who had seen a spirit from some world beyond the grave." 19

—*humanity?* "To say that Ralph loved or cared for—in the most ordinary acceptation of those terms—any one of God's creatures, would be the wildest fiction. Still, there had somehow stolen upon him from time to time a thought of his niece which was tinged with compassion and pity; breaking through the dull cloud of dislike or indifference which darkened men and women in his eyes, there was, in her case, the faintest gleam of light—a most feeble and sickly ray at the best of times—but there it was, and it showed the poor girl in a better and purer aspect than any in which he had looked on human nature yet." 26

" . . . notwithstanding the baseness with which he had behaved, and was then behaving, and would behave again if his interest prompted him, towards **Kate** herself—still there was, strange though it may seem, something humanizing and even gentle in his thoughts . . . . He thought of what his home might be if Kate were there; he placed her in the empty chair, looked upon her, heard her speak; he felt again upon his arm the gentle pressure of the trembling hand; he strewed his costly rooms with the hundred silent tokens of feminine presence and occupation . . . in that one glimpse of a better nature, born as it was in selfish thoughts, the rich man felt himself friendless, childless, and alone." 31

—*seen by a mountebank:* "' . . . what a demneble fierce old evil genius you are. You're enough to frighten my life and soul out of her little delicious wits— flying all at once into such a glazing, ravaging, raging passion as never was, demmit.'

"'Pshaw,' rejoined Ralph, forcing a smile. 'It is but manner.'

"'It is a demd uncomfortable and private-madhouse-sort of manner,' said Mr **Mantalini** . . . ." 34

—*nourished by hatred:* "In exact proportion as Ralph Nickleby became conscious of a struggling and lingering regard for **Kate**, had his detestation of **Nicholas** augmented. It might be, that to atone for the weakness of inclining to any one person, he held it necessary to hate some other more intensely than before; but such had been the course of his feelings." 34

—*no hypocrite:* "Stern, unyielding, dogged, and impenetrable, Ralph cared for nothing in life, or beyond it, save the gratification of two passions, avarice, the first and predominant appetite of his nature, and hatred, the second.

Affecting to consider himself but a type of all humanity, he was at little pains to conceal his true character from the world in general, and in his own heart he exulted over and cherished every bad design as it had birth. The only scriptural admonition that Ralph Nickleby heeded, in the letter, was 'know thyself.' He knew himself well, and choosing to imagine that all mankind were cast in the same mould, hated them . . . ." 44

—*his clientele:*   "He appeared to have a very extraordinary and miscellaneous connexion, and very odd calls he made—some at great rich houses, and some at small poor ones—but all upon one subject: money. His face was a talisman to the porters and servants of his more dashing clients, and procured him ready admission, though he trudged on foot, and others, who were denied, rattled to the door in carriages. Here he was all softness and cringing civility; his step so light, that it scarcely produced a sound upon the thick carpets; his voice so soft, that it was not audible beyond the person to whom it was addressed.

"But in the poorer habitations Ralph was another man; his boots creaked upon the passage floor as he walked boldly in, his voice was harsh and loud as he demanded the money that was overdue; his threats were coarse and angry.

"With another class of customers, Ralph was again another man. These were **attorneys** of more than doubtful reputation, who helped him to new business, or raised fresh profits upon old. With them Ralph was familiar and jocose—humorous upon the topics of the day, and especially pleasant upon bankruptcies and pecuniary difficulties that made good for trade.

"In short, it would have been difficult to have recognised the same man under these various aspects, but for the bulky leather case full of bills and notes which he drew from his pocket at every house, and the constant repetition of the same complaint (varied only in tone and style of delivery), that the world thought him rich, and that perhaps he might be if he had his own; but there was no getting money in when it was once out, either principal or interest, and it was a hard matter to live—even to live from day to day." 44

—*beside himself:*   "There was something so unnatural in the constrained calmness with which Ralph Nickleby spoke, when coupled with the livid face, the horrible expression of the features to which every nerve and muscle as it twitched and throbbed with a spasm whose workings no effort could conceal, gave every instant some new and frightful aspect—there was something so unnatural and ghastly in the contrast between his harsh, slow, steady voice (only altered by a certain halting of the breath which made him pause between almost every word like a drunken man bent upon speaking plainly), and these evidences of the most intense and violent passions, and the struggle he made to keep them under, that if [**Bray**'s] dead body which lay above had stood instead of him before the cowering **Gride**, it could scarcely have presented a spectacle which would have terrified [the latter] more." 56

The Damsel in Distress

Madeline Bray. " . . . a young lady who could be scarcely eighteen, of very slight and delicate figure, but exquisitely shaped, who, walking timidly up to the desk, made an inquiry. . . . She raised her veil for an instant . . .and disclosed a countenance of most uncommon beauty, although shaded by a cloud of sadness, which in one so young was doubly remarkable . . . .

"She was neatly, but very quietly attired; so much so, indeed, that it seemed as though her dress, if it had been worn by one who imparted fewer graces of her own to it, might have looked poor and shabby." 16

—her occupation: " . . . proudly resisting all offers of permanent aid and support from her late mother's friends, because they were made conditional upon her quitting the wretched man, her father, who had no friends left, and shrinking with instinctive delicacy from appealing in their behalf to that true and noble heart [of **Charles Cheeryble**] which he hated, and had . . . deeply wronged by misconstruction and ill report, this young girl had struggled alone and unassisted to maintain him by the labour of her hands . . . never wearied by the petulant gloom of a sick man sustained by no consoling recollections of the past or hopes of the future; never repining for the comforts she had rejected, or bewailing the hard lot she had voluntarily incurred." 46

—*her home:* "But how the graces and elegancies which she had dispersed about the poorly-furnished room, went to the heart of **Nicholas**! Flowers, plants, birds, the harp, the old piano whose notes had sounded so much sweeter in bygone times—how many struggles had it cost her to keep these two last links of that broken chain which bound her yet to home! With every slender ornament, the occupation of her leisure hours, replete with that graceful charm which lingers in every little tasteful work of woman's hands, how much patient endurance and how many gentle affections were entwined!" 46

—*to be sold:* "There are no words which can express, nothing with which can be compared, the perfect pallor, the clear transparent cold ghastly white-ness, of the beautiful face which turned towards [**Nicholas**] when he entered. Her hair was a rich deep brown, but shading that face, and straying upon a neck that rivalled it in whiteness, it seemed by the strong contrast raven black. Something of wildness and restlessness there was in the dark eye, but there was the same patient look, the same expression of gentle mournfulness which he well remembered, and no trace of a single tear. Most beautiful—more beautiful perhaps in appearance than ever—there was something in her face which quite unmanned him, and appeared far more touching than the wildest agony of grief. It was not merely calm and composed, but fixed and rigid, as though the violent effort which had summoned that composure beneath her father's eye, while it mastered all other thoughts, had prevented even the momentary expression they had communicated to the features from subsiding, and had fastened it there as an evidence of its triumph." 52

The Pure Sister

Kate Nickleby, "slight but very beautiful girl of about seventeen . . . . " 3

—*feeling demeaned:* "Kate shed many bitter tears when [the rich lady and the rich daughter] were gone, and felt, for the first time, humbled by her occupation. She had, it is true, quailed at the prospect of drudgery and hard service; but she had felt no degradation in working for her bread, until she found herself exposed to insolence and the coarsest pride. Philosophy would have taught her that the degradation was on the side of those who had sunk so low as to display such passions habitually, and without cause; but she was too young for such consolation, and her honest feeling was hurt." 17

—*aroused:* "'The matter which brings me to you, sir . . . is one which should call the blood up into your cheeks, and make you burn to hear, as it does me to tell. I have been wronged; my feelings have been outraged, insulted, wounded past all healing, and by your friends.'

"'Friends!' cried **Ralph**, sternly. '*I* have no friends, girl.'

"'By the men I saw here, then,' returned Kate quickly. 'If they were no friends of yours, and you knew what they were—oh, the more shame on you, uncle, for bringing me among them. To have subjected me to what I was exposed to here, through any misplaced confidence or imperfect knowledge of your guests, would have required some strong excuse; but if you did it—as I now believe you did—knowing them well, it was most dastardly and cruel.'

"Ralph drew back in utter amazement at this plain speaking, and regarded Kate with his sternest look. But she met his gaze proudly and firmly, and although her face was very pale, it looked more noble and handsome, lighted up as it was, than it had ever appeared before." 28

The Well-meaning Mother

Mrs Nickleby. "'My brother was a thoughtless, inconsiderate man, Mrs Nickleby, and nobody, I am sure, can have better reason to feel that, than you [said **Ralph**].'

"This appeal set the widow upon thinking that perhaps she might have made a more successful venture with her one thousand pounds, and then she began to reflect what a comfortable sum it would have been just then; which dismal thoughts made her tears flow faster, and in the excess of these griefs she (being a well-meaning woman enough, but rather weak withal) fell first to deploring her hard fate, and then to remarking, with many sobs, that to be sure she had been a slave to poor **Nicholas**, and had often told him she might have married better (as indeed she had, very often), and that she never knew in his lifetime how the money went, but that if he had confided in her they might all have been better off that day; with other bitter recollections common to most married ladies either during their coverture, or afterwards, or at both periods. Mrs Nickleby concluded by lamenting that the dear departed had never deigned to profit by her advice, save on one occasion: which was a strictly veracious statement, inasmuch as he had only acted upon it once, and had ruined himself in consequence . . . .

" . . . [Ralph] had struck so successfully on one of those little jarring chords in the human heart (Ralph was well acquainted with its worst weaknesses, though he knew nothing of its best), that she had already begun seriously to consider herself the amiable and suffering victim of her late husband's imprudence." 3

—*talking:* " . . . Miss **Knag** fell into many more recollections, no less interesting than true, the full tide of which Mrs Nickleby in vain attempting to stem, at length sailed smoothly down, by adding an undercurrent of her own recollections; and so both ladies went on talking together in perfect contentment; the only difference between them being, that whereas Miss Knag addressed herself to **Kate**, and talked very loud, Mrs Nickleby kept on in one unbroken monotonous flow, perfectly satisfied to be talking, and caring very little whether anybody listened or not." 18

—*comprehending:* "Mrs Nickleby was not the sort of person to be told anything in a hurry, or rather to comprehend anything of peculiar delicacy or importance on a short notice. Wherefore, although the good lady had been subjected to a full hour's preparation by little **Miss La Creevy**, and was now addressed in most lucid terms both by **Nicholas** and his sister, she was in a state of singular bewilderment and confusion . . . ." 33

—*vanity:* "To do Mrs Nickleby justice, her attachment to her children would have prevented her seriously contemplating a second marriage, even if she could have so far conquered her recollections of her late husband as to have any strong inclinations that way. But although there was no evil and little real selfishness in Mrs Nickleby's heart, she had a weak head and a vain one; and there was something so flattering in being sought (and vainly sought) in marriage at this time of day, that she could not dismiss the passion of the unknown gentleman quite so summarily or lightly as Nicholas appeared to deem becoming." 37

—*dressed to kill:* " . . . Mrs Nickleby had by little and little begun to display unusual care in the adornment of her person, gradually superadding to those staid and matronly habiliments, which had up to that time formed her ordinary attire, a variety of embellishments and decorations, slight perhaps in themselves, but, taken together . . . of no mean importance. Even her black dress assumed something of a deadly-lively air from the jaunty style in which it was worn; and, eked out as its lingering attractions were, by a prudent disposal here and there of certain juvenile ornaments of little or no value, which had for that reason alone escaped the general wreck and been permitted to slumber peacefully in odd corners of old drawers and boxes where daylight seldom shone, her mourning garments assumed quite a new character, and from being the outward tokens of respect and sorrow for the dead, were converted into signals of very slaughterous and killing designs upon the living.

"Mrs Nickleby might have been stimulated to this proceeding by a lofty sense of duty, and impulses of unquestionable excellence. She might by this time have become impressed with the sinfulness of long indulgence in unavailing woe, or the necessity of setting a proper example of neatness and decorum to her blooming daughter. Considerations of duty and responsibility apart, the change might have taken its rise in feelings of the purest and most disinterested charity. The gentleman next door had been vilified by **Nicholas**; rudely stigmatised as a dotard and an idiot; and for these attacks upon his understanding, Mrs Nickleby was in some sort accountable. She might have felt that it was the act of a good Christian to show, by all means in her power, that the abused gentleman was neither the one nor the other. And what better means could she adopt towards so virtuous and laudable an end, than proving to all men, in her own person, that his passion was the most rational and reasonable in the world, and just the very result of all others which discreet and thinking persons might have foreseen, from her incautiously displaying her matured charms, without reserve, under the very eye, as it were, of an ardent and too-susceptible man?" 41

—*an unexpected outcome:* "'. . . I do beg and entreat of him to go quietly away, if it's only for'—here Mrs Nickleby simpered and hesitated—'for *my* sake.'

"It might have been expected that the old gentleman would have been penetrated to the heart by the delicacy and condescension of this appeal, and that he would at least have returned a courteous and suitable reply. What, then, was the shock which Mrs Nickleby received, when, accosting *her* in the most unmistakable manner, he replied in a loud and sonorous voice: 'Avaunt— Cat!'

"'Sir!' cried Mrs Nickleby, in a faint tone.

"'Cat!' repeated the old gentleman. 'Puss, Kit, Tit, Grimalkin, Tabby, Brindle—Whoosh!' with which last sound, uttered in a hissing manner between his teeth, the old gentleman swung his arms violently round and round, and at the same time alternately advanced on Mrs Nickleby, and retreated from her, in that species of savage dance with which boys on market-days may be seen to frighten pigs, sheep, and other animals, when they give out obstinate indications of turning down a wrong street.

"Mrs Nickleby wasted no words, but uttered an exclamation of horror and surprise, and immediately fainted away." 49 *And see* **Lunatic**, in Small-Clothes SR

—*punctilious:* "Mrs Nickleby, knowing of her son's obligations to the honest Yorkshireman, had, after some demur, yielded her consent to Mr and **Mrs Browdie** being invited out to tea; in the way of which arrangement, there were at first sundry difficulties and obstacles, arising out of her not having had an opportunity of 'calling' upon Mrs Browdie first; for although Mrs Nickleby very often observed with much complacency (as most punctilious people do), that she had not an atom of pride or formality about her, still she was a great stickler for dignity and ceremonies; and as it was manifest that, until a call had been made, she could not be (politely speaking, and according to the laws of society) even cognizant of the fact of Mrs Browdie's existence, she felt her situation to be one of peculiar delicacy and difficulty.

"'The call *must* originate with me, my dear,' said Mrs Nickleby, 'that's indispensable. The fact is, my dear, that it's necessary there should be a sort of condescension on my part, and that I should show this young person that I am willing to take notice of her." 45

Heroes and Heroines of her Illustrative Reminiscence

Mrs Bevan. "'I recollect dining once at Mrs Bevan's in that broad street, round the corner by the coach-maker's, where the tipsy man fell through the cellar-flap of an empty house nearly a week before quarter-day, and wasn't found till the new tenant went in—and we had roast pig there.'" 41

Miss Biffin. "'The Prince Regent was proud of his legs, and so was **Daniel Lambert**, who was also a fat man; he was proud of his legs. So was Miss Biffin: she was—no,' added Mrs Nickleby, correcting herself, 'I think she had only toes, but the principle is the same.'" 37

Miss Browndock. "'Why your poor dear papa's cousin's sister-in-law—a Miss Browndock—was taken into partnership by a lady that kept a school at Hammersmith, and made her fortune in no time at all; I forget, by the bye, whether that Miss Browndock was the same lady that got the ten thousand pounds prize in the lottery, but I think she was; indeed, now I come to think of it, I am sure she was.'" 17

Clergyman. "'I forget . . . whether it was my great-grandfather who went to school with the Cock-lane Ghost, or the Thirsty Woman of Tutbury who went to school with my grandmother . . . . Which was it that didn't mind what the clergyman said? The Cock-lane Ghost, or the Thirsty Woman of Tutbury?'

"'The Cock-lane Ghost, I believe.'

"'Then I have no doubt,' said Mrs Nickleby, 'that it was with him my great-grandfather went to school; for I know the master of his school was a dissenter, and that would, in a great measure, account for the Cock-lane Ghost's behaving in such an improper manner to the clergyman when he grew up." 49

Coachman. " . . . supposing that the man who drove must have been either the man in the shirt-sleeves or the man with the black eye; that whoever he was, he hadn't found that parasol she left inside last week . . . . " 49

Companion. "'Did you never hear your poor dear papa speak of the young lady who was the daughter of the old lady who boarded in the same house that he boarded in once, when he was a bachelor—what was her name again? I know it began with a B, and ended with a g, but whether it was Waters or—no it couldn't have been that either . . . . '" 21

Conductor. "'There's a very respectable-looking young man,' added Mrs Nickleby, after a short consideration, 'who is conductor to one of the omnibuses that go by here, and who wears a glazed hat—your sister and I have noticed him very often—he has a wart upon his nose, **Kate**, you know, exactly like a gentleman's servant.'" 45

Jane Dibabs. "'Jane Dibabs—the Dibabses lived in the beautiful little thatched white house one story high, covered all over with ivy and creeping plants, with an exquisite little porch with twining honeysuckles and all sorts of things, where the earwigs used to fall into one's tea on a summer evening, and always fell upon their backs and kicked dreadfully, and where the frogs used to get into the rushlight shades when one stopped all night, and sit up and look through the little holes like Christians—Jane Dibabs, *she* married a man who was a great deal older than herself, and would marry him notwithstanding all that could be said to the contrary, and she was so fond of him that nothing was ever equal to it.'" 55

Footboy. "' . . . we had a footboy once, who had not only a wart, but a wen also, and a very large wen too, and he demanded to have his wages raised in consequence, because he found it came very expensive.'" 45

Sir **Thomas Grimble**, "'You don't happen, Mr **Smike**, ever to have dined with the Grimbles of Grimble Hall, somewhere in the North Riding, do you? . . . A very proud man, Sir Thomas Grimble, with six grown-up and most lovely daughters, and the finest park in the county.'

"'My dear mother,' reasoned **Nicholas**, 'do you suppose that the unfortunate outcast of a Yorkshire school was likely to receive many cards of invitation from the nobility and gentry in the neighbourhood?'" 35 *See* **Hawkinses**

Hairdresser. "'The least excitement, the slightest surprise, your **grandmama, Kate**, fainted away directly. . . before she was married, she was turning a corner into Oxford Street one day, when she ran against her own hairdresser, who, it seems, was escaping from a bear—the suddenness of the encounter made her faint away directly.'" 35

Hawkinses. "'Really, my dear, I don't know why it should be so very extraordinary,' said Mrs Nickleby. 'I know that when *I* was at school, I always went at least twice every half-year to the Hawkinses at Taunton Vale, and they are much richer than the **Grimbles**, and connected with them in marriage; so you see it's not so very unlikely, after all.'" 35

Milliner. "'I recollect when your poor papa and I came to town after we were married, that a young lady brought me home a chip cottage bonnet, with white and green trimming, and green persian lining, in her own carriage, which drove up to the door full gallop; —at least, I am not quite certain whether it was her own carriage or a hackney chariot, but I remember very well that the horse dropped down dead as he was turning round . . . . '" 10

Milliners. "'I recollect getting three young milliners to sit to me when I first began to paint, [said **Miss La Creevy**], and I remember that they were all very pale and sickly.'

"'Oh! that's not a general rule, by any means,' observed Mrs Nickleby; 'for I remember as well as if it was only yesterday, employing one that I was particularly recommended to, to make me a scarlet cloak at the time when scarlet cloaks were fashionable, and she had a very red face—a very red face, indeed.'

"'Perhaps she drank,' suggested Miss La Creevy.

"'I don't know how that may have been,' returned Mrs Nickleby; 'but I know she had a very red face, so your argument goes for nothing.'" 11

Nurse. "' . . . that well-behaved nurse who ran away with the linen and the twelve small forks . . . .'" 61

Peltiroguses. "'There was one family in particular, that used to live about a mile from us—not straight down the road, but turning sharp off to the left by the turnpike where the Plymouth mail ran over the donkey—that were quite extraordinary people for giving the most extravagant parties, with artificial flowers and champagne, and variegated lamps, and, in short, every delicacy of eating and drinking that the most singular epicure could possibly require—I don't think there ever were such people as those Peltiroguses.'" 45

Horatio Peltirogus. " . . . she even went so far as to hint obscurely at an attachment entertained for her daughter by the son of an old neighbour of theirs, one Horatio Peltirogus (a young gentleman who might have been at the time four years old, or thereabouts), and to represent it indeed as almost a settled thing between the families—only waiting for her daughter's final decision to come off with the sanction of the church, and to the unspeakable happiness and content of all parties." 55

Reverend. "' . . . the reverend Mr what's his name, who used to read prayers in that old church with the curious little steeple that the weathercock was blown off the night week before you were born . . . .'" 37

Mrs Rogers. "'There was a lady in our neighbourhood,' said Mrs Nickleby, 'speaking of sons puts me in mind of it—a lady in our neighbourhood when we lived near Dawlish, I think her name was Rogers; indeed I am sure it was if it wasn't **Murphy**, which is the only doubt I have . . . ." 37

Shoemaker. "' . . . I am sure there was a case in the day before yesterday's paper, extracted from one of the French newspapers, about a journeyman shoemaker who was jealous of a young girl in an adjoining village, because she wouldn't shut herself up in an airtight three-pair-of-stairs and charcoal herself to death with him, and who went and hid himself in a wood with a sharp-pointed knife, and rushed out as she was passing by with a few friends, and killed himself first, and then all the friends, and then her—no, killed all the friends first, and then herself, and then *himself*—which it is quite frightful to think of. Somehow or other,' added Mrs Nickleby, after a momentary pause, 'they always *are* journeyman shoemakers who do these things in France, according to the papers. I don't know how it is—something in the leather, I suppose.'" 37

Slammons. " . . . Mrs Nickleby was suddenly seized with a forgetfulness of **Smike**'s real name, and an irresistible tendency to call him Mr Slammons; which circumstance she attributed to the remarkable similarity of the two names in point of sound, both beginning with an S, and moreover being spelt with an M." 35

Watkins, "'You know, **Kate**, my dear, that your poor papa went bail for, who afterwards ran away to the United States, and sent us a pair of snow shoes, with such an affectionate letter that it made your poor dear father cry for a week.'" 18

Young gentleman, suitor, "who used to go at that time to the same dancing-school, and who would send gold watches and bracelets to our house in gilt-edged paper, (which were always returned), and who afterwards unfortunately went out to Botany Bay in a cadet ship—a convict ship I mean—and escaped into a bush and killed sheep (I don't know how they got there) and was going to be hung, only he accidentally choked himself, and the government pardoned him.'" 41

Other Principals

Sir Mulberry Hawk. " . . . another superlative gentleman, something older, something stouter, something redder in the face, and something longer upon town . . . .

"'Introduce me, **Nickleby**,' said this second gentleman, who was lounging with his back to the fire, and both elbows on the chimney-piece.

"'Sir Mulberry Hawk,' said **Ralph**.

"'Otherwise the most knowing card in the pa-ack, Miss Nickleby,' said Lord **Frederick Verisopht**." 19

" . . . Sir Mulberry Hawk leered upon his friends most facetiously, and led **Kate** down-stairs with an air of familiarity, which roused in her gentle breast such disgust and burning indignation, as she felt it almost impossible to repress." 19

—*his occupation:* Sir Mulberry Hawk was remarkable for his tact in ruining, by himself and his creatures, young gentlemen of fortune—a genteel and elegant profession, of which he had undoubtedly gained the head. With all the boldness of an original genius, he had struck out an entirely new course of treatment quite opposed to the usual method, his custom being, when he had gained the ascendancy over those he took in hand, rather to keep them down than to give them their own way; and to exercise his vivacity upon them openly and without reserve. Thus he made them butts in a double sense, and while he emptied them with great address, caused them to ring with sundry well-administered taps for the diversion of society." 19

—*priorities:* "The reflections of Sir Mulberry Hawk—if such a term can be applied to the thoughts of the systematic and calculating man of dissipation, whose joys, regrets, pains, and pleasures, are all of self, and who would seem to retain nothing of the intellectual faculty but the power to debase himself, and to degrade the very nature whose outward semblance he wears . . . . " 28

—*envoi:* "Sir Mulberry Hawk lived abroad for some years, courted and caressed, and in high repute as a fine dashing fellow. Ultimately, returning to this country, he was thrown into jail for debt, and there perished miserably, as such high spirits generally do." 65

See **Nicholas Nickleby** H—*a brother's moment*

Newman Noggs. " . . . a sallow-faced man in rusty brown, who . . . always had a pen behind his ear . . . .

"He was a tall man of middle-age with two goggle eyes whereof one was a fixture, a rubicund nose, a cadaverous face, and a suit of clothes (if the term be allowable when they suited him not at all) much the worse for wear, very much too small, and placed upon such a short allowance of buttons that it was quite marvelous how he contrived to keep them on . . . ." 2

—*reflecting:* "Noggs gave a peculiar grunt . . . and (as he rarely spoke to anybody unless somebody spoke to him) fell into a grim silence, and rubbed his hands slowly over each other, cracking the joints of his fingers, and squeezing them into all possible distortions. The incessant performance of this routine on every occasion, and the communication of a fixed and rigid look to his unaffected eye, so as to make it uniform with the other, and to render it impossible for anybody to determine where or at what he was looking, were two among the numerous peculiarities of Mr Noggs, which struck an inexperienced observer at first sight." 2

—*his suitability:* "' . . . Newman Noggs kept his horses and hounds once [said **Ralph**] . . . and not many years ago either; but he squandered his money, invested it anyhow, borrowed at interest, and in short made a thorough fool of himself, and then a beggar. He took to drinking, and had a touch of paralysis, and then came here to borrow a pound . . . '

"The kind-hearted gentleman omitted to add that Newman Noggs, being utterly destitute, served him for rather less than the usual wages of a boy of thirteen; and likewise failed to mention in his hasty chronicle, that his eccentric taciturnity rendered him an especially valuable person in a place where much business was done, of which it was desirable no mention should be made out of doors." 2

—*his expression:* " . . . his face was curiously twisted as by a spasm, but whether of paralysis, or grief, or inward laughter, nobody but himself could possibly explain . . . the countenance of Newman Noggs, in his ordinary moods, was a problem which no stretch of ingenuity could solve." 3

—*"no":* " . . . not having the courage to say no, a word which in all his life he never could say at the right time, either to himself or anyone else . . . . " 14

—*aroused (circumspectly):* "He stood at a little distance from the door, with his face towards it; and with the sleeves of his coat turned back at the wrists, was occupied in bestowing the most vigorous, scientific, and straightforward blows upon the empty air.

" . . . the intense eagerness and joy depicted in the face of Newman Noggs, which was suffused with perspiration; the surprising energy with which he directed a constant succession of blows towards a particular panel about five feet eight from the ground, and still worked away in the most untiring and persevering manner, would have sufficiently explained to the attentive observer, that his imagination was threshing, to within an inch of his life, his body's most active employer, Mr **Ralph Nickleby**." 28

Smike. "Although he could not have been less than eighteen or nineteen years old, and was tall for that age, he wore a skeleton suit, such as is usually put upon very little boys, and which, though most absurdly short in the arms and legs, was quite wide enough for his attenuated frame. In order that the lower part of his legs might be in perfect keeping with this singular dress, he had a very large pair of boots originally made for tops, which might have been once worn by some stout farmer, but were now too patched and tattered for a beggar. God knows how long he had been there, but he still wore the same linen which he had first taken down; for round his neck was a tattered child's frill, only half concealed by a coarse man's neckerchief. He was lame; and as he feigned to be busy in arranging the table, glanced at the letters with a look so keen, and yet so dispirited and hopeless, that **Nicholas** could hardly bear to watch him." 7

—*with a friend:* "The wretched creature, Smike, since the night **Nicholas** had spoken kindly to him in the school-room, had followed him to and fro with an ever restless desire to serve or help him, anticipating such little wants as his humble ability could supply, and content only to be near him. He would sit beside him for hours looking patiently into his face, and a word would brighten up his care-worn visage, and call into it a passing gleam even of happiness. He was an altered being; he had an object now, and that object was to show his attachment to the only person—that person a stranger—who had treated him, not to say with kindness, but like a human creature." 12

Fanny Squeers. "Miss Fanny Squeers was in her three-and-twentieth year. If there be any one grace or loveliness inseparable from that particular period of life, Miss Squeers may be presumed to have been possessed of it, as there is no reason to suppose that she was a solitary exception to a universal rule. She was not tall like her mother, but short like her father; from the former she inherited a voice of harsh quality, and from the latter a remarkable expression of the right eye, something akin to having none at all." 9

—*dressed for tea:* "To be sure Miss Squeers was in a desperate flutter as the time approached, and to be sure she was dressed out to the best advantage: with her hair—it had more than a tinge of red, and she wore it in a crop—curled in five distinct rows up to the very top of her head, and arranged dexterously over the doubtful eye; to say nothing of the blue sash which floated down her back, or the worked apron, or the long gloves, or the green gauze scarf worn over one shoulder and under the other, or any of the numerous devices which were to be as so many arrows to the heart of **Nicholas**." 9

—*correspondent:*

"'Dotheboys Hall

"'Thursday Morning

"'SIR,

"'My pa requests me to write to you, the doctors considering it doubtful whether he will ever recuvver the use of his legs which prevents his holding a pen.

"'We are in a state of mind beyond everything, and my pa is one mask of brooses both blue and green likewise two forms are steepled in his Goar. We were kimpelled to have him carried down into the kitchen where he now lays. You will judge from this that he has been brought very low.

"'When your nevew that you recommended for a teacher had done this to my pa and jumped upon his body with his feet and also langwedge which I will not pollewt my pen with describing, he assaulted my ma with dreadful violence, dashed her to the earth, and drove her back comb several inches into her head. A very little more and it must have entered her skull. We have a medical certifiket that if it had, the tortershell would have affected the brain. . . .

"The monster having sasiated his thirst for blood ran away, taking with him a boy of desperate caracter that he had excited to rebellyon, and a garnet ring belonging to my ma, and not having been apprehended by the constables is supposed to have been took up by some stage-coach. My pa begs that if he comes to you the ring may be returned, and that you will let the thief and assassin go, as if we prosecuted him he would only be transported, and if he is let go he is sure to be hung before long, which will save us trouble, and be much more satisfactory. Hoping to hear from you when convenient

"'I remain

"'Yours and cetrer

"'FANNY SQUEERS.

"'P. S. I pity his ignorance and despise him.'" 15

—*decked out:* "To have seen Miss Squeers now, divested of the brown beaver, the green veil, and the blue curl-papers, and arrayed in all the virgin splendour of a white frock and spencer, with a white muslin bonnet, and an imitative damask rose in full bloom on the inside thereof: her luxuriant crop of hair arranged in curls so tight that it was impossible they could come out by any accident, and her bonnet-cap trimmed with little damask roses, which might be supposed to be so many promising scions of the big one—to have seen all this, and to have seen the broad damask belt, matching both the family rose and the little ones, which encircled her slender waist, and by a happy ingenuity took off from the shortness of the spencer behind—to have beheld all this, and to have taken further into account the coral bracelets (rather short of beads, and with a very visible black string) which clasped her wrists, and the coral necklace which rested on her neck, supporting outside her frock a lonely cornelian heart, typical of her own disengaged affections—to have contemplated all these mute but expressive appeals to the purest feelings of our nature, might have thawed the frost of age, and added new and inextinguishable fuel to the fire of youth." 39

Wackford Squeers. "Mr Squeers's appearance was not prepossessing. He had but one eye, and the popular prejudice runs in favour of two. The eye he had was unquestionably useful, but decidedly not ornamental, being of a greenish grey, and in shape resembling the fanlight of a street door. The blank side of his face was much wrinkled and puckered up, which gave him a very sinister appearance, especially when he smiled, at which times his expression bordered closely on the villainous. His hair was very flat and shiny, save at the ends, where it was brushed stiffly up from a low protruding forehead, which assorted well with his harsh voice and coarse manner. He was about two or three and fifty, and a trifle below the middle size; he wore a white neckerchief with long ends, and a suit of scholastic black, but his coat sleeves being a great deal too long, and his trousers a great deal too short, he appeared ill at ease in his clothes, and as if he were in a perpetual state of astonishment at finding himself so respectable."4

—*pedagogy:* "'This is the first class in English spelling and philosophy, Nickleby,' said Squeers, beckoning **Nicholas** to stand beside him. 'We'll get up a Latin one, and hand that over to you. Now, then, where's the first boy?'

"'Please sir, he's cleaning the back parlour window,' said the temporary head of the philosophical class.

"'So he is, to be sure,' rejoined Squeers. 'We go upon the practical mode of teaching, Nickleby; the regular education system. C-l-e-a-n, clean, verb active, to make bright, to scour. W-i-n, win, d-e-r, der, winder, a casement. When the boy knows this out of book, he goes and does it. It's just the same principle as the use of the globes. Where's the second boy?'

"'Please, sir, he's weeding the garden,' replied a small voice.

"'To be sure,' said Squeers, by no means disconcerted. 'So he is. B-o-t, bot, t-i-n, tin, bottin, n-e-y, ney, bottinney, noun substantive, a knowledge of plants. When he has learned that bottinney means a knowledge of plants, he goes and knows 'em. That's our system, Nickleby: what do you think of it?'

"'It's a very useful one, at any rate,' answered Nicholas significantly." 8
And see **Mrs Squeers** SR—*priorities*

The Boys at Dotheboys Hall

"Pale and haggard faces, lank and bony figures, children with the countenances of old men, deformities with irons upon their limbs, boys of stunted growth, and others whose long meagre legs would hardly bear their stooping bodies, all crowded on the view together; there were the bleared eye, the hare-lip, the crooked foot, and every ugli-ness or distortion that told of unnatural aversion conceived by parents for their offspring, or of young lives which, from the earliest dawn of infancy, had been one horrible endurance of cruelty and neglect.

"There were little faces which should have been handsome, darkened with the scowl of sullen dogged suffering; there was childhood with the light of its eye quenched, its beauty gone, and its helplessness alone remaining; there were vicious-faced boys brooding, with leaden eyes, like malefactors in a jail; and there were young creatures on whom the sins of their frail parents had descended, weeping even for the mercenary nurses they had known, and lonesome even in their loneliness.

"With every kindly sympathy and affection blasted in its birth, with every young and healthy feeling flogged and starved down, with every revengeful passion that can fester in swollen hearts, eating its evil way to their core in silence, what an incipient Hell was breeding there!" ¶8

—*asleep:* "It needed a quick eye to detect from among the huddled mass of sleepers, the form of any given individual. As they lay closely packed together, covered, for warmth's sake, with their patched and ragged clothes, little could be distinguished but the sharp outlines of pale faces, over which the sombre light shed the same dull heavy colour, with here and there a gaunt arm thrust forth: its thinness hidden by no covering, but fully exposed to view in all its shrunken ugliness.

"There were some who, lying on their backs with upturned faces and clenched hands, just visible in the leaden light, bore more the aspect of dead bodies than of living creatures, and there were others coiled up into strange and fantastic postures, such as might have been taken for the uneasy efforts of pain to gain some temporary relief, rather than the freaks of slumber.

"A few—and these were among the youngest of the children—slept peacefully on with smiles upon their faces, dreaming perhaps of home; but ever and again a deep and heavy sigh, breaking the stillness of the room, announced that some new sleeper had awakened to the misery of another day, and, as morning took the place of night, the smiles gradually faded away with the friendly darkness which had given them birth." ¶13

—**Belling**. "In a corner of the seat was a very small deal trunk, tied round with a scanty piece of cord; and on the trunk was perched—his lace-up half-boots and corduroy trousers dangling in the air—a diminutive boy, with his shoulders drawn up to his ears, and his hands planted on his knees, who glanced timidly at the school-master from time to time with evident dread and apprehension." 4

—**Bolder**. "An unhealthy-looking boy, with warts all over his hands, stepped from his place to the master's desk, and raised his eyes imploringly to **Squeers**'s face; his own quite white from the rapid beating of his heart." 8

—**Cobbey**. "Another boy stood up, and eyed the letter very hard while **Squeers** made a mental abstract of the same.

". . . 'Cobbey's grandmother is dead, and his uncle John has took to drinking, which is all the news his sister sends, except eighteenpence, which will just pay for that broken square of glass . . . my dear, will you take the money?'" 8

—**Dorker**. "' . . . who unfortunately—' '—unfortunately died at Dotheboys Hall,' said **Ralph** . . . . " 4

—**Graymarsh**. "'Graymarsh's maternal aunt . . . . Hopes above all, that he will study in everything to please Mr and **Mrs Squeers**, and look upon them as his only friends; and that he will love **Master Squeers**, and not object to sleeping five in a bed, which no Christian should.' . . . Graymarsh's maternal aunt was strongly supposed, by her more intimate friends, to be no other than his maternal parent . . . . " 8

—**Mobbs**. "'Mobbs's [**stepmother**] took to her bed on hearing that he would not eat fat, and has been very ill ever since . . . . A sulky state of feeling,' said **Squeers**, after a terrible pause, during which he had moistened the palm of his right hand again, 'won't do; cheerfulness and contentment must be kept up. Mobbs, come to me.'" 8

—**Palmer**. "'"The juniorest Palmer said he wished he was in Heaven," —I really don't know, I do not know what's to be done with that young fellow; he's always a-wishing something horrid.'" 57

—**Pitcher**. "'That young Pitcher's had a fever.' 'No!' exclaimed **Squeers**. 'Damn that boy, he's always at something of that sort.'

"'Never was such a boy, I do believe . . . whatever he had, is always catching too. I say it's obstinacy, and nothing shall ever convince me that it isn't. I'd beat it out of him, and I told you that six months ago.'" 7

—**Snawley** boys. "'How do you do, my little gentlemen? . . . . With this salutation Mr **Squeers** patted the heads of two hollow-eyed, small-boned little boys . . . . " 4

—**Sprouter**. "'Young Sprouter has been a-winking, has he? I'll wink him when I get back.'" 57

—**Tomkins**. "'Please, sir, I think **Smike**'s run away, sir' . . . Mr **Squeers** made a plunge into the crowd, and at one dive caught a very little boy habited still in his night gear, and the perplexed expression of whose countenance as he was brought forward, seemed to intimate that he was as yet uncertain whether he was about to be punished or rewarded for the suggestion. He was not long in doubt." 13

Other Supporting Roles

John Browdie. " . . . the expected swain arrived with his hair very damp from recent washing; and a clean shirt, whereof the collar might have belonged to some giant ancestor, forming, together with a white waistcoat of similar dimensions, the chief ornament of his person. . . . 'Weel,' said John, with a grin that even the collar could not conceal. . . . 'Servant, sir,' said John, who was something over six feet high, with a face and body rather above the due proportion than below it . . . .

"Mr Browdie was not a gentleman of great conversational powers, so he grinned twice more, and having now bestowed his customary mark of recognition on every person in company, grinned at nothing particular and helped himself to food." 9

—*delighted:* "'The fact is,' said **Nicholas**, not very well knowing how to make the avowal, 'the fact is, that I have been ill-treated . . . by that man **Squeers**, and I have beaten him soundly, and am leaving this place in consequence.'

"'What!' cried John Browdie, with such an ecstatic shout, that the horse quite shied at it. 'Beatten the schoolmeasther! Ho! ho! ho! Beatten the schoolmeasther! who ever heard 'o the loike o' that noo! Giv' us thee hond agean, yoongster. Beatten the schoolmeasther! Dang it, I loove thee for't.'" 13

—*amused:* "Never was man so tickled with a respectable old joke, as John Browdie . . . . He chuckled, roared, half suffocated himself by laughing large pieces of beef into his windpipe, roared again, persisted in eating at the same time, got red in the face and black in the forehead, coughed, cried, got better, went off again laughing inwardly, got worse, choked, had his back thumped, stamped about, frightened his wife, and at last recovered in a state of the last exhaustion and with the water streaming from his eyes, but still faintly ejaculating 'A godfeyther—a godfeyther, **Tilly**!' in a tone bespeaking an exquisite relish of the sally, which no suffering could diminish." 42

Charles Cheeryble, German-merchant. "He was a sturdy old fellow in a broad-skirted blue coat, made pretty large, to fit easily, and with no particular waist; his bulky legs clothed in drab breeches and high gaiters, and his head protected by a low-crowned broad-brimmed white hat, such as a wealthy grazier might wear. He wore his coat buttoned; and his dimpled double-chin rested in the folds of a white neckerchief—not one of your stiff starched apoplectic cravats, but a good easy old-fashioned white neckcloth that a man might go to bed in and be none the worse for it.

"But what principally attracted the attention of **Nicholas**, was the old gentleman's eye,—never was such a clear, twinkling, honest, merry, happy eye, as that. And there he stood, looking a little upward, with one hand thrust into the breast of his coat, and the other playing with his old-fashioned gold watch-chain: his head thrown a little on one side, and his hat a little more on one side than his head (but that was evidently accident; not his ordinary way of wearing it), with such a pleasant smile playing about his mouth, and such a comical expression of mingled slyness, simplicity, kind-heartedness, and good-humour, lighting up his jolly old face, that Nicholas would have been content to have stood there and looked at him until evening, and to have forgotten meanwhile that there was such a thing as a soured mind or a crabbed countenance to be met with in the whole wide world." ¶35

Edwin (Ned) Cheeryble. " . . . . the same face, the same figure, the same coat, waistcoat, and neckcloth, the same breeches and gaiters—nay, there was the very same white hat hanging against the wall!

"As they shook each other by the hand, the face of each lighted up by beaming looks of affection, which would have been most delightful to behold in infants, and which, in men so old, was inexpressibly touching, Nicholas could observe that the last old gentleman was something stouter than his brother; this, and a slight additional shade of clumsiness in his gait and stature, formed the only perceptible difference between them. Nobody could have doubted their being twin brothers . . . .

"Both the brothers it may be here remarked, had a very emphatic and earnest delivery, both had lost nearly the same teeth, which imparted the same peculiarity to their speech; and both spoke as if, besides possessing the utmost serenity of mind that the kindliest and most unsuspecting nature could bestow, they had, in collecting the plums from Fortune's choicest pudding, retained a few for present use, and kept them in their mouths." 35

Frank Cheeryble. " . . . a young man who from his appearance might have been a year or two older than **Nicholas** . . . although, to judge from what had recently taken place, a hot-headed young man, (which is not an absolute miracle and phenomenon in nature) was a sprightly, good-humoured, pleasant fellow, with much both in his countenance and disposition that reminded Nicholas very strongly of the kind-hearted brothers. His manner was as unaffected as theirs, and his demeanour full of that heartiness which, to most people who have anything generous in their composition, is peculiarly prepossessing.

"Add to this, that he was good-looking and intelligent, had a plentiful share of vivacity, was extremely cheerful, and accommodated himself in five minutes' time to all **John Browdie**'s oddities with as much ease as if he had known him from a boy; and it will be a source of no great wonder that, when they parted for the night, he had produced a most favourable impression . . . . " ¶53

Arthur Gride, usurer. " . . . a little old man, of about seventy or seventy-five years of age, of a very lean figure, much bent, and slightly twisted. He wore a grey coat with a very narrow collar, an old-fashioned waistcoat of ribbed black silk, and such scanty trousers as displayed his shrunken spindle-shanks in their full ugliness. The only articles of display or ornament in his dress, were a steel watch-chain to which were attached some large gold seals; and a black ribbon into which, in compliance with an old fashion scarcely ever observed in these days, his grey hair was gathered behind.

"His nose and chin were sharp and prominent, his jaws had fallen inwards from loss of teeth, his face was shrivelled and yellow, save where the cheeks were streaked with the colour of a dry winter apple; and where his beard had been, there lingered yet a few grey tufts which seemed, like the ragged eyebrows, to denote the badness of the soil from which they sprung. The whole air and attitude of the form, was one of stealthy cat-like obsequiousness; the whole expression of the face was concentrated in a wrinkled leer, compounded of cunning, lecherousness, slyness, and avarice.

"Such was old Arthur Gride, in whose face there was not a wrinkle, in whose dress there was not one spare fold or plait, but expressed the most covetous and griping penury, and sufficiently indicated his belonging to that class of which **Ralph Nickleby** was a member." 47

The **Kenwigses**. "The lodgers . . . were the wife and olive branches of one Mr **Kenwigs**, a turner in ivory, who was looked upon as a person of some consideration on the premises, inasmuch as he occupied the whole of the first floor, comprising a suite of two rooms. **Mrs [Susan]** Kenwigs, too, was quite a lady in her manners, and of a very genteel family, having an uncle who collected a water-rate; besides which distinction, the two eldest of her [four] little girls went twice a week to a dancing school in the neighbourhood, and had flaxen hair tied with blue ribands hanging in luxuriant pigtails down their backs, and wore little white trousers with frills round the ankles—for all of which reasons and many more, equally valid but too numerous to mention, Mrs Kenwigs was considered a very desirable person to know, and was the constant theme of all the gossips in the street, and even three or four doors round the corner at both ends." 14

—on hearing bad news: "'[Mr **Lillyvick**] was married to **Miss Petowker**.'

"Mr **Kenwigs** started from his seat with a petrified stare, caught his second daughter by the flaxen tail, and covered his face with his pocket-handkerchief. **Morleena** fell, all stiff and rigid, into the baby's chair, as she had seen her mother fall when she fainted away, and the two remaining little Kenwigses shrieked in affright.

"'My children, my defrauded, swindled infants!' cried Mr Kenwigs, pulling so hard, in his vehemence, at the flaxen tail of his second daughter, that he lifted her up on tiptoe, and kept her for some seconds in that attitude. 'Villain, ass, traitor!' . . the exertion of speaking with so much vehemence, and yet in such a tone as should prevent his lamentations reaching the ears of Mrs **Kenwigs**, had made him very black in the face; besides which, the excitement of the occasion, and an unwonted indulgence in various strong cordials to celebrate it, had swollen and dilated his features to a most unusual extent . . . .

"'The attention,' said Mr Kenwigs, looking around with a plaintive air, 'the attention that I've shown to that man. 'The hyseters he has eat, and the pints of ale he has drank, in this house—!'" 36

—reconciled: "'When I see that man . . . a mingling once again in the spear which he adorns, and see his affections developing themselves in legitimate sitivations, I feel that his natur is as elewated and expanded as his standing

afore society as a public character is unimpeached, and the woices of my infant children purvided for in life, seem to whisper to me softly, "This is an ewent at which Evins itself looks down!"'" 52

—*offspring:* ". . . the four little Kenwigses disposed on a small form in front of the company with their flaxen tails towards them, and their faces to the fire; an arrangement which was no sooner perfected than **Mrs Kenwigs** . . . dissolved in tears. . . .'I can—not help it . . . they're too beautiful to live, much too beautiful.'

" . . . the ladies and gentlemen united in prophesying that they would live for many, many years, and that there was no occasion at all for Mrs Kenwigs to distress herself; which in good truth there did not appear to be, the loveliness of the children by no means justifying her apprehensions." 14

Miss Knag. " . . . a short, bustling, over-dressed female, full of importance . . . . Miss Knag bestowed a reverential smile upon **Madame Mantalini**, which she dexterously transformed into a gracious one for **Kate** . . . ." 17

" . . . it may be observed—not that she was marvellously loquacious and marvellously deferential to Madame Mantalini . . . but that every now and then she was accustomed, in the torrent of her discourse, to introduce a loud, shrill, clear 'hem!' the import and meaning of which was variously interpreted by her acquaintance . . . . It may be further remarked, that Miss Knag still aimed at youth, though she had shot beyond it years ago; and that she was weak and vain, and one of those people who are best described by the axiom, that you may trust them as far as you can see them, and no farther." 17

—*distressed:* "'Have I lived to this day to be called a fright! cried Miss Knag, suddenly becoming convulsive, and making an effort to tear her front off.

"'Oh no, no,' replied the chorus, 'pray don't say so; don't, now!'

"'Have I deserved to be called an elderly person?' screamed Miss Knag, wrestling with the supernumeraries.

"'Don't think of such things, dear,' answered the chorus.

"' . . . . Having denounced the object of her wrath . . . Miss Knag screamed once, hiccuped thrice, and gurgled in her throat several times: slumbered, shivered, woke, came to, composed her head-dress, and declared herself quite well again." 18 *And see* Lively **young lady** O

Miss La Creevy. "'Creevy—La Creevy,' replied the voice, as a yellow head-dress bobbed over the bannisters . . . the wearer . . . had a gown to correspond, and was of much the same colour herself. Miss La Creevy was a mincing young lady of fifty . . . . " 3

—*her heart:* "'. . . if in all London, or all the wide world besides, there is no other heart that takes an interest in your welfare [she said to **Kate** and **Mrs Nickleby**], there will be one little lonely woman that prays for it night and day.'

"With this the poor soul, who had a heart big enough for Gog, the guardian genius of London, and enough to spare for Magog to boot, after making a great many extraordinary faces which would have secured her an ample fortune, could she have transferred them to ivory or canvas, sat down in a corner, and had what she termed 'a real good cry.'" 11

Lillyvick, "who collected a water-rate . . . . 'He is so particular,' said **Mrs Kenwigs** . . . 'that if we began without him, I should be out of his will for ever. . . . You've no idea what he is . . . and yet as good a creature as ever breathed.'" 14

" . . . a short old gentleman, in drabs and gaiters, with a face that might have been carved out of *lignum vitae*, for anything that appeared to the contrary, was led playfully in . . . . "

"Now this was an interesting thing. Here was a collector of water-rates without his book, without his pen and ink, without his double knock, without his intimidation, kissing—actually kissing—an agreeable female, and leaving taxes, summonses, notices that he had called, or announcements that he would never call again for two quarters' due, wholly out of the question. It was pleasant to see how the company looked on, quite absorbed in the sight, and to behold the nods and winks with which they expressed their gratification at finding so much humanity in a tax-gatherer." 14

—*his bachelorhood:* "'The great reason for not being married . . . is the expense; that's what's kept me off, or else—Lord!' said Mr Lillyvick, snapping his fingers, 'I might have had fifty women . . . not so fine as **Henrietta Petowker**, for she is an uncommon specimen, but such women as don't fall into every man's way, I can tell you that. Now suppose a man can get a fortune *in* his wife instead of with her—eh?' . . . Henrietta Petowker, the talented Henrietta Petowker, has a fortune in herself, and I am going to . . . marry her; and the day after to-morrow, too . . . . I shall draw her salary, of course, and I hope after all it's nearly as cheap to keep two as it is to keep one; that's a consolation.'" 25 *And see* **Snevellicci** CTT

—*cast down:* "If ever an old gentleman had made a point of appearing in public, shaved close and clean, that old gentleman was Mr Lillyvick. If ever a collector had borne himself like a collector, and assumed before all men a solemn and portentous dignity as if he had the world on his books and it was all two quarters in arrear, that collector was Mr Lillyvick. And now, there he sat with the remains of a beard at least a week old encumbering his chin, a soiled and crumpled shirt-frill crouching as it were upon his breast instead of standing boldly out; a demeanour so abashed and drooping, so despondent, expressive of such humiliation, grief, and shame, that if the souls of forty unsubstantial housekeepers all of whom had had their water cut off for non-payment of the rate, could have been concentrated in one body, that one body could hardly have expressed such mortification and defeat as were now expressed in the person of Mr Lillyvick the collector . . . .

"'Eloped with a **half-pay captain** . . . basely and falsely eloped with a . . . bottle-nosed captain that any man might have considered himself safe from. It was in this room,' said Mr Lillyvick, looking sternly round, 'that I first see **Henrietta Petowker**. It is in this room that I turn her off for ever.'" 52

Tim Linkinwater. "Tim . . . drew himself up and looked particularly fat and very important. After which there was a profound silence.

"'I'm not coming an hour later in the morning you know,' said Tim, breaking out all at once, and looking very resolute. 'I'm not going to sleep in the fresh air—no, nor I'm not going into the country either. A pretty thing at this time of day, certainly. Pho!' . . . .

"'It's forty-four year,' said Tim, making a calculation in the air with his pen, and drawing an imaginary line before he cast it up, 'forty-four year, next May, since I first kept the books of **Cheeryble**, Brothers. I've opened the safe every morning all that time (Sundays excepted) as the clock struck nine, and gone over the house every night at half-past ten (except on Foreign Post nights, and then twenty minutes before twelve) to see the doors fastened and the fires out. I've never slept out of the back attic one single night . . . . There's not such a view in England as the view out of my window; I've seen it every morning before I shaved, and I ought to know something about it. I have slept in that room,' added Tim, sinking his voice a little, 'for four-and-forty year; and if it wasn't inconvenient, and didn't interfere with business, I should request leave to die there.' . . . .

" . . . . 'This isn't the first time you've talked about superannuating me; but if you please we'll make it the last, and drop the subject for evermore.'" 35

—*well pleased:* "Tim Linkinwater turned pale, and tilting up his stool on the two legs nearest **Nicholas**, looked over his shoulder in breathless anxiety [and] . . . without looking round, impatiently waved his hand as a caution that profound silence must be observed, and followed the nib of the inexperienced pen with strained and eager eyes . . . .

" . . . just then Nicholas stopped to refer to some other page, and Tim Linkinwater, unable to contain his satisfaction any longer, descended from his stool and caught him rapturously by the hand.

"'He has done it,' said Tim, looking round at his employers and shaking his head triumphantly. 'His capital B's and D's are exactly like mine; he dots all his small i's and crosses every t as he writes it. There an't such a young man as this in all London,' said Tim, clapping Nicholas on the back; 'not one. Don't tell me. The City can't produce his equal. I challenge the City to do it! . . . ." 37

Lunatic, in small-clothes. "'A—hem!' cried the same voice; and that not in the tone of an ordinary clearing of the throat, but in a kind of bellow, which woke up all the echoes in the neighbourhood, and was prolonged to an extent which must have made the unseen bellower quite black in the face . . . a shouting and scuffling noise, as of an elderly gentleman whooping, and kicking up his legs on loose gravel with great violence, was heard to proceed from the same direction as the former sounds; and, before they had subsided, a large cucumber was seen to shoot up in the air with the velocity of a sky-rocket, whence it descended, tumbling over and over, until it fell at Mrs **Nickleby**'s feet." 41

" . . . [**Kate**] was quite terrified by the apparition of an old black velvet cap, which . . . rose above the wall dividing their garden from that of the next cottage . . . and was gradually followed by a very large head, and an old face, in which were a pair of most extraordinary grey eyes, very wild, very wide open, and rolling in their sockets with a dull, languishing, and leering look, most ugly to behold." 41

—*warming:* "'Why is it,' said the old gentleman, coming up a step higher, and leaning his elbows on the wall, with as much complacency as if he were looking out of window, 'why is it that beauty is always obdurate, even when admiration is as honourable and respectful as mine?' . . .

"'I do know,' said the old gentleman, laying his finger on his nose with an air of familiarity most reprehensible, 'that this is a sacred and enchanted spot, where the most divine charms'—here he kissed his hand and bowed again— 'waft mellifluousness over the neighbours' gardens, and force the fruit and vegetables into premature existence. That fact I am acquainted with. But will you permit me, fairest creature, to ask you one question . . . .

"'Are you a princess?'" 41

—*wooing:* "'I have estates, ma'am,' said the old gentleman, flourishing his right hand negligently, as if he made very light of such matters, and speaking very fast; 'jewels, lighthouses, fishponds, a whalery of my own in the North Sea, and several oyster-beds of great profit in the Pacific Ocean. If you . . . bless me with your hand and heart, you can apply to the Lord Chancellor or call out the military if necessary—sending my toothpick to the commander-in-chief will be sufficient—and so clear the house of them before the ceremony is performed. After that, love bliss and rapture; rapture love and bliss. Be mine, be mine!'" 41

—*in his glory:* " . . . he suddenly flung off his coat, and springing on the top of the wall, threw himself into an attitude which displayed his small-clothes and grey worsteds to the fullest advantage, and concluded by standing on one leg, and repeating his favourite bellow with increased vehemence." 41

—*described:* "'Beg your pardon, ladies,' said [the **keeper**]. 'Has he been making love to either of you? .... Ah!,' rejoined the man ... 'he always will, you know. Nothing will prevent his making love .... He's a deal pleasanter without his senses than with 'em. He was the cruellest, wickedest, out-and-outerest old flint that ever drawed breath. ...

"'.... Broke his poor wife's heart, turned his daughters out of doors, drove his sons into the streets—it was a blessing he went mad at last, through evil tempers, and covetousness, and selfishness, and guzzling, and drinking, or he'd have drove many others so. Hope for *him*, an old rip! There isn't too much hope going, but I'll bet a crown that what there is, is saved for more deserving chaps than him, anyhow.'" 41 *See* **Keeper** O

Alfred Mantalini (formerly **Muntle**). " ... the head reappeared, and the mouth displaying a very long row of very white teeth, uttered in a mincing tone the words, 'Demmit. What, Nickleby! oh, demmit!' Having uttered which ejaculations, the gentleman advanced, and shook hands with **Ralph** with great warmth. He was dressed in a gorgeous morning gown, with a waistcoat and Turkish trousers of the same pattern, a pink silk neckerchief, and bright green slippers, and had a very copious watch-chain wound round his body. Moreover, he had whiskers and a moustache, both dyed black and gracefully curled." 10

—*his occupation:* " .... He had married on his whiskers, upon which property he had previously subsisted in a genteel manner for some years, and which he had recently improved after patient cultivation by the addition of a moustache, which promised to secure him an easy independence: his share in the labours of the business being at present confined to spending the money, and occasionally when that ran short, driving to Mr **Ralph Nickleby** to procure discount—at a percentage— for the customers' bills." 10

—*suicidal:* "The dressing-room door being hastily flung open, Mr Mantalini was disclosed to view with his shirt-collar symmetrically thrown back, putting fine edge to a breakfast knife by means of his razor strop.

"'Ah!' cried Mr Mantalini, 'interrupted!' and whisk went the breakfast knife into Mr Mantalini's dressing-gown pocket, while Mr Mantalini's eyes rolled wildly, and his hair floating in wild disorder, mingled with his whiskers .... 'Ruined!' cried Mr Mantalini. 'Have I brought ruin upon the best and purest creature that ever blessed a demnition vagabond! Demmit, let me go.' At this crisis of his ravings Mr Mantalini made a pluck at the breakfast knife, and being restrained by his wife's grasp, attempted to dash his head against the wall—taking very good care to be at least six feet from it, however ....

" ... after calling several times for poison, and requesting some lady or gentleman to blow his brains out, gentler feelings came upon him, and he wept pathetically. In this softened frame of mind he did not oppose the capture of the knife—which, to tell the truth, he was rather glad to be rid of, as an inconvenient and dangerous article for a shirt pocket—and finally he suffered himself to be led away by his affectionate partner." 31

—*in extremis:* " ... Mr Mantalini's legs were extended at full length upon the floor ... and [his] eyes were closed, and his face was pale, and his hair was comparatively straight, and his whiskers and moustache were limp, and his teeth were clenched, and he had a little bottle in his right hand, and a little tea-spoon in his left; and his hands, arms legs, and shoulders, were all stiff and powerless. And yet **Madame Mantalini** was not weeping upon the body, but was scolding violently upon her chair . . . . " 44

—*at the last:* "There, amidst clothes-baskets and clothes, stripped to his shirt-sleeves, but wearing still an old patched pair of pantaloons of superlative make, a once brilliant waistcoat, and moustache and whiskers as of yore, but lacking their lustrous dye—there, endeavouring to mollify the wrath of a buxom **female**, the proprietress of the concern, and grinding meanwhile as if for very life at the mangle, whose creaking noise, mingled with her shrill tones, appeared almost to deafen him—there was the graceful, elegant, fascinating, and once dashing Mantalini." 64

Madame Mantalini. "The dress-maker was a buxom person, handsomely dressed and rather good-looking, but much older than the gentleman in the Turkish trousers, whom she had wedded some six months before."10

—*under execution:* "'My cup of happiness's sweetener,' said **Mantalini**, approaching his wife with a penitent air; 'will you listen to me for two minutes?'

"'Oh! don't speak to me,' replied his wife, sobbing. 'You have ruined me, and that's enough.'

"Mr Mantalini . . . assumed an expression of consuming mental agony, rushed headlong from the room, and was soon afterwards heard to slam the door of an up-stairs dressing-room with great violence.

"Miss **Nickleby**,' cried Madame Mantalini, when this sound met her ear, 'make haste for Heaven's sake, he will destroy himself! I spoke unkindly to him, and he cannot bear it from me. Alfred, my darling Alfred.'·

"With such exclamations she hurried up-stairs . . . . 'Alfred,' cried his wife, flinging her arms about him, 'I didn't mean to say it, I didn't mean to say it!'" 21

—*eyes opened:* "'I will . . . say before you [**Ralph Nickleby**], and before everybody here, for the first time, and once for all, that I never will supply that man's extravagances and viciousness again. I have been a dupe and a fool to him long enough. In future, he shall support himself if he can, and then he may spend what money he pleases, upon whom and how he pleases; but it shall not be mine, and therefore you had better pause before you trust him further.'" 44

Henrietta Petowker, of the Theatre Royal, Drury Lane; "who, next to the collector, perhaps was the great lion of the party, being the daughter of a theatrical **fireman**, who 'went on' in the pantomime, and had the greatest turn for the stage that was ever known, being able to sing and recite in a manner that brought the tears into **Mrs Kenwigs**'s eyes." 14

—*to be married:* "**Miss Snevellicci** and **Miss Ledrook**, who knew perfectly well that their fair friend's mind had been made up for three or four years, at any period of which time she would have cheerfully undergone the desperate trial now approaching if she could have found any eligible gentleman disposed for the venture, began to preach comfort and firmness, and to say how very proud she ought to feel that it was in her power to confer lasting bliss on a deserving object, and how necessary it was for the happiness of mankind in general that women should possess fortitude and resignation on such occasions; and that although for their parts they held true happiness to consist in a single life, which they would not willingly exchange—no, not for any worldly consideration—still (thank God), if ever the time *should* come, they hoped they knew their duty too well to repine, but would the rather submit with meekness and humility of spirit to a fate for which Providence had clearly designed them with a view to the contentment and reward of their fellow-creatures . . . .

"This pious reasoning, and perhaps the fear of being too late, supported the bride through the ceremony of robing, after which, strong tea and brandy were administered in alternate doses as a means of strengthening her feeble limbs and causing her to walk steadier . . . .

"There is no knowing in what this burst of feeling might have ended . . . the arrival of the fly . . . so astounded the bride that she shook off divers alarming symptoms which were coming on very strong, and running to the glass adjusted her dress, and calmly declared that she was ready for the sacrifice." 25

Matilda Price. She "was a miller's daughter of only eighteen, who had contracted herself unto the son of a small corn-factor resident in the nearest market town. **Miss Squeers** and the miller's daughter being fast friends, had covenanted together some two years before, according to a custom prevalent among young ladies, that whoever was first engaged to be married should straightway confide the mighty secret to the bosom of the other, before communicating it to any living soul, and bespeak her as bridesmaid without loss of time; in fulfilment of which pledge the miller's daughter, when her engagement was formed, came out express at eleven o'clock at night as the corn-factor's son made an offer of his hand and heart at twenty-five minutes past ten by the

Dutch clock in the kitchen, and rushed into Miss Squeers's bedroom with the gratifying intelligence." 9

Peg Sliderskew. " . . . a short, thin, weasen, blear-eyed old woman, palsy-stricken and hideously ugly, who, wiping her shrivelled face upon her dirty apron, inquired, in that subdued tone in which deaf people commonly speak:

"'Was that you a calling, or only the clock striking? My hearing gets so bad, I never know which is which; but when I hear a noise I know it must be one of you, because nothing else ever stirs in the house.'" 51

Mrs Squeers. " . . . a female bounced into the room, and seizing Mr **Squeers** by the throat gave him two loud kisses, one close after the other like a postman's knock. The lady, who was of a large raw-boned figure, was about half a head taller than Mr Squeers, and was dressed in a dimity night-jacket with her hair in papers; she had also a dirty night-cap on, relieved by a yellow cotton handkerchief which tied it under the chin.

"'How is my Squeery?' said this lady, in a playful manner, and a very hoarse voice." 7

—*priorities:* "Now the fact was, that both Mr and Mrs Squeers viewed the boys in the light of their proper and natural enemies; or, in other words, they held and considered that their business and profession was to get as much from every boy as could by possibility be screwed out of him. On this point they were both agreed, and behaved in unison accordingly. The only difference between them was, that Mrs Squeers waged war against the enemy openly and fearlessly, and that Squeers covered his rascality, even at home, with a spice of his habitual deceit, as if he really had a notion of some day or other being able to take himself in, and persuade his own mind that he was a very good fellow." 8

Wackford Squeers, Jr " . . . a striking likeness of his father—kicking with great vigour under the hands of **Smike**, who was fitting upon him a pair of new boots that bore a most suspicious resemblance to those which the least of the little boys had worn on the journey down . . . . " 8

"'Am I to take care of the school when I grow up a man, father?' said Wackford junior, suspending in the excess of his delight, a vicious kick which he was administering to his sister.

"'You are, my son,' replied Mr **Squeers**, in a sentimental voice.

"'Oh my eye, won't I give it to the boys!' exclaimed the interesting child . . . . 'Oh, father, won't I make 'em squeak again!'" 9

—*in stout health:* "'My son, sir, little Wackford. What do you think of him, sir, for a specimen of the Dotheboys Hall feeding? ain't he fit to bust out of his clothes, and start the seams, and make the very buttons fly off with his fatness. Here's flesh!' cried **Squeers**, turning the boy about, and indenting the plumpest parts of his figure with divers pokes and punches, to the great discomposure of his son and heir. 'Here's firmness, here's solidness! why you can hardly get up enough of him between your finger and thumb to pinch him anywheres.'" 34

—*behaving in character:* " . . . Master Wackford, finding himself unnoticed, and feeling his preponderating inclinations strong upon him, had by little and little sidled up to the table and attacked the food with such slight skirmishing as drawing his fingers round and round the inside of the plates, and afterwards sucking them with infinite relish—picking the bread, and dragging the pieces over the surface of the butter—pocketing lumps of sugar, pretending all the time to be absorbed in thought—and so forth. Finding that no interference was attempted with these small liberties, he gradually mounted to greater, and, after helping himself to a moderately good cold collation, was, by this time, deep in the pie." 42

Lord Frederick Verisopht. "The gentleman addressed, turning round, exhibited a suit of clothes of the most superlative cut, a pair of whiskers of similar quality, a moustache, a head of hair, and a young face." 19

"Indeed, it was not difficult to see, that the majority of the company preyed upon the unfortunate young lord, who, weak and silly as he was, appeared by far the least vicious of the party." 19

—*not so soft:* "'I never will be a party to, or permit, if I can help it, a cowardly attack upon this young fellow . . . you [**Hawk**] did wrong. I did wrong too, not to interfere, and I am sorry for it. What happened to you afterwards was as much the consequence of accident as design, and more your fault than his; and it shall not, with my knowledge, be cruelly visited upon him—it shall not indeed . . . . I do believe now, upon my honour I do believe, that the sister is as virtuous and modest a young lady as she is a handsome one; and of the brother, I say this, that he acted as her brother should, and in a manly and spirited manner. And I only wish with all my heart and soul that any one of us came out of this matter half as well as he does.'" 38

—*an end:* "So died Lord Frederick Verisopht, by the hand which he had loaded with gifts and clasped a thousand times; by the act of him but for whom and others like him he might have lived a happy man, and died with children's faces round his bed." 50

Henry Wititterly, "an important gentleman of about eight-and-thirty, of rather plebeian countenance and with a very light head of hair, who leant over **Mrs Wititterly** . . . and conversed with her in whispers." 21

—*uxorious:* "'Oh!' he said, turning round, 'yes. This is a most important matter. **Mrs Wititterly** is of a very excitable nature, very delicate, very fragile; a hothouse plant, an exotic. . . .You are my love, you know you are; one breath—' said Mr W. blowing an imaginary feather away. 'Pho! you're gone . . . . Your soul is too large for your body . . . . Your intellect wears you out; all the medical men say so; you know that there is not a physician who is not proud of being called in to you . . . . The society in which you move—necessarily move, from your station, connexion, and endowments—is one vortex and whirlpool of the most frightful excitement. Bless my heart and body, can I ever forget the night you danced with the **baronet's nephew**, at the election ball, at Exeter! it was tremendous.'

"'I always suffer for these triumphs afterwards,' said Mrs Wititterly.

"'And for that very reason,' rejoined her husband, 'you must have a companion, in whom there is great gentleness, great sweetness, excessive sympathy, and perfect repose.'

"Here both Mr and Mrs Wititterly, who had talked rather at [**Kate** and her mother] than to each other, left off speaking, and looked at their two hearers, with an expression of countenance which seemed to say, 'What do you think of all that!'" 21

—*his fiscal way:* "'With regard to the trifle of salary that is due,' said Mr Wititterly, 'I will'—here he was interrupted by a violent fit of coughing—'I will— owe it to **Miss Nickleby**.'

"Mr Wititterly, it should be observed, was accustomed to owe small accounts, and to leave them owing. All men have some little pleasant way of their own; and this was Mr Wititterly's." 33

Mrs Julia Wititterly, of Cadogan Place, Sloane Street. "The lady had an air of sweet insipidity, and a face of engaging paleness; there was a faded look about her, and about the furniture, and about the house altogether. She was reclining on a sofa in such a very unstudied attitude, that she might have been taken for an actress all ready for the first scene in a ballet, and only waiting for the drop curtain to go up." 21

—*her acuity:* "That any but the weakest and silliest of people could have seen in one interview that [**Verisopht** and **Hawk**] . . . were not persons accustomed to be the best possible companions, and were certainly not calculated by habits, manners, tastes, or conversation, to shine with any very great lustre in the society of ladies, need scarcely be remarked. But with Mrs Wititterly the two titles were all-sufficient; coarseness became humour, vulgarity softened itself down into the most charming eccentricity; insolence took the guise of an easy absence of reserve, attainable only by those who had had the good fortune to mix with high folks." 28

The Crummles Theatrical Troupe *(in order of appearance)*

Combatants (Master **Vincent Crummles** and **Percy Crummles**). "At the upper end of the room were a couple of boys, one of them very tall and the other very short, both dressed as sailors—or at least as theatrical sailors, with belts, buckles, pigtails, and pistols complete—fighting what is called in play-bills a terrific combat with two of those short broad-swords with basket hilts which are commonly used at our minor theatres . . . when the short sailor made a vigorous cut at the tall sailor's legs, which would have shaved them clean off if it had taken effect, the tall sailor jumped over the short sailor's sword, wherefore to balance the matter and make it all fair, the tall sailor administered the same cut and the short sailor jumped over *his* sword.

"After this there was a good deal of dodging about and hitching up of the inexpressibles in the absence of braces, and then the short sailor (who was the moral character evidently, for he always had the best of it) made a violent demonstration and closed with the tall sailor, who, after a few unavailing struggles, went down and expired in great torture as the short sailor put his foot upon his breast and bored a hole in him through and through." ¶ 22

Vincent Crummles (of Provincial Celebrity). The combatants "were overlooked by a large heavy man, perched against the corner of a table, who emphatically adjured them to strike a little more fire out of the swords, and they couldn't fail to bring the house down on the very first night . . . Mr Vincent Crummles received **Nicholas** with an inclination of the head, something between the courtesy of a Roman emperor and the nod of a pot companion; and bade the landlord shut the door and begone." 22

" . . . the face of Mr Crummles was quite proportionate in size to his body . . . he had a very full under-lip, a hoarse voice, as though he were in the habit of shouting very much, and very short black hair, shaved off nearly to the crown of his head—to admit . . . of his more easily wearing character wigs of any shape or pattern . . . .

"He was very talkative and communicative, stimulated perhaps not only by his natural disposition, but by the spirits and water he sipped very plentifully, or the snuff which he took in large quantities from a piece of whitey-brown paper in his waistcoat pocket." 22

—*impressed:* " ' . . . what a capital countenance your friend [**Smike**] has got!' . . . Why, as he is now,' said the manager, striking his knee emphatically; 'without a pad upon his body, and hardly a touch of paint upon his face, he'd make such an actor for the starved business as was never seen in this country. Only let him be tolerably well up in the Apothecary in Romeo and Juliet with the slightest possible dab of red on the tip of his nose, and he'd be certain of three rounds the moment he put his head out of the practicable door in the front grooves O. P. . . . I never saw a young fellow so regularly cut out for that line since I've been in the profession, and I played the heavy children when I was eighteen months old.'" 22

—*recruiting:* " 'The stage! . . . . The theatrical profession. . . . I am in the theatrical profession myself, my wife is in the theatrical profession, my children are in the theatrical profession. I had a dog that lived and died in it from a puppy; and my chaise-pony goes on in Timour the Tartar. I'll bring you out, and your friend too. Say the word. I want a novelty . . . .

"There's genteel comedy in your walk and manner, juvenile tragedy in your eye, and touch-and-go farce in your laugh,' said Mr Vincent Crummles [to **Nicholas**]. 'You'll do as well as if you had thought of nothing else but the lamps, from your birth downwards.'" 22

—*saying farewell:* "Mr Crummles, who could never lose any opportunity for professional display, had turned out for the express purpose of taking a public farewell of **Nicholas**; and to render it the more imposing, he was now, to that young gentleman's most profound annoyance, inflicting upon him a rapid succession of stage embraces, which, as everybody knows, are performed by the embracer's laying his or her chin on the shoulder of the object of affection, and looking over it." 30

Pony, and forbears. " . . . Mr **Crummles** had a strange four-legged animal in the inn stables, which he called a pony, and a vehicle of unknown design, on which he bestowed the appellation of a four-wheeled phaeton . . . .

"The pony took his time upon the road, and—possibly in consequence of his theatrical education—evinced every now and then a strong inclination to lie down . . . .

"'He's a good pony at bottom,' said Mr Crummles . . . .

"He might have been at bottom, but he certainly was not at top, seeing that his coat was of the roughest and most ill-favoured kind . . . .

" . . . 'He is quite one of us. His mother was on the stage . . . she ate apple-pie at a circus for upwards of fourteen years,' said the manager; 'fired pistols, and went to bed in a nightcap; and in short, took the low comedy entirely. His father was a dancer.'

"'Was he at all distinguished?'

"'Not very,' said the manager. 'He was rather a low sort of pony. The fact is, that he had been originally jobbed out by the day, and he never quite got over his old habits. He was clever in melodrama too, but too broad—too broad. When his mother died, he took the port-wine business.'

"'The port-wine business!' cried **Nicholas**.

"'Drinking port-wine with the clown,' said the manager; 'but he was greedy, and one night bit off the bowl of the glass, and choked himself, so that his vulgarity was the death of him at last.'" 23

Mrs Crummles. " . . . a stout, portly female, apparently between forty and fifty, in a tarnished silk cloak, with her bonnet dangling by the strings in her hand, and her hair (of which she had a great quantity) braided in a large festoon over each temple . . . .

"'I am glad to see you, sir,' said Mrs Vincent Crummles, in a sepulchral voice. "I am very glad to see you, and still more happy to hail you as a promising member of our corps.'

"The lady shook Nicholas by the hand as she addressed him in these terms; he saw it was a large one, but had not expected quite such an iron grip as that with which she honoured him." 23

—*her early career:* "'Mrs Crummles was the original Blood-Drinker. . . . She was obliged to give it up though.'

"'Did it disagree with her?' asked **Nicholas**, smiling.

"'Not so much with her, as with her audiences,' replied Mr **Crummles**. 'Nobody could stand it. It was too tremendous . . . . The very first time I saw that admirable woman, **Johnson**,' said Mr Crummles, drawing a little nearer, and speaking in the tone of confidential friendship, 'she stood upon her head on the butt-end of a spear, surrounded with blazing fireworks.'

"'You astonish me!' said Nicholas.

"'*She* astonished *me*!'returned Mr Crummles, with a very serious countenance. 'Such grace, coupled with such dignity! I adored her from that moment.'" 25

Ninetta Crummles (The **Infant Phenomenon**). " . . . there bounded on to the stage from some mysterious inlet, a little girl in a dirty white frock with tucks up to the knees, short trousers, sandaled shoes, white spencer, pink gauze bonnet, green veil and curl-papers, who turned a pirouette, cut twice in the air, turned another pirouette, then looking off at the opposite wing shrieked, bounded forward to within six inches of the footlights, and fell into a beautiful attitude of terror . . . . " 23

"'May I ask how old she is?' inquired **Nicholas**.

"'You may, sir,' replied Mr **Crummles**, looking steadily in his questioner's face as some men do when they have doubts about being implicitly believed in what they are going to say. 'She is ten years of age, sir.'

"'Not more!'

"'Not a day.'

"'Dear me! said Nicholas, 'it's extraordinary.'

"It was; for the infant phenomenon, though of short stature, had a comparatively aged countenance, and had moreover been precisely the same age—not perhaps to the full extent of the memory of the oldest inhabitant, but certainly for five good years. But she had been kept up late every night, and put upon an unlimited allowance of gin-and-water from infancy, to prevent her growing tall, and perhaps this system of training had produced in the infant phenomenon these additional phenomena." 23 ["This character was drawn from life; and the original is now [1894] the wife of a distinguished American general." —HMCD XXXII p 126]

Tommy Folair. " . . . a shabby gentleman in an old pair of buff slippers came in at one powerful slide, and chattering his teeth fiercely brandishing a walking-stick . . . after a little more ferocity and chasing of the maiden into corners, he began to relent, and stroked his face several times with his right thumb and four fingers, thereby intimating that he was struck with admiration of the maiden's beauty." 23

—*dressed for ceremony:* "Mr Folair's head was usually decorated with a very round hat, unusually high in the crown, and curled up quite tight in the brims. On the present occasion he wore it very much on one side, with the back part forward in consequence of its being the least rusty; round his neck he wore a flaming red worsted comforter, whereof the straggling ends peeped out beneath his threadbare Newmarket coat,which was very tight and buttoned all the way up. He carried in his hand one very dirty glove, and a cheap dress cane with a glass handle; in short, his whole appearance was unusually dashing, and demonstrated a far more scrupulous attention to his toilet, than he was in the habit of bestowing upon it." 29

Lenville. " . . . a dark-complexioned man, inclining indeed to sallow, with long thick black hair, and very evident indications (although he was close shaved) of a stiff beard, and whiskers of the same deep shade. His age did not appear to exceed thirty, although many at first sight would have considered him much older, as his face was long and very pale, from the constant application of stage paint. He wore a checked shirt, an old green coat with new gilt buttons, a neckerchief of broad red and green stripes, and full blue trousers; he carried too a common ash walking-stick, apparently more for show than use, as he flourished it about with the hooked end downwards, except when he raised it for a few seconds, and throwing himself into a fencing attitude, made a pass or two at the side-scenes, or at any other object, animate or inanimate, that chanced to afford him a pretty good mark at the moment." 23

Slim **young gentleman**. " . . . with weak eyes, who played the low-spirited lovers and sang tenor songs . . . . " 23

Comic **countryman**. " . . . a man with a turned-up nose, large mouth, broad face, and staring eyes." 23

Elderly **gentleman**. "Making himself very amiable to the **infant phenomenon**, was an inebriated elderly gentleman in the last depths of shabbiness, who played the calm and virtuous old men . . . . " 23

Elderly **gentleman**. " . . . paying especial court to **Mrs Crummles** was another elderly gentleman, a shade more respectable, who played the irascible old men—those funny fellows who have nephews in the army, and perpetually run about with thick sticks to compel them to marry heiresses." 23

Hero, of comedy. " . . . there was a roving-looking person in a rough great-coat, who strode up and down in front of the lamps, flourishing a dress-cane, and rattling away in an undertone with great vivacity for the amusement of an ideal audience. He was not quite so young as he had been, and his figure was rather running to seed; but there was an air of exaggerated gentility about him, which bespoke the hero of swaggering comedy." 23

Young men. "There was . . . a little group of three or four young men, with lantern jaws and thick eyebrows, who were conversing in one corner; but they seemed to be of secondary importance, and laughed and talked together without attracting any very marked attention." 23

Miss Snevellicci, "who always played some part in blue silk knee-smalls at her benefit, glancing from the depths of her coal-scuttle straw bonnet at **Nicholas**, and affecting to be absorbed in the recital of a diverting story . . . . " 23

Miss Ledrook, "who had brought her work, and was making up a ruff in the most natural manner possible." 23

Miss Belvawney "seldom aspired to speaking parts, and usually went on as a page in white silk hose, to stand with one leg bent and contemplate the audience . . . ." 23

Miss Bravassa "who had once had her likeness taken 'in character' by an engraver's apprentice, whereof impressions were hung up for sale . . . whenever the announce bills came out for her annual night." 23

Mrs Lenville. " . . . in a very limp bonnet and veil, decidedly in that way in which she would wish to be if she truly loved Mr **Lenville**. . . . " 23

Miss Gazingi. " . . . with an imitation ermine boa tied in a loose knot round her neck, flogging Mr **Crummles**, junior, with both ends in fun." 23

Mrs Grudden. " . . . in a brown cloth pelisse and a beaver bonnet, who . . . took money at the doors, and dressed the ladies, and swept the house, and held the prompt book when everybody else was on for the last scene, and acted any kind of part on any emergency without ever learning it . . . . " 23

Fluggers "does the heavy business . . . . " 30

Snevellicci. "And an uncommonly fine man [he] was, with a hook nose, and a white forehead, and curly black hair, and high cheek bones, and altogether quite a handsome face, only a little pimply as though with drinking. He had a very broad chest . . . and he wore a threadbare blue dress coat buttoned with gilt buttons tight across it . . . .

"[He] had been in the profession ever since he had first played the ten-year-old imps in the Christmas pantomimes; who could sing a little, dance a little, fence a little, act a little, and do everything a little, but not much; who had been sometimes in the ballet, and sometimes in the chorus, at every theatre in London; who was always selected in virtue of his figure to play the military visitors and the speechless noblemen; who always wore a smart dress, and came on arm-in-arm with a smart lady in short petticoats—and always did it too with such an air that people in the pit had been several times known to cry out 'Bravo!' under the impression that he was somebody." 30

—*spiritously admiring:* "Mr Snevellicci had no sooner swallowed another glassful than he smiled upon all present in happy forgetfulness of having exhibited symptoms of pugnacity, and proposed 'The ladies—bless their hearts! . . . I love 'em . . . I love 'em, every one.'

"'Not every one,' reasoned Mr **Lillyvick**, mildly. . . . "That would include the married ladies, you know . . . . "

"'I love them too, sir,' said Mr Snevellicci.

"The collector looked into the surrounding faces with an aspect of grave astonishment, seeming to say, 'This is a nice man!' and appeared a little surprised that Mrs Lillyvick's manner yielded no evidences of horror and indignation." 30

Mrs Snevellicci , "who was still a dancer, with a neat little figure and some remains of good looks; and who now sat, as she danced—being rather too old for the full glare of the foot-lights,—in the background." 30

Robber, "with a very large belt and buckle round his waist, and very large leather gauntlets on his hands . . . . " 48

Snittle Timberry. " . . . having recovered from his late severe indisposition, would have the honour of appearing that evening . . . . " 48

African Swallower "looked and spoke remarkably like an Irishman." 48

Others

Captain **Adams**, second to Lord **Verisopht**. "Both [with **Westwood**] utterly heartless, both men upon town, both thoroughly initiated in its worst vices, both deeply in debt, both fallen from some higher estate, both addicted to every depravity for which society can find some genteel name and plead its most depraving conventionalities as an excuse, they were naturally gentlemen of most unblemished honour themselves, and of great nicety concerning the honour of other people." 50

Alphonse, "so little indeed that his body would not hold, in ordinary array, the number of small buttons which are indispensable to a page's costume, and they were consequently obliged to be stuck on four abreast . . . if ever there were an Alphonse who carried plain Bill in his face and figure, that page was the boy." 21

—*awakened:* "[He] appeared with dishevelled hair and a very warm and glossy face, as of a page who had just got out of bed . . . . On the question being propounded whether he could go and find [**Kate**], the page desponded and thought not; but being stimulated with a shilling, the page grew sanguine and thought he could . . . . The plated buttons disappeared with an alacrity most unusual to them . . . . " 33

Attendant. "[**Madeline**'s] attendant . . . was a red-faced, round-eyed, slovenly girl, who, from a certain roughness about the bare arms that peeped from under her draggled shawl, and the half-washed-out traces of smut and blacklead which tattooed her countenance, was clearly of a kin with the servants-of-all-work . . . . " 16

Bachelor. " . . . the company in some degree recovered from their fears, which had been productive of some most singular instances of a total want of presence of mind; thus the bachelor friend had for a long time supported in his arms Mrs Kenwigs's **sister**, instead of **Mrs Kenwigs** . . . . " 15

Bank clerk. " . . . a ruddy-faced, white-headed friend . . . ." 37 "The Brothers . . . gave occasion to the superannuated bank clerk to say so many good things that he quite outshone himself, and was looked upon as a prodigy of humour." 63

Bar-maid. "'A pretty state of things, if a man isn't to admire a handsome girl without being beat to pieces for it!'

"This reflection appeared to have great weight with the young lady in the bar, who (adjusting her cap as she spoke, and glancing at a mirror) declared that it would be a very pretty state of things indeed . . . ." 43

Mrs Blockson, charwoman. "'Will you hold your tongue— female?' said Mr **Mortimer Knag** . . . .

"'By your leave, Mr Knag,' retorted the charwoman, turning sharp round. 'I'm only too glad not to speak in this house, excepting when and where I'm spoke to, sir; and with regard to being a female, sir, I should wish to know what you considered yourself?'" 18

Cecilia Bobster. "At the sight of the young lady, **Nicholas** started and changed colour; his heart beat violently, and he stood rooted to the spot . . . . '[It] was the wrong lady . . . .'" 40

Augustus Borum. " . . . a young gentleman who was pinching the **phenomenon** behind, apparently with the view of ascertaining whether she was real." 24

Mrs Borum. The mother of "the six children who were so enraptured with the public actions of the **phenomenon** . . . ." 24

"Mrs Borum and the **governess** cast wreaths upon the stage, of which some fluttered into the lamps, and one crowned the temples of a fat gentleman in the pit, who . . . remained unconscious of the honour. . . ." 24

Mrs Bray. "'The mother was a gentle, loving, confiding creature, and although [her husband] wounded her from their marriage till her death as cruelly and wantonly as ever man did, she never ceased to love him. She commended him on her death-bed to her child's care. Her child has never forgotten it, and never will.'" 46

Walter Bray. "He was scarce fifty, perhaps, but so emaciated as to appear much older. His features presented the remains of a handsome countenance, but one in which the embers of strong and impetuous passions were easier to be traced than any expression which would have rendered a far plainer face much more prepossessing. His looks were very haggard, and his limbs and body literally worn to the bone, but there was something of the old fire in the large sunken eye notwithstanding . . . ." 46

Brooker. " . . . a shambling figure, which at one time stole behind [**Ralph**] with noiseless footsteps, at another crept a few paces before him, and at another glided along by his side; at all times regarding him with an eye so keen, and a look so eager and attentive, that it was more like the expression of an intrusive face in some powerful picture or strongly-marked dream . . . .

"A spare, dark, withered man, of about [Ralph's] own age, with a stooping body, and a very sinister face rendered more ill-favoured by hollow and hungry cheeks, deeply sun-burnt, and thick black eyebrows, blacker in contrast with the perfect whiteness of his hair; roughly clothed in shabby garments, of a strange and uncouth make; and having about him an indefinable manner of depression and degradation;—this, for a moment, was all [Ralph] saw. But he looked again, and the face and person seemed gradually to grow less strange; to change as he looked, to subside and soften into lineaments that were familiar, until at last they resolved themselves, as if by some strange optical illusion, into those of one whom he had known for many years, and forgotten and lost sight of for nearly as many more." 44

Bulph, a pilot, "who sported a boat-green door, with window-frames of the same colour, and had the little finger of a drowned man on his parlour mantel-shelf, with other maritime and natural curiosities. He displayed also a brass knocker, a brass plate, and a brass bell-handle, all very bright and shining; and had a mast, with a vane on the top of it, in his back yard." 23

Croupier. " . . . a plump, paunchy, sturdy-looking fellow, with his under-lip a little pursed from a habit of counting money inwardly as he paid it, but with no decidedly bad expression in his face, which was rather an honest and jolly one than otherwise." 50

Crowl. " . . . a hard-featured square-faced man, elderly and shabby . . . wore a wig of short, coarse, red hair, which he took off with his hat, and hung upon a nail. Having adopted in its place a dirty cotton nightcap, and groped about in the dark till he found a remnant of candle, he knocked at the partition which divided the two garrets . . . [his] harsh countenance was the very epitome of selfishness . . . ." 14

Curdle, "who had written a pamphlet of sixty-four pages, post octavo, on the character of the Nurse's deceased husband in Romeo and Juliet . . . [he] wore a loose robe on his back, and his right forefinger on his forehead after the portraits of **Sterne**, to whom somebody or other had once said he bore a striking resemblance." 24

Mrs Curdle "who was supposed, by those who were best informed on such points, to possess quite the London taste in matters relating to literature and the drama . . . . Mrs Curdle was dressed in a morning wrapper, with a little cap stuck upon the top of her head . . . ." 24

Cutlers, a newly married couple. " . . . Mr Cutler, having kept house in Mr **Lillyvick**'s parish, had heard of him very often indeed. His attention in calling [to collect the water-rate] had been quite extraordinary." 14

David. " . . . an ancient butler of apoplectic appearance, and with very short legs . . . .

"Instantly, by a feat of dexterity . . . the apoplectic butler bringing his left hand from behind the small of his back, produced the bottle with the corkscrew already inserted; uncorked it at a jerk and placed the magnum and the cork before his master with the dignity of conscious cleverness." 37

Dick. "When the guard (who was a stout old Yorkshireman) had blown himself quite out of breath, he put the horn into a little tunnel of a basket fastened to the coach-side for the purpose, and giving himself a plentiful shower of blows on the chest and shoulders, observed it was uncommon cold, after which he demanded of every person separately whether he was going right through, and if not where he *was* going . . . he took another blow at the horn by way of refreshment, and having how exhausted his usual topics of conversation folded his arms as well as he could in so many coats, and falling into a solemn silence . . . the only things he seemed to care for, being horses and droves of cattle, which he scrutinised with a critical air as they were passed upon the road." 5

Buxom **female**. "'You're never to be trusted,' screamed the woman . . . . Isn't it enough that I paid two pound fourteen for you, and took you out of prison and let you live here like a gentleman, but must you go on like this: breaking my heart besides?' . . . she suddenly, and with a dexterity which could only have been acquired by long practice, flung a pretty heavy clothes-basket at [**Mantalini**], with so good an aim that he kicked more violently than before, though without venturing to make any effort to disengage his head, which was quite extinguished." 64

Fly-driver. "There was some singing . . . and very likely there might have been more, if the fly-driver, who stopped to drive the happy pair [of newly-married **Lillyvicks**] . . . had not sent in a peremptory message intimating, that if they didn't come directly he should infallibly demand eighteen-pence over and above his agreement." 25

Footman. "'Is Madame **Mantalini** in?' faltered **Kate**.

"'Not often out at this time, Miss,' replied the man in a tone which rendered 'Miss,' something more offensive than 'My dear.'"17

" . . . Mr **Mantalini**'s legs were extended at full length upon the floor, and his head and shoulders were supported by a very tall footman, who didn't seem to know what to do with them . . . being startled to hear such awful tones proceeding, as it were, from between his very fingers, [he] dropped his master's head upon the floor with a pretty loud crash, and then, without an effort to lift it up, gazed upon the by-standers, as if he had done something rather clever than otherwise." 44

Footman. " . . . [**Hawk**'s] private chariot, having behind it a footman, whose legs, although somewhat large for his body, might, as mere abstract legs, have set themselves up for models at the Royal Academy." 27

Mr **Gallanbile**, M. P. ""Fifteen guineas, tea and sugar, and servants allowed to see male cousins, if godly. Note. Cold dinner in the kitchen on the Sabbath. Mr Gallanbile being devoted to the Observance question. No victuals whatever cooked on the Lord's Day, with the exception of dinner for Mr and Mrs Gallanbile, which, being a work of piety and necessity, is exempted. Mr Gallanbile dines late on the day of rest, in order to prevent the sinfulness of the cook's dressing herself."' [read **Tom**]" 16

Literary **gentleman**. "There was a literary gentleman present who had dramatised in his time two hundred and forty-seven novels as fast as they had come out—some of them faster than they had come out—and was a literary gentleman in consequence." 48

George. " . . . a young man, who had known Mr **Kenwigs** when he was a bachelor, and was much esteemed by the ladies, as bearing the reputation of a rake . . . .

"'It goes to [Mr **Lillyvick**'s] heart, I believe, to be forced to cut the water off when the people don't pay,' observed the bachelor friend, intending a joke.

"'George,' said Mr **Kenwigs**, solemnly, 'none of that, if you please.'" 14

Miss **Green**, "who had made Mrs **Kenwigs**'s dress . . . which gown, being of a flaming colour and made upon a juvenile principle, was so successful that Mr **Kenwigs** said the eight years of matrimony and the five children seemed all a dream, and Mrs Kenwigs younger and more blooming than the very first Sunday he kept company with her." 14

Mr **Gregsbury**, M.P. "For a gentleman who was rejoiced to see a body of visitors, Mr Gregsbury looked as uncomfortable as might be; but perhaps this was occasioned by senatorial gravity, and a statesmanlike habit of keeping his feelings under control. He was a tough, burly, thick-headed gentleman, with a loud voice, a pompous manner, a tolerable command of sentences with no meaning in them, and in short every requisite for a very good member indeed." 16

Hairdresser. " . . . there were displayed . . . waxen busts of a light lady and a dark gentleman . . . some ladies had gone so far as to assert, that the dark gentleman was actually a portrait of the spirited young proprietor, and the great similarity between their head-dresses—both wore very glossy hair with a narrow walk straight down the middle, and a profusion of flat circular curls on both sides—encouraged the idea." 52

Hannah. " . . . a servant girl with an uncommonly dirty face . . . .

"'Somebody went out just now, but I think it was the attic which had been a cleaning of himself,' replied the girl." 3

Keeper. " . . . a dirty hand was observed to glide, stealthily and swiftly along the top of the wall, as if in pursuit of a fly, and then to clasp with the utmost dexterity one of the old gentleman's ankles. This done, the companion hand appeared, and clasped the other ankle . . . .

"One of the hands being then cautiously unclasped, the old gentleman dropped into a sitting posture, and was looking round to smile and bow to Mrs **Nickleby**, when he disappeared with some precipitation, as if his legs had been pulled from below.

" . . . the dirty hands again became visible, and were immediately followed by the figure of a coarse squat man, who ascended by the steps which had been recently occupied by their singular neighbour." 41

Lillyvick Kenwigs. "'My baby, my blessed, blessed, blessed, blessed baby,' screamed **Mrs Kenwigs**, making every blessed louder than the last. 'My own darling, sweet, innocent Lillyvick—Oh let me go to him. Let me go-o-o-o!'" 15

Morleena Kenwigs. " . . . regarding whose uncommon Christian name . . . it was invented and composed by **Mrs Kenwigs** previous to her first lying-in, for the special distinction of her eldest child, in case it should prove a daughter."14

Mortimer Knag. " . . . an ornamental stationer and small circulating library keeper, in a by-street off Tottenham Court Road . . . and as [he] was a tall lank gentleman of solemn features, wearing spectacles, and garnished with much less hair than a gentleman bordering on forty or thereabouts usually boasts, Mrs **Nickleby** whispered her daughter that she thought he must be literary." 18

Elderly **lady** guest, "who was very fat, and turned of sixty, [and who] came in a low book-muslin dress and short kid gloves, which so exasperated **Mrs Kenwigs**, that that lady assured her sister in private, that if it hadn't happened that the supper was cooking at the back-parlour grate at that moment, she certainly would have requested its representative to withdraw." 14

Fastidious **lady**, "[with] an infinite variety of cloaks and small parcels, who loudly lamented for the behoof of the outsides the non-arrival of her own carriage which was to have taken her on, and made the guard solemnly promise to stop every green chariot he saw coming . . . . " 5

Rich **lady**. " . . . some great lady—or rather rich one, for there is occasionally a wide distinction between riches and greatness—who had come with her **daughter** to approve of some court-dresses . . . [they] were both out of temper that day, and [Kate] came in for her share of their revilings. She was awkward—her hands were cold—dirty—coarse—she could do nothing right; they wondered how Madame **Mantalini** could have such people about her, requested they might see some other young woman the next they came, and so forth." 17

John La Creevy. "'But what do you think . . . of that very same brother coming up to London at last, and never resting till he found me out . . . and making me stay a whole month, and pressing me to stop there all my life—yes, all my life—and so did his wife, and so did the children—and there were four of them, and one, the eldest girl of all, they—they had named her after me eight good years before, they had indeed.'" 31

Miss Linkinwater. ". . . a great to-do there was . . . respecting [her] cap, which had been despatched, per [**messenger**] boy, from the house of the family where [she] boarded, and had not yet come to hand . . . ." 37 " . . . a chubby old lady . . . ." 63

Little girl. "' . . . the little girl, who was watching the child, being tired I suppose, fell asleep and set her hair on fire.'

"'Oh you malicious little wretch!' cried **Mrs Kenwigs**, impressively shaking her forefinger at the small unfortunate, who might be thirteen years old and was looking on with a singed head and a frightened face." 15

Lumbey. " . . . Doctor Lumbey sat in the first floor front . . . nursing the deposed baby, and talking to Mr **Kenwigs**. He was a stout bluff-looking gentleman, with no shirt-collar, to speak of, and a beard that had been growing since yesterday morning; for Doctor Lumbey was popular, and the neighbourhood was prolific; and there had been no less than three other knockers muffled, one after the other, within the last forty-eight hours." 36

Man, a coach passenger. " . . . the broken-headed inside, who was a man of very genteel appearance, dressed in mourning. He was not past the middle age, but his hair was grey; it seemed to have been prematurely turned by care or sorrow." 6

Messenger. " . . . when he was least expected, the messenger, carrying the band-box with elaborate caution, appeared in an exactly opposite direction, puffing and panting for breath, and flushed with recent exercise . . . ." 37 *See* **Miss Linkinwater**

Godfrey Nickleby, grandfather of **Nicholas**. " . . . a worthy gentleman, who taking it into his head rather late in life that he must get married, and not being young enough or rich enough to aspire to the hand of a lady of fortune, had wedded an old flame out of mere attachment . . . ." 1

Grandmother **Nickleby**, wife of **Godfrey**. She "presented her husband with a couple of sons . . . ." 1

Nicholas Nickleby, Sr. He "was of a timid and retiring disposition [and] gleaned . . . forewarnings to shun the great world and attach himself to the quiet routine of a country life . . . ." 1

"The run of luck went against Mr Nickleby; a mania prevailed, a bubble burst, four **stockbrokers** took villa residences at Florence, four hundred nobodies were ruined, and among them Mr Nickleby . . . he took at once to his bed, apparently resolved to keep that, at all events. . . [he] embraced his wife and children, and having pressed them by turns to his languidly beating heart . . . solemnly commended them to One who never deserted the widow or her fatherless children, and smiling gently on them, turned upon his face, and observed, that he thought he could fall asleep." 1

Ralph Nickleby, uncle of **Godfrey**. "The amiable old gentleman, it seemed, had intended to leave the whole to the Royal Human Society . . . but the Institution having been unfortunate enough . . . to save the life of a poor relation to whom he paid a weekly allowance of three shillings and six-pence, he had in a fit of very natural exasperation, revoked the bequest in a codicil, and left it all to Mr Godfrey Nickleby . . . ." 1

Nurse. "'Drat the man!' cried the nurse, looking angrily round. 'What does he mean by making that noise here?' 'Silence, woman!' said Mr **Kenwigs** fiercely. 'I won't be silent,' returned the nurse. 'Be silent yourself, you wretch. Have you no regard for your baby?' 'No,' returned Mr Kenwigs. 'More shame for you,' retorted the nurse. 'Ugh! you unnatural monster.'" 36

Old lord, "who was a *very* old lord . . . mumbled and chuckled in a state of great delight . . . with his own address in getting such a fine woman for his wife; and the young lady, who was a very lively young lady, seeing the old lord in this rapturous condition, chased the old lord behind a cheval-glass, and then and there kissed him . . . ." 18

Passenger, in a coach. **Nicholas** "was still more relieved when a hearty-looking gentleman, with a very good-humoured face, and a very fresh colour, got up behind and proposed to take the other corner of the seat.

"'If we put some of these youngsters in the middle,' said the newcomer, 'they'll be safer in case of their going to sleep; eh?'" 5

Phib (**Phoebe**). "The hungry servant attended **Miss Squeers** in her own room according to custom, to curl her hair, perform the other little offices of her toilet, and administer as much flattery as she could get up for the purpose. . . . " 12

Pluck is one of Sir **Mulberry Hawk**'s "toads in ordinary." 19 *See* **Pyke**

Porter. ". . . [Nicholas] walked slowly on, a little in advance of the porter, and very probably with not half as light a heart in his breast as the man had, although he had no waistcoat to cover it with, and had evidently, from the appearance of his other garments, been spending the night in a stable, and taking his breakfast at a pump." 5

Proprietor, of a gambling establishment. " . . . a man of six or eight and fifty . . . with his hands folded on the top of his stick and his chin appearing above them. He was a tall, fat, long-bodied man, buttoned up to the throat in a light green coat, which made his body look still longer than it was, and wore besides drab breeches and gaiters, a white neckerchief, and a broad-brimmed white hat." 50

Proprietress, of a General Agency Office. **Tom**'s "eyes fixed on a very fat old lady in a mob-cap . . . who was airing herself at the fire . . . ." 16

Pugstyles. "'Now gentlemen. . . [said Mr **Gregsbury**] you are dissatisfied with my conduct, I see by the newspapers.'

"'Yes, Mr Gregsbury, we are,' said a plump old gentleman in a violent heat, bursting out of the throng, and planting himself in the front. . . . 'I am very sorry to be here, sir . . . but your conduct . . . has rendered this deputation from your constituents imperatively necessary.'" 16

Pyke. One of Sir **Mulberry Hawk**'s "toads in ordinary . . . [he was] a sharp-faced gentleman, who was sitting on a low chair with a high back, reading the paper." 19

—*condescending:* "'And I'll tell you what,' said Mr Pyke; 'if you'll send round to the public-house for a pot of mild half-and-half, positively and actually I'll drink it.'

"And positively and actually Mr Pyke *did* drink it, and Mr **Pluck** helped him, while **Mrs Nickleby** looked on in divided admiration of the condescension of the two, and the aptitude with which they accommodated themselves to the pewter-pot . . . ." 27

Rival. "'Ah! **Hawk**,' said one very sprucely-dressed personage in a Newmarket coat, a choice neckerchief, and all other accessories of the most unexceptionable kind. 'How d'ye do, old fellow?'

"This was a rival trainer of young noblemen and gentlemen, and the person of all others whom Sir **Mulberry** most hated and dreaded to meet. They shook hands with excessive cordiality." 50

Scaley. **Kate** "started again to observe, on looking round, that a white hat, and a red neckerchief and a broad round face, and large head, and part of a green coat, were in the room too . . . . 'Mr **Muntlehiney**,' said the man 'Wot's come of him? Is he at home?'" 21

Sister, of a fox-hunter. "'The gentlewoman was not a girl, but she was . . . handsome, and entitled to a pretty large property. In course of time [**Ralph Nickleby**] married her . . . when they had been married nearly seven years, and were within a few weeks of the time when the brother's death would have adjusted all, she eloped with a younger man and left him.'" 60

Snawley, "who was a sleek flat-nosed man, clad in sombre garments, and long black gaiters, and bearing in his countenance an expression of much mortification and sanctity, so that his smiling without any obvious reason was the more remarkable." 4

—*on parental instinct:* "'That's what it was, sir. . . the elevated feeling—the feeling of the ancient Romans and Grecians, and of the beasts of the field and birds of the air, with the exception of rabbits and tom-cats, which sometimes devour their offspring. My heart yearned towards [**Smike**]. I could have—I don't know what I couldn't have done to him in the anger of a father.'" 45

Mrs Snawley. "'You see I have married the mother,' pursued **Snawley**; 'it's expensive keeping boys at home, and as she has a little money in her own right, I am afraid (women are so very foolish, Mr **Squeers**) that she might be led to squander it on them, which would be their ruin, you know.'" 4

"'Stop! You don't come in here,' said Mr Snawley's better half, interposing her person, which was a robust one, in the doorway. . . .

"'You set me at defiance, do you?' said **Ralph**.

"'Yes,' was the answer. 'I do.'" 59

Sir Tumley Snuffim, physician. "'"My dear fellow," he said, "be proud of that woman; make much of her; she is an ornament to the fashionable world, and to you. Her complaint is soul. It swells, expands, dilates—the blood fires, the pulse quickens, the excitement increases—Whew!"'" 21

Spinster. " . . . she was to the full as good-looking as she had been described—more so, indeed—but that she was in too much of a hurry to change her condition, and consequently, while **Tim** was courting her and thinking of changing his, got married to somebody else." 37

Tom Tix. **Scaley** "was closely followed by a little man in brown, very much the worse for wear, who brought with him a mingled fumigation of stale tobacco and fresh onions. The clothes of this gentleman were much bespeckled with flue; and his shoes, stockings, and nether garments, from his heels to the waist buttons of his coat inclusive, were profusely embroidered with splashes of mud, caught a fortnight previous—before the setting-in of the fine weather." 21

Tom, a clerk in a General Agency Office. **Nicholas** "found himself in a little floor-clothed room, with a high desk railed off in one corner, behind which sat a lean youth with cunning eyes and a protruding chin, whose performances in capital-text darkened the window. "16

Waiter. " . . . a waiter who had been rubbing his hands in excessive enjoyment . . . so long as only the breaking of heads was in question, adjured the spectators with great earnestness to fetch the police, declaring that otherwise murder would be surely done, and that he was responsible for all the glass and china on the premises." 43

Waiter, in a handsome hotel. "**Nicholas** sat himself down, directly opposite to the party, and summoning the waiter, paid his bill.

"'Do you know that person's name?' he inquired of the man in an audible voice; pointing out **Sir Mulberry** as he put the question . . . .

"'That gentleman, sir?' replied the waiter, who, no doubt, knew his cue, and answered with just as little respect, and just as much impertinence as he could safely show: 'no, sir, I do not, sir.'" 32

Warehouseman. " . . . the sturdiest and jolliest subordinate . . . exhibiting a very hot and flushed countenance, pulled a single lock of grey hair in the middle of his forehead as a respectful salute to the company . . . . " 37

Westwood. "'Captain **Adams**,' cried Westwood, hastily, 'I call you to witness that this was fairly done. **Hawk**, we have not a moment to lose. We must leave this place immediately, push for Brighton, and cross to France with all speed. This has been a bad business, and may be worse if we delay a moment. Adams, consult your own safety, and don't remain here; the living before the dead—good-bye.'" 50

Mrs Wrymug. "'''Three serious footmen,'" said **Tom**, impressively.

"'Three, did you say? ' asked the **client**, in an altered tone.

"'Three serious footmen,' replied Tom. "'Cook, housemaid, and nursemaid; each female servant required to join the Little Bethel Congregation three times every Sunday—with a serious footman. If the cook is more serious than the footman, she will be expected to improve the footman; if the footman is more serious than the cook, he will be expected to improve the cook.'" 16

Yardmen. "**Nicholas** . . . thrust himself at once into the centre of the group, and in a more emphatic tone perhaps than circumstances might seem to warrant, demanded what all that noise was about.

"'Hallo!' said one of the men from the yard, 'this is somebody in disguise, this is.'

"'Room for the eldest son of the Emperor of Roosher, gen'lmen!' cried another fellow." 43

Lively young lady. " . . . Miss **Knag**, who was tinged with curiosity, stepped accidentally behind the glass, and encountered the lively young lady's eye just at the very moment when she kissed the old lord; upon which the young lady in a pouting manner murmured something about 'an old thing,' and 'great impertinence,' and finished by darting a look of displeasure at Miss Knag and smiling contemptuously.

"'**Madame Mantalini**,' said the young lady. . . 'Pray have up that pretty young creature we saw yesterday. . . . Of all things in the world, Madame Mantalini,' said the lord's intended, throwing herself languidly on a sofa, 'I hate being waited upon by frights or elderly persons. Let me always see that young creature, I beg, whenever I come. . . . Everyone is talking about her . . . and my lord, being a great admirer of beauty, must positively see her.'" 18

Walk-ons

Bobster. " . . . **Newman** . . . had been led to suspect that the young lady led a very miserable and unhappy life, under the strict control of her only parent, who was of a violent and brutal temper . . . . " 40

Borum boys. "The **phenomenon** was really in a fair way of being torn limb from limb, for two strong little boys . . . were dragging her in different directions as a trial of strength." 24

Charlotte Borum. " . . . having filched the **phenomenon**'s little green parasol, [he] was now carrying it bodily off, while the distracted infant looked helplessly on." 24

Emma Borum. "'Emma, don't stare so.'" 24

Assistant **box-keeper**. " . . . they reached their box with no more serious interruption by the way, than a desire on the part of the same pugnacious gentleman [**Pyke**] to 'smash' the assistant box-keeper for happening to mistake the number." 27

Hump-backed **boy**. "'There were hyacinths there this last spring, blossoming in . . . old blacking-bottles,' said **Tim** . . . . 'They belong to a sickly bed-ridden hump-backed boy, and seem to be the only pleasures . . . of his sad existence.'" 40

Two **bricklayers.** "'What's he [**Smike**] been a doing of?' asked a labourer, with a hod of bricks, against whom and a fellow-labourer Mr **Squeers** had backed, on the first jerk of the umbrella." 38

Mrs **Cheeryble** (the late). "' . . . the kindest and very best of parents—the very best of parents to us both. I wish that she could have seen us in our prosperity, and shared it, and had the happiness of knowing how dearly we loved her in it . . . .'" 37

Colonel **Chowser**. " . . . of the Militia—and the race-courses . . . a white-headed person . . . was in conversation with somebody, who appeared to be a **make-weight**, and was not introduced at all." 19

Mrs Clark. "'Where have you sent [**Madeline Bray**] to?' asked the fat lady.

"'Mrs Clark's,' replied **Tom**.

"'She'll have a nice life of it, if she goes there,' observed the fat lady, taking a pinch of snuff from a tin box." 16

Client in a General Agency Office. " . . . a genteel female in shepherd's-plaid boots, who appeared to be the client." 16

Coachman. " . . . brother **Charles** [**Cheeryble**] imparted the fullest directions to the coachman, and, besides paying the man a shilling over and above his fare in order that he might take the utmost care of the lady [**Miss Linkinwater**], all but choked him with a glass of spirits of uncommon strength, and then nearly knocked all the breath out of his body in his energetic endeavours to knock it in again." 37

Coachman, in the stage to Greta Bridge. "'All right behind there, **Dick**?' cried the coachman." 5

Coachman, London hackney. "And the coach, and the coachman, and the horses, rattled, and jangled, and whipped, and cursed, and swore, and tumbled on together, till they came to Golden Square." 19

Coachman, London hackney. "To the City they went accordingly, with all the speed the hackney-coach could make; and as the horses happened to live at Whitechapel and to be in the habit of taking their breakfast there, when they breakfasted at all, they performed the journey with greater expedition than could reasonably have been expected." 33

Coachman, London hackney. "The coach came up; Master **Wackford** entered; **Squeers** pushed in his prize [**Smike**], and following close at his heels, pulled up the glasses. The coachman mounted his box and drove slowly off . . . ." 38

Coachman, London hackney. "'Noo,' said **John** [**Browdie**], when a hackney-coach had been called and the ladies and the luggage hurried in, 'gang to the Sarah's Head, mun.'

"'To the *vere*?' cried the coachman." 39

Coachman, London hackney. " . . . carrying **Madeline** in his great excitement as easily as if she were an infant, [**Nicholas**] reached the coach in which **Kate** and the girl were already waiting, and confiding his charge to them, jumped up beside the coachman and bade him drive away." 54

Coachman, London hackney. "The man rang and rang again; then knocked until the street re-echoed with the sounds; then listened at the key-hole of the door. Nobody came, and the [**Gride**] house was as silent as the grave." 56

Coachman, in the Portsmouth stage to London. " . . . he let out his whip-lash and touched up a little boy on the calves of his legs by way of emphasis." 32

Coal-heaver. " . . . there presented himself for shaving a big, burly, good-humoured coal-heaver with a pipe in his mouth, who drawing his hand across his chin, requested to know when a shaver would be disengaged." 52

Dancer. " . . . a little, weazen, hump-backed man, began to dance. He was a grotesque, fantastic figure, and the few bystanders laughed." 62

Tailor's **daughter**, "who opened the door, appeared in that flutter of spirits which is so often attendant upon the periodical getting up of a family's linen." 24

Decoys. " . . . another proprietor with his confederates in various disguises—one man in spectacles, another, with an eye-glass and a stylish hat; a third, dressed as a farmer well to do in the world, with his top-coat over his arm and his flash notes in a large leathern pocket-book; and all with heavy-handled whips to represent most innocent country fellows who had trotted there on horseback—sought, by loud and noisy talk and pretended play, to entrap some unwary customer, while the gentlemen confederates (of more villanous aspect still, in clean linen and good clothes) betrayed their close inter-est in the concern by the anxious furtive glance they cast on all new comers." 50

Dick, a blackbird. "There was not a bird of such methodical and businesslike habits in all the world as the blind blackbird, who dreamed and dozed away his days in a large snug cage, and had lost his voice from old age years before **Tim** [**Linkinwater**] first bought him." 37

Digby. "'What a dear that Mr Digby is!' said **Miss Snevellicci** . . . . (**Smike**'s theatrical name was Digby.)" 30

Big **footman**. "The [**Wititterly**] door was opened by a big footman with his head floured, or chalked, or painted in some way (it didn't look genuine powder) . . ." 21

Fox-hunter. "' . . . there was . . . a rough fox-hunting, hard-drinking gentleman, who had run through his own fortune, and wanted to squander away that of his sister [who was **Mrs Ralph Nickleby** for a while]; they were both orphans, and she lived with him and managed his house.'" 60

Gamblers. " . . . one or two men who, each with a long roll of half-crowns chequered with a few stray sovereigns, in his left hand, staked their money at every roll of the ball with a business-like sedateness which showed that they were used to it, and had been playing all day, and most probably all the day before . . . . " 50

Glavormelly. "'You never saw my friend Glavormelly, sir! . . . Then you have never seen acting yet. . . . He is gone to that bourne from whence no traveller returns. I hope he is appreciated *there*.'" 33

Journeyman **hairdresser**. " . . . (who was not very popular among the ladies, by reason of his obesity and middle age). . . . " 52

Mrs Knag. "'My mamma—hem—was the most lovely and beautiful creature, with the most striking and exquisite—hem—the most exquisite nose that ever was put upon a human face . . . (here Miss Knag rubbed her own nose sympathetically). . . . '" 18

Country **lady**. "But it was London; and the old country lady inside, who had put her head out of the coach-window a mile or two this side Kingston, and cried out to the driver that she was sure he must have passed it and forgotten to set her down, was satisfied at last." 32

Landlord, on the road to Portsmouth. "The landlord led [**Nicholas** and **Smike**] into the kitchen, and as there was a good fire he remarked that it was very cold. If there had happened to be a bad one he would have observed that it was very warm." 22

Lawyer. "'Such things happen every day,' remarked the lawyer." 1

Lawyer. "[**Nicholas** and the **Cheerybles**] had been advised by a lawyer, eminent for his sagacity and acuteness in such practice, to resist the proceedings taken on the other side for the recovery of [**Smike**] as slowly and artfully as possible . . . . " 59

Parlour **lodger**. " . . . being deputed by the landlord to dispose of the rooms as they became vacant, and to keep a sharp look-out that the lodgers didn't run away . . . he was permitted to live rent-free, lest he should at any time be tempted to run away himself." 16

London manager. "'I have not the smallest doubt it's the fame of the **phenomenon**—that's the man; him in the great-coat and no shirt-collar.'" 30

Very fat **man**. " . . . some held that [**Peg Sliderskew**] had fallen asleep, some that she had burnt herself to death, some that she had got drunk; and one very fat man that she had seen something to eat which had frightened her so much (not being used to it) that she had fallen into a fit." 56

Manservant, for **Hawk**. "The fact was, that **Ralph Nickleby** had bribed the man, who, being anxious to earn his money with a view to future favours, held the door in his hand, and ventured to linger still." 38

Mrs Marker. "'"Russell Place, Russell Square; offers eighteen guineas, tea and sugar found. Two in family, and see very little company. Five servants kept. No man. No followers."'" 14

Matthews. " . . . a very pale, shabby boy, who looked as if he had slept underground from his infancy, as very likely he had." 16

Matrons. " . . . the [**Kenwigs**] baby had been exhibited to a score or two of deputations from a select body of female friends, who had assembled in the passage, and about the street-door, to discuss the event in all its bearings." 35

Officer. " . . . a young officer, supposed to entertain a passion for Miss Snevellicci, stuck his glass in his eye as though to hide a tear." 24

Very **old man**. " . . . **Pyke** threatened with many oaths to 'smifligate' a very old man with a lantern who accidentally stumbled in her way—to the great terror of **Mrs Nickleby** . . . . " 27

Omnibus conductor. " . . . 'the omnibus,' as **Miss La Creevy** protested, 'swore so dreadfully, that it was quite awful to hear it.'" 38

Porters and **warehousemen**, for **Cheeryble** Brothers. "There were four in all, and as they came in, bowing and grinning, and blushing, the housekeeper and **cook** and **housemaid** brought up the rear." 37

Seamstresses. ". . . **Miss Knag**'s friendship [for **Kate**] remained for three whole days, much to the wonderment of **Madame Mantalini**'s young ladies who had never beheld such constancy in that quarter before . . . . " 19 *And see* **Miss Knag** —*distressed*

Servant, for the **Knags**. "'. . . our last servant went to the hospital a week ago, with Saint Anthony's fire in her face . . . '" 18

Servant, at Miss **La Creevy**'s. ". . . on whom the odd figure of [**Noggs**] did not appear to make the most favourable impression possible, inasmuch as she no sooner saw him than she very nearly closed [the door], and placing herself in the narrow gap, inquired what he wanted." 31

Servant, for the **Mantalinis**. ". . . while [**Ralph Nickleby**] was hesitating whether to knock at the door or listen at the key-hole a little longer, a female servant . . . opened it abruptly and bounced out, with her blue cap-ribands streaming in the air. . . ." 44

Servant, for **Mrs Nickleby**, "who contented herself with holding out sundry vague and mysterious hopes of preferment to the servant girl, who received these obscure hints of dawning greatness with much veneration and respect." 27

Servant-girls and **little boys**. "Indeed, divers servant-girls who came to draw water, and sundry little boys who stopped to drink at the ladle, were almost scared out of their senses by the apparition of **Newman Noggs** looking stealthily round the pump, with nothing of him visible but his face, and that wearing the expression of a meditative Ogre." 40

Servants-of-all-work. ". . . some half-dozen strong young women, each with pattens and an umbrella . . . in attendance for [hire]. . . the poor things looked anxious and weary." 16

Miss Simmonds. "'I am very sorry to have wounded you by my thoughtless speech,' said [**Kate**'s] companion. 'I did not think of it. You are in mourning for some near relation?'" 17

Slopseller. ". . . **Nicholas** hurried into a slopseller's hard by, and bought **Smike** a great-coat. It would have been rather large for a substantial yeoman, but the shopman averring (and with considerable truth) that it was a most uncommon fit, Nicholas would have purchased it in his impatience if it had been twice the size." 30

Snewkes. ". . . another young man supposed to entertain honourable designs upon [**Mrs Kenwigs**'s sister] . . . . " 14

Snobb, the Honourable Mr. ". . . a gentleman with the neck of a stork and the legs of no animal in particular . . . . " 19

Ticket-porter. "The ticket-porter leans idly against the post at the corner, comfortably warm, but not hot, although the day is broiling. His white apron flaps languidly in the air, his head gradually droops upon his breast, he takes very long winks with both eyes at once; even he is unable to withstand the soporific influce of the place, and is gradually falling asleep. But now, he starts into full wakefulness, recoils a step or two, and gazes out before him with eager wildness in his eye. Is it a job, or a boy at marbles? Does he see a ghost, or hear an organ? No; sight more unwonted still—there is a butterfly in the square—a real, live butterfly! astray from flowers and sweets, and fluttering among the iron heads of the dusty area railings." 37

Trimmers. "'Trimmers is one of the best friends we have [said **Charles Cheeryble**]. He makes a thousand cases known to us that we should never discover ourselves. I am *very* much obliged to Trimmers.'" 35

Uncle, of **Miss Knag**. "'I had an uncle once . . . who . . . had a most excellent business as a tobacconist— hem—who had such small feet, that they were no bigger than those which are usually joined to wooden legs—the most symmetrical feet, **Madame Mantalini**, that even you can imagine.'

"'They must have had something the appearance of club feet, Miss Knag,' said Madame." 17

Waiter. "The waiter was touched. Waiter as he was, he had human passions and feelings, and he looked very hard at Miss **Squeers** as he handed the muffins." 39 *See* **Fanny Squeers** P—*decked out*

William, waiter at the Saracen's Head. "'Oh! that's the milk and water, is it, William?' said **Squeers**. 'Very good; don't forget the bread and butter presently.'" 5

United Metropolitan Improved Hot Muffin and Crumpet Baking and Punctual Delivery Company

Bonney. " . . . a pale gentleman in a violent hurry, who, with his hair standing up in great disorder all over his head, and a very narrow white cravat tied loosely round his throat, looked as if he had been knocked up in the night and had not dressed himself since.

"'My dear [**Ralph**] **Nickleby**,' said the gentleman, taking off a white hat which was so full of papers that it would scarcely stick upon his head, 'there's not a moment to lose; I have a cab at the door.'" 2

—*in action:* "Mr Bonney then presented himself to move the first resolution, and having run his right hand through his hair, and planted his left in an easy manner in his ribs, he consigned his hat to the care of the gentleman with the double-chin (who acted as a species of bottle-holder to the orators generally), and said he would read to them the first resolution . . . . " 2

Grievous **gentleman**. " . . . of semi-clerical appearance, who went at once into such deep pathetics, that he knocked the first speaker clean out of the course in no time. You might have heard a pin fall—a pin! a feather—as he described the cruelties inflicted on muffin boys by their masters . . . . " 2

Man, in the crowd. " . . . [a] gentleman having moved that [the resolution] be amended by the insertion of the words 'and crumpet' after the word 'muffin,' whenever it occurred, it was carried triumphantly; only one man in the crowd cried 'No!' and he was promptly taken into custody, and straightway borne off." 2

Two **Members**, of Parliament. " . . . there came forward the **Irish** member (who was a young gentleman of ardent temperament), with such a speech as only an Irish member can make, breathing the true soul and spirit of poetry, and poured forth with such fervour, that it made one warm to look at him . . . . And after him came the **Scotch** member, with various pleasant allusions to the probable amount of profits, which increased the good humour that the poetry had awakened . . . . " 2

Third **Member**, of Parliament. "'[He] has just gone home to put a clean shirt on, and take a bottle or two of sodawater, and will certainly be with us in time to address the meeting [said **Bonney**]. He is a little excited by last night, but never mind that; he always speaks the stronger for it.' . . . [he] grew jocular; and as patent boots, lemon-coloured kid gloves, and a fur coat-collar, assist jokes materially, there was immense laughter and much cheering . . . . " 2

Sir **Matthew Pupker**. He "had a little round head with a flaxen wig on the top of it [and] fell into such a paroxysm of bows, that the wig threatened to be jerked off every instant." 2

Waiter, in Bishopsgate Street Within, "feverish with agitation, tore into the room, and [threw] the door open with a crash . . . . " 2

Figures in Interludes

The Five Sisters of York 6

Alice, the youngest. "The blushing tints in the soft bloom on the fruit, or the delicate painting on the flower, are not more exquisite than was the blending of the rose and lily in her gentle face, or the deep blue of her eye. The vine in all its elegant luxuriance is not more graceful than were the clusters of rich brown hair that sported around her brow. . . . The heart of this fair girl bounded with joy and gladness. Devoted attachment to her sisters, and a fervent love of all beautiful things in nature, were its pure affections. Her gleesome voice and merry laugh were the sweetest music of their home. She was its very light and life. The brightest flowers in the garden were reared by her; the caged birds sang when they heard her voice, and pined when they missed its sweetness . . . what living thing within the sphere of her gentle witchery, could fail to love her!'"

Monk. "Everything looked gay and smiling; but the holy man walked gloomily on, with his eyes bent upon the ground. The beauty of the earth is but a breath, and man is but a shadow. What sympathy should a holy preacher have with either?"

Four sisters. "The eldest was in her twenty-third year, the second a year younger, the third a year younger than the second, and the fourth a year younger than the third . . . tall stately figures, with dark flashing eyes and hair of jet; dignity and grace were in their every movement . . . . "

The Baron of Grogzwig 6

Ancestor. " . . . short of money, had inserted a dagger in a gentleman who called one night to ask his way . . . [he being] an amiable man, felt very sorry afterwards for having been so rash, and laying violent hands upon a quantity of stone and timber which belonged to a weaker baron, built a chapel as an apology, and so took a receipt from Heaven in full of all demands."

Genius of Despair and Suicide. " . . . a wrinkled hideous figure, with deeply sunk and bloodshot eyes, and an immensely long cadaverous face, shadowed by jagged and matted locks of coarse black hair. He wore a kind of tunic of a dull bluish colour, which . . . was clasped or ornamented down the front with coffin-handles. His legs, too, were encased in coffin-plates as though in armour, and over his left shoulder he wore a short dusky cloak, which seemed made of a remnant of some pall."

Baron **Von Koeldwethout**. " . . . a fine swarthy fellow, with dark hair and large mustachios, who rode a-hunting in clothes of Lincoln green, with russet boots on his feet, and a bugle slung over his shoulder like the guard of a long stage. When he blew this bugle, four-and-twenty other gentlemen of inferior rank, in Lincoln green a little coarser, and russet boots with a little thicker soles, turned out directly, and away galloped the whole train, with spears in their hands like lackered area railings, to hunt down the boars, or perhaps encounter a bear, in which latter case the baron killed him first and greased his whiskers with him afterwards."

—**Baroness**. "'My dear . . . . Those coarse, noisy men—' . . . . 'My hunting train, ma'am,' said the baron. 'Disband them, love,' murmured the baroness. 'Disband them!' cried the baron, in amazement. 'To please me, love,' replied the baroness. 'To please the devil, ma'am,' answered the baron. Whereupon the baroness uttered a great cry, and swooned away at the baron's feet."

Baron **Von Swillenhausen**. His daughter "was no sooner assured that the horseman with the large mustachios was her proffered husband, than she hastened to her father's presence, and expressed her readiness to sacrifice herself to secure his peace. The venerable baron caught his child to his arms, and shed a wink of joy."

—**Baroness**. " . . . the baron [**Von Koeldwethout**] found himself the father of a small family of twelve. Upon every one of these anniversaries the venerable Baroness . . . was nervously sensitive for the well-being of her child . . . and although it was not found that the good lady ever did anything material towards contributing to her child's recovery, still she made it a point of duty to be as nervous as possible at the castle of Grogzwig, and to divide her time between moral observations on the baron's house-keeping, and bewailing the hard lot of her unhappy daughter."

Contributions to
The Examiner,
a Weekly Paper on Politics, Literature and the Fine Arts

CD's particular friend and advisor, John Forster, was literary and dramatic critic at *The Examiner* when they met in 1836. He became Editor in 1847-48.

The Dickensian's first editor, B. W. Matz, in 1908 identified and assembled previously uncollected, anonymous articles written by CD for various publications including *The Examiner,* as well as the two principal periodicals CD led beginning 1850: *Household Words* and *All the Year Round* (*see* entries in Volume II). Included here are Matz' twenty items (another has been undermined: *see* E/L), plus a group of verse parodies and twenty-eight reviews and other pieces which CD's letters in PE and other scholarship indicate are or probably (possibly) are by CD, in collaboration where indicated.

Except for the parodies, which mention specific people, we omit the verse. Quotation marks around a title mean that it has been supplied, by Matz or by the editor (in the original, book and drama reviews appear under the rubrics *Literary Examiner* and *Theatrical Examiner,* respectively.) Michael Slater supplied several important contributions and corrections for this section of EID, and David Parker also made useful suggestions.

In the Contents following, * indicates that the piece is "possibly" by CD. E/L is a special case: the other "possiblys," as well as the "probablys" in the headings to some pieces, are the judgments of the Pilgrim Edition editors as noted (there is a table of the 1848-49 pieces at PE V p 710). None of the questioned pieces included here lacks meaningful indicia of CD's authorship, commented on in particular cases.

CONTENTS

PERSONS MENTIONED

[CD coinages in **bold**, others' in *italics*].

E 1 December 3, 1837 (PE I 336)   **TE1**

Theatrical Examiner

A report on what was going on in three London theatres at the height of the Season. Astonishingly, we get a prefiguring of, of all people, TTC's **Madame Defarge** in CD's summary of the *Maid of Orleans:* the fictional family atrocities enumerated are identical. As with *The Morning Chronicle*, scholarship on the basis of which a piece is included in EID is cited after its date.

Peasant Girl, in Serle's play. " . . . one of the most extraordinary beings the world has known . . . . In her sister's wrong, her brother's murder, and her father's agony, she sees all France, visions and dreams—the first of her lonely watchings and prayers for the rescue of her country—complete the work oppression and outrage had begun, and the solitary musing girl bursts into the inspired leader of a conquering army."

O. Smith. "Even O. Smith, who in his Vandyke armour looks like some magnificent old portrait which has walked out of its frame, is unable to conquer the excessive absurdity of what is set down for him [in *Valsha*]."

Wright. "There is an actor of the name of Wright here [at St James's Theatre], who appears to think a great deal of himself. On the whole we are sorry for him."

> Anderson, whose impersonation of *Sir Lionel* is "finished and masterly"
> Braham, acting in *The Cabinet*: "stout heart and spirit unquenched"
> [J. S. Coyne] author of *Valsha* at the Adelphi
> [T. J. Dibdin] author of *The Cabinet* at the St James's
> Harley in *The Cabinet*: "lively and comical"
> Miss Huddart, whose acting of the *Peasant Girl* is highly praised
> *Sir Lionel,* a wounded English knight in Serle's play: Joan's weakness
> Miss Rainforth, whose study and application should raise her to the summit
> Serle, Thomas James; author of *Joan of Arc, the Maid of Orleans:* the Covent Garden
> Mrs Sterling: an actress who wakes up the dullest of all dull audiences

E 2 December 17, 1837 (PE I 344) **PB**

Pierre Bertrand

Detailed summary and caustic review of **Frederic Lawrance**'s play.

Pierre Bertrand, "an amiable Frenchman, reduced to the small but honourable independence derivable from breaking stones for the parish . . . ."

Frederic Lawrance. "'What's in a name?' [he] observes . . . indignantly. 'Everything. Nothing is to be done without one.' We know one, at all events, by which nothing will ever be done, and that is the name of Mr Frederic Lawrance."

Mrs Glover plays *Madame Clement,* "a mourning bride of 28 years standing"
Hutchings plays *Albert,* a friend of the protagonist
T. F. Mathews plays *Trusty,* a servant
Ranger, playing the title role: great intelligence; every requisite for genteel comedy
Ray plays *Hardheart,* "nobody's friend and an overseer"
Strickland plays *Colonel Lacy,* "everybody's friend"
Mrs Waylett plays *Agnes Lacy,* "a ballad singer of private life"
Worrell plays a landlord

E 3 January 28, 1838 (PE I 360n) **FB**

The Ages of Female Beauty

Favourable review of of a book of engravings, **Frederic Montagu**, editor, depicting the nine stages of a woman's life.

Miss H. Corbeaux, illustrator of infancy and childhood
Chalon, "the bride"; Mrs G. Ward, "the schoolgirl"; J. W. Wright, "the widow"
H. Rochard: handled well the not so attractive subject of the "old lady"

E 4 January 28, 1838 (PE I 360n) **S**

Sporting. Edited by Nimrod

Review of a book of sport commentary anchored by thirty-eight "embellishments"—engravings from **Edwin Landseer**, **Gainsborough** and others. "Nimrod" was **Charles Apperley**.

Baroness de Dracek, whose story *Nimrod* tells: " . . . a celebrated French sportswoman, who had cock fights at her house and had been at the death of six hundred and seventy-three wolves . . . . "

Barraud, Cooper, Hancock and Lewis: artists whose work is reflected
Goodlake of Berkshire: a letter to him from Scott extracted
Thomas Hood, who contributed a humorous extravaganza on fishing
Sir Walter Scott, extensively extracted

E 5 January 28 1838 (probably; William J. Carlton D 61 p133)   **L**

Macready's *Lear* at Covent Garden

Matz (*see* headnote) ascribed to CD an *Examiner* review dated February 4, 1838 of a reconstituted *Lear* with the *Fool* restored, presented at Covent Garden Theatre. Carlton shows the attribution to CD was a mistake. It appears beyond question that the February review was by John Forster. Earlier, however, Forster had quoted a brief notice on the subject as by "A friend, on whose judgement we have thorough reliance." Given CD's 1849 statement in E/ML (page 408) that he had "noticed" Miss Horton as the *Fool* several years before, it seems appropriate to excerpt the "friend" below even though his remarks did not achieve the status of a free-standing review:

Miss P[riscilla] Horton, as the *Fool,* in *Lear.* "The restoration of the Fool points some of *Lear's* finest and most touching passages. The character was exquisitely played by Miss P. Horton; the face, gait, voice, and manner were alike in perfect keeping with the part; the attachment and fidelity of the poor *Fool* to the houseless, broken-hearted King, in his sorrow and destitution, were most affectionately and beautifully portrayed. A more finished and delicate performance of a very difficult part cannot be imagined."

William Charles Macready. "[He] has played *Lear* before, and the extraordinary beauties of his impersonation of the character are known. Surrounded as he is now, however, by competent performers, and possessed of all the aids derivable from the most careful attention to the minutest points of stage effect and arrangement, it is impossible to form from mere description an adequate conception of his very masterly performance. The reception of the tragedy was indeed a triumph and one which will be long and deservedly remembered."

E 6 July 1, 1838 (PE I 408 & n)   **QC**

The Queen's Coronation

CD wrote at least the portion of this long article which describes a fair at Hyde Park. He *may* have written at least some of the balance of the piece. (He engaged a house on the procession route, but only internal "evidence," if such it is, suggests he went on to the Abbey.) We cannot categorically attribute the comments on foreign visitors and the Queen to CD, but the sentiments expressed are as characteristic as his social commentary on the labouring classes.

Foreign lady. " . . . the beauty of one of the ladies of a foreign embassy, who entered unadorned with a single jewel, but in all the lustre of a most radiant face and the most glorious form ever possessed by a woman, which flung a perfect blaze of light around her as she appeared, and gave to eyes, palled with long endurance of the most gorgeous colours, a new and delicious sense of unimaginable pleasure."

Foreign nobleman. " . . . preposterous appearance. . . covered with fur, and looking as if he had just been sitting to Mr **Waterton** for a new nondescript, went dancing up the aisle with a mincing fierceness . . . . "

Populace. "The fair in Hyde Park—which covered some fifty acres of ground—swarmed with an eager, busy crowd from morning until night. There were booths of all kinds and sizes, from **Richardson**'s theatre, which is always the largest, to the canvas residences of the **giants**, which are always the smallest; and exhibitions of all sorts, from tragedy to tumbling."

" . . . the many are at least as capable of decent enjoyment as the few. There were no **thimble-rigmen**, who are plentiful at race-courses, as at Epsom, where only *gold* can be staked; no gambling tents, roulette tables, hazard booths or dice shops. There was beer drinking, no doubt, such beer drinking as **Hogarth** has embodied in his happy, hearty picture, and there were faces as jovial as ever he could paint. These may be, and are, sore sights to the bleared eyes of bigotry and gloom . . . so unanswerable a refutation of the crude and narrow statements of those, who, deducing their facts from the very worst members of society, let loose on the very worst opportunities, and under the most disadvantageous circumstances, would apply their inferences to the whole mass of the people."

Queen Victoria "looked pale . . . and worn with fatigue; the weight of her gorgeous robe, partially borne by eight of the loveliest daughters of our English nobles, seemed still to oppress her; but she moved with quiet grace and a wonderful collectedness . . . [we felt] a strong sense of the probable injuriousness of [the coronation] at all times to the individual, but especially to a *young* individual, whose royalty is all to come, and who thus has it intensely burnt in upon her at the outset, so as to give her a preposterous sense of her 'sacredness' . . . . "

Victuallers, "relying on their well-earned fame, scorned to adopt any *nom de guerre,* and boldly put forth themselves for signs—as the **Gravesend Pet**, the **Middlesex Favourite** [pugilists], and many other gentlemen no less celebrated for their convivial virtues and hospitality. There . . . were tents so spacious, so complete in their appointments, and so quickly raised, that they might have come fresh from the hands of Arabian Genii."

E 7 February 3, 1839 (PE I 505n) CA

Hood's *Tenth Comic Annual*

CD wrote Forster, apparently about this book, calling it "rather poor, but I have not said so, because Hood is too, and ill besides."

Thomas Hood. " . . . of the originality of these ten little tomes, and of the pleasant and inoffensive nature of their sparkling humour, all men must be satisfied."

Francis Moore, "or even Mr **Murphy**, might safely prophesy a good twelvemonths beforehand, 'about such and such a period there will be a heavy fall of annuals—literature at its lowest temperature.'"

E 8-10 September 2, 1838 (PE I 428n)   **SP**
    March 31, September 29, 1839 (Matz)

"Scott and his Publishers"

The pieces analyze the *Refutation of the Misstatements and Calumnies contained in Mr Lockhart's Life of Sir Walter Scott, Bart., respecting the Messrs
Ballantyne.* **John Gibson Lockhart**, Scott's son-in-law, wrote a reply, *The
Ballantyne Humbug Handled,* in a letter which was then published in pamphlet
form and became the occasion for these articles. CD takes Lockhart's side. His
acute, hardheaded financial analysis might have given his own publishers food
for thought. He excoriates **James Ballantyne**, Scott's printer and partner.

The **Ballantynes**. " . . . the refutation originated in the overweening vanity
of the Ballantyne family, who, confounding their own importance with that of
the great man who condescended (to his cost) to patronise them, sought to
magnify and exalt themselves with a degree of presumption and conceit which
leaves the fly on the wheel, the organ bellows-blower, and the aspiring frog of
the fable, all at an immeasurable distance behind." 2

—father **James**. "Mr James Ballantyne was a respectable small tradesman, doing business originally in the small town of Kelso, whence he gladly removed to Edinburgh—in compliance with the invitation of **Sir Walter Scott**." 1

—son **James**. " . . . the needy and embarrassed printer of Kelso . . . ." 2

"[He] corrected the proof-sheets of the Waverley Novels, and wrote
criticisms thereupon to Scott as they passed through the press—not always,
we think, with a precise recollection of their relative positions in the world of
letters or with the most delicate regard to Sir Walter's state of health or spirits
at the moment. He was, however, a gentleman by manners and accomplishments . . . . " 1

—**John**: "' . . . a dealer in goods of all sorts.'"

"Of Mr John Ballantyne, the less said the better. If he were an honest,
upright, honourable man, it is a comfort to know that there are plentiful store
of such characters living at this moment in the rules of our Debtors' Prison, and
passing through the Insolvent Court by dozens every day." 2

" . . . the extravagance, thoughtlessness, recklessness, and wrong have
been upon the part of these pigmies, and the truest magnanimity and
forbearance on the side of the giant who upheld them, and under the shadow of
whose protection they gradually came to lose sight of their own stature, and to
imagine themselves as great as he . . . . " 2

Sir Walter Scott. " . . . it is no great stretch of the imagination to assume
that knowing [his nicknames for the **Ballantynes**] to have been bestowed by
Scott in moments of thoughtlessness and good humour, [**Lockhart**] preserved
them rather as little traits of his cheerfulness and hilarity to those by whom he
was surrounded, than as throwing any slight or disparagement upon those
gentlemen." 1

"Foremost and unapproachable in the bright world of fiction, gifted with a
vivacity and range of invention scarcely if ever equalled, and never (but in the
case of **Shakspeare**) exceeded; endowed, as never fabled enchanter was, with
spells to conjure of the past, and to give days and men of old the spirit and

freshness of yesterday; to strip Religion of her gloom, Virtue of her austerity—
and to present them both in such attractive forms that you could not choose
but love them—combining with all these things a degree of worldly success
never before attained through the same path, and coining gold with even the
rapidity of *his* thought—who ever had a right, if Scott had not, to look to the
endowment of those who bore his great name . . . . " 1

"There is nothing in the whole of these transactions, which, to our mind,
casts the smallest doubt or suspicion upon Sir Walter Scott, save in one single
particular. His repeated forgiveness of his careless partners, and his constant
and familiar association with persons so much beneath a man of his transcendent abilities and elevated station, lead us to fear that he turned a readier
ear than became him to a little knot of toad-eaters and flatterers." 3

Messrs Blackwood, suppliers (mercers) to Sir Walter Scott	3
Brown, a partner with Jollie as suppliers to Scott	3
Cadell, publisher of Lockhart's *Memoirs of the Life of Sir Walter Scott*	all
Sheriff Cay, resident of Edinburgh	2
David Garrick, great actor	3
George Hogarth, brother-in-law of young James; father-in-law of CD	3
Jollie and Brown: supplier to Scott: giving up business	3
John Gibson Lockhart, acerbic son-in-law and biographer of Scott	all
Pringle, a butcher: supplier to Scott	3
Robertson, Peter: resident of Edinburgh	2
Nathan Mayer Rothschild, established English branch of family business	2
Lady Margaret Scott, correspondent with James Ballantyne	3
Miss Scott: two of her bills to be paid by James Ballantyne	3
son of Scott: received Abbotsford, the Scott estate, upon his marriage	2
Mrs Siddons, great actress	2
Thompson, supplier of hay and corn to Scott	3
Professor John Wilson, resident of Edinburgh and Lockhart ally	2

E 11 April 7, 1839 (PE I 536)   **CB**

The Boy's Country Book: being the
Real Life of a Country Boy. Written by Himself

The book claims to be "edited" by its author, **William Howitt**. One does not
know how to take CD in this piece: is he sarcastic? sentimental? schizophren-
ic? After admiring the book's "sparkling in every page with fresh morning dew
and sun-light," CD's first example quotes Howitt's scarifying picture of the
desolation and hideousness of the coal-pits, including a father's discovery of his
daughter, dead from a fall to the bottom (a foreshadowing of HT?). There follow
saccharine quotations captioned "Summer Mornings" and a "Dogged Lecture"
involving Man's Best Friend. The finish might be deemed "reviewer's license,"
but knowing something of CD's childhood one wishes he had restrained himself.

Ned Tunstal, leading an expedition to a ruined chapel, "under false pretences, and at the special instigation and temptation of one Ned Tunstal, who,
in all human probability, has been since hung, or transported at least . . . . "

*"And here we must leave **Will Middleton, Joe Garner, Cris Newton,
Tom Smith,** and all the country boy's companions, commending them to the ac-*

*quaintance and good-fellowship of all town and country boys and men likewise.
We have read this book as if it were some fairy chronicle of boyish days of our
own, and have closed it with a sigh for the memory of those brief but sweetest
pleasures which boyhood only knows.*" [fadeout with violins]

E 12 July 26, 1840 (PE II 103n)   **TE2**

Theatrical Examiner

Tour d'horizon of six theatres: Drury Lane, Haymarket, Astley's, St James's,
the Pavilion and the Strand. Plays mentioned: *The Lady of Lyons, Glencoe* and
The Courier of St Petersburg.

Carter the Lion King "puts his legs and arms into their jaws, when he
would go to sleep comfortably, with a coolness most remarkable."

Power, "as rattling and vivacious as ever, has sent merry audiences
laughing to their beds, and is now on the eve of another trip to America, whence
let all lovers of rich humour pray for his speedy and safe return."

Van Amburgh and **lion**. " . . . but who can wonder at the docility of the
latter? Time was when one virgin was more than a match for the boldest forest
lion, who crouched at her tender feet; but one hundred virgins flocking around a
captive lion, half blind and stupefied already by sleeping behind dark scenes all
day, and gaping and winking in the gas by night! Let Mr Van Amburgh no
longer be prevailed upon to delay his journey to Saint Petersburg, but fly with
his prostrate lion ere the virgins prove too many for him, and he dies."

> Bullock, a very humorous clown with an untheatrical name
> Butler, "the great tragedian"
> Ducrow, manager at Astley's
> Signor Frangiopoulos, an impostor, whose performances would disgrace a race-course
> Hiller, an actor who played the *Courier*

E 13 August 7, 14, 21, 1841   **VP**

Three Verse Parodies

If after reading such as MC/NE1 and /NE2, any doubt lingers that CD was a
passionate partisan of the Whigs and Radicals, zinging the Tories when he was
in the mood with a gusto he would have been repulsed by in an American (see
AN and MC—*the Americans*), we have these effusions to disabuse us.

Fine Old English Gentleman—contains a reference to "The good old times,
when **William Pitt,** as all good men agreed/Came down direct from Paradise at
more than railroad speed . . . . "

The Quack Doctor's Proclamation—contains this: "Homœopathy too, he
has practised for ages/(You'll find his prescriptions in **Luke Hansard's**
pages)/He has only to add he's the real doctor **Flam**/All others being purely
fictitious and sham . . . . "

Subjects for Painters—is dedicated to **Sir Martin Arthur Shee**, PRA and

> *To you, MACLISE, who Eve's fair daughters paint*
> *With Nature's hand, and want the maudlin taint*
> *Of the sweet Chalon school of silk and ermine:*
> *To you, E. LANDSEER, who from year to year*
> *Delight in beasts and birds, and dogs and deer,*
> *And seldom give us any human vermin . . . .*

> *"Great Sibthorp and his butler, in debate*
> *(Arcades ambo*) on affairs of state*
> *Not altogether 'gone,' but rather funny;*
> *Cursing the Whigs for leaving in the lurch*
> *Our d——d good, pleasant, gentlemanly Church,*
> *Would make a picture—cheap at any money.*

> *"Fame with her trumpet blowing very hard,*
> *And making earth rich with celestial lard,*
> *In puffing deeds done through Lord Chamberlain Howe,*
> *While some few thousand persons of small gains,*
> *Who give their charities without such pains,*
> *Look up, much wondering what may be the row . . . .*

> *"Behind them Joseph Hume, who turns his pate*
> *To where great Marlbro' House in princely state*
> *Shelters a host of lacqueys, lords and pages,*
> *And says he knows of dowagers a crowd,*
> *Who, without trumpeting so very loud,*
> *Would do so much, and more, for half the wages . . . .*

> *"Limn, sirs, the highest lady in the land,*
> *When Joseph Surface, fawning cap in hand,*
> *Delivers in his list of patriot mortals;*
> *Those gentlemen of honour, faith and truth,*
> *Who, foul-mouthed, spat upon her maiden youth,*
> *And dog-like did deface her palace portals . . . .*

> *"Paint me the Tories, full of grief and woe,*
> *Weeping (to voters) over Frost and Co.,*
> *Their suff'ring, erring, much-enduring brothers.*
> *And in the background don't forget to pack,*
> *Each grinning ghastly from its bloody sack*
> *The heads of Thistlewood, Despard, and others."*

[*Arcades ambo is from Virgil's seventh *Eclogue*. The full line is *Ambo florentes aetatibus, Arcades ambo,* meaning "Both in the flower of youth, Arcadians both." It was customary to use it to indicate two persons having tastes or habits in common. (With thanks to David Parker)]

E 14 July 16, 1842 (Matz)   Also in the *Athenæum* and other papers **IC**

"International Copyright"

CD circular letter to English authors urging a boycott of unethical American editors and publishers. Many eminent American men of letters supported him in the effort, but it was vastly unpopular in American press circles.

Newspaper editors and **publishers**, in the United States. "They are, for the most part, men of very low attainments, and of more than indifferent reputation; and I have frequently seen them, in the same sheet in which they boast of the rapid sale of many thousand copies of an English reprint, coarsely and insolently attacking the author of that very book, and heaping scurrility and slander upon his head."

William Prescott, American author and historian, "who commented, with the natural indignation of a gentleman and a man of letters, upon [the] extraordinary dishonesty [of attempts to lobby Congress by claiming] that if English authors were invested with any control over the republication of their own books, it would be no longer possible for American editors to alter and adapt them (as they do now) to the American taste!"

> Henry Clay: presented international CD's copyright petition in Congress
> James Fenimore Cooper: signed international copyright petition
> Washington Irving: American author who signed international copyright petition

E 15 December 24, 1842 (PE 399 & n, 401 & n)   **SM**

Snoring for the Million

Michael Slater provided essential clarification of the facts underlying this piece. An official policy was promulgated in 1841 to encourage elementary school-teachers to attend singing classes. CD lampoons the sleepyheads in government, with the recommendation that they be taught how to snore.

> *"The Government seeing the million with their mouths wide open, naturally thinks that they must want to sing;; for it only recognizes two kinds of forks, the silver fork and the tuning fork, between which opposite extremes there is nothing."*

Bishops. "It is unnecessary to make any separate and distinct provision for the Bishops, as they are pretty well known to be sound sleepers and very heavy snorers already."

Lord Ellenborough. " . . . consider how much more honourably for the credit and renown of Britain affairs in India would be managed, if Lord Ellenborough were comfortably tucked up in bed, in which case he would be worth at least double his present salary."

Doctor Gardner, "sole keeper and warder of the leaden gate to that great science hypnology, is lately dead; but . . . has, happily for the world, left his key behind him."

Home Secretary. " . . . what a blessing it would be, if the Home Secretary, instead of occasionally bestirring himself in that somnambulistic state, in which people, with a muddled remembrance of their real duties, are apt to do things by halves and then to do them wrong, were but sound asleep and incapable of mischief."

Prime Minister. " . . . it is impossible to set a price upon the luxury of forgetting the existence of a Minister who so handsomely cajoled and so worthily deceived them [the people], as did the Right Hon. Baronet [**Sir Robert Peel**] who is now at the head of her Majesty's Government."

> John, type of husband; type of poor man   Lord Wharncliffe

E 16 December 31, 1842   **TE3**

Theatrical Examiner

Report on a burlesque based on *William Tell;* pantomimes and operas (**Arne**'s *Artaxerxes,* **Bellini**'s *La Sonnambula); * **Congreve**'s *Riquet* and other attractions. CD provides some detailed commentary on opera vocalism, the most ambitious music criticism we have found in his work.

Albert. " . . . an obstinate, gluttonous, mischief-making, incorrigible young vagabond, who lodges arrows in his father' [*William Tell*]'s rear instead of the target, and can only with the greatest difficulty be made to stand still when the apple is to be shot from his head."

Gesler. "When disturbed at his toilet by what he supposes the too flattering evidence outside his window of a somewhat inconvenient popularity, and, presenting himself at the casement with fond and gratified reluctance, receives a sudden shower of turnips, cabbages and other vegetable decomposition, there is nothing in the incident that offends historic propriety."

Strickland "[did] the Old Uncle [in **Congreve**'s *Riquet*] in just that ungainly, unreal way which an upper footman was sure to have assumed."

Messrs Balls, Oxberry and Salter, singers in *La Sonnambula*
Benedict, Bishop or T. Cook sought to update Arne orchestration
Buckstone, acting in Congreve: "utterly gross"
Mme Celeste in *The Bastile* at the Haymarket
Miss Fairbrother, "the prettiest *Columbine*"
Farron, whose acting is "real, full, vigorous, broad and hearty" in the Congreve
Eugenia Garcia, singing *La Sonnambula* at the Princess's Theatre
Mrs Glover: acting *Lady Wishfort* in Congreve is "real, full, vigorous, broad, hearty"
Hance as *Albert:* "exquisite burlesque acting"
Harrison as *Artabanes* in Arne opera: "most wooden and inanimate"
Holl: his acting in Congreve is "utterly gross"
Manvers, *Artaces* in Arne
Mathews, "incapably feeble" in Congreve
Mrs F. Matthews, considered "utterly gross" in the Congreve
T. Matthews, "the best *Clown* left to the stage"
Melchtel, to pay *Gesler's* tax with his ears instead of his eyes
Mozart, composer of an "effective march"
Payne as a pantomime's lead *King John:* "not very ludicrous"
Miss Poole "makes *Semira* a nonentity" (*Artaxerxes*)
Miss Ransforth, as the *Mandane* in *Artaxerxes*
Rice, "of American notoriety;" in a pantomime at the Adelphi
Sacchini, composer of a "fine chorus" interpolated in the Arne
Mrs Shaw as *Artaxerxes:* "chaste and powerful"
C. J. Smith, as *Tell:* "exquisite burlesque acting"
Miss Stephens, an important vocalist in Arne
Stilt, a posture-maker "whose exertions are surprisingly successful"
Stuart, who played *Mr Marwood* (formerly Mrs) in Congreve
Templeton, the tenor lead in *La Sonnambula*
Mme Vestris resorted to "trickery to gain applause" in Congreve: incapably feeble
Webster, acting in *The Bastile* at the Haymarket
Wieland, the chief attraction in a pantomime at the Adelphi
Miss Wilson, an important vocalist in Arne

E 17 March 4, 1843 (Matz)   **MB**

"Macready as 'Benedick'"

Theatrical review highly laudatory of Macready in Shakespeare's comic part.
Its comment on the low tastes of the "nobility and gentry" is a classic.

    Anderson. "*Claudio,* in the gay and gallant scenes, has an efficient repre-
sentative in Mr Anderson; but his perfect indifference to *Hero*'s supposed death
is an imputation on his good sense, and a disagreeable circumstance in the representation of the play, which we should be heartily glad to see removed."

    William Charles Macready. " . . . before his very first scene was over . . .
the whole house felt that there was before them a presentment of the character so fresh, distinct, vigorous, and enjoyable, as they could not choose but
relish, and go along with delightedly, to the fall of the curtain."

    Nobility and gentry, "who seldom enter a theatre unless it be a foreign
one; or who, when they do repair to an English temple of the drama, would seem
to be attracted thither solely by an amiable desire to purify, by their presence,
a scene of vice and indecorum; and who select their place of entertainment
accordingly."

> Authors: Fielding, Goldsmith, Smollett, Sterne, Swift
> W. Bennett: acted *Much Ado* "at once with great spirit and great discretion"
> Compton provided glimpses of *Dogberry,* though iron was never harder than he
> Mrs Fortescue, actress in Macready's *Much Ado*
> [Robert] Keeley, performer in Macready's *Much Ado*
> Leslie, a painter
> Mrs Nisbett, in *Much Ado:* "no less charming than at first"
> Phelps: acted in *Much Ado* "at once with great spirit and great discretion"

E 18 June 3, 1843 (Matz)   **UO**

The Oxford Commission

Report of the Commissioners
Appointed to Inquire into the Condition of the Persons
Variously Engaged in the University of Oxford

Satire on the report of a Parliamentary Children's Employment Commission.

    Boy, "who had been three years at school, and could not spell 'Church';
whereas there is no doubt that the persons employed in the University of
Oxford can all spell Church with great readiness, and, indeed, very seldom spell
anything else."

    Boy. "One young person, employed in a Mine, had no other idea of a
Supreme Being than 'that he had heard him constantly damned at' . . . . "

    Sir Robert Inglis. "And one boy (quite an old boy, too, who might have
known better) being interrogated in a public class, as to whether it was his
opinion that a man who professed to go to church was of necessity a better

man than one who went to chapel, also answered 'Yes'; which . . . is an example of ignorance, besotted dulness, and obstinacy, wholly without precedent in the inquiry . . . . "

[Edward Bouverie] Pusey. " . . . being asked if [he] deemed it to be a matter of great interest in Heaven, and of high moment in the vast scale of creation, whether a poor human priest should put on, at a certain time, a white robe or a black one; or should turn his face to the East or to the West; or should bend his knees of clay; or stand, or worm on end upon the earth, said, 'Yes . . .' and being further questioned, whether a man could hold such mummeries in his contempt, and pass to everlasting rest, said boldly, 'No.'"

> Leonard Horner, member of the Children's Employment Commission
> Robert J. Saunders, member of the Commission
> T. Southwood Smith, Unitarian minister and social reformer
> Thomas Tooke, member of the Commission

E 19 September 16, 1843 ("possibly" PE III 562n)   **JI**

Juvenile Imprisonment in the Metropolis

This piece unquestionably represents CD's view. The writing is mercilessly penetrating and vivid. The **Chairman** at the Surrey Sessions has sentenced three **boys**, the eldest nine years old, to seven years transportation for stealing a box of toys. The boys cannot read or write and have already spent years in London jails. The fierce polemic is made concrete in human terms.

> *"To spend two years of childhood in confinement; in the custody of the law that cares so anxiously for the correction of rogues and for the protection of the honest; under the watchful eyes of **Magistrates** half clerical or wholly, and **Chaplains** paid for the discharge of their holy offices; and yet to be, at the end of this time, as innocent of reading as of writing—as destitute of both as of the 'slightest idea of God or religion!' Here is matter for more than the bench of Justices, in whose presence the announcement was made, to reflect upon deeply."*

> *"What a world of trouble and loss might have been spared to chairmen of quarter sessions, to **keepers** of toy shops, and **prosecutors** of all kinds, to magistrates and **witnesses**, **gaolers** and **policemen**, fifty deep, had the urchin felons, on their first imprisonment, been doomed to undergo the utmost rigours of the horn-book, and been taught the existence of a providence beyond the policeman."*

E 20 October 21, 1843   **TE4**

Theatrical Examiner

Reviews of **Donizetti's** *La Favorita* presented in English; *Old Parr,* a drama produced by CD's dear friend **Mark Lemon**; two farces, an opera, a play and a ballet. The risk in presenting opera in the vernacular is vividly demonstrated:

"*[The Favourite] is a very long opera, in four acts; the first three very heavy, very cold and very noisy; the latter quality being particularly illustrated when the nobles of Castile resolve, in a chorus, to console themselves with 'silence and sneers;' at which secret time, there came a clanging of cymbals in the orchestra that fairly electrified the whole house.*"

Eugenia Garcia, in the opera *Geraldine*. " . . . we found [her] exhibiting few traces as ever, whether in action or in accent, of a more mature acquaintance with anything English."

Harley, in the farce *My Wife's come,* "in a perpetual dread of being detected in a secret marriage; taking pills to compose his agitation; staggering against everybody for support in unexpected alarms; and doing everything on his toes, like a puppet whose wires are too short for him, was irresistibly ridiculous."

Miss Romer, "walking upon her knees [in *The Favourite*] to an extent which we never saw equalled, saving by the **clown** at Astley's . . . . "

James Russell, in a round of Irish characters. "[His admirers] may know little of his later acquisition, the brogue. This is vastly recommended by his singing, an accomplishment in which he is alone."

Miss Ballin in *Giselle,* "is triumphant in her magic fall into the lake"
Morris Barnett, effective "in characters of the *Jacques* class (*The Old Guard*)
Paul Bedford, a 'radiance of feature' and a 'broad self-enjoying humour'
Miss Bennett and Mr Buckstone were "very effective" in *Old Parr*
Bourcicault [*sic.*], author of The Old Guard, a drama
Farron: played two different old men "just up to the point of dotage and drivelling"
Carlotta Grisi, "immeasurably the best, of course" in the opera ballet
Keeley, who fulfilled every hope of merriment in the Morton farce
Lyon had "energy" in the Stanley novelties at the Adelphi
Macready's rapturous reception in New York City is quoted at the end of the piece
Meadows and Mrs Stirling, "like Goldsmith's Bear-leader, in a concatenation"
Petipa, in an opera divertissement
Eugenie Prosper, a new actress from France in *The Old Guard*
Selby, "capital" in farce: his "dressing and making-up quite perfect"
Miss Emma Stanley presented several novelties in an "often too careless manner"
Clara Webster, dancing in opera ballet
Miss Woolgar provided "pathetic touches" in the Adelphi novelties

This was CD's last work published in the Examiner for nearly five years. When he resumed his contributions, they were largely oriented toward law and justice.

E 21 February 26, 1848 (PE V 255nn)   **NN**

The Night Side of Nature; or, Ghosts and Ghost Seers

CD says at the outset that the author, **Catherine Crowe**, "can never be read without pleasure and profit, and can never write otherwise than sensibly and well," and goes on to impugn her judgment mortally for summarizing as though factual a long series of mostly discredited stories of apparitions. His discourse is substantive, thorough, and important. Evidently he literally believed in the "power of the mother" to mark his **Barnaby Rudge** in the womb.

Lord Londonderry. "That sage statesman . . . when it was suggested that the occupation of a **trapper** (a little child who sits alone in the dark, at the bottom of a mine, all day, opening and shutting a door) had something dreary in it, could conceive nothing jollier than 'a jolly little trapper,' and could, in fact, recognise the existence of no greater jollity in this imperfect state of existence, than that which was inseparable from a trapper's occupation . . . . "

Francis Moore. "**Mrs Crowe'**s idea that the predictions of soothsayers, and their oracular solutions of dreams, and so forth, must have been true, because the craft did not lose ground by failure, would make the almanack of Francis Moore, Physician, at its sale of twenty years ago, one of the lost books of the **Sybil**."

Mother. " . . . the power a mother has, of marking the body of her unborn child, with the visible stamp of any image strongly impressed on her imagination."

Addison quoted on the dream of Josephus
Ann and Colonel M., alarmed by a soldier in the orchard and a terrified dog
Belshazzar and Nebuchadnezzar, cited for sending for soothsayers
Lady Beresford, visited in the night by a ghost: her wrist withered ever after
Captain Bligh and Lord Nelson: their substantial histories one fact could not change
Caesar, actual; seen by millions: contrasted with his ghost, seen by few
De Foe [*sic.*] who discusses strange wickedness
Fielding quoted on the power of early training to create superstitious belief
Robin Goodfellow: Crowe does not shrink from him, or from anything else
Hone, who got the truth of the Stockwell Ghost from Brayfield
Imlac, who believed ghosts were real because there had been so many sightings
A. W. N. Pugin, mediaevalist and architect; thought taste was decaying
Dr Samuel Johnson, whose views on ghosts are touched on
Dr Locock, sent for "towards the happy introduction of another approaching body"
Newman, "on his way to Rome," writing pamphelts against Dr Hampden
Nicolai, a Berlin bookseller plagued by spectral illusions
Ann Robinson, who confessed the Stockwell hoax to Brayfield
Professor Simson of Edinburgh, consulted by the Queen along with Locock
Stockwell Ghost of 1772, long since debunked
Queen Victoria talks to Dr Southwood Smith on fever, Palmerston on foreign matters

E 22 April 22, 1848 (Matz)   I&C

Ignorance and Crime

London police and criminal court activity in 1847. Passionate observations on the need for education "deep as the lowest depth of Society."

Sir Peter Laurie. " . . . [his] sagacity does not appear by these returns to have quite 'put down' suicide yet. It has remained almost as steady, indeed, as if the world rejoiced in no such magnate."

Thomas More, quoted: "'Let the State prevent vices, and take away the occasions for offences by well ordering its subjects, and not by suffering wickedness to increase, afterward to be punished.'"

E 23 April 29, 1848 (PE V vii n)   **IV**

Ignorance and its Victims

A startling case study in ignorance and credulity: a gipsy gets silver, gold, and
substantial clothing from a lady with her promise to 'rule the planets' for her.
In convicting the gipsy, **Alice Lee**, the **judge** expressed surprise at the plaintiff's being taken in, for she had been "educated."

> " . . . *if [**Susan Grant**] had left Kensington National School with the
> religious belief that the moon was an immense agglomeration of green
> cheese, and the whole solar system so many myriads of small stiltons, the
> results of her 'education' need not have been more surprising . . . .* "

Aladdin. "When Aladdin went down into the cave leading to the gardens
where the wonderful lamp was burning, the **magician**, keeping watch over the
entrance, charged him not to touch the walls about him by so much as the
skirt of his garment, or he would die. Some of the magicians who keep watch
over the wonderful lamp of knowledge in the nineteenth century, still proceed on
the same plan; and taboo all approach on the part of their pupils to an acquaintance with the commonest objects that surround them in the blind dark journey, from which they never grope their way into the light."

E 24 June 24, 1848 (Matz)   **CJ**

The Chinese Junk

A reporter's visit to and description of an outlandish vessel.

Chinese crew. "Of all unlikely callings with which imagination could
connect the Chinese lounging on the deck, the most unlikely and the last would
be the mariner's craft. Imagine a ship's crew, without a profile among them, in
gauze pinafores and plaited hair; wearing stiff clogs, a quarter of a foot thick in
the sole; and lying at night in little scented boxes, like backgammon men or
chess pieces, or mother of pearl counters!"

> English sailors, who sailed the junk to safety with "skill and coolness"
> He Sing, never more than ten miles from home before, giving autographs
> Sam Sing, the "artist" of the junk

E 25 July 8, 1848 (Matz)   **DC**

Cruikshank's *The Drunkard's Children*

Critique, favourable as to technique but not as to philosophy, of an eight-plate
sequence of engravings sequel to an earlier series, 'The Bottle.' CD had a lot of
difficulty with the lengths Cruikshank went to in his whole-hogged condemna-
tion of drinking. *See* HW/FF

George Cruikshank. "Few men have a better right to erect themselves into teachers of the people than Mr George Cruikshank. Few men have observed the people as he has done, or know them better; few are more earnestly and honestly disposed to teach them for their good; and there are very, very few artists, in England or abroad, who can approach him in his peculiar and remarkable power."

"In the trial scene at the Old Bailey the eye may wander round the court, and observe everything that is a part of the place. The very light and atmosphere of the reality are reproduced with astonishing truth. So in the gin-shop and the beer-shop; no fragment of the fact is indicated and slurred over, but every shred of it is honestly made out. It is curious, in closing the book, to recall the number of faces we have seen that have as much individual character and identity in our remembrance as if we had been looking at so many living people of flesh and blood . . . . May Mr Cruikshank linger long behind to give us many more of such realities, and to do with simple means, such as are used here, what the whole paraphernalia and resources of Art could not effect, without a master hand!"

Hero of the Bottle. " . . . [he] lived in undoubted comfort and good esteem until he was some five-and-thirty years of age, when, happening, unluckily, to have a goose for dinner one day, in the bosom of his thriving family, he jocularly sent out for a bottle of gin, and persuaded his **wife** (until then a pattern of neatness and good housewifery) to take a little drop, after the stuffing, from which moment the family never left off drinking gin, and rushed downhill to destruction, very fast."

William Hogarth. "Hogarth avoided the Drunkard's Progress, we conceive, precisely because the causes of drunkenness among the poor were so numerous and widely spread, and lurked so sorrowfully deep and far down in all human misery, neglect, and despair, that even *his* pencil could not bring them fairly and justly into the light."

> *Daughter of the Hero,* desolate and mad: flings herself into the Thames
>   *son,* who is convicted for robbery and transported
> *Idle, Thomas:* character in William Hogarth's engravings
> Lamb, Charles: essayist
> Spanish Friar: who spoke of pictures to Wilkie
> Wilkie, to whom the Spanish Friar spoke of vivid figures in pictures

E 26 August 19, 1848 (Matz)   **NE**

The Niger Expedition

Summary of the contents of a report of an ill-fated expedition to discourage the slave trade and establish Christianity. Many Englishmen died of malaria.

> *"To change the customs even of civilised and educated men, and impress them with new ideas, is—we have good need to know it—a most difficult and slow proceeding; but to do this by ignorant and savage races, is a work which, like the progressive changes of the globe itself, requires a stretch of years that dazzles in the looking at."*

> *"Gently and imperceptibly the widening circle of enlightenment must stretch and stretch, from man to man, from people on to people, until there*

is a girdle round the earth; but no convulsive effort, or far-off aim, can
make the last great outer circle first, and then come home at leisure to trace
out the inner one."

Captain William Allen. "As a most distinguished officer and a highly
accomplished gentleman, than whom there is no one living so well entitled to be
heard on all that relates to Africa, [his scheme of future operations] merits, and
assuredly will receive, great attention . . . there is sound wisdom in his idea of
approaching the black man through the black man, and in his conviction that
he can only be successfully approached by a studied reference to the current of
his own opinions and customs instead of ours."

Attah of Iddah, "'whose feet, enclosed in very large red leather boots,
surrounded with little bells, dangled carelessly over the side of the throne,' who
spoke through a State functionary, called the King's mouth, and who had this
very orthodox notion of the Divine right: 'God made me after His image; I am all
the same as God; and He appointed me a King' . . . he, too, promised everything
that was asked, and was particularly importunate to see the presents. He also
was very much amused by the missionary's spectacles . . . and as royalty in
these parts must not smile in public, the fan-bearers found it necessary to hide
his face very often."

The **Kru**, a West African tribe. " . . . a large gang of Krumen to assist in
working the vessels, and to save the white men as much as possible from exposure to the sun and heavy rains. Of these negroes—a faithful, cheerful, active, affectionate race—a very interesting account is given; which seems to
render it clear that they, under civilised direction, are the only hopeful human
agents to whom recourse can ultimately be had for aid in working out the slow
and gradual raising up of Africa. These eminent Krumen, Jack Frying Pan,
King George, Prince Albert, Jack Sprat, Bottle-of-Beer, Tom Tea Kettle, the
Prince of Wales, the Duke of York, and some four-score others . . . . "

Drs McWilliam and **Stanger**, "names that should ever be memorable and
honoured in the history of truly heroic enterprise—took upon themselves, in
addition to the duty of attending the sick, the task of navigating the ship down
the river. The former took charge of her, the latter worked the engines, and,
both persevering by day and night—through all the horrors of such a voyage,
with their friends raving and dying around them, and some, in the madness of
the fever, leaping overboard—brought her in safety to the sea."

King Obi. "His Majesty was dressed in a sergeant-major's coat . . . and a
loose pair of scarlet trousers . . . and a conical black velvet cap was stuck on
his head in a slanting manner . . . [he] agreed to every article of the proposed
treaty, and plighted his troth to it then and there amidst a prodigious beating of
tom-toms, which lasted all night. Of course he broke the treaty on the first
opportunity (being one of the falsest rascals in Africa), and went on slave-
dealing vigorously."

"Obi . . . came out in his true colours on the *Wilberforce*'s return, and, not
being by any means awakened to a proper sense of his own degradation,
appears to have evinced an amiable intention of destroying the crew and
seizing the ship . . . he is no doubt ready at this moment, if still alive, to enter
into any treaty that may be proposed to him., with presents to follow; and to be
highly amused again on the subject of the slave-trade, and to beat his tom-
toms all night long for joy."

Albert, Prince Consort: presented gold chronometers to Expeditionists
Jack Andrews, head-man of Sierra Leone negroes with the Expedition
Beecroft, pilot of an expeditionary ship
James Bruce, African traveller who discovered the Blue Nile's source
Thomas Fowell Buxton, supporter of the Expedition
Alfred Carr, West Indian designated to supervise a model farm on the Niger
Clapperton: expeditionary sought unsuccessfully to abolish the slave trade
Chief Ju-juman, attendant upon King Obi on the Niger
King Boy, son of Old King: murdered Carr
Lander: supplied King Obi with a sergeant-major's coat; held captive
Dr Lushington, supporter of the Expedition
MacLean [should be McLean], Governor at Cape Coast Castle, Africa
    Mrs Letitia Elizabeth: deceased and memorialized at Cape Coast Castle
Ralph Moore, an American negro immigrant left in charge of a model farm
Officer, in a ship on the Niger
Dr Pritchett, ship's surgeon
Dr Reid: provided ventilating apparatus which "smothered" the crews
Lord John Russell, Colonial Secretary
Schoen, missionary to the Niger
Jack Smoke, faithful servant and attendant in illness to Captain Allen
T. R. H. Thomson, M.D.: co-author of narrative of the Niger Expedition
Captain H. D. Trotter, who commanded an expedition to the Niger in 1841
Lieutenant Webb,: first officer for Captain Allen on the Niger

E 27 August 19, 1848 ("probably" PE V 710n)								**BJ**

A Truly British Judge
(From a Correspondent)

This piece is presented as a "letter to the editor." A notorious judge (*see* E/VD) keeps changing his mind about the sentence in a case of purse-stealing.

Richard Hooper, age ten. "Of course one cannot irreverently assume that [the Judge] separated him, at his tender years, from the sweet face of green and flowery nature, and the sweeter sympathies of kindred—and consigned him for two tedious years to the contamination, the stone cells and passages, the chilling damps, the rugged turnkeys, stolid chaplains, and staring red brick walls of the great Gloucester Penitentiary, out of a *tender regard* [the judge's words] for the child's future morals."

Baron Platt. "We cannot help thinking that the Judge who thus lightly deals out, recals, increases, revokes, and remodels such sentences, has no true sense of the value of human liberty, nor sympathies with human and erring nature."

Mrs Albinia Cooke, whose purse was stolen
Hemp, court clerk; he pointed out that flogging was not an option for a felon

E 28 December 9, 1848 (Matz)   **PS**

The Poetry of Science

Favourable review of *The Poetry of Science, or Studies of the Physical Phenomena of Nature,* by **Robert Hunt**.

> *"To show that the facts of science are at least as full of poetry, as the most poetical fancies ever founded on an imperfect observation and a distant suspicion of them (as, for example, among the ancient Greeks); to show that . . . there is, in every forest, in every tree, in every leaf, and in every ring on every sturdy trunk, a beautiful and wonderful creation, always changing, always going on, always bearing testimony to the stupendous workings of Almighty Wisdom, and always leading the student's mind from wonder on to wonder . . . is a purpose worthy of the natural philosopher, and salutary to the spirit of the age."*

Urbain Le Verrier [*sic.*] and **John Couch Adams**. " . . . two astronomers, far apart, each looking from his solitary study up into the sky, observe, in a known star, a trembling which forewarns them of the coming of some unknown body through the realms of space, whose attraction at a certain period of its mighty journey causes that disturbance. In due time it comes, and passes out of the disturbing path; the old star shines at peace again; and the new one, evermore to be associated with the honoured names of Le Verrier [*sic.*] and Adams, is called Neptune!"

[Robert Chambers (1802-71)], author of *Vestiges of the Natural History of Creation*

E 29 December 16, 1848 (Matz)   **AP**

The American Panorama

Praise for a three-mile long painting by an unheralded American depicting scenes on the length of the combined Mississippi and Missouri Rivers.

Banvard. "Poor, untaught, wholly unassisted, he conceives the idea—a truly American idea—of painting 'the largest picture in the world' . . . . There is a mixture of shrewdness and simplicity . . . which is very prepossessing; a modesty, and honesty, and an odd original humour, in his manner of telling what he has to tell, that give it a peculiar relish. The picture itself, as an indisputably true and faithful representation of a wonderful region—wood and water, river and prairie, lonely log hut and clustered city rising in the forest—is replete with interest throughout."

Stanfield, Clarkson: painter, set designer, illustrator; friend of CD

E 30 December 23, 1848 (Matz) **JP**

Judicial Special Pleading

CD scolds a judge for inaccurate citations of conditions in Revolutionary France in making arguments against Chartism in England.

Baron Alderson. "Mr Baron [Judge] Alderson's proof of his position would be a strange one, by whomsoever addressed, but is an especially strange one to be put forward by a high functionary, one of whose most important duties is the examination and sifting of evidence, with a view to its being better understood by minds unaccustomed to such investigations."

> Isaac Bickerstaff, a magic thermometer scale from zeal to moderation
> Philippe Egalité (of Orleans): French prince who supported the Revolution
> François Fenelon, French churchman and philosopher; of "immortal charity"
> Louis XIV: 1789 the hardest year known by the French since his "disasters"
> Honoré Mirabeau, French orator and politican of the Revolution
> Adolphe Thiers, French statesman and historian

E 31 December 30, 1848 (Matz) **EA**

Edinburgh Apprentice School Association

Comments on the Association's annual report and on the Edinburgh Sheriff.

Sheriff Gordon. "If we had had a few sheriffs like Mr Sheriff Gordon on this side of the Tweed, years ago, our sheriffs would have had less to do at the foot of the gallows. He is a good and earnest man, and his earnestness begins at the right end."

E 32 December 30, 1848 (Matz) **RG**

Leech's *The Rising Generation*

Review of a series of twelve drawings on stone, originally in *Punch*.

John Leech. " . . . he is the very first English caricaturist (we use the word for want of a better) who has considered beauty as being perfectly compatible with his art . . . . His wit is good-natured, and always the wit of a true gentleman. He has a becoming sense of responsibility and self-restraint; he delights in pleasant things; he imparts some pleasant air of his own to things not pleasant in themselves; he is suggestive and full of matter, and he is always improving . . . . He is an acquisition to popular art in England who has already done great service, and will, we doubt not, do a great deal more."

Thomas Rowlandson and **James Gilray**. "If we turn back to a collection of the works of Rowlandson or Gilray, we shall find, in spite of the great humour displayed in many of them, that they are rendered wearisome and unpleasant by a vast amount of personal ugliness."

Barnwell: George Lillo's famous fictional murderer in Camberwell
George Cruikshank, eminent illustrator

E 33 January 20, 1849 (Matz)   PT

The Paradise at Tooting

First of a four-part series on a cholera epidemic at a farming establishment for pauper children conducted by **Benjamin Drouet**, and consequent litigation.

"... *the Board of Health ... has settled the question .... The cholera, or some unusually malignant form of typhus assimilating itself to that disease, broke out in Mr Drouet's farm for children, because it was brutally conducted, vilely kept, preposterously inspected, dishonestly defended, a disgrace to a Christian community, and a stain upon a civilised land.*"

Coroner. "The learned coroner for the county of Surrey deemed it quite unnecessary to hold any inquests on these dead children, being as perfectly satisfied in his own mind that Mr **Drouet**'s farm was the best of all possible farms .... "

Benjamin Drouet. "He has a bad habit of putting four cholera patients in one bed. He has a weakness in respect of leaving the sick to take care of themselves .... He is so ignorant, or so criminally careless, that he has taken none of the easy precautions, and provided himself with none of the simple remedies ... of all conceivable places in which pestilence might—or rather *must* —be expected to break out, and to make direful ravages, Mr Drouet's model farm stands foremost."

—*his brother:* "He has a pleasant brother—a man of an amiable eccentricity—who besides being active, for all improper purposes, in the farm, is 'with difficulty restrained' from going to Kensington 'to thrash the guardians' of that Union for proposing to remove their children!"

Pauper children. "The boys under Mr **Drouet**'s fostering protection are habitually knocked down, beaten, and brutally used. They are put on short diet if they complain. They are 'very lean and emaciated.' Mr Drouet's system is admirable, but it entails upon them such slight evils as 'wasting of the limbs, debility, boils, etc.' and a more dreadful aggravation of the itch than a medical witness of great experience has ever beheld in thirty years' practice."

"The boys had had ample encouragement to complain. They had seen Mr Drouet standing glowering by, on the previous occasion. They had heard him break out about liars, and scoundrels, and rascals. They had understood that his precious character—immeasurably more precious than the existence of any number of pauper children—was at stake. They had had the benefit of a little fatherly advice and caution from him, in the interval. They were in a position, moral and physical, to be high-spirited, bold and open. Yet not a boy complained."

Wakley: " . . . a very different kind of coroner . . . being of little faith, holds inquests, and even manifests a disposition to institute a very searching inquiry into the causes of these horrors; rather thinking that such grievous effects must have some grievous causes."

> Assistants, of Drouet: bullied when inclined to reveal "disagreeable truths"
> *Candide,* Voltaire's innocent
> Dr Grainger, an inspector for the Board of Health who investigated Drouet
> William Robert James, solicitor who whitewashed Drouet's establishment
> Elizabeth Male, her complaints concerning Drouet discounted by James Drouet
> Mayes, a guardian of the poor who visited Tooting Farm
> Mills, deputy coroner on Wakley's staff
> Parish authorities, who sent children to Drouet
> Poor-Law Commissioners: culpable if they could have ordered improvements
> Poor-Law Inspector, who visited but did not condemn the Drouet establishment
> Rebbeck, a guardian of the poor who visited Tooting Farm
> Schoolmaster at Tooting Farm, present for visit by guardians of the poor
> Hannah Sleight, her complaints concerning Drouet discounted by James Drouet
> Sydney Smith, social reformer and friend of CD
> Surgeon, from St Pancras Hospital: reported on Drouet's "severity"
> *Baron Thunder-te Trouekh,:* kept the best of all possible chateaux, in *Candide*
> Winch, a guardian of the poor for the Holborn Union, who visited Tooting Farm

E 34 January 27, 1849 (Matz)   TF

The Tooting Farm

Comments on a coroner's jury manslaughter verdict against **Drouet**. *See* E/PT

Chartists. "The chartist leaders who are now undergoing their various sentences in various prisons, found the mass of their audience among the discontented poor. The foremost of them had not the plea of want to urge for themselves; but their misrepresentations were addressed to the toiling multitudes . . . . "

Guardians of the Poor. " . . . while we recognise a broad distinction between the culpability of those who consigned hundreds of children to this hateful place, too easily satisfied by formal, periodical visitation of it—and the guilt of its administrator [**Drouet**], who knew it at all hours and times, at its worst as well as at its best, and who drove a dangerous and cruel traffic, for his own profit, at his own peril—we must take leave to repeat that the Board of Guardians concerned are grossly in the wrong . . . they took for granted what they should have thoroughly sifted and ascertained."

> Thomas Thurtell, murderer: objected to uncomplimentary newspaper remark
> Greenacre, who was and did the same

E 35 March 3, 1849 (PE V 604n)   RC

A Recorder's Charge

Attacks the premise of this charge to the grand jury as requiring a proximate act causing death, general gross negligence being inadequate. Cites a theoretical engine-driver who disregards warnings, drives too fast and kills many.

Charles Cochrane and **G. W. M. Reynolds**, defenders of **Drouet**. "[They] appeared upon the hustings in hopes to inclose and cultivate for themselves a snug little farm of a grievance, out of the Tooting paradise. It is so peculiarly the misfortune of these illustrious patriots to damage and debase any cause with which they connect themselves, that we should hail their expatriation for life on any constitutional grounds, with unbounded satisfaction."

Engine-driver. " . . . are we to be told that before he could be tried for the manslaughter of four of these unfortunates, it would be necessary to show that he had put a luggage-van across the railway, or a hundredweight of gunpowder into the boiler?"

Recorder. " . . . the learned Recorder of the city of London, who, as medicine man, danced round and round them [the grand **jurymen**] and the general question of the Tooting case, in the following wild manner: [quoting the charge *in extenso*]."

EC 36 March 10, 1849 ("possibly partly" PE V 710n)   PC

Prison and Convict Discipline

Whether or not CD wrote this piece, it certainly expresses a view he took more and more strongly with the passage of time: that felons (particularly as compared with the poor) were coddled in the justice and penal processes. The writer(s) deplore abolishing the treadmill, the prison governors' "only hold upon the fears of a large class of prisoners." The ticket-of-leave system described.

Felon. "The lucky felon has now three chances. There is the jury lottery, which enables on obstinate juryman to repeal at his pleasure the law against the gravest offences. There is the chance of the judge finding it 'dreadful' to pass a sentence of salutary severity. And at the worst there are the certain comforts of prison to set against its occasional hardships. Is it wonderful that crime should be increasing on every hand?"

Sages. "[There are] one or two active sages of Clerkenwell who had crotchets about non-productive labour, and who are for setting up workshops in the place of treadmills, and for teaching instead of punishing prisoners."

> Lord Mahon: a House of Commons speech on convict discipline
> Phillips, a prisoner who laughed when sentenced to ten years' transportation
> Magistrate Rotch, castigated for favouring training convicts in sheep-shearing
> Sergeant, a sentencing judge

E 37 April 7, 1849 ("probably" PE V 710n)   R

Rush's Conviction

A study of a murderer's psychology, always a matter of fascination for CD. But there is at least one flagrant stylistic solecism which makes his authorship suspect: speaking of **Emily Sandford**, the writer says "she was as little without scruples as without intelligence." A double negative by CD???

Eliza Chestney, wounded but survived to be "one of the best witnesses that ever gave evidence the most trying in a criminal court. The truth of that woman, the service she rendered to society in going through an ordeal of moral torture the most exquisite with inflexible veracity, expiates a thousand-fold her frailty."

[James Blomfield] Rush. "We see in the conduct of this man the not unusual mixture of cunning and imprudence. It would seem as if he had been carrying on two distinct plots, one against his victims and the other against himself, one for the perpetration of the murders, and the other for the discovery of the assassin."

> Judge Balfe "performed his duty . . . with transcendent uprightness and ability"
> Jermy, one of the two males murdered

E 38 April 21, 1849 (Matz)   **VD**

The Verdict for Drouet

Finds a silver lining in the outcome, despite the Judge's biased conduct and direction of an acquittal of the notorious child-farmer. *See* E/PT, /TF and /RC

> " . . . *no one doubts that the child-farming system is effectually broken up by this trial. And every one must recognise that a trade which derived its profits from the deliberate torture and neglect of a class the most innocent on earth, as well as the most wretched and defenceless, can never on any pretence be resumed.*"

Andrews. "'Oh, nurse!' says the poor little fellow, with an eager sense that what he had longed for had come too late; 'what a big bit of bread this is!' Yes, Mr **Baron Platt**, it is clear that it was too much for him. His head was lifted up for an instant, but it sank again. He could not but be full of wonder and pleasure that the big bit of bread had come, though he could not eat it."

Baron Platt. He "declared himself early. The prosecution being less strongly represented than the defence, he took the very first opportunity of siding with the stronger. Witnesses that required encouragement, he browbeated; and witnesses that could do without it, he insulted or ridiculed."

Poet. "An English poet in the days when poetry and poverty were inseparable companions, received a bit of bread . . . which proved too much for him, and he died in the act of swallowing it."*

> Clarkson, a barrister in the case against Drouet
> Deputy-matron, a witness against Drouet
> Mary Harris, a nurse who was a witness against Drouet

[*We paged the four volumes of **Samuel Johnson's** *Lives of the Poets* and looked at over one thousand deaths without feeling we had found this poet. But at last we found in S/LS CD's mention of **Thomas Otway** (1652-85), who (in the words of the *Oxford Companion to English Literature* fifth edition 1985) wrote "three great tragedies" in verse: *Don Carlos, The Orphan*, and *Venice Preserv'd*, and, at only thirty-three, "died in destitution."]

E 39 May 5, 1849 ("possibly" PE V 710n)   **CP**

Capital Punishment

One of CD's favourite subjects was the question of public, as opposed to private (within prison walls), executions of the condemned. The story of **Rush**'s execution is told. *See* E/R

Jeremy Bentham "admits that some portion of the vindictive sentiment is essential to stir justice to its great ends."

Rush "might have gone out of the world without the addition of the last false show and pretences of innocence, and mockeries of appeal to heaven even on the threshold of eternity, if it had not been for the public exhibition which moved him to keep up his hypocritical part. The drop is literally the stage of crime for its last theatrical performance."

> Ewart, who argued against the death penalty
> Girl, wretched; shrieking and struggling with the executioners
> Sir George Grey, judge
> Mutes, who strangled the girl "in the eastern style of barbarity"
> Sheriff "provided a black banner to heighten the picturesque horror"

E 40 May 12, 1849 (Matz)   **VS**

Virginie and *Black-Eyed Susan*

Douglas Jerrold. " . . . the audience laughed and wept with all their hearts . . . a remarkable illustration of what a man of genius may do with a common-enough thing, and how what he does will remain a thing apart from all imitation."

Mowatt, Mrs. " . . . the character [*Virginie*] was rendered in a touching, truthful, and womanly manner, that might have furnished a good lesson to some actresses of high pretensions we could name. There is great merit in all this lady does. She very rarely oversteps the modesty of nature. She is not a conventional performer. She has a true feeling for nature and for her art; and we question whether any one now upon the stage could have acted this part better, or have acted it so well."

> *Appius Claudius,* character in *Virginie,* by St Ytres
> Davenport, actor praised; played *Virginius*
> *Icilius:* character in *Virginie*
> Sheridan Knowles, playwright
> Latour de St Ytres, French playwright; author of *Virginie*
> Mrs Vining, praised for her acting of *Susan* in the Jerrold play
> *Virginius:* character in *Virginie*

E 41 June 2, 1849 ("possibly" PE V 710n) **FR**

False Reliance

Bizarre sequel to the **Rush** story: the murder weapon was discovered after being concealed by Rush's son, who threatened police with a suit for trespass.

"When we see such an example as this, what a marvel it appears that the machinery of justice works under such numskull direction."

Eliza Chestney, the crucial witness
Colonel Oakes, Chief Constable of Norwich; buffaloed by the young Rush
James Blomfield Rush, a convicted murderer
Rush, junior: he "had a veto" on the proceedings of the Constable

EC 42 July 14, 1849 ("probably" PE V 710n) **DH**

Drainage and Health of the Metropolis

If CD participated in this piece, PE's editors (Graham Storey and K. J. Fielding) say it was with **Henry Austin**, secretary of the General Board of Health; and the *Examiner*'s editor, his friend **John Forster**. There were substantial disagreements within the Sewers' Commission as to the proper master plan to choose: that of Austin or that of **John Phillips**, chief surveyor to the Commission, which as described sounds impracticably grandiose. CD was immensely concerned with sanitation, and to take a hand in this piece would doubtless have been congenial to him. *See also* E/SC

"The unpaid are the most expensive of state functionaries. The public has to consider itself fortunate when it gets from them only as much as it gives." [In his family farce *O'thello,* CD's father was *The Great Unpaid.*]

Henry Fielding: a reminder of his phrase, "Burst of warlike music"

E 43 July 21, 1849 (Matz) **AE**

An American in Europe

Commentary, sometimes hilarious, on a fulsome two-volume report by an American on *European Life and Manners, in Familiar Letters to Friends.*

Henry Colman. "Why an honest republican, coming from the United States to England . . . cannot be easy unless he is for ever exhibiting himself to his admiring countrymen, with a countess hanging on each arm, a duke or two walking deferentially behind, and a few old English barons (all his very particular friends) going on before, we cannot, to our satisfaction, comprehend."

—*his acquaintance:* "Neither is his facility of getting into such company quite intelligible; unless something of the spirit which rushes into print with a record of these genteel processions, pervades the aristocratic as well as the republican breast, and tickles the noble fancy with a bird's-eye view of some thousands of American readers across the water, poring, with open mouths and goggle-eyes, over descriptions of its owner's domestic magnificence. We are bound to confess . . . we are not altogether free from a suspicion of this kind."

—*his friends at home:* "Mr Colman's letters have one very remarkable feature which our readers will probably never have observed before in any similar case. They were not intended for publication. Of this unprecedented fact, there is no doubt. He wrote them, without a twinkle of his eye at the public, to some partial friends; who were so delighted with them and talked so much about them, that all his other friends cried out for copies. They *would have* copies. Now these may be excellent friends, but they are bitter bad judges: still they may be turned to good account; for if Mr Colman should ever, in future, write anything that is particularly agreeable to this audience, he may rely upon it that the nearest fire will be its fittest destination."

—*sentiment:* " . . . there are parts of these letters which exhibit the writer in the character of a good-natured, kind-hearted private individual, though of a somewhat cumbrous and elephantine jocularity, and of a rather startling sentimentality—as when he goes to see the charity children assembled at St Paul's, and has impulses, on account of their extraordinary beauty, to pitch himself out of the whispering-gallery head foremost into the midst of those young Christians; a homage to youth and innocence necessarily involving the annihilation of the wearers of several undersized pairs of leather-breeches."

Ladies. " . . . we have a dim vision of the agitation of the tremendous depths of this social sea which looks so smooth at top, when we are informed that 'some of them (the ladies) if they find, on going into society, *another person of inferior rank wearing the same dress as themselves*'—which would certainly appear an inconvenient proceeding—'the dress, upon being taken off, is at once thrown aside, and the lady's maid perfectly understands her perquisite.'

"Having recovered our breath, impeded in the contemplation of this awful picture, and the mysterious shadow thrown around the lady's maid, we expect to find our American friend in some new scene . . . . "

—*emulated:* "'The Duke' meantime [during all meals described], it is to be presumed, keeping his noble eyes on Mr **Colman**'s waistcoat, until he satisfies his noble mind that it is not a waistcoat, like his waistcoat; which would render it indispensable for his Grace instantly to depart from table, take it off in desperation, and bestow it on his valet."

Lady Byron, to whom Henry Colman dedicated *European Life and Manners*
William Cobbett, English writer on agricultural matters
Duke and Duchess, unnamed; who were hosts to Henry Colman
Judge George Jeffreys, of the "Bloody Assize"
Judge, of sanguinary temperament: observed by Henry Colman at Old Bailey
Marquess of Rockingham, former owner of a property visited by Henry Colman
Lord Spencer, a host of Henry Colman
N. P. Willis: his rights outraged by Henry Colman's dedication to Lady Byron

EC 44 August 4, 1849 ("possibly" PE V 710n)   **SC**

The Sewers' Commission

Sequel to E/DH, detailing the controversy over the proper path to follow. The style, particularly the literary references, is redolent of CD.

Civil engineers. **[John] Phillips** "is in the lists against Mr **[Henry] Austin**, Mr Austin couches lance against Mr Phillips, and Mr **Byng** pushes hard against Mr **Buller**. Mr **[Edwin] Chadwick**, with visor up, takes the field against all comers . . . . Mr **Hertslet**, with a parade of indignant virtue, throws up his appointment, assigning reasons which might have had some weight if alleged for not accepting it at all . . . . The discord in the camp of **King Agramont** was a trifle to the quarrelling and brawling in Greek street Soho."

Phillips' plan "is a very Arabian Nights fable of city sewerage."

> Sir Henry de la Beche and Doctor Buckland: warn of difficulty tunneling
> Brunel, engineer over the only sub-Thames tunnel: "genius and pertinacity"
> Doctor Southwood Smith, distinguished physician and public servant

E 45 September 8, 1849 (PE V 710)   **IR**

Address Issued by the Committee of the Italian Refugee Fund

Refugees. "Hunted by their and the world's enemies; forlorn and penniless; reduced to indigence, bereft of almost all that makes life dear, and bringing nothing from the wreck beyond the Mediterranean Sea but Hope in the eternal might of the principles they have upheld; the Committee appeals in their behalf to Englishmen, for present help. That they may not die of want where they have found a home; that their noble spirits may not sink into despair; that they may connect with this free country in their Future, be it which it may, such associations as such men should connect with it, and ever love and honour it with grateful hearts, as worthy of its freedom and its high renown; the Committee issues this address, earnestly soliciting subscriptions for their aid."

E 46 October 27, 1849 ("probably" PE V 46n)   **DA**

Demoralisation and Total Abstinence

In all his years and many efforts for his friend Forster, CD never was given the "lead" in the *Examiner* until this piece, which attacks the movement for disarmament and, by extension, other forms of "whole-hoggism." One **Beggs** had written a pamphlet against "juvenile depravity," and here is its refutation.

> *"For the condition of the lowest classes in this country, and the ever-rising, ever-increasing generation of unhappy beings included under that denomination, is a question far too momentous to be trifled with, by the weakness or the unscrupulous devotion to one idea, of any order of men.*

> *'There is a poor blind **Samson** in this land,'*
>
> writes Mr **Longfellow** *of slavery in America; but there is a poor, blind Samson in <u>this</u> land, as dangerous as he. Like the strong man of old, he is led by a child—an ignorant child. Like him, he has his sinewy arms—one branded Pauperism, the other Crime—already round the pillars whereupon the house standeth. Let us beware of him in time, before he makes his awful prayer to be avenged upon us for his blindness, and brings the edifice upon himself, and us—a heap of ruins!"*

Bill Brute, "the robber of Newgate" and **Brallaghan of Killaloo**, "resident down the next court, make a wild beast of themselves under the influence of strong liquor."

Elihu Burritt, "as a choice of two evils, [we] would infinitely prefer a fleet and an army to any amount of Mr Elihu Burritt—though we have no doubt he is a very honest man in his way."

Tee-totallers. "If they would rest their case on the fair ground of temperance for those who can be temperate, and total abstinence for those who cannot . . . and would be content to parade the good they have done (which we do not dispute) in the exceptional cases where persons having no excuse for such misconduct, have yielded to a depraved passion for strong liquor and fallen into a gulf of misery, we should regard them as a good example and as a public benefit. But, running amuck like mad Malays, we look upon them as a bad example, and a public evil, only less intolerable than drunkenness it-self."

> Hudson, inclined to "cook accounts"
> Jones, theoretical "decent and industrious mechanic"
> Professor Holloway, and Morison, pill-makers
> Rotch: "we had almost written Mr Botch, remembering his sheep-shearing"

E 47 October 27, 1849 [Leslie C. Staples D 44 p78]   **LH**

Macready's *Lear* at the Haymarket

Staples found the piece in the Forster collection at the Victoria & Albert Museum, and Michael Slater put us on its track. It is in CD's hand.

Miss [Priscilla] Horton, as the *Fool*. "It has been several years since we first noticed Miss Horton's acting of the *Fool* [page 382], restored to the play, as one of its most affecting and necessary features . . . . It would be difficult indeed to praise so exquisite and delicate an assumption too highly."

William Charles Macready. "Of the many great impersonations with which Mr Macready is associated . . . perhaps his *Lear* is the finest. The deep and subtle consideration he has given to the whole noble play, is visible in all he says and does. From his rash renunciation of the gentle daughter who can only love him and be silent, to his falling dead beside her, unbound from the rack of this tough world, a more affecting, truthful and awful picture never surely was presented . . . .

"It was the mind of *Lear* on which we looked. The heart, soul and brain of the ruin'd piece of nature, in all the stages of its ruining, were bare before us."

Howe "played with great spirit"
Miss Reynolds, as *Cordelia,* "was not (except in her appearance) very effective."
Stuart as *Kent* justifed his banishment by his uproarious demeanour toward *Lear*
Wallack as *Edgar* was "highly meritorious." CD had never seen it done better.
Mrs Warner "was most wickedly beautiful in *Goneril.* "

E 48 December 8, 1849 ("possibly" PE V 711 & n)   **C**

Central Criminal Court

An apparent miscarriage of justice through a fatuous ruling by a judge about to
try **Thomas Edward Hall** for "an atrocious offense upon the person of his
young daughter, a girl 12 years of age." The daughter had no idea who or what
"God" was. *See* **Jo** and the **Coroner** BH 11

Baron Alderson "said he could not permit a child who betrayed such
ignorance to be examined upon oath, and as there was no evidence without her
testimony to support the charge, the prisoner must be acquitted."

Jeremy Bentham cited: natural safeguards of sagacity of jury, judge, defense counsel
Huddlestone, prosecutor: suggested educating the girl, then calling her as witness

E 49 December 15, 1849 (Matz)   **CC**

Court Ceremonies

CD likes Dowager **Queen Adelaide's** request for a simple funeral, noting "the
preposterous constraints and forms that set a mark upon the English Court
among the nations of Europe, and amaze European Sovereigns . . . . "

Queen Adelaide, "whose death has given occasion for many public trib-
utes to exalted worth, often formally and falsely rendered on similar occasions,
and rarely, if ever, better deserved than on this . . . . "

Lord Chamberlain. " . . . [his] office is the last stronghold of an enormous
amount of tomfoolery, which is infinitely better done upon the stage in **Tom
Thumb,** which is cumbrous and burdensome to all outside the office itself, and
which is negative for any good purpose and often positive for much harm, as
making things ridiculous or repulsive which can only exist beneficially in the
general love and respect . . . . "

Invited to Queen Adelaide's funeral: Duchess of Norfolk, chief mourner
    Hon William Ashley   Lord Denbigh
    Sir Andrew Barnard   Lord Howe
    Sir D. Davies   Wood
Ducrow, deceased manager of Astley's
Edward, Prince of Saxe Weimar: nephew of the Queen Adelaide
Stephenson, throwing a tube across the Menai Straits
Duke of Sussex, who gave an example of an unpretentious funeral

April 1840-December 1841 (88 weekly nos.)   sponsored by C&H **MHC MH/**
Three volumes by Chapman & Hall October, 1840 and April and December 1841
Simultaneous American publication in monthly parts by Lea & Blanchard, Philadelphia

Master Humphrey's Clock

After leaving *Bentley's Miscellany,* CD started his own paper, backed by his publishers Chapman and Hall (C&H). The old clock was to be the depository of narratives and literary oddities by various writers, but in fact only CD contributed. **Mr Pickwick** and the **Wellers** appear (with grandson; the only time CD tried to recycle his muse). To stimulate sluggish early response, CD provided two serial novels, OCS and BR, but after eighteen months he felt he had not solved the "problems of editorship." He closed the paper, which *"became one of the lost books of the earth."* —preface to OCS

PRÉCIS*

Lifelong, lonely cripple **Master Humphrey** reminisces on his sad, loving mother, who pitied his infirmity, and describes his best friend: the old clock in his London house. He encounters a sad-looking, lonely deaf man in a tavern dining-room and makes a friend of him. His two other regulars are his factotum **Jack Redburn** and widower **Owen Miles**. Interludes, in the form of stories found in the clock case, and some correspondence. parts I-II (with I, F and C)

Mr Pickwick calls, wishing to join the circle. He contributes a long tale and is voted in. He returns, bringing **Sam Weller** and his father, eminent coachman **Tony Weller**, very proud of his namesake grandson and indignant at the newfangled railroad. Mr Pickwick meets and sits down with Messrs Redburn and Miles. He observes the ceremonies, while housekeeper **Miss Benton** entertains the Wellers in the kitchen. Mr Pickwick suggests **Jack Bamber**, ghost story specialist, for the last vacant chair. III-IV (with PT)

Miss Benton introduces **Slithers**, a barber, and Sam tells of the illness and last days of **Jinkinson**. Sam suggests forming an auxiliary to the group upstairs, and his father rises to the occasion. "Mr Weller's Watch" is inaugurated. Sam tells of the sad love and loss of a hairdresser. V (with W)

Tony Weller, with infinite pride and delight, introduces his grandson, young **Tony**, who winks devastatingly at Miss Benton. Master Humphrey contemplates London, in its wealth and beggary, vice and virtue. He now has ended the regular meetings of the little society, and he sinks to a peaceful death. The deaf gentleman recounts the quiet aftermath. VI

*The original organizational scheme of MHC is shown on page 425.

CONTENTS

Illustrations by *Hablôt K. Browne*

CHARACTERS

Principals

Clock. " . . . my old, cheerful, companionable Clock. How can I ever convey to others an idea of the comfort and consolation that this old Clock has been for years to me!

"It is associated with my earliest recollections. It stood upon the staircase at home . . . nigh sixty years ago . . . it is a quaint old thing in a huge oaken case curiously and richly carved . . . . I incline to it as if it were alive, and could understand and give me back the love I bear it." 1 [numerical citations: *see* page 25]

Deaf gentleman. "He did not look so old as I, but like me he was advanced in life, and his hair was nearly white . . . he did not raise his head, but sat with it resting on his hand, musing over his half-finished meal.

" . . . . sad and thoughtful . . . I never saw so patient and kind a face . . . . "

—*a companion:* "I scarcely know how we communicate as we do; but he has long since ceased to be deaf to me. He is frequently my companion in my walks, and even in crowded streets replies to my slightest look or gesture, as though he could read my thoughts." 6

—*unfortunate:* "Misfortune can never have fallen upon such a man but for some good purpose; and when I see its traces in his gentle nature and his earnest feeling, I am the less disposed to murmur at such trials as I may have undergone myself." 6

Master Humphrey. "I am not a churlish old man. Friendless I can never be, for all mankind are my kindred, and I am on ill terms with no one member of my great family. But for many years I have led a lonely, solitary life—what wound I sought to heal, what sorrow to forget, originally, matters not now; it is sufficient that retirement has become a habit with me, and that I am unwilling to break the spell which for so long a time has shed its quiet influence upon my home and heart." 1

—*home:* "I live . . . in an old house which in bygone days was a famous resort for merry roysterers and peerless ladies, long since departed. It is a silent, shady place, with a paved courtyard . . . .

" . . . . Its worm-eaten doors, and low ceilings crossed by clumsy beams; its walls of wainscot, dark stairs, and gaping closets; its small chambers, communicating with each other by winding passages or narrow steps; its many nooks, scarce larger than its corner-cupboards; its very dust and dulness, are all dear to me." 1

—*misfortune:* " . . . I wish [my readers] to know—and I smile sorrowfully to think that the time has been when the confession would have given me pain—that I am a misshapen, deformed old man.

"I have never been made a misanthrope by this cause. I have never been stung by any insult, nor wounded by any jest upon my crooked figure." 1

—*with a guest:* "**Mr Pickwick** and I must have been a good contrast just then. I leaning quietly on my crutch-stick, with something of a care-worn, patient air; he, having hold of my arm, and bowing in every direction with the most elastic politeness, and an expression of face whose sprightly cheerfulness and good-humour knew no bounds. The difference between us must have been more striking yet, as we advanced towards the table, and the amiable gentleman, adapting his jocund step to my poor tread, had his attention divided between treating my infirmities with the utmost consideration, and affecting to be wholly unconscious that I required any." 12

—*a startling disclosure:* "'The younger brother, the single gentleman, the nameless actor in this little drama [OCS], stands before you now.'" 14 [*Homer nodded. CD elsewhere confirms that Humphrey is the Narrator who wanders London, encounters* **Nell** *and opens the OCS story.*]

—*in death (reported by the deaf gentleman):* "I have often, very often, seen him sleeping, and always peacefully, but I never saw him look so calm and tranquil. His face wore a serene, benign expression, which had impressed me very strongly when we last shook hands; not that he had ever had any other look, God knows; but there was something in this so very spiritual, so strangely and indefinably allied to youth, although his head was gray and venerable, that it was new even in him." 15

—*an obsequy:* "'And the sweet old creetur, sir,' said the elder Mr **Weller** . . . 'has bolted. Him as had no wice, and was so free from temper that a infant might ha' drove him, has been took at last with that 'ere unawoidable fit of staggers as we all must come to, and gone off his feed for ever! I see him,' said the old gentleman, with a moisture in his eye, which could not be mistaken—'I see him gettin', every journey, more and more groggy; I says to **Samivel**, "My boy! the Grey's a-goin' at the knees;" and now my predilictions is fatally werified, and him as I could never do enough to serve or show my likin' for, is up the great uniwersal spout o' natur'.'" 15

Owen Miles, "a most worthy gentleman . . . once a very rich merchant; but receiving a severe shock in the death of his wife, he retired from business, and devoted himself to a quiet, unostentatious life. He is an excellent man, of thoroughly sterling character: not of quick apprehension, and not without some amusing prejudices . . . ." 6

" . . . although Mr Miles never by any chance does anything in the way of assistance, **Jack** could do nothing without him. Whether he is reading, writing, painting, carpentering, gardening, flute-playing, or what not, there is Mr Miles beside him, buttoned up to the chin in his blue coat, and looking on with a face of incredulous delight . . . ." 6

—*the new guest:* " . . . although he had no doubt Mr **Pickwick** was a very worthy man, still he did consider that some of his exploits were unbecoming a gentleman of his years and gravity . . . it is one of his fixed opinions, that the law never can by possibility do anything wrong; he therefore looks upon Mr Pickwick as one who has justly suffered in purse and peace for a breach of his plighted faith to an unprotected female, and holds that he is called upon to regard him with some suspicion on that account. These causes led to a rather cold and formal reception; which Mr Pickwick acknowledged with the same stateliness and intense politeness as was displayed on the other side." 12

Samuel Pickwick. "He was an elderly gentleman, but came tripping along in the pleasantest manner conceivable, avoiding the garden-roller and the borders of the beds with inimitable dexterity, picking his way among the flower-pots, and smiling with unspeakable good humour . . . when he came towards me with his hat in his hand, the sun shining on his bald head, his bland face, his bright spectacles, his fawn-coloured tights, and his black gaiters—then my heart warmed towards him, and I felt quite certain that it was Mr Pickwick." 9

—*visiting:* "His admiration was not confined to the clock either, but extended itself to every article in the room; and really, when he had gone through them every one, and at last sat himself down in all the six chairs, one after another, to try how they felt, I never saw such a picture of good-humour and happiness as he presented, from the top of his shining head down to the very last button of his gaiters." 9

—*a vanity:* "'No, really!' cried Mr Pickwick, with manifest pleasure. 'Do you think they care about my gaiters? Do you seriously think that they identify me at all with my gaiters?'

"'I am sure they do,' I replied.

"'Well, now,' said Mr Pickwick, 'that is one of the most charming and agreeable circumstances that could possibly have occurred to me!'

" . . . . He has a secret pride in his legs. The manner in which he spoke, and the accompanying glance he bestowed upon his tights, convince me that Mr Pickwick regards his legs with much innocent vanity." 12

Jack Redburn. " . . . one of that easy, wayward, truant class whom the world is accustomed to designate as nobody's enemies but their own. Bred to a profession for which he never qualified himself, and reared in the expectation of a fortune he has never inherited, he has undergone every vicissitude of which such an existence is capable . . . . " 6

"I should be puzzled to say how old he is. His health is none of the best, and he wears a quantity of iron-gray hair, which shades his face and gives it rather a worn appearance; but we consider him quite a young fellow notwithstanding; and if a youthful spirit, surviving the roughest contact with the world, confers upon its possessor any title to be considered young, then he is a mere child." 6

—*his dress:* " . . . we seldom see him in any other upper garment than an old spectral-looking dressing-gown, with very disproportionate pockets, full of a miscellaneous collection of odd matters, which he picks up wherever he can lay his hands upon them." 6

—*factotum:* "He is my librarian, secretary, steward, and first minister; director of all my affairs, and inspector-general of my household. He is something of a musician, something of an author, something of an actor, something of a painter, very much of a carpenter, and an extraordinary gardener, having had all his life a wonderful aptitude for learning everything that was of no use to him. He is remarkably fond of children, and is the best and kindest nurse in sickness that ever drew the breath of life. He has mixed with every grade of society, and known the utmost distress; but there never was a less selfish, a more tender-hearted, a more enthusiastic, or a more guileless man . . . . " 6

Sam Weller. "'Samivel Veller, sir,' said the old gentleman, 'has conferred upon me the ancient title o' grandfather vich had long laid dormouse, and wos s'posed to be nearly hextinct in our family.'" 11

—*Wellerism:* "'Well, I'm agreeable to do it,' said Sam, 'but not if you go cuttin' away like that, as the bull turned round and mildly observed to the drover ven they wos a goadin' him into the butcher's door.'" 11

—valet: "'All right, sir . . . . Hold hard, sir. Right arm fust—now the left—now one strong convulsion, and the great-coat's on, sir.'" 12

Tony Weller. "It was a warm evening, but the elder Mr Weller was attired, notwithstanding, in a most capacious greatcoat, and his chin enveloped in a large speckled shawl, such as is usually worn by stage coachmen on active service. He looked very rosy and very stout, especially about the legs, which appeared to have been compressed into his top-boots with some difficulty. His broad-brimmed hat he held under his left arm, and with the forefinger of his right hand he touched his forehead a great many times . . . ." 11

—rescued: "Mr Weller . . . fell into a most alarming fit of coughing, which must certainly have been attended with some fatal result, but for the dexterity and promptitude of **Sam**, who, taking a firm grasp of the shawl just under his father's chin, shook him to and fro with great violence, at the same time administering some smart blows between his shoulders. By this curious mode of treatment Mr Weller was finally recovered, but with a very crimson face, and in a state of great exhaustion." 11

—laughing: "In fact, Mr Weller, whose mind was still running upon his precocious grandson, was seen to shake his head from side to side, while a laugh, working like an earthquake, below the surface, produced various extraordinary appearances in his face, chest, and shoulders—the more alarming because unaccompanied by any noise whatever. These emotions . . . gradually subsided, and after three or four short relapses he wiped his eyes with the cuff of his coat, and looked about him with tolerable composure." 11

—a semanticist: "'A wot?' said his father, with deep scorn.

"'A spinster,' replied **Sam**.

"Mr Weller looked very hard at his son for a minute or two, and then said,

"'Never mind vether she makes jokes or not, that's no matter. Wot I say is, is that 'ere female a widder, or is she not?'

"'Wot do you mean by her making jokes?' demanded Sam, quite aghast at the obscurity of his parent's speech.

"'Never you mind, Samivel,' returned Mr Weller gravely; 'puns may be wery good things or they may be wery bad 'uns, and a female may be none the better or she may be none the vurse for making of 'em; that's got nothin' to do vith vidders.'

"'Vy now,' said Sam, looking round, 'would anybody believe as a man at his time o' life could be running his head agin spinsters and punsters being the same thing?'

"'There an't a straw's difference between 'em,' said Mr Weller. 'Your father didn't drive a coach for so many years, not to be ekal to his own langvidge as far as *that* goes, Sammy.'" 11

—chivalry: "'There is no call for any hock'erdness, mum,' said Mr Weller with the utmost politeness; 'no call wotsumever. A lady,' added the old gentleman, looking about him with the air of one who establishes an incontrovertible position—'a lady can't be hock'erd. Natur' has otherwise purwided.'" 13

—forming an auxiliary: "Mr Weller said nothing, but he laid down his pipe as if in a fit of inspiration, and performed the following manœuvres.

"Unbuttoning the three lower buttons of his waistcoat and pausing for a moment to enjoy the easy flow of breath consequent upon this process, he laid violent hands upon his watch-chain, and slowly and with extreme difficulty drew from his fob an immense double-cased silver watch, which brought the lining of the pocket with it, and was not to be disentangled but by great exertions and an amazing redness of face. Having fairly got it out at last, he detached the outer case and wound it up with a key of corresponding magnitude; then put the case on again, and having applied the watch to his ear to ascertain that it was still going, gave it some half-dozen hard knocks on the table to improve its performance.

"'That,' said Mr Weller, laying it on the table with its face upwards, 'is the title and emblem o' this here society. **Sammy**, reach them two stools this vay for the wacant cheers. Ladies and gen'lmen, Mr Weller's Watch is vound up and now a-going'. Order!'" 13

—*shining:* "'Well, but suppose he wasn't a hairdresser,' suggested **Sam**.

"'Wy then, sir, be parliamentary and call him vun all the more,' returned his father. 'In the same vay as ev'ry gen'lman in another place is a *h*onourable, ev'ry barber in this place is a hairdresser. Ven you read the speeches in the papers, and see as vun gen'lman says of another, "the *h*onourable member, if he vill allow me to call him so," you vill understand, sir, that that means "if he vill allow me to keep up that 'ere pleasant and uniwersal fiction."'

"It is a common remark, confirmed by history and experience, that great men rise with the circumstances in which they are placed. Mr Weller came out so strong in his capacity of chairman, that Sam was for some time prevented from speaking by a grin of surprise, which held his faculties enchained, and at last subsided in a long whistle of a single note. Nay, the old gentleman appeared even to have astonished himself, and that to no small extent, as was demonstrated by the vast amount of chuckling in which he indulged, after the utterance of these lucid remarks." 13

Supporting Roles

Miss Benton. " . . . I know that my housekeeper, while she holds [the **deaf gentleman**'s pipe] in high veneration, has a superstitious feeling connected with it which would render her exceedingly unwilling to be left alone in its company after dark." 6

Doctor. "' . . . **Jinkinson** . . . wos took wery ill with some inn'ard disorder, lost the use of his legs, and wos confined to his bed, vere he laid a wery long time . . . "Doctor," he says, "will you grant me one favour?" "I will, Jinkinson," says the doctor. "Then, doctor," says Jinkinson, "vill you come unshaved, and let me shave you?" "I will," says the doctor. "God bless you," says Jinkinson.

"'Next day the doctor came, and arter he'd been shaved all skilful and reg'lar, he says, "Jinkinson," he says, "it's wery plain this does you good. Now," he says, "I've got a coachman as has got a beard that it 'ud warm your heart to work on, and though the footman," he says, "hasn't got much of a beard, still he's a trying it on vith a pair o' viskers to that extent that razors is Christian charity . . . you've got six **children**," he says, "wot's to hinder you from shavin' all their heads and keepin' 'em shaved? You've got two **assistants** in the shop down-stairs, wot's to hinder you from cuttin' and curlin' them as often as you like? Do this," he says, "and you're a man agin."

"'Jinkinson squeedged the doctor's hand and begun that wery day; he kept his tools upon the bed, and wenever he felt his-self gettin' worse, he turned to at vun o' the children who wos a runnin' about the house vith heads like clean Dutch cheeses, and shaved him agin."' ¶13

William Gibbs.—*his dummies:* "' . . . a wery smart little shop with four wax dummies in the winder, two gen'lmen and two ladies—the gen'lmen vith blue dots for their beards, wery large viskers, oudacious heads of hair, uncommon clear eyes, and nostrils of amazin' pinkness; the ladies with their heads o' one side, their right forefingers on their lips, and their forms developed beautiful, in vich last respect they had the adwantage over the gen'lmen, as wasn't allowed but wery little shoulder, and terminated rayther abrupt in fancy drapery . . . the great attraction and ornament wos the dummies, which this here young hairdresser wos constantly a runnin' out in the road to look at, and constantly a runnin' in again to touch up and polish . . . .'" 13

—*in love:* "'"I never vill enter into the bonds of vedlock," he says, "until I meet vith a young 'ooman as realises my idea o' that 'ere fairest dummy vith the light hair. Then, and not till then", he says, "I vill approach the altar."'" 13

Jinkinson, a barber. "'Was he in the easy shaving way, sir,' inquired **Mr Slithers**, 'or in the cutting and curling line?'

"'Both,' replied **Sam**; 'easy shavin' was his natur', and cuttin' and curlin' was his pride and glory. His whole delight wos in his trade. He spent all his money in bears, and run in debt for 'em besides, and there they wos a growling avay down in the front cellar all day long, and ineffectooally gnashing their teeth, vile the grease o' their relations and friends wos being retailed in gallipots in the shop above, and the first-floor winder wos ornamented vith their heads . . . .'" 13

—his passing: "' . . . at last vun day he has in all the children vun arter another, shaves each on 'em wery clean, and gives him vun kiss on the crown o' his head; then he has in the two **assistants**, and arter cuttin' and curlin' of 'em in the first style of elegance, says he should like to hear the woice o' the greasiest bear, vich rekvest is immediately complied with; then he says that he feels wery happy in his mind and vishes to be left alone; and then he dies, previously cuttin' his own hair and makin' one flat curl in the wery middle of his forehead.'" 13 *And see* **Doctor**

Redburn, "the younger, who did not fail to improve his opportunity, now triumphs in the possession of enormous wealth . . . to hoard it in solitary wretchedness, and probably to feel with the expenditure of every shilling a greater pang than the loss of his whole inheritance ever cost his brother." 6

Slithers. "My barber is at all times a very brisk, bustling, active little man—for he is, as it were, chubby all over, without being stout or unwieldy— but yesterday his alacrity was so very uncommon that it quite took me by surprise. For could I fail to observe when he came up to me that his gray eyes were twinkling in a most extraordinary manner, that his little red nose was in an unusual glow, that every line in his round bright face was twisted and curved into an expression of pleased surprise, and that his whole countenance was radiant with glee?" 9

Tony Weller, the younger. " . . . something outside the door about two feet six from the ground, Mr **Weller** introduced a very small boy firmly set upon a couple of very sturdy legs, who looked as if nothing could ever knock him down. Besides having a very round face strongly resembling Mr Weller's, and a stout little body of exactly his build, this young gentleman, standing with his little legs very wide apart, as if the top-boots were familiar to them, actually winked upon the housekeeper with his infant eye, in imitation of his grandfather.

"'There's a naughty boy, mum,' said Mr Weller, bursting with delight, 'there's a immoral Tony. Wos there ever a little chap o' four year and eight months old as vinked his eye at a strange lady afore?'" 14

Young lady. "'The young hairdresser . . . encountered a young lady as wos the wery picter o' the fairest dummy. "Now," he says, "it's all up. I am a slave!" . . . d'rectly she sees the dummies she changes colour and falls a tremblin' wiolently. "Look up, my love," says the hairdresser, "behold your imige in my winder, but not correcter than in my art!" "My imige!" she says. "Yourn!" replies the hairdresser. "But whose imige is that?" she says a pinting at vun o'the gen'lemn. "No vun's, my love," he says, "it is but a idea." "A idea!" she cries: "it is a portrait, I feel it is a portrait, and that 'ere noble face must be in the millingary!" "Wot do I hear!" says he, a crumplin' his curls. "**Villiam Gibbs**," she says, quite firm, "never renoo the subject. I respect you as a friend," she says, "but my affections is set upon that manly brow."'" 13

Others

[**Jack**] **Bamber**. "' . . . he is a very extraordinary and remarkable person [said Mr **Pickwick**]; living, and talking, and looking, like some strange spirit, whose delight is to haunt old buildings; and absorbed in that one subject . . . the more I see of him, the more strongly I am impressed with the strange and dreamy character of his mind . . . he is a strange secluded visionary, in the world but not of it; and as unlike anybody here as he is unlike anybody elsewhere that I have ever met or known.'" 12

Belinda: *see* Second **Correspondent**

Bill Blinder, "'as is now at grass, as all on us vill be in our turns. Bill, mum, wos the hostler as had charge o' them two vell-known piebald leaders that run in the Bristol fast coach, and vould never go to no other tune but a sutherly vind and a cloudy sky, which wos consekvently played incessant, by the guard, wenever they wos on duty.'" 12

First **correspondent** (rejected). "I am considered a devilish gentlemanly fellow . . . ask any of the men at our club. Ask any fellow . . . what sort of conversation mine is. Ask him if he thinks I have the sort of voice that will suit your deaf friend and make him hear, if he can hear anything at all. Ask the servants what they think of me. There's not a rascal among 'em, sir, but will tremble to hear my name." 5

Second **correspondent**, with a letter "on strongly-scented paper, and sealed in light-blue wax with the representation of two very plump doves interchanging beaks." [*signing* **Belinda**] 8

—*referring to the first* **correspondent**: "He raised his eyes (luminous in their seductive sweetness) to my agitated face. '*Can* you?' said he, with peculiar meaning. I felt the gentle pressure of his foot on mine; our corns throbbed in unison. '*Can* you?' he said again; and every lineament of his expressive countenance added the words 'resist me?' I murmured 'No,' and fainted . . . .

"Faithless, inconstant man! How many ages seem to have elapsed since his unaccountable and perfidious disappearance! Could I still forgive him both that and the borrowed lucre that he promised to pay next week! Could I spurn him from my feet if he approached in penitence, and with a matrimonial object! Would the blandishing enchanter still weave his spells around me, or should I burst them all and turn away in coldness! I dare not trust my weakness with the thought." 8

Lawyer, "'come to make [**Jinkinson**'s] vill; all the time he wos a takin' it down, Jinkinson was secretly a clippin' avay at his hair vith a large pair of scissors. "Wot's that 'ere snippin' noise?' says the lawyer every now and then; "it's like a man havin' his hair cut." "It is wery like a man having his hair cut," says poor Jinkinson, hidin' the scissors, and lookin' quite innocent. By the time the lawyer found it out, he was wery nearly bald.'" 13

Mother. "I was but a very young creature when my poor mother died, and yet I remember that often when I hung around her neck, and oftener still when I played about the room before her, she would catch me to her bosom, and bursting into tears, would soothe me with every term of fondness and affection . . . I knew, while watching my awkward and ungainly sports, how keenly she had felt for her poor crippled boy." 1

Working man. " . . .I admired how carefully the working man carried the **baby** in its gaudy hat and feathers, and how his **wife**, trudging patiently on behind, forgot even her care of her gay clothes, in exchanging greetings with the child as he crowed and laughed over the father's shoulder . . . ." 6

Jinkinson children
Money-taker, in St Pauls'
Tobacconist, who receives a visit from two Tonys
Waiter,a poor, lean, hungry man

MH I

From the Clock-case: Introduction to the Giant Chronicles

A pompous, self-important Lord Mayor-elect is called upon by an old school-fellow, **Joe Toddyhigh**. He receives him rudely but deigns to give him a ticket to his investiture banquet at Guildhall. Joe attends, falls asleep and dreams. He sees the giant statues of Gog and Magog awake and talking. 3

Alderman ["**Jack**"]. " . . . there dwelt in the city of London a substantial citizen, who united in his single person the dignities of wholesale fruiterer, alderman, common-councilman, and member of the worshipful Company of Patten-makers; who had superadded to these extraordinary distinctions the important post and title of Sheriff, and who . . . stood next in rotation for the high and honourable office of Lord Mayor.

" . . . . His face was like the full moon in a fog, with two little holes punched out for his eyes, a very ripe pear stuck on for his nose, and a wide gash to serve for a mouth. The girth of his waistcoat was hung up and lettered in his tailor's shop as an extraordinary curiosity. He breathed like a heavy snorer, and his voice in speaking came thickly forth, as if it were oppressed and stifled by feather-beds. He trod the ground like an elephant, and eat [*sic.*]and drank like—like nothing but an alderman, as he was."

Gog and **Magog**, "each above fourteen feet in height . . . were endowed with life and motion . . . and reclined in easy attitudes in the great stained glass window. Between them was an ancient cask, which seemed to be full of wine; for the younger Giant [Magog], clapping his huge hand upon it, and throwing up his mighty leg, burst into an exulting laugh, which reverberated through the hall like thunder."

" . . . the elder Giant [Gog], who had a flowing grey beard . . . [and] a grave and solemn voice . . . . "

Patten-maker. "The next moment [**Joe Toddyhigh**] cursed his weakness in behalf of a man so changed and selfish [as the **alderman**], and quite hated a jolly-looking old gentleman opposite for declaring himself in the pride of his heart a Patten-maker."

Recorder, "for the city of London . . . a man of birth and education, of the Honourable Society of the Middle Temple, Barrister-at-Law—he who had an uncle in the House of Commons, and an aunt almost but not quite in the House of Lords (for she had married a feeble peer, and made him vote as she liked) . . . ."

Joe Toddyhigh. "The strange man was not over and above well dressed, and was very far from being fat or rich-looking in any sense of the word, yet he spoke with a kind of modest confidence, and assumed an easy, gentlemanly sort of an air, to which nobody but a rich man can lawfully presume . . . sunburnt face and grey hair were present to the citizen's mind for a moment . . . . "

Attendants clearing away feast fragments, and drinking same

From the Clock-case: First Night of the Giant Chronicles

Magog tells Gog the Elizabethan story of the seduction of beautiful **Alice** by a cavalier. She leaves faithful **Hugh Graham**, who lives stoically on. She returns in the night, and he hides her in her old house. The Queen issues an edict against the wearing of long rapiers, and in enforcing it Hugh recognizes the haughty cavalier, who picks a fight with him and dies. Hugh is shot in the ensuing melee. Alice is dead. They are buried together. 4

Alice. " . . . Mistress Alice [the **Bowyer**'s] only daughter, was the richest heiress in all his wealthy ward. Young **Hugh** had often maintained with staff and cudgel that she was the handsomest. To do him justice, I believe she was. . . . A glance of her dark eye . . . would fire Hugh's blood so that none could stand before him . . . . "

—*returned:* "Yes, there she was . . . there, in her old innocent happy home, so changed that none but he could trace one gleam of what she had been— there upon her knees—with her hands clasped in agony and shame before her burning face."

Bowyer [bow-maker] " dwelt in the ward of Cheype, and was rumoured to possess great wealth . . . . His trade had been a profitable one in the time of King Henry the Eighth, who encouraged English archery to the utmost, and he had been prudent and discreet."

Cavalier. "He was nobly mounted, and, having no attendant, gave his horse in charge to **Hugh** while he and the **Bowyer** were closeted within. Once as he sprung into the saddle Mistress **Alice** was seated at an upper window, and before she could withdraw he had doffed his jewelled cap and kissed his hand . . . .

"He came again and often, each time arrayed more gaily than before, and still the little casement showed him Mistress Alice. At length one heavy day, she fled from home."

Hugh Graham, "a bold young 'prentice who loved his master's daughter. . . . From the time of **Alice**'s flight, the tilting-ground, the fields, the fencing-school, the summer-evening sports, knew Hugh no more. His spirit was dead within him. He rose to great eminence and repute among the citizens, but was seldom seen to smile . . . . Brave, humane, and generous, he was beloved by all."

—*mature:* "He was now a grey-haired man, though still in the prime of life. . . .The citizen . . . preserved the resolute bearing of one who was not to be frowned down or daunted, and who cared very little for any nobility but that of worth and manhood."

> Attendant, to a cavalier
> Courtier, showed a sword exactly three feet long and got it back
> -with a sword only two feet long and corresponding loss of dignity
> Fellow, with a sword too long: turned back again
> Females, well-conducted: they agreed there could be no woman there
> Officer, at the barrier, measuring swords
> -with a rapier at least four and a half feet long; sent it home
> Servant, of an officer; took home his rapier
> Waiting-woman: reported Alice's smiles to Hugh

MH C

The Clock-case: A Confession found in a Prison
in the Time of Charles the Second

A condemned man tells how he murdered his orphaned nephew out of envy and feelings of inferiority. He buries the body in his garden. An old comrade-in-arms calls with another, and the murderer entertains them, placing his heavy chair right over the corpse. A pack of bloodhounds, escaped from their keeper, enter the yard and sniff out the grave. The murderer is caught and admits his guilt. His wife goes mad. The writer of the Confession will die in the morning. 7

Brother, "open-hearted and generous, handsomer than I, more accomplished, and generally beloved. Those who sought my acquaintance abroad or at home, because they were friends of his, seldom attached themselves to me long, and would usually say, in our first conversation, that they were surprised to find two brothers so unlike in their manners and appearance."

Narrator. "I held a lieutenant's commission in his Majesty's army, and served abroad in the campaigns of 1677 and 1678."

"I was never a brave man, and had always been from my childhood of a secret, sullen and distrustful nature . . . while I write this, my grave is digging and my name is written in the black-book of death."

" . . . I have not the courage to anticipate my doom, or to bear up manfully against it . . . I have no compassion, no consolation, no hope, no friend . . . I am alone in this stone dungeon with my evil spirit, and . . . I die tomorrow."

Nephew. "The child was ardently attached to [my **wife**]; but he was his mother's image in face and spirit, and always mistrusted me."

"He feared me, but seemed by some instinct to despise me while he did so; and even when he drew back beneath my gaze—as he would when we were alone . . . he would keep his bright eyes upon me still."

Men, who laid down the grass, frantically expedited by the prisoner
Officers visiting after a long separation
Servant who walked over a grave
Wife of narrator's brother who knew his jealousy: a fixed, steady look

MH **PT**

Mr Pickwick's Tale

John Podgers, a hard eater and sleeper in the days of James I, is plagued by fears of witches and causes the deaths of many old women. His nephew **Will Marks** is not impressed. When John is summoned to assist in an ominous case of suspected witchcraft, Will agrees to take on the task of watching all night beside a gibbet. He notes with relief that it is empty. 10 i

Two women, shrieking in horror that there is no body to be buried, rouse Will, who is touched and offers his help. A masked cavalier recruits him to drive the corpse, taken down earlier, to the city for burial. After a harrowing journey, he consigns the coffin to shrouded figures. Returned home, he fabricates a colourful witch story to universal approbation. 10 ii

Cavalier. " . . . a man pretty far advanced in life, but of a firm and stately carriage. His dress was of a rich and costly kind, but so soiled and disordered that it was scarcely to be recognised for one of those gorgeous suits which the expensive taste and fashion of the time prescribed for men of any rank or station. He was booted and spurred, and bore about him even as many tokens of the state of the roads as **Will** himself." ii

Fellows. " . . . ill-favoured fellows lurked in knots of three or four; some standing upright against the wall, lying in wait; others skulking in gateways, and thrusting out their uncombed heads and scowling eyes: others crossing and recrossing, and constantly jostling both horse and man to provoke a quarrel; others stealing away and summoning their companions in a low whistle." ii

Will Marks, nephew of **Podgers**. " . . . a wild, roving young fellow of twenty who had been brought up in his uncle's house and lived there still . . . he was an apt scholar . . . . " i

"As it was plain that he set his mind upon it, and would go, **John Podgers** offered him a few first-rate charms out of his own pocket, which he dutifully declined to accept; and the **young lady** gave him a kiss, which he also returned." i

John Podgers. "John Podgers was broad, sturdy, Dutch-built, short, and a very hard eater, as men of his figure often are. Being a hard sleeper likewise, he divided his time pretty equally between these two recreations, always falling asleep when he had done eating, and always taking another turn at the trencher when he had done sleeping, by which means he grew more corpulent and more drowsy every day of his life." i

" . . . strong, sound sense, not what is called smart . . . of a rather lazy and apoplectic turn, but still a man of solid parts, and one who meant much more than he cared to show. This impression was confirmed by a very dignified way he had of shaking his head and imparting, at the same time, a pendulous motion to his double chin. . . ." i

Two **women**. "**Will** threw off his cloak, drew his sword, and darting swiftly round, seized a woman by the wrist, who, recoiling from him with a dreadful shriek, fell struggling upon her knees. Another woman, clad, like her whom he had grasped, in mourning garments, stood rooted to the spot on which they were, gazing upon his face with wild and glaring eyes . . . ." ii

" . . . Both were deadly pale, their garments wet and worn, their hair dishevelled and streaming in the wind, themselves bowed down with grief and misery; their whole appearance most dejected, wretched, and forlorn." ii

Attendants with three saddled horses
Bully, stout; taking a seat in the cart and insisting on being driven home
Cleric, severe on a sentinel for levity and youthful folly
Farrier, in the habit of beating his lady
Functionaries, grave: trod on Will's toes, tripped on his ankles; in fear
Gentleman, red-faced with a gruff voice
-masked, like a cavalier
-*pl* in cloaks, on the brink of a vault, supporting female figures
Hopkins[H]: the greatest witch-finder of the age
Housekeeper, afflicted with rheumatism: therefore burnt as a witch

Man, little; with a yellow face, taunting nose and chin
-long, under whose arm the little man thrust his face
-mounted a cart and drove briskly away
Mask, the: a shrouded cavalier who recruits Will Marks to convey a body
Men, came down on Will Marks demanding to be shown what was inside
Men, who removed a coffin: appeared suddenly as though started from the earth
Messenger: horseman dashed up to the porch and inquired for Podgers
Old woman: type of female drowned for a witch
Robbers, drunken, desperate; staggering through open streets
Ruffians: bands who pursued men with naked weapons
Sentinel, lonely; castigated by a cleric
Servitors, returning from the Bear Garden, dragging bleeding dogs
Watch, drawn across the road: questioned Will closely with cuffing
Young lady, pretty; an arm coiled around her waist; married Will Marks

The original organization of MHC is divided into six main sections comprising fifteen subdivisions, which we have numbered to facilitate reference from the extracts quoted above:

"As a triumph of Dickens, at least, [MHC] is not of great importance. But as a sample of Dickens it happens to be of quite remarkable importance. The very fact that it is for the most part somewhat more level and even monotonous than most of his creations, makes us realise, as it were, against what level and monotony those creations commonly stand out. This book is the background of his mind. It is the basis and minimum of him which was always there. Alone, of all written things, this shows how he felt when he was not writing. Dickens might have written it in his sleep. That is to say, it is written by a sluggish Dickens, a half automatic Dickens, a dreaming and drifting Dickens; but still by the enduring Dickens." GKC p229

N 4 Apr 1840-Feb 1841 wkly and monthly by C&H in MHC   1 vol 1841 **OCS**
Simultaneous U. S. publication in monthly parts by Lea & Blanchard, Philadelphia

The Old Curiosity Shop

Disconcerted by disappointing sales of MHC, his first very own periodical, CD sought to stimulate interest with a serialized piece, which grew and grew.

"Once having come into the society of Swiveller it is not unnatural that Dickens stayed there for a whole book. The essential point . . . is that Master Humphrey's Clock was stopped by the size and energy of the thing that had come of it. It died in childbirth." GKC p231

"MASTER HUMPHREY *(before his devotion to the trunk and butter business) was originally supposed to be the narrator of the story."* —preface [discarded newspapers lined trunks and wrapped butter in CD's day]

PRÉCIS

A gentleman on a London street guides a young girl to her home with her **grandfather** (G), who keeps a curiosity shop, employing **Kit Nubbles** as shop boy. G leaves on a mysterious night errand. A week later, the gentleman meets **Nell**'s brother **Fred** and **Dick Swiveller**. **Daniel Quilp**, malevolent dwarf, appears. All visitors leave, and G speaks of his dreams of a fortune for Nell, who gives Kit a writing lesson. 1-3

Quilp finds **Mrs Quilp**, her mother **Mrs Jiniwin** and lady neighbours discussing him. He makes his wife sit up all night while he enjoys a redly glowing cigar. At his office Quilp roughs up his boy **Tom Scott**. Nell arrives with a note from G. 4-5

The leeringly admiring Quilp takes Nell to his home and eavesdrops on her conversation with Mrs Quilp, getting a clue to G's activities. He sends her home after banter about making her his second wife. Fred urges Dick to marry her, to get at G's supposed fortune. 6-7

Swiveller dances at the **Wackles'**, whose daughter **Sophy** he admires. His rival is **Cheggs**. Dick disdains the competition and leaves. 8

Nell implores G to take her away. Quilp overhears and, Nell absent, taxes G with gambling away the money he has lent him. He hints that Kit has given him away and declines more advances. Nell, deeply distressed, appears at Kit's home, saying G is raving against him. 9-10

G ill, Quilp, with his lawyer, **Sampson Brass**, takes creditor's possession. Recovered but foolish, G steals away with Nell. Quilp is frantic to see his victims fled. Kit is mystified. He luckily is asked to hold the **Garlands'** pony and, overpaid, promises to work it off. Notary **Witherden**'s employee, **Chuckster**, is not impressed. 11-14

G and Nell walk to the country. A Punch and Judy troupe led by **Short** and **Codlin** take them in. They meet other performers and journey together. Alarmed by the keenness of their new friends' interest, they slip away. 15-19

Kit delivers as promised and, impressed, the Garlands engage him. Quilp and Swiveller turn up, looking for Nell. They and Fred conspire. Kit meets **Barbara**, a pretty servant at the Garlands'. 20-23

Nell and G come to a village school, whose kind **schoolmaster** witnesses a loved pupil's death. Pushing on, Nell and G meet **Mrs Jarley** and her caravan of wax-works. 24-26

Nell is now the wax-work girl. The Jarley caravan progresses. Out for a stroll, Nell and G take refuge from a storm at a wayside inn, where **Jowl** and **List** gamble. G begs a stake from Nell, which he loses. In the night, Nell sees him steal the rest of her precious hoard and knows the worst. 27-30

Making calls for Mrs Jarley, Nell meets Miss **Monflathers** and her pupils. She learns how wax-works are advertised and presented. 31-32

To keep an eye on him, Quilp has Brass hire Swiveller as clerk. Dick meets **Sally Brass** and their little servant. A **single gentleman** (SG) hires lodgings upstairs and sleeps alarmingly well. 33-35

Swiveller and Sally get along, but the little servant, "The **Marchioness**," intrigues Dick. He observes her fed and abused. The SG interviews all Punch and Judy proprietors. He is seeking Nell. 36-38

Kit gets his first pay and takes Barbara and their families out for entertainment and oysters. Mr Garland tells him the SG wants to borrow him and his mother to go after Nell. Kit finds and extracts his mother, at chapel. 39-41

Nell overhears the gamblers urging G to rob Mrs Jarley so he can resume play. She persuades G to flee with her instead, and they are taken onto a canal boat. Further wanderings and privations are ended when the schoolmaster, re-encountered on the road, takes them on with him. 42-46

SG, with **Mrs Nubbles**, is in hot pursuit of Nell. They meet Mrs Jarley and a dead end. Quilp has contrived to follow. Returning to London, Quilp frightens Mrs Nubbles, and Kit threatens him with a beating. 47-48

Quilp comes upon his family and his lawyer enjoying a wake. Believed drowned, he disabuses them, to mixed reaction. Aggrieved, he moves to bachelor quarters on the wharf. He plans to use the Brasses to injure Kit. 49-51

Nell and G have a refuge at last, near an old church with the schoolmaster and a kind old **Bachelor**. Nell is cherished, but she is in decline. 52-55

The Brasses start their scheme to frame Kit for theft, unaware that the Marchioness has overheard. Dick and the servant are friends. The trap is sprung, with Dick's unwitting aid, and Kit is arrested. He is visited by his family in the jail. Swiveller sends him beer. 56-61

Sampson reports to Quilp. Kit is tried and convicted, and Swiveller, no longer needed, is dismissed. He falls very ill and wakes to realize that the Marchioness, alerted by his landlady, has come and nursed him. She describes the Quilp-Brass plot against Kit. 62-64

Dick sends her to Witherden to find the Garlands, and she brings them to him. They plan to confront the Brasses, starting with Sally, but Sampson is the turncoat. Dick's aunt has died and he has an annuity. 65-66

Sally sends to warn Quilp. The police arrive. Attempting to flee, he falls in the river and drowns. Kit is exonerated and released. Nell and G have been found through the Bachelor, revealed to be Mr Garland's brother. 67-68

The SG reveals he is G's younger brother. He went abroad to leave the lady they both loved to the elder. He has come home and now seeks both G and Nell. They journey to the church enclave but are too late: Nell has died two days before. G is insane with grief. 69-71

Nell is buried. (All the English-speaking world mourned.) G dies. Sampson goes to jail, Sally into hiding. The widow Quilp, now rich, marries a smart young man who insists on separate accommodation for Mrs Jiniwin. Swiveller marries the Marchioness after sending her to school and rechristening her. (Chesterton thought this the truest romance CD ever created.) Kit and Barbara unite. 72-73

CONTENTS

Illustrations by (with one exception) *Hablôt K. Browne*

CHARACTERS

Brass, Old Foxey: father of Sampson and Sally	W	462
Sally; an amazon of common law	P	436
Sampson; a gentleman by law	P	437
Brown, a prospective character reference for Kit	W	462
Butcher, to Miss Monflathers	W	462
Carrier who took and kept Kit's box	W	462
Carter who gives a lift	W	462
-pl inveiglers for Mrs Jarley	W	462
Chambermaid, attractive to a dwarf	W	463
Cheggs, Alick; market gardener	O	454
Miss, his supportive sister	O	454
Child: his brother is buried; his grief is the first intimation of Nell's death	O	454
Chuckster, notary's clerk	SR	445
Clergyman, simple and shrinking	O	455
Coachman, dealing with the Single Gentleman's trunk	W	463
Codlin, Thomas; Punch & Judy operator	G	451
Constable, with a regular course of business	O	455
Cottagers: father, old man, wife; three children, brown as berries	W	463
Daughter, of a Baronet: life is unfair	W	463
Davy, a grave digger	O	455
Day-scholars at the Wackles school	W	463
Defense attorney for Kit Nubbles	W	463
Doctor, apparently very wise	O	455
Dogs, trained well-behaved: *see* Jerry		
Edwards, Miss; sweet but poor Monflathers student	O	455
Miss; her younger sister	O	455
Evans, Richard; schoolboy psalm singer	O	455
Furnace watcher, partial orphan (his mother): kind to Nell	G	451
Garland, Abel; son like his father	O	455
Mr; employs Kit Nubbles with a pony	SR	446
Mrs; as comfortable as the others	SR	446
George, driver and factotum, later bridegroom, for Mrs Jarley	O	455
George, Mrs; friend of Mrs Jiniwin	O	455
Gipsy: watchful and interested (a red herring)	W	463
Grandfather (no surname) of Nell Trent; has an addiction	Pr	433
Green, prospective character reference	W	463
Grinder, proprietor of a stilt-walking team	G	451
-his lot: young gentleman and young lady on stilts	G	451
Groves, "honest" Jem; landlord	O	456
Harris (**Short Trotters**), Punch & Judy proprietor	G	452
Harry, beloved and dying boy	O	456
Jarley, Mrs; waxworks exhibition proprietor	SR	446
Jerry, with a dog act	G	452
Jiniwin, Mrs; mother of Mrs Quilp	SR	448
Jowl, Joe or Mat: a gambler	G	452
Kit (Christopher Nubbles)	P	439
Ladies, from the neighbourhood	O	456
Lady, alone: she aids Nell, declines a fortune-teller	W	463
-from the Minories [a London district]; she does not admire Quilp	O	456
Landlady, decisive with medication	W	463
Landlord, and Landlady: in a country town; they admire Nell	W	463
-who loves to cook	O	456
List, Isaac; gambler	G	453
"Little Nell"	Pr	434

Spear-carriers

The Proprietors

Grandfather. ". . . a little old man with long grey hair . . . . Though much altered by age, I fancied I could recognise in his spare and slender form something of that delicate mould which I had noticed in [**Nell**]. Their bright blue eyes were certainly alike, but his face was so deeply furrowed and so very full of care, that here all resemblance ceased . . . coupled with something feeble and wandering in his manner, there were in his face marks of deep and anxious thought which convinced me that he could not be, as I had been at first inclined to suppose, in a state of dotage or imbecility." 1

—*once upon a time:* "' . . . he told me about my mother, and how she once looked and spoke just like me when she was a little child. Then, he used to take me on his knee, and try to make me understand that she was not lying in her grave, but had flown to a beautiful country beyond the sky, where nothing died or ever grew old—we were very happy once!'" 6

—*his dream:* "'All is for her sake. I have borne great poverty myself, and would spare her the sufferings that poverty carries with it. I would spare her the miseries that brought her mother, my own dear child, to an early grave. I would leave her—not with resources which could be easily spent or squandered away, but with what would place her beyond the reach of want for ever . . . . She shall have no pittance, but a fortune . . . . '" 3

—*driven, in the night:* "A figure was there . . . it crouched and slunk along, groping its way with noiseless hands, and stealing round the bed. [**Nell**] had no voice to cry for help, no power to move, but lay still, watching . . . .

"The dark form was a mere blot upon the lighter darkness of the room, but she saw the turning of the head, and felt and knew how the eyes looked and the ears listened. There it remained, motionless as she. At length, still keeping the face towards her, it busied its hands in something, and she heard the chink of money.

"Then, on it came again, silent and stealthy as before, and, replacing the garments it had taken from the bedside, dropped to its hands and knees, and crawled away. How slowly it seemed to move, now that she could hear but not see it, creeping along the floor! It reached the door at last, and stood upon its feet. The steps creaked beneath its noiseless tread, and it was gone." 30

—*guilt:* "'Nothing but flight can save us. Up!'

"The old man rose from his bed: his forehead bedewed with the cold sweat of fear; and, bending before the child as if she had been an angel messenger sent to lead him where she would, made ready to follow her. She took him by the hand and led him on. As they passed the door of the room he had proposed to rob, she shuddered and looked up into his face. What a white face was that, and with what a look did he meet hers!'" 42

—*petulance:* "'Why did you bring me here?' returned the old man fiercely. 'I cannot bear these close eternal streets. We came from a quiet part. Why did you force me to leave it?'" 44

—*mourning:* "There was a curious noise inside . . . .It bore a resemblance to the low moaning of one in pain, but it was not that, being too regular and constant. Now it seemed a kind of song, now a wail . . . in its tone there was something fearful, chilling, and unearthly . . . . The dull, red glow of a wood fire . . . showed [**Kit**] a figure, seated on the hearth with its back towards him, bending over the fitful light. The attitude was that of one who sought the heat. It was, and yet was not. The stooping posture and the cowering form were there, but no hands were stretched out to meet the grateful warmth, no shrug or shiver compared its luxury with the piercing cold outside. With limbs huddled together, head bowed down, arms crossed upon the breast, and fingers tightly clenched, it rocked to and fro upon its seat without a moment's pause, accompanying the action with the mournful sound he had heard.

" . . . . The form was that of an old man, his white head akin in colour to the mouldering embers upon which he gazed. And the failing light and dying fire, the time-worn room, the solitude, the wasted life, and gloom, were all in fellowship. Ashes, and dust, and ruin!" 71

Nell Trent. ". . . a pretty little girl . . . a soft sweet voice . . . her small and delicate frame imparted a peculiar youthfulness to her appearance. Though more scantily attired than she might have been she was dressed with perfect neatness, and betrayed no marks of poverty or neglect . . . . Bright blue eyes [and] light brown hair . . . . " 1

—*her constant preoccupation:* " . . . it was not the monotonous day unchequered by variety and uncheered by pleasant companionship, it was not the dark dreary evenings or the long solitary nights, it was not the absence of every slight and easy pleasure for which young hearts beat high, or the knowing nothing of childhood but its weakness and its easily wounded spirit, that had wrung such tears from Nell.

"To see the old man struck down beneath the pressure of some hidden grief, to mark his wavering and unsettled state, to be agitated at times with a dreadful fear that his mind was wandering, and to trace in his words and looks the dawning of despondent madness; to watch and wait and listen for confirmation of these things day after day, and to feel and know that, come what might, they were alone in the world with no one to help or advise or care about them—these were causes of depression and anxiety that might have sat heavily on an older breast with many influences at work to cheer and gladden it, but how heavily on the mind of a young child to whom they were ever present, and who was constantly surrounded by all that could keep such thoughts in restless action!" ¶9

—*seen by a lecher:* "'Such a fresh, blooming, modest little bud . . . such a chubby, rosy, cosy, little Nell! . . . She's so . . . so small, so compact, so beautifully modelled, so fair, with such blue veins and such a transparent skin, and such little feet, and such winning ways . . . .'" 9 *[This and two other Quilp remarks are the only usages of the term "little Nell" in the novel. See Vol III p149.]*

—*her eyes opened:* " . . . meaning to preserve [her **grandfather**] or be killed herself, she staggered forward and looked in. What sight was that which met her view!

"The bed had not been lain on, but was smooth and empty. And at a table sat the old man himself, the only living creature there, his white face pinched and sharpened by the greediness which made his eyes unnaturally bright, counting the money of which his hands had robbed her." 30

—*resolved:* She "was sensible of a new feeling within her, which elevated her nature, and inspired her with an energy and confidence she had never known. There was no divided responsibility now; the whole burden of their two lives had fallen upon her, and henceforth she must think and act for both. . . . In the pale moonlight, which lent a wanness of its own to the delicate face where thoughtful care already mingled with the winning grace and loveliness of youth, the too bright eye, the spiritual head, the lips that pressed each other with such high resolve and courage of the heart, the slight figure, firm in its bearing and yet so very weak, told their silent tale . . . ." 43

—*at last*: "There, upon her little bed, she lay at rest. The solemn stillness was no marvel now.

"She was dead. No sleep so beautiful and calm, so free from trace of pain, so fair to look upon. She seemed a creature fresh from the hand of God, and waiting for the breath of life; not one who had lived and suffered death.

"Her couch was dressed with here and there some winter berries and green leaves, gathered in a spot she had been used to favour. 'When I die, put near me something that has loved the light, and had the sky above it always.' Those were her words.

"She was dead. Dear, gentle, patient, noble Nell, was dead. Her little bird— a poor slight thing the pressure of a finger would have crushed—was stirring nimbly in its cage; and the strong heart of its child-mistress was mute and motionless for ever.

"Where were the traces of her early care, her sufferings, and fatigues? All gone. Sorrow was dead indeed in her, but peace and perfect happiness were born; imaged in her tranquil beauty and profound repose.

"And still her former self lay there, unaltered in this change. Yes. The old fireside had smiled upon that same sweet face; it had passed like a dream through haunts of misery and care; at the door of the poor schoolmaster on the summer evening, before the furnace fire upon the cold wet night, at the still bedside of the dying boy, there had been the same mild lovely look. So shall we know the angels in their majesty, after death . . . .

"She was dead, and past all help, or need of it. The ancient rooms she had seemed to fill with life, even while her own was waning fast—the garden she had tended—the eyes she had gladdened—the noiseless haunts of many a thoughtful hour—the paths she had trodden as it were but yesterday—could know her no more." 71

Other Principals

Sally Brass: " . . . clerk, assistant, housekeeper, secretary, confidential plotter, adviser, intriguer, and bill of cost increaser, Miss Brass—a kind of amazon at common law . . . was a lady of thirty-five or thereabouts, of a gaunt and bony figure, and a resolute bearing, which if it repressed the softer emotions of love, and kept admirers at a distance, certainly inspired a feeling akin to awe in the breasts of those male strangers who had the happiness to approach her.

"In face she bore a striking resemblance to her brother, Sampson—so exact, indeed, was the likeness between them, that had it consorted with Miss Brass's maiden modesty and gentle womanhood to have assumed her brother's clothes in a frolic and sat down beside him, it would have been difficult for the oldest friend of the family to determine which was **Sampson** and which Sally, especially as the lady carried upon her upper lip certain reddish demonstrations, which, if the imagination had been assisted by her attire, might have been mistaken for a beard. These were, however, in all probability nothing more than eyelashes in a wrong place, as the eyes of Miss Brass were quite free from any such natural impertinencies.

"In complexion Miss Brass was sallow—rather a dirty-sallow, so to speak—but this hue was agreeably relieved by the healthy glow which mantled in the extreme tip of her laughing nose. Her voice was exceedingly impressive—deep and rich in quality, and, once heard, not easily forgotten. Her usual dress was a green gown, in colour not unlike the curtain of the office window, made tight to the figure, and terminating at the throat, where it was fastened behind by a peculiarly large and massive button. Feeling, no doubt, that simplicity and plainness are the soul of elegance, Miss Brass wore no collar or kerchief except upon her head, which was invariably ornamented with a brown gauze scarf, like the wing of the fabled vampire, and which, twisted into any form that happened to suggest itself, formed an easy and graceful head-dress.

"Such was Miss Brass in person. In mind, she was of a strong and vigorous turn, having from her earliest youth devoted herself with uncommon ardour to the study of the law; not wasting her speculation upon its eagle flights, which are rare, but tracing it attentively through all the slippery and eel-like crawlings in which it commonly pursues its way.

"Nor had she, like many persons of great intellect, confined herself to theory, or stopped short where practical usefulness begins; inasmuch as she could engross, fair-copy, fill up printed forms with perfect accuracy, and in short transact any ordinary duty of the office down to pouncing a skin of parchment or mending a pen.

"It is difficult to understand how, possessed of these combined attractions, she should remain Miss Brass; but whether she had steeled her heart against mankind, or whether those who might have wooed and won her, were deterred

by fears that, being learned in the law, she might have too near her fingers'
ends those particular statutes which regulate what are familiarly termed
actions for breach, certain it is that she was still in a state of celibacy, and still
in daily occupation of her old stool opposite to that of her brother Sampson.
And equally certain it is, by the way, that between these two stools a great
many people had come to the ground." ¶33

—as a child: "She had been remarkable, when a tender prattler, for an uncommon talent in counterfeiting the walk and manner of a bailiff; in which
character she had learned to tap her little playfellows on the shoulder, and to
carry them off to imaginary sponging-houses, with a correctness of imitation
which was the surprise and delight of all who witnessed her performances, and
which was only to be exceeded by her exquisite manner of putting an execution
into her doll's house, and taking an exact inventory of the chairs and tables." 36

—to her clerk: "'She's the sphynx of private life is Sally B.'" 50

—sibling sentiment: " . . . she no sooner beheld the latent uneasiness and
misery of her brother than she developed a grim satisfaction, and began to
enjoy herself after her own manner . . . unmindful of the wet which dripped down
upon her own feminine person and fair apparel, [she] sat placidly behind the
teaboard, erect and grizzly, contemplating the unhappiness of her brother with
a mind at ease, and content, in her amiable disregard of self, to sit there all
night, witnessing the torments which his avaricious and grovelling nature compelled him to endure and forbade him to resent." 51

—in the end: " . . . two wretched people were more than once observed to
crawl at dusk from the inmost recesses of St Giles's, and to take their way
along the streets, with shuffling steps and cowering shivering forms, looking
into the roads and kennels as they went in search of refuse food or disregarded
offal. These forms were never beheld but in those nights of cold and gloom,
when the terrible spectres, who lie at all other times in the obscene hiding-
places of London, in archways, dark vaults and cellars, venture to creep into
the streets; the embodied spirits of Disease, and Vice, and Famine. It was
whispered by those who should have known, that these were **Sampson** and his
sister Sally . . . ." 73

Sampson Brass. "This Brass was an attorney of no very good repute
from Bevis-Marks in the city of London; he was a tall, meagre man, with a
nose like a wen, a protruding forehead, retreating eyes, and hair of a deep red.
He wore a long black surtout reaching nearly to his ankles, short black
trousers, high shoes, and cotton-stockings of a blueish grey. He had a cringing
manner but a very harsh voice, and his blandest smiles were so extremely
forbidding, that to have had his company under the least repulsive
circumstances, one would have wished him to be out of temper that he might
only scowl." 11

—his office: "In the parlour window of this little habitation, which is so
close upon the footway that the passenger who takes the wall brushes the dim
glass with his coat sleeve—much to its improvement, for it is very dirty . . .
there hung, all awry and slack, and discoloured by the sun, a curtain of faded
green, so threadbare from long service as by no means to intercept the view of
the little dark room, but rather to afford a favourable medium through which to
observe . . . .

"A rickety table, with spare bundles of papers, yellow and ragged from long
carriage in the pocket, ostentatiously displayed upon its top; a couple of stools
set face to face on opposite sides of this crazy piece of furniture; a treacherous
old chair by the fireplace, whose withered arms had hugged full many a client

and helped to squeeze him dry; a second-hand wig box, used as a depository for blank writs and declarations and other small forms of law . . . two or three common books of practice; a jar of ink, a pounce box, a stunted hearth-broom, a carpet trodden to shreds but still clinging with the tightness of desperation to its tacks . . . the yellow wainscot of the walls, the smoke-discoloured ceiling, the dust and cobwebs . . . .

"Its atmosphere was of a close and earthy kind, and, besides being frequently impregnated with strong whiffs of the second-hand wearing apparel exposed for sale in Duke's Place and Houndsditch, had a decided flavour of rats and mice, and a taint of mouldiness." ¶33

—*his sycophancy:* "It was a maxim with Mr. Brass that the habit of paying compliments kept a man's tongue oiled without any expense; and, as that useful member ought never to grow rusty or creak in turning on its hinges in the case of a practitioner of the law, in whom it should be always glib and easy, he lost few opportunities of improving himself by the utterance of handsome speeches and eulogistic expressions. And this had passed into such a habit with him, that, if he could not be correctly said to have his tongue at his fingers's ends, he might certainly be said to have it anywhere but in his face: which being . . . of a harsh and repulsive character, was not oiled so easily, but frowned above all the smooth speeches; one of nature's beacons, warning off those who navigated the shoals and breakers of the World, or of that dangerous strait the Law, and admonishing them to seek less treacherous harbours and try their fortune elsewhere." 35

—*dissembling:* "'I respect *you,* **Kit**,' said Brass with emotion. 'I saw enough of your conduct . . . to respect you, though your station is humble, and your fortune lowly. It isn't the waistcoat that I look at. It is the heart. The checks in the waistcoat are but the wires of the cage. But the heart is the bird. Ah! How many sich birds are perpetually moulting, and putting their beaks through the wires to peck at all mankind!'" 56

—*requited:* " . . . he was permitted to grace the mother country under certain insignificant restrictions.

"These were that he should, for a term of years, reside in a spacious mansion where several other gentlemen were lodged and boarded at the public charge, who went clad in a sober uniform of grey turned up with yellow, had their hair cut extremely short, and chiefly lived on gruel and light soup. It was also required of him that he should partake their exercise of constantly ascending an endless flight of stairs [a treadmill]; and lest his legs, unused to such exertion, should be weakened by it, that he should wear upon one ankle an amulet or charm of iron." 73

Christopher (Kit) Nubbles: "Kit was a shock-headed shambling awkward lad with an uncommonly wide mouth, very red cheeks, a turned-up nose, and certainly the most comical expression of face I ever saw. He stopped short at the door on seeing a stranger, twirled in his hand a perfectly round old hat without any vestige of a brim, and resting himself now on one leg and now on the other and changing them constantly, stood in the doorway, looking into the parlour with the most extraordinary leer I ever beheld." 1

"The lad had a remarkable manner of standing sideways as he spoke, and thrusting his head forward over his shoulder, as if he could not get at his voice without that accompanying action. I think he would have amused one anywhere, but [**Nell**'s] exquisite enjoyment of his oddity, and the relief it was to find that there was something she associated with merriment in a place that appeared so unsuited to her, were quite irresistible. It was a great point too that Kit himself was flattered by the sensation he created, and after several efforts to preserve his gravity, burst into a loud roar, and so stood with his mouth wide open and his eyes nearly shut, laughing violently." 1

—*eating:* "Kit . . . in despatching his bread and meat had been swallowing two-thirds of his knife at every mouthful with the coolness of a juggler . . . incapacitated himself for further conversation by taking a most prodigious sandwich at one bite." 1

—*on seeing his adored's home empty:* "It must be specially observed in justice to poor Kit that he was by no means of a sentimental turn . . . . He was only a soft-hearted grateful fellow, and had nothing genteel or polite about him; consequently instead of going home again in his grief to kick the children and abuse his mother . . . he turned his thoughts to the vulgar expedient of making them more comfortable if he could." 14

—*in uniform:* " . . . he wore no livery, but was dressed in a coat of pepper-and-salt with waistcoat of canary colour, and nether garments of iron-grey; besides these glories, he shone in the lustre of a new pair of boots and an extremely stiff and shiny hat, which on being struck anywhere with the knuckles, sounded like a drum." 22

—*tact:* "**Barbara**'s thoughts seemed to have been running upon what Kit had said at tea-time, for when they were coming out of the play, she asked him, with an hysterical simper, if Miss **Nell** was as handsome as the lady who jumped over the ribbons. 'As handsome as *her*?' said Kit. 'Double as handsome.' 'Oh, Christopher! I'm sure she was the beautifullest creature ever was.' said Barbara. 'Nonsense!' returned Kit. 'She was well enough, I don't deny that; but think how she was dressed and painted, and what a difference that made. Why *you* are a good deal better-looking than her, Barbara.' 'Oh Christopher!' said Barbara, looking down. 'You are any day,' said Kit '—and so's your mother.'" 39

—*and see* **Quilp**—*appreciation of virtue*

Daniel Quilp. " . . . an elderly man of remarkably hard features and for-bidding aspect, and so low in stature as to be quite a dwarf, though his head and face were large enough for the body of a giant. His black eyes were restless, sly, and cunning; his mouth and chin, bristly with the stubble of a coarse hard beard; and his complexion was one of that kind which never looks clean or wholesome. But what added most to the grotesque expression of his face, was a ghastly smile, which, appearing to be the mere result of habit and to have no connexion with any mirthful or complacent feeling, constantly revealed the few discoloured fangs that were yet scattered in his mouth, and gave him the aspect of a panting dog.

"His dress consisted of a large high-crowned hat, a worn dark suit, a pair of capacious shoes, and a dirty white neckerchief sufficiently limp and crumpled to disclose the greater portion of his wiry throat. Such hair as he had, was of a grizzled black, cut short and straight upon his temples, and hanging in a frowzy fringe about his ears. His hands, which were of a rough, coarse grain, were very dirty; his finger-nails were crooked, long, and yellow." ¶3

—*uxorious:* "'Ask **Mrs Quilp**, pretty Mrs Quilp, obedient, timid, loving Mrs Quilp. But that reminds me—I have left her all alone, and she will be anxious and know not a moment's peace till I return. I know she's always in that condition when I'm away, though she doesn't dare to say so, unless I lead her on and tell her she may speak freely and I won't be angry with her. Oh! well-trained Mrs Quilp.'

"The creature appeared quite horrible with his monstrous head and little body, as he rubbed his hands slowly round, and round, and round again—with something fantastic even in his manner of performing this slight action—and, dropping his shaggy brows and cocking his chin in the air, glanced upward with a stealthy look of exultation that an imp might have copied and appropriated to himself." 3

—*his occupation:* "Mr. Quilp could scarcely be said to be of any particular trade or calling, though his pursuits were diversified and his occupations numerous. He collected the rents of whole colonies of filthy streets and alleys by the waterside, advanced money to the seamen and petty officers of merchant vessels, had a share in the ventures of divers mates of East Indiamen, smoked his smuggled cigars under the very nose of the Custom House, and made appointments on 'Change with men in glazed hats and round jackets pretty well every day." 4

—*an all-night smoke:* ". . . the small lord of creation took his first cigar and mixed his first glass of grog. The sun went down, and the stars peeped out, the Tower turned from its own proper colours to grey and from grey to black, the room became perfectly dark and the end of the cigar a deep fiery red, but still Mr. Quilp went on smoking and drinking in the same position, and staring listlessly out of the window with the dog-like smile always on his face, save when Mrs. Quilp made some involuntary movement of restlessness or fatigue; and then it expanded into a grin of delight.

"Whether Mr. Quilp took any sleep by snatches of a few winks at a time, or whether he sat with his eyes wide open all night long, certain it is that he kept his cigar alight, and kindled every fresh one from the ashes of that which was nearly consumed, without requiring the assistance of a candle. Nor did the striking of the clocks, hour after hour, appear to inspire him with any sense of drowsiness or any natural desire to go to rest, but rather to increase his wakefulness, which he showed, at every such indication of the progress of the night, by a suppressed cackling in his throat, and a motion of his shoulders, like one who laughs heartily but at the same time slyly and by stealth." 4, 5

—*at the breakfast table:* " . . . he ate hard eggs, shell and all, devoured gigantic prawns with the heads and tails on, chewed tobacco and watercresses at the same time and with extraordinary greediness, drank boiling tea without winking, bit his fork and spoon till they bent again, and in short performed so many horrifying and uncommon acts that the women were nearly frightened out of their wits, and began to doubt if he were really a human creature." 5

—his usual expression: "Mr Quilp . . . subsided into the panting look which was customary with him, and which, whether it were assumed or natural, had equally the effect of banishing all expression from his face, and rendering it, as far as it afforded any index to his mood or meaning, a perfect blank." 48

—a wake: " . . . Mrs **Jiniwin**; no longer sipping other people's punch feloniously with tea-spoons, but taking deep draughts from a jorum of her own; while her daughter—not exactly with ashes on her head, or sackcloth on her back, but preserving a very decent and becoming appearance of sorrow never-the-less—was reclining in an easy chair, and soothing her grief with a smaller allowance of the same glib liquid.

"'If I could poison that dear old lady's rum and water,' murmured Quilp, 'I'd die happy.'" 49

—appreciation of virtue: "'This **Kit** is one of your honest people; one of your fair characters; a prowling prying hound; a hypocrite; a double-faced, white-livered, sneaking spy; a crouching cur to those that feed and coax him, and a barking yelping dog to all besides.'" 51

And see **Tom Scott** SR—*employer relations*

Single gentleman. " . . .when the trunk was at last got into the bedroom, [he] sat down upon it and wiped his bald head and face with his handkerchief. He was very warm, and well he might be; for, not to mention the exertion of getting the trunk upstairs, he was closely muffled up in winter garments, though the thermometer had stood all day at eighty-one in the shade." 34

—impatient: "To have been indifferent to the companionship of the single gentleman would have been tantamount to being gifted with nerves of steel. Never did chaise inclose, or horses draw, such a restless gentleman as he. He never sat in the same position for two minutes together, but was perpetually tossing his arms and legs about, pulling up the sashes and letting them violently down, or thrusting his head out of one window to draw it in again and thrust it out of another.

"He carried in his pocket, too, a fire-box of mysterious and unknown construction; and sure as ever **Kit**'s mother closed her eyes, so surely—whisk, rattle, fizz—there was the single gentleman consulting his watch by a flame of fire, and letting the sparks fall down among the straw as if there were no such thing as a possibility of himself and Kit's mother being roasted alive before the boys could stop their horses.

"Whenever they halted to change, there he was—out of the carriage without letting down the steps, bursting about the inn-yard like a lighted cracker, pulling out his watch by lamplight and forgetting to look at it before he put it up again, and in short committing so many extravagances that Kit's mother was quite afraid of him." ¶47

Dick Swiveller. "A figure conspicuous for its dirty smartness . . . took occasion to apologise for any negligence that might be perceptible in his dress, on the ground that last night he had had 'the sun very strong in his eyes;' by which expression he was understood to convey to his hearers in the most delicate manner possible, the information that he had been extremely drunk . . . if no such suspicion had been awakened by his speech, his wiry hair, dull eyes, and sallow face, would still have been strong witnesses against him.

"His attire was not, as he had himself hinted, remarkable for the nicest arrangement, but was in a state of disorder which strongly induced the idea that he had gone to bed in it. It consisted of a brown body-coat with a great many brass buttons up the front and only one behind, a bright check neckerchief, a plaid waistcoat, soiled white trousers, and a very limp hat, worn with the wrong side foremost, to hide a hole in the brim.

"The breast of his coat was ornamented with an outside pocket from which there peeped forth the cleanest end of a very large and very ill-favoured handkerchief; his dirty wristbands were pulled down as far as possible and ostentatiously folded back over his cuffs; he displayed no gloves, and carried a yellow cane having at the top a bone hand with the semblance of a ring on its little finger and a black ball in its grasp.

"With all these personal advantages (to which may be added a strong savour of tobacco-smoke and a prevailing greasiness of appearance) Mr. Swiveller leant back in his chair with his eyes fixed on the ceiling, and occasionally pitching his voice to the needful key, obliged the company with a few bars of an intensely dismal air, and then, in the middle of a note, relapsed into his former silence." ¶2

—*philosophy:* "'What is the odds so long as the fire of soul is kindled at the taper of conwiviality . . . . What is the odds so long as the spirit is expanded by means of rosy wine, and the present moment is the least happiest of our existence! . . . . If the wing of friendship should never moult a feather, the wing of relationship should never be clipped but be always expanded and serene.'" 2

—*dancing:* " . . . determining to show the family what quality of man they trifled with, and influenced perhaps by his late libations, he performed such feats of agility and such spins and twirls as filled the company with astonishment, and in particular caused a very long gentleman . . . to stand quite transfixed by wonder and admiration. Even **Mrs Wackles** forgot for the moment to snub three small young ladies who were inclined to be happy, and could not repress a rising thought that to have such a dancer as that in the family would be a pride indeed." 8

—*Swivelloggerel:* "'It's rather sudden,' said Dick, shaking his head with a look of infinite wisdom, and running on (as he was accustomed to do) with scraps of verse as if they were only prose in a hurry;

> *when the heart of a man is depressed with fears,*
> *the mist is dispelled when Miss Wackles appears . . . .* ' 8

—*leaving a message:* "'And say . . . sir, that I was wafted here upon the pinions of concord, that I came to remove, with the rake of friendship, the seeds of mutual wiolence and heart-burning, and to sow in their place, the germs of social harmony. Will you have the goodness to charge yourself with that commission, sir?'" 13

—*representing a client:* He inquired "whether the [**single gentleman**] held it to be consistent with the conduct and character of a gentleman to go to sleep for six-and-twenty hours at a stretch, and, whether the peace of an amiable and virtuous family was to weigh as nothing in the balance . . . . ' . . .if ever you do that again, take care you're not sat upon by the coroner and buried in a cross road before you wake. We have been distracted with fears that you were dead, sir. . . and the short and the long of it is, that we cannot allow single gentlemen to come into this establishment and sleep like double gentlemen without paying extra for it . . . an equal quantity of slumber was never got out of one bed and bedstead, and if you're going to sleep in that way, you must pay for a double-bedded room.'" 35

—*discretion undermined:* "[He] chanced at the moment to be sprinkling a glass of warm gin and water on the dust of the law, and to be moistening his clay, as the phrase goes, rather copiously. But as clay in the abstract, when too much moistened, becomes of a weak and uncertain consistency, breaking down in unexpected places, retaining impressions but faintly, and preserving no strength or steadiness of character, so Mr Swiveller's clay, having imbibed a considerable quantity of moisture, was in a very loose and slippery state, insomuch that the various ideas impressed upon it were fast losing their distinctive character, and running into each other.

"It is not uncommon for human clay in this condition to value itself above all things upon its great prudence and sagacity; and Mr Swiveller, especially, prizing himself upon these qualities, took occasion to remark that he had made strange discoveries in connection with the single gentleman who lodged above, which he had determined to keep within his own bosom, and which neither tortures nor cajolery should ever induce him to reveal." 48

—*grieving in prose:* "'I shall wear,' added Richard, taking off his hat again and looking hard at it, as if he were only deterred by pecuniary considerations from spurning it with his foot, 'I shall wear this emblem of woman's perfidy, in remembrance of her with whom I shall never again thread the windings of the mazy; whom I shall never more pledge in the rosy; who, during the short remainder of my existence, will murder the balmy.'" 56

And see **Marchioness** SR

Supporting Roles

The Bachelor (another **Garland**). "The little old gentleman was the active spirit of the place; the adjuster of all differences, the promoter of all merry-makings . . . the universal mediator, comforter, and friend. None of the simple villagers had cared to ask his name, or, when they knew it, to store it in their memory. Perhaps from some vague rumour of his college honours which had been whispered abroad on his first arrival, perhaps because he was an unmarried, unencumbered gentleman, he had been called the bachelor.

"The bachelor, then . . . lifted the latch, showed his little round mild face for a moment at the door, and stepped into the room like one who was no stranger to it." 52

" . . . the little old gentleman, disappearing for some five or ten minutes, presently returned, laden with old shelves, rugs, blankets, and other household gear, and followed by a **boy** bearing a similar load. These being cast on the floor in a promiscuous heap, yielded a quantity of occupation in arranging, erecting, and putting away; the superintendence of which task evidently afforded the old gentleman extreme delight, and engaged him for some time with great briskness and activity." 52

Barbara. A "little servant girl, very tidy, modest, and demure, but very pretty too . . ." 22

—*with a visitor:* "It did not appear, however, that there was anything remarkably tremendous about this strange Barbara, who having lived a very quiet life, blushed very much and was quite as embarrassed and uncertain what she ought to say or do, as **Kit** could possibly be. When he had sat for some little time, attentive to the ticking of the sober clock, he ventured to glance curiously at the dresser, and there, among the plates and dishes, were Barbara's little work-box with a sliding lid to shut in the balls of cotton, and Barbara's prayer-book and Barbara's hymn-book, and Barbara's Bible. Barbara's little looking-glass hung in a good light near the window, and Barbara's bonnet was on a nail behind the door.

"From all these mute signs and tokens of her presence, he naturally glanced at Barbara herself, who sat as mute as they, shelling peas into a dish; and just when Kit was looking at her eyelashes and wondering—quite in the simplicity of his heart—what colour her eyes might be, it perversely happened that Barbara raised her head a little to look at him, when both pair of eyes were hastily withdrawn, and Kit leant over his plate, and Barbara over her pea-shells, each in extreme confusion at having been detected by the other." ¶22 *And see* **Kit Nubbles** OP—*tact*

Chuckster. " . . . with his hat extremely on one side, and his hair a long way beyond it, [he] came swaggering up the walk [and] exerted his utmost abilities to enchant his entertainers, and impress them with a conviction of the mental superiority of those who dwelt in town; with which view he led the discourse to the small scandal of the day, in which he was justly considered by his friends to shine prodigiously [and] entertained them with theatrical chit-chat and the court circular; and so wound up a brilliant and fascinating conversation which he had maintained alone, and without any assistance whatever, for upwards of three-quarters of an hour." 40

—*ladykiller:* "Having had great experience of the [female] sex, and being perfectly acquainted with all those little artifices which find the readiest road to their hearts, Mr. Chuckster, on taking his ground, planted one hand on his hip, and with the other adjusted his flowing hair. This is a favourite attitude in the polite circles, and accompanied with a graceful whistling has been known to do immense execution." 69

The **Garlands** of Abel Cottage, Finchley. A "little fat placid-faced old gentleman (who had a club-foot) . . . [and a] little old lady, plump and placid like [her husband]." 14

—*their home:* "To be sure, it was a beautiful little cottage with a thatched roof and little spires at the gable-ends, and pieces of stained glass in some of the windows, almost as large as pocket-books. On one side of the house was a little stable, just the size for the pony, with a little room over it, just the size for **Kit**. White curtains were fluttering, and birds, in cages that looked as bright as if they were made of gold, were singing, at the windows; plants were arranged on either side of the path, and clustered about the door; and the garden was bright with flowers in full bloom, which shed a sweet odour all round, and had a charming and elegant appearance. Everything, within the house and without, seemed to be the perfection of neatness and order. In the garden there was not a weed to be seen, and to judge from some dapper gardening-tools, a basket, and pair of gloves which were lying in one of the walks, old Mr Garland had been at work in it that very morning." 22

Mrs Jarley.—*her caravan:* "It was not a shabby, dingy, dusty cart, but a smart little house upon wheels, with white dimity curtains festooning the windows, and window-shutters of green picked out with panels of a staring red, in which happily-contrasted colours the whole concern shone brilliant. Neither was it a poor caravan drawn by a single donkey or emaciated horse, for a pair of horses in pretty good condition were released from the shafts and grazing on the frowzy grass.

"Neither was it a gipsy caravan, for at the open door (graced with a bright brass knocker) sat a Christian lady, stout and comfortable to look upon, who wore a large bonnet trembling with bows. And that it was not an unprovided or destitute caravan was clear from this lady's occupation, which was the very pleasant and refreshing one of taking tea. The tea-things, including a bottle of rather suspicious character and a cold knuckle of ham, were set forth upon a drum, covered with a white napkin; and there, as if at the most convenient round-table in all the world, sat this roving lady, taking her tea and enjoying the prospect." ¶26

—*on her collection:* "'I never saw any wax-work, ma'am,' said **Nell**. 'Is it funnier than Punch?' . . .

"'It isn't funny at all,' repeated Mrs Jarley. 'It's calm and—what's that word again—critical?—no—classical, that's it—it's calm and classical. No low beatings and knockings about, no jokings and squeakings like your precious Punches, but always the same, with a constantly unchanging air of coldness and gentility; and so like life, that if wax-work only spoke and walked about, you'd hardly know the difference. I won't go so far as to say, that, as it is, I've seen wax-work quite like life, but I've certainly seen some life that was exactly like wax-work.'" 27

" . . . 'it's Jarley's wax-work, remember. The duty's very light and genteel, the company particular select, the exhibition takes place in assembly rooms, town-halls, large rooms at inns, or auction galleries. There is none of your open-air wagrancy at Jarley's, recollect; there is no tarpaulin and sawdust at Jarley's, remember. Every expectation held out in the handbills is realised to the utmost, and the whole forms an effect of imposing brilliancy hitherto unrivalled in this kingdom. Remember that the price of admission is only sixpence, and that this is an opportunity which may never occur again!'" 27

Mrs Jiniwin. "[She was] known to be laudably shrewish in her disposition and inclined to resist male authority. . . ." 4

—*her late husband:* "'When my poor husband, her dear father, was alive, if he had ever ventur'd a cross word to *me*, I'd have ——' the good old lady did not finish the sentence, but she twisted off the head of a shrimp with a vindictiveness which seemed to imply that the action was in some degree a substitute for words." 4

"'Her father was a blessed creetur, **Quilp**, and worth twenty thousand of some people,' said Mrs Jiniwin; 'twenty hundred million thousand.'

"'I should like to have known him,' remarked the dwarf. 'I dare say he was a blessed creature then; but I'm sure he is now. It was a happy release. I believe he had suffered a long time?'

"The old lady gave a gasp, but nothing came of it . . . . " 4

—*tormented:* "Mrs Jiniwin being very fond of cards was carefully excluded by her son-in-law from any participation in the game, and had assigned to her the duty of occasionally replenishing the glasses from the case-bottle; Mr **Quilp** from that moment keeping one eye constantly upon her, lest she should be any means procure a taste of the same, and thereby tantalising the wretched old lady (who was as much attached to the case-bottle as the cards) in a double degree and most ingenious manner." 23

The Marchioness. A "small slipshod girl in a dirty coarse apron and bib, which left nothing of her visible but her face and feet. She might as well have been dressed in a violin-case. . . . There never was such an old-fashioned child in her looks and manner. She must have been at work from her cradle." 34

—*her mystery:* " . . . the small servant always remained somewhere in the bowels of the earth under Bevis Marks, and never came to the surface unless the single gentleman rang his bell, when she would answer it and immediately disappear again. She never went out, or came into the office, or had a clean face, or took off the coarse apron, or looked out of any one of the windows, or stood at the street-door for a breath of air, or had any rest or enjoyment whatever. Nobody ever came to see her, nobody spoke of her, nobody cared about her. Mr **Brass** had said once, that he believed she was 'a love-child,' (which means anything but a child of love) and that was all the information **Richard Swiveller** could obtain." 36

—*as nurse:* " . . . the patient applied himself to his food with a keen appetite, though evidently not with a greater zest in the eating than his nurse appeared to have in seeing him eat. The manner of his meal was this:—Mr **Swiveller**, holding the slice of toast or cup of tea in his left hand, and taking a bite or drink as the case might be, constantly kept, in his right, one palm of the Marchioness tight locked; and to shake, or even to kiss this imprisoned hand, he would stop every now and then, in the very act of swallowing, with perfect seriousness of intention, and the utmost gravity.

"As often as he put anything into his mouth, whether for eating or drinking, the face of the Marchioness lighted up beyond all description; but whenever he gave her one or other of these tokens of recognition, her countenance became overshadowed, and she began to sob. Now, whenever she was in her laughing joy, or in her crying one, the Marchioness could not help turning to the visitors with an appealing look, which seemed to say, 'You see this fellow—can I help this?'—and they being thus made, as it were, parties to the scene, as regularly answered by another look, 'No. Certainly not.'" 66

—*later:* "Mr **Swiveller** kept the Marchioness at [a school of his selection] until she was, at a moderate guess, full nineteen years of age—good-looking, clever, and good-humoured; when he began to consider seriously what was to be done next. On one of his periodical visits, while he was revolving this question in his mind, the Marchioness came down to him, alone, looking more smiling and more fresh than ever. Then it occurred to him, but not for the first time, that if she would marry him, how comfortable they might be! So Richard asked her; whatever she said, it wasn't No . . . ." 73

—*renamed:* "After casting about for some time for a name which should be worthy of her, [**Dick**] decided in favour of **Sophronia Sphynx**, as being euphonious and genteel, and furthermore indicative of mystery." 73 *And see* **Sally Brass** OP—*to her clerk*

Mrs (**Betsy**) **Quilp**. "—a pretty little, mild-spoken, blue-eyed woman, who having allied herself in wedlock to the dwarf in one of those strange infatuations of which examples are by no means scarce, performed a sound practical penance for her folly, every day of her life." 4

—*complimented:* "'Oh you nice creature!' were the words with which [her husband] broke silence; smacking his lips as if this were no figure of speech, and she were actually a sweetmeat. 'Oh you precious darling! oh you delicious charmer!'

"Mrs Quilp sobbed; and knowing the nature of her pleasant lord, appeared quite as much alarmed by these compliments, as she would have been by the most extreme demonstrations of violence.

"'She's such,' said the dwarf, with a ghastly grin, 'such a jewel, such a diamond, such a pearl, such a ruby, such a golden casket set with gems of all sorts! She's such a treasure! I'm so fond of her!'

"The poor little woman shivered from head to foot; and raising her eyes to his face with an imploring look, suffered them to droop again, and sobbed once more.

"'The best of her is,' said the dwarf, advancing with a sort of skip, which, what with the crookedness of his legs, the ugliness of his face, and the mockery of his manner, was perfectly goblin-like;—'the best of her is that she's so meek, and she's so mild, and she never has a will of her own, and she has such an insinuating mother!'" 4

Tom Scott. ". . . an amphibious boy in a canvas suit, whose sole change of occupation was from sitting on the head of a pile and throwing stones into the mud when the tide was out, to standing with his hands in his pockets gazing listlessly on the motion and on the bustle of the river at high-water." 4

"Arrived at his destination, the first object that presented itself to [**Quilp's**] view was a pair of very imperfectly shod feet elevated in the air with the soles upwards, which remarkable appearance was referable to the boy, who being of an eccentric spirit and having a natural taste for tumbling was now standing on his head and contemplating the aspect of the river under these uncommon circumstances." 5

—*employer relations:* "'Why don't you hit one of your size?' . . .

"'Where is there one of my size, you dog?' returned Quilp. 'Take the key, or I'll brain you with it'—indeed he gave him a smart rap with the handle as he spoke. 'Now, open the counting-house.'

"The boy sulkily complied, muttering at first, but desisting when he looked round and saw that Quilp was following him with a steady look. And here it may be remarked, that between this boy and the dwarf there existed a strange kind of mutual liking. How born or bred, or how nourished upon blows and threats on one side, and retorts and defiances on the other, is not to the purpose. Quilp would certainly suffer nobody to contradict him but the boy, and the boy would assuredly not have submitted to be so knocked about by anybody but Quilp, when he had the power to run away at any time he chose." 5

Sophy Wackles. "Miss Sophy was a fresh, good-humoured, buxom girl of twenty . . . arrayed in virgin white, embellished by no ornament but one blushing rose, [she] received [**Dick Swiveller**]." 8

—*last words:* "'Are you going?' said Miss Sophy, whose heart sunk within her at the result of her stratagem, but who affected a light indifference notwithstanding.

"'Am I going!' echoed **Dick** bitterly. 'Yes, I am. What then?'

"'Nothing, except that it's very early,' said Miss Sophy, 'but you are your own master, of course.'

"'I would that I had been my own mistress too,' said Dick, 'before I had ever entertained a thought of you. Miss Wackles, I believed you true, and I was blest in so believing, but now I mourn that e'er I knew, a girl so fair yet so deceiving.'

"Miss Sophy bit her lip and affected to look with great interest after Mr **Cheggs**, who was quaffing lemonade in the distance." 8

The Grotesques

"'*It would be a curious speculation,*' said [the **Narrator**], *after some restless turns across and across the room, 'to imagine [**Nell**] in her future life, holding her solitary way among a crowd of wild grotesque companions; the only pure, fresh, youthful object in the throng. It would be curious to find —'*" 1

Thomas Codlin. "[He] took the money—had rather a careful and cautious look, which was perhaps inseparable from his occupation . . . a surly, grumbling manner . . . the air of a discontented philosopher." 16

—*on duty:* "And now Mr Thomas Codlin, the misanthrope, after blowing away at the Pan's pipes until he was intensely wretched, took his station on one side of the checked drapery which concealed the mover of the figures, and putting his hands in his pockets prepared to reply to all questions and remarks of Punch, and to make a dismal feint of being his most intimate private friend, of believing in him to the fullest and most unlimited extent, of knowing that he enjoyed day and night a merry and glorious existence in that temple, and that he was at all times and under every circumstance the same intelligent and joyful person that the spectators then beheld him. All this Mr Codlin did with the air of a man who had made up his mind for the worst and was quite resigned . . . ." 16

Furnace watcher. A man "miserably clad and begrimed with smoke, which, perhaps by its contrast with the natural colour of his skin, made him look paler than he really was. That he was naturally of a very wan and pallid aspect, however, his hollow cheeks, sharp features, and sunken eyes, no less than a certain look of patient endurance, sufficiently testified. His voice was harsh by nature, but not brutal; and though his face . . . was overshadowed by a quantity of long dark hair, its expression was neither ferocious nor cruel." 44

Grinder, and his Lot. "Mr. Grinder's company, familiarly termed a lot, consisted of a young gentleman and a young lady on stilts, and Mr. Grinder himself, who used his natural legs for pedestrian purposes and carried at his back a drum. The public costume of the young people was of the Highland kind, but the night being damp and cold, the young gentleman wore over his kilt a man's pea jacket reaching to his ankles, and a glazed hat; the young lady too was muffled in an old cloth pelisse and had a handkerchief tied about her head. Their Scotch bonnets, ornamented with plumes of jet black feathers, Mr Grinder carried on his instrument.

"'Bound for the races, I see,' said Mr Grinder, coming up out of breath. 'So are we. How are you, **Short**?' With that they shook hands in a very friendly manner. The young people being too high up for the ordinary salutations, saluted Short after their own fashion. The young gentleman twisted up his right stilt and patted him on the shoulder, and the young lady rattled her tambourine.

"'Practice?' said Short, pointing to the stilts.

"'No, returned Grinder. 'It comes either to walkin' in 'em or carryin' of 'em, and they like walkin' in 'em best. It's wery pleasant for the prospects.'" 17

Harris ("Short Trotters"). ". . . the actual exhibitor . . . was a little, merry-faced man with a twinkling eye and a red nose, who seemed to have unconsciously imbibed something of [Punch] his hero's character." 14

"[His surname] had gradually merged into the less euphonious one of Trotters, which, with the prefatory adjective, Short, had been conferred upon him by reason of the small size of his legs . . . [he] was known among his intimates either as 'Short,' or 'Trotters,' and was seldom accosted at full length as Short Trotters, except in formal conversations and on occasions of ceremony." 17

Jerry, and his **dogs**. A "tall black-whiskered man in a velveteen coat [and] four very dismal dogs . . . who immediately stood upon their hind legs, in a grave and melancholy row . . . each of them wore a kind of little coat of some gaudy colour trimmed with tarnished spangles, and one of them had a cap fallen down upon his nose and completely obscured one eye. . . . So there the dogs stood, patiently winking and gaping and looking extremely hard at the boiling pot, until Jerry himself appeared, when they all dropped down at once and walked about the room in their natural manner. This posture it must be confessed did not much improve their appearance, as their own personal tails and their coat tails—both capital things in their way—did not agree together." 18

Joe (or **Mat**) **Jowl**, gambler. "The man with the rough voice was a burly fellow of middle age, with large black whiskers, broad cheeks, a coarse wide mouth, and bull neck, which was pretty freely displayed as his shirt-collar was only confined by a loose red neckerchief. He wore his hat, which was of a brownish-white, and had beside him a thick knotted stick." 29 (Mat) and 42 (Joe)

Isaac List, gambler. "[He had a] sharp, cracked voice of most disagreeable quality . . . a slender figure—stooping, and high in the shoulders—with a very ill-favoured face, and a most sinister and villanous squint." 29

Maunders, menagerie proprietor. "' . . . Maunders had in his cottage . . . eight male and female **dwarfs** setting down to dinner every day, who was waited on by eight old **giants** in green coats, red smalls, blue cotton stockings, and high-lows: and there was one dwarf as had grown elderly and wicious who whenever his giant wasn't quick enough to please him, used to stick pins in his legs, not being able to reach up any higher.'" 19

Sweet William. A "silent gentleman who earned his living by showing tricks upon the cards, and who had rather deranged the natural expression of his countenance by putting small leaden lozenges into his eyes and bringing them out of his mouth, which was one of his professional accomplishments [and] probably as a satire on his ugliness was called Sweet William." 19

Vuffin, giant proprietor. "'The older a dwarf is, the better worth he is. A grey-headed dwarf, well wrinkled, is beyond all suspicion. But a giant weak in the legs and not standing upright!—keep him in the carawan, but never show him, never show him, for any persuasion that can be offered.'" 19

Others

Boy. "A small white-headed boy with a sunburnt face appeared at the door while [the schoolmaster] was speaking, and stopping there to make a rustic bow, came in and took his seat upon one of the forms. The white-headed boy then put an open book, astonishingly dog's-eared, upon his knees, and thrusting his hands into his pockets began counting the marbles with which they were filled; displaying in the expression of his face a remarkable capacity of totally abstracting his mind from the spelling on which his eyes were fixed." 25

Boys. " . . . another white-headed little boy came straggling in, and after him a red-headed lad, and after him two more with white heads, and then one with a flaxen poll, and so on until the forms were occupied by a dozen boys or thereabouts, with heads of every colour but grey, and ranging in their ages from four years old to fourteen years or more; for the legs of the youngest were a long way from the floor when he sat upon the form, and the eldest was a heavy good-tempered foolish fellow, about half a head taller than the schoolmaster." 25

Alick Cheggs. "A stricken market-gardener known to be ready with his offer [for **Sophy**'s hand] on the smallest encouragement [who] came not alone or unsupported, for he prudently brought along with him his sister, **Miss Cheggs**. . ." 8

—*moved:* " . . . [his sister] declaring that she was frightened to death lest Alick should fall upon, and beat [**Swiveller**], in the fullness of his wrath, and entreating **Miss Sophy** to observe how the eyes of the said Alick gleamed with love and fury; passions, it may be observed, which being too much for his eyes rushed into his nose also, and suffused it with a crimson glow." 8

Miss Cheggs. " . . .not confining herself to expressing by scornful smiles a contempt for Mr. **Swiveller**'s [terpsichorean] accomplishments, she took every opportunity of whispering into Miss **Sophy**'s ear expressions of condolence and sympathy on her being worried by such a ridiculous creature . . . . " 8 *And see* **Alick Cheggs**—*moved*

Child. **Nell** "drew near and asked one of [the children] whose grave it was. The child answered that that was not its name; it was a garden—his brother's. It was greener, he said, than all the other gardens, and the birds loved it better because he had been used to feed them. When he had done speaking, he looked at her with a smile, and kneeling down and nestling for a moment with his cheek against the turf, bounded merrily away." 53 *And see* **Willy**

" . . . he would often come, even in the dark evenings, and call in a timid voice outside the door to know if she were safe within; and being answered yes, and bade to enter, would take his station on a low stool at her feet, and sit there patiently until they came to seek, and take him home. Sure as the morning came, it found him lingering near the house to ask if she were well; and, morning, noon, or night, go where she would, he would forsake his playmates and his sports to bear her company." 55

Clergyman. "He was a simple-hearted old gentleman, of a shrinking, subdued spirit, accustomed to retirement, and very little acquainted with the world . . ." 52

Constable. "This functionary . . . looking upon all kinds of robbery from petty larceny up to housebreaking or ventures on the highway as matters in the regular course of business, and regarding the perpetrators in the light of so many customers coming to be served at the wholesale and retail shop of criminal law where he stood behind the counter . . . took **Kit** into custody with a decent indifference." 60

Davy, a deaf gravedigger. "[He] did the sexton's duty [and] was a little older than he, though much more active." 54 *See* **Becky Morgan**

Doctor. " . . . a red-nosed gentleman with a great bunch of seals dangling below a waistcoat of ribbed black satin . . . looked at [**Nell**'s] tongue, then he felt her pulse again, and while he did so, he eyed the half-emptied wine-glass as if in profound abstraction. 'I should give her,' said the doctor at length, 'a teaspoonful every now and then, of hot brandy and water.' 'Why, that's exactly what we've done sir!' said the delighted landlady . . . .

" . . . . Everybody said he was a very shrewd doctor indeed, and knew perfectly what people's constitutions were; which there appears some reason to suppose he did." 46

Miss Edwards. A "young lady of about fifteen or sixteen" with "a sweet voice . . . who only paid a small premium which had been spent long ago . . . . " 32

Miss Edwards the younger. " . . . much younger than **Nell**, whom [Miss **Edwards**] had not seen for five years, and to bring whom to that place on a short visit, she had been saving her poor means all that time." 32

Richard Evans. "'Now look at that lad, sir,' said the **bachelor** . . . . 'An amazing boy to learn, blessed with a good memory, and a ready understanding, and moreover with a good voice and ear for psalm-singing, in which he is the best among us. Yet, sir, that boy will come to a bad end; he'll never die in his bed; he's always falling asleep in church in sermon-time . . . ." 52

Abel Garland. "[He] had a quaint old-fashioned air about him, looked nearly of the same age as his father, and bore a wonderful resemblance to him in face and figure, though wanting something of his full, round cheerfulness, and substituting in its place a timid reserve. In all other respects, in the neatness of the dress, and even in the club-foot, he and the old gentleman were precisely alike." 14

George, a driver. " . . . in a carter's frock . . . [he] appeared in a sitting attitude, supporting on his legs a baking-dish and a half-gallon stone bottle, and bearing in his right hand a knife, and in his left a fork . . . after scraping the dish all round with his knife and carrying the choice brown morsels to his mouth, and after taking such a scientific pull at the stone bottle that, by degrees almost imperceptible to the sight, his head went further and further back until he lay nearly at his full length upon the ground, this gentleman declared himself quite disengaged, and came forth from his retreat. 'I hope I haven't hurried you, George,' said [**Mrs. Jarley**] . . . . " 26

Mrs George. " . . . a stout lady opened the proceedings by inquiring, with an air of great concern and sympathy, how Mr **Quilp** was . . . .'I wish you'd give her a little of your advice, Mrs **Jiniwin** . . . nobody knows better than you, ma'am, what us women owe to ourselves.'" 4

Jem Groves, landlord. "' . . .honest Jem Groves, as is a man of unblemished moral character, and has a good dry skittle-ground. If any man has got anything to say against Jem Groves, let him say it *to* Jem Groves, and Jem Groves can accommodate him with a customer on any terms from four pounds a side to forty.'

"With these words, the speaker tapped himself on the waist-coat to intimate that he was the Jem Groves so highly eulogized, sparred scientifically at a counterfeit Jem Groves, who was sparring at society in general from a black frame over the chimney-piece, and applying a half-emptied glass of spirits and water to his lips, drank Jem Groves's health." 29

Harry. "He was a very young boy; quite a little child. His hair still hung in curls about his face, and his eyes were very bright; but their light was of Heaven, not earth . . . the little scholar turned his face towards the wall, and fell asleep.

"The poor schoolmaster sat in the same place, holding the small cold hand in his, and chafing it. It was but the hand of a dead child. He felt that; and yet he chafed it still, and could not lay it down." 25

Ladies of the neighbourhood. " . . . it is no wonder that the ladies felt an inclination to talk and linger, especially when there are taken into account the additional inducements of fresh butter, new bread, shrimps, and water-cresses.

"Now, the ladies being together under these circumstances, it was extremely natural that the discourse should turn upon the propensity of mankind to tyrannise over the weaker sex, and the duty that devolved upon the weaker sex to resist that tyranny and assert their rights and dignity. It was natural for four reasons: firstly because **Mrs Quilp** being a young woman and notoriously under the dominion of her husband ought to be excited to rebel, secondly because Mrs Quilp's parent was known to be laudably shrewish in her disposition and inclined to resist male authority, thirdly because each visitor wished to show for herself how superior she was in this respect to the generality of her sex, and fourthly because the company being accustomed to scandalise each other in pairs were deprived of their usual subject of conversation now that they were all assembled in close friendship, and had consequently no better employment than to attack the common enemy." 4

Lady (from the Minories). "'Mr **Quilp** may be a very nice man,' said this lady, 'and I suppose there's no doubt he is, because **Mrs Quilp** says he is, and **Mrs Jiniwin** says he is, and they ought to know, or nobody does. But still he is not quite a—what one calls a handsome man, nor quite a young man neither, which might be a little excuse for him if anything could be; whereas his wife is young, and is good-looking, and is a woman— which is the great thing, after all.'" 4

Landlord. " . . . with a roguish look he held the cover in his hand, and, feigning that his doing so was needful to the welfare of the cookery, suffered the delightful steam to tickle the nostrils of his guest. The glow of the fire was upon the landlord's bald head, and upon his twinkling eye, and upon his watering mouth, and upon his pimpled face, and upon his round fat figure." 18

Marton, schoolmaster. "He was a pale, simple-looking man, of a spare and meagre habit, and sat among his flowers and beehives, smoking his pipe, in the little porch before his door. . . . He had a kind face . . . . They fancied, too, a lonely air about him and his house . . . . " 24

Miss Monflathers, school proprietor. Her "awful door . . . turned slowly upon its hinges with a creaking noise, and, forth from the solemn grove beyond, came a long file of young ladies, two and two, all with open books in their hands, and some with parasols likewise. And last of the goodly procession came Miss Monflathers, bearing herself a parasol of lilac silk, and supported by two smiling teachers, each mortally envious of the other, and devoted unto Miss Monflathers." 31

—on work for the poor: "' . . . don't you think you must be a very wicked little child,' said Miss Monflathers, who was of rather uncertain temper, and lost no opportunity of impressing moral truths upon the tender minds of the young ladies, 'to be a wax-work child at all? . . . . Don't you know that it's very naughty and unfeminine, and a perversion of the properties wisely and benignantly transmitted to us, with expansive powers to be roused from their dormant state through the medium of cultivation? . . . Don't you feel how naughty it is of you to be a wax-work child, when you might have the proud consciousness of assisting, to the extent of your infant powers, the manufactures of your country; of improving your mind by the constant contemplation of the steam-engine; and of earning a comfortable and independent subsistence of from two-and-ninepence to three shillings per week? Don't you know that the harder you are at work, the happier you are?'" 31 *And see* **Parlourmaid**

Becky Morgan. "'I have been thinking, **Davy**,' replied the sexton, 'that she,' he pointed to the grave, 'must have been a deal older than your or me . . . Davy, women don't always tell the truth about their age . . . . I call to mind the time her daughter died. She was eighty-nine if she was a day, and tries to pass upon us now, for ten year younger. Oh! human vanity!'" 54

Mother, of **Barbara**. "Barbara's mother came in with astonishing accounts of the fineness of the weather out of doors (but with a very large umbrella notwithstanding, for people like Barbara's mother seldom make holiday without one) . . . . " 39

Narrator (Master Humphrey). "Night is generally my time for walking . . . saving in the country I seldom go out until after dark . . . .

"I have fallen insensibly into this habit, both because it favours my infirmity and because it affords me greater opportunity of speculating on the characters and occupations of those who fill the streets." 1

"'You are such a very old gentleman, [said **Nell**] and walk so slow yourself.'" 1

Baby Nubbles. " . . . a sturdy boy of two or three years old, very wide awake, with a very tight night-cap on his head, and a night-gown very much too small for him on his body, was sitting bolt upright in a clothes- basket, staring over the rim with his great round eyes, and looking as if he had thoroughly made up his mind never to go to sleep any more; which, as he had been brought out of bed in consequence, opened a cheerful prospect for his relations and friends." 10

—at celebration: "There was the baby too, who had never closed an eye all night, but had sat as good as gold, trying to force a large orange into his mouth, and gazing intently at the lights in the chandelier—there he was, sitting up in his mother's lap, staring at the gas without winking, and making indentations in his soft visage with an oyster-shell, to that degree that a heart of iron must have loved him." 39

Jacob Nubbles. "[He was] the greatest miracle of the night . . . who ate oysters as if he had been born and bred to the business, sprinkled the pepper and the vinegar with a discretion beyond his years, and afterwards built a grotto on the table with the shells." 39

Mrs Nubbles. "The room in which **Kit** sat himself down . . . was extremely poor and homely place, but with that air of comfort about it, nevertheless, which . . . cleanliness and order can always impart in some degree. Late as the Dutch clock showed it to be, the poor woman was still hard at work at an ironing table . . ." 10

Old lady. " . . . finding that she could not inflame or irritate the peaceable schoolmaster by talking to him, [she] bounced out of his house and talked at him for half-an-hour outside his own window, to another old lady, saying that of course he would deduct this half-holiday from his weekly charge, or of course he would naturally expect to have an opposition started against him; there was no want of idle chaps in that neighbourhood (here the old lady raised her voice), and some chaps who were too idle even to be schoolmasters, might soon find that there were other chaps put over their heads, and so she would have them take care, and look pretty sharp about them." 25

John Owen. "' . . . a lad of good parts, sir, and frank, honest temper; but too thoughtless, too playful, too light-headed by far. That boy, my good sir, would break his neck with pleasure, and deprive his parents of their chief comfort—and between ourselves, when you come to see him at hare and hounds, taking the fence and ditch by the finger-post, and sliding down the face of the little quarry, you'll never forget it. It's beautiful!'" 52

Parents. " . . . in the course of the afternoon several mothers and aunts of pupils looked in to express their entire disapproval of the schoolmaster's proceeding [in giving the boys the afternoon off]. A few confined themselves to hints, such as politely inquiring what red-letter day or saint's day the almanack said it was; a few (these were the profound village politicians) argued that it was a slight to the Throne and an affront to Church and State, and savoured of revolutionary principles, to grant a half-holiday upon any lighter occasion than the birthday of the Monarch; but the majority expressed their displeasure on private grounds and in plain terms, arguing that to put the pupils on this short allowance of learning was . . . downright robbery and fraud . . . . " 25

Parlourmaid. "**Miss Monflathers's** . . . was a large house, with a high wall, and large garden-gate with a large brass plate, and a small grating through which [her] parlourmaid inspected all visitors before admitting them; for nothing in the shape of a man—no, not even a milkman—was suffered, without special licence, to pass that gate." 31

Porter. " . . . there stood a strong man, with a mighty hamper, which being hauled into the room and presently unpacked, disgorged . . . treasures of tea, and coffee, and wine, and rusks, and oranges, and grapes, and fowls ready trussed for boiling, and calves'-foot jelly, and arrow-root, and sago, and other delicate restoratives . . . . " 66

Preacher. He held forth at Little Bethel Chapel, which "was not badly named in one respect, being in truth a particularly little Bethel—a Bethel of the smallest dimensions—with a small number of small pews, and a small pulpit, in which a small gentleman (by trade a Shoemaker, and by calling a Divine) was delivering in a by no means small voice, a by no means small sermon, judging of its dimensions by the condition of his audience, which, if their gross amount were but small, comprised a still smaller number of hearers, as the majority were slumbering." 41

Sexton. He admitted to "'seventy-nine years old—next summer,'" whose memory was a poor one: "'That's nothing new,' he added hastily. 'It always was.'" 53

" . . . both [sexton and **Davy**] adduced a mass of evidence; of such weight as to render it doubtful—not whether the deceased was of the age suggested, but whether she had not almost reached the patriarchal term of a hundred . . . .

"And so they parted: each persuaded that the other had less life in him than himself; and both greatly consoled and comforted by the little fiction they had agreed upon, respecting Becky Morgan, whose decease was no longer a precedent of uncomfortable application, and would be no business of theirs for half-a-score of years to come." 54

Henrietta Simmons. "**Mrs George** remarked that people would talk, that people had often said this [concerning **Quilp**'s tyranny] to her before, that . . . she had always said, 'No, Henrietta Simmons, unless I see it with my own eyes and hear it with my own ears, I never will believe it.' Mrs Simmons corroborated this testimony . . . . " 4

Slum. A poet with an "insinuating manner" — a "tallish gentleman with a hook nose and black hair, dressed in a military surtout very short and tight in the sleeves, and which had once been frogged and braided all over but was now sadly shorn of its garniture and quite threadbare —dressed too in ancient grey pantaloons fitting tight to the leg, and a pair of pumps in the winter of their existence . . ." 28

Swimmer. "'But if we talk of examples to be shunned . . . this one with the blue eyes and light hair. This is a swimmer, sir, this fellow—a diver, Lord save us! This is a boy, sir, who had a fancy for plunging into eighteen feet of water with his clothes on and bringing up a blind man's dog, who was being drowned by the weight of his chain and collar, while his master stood wringing his hands upon the bank, bewailing the loss of his guide and friend.'" 52

Frederick Trent. " . . . [he] stood lounging with his foot upon a chair, and regarded [his grandfather] with a contemptuous sneer. He was a young man of one-and-twenty or thereabouts; well made, and certainly handsome, though the expression of his face was far from prepossessing, having in common with his manner and even his dress, a dissipated, insolent air which repelled one." 2

—*described by his grandfather:* "'A profligate, sir, who has forfeited every claim not only upon those who have the misfortune to be of his blood, but upon society which knows nothing of him but his misdeeds. A liar too . . . .'" 2

Turnkey. " . . . the turnkey read his newspaper with a waggish look (he had evidently got among the facetious paragraphs) until, happening to take his eyes off it for an instant, as if to get by dint of contemplation at the very marrow of some joke of a deeper sort than the rest, it appeared to occur to him for the first time that somebody was crying.

"'Now, ladies, ladies,' he said, looking round with surprise, 'I'd advise you not to waste time like this. It's allowanced here, you know. You mustn't let that child make that noise either. It's against all rules.'" 61

Wackles family and its Ladies Seminary. "The spot was at Chelsea, for there Miss Sophia [**Sophy**] Wackles resided with her widowed mother and two sisters, in conjunction with whom she maintained a very small day-school for young ladies of proportionate dimensions . . . . The several duties of instruction in this establishment were thus discharged. English grammar, composition, geography, and the use of the dumbbells, by Miss **Melissa** Wackles; writing, arithmetic, dancing, music, and general fascination, by Miss Sophy Wackles; the art of needle-work, marking and samplery, by Miss **Jane** Wackles; corporal punishment, fasting, and other tortures and terrors, by **Mrs Wackles**." 8

—**Jane**, "who had kept her head during the whole of the preceding day screwed up tight in a yellow play-bill. . . . being one of those young ladies who are prematurely shrill and shrewish, gave such undue importance to her part that Mr **Swiveller** retired in dudgeon . . . . " 8

—**Melissa** "was the eldest daughter, Miss **Sophy** the next, and Miss **Jane** the youngest. Miss Melissa might have seen five-and-thirty summers or thereabouts, and verged on the autumnal . . . . " 8

—**Mrs Wackles** "was an excellent but rather venomous old lady of threescore." 8

Waiter. "[Kit] ordered a fierce gentleman with whiskers, who acted as waiter and called him, him, Christopher Nubbles, 'sir,' to bring three dozen of his largest-sized oysters, and to look sharp about it . . . and both Kit's mother and **Barbara**'s mother declared as he turned away that he was one of the slimmest and gracefullest young men she had ever looked upon." 39

Dame West. "'He's going fast,' cried the old woman; [**Harry**], 'my grandson's dying. It's all along of you. You shouldn't see him now, but for his being so earnest on it. This is what his learning has brought him to. Oh dear, dear, dear, what can I do! . . . .If he hadn't been poring over his books out of fear of you, he would have been well and merry now, I know he would.'" 25

Whisker. A "little obstinate-looking rough-coated pony . . . the utmost the pony would consent to do, was to go in his own way up any street that [Mr **Garland**] particularly wished to traverse, but that it was an understanding between them that he must do this after his own fashion or not at all." 14

" . . . there came dancing up the street, with his legs all wrong, and his head everywhere by turns, a pony . . . neither man nor phaeton seemed to embarrass him in the least, as he reared up on his hind legs, or stopped or went on, or stood still again, or backed, or went sideways, without the smallest reference to them, just as the fancy seized him, and as if he was the freest animal in the creation." 65

Widow. "' . . . I know that if I was to die to-morrow, **Quilp** could marry anybody he pleased . . . . '

" . . . . Marry whom he pleased! They would like to see him dare to think of marrying any of them . . . . One lady (a widow) was quite certain she should stab him if he hinted at it." 4

Willy. "'Willy went away, to join [the angels]; but if he had known how I should miss him in our little bed at night, he never would have left me, I am sure [said the child].'" 55

Witherden, the Notary, "who was short, chubby, fresh-coloured, brisk, and pompous . . . ." 14

—*in high legal form*: "'Come, come, **Miss Brass**,' said the Notary, 'you have great command of feature, but you feel, I see, that by a chance which never entered your imagination, this base design is revealed, and two of its plotters must be brought to justice. Now, you know the pains and penalties you are liable to, and so I need not dilate upon them, but I have a proposal to make to you . . . do us the favour to reveal the whole history of this affair. Let me remind you that your doing so, at our instance, will place you in a safe and comfortable position—your present one is not desirable—and cannot injure your brother . . . . " 66

Young lady. " . . . the most bashful young lady that was ever seen, with whom Mr **Abel** happened to fall in love. How it happened, or how they found it out, or which of them first communicated the discovery to the other, nobody knows . . . . " 73

Walk-ons

Barber. "Certain machinery in the body of the nun on the leads over the doors was cleaned up and put in motion, so that the figure shook its head paralytically all day long, to the great admiration of a drunken, but very Protestant, barber over the way, who looked upon the said paralytic motion as typical of the degrading effect wrought upon the human mind by the ceremonies of the Romish Church, and discoursed upon that theme with great eloquence and morality." 32

Bargemen. "A man of very uncouth and rough appearance was standing over [**Nell** and her **grandfather**], and two of his companions were looking on from a long heavy boat which had come close to the bank while they were sleeping . . . . " 43

Boy, deaf and dumb. "'Here, woman [said the **magistrate**] . . . . He was brought before me this morning charged with theft; and with any other boy it would have gone hard, I assure you. But as I had compassion on his infirmities, and thought he might have learnt no better, I have managed to bring him back to you. Take more care of him for the future.'" 45

Foxey Brass. "'You will not have forgotten [said **Sampson Brass**] that it was a maxim with Foxey—our revered father, gentlemen—"Always suspect everybody." That's the maxim to go through life with! . . . '" 66

Brown. "(. . . who was supposed to be then a corporal in the East Indies, and who could of course be found with very little trouble), [to be a character reference for **Kit**]". 21

Butcher. "The very butcher respected [**Miss Monflathers**'s gate] as a gate of mystery, and left off whistling when he rang the bell." 31

Carrier. "**Kit** arrived in course of time at the carrier's house, where, to the lasting honour of human nature, he found the box in safety. Receiving from the wife of this immaculate man, a direction to Mr **Garland**'s, he took the box upon his shoulder and repaired thither directly." 22

Carter. "The driver on coming up to them stopped his horse and looked earnestly at **Nell**.

"'Didn't you stop to rest at a cottage yonder?' he said. . . . 'They asked me to look out for you . . . I'm going your way. Give me your hand—jump up, master.'" 16

Two **carters**. They "constantly passed in and out of the exhibition-room, under various disguises, protesting aloud that the [wax-works] sight was better worth the money than anything they had beheld in all their lives, and urging the bystanders, with tears in their eyes, not to neglect such a brilliant gratification." 32

Chambermaid. "'When the chambermaid asked [**Quilp**] just now if he should want a bed, sir, he first made faces at her, and then wanted to kiss her.'" 48

Coachman. " . . . the single gentleman's trunk . . . being nearly twice as wide as the staircase, and exceedingly heavy withal, it was no easy matter for the united exertions of the single gentleman and the coachman to convey up the steep ascent." 34

Cottagers. " . . . there was an old man sitting in a cushioned chair beside the hearth . . . . There were besides, the cottager and his wife, and three young sturdy children, brown as berries . . . . The eldest boy ran out to fetch some milk, the second dragged two stools towards the door, and the youngest crept to his mother's gown and looked at the strangers from beneath his sunburnt hand." 15

Daughter, of a Baronet, "who learned all the extras (or was taught them all) and whose half-yearly bill came to double that of any other young lady's in the school . . . [and] who, by some extraordinary reversal of the Laws of Nature, was not only plain in features but dull in intellect, while the poor apprentice had both a ready wit, and a handsome face and figure." 31

Day scholars. "Looking into the eyes of Mrs and Miss **Wackles** for encouragement, and sitting very upright and uncomfortable on a couple of hard stools, were two of the day-scholars . . . ." 8

Defense attorney. " . . . when one of the gentlemen in wigs got up and said 'I am for the prisoner my Lord,' **Kit** made him a bow . . . . Then, Kit's gentleman takes [**Brass**] in hand, but can make nothing of him; and after a great many very long questions and very short answers, Mr Sampson Brass goes down in glory." 63

Gipsy. " . . . a tall, athletic man, who stood with his arms folded, leaning against a tree a little distance off, looking now at the fire, and now, under his black eyelashes, at three other men who were there, with a watchful but half-concealed interest in their conversation." 42 [*This is a rare CD loose end: nothing more is heard of this character.*]

Green. A "lodger, at the cheesemonger's round the corner," character reference for **Kit**. 21

Lady, alone. "There was but one lady who seemed to understand the child, and she was one who sat alone in a handsome carriage . . . . She motioned away a **gipsy-woman** urgent to tell her fortune, saying that it was told already and had been for some years, but called [**Nell**] towards her, and taking her flowers put money into her trembling hand, and bade her go home and keep at home for God's sake." 19

Landlady of a small inn, "who possessed more readiness and activity than [the rest], and who had withal a quicker perception of the merits of the case, soon came running in with a little hot brandy and water [for **Nell**]." 46

Landlord and **landlady** in a country town. "The public-house was kept by a fat old landlord and landlady who made no objection to receiving their new guests, but praised **Nelly**'s beauty and were at once prepossessed in her behalf." 16

Magistrate. "In the centre [of the room] stood a grave gentleman in black who . . . held by the arm a boy." 45 *See* **Boy**, deaf and dumb.

Mail-guard. " . . . the mail came dashing past like a highway comet, with gleaming lamps and rattling hoofs, and visions of a guard behind, standing up to keep his feet warm . . . . " 46

Man, starving. "'What would you have here?' said a gaunt miserable man. . . . 'Do you see that?' returned the man hoarsely, pointing to a kind of bundle on the ground. 'That's a dead child. I and five hundred other men were thrown out of work three months ago. That is my third dead child, and last. Do you think I have charity to bestow, or a morsel of bread to spare?'" 45

Two **mothers**. "It seemed that a couple of poor families lived in this hovel, for two women, each among children of her own, occupied different portions of the room." 45

Movers. " . . . divers strong men in carpet caps were balancing chests of drawers and other trifles of that nature upon their heads, and performing muscular feats which heightened their complexions considerably." 13

Newsmonger. "As they pass through the dismal passages, some officers of the jail who are in waiting there, congratulate [**Kit**] in their rough way on his release. The newsmonger is of the number, but his manner is not quite hearty—there is something of surliness in his compliments. He looks upon Kit as an intruder, as one who has obtained admission to that place on false pretences; who had enjoyed a privilege without being duly qualified." 68

Nurses. "There was watching enough, now, but it was the watching of strangers who made a greedy trade of it, and who, in the intervals of their attendance upon the sick man [**Nell's Grandfather**] huddled together with a ghastly good-fellowship, and ate and drank and made merry; for disease and death were their ordinary household gods." 11

Old gentleman. "Miss **Jane Wackles** . . . in all the glory of her curls was holding a flirtation (as good practice when no better was to be had) with a feeble old gentleman who lodged in the parlour." 8

Performers at Astley's. " . . . the forlorn lady, who made [**Barbara**] cry— the tyrant, who made her tremble—the man who sang the song with the lady's-maid and danced the chorus, who made her laugh—the pony who reared up on his hind legs when he saw the murderer, and wouldn't hear of walking on all-fours again until he was taken into custody—the clown who ventured on such familiarities with the military man in boots—the lady who jumped over the nine-and-twenty ribbons and came down safe upon the horse's back. . . ." 39

Post-boy. "The boy on the wheeler touched his hat, and setting spurs to his horse, to the end that they might go in brilliantly, all four broke into a smart canter . . . . " 47

Prosecuting attorney. "The gentleman who was against [**Kit**] had to speak first, and being in dreadfully good spirits (for he had, in the last trial, very nearly procured the acquittal of a young gentleman who had had the misfortune to murder his father) he spoke up, you may be sure; telling the Jury that if they acquitted this prisoner they must expect to suffer no less pangs and agonies than he had told the other Jury they would certainly undergo if they convicted that prisoner." 63

Servant-girl, at a small inn. "[The landlady was] followed by her servant-girl, carrying vinegar, hartshorn, smelling salts, and such other restoratives [for **Nell**]. . . . " 46

Violetta Stretta. Notedly "of the Italian opera," in **Chuckster**'s gossip. 40

Rebecca Swiveller, spinster aunt of Cheselbourne in Dorsetshire. "'Deceased!' cried **Dick**." 66

Tax-gatherer. " . . . stout, and wore spectacles and a broad-brimmed hat, had the taxes handed through the grating." 31

Toby. "In some versions of the great drama of Punch there is a small dog . . . . This Toby has been stolen in youth from another gentleman, and fraudulently sold to the confiding hero, who having no guile himself has no suspicion that it lurks in others; but Toby, entertaining a grateful recollection of his old master, and scorning to attach himself to any new patrons, not only refuses to smoke a pipe at the bidding of Punch, but to mark his old fidelity more strongly, seizes him by the nose and wrings the same with violence, at which instance of canine attachment the spectators are deeply affected." 18

Turnpike collector. " . . . [the Punch and Judy show] . . . once exhibited by particular desire at a turnpike, where the collector, being drunk in his solitude, paid down a shilling to have it to himself." 17

Turnpike-man. " . . . he answered with a smothered shout from under the bedclothes in the little room above, where the faint light was burning, and presently came down, nightcapped and shivering, to throw the gate wide open, and wish all waggons off the road except by day." 46

Waterside men. "There were also present a couple of waterside men, bearing between them certain machines called drags; even these fellows were accommodated with a stiff glass a-piece; and as they drank with a great relish, and were naturally of a red-nosed, pimple-faced, convivial look, their presence rather increased than detracted from that decided appearance of comfort . . . of the [mourning] party." 49

Widow, "bent with the weight of years, who tottered to the foot of that same grave and asked [**Nell**] to read the writing on the stone . . . . 'Yes, I was his wife. Death doesn't change us more than life, my dear.'" 17

Luke Withers. "'I haven't seen such a storm as this . . . since the night when old Luke Withers won thirteen times running, upon the red. We all said he had the Devil's luck and his own, and as it was the kind of night for the Devil to be out and busy, I suppose he *was* looking over his shoulder, if anybody could have seen him.'" 29

Smart **young fellow**. "Having married the first time at her mother's instigation, [**Mrs Quilp**] consulted in her second choice nobody but herself. It fell upon a smart young fellow enough; and as he made it a preliminary condition that Mrs **Jiniwin** should be thenceforth an out-pensioner, they lived together after marriage with no more than the average amount of quarrelling, and led a merry life upon the dead dwarf's money." 73

The Lamplighter

CD tried the farce on actor William Macready, who thought its plot meagre. It was CD's last attempt to be a playwright. He included the story version (below) in a three-volume collection of pieces by various writers, which he edited.

Tom Grig, exemplary lamplighter, is collared by an eccentric astrologer, who casts his horoscope and identifies him as the intended of his niece **Fanny Barker**, heiress to £5,000 He has picked his colleague, **Mooney,** to marry his daughter **Emma.** The ladies object: Emma loves Mooney, and Fanny turns to Tom, but he is willing to take the fortune even though his death in two months is part of the prediction.

The crucible explodes, destroying the £5,000 investment; the prediction is erroneous. Tom keeps his freedom. A sub-plot touches the transition, from lamps requiring hand lighting by the likes of the hero, to piped Gas.

CONTENTS

CHARACTERS

Principals

Astrologer. "'Gentlemen [said the **Narrator**], he was one of the strangest and most mysterious-looking files that ever **Tom** clapped his eyes on. He was dressed all slovenly and untidy, in a great gown of a kind of bed-furniture pattern, with a cap of the same on his head; and a long old flapped waistcoat; with no braces, no strings, very few buttons—in short, with hardly any of those artificial contrivances that hold society together. Tom knew by these signs, and by his not being shaved, and by his not being over-clean, and by a sort of wisdom not quite awake, in his face, that he was a scientific old gentleman. He often told me that if he could have conceived the possibility of the whole Royal Society being boiled down into one man, he should have said the old gentleman's body was that Body.'"

Fanny Barker, the Astrologer's niece. "'"She's beautiful! . . . She has a graceful carriage, an exquisite shape, a sweet voice, a countenance beaming with animation and expression; and the eye," he says, rubbing his hands, "of a startled fawn."'"

Emma, the astrologer's daughter. "'"The maddening interview of this one night has filled my soul with love . . . for thee, for thee, young man,' she cries to **Tom**. 'As **Monk Lewis**[H] finely observes, Thomas, Thomas, I am thine, Thomas, Thomas, thou art mine: thine for ever, mine for ever!' with which words, she became very tender likewise.'"

Tom Grig. "[He had] a bran-new ladder, a white hat, a brown holland jacket and trousers, a blue neckerchief, and a sprig of full-blown double wallflower in his button-hole. Tom was always genteel in his appearance, and I have heard from the best judges, that if he had left his ladder at home that afternoon, you might have took him for a lord.'"

—*his origin:* "'There *was* a mystery about his birth. His mother had always admitted it. Tom had never known who was his father, and some people had gone so far as to say that even she was in doubt.'"

—*a dream:* "' . . . to have a country-house and a park; and to plant a bit of it with a double row of gas-lamps a mile long, and go out every night with a French-polished mahogany ladder, and two servants in livery behind him, to light 'em for his own pleasure.'"

Supporting Roles

Galileo Isaac Newton Flamstead, the Salamander. "' . . . a tall, thin, dismal-faced young gentleman, half man and half boy, dressed in a childish suit of clothes very much too short in the legs and arms; and looking, according to **Tom**'s comparison, like one of the wax juveniles from a tailor's door, grown up and run to seed.'"

Mooney, the Gifted. "' . . . even more scientific in appearance than his friend; and had . . . the dirtiest face we can possibly know of, in this imperfect state of existence . . . . Mr Mooney was so absent, that when the old gentleman said to him, "Shake hands with Mr **Grig**," he put out his leg.'"

Uncle, of **Tom Grig**. "'Gas was the death of him. When it was first talked of, he laughed. He wasn't angry;' he laughed at the credulity of human nature.

"They might as well talk," he says, "of laying on an everlasting succession of glow-worms;" and then he laughed again, partly at his joke, and partly at poor humanity.'"

"'. . . he got very fond of his country all at once, and went about saying that gas was a death-blow to his native land, and that it was a plot of the radicals to ruin the country and destroy the oil and cotton trade for ever, and that the whales would go and kill themselves privately, out of sheer spite and vexation at not being caught. At last he got right-down cracked; called his tobacco-pipe a gas-pipe; thought his tears were lamp-oil . . . till one night he hung himself on a lamp-iron in Saint Martin's Lane, and there was an end of *him.*'"

Waiting-maid, "'that under any other circumstances **Tom** would have looked upon as a Venus . . . . '"

"'. . . she couldn't abear Mr Grig should think she wanted him to marry her; and that she had even gone so far as to refuse the last lamplighter, who was now a literary character (having set up as a bill-sticker) . . . . "

Spear-carriers

Baker: very strong in his attentions to the waiting-maid at the moment
Butcher: frantic in his interest in the waiting-maid
Lamplighter, in the chair: narrator
-vice-chairman and auditor
-wooed the waiting-maid; now a bill-sticker
Monk Lewis[H]: gothic novelist
Magistrate, who fined Tom, if he could conveniently spare the money
Father Mathew[H], known for his predictions; cited as free from fever
Francis Moore[H], physician, with a name in forecasting
Murphy: cited by the lamplighters on the question of belief in himself

N 5 Feb-Nov 1841 wkly (and monthly) by C&H in MHC   1 vol 1841 **BR**
U.S. publication 1841-42 in monthly parts by Lea & Blanchard, Philadelphia

Barnaby Rudge

A Tale of the Riots of 'Eighty

"*It is unnecessary to say, that those shameful tumults, while they reflect indelible disgrace upon the time in which they occurred, and all who had act or part in them, teach a good lesson. That what we falsely call a religious cry is easily raised by men who have no religion, and who in their daily practice set at nought the commonest principles of right and wrong; that it is begotten of intolerance and persecution; that it is senseless, besotted, inveterate and unmerciful; all History teaches us. But perhaps we do not know it in our hearts too well, to profit by even so humble an example as the 'No Popery' riots of Seventeen Hundred and Eighty.*"

—preface

" . . . in one book Dickens suddenly confesses that he likes the grotesque even without the comic. In one case he makes clear that he enjoys pure pictures with a pure love of the picturesque. That place is *Barnaby Rudge*." GKC pp69-70

"Now we might very well take the type of Mr Chester on the one hand, and of Sim Tappertit on the other, as marking the issue, the conflict, and the victory which really ushered in the nineteenth century. Dickens was very like Sim Tappertit. The Liberal Revolution was very like a Sim Tappertit revolution. It was vulgar, it was overdone, it was absurd, but it was alive. Dickens was vulgar, was absurd, overdid everything, but he was alive. The aristocrats were perfectly correct, but quite dead; dead long before they were guillotined. The classics and critics who lamented that Dickens was no gentleman were quite right, but quite dead. The revolution thought itself rational; but so did Sim Tappertit. It was really a huge revolt of romanticism against a reason which had grown sick even of itself. Sim Tappertit rose against Mr Chester; and, thank God! he put his foot upon his neck." GKC p75

The Maypole Inn

The Bar and its Licensee

PRÉCIS

Exposition at **John Willet**'s Maypole Inn in 1775: **Solomon Daisy** retells the story of a double murder in 1753 at The Warren, a great house nearby. **Reuben Haredale**, brother of the current master, **Geoffrey**, was found dead and the steward **Rudge** and a gardener missing. Months later a body, identified as Rudge's, was found. Auditors include the stolid Willet's son **Joe**; **Edward Chester**, who has vainly sought a meeting with **Emma**, Haredale's niece; and an ill-looking **Stranger** in an obscuring hat. 1

Riding furiously, the Stranger collides with **Gabriel Varden**'s chaise. Varden stops in at the Maypole for repairs. Joe complains to him of his father's dictatorial ways. Headed for London, locksmith Varden comes on simpleton **Barnaby Rudge** standing over Edward, who has been waylaid and hurt by a highwayman. Varden carries him to **Mrs Rudge**'s and goes home to his difficult wife; pretty, spoiled daughter **Dolly**; impossible maid-servant **Miggs** and tiny, grandiose apprentice **Simon Tappertit**, who yearns for Dolly. 2-4

Checking on Edward at Mrs Rudge's, Varden hears a familiar voice at the window, but the widow forestalls investigation. Edward's assailant evidently was the Stranger. Barnaby's raven **Grip** speaks out. 5-6

Tappertit uses a key he has made to sneak off to a clandestine cabal of disgruntled apprentices. Miggs plugs the keyhole, obliging him to summon her aid to reenter. She appears to faint with relief at his safety. 7-9

The elegant **John Chester**, Edward's father, visits the Maypole to confer with his ancient enemy, Geoffrey Haredale, whose beloved Chester married. They agree that their children must be kept apart. 10-12

On an errand in London, Joe visits Dolly, but she will be out for the evening. Heading home disconsolate, he encounters Edward, who sees Emma momentarily before Geoffrey bars further intercourse. Returning home, Edward confronts and defies his cynical father. He says he will not marry for money. They sever all ties. 13-15

The ill-looking stranger invades Mrs Rudge's home for warmth and food and hides when Barnaby comes in. Seeing Barnaby asleep and realising who he is, he claims new power over the widow, threatens her and leaves. 16-18

Edward enlists Gabriel's aid to get a note to Emma. The Vardens visit the cosy Maypole bar, and Dolly goes to Emma and receives a letter for Edward. Dolly is intercepted by the Maypole hostler, **Hugh**, who snatches the letter, a bracelet and a kiss. Joe appears. Dolly feigns ignorance of her attacker's identity. Joe escorts the Vardens part way home. His love grows. 19-22

Hugh brings Emma's letter to John Chester and admits the bracelet theft (men were hanged for less). Tappertit visits Chester, suggesting that he call on Mrs Varden and spike Dolly's friendship with Emma. He warns him of Joe's partisanship of Edward and Emma. 23-24

Mrs Rudge disappears with Barnaby. Chester visits first Mrs Varden and then, with further intelligence from Hugh, Emma. He tries but fails to turn her against his son. 25-29

Humiliated by his father again, Joe will take no more. After thrashing **Tom Cobb**, a teasing Maypole hanger-on, he steals away and visits Dolly to say good-bye. Her coquetry keeps her tongue-tied, and she bitterly regrets it afterward, for Joe goes for a soldier and does not return. 30-3

Five years pass.

Solomon Daisy staggers into the Maypole bar, white with fright at having seen Rudge, or his ghost. John Willet goes with Hugh to tell Geoffrey the news. On the way home they are overtaken by Lord **George Gordon**, his secretary **Gashford** and man **John Grueby**,. The visitors sleep at the Maypole. 33-36

Hugh finds Gashford's "No Popery" flyer and follows the Gordon group to London, where he meets **Ned Dennis** the hangman and Tappertit, to whose leadership he finds it amusing to submit. 37-39

John Chester, now knighted, plans to use Hugh against Catholic Haredale. The smitten Mrs Varden is collecting funds for the Protestants, to her husband's disgust. Gashford, formerly a Catholic, hates Haredale, who confronts and exposes him to an indifferent Lord Gordon. 40-44

Mrs Rudge and Barnaby, whose country wanderings have been sustained by Grip's exhibitions, are tracked down by the blind **Stagg** acting for the Stranger. The widow seeks obscurity in London. A procession of "No Popery" rioters passes, and Barnaby goes off with Hugh, who gives him a banner to carry. He defends it stoutly, unhorsing a soldier. The mob cheers him. 45-49

Tappertit gives Mrs Varden a paper exempting the house from mob reprisal, but Gabriel tears it up. He plans work as usual. Mounting riots destroy much Catholic and other property. Hugh and Barnaby reconnect. 50-53

A mob, egged on by Gashford and led by Hugh, pillage the Maypole. John Willet's life is spared but his mind softens. The rioters burn The Warren. The Stranger reappears but flees at the sound of the Warren alarm bell. Emma and Dolly are prisoners of Hugh and Dennis and fear the worst. 54-55

Haredale comes to his ruined house. He traps and seizes the Stranger, now identified as the murderer Rudge. The riots spread. Barnaby is captured. Emma and Dolly are missing. Haredale gets Rudge to a London prison. 56-61

Varden's gun has been sabotaged by Miggs. The mob try to extort his help to open Newgate Prison. He refuses and is rescued from death by Edward Chester and one-armed **Tom Green**. Fire brings down the prison gates, and the mob frees all prisoners, including Barnaby and his father Rudge. 62-65

Haredale, shelterless, is aided by the vintner, **Langdale**, whose house is assaulted by rioters led by Hugh. They escape out the back way with Edward and Green, now revealed as Joe Willet. 66-68

Hugh falls wounded, but Barnaby carries him off. Dennis has turned his coat and leads soldiers to capture them and Rudge. 69-70 The mob has been dispersed by the militia, under proper orders at last. The ladies are rescued by Varden and Joe, on whose bosom a transformed Dolly falls. 71-72

Mrs Rudge goes to her son in prison. Dennis's treachery has not availed him, and he is marked for execution, but his recollections reveal Hugh's paternity. Varden goes to the father, Sir John Chester, who masks his shock and leaves Hugh to the rope. Pleas to reprieve Barnaby fail. 73-75

Hugh is hanged after a brave final statement. Dennis and Rudge meet death cringingly, and Barnaby is reprieved to general rejoicing. 76-77

Geoffrey kills Sir John in a sword fight. He flees to French monastery. Joe and Dolly marry and take over the Maypole. His addled father keeps imaginary bar accounts for his cronies. Edward and Emma unite. Explicitly not invited to return to the Vardens', Miggs finds her niche warding women prisoners. Tappertit, now legless, shines shoes. Gashford lives, dies wretchedly. Gordon's long tale is told, to its prison end. The Vardens find domestic bliss. 78-82

CD's thoroughly researched depiction of the 1780 London rising is excerpted in the Panorama. A historic event of major (unintended), no longer remembered importance to the American Revolution, the Gordon Riots cost many hundred deaths. A proportional uprising in London or New York City today would kill several thousand. Though the description is vivid, brilliant and authoritative, it goes unread today because BR is largely overlooked. Scholars believe it has essentially formed the way we think about the "madness of crowds." The mob, like the Maypole, is too much a "Character" not to be in "Everyone in Dickens."

CONTENTS

Illustrations by *Hablôt K. Browne and George Cattermole*

CHARACTERS

Akerman[H], head jailer at Newgate Prison	RA	505
Apprentice, a novice conspirator	W	500
Assistant, to a chaplain	RA	505
Attendants, at a hanging	RA	505
Beggar, disappointed	O	498
Benjamin, tall and resentful apprentice	O	498
Black Lion, a landlord (sometimes called Lion)	W	500
Body-snatchers, observing the Stranger	W	500
Boys demanding money for the rioters	RA	505
Burgesses, making a show	RA	505
Chairmen, bearing Dolly	O	498
Chester, Edward; Emma Haredale's admirer	P	479
John; hypocrite subsequently knighted; unnatural and unknowing father	P	479, 481
Coachmaker, languishing swain of Dolly Varden	O	498
Cobb, Tom; fixture at The Maypole	O	498
Commanding officer of the Guards, at the reading of the Riot Act	RA	505
Convicts, in their cells and freed	RA	505
Conway, General[H]; protecting Parliament	RA	505
Cook, at the Maypole	RA	505
Corporals, of the militia	W	500
Country squire, brother of the Lord Mayor; he covets Grip	O	498
wife, who sent Barnaby money	O	500
Cripples, two boys; victims of retribution	RA	507
Daisy, Solomon; a fixture at the May-Pole	SR	493
Dennis, Ned; cowardly hangman	GPA	501
Fielding, Sir John[H]; magistrate	RA	506
Gardener, to Reuben Haredale; murdered because he saw too much	W	500
Gashford, villain serving Lord George Gordon	GPA	502
Gilbert, Mark; revolutionary apprentice	O	498
Gipsy, who cut an image on a stick	O	498
Gipsy woman, hanged having left a child	SR	493
Gordon, Colonel; protecting Parliament	RA	506
Gordon, Lord George[H]; "No Popery!!"	GPA	503
Grave-digger, gone to bed	W	500
Green, Tom; name assumed by Joe Willet	RA	506
Grip, a raven	SR	493
Grueby, John; Lord George Gordon's man	GPA	505
Haredale, Emma; in love with Edward Chester	P	481
Geoffrey, her misanthropic uncle	P	482
Reuben; Geoffrey's murdered brother	O	498
Herbert, Mr, M. P.[H]; critical of Lord George Gordon	RA	506
Hugh, unfathered revolutionary	P	482
Jewess, comfort to Lord Gordon	RA	506
Jones, Mary[H]; hanged for apparently intending to shop-lift	W	500
Kennet, Brackley[H]; the (unnamed) Lord Mayor during the Riots	RA	506
Lamplighter, leaving a trail of smoke	W	500
Landlord, of the Lion (later called the Black Lion)	O	499
Langdale[H], vintner who saves the day	O	499
Lion (also Black Lion), a landlord called by his inn's name	O	499
Lord Mayor of London [Brackley Kennet], coward and fool	RA	506
Mansfield, Lord[H]; a great law library lost	RA	506
Miggs, Miss; sharp of tongue and profile	SR	494
a nephew, the butt of recrimination	W	500

Barnaby and Grip after the Riots

Title Role

Barnaby Rudge. "He was about three-and-twenty years old, and though rather spare, of a fair height and strong make. His hair, of which he had a great profusion, was red, and hanging in disorder about his face and shoulders, gave to his restless looks an expression quite unearthly—enhanced by the paleness of his complexion, and the glassy lustre of his large protruding eyes. Startling as his aspect was, the features were good, and there was something even plaintive in his wan and haggard aspect . . . .

"His dress was of green, clumsily trimmed here and there—apparently by his own hands—with gaudy lace; brightest where the cloth was most worn and soiled, and poorest where it was at the best. A pair of tawdry ruffles dangled at his wrists, while his throat was nearly bare. He had ornamented his hat with a cluster of peacock's feathers, but they were limp and broken; and now trailed negligently down his back. Girt to his side was the steel hilt of an old sword without blade or scabbard; and some parti-coloured ends of ribands and poor glass toys completed the ornamental portion of his attire. The fluttered and confused disposition of the motley scraps that formed his dress, bespoke, in a scarcely less degree than his eager and unsettled manner, the disorder of his mind, and by a grotesque contrast set off and heightened the more impressive wildness of his face." 3

—*seen by his mother:* "Two-and-twenty years. Her boy's whole life and history . . . . How often . . . had she sat beside him night and day, watching for the dawn of mind that never came; how had she feared, and doubted, and yet hoped, long after conviction forced itself upon her! The little stratagems she had devised to try him, the little tokens he had given in his childish way—not of dullness but of something infinitely worse, so ghastly and unchild-like in its cunning—came back as vividly as if but yesterday had intervened . . . he, old and elfin-like in face, but ever dear to her, gazing at her with a wild and vacant eye, and crooning some uncouth song as she sat by and rocked him; every circumstance of his infancy came thronging back, and the most trivial, perhaps, the most distinctly.

"His older childhood, too; the strange imaginings he had; his terror of certain senseless things—familiar objects he endowed with life; the slow and gradual breaking out of that one horror, in which, before his birth, his darkened intellect began [*see* E/NN]; how, in the midst of all, she had found some hope and comfort in his being unlike another child, and had gone on almost believing in the slow development of his mind until he grew a man, and then his childhood was complete and lasting . . . these old thoughts sprung up within her, strong after their long slumber and bitterer than ever." 25

—*spirit:* "He, a poor idiot, caged in his narrow cell, was as much lifted up to God, while gazing on the mild [moon and star] light, as the freest and most favoured man in all the spacious city; and in his ill-remembered prayer, and in the fragment of the childish hymn, with which he sung and crooned himself asleep, there breathed as true a spirit as ever studied homily expressed, or old cathedral arches echoed." 73

—*in extremis:* "He was the only one of the three who had washed or trimmed himself that morning . . . . He still wore the broken peacock's feathers in his hat; and his usual scraps of finery were carefully disposed about his person. His kindling eye, his firm step, his proud and resolute bearing, might have graced some lofty act of heroism; some voluntary sacrifice, born of a noble cause and pure enthusiasm; rather than that felon's death." 77

Other Principals

Edward Chester. "This was a young man of about eight-and-twenty, rather above the middle height, and though of a somewhat slight figure, gracefully and strongly made. He wore his own dark hair, and was accoutred in a riding dress . . . travel-stained though he was, he was well and even richly attired, and without being over-dressed looked a gallant gentleman.

"Lying upon the table beside him . . . were a heavy riding-whip and a slouched hat, the latter worn no doubt as being best suited to the inclemency of the weather. There, too, were a pair of pistols in a holster-case, and a short riding-cloak. Little of his face was visible, except the long dark lashes which concealed his downcast eyes, but an air of careless ease and natural gracefulness of demeanour pervaded the figure, and seemed to comprehend even those slight accessories, which were all handsome, and in good keeping." 1

—manly defiance: "'Your cold and sullen temper, which chills every breast about you, which turned affection into fear, and changes duty into dread, has forced us on this secret course, repugnant to our nature and our wish, and far more foreign, sir, to us than you. I am not a false, a hollow, or a heartless man; the character is yours, who poorly venture on these injurious terms, against the truth . . . . You shall not cancel the bond between us. I will not abandon this pursuit. I rely upon your niece's truth and honour, and set your influence at nought. I leave her with a confidence in her pure faith, which you will never weaken, and with no concern but that I do not leave her in some gentler care.'" 13

—confronting his father: "'It is . . . sad when a son, proffering him his love and duty in their best and truest sense, finds himself repelled at every turn, and forced to disobey. Dear father,' he added, more earnestly though in a gentler tone . . . 'Let there be a confidence between us; not in terms, but truth. Hear what I have to say.'" 32

John Chester. "He was a staid, grave, placid gentleman, something past the prime of life, yet upright in his carriage, for all that, and slim as a greyhound. He was well-mounted upon a sturdy chestnut cob, and had the graceful seat of an experienced horseman; while his riding gear, though free from such fopperies as were then in vogue, was handsome and well chosen. He wore a riding-coat of a somewhat brighter green than might have been expected . . . with a short, black velvet cape, and laced pocket-holes and cuffs, all of a jaunty fashion; his linen, too, was of the finest kind, worked in a rich pattern at the wrists and throat, and scrupulously white. Although he seemed . . . to have come from London, his horse was as smooth and cool as his own iron-grey periwig and pigtail. Neither man nor beast had turned a single hair; and saving for his soiled skirts and spatter-dashes, this gentleman, with his blooming face, white teeth, exactly-ordered dress, and perfect calmness, might have come from making an elaborate and leisurely toilet, to sit for an equestrian portrait at old **John Willet**'s gate." 10

—on murder: "' . . . . The very idea of marrying a girl whose father was killed, like meat! Good God, **Ned**, how disagreeable! Consider the impossibility of having any respect for your father-in-law under such unpleasant circumstances—think of his having been "viewed" by jurors, and "sat upon" by coroners, and of his very doubtful position in the family ever afterwards. It seems to me such an indelicate sort of thing that I really think the girl ought to have been put to death by the state to prevent its happening.'" 15

—on the world: "'The world is a lively place enough, in which we must accommodate ourselves to circumstances, sail with the stream as glibly as we can, be content to take froth for substance, the surface for the depth, the counterfeit for the real coin. I wonder no philosopher has ever established that our globe itself is hollow. It should be, if Nature is consistent in her works.'" 12

—on fortune hunting: "'All men are fortune-hunters, are they not? The law, the church, the court, the camp—see how they are all crowded with fortune-hunters, jostling each other in the pursuit. The Stock Exchange, the pulpit, the counting-house, the royal drawing-room, the senate—what but fortune-hunters are they filled with? . . . you would be nothing else, my dear **Ned**, if you were the greatest courtier, lawyer, legislator, prelate, or merchant, in existence.'" 15

—the social lion: "How the accomplished gentleman spent the evening in the midst of a dazzling and brilliant circle; how he enchanted all those with whom he mingled by the grace of his deportment, the politeness of his manner, the vivacity of his conversation, and the sweetness of his voice; how it was observed in every corner, that Chester was a man of that happy disposition that nothing ruffled him, that he was one on whom the world's cares and errors sat lightly as his dress, and in whose smiling face a calm and tranquil mind was constantly reflected; how honest men, who by instinct knew him better, bowed down before him nevertheless, deferred to his every word, and courted his favourable notice; how people, who really had good in them, went with the stream, and fawned and flattered, and approved, and despised themselves while they did so, and yet had not the courage to resist; how, in short, he was one of those who are received and cherished in society (as the phrase is) by

scores who individually would shrink from and be repelled by the object of their lavish regard; are things of course, which will suggest themselves. Matter so common-place needs but a passing glance, and there an end." 24

Sir John Chester, M. P. "The old face, calm and pleasant as ever; the complexion, quite juvenile in its bloom and clearness; the same smile; the wonted precision and elegance of dress; the white, well-ordered teeth; the delicate hands; the composed and quiet manner; everything as it used to be: no mark of age or passion, envy, hate, or discontent: all unruffled and serene, and quite delightful to behold . . . .

"But how Sir John? Nothing so simple, or so easy . . . . John Chester, Esquire, M. P., attended court—went up with an address—headed a deputation. Such elegance of manner, so many graces of deportment, such powers of conversation, could never pass unnoticed. Mr was too common for such merit. A man so gentlemanly should have been—but Fortune is capricious—born a duke . . . . He caught the fancy of the king, knelt down a grub, and rose a butterfly." 40

—in violent death: **Haredale** "put his arm about the dying man, who repulsed him, feebly, and dropped upon the turf. Raising himself upon his hands, he gazed at him for an instant, with scorn and hatred in his look, but, seeming to remember, even then, that this expression would distort his features after death, he tried to smile, and faintly moving his right hand, as if to hide his bloody linen in his vest, fell back dead . . . ." 81

Emma Haredale. " . . . a lovely girl appeared, whose dark hair next moment rested on [**Edward**'s] breast." 13

—with a friend: " . . . they were both so very handsome, and it was such a breezy day, and their light dresses and dark curls appeared so free and joyous in their abandonment, and Emma was so fair, and **Dolly** so rosy, and Emma so delicately shaped, and Dolly so plump, and—in short, there are no flowers for any garden like such flowers . . . and both house and garden seemed to know it, and to brighten up sensibly." 20

—horrified: "Miss Haredale, whose feelings were usually of a quieter kind than **Dolly**'s, and not so much upon the surface, was dreadfully alarmed, and indeed had only just recovered from a swoon. She was very pale, and the hand which Dolly held was quite cold; but she bade her, nevertheless, remember that, under Providence, much must depend upon their own discretion . . . the idea that [her uncle] had fallen in a general massacre of the Catholics that night—no very wild or improbable supposition after what they had seen and undergone—struck her dumb; and, lost in the horrors they had witnessed, and those they might be yet reserved for, she sat incapable of thought, or speech, or outward show of grief: as rigid, and almost as white and cold, as marble." 59

—her courage: "Emma had known grief, and could bear it better [than **Dolly**]. She had little comfort to impart, but she could soothe and tend her, and she did so; and Dolly clung to her like a child to its nurse. In endeavouring to inspire her with some fortitude, she increased her own; and though the nights were long, and the days dismal, and she felt the wasting influence of watching and fatigue, and had perhaps a more defined and clear perception of their destitute condition and its worst dangers, she uttered no complaint. Before the ruffians, in whose power they were, she bore herself so calmly, and with such an appearance, in the midst of all her terror, of a secret conviction that they dared not harm her, that there was not a man among them but held her in some degree of dread; and more than one believed she had a weapon hidden in her dress, and was prepared to use it." 71

Geoffrey Haredale." . . . a burly square-built man, negligently dressed, rough and abrupt in manner, stern . . . forbidding both in look and speech . . . a distrustful frown . . . bent on showing by his every tone and gesture his determined opposition and hostility to the man he had come to meet." 12

—*hard-earned wisdom:* "'I have had my share of sorrows—more than the common lot, perhaps, but I have borne them ill. I have broken where I should have bent; and have mused and brooded, when my spirit should have mixed with all God's great creation. The men who learn endurance, are they who call the whole world, brother. I have turned *from* the world, and I pay the penalty. . . . It is too late to evade it now. I sometimes think, that if I had to live my life once more, I might amend this fault—not so much, I discover when I search my mind, for the love of what is right, as for my own sake. But even when I make these better resolutions, I instinctively recoil from the idea of suffering again what I have undergone . . . I should still be the same man, though I could cancel the past, and begin anew, with its experience to guide me.'" 79

—*alone, and lonely:* " . . . his appearance was greatly altered. He looked much older, and more care-worn. Agitation and anxiety of mind scatter wrinkles and grey hairs with no unsparing hand; but deeper traces follow on the silent uprooting of old habits, and severing of dear, familiar ties. . . . He was now a solitary man, and the heart within him was dreary and lonesome." 81

Hugh. " . . . a young man, of a hale athletic figure, and a giant's strength, whose sunburnt face and swarthy throat, overgrown with jet black hair, might have served a painter for a model. Loosely attired, in the coarsest and roughest garb, with scraps of straw and hay—his usual bed—clinging here and there, and mingling with his uncombed locks, he had fallen asleep in a posture as careless as his dress. The negligence and disorder of the whole man, with something fierce and sullen in his features, gave him a picturesque appearance ... like a poaching rascal [to **Parkes**] ...." 11

—*his story:* "' ... whose mother was hung when he was a little boy, along with six others, for passing bad notes ... that chap was then turned loose, and had to mind cows, and frighten birds away, and what not, for a few pence to live on, and so got on by degrees to mind horses, and to sleep in course of time in lofts and litter, instead of under haystacks and hedges, till at last he come to be hostler at the Maypole for his board and lodging and an annual trifle ...." 11

—*intimidated:* "Hard words he could have returned, violence he would have repaid with interest; but [**Chester**'s] cool, complacent, contemptuous, self-possessed reception, caused him to feel his inferiority more completely than the most elaborate arguments. Everything contributed to this effect. His own rough speech, contrasted with the soft persuasive accents of the other; his rude bearing, and Mr Chester's polished manner; the disorder and negligence of his ragged dress, and the elegant attire he saw before him; with all the unaccustomed luxuries and comforts of the room, and the silence that gave him leisure to observe these things, and feel how ill at ease they made him; all these influences, which have too often some effect on tutored minds and become of almost resistless power when brought to bear on such a mind as his, quelled Hugh completely." 23

—*in his element:* "Full twenty times, the rioters, headed by one man who wielded an axe in his right hand, and bestrode a brewer's horse of great size and strength, caparisoned with fetters taken out of Newgate, which clanked and jingled as he went, made an attempt to force a passage . . . and fire the vintner's house. Full twenty times they were repulsed with loss of life, and still came back again; and though the fellow at their head was marked and singled out by all, and was a conspicuous object as the only rioter on horseback, not a man could hit him. So surely as the smoke cleared away, so surely there was he; calling hoarsely to his companions, brandishing his axe above his head, and dashing on as though he bore a charmed life, and was proof against ball and powder. . . ." 67

—*in extremis:* "[He] displayed, in his speech and bearing, the most reckless hardihood . . . . Hugh's was the dogged desperation of a savage at the stake . . . . 'Ha ha ha! Courage, bold **Barnaby**, what care we? Your hand! They do well to put us out of the world, for if we got loose a second time, we wouldn't let them off so easy, eh? Another shake! A man can die but once. If you wake in the night, sing that out lustily, and fall asleep again. Ha ha ha!'" 76

—*heart revealed?* "'Bless you . . . I'm not frightened, Hugh. I'm quite happy. I wouldn't desire to live now, if they'd let me. Look at me! Am I afraid to die? Will they see *me* tremble?'

"Hugh gazed for a moment at [**Barnaby**'s] face, on which there was a strange, unearthly smile; and at his eye, which sparkled brightly; and interposing between him and the Ordinary, gruffly whispered to the latter:

"'I wouldn't say much to him, master, if I was you. He may spoil your appetite for breakfast, though you *are* used to it.'" 77

—*conscience:* "There was, for the moment, something kind, and even tender, struggling in his fierce aspect, as he wrung his poor companion [**Barnaby**] by the hand.

"' . . . if I had ten lives to lose, and the loss of each would give me ten times the agony of the hardest death, I'd lay them all down—ay I would, though you gentlemen may not believe it—to save this one. This one . . . that will be lost through me . . . . I took him from her in a reckless mood, and didn't think what harm would come of it . . . . I ask her pardon, and his . . . . '" 77

Mary Rudge. "She was about forty—perhaps two or three years older— with a cheerful aspect, and a face that had once been pretty. It bore traces of affliction and care, but they were of an old date, and Time had smoothed them. Any one who had bestowed but a casual glance on **Barnaby** might have known that this was his mother, from the strong resemblance between them; but where in his face there was wildness and vacancy, in hers there was the patient composure of long effort and quiet resignation.

"One thing about this face was very strange and startling. You could not look upon it in its most cheerful mood without feeling that it had some extraordinary capacity of expressing terror. It was not on the surface. It was in no one feature that it lingered. You could not take the eyes, or mouth, or lines upon the cheek, and say, if this or that were otherwise, it would not be so. Yet there it always lurked—something for ever dimly seen, but ever there, and never absent for a moment. It was the faintest, palest shadow of some look, to which an instant of intense and most unutterable horror only could have given birth; but indistinct and feeble as it was, it did suggest what that look must have been, and fixed it in the mind as if it had had an existence in a dream." 4

Stranger. " . . . wrapped in a loose riding-coat with huge cuffs ornamented with tarnished silver lace and large metal buttons, who sat apart from the regular frequenters of the [Maypole], and wearing a hat flapped over his face, which was still further shaded by the hand on which his forehead rested, [he] looked unsociable enough." 1

"The stranger took off his hat, and disclosed the hard features of a man of sixty or thereabouts, much weatherbeaten and worn by time, and the naturally harsh expression of which was not improved by a dark handkerchief which was bound tightly round his head, and, while it served the purpose of a wig, shaded his forehead, and almost hid his eyebrows. If it were intended to conceal or divert attention from a deep gash, now healed into an ugly seam, which when it was first inflicted must have laid bare his cheekbone, the object was but indifferently attained, for it could scarcely fail to be noted at a glance. His complexion was of a cadaverous hue, and he had a grizzly jagged beard of some three weeks' date . . . [he was] very meanly and poorly clad . . . . " 1

—*a meeting:* "Perhaps two men more powerfully contrasted, never opposed each other face to face. The ruddy features of the locksmith so set off and heightened the excessive paleness of the man on horseback, that he looked like a bloodless ghost . . . . [His] face . . . sullen and fierce, but shrinking too, was that of a man who stood at bay; while his firmly closed jaws, his puckered mouth, and more than all a certain stealthy motion of the hand within his breast, seemed to announce a desperate purpose very foreign to acting, or child's play. . . . 'to be plain with you, friend, you don't carry in your countenance a letter of recommendation.'" 2

—in London: "Among all the dangerous characters who . . . prowled and skulked in the metropolis at night, there was one man from whom many as uncouth and fierce as he, shrunk with an involuntary dread . . . .

"His voice, and look, and bearing—all expressive of the wildest recklessness and desperation—daunted while they repelled the bystanders . . . .

"'I am what you all are, and live as you all do,' said the man sternly, after a short silence. 'I am in hiding here like the rest, and if we were surprised would perhaps do my part with the best of ye. If it's my humour to be left to myself, let me have it. Otherwise,'—and here he swore a tremendous oath—'there'll be mischief done in this place, though there *are* odds of a score against me.'" 16

—on hearing an alarm bell: "If the ghastliest shape the human mind has ever pictured in its wildest dreams had risen up before him, he could not have staggered backward from its touch, as he did from the first sound of that loud iron voice. With eyes that started from his head, his limbs convulsed, his face most horrible to see, he raised one arm high up into the air, and holding something visionary back and down, with his other hand, drove at it as though he held a knife and stabbed it to the heart. He clutched his hair, and stopped his ears, and travelled madly round and round; then gave a frightful cry, and with it rushed away . . . . " 55 *And see* **Rudge** OC

Simon Tappertit. "Sim, as he was called in the locksmith's family, or Mr Simon Tappertit, as he called himself, and required all men to style him out of doors, on holidays, and Sundays out—was an old-fashioned, thin-faced, sleek-haired, sharp-nosed, small-eyed little fellow, very little more than five feet high, and thoroughly convinced in his own mind that he was above the middle size; rather tall, in fact, than otherwise. Of his figure, which was well enough formed, though somewhat of the leanest, he entertained the highest admiration; and with his legs, which, in knee- breeches, were perfect curiosities of littleness, he was enraptured to a degree amounting to enthusiasm." 4

—grandiosity: He also had some majestic, shadowy ideas . . . concerning the power of his eye. Indeed he had been known to go so far as to boast that he could utterly quell and subdue the haughtiest beauty by a simple process, which he termed 'eyeing her over;' but it must be added, that neither of this faculty, nor of the power he claimed to have, through the same gift, of vanquishing and heaving down dumb animals, even in a rabid state, had he ever furnished evidence which could be deemed quite satisfactory and conclusive.

"It may be inferred from these premises, that in the small body of Mr Tappertit there was locked up an ambitious and aspiring soul. As certain liquors, confined in casks too cramped in their dimensions, will ferment, and fret, and chafe in their imprisonment, so the spiritual essence or soul of Mr Tappertit would sometimes fume within that precious cask, his body, until, with great foam and froth and splutter, it would force a vent, and carry all before it. It was his custom to remark, in reference to any one of these occasions, that his soul had got into his head; and in this novel kind of intoxication many scrapes and mishaps befell him which he had frequently concealed with no small difficulty from his worthy master." 4

—garb: "In respect of dress and personal decoration, Sim Tappertit was no less of an adventurous and enterprising character. He had been seen, beyond dispute, to pull off ruffles of the finest quality at the corner of the street on Sunday night, and to put them carefully in his pocket before returning home;

and it was quite notorious that on all great holiday occasions it was his habit to
exchange his plain steel knee-buckles for a pair of glittering paste, under cover
of a friendly post, planted most conveniently in that same spot. Add to this
that he was in years just twenty, in his looks much older, and in conceit at
least two hundred . . . . " 4

—*smitten: See* **Dolly Varden** *dressed for an outing*

—*his card:* "'In the first place, sir,' said Mr Tappertit, producing a small
pocket-handkerchief, and shaking it out of the folds, 'as I have not a card about
me (for the envy of masters debases us below that level) allow me to offer the
best substitute that circumstances will admit of. If you will take that in your
own hand, sir, and cast your eye on the right-hand corner,' said Mr Tappertit,
offering it with a graceful air, 'you will meet with my credentials.'

"'Thank you,' answered Mr **Chester**, politely accepting, and turning to
some blood-red characters at the end. ' "Four. Simon Tappertit. One." Is that
the—'

"'Without the numbers, sir, that is my name,' replied the 'prentice. 'They
are merely intended as directions to the washerwoman, and have no connection
with myself or family.'" 24

—*after five years:* " . . . [he] seemed, physically speaking, to have grown
smaller with years (particularly as to his legs, which were stupendously little),
but . . . in personal dignity and self-esteem, had swelled into a giant . . . it not
only proclaimed itself impressively and beyond mistake in his majestic walk

and kindling eye, but found a striking means of revelation in his turned-up nose, which scouted all things of earth with deep disdain, and sought communion with its kindred skies." 39

—*after the Riots:* "Many months after . . . the United Bulldogs were to a man all killed, imprisoned, or transported, Mr Simon Tappertit . . . was discharged by proclamation, on two wooden legs . . . he was established in business as a shoe-black, and opened shop under an archway near the Horse Guards . . . [taking] for his wife the widow of an eminent bone and rag collector . . . he lived in great domestic happiness, only checkered by those little storms which serve to clear the atmosphere of wedlock, and brighten its horizon. In some of these gusts of bad weather, Mr Tappertit would, in the assertion of his prerogative, so far forget himself as to correct his lady with a brush, or boot, or shoe; while she (but only in extreme cases) would retaliate by taking off his legs, and leaving him exposed to the derision of those urchins who delight in mischief." LAST

Dolly Varden. " . . . a roguish face . . . lighted up by the loveliest pair of sparkling eyes that ever locksmith looked upon; the face of a pretty, laughing girl; dimpled and fresh, and healthful—the very impersonation of good-humour and blooming beauty." 4

—*going to a party:* "Never had Dolly looked so handsome as she did then, in all the glow and grace of youth, with all her charms increased a hundredfold by a most becoming dress, by a thousand little coquettish ways which nobody could assume with a better grace . . . . To see her seat herself inside [the chair], with her laughing eyes brighter than diamonds, and her hand— surely she had the prettiest hand in the world—on the ledge of the open window, and her little finger provokingly and pertly tilted up, as if it wondered why **Joe** didn't squeeze or kiss it! . . . . To hear that provoking precious little scream when the chair was hoisted on its poles, and to catch that transient but not-to-be-forgotten vision of the happy face within—what torments and aggravations, and yet what delights were these!" 13

—*dressed for an outing:* " . . . in a smart little cherry-coloured mantle, with a hood of the same drawn over her head, and upon the top of that hood, a little straw hat trimmed with cherry-coloured ribbons, and worn the merest trifle on one side—just enough in short to make it the wickedest and most provoking headdress that ever malicious milliner devised. And not to speak of the manner in which these cherry-coloured decorations brightened her eyes, or vied with her lips, or shed a new bloom on her face, she wore such a cruel little muff, and such a heart-rending pair of shoes, and was so surrounded and hemmed in, as it were, by aggravations of all kinds, that when Mr **Tappertit**, holding the horse's head, saw her come out of the house alone, such impulses came over him to decoy her into the chaise and drive off like mad, that he would unquestionably have done it, but for certain uneasy doubts besetting him as to the shortest way to Gretna Green . . . ." 19

—*saying goodbye:* "'Say something kind to me [said **Joe**]. I have no right to expect it of you, I know, but I ask it because I love you, and shall treasure the slightest word from you all through my life. Dolly, dearest, have you nothing to say to me?'

"No. Nothing. Dolly was a coquette by nature, and a spoilt child. She had no notion of being carried by storm in this way . . . . Joe had no business to be going abroad. He had no right to be able to do it. If he was in adamantine chains, he couldn't. . . .

"He was gone, actually gone. Dolly waited a little while, thinking he would return, peeped out at the door, looked up the street and down as well as the increasing darkness would allow, came in again, waited a little longer, went upstairs humming a tune, bolted herself in, laid her head down on her bed, and cried as if her heart would break. And yet such natures are made up of so many contradictions, that if Joe Willet had come back that night, next day, next week, next month, the odds are a hundred to one she would have treated him in the very same manner, and have wept for it afterwards with the very same distress." 31

—*after five years:* "When and where was there ever such a plump, roguish, comely, bright-eyed, enticing, bewitching, captivating, maddening little puss in all this world, as Dolly! What was the Dolly of five years ago, to the Dolly of that day! How many coachmakers, saddlers, cabinet-makers, and professors of other useful arts, had deserted their fathers, mothers, sisters, brothers, and, most of all, their cousins, for the love of her! How many unknown gentlemen—supposed to be of mighty fortunes, if not titles—had waited round the corner after dark, and tempted **Miggs** the incorruptible, with golden guineas, to deliver offers of marriage folded up in love-letters! . . .

" . . . . How many young ladies had publicly professed, with tears in their eyes, that for their tastes she was much too short, too tall, too bold, too cold, too stout, too thin, too fair, too dark—too everything but handsome!

"How many old ladies, taking counsel together, had thanked Heaven their daughters were not like her, and had hoped she might come to no harm, and had thought she would come to no good . . . and that she was a thorough imposition and a popular mistake!" ¶ 41

—*a captive:* " . . . Dolly—beautiful, bewitching, captivating, little Dolly—her hair dishevelled, her dress torn, her dark eyelashes wet with tears, her bosom heaving—her face, now pale with fear, now crimsoned with indignation—her whole self a hundred times more beautiful in this heightened aspect than ever she had been before—vainly strove to comfort **Emma Haredale**, and to impart to her the consolation of which she stood in so much need herself." 59

"Poor Dolly! Do what she would, she only looked the better for it, and tempted them the more. When her eyes flashed angrily, and her ripe lips slightly parted, to give her rapid breathing vent, who could resist it? When she wept and sobbed as though her heart would break, and bemoaned her miseries in the sweetest voice that ever fell upon a listener's ear, who could be insensible to the little winning pettishness which now and then displayed itself, even in the sincerity and earnestness of her grief? When, forgetful for a moment of herself, as she was now, she fell on her knees beside her friend, and bent over her, and laid her cheek to hers, and put her arms about her, what mortal eyes could have avoided wandering to the delicate bodice, the streaming hair, the neglected dress, the perfect abandonment and unconsciousness of the blooming little beauty? Who could look on and see her lavish caresses and endearments, and not desire to be in Emma Haredale's place; to be either her or Dolly; either the hugging or the hugged? Not **Hugh**. Not **Dennis**." 59

—*heart-sunk:* "With all her old horror of [**Hugh**] revived, and deepened into a degree of aversion and abhorrence which no language can describe . . . poor Dolly Varden . . . began to hang her head, and fade, and droop, like a beautiful flower. The colour fled from her cheeks, her courage forsook her, her gentle heart failed. Unmindful of all her provoking caprices, forgetful of all her conquests and inconstancy, with all her winning little vanities quite gone, she nestled all the livelong day in **Emma Haredale**'s bosom; and . . . pined slowly away, like a poor bird in its cage." 71

—*enlightened:* "'I shall bless your name,' sobbed the locksmith's little daughter, 'as long as I live. I shall never hear it spoken without feeling as if my heart would burst. I shall remember it in my prayers, every night and morning till I die!' . . . .

"Oh! how much, and how keenly, the little coquette of five years ago, felt now! She had found her heart at last. Never having known its worth till now, she had never known the worth of his. How priceless it appeared!" 72

Gabriel Varden. He "was a round, red-faced, sturdy yeoman, with a double chin, and a voice husky with good living, good sleeping, good humour, and good health. He was past the prime of life . . . .

". . . [He was] bluff, hale, hearty, and in a green old age: at peace with himself, and evidently disposed to be so with all the world. Although muffled up in divers coats and handkerchiefs—one of which, passed over his crown, and tied in a convenient crease of his double chin, secured his three-cornered hat and bob-wig from blowing off his head—there was no disguising his plump and comfortable figure; neither did certain dirty finger-marks upon his face give it any other than an odd and comical expression, through which its natural good humour shone with undiminished lustre." 2

—*triumphant:* "Among a dense mob of persons, of whom not one was for an instant still, the locksmith's ruddy face and burly form could be descried, beating about as though he was struggling with a rough sea . . . . Though he was really in a fair way to be torn to pieces in the general enthusiasm, the lock-smith, nothing discomposed, echoed their shouts till he was as hoarse as they, and in a glow of joy and right good-humour, waved his hat until the daylight shone between its brim and crown.

" . . . all the bandyings from hand to hand, and strivings to and fro, and sweepings here and there . . . saving that he looked more jolly and more radiant after every struggle—troubled his peace of mind no more than if he had been a straw upon the water's surface . . . ." 79

—*in bliss:* " . . . the locksmith sat himself down at the tea-table in the little back-parlour: the rosiest, cosiest, merriest, heartiest, best-contented old buck, in Great Britain or out of it.

"There he sat, with his beaming eye on **Mrs V.**, and his shining face suf-fused with gladness, and his capacious waistcoat smiling in every wrinkle, and his jovial humour peeping from under the table in the very plumpness of his legs; a sight to turn the vinegar of misanthropy into purest milk of human kindness . . . there sat the locksmith among all and every these delights, the sun that shone upon them all: the centre of the system: the source of light, heat, life and frank enjoyment in the bright household world." 80

Joe Willet, "the landlord's son Joe, a broad-shouldered strapping young fellow of twenty, whom it pleased his father still to consider a little boy, and to treat accordingly." 1

"'Father . . . I can bear with you, but I cannot bear the contempt that your treating me in the way you do, brings upon me from others every day. Look at other young men of my age. Have they no liberty, no will, no right to speak? Are they obliged to sit mumchance, and to be ordered about till they are the laughing-stock of young and old? I am a bye-word all over Chigwell, and I say— and it's fairer my saying so now, than waiting till you are dead, and I have got your money—I say, that before long I shall be driven to break such bounds, and that when I do, it won't be me that you'll have to blame . . . '" 3

—*leaving home:* "Joe, with his stick and bundle on his shoulder, quickly stood on the firm earth, and looked up at the old Maypole, it might be for the last time.

"He didn't apostrophise it, for he was no great scholar. He didn't curse it, for he had little ill-will to give to anything on earth. He felt more affectionate and kind to it than ever he had done in all his life before, so said with all his heart, 'God bless you! as a parting wish, and turned away." 31 *And see* **Tom Green** RA

John Willet was "a burly, large-headed man with a fat face, which betokened profound obstinacy and slowness of apprehension, combined with a very strong reliance upon his own merits. It was John Willet's ordinary boast in his more placid moods that if he were slow he was sure; which assertion could, in one sense at least, be by no means gainsaid, seeing that he was in everything unquestionably the reverse of fast, and withal one of the most dogged and positive fellows in existence—always sure that what he thought or said or did was right, and holding it as a thing quite settled and ordained by the laws of nature and Providence, that anybody who said or did or thought otherwise must be inevitably and of necessity wrong . . . a large pair of dull fish-like eyes . . . . " 1

—*laughing:* " . . . without any visible alteration of feature, [he] chuckled thrice audibly. This nearest approach to a laugh in which he ever indulged . . . never even curled his lip or effected the smallest change in—no, not so much as a slight wagging of—his great, fat, double chin, which at these times, as at all others, remained a perfect desert in the broad map of his face; one changeless, dull, tremendous blank." 29

—*thinking:* " . . . Mr Willet sat close to the fire. He was in a state of profound cogitation, with his own thoughts, and it was his custom at such times to stew himself slowly, under the impression that that process of cookery was favourable to the melting out of his ideas, which, when he began to simmer, sometimes oozed forth so copiously as to astonish even himself." 68

—*surprised:* "If a roc, an eagle, a griffin, a flying elephant, a winged seahorse, had suddenly appeared, and, taking him on its back, carried him bodily into the heart of the 'Salwanners,' [*see* **Black Lion** W] it would have been to him as an everyday occurrence, in comparison with what he now beheld. To be sitting quietly by, seeing and hearing these things; to be completely overlooked, unnoticed, and disregarded, while his son and a young lady were talking to each other in the most impassioned manner, kissing each other, and making themselves in all respects perfectly at home; was a position so tremendous, so inexplicable, so utterly beyond the widest range of his capacity of comprehension, that he fell into a lethargy of wonder, and could no more rouse himself than an enchanted sleeper in the first year of his fairy lease, a century long." 78

Supporting Roles

Solomon Daisy. " . . . the little man who . . . was the parish-clerk and bell-ringer of Chigwell . . . had little round black shiny eyes like beads; moreover this little man wore at the knees of his rusty black breeches, and on his rusty black coat, and all down his long flapped waistcoat, little queer buttons like nothing except his eyes; but so like them, that as they twinkled and glistened in the light of the fire, which shone too in his bright shoe-buckles, he seemed all eyes from head to foot . . . . " 1

—*frightened:* "A more complete picture of terror than the little man presented, it would be difficult to imagine. The perspiration stood in beads upon his face, his knees knocked together, his every limb trembled, the power of articulation was quite gone; and there he stood, panting for breath, gazing on [his friends] with such livid ashy looks, that they were infected with his fear, though ignorant of its occasion, and reflecting his dismayed and horror-stricken visage, stared back again without venturing to question him . . . . " 33

Gipsy woman, mother of **Hugh**. "'She had been tempted by want—as so many people are—into the easy crime of passing forged notes. She was young and handsome; and the traders who employ men, women, and children in this traffic, looked upon her as one who was well adapted for their business, and who would probably go on without suspicion for a long time. But they were mistaken; for she was stopped in the commission of her very first offence, and died for it. . . . She was of gipsy blood . . . and had a high, free spirit. This, and her good looks, and her lofty manner, interested some gentlemen who were easily moved by dark eyes; and efforts were made to save her.'" 75

Grip, "a large raven, who . . . listened with a polite attention and a most extraordinary appearance of comprehending every word . . . turning his head from one to the other, as if his office were to judge between them, and it were of the very last importance that he should not lose a word . . . the bird, balancing himself on tiptoe, as it were, and moving his body up and down in a sort of grave dance, rejoined, 'I'm a devil, I'm a devil, I'm a devil,' and flapped his wings against his sides as if he were bursting with laughter. **Barnaby** clapped his hands, and fairly rolled upon the ground in an ecstasy of delight.

"'Strange companions, sir,' said the locksmith, shaking his head, and looking from one to the other. 'The bird has all the wit.'

" . . . he fluttered to the floor, and went to Barnaby—not in a hop, or walk, or run, but in a pace like that of a very particular gentleman with exceedingly tight boots on, trying to walk fast over loose pebbles. Then stepping into his extended hand, and condescending to be held out at arm's length, he gave vent to a succession of sounds, not unlike the drawing of some eight or ten dozen of long corks, and asserted his brimstone birth and parentage with great distinctness." 6

—*after five years:* "Grip was by no means an idle or unprofitable member of the humble household. Partly by dint of **Barnaby**'s tuition, and partly by pursuing a species of self-instruction common to his tribe, and exerting his powers of observation to the utmost, he had acquired a degree of sagacity which rendered him famous for miles round. His conversational powers and surprising performances were the universal theme . . . though he was perfectly free and unrestrained in the presence of Barnaby and his mother, he maintained in public an amazing gravity, and never stooped to any other gratuitous performances than biting the ankles of vagabond boys (an exercise in which he much delighted), killing a fowl or two occasionally, and swallowing the dinners of various neighbouring dogs, of whom the boldest held him in great awe and dread." 45

Miggs. "**Mrs Varden**'s chief aider and abettor, and at the same time her principal victim and object of wrath, was her single domestic servant . . . . This Miggs was a tall young lady, very much addicted to pattens in private life; slender and shrewish, of a rather uncomfortable figure, and though not absolutely ill-looking, of a sharp and acid visage. As a general principle and abstract proposition, Miggs held the male sex to be utterly contemptible and unworthy of notice; to be fickle, false, base, sottish, inclined to perjury, and wholly undeserving. When particularly exasperated against them . . . she was accustomed to wish with great emphasis that the whole race of women could but die off, in order that the men might be brought to know the real value of the blessings by which they set so little store . . . she sometimes declared, if she could only have good security for a fair, round number—say ten thousand—of young virgins following her example, she would, to spite mankind, hang, drown, stab, or poison herself, with a joy past all expression." 7

—*her figure:* "Mr Tappertit . . . disliked Miss Miggs more when she laid her hand on her heart and panted for breath than at any other time, as her deficiency of outline was most apparent under such circumstances . . . . " 22

—*in a snit:* "Miggs howled . . . in a peculiarly dismal way, and said she knowed that master hated her. That it was a dreadful thing to live in families and have dislikes, and not give satisfactions. That to make divisions was a thing she could not abear to think of, neither could her feelings let her do it. That if it was master's wishes as she and him should part, it was best they should part, and she hoped he might be the happier for it, and always wished him well, and that he might find somebody as would meet his dispositions. It would be a hard trial, she said, to part from such a missis, but she could meet any suffering when her conscience told her she was in the rights, and therefore she was willing even to go that lengths. She did not think, she added, that she could long survive the separations, but, as she was hated and looked upon unpleasant, perhaps her dying as soon as possible would be the best endings for all parties. With this affecting conclusion, Miss Miggs shed more tears, and sobbed abundantly." 41

—*distraught:* " . . . her nightcap had been knocked off in the scuffle, and she was on her knees upon the floor, making a strange revelation of blue and yellow curl-papers, straggling locks of hair, tags of staylaces, and strings of it's impossible to say what; panting for breath, clasping her hands, turning her eyes upwards, shedding abundance of tears, and exhibiting various other symptoms of the acutest mental suffering." 51

—*comeuppance:* "'Let her leave the house this moment.'

"Miggs, hearing this, let her end of the box fall heavily to the floor, gave a very loud sniff, crossed her arms, screwed down the corners of her mouth, and cried, in an ascending scale, 'Ho, good gracious!' three distinct times . . . .

"Again, Miggs paused for a reply; and none being offered, was so oppressed with teeming spite and spleen, that she seemed like to burst . . . her vexation and chagrin being of that internally bitter sort which finds no relief in words, and is aggravated to madness by want of contradiction, she could hold out no longer, and burst into a storm of sobs and tears.

"In this extremity she fell on the unlucky **nephew,** tooth and nail, and plucking a handful of hair from his head, demanded to know how long she was to stand there to be insulted . . . . Somehow or other, by dint of pushing and pulling, they did attain the street at last; where Miss Miggs, all blowzed with the exertion of getting there, and with her sobs and tears, sat down upon her property to rest and grieve, until she could ensnare some other youth to help her home." 80

—*her niche:* "It chanced . . . that the justices of the peace for Middlesex proclaimed by public placard that they stood in need of a female turnkey for the County Bridewell . . . [She] was instantly chosen and selected from one hundred and twenty-four competitors, and at once promoted to the office; which she held until her decease, more than thirty years afterwards, remaining single all that time. It was observed of this lady that while she was inflexible and grim to all her female flock, she was particularly so to those who could establish any claim to beauty: and it was often remarked as a proof of her indomitable virtue and severe chastity, that to such as had been frail she showed no mercy; always falling upon them on the slightest occasion, or on no occasion at all, with the fullest measure of her wrath. Among other useful inventions which she practised upon this class of offenders and bequeathed to posterity, was the art of inflicting an exquisitely vicious poke or dig with the wards of a key in the small of the back, near the spine. She likewise originated a mode of treading by accident (in pattens) on such as had small feet; also very remarkable for its ingenuity, and previously quite unknown." LAST

Stagg. "The proprietor . . . and owner of the ragged head . . . wore an old tie-wig as bare and frowzy as a stunted hearth-broom. . . and stood a little apart, rubbing his hands, wagging his hoary bristled chin, and smiling in silence. His eyes were closed; but had they been wide open, it would have been easy to tell, from the attentive expression of the face he turned towards them—pale and unwholesome as might be expected in one of his underground existence— and from a certain anxious raising and quivering of the lids, that he was blind." 8

—*sarcastic:* "'Good night, noble captain [**Tappertit**],' whispered the blind man as he held [the grating] open for his passage out. 'Farewell, brave general. Bye, bye, illustrious commander. Good luck go with you for a—conceited, bragging, empty-headed, duck-legged idiot.'" 8

—*a quest completed:* "The change in his manner was so unexpected, the craft and wickedness of his deportment were so much aggravated by his condition . . . and this alteration bred so many fears in her whom he addressed, that she could not pronounce one word." 45

—*his end:* "He was called loudly on, to surrender. He ran the harder, and in a few seconds would have been out of gunshot. The word was given, and the men fired.

"There was a breathless pause and a profound silence, during which all eyes were fixed upon him. He had been seen to start at the discharge, as if the report had frightened him. But he neither stopped nor slackened his pace in the least, and ran on full forty yards further. Then, without one reel or stagger, or sign of faintness, or quivering of any limb, he dropped." 69

Martha Varden. "Mrs Varden was a lady of what is commonly called an uncertain temper—a phrase which being interpreted signifies a temper tolerably certain to make everybody more or less uncomfortable . . . when other people were merry, Mrs Varden was dull; and . . . when other people were dull, Mrs Varden was disposed to be amazingly cheerful . . . she not only attained a higher pitch of genius than Macbeth, in respect of her ability to be wise, amazed, temperate and furious, loyal and neutral in an instant, but would sometimes ring the changes backwards and forwards on all possible moods and flights in one short quarter of an hour; performing, as it were, a kind of triple bob major on the peal of instruments in the female belfry, with a skilfulness and rapidity of execution that astonished all who heard her.

"It has been observed in this good lady (who did not want for personal attractions, being plump and buxom to look at, though like her fair daughter, somewhat short in stature) that this uncertainty of disposition strengthened and increased with her temporal prosperity; and divers wise men and matrons, on friendly terms with the locksmith and his family, even went so far as to assert, that a tumble down some half-dozen rounds in the world's ladder—such as the breaking of the bank in which her husband kept his money, or some little fall of that kind—would be the making of her, and could hardly fail to render her one of the most agreeable companions in existence." 7

—at mealtime: "Mrs Varden was seldom very Protestant at meals, unless it happened that they were under-done, or over-done, or indeed that anything occurred to put her out of humour. Her spirits rose considerably on beholding [**John Willet**'s] goodly preparations, and from the nothingness of good works, she passed to the somethingness of ham and toast with great cheerfulness . . . .

"The proceedings of such a day occasion various fluctuations in the human thermometer, and especially in instruments so sensitively and delicately constructed as Mrs Varden. Thus, at dinner Mrs V stood at summer heat; genial, smiling, and delightful. After dinner, in the sunshine of the wine, she went up at least half-a-dozen degrees, and was perfectly enchanting. As its effect subsided, she fell rapidly, went to sleep for an hour or so at temperate, and woke at something below freezing. Now she was at summer heat again, in the shade; and when tea was over, and old John, producing a bottle of cordial from one of the oaken cases, insisted on her supping two glasses thereof in slow succession, she stood steadily at ninety for one hour and a quarter. Profiting by experience, the locksmith took advantage of this genial weather to smoke his pipe in the porch, and in consequence of this prudent management, he was fully prepared, when the glass went down again, to start homewards directly." 21

—transformed by tribulation: " . . . Mrs V. herself had grown quite young, and stood there in a gown of red and white: symmetrical in figure, buxom in bodice, ruddy in cheek and lip, faultless in ankle, laughing in face and mood, in all respects delicious to behold . . . . " 80

Others

Beggar. "[Mr **Chester**] smiled so very pleasantly as he communed with himself . . . that a beggar was emboldened to follow for alms, and to dog his footsteps for some distance. He was gratified . . . feeling it complimentary to his power of feature, and as a reward suffered the man to follow him until he called a chair, when he graciously dismissed him with a fervent blessing." 26

Benjamin. "'Welcome, noble captain!' cried a lanky figure, rising as from a nap . . . stretching himself—and he was so long already that it was quite alarming to see him do it . . . ." 8

Chairmen. "The very chairmen seemed favoured rivals as they bore [**Dolly**] down the street." 13

"The chairmen were rendered quite vivacious by having such a courteous burden [as **Chester**], and to Clerkenwell they went at a fair round trot." 27

Coachmaker. " . . . a young coachmaker (a master in his own right) who had given [**Dolly**] to understand, when he handed her into the chair at parting, that it was his fixed resolve to neglect his business from that time, and die slowly for the love of her . . . ." 19

Tom Cobb. " . . . short Tom Cobb the general chandler and post-office keeper. . . ." 1

" . . . Mr Cobb would acquaint [**Joe Willet**], that when he was his age, his father thought no more of giving him a parental kick, or a box on the ears, or a cuff on the head, or some little admonition of that sort, than he did of any other ordinary duty of life; and he would further remark . . . that but for this judicious bringing up, he might have never been the man he was at that present speaking; which was probable enough, as he was, beyond all question, the dullest dog of the party." 30

Country squire, brother of the **Lord Mayor** of London. " . . . a stout gentleman with a long whip in his hand, and a flushed face which seemed to indicate that he had had his morning's draught, rode up to the gate, and called in a loud voice and with more oath than the occasion seemed to warrant to have it opened directly." 47

Mark Gilbert. " . . . a third [apprentice], whose eyes were bandaged, and who was attired in a bag-wig, and a broad-skirted coat, trimmed with tarnished lace; and who was girded with a sword, in compliance with the laws of the Institution regulating the introduction of candidates . . . . 'Mark Gilbert. Age, nineteen. Bound to **Thomas Curzon**, hosier . . . . Loves Curzon's daughter . . . . Curzon pulled his ears last Tuesday week.'" 8

" . . . an ill-looking, one-sided, shambling lad, with sunken eyes set close together in his head—'if the society would burn his house down—for he's not insured—or beat him as he comes home from his club at night, or help me to carry off his daughter, and marry her at the Fleet, whether she gave consent or not—'" 8

Gipsy. "' . . . a sunburnt, swarthy fellow, almost a wild man; and while he lay in prison, under sentence, he, who had seen the hangman more than once while he was free, cut an image of him on his stick, by way of braving death . . . .'" 75

Reuben Haredale, elder brother of **Geoffrey**. He "'was found murdered in his bedchamber; and in his hand was a piece of the cord attached to an alarm-bell outside the roof, which hung in his room and had been cut asunder, no doubt by the murderer, when he seized it.'" 1

Landlord, of The Lion. "This Lion or landlord—for he was called both man and beast, by reason of his having instructed the artist who painted his sign, to convey into the features of the lordly brute whose effigy it bore, as near a counterpart of his own face as his skill could compass and devise—was a gentleman almost as quick of apprehension, and of almost as subtle a wit, as the mighty **John** himself. But the difference between them lay in this; that whereas Mr **Willet's** extreme sagacity and acuteness were the efforts of unassisted nature, the Lion stood indebted, in no small amount, to beer; of which he swigged such copious draughts, that most of his faculties were utterly drowned and washed away, except the one great faculty of sleep, which he retained in surprising perfection." 31 [*CD makes this inn and its owner the* "**Black Lion**" W in 72]

Langdale[H]. " . . . whose place of business was down in some deep cellars hard by Thames Street, and who was as purple-faced an old gentleman as if he had all his life supported their arched roof on his head . . . . " 13

" . . . a portly old man . . . with an anxious expression of countenance, was remonstrating with some unseen personage up-stairs, while the porter essayed to close the door by degrees and get rid of him. . . . " 61

Night-porter. "[He] looked through a small grating in the portal with a surly eye, and cried 'Halloa! . . . We don't sell beer here . . . what else do you want?'

"'To come in,' **Hugh** replied, with a kick at the door." 39

Old gentleman. " . . . a weazen old gentleman, ogling the nursery-maid, looked with like scorn upon the spinster, and wondered she didn't know she was no longer young." 14

Phil Parkes. " . . . long Phil Parkes the ranger . . . . " 1 "'It's as plain . . . as the nose on Parkes's face'—Mr Parkes, who had a large nose, rubbed it, and looked as if he considered this a personal allusion . . . . " 11

Peak. " . . . the servant, who was to the full as cool and negligent in his way as his master [**Chester**] . . . . " 23

—*at the last:* "As soon as [his master's body] was recognised and carried home, the faithful valet . . . eloped with all the cash and movables he could lay his hands on, and started as a finished gentleman upon his own account. In this career he met with great success, and would certainly have married an heiress in the end, but . . . . He sank under a contagious disorder, very prevalent at that time, and vulgarly termed the jail fever." LAST

Rudge. "'Villain!' cried Mr **Haredale**, in a terrible voice . . . . 'Dead and buried, as all men supposed through your infernal arts, but reserved by Heaven for this—at last—at last—I have you. You, whose hands are red with my brother's blood, and that of his faithful servant . . . . You, Rudge, double murderer and monster, I arrest you in the name of God . . . . Though you had the strength of twenty men,' he added, as the murderer writhed and struggled, 'you could not escape me or loosen my grasp to-night!'" 56

Serjeant. "The serjeant was describing a military life. It was all drinking, he said, except that there were frequent intervals of eating and lovemaking. A battle was the finest thing in the world—when your side won it—and Englishmen always did that." 31

Servant, of stout gentleman. "[He] feigned to be very active in ordering [**Mary** and **Barnaby**] off, but this man put a crown into the widow's hand, and whispering that his lady sent it, thrust them gently from the gate." 47

Waiter, from an inn in Bristol. " . . . [he] stood looking after [**Haredale**'s] retreating figure, doubtful whether he ought not to follow . . . he feared the gentleman intended to destroy himself . . . ." 81

Wife, of **country squire**. " . . . presently there appeared, a little flurried, as it seemed, by the unwonted summons, a lady much younger than himself, who had the appearance of being in delicate health, and not too happy." 47

Walk-ons

Apprentice, novice. "[His] eyes were bandaged, and who was attired in a bag-wag, and a broad skirted-coat, trimmed with tarnished lace; and who was girded with a sword, in compliance with the laws of the Institution regulating the introduction of candidates, which required them to assume this courtly dress, and kept it constantly in lavender, for their convenience." 8

Black Lion. "'Tell him where it was done [where you lost your arm]' said the Black Lion to **Joe**.

"'At the defence of the Savannah,* father.'" 72 [*Savannah, Georgia, in the U.S. was captured by the British in 1778 and held until the end of the Revolutionary War] *See* **Landlord** of the Lion

Body-snatchers. " . . . they who dealt in bodies with the surgeons could swear [the **Stranger**] slept in churchyards, and that they had beheld him glide away among the tombs on their approach." 16

Corporals. " . . . being gentlemen of sedentary pursuits in private life and excitable out of doors, broke several windows with their bayonets, and rendered it imperative on the commanding **officer** to deliver them over to a strong guard, with whom they fought at intervals as they came along . . . . " 42

Gardener, to **Reuben Haredale**. "'Do I fancy that as I left the chamber where [Reuben] lay, I saw the face of a man peeping from a dark door, who plainly showed me by his fearful looks that he suspected what I had done? Do I remember that I spoke fairly to him—that I drew nearer—nearer yet—with the hot knife in my sleeve? Do I fancy how he died? Did he stagger back into the angle of the wall into which I had hemmed him, and, bleeding inwardly, stand, not fall, a corpse before me? Did I see him, for an instant . . . erect and on his feet—but dead!'" 62

Grave-digger. He "'was laid up in his bed, from long working in a damp soil and sitting down to take his dinner on cold tombstones. . . . '" 1

Mary Jones. "'I got Mary Jones [said **Dennis**], a young woman of nineteen who . . . was worked off for taking a piece of cloth off the counter of a shop . . . and putting it down again when the shopman see her; and who had never done any harm before, and only tried to do that, in consequence of her husband having been pressed three weeks previous, and she being left to beg, with two young children . . . .'" 37

Lamplighter. " . . . on his rounds [he] went flashing past, leaving behind a little track of smoke mingled with glowing morsels of his hot red link." 18

Nephew of **Miggs**. " . . . the small boy, who had been all this time gradually lashed into rebellion by the sight of unattainable pastry, walked off indignant, leaving his aunt and the box to follow at their leisure." 80 *See* **Miggs** SR—*comeuppance*

Royal East London Volunteers. "[They] made a brilliant sight that day: formed into lines, squares, circles, triangles, and what not, to the beating of drums, and the streaming of flags; and performed a vast number of complex evolutions, in all of which Serjeant **Varden** bore a conspicuous share. Having displayed their military prowess to the utmost in these warlike shows, they marched in glittering order to the Chelsea Bunhouse, and regaled in the adjacent taverns until dark." 42

Running-footmen. "Many a private chair . . . preceded by running-footmen bearing flambeaux . . . made the way gay and light as it danced along, and darker and more dismal when it had passed. It was not unusual for these running gentry, who carried it with a very high hand, to quarrel in the servants' hall while waiting for their masters and mistresses; and, falling to blows either there or in the street without, to strew the place of skirmish with hair-powder, fragments of bag-wigs, and scattered nosegays." 16

Tambourine-player. "'Even **Miggs** would go [said **Varden**]. Some black tambourine-player, with a great turban on, would be bearing her off, and, unless the tambourine-player was proof against kicking and scratching, it's my belief he'd have the worst of it. Ha ha ha! I'd forgive the tambourine-player. I wouldn't have him interfered with on any account, poor fellow.'" 41

Watch, in London. "Then there was the watch with staff and lantern crying the hour, and the kind of weather; and those who woke up at his voice and turned them round in bed, were glad to hear it rained, or snowed, or blew, or froze, for very comfort's sake." 16

The Great Protestant Association and All Its Works

Ned Dennis, the hangman. "The man who now confronted **Gashford**, was a squat, thick-set personage, with a low, retreating forehead, a coarse shock head of hair, and eyes so small and near together, that his broken nose alone seemed to prevent their meeting and fusing into one of the usual size. A dingy handkerchief twisted like a cord about his neck, left its great veins exposed to view, and they were swollen and starting, as though with gulping down strong passions, malice, and ill-will. His dress was of threadbare velveteen—a faced, rusty, whitened black, like the ashes of a pipe or a coal fire after a day's extinction; discoloured with the soils of many a stale debauch, and reeking yet with pot-house odours. In lieu of buckles at his knees, he wore unequal loops of packthread; and in his grimy hands he held a knotted stick, the knob of which was carved into a rough likeness of his own vile face." 37

—*complimentary*: "'Did you ever . . . ' whispered Dennis, with a horrible kind of admiration, such as that with which a cannibal might regard his intimate friend, when hungry—'did you ever'—and here he drew still closer to [**Gashford**'s] ear, and fenced his mouth with both his open hands—'see such a throat as his? Do but cast your eye upon it. There's a neck for stretching . . . !'" 37

—*his occupation*: "'I'm of as genteel a calling, brother, as any man in England—as light a business as any gentleman could desire.'

"'Was you 'prenticed to it?' asked Mr **Tappertit**.

"'No. Natural genius,' said Mr Dennis. 'No 'prenticing. It comes by natur'. . . . Look at that hand of mine—many and many a job that hand has done, with a neatness and dexterity, never known afore. When I look at that hand,' said Mr Dennis, shaking it in the air, 'and remember the helegant bits of work it has turned off, I feel quite molloncholy to think it should ever grow old and feeble. But sich is life!'

"He heaved a deep sigh as he indulged in these reflections, and putting his fingers with an absent air on **Hugh**'s throat, and particularly under his left ear, as if he were studying the anatomical development of that part of his frame, shook his head in a despondent manner and actually shed tears.

"'You're a kind of artist, I suppose—eh!' said Mr Tappertit.

"'Yes,' rejoined Dennis; 'yes—I may call myself a artist—a fancy workman—art improves natur'—that's my motto.'" 39

—*refurbished:* "He was rather better dressed than usual: wearing the same suit of threadbare black, it is true, but having round his neck an un-wholesome-looking cravat of yellowish white; and, on his hands, great leather gloves, such as a gardener might wear in following his trade. His shoes were newly greased, and ornamented with a pair of rusty iron buckles; the pack-thread at his knees had been renewed; and where he wanted buttons, he wore pins. Altogether, he had something the look of a tipstaff, or a bailiff's follower, desperately faded, but who had a notion of keeping up the appearance of a pro-fessional character, and making the best of the worst means." 69

—*disconcerted:* "'I was formed for society, I was.'

"'That's rather a pity, an't it? said the [jail officer].

"'No,' answered Dennis, 'I'm not aware that it is. Why should it be a pity, brother?'

"'Oh! I don't know,' said the man carelessly. 'I thought that was what you meant. Being formed for society, and being cut off in your flower, you know—'

"'I say,' interposed the other quickly. 'what are you talking of? Don't. Who's a-going to be cut off in their flowers?'

"'Oh, nobody particular. I thought you was, perhaps,' said the man.

"Mr Dennis wiped his face, which had suddenly grown very hot, and re-marking in a tremulous voice to his conductor that he had always been fond of a joke, followed him in silence until he stopped at a door." 74

—*condemned:* "'Somebody tell me what he thinks!' cried the wretched ob-ject—so mean, and wretched, and despicable, that even Pity's self might have turned away, at sight of such a being in the likeness of a man—'isn't there a chance for me—isn't there a good chance for me? Isn't it likely they may be doing this to frighten me? Don't you think it is? Oh!' he almost shrieked, as he wrung his hands, 'won't anybody give me comfort!'" 76

Gashford. " . . . the secretary . . . angularly made, high-shouldered, bony, and ungraceful. His dress, in imitation of his superior, was demure and staid in the extreme; his manner, formal and constrained. This gentleman had an overhanging brow, great hands and feet and ears, and a pair of eyes that seemed to have made an unnatural retreat into his head, and to have dug themselves a cave to hide in. His manner was smooth and humble, but very sly and slinking. He wore the aspect of a man who was always lying in wait for something that wouldn't come to pass; but he looked patient—very patient—and fawned like a spaniel dog. Even now, while he warmed and rubbed his hands before the blaze, he had the air of one who only presumed to enjoy it in his degree as a commoner; and though he knew his lord was not regarding him, he looked into his face from time to time, and with a meek and deferential manner, smiled as if for practice." 35

"There was a remarkable contrast between this man's occupation at the moment, and the expression of his countenance, which was singularly repulsive and malicious. His beetling brow almost obscured his eyes; his lip was curled contemptuously; his very shoulders seemed to sneer in stealthy whisperings with his great flapped ears." 36

—*sycophant:* "'No, no, my lord . . . your life is of far too much importance to the nation in these portentous times, to be placed upon a level with one so useless and so poor as mine. A great cause, my lord, a mighty cause, depends on you. You are its leader and its champion, its advanced guard and its van. It is the cause of our altars and our homes, our country and our faith . . . .My lord,' said the speaker, rising in his stirrups, 'it is a glorious cause, and must not be forgotten. My lord, it is a mighty cause, and must not be endangered. My lord, it is a holy cause, and must not be deserted.'" 35

—*unmasked:* "'This man,' said Mr **Haredale** . . . 'who in his boyhood was a thief, and has been from that time to this, a servile, false, and truckling knave: this man, who has crawled and crept through life, wounding the hands he licked, and biting those he fawned upon: this sycophant, who never knew what honour, truth, or courage meant; who robbed his benefactor's daughter of her virtue, and married her to break her heart, and did it, with stripes and cruelty: this creature, who has whined at kitchen windows for the broken food, and begged for half-pence at our chapel doors: this apostle of the faith, whose tender conscience cannot bear the altars where his vicious life was publicly denounced . . . .'" 43

Lord George Gordon. "The lord . . . was about the middle height, of a slender make, and sallow complexion, with an aquiline nose, and long hair of a reddish brown, combed perfectly straight and smooth about his ears, and slightly powdered, but without the vestige of a curl. He was attired, under his great-coat, in a full suit of black, quite free from any ornament, and of the most precise and sober cut. The gravity of his dress, together with a certain lankness of cheek and stiffness of deportment, added nearly ten years to his age, but his figure was that of one not yet past thirty.

"As he stood musing in the red glow of the fire, it was striking to observe his very bright large eye, which betrayed a restlessness of thought and purpose, singularly at variance with the studied composure and sobriety of his mien, and with his quaint and sad apparel. It had nothing harsh or cruel in its expression; neither had his face, which was thin and mild, and wore an air of melancholy; but it was suggestive of an air of indefinable uneasiness, which infected those who looked upon him, and filled them with a kind of pity for the man: though why it did so, they would have had some trouble to explain." ¶35

"It would be difficult to convey an adequate idea of the excited manner in which he gave [his] answers to the secretary's promptings; of the rapidity of his utterance, or the violence of his tone and gesture in which, struggling through his Puritan's demeanour, was something wild and ungovernable which broke through all restraint." 35

—*his character:* "Although there was something very ludicrous in his vehement manner, taken in conjunction with his meagre aspect and ungraceful presence, it would scarcely have provoked a smile in any man of kindly feeling; or even if it had, he would have felt sorry and almost angry with himself next moment, for yielding to the impulse. This lord was sincere in his violence and in his wavering. A nature prone to false enthusiasm, and the vanity of being a leader, were the worst qualities apparent in his composition. All the rest was weakness—sheer weakness . . . . " 36

—*on horseback:* "If Lord George Gordon had appeared . . . overnight, a nobleman of somewhat quaint and odd exterior, the impression was confirmed this morning, and increased a hundred-fold. Sitting bolt upright upon his bony steed, with his long, straight hair, dangling about his face and fluttering in the wind; his limbs all angular and rigid, his elbows stuck out on either side ungracefully, and his whole frame jogged and shaken at every motion of his horse's feet; a more grotesque or more ungainly figure can hardly be conceived.

"In lieu of whip, he carried in his hand a great gold-headed cane, as large as any footman carries in these days, and his various modes of holding this unwieldy weapon—now upright before his face like the sabre of a horse-soldier, now over his shoulder like a musket, now between his finger and thumb, but always in some uncouth and awkward fashion—contributed in no small degree to the absurdity of his appearance.

"Stiff, lank, and solemn, dressed in an unusual manner, and ostentatiously exhibiting—whether by design or accident—all his peculiarities of carriage, gesture, and conduct, all the qualities, natural and artificial, in which he differed from other men; he might have moved the sternest looker-on to laughter, and fully provoked the smiles and whispered jests which greeted his departure from the Maypole inn." ¶37 *And see* **Panorama**—*the leader thereafter*

John Grueby. "He was a square-built, strong-made, bull-necked fellow, of the true English breed . . . . five-and-forty; but was one of those self-possessed, hard-headed, imperturbable fellows, who, if they are ever beaten at fisticuffs, or other kind of warfare, never know it, and go on coolly till they win." 35

The Riots and Their Aftermath: *Dramatis Personae*

Akerman, head jailer, Newgate. " . . . a man appeared upon the roof of the governor's house, and asked what it was [the rioters] wanted." 64

Assistant, to a Chaplain. "[He] and some members [of Parliament] who were imploring the people to retire, immediately withdrew . . . . " 49

Attendants, at a hanging. "[**Dennis**] sank down a mere heap of clothes between the two attendants." 77

Two **boys**. "[They] went down Holborn alone, armed with bars taken from the railings of Lord **Mansfield**'s house, and demanded money for the rioters." 67

Burgesses. " . . . without making a very fierce show, [they] looked brave enough." 67

Commanding officer, of the Guards. " . . . rode hastily into the open space between [the soldiers and the rioters], accompanied by a **magistrate** and an **officer** of the House of Commons, for whose accommodation a couple of troopers had hastily dismounted. The Riot Act was read, but not a man stirred." 49

Convicts. " . . . the four men in the cells . . . gave vent to such piteous entreaties as wretches in their miserable condition may be supposed to have been inspired with: urging, whoever it was, to set them at liberty, for the love of Heaven; and protesting, with great fervour, and truly enough, perhaps, for the time, that if they escaped, they would amend their ways, and would never, never, never again do wrong before God or man, but would lead penitent and sober lives, and sorrowfully repent the crimes they had committed." 65

—*free:* "Their pale and haggard looks and hollow eyes; their staggering feet, and hands stretched out as if to save themselves from falling; their wandering and uncertain air; the way they heaved and gasped for breath, as though in water, when they were first plunged into the crowd; all marked them for the men. No need to say 'this one was doomed to die;' for there were the words broadly stamped and branded on his face. The crowd fell off, as if they had been laid out for burial, and had risen in their shrouds; and many were seen to shudder, as though they had been actually dead men, when they chanced to touch or brush against their garments." 65

General Conway, "turning to Lord **George**, spoke thus—in a loud voice that they might hear him well, but quite coolly and collectedly.

"'You may tell these people, if you please, my lord, that I am General Conway of whom they have heard; and that I oppose this petition, and all their proceedings, and yours. I am a soldier, you may tell them, and I will protect the freedom of this place [Parliament] with my sword.'" 49

Cook, at the Maypole. "[She and the **housemaid**] ran screaming upstairs and locked themselves into one of the old garrets—shrieking dismally when they had done so, by way of rendering their place of refuge perfectly secret and secure." 54

Sir John Fielding. He "had the reputation of being a bold and active magistrate . . . . " 61

Colonel Gordon. "'And my Lord **George** . . . If a man among this crowd, whose uproar strikes us deaf, crosses the threshold of the House of Commons, I swear to run my sword that moment—not into his, but into your body!'" 49

Tom Green (Joe Willet). " . . . he was a gallant, manly, handsome fellow, but he had lost his left arm. It had been taken off between the elbow and the shoulder, and his empty coat-sleeve hung across his breast . . . . There was something soldierly in his bearing, and he wore a jaunty cap and jacket. Perhaps he had been in the service at one time or other . . . it could not have been very long ago, for he was but a young fellow now." 58

Herbert. " . . . one of the members present, indignantly rose and called upon the House to observe that Lord **George Gordon** was then sitting under the gallery with the blue cockade, the signal of rebellion, in his hat."73

Jewess. " . . . constant attendant . . . a beautiful Jewish girl, who attached herself to [**Gordon**] from feelings half religious, half romantic, but whose virtuous and disinterested character appears to have been beyond the censure even of the most censorious." LAST

Lord Mansfield. " . . . the mob gathering round Lord Mansfield's house, had called on those within to open the door, and receiving no reply . . . forced an entrance . . . [and] began to demolish the house with great fury, and setting fire to it in several parts, involved in a common ruin . . . the rarest collection of manuscripts ever possessed by any one private person in the world, and worse than all, because nothing could replace this loss, the great Law Library, on almost every page of which were notes in the judge's own hand, of inestimable value—being the results of the study and experience of his whole life." 66

Lord Mayor of London [Brackley Kennet]. "'Am I citizen of England? Am I to have the benefit of the laws? Am I to have any return for the King's taxes?' [said **Langdale**]

"' . . . . Oh dear me, what a thing it is to be a public character!—You must look in again in the course of the day.—Would a javelin-man do?—Or there's **Philips** the constable—he's disengaged—he's not very old for a man at his time of life, except in his legs, and if you put him up at a window he'd look quite young by candle-light, and might frighten 'em very much.—Oh dear!—well!— we'll see about it.'" 61

And see **Rioters** *and* **Panorama of the Riots**—*The Mob Ascendant*

Officer, of the Foot Guards. ". . . desirous to avoid rousing the people by the display of military force in the streets, [he] was humanely anxious to give as little opportunity as possible for any attempt at rescue [of **Barnaby**]; knowing that it must lead to bloodshed and loss of life . . . . " 58

Old man, servant at The Warren. "[He] was never heard of again, and was said to have had his brains beaten out with an iron bar . . . and to have been afterwards burnt in the flames." 55

Ordinary [prison Chaplain] "The Ordinary . . . reproved [**Hugh**] for his indecent mirth, and advised him to alter his demeanour." 77

Sir Algernon Percy[H], commander of the Northumberland Militia. 67

Post-boy. "[Haredale] would have harnessed the horses, but that the post-boy of the village—a soft-hearted, good-for-nothing, vagabond kind of fellow—was moved by his earnestness and passion, and throwing down a pitchfork with which he was armed, swore that the rioters might cut him into mincemeat if they liked, but he would not stand by and see an honest gentleman who had done no wrong, reduced to such extremity, without doing what he could to help him." 61

Priest. "One mild old man—a priest, whose chapel was destroyed; a very feeble, patient, inoffensive creature—who was trudging away . . . ." 61

Prisoner. "Now a party of a dozen men . . . dragging a prisoner along the ground whose dress they had nearly torn from his body in their mad eagerness to set him free, and who was bleeding and senseless in their hands." 64

Rioter. " . . . one tall fellow, fresh from a slaughter-house, whose dress and great thigh-boots smoked hot with grease and blood, raised a pole-axe, and swearing a horrible oath, aimed it at the old man's [**Gabriel Varden**] uncovered head. At that instant, and in the very act, he fell himself, as if struck by lightning . . . . " 64

Rioters. " . . . one of the fellows who went through the rooms, breaking the furniture and helping to destroy the building, found a child's doll—a poor toy— which he exhibited at the window to the mob below, as the image of some unholy saint which the late occupants had worshipped. While he was doing this, another . . . harangued the crowd . . . [on] the true principles of Christianity. Meanwhile the **Lord Mayor**, with his hands in his pockets, looked on as an idle man might look at any other show, and seem mightily satisfied to have got a good place." 66

Serjeant, of the Foot Guards. "'. . . I'll tell you what. I wish . . . that I was a commissioned instead of a non-commissioned officer . . . . Call me out to stop these riots—give me the needful authority, and half-a-dozen rounds of ball cartridge . . .'" 58

Servant-men. "A few armed servant-men were posted in the hall [of The Warren], and when the rioters forced an entrance there, they fired some half-a-dozen shots." 55

Sexton. "Directing the sexton to lead the horse, [**Haredale**] walked close by the murderer's side . . . . " 61

Soldier. "The soldier came spurring on, making his horse rear as the people pressed about him . . . and still **Barnaby**, without retreating an inch, waited for his coming . . . the pole swept into the air above the people's heads, and the man's saddle was empty in an instant." 49

Sons, of a man on death-row. " . . . the anguish and suffering of the two sons . . . when they heard . . . their father's voice, is past description . . . . At last, they cleft their way among the mob about the door, though many men, a dozen times their match, had tried to do so, and were seen, in—yes, in—the fire, striving to prize it down, with crowbars." 64

Stragglers. " . . . two or three figures appeared . . . motioning with their hands as though they urged . . . retreat from some approaching danger." 57

Toll-keeper. " . . . the man with a lantern in his hand, came running out . . . and was about to throw the gate open . . . . " 56

Victims of Retribution. " . . . there had been many [sad] sights since the riots were over—some so moving in their nature, and so repulsive too, that they were far more calculated to awaken pity for the sufferers, than respect for that law whose strong arm seemed in more than one case to be as wantonly stretched forth now that all was safe, as it had been basely paralysed in time of danger.

—"Two **cripples**—both mere boys—one with a leg of wood, one who dragged his twisted limb along by the help of a crutch, were hanged in this same Bloomsbury Square . . . . Another **boy** was hanged in Bow Street; other young lads in various quarters of the town. Four wretched **women**, too, were put to death. In a word, those who suffered as rioters were, for the most part, the weakest, meanest, and most miserable among them . . . some of these people owned themselves to be Catholics . . . .

—"One **young man** was hanged in Bishopsgate Street, whose aged grey-headed **father** waited for him at the gallows, kissed him at its foot when he arrived, and sat there, on the ground, till they took him down. They would have given him the body of his child; but he had no hearse, no coffin, nothing to remove it in, being too poor—and walked meekly away beside the cart that took it back to prison . . . ." 77

Villagers. "They were assembled for their own protection, and could not endanger themselves by lending any aid to [**Haredale**]." 61

Prison **watchman**. " . . . could be seen upon [Newgate Prison's] roof, stopping to look down upon the preparations in the street." 77

Panorama of the Riots (June 2-9, 1780)

The Infection. "If a man had stood on London Bridge, calling till he was hoarse, upon the passers-by, to join with **Lord George Gordon**, although for an object which no man understood, and which in that very incident had a charm of its own—the probability is, that he might have influenced a score of people in a month.

"If all zealous Protestants had been publicly urged to join an association for the avowed purpose of singing a hymn or two occasionally, and hearing some indifferent speeches made, and ultimately of petitioning Parliament not to pass an act for abolishing the penal laws against Roman Catholic priests, the penalty of perpetual imprisonment denounced against those who educated children in that persuasion, and the disqualification of all members of the Romish church to inherit real property in the United Kingdom by right of purchase or descent—matters so far removed from the business and bosoms of the mass, might perhaps have called together a hundred people.

"But when vague rumours got abroad, that in this Protestant association a secret power was mustering against the government for undefined and mighty purposes; when the air was filled with whispers of a confederacy among the Popish powers to degrade and enslave England, establish an inquisition in London, and turn the pens of Smithfield market into stakes and cauldrons; when terrors and alarms which no man understood were perpetually broached, both in and out of Parliament, by one enthusiast who did not understand himself, and bygone bugbears which had lain quietly in their graves for centuries, were raised again to haunt the ignorant and credulous; when all this was done, as it were, in the dark, and secret invitations to join the Great Protestant Association in defence of religion, life, and liberty, were dropped in the public ways, thrust under the house-doors, tossed in at windows, and pressed into the hands of those who trod the streets by night; when they glared from every wall, and shone on every post and pillar, so that stocks and stones appeared infected with the common fear, urging all men to join together blindfold in resistance of they knew not what, they knew not why;—then the mania spread indeed, and the body, still increasing every day, grew forty thousand strong." ¶37

The Crowd Gathers. " . . . the stream of life was all pouring one way . . . a vast throng of persons were crossing the river from the Middlesex to the Surrey shore, in unusual haste and evident excitement. They were, for the most part, in knots of two or three, or sometimes half-a-dozen; they spoke little together— many of them were quite silent; and hurried on as if they had one absorbing object in view, which was common to them all.

" . . . nearly every man in this great concourse, which still came pouring past, without slackening in the least, wore in his hat a blue cockade . . . chance passengers who were not so decorated, appeared timidly anxious to escape observation or attack, and gave them the wall as if they would conciliate them. This, however, was natural enough, considering their inferiority in point of numbers; for the proportion of those who wore blue cockades, to those who were dressed as usual, was at least forty or fifty to one . . . .

"At first, the current of people had been confined to the two pathways, and but a few more eager stragglers kept the road. But after half an hour or so, the passage was completely blocked up by the great press, which, being now closely wedged together, and impeded by the carts and coaches it encountered, moved but slowly, and was sometimes at a stand for five or ten minutes together.

"After the lapse of nearly two hours, the numbers began to diminish visibly, and gradually dwindling away, by little and little, left the bridge quite clear, save that, now and then, some hot and dusty **man**, with the cockade in his hat, and his coat thrown over his shoulder, went panting by, fearful of being too late, or stopped to ask which way his friends had taken, and being directed, hastened on again like one refreshed." 48

An Assembly. "[The **Gordon** party] passed quickly through the Bridge Road, where the shops were all shut up (for the passage of the great crowd and the expectation of their return had alarmed the tradesmen for their goods and windows), and where, in the upper stories, all the inhabitants were congregated, looking down into the street below, with faces variously expressive of alarm, of interest, expectancy, and indignation. Some of these applauded, and some hissed; but regardless of these interruptions —for the noise of a vast congregation of people at a little distance, sounded in his ears, like the roaring of the sea—Lord George Gordon quickened his pace, and presently arrived before St George's Fields.

"They were really fields at that time, and of considerable extent. Here an immense multitude was collected, bearing flags of various kinds and sizes, but all of the same colour—blue, like the cockades—some sections marching to and fro in military array, and others drawn up in circles, squares, and lines. A large portion, both of the bodies which paraded the ground, and of those which remained stationary, were occupied in singing hymns or psalms. With whomsoever this originated, it was well done; for the sound of so many thousand voices in the air must have stirred the heart of any man within him, and could not fail to have a wonderful effect upon enthusiasts, however mistaken.

"Scouts had been posted in advance of the great body, to give notice of their leader's coming. These falling back, the word was quickly passed through the whole host, and for a short interval there ensued a profound and deathlike silence, during which the mass was so still and quiet, that the fluttering of a banner caught the eye, and became a circumstance of note. Then they burst into a tremendous shout, into another, and another; and the air seemed rent and shaken, as if by the discharge of cannon." 48

On to Parliament. "The mob had been divided from its first assemblage into four divisions; the London, the Westminster, the Southwark, and the Scotch. Each of these divisions being subdivided into various bodies, and these bodies being drawn up in various forms and figures, the general arrangement was, except to the few chiefs and leaders, as unintelligible as the plan of a great battle to the meanest soldier in the field. It was not without its method, however; for, in a very short space of time after being put in motion, the crowd had resolved itself into three great parties, and were prepared, as had been arranged, to cross the river by different bridges, and make for the House of Commons in separate detachments.

"At the head of that division which had Westminster Bridge for its approach to the scene of action, **Lord George Gordon** took his post; with **Gashford** at his right hand, and sundry ruffians, of most unpromising appearance, forming a kind of staff about him. The conduct of a second party, whose route lay by Blackfriars, was entrusted to a committee of management, including perhaps a dozen men: while the third, which was to go by London Bridge, and through the main streets, in order that their numbers and their serious intentions might be the better known and appreciated by the citizens, were led by **Simon Tappertit** . . . **Dennis** the hangman, **Hugh**, and some others.

"The word of command being given, each of these great bodies took the road assigned to it, and departed on its way, in perfect order and profound silence. That which went through the city greatly exceeded the others in number, and was of such prodigious extent that when the rear began to move, the front was nearly four miles in advance, notwithstanding that the men marched three abreast and followed very close upon each other." 49

"It was between two and three o'clock in the afternoon when the three great parties met at Westminster, and, uniting into one huge mass, raised a tremendous shout. This was not only done in token of their presence, but as a signal to those on whom the task devolved, that it was time to take possession of the lobbies of both Houses, and of the various avenues of approach, and of the gallery stairs. To the last-named place, Hugh and Dennis, still with their pupil between them rushed straightway; **Barnaby** having given his flag into the hands of one of their own party, who kept them at the outer door. Their followers pressing on behind, they were borne as on a great wave to the very doors of the gallery, whence it was impossible to retreat, even if they had been so inclined, by reason of the throng which choked up the passages.

"It is a familiar expression in describing a great crowd, that a person might have walked upon the people's heads. In this case it was actually done; for a boy who had by some means got among the concourse, and was in imminent danger of suffocation, climbed to the shoulders of a man beside him and walked upon the people's hats and heads into the open street; traversing in his passage the whole length of two staircases and a long gallery. Nor was the swarm without less dense; for a basket which had been tossed into the crowd, was jerked from head to head, and shoulder to shoulder, and went spinning and whirling on above them, until it was lost to view, without even once falling in among them or coming near the ground.

"Through this vast throng, sprinkled doubtless here and there with honest zealots, but composed for the most part of the very scum and refuse of London, whose growth was fostered by bad criminal laws, bad prison regulations, and the worst conceivable police, such of the members of both Houses of Parliament as had not taken the precaution to be already at their posts, were compelled to fight and force their way. Their carriages were stopped and broken; the wheels wrenched off; the glasses shivered to atoms; the panels beaten in; drivers, footmen, and masters, pulled from their seats and rolled in the mud.

"Lords, commoners, and reverend bishops, with little distinction of person or party, were kicked and pinched and hustled; passed from hand to hand through various stages of ill-usage; and sent to their fellow-senators at last with their clothes hanging in ribands about them, their bagwigs torn off, themselves speechless and breathless, and their persons covered with the powder which had been cuffed and beaten out of their hair. One **lord** was so long in the hands of the populace, that the Peers as a body resolved to sally forth and rescue him, and were in the act of doing so, when he happily appeared among them covered with dirt and bruises, and hardly to be recognised by those who knew him best. The noise and uproar were on the increase every moment. The air was filled with execrations, hoots, and howlings. The mob raged and roared, like a mad monster as it was, unceasingly, and each new outrage served to swell its fury.

"Within doors, matters were even yet more threatening. Lord George —preceded by a man who carried the immense petition on a porter's knot through the lobby to the door of the House of Commons, where it was received by two officers of the House who rolled it up to the table ready for presentation—had taken his seat at an early hour, before the Speaker went to prayers. His followers pouring in at the same time, the lobby and all the avenues were immediately filled, as we have seen.

"Thus the members were not only attacked in their passage through the streets, but were set upon within the very walls of Parliament; while the tumult, both within and without, was so great, that those who attempted to speak could scarcely hear their own voices: far less, consult upon the course it would be wise to take in such extremity, or animate each other to dignified and firm resistance. So sure as any member, just arrived, with dress disordered and dishevelled hair, came struggling through the crowd in the lobby, it yelled and screamed in triumph; and when the door of the House, partially and cautiously opened by those within for his admission, gave them a momentary glimpse of the interior, they grew more wild and savage, like beasts at the sight of prey, and made a rush against the portal which strained its locks and bolts in their staples, and shook the very beams." ¶49

The First Night. "[The streets] were filled with people, for the rumour of that day's proceedings had made a great noise. Those persons who did not care to leave home, were at their doors or windows, and one topic of discourse prevailed on every side. Some reported that the riots were effectually put down; others that they had broken out again: some said that Lord **George Gordon** had been sent under a strong guard to the Tower; others that an attempt had been made upon the King's life, that the soldiers had been again called out, and that the noise of musketry in a distant part of the town had been plainly heard within an hour.

"As it grew darker, these stories became more direful and mysterious; and often, when some frightened passenger ran past with tidings that the rioters were not far off, and were coming up, the doors were shut and barred, lower windows made secure, and as much consternation engendered, as if the city were invaded by a foreign army. ¶50

"[The crowd] had torches among them, and the chief faces were distinctly visible. That they had been engaged in the destruction of some building was sufficiently apparent, and that it was a Catholic place of worship was evident from the spoils they bore as trophies, which were easily recognisable for the vestments of priests, and rich fragments of altar furniture.

"Covered with soot, and dirt, and dust, and lime; their garments torn to rags; their hair hanging wildly about them; their hands and faces jagged and bleeding with the wounds of rusty nails . . . the dense throng came fighting on: some singing; some shouting in triumph; some quarrelling among themselves; some menacing the spectators as they passed; some with great wooden fragments, on which they spent their rage as if they had been alive, rending them limb from limb, and hurling the scattered morsels high into the air; some in a drunken state, unconscious of the hurts they had received from falling bricks, and stones, and beams; one borne upon a shutter, in the very midst, covered with a dingy cloth, a senseless, ghastly heap.

"Thus—a vision of coarse faces, with here and there a blot of flaring, smoky light; a dream of demon heads and savage eyes, and sticks and iron bars uplifted in the air, and whirled about; a bewildering horror, in which so much was seen, and yet so little, which seemed so long, and yet so short, in which there were so many phantoms, not to be forgotten all through life, and yet so many things that could not be observed in one distracting glimpse—it flitted onward, and was gone." ¶50

A Respite. "The soldiers were again called out, again they took half-a-dozen prisoners, and again the crowd dispersed after a short and bloodless scuffle. Hot and drunken though they were, they had not yet broken all bounds and set all law and government at defiance. Something of their habitual deference to the authority erected by society for its own preservation yet remained among them . . . .

"By midnight, the streets were clear and quiet, and, save that there stood in two parts of the town a heap of nodding walls and pile of rubbish, where there had been at sunset a rich and handsome building, everything wore its usual aspect.

"Even the Catholic gentry and tradesmen, of whom there were many resident in different parts of the City and its suburbs, had no fear for their lives or property, and but little indignation for the wrong they had already sustained in the plunder and destruction of their temples of worship. An honest confidence in the government under whose protection they had lived for many years, and a well-founded reliance on the good feeling and right thinking of the great mass of the community, with whom, notwithstanding their religious differences, they were every day in habits of confidential, affectionate, and friendly intercourse, reassured them, even under the excesses that had been committed; and convinced them that they who were Protestants in anything but the name, were no more to be considered as abettors of these disgraceful occurrences, than they themselves were chargeable with the uses of the block, the rack, the gibbet, and the stake in cruel Mary's reign." ¶51

The Mob in Suspension. "The people who were boisterous at Westminster upon the Friday morning, and were eagerly bent upon the work of devastation in Duke Street and Warwick Street at night, were, in the mass, the same. Allowing for the chance accession of which any crowd is morally sure in a town where there must always be a large number of idle and profligate persons, one and the same mob was at both places. Yet they spread themselves in various directions when they dispersed in the afternoon, made no appointment for re-assembling, had no definite purpose or design, and indeed, for anything they knew, were scattered beyond the hope of future union.

"At . . . the headquarters of the rioters, there were not, upon this Friday night, a dozen people. Some slept in the stable and outhouses, some in the common room, some two or three in beds. The rest were in their usual homes or haunts. Perhaps not a score in all lay in the adjacent fields and lanes, and under haystacks, or near the warmth of brick-kilns, who had not their accustomed place of rest beneath the open sky. As to the public ways within the town, they had their ordinary nightly occupants, and no others; the usual amount of vice and wretchedness, but no more.

"The experience of one evening, however, had taught the reckless leaders of disturbance, that they had but to show themselves in the streets, to be immediately surrounded by materials which they could only have kept together when their aid was not required, at great risk, expense, and trouble. Once possessed of this secret, they were as confident as if twenty thousand men, devoted to their will, had been encamped about them, and assumed a confidence which could not have been surpassed, though that had really been the case." ¶52

Looting Freely. "Without the slightest preparation, saving that they carried clubs and wore the blue cockade, [the leaders] sallied out into the streets; and, with no more settled design than that of doing as much mischief as they could, paraded [the crowd] at random. Their numbers rapidly increasing, they soon divided into parties; and agreeing to meet by-and-by, in the fields near Welbeck Street, scoured the town in various directions. The largest body, and that which augmented with the greatest rapidity . . . took its way towards Moorfields, where there was a rich chapel, and in which neighbourhood several Catholic families were known to reside.

"Beginning with the private houses so occupied, they broke open the doors and windows; and while they destroyed the furniture and left but the bare walls, made a sharp search for tools and engines of destruction, such as hammers, pokers, axes, saws, and such like instruments. Many of the rioters made belts of cord, of handkerchiefs, or any material they found at hand, and wore these weapons as openly as pioneers upon a field-day. There was not the least disguise or concealment—indeed, on this night, very little excitement or hurry. From the chapels, they tore down and took away the very altars, benches, pulpits, pews, and flooring; from the dwelling-houses, the very wainscoting and stairs. This Sunday evening's recreation they pursued like mere workmen who had a certain task to do, and did it.

"Fifty resolute men might have turned them at any moment; a single company of soldiers could have scattered them like dust; but no man interposed, no authority restrained them, and, except by the terrified persons who fled from their approach, they were as little heeded as if they were pursuing their lawful occupation with the utmost sobriety and good conduct.

"In the same manner, they marched to the place of rendezvous agreed upon, made great fires in the fields, and reserving the most valuable of their spoils, burnt the rest. Priestly garments, images of saints, rich stuffs and ornaments, altar-furniture and household goods, were cast into the flames, and shed a glare on the whole country round; but they danced and howled, and roared about these fires till they were tired, and were never for an instant checked." ¶52

No Turning Back. "The leaders of the riot, rendered still more daring by the success of last night and by the booty they had acquired, kept steadily together, and only thought of implicating the mass of their followers so deeply that no hope of pardon or reward might tempt them to betray their more notorious confederates into the hands of justice.

"Indeed, the sense of having gone too far to be forgiven, held the timid together no less than the bold. Many who would readily have pointed out the foremost rioters and given evidence against them, felt that escape by that means was hopeless, when their every act had been observed by scores of people who had taken no part in the disturbances; who had suffered in their persons, peace, or property, by the outrages of the mob; who would be most willing witnesses; and whom the government would, no doubt, prefer to any King's evidence that might be offered.

"Many of this class had deserted their usual occupations on the Saturday morning; some had been seen by their employers active in the tumult; others knew they must be suspected, and that they would be discharged if they returned; others had been desperate from the beginning, and comforted themselves with the homely proverb, that, being hanged at all, they might as well be hanged for a sheep as a lamb.

"They all hoped and believed, in a greater or less degree, that the government they seemed to have paralysed, would, in its terror, come to terms with them in the end, and suffer them to make their own conditions. The least sanguine among them reasoned with himself that, at the worst, they were too many to be all punished, and that he had as good a chance of escape as any other man. The great mass never reasoned or thought at all, but were stimulated by their own headlong passions, by poverty, by ignorance, by the love of mischief, and the hope of plunder." 53

The Mob a Force of Nature. " . . . from the moment of their first outbreak at Westminster, every symptom of order or preconcerted arrangement among them vanished. When they divided into parties and ran to different quarters of the town, it was on the spontaneous suggestion of the moment. Each party swelled as it went along, like rivers as they roll towards the sea; new leaders sprang up as they were wanted, disappeared when the necessity was over, and reappeared at the next crisis.

"Each tumult took shape and form from the circumstances of the moment; sober workmen, going home from their day's labour, were seen to cast down their baskets of tools and become rioters in an instant; mere boys on errands did the like. In a word, a moral plague ran through the city. The noise, and hurry, and excitement, had for hundreds and hundreds an attraction they had no firmness to resist. The contagion spread like a dread fever: an infectious madness, as yet not near its height, seized on new victims every hour, and society began to tremble at their ravings." 53

Madness at a House-burning. "If Bedlam gates had been flung open wide, there would not have issued forth such maniacs as the frenzy of that night had made. There were men there, who danced and trampled on the beds of flowers as though they trod down human enemies, and wrenched them from the stalks, like savages who twisted human necks. There were men who cast their lighted torches in the air, and suffered them to fall upon their heads and faces, blistering the skin with deep unseemly burns.

"There were men who rushed up to the fire, and paddled in it with their hands as if in water; and others who were restrained by force from plunging in, to gratify their deadly longing. On the skull of one drunken **lad**—not twenty, by his looks—who lay upon the ground with a bottle to his mouth, the lead from the roof came streaming down in a shower of liquid fire, white hot; melting his head like wax.

"When the scattered parties were collected, men—living yet, but singed as with hot irons—were plucked out of the cellars, and carried off upon the shoulders of others, who strove to wake them as they went along, with ribald jokes, and left them, dead, in the passages of hospitals. But of all the howling throng not one learnt mercy from, nor sickened at, these sights; nor was the fierce, besotted, senseless rage of one man glutted." ¶55

The Mob Ascendant. "During the whole of this day, every regiment in or near the metropolis was on duty in one or other part of the town; and the regulars and militia, in obedience to the orders which were sent to every barrack and station within twenty-four hours' journey, began to pour in by all the roads. But the disturbance had attained to such a formidable height, and the rioters had grown, with impunity, to be so audacious, that the sight of their great force, continually augmented by new arrivals, instead of operating as a check, stimulated them to outrages of greater hardihood than any they had yet committed; and helped to kindle a flame in London, the like of which had never been beheld, even in its ancient and rebellious times.

"All yesterday, and on this day likewise, the **commander-in-chief** endeavoured to arouse the magistrates to a sense of their duty, and in particular the **Lord Mayor**, who was the faintest-hearted and most timid of them all. With this object, large bodies of the soldiery were several times despatched to the Mansion House to await his orders: but as he could, by no threats or persuasions, be induced to give any, and as the men remained in the open street, fruitlessly for any good purpose, and thrivingly for a very bad one; these laudable attempts did harm rather than good. For the crowd, becoming speedily acquainted with the Lord Mayor's temper, did not fail to take advantage of it by boasting that even the civil authorities were opposed to the Papists, and could not find in their hearts to molest those who were guilty of no other offence.

"These vaunts they took care to make within the hearing of the soldiers; and they, being naturally loth to quarrel with the people, received their advances kindly enough: answering, when they were asked if they desired to fire upon their countrymen, 'No, they would be damned if they did;' and showing much honest simplicity and good nature. The feeling that the military were No Popery men, and were ripe for disobeying orders and joining the mob, soon became very prevalent in consequence. Rumours of their disaffection, and of their leaning towards the popular cause, spread from mouth to mouth with astonishing rapidity; and whenever they were drawn up idly in the streets or squares, there was sure to be a crowd about them, cheering and shaking hands, and treating them with a great show of confidence and affection.

"By this time, the crowd was everywhere; all concealment and disguise were laid aside, and they pervaded the whole town. If any man among them wanted money, he had but to knock at the door of a dwelling-house, or walk into a shop, and demand it in the rioters' name; and his demand was instantly complied with. The peaceable citizens being afraid to lay hands upon them, singly and alone, it may be easily supposed that when gathered together in bodies, they were perfectly secure from interruption.

"They assembled in the streets, traversed them at their will and pleasure, and publicly concerted their plans. Business was quite suspended; the greater part of the shops were closed; most of the houses displayed a blue flag in token of their adherence to the popular side; and even the Jews in Houndsditch, Whitechapel, and those quarters, wrote upon their doors or window-shutters: 'This House is a True Protestant.' The crowd was the law, and never was the law held in greater dread, or more implicitly obeyed." ¶63

Invasion and Fire at Newgate. "And now the strokes began to fall like hail upon the gate, and on the strong building; for those who could not reach the door, spent their fierce rage on anything—even on the great blocks of stone, which shivered their weapons into fragments, and made their hands and arms to tingle as if the walls were active in their stout resistance, and dealt them back their blows.

"The clash of iron ringing upon iron, mingled with the deafening tumult and sounded high above it, as the great sledge-hammers rattled on the mailed and plated door: the sparks flew off in showers; men worked in gangs, and at short intervals relieved each other, that all their strength might be devoted to the work; but there stood the portal still, as grim and dark and strong as ever, and, saving for the dints upon its battered surface, quite unchanged.

"While some brought all their energies to bear upon the toilsome task; and some, rearing ladders against the prison, tried to clamber to the summit of the walls they were too short to scale; and some again engaged a body of police a hundred strong, and beat them back and trod them under foot by force of numbers; others besieged the house on which the jailer had appeared, and driving in the door, brought out his furniture, and piled it up against the prison-gate, to make a bonfire which should burn it down.

"As soon as this device was understood, all those who had laboured hitherto, cast down their tools and helped to swell the heap; which reached halfway across the street, and was so high, that those who threw more fuel on the top, got up by ladders. When all the keeper's goods were flung upon this costly pile, to the last fragment, they smeared it with the pitch, and tar, and rosin they had brought, and sprinkled it with turpentine. To all the woodwork round the prison-doors they did the like, leaving not a joist or beam untouched. This infernal christening performed, they fired the pile with lighted matches and with blazing tow, and then stood by, awaiting the result . . . .

" . . . .They never slackened in their zeal, or kept aloof, but pressed upon the flames so hard, that those in front had much ado to save themselves from being thrust in; if one man swooned or dropped, a dozen struggled for his place, and that although they knew the pain, and thirst, and pressure to be unendurable. Those who fell down in fainting-fits, and were not crushed or burnt, were carried to an inn-yard close at hand, and dashed with water from a pump; of which buckets full were passed from man to man among the crowd; but such was the strong desire of all to drink, and such the fighting to be first, that for the most part, the whole contents were spilled upon the ground, without the lips of one man being moistened.

"Meanwhile, and in the midst of all the roar and outcry, those who were nearest to the pile, heaped up again the burning fragments that came toppling down, and raked the fire about the door, which although a sheet of flame, was still a door fast locked and barred, and kept them out. Great pieces of blazing wood were passed, besides, above the people's heads to such as stood about the ladders, and some of these, climbing up to the topmost stave, and holding on with one hand by the prison wall, exerted all their skill and force to cast these fire-brands on the roof, or down into the yards within.

"In many instances their efforts were successful; which occasioned a new and appalling addition to the horrors of the scene: for the prisoners within, seeing from between their bars that the fire caught in many places and thrived fiercely, and being all locked up in strong cells for the night, began to know that they were in danger of being burnt alive. This terrible fear, spreading from cell to cell and from yard to yard, vented itself in such dismal cries and wailings, and in such dreadful shrieks for help, that the whole jail resounded with the noise; which was loudly heard even above the shouting of the mob and roaring of the flames, and was so full of agony and despair, that it made the boldest tremble.

" . . . . The women who were looking on, shrieked loudly, beat their hands together, stopped their ears; and many fainted; the men who were not near the walls and active in the siege, rather than do nothing, tore up the pavement of the street, and did so with a haste and fury they could not have surpassed if that had been the jail, and they were near their object. Not one living creature in the throng was for an instant still. The whole great mass were mad.

"A shout! Another! Another yet, though few knew why, or what it meant. But those around the gate had seen it slowly yield, and drop from its topmost hinge. It hung on that side by but one, but was upright still, because of the bar, and its having sunk, of its own weight, into the heap of ashes at its foot. There was now a gap at the top of the doorway, through which could be descried a gloomy passage, cavernous and dark. Pile up the fire!

"It burnt fiercely. The door was red-hot, and the gap wider. They vainly tried to shield their faces with their hands, and standing as if in readiness for a spring, watched the place. Dark figures, some crawling on their hands and knees, some carried in the arms of others, were seen to pass along the roof. It was plain the jail could hold out no longer. The keeper, and his officers, and their wives and children, were escaping. Pile up the fire!

"The door sank down again: it settled deeper in the cinders—tottered —yielded—was down!

"As they shouted again, they fell back a moment, and left a clear space about the fire that lay between them and the jail entry. **Hugh** leapt upon the blazing heap, and scattering a train of sparks into the air, and making the dark lobby glitter with those that hung upon his dress, dashed into the jail.

"The hangman followed. And then so many rushed upon their track, that the fire got trodden down and thinly strewn about the street; but there was no need of it now, for, inside and out, the prison was in flames." ¶64

The Crisis. "At last, at seven o'clock in the evening, the Privy Council issued a solemn proclamation that it was now necessary to employ the military, and that the officers had most direct and effectual orders, by an immediate exertion of their utmost force, to repress the disturbances; and warning all good subjects of the King to keep themselves, their servants, and apprentices, within doors that night. There was then delivered out to every soldier on duty, thirty-six rounds of powder and ball; the drums beat; and the whole force was under arms at sunset.

"The City authorities, stimulated by the vigorous measures, held a Common Council; passed a vote thanking the military associations who had tendered their aid to the civil authorities; accepted it; and placed them under the direction of the two sheriffs.

"At the Queen's palace, a double guard, the yeomen on duty, the groom-porters, and all other attendants, were stationed in the passages and on the staircases at seven o'clock, with strict instructions to be watchful on their posts all night; and all the doors were locked.

"The gentlemen of the Temple, and the other Inns, mounted guard within their gates, and strengthened them with the great stones of the pavement, which they took up for the purpose. In Lincoln's Inn, they gave up the hall and commons to the Northumberland Militia, under the command of Lord

Algernon Percy; in some few of the city wards, the **burgesses** turned out, and without making a very fierce show, looked brave enough.

"Some hundreds of stout gentlemen threw themselves, armed to the teeth, into the halls of the different companies, double-locked and bolted all the gates, and dared the rioters (among themselves) to come on at their peril. These arrangements being all made simultaneously, or nearly so, were completed by the time it got dark; and then the streets were comparatively clear, and were guarded at all the great corners and chief avenues by the troops: while parties of the officers rode up and down in all directions, ordering chance stragglers home, and admonishing the residents to keep within their houses, and, if any firing ensued, not to approach the windows.

"More chains were drawn across such of the thoroughfares as were of a nature to favour the approach of a great crowd, and at each of these points a considerable force was stationed. All these precautions having been taken, and it being now quite dark, those in command awaited the result in some anxiety: and not without a hope that such vigilant demonstrations might of themselves dishearten the populace, and prevent any new outrages.

"But in this reckoning they were cruelly mistaken, for in half an hour, or less, as though the setting in of night had been their preconcerted signal, the rioters having previously, in small parties, prevented the lighting of the street lamps, rose like a great sea; and that in so many places at once, and with such inconceivable fury, that those who had the direction of the troops knew not, at first, where to turn or what to do.

"One after another, new fires blazed up in every quarter of the town, as though it were the intention of the insurgents to wrap the city in a circle of flames, which, contracting by degrees, would burn the whole to ashes; the crowd swarmed and roared in every street; and none but rioters and soldiers being out of doors, it seemed to the latter as if all London were arrayed against them, and they stood alone against the town.

"In two hours, six-and-thirty fires were raging—six-and-thirty great conflagrations; among the Borough Clink in Tooley Street, the King's Bench, the Fleet, and the New Bridewell. In almost every street, there was a battle; and in every quarter the muskets of the troops were heard above the shouts and tumult of the mob. The firing began in the Poultry, where the chain was drawn across the road, where nearly a score of people were killed on the first discharge. Their bodies having been hastily carried into St Mildred's Church by the soldiers, the latter fired again, and following fast upon the crowd, who began to give way when they saw the execution that was done, formed across Cheapside, and charged them at the point of the bayonet.

"The streets were now a dreadful spectacle. The shouts of the rabble, the shrieks of women, the cries of the wounded, and the constant firing, formed a deafening and an awful accompaniment to the sights which every corner presented. Wherever the road was obstructed by chains, there the fighting and the loss of life was greatest; but there was hot work and bloodshed in almost every leading thoroughfare." ¶67

Depth of Horror. "The vintner's house, with half-a-dozen others near at hand, was one great, glowing blaze. All night, no one had essayed to quench the flames, or stop their progress; but now a body of soldiers were actively engaged in pulling down two old wooden houses, which were every moment in danger of taking fire, and which could scarcely fail, if they were left to burn, to extend the conflagration immensely.

"The tumbling down of nodding walls and heavy blocks of wood, the hooting and the execrations of the crowd, the distant firing of other military detachments, the distracted looks and cries of those whose habitations were in danger, the hurrying to and fro of frightened people with their goods; the reflections in every quarter of the sky, of deep, red, soaring flames, as though the last day had come and the whole universe was burning; the dust, and smoke, and drift of fiery particles, scorching and kindling all it fell upon; the hot unwholesome vapour, the blight on everything; the stars, and moon, and very sky, obliterated;—made up such a sum of dreariness and ruin, that it seemed as if the face of Heaven were blotted out, and night, in its rest and quiet, and softened light, never could look upon the earth again.

"But there was a worse spectacle than this—worse by far than fire and smoke, or even the rabble's unappeasable and maniac rage. The gutters of the street, and every crack and fissure in the stones, ran with scorching spirit, which being dammed up by busy hands, overflowed the road and pavement, and formed a great pool, into which the people dropped down dead by dozens. They lay in heaps all round this fearful pond, husbands and wives, fathers and sons, mothers and daughters, women with children in their arms and babies at their breasts, and drank until they died. While some stooped with their lips to the brink and never raised their heads again, others sprang up from their fiery draught, and danced, half in a mad triumph, and half in the agony of suffocation, until they fell, and steeped their corpses in the liquor that had killed them.

"Nor was even this the worst or most appalling kind of death that happened on this fatal night. From the burning cellars, where they drank out of hats, pails, buckets, tubs, and shoes, some men were drawn, alive, but all alight from head to foot; who, in their unendurable anguish and suffering, making for anything that had the look of water, rolled, hissing, in this hideous lake, and splashed up liquid fire which lapped in all it met with as it ran along the surface, and neither spared the living nor the dead. On this last night of the great riots—for the last night it was—the wretched victims of a senseless outcry, became themselves the dust and ashes of the flames they had kindled, and strewed the public streets of London." ¶68

Aftermath. "By this Friday night . . . the disturbances were entirely quelled, and peace and order were restored to the affrighted city . . . in spite of the melancholy forebodings of that numerous class of society who see with the greatest clearness into the darkest perspectives, the town remained profoundly quiet. The strong military force disposed in every advantageous quarter, and stationed at every commanding point, held the scattered fragments of the mob in check; the search after rioters was prosecuted with unrelenting vigour; and if there were any among them so desperate and reckless as to be inclined, after the terrible scenes they had beheld, to venture forth again, they were so daunted by these resolute measures, that they quickly shrunk into their hiding-places, and had no thought but for their own safety.

"In a word, the crowd was utterly routed. Upwards of two hundred had been shot dead in the streets. Two hundred and fifty more were lying, badly wounded, in the hospitals; of whom seventy or eighty died within a short time afterwards. A hundred were already in custody, and more were taken every hour. How many perished in the conflagrations, or by their own excesses, is unknown; but that numbers found a terrible grave in the hot ashes of the flames they had kindled, or crept into vaults and cellars to drink in secret or to nurse their sores, and never saw the light again, is certain. When the embers of the fires had been black and cold for many weeks, the labourers' spades proved this, beyond a doubt.

"Seventy-two private houses and four strong jails were destroyed in the four great days of these riots. The total loss of property, as estimated by the sufferers, was one hundred and fifty-five thousand pounds; at the lowest and least partial estimate of disinterested persons, it exceeded one hundred and twenty-five thousand pounds., For this immense loss, compensation was soon afterwards made out of the public purse, in pursuance of a vote of the House of Commons; the sum being levied on the various wards in the city, on the county, and the borough of Southwark. Both Lord **Mansfield** and Lord **Saville**, however, who had been great sufferers, refused to accept of any compensation whatever.

"The House of Commons, sitting on Tuesday with locked and guarded doors, had passed a resolution to the effect that, as soon as the tumults subsided, it would immediately proceed to consider the petitions presented from many of his Majesty's Protestant subjects, and would take the same into its serious consideration." ¶73

The Leader's Fate. "And in the Tower, in a dreary room whose thick stone walls shut out the hum of life, and made a stillness which the records left by former prisoners with those silent witnesses seemed to deepen and intensify; remorseful for every act that had been done by every man among the cruel crowd; feeling for the time their guilt his own, and their lives put in peril by himself; and finding, amidst such reflections, little comfort in fanaticism, or in his fancied call; sat the unhappy author of all—**Lord George Gordon**.

"He had been made prisoner that evening. 'If you are sure it's me you want,' he said to the officers, who waited outside with the warrant for his arrest on a charge of High Treason, 'I am ready to accompany you—' which he did without resistance. He was conducted first before the Privy Council, and afterwards to the Horse Guards, and then was taken by way of Westminster Bridge, and back over London Bridge (for the purpose of avoiding the main streets), to the Tower, under the strongest guard ever known to enter its gates with a single prisoner.

"Of all his forty thousand men, not one remained to bear him company. Friends, dependents, followers—none were there. His fawning secretary had played the traitor; and he whose weakness had been goaded and urged on by so many for their own purposes, was desolate and alone." 73

"Lord George Gordon, remaining in his prison in the Tower until Monday the fifth of February in the following year, was on that day solemnly tried at Westminster for High Treason. Of this crime he was, after a patient investigation, declared Not Guilty; upon the ground that there was no proof of his having called the multitude together with any traitorous or unlawful intentions. Yet so many people were there, still, to whom those riots taught no lesson of reproof or moderation, that a public subscription was set on foot in Scotland to defray the cost of his defence.

"For seven years afterwards he remained, at the strong intercession of his friends, comparatively quiet . . . . In the year 1788 he was stimulated by some new insanity to write and publish an injurious pamphlet, reflecting on the Queen of France, in very violent terms. Being indicted for the libel, and . . . found guilty, he fled into Holland in place of appearing to receive sentence; from whence . . . he was sent home again with all speed . . . [at] Birmingham he made . . . a public profession of the Jewish religion; and figured there as a Jew until he was arrested, and brought back to London to receive the sentence he had evaded. By virtue of this sentence he was . . . cast into Newgate for five years and ten months, and required besides to pay a large fine, and to furnish heavy securities for his future good behaviour.

" . . . suffering his beard to grow nearly to his waist, and conforming in all respects to the ceremonies of his new religion, he applied himself to the study of history, and occasionally to the art of painting, in which, in his younger days, he had shown some skill. Deserted by his former friends, and treated in all respects like the worst criminal in the jail, he lingered on, quite cheerful and resigned, until the 1st of November 1793, when he died in his cell, being then only three-and-forty years of age." LAST

"Many men with fewer sympathies for the distressed and needy, with less abilities and harder hearts, have made a shining figure and left a brilliant fame. He had his mourners. The prisoners bemoaned his loss, and missed him; for though his means were not large, his charity was great, and in bestowing alms among them he considered the necessities of all alike, and knew no distinction of sect or creed. There are wise men in the highways of the world who may learn something, even from this poor crazy lord who died in Newgate." LAST

October 1842   2 vols C&H **AN**
U.S. publication 1842 by Wilson & Co., New York, as an extra number of *Brother Jonathan*

American Notes

(for General Circulation) *

CD and his wife Catherine journeyed to North America on the *Britannia*, leaving Liverpool on January 3, 1842. The crossing was tumultuous, more so than normal even for that wintry season. Their landfall was Halifax. On to Boston, Lowell, Worcester, Hartford, New Haven, New York and Philadelphia; then Washington, Richmond, Baltimore and Harrisburg. 1-9

Then across the Alleghenies to Pittsburgh, Cincinnati, Louisville, Cairo (the Eden of MC) and St Louis, with an excursion to look at the Prairie. Returning to Cincinnati, the Dickenses headed north to Columbus, Sandusky, Cleveland, Buffalo, Lake Erie and Niagara. 10-14

Canadian cities Toronto, Kingston, Montreal, Quebec and St John's came next, and then back to the U.S.: Burlington, Albany, the Shaker Village near Lebanon (NY), the Hudson Highlands and West Point. The Dickenses left for home from New York on June 7, 1842. The crossing was uneventful. 15-16

By addendum, CD adverts to Slavery and its endemic connective, Violence, in the United States, primarily by direct quotation of newspaper advertisements and articles. CD comments on the venomous international copyright question he had raised in speeches, and on public health. 17 He concludes with a cautionary tale for Britons purchasing shoes in New York. 18

AN was not welcomed everywhere in the U.S., but later many American observers acknowledged that CD's criticisms had importantly affected American mores in journalism, table manners and chewing (and spitting) tobacco. His strictures might have been more resented and less salutary in ultimate impact had not John Forster (so he tells us) persuaded CD to change part of his plan. See the following.

*The Panic of 1837, which caused many states to repudiate their debts, was much criticized in England. GC says CD's title is "another snide pun about the erratic reliability of the American financial system." (I p846)

"Dickens is cross with America because he is worried about America; as if he were its father. He explores its industrial, legal, and educational arrangements like a mother looking at the housekeeping of a married son; he makes suggestions with a certain acidity; he takes a strange pleasure in being pessimistic. He advises them to take note of how much better certain things are done in England. All this is very different from Dickens's characteristic way of dealing with a foreign country. . . . . He does not go carefully with a notebook through Jesuit schools nor offer friendly suggestions to the governors of Parisian prisons. Or if he does, it is in a different spirit; it is in the spirit of an ordinary tourist being shown over the Coliseum or the Pyramids. But he visited America in the spirit of a Government inspector dealing with something it was his duty to inspect." GKC pp78-9

A Suppressed Introduction

By his account, John Forster with difficulty persuaded CD not to include the following in AN's first publication. He thus suppressed CD's worst-tempered lashing at the trans-Atlantic Press and effectively excluded it from subsequent AN editions (we know of none which gives it).

"INTRODUCTORY. AND NECESSARY TO BE READ.

"I have placed the foregoing title at the head of this page, because I challenge and deny the right of any person to pass judgment on this book, or to arrive at any reasonable conclusion in reference to it, without first being at the trouble of becoming acquainted with its design and purpose.

"It is not statistical. Figures of arithmetic have already been heaped upon America's devoted head, almost as lavishly as figures of speech have been piled above Shakespeare's grave.

"It comprehends no small talk concerning individuals, and no violation of the social confidences of private life. The very prevalent practice of kidnapping live ladies and gentlemen, forcing them into cabinets, and labelling and ticketing them whether they will or no, for the gratification of the idle and the curious, is not to my taste. Therefore I have avoided it.

"It has not a grain of any political ingredient in its whole composition.

"Neither does it contain, nor have I intended that it should contain, any lengthened and minute account of my personal reception in the United States: not because I am, or ever was, insensible to that spontaneous effusion of affection and generosity of heart, in a most affectionate and generous-hearted people; but because I conceive that it would ill become me to flourish matter necessarily involving so much of my own praises, in the eyes of my unhappy readers.

"This book is simply what it claims to be—a record of the impressions I received from day to day, during my hasty travels in America, and sometimes (but not always) of the conclusions to which they, and after-reflection on them, have led me; a description of the country I passed through; of the institutions I visited; of the kind of people among whom I journeyed; and of the manners and customs that came within my observation. Very many works having just the same scope and range, have been already published, but I think that these two volumes stand in need of no apology on that account. The interest of such productions, if they have any, lies in the varying impressions made by the same novel things on different minds; and not in new discoveries or extraordinary adventures.

"I can scarcely be supposed to be ignorant of the hazard I run in writing of America at all. I know perfectly well that there is, in that country, a numerous mass of well-intentioned persons prone to be dissatisfied with all accounts of the Republic whose citizens they are, which are not couched in terms of exalted and extravagant praise. I know perfectly well that there is in America, as in most other places laid down in maps of the great world, a numerous class of persons so tenderly and delicately constituted, that they cannot bear the truth in any form. And I do not need the gift of prophecy to discern afar off, that they who will be aptest to detect malice, ill-will, and all uncharitableness in these pages, and to show, beyond any doubt, that they are perfectly inconsistent with that grateful and enduring recollection which I profess to entertain of the welcome I found awaiting me beyond the Atlantic—will be certain native **journalists**, veracious and gentlemanly, who were at geat pains to prove to me, on all occasions during my stay there, that the aforesaid welcome was utterly worthless.

"But, venturing to dissent even from these high authorities, I formed my own opinion of its value in the outset, and retain it to this hour; and in asserting (as I invariably did on all public occasions) my liberty and freedom of speech while I was among the Americans, and in maintaining it at home, I believe that I best show my sense of the high worth of that welcome, and of the honourable singleness of purpose with which it was extended to me. From first to last I saw, in the friends who crowded round me in America, old readers, over-grateful and over-partial perhaps, to whom I had happily been the means of furnishing pleasure and entertainment; not a vulgar herd who would flatter and cajole a stranger into turning with closed eyes from all the blemishes of the nation, and into chaunting its praises with the discrimination of a street ballad-singer. From first to last I saw, in those hospitable hands, a home-made wreath of laurel; and not an iron muzzle disguised beneath a flower or two.

"Therefore I take—and hold myself not only justified in taking, but bound to take—the plain course of saying what I think, and noting what I saw; and as it is not my custom to exalt what in my judgment are foibles and abuses at home, so I have no intention of softening down, or glozing [*sic.*] over, those that I have observed abroad.

"If this book should fall into the hands of any sensitive American who cannot bear to be told that the working of the institutions of his country is far from perfect; that in spite of the advantage she has over all other nations in the elastic freshness and vigour of her youth, she is far from being a model for the earth to copy; and that even in those pictures of the national manners with which he quarrels most, there is still (after the lapse of several years, each of which may be fairly supposed to have had its stride in improvement) much that is just and true at this hour; let him lay it down, now, for I shall not please him. Of the intelligent, reflecting, and educated among his countrymen, I have no fear; for I have ample reason to believe, after many delightful conversations snot easily to be forgotten, that there are very few topics (if any) on which their sentiments differ materially from mine.

"I may be asked—'If you have been in any respect disappointed in America, and are assured beforehand that the expression of your disappointment will give offence to any class, why do you write at all?' My answer is, that I went there expecting greater things than I found, and resolved as far as in me lay to do justice to the country, at the expense of any (in my view) mistaken or prejudiced statements that might have been made to its disparagement. Coming home with a corrected and sobered judgment, I consider myself no less bound to do justice to what, according to my best means of judgment, I found to be the truth." JF II pp13-17

On his second visit, CD expressed a profound change of heart at a public dinner in New York City April 18, 1868 (the essence is provided to the current reader in many but not all AN editions):

"[It is] a duty with which I henceforth charge myself, not only here but on every suitable occasion, whatsoever and wheresoever, to express my high and grateful sense of my second reception in America, and to bear my honest testimony to the national generosity and magnanimity. Also, to declare how astounded I have been by the amazing changes I have seen around me on every side—changes moral, changes physical, changes in the amount of land subdued and peopled, changes in the rise of vast new cities, changes in the growth of older cities almost out of recognition, changes in the graces and amenities of life, changes in the Press, without whose advancement no advancement can take place anywhere.

"Nor am I, believe me, so arrogant as to suppose that in five-and-twenty years there have been no changes in me, and that I had nothing to learn and no extreme impressions to correct when I was here first . . . what I have resolved upon . . . is, on my return to England, in my own person, in my own Journal, to bear, for the behoof of my countrymen, such testimony to the gigantic changes in this country as I have hinted at to-night. Also, to record that wherever I have been, in the smallest places equally with the largest, I have been received with unsurpassable politeness, delicacy, sweet temper, hospitality, considera-tion, and with unsurpassable respect for the privacy daily enforced upon me by the nature of my avocation here and the state of my health.

"This testimony, so long as I live, and so long as my descendants have any legal right in my books, I shall cause to be republished, as an appendix to every copy of those two books of mine [AN and MC] in which I have referred to America. And this I will do and cause to be done, not in mere love and thankful-ness, but because I regard it as an act of plain justice and honour." ¶

In May 1868, he included this statement as a Postscript to AN, adding:

"I said these words with the greatest earnestness that I could lay upon them, and I repeat them in print here with equal earnestness. So long as this book shall last, I hope that they will form a part of it, and will be fairly read as inseparable from my experiences and impressions of America.

"CHARLES DICKENS"

CONTENTS

Going to America: On Shipboard

Captain. "Now, by all our hopes and wishes, the very man he ought to be! A well-made, tight-built, dapper little fellow; with a ruddy face, which is a letter of invitation to shake him by both hands at once; and with a clear, blue honest eye, that it does one good to see one's sparkling image in." 1

" . . . the captain comes down again, in a sou'-wester hat tied under his chin, and a pilot-coat: making the ground wet where he stands . . . after an hour's pleasant conversation about the ship, the passengers, and things in general, the captain (who never goes to bed, and is never out of humour) turns up his coat collar for the deck again; shakes hands all round; and goes laughing out into the weather as merrily as to a birthday party." 2

Couple. " . . . newly married too, if one might judge from the endearments they frequently interchanged . . . a mysterious, runaway kind of couple; that the lady had great personal attractions also; and that the gentleman carried more guns with him than Robinson Crusoe, wore a shooting-coat, and had two great dogs on board . . . he tried hot roast pig and bottled ale as a cure for seasickness; and that he took these remedies (usually in bed) day after day, with astonishing perseverance . . . they decidedly failed." 2

Lazy gentleman. With "his hat on one side and his hands in his pockets . . . [he] condescends to look that way . . . and not even the sage **Lord Burleigh** on his nod, included half so much as this lazy gentleman of might who has made the passage (as everybody on board has found out already; it's impossible to say how) thirteen times without a single accident!" 1

Passenger. "There is another passenger very much wrapped-up, who has been frowned down by the rest, and morally trampled upon and crushed, for presuming to inquire with a timid interest how long it is since the poor President went down." 1

Passengers. " . . . nor were there wanting (as there never are) sagacious doubters of the captain's calculations, who, so soon as his back was turned, would, in the absence of compasses, measure the chart with bits of string, and ends of pocket-handkerchiefs, and points of snuffers, and clearly prove him to be wrong by an odd thousand miles or so." 16

"There are always on board ship, a Sanguine One, and a Despondent One. The latter character carried it hollow at this period of the voyage, and triumphed over the Sanguine One at every meal . . . . " 16

Pilot. " . . . how desperately unpopular the poor pilot became in one short minute. He had had his passage out from Liverpool, and during the whole voyage had been quite a notorious character, as a teller of anecdotes and cracker of jokes. Yet here were the very men who had laughed the loudest at his jests, now flourishing their fists in his face, loading him with imprecations, and defying him to his teeth as a villain!" 2

Sailor. " . . . an English sailor, a smart, thorough-built, English man-of-war's-man from his hat to his shoes, who was serving in the American navy, and having got leave of absence was on his way home to see his friends . . . all through the passage there he was, first at the braces, outermost on the yards, perpetually lending a hand everywhere, but always with a sober dignity in his manner, and a sober grin on his face, which plainly said, 'I do it as a gentleman. For my own pleasure, mind you!'" 16

Stewardess. "God bless [her] for her piously fraudulent account of January voyages! God bless her for her clear recollection of the companion passage of last year, when nobody was ill, and everybody dancing from morning to night, and it was 'a run' of twelve days, and a piece of the purest frolic, and delight, and jollity!

"All happiness be with her for her bright face and her pleasant Scotch tongue, which had sounds of old Home in it for my fellow-traveller; and for her predictions of fair winds and fine weather (all wrong, or I shouldn't be half so fond of her); and for the ten thousand small fragments of genuine womanly tact, by which, without piecing them elaborately together, and patching them up into shape and form and case and pointed application, she nevertheless did plainly show that all young mothers on one side of the Atlantic were near and close at hand to their little children left upon the other; and that what seemed to the uninitiated a serious journey, was, to those who were in the secret, a mere frolic, to be sung about and whistled at! Light be her heart, and gay her merry eyes, for years!" ¶1

America: the East and the South

Boy, in a coach. " . . . I observed a new parcel lying on the coach roof, which I took to be a rather large fiddle in a brown bag. In the course of a few miles, however, I discovered that it had a glazed cap at one end and a pair of muddy shoes at the other; and further observation demonstrated it to be a small boy in a snuff-coloured coat, with his arms quite pinioned to his sides, by deep forcing into his pockets . . . he lay a-top of the luggage with his face towards the rain . . . . At last, on some occasion of our stopping, this thing slowly upreared itself to the height of three feet six, and fixing its eyes on me, observed in piping accents, with a complaisant yawn, half quenched in an obliging air of friendly patronage, 'Well now, stranger, I guess you find this a'most like an English arternoon, hey?'" 9

Laura Bridgman. " . . . a girl, blind, deaf, and dumb; destitute of smell; and nearly so of taste: before a fair young creature with every human faculty, and hope, and power of goodness and affection, inclosed within her delicate frame, and but one outward sense—the sense of touch . . . .

" . . . .Her face was radiant with intelligence and pleasure. Her hair, braided by her own hands, was bound about a head, whose intellectual capacity and development were beautifully expressed in its graceful outline, and its broad open brow; her dress, arranged by herself, was a pattern of neatness and simplicity; the work she had knitted, lay beside her; her writing-book was on the desk she leaned upon.—From the mournful ruin of such bereavement, there had slowly risen up this gentle, tender, guileless, grateful-hearted being." 3

Oliver Caswell. " . . . a small laughing fellow, who stood aloof, entertaining himself with a gymnastic exercise for bringing the arms and chest into play; which he enjoyed mightily; especially when, in thrusting out his right arm, he brought it into contact with another boy . . . this young child was deaf, and dumb, and blind." 3

Dr [William Ellery] Channing. " . . . I was reluctantly obliged to forego the delight of hearing Dr. Channing, who happened to preach that morning for the first time in a very long interval. I mention the name of this distinguished and accomplished man (with whom I soon afterwards had the pleasure of becoming personally acquainted), that I may have the gratification of recording my humble tribute of admiration and respect for his high abilities and character; and for the bold philanthropy with which he has ever opposed himself to that most hideous blot and foul disgrace—Slavery." 3

Coachmen, in New York. "Negro coachmen and white; in straw hats, black hats, white hats, glazed caps, fur caps; in coats of drab, black, brown, green, blue, nankeen, striped jean and linen; and there, in that one instance (look while it passes, or it will be too late), in suits of livery. Some southern republican that, who puts his blacks in uniform, and swells with Sultan pomp and power." 6

Coachmen, in western Pennsylvania. "The coachmen always change with the horses, and are usually as dirty as the coach. The first was dressed like a very shabby English baker; the second like a Russian peasant: for he wore a loose purple camlet robe, with a fur collar, tied round his waist with a parti-coloured worsted sash; grey trousers; light blue gloves: and a cap of bearskin." 9

Congressman. "It was not a month, since this same body had sat calmly by, and heard a man, one of themselves, with oaths which beggars in their drink reject, threaten to cut another's throat from ear to ear. There he sat, among them; not crushed by the general feeling of the assembly, but as good a man as any."

Dancer. "Five or six couples come upon the floor, marshalled by a lively young negro, who is the wit of the assembly, and the greatest dancer known. He never leaves off making queer faces, and is the delight of all the rest, who grin from ear to ear, incessantly . . . .

—*his dancing:* "Single shuffle, double shuffle, cut and cross-cut; snapping his fingers, rolling his eyes, turning in his knees, presenting the backs of his legs in front, spinning about on his toes and heels like nothing but the man's fingers on the tambourine; dancing with two left legs, two right legs, two wooden legs, two wire legs, two spring legs—all sorts of legs and no legs—what is this to him? And in what walk of life, or dance of life, does man ever get such stimulating applause as thunders about him, when, having danced his partner off her feet, and himself too, he finishes by leaping gloriously on the bar-counter, and calling for something to drink, with the chuckle of a million of counterfeit Jim Crows, in one inimitable sound!" 6

Driver. "He is a negro—very black indeed. He is dressed in a coarse pepper-and-salt suit excessively patched and darned (particularly at the knees), grey stockings, enormous unblacked high-low shoes, and very short trousers. He has two odd gloves: one of parti-coloured worsted, and one of leather. He has a very short whip, broken in the middle and bandaged up with string. And yet he wears a low-crowned, broad-brimmed, black hat: faintly shadowing forth a kind of insane imitation of an English coachman!"

Ralph Waldo Emerson. "This gentleman has written a volume of Essays, in which, among much that is dreamy and fanciful (if he will pardon me for saying so), there is much more that is true and manly, honest and bold." 3

Farmer. " . . . a Kentucky farmer, six-feet-six in height, with his hat on, and his hands under his coat-tails, who leaned against the wall and kicked the floor with his heel, as though he had Time's head under his shoe, and were literally 'killing' him." 8

Horatio Greenough. "In [the Capitol rotunda] Mr Greenough's large statue of Washington has been lately placed. It has great merits of course, but it struck me as being rather strained and violent for its subject. I could wish, however, to have seen it in a better light than it can ever be viewed in, where it stands." 8

Insane. "The moping **idiot**, cowering down with long dishevelled hair; the gibbering **maniac**, with his hideous laugh and pointed finger; the vacant eye, the fierce wild face, the gloomy picking of the hands and lips, and munching of the nails: there they were all, without disguise, in naked ugliness and horror. In the dining-room, a bare, dull, dreary place, with nothing for the eye to rest on but the empty walls, a **woman** was locked up alone. She was bent, they told me, on committing suicide. If anything could have strengthened her in her resolution, it would certainly have been the insupportable monotony of such an existence." 6

Two **Irishmen**. " . . . those two labourers in holiday clothes, of whom one carries in his hand a crumpled scrap of paper from which he tries to spell out a hard name, while the other looks about for it on all the doors and windows.

"Irishmen both! You might know them, if they were masked, by their long-tailed blue coats and bright buttons, and their drab trousers, which they wear like men well used to working dresses, who are easy in no others." 6

Washington Irving. "I sincerely believe that in all the madness of American politics, few public men would have been so earnestly, devotedly, and affectionately caressed, as this most charming writer: and I have seldom respected a public assembly more, than I did this eager throng, when I saw them turning with one mind from noisy orators and officers of state, and flocking with a generous and honest impulse round the man of quiet pursuits: proud in his promotion as reflecting back upon their country: and grateful to him with their whole hearts for the store of graceful fancies he had poured out among them. Long may he dispense such treasures with unsparing hand; and long may they remember him as worthily!" 8

Lawyer. "The learned gentleman (like a few of his English brethren) was desperately long-winded, and had a remarkable capacity of saying the same thing over and over again . . . . I listened to him for about a quarter of an hour; and, coming out of court at the expiration of that time, without the faintest ray of enlightenment as to the merits of the case, felt as if I were at home again." 3

First **madwoman**, the 'lady of the house.' "Leaning her head against the chimneypiece, with a great assumption of dignity and refinement of manner, sat an elderly female, in as many scraps of finery as **Madge Wildfire** herself. Her head in particular was so strewn with scraps of gauze and cotton and bits of paper, and had so many queer odds and ends stuck all about it, that it looked like a bird's-nest. She was radiant with imaginary jewels; wore a rich pair of undoubted gold spectacles; and gracefully dropped upon her lap, as we approached, a very old greasy newspaper, in which I dare say she had been reading an account of her own presentation at some Foreign Court." 3

Second **madwoman**. "There was one little prim old lady, of very smiling and good-humoured appearance, who came sidling up to me from the end of a long passage, and with a curtsey of inexpressible condescension, propounded this unaccountable inquiry:

"'Does Pontefract still flourish, Sir, upon the soil of England?'

" . . . . After glancing at me for a moment, as if to be quite sure that I was serious in my respectful air, she sidled back some paces; sidled forward again; made a sudden skip (at which I precipitately retreated a step or two); and said:

"'*I* am an antediluvian, Sir . . . . It is an extremely proud and pleasant thing, Sir, to be an antediluvian,' said the old lady.

"'I should think it was, ma'am,' I rejoined.

"The old lady kissed her hand, gave another skip, smirked and sidled down the gallery in a most extraordinary manner, and ambled gracefully into her own bedchamber." 5

Mother. " . . . the poor old crone is restless in a strange land, and yearns to lay her bones, she says, among her people in the old graveyard at home: and so they go to pay her passage back: and God help her and them, and every simple heart, and all who turn to the Jerusalem of their younger days, and have an altar-fire upon the cold hearth of their fathers." 6

Old man. "One [White House visitor], a tall, wiry, muscular old man, from the west; sunburnt and swarthy; with a brown white hat on his knees, and a giant umbrella resting between his legs; who sat bolt upright in his chair, frowning steadily at the carpet, and twitching the hard lines about his mouth, as if he had made up his mind 'to fix' the President on what he had to say, and wouldn't bate him a grain." 8

Coach **passengers**. "'Any room, Sir?' cries the new passenger to the **coachman.**

"'Well there's room enough,' replies the coachman, without getting down, or even looking at him.

"'There an't no room at all, Sir,' bawls a gentleman inside. Which another gentleman (also inside) confirms, by predicting that the attempt to introduce any more passengers 'won't fit nohow.'

"The new passenger, without any expression of anxiety, looks into the coach, and then looks up at the coachman: 'Now, how do you mean to fix it?' says he, after a pause: 'for I *must* go.'

" . . . . In this state of things, matters seem to be approximating to a fix of another kind, when another inside passenger in a corner, who is nearly suffocated, cries faintly, 'I'll get out.'" 9

Physician. " . . . [the first **madwoman**] will serve to exemplify the physician's manner of acquiring and retaining the confidence of his patients.

"'This,' he said aloud, taking me by the hand, and advancing to the fantastic figure with great politeness—not raising her suspicions by the slightest look or whisper, or any kind of aside, to me: 'This lady is the hostess of this mansion, Sir. It belongs to her. Nobody else has anything whatever to do with it. It is a large establishment, as you see, and requires a great number of attendants. She lives, you observe, in the very first style. She is kind enough to receive my visits, and to permit my wife and family to reside here; for which it is hardly necessary to say, we are much indebted to her. She is exceedingly courteous, you perceive,' on this hint she bowed condescendingly, 'and will permit me to have the pleasure of introducing you: a gentleman from England, ma'am: newly arrived from England, after a very tempestuous passage: Mr Dickens,—the lady of the house!'" 3

Prisoners, in Philadelphia.

—[in solitary confinement]. "He stopped his work when we went in, took off his spectacles, and answered freely to everything that was said to him, but always with a strange kind of pause first, and in a low thoughtful voice. He wore a paper hat of his own making, and was pleased to have it noticed and commended . . . I saw that his lip trembled, and could have counted the beating of his heart. I forget how it came about, but some allusion was made to his having a wife. He shook his head at the word, turned aside, and covered his face with his hands." 7

—[in solitary confinement]. "In another cell, there was a German, sentenced to five years' imprisonment for larceny, two of which had just expired. With colours . . . he had painted every inch of the walls and ceiling quite beautifully. He had laid out the few feet of ground, behind, with exquisite neatness, and had made a little bed in the centre, that looked by-the-bye like a grave. The taste and ingenuity he had displayed in everything were most extraordinary; and yet a more dejected, heart-broken, wretched creature, it would be difficult to imagine." 7

—[in solitary confinement]. " . . . a tall strong black, a burglar, working at his proper trade of making screws and the like. His time was nearly out. He was not only a very dexterous thief, but was notorious for his boldness and hardihood, and for the number of his previous convictions . . . . This fellow, upon the slightest encouragement, would have mingled with his professional recollections the most detestable cant; but I am very much mistaken if he could have surpassed the unmitigated hypocrisy with which he declared that he blessed the day on which he came into that prison, and that he never would commit another robbery as long as he lived." 7

—[in solitary confinement]. "There was one man who was allowed, as an indulgence, to keep rabbits . . . . [He] stood shading his haggard face in the unwonted sunlight of the great window, looking as wan and unearthly as if he had been summoned from the grave. He had a white rabbit in his breast; and when the little creature, getting down upon the ground, stole back into the cell, and he, being dismissed, crept timidly after it, I thought it would have been very hard to say in what respect the man was the nobler animal of the two." 7

—"There was an English thief, who had been there but a few days out of seven years: a villainous, low-browed, thin-lipped fellow, with a white face; who had as yet no relish for visitors, and who, but for the additional penalty, would have gladly stabbed me with his shoemaker's knife." 7

—"There was another German who had entered the jail but yesterday, and who started from his bed when we looked in, and pleaded, in his broken English, very hard for work." 7

—"There was a poet, who after doing two days' work in every four-and-twenty hours, one for himself and one for the prison, wrote verses about ships (he was by trade a mariner), and 'the maddening winecup,' and his friends at home." 7

—" . . . a fat old negro whose leg had been taken off within the jail, had for his attendant a classical scholar and an accomplished surgeon, himself a prisoner likewise." 7

—"Eleven years of solitary confinement!

"'I am very glad to hear your time is nearly out.' What does he say? Nothing. Why does he stare at his hands, and pick the flesh upon his fingers, and raise his eyes for an instant, every now and then, to those bare walls which have seen his head turn grey? It is a way he has sometimes.

"Does he never look men in the face, and does he always pluck at those hands of his, as though he were bent on parting skin and bone? It is his humour: nothing more.

"It is his humour too, to say that he does not look forward to going out; that he is not glad the time is drawing near; that he did look forward to it once, but that was very long ago; that he has lost all care for everything. It is his humour to be a helpless, crushed, and broken man. And, Heaven be his witness that he has his humour thoroughly gratified!" 7

—"I have the face of this man, who was going to be released next day, before me now. It is almost more memorable in its happiness than the other faces in their misery. How easy and how natural it was for him to say that the [solitary confinement] system was a good one; and that the time went 'pretty quick—considering;' and that when a man once felt that he had offended the law, and must satisfy it, 'he got along, somehow:' and so forth!" 7

Quaker. "[He was] mild and modest . . . [he] opened the discourse by informing me, in a grave whisper, that his grandfather was the inventor of cold-drawn castor oil. I mention the circumstance here, thinking it probable that this is the first occasion on which the valuable medicine in question was ever used as a conversational aperient." 7 [aperient: ppr of *aperire,* to open, uncover; *ab,* from, and *parire,* to produce: laxative—Webster's New Universal Unabridged Dictionary]

Captain Sherman. "This steamboat [on Lake Champlain], which is called 'The Burlington,' is a perfectly exquisite achievement of neatness, elegance, and order. The decks are drawing-rooms; the cabins are boudoirs, choicely furnished and adorned with prints, pictures, and musical instruments; every nook and corner in the vessel is a perfect curiosity of graceful comfort and beautiful contrivance. Captain Sherman, her commander, to whose ingenuity and excellent taste these results are solely attributable, has bravely and worthily distinguished himself on more than one trying occasion . . . . He and his vessel are held in universal respect, both by his own countrymen and ours; and no man ever enjoyed the popular esteem, who, in his sphere of action, won and wore it better than this gentleman." 15

Slave. " . . . a wretched drudge, who, after running to and fro all day till midnight, and moping in his stealthy winks of sleep upon the stairs between-whiles, was washing the dark passages at four o'clock in the morning; and [I] went upon my way with a grateful heart that I was not doomed to live where slavery was, and had never had my senses blunted to its wrongs and horrors in a slave-rocked cradle." 9

Slavemaster. "The champion of Life, Liberty, and the Pursuit of Happiness, who had bought [the slaves], rode in the same train; and, every time we stopped, got down to see that they were safe. The **black** in **Sinbad's**

Travels with one eye in the middle of his forehead which shone like a burning coal, was nature's aristocrat compared with this white gentleman." 9

Edward Thompson Taylor. "The only preacher I heard in Boston was Mr Taylor, who addresses himself peculiarly to seamen, and who was once a mariner himself . . . . He looked a weather-beaten hard-featured man, of about six or eight and fifty; with deep lines graven as it were into his face, dark hair, and a stern, keen eye. Yet the general character of his countenance was pleasant and agreeable." 3

—*his preaching:* "It is possible, however, that my favourable impression of him may have been greatly influenced and strengthened, firstly, by his impressing upon his hearers that the true observance of religion was not inconsistent with a cheerful deportment and an exact discharge of the duties of their station, which, indeed, it scrupulously required of them; and secondly, by his cautioning them not to set up any monopoly in Paradise and its mercies. I never heard these two points so wisely touched (if indeed I have ever heard them touched at all), by any preacher of that kind before." 3

John Tyler. " . . . at a business-like table covered with papers, sat the President himself. He looked somewhat worn and anxious, and well he might; being at war with everybody—but the expression of his face was mild and pleasant, and his manner was remarkably unaffected, gentlemanly, and agreeable. I thought that in his whole carriage and demeanour, he became his station singularly well." 8

Young gentlemen. "On board this steamboat, there were two young gentlemen, with shirt-collars reversed as usual, and armed with very big walking-sticks; who planted two seats in the middle of the deck, at a distance of some four paces apart; took out their tobacco-boxes; and sat down opposite each other, to chew. In less than a quarter of an hour's time, these hopeful youths had shed about them on the clean boards, a copious shower of yellow rain; clearing, by that means, a kind of magic circle, within whose limits no intruders dared to come, and which they never failed to refresh and re-refresh before a spot was dry." 8

Young girl, a prisoner. " . . . not twenty, as I recollect . . . upon whose downcast face the sun in all its splendour shone down through the high chink in the wall, where one narrow strip of bright blue sky was visible. She was very penitent and quiet; had come to be resigned, she said (and I believe her); and had a mind at peace. 'In a word, you are happy here?' said one of my companions. She struggled—she did struggle very hard—to answer, Yes; but raising her eyes, and meeting that glimpse of freedom overhead, she burst into tears, and said, 'She tried to be; she uttered no complaint; but it was natural that she should sometimes long to go out of that one cell; she could not help that,' she sobbed, poor thing!" 7

Prisoner, in New York; murdered his wife and will probably be hanged   6
Shaker, female: stock was presided over by something alive in a russet case   15
-male; eyes as hard, dull and cold, as the buttons on his coat: a calm goblin   15
-*pl* very wooden, like the figure-heads of ships; broadest of brims on hats   15
Sinbad: encountered a black with one eye in the middle of his forehead   9
Slaves in the train: mother and children separated from their husband and father   9
Slave owner: considerate, excellent master; inherited slaves and not buyer or seller   9
Steward, black and hospitable; awakened, led CD to his berth   9
Tambourinist, friend of the fiddler: playing a lively measure   6
John Trumbull, painter   8
John Tyler's daughter-in-law: acted as lady of the mansion: graceful and accomplished   8
Madge Wildfire (Magdalen Murdockson): character in Scott's *Heart of Midlothian*   3
Young lady, who praised the banks of the Connecticut River: very beautiful   4
Young man, whose madness was love and music   4

America: the West and the Mid-West

Bride and Bridegroom, headed for the Far West   536
Captain, a whittler   536
Crocus, Dr; phrenologist from Scotland   537
Forester, who did not like overcrowding   537
Gentleman, droning   537
-passenger, who had read Boz   537
Girl, with a loquacious chin   537
Husband, of a little woman   538
Inquisitor, on shipboard   538
Irishmen, of a temperance persuasion   538
Lady, with a lap-dog, but tender   538
Landlord and landlady in St Louis   538
Magistrate, lazy and relaxed office   539
Miner, and employees   539
Passengers, on a boat   539
Pitchlynn, chief of the Choctaw tribe   539
Porter: a Kentucky Giant   539
Settler, near the Prairie   540
Temperance officers: a procession of several thousand   540
Traveller: a great politician   540
Wife: of a sergeant   540
Woman, little, with a little baby   540

Bride and **bridegroom**. "The beautiful girl . . . married the young man with the dark whiskers, who sits beyond *her,* only last month. They are going to settle in the very Far West, where he has lived four years, but where she has never been. They were both overturned in a stage-coach the other day (a bad omen anywhere else, where overturns are not so common), and his head, which bears the marks of a recent wound, is bound up still. She was hurt too, at the same time, and lay insensible for some days; bright as her eyes are, now." 11

Captain. "The captain coming up to have a little conversation, and to introduce a friend, seated himself astride of one of these barrels [of flour], like a Bacchus of private life; and pulling a great clasp-knife out of his pocket, began to 'whittle' it as he talked, by paring thin slices off the edges. And he whittled with such industry and hearty good will, that but for his being called away very soon, it must have disappeared bodily, and left nothing in its place but grist and shavings." 14

Doctor Crocus, phrenologist. "'Mr Dickens,' says the colonel, 'Doctor Crocus.'

"Upon which Doctor Crocus, who is a tall, fine-looking Scotchman, but rather fierce and warlike in appearance for a professor of the peaceful art of healing, bursts out of the concourse with his right arm extended, and his chest thrown out as far as it will possibly come, and says:

"'Your countryman, Sir!'" 13 ['*Crocus*' means *Quack*]

Forester. "This was a thin-faced, spare-figured man of middle age and stature, dressed in a dusty drabbish-coloured suit, such as I never saw before. He was perfectly quiet during the first part of the journey: indeed I don't re-member having so much as seen him until he was brought out by circum-stances, as great men often are . . . .

" . . . At home, I should have protested lustily [at the overcrowding], but being a foreigner here, I held my peace. Not so this passenger. He cleft a path among the people on deck (we were nearly all on deck), and without addressing anybody whomsoever, soliloquised as follows:

"'This may suit *you*, this may, but it don't suit *me*. This may be all very well with Down Easters, and men of Boston raising, but it won't suit my figure no-how; and no two ways about *that*; and so I tell you. Now! I'm from the brown forests of the Mississippi, *I* am, and when the sun shines on me, it does shine— a little. It don't glimmer where *I* live, the sun don't. No. I'm a brown forester, I am. I an't a Johnny Cake. There are no smooth skins where I live. We're rough men there. Rather. If Down Easters and men of Boston raising like this, I'm glad of it, but I'm none of that raising nor of that breed. No. This company wants a little fixing, *it* does. I'm the wrong sort of man for 'em, *I* am. They wont like me, *they* won't. This is piling of it up, a little too mountainous, this is.' At the end of every one of these short sentences he turned upon his heel, and walked the other way; checking himself abruptly when he had finished another short sentence, and turning back again.

"It is impossible for me to say what terrific meaning was hidden in the words of this brown forester, but I know that the other passengers looked on in a sort of admiring horror, and that presently the boat was put back to the wharf, and as many of the [excess crowd] as could be coaxed or bullied into go-ing away, were got rid of." 10

Gentleman. " . . . a droning gentleman, who talks arithmetically and sta-tistically on all subjects, from poetry downwards; and who always speaks in the same key, with exactly the same emphasis, and with very grave delibera-tion." 14

Gentleman, passenger. "I don't know why or wherefore, but I appeared to run in his mind perpetually, and to dissatisfy him very much . . . he broke out again, with 'I suppose *that* Boz will be writing a book by-and-by, and putting all our names in it!' at which imaginary consequence of being on board a boat with Boz, he groaned, and became silent." 14

Girl. "It is quite a relief to have, sitting opposite, that little girl of fifteen with the loquacious chin: who, to do her justice, acts up to it, and fully identifies nature's handwriting, for of all the small chatterboxes that ever invaded the repose of a drowsy ladies' cabin, she is the first and foremost." 11

Husband, of the little **woman**. " . . . there was the little woman clinging with both arms tight round the neck of a fine, good-looking, sturdy young fellow! and in a moment afterwards, there she was again, actually clapping her little hands for joy, as she dragged him through the small door of her small cabin, to look at the baby as he lay asleep!" 12

Inquisitor. "There was a man on board this boat, with a light fresh-coloured face, and a pepper-and-salt suit of clothes, who was the most inquisitive fellow that can possibly be imagined. He never spoke otherwise than interrogatively. He was an embodied inquiry. Sitting down or standing up, still or moving, walking the deck or taking his meals, there he was, with a great note of interrogation in each eye, two in his cocked ears, two more in his turned-up nose and chin, at least half-a-dozen more about the corners of his mouth, and the largest one of all in his hair, which was brushed pertly off his forehead in a flaxen clump.

"Every button in his clothes said, 'Eh? What's that? Did you speak? Say that again, will you?' He was always wide awake, like the enchanted bride who drove her husband frantic; always restless; always thirsting for answers; perpetually seeking and never finding. There never was such a curious man." ¶10

Irishmen. "I was particularly pleased to see the Irishmen, who formed a distinct [Temperance] society among themselves, and mustered very strong with their green scarves; carrying their national Harp and their Portrait of **Father Mathew** high above the people's heads. They looked as jolly and good-humoured as ever; and, working (here) the hardest for their living and doing any kind of sturdy labour that came in their way, were the most independent fellows there, I thought." 11

Lady. " . . . there was another lady (with a lap-dog) old enough to moralize on the lightness of human affections, and yet not so old that she could help nursing the baby, now and then, or laughing with the rest, when the little **woman** called it by its father's name, and asked it all manner of fantastic questions concerning him in the joy of her heart." 12

Landlord and **Landlady**, near St Louis. "The house was kept by a characteristic old couple, with whom we had a long talk, and who were perhaps a very good sample of that kind of people in the West.

"The landlord was a dry, tough, hard-faced old fellow (not so very old either, for he was but just turned sixty, I should think), who had been out with the militia in the last war with England, and had seen all kinds of service—except a battle . . . . He had all his life been restless and locomotive, with an irresistible desire for change; and was still the son of his old self: for if he had nothing to keep him at home, he said (slightly jerking his hat and his thumb towards the window of the room in which the old lady sat . . .), he would clean up his musket, and be off to Texas to-morrow morning. He was one of the very many descendants of Cain proper to this continent, who seem destined from their birth to serve as pioneers in the great human army: who gladly go on from year to year extending its outposts, and leaving home after home behind them; and die at last, utterly regardless of their graves being left thousands of miles behind, by the wandering generation who succeed.

"His wife was a domesticated kind-hearted old soul, who had come with him 'from the queen city of the world,' which, it seemed, was Philadelphia; but had no love for this Western country, and indeed had little reason to bear it any; having seen her children, one by one, die here of fever, in the full prime and beauty of their youth. Her heart was sore, she said, to think of them; and to talk on this theme, even to strangers, in that blighted place, so far from her old home, eased it somewhat, and became a melancholy pleasure." 14

Magistrate. " . . . we passed a 'Magistrate's office,' which amused me, as looking far more like a dame school than any police establishment: for this awful Institution was nothing but a little lazy, good-for-nothing front parlour, open to the street; wherein two or three figures (I presume the magistrate and his myrmidons) were basking in the sunshine, the very effigies of languor and repose. It was a perfect picture of Justice retired from business for want of customers; her sword and scales sold off; napping comfortably with her legs upon the table." 12

Miner, and employees. " . . . a man who is going some miles . . . to 'improve' a newly-discovered copper mine. He carries the village—that is to be—with him: a few frame-cottages, and an apparatus for smelting the copper. He carries its people too. They are partly American and partly Irish, and herd together on the lower deck; where they amused themselves last evening till the night was pretty far advanced, by alternately firing off pistols and singing hymns." 11

Passengers. " . . . nothing could have made head against the depressing influence of the general body. There was a magnetism of dulness in them which would have beaten down the most facetious companion that the earth ever knew. A jest would have been a crime, and a smile would have faded into a grinning horror. Such deadly leaden people; such systematic plodding weary insupportable heaviness; such a mass of animated indigestion in respect of all that was genial, jovial, frank, social, or hearty; never, sure, was brought together elsewhere since the world began." 12

Pitchlynn. "There chanced to be on board this boat [from Cincinnati to Louisville], in addition to the usual dreary crowd of passengers, one Pitchlynn, a chief of the Choctaw tribe of Indians, who *sent in his card* to me, and with whom I had the pleasure of a long conversation.

"He spoke English perfectly well, though he had not begun to learn the language, he told me, until he was a young man grown. He had read many books; and Scott's poetry appeared to have left a strong impression on his mind . . . .

"I asked him what he thought of Congress? He answered, with a smile, that it wanted dignity, in an Indian's eyes." 12

"He was a remarkably handsome man; some years past forty, I should judge; with long black hair, an aquiline nose, broad cheek-bones, a sunburnt complexion, and a very bright, keen, dark, and piercing eye. There were but twenty thousand of the Choctaws left, he said, and their number was decreasing every day. A few of his brother chiefs had been obliged to become civilised, and to make themselves acquainted with what the whites knew, for it was their only chance of existence. But they were not many; and the rest were as they always had been. He dwelt on this: and said several times that unless they tried to assimilate themselves to their conquerors, they must be swept away before the strides of civilised society." 12

"He took his leave; as stately and complete a gentleman of Nature's making, as ever I beheld; and moved among the people in the boat, another kind of being." 12

Porter. " . . . a certain Kentucky Giant whose name is Porter, and who is of the moderate height of seven feet eight inches, in his stockings . . . . He had a weakness in the region of the knees, and a trustfulness in his long face, which appealed even to five-feet nine for encouragement and support. He was only twenty-five years old, he said, and had grown recently, for it had been found necessary to make an addition to the legs of his inexpressibles." 12

Settler, near the Prairie. " . . . a log inn in the wood, far removed from any other residence. It consisted of one room, bare-roofed and bare-walled of course, with a loft above. The ministering priest was a swarthy young savage, in a shirt of cotton print like bed-furniture, and a pair of ragged trousers." 13

Temperance officers. "[The procession] comprised several thousand men; the members of various 'Washington Auxiliary Temperance Societies;' and was marshalled by officers on horseback, who cantered briskly up and down the line, with scarves and ribbons of bright colours fluttering out behind them gaily." 11

Traveller. "The traveller was an old man with a grey grizzly beard two inches long, a shaggy moustache of the same hue, and enormous eyebrows; which almost obscured his lazy, semi-drunken glance, as he stood regarding us with folded arms: poising himself alternately upon his toes and heels. On being addressed by one of the party, he drew nearer, and said, rubbing his chin (which scraped under his horny hand like fresh gravel beneath a nailed shoe), that he was from Delaware . . . .

"He was a great politician of course, and explained his opinions at some length to one of our company; but I only remember that he concluded with two sentiments, one of which was, Somebody for ever; and the other, Blast everybody else! which is by no means a bad abstract of the general creed in these matters." ¶13

Wife. "I was standing on the wharf . . . participating in the anxiety with which a sergeant's wife was collecting her few goods together—keeping one distracted eye hard upon the porters, who were hurrying them on board, and the other on a hoopless washing-tub for which, as being the most utterly worthless of all her movables, she seemed to entertain particular affection . . . . " 15

Little **woman**. "There was a little woman on board, with a little baby; and both little woman and little child were cheerful, good-looking, bright-eyed, and fair to see." 12

"Well, to be sure, there never was a little woman so full of hope, and tenderness, and love, and anxiety, as this little woman was: and all day long she wondered whether 'He' would be at the wharf; and whether 'He' had got her letter; and whether, if she sent the baby ashore by somebody else, 'He' would know it, meeting it in the street: which, seeing that he had never set eyes upon it in his life, was not very likely in the abstract, but was probable enough, to the young mother. She was such an artless little creature; and was in such a sunny, beaming, hopeful state; and let out all this matter clinging close about her heart, so freely; that all the other lady passengers entered into the spirit of it as much as she . . . . " 12

Canada

Girl, prisoner. "The female prisoners were occupied in needlework. Among them was a beautiful girl of twenty, who had been there nearly three years. She acted as a bearer of secret dispatches for the self-styled Patriots on Navy Island, during the Canadian Insurrection: sometimes dressing as a girl, and carrying them in her stays; sometimes attiring herself as a boy, and secreting them in the lining of her hat. In the latter character she always rode as a boy would, which was nothing to her, for she could govern any horse that any man could ride, and could drive four-in-hand with the best whip in those parts . . . . She had quite a lovely face, though . . . there was a lurking devil in her bright eye, which looked out pretty sharply from between her prison bars." 15

Recruit. "The recruit was a likely young fellow enough, strongly built and well made, but by no means sober: indeed he had all the air of a man who had been more or less drunk for some days. He carried a small bundle over his shoulder, slung at the end of a walking-stick, and had a short pipe in his mouth. He was as dusty and dirty as recruits usually are, and his shoes betokened that he had travelled on foot some distance, but he was in a very jocose state, and shook hands with this soldier, and clapped that one on the back, and talked and laughed continually, like a roaring idle dog as he was." 15

Soldiers. " . . . suddenly the novice [**recruit**], who had been backing towards the gangway in his noisy merriment, fell overboard before their eyes, and splashed heavily down into the river between the vessel and the dock.

"I never saw such a good thing as the change that came over these soldiers in an instant. Almost before the man was down, their professional manner, their stiffness and constraint, were gone, and they were filled with the most violent energy. In less time than is required to tell it, they had him out again, feet first, with the tails of his coat flapping over his eyes, everything about him hanging the wrong way, and the water streaming off at every thread in his threadbare dress. But the moment they set him upright and found that he was none the worse, they were soldiers again, looking over their glazed stocks more composedly than ever." 15

Waiter. "'Dinner, if you please,' said I to the waiter.

"'When?' said the waiter.

"'As quick as possible,' said I.

"'Right away?' said the waiter.

"After a moment's hesitation, I answered 'No,' at hazard.

"'*Not* right away?' cried the waiter, with an amount of surprise that made me start."

"I looked at him doubtfully, and returned, 'No; I would rather have it in this private room.'" 15

Slavery and Violence

"Let us try this public opinion by another test . . . as showing how desperately timid of the public opinion slave-owners are, in their delicate descriptions of fugitive slaves in widely circulated newspapers; secondly, as showing how perfectly contented the slaves are, and how very seldom they run away; thirdly, as exhibiting their entire freedom from scar, or blemish, or any mark of cruel infliction, as their pictures are drawn, not by lying abolitionists, but by their own truthful masters." 17

CD quotes actual advertisements concerning runaway slaves.

Anthony. "'One of his ears cut off, and his left hand cut with an axe.'"

Arthur. "'Has a considerable scar across his breast and each arm, made by a knife . . . .'"

Ben. "'Has a scar on his right hand: his thumb and forefinger being injured by being shot last fall. A part of the bone came out. He has also one or two large scars on his back and hips.'"

Betsy. "'Had an iron bar on her right leg.'"

Jim Blake. "'Has a piece cut out of each ear, and the middle finger of the left hand cut off to the second joint.'"

Bob, "'has lost one eye . . . .'"

Caroline. "'Had on a collar with one prong turned down.'"

De Lampert. "'Ran away, a negro boy about twelve years old. Had round his neck a chain dog-collar with "De Lampert" engraved on it.'"

Dennis. "'Said negro has been shot in the left arm between the shoulder and elbow, which has paralysed the left hand.'"

Joe Dennis. "'Has a small notch in one of his ears.'"

Edward. "'He has a scar on the corner of his mouth, two cuts on and under his arm, and the letter E on his arm.'"

Ellie. "'Has a scar on one of his arms from the bite of a dog.'"

Fanny. "'Had on an iron band about her neck.'"

Fountain. "'Has holes in his ears, a scar on the right side of his forehead, has been shot in the hind parts of his legs, and is marked on the back with the whip.'"

Grise. "' . . . having a ring and chain on the left leg.'"

Henry. "' . . . his left eye out, some scars from a dirk on and under his left arm, and much scarred with the whip.'"

Hown. "'Has a ring of iron on his left foot.'"

Ivory. "'Has a small piece cut out of the top of each ear.'"

Isaac. "'He has a scar on his forehead, caused by a blow; and one on his back, made by a shot from a pistol.'"

Jack. "'Has a small crop out of his left ear.'"

James. "'Said boy was ironed when he left me.'"

Jim. "'He is much marked with shot in his right thigh. The shot entered on the outside, halfway between the hip and knee joints.'"

John. "'He has a clog of iron on his right foot which will weigh four or five pounds.'"

John. "'Left ear cropt.'"

John. "'The tip of his nose is bit off.'"

Josiah. "'His back very much scarred by the whip; and branded on the thigh and hips in three or four places, thus (J M). The rim of his right ear has been bit or cut off.'"

Judy. "'She has had her right arm broke.'"

Kentucky Tom, "'has one jaw broken.'"

Levi. "'His left hand has been burnt, and I think the end of his forefinger is off.'"

Manuel. "'Much marked with irons.'"

Maria. "'Has a scar on one side of her cheek, by a cut. Some scars on her back.'"

Mary. "'Has a small scar over her eye, a good many teeth missing, the letter A is branded on her cheek and forehead.'"

Mary, a mulatto. "'Has a cut on the left arm, a scar on the left shoulder, and two upper teeth missing.'"

Mary. "'Has a scar on her cheek, and the end of one of her toes cut off.'"

Myra. "'Has several marks of LASHING, and has irons on her feet.'"

Ned. "'Three of his fingers are drawn into the palm of his hand by a cut. Has a scar on the back of his neck, nearly half round, done by a knife.'"

Negro man. "'Has no toes on the left foot.'"

Negro man. "'Is very much scarred about the face and body, and has the left ear bit off.'"

Negro woman. "'A few days before she went off, I burnt her with a hot iron, on the left side of her face. I tried to make the letter M.'"

Pompey. "'He is branded on the left jaw.'"

Rachel. "'Has lost all her toes except the large one.'"

Randal, "'has one ear cropped . . . . '"

Sally. "'Walks *as though* crippled in the back.'"

Sam. "He was shot a short time since through the hand, and has several shots in his left arm and side.'"

Simon. "'He has been shot badly, in his back and right arm.'"

James Surgette, advertiser for **Bob**, **Kentucky Tom** and **Randal**.

Tom. "'Has a scar on the right cheek, and appears to have been burned with powder on the face.'"

Washington. "'Has lost a part of his middle finger, and the end of his little finger.'"

" . . . it may be worth while to inquire how the slave-owners, and the class of society to which great numbers of them belong, defer to public opinion in their conduct, not to their slaves but to each other; how they are accustomed to restrain their passions; what their bearing is among themselves; whether they are fierce or gentle; whether their social customs be brutal, sanguinary, and violent, or bear the impress of civilisation and refinement." 17

CD collected the following newspaper extracts on manners. Italics are his.

Major Allison "'has stated to some of our citizens in town that Mr **Loose** gave the first blow.'"

C. P. Arndt. "' . . . Member of the Council for Brown county [Wisconsin], was shot dead on the floor of the Council chamber, by **James R. Vinyard**, Member from Grant County.'"

Lilburn W. Baggs, late Governor of Missouri. "'Gov. Baggs was shot by some villain on Friday, 6th inst., in the evening, while sitting in a room in his own house in Independence.'"

E. S. Baker. "'The affair grew out of a nomination for Sheriff of Grant county. Mr E. S. Baker was nominated and supported by Mr **Arndt**.'"

Bridgman. "'A Mr Bridgman having had a difficulty with a citizen of the place [in Iowa], Mr **Ross**; a brother-in-law of the latter . . . *discharged the contents of five of the barrels at him: each shot taking effect*. Mr B., though horribly wounded, and dying, returned the fire, and killed Ross on the spot.'"

James Cottingham. "' . . . in an affray near Carthage, Leake county, Mississippi, between James Cottingham and **John Wilburn**, the latter was shot by the former, and so horribly wounded, that there was no hope of his recovery.'"

Judge Dunn "'*has discharged **Vinyard** on bail.*'"

Fall, of Tennessee "'fired two pistols without effect. Mr **Robbins**' first shot took effect in Fall's thigh, who fell, and was unable to continue the combat.'"

Major C. Gally, of Louisiana, "'having a cane in his hands, struck Mr **Arpin** across the face, and the latter drew a poignard from his pocket and stabbed Major Gally in the abdomen.'"

William Hine, aged thirteen. "' . . . the ball of **Thurston**'s gun passing through the crown of Hine's hat.'"

Mr Loose, of Arkansas. "'It is said that **Major Gillespie** brought on the attack with a cane. A severe conflict ensued, during which two pistols were fired by Gillespie and one by Loose. Loose then stabbed Gillespie with one of those never-failing weapons, a bowie-knife.'"

M'Kane, of Missouri, "'who had been engaged in the business of distilling, and resulted in the death of [**M'Allister**], who was shot down by Mr M'Kane, because of his attempting to take possession of seven barrels of whiskey . . . . '"

Colonel Robert Potter. "'He was beset in his house [in Caddo County, Louisiana] by an enemy, named **Rose** . . . . His first impulse was to jump in the water and dive for it, which he did . . . scarce had his head reached the surface of the water when it was completely riddled with the shot of their guns, and he sunk, to rise no more!'"

A. C. Sharkey. "'On the 2nd instant, there was an affray at Carthage [Mississippi] between A. C. Sharkey and **George Goff**, in which the latter was shot, and thought mortally wounded.'"

Samuel Thurston, aged fifteen. "'The weapons used on the occasion, were a couple of Dickson's best rifles; the distance, thirty yards.'" *See* **Hine**

James R. Vinyard. "'Mr **Arndt** then made a blow at Vinyard, who stepped back a pace, drew a pistol, and shot him dead.'"

The Democratic Tale of a Shoemaker

"The Republican Institutions of America undoubtedly lead the people to assert their self-respect and their equality; but a traveller is bound to bear those Institutions in his mind, and not hastily to resent the near approach of a class of strangers, who, at home, would keep aloof. This characteristic, when it was tinctured with no foolish pride, and stopped short of no honest service, never offended me; and I very seldom, if ever, experienced its rude or unbecoming display. Once or twice it was comically developed . . . .

"I wanted a pair of boots at a certain town, for I had none to travel in, but those with the memorable cork soles, which were much too hot for the fiery decks of a steamboat. I therefore sent a message to an artist in boots, importing, with my compliments, that I should be happy to see him, if he would do me the polite favour to call. He very kindly returned for answer, that he would 'look round' at six o'clock that evening.

" . . . the door opened, and a gentleman in a stiff cravat, within a year or two on either side of thirty, entered, in his hat and gloves; walked up to the looking-glass; arranged his hair; took off his gloves; slowly produced a measure from the uttermost depths of his coat-pocket; and requested me, in a languid tone, to 'unfix' my straps. I complied, but looked with some curiosity at his hat, which was still upon his head. It might have been that, or it might have been the heat—but he took it off.

"Then, he sat himself down on a chair opposite to me; rested an arm on each knee; and, leaning forward very much, took from the ground, by a great effort, the specimen of metropolitan workmanship which I had just pulled off: whistling, pleasantly, as he did so. He turned it over and over; surveyed it with a contempt no language can express; and inquired if I wished him to fix me a boot like *that?*

"I courteously replied, that provided the boots were large enough, I would leave the rest to him; that if convenient and practicable, I should not object to their bearing some resemblance to the model then before him; but that I would be entirely guided by, and would beg to leave the whole subject to, his judgment and discretion. 'You an't partickler, about this scoop in the heel, I suppose then?' says he: 'we don't foller that, here.'

"I repeated my last observation.

"He looked at himself in the glass again; went closer to it to dash a grain or two of dust out of the corner of his eye; and settled his cravat. All this time, my leg and foot were in the air. 'Nearly ready, Sir?' I inquired. 'Well, pretty nigh,' he said; 'keep steady.' I kept as steady as I could, both in foot and face; and having by this time got the dust out, and found his pencil-case, he measured me, and made the necessary notes.

"When he had finished, he fell into his old attitude, and taking up the boot again, mused for some time. 'And this,' he said, at last, 'is an English boot, is it? This is a London boot, eh?' . . . He mused over it again, after the manner of Hamlet with Yorick's skull; nodded his head, as who should say, 'I pity the Institutions that led to the production of this boot;' rose; put up his pencil, notes, and paper—glancing at himself in the glass, all the time—put on his hat; drew on his gloves very slowly; and finally walked out.

"When he had been gone about a minute, the door reopened, and his hat and his head reappeared. He looked round the room, and at the boot again, which was still lying on the floor; appeared thoughtful for a minute; and then said 'Well, good arternoon' . . . . that was the end of the interview."¶18

Frontispiece for *Martin Chuzzlewit*. Clockwise from top: Tom Pinch drafting, Pecksniff posing; *Sic vos non vobis:* "Thus you labour, but not for yourselves" (i.e., you do the work, and another gets the credit); *Si monumentum requiris (requiras* is a mistake) *circumspice:* "If you seek a monument, look around;" Jonas Chuzzlewit in Hell, taunted by filthy lucre; Tom knocks Jonas down at the stile; Charity Pecksniff, Tom and Mercy Pecksniff; Tom and 'Merry' Chuzzlewit; Mrs Todgers and cat; Pecksniff takes a fall; allegory of hypocrisy with the mask of Pecksniff; four couples (l to r): John Westlock and Ruth Pinch, young Martin and Mary Graham, Mark Tapley and Mrs Lupin, Charity and reluctant Moddle; Mrs Gamp in straits; Montague Tigg hand in hand with the Spirit of Mummery; Mrs Lupin; Poll Sweedlepipe; Bill Bailey. At organ, Tom dreams of Mary(?), observed by Martin(?).

N 6 January 1843-July 1844 monthly by C&H   1 vol 1844 **MC**
   U.S. publication 1844 in seven parts by Harper & Bros., New York

The Life and Adventures of
Martin Chuzzlewit,
his Relatives, Friends and Enemies:

Comprising all his Wills and his Ways, with an
Historical Record of What he did, and What he didn't;
showing, moreoever, who inherited the Family Plate,
who came in for the Silver Spoons, and who for the Wooden Ladles:
the Whole forming a Complete key to the House of Chuzzlewit,
edited by Boz

"This history . . . at present contents itself with remarking . . . Firstly, that it may be safely asserted, and yet without implying any direct participation in the **Monboddo** doctrine touching the probability of the human race having once been monkeys, that men do play very strange and extraordinary tricks. Secondly, and yet without trenching on the **Blumenbach** theory as to the descendants of Adam having a vast number of qualities which belong more particularly to swine than to any other class of animals in the creation, that some men certainly are remarkable for taking uncommon good care of themselves." 1

"There are grotesque figures of the most gorgeous kind; there are scenes that are farcical even by the standard of the farcical license of Dickens; there is humour both of the heaviest and of the lightest kind; there are two great comic personalities who run like a rich vein through the whole story, Pecksniff and Mrs Gamp; there is one blinding patch of brilliancy, the satire on American cant; there is Todgers's boarding-house; there is Bailey; there is Mr Mould, the incomparable undertaker. But yet in spite of everything, in spite even of the undertaker, the book is sad." GKC p90

PRÉCIS

After tracing the Chuzzlewit line since Adam, we meet architect **Seth Pecksniff**, home on a windy night with his daughters **Charity** and **Mercy**. His student **John Westlock** departs in dudgeon, despite acolyte **Tom Pinch**'s peace-making effort. 1-2

Old **Martin Chuzzlewit**, ill and disillusioned at the local inn, is attended by **Mary Graham** and landlady **Mrs Lupin**, who enlists help from Pecksniff. Thinking his old relative may be dying, Pecksniff hosts a meeting of the Chuzzlewit clan, including the indigent **Chevy Slyme**, whose companion, **Montague Tigg**, sniffs about. 3-4

Tom Pinch goes to welcome a new pupil, taking along **Mark Tapley**, factotum at the inn and an aspirer to spiritual merit. The pupil is young **Martin Chuzzlewit**, selfish and handsome. Pinch confides in him, and they become friends. Peckniff and daughters go to London for a week. Martin is in love and feels frustrated by his grandfather. 5-6

Tigg turns up, under Tapley escort, looking for a loan for Slyme. Young Martin persuades Pinch to help his kinsman pay his inn bill. Tigg borrows from the soft Pinch. Tapley announces his plan to leave to seek his fortune, despite Mrs Lupin's attractions. 7

En route to London, the Pecksniffs fall in with **Anthony** Chuzzlewit and his son **Jonas**, who flirts with the ladies. The Pecksniffs lodge at **Mrs Todgers'** commercial boarding-house. They call on the haughty employers (connected with a brass and copper foundry) of Pinch's sister, **Ruth**. The ladies are lionized by **Jinkins** (the oldest boarder) and **Augustus Moddle** (the Youngest Gentleman), all served by impudent **Benjamin Bailey**. 8-9

Old Martin turns up at Todgers's and seems to embrace Pecksniff. He demands that Pecksniff expel his grandson. Mrs Todgers pacifies Moddle, who is jealous of Jinkins. Jonas comes calling and shows the sisters the town. Anthony's supper for them includes his devoted clerk **Chuffey**. 10-11

The departing Pecksniffs are serenaded by the Commercials. Westlock entertains Pinch and Martin. Pecksniff snubs Martin, who stalks out penniless and gets to London. He pawns his watch at **David Crimp**'s, where he sees Tigg. He receives a mystery gift of twenty pounds. Tapley turns up (another mystery) and signs on as his man. He takes a letter to Mary, who meets Martin, hears his plan to go to America and sends him a diamond, convincing him she is worthy of him. Tapley is tickled at Martin's egotism.12-14

Mark and Martin have a miserable voyage in steerage. Mark aids immigrants. In New York, **Colonel Diver**, newspaper publisher, accosts Martin and invites him for champagne. He meets **Jefferson Brick**, war correspondent, and observes American manners at **Major Pawkins'** boarding-house. 15-16

Mark has met **Cicero**, a former slave, who takes their baggage to the boarding-house. **Bevan**, sympathetic new friend, introduces Martin to the **Norrises** and their daughters. A guest, **General Fladdock**, was on Martin's ship and does not remember him. When it comes out that he sailed in steerage, the Norrises are appalled. Martin withdraws in heat. 17

Jonas wants to inherit. Pecksniff catches him reading Anthony's Will. Jonas goes out, Anthony and Pecksniff confer, and Jonas returns to see his father fall in a fit and shortly die. Jonas is unreasonably panicked and pays for elaborate obsequies. Pecksniff fetches **Sairey Gamp** for the laying-out. The undertaker **Mould** presides, and only Chuffey seems to sorrow. Jonas accompanies Pecksniff home and, bypassing the expectant Charity, surprisingly proposes marriage to flirtatious Mercy. 18-20

Martin and Mark journey west. They meet **La Fayette Kettle** and other American characters on the train. With his savings Martin buys a choice lot from **Zephaniah Scadder**, agent for the garden spot of Eden. Martin is the involuntary object of a great levee. A deadly swamp, Eden seems the likely burial ground of his hopes. Mark anticipates much spiritual growth. 21-23

Old Martin and Mary are at Pecksniff's. Jonas waylays Tom, who knocks him down, pleasing Charity. Mercy ignores the old man's warnings and agrees to marry Jonas, to tease him and torment Charity. Bibulous Mrs Gamp tends the feverish **Lewsome**, who babbles of Jonas. She roughly nurses Chuffey. 24-25

Poll Sweedlepipe, Sairey's landlord, has a new friend—Bailey, now working for **Tigg Montague**, chairman of an insurance company whose secretary is David **Crimple** (formerly Crimp). **Jobling**, the society doctor who attended Anthony, and **Nadgett**, an investigating officer, are on the staff. Jonas comes to buy a policy and is blandished by Montague. His brutal treatment of Mercy pains Bailey. Mrs Gamp's patient Lewsome has something on his mind. 26-29

The jilted Charity leaves home to live at Todgers's. Oleaginous Pecksniff lays deep plans, sure of his influence with old Martin. He greasily proposes to Mary Graham, who, revolted, confides in Pinch. Pecksniff overhears. To cover himself, he expels Pinch, ostensibly for wooing Mary. Pinch leaves stoically. Charity corners Moddle, to be her consolation, her nose to be his. 30-32

Young Martin is very ill in Eden. Mark tends him. These roles reverse, and the invalid gains insight and resolves to be a better man. They escape Eden with Bevan's aid and embark for England after meeting the expectorating **Hannibal Chollop**, **Elijah Pogram**, and other local colour. On landing, they chance on a cornerstone laying honouring Pecksniff for work Martin recognises as his own. 33-35

Pinch in London connects with Westlock and collects his sister, who has been treated unworthily. Pinch sees the Pecksniff sisters and is brought up to date. Westlock glimpses sparkling Ruth Pinch. Nadgett has been investigating. He reports to Montague, whose hints terrify Jonas. 36-38

Tom and Ruth keep delightful house together. Unknown lawyer **Fips** offers a perfect job for Tom: reorganising a library for an unknown client. The Pinches meet Mrs Gamp at a ship pier. Their landlord, who is Nadgett, gives Tom a missive for some passengers. They turn out to be Jonas and Mercy. The livid Jonas abandons his trip and surrenders to Montague. 39-41

Montague extorts Jonas's help to gull Pecksniff, and Jonas insists Tigg go with him. He nearly gets Tigg killed under the horses' hooves when the coach overturns in a terrible storm. Bailey is critically hurt. 42

Mark's return from America overjoys Mrs Lupin. She reports odd events at the Pecksniffs', and young Martin presents himself. His grandfather ignores him: he seems guided solely by Pecksniff. Montague and Jonas gain Pecksniff's confidence and a major investment. 43-44

Tom and Ruth visit Mercy, meeting Charity and a disconsolate Moddle on the way. Chuffey babbles of the dead, and Jonas appears. Tom's role in delivering the missive on the boat creates embarrassment, and he leaves with it unexplained. Jonas thus remains oblivious of Nadgett's interest in him. Jonas orders that he not be disturbed and locks himself in his room. He steals away in disguise and travels incognito to the country. He waylays and murders Montague and returns home, strangely fearful of himself. Only Nadgett has inquired for him. 45-47

Martin and Mark visit the Pinches and take Tom to see Westlock, who is with Lewsome, a medical man who confesses supplying Jonas with a poison he fears ended Anthony's life. Tom and the others plan to interview Chuffey, with Gamp aid, to clarify things. 48

A deeply distressed Sweedlepipe reports Bailey's supposed death to Mrs Gamp and colleague **Betsey Prig**. Montague is missing, and Crimple has disappeared with the insurance company assets. But, most seriously, Mrs Prig flaunts her disbelief in Mrs Gamp's cherished confidante, **Mrs Harris**. 49

Young Martin bitterly reproaches Tom for treachery, to his bewilderment. Tom has confessed to Ruth that he loves Mary and knows it is hopeless. At his library office next day, Tom is visited by a transformed Old Martin and recognises his mysterious employer, and much more, in a flash. 50

Jonas fears Chuffey will reveal a terrible secret. He consigns him to Mrs Gamp, and a general confrontation follows. Nadgett followed Jonas and knows he is a murderer. Chuffey shows the murder had been unnecessary. Jonas bribes police officer Chevy Slyme (now gainfully, if embarrassingly, employed) for privacy and takes poison. 51

Pecksniff appears at old Martin's apartment and is struck down and dumb, as the grandfather excoriates his dissembling hypocrisy. Charity is humiliated at the altar, where Moddle is present only by letter reporting his flight, but young Martin and Mary, Mark and Mrs Lupin, Westlock and Ruth all pair off happily. Seth Pecksniff improbably ends in penury. 52-54

CONTENTS

CHARACTERS

Spear-carriers   chapter

Title Role(s)

Martin Chuzzlewit the elder. "[He] was a strong and vigorous old man, with a will of iron, and a voice of brass." 3

—*his suspicious nature:* " . . . fixing on [**Mrs Lupin**] two dark eyes whose brightness was exaggerated by the paleness of his hollow cheeks, as they in turn, together with his straggling locks of long grey hair, were rendered whiter by the tight black velvet skull-cap which he wore, he searched her face intently.

"'Ah! you begin too soon,' he said . . . .'But you lose no time. You do your errand, and you earn your fee. Now, who may be *your* client?'" 3

—*truth from a relation:* "'There is nothing in your possession that I know of, Mr Chuzzlewit [said **Pecksniff**], which is much to be coveted for the happiness it brings you.'" 3

—*The Midas Curse:* "'I have gone, a rich man, among people of all grades and kinds; relatives, friends, and strangers; among people in whom, when I was poor, I had confidence, and justly, for they never once deceived me then, or, to me, wronged each other. But I have never found one nature, no, not one, in which, being wealthy and alone, I was not forced to detect the latent corruption that lay hid within it, waiting for such as I to bring it forth.

"Treachery, deceit, and low design; hatred of competitors, real or fancied, for my favour; meanness, falsehood, baseness, and servility; or . . . an assumption of honest independence, almost worse than all; these are the beauties which my wealth has brought to light. Brother against brother, child against parent, friends treading in the faces of friends, this is the social company by whom my way has been attended." ¶3

—*his hurt:* " . . . the last link in the chain of grateful love and duty, that held me to my race, was roughly snapped asunder; roughly, for I loved him [young **Martin**] well; roughly, for I had ever put my trust in his affection; roughly, for that he broke it when I loved him most, God help me! and he without a pang could throw me off, while I clung about his heart!'" 10

—*apathy:* "Old Martin Chuzzlewit had gradually undergone an important change . . . his character seemed to have modified by regular degrees, and to have softened down into a dull indifference for almost every one but Mr **Pecksniff**. His looks were much the same as ever, but his mind was singularly altered. It was not that this or that passion stood out in brighter or in dimmer hues; but that the colour of the whole man was faded. As one trait disappeared, no other trait sprung up to take its place. His sense dwindled too. He was less keen of sight; was deaf sometimes; took little notice of what passed before him; and would be profoundly taciturn for days together." 30

—*revealed:* "Old Martin Chuzzlewit! The same whom he had left at Mr **Pecksniff**'s, weak and sinking!

"The same? No, not the same, for this old man, though old, was strong, and leaned upon his stick with a vigorous hand, while with the other he signed to **Tom** to make no noise. One glance at the resolute face, the watchful eye, the vigorous hand upon the staff, the triumphant purpose in the figure, and such a light broke in on Tom as blinded him." 50

Martin Chuzzlewit the younger. "[He was] one-and-twenty, perhaps—and handsome; with a keen dark eye, and a quickness of look and manner. . . ." 5

—*his self-knowledge:* "'I told you obstinacy was no part of my character, did I not? I was going to say, if you had given me leave, that a chief ingredient in my composition is a most determined firmness . . . . And being firm,' pursued Martin, 'of course I was not going to yield to him [old **Martin**], or give way by so much as the thousandth part of an inch.'" 6

—*as seen by his servant:* "'I want a man as is always a-sliding off his legs when he ought to be on 'em. I want a man as is so low down in the school of life that he's always a-making figures of one in his copy-book, and can't get no further. I want a man as is his own great-coat and cloak, and is always a-wrapping himself up in himself. And I have got him too,' said Mr **Tapley**, after a moment's silence. 'What a happiness!' " 33

—*a sea-change:* "If any one had taxed him with the vice [of selfishness], he would have indignantly repelled the accusation, and conceived himself un-

worthily aspersed. He never would have known it, but that being newly risen
from a bed of dangerous sickness, to watch by such another couch, he felt how
nearly Self had dropped into the grave, and what a poor dependent, miserable
thing it was.

"It was natural for him to reflect . . . upon his own escape, and **Mark**'s extremity. This led him to consider which of them could be the better spared, and
why? Then the curtain slowly rose a very little way; and Self, Self, Self, was
shown below.

"He asked himself, besides, when dreading Mark's decease (as all men do
and must, at such a time), whether he had done his duty by him, and had deserved and made a good response to his fidelity and zeal. No. Short as their
companionship had been, he felt in many, many instances, that there was
blame against himself; and still inquiring why, the curtain slowly rose a little
more, and Self, Self, Self, dilated on the scene.

"It was long before he fixed the knowledge of himself so firmly in his mind
that he could thoroughly discern the truth; but in the hideous solitude of that

most hideous place, with Hope so far removed, Ambition quenched, and Death beside him rattling at the very door, reflection came, as in a plague-beleaguered town; and so he felt and knew the failing of his life, and saw distinctly what an ugly spot it was . . . .

"He made a solemn resolution that when his strength returned he . . . would look upon it as an established fact, that selfishness was in his breast, and must be rooted out. He was so doubtful (and with justice) of his own character, that he determined not to say one word of vain regret or good resolve to Mark, but steadily to keep his purpose before his own eyes solely: and there was not a jot of pride in this; nothing but humility and steadfastness: the best armour he could wear. So low had Eden brought him down. So high had Eden raised him up." 33

—*manful apology:* "'Upon that subject,' said Martin, looking calmly at the old man as he spoke, but glancing once at **Mary**, whose face was now buried in her hands, upon the back of his easy-chair: 'upon that subject, which first occasioned a division between us, my mind and heart are incapable of change. Whatever influence they have undergone, since that unhappy time, has not been one to weaken but to strengthen me. I cannot profess sorrow for that, nor irresolution in that, nor shame in that. Nor would you wish me, I know.

"But that I might have trusted to your love, if I had thrown myself manfully upon it; that I might have won you over with ease, if I had been more yielding and more considerate; that I should have best remembered myself in forgetting myself, and recollecting you; reflection, solitude, and misery, have taught me. I came resolved to say this, and to ask your forgiveness: not so much in hope for the future, as in regret for the past: for all that I would ask of you is, that you would aid me to live.

"Help me to get honest work to do, and I would do it. My condition places me at the disadvantage of seeming to have only my selfish ends to serve, but try if that be so or not. Try if I be self-willed, obdurate, and haughty, as I was; or have been disciplined in a rough school. Let the voice of nature and association plead between us, Grandfather; and do not, for one fault, however thankless, quite reject me!'" ¶43

Other Principals

Jonas Chuzzlewit. "[He] had so well profited by the precept and example of the father [**Anthony**], that he looked a year or two the elder of the twain, as they stood winking their red eyes, side by side . . . ." 5

—*an uncle's view:* "'My brother had in his wealth the usual doom of wealth, and root of misery . . . . It made of his own child a greedy expectant, who measured every day and hour the lessening distance between his father and the grave, and cursed his tardy progress on that dismal road.'" 24

—*avarice:* "The education of Mr. Jonas had been conducted from his cradle on the strictest principles of the main chance. The very first word he learnt to spell was 'gain' and the second (when he got into two syllables), 'money.' But for two results, which were not clearly foreseen perhaps by his watchful parent in the beginning, his training may be said to have been unexceptionable. One of these flaws was, that having been long taught by his father to over-reach everybody, he had imperceptibly acquired a love of over-reaching that venerable monitor himself. The other, that from his early habits of considering everything as a question of property, he had gradually come to look, with impatience, on his parent as a certain amount of personal estate, which had no right whatever to be going at large, but ought to be secured in that particular description of iron safe which is commonly called a coffin, and banked in the grave." 8

"'Liveliness is a pleasant thing—when it don't lead to spending money. An't it?'; asked Mr Jonas." 11

—*his ingratiating nature:* "An ancient proverb warns us that we should not expect to find old heads upon young shoulders; to which it may be added that we seldom meet with that unnatural combination, but we feel a strong desire to knock them off; merely from an inherent love we have of seeing things in their right places. It is not improbable that many men, in no wise choleric by nature, felt this impulse rising up within them, when they first made the acquaintance of Mr Jonas; but if they had known him more intimately in his own house, and had sat with him at his own board, it would assuredly have been paramount to all other considerations." 11

—*his poise:* " . . . so singular a mixture of defiance and obsequiousness, of fear and hardihood, of dogged sullenness and an attempt at cringing and propitiation, never was expressed in any one human figure as in that of Jonas, when, having raised his downcast eyes to [old] **Martin**'s face, he let them fall again, and uneasily closing and unclosing his hands without a moment's intermission, stood swinging himself from side to side, waiting to be addressed." 24

—*a weak point:* " . . . conscious that there was nothing in his person, conduct, character, or accomplishments, to command respect, he was greedy of power, and was, in his heart, as much a tyrant as any laurelled conqueror on record." 28

—*appalled:* "[**Montague**] beckoned to Jonas to bring his chair nearer; and looking slightly round, as if to remind him of the presence of **Nadgett**, whispered in his ear.

"From red to white; from white to red again; from red to yellow; then to a cold, dull, awful, sweat-bedabbled blue. In that short whisper, all these changes fell upon the face of Jonas Chuzzlewit; and when at last he laid his hand upon the whisperer's mouth, appalled, lest any syllable of what he said should reach the ears of the third person present, it was as bloodless and as heavy as the hand of Death.

"He drew his chair away, and sat a spectacle of terror, misery, and rage. He was afraid to speak, or look, or move, or sit still. Abject, crouching, and miserable, he was a greater degradation to the form he bore, than if he had been a loathsome wound from head to heel." 38

—*steeling himself:* "He had the aspect of a man found out and held at bay; of being baffled, hunted, and beset; but there was now a dawning and increasing purpose in his face, which changed it very much. It was gloomy, distrustful, lowering; pale with anger and defeat; it still was humbled, abject, cowardly, and mean; but, let the conflict go on as it would, there was one strong purpose wrestling with every emotion of his mind, and casting the whole series down as they arose.

"Not prepossessing in appearance at the best of times, it may be readily supposed that he was not so now. He had left deep marks of his front teeth in his nether lip; and those tokens of the agitation he had lately undergone improved his looks as little as the heavy corrugations in his forehead. But he was self-possessed now; unnaturally self-possessed, indeed, as men quite otherwise than brave are known to be in desperate extremities . . . ." 41

—*steeled:* "The boisterous manner which Jonas had exhibited . . . which had gone on rapidly increasing with almost every word he had spoken; from the time when he looked his honourable friend [**Montague**] in the face until now; did not now subside, but, remaining at its height, abided by him. Most unusual with him at any period; most inconsistent with his temper and constitution; especially unnatural it would appear in one so darkly circumstanced; it abided by him. It was not like the effect of wine, or any ardent drink, for he was perfectly coherent. It even made him proof against the usual influence of such means of excitement; for, although he drank deeply several times that day, with no reserve or caution, he remained exactly the same man, and his spirits neither rose nor fell in the least observable degree." 41

—*a crime committed:* " . . . he was not sorry for what he had done. He was frightened when he thought of it—when did he not think of it!—but he was not sorry. He had had a terror and dread of the wood when he was in it; but being out of it, and having committed the crime, his fears were now diverted, strangely, to the dark room he had left shut up at home. He had a greater horror, infinitely greater, of that room than of the wood. Now that he was on his return to it, it seemed beyond comparison more dismal and more dreadful than the wood. His hideous secret was shut up in the room, and all its terrors were there; to his thinking it was not in the wood at all." 47

"Dread and fear were upon him, to an extent he had never counted on, and could not manage in the least degree. He was so horribly afraid of that infernal room at home. This made him, in a gloomy, murderous, mad way, not only fearful *for* himself but *of* himself; for being, as it were, a part of the room: a something supposed to be there, yet missing from it: he invested himself with its mysterious terrors; and when he pictured in his mind the ugly chamber, false and quiet, false and quiet, through the dark hours of two nights; and the tumbled bed, and he not in it, though believed to be; he became in a manner his own ghost and phantom, and was at once the haunting spirit and the haunted man." 47

Sairey Gamp, midwife. "She was a fat old woman, this Mrs. Gamp, with a husky voice and a moist eye, which she had a remarkable power of turning up, and only showing the white of it. Having very little neck, it cost her some trouble to look over herself, if one may say so, at those to whom she talked.

"She wore a very rusty black gown, rather the worse for snuff, and a shawl and bonnet to correspond. In these dilapidated articles of dress she had, on principle, arrayed herself, time out of mind, on such occasions as the present; for this at once expressed a decent amount of veneration for the deceased, and invited the next of kin to present her with a fresher suit of weeds; an appeal so frequently successful, that the very fetch and ghost of Mrs. Gamp, bonnet and all, might be seen hanging up, any hour in the day, in at least a dozen of the second-hand clothes shops about Holborn.

"The face of Mrs. Gamp—the nose in particular—was somewhat red and swollen, and it was difficult to enjoy her society without becoming conscious of a smell of spirits. Like most persons who have attained to great eminence in their profession, she took to hers very kindly; insomuch that, setting aside her natural predilections as a woman, she went to a lying-in or a laying-out with equal zest and relish." ¶19

—*her intake:* "Mrs. Gamp proved to be very choice in her eating, and repudiated hashed mutton with scorn. In her drinking too, she was very punctual and particular, requiring a pint of mild porter at lunch, a pint at dinner, half-a-pint as a species of stay or holdfast between dinner and tea, and a pint of the celebrated staggering ale, or Real Old Brighton Tipper, at supper; besides the bottle on the chimney-piece, and such casual invitations to refresh herself with wine as the good breeding of her employers might prompt them to offer." 19

"'I think, young woman,' said Mrs Gamp . . . in a tone expressive of weakness, 'that I could pick a little bit of pickled salmon, with a nice little sprig of fennel, and a sprinkling of white pepper. I take new bread, my dear, with jest a little pat of fresh butter, and a mossel of cheese. In case there should be such a thing as a cowcumber in the 'ouse, will you be so kind as to bring it, for I'm rather partial to 'em, and they does a world of good in a sick room. If they draws the Brighton Old Tipper here, I takes *that* ale at night, my love; it bein' considered wakeful by the doctors. And whatever you do, young woman, don't bring more than a shilling's-worth of gin and water-warm when I rings the bell a second time; for that is always my allowance, and I never take a drop beyond!'" 25

—*death watch dress:* ". . . she took out of her bundle a yellow night-cap, of prodigious size, in shape resembling a cabbage; which article of dress she fixed and tied on with the utmost care, previously divesting herself of a row of bald

old curls that could scarcely be called false, they were so very innocent of anything approaching to deception . . . she brought forth a night-jacket . . . [and] a
watchman's coat, which she tied round her neck by the sleeves, so that she became two people; and looked, behind, as if she were in the act of being embraced by one of the old patrol." 25

—*marketing:* " . . . the ecstasies of Mrs Gamp were sufficient to have furnished forth a score of young lovers: and they were chiefly awakened by the
sight of **Tom Pinch** and his sister. Mrs Gamp was a lady of that happy temperament which can be ecstatic without any other stimulating cause than a
general desire to establish a large and profitable connexion. She added daily so
many strings to her bow, that she made a perfect harp of it; and upon that instrument she now began to perform an extemporaneous concerto." 46

—*her nursing craft:* "Mrs. Gamp took [**Chuffey**] by the collar of his coat,
and gave him some dozen or two of hearty shakes backward and forward in his
chair; that exercise being considered by the disciples of the **Prig** school of
nursing (who are very numerous among professional ladies) as exceedingly

conducive to repose, and highly beneficial to the performance of the nervous functions. Its effect in this instance was to render the patient so giddy and ad- dle-headed, that he could say nothing more; which Mrs. Gamp regarded as the triumph of her art." 46

—*her precept:* "'To wotever place I goes, I sticks to this mortar, "I'm easy pleased; it is but little as I wants' but I must have that little of the best, and to the minute when the clock strikes, else we do not part as I could wish, but bearin' malice in our arts.""' 49

—*a sideline:* " . . . Mrs Gamp performed swoons of different sorts, upon a moderate notice, as Mr **Mould** did Funerals." 51

—*a truth told:* "' . . . give her a word or two of good advice now and then. Such [said old **Martin**] . . . as hinting at the expediency of a little less liquor, and a little more humanity, and a little less regard for herself, and a little more re- gard for her patients, and perhaps a trifle of additional honesty. Or when Mrs Gamp gets into trouble . . . it had better not be at a time when I am near enough to the Old Bailey to volunteer myself as a witness to her character." 52

And see **Mrs Gamp and Mrs Harris**

Tigg Montague. "[He] had a world of jet-black shining hair upon his head, upon his cheeks, upon his chin, upon his upper lip. His clothes, symmetrically made, were of the newest fashion and the costliest kind. Flowers of gold and blue, and green and blushing red, were on his waistcoat; precious chains and jewels sparkled on his breast; his fingers, clogged with brilliant rings, were as unwieldy as summer flies but newly rescued from a honey-pot. The daylight mantled in his gleaming hat and boots as in a polished glass. And yet, though changed his name, and changed his outward surface, it was Tigg. Though turned and twisted upside down, and inside out, as great men have been sometimes known to be; though no longer **Montague Tigg,** but Tigg Montague; still it was Tigg; the same Satanic, gallant, military Tigg. The brass was burnished, lacquered, newly-stamped; yet it was the true Tigg metal notwithstanding." 27

—*his genius:* "'Who said, that if we put the money together we could furnish an office, and make a show [said **David Crimple**]?'

"'And who said,' retorted Mr Tigg, 'that, provided we did it on a sufficiently lartge scale, we could furnish an office and make a show, without any money at all? Be rational, and just, and calm, and tell me whose idea was that.'" 27

Charity Pecksniff.—*and her sister:* "Charity, with her fine strong sense, and her mild, yet not reproachful gravity, was so well named, and did so well set off and illustrate her sister! What a pleasant sight was that, the contrast they presented: to see each loved and loving one sympathising with, and devoted to, and leaning on, and yet correcting and counter-checking, and, as it were, antidoting, the other! To behold each damsel, in her very admiration of her sister, setting up in business for herself on an entirely diffcrcnt principle, and announcing no connexion with over-the-way, and if the quality of goods at that establishment don't please you, you are respectfully invited to favour ME with a call! And the crowning circumstance of the whole delightful catalogue was, that both the fair creatures were so utterly unconscious of all this! They had no idea of it. They no more thought or dreamed of it than Mr **Pecksniff** did. Nature played them off against each other: *they* had no hand in it, the two Miss Pecksniffs." 2

—*innocently discovered:* "Truly Mr **Pecksniff** is blessed in his children. In one of them, at any rate. The prudent Cherry—staff and scrip, and treasure of her doting father—there she sits, at a little table white as driven snow, before the kitchen fire, making up accounts! See the neat maiden, as with pen in hand, and calculating look addressed towards the ceiling, and bunch of keys within a little basket at her side, she checks the housekeeping expenditure! From flat-iron, dish-cover, and warming-pan; from pot and kettle, face of brass footman, and black-leaded stove; bright glances of approbation wink and glow upon her. The very onions dangling from the beam, mantle and shine like cherubs' cheeks. Something of the influence of those vegetables sinks into Mr Pecksniff's nature. He weeps." 20

—*disappointed:* "As [**Jonas**] released his hold of Charity, to put [his proposal to **Mercy**] with better effect, she started up and hurried away to her own room, marking her progress as she went by such a train of passionate and incoherent sound, as nothing but a slighted woman in her anger could produce." 20

"The beauteous Merry, too, with all the glory of her conquest fresh upon her, so probed and lanced the rankling disappointment of her sister by her capricious airs and thousand little trials of Mr **Jonas**'s obedience, that she almost goaded her into a fit of madness, and obliged her to retire from table in a burst of passion, hardly less vehement than that to which she had abandoned herself in the first tumult of her wrath." 24

—*triumphant:* "Miss Pecksniff was in a frame of mind equally becoming to herself and the occasion. She was full of clemency and conciliation. She had laid in several chaldrons of live coals, and was prepared to heap them on the heads of her enemies. She bore no spite nor malice in her heart. Not the least." 54

—*overthrown:* " . . . Miss Pecksniff really had fainted away. The bitterness of her mortification; the bitterness of having summoned witnesses, and such witnesses, to behold it; the bitterness of knowing that the strong-minded **woman** and the red-nosed **daughters** towered triumphant in this hour of their anticipated overthrow; was too much to be borne. Miss Pecksniff had fainted away in earnest." 54 *See* **Youngest Gentleman**

Mercy Pecksniff. "[She] sat upon the stool because of her simplicity and innocence, which were very great: very great. Miss Pecksniff sat upon a stool because she was all girlishness, and playfulness, and wildness, and kittenish buoyancy. She was the most arch and at the same time the most artless creature, was the youngest Miss Pecksniff, that you can possibly imagine. It was her great charm. She was too fresh and guileless, and too full of child-like vivacity, was the youngest Miss Pecksniff, to wear combs in her hair, or to turn it up, or to frizzle it, or braid it. She wore it in a crop, a loosely flowing crop, which had so many rows of curls in it, that the top row was only one curl. Moderately buxom was her shape, and quite womanly too . . . ." 2

—*cast down:* "It was the merry one herself. But sadly, strangely altered! So careworn and dejected, so faltering and full of fear; so fallen, humbled, broken; that to have seen her quiet in her coffin would have been a less surprise.

"She set the light upon a bracket in the hall, and laid her hand upon her heart; upon her eyes; upon her burning head. Then she came on towards the door with such a wild and hurried step that Mr **Bailey** lost his self-possession, and still had his eye where the keyhole had been, when she opened it." 28 *See* **Charity Pecksniff**—*disappointed*

—*suffering and outcome:* "'I know how obdurate I was! I never thought at all; dear **Mr Chuzzlewit**, I never thought at all; I had no thought, no heart, no care to find one; at that time. It has grown out of my trouble. I have felt it in my trouble. I wouldn't recall my trouble, such as it is and has been—and it is light in comparison with trials which hundreds of good people suffer every day, I know—I wouldn't recall it to-morrow, if I could. It has been my friend, for without it no one could have changed me; nothing could have changed me. Do not mistrust me because of these tears; I cannot help them. I am grateful for it, in my soul. Indeed I am!'" 54

Seth Pecksniff. "Perhaps there never was a more moral man than Mr. Pecksniff: especially in his conversation and correspondence. It was once said of him by a homely admirer, that he had a Fortúnatus's purse of good sentiments in his inside. In this particular he was like the girl in the fairly tale, except that if they were not actual diamonds which fell from his lips, they were the very brightest paste, and shone prodigiously.

"He was a most exemplary man: fuller of virtuous precept than a copybook. Some people likened him to a direction-post, which is always telling the way to a place, and never goes there: but these were his enemies; the shadows cast by his brightness; that was all.

"His very throat was moral. You saw a good deal of it. You looked over a very low fence of white cravat (whereof no man had ever beheld the tie, for he fastened it behind), and there it lay, a valley between two jutting heights of collar, serene and whiskerless before you. It seemed to say, on the part of Mr. Pecksniff, 'There is no deception, ladies and gentlemen, all is peace, a holy calm pervades me.'

"So did his hair, just grizzled with an iron-grey, which was all brushed off his forehead, and stood bolt upright, or slightly drooped in kindred action with his heavy eyelids. So did his person, which was sleek though free from corpulency. So did his manner, which was soft and oily. In a word, even his plain black suit, and state of widower, and dangling double eyeglass, all tended to the same purpose, and cried aloud, 'Behold the moral Pecksniff!' " 2

—*his occupation:* "The brazen plate upon the door (which being Mr Pecksniff's, could not lie) bore this inscription, 'PECKSNIFF, ARCHITECT' . . . he had never designed or built anything; but it was generally understood that his knowledge of the science was almost awful in its profundity.

"Mr Pecksniff's professional engagements, indeed, were almost, if not entirely, confined to the reception of pupils; for the collection of rents, with which pursuit he occasionally varied and relieved his graver toils, can hardly be said to be a strictly architectural employment. His genius lay in ensnaring parents and guardians, and pocketing premiums." 2

" . . . there were cases on record in which the masterly introduction of an additional back window, or a kitchen door, or half-a-dozen steps, or even a water-spout, had made the design of a pupil Mr Pecksniff's own work, and had brought substantial rewards into that gentleman's pocket. But such is the magic of genius, which changes all it handles into gold!" 6

—*his nature:* " . . . the enemies of this worthy man unblushingly maintained that he always said of what was very bad, that it was very natural; and that he unconsciously betrayed his own nature in doing so." 3

—*his manner:* "Mr. Pecksniff's manner was so bland, and he nodded his head so soothingly, and showed in everything such an affable sense of his own excellence, that anybody would have been, as **Mrs Lupin** was, comforted by the mere voice and presence of such a man; and, though he had merely said 'a verb must agree with its nominative case in number and person, my good friend,' or 'eight times eight are sixty-four, my worthy soul,' must have felt deeply grateful to him for his humanity and wisdom." 3

" . . . Mr Pecksniff presented himself at dinner-time in such a state of suavity, benevolence, cheerfulness, politeness, and cordiality, as even he had perhaps never attained before. The frankness of the country gentleman, the refinement of the artist, the good-humoured allowance of the man of the world; philanthropy, forbearance, piety, toleration, all blended together in a flexible adapatability to anything and everything; were expressed in Mr Pecksniff . . . ." 44

—*tenderness:* "To a gentleman of Mr Pecksniff's tenderness, [old **Martin**] was a very mournful sight. He could not but foresee the probability of his respected relative being made the victim of designing persons, and of his riches falling into worthless hands. It gave him so much pain that he resolved to secure the property to himself; to keep bad testamentary suitors at a distance: to wall up the old gentleman, as it were, for his own use." 30

—*and the fair sex:* "Mr Pecksniff had a lively sense of the Beautiful: especially in women. His manner towards the sex was remarkable for its insinuating character. It is recorded of him in another part of these pages, that he embraced Mrs Todgers on the smallest provocation: and it was a way he had: it was a part of the gentle placidity of his disposition. Before any thought of matrimony was in his mind, he had bestowed on **Mary [Graham]** many little tokens of his spiritual admiration. They had been indignantly received, but that was nothing. True, as the idea expanded within him, these had become too ardent to escape the piercing eye of Cherry [**Charity Pecksniff**], who read his scheme at once; but he had always felt the power of Mary's charms. So Interest and Inclination made a pair, and drew the curricle of Mr Pecksniff's plan." 30

—*by woman spurned:* "Gallantry in its true sense is supposed to ennoble and dignify a man; and love has shed refinements on innumerable **Cymons**. But Mr. Pecksniff: perhaps because to one of his exalted nature these were mere grossnesses: certainly did not appear to any unusual advantage, now that he was left alone. On the contrary, he seemed to be shrunk and reduced; to be trying to hide himself within himself; and to be wretched at not having the power to do it. His shoes looked too large; his sleeve looked too long; his hair looked too limp; his features looked too mean; his exposed throat looked as if a halter would have done it good. For a minute or two, in fact, he was hot, and pale, and mean, and shy, and slinking, and consequently not at all

Pecksniffian. But after that, he recovered himself, and went home with as beneficent an air as if he had been the High Priest of the summer weather." 30

—*scorn:* "'Oh vermin!' said Mr. Peckniff. 'Oh, bloodsuckers! Is it not enough that you have embittered the existence of an individual, wholly unparalleled in the biographical records of amiable persons; but must you now, even now, when he has made his election, and reposed his trust in a Numble, but at least sincere and disinterested relative; must you now, vermin and swarmers (I regret to make use of these strong expressions, my dear sir, but there are times when honest indignation will not be controlled), must you now, vermin and swarmers (for I WILL repeat it), taking advantage of his unprotected state, assemble round him from all quarters, as wolves and vultures, and other animals of the feathered tribe assemble round—I will not say round carrion or a carcass, for Mr **Chuzzlewit** is quite the contrary—but round their prey—their prey—to rifle and despoil; gorging their voracious maws, and staining their offensive beaks, with every description of carnivorous enjoyment ! '" 52

—*exposed:* "[He] stood with his eyes fixed upon the floor and his hands clasping one another alternately, as if a host of penal sentences were being passed upon him. Not only did his figure appear to have shrunk, but his discomfiture seemed to have extended itself even to his dress. His clothes seemed to have grown shabbier, his linen to have turned yellow, his hair to have become lank and frowsy; his very boots looked villainous and dim, as if their gloss had departed with his own." 52

Ruth Pinch. "[She] was not at all ugly. On the contrary, she had a good face; a very mild and prepossessing face; and a pretty little figure—slight and short, but remarkable for its neatness. There was something of her brother, much of him indeed, in a certain gentleness of manner, and in her look of timid trustfulness; but she was so far from being a fright, or a dowdy, or a horror, or anything else, predicted by the two Miss **Pecksniffs**, that those young ladies naturally regarded her with great indignation . . . . [She] had a chatty, cheerful way with her, and a single-hearted desire to look upon the best side of everything, which was the very moral and image of **Tom** . . . . " 9

—*in the kitchen:* "Well, she *was* a cheerful little thing; and had a quaint, bright quietness about her that was infinitely pleasant. Surely she was the best sauce for chops ever invented. The potatoes seemed to take a pleasure in sending up their grateful steam before; the froth upon the pint of porter pouted to attract her notice." 37

—*pedestrian in London:* "Whether there was life enough left in the slow vegetation of Fountain Court for the smoky shrubs to have any consciousness of the brightest and purest-hearted little woman in the world, is a question for gardeners, and those who are learned in the loves of plants. But, that it was a good thing for that same paved yard to have such a delicate little figure flitting through it; that it passed like a smile from the grimy old houses, and the worn flagstones, and left them duller, darker, sterner than before; there is no sort of doubt.

"The Temple fountain might have leaped up twenty feet to greet the spring of hopeful maidenhood, that in her person stole on, sparkling, through the dry and dusty channels of the Law; the chirping sparrows, bred in Temple chinks and crannies, might have held their peace to listen to imaginary skylarks, as so fresh a little creature passed; the dingy boughs, unused to droop, otherwise than in their puny growth, might have bent down in a kindred gracefulness to shed their benedictions on her graceful head . . . . Anything might have happened that did not happen, and never will, for love of Ruth." 14

—*fluttered:* " . . . was anybody else there, that she blushed so deeply, after looking round, and tripped off down the steps with such unusual expedition?

"Why, the fact is, that Mr **Westlock** was passing at that moment. The Temple is a public thoroughfare; they may write up on the gates that it is not, but so long as the gates are left open it is, and will be; and Mr Westlock had as good a right to be there as anybody else. But why did she run away, then? Not being ill dressed, for she was much too neat for that, why did she run away? The brown hair that had fallen down beneath her bonnet, and had one impertinent imp of a false flower clinging to it, boastful of its licence before all men, *that* could not have been the cause, for it looked charming. Oh! foolish, panting, frightened little heart, why did she run away!" 14

Tom Pinch. "An ungainly, awkward-looking man, extremely shortsighted, and prematurely bald . . . stood hesitating, with the door in his hand. He was far from handsome certainly; and was dressed in a snuff-coloured suit, of an uncouth make at the best, which, being shrunk with long wear, was twisted and tortured into all kinds of odd shapes; but notwithstanding his attire, and his clumsy figure, which a great stoop in his shoulders, and a ludicrous habit he had of thrusting his head forward, by no means redeemed, one would not have been disposed . . . to consider him a bad fellow by any means. He was perhaps about thirty, but he might have been almost any age between sixteen and sixty: being one of those strange creatures who never decline into an ancient appearance, but look their oldest when they are very young, and get it over at once." 2

—*value to an employer:* "'He doesn't keep you as his assistant because you are of any use to him; because your wonderful faith in his pretensions is of inestimable service in all his mean disputes; because your honesty reflects honesty on him; because your wandering about this little place all your spare hours, reading in ancient books and foreign tongues, gets noised abroad, even as far as Salisbury, making of him, **Pecksniff** the master, a man of learning and of vast importance. *He* gets no credit from you, Tom, not he [said **John Westlock**].'" 2

—*happiness:* "If Diogenes coming to life again could have rolled himself, tub and all, into Mr **Pecksniff**'s parlour, and could have seen Tom Pinch as he sat on **Mercy** Pecksniff's stool, with his plate and glass before him, he could not have faced it out, though in his surliest mood, but must have smiled good-temperedly. The perfect and entire satisfaction of Tom; his surpassing appreciation of the husky sandwiches, which crumbled in his mouth like saw-dust; the unspeakable relish with which he swallowed the thin wine by drops, and smacked his lips, as though it were so rich and generous that to lose an atom of its fruity flavour were a sin; the look with which he paused sometimes, with his glass in his hand, proposing silent toasts to himself . . . no cynic in the world, though in his hatred of its men a very griffin, could have withstood these things in Thomas Pinch." 6

Mark Tapley. "He was a young fellow, of some five or six-and-twenty perhaps, and was dressed in such a free and fly-away fashion, that the long ends of his loose red neckcloth were streaming out behind him quite as often as before; and the bunch of bright winter berries in the buttonhole of his velveteen coat was as visible to Mr **Pinch**'s rearward observation, as if he had worn that garment wrong side foremost. He continued to sing with so much energy that he did not hear the sound of wheels until it was close behind him. . . ." 5

—*seeking spiritual growth:* "'I was thinking . . . of something in the grave-digging way. . . . It's a good damp, wormy sort of business . . . and there might be some credit in being jolly, with one's mind in that pursuit, unless grave-diggers is usually given that way; which would be a drawback . . . . In case of that not turning out as well as one could wish . . . there's other businesses. Undertaking now. That's gloomy. There might be credit to be gained there. A broker's man in a poor neighbourhood wouldn't be bad perhaps. A jailor sees a deal of misery. A doctor's man is in the very midst of murder. A bailiff's an't a lively office nat'rally. Even a tax-gatherer must find his feelings rather worked upon, at times. There's lots of trades in which I should have an opportunity, I think.'" 5

—*love in action:* "It cannot be said that as his illness wore off, his cheerfulness and good nature increased, because they would hardly admit of augmentation; but his usefulness among the weaker members of the party was much enlarged; and at all times and seasons there he was exerting it.

"If a gleam of sun shone out of the dark sky, down Mark tumbled into the cabin, and presently up he came again with a woman in his arms, or half-a-dozen children, or a man, or a bed, or a saucepan, or a basket, or something animate or inanimate, that he thought would be the better for the air. If an hour or two of fine weather in the middle of the day tempted those who seldom or never came on deck at other times to crawl into the long-boat, or lie down upon the spare spars, and try to eat, there, in the centre of the group, was Mr Tapley, handing about salt beef and biscuit, or dispensing tastes of grog, or

cutting up the children's provisions with his pocket-knife, for their greater ease
and comfort, or reading aloud from a venerable newspaper, or singing some
roaring old song to a select party, or writing the beginnings of letters to their
friends at home for people who couldn't write, or cracking jokes with the crew,
or nearly getting blown over the side, or emerging, half-drowned, from a shower
of spray, or lending a hand somewhere or other: but always doing something
for the general entertainment.

"At night, when the cooking-fire was lighted on the deck, and the driving
sparks that flew among the rigging, and the cloud of sails, seemed to menace
the ship with certain annihilation by fire, in case the elements of air and water
failed to compass her destruction; there, again, was Mr Tapley, with his coat
off and his shirt-sleeves turned up to his elbows, doing all kinds of culinary offices; compounding the strangest dishes; recognised by every one as an established authority; and helping all parties to achieve something which, left to
themselves, they never could have done, and never would have dreamed of.

"In short, there never was a more popular character than Mark Tapley
became, on board that noble and fast-sailing line-of-packet ship, *The Screw*;
and he attained at last to such a pitch of universal admiration, that he began
to have grave doubts within himself whether a man might reasonably claim
any credit for being jolly under such exciting circumstances.

"'If this was going to last,' said Tapley, 'there'd be no great difference as I
can perceive, between *The Screw* and the Dragon. I never *am* to get credit, I
think. I begin to be afraid that the Fates is determined to make the world easy
to me.'" ¶15

—*surrender:* "'My constitution is, to be jolly; and my weakness is, to wish
to find a credit in it. Wery good, sir. In this state of mind, I gets a notion in my
head that [**Mrs Lupin**] looks on me with a eye of—with what you may call a
favourable sort of eye in fact . . . . But bein' at that time full of hopeful wisions,
I arrives at the conclusion that no credit is to be got out of such a way of life as
that, where everything agreeable would be ready to one's hand.

"'Lookin' on the bright side of human life in short, one of my hopeful wisions
is, that there's a deal of misery a-waitin' for me; in the midst of which I may
come out tolerable strong, and be jolly under circumstances as reflects some
credit . . . . I gets to the U-nited States; and then I *do* begin, I won't deny it, to
feel some little credit in sustaining my spirits. What follows? Jest as I'm a-
beginning to come out, and am a-treadin' on the werge, my master deceives me
. . . leaves me, high and dry, without a leg to stand upon. In which state I returns home.

"'Wery good. Then all my hopeful wisions bein' crushed; and findin' that
there ain't no credit for me nowhere; I abandons myself to despair, and says,
"Let me do that as has the least credit in it of all; marry a dear, sweet creetur,
as is wery fond of me: me bein', at the same time, wery fond of her: lead a
happy life, and struggle no more again' the blight which settles on my
prospects."'" ¶48

Montague Tigg. " . . . Mr **Pecksniff** found himself immediately collared
by something which smelt like several damp umbrellas, a barrel of beer, a cask
of warm brandy-and-water, and a small parlour-full of stale tobacco smoke,
mixed . . . .

—*shabby-genteel:* "The gentleman was of that order of appearance which
is currently termed shabby-genteel, though in respect of his dress he can
hardly be said to have been in any extremities, as his fingers were a long way

out of his gloves, and the soles of his feet were at an inconvenient distance from the upper leather of his boots. His nether garments were of a bluish grey—violent in its colours once, but sobered now by age and dinginess—and were so stretched and strained in a tough conflict between his braces and his straps, that they appeared every moment in danger of flying asunder at the knees.

"His coat, in colour blue and of a military cut, was buttoned and frogged up to his chin. His cravat was, in hue and pattern, like one of those mantles which hairdressers are accustomed to wrap about their clients, during the progress of the professional mysteries. His hat had arrived at such a pass that it would have been hard to determine whether it was originally white or black.

"But he wore a moustache—a shaggy moustache too: nothing in the meek and merciful way, but quite in the fierce and scornful style: the regular Satanic sort of thing—and he wore, besides, a vast quantity of unbrushed hair. He was very dirty and very jaunty; very bold and very mean; very swaggering and very slinking; very much like a man who might have been something better, and unspeakably like a man who deserved to be something worse." ¶4 *And see* **Tigg Montague**

The Rest of the Chuzzlewits

Anthony. "Then there were Anthony Chuzzlewit, and his son **Jonas**: the face of the old man so sharpened by the wariness and cunning of his life, that it seemed to cut him a passage through the crowded room, as he edged away behind the remotest chairs . . ." 4

Diggory. An ancestor who "was in the habit of perpetually dining with Duke Humphrey. So constantly was he a guest at that nobleman's table indeed; and so unceasingly were His Grace's hospitality and companionship forced, as it were, upon him; that we find him uneasy, and full of constraint and reluctance: writing his friends to the effect that if they fail to do so and so by bearer, he will have no choice but to dine again with Duke Humphrey: and expressing himself in a very marked and extraordinary manner as one surfeited of High Life and Gracious Company." 1

George. "[He was] a gay bachelor cousin, who claimed to be young but had been younger, and was inclined to corpulency, and rather over-fed himself: to that extent, indeed, that his eyes were strained in their sockets, as if with constant surprise; and he had such an obvious disposition to pimples, that the bright spots on his cravat, the rich pattern on his waistcoat, and even his glittering trinkets, seemed to have broken out upon him, and not to have come into existence comfortably." 4

Grandmother. "The old lady, naturally strong-minded, was nevertheless frail and fading; she was notoriously subject to that confusion of ideas, or, to say the least, of speech, to which age and garrulity are liable." 1

Ned, deceased. *See* **Widow**, strong-minded

Toby. When he "lay upon his deathbed, this question was put to him in a distinct, solemn, and formal way: 'Toby Chuzzlewit, who was your grandfather?' To which he, with his last breath, no less distinctly, solemnly, and formally replied: and his words were taken down at the time, and signed by six witnesses, each with his name and address in full: 'The **Lord No Zoo**.'" 1

Chevy Slyme. "'Every man of true genius has his peculiarity. Sir, the peculiarity of my friend Slyme is, that he is always waiting round the corner. He is perpetually around the corner, sir. He is round the corner at this instant.'

... [**Tigg**] returned with a companion shorter than himself, who was wrapped in an old blue camlet cloak with a lining of faded scarlet. His sharp features being much pinched and nipped by long waiting in the cold, and his straggling red whiskers and frowzy hair being more than usually dishevelled from the same cause, he certainly looked rather unwholesome and uncomfortable than Shakespearian or Miltonic. ... [His] great abilities seemed one and all to point towards the sneaking quarter of the moral compass ...." 4

—*frustrated:* "'I swear,' cried Mr Slyme, giving the table an imbecile blow with his fist, and then feebly leaning his head upon his hand, while some drunken drops oozed from his eyes, 'that I am the wretchedest creature on record. Society is in a conspiracy against me. I'm the most literary man alive. I'm full of scholarship; I'm full of genius; I'm full of information; I'm full of novel views on every subject; yet look at my condition! I'm at this moment obliged to two strangers for a tavern bill!'" 7

—*gainfully employed:* "'Steady, kinsman!' said the chief officer of the party [of three policemen]. 'Don't be violent' ....

"'Aye,' he said, with a sulky nod. 'You may deny your nephews till you die, but Chevy Slyme is Chevy Slyme still, all the world over. Perhaps even you may feel it some disgrace to your own blood to be employed in this way. I'm to be bought off.'" 51

The **Spottletoes**. "First, there was Mr. Spottletoe, who was so bald and had such big whiskers, that he seemed to have stopped his hair, by the sudden application of some powerful remedy, in the very act of falling off his head, and to have fastened it irrevocably on his face. Then there was Mrs Spottletoe, who being much too slim for her years, and of a poetical constitution, was accustomed to inform her more intimate friends that the said whiskers were 'the lodestar of her existence ....'" 4

Widow, strong-minded. "Then there was the widow of a deceased brother [**Ned**] of Mr. **Martin Chuzzlewit**, who being almost supernaturally disagreeable, and having a dreary face and a bony figure and a masculine voice, was, in right of these qualities, what is commonly called a strong-minded woman; and who, if she could, would have established her claim to the title, and have shown herself, mentally speaking, a perfect Samson, by shutting up her brother-in-law in a private mad-house, until he proved his complete sanity by loving her very much." 4

—*her daughters:* "Beside her sat her spinster daughters, three in number, and of gentlemanly deportment, who had so mortified themselves with tight stays, that their tempers were reduced to something less than their waists, and sharp lacing was expressed in their very noses." 4

—*characterized by a relation:* "' ... naming no names ... I think it would be much more decent and becoming, if those who hooked and crooked themselves into this family by getting on the blind side of some of its members before marriage, and manslaughtering them afterwards by crowing over them to that strong pitch that they were glad to die, would refrain from acting the part of vultures in regard to other members of this family who are living. I think it would be full as well, if not better, if those individuals would keep at home, contenting themselves with what they have got (luckily for them) already; instead of hovering about, and thrusting their fingers into, a family pie, which they flavour much more than enough, I can tell them, when they are fifty miles away.'"4

Young man. " . . . a young gentleman, grand-nephew of Mr. **Martin Chuzzlewit**, very dark and very hairy, and apparently born for no particular purpose but to save looking-glasses the trouble of reflecting more than just the first idea and sketchy notion of a face, which had never been carried out." 4

Supporting Roles

Benjamin Bailey. "[He was] a small boy with a large red head, and no nose to speak of, and a very dirty Wellington boot on his left arm, appeared; who (being surprised) rubbed the nose just mentioned with the back of a shoe-brush, and said nothing." 8

—*candor on duty:* " . . . he . . . expressed his belief that the approaching collation would be of 'rather a spicy sort.'

"'Will it be long before it's ready, Bailey?' asked **Mercy**.

"'No,' said Bailey, 'it *is* cooked. When I come up, she was dodging among the tender pieces with a fork, and eating of 'em.'

"But he had scarcely achieved the utterance of these words, when he received a manual compliment on the head, which sent him staggering against the wall; and **Mrs Todgers**, dish in hand, stood indignantly before him.

"'Oh you little villain!' said that lady. 'Oh you bad, false boy!'

"'No worse than yerself,' retorted Bailey, guarding his head, on a principle invented by Mr **Thomas Cribb**. 'Ah! Come now! Do that agin, will yer?'

"'He's the most dreadful child,' said Mrs Todgers, setting down the dish, 'I ever had to deal with. The gentlemen spoil him to that extent, and teach him such things, that I'm afraid nothing but hanging will ever do him any good.'" 9

—*in full dress:* "When the hour [of the party] drew nigh, Bailey junior, testifying great excitement, appeared in a complete suit of cast-off clothes several sizes too large for him, and in particular, mounted a clean shirt of such extraordinary magnitude, that one of the gentlemen (remarkable for his ready wit) called him 'collars' on the spot." 9

" . . . this remarkable boy . . . nothing disconcerted or put out of his way. If any piece of crockery, a dish or otherwise, chanced to slip through his hands (which happened once or twice), he let it go with perfect good breeding, and never added to the painful emotions of the company by exhibiting the least regret. Nor did he, by hurrying to and fro, disturb the repose of the assembly, as many well-trained servants do; on the contrary, feeling the hopelessness of waiting upon so large a party, he left the gentlemen to help themselves to what they wanted, and seldom stirred from behind Mr **Jinkins**'s chair: where, with his hands in his pockets, and his legs planted pretty wide apart, he led the laughter, and enjoyed the conversation." 9

—*a case of accelerated development:* He was "a highly-condensed embodiment of all the sporting grooms in London; an abstract of all the stable-knowledge of the time; a something at a high-pressure that must have had existence many years, and was fraught with terrible experiences . . . Mr Bailey's genius . . . now eclipsed both time and space, cheated beholders of their senses, and worked on their belief in defiance of all natural laws. He walked along the tangible and real stones of Holborn Hill, an under-sized boy; and yet he winked the winks, and thought the thoughts, and did the deeds, and said the sayings of an ancient man. There was an old principle within him, and a young surface without. He became an inexplicable creature: a breeched and booted Sphinx." 26

And see **Poll Sweedlepipe**—*professionally challenged*

Chuffey. " . . . a little blear-eyed, weazen-faced, ancient man came creeping out. He was of a remote fashion, and dusty, like the rest of the furniture; he was dressed in a decayed suit of black; with breeches garnished at the knees with rusty wisps of ribbon, the very paupers of shoe-strings; on the lower portion of his spindle legs were dingy worsted stockings of the same colour. He looked as if he had been put away and forgotten half a century before, and somebody had just found him in a lumber-closet." 11

" . . . some dregs of a better nature unawakened, might perhaps have been descried through that very medium, melancholy though it was, yet lingering at the bottom of the worn-out cask called Chuffey." 11

Mary Graham. "She was very young; apparently no more than seventeen; timid and shrinking in her manner, and yet with a greater share of self-possession and control over her emotions than usually belongs to a far more advanced period of female life . . . . She was short in stature; and her figure was slight, as became her years; but all the charms of youth and maidenhood set it off, and clustered on her gentle brow. Her face was very pale, in part no doubt from recent agitation. Her dark brown hair, disordered from the same cause, had fallen negligently from its bonds, and hung upon her neck: for which instance of its waywardness no male observer would have had the heart to blame it.

"Her attire was that of a lady, but extremely plain; and in her manner, even when she sat as still as she did then, there was an indefinable something which appeared to be in kindred with her scrupulously unpretending dress." 3

—*character:* " . . . she had been reared up in a sterner school than the minds of most young girls are formed in; she had had her nature strengthened by the hands of hard endurance and necessity; had come out from her young trials constant, self-denying, earnest, and devoted: had acquired in her maidenhood . . . something of that nobler quality of gentle hearts which is developed often by the sorrows and struggles of matronly years, but often by their lessons only. Unspoiled, unpampered in her joys or griefs; with frank and full, and deep affection for the object of her early love; she saw in [young **Martin**] one who for her sake was an outcast from his home and fortune, and she had no more idea of bestowing that love upon him in other than cheerful and sustaining words, full of high hope and grateful trustfulness, than she had of being unworthy of it, in her lightest thought or deed, for any base temptation that the world could offer." 14

Mrs. Lupin. "The mistress of the Blue Dragon was in outward appearance just what a landlady should be: broad, buxom, comfortable, and good-looking, with a face of clear red and white, which, by its jovial aspect, at once bore testimony to her hearty participation in the good things of the larder and cellar, and to their thriving and healthful influences.

"She was a widow, but years ago had passed through her state of weeds, and burst into flower again; and in full bloom she had continued ever since; and in full bloom she was now; with roses on her ample skirts, and roses on her bodice, roses in her cap, roses in her cheeks—ay, and roses, worth the gathering too, on her lips, for that matter.

"She had still a bright black eye, and jet black hair, was comely, dimpled, plump, and tight as a gooseberry; and though she was not exactly what the world calls young, you may make an affidavit, on trust, before any mayor or magistrate in Christendom, that there are a great many young ladies in the world (blessings on them, one and all!) whom you wouldn't like half as well, or admire half as much, as the beaming hostess of the Blue Dragon." ¶3

—*on the USA*: "'[**Mark Tapley**] went,' said Mrs. Lupin, with increased distress, 'to America. He was always tender-hearted and kind, and perhaps at this moment may be lying in prison under sentence of death, for taking pity on some miserable black, and helping the poor runaway creetur to escape. How could he ever go to America! Why didn't he go to some of those countries where the savages eat each other fairly, and give an equal chance to every one!'" 43

Mould. "In the passage they encountered Mr Mould the undertaker: a little elderly gentleman, bald, and in a suit of black; with a note-book in his hand, a massive gold watch-chain dangling from his fob, and a face in which a queer attempt at melancholy was at odds with a smirk of satisfaction; so that he looked as a man might, who, in the very act of smacking his lips over choice old wine, tried to make believe it was physic." 19

—*the ultimate accolade:* "' . . . [**Mrs Gamp**]'s a ve-ry shrewd woman. That's a woman whose intellect is immensely superior to her station in life. . . . She's the sort of woman now,' said Mould, drawing his silk handkerchief over his head again, and composing himself for a nap, 'one would almost feel disposed to bury for nothing: and do it neatly too!'" 25

—*professionally blissful:* "'This is one of the most impressive cases, sir . . . that I have seen in the whole course of my professional experience. . . . Such affectionate regret, sir, I never saw. There is no limitation, there is positively NO limitation:' opening his eyes wide, and standing on tiptoe: 'in point of expense! I have orders, sir, to put on my whole establishment of mutes; and mutes come very dear . . . not to mention their drink. To provide silver-plated handles of the very best description, ornamented with angels' heads from the most expensive dies. To be perfectly profuse in feathers. In short, sir, to turn out something absolutely gorgeous.'" 19

" . . . an afflicted gentleman, an affectionate gentleman, who knows what it is in the power of money to do, in giving him relief, and in testifying his love and veneration for the departed. It can give him . . . four horses to each vehicle; it can give him velvet trappings; it can give him drivers in cloth cloaks and topboots; it can give him the plumage of the ostrich, dyed black; it can give him any number of walking attendants, dressed in the first style of funeral fashion, and carrying batons tipped with brass; it can give him a handsome tomb; it can give him a place in Westminster Abbey itself, if he choose to invest it in such a purchase. Oh! do not let us say that gold is dross, when it can buy such things as these.'" 19

—*professionally offended:* "'You wouldn't be inclined to take a walking one of two, with the plain wood and a tin plate, I suppose?'

"'Certainly not,' replied Mr Mould, 'much too common. Nothing to say to it.'

"'I told 'em it was precious low,' observed Mr **Tacker**.

"'Tell 'em to go somewhere else. We don't do that style of business here,' said Mr Mould. 'Like their impudence to propose it. Who is it?'

"'Why,' returned Tacker, pausing, 'that's where it is, you see. It's the **beadle's son-in-law**.'

"'The beadle's son-in-law, eh?' said Mould. 'Well! I'll do it if the beadle follows in his cocked hat; not else. We carry it off that way, by looking official, but it'll be low enough then. His cocked hat, mind!'" 25

Nadgett. "He was a short-dried-up, withered old man, who seemed to have secreted his very blood; for nobody would have given him credit for the possession of six ounces of it in his whole body. How he lived was a secret; where he lived was a secret; and even what he was, was a secret. In his musty old pocket-book he carried contradictory cards, in some of which he called himself a coal-merchant, in others a wine-merchant, in others a commission-agent, in

others a collector, in others an accountant: as if he really didn't know the secret himself.

"He was always keeping appointments in the City, and the other man
never seemed to come. He would sit on 'Change for hours, looking at everybody
who walked in and out, and would do the like at Garraway's, and in other business coffee-houses, in some of which he would be occasionally seen drying a
very damp pocket-handkerchief before the fire, and still looking over his shoulder for the man who never appeared.

"He was mildewed, threadbare, shabby; always had flue upon his legs and
back; and kept his linen so secret by buttoning up and wrapping over, that he
might have had none—perhaps he hadn't. He carried one stained beaver glove,
which he dangled before him by the forefinger as he walked or sat; but even its
fellow was a secret. Some people said he had been a bankrupt, others that he
had gone an infant into an ancient Chancery suit which was still depending, but
it was all a secret.

"He carried bits of sealing-wax and a hieroglyphical old copper seal in his
pocket, and often secretly indited letters in corner boxes of the trysting-places
before mentioned; but they never appeared to go to anybody, for he would put
them into a secret place in his coat, and deliver them to himself weeks afterwards, very much to his own surprise, quite yellow.

"He was that sort of man that if he had died worth a million of money, or
had died worth twopence half-penny, everybody would have been perfectly
satisfied, and would have said it was just as they expected. And yet he belonged to a class; a race peculiar to the City; who are secrets as profound to
one another, as they are to the rest of mankind." ¶27

—*on duty:* ". . . that amiable and worthy orphan [**Jonas Chuzzlewit**] had
become a part of the mystery of Mr Nadgett's existence. Mr Nadgett took an
interest in his lightest proceedings; and it never flagged or wavered . . . . Jonas
had no more idea that Mr Nadgett's eyes were fixed on him, than he had that
he was living under the daily inspection and report of a whole order of Jesuits.
Indeed Mr Nadgett's eyes were seldom fixed on any other objects than the
ground, the clock, or the fire; but every button on his coat might have been an
eye: he saw so much.

"The secret manner of the man disarmed suspicion in this wise; suggesting,
not that he was watching any one, but that he thought some other man was
watching him. He went about so stealthily, and kept himself so wrapped up in
himself, that the whole object of his life appeared to be, to avoid notice and preserve his own mystery. Jonas sometimes saw him in the street, hovering in
the outer office, waiting at the door for the man who never came, or slinking off
with his immovable face and drooping head, and the one beaver glove dangling
before him; but he would as soon have thought of the cross upon the top of St
Paul's Cathedral taking note of what he did, or slowly winding a great net about
his feet, as of Nadgett's being engaged in such an occupation.

" . . . Mr **Mould** himself . . . openly said he was a long-headed man, a dry
one, a salt fish, a deep file, a rasper; and made him the subject of many other
flattering encomiums." 38

Betsey Prig. "Mrs Prig was of the **Gamp** build, but not so far; and her
voice was deeper and more like a man's. She had also a beard." 25

"Mrs Prig, of Bartlemy's: or as some said Barklemy's, or as some said
Bardlemy's; for by all these endearing and familiar appellations, had the hospi-

tal of Saint Bartholomew become a household word among the sisterhood which Betsey Prig adorned." 49

—*primping:* "Her toilet was simple. She had merely to 'chuck' her bonnet and shawl upon the bed; give her hair two pulls, one upon the right side and one upon the left, as if she were ringing a couple of bells; and all was done." 49

—*acidic:* "The best among us have their failings, and it must be conceded of Mrs Prig, that if there were a blemish in the goodness of her disposition, it was a habit she had of not bestowing all its sharp and acid properties upon her patients (as a thoroughly amiable woman would have done), but of keeping a considerable remainder for the service of her friends . . . she was most contradictory when most elevated. It is certain that her countenance became . . . derisive and defiant, and that she sat with her arms folded, and one eye shut up, in a somewhat offensive, because obtrusively intelligent, manner." 49

—*in vino:* "'Bother **Mrs Harris**!' said Betsy Prig.

"**Mrs Gamp** looked at her with amazement, incredulity, and indignation; when Mrs Prig, shutting her eye still closer, and folding her arms still tighter, uttered these memorable and tremendous words:

"'I don't believe there's no sich a person!'

"After the utterance of which expressions, she leaned forward, and snapped her fingers once, twice, thrice; each time nearer to the face of Mrs Gamp, and then rose to put on her bonnet, as one who felt that there was now a gulf between them, which nothing could ever bridge across." 49

Paul ("Poll") Sweedlepipe. "He was a little elderly man, with a clammy cold right hand, from which even [his] rabbits and birds could not remove the smell of shaving-soap. Poll had something of the bird in his nature; not of the hawk or eagle, but of the sparrow, that builds in chimney-stacks and inclines to human company. He was not quarrelsome, though, like the sparrow; but peaceful, like the dove. In his walk he strutted; and, in this respect, he bore a faint resemblance to the pigeon, as well as in a certain prosiness of speech, which might, in its monotony, be likened to the cooing of that bird.

"He was very inquisitive; and when he stood at his shop-door in the evening-tide, watching the neighbours, with his head on one side, and his eye cocked knowingly, there was a dash of the raven in him. Yet there was no more wickedness in Poll than in a robin. Happily, too, when any of his ornithological properties were on the verge of going too far, they were quenched, dissolved, melted down, and neutralised in the barber; just as his bald head—otherwise, as the head of a shaved magpie—lost itself in a wig of curly black ringlets, parted on one side, and cut away almost to the crown, to indicate immense capacity of intellect.

"Poll had a very small, shrill, treble voice . . . a tender heart, too . . . [and] wore in his sporting character, a velveteen coat, a great deal of blue stocking, ankle boots, a neckerchief of some bright colour, and a very tall hat. Pursuing his more quiet occupation of barber, he generally subsided into an apron not over-clean, a flannel jacket, and corduroy knee-shorts." ¶26

—*professionally challenged:* "'Poll,' [**Bailey**] said, 'I ain't as neat as I could wish about the gills. Being here, I may as well have a shave, and get trimmed close.'

"The barber stood aghast; but Mr Bailey divested himself of his neck-cloth, and sat down in the easy shaving chair with all the dignity and confidence in life. There was no resisting his manner. The evidence of sight and touch became as nothing. His chin was as smooth as a new-laid egg or a scraped Dutch cheese; but Poll Sweedlepipe wouldn't have ventured to deny, on affidavit, that he had the beard of a Jewish rabbi."

Mrs Todgers. "[She] was a lady, rather a bony and hard-featured lady, with a row of curls in front of her head, shaped like little barrels of beer; and on the top of it something made of net—you couldn't call it a cap exactly—which looked like a black cobweb. She had a little basket on her arm, and in it a bunch of keys that jingled as she came." 8

"Commercial gentlemen and gravy had tried Mrs. Todgers's temper; the main chance—it was such a very small one in her case, that she might have been excused for looking sharp after it, lest it should entirely vanish from her sight—had taken a firm hold on Mrs. Todgers's attention. But in some odd nook in Mrs. Todgers's breast, up a great many steps, and in a corner easy to be overlooked, there was a secret door, with 'Woman' written on the spring, which, at a touch from **Mercy's** hand, had flown wide open, and admitted her for shelter. . . she was poor, and . . . this good had sprung up in her from among the sordid strivings of her life . . . ." 37

"She had a lean lank body, Mrs Todgers, but a well-conditioned soul within. Perhaps the Good Samaritan was lean and lank, and found it hard to live. Who knows!" 54

John Westlock.—*giving a party:* " . . . nobody ever dreamed such soup as was put upon the table directly afterwards; or such fish; or such side-dishes; or such a top and bottom; or such a course of birds and sweets; or in short anything approaching the reality of that entertainment at ten-and-sixpence a head, exclusive of wines. As to *them*, the man who can dream such iced champagne, such claret, port, or sherry, had better go to bed and stop there.

"But perhaps the finest feature of the banquet was, that nobody was half so much amazed by everything as John himself, who in his high delight was constantly bursting into fits of laughter, and then endeavouring to appear preternaturally solemn, lest the waiters should conceive he wasn't used to it." 12 *And see* **Ruth Pinch** OP—*fluttered*

Youngest gentleman (**Augustus Moddle**). "The youngest gentleman in company is pale, but collected, and still sits apart; for his spirit loves to hold communion with itself, and his soul recoils from noisy revellers. [**Mercy**] has a consciousness of his presence and adoration. He sees it flashing sometimes in the corner of her eye. Have a care, **Jinkins**, ere you provoke a desperate man to frenzy!" 9

—*fulmination:* "'I should think no more of admitting daylight into the fellow,' said the youngest gentleman, in a desperate voice, 'than if he was a bulldog . . . . Let him be careful . . . I give him warning. No man shall step between me and the current of my vengeance . . . . I have borne this long enough . . . but now my soul rebels against it, and I won't stand it any longer. I left home originally, because I had that within me which wouldn't be domineered over by a sister; and do you think I'm going to be put down by *him?* . . . Does he make a point of always pretending to forget me, when he's pouring out the beer? Does he make bragging remarks about his razors, and insulting allusions to people who have no necessity to shave more than once a week? But let him look out! He'll find himself shaved, pretty close, before long, and so I tell him.'

"The young gentleman was mistaken in this closing sentence, inasmuch as he never told it to **Jinkins**, but always to **Mrs Todgers**." 10

—*defeated:* "'But when the marriage took place . . . . The violence of that young man . . . the frightful opinions he expressed upon the subject of self-destruction; the extraordinary actions he performed with his tea; the clenching way in which he bit his bread and butter . . . all combined to form a picture never to be forgotten . . . .

"' . . . .The turn I experienced only yesterday,' said **Mrs Todgers**, putting her hand to her side, 'when the house-maid threw his bedside carpet out of the window of his room, while I was sitting here, no one can imagine. I thought it was him, and that he had done it at last!'" 32

—*a new interest:* "'Oh, **Mrs Todgers**, if you knew what a comfort her nose is to me!'

"'Her nose, sir!' Mrs Todgers cried.

"'Her profile, in general,' said the youngest gentleman, 'but particularly her nose. It's so like;' here he yielded to a burst of grief; 'it's so like hers who is Another's, Mrs Todgers!'" 32

—*wooing:* " 'I am sure I don't know what encouragement he would have [said **Charity**]. . . . He walks with me, and plays cards with me, and he comes and sits alone with me.'

"'Quite right,' said **Mrs Todgers**. 'That's indispensable, my dear.'

"'And he sits very close to me.'

"'Also quite correct,' said Mrs Todgers.

"'And he looks at me.'

"'To be sure he does,' said Mrs Todgers.

"'And he has his arm upon the back of the chair or sofa, or whatever it is—behind me, you know.'

"'I should think so,' said Mrs Todgers.

"'And then he begins to cry!'" 32

—*success:* "Moddle . . . inferred . . . that, being a kind of unintentional Vampire, he had had Miss Pecksniff assigned to him by the Fates, as Victim Number One. Miss Pecksniff controverting this opinion as sinful, Moddle was goaded on to ask whether she could be contented with a blighted heart; and it appearing on further examination that she could be, plighted his dismal troth, which was accepted and returned.

"He bore his good fortune with the utmost moderation. Instead of being triumphant, he shed more tears than he had ever been known to shed before: and sobbing, said:

"'O! what a day this has been! I can't go back to the office this afternoon. Oh, what a trying day this has been, Good Gracious!'" 32

—*his last word:*

> *Off Gravesend*
> *Clipper Schooner, Cupid*
> *Wednesday night*

"*Ever-injured Miss Pecksniff,*

"'Ere this reaches you, the undersigned will be—if not a corpse—on the way to Van Dieman's Land. Send not in pursuit. I never will be taken alive! . . . .

"Oh! Miss Pecksniff, why didn't you leave me alone! Was it not cruel, *cruel!* Oh, my goodness, have you not been a witness of my feelings—have you not seen them flowing from my eyes—did you not, yourself, reproach me with weeping more than usual on that dreadful night when last we met—in that house—where I once was peaceful—though blighted—in the society of **Mrs Todgers**!

"But it was written—in the Talmud—that you should involve yourself in the inscrutable and gloomy Fate which it is my mission to accomplish, and which wreathes itself—e'en now—about my—temples. I will not reproach, for I have wronged you. May the furniture make some amends!

"Farewell! Be the proud bride of a ducal coronet, and forget me! Long may it be before you know the anguish with which I now subscribe myself—amid the tempestuous howlings of the— sailors,

"Unalterably, never yours,

"*Augustus*" 54

The Americans

"I am inclined to think . . . that Dickens was never in all his life so strictly clever as he is in the American part of Martin Chuzzlewit. There are places where he was more inspired . . . there are places where he wrote more carefully and cunningly . . . there are places where he wrote very much more humanly, more close to the ground and to growing things . . . .But I do not think that his mere abstract acuteness and rapidity of thought were ever exercised with such startling exactitude as they are in this place in Martin Chuzzlewit." GKC pp94-5

American gentleman, on the boat to New York. "An American gentleman in the after-cabin, who had been wrapped up in fur and oilskin the whole passage, unexpectedly appeared in a very shiny, tall, black hat, and constantly overhauled a very little valise of pale leather, which contained his clothes, linen, brushes, shaving apparatus, books, trinkets, and other baggage. He likewise stuck his hands deep into his pockets, and walked the deck with his nostrils dilated, as already inhaling the air of Freedom which carries death to all tyrants, and can never (under any circumstances worth mentioning) be breathed by slaves." 15

Americans, as debtors. "'If ever the defaulting part of this here country pays its debts—along of finding that not paying 'em won't do in a commercial point of view, you see, and is inconvenient in its consequences—they'll take such a shine out of it, and make such bragging speeches, that a man might suppose no borrowed money had ever been paid afore, since the world was first begun. That's the way they gammon each other, sir [said **Mark Tapley**]. Bless you, *I* know 'em.'" 23

Bevan. " . . . a middle-aged man with a dark eye and a sunburnt face, who had attracted [young] **Martin's** attention by having something very engaging and honest in the expression of his features . . . .

"There was a cordial candour in his manner, and an engaging confidence that it would not be abused; a manly bearing on his own part, and a simple reliance on the manly faith of a stranger; which Martin had never seen before. He linked his arm readily in that of the American gentleman, and they walked out together." 16

Julius Washington Merryweather Bib. "'. . . a gentleman in the lumber line, sir, and much esteemed.'" 34

Jefferson Brick. "[He] was a small young gentleman of very juvenile appearance, and unwholesomely pale in the face; partly, perhaps, from intense thought, but partly, there is no doubt, from the excessive use of tobacco, which he was at that moment chewing vigorously.

"He wore his shirt-collar turned down over a black ribbon; and his lank hair, a fragile crop, was not only smoothed and parted back from his brow, that none of the poetry of his aspect might be lost, but had, here and there, been grubbed up by the roots: which accounted for his loftiest developments being somewhat pimply.

"He had that order of nose on which the envy of mankind has bestowed the appellation 'snug,' and it was very much turned up at the end, as with a lofty scorn. Upon the upper lip of this young gentleman were tokens of a sandy down: so very, very smooth and scant, that, though encouraged to the utmost, it looked more like a recent trace of gingerbread than the fair promise of a moustache; and this conjecture his apparently tender age went far to strengthen . . . .

"**Martin** . . . had begun to say that he presumed this was the colonel's little boy, and that it was very pleasant to see him playing at Editor in all the guile-lessness of childhood, when the colonel proudly interposed and said:

"'My War Correspondent, sir. Mr. Jefferson Brick!'" 16

Mrs Jefferson Brick. "'Pray,' said **Martin**, 'who is that sickly little girl opposite, with the tight round eyes? I don't see anybody here, who looks like her mother, or who seems to have charge of her.'

"'Do you mean the matron in blue, sir?' asked the **colonel**, with emphasis. 'That is Mrs Jefferson Brick, sir.'

"'No, no,' said Martin, 'I mean the little girl, like a doll; directly opposite.'

"'Well, sir!' cried the colonel. '*That* is Mrs Jefferson Brick.'" 16

—*improving:* "'What course of lectures are you attending now, ma'am?' said [**Bevan**], turning again to Mrs Brick.

"'The Philosophy of the Soul, on Wednesdays.'

"'On Mondays?'

"'The Philosophy of Crime.'

"'On Fridays?'

"'The Philosophy of Vegetables.'

"'You have forgotten Thursdays; the Philosophy of Government, my dear,' observed the third lady.

"'No,' said Mrs Brick. 'That's Tuesdays.'

"'So it is!' cried the lady. 'The Philosophy of Matter on Thursdays, of course.'" 17

Captain of the *Esau Slodge*. ". . . waiting anxiously to see the boat depart, [**Martin** and **Mark**] stopped up the gangway: an instance of neglect which caused the 'Capting' of the Esau Slodge to 'wish he might be sifted fine as flour, and whittled small as chips; that if they didn't come off that there fixing right smart too, he'd spill 'em in the drink' . . . ." 33

Captain of *The Screw*. "'A good passage, cap'en?' inquired the colonel, taking him aside.

"'Well now! It was a pretty spanking run, sir,' said, or rather sung, the captain, who was a genuine New Englander: 'considerin the weather.'

"' . . . —A first-rate spanker, cap'en, was it? Yes?'

"'A most e—ternal spanker,' said the skipper . . . . " 16

Chiggle, sculptor. "'Our own immortal Chiggle, sir, is said to have observed, when he made the celebrated **Pogram** statter in marble, which rose so much con-test and preju-dice in Europe, that the brow was more than mortal.'" 34

General **Cyrus Choke**. "One very lank gentleman, in a loose limp white cravat, long white waistcoat, and a black great-coat, who seemed to be in authority among them . . . . 'I would say, sir, may the British Lion have his talons eradicated by the noble bill of the American Eagle, and be taught to play upon the Irish Harp and the Scotch Fiddle that music which is breathed in every empty shell that lies upon the shores of green Co-lumbia !'" 21

Hannibal Chollop. " . . . a lean person in a blue frock and a straw hat, with a short black pipe in his mouth, and a great hickory stick, studded all over with knots, in his hand; who smoking and chewing as he came along, and spitting frequently, recorded his progress by a train of decomposed tobacco on the ground. . . His face was almost as hard and knobby as his stick; and so were his hands. His head was like an old black hearth-broom." 33

—*his occupation:* "Mr Chollop was a man of a roving disposition; and, in any less advanced community, might have been mistaken for a violent vagabond. But his fine qualities being perfectly understood and appreciated in those regions where his lot was cast, and where he had many kindred spirits to consort with, he may be regarded as having been born under a fortunate star, which is not always the case with a man so much before the age in which he lives.

"Preferring, with a view to the gratification of his tickling and ripping fancies, to dwell upon the outskirts of society, and in the more remote towns and cities, he was in the habit of emigrating from place to place, and establishing in each some business—usually a newspaper—which he presently sold: for the most part closing the bargain by challenging, stabbing, pistolling, or gouging the new editor, before he had quite taken possession of the property.

"He always introduced himself to strangers as a worshipper of Freedom; was the consistent advocate of Lynch law, and slavery; and invariably recommended . . . the 'tarring and feathering' of any unpopular person who differed from himself. He called this 'planting the standard of civilisation in the wilder gardens of My country.'" 33

—*peer appraisal:* "'Our fellow-countryman is a model of a man, quite fresh from Natur's mould!' . . . 'He is a true-born child of this free hemisphere! Verdant as the mountains of our country; bright and flowing as our mineral Licks; unspiled by withering conventionalities as air our broad and boundless Perearers! Rough he may be. So air our Barrs. Wild he may be. So air our Buffalers. But he is a child of Natur', and a child of Freedom; and his boastful answer to the Despot and the Tyrant is, that his bright home is in the Settin Sun.'" 34

Cicero. " . . . they found [**Mark**] recumbent in the midst of a fortification of luggage, apparently performing his national anthem for the gratification of a grey-haired black man, who sat . . . staring intently . . . while Mark, with his head reclining on his hand, returned the compliment in a thoughtful manner, and whistled all the time." 17

Miss Codger. "Sticking on [her] forehead . . . by invisible means, was a massive cameo, in size and shape like the raspberry tart which is ordinarily sold for a penny, representing on its front the Capitol at Washington.

"'**Miss Toppit** and Miss Codger!' said **Mrs Hominy**.

"'Codger's the lady so often mentioned in the English newspapers, I should think, sir,' whispered **Mark**. 'The oldest inhabitant as never remembers anything.

"'To be presented to a **Pogram**,' said Miss Codger, 'by a **Hominy**, indeed, a thrilling moment is it in its impressiveness on what we call our feelings. But why we call them so, or why impressed they are, or if impressed they are at all, or if at all we are, or if there really is, oh gasping one ! a Pogram or a Hominy, or any active principle to which we give those titles, is a topic, Spirit searching, light abandoned, much too vast to enter on, at this unlooked-for crisis.'" 34

Colonel Diver. "[He was] a sallow gentleman, with sunken cheeks, black hair, small twinkling eyes, and a singular expression hovering about that region of his face, which was not a frown, nor a leer, and yet might have been mistaken at the first glance for either. Indeed it would have been difficult, on a much closer acquaintance, to describe it in any more satisfactory terms than as a mixed expression of vulgar cunning and conceit.

"This gentleman wore a rather broad-brimmed hat for the greater wisdom of his appearance; and had his arms folded for the greater impressiveness of his attitude. He was somewhat shabbily dressed in a blue surtout reaching nearly to his ankles, short loose trousers of the same colour, and a faded buff waistcoat, through which a discoloured shirt-frill struggled to force itself into notice, as asserting an equality of civil rights with the other portions of his dress, and maintaining a declaration of Independence on its own account.

"His feet, which were of unusually large proportions, were leisurely crossed before him as he half leaned against, half sat upon, the steamboat's bulwark; and his thick cane, shod with a mighty ferule at one end and armed with a great metal knob at the other, depended from a line-and-tassel on his wrist." ¶16

Ginery Dunkle. "'Mr **Pogram!**' cried the shrill boy.

"The spokesman thus reminded of the shrill boy's presence, introduced him. 'Doctor Ginery Dunkel, sir. A gentleman of great poetical elements. He has recently jined us here, sir, and is an acquisition to us, sir, I do assure you.'" 34

Edener. " . . . he was pale and worn . . . his anxious eyes were deeply sunken in his head. His dress of homespun blue hung about him in rags; his feet and head were bare. He sat down on a stump half-way, and . . . put his hand upon his side as if in pain, and while he fetched his breath stared at [**Martin** and **Mark**], wondering . . . .

"'My eldest son would [help] if he could . . . but to-day he has his chill upon him, and is lying wrapped up in the blankets. My youngest died last week.'" 23

Edeners. "[**Martin**] found some half-dozen men—wan and forlorn to look at, but ready enough to assist—who helped him . . . to the log-house. They shook their heads in speaking of the settlement, and had no comfort to give him. Those who had the means of going away had all deserted it. They who were left had lost their wives, their children, friends, or brothers there, and suffered much themselves. Most of them were ill then; none were the men they had been once." 23

Elderly gentleman. "'I go back Toe my home, sir,' pursued the gentleman, 'by the return train, which starts immediate. Start is not a word you use in your country, sir.'

"'Oh yes, it is,' said Martin.

"'You air mistaken, sir,' returned the gentleman, with great decision: 'but we will not pursue the subject, lest it should awake your prejudice. Sir, **Mrs Hominy**.'" 22

Engine-driver. "The engine-driver of the train . . . leaned with folded arms and crossed legs against the side of the carriage, smoking: and, except when he expressed, by a grunt as short as his pipe, his approval of some particularly dexterous aim on the part of his colleague, the **fireman**, who beguiled his leisure by throwing logs of wood from the tender at the numerous stray cattle on the line, he preserved a composure so immovable, and an indifference so complete, that if the locomotive had been a sucking-pig, he could not have been more perfectly indifferent to its doings."21

General Fladdock. "'Jiniral Fladdock!'

"'My!' cried the sisters . . . 'The general come back!'

"As they made the exclamation, the general, attired in full uniform for a ball, came darting in with such precipitancy that, hitching his boot in the carpet, and getting his sword between his legs, he came down headlong, and presented a curious little bald place on the crown of his head to the eyes of the astonished company. Nor was this the worst of it; for being rather corpulent and very tight, the general, being down, could not get up again, but lay there writhing and doing such things with his boots, as there is no other instance of in military history.

"Of course there was an immediate rush to his assistance; and the general was promptly raised. But his uniform was so fearfully and wonderfully made, that he came up stiff and without a bend in him, like a dead clown, and had no command whatever of himself until he was put quite flat upon the soles of his feet, when he became animated as by a miracle, and moving edgewise that he might go in a narrower compass and be in less danger of fraying the gold lace on his epaulettes by brushing them against anything, advanced with a smiling visage to salute the lady of the house.

" . . . . The general was as warmly received as if New York had been in a state of siege and no other general was to be got for love or money. He shook hands with the Norrises three times all round, and then reviewed them from a little distance as a brave commander might, with his ample cloak drawn forward over the right shoulder and thrown back upon the left side to reveal his manly breast." 17

—*disconcerted:* "'I took my passage in the steerage.'

"If the general had been carried up bodily to a loaded cannon, and required to let it off that moment, he could not have been in a state of greater consternation than when he heard these words. He, Fladdock, Fladdock in full militia uniform, Fladdock the General, Fladdock the caressed of foreign noblemen, expected to know a fellow who had come over in the steerage of a line-of-packet ship, at the cost of four pound ten! And meeting that fellow in the very sanctuary of New York fashion, and nestling in the bosom of the New York aristocracy! He almost laid his hand upon his sword." 17 *See* **American Gentleman**

Gentleman, in a bar. "[Martin] encountered more weeds in the bar-room, some of whom (being thirsty souls as well as dirty) were pretty stale in one sense, and pretty fresh in another. Among them was a gentleman who . . . started that afternoon for the Far West on a six months' business tour; and who, as his outfit and equipment for this journey, had just such another shiny hat and just such another little pale valise as had composed the luggage of the gentleman who came from England . . . ." 16

Gentleman, at a levee. " . . . one silent gentleman with glazed and fishy eyes, and only one button on his waistcoat (which was a very large metal one, and shone prodigiously), got behind the door, and stood there, like a clock, long after everybody else was gone." 22

Gentleman, with a spittoon. "In the further region of [the] banqueting hall was a stove, garnished on either side with a great brass spittoon . . . . Before it, swinging himself in a rocking-chair, lounged a large gentleman with his hat on, who amused himself by spitting alternately into the spittoon on the right hand of the stove, and the spittoon on the left, and then working his way back again in the same order." 16

Miss Hominy and **husband**. "'. . . work it which way you will, [New Thermopylae] beats Eden,' said **Mrs Hominy**, nodding her head with great expression.

"The married Miss Hominy, who had come on board with her husband, gave to this statement her most unqualified support, as did that gentleman also." 23

Mrs. Hominy. "[She was] a lady who certainly could not be considered young—that was matter of fact; and probably could not be considered handsome—but that was matter of opinion. She was very straight, very tall, and not at all flexible in face or figure. On her head she wore a great straw bonnet, with trimmings of the same, in which she looked as if she had been thatched by an unskilful labourer; and in her hand she held a most enormous fan." 21

"'Our institutions make our people smart much, sir,' Mrs Hominy remarked.

"'The most short-sighted man could see that at a glance, with his naked eye,' said **Martin**.

"Mrs Hominy was a philosopher and an authoress, and consequently had a pretty strong digestion; but this coarse, this indecorous phrase, was almost too much for her. For a gentleman sitting alone with a lady—although the door was open—to talk about a naked eye!

"A long interval elapsed before even she, woman of masculine and towering intellect though she was, could call up fortitude enough to resume the conversation. But Mrs Hominy was a traveller. Mrs Hominy was a writer of reviews and analytical disquisitions. Mrs Hominy had had her letters from abroad, beginning 'My ever dearest blank,' and signed 'The Mother of the Modern Gracchi' (meaning the married **Miss Hominy**), regularly printed in a public journal, with all the indignation in capitals, and all the sarcasm in italics. Mrs Hominy had looked on foreign countries with the eye of a perfect republican hot from the model oven; and Mrs Hominy could talk (or write) about them by the hour together. So Mrs Hominy at last came down on Martin heavily, and as he was fast asleep, she had it all her own way, and bruised him to her heart's content." 22

Irishman. " . . . with such a thoroughly Irish face, that it seemed as if he ought, as a matter of right and principle, to be in rags, and could have no sort of business to be looking cheerfully at anybody out of a whole suit of clothes." 17

Captain Kedgick. "The Captain sat down upon the bed before he spoke; and finding it rather hard, moved to the pillow.

"'Well, sir!' said the Captain, putting his hat a little more on one side, for it was rather tight in the crown. 'You're quite a public man I calc'late.'

"'So it seems,' retorted **Martin**, who was very tired.

"'Our citizens, sir,' pursued the Captain, 'intend to pay their respects to you. You will have to hold a sort of le—vee, sir, while you're here.' . . .

"'. . . . What do they want to see me for? what have I done? and how do they happen to have such a sudden interest in me?'

"Captain Kedgick put a thumb and three fingers to each side of the brim of his hat; lifted it a little way off his head, put it on again carefully; passed one hand all down his face, beginning at the forehead and ending at the chin; looked at Martin; then at Mark; then at Martin again; winked; and walked out." 22 *And see A Levee*

La Fayette Kettle. "[He] was as languid and listless in his looks, as most of the gentlemen [**Martin** and **Mark**] had seen; his cheeks were so hollow that he seemed to be always sucking them in; and the sun had burnt him, not a wholesome red or brown, but dirty yellow. He had bright dark eyes, which he kept half closed; only peeping out of the corners, and even then with a glance that seemed to say, 'Now you won't overreach me: you want to, but you won't.' His arms rested carelessly on his knees as he leant forward; in the palm of his left hand, as English rustics have their slice of cheese, he had a cake of tobacco; in his right a penknife. He struck into the dialogue with as little reserve as if he had been specially called in, days before, to hear the arguments on both sides, and favour them with his opinion; and he no more contemplated or cared for the possibility of their not desiring the honour of his acquaintance or interference in their private affairs, than if he had been a bear or a buffalo." 21

Lad, black. "[The lad] in a soiled white jacket was busily engaged in placing on the table two long rows of knives and forks, relieved at intervals by jugs of

water; and as he travelled down one side of this festive board, he straightened
with his dirty hands the dirtier cloth . . . ." 16

Military officer. """Oh!" says he, "if you should ever happen to go to bed
[in Eden] . . . don't forget as to take a axe with you." I looks at him tolerable
hard [said **Mark**]. "Fleas?" says I. "And more," says he. "Wampires?" says I.
"And more," says he. "Musquitoes, perhaps?" says I. "And more," says he.
"What more?" says I. "Snakes more," says he; "rattlesnakes. You're right to a
certain extent, stranger. There air some catawampous chawers in the small
way too, as graze upon a human pretty strong; but don't mind *them*, they're
company. It's snakes," he says, "as you'll object to: and whenever you wake
and see one in a upright poster on your bed," he says, "like a corkscrew with
the handle off a-sittin' on its bottom ring, cut him down, for he means wenom."""
21

Professor Mullit. " . . . 'who is that:' [**Martin**] was going to say 'young'
but thought it prudent to eschew the word: 'that very short gentleman yonder,
with the red nose?'

"'That is Pro-fessor Mullit, sir . . . . He is a man of fine moral elements, sir,
and not commonly endowed . . . . He felt it necessary, at the last election for
President, to repudiate and denounce his father, who voted on the wrong interest. He has since written some powerful pamphlets, under the signature of
'**Suturb**,' or Brutus reversed. He is one of the most remarkable men in our
country, sir.'"16

Negro. "Martin . . . burst into a hearty laugh; to which the negro, out of
his natural good humour and desire to please, so heartily responded, that his
teeth shone like a gleam of light. 'You're the pleasantest fellow I have seen yet,'
said Martin, clapping him on the back, 'and give me a better appetite than bitters.'" 16

Norris family. "There were two **young ladies**—one eighteen; the other
twenty—both very slender, but very pretty; their **mother**, who looked . . .
much older and more faded than she ought to have looked; and their **grandmother**, a little sharp-eyed, quick old woman, who seemed to have got past
that stage, and to have come all right again. Besides these, there were the
young ladies' **father**, and the young ladies' **brother**; the first engaged in mer-
cantile affairs; the second, a student at college [but] the two young ladies . . .
were foremost in [**Martin**'s] thoughts; not only from being, as aforesaid, very
pretty, but by reason of their wearing miraculously small shoes, and the
thinnest possible silk stockings; the which their rocking-chairs developed to a
distracting extent. . . . " 17

—*social taste:* "The whole family had been in England. There was a pleasant thing! But Martin was not quite so glad of this, when he found that they
knew all the great dukes, lords, viscounts, marquesses, duchesses, knights, and
baronets, quite affectionately and were beyond everything interested in the
least particular concerning them . . .

"Martin thought it rather strange, and in some sort inconsistent, that during the whole of these narrations, and in the very meridian of their enjoyment
thereof, both Mr Norris the father, and Mr Norris Junior, the son (who corre-
sponded, every post, with four members of the English Peerage), enlarged upon
the inestimable advantage of having no such arbitrary distinctions in that enlightened land, where there were no noblemen but nature's noblemen, and
where all society was based on one broad level of brotherly love and national
equality." 17

—on race: "**Martin** was so much encouraged on finding himself in such company, that he expressed his sympathy with the oppressed and wretched blacks. Now, one of the young ladies—the prettiest and most delicate—was mightily amused at the earnestness with which he spoke; and on his craving leave to ask her why, was quite unable for a time to speak for laughing. As soon however as she could, she told him that the negroes were such a funny people, so excessively ludicrous in their manners and appearance, that it was wholly impossible for those who knew them well, to associate any serious ideas with such a very absurd part of the creation. Mr Norris the father, and Mrs Norris the mother, and Miss Norris the sister, and Mr Norris Junior the brother, and even Mrs Norris Senior the grandmother, were all of this opinion, and laid it down as an absolute matter of fact." 17

—disconcerted: "'I took my passage in the steerage.' . . .

"A death-like silence fell upon the Norrises. If this story should get wind, their country relation had, by his imprudence, for ever disgraced them. They were the bright particular stars of an exalted New York sphere. There were other fashionable spheres above them, and other fashionable spheres below, and none of the stars in any one of these spheres had anything to say to the stars in any other of these spheres. But, through all the spheres it would go forth, that the Norrises, deceived by gentlemanly manners and appearances, had, falling from their high estate, 'received' a dollarless and unknown man. O guardian eagle of the pure Republic, had they lived for this!

"'You will allow me,' said **Martin**, after a terrible silence, 'to take my leave.'" 17

Obnoxious gentleman. " . . . the friends of the disappointed candidate had found it necessary to assert the great principles of Purity of Election and Freedom of Opinion by breaking a few legs and arms, and furthermore pursuing one obnoxious gentleman through the streets with the design of slitting his nose." 16

Officers and **gentlemen**. " . . . Martin found that there were no fewer than four **majors** present, two **colonels**, one **general**, and a **captain**, so that he could not help thinking how strongly officered the American militia must be; and wondering very much whether the officers commanded each other; or if they did not, where on earth the privates came from. There seemed to be no man there without a title: for those who had not attained to military honours were either doctors, professors, or reverends. Three very hard and disagreeable **gentlemen** were on missions from neighbouring States; one on monetary affairs, one on political, one on sectarian." 16

Major Pawkins. " . . . (a gentleman of Pennsylvania origin) was distinguished by a very large skull, and a great mass of yellow forehead; in deference to which commodities it was currently held in bar-rooms and other such places of resort that the major was a man of huge sagacity. He was further to be known by a heavy eye and a dull slow manner; and for being a man of that kind who, mentally speaking, requires a deal of room to turn himself in. But, in trading on his stock of wisdom, he invariably proceeded on the principle of putting all the goods he had (and more) into his window; and that went a great way with his constituency of admirers." 16

—his bouquet: "When the major arose from his rocking-chair before the stove, and so disturbed the hot air and balmy whiff of soup which fanned their brows, the odour of stale tobacco became so decidedly prevalent as to leave no doubt of its proceeding mainly from that gentleman's attire. Indeed, as **Martin** walked behind him to the bar-room, he could not help thinking that the great

square major, in his listlessness and languor, looked very much like a stale weed himself: such as might be hoed out of the public garden, with great advantage to the decent growth of that preserve, and tossed on some congenial dung-hill." 16

Mrs. Pawkins, landlady. "What Mrs Pawkins felt each day at dinner-time is hidden from all human knowledge. But she had one comfort. It was very soon over." 16

Pilot. " . . . upon a certain starlight night, they took a pilot on board, and within a few hours afterwards lay to until the morning, awaiting the arrival of a steamboat in which the passengers were to be conveyed ashore." 15

Elijah Pogram. "Among the passengers on board the steamboat, there was a faint gentleman sitting on a low camp-stool, with his legs on a high barrel of flour, as if he were looking at the prospect with his ankles . . . . He had straight black hair, parted up the middle of his head and hanging down upon his coat; a little fringe of hair upon his chin; wore no neckcloth; a white hat; a suit of black, long in the sleeves and short in the legs; soiled brown stockings and laced shoes. His complexion, naturally muddy, was rendered muddier by too strict an economy of soap and water; and the same observation will apply to the washable part of his attire, which he might have changed with comfort to himself and gratification to his friends. He was about five and thirty; was crushed and jammed up in a heap, under the shade of a large green cotton umbrella; and ruminated over his tobacco-plug like a cow." 34

"The languid Mr. Pogram shook hands with **Martin**, like a clock-work figure that was just running down. But he made amends by chewing like one that was just wound up." 34

—*receiving:* "'Yes, sir. Mr **Jodd**, sir. Mr **Izzard**, sir. Mr. **Julius Bib**, sir.'

"'**Julius Washington Merryweather Bib**,' said the gentleman himself *to* himself.

"'I beg your pardon, sir. Excuse me . . . . **Colonel Groper**, sir. **Professor Piper**, sir. My own name, sir, is **Oscar Buffum**.'

"Each man took one slide forward as he was named; butted at the Honourable Elijah Pogram with his head; shook hands, and slid back again." 34

Postmaster. " . . . a Western postmaster, who, being a public defaulter not very long before (a character not at all uncommon in America), had been removed from office . . . . " 34

Zephaniah Scadder. " . . . [he was] no doubt a tremendous fellow to get through his work, for he seemed to have no arrears, but was swinging backwards and forwards in a rocking-chair, with one of his legs planted high up against the door-post, and the other doubled up under him, as if he were hatching his foot.

"He was a gaunt man in a huge straw hat, and a coat of green stuff. The weather being hot, he had no cravat, and wore his shirt collar wide open; so that every time he spoke something was seen to twitch and jerk up in his throat, like the little hammers in a harpsichord when the notes are struck. Perhaps it was the Truth feebly endeavouring to leap to his lips. If so, it never reached them.

"Two grey eyes lurked deep within this agent's head, but one of them had no sight in it, and stood stock still. With that side of his face he seemed to listen to what the other side was doing. Thus each profile had a distinct expression;

and when the movable side was most in action, the rigid one was in its coldest state of watchfulness. It was like turning the man inside out, to pass to that view of his features in his liveliest mood, and see how calculating and intent they were.

"Each long black hair upon his head hung down as straight as any plummet line; but rumpled tufts were on the arches of his eyes, as if the crow whose foot was deeply printed in the corners had pecked and torn them in a savage recognition of his kindred nature as a bird of prey." 21

Ship's boys. "'I've just now sent a boy up to your office with the passenger-list, colonel [said the captain of *The Screw*].'

"'You haven't got another boy to spare, p'raps, cap'en?' said the colonel, in a tone almost amounting to severity.

"'I guess there air a dozen if you want 'em, colonel,' said the captain.

"'One moderate big 'un could convey a dozen of champagne, perhaps,' observed the colonel, musing, 'to my office.'" 16

Esau Slodge. " . . . the high-pressure snorting of the 'Esau Slodge;' named after one of the most remarkable men in the country, who had been very eminent somewhere." 33

Putnam Smif. An American correspondent of **Martin**'s. 22

Steamboat passengers. "There happened to be on board the steamboat several gentlemen passengers, of the same stamp as Martin's New York friend Mr **Bevan**; and in their society he was cheerful and happy. They . . . exhibited, in all they said and did, so much good sense and high feeling, that he could not like them too well." 23

Tobacco-user. " . . . a gentleman in a high state of tobacco, who wore quite a little beard, composed of the overflowings of that weed, as they had dried about his mouth and chin: so common an ornament that it would scarcely have attracted **Martin**'s observation, but that this good citizen, burning to assert his equality against all comers, sucked his knife for some moments, and made a cut with it at the butter, just as Martin was in the act of taking some. There was a juiciness about the deed that might have sickened a scavenger." 34

Miss Toppit. "'Mind and matter,' said the lady in the wig [of uncommon size], 'glide swift into the vortex of immensity. Howls the sublime, and softly sleeps the calm Ideal, in the whispering chambers of Imagination. To hear it, sweet it is. But then, outlaughs the stern philosopher, and saith to the Grotesque, "What ho! arrest for me that Agency. Go, bring it here!" And so the vision fadeth.'" 34

—Levee

"Punctually, as the hour struck, **Captain Kedgick** returned to hand [young **Martin**] to the room of state; and he had no sooner got him safe there, than he bawled down the stair-case to his fellow-citizens below, that Mr. Chuzzlewit was 'receiving.'

"Up they came in a rush. Up they came until the room was full, and, through the open door, a dismal perspective of more to come, was shown upon the stairs. One after another, one after another, dozen after dozen, score after score, more, more, more, up they came: all shaking hands with Martin. Such varieties of hands, the thick, the thin, the short, the long, the fat, the lean, the coarse, the fine; such differences of temperature, the hot, the cold, the dry, the moist, the flabby; such diversities of grasp, the tight, the loose, the short-lived, and the lingering! Still up, up, up, more, more, more: and ever and anon the Captain's voice was heard above the crowd: 'There's more below! there's more below. Now gentlemen, you that have been introduced to Mr. Chuzzlewit, will you clear, gentlemen? Will you clear? Will you be so good as clear, gentlemen, and make a little room for more?'

"Regardless of the Captain's cries, they didn't clear at all, but stood there, bolt upright and staring. Two gentlemen [**reporters**] connected with the Watertoast Gazette had come express to get the matter for an article on Martin. They had agreed to divide the labour. One of them took him below the waistcoat; one above. Each stood directly in front of his subject with his head a little on one side, intent on his department. If Martin put one boot before the other, the lower gentleman was down upon him; he rubbed a pimple on his nose, and the upper gentleman booked it. He opened his mouth to speak, and the same gentleman was on one knee before him, looking in at his teeth, with the nice scrutiny of a dentist.

"Amateurs in the physiognomical and phrenological sciences roved about him with watchful eyes and itching fingers, and sometimes one [**phrenologist**], more daring than the rest, made a mad grasp at the back of his head, and vanished in the crowd. They had him in all points of view: in front, in profile, three-quarter face, and behind. Those who were not professional or scientific, audibly exchanged opinions on his looks. New lights shone in upon him, in respect of his nose. Contradictory rumours were abroad on the subject of his hair. And still the Captain's voice was heard—so stifled by the concourse, that he seemed to speak from underneath a feather-bed, exclaiming, 'Gentlemen, you that have been introduced to Mr. Chuzzlewit, *will* you clear?'

"Even when they began to clear it was no better; for then a stream of gentlemen, every one with a lady on each arm (exactly like the chorus to the National Anthem when Royalty goes in state to the play), came gliding in: every new group fresher than the last, and bent on staying to the latest moment. If they spoke to him, which was not often, they invariably asked the same questions, in the same tone: with no more remorse, or delicacy, or consideration, than if he had been a figure of stone, purchased, and paid for, and set up there for their delight.

"Even when, in the slow course of time, these died off, it was as bad as ever, if not worse; for then the boys grew bold, and came in as a class of themselves, and did everything that the grown-up people had done. Uncouth stragglers, too, appeared; men of a ghostly kind, who being in, didn't know how to get out again: insomuch that one **silent gentleman** with glazed and fishy eyes, and only one button on his waist-coat (which was a very large metal one, and shone prodigiously), got behind the door, and stood there, like a clock, long after everybody else was gone." ¶32

—Mealtime

" . . . they heard a bell ringing violently. The instant this sound struck upon their ears, the colonel and the major darted off, dashed up the steps and in at the streetdoor . . . like lunatics . . . three more gentlemen, with horror and agitation depicted in their faces, came plunging wildly round the street corner; jostled each other on the steps; struggled for an instant; and rushed into the house, a confused heap of arms and legs. . . . [**Martin**] walked into the dining-room and slipped into a chair next the colonel, which that gentleman (by this time nearly through his dinner) had turned down in reserve for him, with its back against the table.

"It was a numerous company, eighteen or twenty perhaps. Of these some five or six were ladies, who sat wedged together in a little phalanx by themselves. All the knives and forks were working away at a rate that was quite alarming; very few words were spoken; and everybody seemed to eat his utmost in self-defence, as if a famine were expected to set in before breakfast time to-morrow morning, and it had become high time to assert the first law of nature.

"The poultry, which may perhaps be considered to have formed the staple of the entertainment, for there was a turkey at the top, a pair of ducks at the bottom, and two fowls in the middle—disappeared as rapidly as if every bird had had the use of its wings, and had flown in desperation down a human throat. The oysters, stewed and pickled, leaped from their capacious reservoirs, and slid by scores into the mouths of the assembly. The sharpest pickles vanished, whole cucumbers at once, like sugar-plums, and no man winked his eye. Great heaps of indigestible matter melted away as ice before the sun. It was a solemn and an awful thing to see.

"Dyspeptic individuals bolted their food in wedges; feeding, not themselves, but broods of nightmares, who were continually standing at livery within them. Spare men, with lank and rigid cheeks, came out unsatisfied from the destruction of heavy dishes, and glared with watchful eyes upon the pastry . . . ." 16

Others

➤   **Bill**, a coach guard. "Seventy breezy miles a day were written in his very whiskers. His manners were a canter; his conversation a round trot. He was a fast coach upon a down-hill turnpike road; he was all pace. A waggon couldn't have moved slowly, with that guard and his key-bugle on the top of it." 36 *And see* **Coachman**

Brass and Copper Family.—*approached:* "**Tom Pinch**'s sister was governess in a family, a lofty family, perhaps the wealthiest brass and copper founder's family known to mankind. They lived at Camberwell; in a house so big and fierce, that its mere outside, like the outside of a giant's castle, struck terror into vulgar minds and made bold persons quail. There was a great front gate; with a great bell, whose handle was in itself a note of admiration; and a great lodge; which being close to the house, rather spoilt the look-out certainly, but made the look-in tremendous. At this entry, a great **porter** kept constant watch and ward; and when he gave the visitor high leave to pass, he rang a second great bell, responsive to whose note a great **footman** appeared in due time at the great hall-door, with such great tags upon his liveried shoulder that he was perpetually entangling and hooking himself among the chairs and tables, and led a life of torment which could scarcely have been surpassed, if he had been a blue-bottle in a world of cobwebs." 9

—**mistress**. " . . . the lady of the establishment was curious in the natural history and habits of the animal called Governess, and encouraged her daughters to report thereon whenever occasion served; which was, in reference to all parties concerned, very laudable, improving, and pleasant." 9

—**master**. " . . . [Mr **Pecksniff**] very politely bowed to a middle-aged gentleman at an upper window . . . . 'Is he looking this way, **Charity**?'

"'He is opening the window, pa!'

"'Ha, ha!' cried Mr Pecksniff softly. 'All right! He has found I'm professional. He heard me inside just now, I have no doubt. Don't look! With regard to the fluted pillars in the portico, my dears——'

"'Hallo!' cried the gentleman.

"'Sir, your servant!' said Mr Pecksniff, taking off his hat. 'I am proud to make your acquaintance.'

"'Come off the grass, will you!' roared the gentleman.

"'I beg your pardon, sir,' said Mr Pecksniff, doubtful of his having heard aright. 'Did you—?'

"'Come off the grass!' repeated the gentleman, warmly.

"'We are unwilling to intrude, sir,' Mr Pecksniff smilingly began.

"'But you *are* intruding,' returned the other, 'unwarrantably intruding. Trespassing. You see a gravel walk, don't you? What do you think it's meant for? Open the gate there! Show that party out!'

"With that he clapped down the window again, and disappeared." 9

—*assembled:* " . . . a middle-aged gentleman, with a pompous voice and manner, and a middle-aged lady, with what may be termed an exciseable face, or one in which starch and vinegar were decidedly employed. There was likewise present that eldest pupil . . . whom **Mrs. Todgers**, on a previous occasion, had called a syrup, and who was now weeping and sobbing spitefully." 36 *And see* **Sophia**

Bullamy. "There was a porter on the premises [of the Anglo-Bengalee Disinterested Loan and Life Assurance Company]—a wonderful creature, in a vast red waistcoat and short-tailed pepper-and-salt coat—who carried more conviction to the minds of sceptics than the whole establishment without him. No confidences existed between him and the Directorship; nobody knew where he had served last; no character or explanation had been given or required. No questions had been asked on either side.

"This mysterious being, relying solely on his figure, had applied for the situation, and had been instantly engaged on his own terms. They were high; but he knew, doubtless, that no man could carry such an extent of waistcoat as himself, and felt the full value of capacity to such an institution. When he sat upon a seat erected for him in a corner of the office, with his glazed hat hanging on a peg over his head, it was impossible to doubt the respectability of the concern. It went on doubling itself with every square inch of his red waist-coat until, like the problem of the nails in the horse's shoes, the total became enormous.

"People had been known to apply to effect an insurance on their lives for a thousand pounds, and looking at him, to beg, before the form of proposal was filled up, that it might be made two . . . . Whether he was a deep rogue, or a stately simpleton, it was impossible to make out, but he appeared to believe in the Anglo-Bengalee. He was grave with imaginary cares of office; and having nothing whatever to do and something less to take care of, would look as if the pressure of his numerous duties, and a sense of the treasure in the company's strong-room, made him a solemn and a thoughtful man." ¶27

Butcher. "To see the butcher slap the steak, before he laid it on the block, and give his knife a sharpening, was to forget breakfast instantly. It was agreeable, too—it really was—to see him cut it off, so smooth and juicy. There was nothing savage in the act, although the knife was large and keen; it was a piece of art, high art; there was delicacy of touch, clearness of tone, skilful handling of the subject, fine shading. It was the triumph of mind over matter, quite.

" . . . the butcher had a sentiment for his business, and knew how to refine upon it. When he saw **Tom** putting the cabbage-leaf into his pocket awkwardly, he begged to be allowed to do it for him; 'for meat,' he said with some emotion, 'must be humoured, not drove.'" 39

Coachman. " . . . of all the swells that ever flourished a whip, professionally, he might have been elected emperor. He didn't handle his gloves like another man, but put them on—even when he was standing on the pavement, quite detached from the coach—as if the four greys were, somehow or other, at the ends of the fingers. It was the same with his hat. He did things with his hat, which nothing but an unlimited knowledge of horses and the wildest freedom of the road, could ever have made him perfect in. Valuable little parcels were brought to him with particular instructions, and he pitched them into this hat, and stuck it on again; as if the laws of gravity did not admit of such an event as its being knocked off or blown off, and nothing like an accident could befall it." 36

Commercial gentleman, of a debating turn. "[He] rises in the midst, and suddenly lets loose a tide of eloquence which bears down everything before it . . . . There is a gentleman in company whom two accomplished and delightful females regard with veneration, as the fountain of their existence. Yes, when yet the two Miss **Pecksniffs** lisped in language scarce intelligible, they called that individual 'Father!'" 9

David Crimp. "'You're always full of your chaff,' said the shopman, rolling up the article (which looked like a shirt) quite as a matter of course, and nibbed his pen upon the counter. . . . 'I'm making it . . . what it always has been—two shillings. Same name as usual, I suppose?'

"'Still the same name,' said Mr **Tigg**; 'my claim to the dormant peerage not being yet established by the House of Lords.'

"'The old address?'

"'Not at all,' said Mr Tigg; 'I have removed my town establishment from thirty-eight Mayfair, to number fifteen-hundred-and-forty-two Park Lane.'

"'Come, I'm not going to put that down, you know,' said the shopman with a grin . . . . The shopman was so highly entertained by his humour that Mr. Tigg himself could not repress some little show of exaltation." 13

—*now* **Crimple**: "Beside [Tigg] sat a smiling gentleman, of less pretensions and of business looks, whom he addressed as David. Surely not the David of the—how shall it be phrased?—the triumvirate of golden balls? . . . Yes. The very man.

"'The Secretary's salary, David,' said Mr Montague, 'the office being now established, is eight hundred pounds per annum, with his house-rent, coals, and candles free. His five-and-twenty shares he holds, of course. Is that enough?'

"David smiled and nodded, and coughed behind a little locked portfolio which he carried; with an air that proclaimed him to be the secretary in question." 27

"This gentleman's name, by the way, had been originally Crimp; but as the word was susceptible of an awkward construction and might be misrepresented, he had altered it to Crimple." 27 ["Crimp": a petty criminal]

Emigrants, in steerage. "There were English people, Irish people, Welsh people, and Scotch people there; all with their little store of coarse food and shabby clothes; and nearly all with their families of children. There were children of all ages; from the baby at the breast, to the slattern-girl who was as much a grown woman as her mother. Every kind of domestic suffering that is bred in poverty, illness, banishment, sorrow, and long travel in bad weather, was crammed into the little space; and yet was there infinitely less of complaint and querulousness, and infinitely more of mutual assistance and general kindness to be found in that unwholesome ark, than in many brilliant ballrooms." 15

Fips, of Austin Friars. "'. . . grave, business-like, sedate-looking . . . small and spare, and looked peaceable, and wore black shorts and powder . . . .'" 39

"And there was Fips, old Fips of Austin Friars, present at the dinner, and turning out to be the jolliest old dog that ever did violence to his convivial sentiments by shutting himself up in a dark office . . . sang songs, did Fips; and made speeches, did Fips; and knocked off his wine pretty handsomely, did Fips; and in short, he showed himself a perfect Trump, did Fips, in all respects." 53

Footman. "'Visitors for **Miss Pinch**!' said the footman. He must have been an ingenious young man, for he said it very cleverly: with a nice discrimination between the cold respect with which he would have announced visitors to the family, and the warm personal interest with which he would have announced visitors to the cook." 9

—*on duty:* "'Pray is Miss Pinch at home?'

"'She's *in*,' replied the footman. As much as to say to **Tom**: 'But if you think she has anything to do with the proprietorship of this place you had better abandon that idea.'

"'I wish to see her, if you please,' said Tom.

"The footman, being a lively young man, happened to have his attention caught at that moment by the flight of a pigeon, in which he took so warm an interest that his gaze was rivetted on the bird until it was quite out of sight. He then invited Tom to come in, and showed him into a parlour.

"'Hany neem?' said the young man, pausing languidly at the door." 36

And see **Brass and Copper Family**—*approached*

Gamp, deceased. "' . . . and as to husbands [said **Mrs Gamp**], there's a wooden leg gone likeways home to its account, which in its constancy of walkin' into wine vaults, and never comin' out again 'till fetched by force, was quite as weak as flesh, if not weaker.'" 40

"'My good young 'ooman [said Mrs Gamp]—to the **servant-girl**—'p'raps somebody would like to try a new-laid egg or two, not biled too hard. Likeways, a few rounds o' buttered toast, first cuttin' off the crust, in consequence of tender teeth, and not too many of 'em; which Gamp himself . . . at one blow, being in liquor, struck out four, two single and two double, as was took by **Mrs Harris** for a keepsake, and is carried in her pocket at this present hour . . . . " 46

Gander. "[He] was of a witty turn, being indeed the gentleman who had originated the sally about 'collars;' which sparkling pleasantry was now retailed from mouth to mouth, under the title of Gander's Last, and was received in all parts of the room with great applause." 9

Grandmother of the **Pinch**es. "' . . . she was a housekeeper, wasn't she, **Tom**? [said **Westlock**]'

"'Yes,' said Mr Pinch, nursing one of his large knees, and nodding his head: 'a gentleman's housekeeper.'

"'*He* [**Pecksniff**] never scraped and clawed into his pouch all her hard savings; dazzling her with prospects of your happiness and advancement, which he knew (and no man better) never would be realised! *He* never speculated and traded on her pride in you, and her having educated you, and on her desire that you at least should live to be a gentleman. Not he, Tom! . . . . *He* didn't take less than he had asked, because that less was all she had, and more than he expected: not he, Tom!'" 2

Mrs Harris. " . . . a fearful mystery surrounded this lady by the name of Harris, whom no one in the circle of **Mrs Gamp**'s acquaintance had ever seen; neither did any human being know her place of residence, though Mrs Gamp appeared on her own showing to be in constant communication with her. There were conflicting rumours on the subject; but the prevalent opinion was that she was a phantom of Mrs. Gamp's brain—as Messrs Doe and Roe are fictions of the law—created for the express purpose of holding visionary dialogues with her on all manner of subjects, and invariably winding up with a compliment to the excellence of her nature." 25

—her father: "'. . . a patient . . . as I once nussed, which his calling was the custom-'us, and his name was Mrs Harris's own father, as pleasant a singer . . . as ever you heerd, with a voice like a Jew's-harp in the bass notes, that it took six men to hold at sech times, foaming frightful.'" 46

See **Mrs Gamp and Mrs Harris**

Tommy Harris. "'Don't I know as that dear woman [**Mrs Harris**] is expecting of me at this minnit [said **Mrs Gamp**] . . . and is a-lookin' out of window down the street, with little Tommy Harris in her arms, as calls me his own Gammy, and truly calls, for bless the mottled little legs of that there precious child (like Canterbury Brawn his own dear father says, which so they are) his own I have been, ever since I found him . . . with his small red worsted shoe a-gurglin' in his throat, where he had put it in his play, a chick, wile they was leavin' of him on the floor a-lookin' for it through the ouse and him a-choakin' sweetly in the parlour!'" 49

Jinkins, senior boarder. "[He] was of a fashionable turn; being a regular frequenter of the Parks on Sundays, and knowing a great many carriages by sight. He spoke mysteriously, too, of splendid women, and was suspected ot having once committed himself with a Countess. . . Mr. Jinkins, it may be added, was much the oldest of the party: being a fish-salesman's book-keeper, aged forty. He was the oldest boarder also; and in right of his double seniority, took the lead in the house . . . ." 9

"Mr Jinkins, the only boarder invited [to **Charity**'s wedding], was on the ground first. He wore a white favour in his button-hole, and a bran new extra super double-milled blue saxony dress coat (that was its description in the bill), with a variety of tortuous embellishments about the pockets, invented by the artist to do honour to the day." 54

John Jobling, MRCS, "had a portentously sagacious chin, and a pompous voice, with a rich huskiness in some of its tones that went directly to the heart, like a ray of light shining through the ruddy medium of choice old burgundy. His neckerchief and shirt-frill were ever of the whitest, his clothes of the blackest and sleekest, his gold watch-chain of the heaviest, and his seals of the largest. His boots, which were always of the brightest, creaked as he walked.

"Perhaps he could shake his head, rub his hands, or warm himself before a fire, better than any man alive; and he had a peculiar way of smacking his lips and saying, 'Ah !' at intervals while patients detailed their symptoms, which inspired great confidence. It seemed to express, 'I know what you're going to say better than you do; but go on, go on.'

"As he talked on all occasions whether he had anything to say or not, it was unanimously observed of him that he was 'full of anecdote;' and his experience and profit from it were considered, for the same reason, to be something much too extensive for description. His female patients could never praise him too highly; and the coldest of his male admirers would always say this for him to their friends, 'that whatever Jobling's professional skill might be (and it could not be denied that he had a very high reputation), he was one of the most comfortable fellows you ever saw in your life !'" ¶27

Landlord, of a port city tavern. "'Pray, landlord!' said **Martin**. 'who is that gentleman who passed just now, and whom you were looking after?'

"The landlord poked the fire as if, in his desire to make the most of his answer, he had become indifferent even to the price of coals; and putting his hands in his pockets, said, after inflating himself to give still further effect to his reply:

"'That, gentlemen, is the great Mr **Pecksniff**! The celebrated architect, gentlemen!'

"He looked from one to the other while he said it, as if he were ready to assist the first man who might be overcome by the intelligence." 35

A **landlord, landlady** and **chambermaid**. "[They] were all on [**Lewsome**'s] threshold together, talking earnestly with [**Westlock**] ... 'No better then?' observed the gentleman.

"'Worse!' said the landlord.

"'Much worse,' added the landlady.

"'Oh! a deal badder,' cried the chambermaid from the background, opening her eyes very wide, and shaking her head." 25

Lewsome. "A young man—dark and not ill-looking—with long black hair, that seemed the blacker for the whiteness of the bedclothes. His eyes were partly open, and he never ceased to roll his head from side to side upon the pillow, keeping his body almost quiet." 25

"He was so wasted, that it seemed as if his bones would rattle when they moved him. His cheeks were sunken, and his eyes unnaturally large. He lay back in the easy-chair like one more dead than living; and rolled his languid eyes towards the door when **Mrs. Gamp** appeared, as painfully as if their weight alone were burdensome to move." 29

Man in the Monument. "[He] had simple tastes; ... stony and artificial as his residence was, he still preserved some rustic recollections ... he liked plants, hung up bird-cages, was not wholly cut off from fresh groundsel, and kept young trees in tubs. The Man in the Monument, himself, was sitting outside the door—his own door: the Monument-door: what a grand idea!—and was actually yawning, as if there were no Monument to stop his mouth, and give him a perpetual interest in his own existence.

"**Tom** was advancing towards this remarkable creature, to inquire the way to Furnival's Inn, when two people came to see the Monument. They were a **gentleman** and a **lady**; and the gentleman said, 'How much a-piece?'"

"The Man in the Monument replied, 'A Tanner.' .... When the gentleman and lady had passed out of view, he ... sat down and laughed.

"'They don't know what a many steps there is! he said. 'It's worth twice the money to stop here. Oh, my eye!'

"The Man in the Monument was a Cynic; a worldly man! Tom couldn't ask his way of *him*. He was prepared to put no confidence in anything he said." 37

Married ladies, neighbours of **Mrs Gamp**. " ... at the first double knock every window in the street became alive with female heads; and before [**Pecksniff**] could repeat the performance whole troops of married ladies (some about to trouble Mrs Gamp themselves very shortly) came flocking round the steps, all crying out with one accord, and with uncommon interest, 'Knock at the winder, sir, knock at the winder. Lord bless you, don't lose no more time than you can help; knock at the winder!' ....

"'He's as pale as a muffin,' said one lady, in allusion to Mr Pecksniff.

"'So he ought to be, if he's the feelings of a man,' observed another.

"A third lady (with her arms folded) said she wished he had chosen any other time for fetching Mrs Gamp, but it always happened so with *her*." 19

Mason. "Mr **Pecksniff** was observed too; closely . . . . When he laid his hand upon the mason's shoulder, giving him directions, how pleasant his demeanour to the working classes: just the sort of man who made their toil a pleasure to them, poor dear souls!

"But now a silver trowel was brought; and when the **member** for the Gentlemanly Interest, tucking up his coat-sleeve, did a little sleight-of-hand with the mortar, the air was rent, so loud was the applause. The workman-like manner in which he did it was amazing. No one could conceive where such a gentlemanly creature could have picked the knowledge up.

"When he had made a kind of dirt-pie under the direction of the mason, they brought a little vase containing coins . . . ." 35

Matron. ". . . a fiery-faced matron attired in a crunched bonnet, with particularly long strings to it hanging down her back . . . . The grim and griffin-like inflexibility with which the fiery-faced matron repelled [**Ruth**'s] engaging advances, as proceeding from a hostile and dangerous power, who could have no business there, unless it were to deprive her of a customer, or suggest what became of the self-consuming tea and sugar, and other general trifles." 45

Mayor, and procession. ". . . the charity school, in clean linen, came filing in two and two, so much to the self-approval of all the people present who didn't subscribe to it, that many of them shed tears. A band of music followed, led by a conscientious **drummer** who never let off. Then came a great many gentlemen with wands in their hands, and bows on their breasts, whose share in the proceedings did not appear to be distinctly laid down, and who trod upon each other, and blocked up the entry for a considerable period. These were followed by the Mayor and Corporation, all clustering round the **member** for the Gentlemanly Interest. . . . " 35

Member for the Gentlemanly Interest. "Silence being restored, the member for the Gentlemanly Interest rubbed his hands, and wagged his head, and looked about him pleasantly; and there was nothing this member did, at which some lady or other did not burst into an ecstatic waving of her pocket handkerchief. When he looked up at the stone, they said how graceful! when he peeped into the hole, they said how condescending! when he chatted with the **Mayor**, they said how easy! when he folded his arms they cried with one accord, how statesman-like!" 35

Mrs Mould and **daughters**. "The partner of his life, and daughters twain, were Mr **Mould**'s companions. Plump as any partridge was each Miss Mould, and Mrs M was plumper than the two together. So round and chubby were their fair proportions, that they might have been the bodies once belonging to the angels' faces in the shop below, grown up, with other heads attached to make them mortal. Even their peachy cheeks were puffed out and distended, as though they ought of right to be performing on celestial trumpets. The bodiless cherubs in the shop, who were depicted as constantly blowing those instruments for ever and ever without any lungs, played, it is to be presumed, entirely by ear." 25

Lummy Ned. "'Ah! said **Bill** [**Simmons**], with a sigh . . . 'Lummy Ned of the Light Salisbury, *he* was the one for musical talents. He *was* a guard. What you may call a Guard'an Angel, was Ned. . . He's no more in England . . . . He went to the U-nited States . . . as he landed without a penny to bless himself with, of course they was very glad to see him in the U-nited States . . . he sent word home that [New York] brought Old York to his mind, quite wivid, in consequence of being so exactly unlike it in every respect. I don't understand what particular business Ned turned his mind to, when he got there; but he wrote home that him and his friends was always a-singing, Ale Columbia, and blowing up the President, so I suppose it was something in the public line, or free-and-easy way again. Anyhow he made his fortune.'

"'No!' cried **Martin**.

"'Yes, he did,' said Bill. 'I know that, because he lost it all the day after, in six-and-twenty banks as broke.'" 13

Organist's assistant. "Now, the organist's assistant was a friend of Mr **Pinch**'s, which was a good thing, for he too was a very quiet gentle soul, and had been, like Tom, a kind of old-fashioned boy at school, though well-liked by the noisy fellows too." 5

Pastrycook's employee, in a white waistcoat. " . . . suddenly there appeared a being in a white waistcoat, carrying under his arm a napkin, and attended by another being with an oblong box upon his head, from which a banquet, piping hot, was taken out and set upon the table.

"Salmon, lamb, peas, innocent young potatoes, a cool salad, sliced cucumber, a tender duckling, and a tart—all there. They all came at the right time. Where they came from, didn't appear, but the oblong box was constantly going and coming, and making its arrival known to the man in the white waistcoat by bumping modestly against the outside of the door; for, after its first appearance, it entered the room no more.

"He was never surprised, this man; he never seemed to wonder at the extraordinary things he found in the box; but took them out with a face expressive of a steady purpose and impenetrable character, and put them on the table. He was a kind man; gentle in his manners, and much interested in what they ate and drank. He was a learned man, and knew the flavour of **John Westlock**'s private sauces, which he softly and feelingly described, as he handed the little bottles round. He was a grave man, and a noiseless; for dinner being done, and wine and fruit arranged upon the board, he vanished, box and all, like something that had never been." 45

Mrs Pecksniff. "'She was beautiful, **Mrs Todgers**,' he said, turning his glazed eye again upon her, without the least preliminary notice. 'She had a small property.'

"'So I have heard,' cried Mrs Todgers with great sympathy.

"'Those are her daughters,' said Mr **Packsniff**, pointing out the young ladies, with increased emotion." 9

Pip. "'[He's a] theatrical man—capital man to know—oh, capital man !'"

"'I've a splendid little trait to tell you of my friend [**Jonas**] **Chuzzlewit**, who is the deepest dog I know [said **Tigg**]. I give you my sacred word of honour he is the deepest dog I know, Pip!'

"Pip swore a frightful oath that he was sure of it already . . . . Pip, in a natural spirit of emulation, then related some instances of his own depth . . . .

"It is so pleasant to find real merit appreciated, whatever its particular walk in life may be, that the general harmony of the company was doubtless much promoted by their knowing that the two men of the world [Pip and **Wolf**] were held in great esteem by the upper classes of society, and by the gallant defenders of their country in the army and navy, but particularly the former. The least of their stories had a colonel in it; lords were as plentiful as oaths; and even the Blood Royal ran in the muddy channel of their personal recollections." 28 *And see* **Wolf**

Porter. "Arriving before the great bell-handle, **Tom** gave it a gentle pull. The porter appeared.

"'Pray does **Miss Pinch** live here?' said Tom.

"'Miss Pinch is governess here,' replied the porter.

"At the same time he looked at Tom from head to foot, as if he would have said, 'You are nice man, *you* are; where did *you* come from?'" 36

And see **Brass and Copper Family**

Postillion. "As [**Jonas**] heard the driver, who had risen and was hurrying up, crying to him to desist, his violence [with the horses] increased.

"'Hillo, Hillo!' cried Jonas.

"'For God's sake!' cried the driver. 'The gentleman—in the road—he'll be killed!'

". . . the man darting in at the peril of his own life, saved **Montague**'s, by dragging him through the mire and water out of the reach of present harm." 42

Bill Simmons. "[He] was a red-faced burly young fellow; smart in his way, and with a good-humoured countenance . . . his spruce appearance was sufficiently explained by his connexion with a large stage-coaching establishment at Hounslow, whither he was conveying his load from a farm belonging to the concern in Wiltshire. He was frequently up and down the road on such errands, he said, and to look after the sick and rest horses, of which animals he had much to relate that occupied a long time in the telling. He aspired to the dignity of the regular box, and expected an appointment on the first vacancy. He was musical besides, and had a little key-bugle in his pocket, on which, whenever the conversation flagged, he played the first part of a great many tunes, and regularly broke down in the second." 13

Chicken Smivey. "'I can lend you three pounds on this, if you like,' said the shopman to **Martin**, confidentially. 'It's very old-fashioned. I couldn't say more.'

"'And devilish handsome, too,' cried Mr **Tigg**. 'Two-twelve-six for the watch, and seven-and-six for personal regard. I am gratified: it may be weakness, but I am. Three pounds will do. We take it. The name of my friend is Smivey: Chicken Smivey, of Holborn, twenty-six-and-a-half B: lodger.' Here he winked at Martin again, to apprise him that all the forms and ceremonies prescribed by law were now complied with, and nothing remained but the receipt of the money." 13

Sophia, daughter of a foundryman. "**Mr Pinch**'s sister was at that moment instructing her eldest pupil: to wit, a premature little woman of thirteen years old, who had already arrived at such a pitch of whalebone and education that she had nothing girlish about her: which was a source of great rejoicing to all her relations and friends." 9

"Both the young [**Pecksniff**] ladies had been in ecstasies with the scion of a wealthy house . . . from the first. **Mrs Todgers** vowed that anything one quarter so angelic she had never seen. 'She wanted but a pair of wings, my dear,' said that good woman, 'to be a young syrup:' meaning, possibly, young sylph, or seraph." 9

Tacker. "**Mrs Gamp** . . . was interrupted by the appearance of one of Mr. **Mould**'s assistants—his chief mourner in fact—an obese person, with his waistcoat in closer connexion with his legs than is quite reconcilable with the established ideas of grace; with that cast of feature which is figuratively called a bottle-nose; and with a face covered all over with pimples. He had been a tender plant once upon a time, but from constant blowing in the fat atmosphere of funerals, had run to seed." 19

Mrs Tamaroo. "This ancient female had been engaged, in fulfilment of a vow, registered by **Mrs Todgers**, that no more boys should darken the commercial doors; and she was chiefly remarkable for a total absence of all comprehension upon every subject whatever. She was a perfect Tomb for messages and small parcels; and when dispatched to the Post Office with letters, had been frequently seen endeavouring to insinuate them into casual chinks in private doors, under the delusion that any door with a hole in it would answer the purpose. She was a very little old woman, and always wore a very coarse apron with a bib before and a loop behind, together with bandages on her wrists, which appeared to be afflicted with an everlasting sprain. She was on all occasions chary of opening the street-door, and ardent to shut it again; and she waited at table in a bonnet." 32

Tavern guests. ". . . the quaint old guests . . . were, in general, ancient inhabitants of that region; born, and bred there from boyhood; who had long since become wheezy and asthmatical, and short of breath, except in the article of story-telling: in which respect they were still marvellously long-winded. These gentry were much opposed to steam and all new-fangled ways, and held ballooning to be sinful, and deplored the degeneracy of the times . . . . " 9

Todgers. "[**Mrs Todgers**] had already communicated the particulars of three early disappointments of a tender nature; and had furthermore possessed her young friends with a general summary of the life, conduct, and character of Mr Todgers. Who, it seemed, had cut his matrimonial career rather short, by unlawfully running away from his happiness, and establishing himself in foreign countries as a bachelor." 9

Tollman and **family**. ". . . when [**Pinch**] came within sight of the turnpike . . . he saw the tollman's **wife**, who had that moment checked a waggon, run back into the little house again like mad, to say (she knew) that Mr Pinch was coming up. And she was right, for when he drew within hail of the gate, forth rushed the tollman's **children**, shrieking in tiny chorus, 'Mr Pinch!' to Tom's intense delight." 5

"The tollman—a crusty customer, always smoking solitary pipes in a Windsor chair, inside, set artfully between two little windows that looked up and down the road, so that when he saw anything coming up, he might hug himself on having toll to take, and when he saw it going down, might hug himself on having taken it—the tollman was out in an instant.

"'Left Mr **Pecksniff**!' cried the tollman.

"'Yes,' said Tom, left him.'

"The tollman looked at his wife, uncertain whether to ask her if she had anything to suggest, or to order her to mind the children. Astonishment making him surly, he preferred the latter, and sent her into the toll-house with a flea in her ear." 31

Travellers.—*the wife:* "'It's a fair division of labour, sir [said **Mark Tapley**]. I wash her **boys**, and she makes our tea. I never *could* make tea, but any one can wash a boy.'

"The woman, who was delicate and ill, felt and understood his kindness, as well she might, for she had been covered every night with his great-coat . . . . " 15

—the husband: "'There was a feeble old shadow come a-creeping down at last, as much like his substance when she know'd him, as your shadow when it's drawn out to its very finest and longest by the sun, is like you. But it was his remains, there's no doubt about that. She took on with joy, poor thing, as much as if it had been all of him! [said **Mark**].'" 17

—in England again: ". . . Mr **Tapley** not only pointed to a decent-looking man and woman standing by, but commenced embracing them alternately, over and over again, in Monument Yard . . . . 'Neighbours in America! Neighbours in Eden! cried Mark. 'Neighbours in the swamp, neighbours in the bush, neighbours in the fever. Didn't she nurse us! Didn't he help us! Shouldn't we both have died without 'em! Hav'n't they come a-strugglin' back, without a single child for their consolation! And talk to me of neighbours!'" 44

Wolf. "'[He's a] literary character—you needn't mention it—remarkably clever weekly paper—oh, remarkably clever !' [said **Tigg**]" 28

" . . . Wolf, not to be left behindhand, recited the leading points of one or two vastly humorous articles he was then preparing Those lucubrations, being of what he called 'a warm complexion,' were highly approved; and all the company agreed that they were full of point." 28 *And see* **Pip**

Walk-ons

Ancient scholar. " . . . an ancient scholar read the inscription, which was in Latin: not in English: that would never do. It gave great satisfaction; especially every time there was a good long substantive in the third declension, ablative case, with an adjective to match; at which periods the assembly became very tender, and were much affected." 35

Child (a **Chuzzlewit**). "And there is one slight creature, **Tom**—her [**Mary**'s] child; not **Ruth**'s —whom thine eyes follow in the romp and dance: who, wondering sometimes to see thee look so thoughtful, runs to climb up on thy knee, and put her cheek to thine: who loves thee, Tom, above the rest, if that can be: and falling sick once, chose thee for her nurse, and never knew impatience, Tom, when thou wert by her side." 54

Coachman, lucky. "'Come, old **Pecksniff**!' Such was his jocose address, as he slapped that gentleman on the back, at the end of the stage; 'let's have something!'

"'With all my heart,' said Mr Pecksniff.

"'Let's treat the driver,' cried **Jonas**.

"'If you think it won't hurt the man, or render him discontented with his station; certainly,' faltered Mr Pecksniff." 20

Coachman and a guard. "'You got up to please yourself, and may get down to please yourself. It won't break our hearts to lose you; and it wouldn't have broken 'em if we'd never found you. Be a little quicker. That's all [said the coachman].' . . .

"'What are you staring at?' said **Jonas**.

"'Not a handsome man,' returned the guard. 'If you want your fortune told, I'll tell you a bit of it. You won't be drowned. That's a consolation for you.'" 47

Commercial gentleman, "of a literary turn, who wrote squibs upon the rest, and knew the weak side of everybody's character but his own." 9

Commercial traveller, "who travelled in the perfumery line, exhibited an interesting nick-nack, in the way of a remarkable cake of shaving soap which he had lately met with in Germany . . . . " 9

Cook, at the Blue Dragon. **Mrs Lupin**, who for [**Martin**'s and **Mark**'s] sakes had dislodged the very cook, high priestess of the temple, with her own genial hands was dressing their repast." 28

Dick, a hostler. ". . . Dick the hostler got [the box] in somehow, and Mr **Chuzzlewit** helped him." 5 [*He is* **Sam** *earlier and* **Sam** *again later.*]

Dragon man. "The man engaged to bear his box—**Tom** knew him well; a Dragon man—came stamping up the stairs, and made a roughish bow to Tom (to whom in common times he would have nodded with a grin) as though he were aware of what had happened, and wished him to perceive it made no difference to *him*. It was clumsily done; he was a mere waterer of horses; but Tom liked the man for it, and felt it more than going away." 31

Two **draymen**. "There were two good-tempered burly draymen letting down big butts of beer into a cellar, somewhere; and when **John** helped [**Ruth**]—almost lifted her—the lightest, easiest, neatest thing you ever saw— across the rope, they said he owed them a good turn for giving him the chance. Celestial draymen!" 53

English gentleman, on the 'Screw.' "An English gentleman who was strongly suspected of having run away from a bank, with something in his possession belonging to its strong-box besides the key, grew eloquent upon the subject of the rights of man, and hummed the Marseillaise Hymn constantly." 15

Father. "'Excuse the weakness of the man,' said **Mrs Gamp**, eyeing **Mr Sweedlepipe** with great indignation . . . 'which not a blessed hour ago he nearly shaved the noge off from the father of as lovely a family as ever, **Mr Chuzzlewit**, was born three sets of twins, and would have done it, only he see it a-goin' in the glass, and dodged the rager.'" 52

Fruit-brokers. "Several . . . had their marts near Todgers's; and one of the first impressions wrought upon the stranger's senses was of oranges—of damaged oranges, with blue and green bruises on them, festering in boxes, or mouldering away in cellars." 9

General practitioner. "'I have been bred a surgeon [said **Lewsome**], and for the last few years have served a general practitioner in the City, as his assistant." 48

Graveyard watchers. "Here, paralysed old watchmen guarded the bodies of the dead at night, year after year, until at last they joined that solemn brotherhood; and, saving that they slept below the ground a sounder sleep than even they had ever known above it, and were shut up in another kind of box, their condition can hardly be said to have undergone any material change when they in turn were watched themselves." 9

Head-waiter, "(who wore powder, and knee-smalls, and was usually a grave man) got to be a bright scarlet in the face, and broke his waistcoat-strings audibly." 53

Idiot emigrant. "The very idiot in the corner who sat mowing there, all day, had his faculty of imitation roused by what he saw about him; and snapped his fingers to amuse a crying child." 15

Irish girl. "The **colonel** knocked at [**Major Pawkins**'s] house with the air of a man who lived there; and an Irish girl popped her head out of one of the top windows to see who it was." 16

Jane. "Miss **Charity** . . . quitted her paternal roof—a blessing, for which the Pecksniffian servant was observed by some profane persons to be particularly active in the thanksgiving at church next Sunday." 30

Landlord, of cheap London lodgings. "[He] called [**Martin**] by his name. Now, as he had never told it to the man, but had scrupulously kept it to himself, he was not a little startled by this; and so plainly showed his agitation that the landlord, to reassure him, said 'it was only a letter.'" 13

Man, in a berth. "'Don't you nor any other friend of mine never go to sleep with his head in a ship any more [said **Tapley**].'

"The man gave a grunt of discontented acquiescence, turned over in his berth, and drew his blanket over his head." 15

Man, in fur cap "was taking down the shutters of an obscure public-house. . . ." 13

Matrons "took it very ill that **Mr Pecksniff**'s mission [to **Mrs Gamp**] was of so unimportant a kind [as a laying-out instead of a lying-in]; and the lady with her arms folded rated him in good round terms, signifying that she would be glad to know what he meant by terrifying delicate females 'with his corpses;' and giving it as her opinion that he was quite ugly enough to know better." 19

Two **men**, in **Jonas**'s courtyard. "They passed on, talking . . . about a skeleton which had been dug up yesterday . . . and was supposed to be that of a murdered man. 'So murder is not always found out, you see,' they said to one another as they turned the corner." 46

Neighbour, "who was mending a pen at an upper window over the way [from **Todgers**'s], became of paramount importance in the scene, and made a blank in it, ridiculously disproportionate in its extent, when he retired." 9

Old grandmother, emigrant. "Here an old grandmother was crooning over a sick child, and rocking it to and fro, in arms hardly more wasted than its own young limbs . . . . " 15

Old men, emigrants. "Here were old men awkwardly engaged in little household offices, wherein they would have been ridiculous but for their goodwill and kind purpose . . . . " 15

Pipesmoking man. "Having called for some beer, and drunk, [**Jonas**] offered it to this companion, who thanked him, and took a draught. He could not help thinking that, if the man had known all, he might scarcely have relished drinking out of the same cup with him." 47

Porters. "All day long, a stream of porters from the wharves beside the river, each bearing on his back a bursting chest of oranges, poured slowly through the narrow passages; while underneath the archway by the public-house, the knots of those who rested and regaled within, were piled from morning until night." 9

Sallow gentleman. **Pinch**'s awe "was not diminished when a sallow gentleman with long dark hair came out [of the theatre] and told a **boy** to run home to his lodgings and bring down his broadsword." 5

Surgeon. "All the service he could render, he rendered promptly and skilfully. But he gave it as his opinion that the boy was labouring under a severe concussion of the brain, and that Mr **Bailey**'s mortal course was run." 42

Tailor. "'There's the old tailor, **Mark**!' whispered **Martin**.

"'There he goes, sir! A little bandier than he was, I think, sir, ain't he? His figure's so far altered, as it seems to me, that you might wheel a rather larger barrow between his legs as he walks, than you could have done conveniently when we know'd him." 43

Whilks and **Mrs Whilks**. "'What, Mr Whilks!' cried **Mrs Gamp**. 'Don't say it's you, Mr Whilks, and that poor creetur Mrs Whilks with not even a pin-cushion ready. Don't say it's you, Mr Whilks!'" 19

Wilkins and **Mrs Wilkins**. "'Not young Wilkins!' cried **Mrs Gamp**. 'Don't say young Wilkins, wotever you do. If young Wilkins's wife is took—'" 4

Woman, emigrant. " . . . here a poor woman with an infant in her lap, mended another little creature's clothes, and quieted another who was creeping up about her from their scanty bed upon the floor." 15

Mrs Gamp and Mrs Harris

Here are the dialogues between these ladies occurring in MC. There are many more in MGS, page 703. Christopher Hibbert, in his introduction to the FS (1988) edition, tells of CD's inspiration:

"Towards the end of March [1843, Dickens] moved out of his London house to a farm at Finchley where . . . he heard of a nurse who wore a yellow night-cap and a rusty black gown, who had a peculiar habit of rubbing her somewhat red and swollen nose along the top of the fender, and who was excessively fond of vinegar, snuff and above all, of gin, a bottle of which she kept conveniently on the 'chimley piece' for when she felt 'dispoged' to taste a drop. Thus was born, in the full glory of her fat awfulness, Mrs Gamp, for whom Dickens supplied the imaginary friend Mrs Harris, and in so doing created the opportunities for dialogue of a telling humour, at once so macabre, salacious, sentimental and knowing that for this alone, Martin Chuzzlewit might be accounted a work of genius." FS/MC xviii-xix (*But see* KJF page 70n)

The indispensable ingredient. "'If it wasn't for the nerve a little sip of liquor gives me (I never was able to do more than taste it), I never could go through with what I sometimes has to do. "**Mrs Harris**," I says, at the very last case as ever I acted in, which it was but a young person, "Mrs Harris," I says, "leave the bottle on the chimley-piece, and don't ask me to take none, but let me put my lips to it when I am so dispoged, and then I will do what I'm engaged to do, according to the best of my ability." "Mrs Gamp," she says, in answer, "if ever there was a sober creetur to be got at eighteen pence a day for working people, and three and six for gentlefolks—night watching,'" said Mrs Gamp, with emphasis, "'being a extra charge—you are that invallable person." "Mrs Harris," I says to her, "don't name the charge, for if I could afford to lay all my feller creeturs out for nothink, I would gladly do it, sich is the love I bears 'em. But what I always says to them as has the management of matters, Mrs Harris . . . be they gents or be they ladies, is, don't ask me whether I won't take none, or whether I will, but leave the bottle on the chimley-piece, and let me put my lips to it when I am so dispoged.'"' 19

The Marks of Age. "'I says to Mrs Harris . . . only t'other day; the last Monday evening fortnight as ever dawned upon this Piljian's Projiss of a mortal wale; I says to Mrs Harris when she says to me, "Years and our trials, Mrs Gamp, sets marks upon us all."—"Say not the words, Mrs Harris, if you and me is to be continual friends, for sech is not the case. **Mrs Mould**," I says, making so free, I will confess, as use the name,' (she curtseyed here,) "'is one of them that goes agen the obserwation straight; and never, Mrs Harris, whilst I've a drop of breath to draw, will I set by, and not stand up, don't think it."—"I ast your pardon, Ma'am," says Mrs Harris, "and I humbly grant your grace; for if ever a woman lived as would see her feller creeturs into fits to serve her friends, well do I know that woman's name is Sairey Gamp."'' 25

Mrs Gamp and Mrs Harris

Offered a glass of rum. "'A thing . . . as hardly ever, **Mrs Mould**, occurs with me unless it is when I am indispoged, and find my half a pint of porter settling heavy on the chest. Mrs Harris often and often says to me, "Sairey Gamp," she says, "you raly do amaze me!" "Mrs Harris," I says to her, "why so? Give it a name, I beg." "Telling the truth, then, ma'am," says Mrs Harris, "and shaming him as shall be nameless betwixt you and me, never did I think till I know'd you, as any woman could sick-nurse and monthly likeways, on the little that you takes to drink." "Mrs Harris," I says to her, "none on us knows what we can do till we tries; and wunst, when me and **Gamp** kept ouse, I thought so too. But now," I says, "my half-pint of porter fully satisfied; perwisin', Mrs Harris, that it is brought reg'lar, and draw'd mild. Whether I sicks or monthlies, ma'am, I hope I does my duty, but I am but a poor woman, and I earns my living hard; therefore I *do* require it, which I makes confession, to be brought reg'lar and draw'd mild."'" 25

Perseverance. "'Talk of constitooshun! . . . . A person's constitooshun need be made of bricks to stand it. Mrs Harris jestly says to me, but t'other day, "Oh! Sairey Gamp," she says, "how is it done?" "Mrs Harris, ma'am," I says to her, "we gives no trust ourselves, and puts a deal o' trust elsevere; these is our religious feelins, and we finds 'em answer." "Sairey," says Mrs Harris, "sech is life. Vich likeways is the hend of all things!"'" 29

Foretelling the future. "'As a good friend of mine has frequent made remark to me, which her name, my love, is Harris, Mrs Harris through the square and up the steps a-turnin' round by the tobacker shop, "Oh, Sairey, Sairey, little do we know wot lays afore us!" "Mrs Harris, ma'am," I says, "not much, it's true, but more than you suppoge. Our calclations, ma'am," I says, "respectin' wot the number of a family will be, comes most times within one, and oftener than you would suppoge, exact." "Sairey," says Mrs Harris, in a awful way,"Tell me wot is my indiwidgle number." "No, Mrs Harris," I says to her, "ex-cuge me, if you please. My own," I says, "has fallen out of three-pair backs, and had damp doorsteps settled on their lungs, and one was turned up smilin' in a bedstead, unbeknown. Therefore, ma'am," I says, "seek not to proticipate, but take 'em as they come and as they go."'" 40

Public thoroughfare. "'I hope sir . . . as no bones is broke by me and Mrs Harris a-walkin' down upon a public wharf. Which was the very words she says to me (although they was the last I ever had to speak) was these: "Sairey," she says, "is it a public wharf?" "Mrs Harris," I makes answer, "can you doubt it? You have know'd me now, ma'am, eight and thirty year; and did you ever know me go, or wish to go where I was not made welcome, say the words." "No, Sairey," Mrs Harris says, "contrairy quite." And well she knows it too.'" 40

A portrait miniature. "'Now, ain't we rich in beauty this here joyful arternoon, I'm sure. I knows a lady, which her name, I'll not deceive you, Mrs Chuzzlewit, is Harris, her husband's brother bein' six foot three, and marked with a mad bull in Wellington boots upon his left arm, on account of his precious mother havin' been worrited by one into a shoemaker's shop, when in a sitiwation which blessed is the man as has his quiver full of sech, as many times I've said to Gamp when words has roge betweixt us on account of the expense—and often have I said to Mrs Harris, "Oh, Mrs Harris, ma'am! your countenance is quite a angel's!" Which, but for Pimples, it would be. "No, Sairey Gamp," says she, "you best of hard-working and industrious creeturs as ever was underpaid at any price, which underpaid you are, quite diff'rent. **Harris** had it done afore marriage at ten and six," she said, "and wore it faithful next his heart 'till the colour run, when the money was declined to be give back, and no arrangement could be come to. But he never said it was a angel's, Sairey, wotever he might have thought." If Mrs Harris's husband was here now . . . he'd speak out plain, he would, and his dear wife would be the last to blame him! For if ever a woman lived as know'd not wot it was to form a wish to pizon them as had good looks, and had no reagion give her by the best of husbands, Mrs Harris is that ev'nly dispogician!'" 46 *And see* **Betsey Prig**—*in vino. For the unpublished dialogues, see* MGS, page 703

CB 1 December 1843 by C&H
First U. S. publication 1844 by Carey & Hart, Philadelphia

𝔄 Christmas Carol

IN PROSE

BEING A GHOST STORY OF CHRISTMAS

"I have endeavoured in this Ghostly little book to raise the Ghost of an Idea which shall not put my readers out of humour with themselves, with each other, with the season, or with me. May it haunt their houses pleasantly, and no one wish to lay it.

"Their faithful Friend and Servant
"December 1843
C. D."

In LL, CD tells the story of Lazarus and the rich man. The latter in Hell sees the beggar he ignored in life safe in Abraham's bosom. He begs the patriarch to send Lazarus to warn his five brothers at home so that they may avoid his fate, for he is tormented in the flame. Abraham replies, "They have Moses and the prophets; let them hear them." Lazarus: "Nay, father Abraham: but if one went to them from the dead, they will repent." Abraham's retort could have come from Scrooge himself: "If they hear not Moses and the prophets, neither will they be persuaded, though one rose from the dead." Luke 16:19-31 CD has the last word.

"Nothing is important except the fate of the soul; and literature is only redeemed from an utter triviality, surpassing that of naughts and crosses, by the fact that it describes not the world around us or the things on the retina of the eye or the enormous irrelevancy of encyclopædias, but some condition to which the human spirit can come." GKC p50

Mr and Mrs Fezziwig are Having a Ball

PRÉCIS

Jacob Marley was dead, to begin with. The late partner of **Ebenezer Scrooge** in their grasping financial firm returns in ghostly form on Christmas Eve, dragging immense chains and adjuring Scrooge to mend his selfish, tight-fisted ways before it is too late. Scrooge has spent the afternoon keeping his poor clerk, **Bob Cratchit**, up to the mark; declining contemptuously to give to the poor; scolding carol singers; and snubbing his cheerful nephew **Fred**'s invitation to dinner. But he sees Marley's face in his door knocker, and a trying interview follows. Scrooge goes to bed, muttering "Humbug!" 1

He wakes to face the Ghost of **Christmas Past**, who insists on taking him for a walk. Scrooge visits his childhood school, reflects on the delights of the tales and myths he once read and sees his sister **Fan** (mother of Fred), come to take him home to his father. He sees his kind old **schoolmaster**, and his employer **Fezziwig**'s joyous Christmas dancing. Then he watches himself, older and cynical, talking with **Belle**, who loves but releases him to his pursuit of Gain. He sees Belle again, now with happy husband and ecstatic children. Keenly discomforted, Scrooge begs the Ghost to take him home. 2

Scrooge wakes, expecting his next visitor. He is bathed in light but no one is to be seen. He discovers the jolly Ghost of **Christmas Present** in the next room seated on a throne of eatables. A humbler Scrooge goes willingly to see London celebrating. He observes the Cratchits' happy Christmas dinner, noting Tiny Tim, a cripple whose days appear to be numbered. He visits a poor mining family keeping Christmas joyfully and crosses the turbulent ocean to a lighthouse and then a ship. The Christmas spirit pervades all. He looks in at Fred's and hears himself unflatteringly discussed. Then, shock: the Ghost shows him **Ignorance** and **Want**, children of Man. 3

Without a break, the dreadful, silent Phantom Ghost of **Christmas Yet To Come** manifests, and Scrooge hears a colleague's death dismissively discussed by men he respects. He then observes three deathbed scavengers selling their loot to **Joe**. He overhears **Caroline** and her family reluctantly overjoyed: an unrelenting creditor's death has given them life and breathing-room. He visits sorrowing Cratchits. Tim is dead. He sees a deathbed, dares not see the dead. The gravestone name is his. Appalled and desperate, he pleads for hope. 4

Scrooge wakes to realize only one night has passed. He cries out to a boy in the street and has him buy a prize turkey for the Cratchits. He meets the previous day's charity solicitor and makes a handsome pledge. He calls on Fred and invites himself to dinner. The next day, he feigns anger when Cratchit is a little late but then reveals his transformation. It has staying power. 5

CONTENTS

CHARACTERS

The Protagonist

Ebenezer Scrooge. " . . . Scrooge's name was good upon 'Change for anything he chose to put his hand to." 1

"Oh! but he was a tight-fisted hand at the grindstone, Scrooge! a squeezing, wrenching, grasping, scraping, clutching, covetous, old sinner! Hard and sharp as flint, from which no steel had ever struck out generous fire; secret, and self-contained, and solitary as an oyster. The cold within him froze his old features, nipped his pointed nose, shrivelled his cheek, stiffened his gait; made his eyes red, his thin lips blue; and spoke out shrewdly in his grating voice. A frosty rime was on his head, and on his eyebrows, and his wiry chin. He carried his own low temperature always about with him; he iced his office in the dog-days, and didn't thaw it one degree at Christmas.

"External heat and cold had little influence on Scrooge. No warmth could warm, no wintry weather chill him. No wind that blew was bitterer than he, no falling snow was more intent upon its purpose, no pelting rain less open to entreaty. Foul weather didn't know where to have him. The heaviest rain, and snow, and hail, and sleet, could boast of the advantage over him in only one respect. They often 'came down' handsomely, and Scrooge never did.

"Nobody ever stopped him in the street to say, with gladsome looks, 'My dear Scrooge, how are you? When will you come to see me?' No beggars implored him to bestow a trifle, no children asked him what it was o'clock, no man or woman ever once in all his life inquired the way to such and such a place, of Scrooge. Even the blind men's **dogs** appeared to know him; and when they saw him coming on, would tug their owners into doorways and up courts; and then would wag their tails as though they said, 'No eye at all is better than an evil eye, dark master!'" 1

—on Christmas: "'Merry Christmas! Out upon Merry Christmas! What's Christmas time to you but a time for paying bills without money; a time for finding yourself a year older, but not an hour richer; a time for balancing your books and having every item in 'em . . . presented dead against you? If I could work my will,' said Scrooge indignantly, 'every idiot who goes about with "Merry Christmas" on his lips should be boiled with his own pudding and buried with a stake of holly through his heart.'" 1

—on the poor: "'Are there no prisons?' asked Scrooge.

"'Plenty of prisons,' said the **gentleman**, laying down the pen again.

"'And the Union workhouses? . . . Are they still in operation?'

"'They are. Still,' returned the gentleman, 'I wish I could say they were not.'

"'The Treadmill and the Poor Law are in full vigour, then?' . . .

"'Both very busy, sir.'

"'Oh! I was afraid, from what you said at first, that something had occurred to stop them in their useful course,' said Scrooge. 'I'm very glad to hear it . . . . I help to support the establishments I have mentioned—they cost enough; and those who are badly off must go there.'

"'Many can't go there; and many would rather die.'

"'If they would rather die,' said Scrooge, 'they had better do it, and decrease the surplus population.'" 1

—home: "They were a gloomy suite of rooms, in a lowering pile of building up a yard . . . . It was old enough now, and dreary enough, for nobody lived in it

but Scrooge, the other rooms being all let out as offices. The yard was so dark that even Scrooge, who knew its every stone, was fain to grope with his hands. The fog and frost so hung about the black old gateway of the house, that it seemed as if the Genius of the Weather sat in mournful meditation on the threshold." 1

—*his senses:* "'. . . a little thing affects them. A slight disorder of the stomach makes them cheats. You [**ghost**] may be an undigested bit of beef, a blot of mustard, a crumb of cheese, a fragment of an under-done potato. There's more of gravy than of grave about you, whatever you are!'" 1

—*in his prime:* "His face had not the harsh and rigid lines of later years; but it had begun to wear the signs of care and avarice. There was an eager, greedy, restless motion in the eye, which showed the passion that had taken root, and where the shadow of the growing tree would fall." 2

—*rebuked:* "'If these shadows remain unaltered by the Future, none other of my race,' returned the Ghost [of **Christmas Present**] 'will find [**Tiny Tim**] here. What then? If he be like to die, he had better do it, and decrease the surplus population.'

"Scrooge hung his head to hear his own words quoted by the Spirit, and was overcome with penitence and grief.

"'Man,' said the Ghost, 'if man you be in heart, not adamant, forbear that wicked cant until you have discovered What the surplus is, and Where it is. Will you decide what men shall live, what men shall die? It may be, that in the sight of Heaven, you are more worthless and less fit to live than millions like this poor man's child. Oh God! to hear the Insect on the leaf pronouncing on the too much life among his hungry brothers in the dust!'" 3

—*an appeal and a vow:* "'Spirit!' he cried, tight clutching at its robe, 'hear me! I am not the man I was. I will not be the man I must have been but for this intercourse. Why show me this, if I am past all hope?'

"For the first time the hand appeared to shake.

"'Good Spirit,' he pursued, as down upon the ground he fell before it. 'Your nature intercedes for me, and pities me. Assure me that I yet may change these shadows you have shown me, by an altered life!'

"The kind hand trembled.

"'I will honour Christmas in my heart, and try to keep it all the year. I will live in the Past, the Present, and the Future. The Spirits of all Three shall strive within me. I will not shut out the lessons that they teach. Oh, tell me I may sponge away the writing on this stone!'

"In his agony, he caught the spectral hand. It sought to free itself, but he was strong in his entreaty, and detained it. The Spirit, stronger yet, repulsed him.

"Holding up his hands in a last prayer to have his fate reversed, he saw an alteration in the Phantom's hood and dress. It shrunk, collapsed, and dwindled down into a bedpost." 4

—*awake:* "His hands were busy with his garments all this time; turning them inside out, putting them on upside down, tearing them, mislaying them, making them parties to every kind of extravagance.

"'I don't know what to do!' cried Scrooge, laughing and crying in the same breath; and making a perfect Laocöon of himself with his stockings. 'I am as light as a feather, I am as happy as an angel, I am as merry as a schoolboy. I am as giddy as a drunken man. A merry Christmas to everybody! A happy New Year to all the world! . . . Ha ha ha!'

"Really, for a man who had been out of practice for so many years, it was a splendid laugh, a most illustrious laugh. The father of a long, long line of brilliant laughs!" 5

—*transformed:* "He became as good a friend, as good a master, and as good a man, as the good old city knew . . . . Some people laughed to see the alteration in him, but he let them laugh, and little heeded them . . . . His own heart laughed; and that was quite enough for him." 5

Other Principals

Bob Cratchit. " . . . the clerk put on his white comforter and tried to warm himself at the candle; in which effort, not being a man of a strong imagination, he failed." 1

—*released:* "The office was closed in a twinkling, and the clerk, with the long ends of his white comforter dangling below his waist (for he boasted no great-coat), went down a slide on Cornhill, at the end of a lane of boys, twenty times, in honour of its being Christmas Eve, and then ran home to Camden Town as hard as he could pelt, to play at blindman's buff." 1

Tiny Tim Cratchit. "Alas for Tiny Tim, he bore a little crutch, and had his limbs supported by an iron frame! . . . 'As good as gold . . . and better. Somehow he gets thoughtful, sitting by himself so much, and thinks the strangest things you ever heard. He told me, coming home, that he hoped the people saw him in the church, because he was a cripple, and it might be pleasant to them to remember upon Christmas Day, who made lame beggars walk, and blind men see.'" 3

—*a toast:* "'A Merry Christmas to us all, my dears. God bless us!'

"Which all the family re-echoed.

"'God bless us every one!' said Tiny Tim, the last of all.

"He sat very close to his father's side upon his little stool. Bob held his withered little hand in his, as if he loved the child, and wished to keep him by his side, and dreaded that he might be taken from him." 3

Ghost of Christmas Past. "It was a strange figure—like a child: yet not so like a child as like an old man, viewed through some supernatural medium, which gave him the appearance of having receded from the view, and being diminished to a child's proportions. Its hair, which hung about its neck and down its back, was white as if with age; and yet the face had not a wrinkle in it, and the tenderest bloom was on the skin. The arms were very long and muscular; the hands the same, as if its hold were of uncommon strength. Its legs and feet, most delicately formed, were, like those upper members, bare. It wore a tunic of the purest white; and round its waist was bound a lustrous belt, the sheen of which was beautiful. It held a branch of fresh green holly in its hand; and, in singular contradiction of that wintry emblem, had its dress trimmed with summer flowers. But the strangest thing about it was, that from the crown of its head there sprung a bright clear jet of light, by which all this was visible; and which was doubtless the occasion of its using, in its duller moments, a great extinguisher for a cap, which it now held under its arm.

"Even this, though, when **Scrooge** looked at it with increasing steadiness, was *not* its strangest quality. For as its belt sparkled and glittered now in one part and now in another, and what was light one instant, at another time was dark, so the figure itself fluctuated in its distinctness: being now a thing with one arm, now with one leg, now with twenty legs, now a pair of legs without a head, now a head without a body: of which dissolving parts, no outline would be visible in the dense gloom wherein they melted away. And in the very wonder of this, it would be itself again, distinct and clear as ever . . . . The voice was soft and gentle. Singularly low, as if instead of being so close beside him, it were at a distance." 2

Ghost of Christmas Present. "It was clothed in one simple green robe, or mantle, bordered with white fur. This garment hung so loosely on the figure, that its capacious breast was bare, as if disdaining to be warded or concealed by any artifice. Its feet, observable beneath the ample folds of the garment, were also bare; and on its head it wore no other covering than a holly wreath, set here and there with shining icicles. Its dark brown curls were long and free; free as its genial face, its sparkling eye, its open hand, its cheery voice, its unconstrained demeanour, and its joyful air." 3

Ghost of Christmas Yet To Come. "It was shrouded in a deep black garment, which concealed its head, its face, its form, and left nothing of it visible save one outstretched hand. But for this it would have been difficult to detach its figure from the night, and separate it from the darkness by which it was surrounded.

"[**Scrooge**] felt that it was tall and stately when it came beside him, and that its mysterious presence filled him with a solemn dread. He knew no more, for the Spirit neither spoke nor moved." 4 *And see* **Ebenezer Scrooge**—*an appeal and a vow*

Ghost of Jacob Marley. "Marley was dead, to begin with. There is no doubt whatever about that. . . . This must be distinctly understood, or nothing wonderful can come of the story I am going to relate." 1

"Marley's face. It was not in impenetrable shadow as the other objects in the yard were, but had a dismal light about it, like a bad lobster in a dark cellar. It was not angry or ferocious, but looked at **Scrooge** as Marley used to look: with ghostly spectacles turned up on its ghostly forehead. The hair was curiously stirred, as if by breath or hot air; and, though the eyes were wide open, they were perfectly motionless. That, and its livid colour, made it horrible; but its horror seemed to be in spite of the face and beyond its control, rather than a part of its own expression." 1

—*at full length:* "Marley in his pigtail, usual waistcoat, tights and boots; the tassels on the latter bristling, like his pigtail, and his coat-skirts, and the hair upon his head. The chain he drew was clasped about his middle. It was long, and wound about him like a tail; and it was made . . . of cash-boxes, keys, padlocks, ledgers, deeds, and heavy purses wrought in steel. His body was transparent; so that **Scrooge**, observing him, and looking through his waistcoat, could see the two buttons on his coat behind . . . he felt the chilling influence of its death-cold eyes; and marked the very texture of the folded kerchief bound about its head and chin . . . . " 1

Supporting Roles

Belle. "[She was] a fair young girl in a mourning-dress: in whose eyes there were tears, which sparkled in the light . . . ' . . . if you [**Ebenezer**] were free today, to-morrow, yesterday, can even I believe that you would choose a dowerless girl—you who, in your very confidence with her, weigh everything by Gain: or, choosing her, if for a moment you were false enough to your one guiding principle to do so, do I not know that your repentance and regret would surely follow? I do; and I release you. With a full heart, for the love of him you once were.'" 2

Boy. "'Do you know the poulterer's, in the next street but one at the corner?' **Scrooge** inquired.

"'I should hope I did,' replied the lad.

"'An intelligent boy!' said Scrooge. 'A remarkable boy! Do you know whether they've sold the prize turkey that was hanging up there?—Not the little prize turkey: the big one?'

"'What, the one as big as me?' returned the boy.

"'What a delightful boy!' said Scrooge. 'It's a pleasure to talk to him. Yes, my buck!'

"'It's hanging there now,' replied the boy.

"'Is it?' said Scrooge. 'Go and buy it.'

"'Walk-ER!' exclaimed the boy.

"'No, no,' said Scrooge, 'I am in earnest. Go and buy it, and tell 'em to bring it here, that I may give them the direction where to take it. Come back with the man, and I'll give you a shilling. Come back with him in less than five minutes and I'll give you half-a-crown!'

"The boy was off like a shot. He must have had a steady hand at a trigger who could have got a shot off half so fast." 5

Fezziwig. " . . . an old gentleman in a Welsh wig, sitting behind such a high desk, that if he had been two inches taller he must have knocked his head against the ceiling . . . . He rubbed his hands; adjusted his capacious waistcoat; laughed all over himself, from his shoes to his organ of benevolence; and called out in a comfortable, oily, rich, fat, jovial voice . . . . " 2

—*dancing:* "A positive light appeared to issue from Fezziwig's calves. They shone in every part of the dance like moons. You couldn't have predicted, at any given time, what would have become of them next. And when old Fezziwig and **Mrs Fezziwig** had gone all through the dance; advance and retire, both hands to your partner, bow and curtsey, corkscrew, thread-the-needle, and back again to your place; Fezziwig 'cut'—cut so deftly, that he appeared to wink with his legs, and came upon his feet again without a stagger." 2

Fred. "He had so heated himself with rapid walking in the fog and frost, this nephew of **Scrooge**'s, that he was all in a glow; his face was ruddy and handsome; his eyes sparkled, and his breath smoked again." 1

—*his laugh:* "If you should happen, by any unlikely chance, to know a man more blest in a laugh than **Scrooge**'s nephew, all I can say is, I should like to know him too. Introduce him to me, and I'll cultivate his acquaintance.

". . . . When Scrooge's nephew laughed in this way: holding his sides, rolling his head, and twisting his face into the most extravagant contortions: Scrooge's niece, by marriage, laughed as heartily as he. And their assembled friends being not a bit behindhand, roared out lustily." 3

Ignorance and Want

Ignorance and **Want**. "They were a boy and girl. Yellow, meagre, ragged, scowling, wolfish; but prostrate, too, in their humility. Where graceful youth should have filled their features out, and touched them with its freshest tints, a stale and shrivelled hand, like that of age, had pinched, and twisted them, and pulled them into shreds. Where angels might have sat enthroned, devils lurked, and glared out menacing. No change, no degradation, no perversion of humanity, in any grade, through all the mysteries of wonderful creation, has monsters half so horrible and dread." 3

Joe. "Far in this den of infamous resort, there was a low-browed, beetling shop, below a pent-house roof, where iron, old rags, bottles, bones, and greasy offal, were bought. Upon the floor within, were piled up heaps of rusty keys, nails, chains, hinges, files, scales, weights, and refuse iron of all kinds. Secrets that few would like to scrutinise were bred and hidden in mountains of unseemly rags, masses of corrupted fat, and sepulchres of bones. Sitting in among the wares he dealt in, by a charcoal stove, made of old bricks, was a grey-haired rascal, nearly seventy years of age; who had screened himself from the cold air without, by a frousy curtaining of miscellaneous tatters, hung upon a line; and smoked his pipe in all the luxury of calm retirement." 4

Fan Scrooge. " . . . a little girl, much younger than the boy, came darting in, and putting her arms about his neck, and often kissing him, addressed [young **Scrooge**] as her 'Dear, dear brother.'" 2

Others

Boys. "Some shaggy ponies now were seen trotting . . . with boys upon their backs, who called to other boys in country gigs and carts . . . . All these boys were in great spirits, and shouted to each other, until the broad fields were so full of merry music, that the crisp air laughed to hear it!" 2

Caroline. "She was expecting some one, and with anxious eagerness; for she walked up and down the room; started at every sound; looked out from the window; glanced at the clock; tried, but in vain, to work with her needle; and could hardly bear the voices of the children in their play." 4

—*husband:* " . . . a man whose face was careworn and depressed, though he was young. There was a remarkable expression in it now; a kind of serious delight of which he felt ashamed, and which he struggled to repress." 4

—*children:* "Soften it as they would, their hearts were lighter. The children's faces, hushed and clustered round to hear what they so little understood, were brighter; and it was a happier house for this man's death!" 4

Charwoman. " . . . a woman with a heavy bundle slunk into the shop . . . threw her bundle on the floor, and sat down in a flaunting manner on a stool; crossing her elbows on her knees, and looking with a bold defiance at the other two." 4

"'Ah!' returned the old woman, laughing and leaning forward on her crossed arms. 'Bed-curtains!'

"'You don't mean to say you took 'em down, rings and all, with him lying there?' said **Joe**.

"'Yes, I do,' replied the woman. 'Why not?'

"'You were born to make your fortune . . . and you'll certainly do it.'" 4

Mrs Cratchit. ". . . dressed out but poorly in a twice-turned gown, but brave in ribbons . . . [she] left the room alone—too nervous to bear witnesses—to take the pudding up and bring it in." 3

Martha Cratchit. "'Here's Martha, mother!' said a girl, appearing as she spoke . . . . Martha, who was a poor apprentice at a milliner's, then told them what kind of work she had to do, and how many hours she worked at a stretch, and how she meant to lie abed tomorrow morning for a good long rest . . . . " 3

Peter Cratchit. "[He] plunged a fork into the saucepan of potatoes, and getting the corners of his monstrous shirt collar . . . into his mouth, rejoiced to find himself so gallantly attired, and yearned to show his linen in the fashionable parks . . . [**Martha**] had seen a countess and a lord some days before, and how the lord 'was much about as tall as Peter;' at which Peter pulled up his collars so high that you couldn't have seen his head if you had been there." 3

Daughter. "Near to the winter fire sat a beautiful young girl, so like that last that **Scrooge** believed it was the same, until he saw *her* [**Belle**], now a comely matron, sitting opposite her daughter." 2

Mrs Dilber. "[The laundress] was next. Sheets and towels, a little wearing apparel, two old-fashioned silver teaspoons, a pair of sugar-tongs, and a few boots." 4

Fiddler. "In came a fiddler with a music-book, and went up to the lofty desk, and made an orchestra of it, and tuned like fifty stomach-aches . . . and the fiddler plunged his hot face into a pot of porter, especially provided for that purpose. But scorning rest, upon his reappearance, he instantly began again, though there were no dancers yet, as if the other fiddler had been carried home, exhausted, on a shutter, and he were a bran-new man resolved to beat him out of sight, or perish." 2

Two portly **gentlemen**, "pleasant to behold . . . now stood, with their hats off, in **Scrooge**'s office. They had books and papers in their hands, and bowed to him." 1 *See* **Scrooge**—*on the poor*

—*one startled:* "'. . . will you have the goodness'—here Scrooge whispered in his ear.

"'Lord bless me!' cried the old gentleman, as if his breath were taken away. 'My dear Mr Scrooge, are you serious? . . . I don't know what to say to such munifi——'

"'Don't say anything, please,' retorted Scrooge. 'Come and see me. Will you come and see me?'

"'I will!' cried the old gentleman . . . it was clear he meant to do it." 5

Ghost. "[Scrooge] had been quite familiar with one old ghost, in a white waistcoat, with a monstrous iron safe attached to its ankle, who cried piteously at being unable to assist a wretched woman with an infant, whom it saw below, upon a door-step." 1

Husband. " . . . having his daughter leaning fondly on him, [he] sat down with her and her mother [**Belle**] at his own fireside . . . ." 2

Lighthouse men. " . . . they wished each other Merry Christmas in their can of grog; and one of them: the elder, too, with his face all damaged and scarred with hard weather, as the figure-head of an old ship might be: struck up a sturdy song that was like a Gale in itself." 3

Merchants. " . . . on 'Change, amongst the merchants; who hurried up and down, and chinked the money in their pockets, and conversed in groups, and looked at their watches, and trifled thoughtfully with their great gold seals; and so forth, as **Scrooge** had seen them often." 4

Miners. " . . . they found a cheerful company assembled round a glowing fire. An old, **old man** and woman, with their children and their children's children, and another generation beyond that, all decked out gaily in their holiday attire." 3

Old man. "The old man, in a voice that seldom rose above the howling of the wind . . . was singing them a Christmas song—it had been a very old song when he was a boy—and from time to time they all joined in the chorus. So surely as they raised their voices, the old man got quite blithe and loud; and so surely as they stopped, his vigour sank again." 3

Phantoms. "The air was filled with phantoms, wandering hither and thither in restless haste, and moaning as they went. Every one of them wore chains like **Marley's Ghost**; some few (they might be guilty governments) were linked together; none were free . . . . The misery with them all was, clearly, that they sought to interfere, for good, in human matters, and had lost the power for ever."1

Porter. " . . . a man laden with Christmas toys and presents . . . the onslaught that was made on the defenceless porter! The scaling him with chairs for ladders to dive into his pockets, despoil him of brown-paper parcels, hold on tight by his cravat, hug him round his neck, pommel his back, and kick his legs in irrepressible affection!" 2

Sailors. "They stood beside the helmsman at the wheel, the look-out in the bow, the officers who had the watch; dark, ghostly figures in their several stations; but every man among them hummed a Christmas tune, or had a Christmas thought, or spoke below his breath to his companion of some bygone Christmas Day, with homeward hopes belonging to it." 3

Schoolmaster. " . . . [he] glared on Master **Scrooge** with a ferocious condescension, and threw him into a dreadful state of mind by shaking hands with him. He then conveyed him and his sister into the veriest old well of a shivering best-parlour that ever was seen, where the maps upon the wall, and the celestial and terrestrial globes in the windows, were waxy with cold. Here he produced a decanter of curiously light wine, and a block of curiously heavy cake ...." 2

Scrooge, sr. "'Father is so much kinder than he used to be [said **Fan**], that home's like Heaven! He spoke so gently to me one dear night when I was going to bed, that I was not afraid to ask him once more if you might come home; and he said Yes, you should; and sent me in a coach to bring you.'" 2

Sisters. " . . . **Scrooge**'s niece's sister—the plump one with the lace tucker: not the one with the roses—blushed." 3

Topper. "[He]. . . answered that a bachelor was a wretched outcast . . . [he] could growl away in the bass like a good one, and never swell the large veins in his forehead, or get red in the face over it." 3

—*playing Blind Man's Buff:* "And I no more believe Topper was really blind than I believe he had eyes in his boots . . . . The way he went after that plump **sister** in the lace tucker, was an outrage on the credulity of human nature. Knocking down the fire-irons, tumbling over the chairs, bumping against the piano, smothering himself among the curtains, wherever she went, there went he! He always knew where the plump sister was . . . . She often cried out that it wasn't fair; and it really was not . . . . " 3

Wife, of **Fred**. "She was very pretty: exceedingly pretty. With a dimpled, surprised-looking, capital face; a ripe little mouth, that seemed made to be kissed—as no doubt it was; all kinds of good little dots about her chin, that melted into one another when she laughed; and the sunniest pair of eyes you ever saw in any little creature's head. Altogether she was what you would have called provoking, you know; but satisfactory, too. Oh, perfectly satisfactory." 3

Walk-ons

Belinda Cratchit. "[She was] second of [the] daughters, also brave in ribbons . . . . " 3

Two smaller **Cratchits**. A "boy and girl, came tearing in, screaming that outside the baker's they had smelt the goose, and known it for their own; and basking in luxurious thoughts of sage and onion. . . . " 3

Gentleman. "'What has he done with his money?' asked a red-faced gentleman with a pendulous excrescence on the end of his nose, that shook like the gills of a turkey-cock." 4

Labourers. "In the main street, at the corner of the court, some labourers were repairing the gas-pipes, and had lighted a great fire in a brazier, round which a party of ragged men and boys were gathered: warming their hands and winking their eyes before the blaze in rapture." 1

Lord Mayor. "The Lord Mayor, in the stronghold of the mighty Mansion House, gave orders to his fifty **cooks** and **butlers** to keep Christmas as a Lord Mayor's household should . . . . " 1

Singer. "The owner of one scant young nose, gnawed and mumbled by the hungry cold as bones are gnawed by dogs, stooped down at **Scrooge**'s keyhole to regale him with a Christmas carol . . . . " 1

Tailor. " . . . even the little tailor, whom [the **Mayor**] had fined five shillings on the previous Monday for being drunk and bloodthirsty in the streets, stirred up tomorrow's pudding in his garret, while his lean **wife** and the **baby** sallied out to buy the beef." 1

Spear-carriers	stave
Ali Baba: with an axe in his belt	2
Baker, cousin of a housemaid at the Fezziwigs'	2
Belle's children, each child conducting itself like forty	2
Boy, suspected of being underfed	
Business man: curious about the time of a death	4
Clergyman, who signed the register of Marley's burial	1
Clerk, who signed the register of Marley's burial	1
Cook, at the Fezziwigs'	2
Cooks and butlers at Mansion House (the Lord Mayor's residence)	1
"Crusoe, Robin"	2
Saint Dunstan[H], who nipped the Evil Spirit's nose	1
Farmers, driving gigs and carts	2
Three or four fellows: good-humoured	5
Three Misses Fezziwig: beaming and lovable	2
Six followers, young: their hearts at risk to the Misses Fezziwig	2
Friday, running for his life to the little creek	2
Girl, from next door but one, whose mistress has pulled her ears	2
-a servant at Fred's: Nice girl! Very.	5

The Ghost of Christmas Present

Miscellaneous Pieces

Part One, 1837-1846

CONTENTS

PERSONS MENTIONED

MP November 1837 **LB**

Preface to
The Loving Ballad of Lord Bateman

Introduction to a facetious verse history of a latter-day Jason, whose Medea (**Sophia**) came to remind him of his promise and got him to jilt the other girl and keep it. Cruikshank's illustrations were the publication's *raison d'être*.

Singer. " . . . a young gentleman who can scarcely have numbered nine-teen summers, and who before his last visit to the treadmill, where he was erroneously incarcerated for six months as a vagrant (being unfortunately mis-taken for another gentleman), had a very melodious and plaintive tone of voice, which, though it is now somewhat impaired by gruel and such a getting up stairs for so long a period, I hope shortly to find restored."

> Black Bear in Piccadilly, alleged commentary on the poem
> Sophia, who got Lord Bateman out of prison in Turkey and came to claim him
> Tripe-skewer, sobriquet for the singer

Introductory Chapter to
Memoirs of Joseph Grimaldi

With some time available, with fond childish memories of the great clown, and having a promise of a reasonable fee from his then publisher, Bentley, CD edited (with considerable compression) the *Memoirs* and wrote an introduction.

Boys. " . . . a long row of small boys, with frills as white as they could be washed, and hands as clean as they would come, were taken to behold the glories . . . . "

Equestrienne, "with a green parasol in her hand, on the outside stage of the next show but one, who supports herself on one foot, on the back of a majestic horse, blotting-paper coloured and white . . . . "

Joseph Grimaldi. "The account of [his] first courtship may appear lengthy in its present form; but it has undergone a double and most comprehensive process of abridgment. The old man was garrulous upon a subject on which the youth had felt so keenly; and as the feeling did him honour in both stages of life, the editor has not had the heart to reduce it further."

Junior usher. " . . . what witchery but a clown's could have caused the junior usher himself to declare aloud, as he shook his sides and smote his knee in a moment of irrepressible joy, that that was the very best thing he had ever heard said!"

Ticket seller. " . . . a stout **gentleman**, "under a Gothic arch, with a hoop of variegated lamps swinging over his head."

Thomas Egerton Wilks, "who was well acquainted with **Grimaldi** and his connections, applied himself to the task of condensing [his manuscript] throughout, and wholly expunging considerable portions . . . . "

Hughes, Richard: Joseph Grimaldi's executor
Richardson, John: self-made promoter of pantomimes

Concerning Grimaldi

Brief rebuttal, making telling analogies, of the criticism that CD had not known **Grimaldi** as an adult and thus was a doubtful commentator on the *Memoirs*.

Gentleman, pleasant. "[He] has made the profound discovery that I can never have seen **Grimaldi** whose life I have edited, and that his biography must therefore and consequently and of necessity be bad."

Lord Braybrooke, who edited the moirs of Samuel Pepys two hundred years later
Hazlitt, not "on close terms of intimacy with Napoleon Bonaparte"
Johnson, not "on visiting terms with the Earl of Rochester"
Plutarch, who did not know many of those about whom he wrote
Scott, not "on close terms of intimacy with Napoleon"

MP June 23 and 29, 1840 (PE II 86-9, 90-1)   MC **LM**

Two Letters from "Manlius"

CD criticises **Charles Phillips**, defense counsel for the murderer **Courvoisier**, for intemperate and disingenuous attacks on prosecution witnesses. His second letter replies to one written in Phillips's defence.

François Courvoisier, convicted murderer. "Whether Mr Phillips was justified in appealing so frequently and solemnly to his God in behalf of a man whose hands he knew were reeking with venerable blood, most savagely, barbarously, and inhumanly shed . . . is a question . . . which I leave between that gentleman and his own conscience." 1

Charles Phillips. "Was Mr Phillips justified in stigmatising the men who, in the discharge of their duty, had been actively and vigilantly employed in tracing the guilty man through all the mazes of his crime, as 'inquisitorial ruffians' and 'miscreant blood-hounds', and in applying to them other wild-flowers of speech of the like nature, which are easily grown, but have a very rank and foul smell in the nostrils of honest men?" 1

"Was Mr Phillips justified . . . in casting disgraceful aspersions on [a witness's] character; thus seeking to render the discharge of that sacred duty to society which she had come there to perform, not matter of consolatory reflection to her, but a most painful and degrading circumstance?" 1

"I recognise the right of any counsel to take a brief from any man, however great his crime, and, keeping within due bounds, to do his best to save him; but I deny his right to defeat the ends of truth and justice by wantonly scattering aspersions upon innocent people, which may fasten a serious imputation upon them for the remainder of their lives—as those so profusely showered by Mr Phillips would have done in this instance, in the not impossible case of **Courvoisier** having been acquitted. In so doing, I maintain that he far oversteps his duty, and renders his office, not a public protection, but a public nuisance." 2

> Lord Erskine, cited by a correspondent defending Charles Phillips   2
> Landlady, of hotel in Leicester Place; a witness against Courvoisier   1,2
> Manlius: pen-name under which CD criticised criminal defense tactics   1,2
> Thomas Paine: his 1792 trial for criminal libel alluded to by CD   2
> Lord William Russell, murdered in his bed by his valet Courvoisier   1

MP July 25, 1842 (PE III 278-285)   MC **MC**

The Mines and Collieries Bill

A vehement letter to the editor of *The Morning Chronicle*, attacking colliery interests in the House of Lords. They opposed **Lord Ashley**'s bill to regulate the employment of women and children in the mines.

Children, and other wretched. "Now, happiness capers and sings on a slave plantation, making it an Eden of ebony. Now, she dwelleth in a roofless cabin, with potatoes thrice a week, buttermilk o' Sundays, a pig in the parlour, a fever in the dungheap, seven naked children on the damp earth-floor, and a wife newly delivered of an eighth, upon a door, brought from the nearest hut that boasts one—five miles off. Now, she rambles through a refreshing grove of steam engines, at midnight, with a Manchester child, patting him occasionally on the head with a billy-roller."

Colliery owners. ". . . it was stoutly contended by their collier lordships that there are no grievances, no discomforts, no miseries whatever, in the mines; that all **labourers** in mines are perpetually singing and dancing, and festively enjoying themselves; in a word, that they lead such rollicking and roystering lives that it is well they work below the surface of the earth, or society would be deafened by their shouts of merriment."

Lord Londonderry. "It is something so new for a rational being to agree with Lord Londonderry on any subject, that I am happy to be enabled to lay claim to that distinction. The pictures on the table of the House of Lords are unquestionably disgusting. They exhibit human beings in a condition which it is horrible to contemplate—which is disgraceful to the country, dangerous to the community, repulsive and offensive to all right-thinking persons, in the highest degree. But Lord Londonderry's objection is not to the existence of this deplor-able state of society; it is confined to the naughty pictures that set it forth and illustrate it; 'Keep it in the mines,' says he, 'but don't lay it on the table. Pre-serve it, but don't paint it. I equally protest against legislation and lithograph.' In like manner the delicacy of the **distillers** of **Hogarth**'s time was grievously outraged by the print of 'Gin Lane,' and nearly all the stout **landladies** dwell-ing about Covent-garden voted ''The Harlot's Progress' indecent and immoral."

Sub-commissioners. —*actual:* " . . . chosen from among barristers, medical gentlemen, and civil engineers . . . . Barristers are not so liable as other men to be easily imposed on by false statements; surgeons cannot be blinded to the present and probable effects of a pernicious atmosphere, and the work of beasts of burden, on tender years and frames. Civil engineers are well acquainted with the dangers that lurk in ill-conducted pits, where no provision is made for the safety of the labourers."

—*theoretical:* "Lord **Littleton**'s **valet**, Lord **Londonderry**'s **butler**, and any **steward** or **overseer** of the Duke of **Hamilton** would have known better. They would have made an excellent commission. With three such sub-commis-sioners (one to form a quorum) the **collier lords** would have got on briskly. Jolly little **trappers** would have been quoted against us by the dozen, and not a whisper would have been heard about their jolly little affidavits."

Trappers. "And now [happiness] sits down in the dark, a thousand feet below the level of the sea, passing the livelong day beside a little trapper six years old. If I were not this great peer, quoth **Lord Londonderry**, I would be that small trapper. If I were not a lord, doomed unhappily in my high place to preserve a solemn bearing, for the wonder and admiration of mankind, and hold myself aloof from innocent sports, I would be a jolly little trapper. Oh, for the cindery days of trapper infancy! The babes in the wood had a rich and cruel uncle. When were the children in the coals ever murdered for their inheritance? Jolly, jolly trappers!" [*See* Glossary and Annotations, Volume III]

Women, in the mines. "It is an interference with the rights of labour to exclude women from the mines—women who work by the side of naked men— (daughters often do this beside their own fathers)—and harnessed to carts in a most revolting and disgusting fashion, by iron chains. Is it among the rights of labour to blot out from that sex all form and stamp, and character of womanhood—to predestine their neglected offspring, from the hour of their conception in the womb, to lives of certain sin and suffering, misery and crime—to divest them of all knowledge of home, and all chance of womanly influence in the humble sphere of a poor peasant's hearth—to make them but so many weaker men, saving in respect of their more rapid and irresistible opportunities of being brutalised themselves, and of brutalizing others; and their capacity of breeding for the scaffold and the gaol?"

Sir John Hope, owner of the worst-conducted mine in the worst Scots district

MP October 20, 1842 (Nonesuch V 13-19)   MC **LA**

A Letter to Lord Ashley M.P. on the
Mines and Collieries Bill,
by C. W. Vane, Marquess of Londonderry, C. C. B.

Responding to **Lord Ashley**'s efforts to regulate working conditions in the collieries, **Lord Londonderry** wrote and promulgated a pamphlet, on which this piece acidly comments.

Lord Londonderry. " . . . it is one of the most charming and graceful characteristics of this remarkable production that it has no one thought, or argument, or line of reasoning, in its whole compass, but is entirely devoted to the display of its noble author's exquisite taste and extreme felicity of expression . . . a triton among the minnows of creation . . . ."

"There be lords who are not born to write one correct sentence in the language of the country they have represented abroad; and who, if they be born to read at all, are born to be never the better for it."

"He has had every possible advantage in the way of station and education; he entertains a high contempt for every thing that is not polite and lofty; his bear never dances but to the genteelest of tunes . . . . "

Colburn, publisher of the pamphlet
Foormen, supposititious, in the waiting room of the House of Lords
Globwog, writer of a book on letter-writing
Mrs Honour
Horner, member of the Children's Employment Commission; zealous in their welfare
Winifred Jankins and *Mrs Malaprop,* cited as literary models for a noble lord
Duke of Marlborough and Lord Nelson, cited as examples of the military hero
Earl of Shaftesbury
Jonathan Swift
Supporters of the Ashley: Earl of Devon, the Duke of Hamilton, Lord Hatherton

MP March 9, 1844   MC **AI**

The Agricultural Interest

Satirical discussion of the competing interests concerned in the effort to repeal the Corn Laws, which supported grain prices.

> "... *the agricultural interest, or what passes by that name ... never thinks of the suffering world, or sees it, or cares to extend its knowledge of it; or, so long as it remains a world, cares anything about it.*"

Engine-driver. "[His] garb, and sympathies, and tastes belong to the factory. His fustian dress, besmeared with coal-dust and begrimed with soot; his oily hands, his dirty face, his knowledge of machinery; all point him out as one devoted to the manufacturing interest. Fire and smoke, and red-hot cinders follow in his wake. He has no attachment to the soil, but travels on a road of iron, furnace wrought."

Police. "Their buttons are made at Birmingham; a dozen of their truncheons would poorly furnish forth a watchman's staff; they have no wooden walls to repose between; and the crowns of their hats are plated with cast-iron."

Stage-coachman. "The old stage-coachman was a farmer's friend. He wore top-boots, understood cattle, fed his horses upon corn, and had a lively personal interest in malt."

Watchmen. "They wore woollen nightcaps to a man; they encouraged the growth of timber, by patriotically adhering to staves and rattles of immense size; they slept every night in boxes, which were but another form of the celebrated wooden walls of Old England; they never woke up till it was too late—in which respect you might have thought them very farmers."

Buckingham, Duke of: a leader of the Agricultural Interest
Cobden, Richard: leader of the Anti-Corn Law League
Dante: first circle would have had representatives of the Agricultural Interest
Exeter, Bishop of: facetiously proposed as a Judge
Ireland, Attorney General for: facetiously proposed as a prosecutor
Morison, related to the medical profession
Moat, related to the medical profession
O'Connell, Daniel: Irish political leader, arrested for plotting sedition

MP May 1844   *Hood's Magazine and Comic Miscellany* **TH**

Threatening Letter to Thomas Hood
From an Ancient Gentleman
By Favour of Charles Dickens

Hood (1799-1845), a friend of CD, founded his Magazine in 1844, and CD contributed this parody on reactionary views to an early issue. The Ancient Gentleman cites the inordinate production of dwarfs by dietary means, and a spreading tendency to emulate native North Americans.

> "*The Constitution is going at last! You needn't laugh, Mr Hood. I am aware that it has been going, two or three times before—perhaps four times; but it is on the move now, sir, and no mistake.*"

Phineas T. Barnum. "If the gallant general [**Tom Thumb**] should decline to treat with you, get Mr Barnum's name, which is the next best in the market."

Female. "There is only one **judge** who knows how to do his duty now. He tried that revolutionary female the other day, who, though she was in full work (making shirts at three halfpence apiece), had no pride in her country, but treasonably took it in her head, in the distraction of having been robbed of her easy earnings, to attempt to drown herself and her young child; and the glorious man went out of his way, sir—out of his way—to call her up for instant sentence of Death . . . . "

Ojibbeway Bride "is on the eve of retiring into a savage fastness, where she may bring forth and educate a wild family who shall in course of time, by the dextrous use of the popularity they are certain to acquire at Windsor and St James's, divide with dwarfs the principal offices of state, of patronage, and power, in the United Kingdom."

> Finlayson, the Government's Actuary
> Judges, used to be admired for dignity and firmness
> Rankin: a promoter
> Schloss: a publisher
> Thumb, Tom: famous dwarf promoted by Barnum

MP 1844   **JO**

Preface to *Evenings of a Working Man*
by John Overs

John Overs. " . . . I state, in the outset, that . . . I have not the smallest intention of comparing him with **Burns**, the exciseman; or with **Bloomfield**, the shoemaker; or with **Ebenezer Elliott**, the worker in iron; or with **James Hogg**, the shepherd."

" . . . he wrote me as manly and straightforward, but withal as modest a letter, as ever I read in my life. He explained to me how limited his ambition was . . . . "

"I have found him from first to last a simple, frugal, steady, upright, honourable man; especially to be noted for the unobtrusive independence of his character, the instinctive propriety of his manner, and the perfect neatness of his appearance . The extent of his information—regard being had to his opportunities of acquiring it—is very remarkable; and the discrimination with which he has risen superior to the mere prejudices of the class with which he is associated, without losing his sympathy for all their real wrongs and grievances— they have a few—impressed me . . . strongly in his favour."

> Bloomfield, Robert; farm labourer and shoemaker: wrote *The Farmer's Boy*
> Burns, Robert; great Scottish poet who held a post as exciseman in Dumfries
> Elliotson, Doctor; to whom the dying John Overs dedicated his book
> Elliott, Ebenezer; Sheffield foundryman and poet: "Corn Law Rhymer"
> Hogg, James; poet discovered by Sir Walter Scott; a shepherd in Ettrick Forest
> Tait, of Edinburgh: published Overs's work in his magazine

MP August 1845 *Douglas Jerrold's Shilling Magazine* **SC**

The Spirit of Chivalry

Daniel Maclise. "Students of art have sat before [his fresco], hour by hour, perusing in its many forms of Beauty, lessons to delight the world, and raise themselves, its future teachers, in its better estimation. Eyes well accustomed to the glories of the Vatican, the galleries of Florence, all the mightiest works of art in Europe, have grown dim before it with the strong emotions it inspires; ignorant, unlettered, drudging men, mere hewers and drawers, have gathered in a knot about it . . . and read it, in their homely language, as it were a Book. In minds, the roughest and the most refined, it has alike found quick response; and will, and must, so long as it shall hold together."

"Is it the Love of Woman, in its truth and deep devotion, that inspires you? See it here! Is it Glory, as the world has learned to call the pomp and circumstance of arms? Behold it at the summit of its exaltation, with its mailed hand resting on the altar where the Spirit ministers. The Poet's laurel-crown, which they who sit on thrones can neither twine or wither—is *that* the aim of thy ambition? It is there, upon his brow; it wreathes his stately forehead, as he walks apart and holds communion with himself. The Palmer and the Bard are there; no solitary wayfarers, now; but two of a great company of pilgrims . . . . And sure, amidst the gravity and beauty of them all—unseen in his own form, but shining in his spirit, out of every gallant shape and earnest thought—the Painter goes triumphant!"

> Eastlake: secretary to the Fine Arts' Commission
> Sterne, Lawrence: "kind Heaven defend me from the cant of Art!"

MP February 4, 1846 Letter to the *Daily News* **CE**

Crime and Education

Urges funding support for the "Ragged Schools," which have been introducing "among the most miserable and neglected outcasts in London, some knowledge of the commonest principles of morality and religion."

Students. "Huddled together on a bench about the room, and shown out by some flaring candles stuck against the walls, were a crowd of boys, varying from mere infants to young men; sellers of fruit, herbs, lucifer-matches, flints; sleepers under the dry arches of bridges; young thieves and beggars—with nothing natural to youth about them: with nothing frank, ingenuous, or pleasant in their faces; low-browed, vicious, cunning, wicked; abandoned of all help but this; speeding downward to destruction; and UNUTTERABLY IGNORANT."

> Chesterton, intelligent and humane prison governor
> Tracey, Lieutenant: intelligent and humane prison governor

Capital Punishment

"[There is a question] Whether an irrevocable Doom—which nothing can recall, which no human power can set right if it be wrong, which may be wrongfully inflicted with the most just intention and which has been wrongfully inflicted with the most just intention, as we all know, more than once— should ever be pronounced by men of fallible and erring judgment, on their fellow-creatures."

Mr Justice Coleridge. " . . . took occasion to lament the presence of serious crimes in the calendar, and to say that he feared that they were referable to the comparative infrequency of Capital Punishment . . . [he] was not supported by facts, but quite the reverse." 5

Courvoisier "might have robbed his master with greater safety and with fewer chances of detection, if he had not murdered him. But, his calculations going to the gain and not to the loss, he had no balance for the consequences of what he did." 3

Thomas Hocker. "Here is an insolent, flippant, dissolute youth: aping the man of intrigue and levity: over-dressed, over-confident, inordinately vain of his personal appearance: distinguished as to his hair, cane, snuff-box, and singing-voice; and unhappily the son of a working shoemaker. Bent on loftier flights than such a poor house-swallow as a teacher in a Sunday-school can take; and having no truth, industry, perseverance, or other dull work-a-day quality, to plume his wings withal; he casts about him, in his jaunty way, for some mode of distinguishing himself—some means of getting that head of hair into the print-shops; of having something like justice done to his singing-voice and fine intellect; of making the life and adventures of Thomas Hocker remarkable; and of getting up some excitement in connection with that slighted piece of biography." 3

Captain G. Johnstone, of the *Tory*. " . . . one of the most cruel murderers of whom we have any record . . . acquitted on a fiction of his being insane . . . ." 1

Thomas Babington Macaulay. " . . . hardly seemed to recognise the possibility of anybody entertainng an honest conviction of the inutility and bad effects of Capital Punishment in the abstract, founded on inquiry and reflection, without being the victim of 'a kind of effeminate feeling.'" 5

Sir James Macintosh. "In Bombay, during [his] Recordership . . . there were fewer crimes in seven years without one execution, than in the preceding seven years with forty-seven executions; notwithstanding that . . . the population had greatly increased, and there had been a large accession to the numbers of the ignorant and licentious soldiery, with whom the more violent offences originated." 5

Lord Melbourne, "[who said] that no class of persons can be shown to be very miserable and oppressed, but some supporters of things as they are will immediately rise up and assert —not that those persons are moderately well to do, or that their lot in life has a reasonably bright side—but that they are, of all sorts and conditions of men, the happiest." 5

Maximilien Robespierre. "What effects a daily increasing familiarity with the scaffold, and with death upon it, wrought in France in the Great Revolution, everybody knows . . . [He] warned the National Assembly that in taking human life, and in displaying before the eyes of the people scenes of cruelty and the bodies of murdered men, the law awakened ferocious prejudices, which gave birth to a long and growing train of their own kind. With how much reason this was said, let his own detestable name bear witness!" 5

B. Seery. " . . . the man just now executed in Ireland: in that unhappy country, where it is considered most essential to assert the law, and make examples through its means . . . set on record, a deliberate and solemn protest against the justice of his sentence, and called upon his Maker before whom he would so soon appear, with all his sins upon his head, to bear witness to his innocence." 1

Wakefield, author, "who, before having personal knowledge of the subject and of Newgate, was quite satisfied that the Punishment of Death should continue, but who, when he gained that experience, exerted himself to the utmost for its abolition, even at the pain of constant public reference in his own person to his own imprisonment." 4

J. Abercromby [CD gives Abercrombie], M.P.: spoke March 1811 on capital punishment 2
Francis Bacon, who strove in his day against excessive death penalties 5
Lord Chief Baron, whose exertions saved innocent men from hanging 5
William Blackstone, who strove in his day against excessive death penalties 5
Madame Blaize, cited for elegance of dress 3
boys, a few score;all young thieves, near the drop at a hanging 2
[Martha Browning], a woman hanged January 1846: "brought out to be killed" 2
Calcraft, the hangman, one of the most manly specimens now in existence 5
Rev Henry Christmas, biblical scholar opposed to death penalty 5
Clergyman, who researched numbers who attended public executions 3
W. Dodd, doctor, executed June 1777 for forgery 2
Lord Eldon, who tearfully opposed abolition of death penalty for forgery 4
Lord Ellenborough, who feared consequences if no death penalty for five shillings 5
H. Fauntleroy, banker, executed November 1824 for fraudulent stock sales and forgery 2, 3
Rev. Peter Fenn, schoolmaster, sentenced to death for uttering forged bills of exchange 2
Eliza Fenning, executed for a crime she did not commit 5
J. Greenacre, executed May 1847 for murdering his affianced, Hannah Brown 2
William Hogarth, artist who satirized public executions 4
J. Hunton, wealthy Quaker: executed December 1828 for a series of forgeries 2
Lord Chancellor: opposed capital punishment abolition for five shillings theft 5
Lord Lyndhurst: opposed abolition of death penalty for forgery 4
Basil Montagu, who opposed excessive use of death penalty 5
W. Montgomery, sentenced to death for issuing forged notes: a suicide in his cell 2
Thomas More, who strove in his day against excessive death penalties 5
Lord Nugent, humane head of Parliamentary committee on public executions 4
Daniel O'Connell, Irish political leader; defended three innocent men who were hanged 5
Old woman, murdered by her female companion 3
Oxford, who fired at Queen Victoria in a park 3
[S. Quennell], hanged January 1846 outside Horsemonger Lane Gaol 2
Recorder, of London: objected capital punishment abolition for pickpockets 5
Sir Samuel Romilly, who in his day opposed excessive death penalties 2, 5
Solicitor General: advocated death for forgery 5
Tawell, a most abhorred villain, but still petitioners opposed death penalty 2, 5
Lord Tenterden, who opposed abolition of death penalty for forgery 4
Thurtell, famous murderer: made a capital speech at his trial and died game 3
Tiddy Doll, character in Hogarth; a ginger-bread seller whose pocket is picked 4
Turnkey, who brought Hocker a glass of water 3
Woman, murderer of old woman companion for what she took to be a bank note 3
Lord Wynford, who opposed abolition of death penalty for forgery 4
Youth, sentenced to death; had been vigilant spectator at public executions 5

The Chimes

Frontispiece by Daniel Maclise

CB 2 December 1844 by Bradbury and Evans (B&E; distributed by C&H)   **C**
U.S. publication 1845 by Lea & Blanchard, Philadelphia

𝕿𝖍𝖊 𝕮𝖍𝖎𝖒𝖊𝖘

A Goblin Story of some Bells
that Rang an Old Year Out and a New One In

PRÉCIS

We meet the Wind, the Steeple and the Chimes—and then **Toby Veck**, ticket-porter familiar with all three, and with the Rain. His daughter **Meg** brings his dinner of tripe, potato and beer, momentarily distracting him from his worries. Meg and **Richard** have decided to be married without waiting for better times. Alderman **Cute** and two colleagues sneer at the dinner and Cute cuttingly lectures against marriage of the Poor. 1

Toby carries Cute's letter to the pontificating **Sir Joseph Bowley**. Cute wants to have **Will Fern**, who had come up from London looking for work, "put down" as a vagrant. Bowley dictates to his secretary **Fish**, urging a short jail term, and Toby takes the note. He runs into Fern, with little **Lilian**. Fern asks the way to Cute's, but Toby warns him off and takes both home. Meg warms Fern's feet and Toby feeds his guests. The newspaper depresses him. The ringing bells draw him to the steeple. He faints. 2

Awake, Toby sees an army of phantoms and elves and is scolded by the **Phantom** of the Great Bell for giving in to despair at the sadness of life. Guided by a child Spirit of the Bells, he sees first himself, dead in a fall from the steeple; then Meg nine years later, blighted, with Lilian a woman. They scrape for bare sustenance. He sees a Bowley fete. Fish tells Cute that banker **Deedles** has shot himself. Fern, just out of jail, cries out against injustice to the Poor. Back at the garret, Meg is alone. A degenerated Richard appears. He has seen Lilian, who has repeatedly tried to send Meg money she has degradedly earned. Lilian appears and dies in Meg's arms. 3

Toby's Vision shows fat **Tugby**, formerly Bowley's footman, and his wife, kind **Anne Chickenstalker**. Their miserable tenants are Meg and Richard. Richard did not marry Meg until he was a castaway—having taken Cute's lecture seriously. He dies, leaving sorrowing Meg with a wretched infant girl. When Tugby forbids her the house, she takes the baby to the River, intending suicide. Galvanized, Toby sees his sin has been despair. He wakes joyously. Meg and Richard will wed. Anne, who had known Lilian's mother, and Fern find each other. The band tunes up. Happy New Year! 4

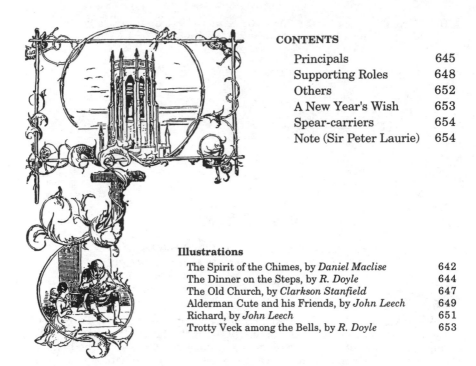

CONTENTS

Illustrations

CHARACTERS

Bowley, child, admired by the Alderman	O	652
Sir Joseph, M.P.; stately and complacent	SR	648
Chickenstalker, Anne; stout and kindly shopkeeper	SR	648
Cute, Alderman; given to lecturing	SR	649
Deedles, the banker; he shoots himself in Trotty's vision	O	652
Drum player, a private friend of Trotty's, and rather drunk	O	652
Fern, Lilian; nine years old, and niece; vision foreshadows a whore	O	650
Will; in trouble with an Alderman	P	645
Filer, in low spirits but an authority on tripe	SR	650
Fish: he wrote to dictation	O	652
Footman, to the Alderman	O	652
Gentleman, red-faced; rather cold about the heart	O	652
Goblins of the Bells	O	652
Margaret, spare, sickly little infant in Toby's vision	O	652
Medical man, officially to serve the poor	O	652
Phantom, of the Great Bell: rather a judging sort	P	645
Richard, a fine smile, briefly discouraged in his wedding plans	SR	651
Spirit of the Chimes, a child; the spirit of little Lilian	O	651
Tugby, fat Porter for Bowley; fond of muffins and crumpets	SR	651
Veck, Margaret (Meg); young bright eyes	P	645
Toby (Trotty); his pace meant speed, did not achieve it	P	646

Principals

Will Fern. " . . . a sun-browned, sinewy, country-looking man, with grizzled hair, and a rough chin . . . . He was so jaded and foot-sore, and so soiled with travel, and looked about him so forlorn and strange, that it was a comfort to him to be able to thank any one: no matter for how little. **Toby** stood gazing after him as he plodded wearily away, with [**Lilian**]'s arm clinging round his neck . . . in the worn shoes—now the very shade and ghost of shoes—rough leather leggings, common frock, and broad slouched hat . . . . " 2

—*character:* "' . . . I never took with that hand'—holding it before him—'what wasn't my own; and never held it back from work, however hard, or poorly paid. Whoever can deny it, let him chop it off!'" 2

—*his story, in a Vision:* "'Gentlefolks, I've lived many a year in this place. You may see the cottage from the sunk fence over yonder. I've seen the ladies draw it in their books, a hundred times. It looks well in a picter, I've heerd say; but there ain't weather in picters, and maybe 'tis fitter for that, than for a place to live in. Well! I lived there. How hard—how bitter hard, I lived there, I won't say . . . .

"'I dragged on . . . somehow. Neither me nor any other man knows how; but so heavy, that I couldn't put a cheerful face upon it, or make believe that I was anything but what I was. Now, gentlemen—you gentlemen that sits at Sessions—when you see a man with discontent writ on his face, you says to one another, "He's suspicious. I has my doubts . . . about Will Fern. Watch that fellow!" I don't say, gentlemen, it ain't quite nat'ral, but I says 'tis so; and from that hour, whatever Will Fern does, or lets alone—all one—it goes against him.'" 3

Phantom, of the Great Bell. " . . . a bearded figure of the bulk and stature of the Bell—incomprehensibly, a figure and the Bell itself. Gigantic, grave, and darkly watchful . . . .

"'Who hears in us, the Chimes, one note bespeaking disregard, or stern regard, of any hope, or joy, or pain, or sorrow, of the many-sorrowed throng; who hears us make response to any creed that gauges human passions and affections, as it gauges the amount of miserable food on which humanity may pine and wither; does us wrong . . . .

"'Lastly, and most of all . . . . Who turns his back upon the fallen and disfigured of his kind; abandons them as vile; and does not trace and track with pitying eyes the unfenced precipice by which they fell from good—grasping in their fall some tufts and shreds of that lost soil, and clinging to them still when bruised and dying in the gulf below; does wrong to Heaven and man, to time and to eternity.'" 3

Margaret (**Meg**) **Veck**. "Bright eyes they were. Eyes that would bear a world of looking in, before their depth was fathomed. Dark eyes, that reflected back the eyes which searched them; not flashingly, or at the owner's will, but with a clear, calm, honest, patient radiance, claiming kindred with that light which Heaven called into being. Eyes that were beautiful and true, and beaming with Hope. With Hope so young and fresh; with Hope so buoyant, vigorous, and bright, despite the twenty years of work and poverty on which they had looked . . . . " 1

—*despairing, in a Vision:* "In her own scanty shawl, she wrapped the baby warm. With her fevered hands she smoothed its limbs, composed its face, arranged its mean attire. In her wasted arms she folded it, as though she never would resign it more. And with her dry lips, kissed it in a final pang, and last long agony of Love.

"Putting its tiny hand up to her neck, and holding it there, within her dress, next to her distracted heart, she set its sleeping face against her: closely, steadily, against her: and sped onward to the River.

"To the rolling River, swift and dim, where Winter Night sat brooding like the last dark thoughts of many who had sought a refuge there before her. Where scattered lights upon the banks gleamed sullen, red, and dull, as torches that were burning there, to show the way to Death. Where no abode of living people cast its shadow on the deep, impenetrable, melancholy shade.

"To the River! To that portal of Eternity, her desperate footsteps tended with the swiftness of its rapid waters running to the sea. [**Toby**] tried to touch her as she passed him, going down to its dark level: but the wild distempered form, the fierce and terrible love, the desperation that had left all human check or hold behind, swept by him like the wind." 4

—the Vision dispelled: "She was working with her needle, at the little table by the fire; dressing her simple gown with ribbons for her wedding. So quietly happy, so blooming and youthful, so full of beautiful promise, that [**Toby**] uttered a great cry as if it were an angel in his house; then flew to clasp her in his arms." 4

Toby (**Trotty**) **Veck**. "They called him Trotty from his pace, which meant speed if it didn't make it. He could have walked faster perhaps; most likely; but rob him of his trot, and Toby would have taken to his bed and died. It bespattered him with mud in dirty weather; it cost him a world of trouble; he could have walked with infinitely greater ease; but that was one reason for his clinging to it so tenaciously. A weak, small, spare old man, he was a very Hercules, this Toby, in his good intentions. He loved to earn his money. He delighted to believe—Toby was very poor, and couldn't well afford to part with a delight—that he was worth his salt. With a shilling or an eighteen-penny message or small parcel in hand, his courage always high, rose higher. As he trotted on, he would call out to fast postmen ahead of him to get out of the way; devoutly believing that in the natural course of things he must inevitably overtake and run them down; and he had perfect faith—not often tested—in his being able to carry anything that man could lift." 1

—and the Wind: "The wind came tearing round the corner—especially the east wind—as if it had sallied forth, express, from the confines of the earth, to have a blow at Toby. And oftentimes it seemed to come upon him sooner than it had expected, for bouncing round the corner, and passing Toby, it would suddenly wheel round again, as if it cried 'Why, here he is!'

"Incontinently his little white apron would be caught up over his head like a naughty boy's garments, and his feeble little cane would be seen to wrestle and struggle unavailingly in his hand, and his legs would undergo tremendous agitation, and Toby himself all aslant, and facing now in this direction, now in that, would be so banged and buffeted, and touzled, and worried, and hustled, and lifted off his feet, as to render it a state of things but one degree removed from a positive miracle, that he wasn't carried up bodily into the air as a colony of frogs or snails or other very portable creatures sometimes are . . . . " 1

—and the weather: "But, windy weather, in spite of its using him so roughly, was, after all, a sort of holiday for Toby. That's the fact. He didn't seem to wait so long for a sixpence in the wind, as at other times; the having to fight with that boisterous element took off his attention, and quite freshened

him up, when he was getting hungry and low-spirited. A hard frost too, or a fall of snow, was an Event; and it seemed to do him good, somehow or other—it would have been hard to say in what respect though, Toby! So wind and frost and snow, and perhaps a good stiff storm of hail, were Toby Veck's red-letter days.

"Wet weather was the worst; the cold, damp, clammy wet, that wrapped him up like a moist great-coat—the only kind of great-coat Toby owned, or could have added to his comfort by dispensing with. Wet days, when the rain came slowly, thickly, obstinately down . . . ." 1

—*and the Chimes:* " . . . they were company to him; and when he heard their voices, he had an interest in glancing at their lodging-place, and thinking how they were moved, and what hammers beat upon them. Perhaps he was the more curious about these Bells, because there were points of resemblance between themselves and him. They hung there, in all weathers, with the wind and rain driving in upon them; facing only the outsides of all those houses; never getting any nearer to the blazing fires that gleamed and shone upon the windows, or came puffing out of the chimney tops; and incapable of participation in any of the good things that were constantly being handed, through the street doors and the area railings, to prodigious cooks . . . .

" . . . being but a simple man, he invested them with a strange and solemn character. They were so mysterious, often heard and never seen; so high up, so far off, so full of such a deep strong melody, that he regarded them with a species of awe; and sometimes when he looked up at the dark arched windows in the tower, he half expected to be beckoned to by something which was not a Bell, and yet was what he had heard so often sounding in the Chimes. . . . . In short, they were very often in his ears, and very often in his thoughts, but always in his good opinion; and he very often got such a crick in his neck by staring with his mouth wide open, at the steeple where they hung, that he was fain to take an extra trot or two, afterwards, to cure it." 1

—*his nose:* " . . . with a face of great interest and some alarm, [he] felt his nose carefully all the way up. It was but a little way (not being much of a nose) and he had soon finished." 1

—the news: " . . . reading of the crimes and violences of the people, he relapsed into his former train . . . .

"'Unnatural and cruel!' Toby cried. 'Unnatural and cruel! None but people who were bad at heart, born bad, who had no business on the earth, could do such deeds. It's too true, all I've heard to-day; too just, too full of proof. We're Bad!'" 2

—awakened: "I don't care where you have lived or what you have seen; you never in all your life saw anything at all approaching him! He sat down in his chair and beat his knees and cried; he sat down in his chair and beat his knees and laughed; he sat down in his chair and beat his knees and laughed and cried together; he got out of his chair and hugged **Meg**; he got out of his chair and hugged **Richard**; he got out of his chair and hugged them both at once; he kept running up to Meg, and squeezing her fresh face between his hands and kissing it, going from her backwards not to lose sight of it, and running up again like a figure in a magic lantern; and whatever he did, he was constantly sitting himself down in his chair, and never stopping in it for one single moment; being—that's the truth—beside himself with joy." 4

Supporting Roles

Sir Joseph Bowley, M. P. " . . . a much statelier gentleman, whose hat and cane were on the table, walked up and down, with one hand in his breast, and looked complacently from time to time at his own picture—a full length; a very full length—hanging over the fireplace." 2

—his role: "'I *am* the Poor Man's Friend,' observed Sir Joseph, glancing at the poor man present . . . .

"'Your only business, my good fellow,' pursued Sir Joseph, looking abstractedly at **Toby**; 'your only business in life is with me. You needn't trouble yourself to think about anything. I will think for you; I know what is good for you; I am your perpetual parent.'" 2

—a fete: "At which Sr Joseph Bowley . . . was to make his great speech. Certain plum-puddings were to be eaten by his Friends and Children in another Hall first; and, at a given signal, Friends and Children flocking in among their Friends and Fathers, were to form a family assemblage, with not one manly eye therein unmoistened by emotion.

"But there was more than this to happen. Even more than this. Sir Joseph Bowley, Baronet and Member of Parliament, was to play a match at skittles—real skittles—with his tenants!" 3

Mrs Anne Chickenstalker, shopkeeper. " . . . stout old lady . . . always inclined to corpulency . . . . " 4

—with her mate, in a Vision: "Fat company, rosy-cheeked company, comfortable company. They were but two, but they were red enough for ten . . . there remained no other visible tokens of the meal just finished, than such as purred and wished their whiskers in the person of the basking cat, and glistened in the gracious, not to say the greasy, faces of her patrons." 4

—her flip: " . . . a good-humoured comely woman of some fifty years of age, or thereabouts, came running in, attended by a man bearing a stone pitcher of terrific size . . . .

"Mrs Chickenstalker's notion of a little flip did honour to her character. The pitcher steamed and smoked and reeked like a volcano; and the man who had carried it was faint." 4

Alderman Cute. " . . . coming out of the house at that kind of light-heavy pace—that peculiar compromise between a walk and a jog-trot—with which a gentleman upon the smooth downhill of life, wearing creaking boots, a watch-chain, and clean linen, *may* come out of his house: not only without any abatement of his dignity, but with an expression of having important and wealthy engagements elsewhere." 1

—*a lecture:* "'You are going to be married you say,' pursued the Alderman. 'Very unbecoming and indelicate in one of your sex! But never mind that. After you are married, you'll quarrel with your husband and come to be a distressed wife. You may think not; but you will, because I tell you so. Now, I give you fair warning, that I have made up my mind to Put distressed wives Down. So, don't be brought before me.

"You'll have children—boys. Those boys will grow up bad, of course, and run wild in the streets, without shoes and stockings. Mind, my young friend! I'll convict 'em summarily, every one, for I am determined to Put boys without shoes and stockings Down.

"Perhaps your husband will die young (most likely) and leave you with a baby. Then you'll be turned out of doors, and wander up and down the streets.

Now, don't wander near me, my dear, for I am resolved to Put all wandering mothers Down. All young mothers, of all sorts and kinds, it's my determination to Put Down.

"Don't think to plead illness as an excuse with me; or babies as an excuse with me; for all sick persons and young children (I hope you know the church-service, but I'm afraid not) I am determined to Put Down. And if you attempt, desperately, and ungratefully, and impiously, and fraudulently attempt, to drown yourself, or hang yourself, I'll have no pity for you, for I have made up my mind to Put all suicide Down! If there is one thing,' said the Alderman, with his self-satisfied smile, 'on which I can be said to have made up my mind more than on another, it is to Put suicide Down. So don't try it on.'" ¶1

—his banker has killed himself: "'Oh the brain, the brain!' exclaimed the pious Alderman, lifting up his hands. 'Oh the nerves, the nerves; the mysteries of this machine called Man! Oh the little that unhinges it: poor creatures that we are! Perhaps a dinner, Mr **Fish**. Perhaps the conduct of his son, who, I have heard, ran very wild . . . . A most respectable man. One of the most respectable men I ever knew! A lamentable instance, Mr Fish. A public calamity! I shall make a point of wearing the deepest mourning. A most respectable man! But there is One above. We must submit, Mr Fish. We must submit!'

"What, Alderman! No word of Putting Down? Remember, Justice, your high moral boast and pride. Come, Alderman! Balance those scales." 3

Lilian Fern. "'She's my brother's child: a orphan. Nine year old, though you'd hardly think it; but she's tired and worn out now.'" 2

—in a Vision: "Looking with awe into its face, he saw a something reigning there: a lofty something, undefined and indistinct, which made it hardly more than a remembrance of that child . . . . " 3

"'Oh **Meg**, Meg!' she raised her voice and twined her arms about her as she spoke, like one in pain. 'How can the cruel world go round, and bear to look upon such lives?'

"'Lilly!' said Meg, soothing her, and putting back her hair from her wet face. 'Why, Lilly! You! So pretty and so young!'

"'Oh Meg!' she interrupted, holding her at arm's-length, and looking in her face imploringly. 'The worst of all, the worst of all! Strike me old, Meg! Wither me, and shrivel me, and free me from the dreadful thoughts that tempt me in my youth!'" 3

—a Vision completed: "'Forgive me, **Meg**! So dear, so dear! Forgive me! I know you do, I see you do, but say so, Meg!'

"She said so, with her lips on Lilian's cheek. And with her arms twined round—she knew it now—a broken heart.

"'His blessing on you, dearest love. Kiss me once more! He suffered her to sit beside His feet, and dry them with her hair. O Meg, what Mercy and Compassion!'

"As she died, the Spirit of the child returning, innocent and radiant touched the old man [**Toby**] with its hand, and beckoned him away." 3

Filer. " . . . a low-spirited gentleman of middle age, of a meagre habit, and a disconsolate face; who kept his hands continually in the pockets of his scanty pepper-and-salt trousers, very large and dog's-eared from that custom; and was not particularly well brushed or washed." 1

"Mr Filer being exceedingly short-sighted, was obliged to go so close to the remnant of **Toby**'s dinner before he could make out what it was, that Toby's heart leaped up into his mouth. But Mr Filer didn't eat it.

"'This is a description of animal food, **Alderman**,' said Filer, making little punches in it with a pencil-case, 'commonly known to the labouring population of this country, by the name of tripe.'" I

Richard. "It was the voice of this same Richard . . . with a face as glowing as the iron on which his stout sledge-hammer daily rung. A handsome, well-made, powerful youngster he was; with eyes that sparkled like the red-hot droppings from a furnace fire; black hair that curled about his swarthy temples rarely; and a smile—a smile that bore out **Meg**'s eulogium on his style of conversation." 1

—degenerated in a Vision: "A man was on the threshold. A slouching, moody, drunken sloven, wasted by intemperance and vice, and with his matted hair and unshorn beard in wild disorder; but with some traces on him, too, of having been a man of good proportion and good features in his youth . . . staring vacantly at the floor with a lustreless and stupid smile . . . deep degradation . . . abject hopelessness . . . a miserable downfall. . . ." 3

—the Vision dispelled: "'You and Richard had some words to-day.'

"'Because he's such a bad fellow, father,' said **Meg**. 'An't you, Richard? Such a headstrong, violent man! He'd have made no more of speaking his mind to that great **Alderman**, and putting him down I don't know where, than he would of—

"'—Kissing Meg,' suggested Richard. Doing it too!" 4

Tugby, porter to **Bowley**. "The door was opened by a Porter. Such a Porter! Not of **Toby**'s order. Quite another thing. His place was the ticket though; not Toby's.

"This Porter underwent some hard panting before he could speak; having breathed himself by coming incautiously out of his chair, without first taking time to think about it and compose his mind. When he had found his voice—which it took him a long time to do, for it was a long way off, and hidden under a load of meat—he said in a fat whisper:

"'Who's it from?'" 2

—married: " 'I'm glad to think we had muffins,' said the former porter, in the tone of one who had set his conscience at rest. 'It's a sort of night that's meant for muffins. Likewise crumpets. Also Sally Lunns.'

"The former porter mentioned each successive kind of eatable, as if he were musingly summing up his good actions. After which he rubbed his fat legs as before, and jerking them at the knees to get the fire upon the yet unroasted parts, laughed as if somebody had tickled him . . . ." 4

Others

Bowley child. "'You'll marry the beautiful ladies, and not murder 'em, eh?' said **Alderman Cute** to the heir of Bowley, aged twelve. 'Sweet boy! We shall have this little gentleman in Parliament now,' said the Alderman, holding him by the shoulders, and looking as reflective as he could, 'before we know where we are.'" 3

Lady **Bowley**. " . . . a stately lady in a bonnet . . . . " 2

Deedles, the banker. "'Shot himself.'

"'Good God!'

"'Put a double-barrelled pistol to his mouth, in his own counting house,' said Mr **Fish**, 'and blew his brains out. No motive. Princely circumstances!'

"'Circumstances!' exclaimed the **Alderman**. 'A man of noble fortune. One of the most respectable of men. Suicide, Mr Fish!' By his own hand!'" 3

Drummer. "'Trotty Veck, my boy! It's got about, that your daughter is to be married to-morrow. There an't a soul that knows you that don't wish you well, or that knows her and don't wish her well. Or that knows you both, and don't wish you both all the happiness the New Year can bring. And here we are, to play it in and dance it in, accordingly.'

"Which was received with a general shout. The Drum was rather drunk, by-the-bye; but never mind." 4

Fish. " . . . a not very stately gentleman in black who wrote from [**Lady Bowley**'s] dictation . . . . " 2

Footman, to the **Alderman Cute**. " . . . the house-door opened without any warning, and a footman very nearly put his foot into the tripe." 1

Goblins, of the Bells. "Then [after the phantoms and elves had vanished] and not before, did Trotty see in every Bell a bearded figure of the bulk and stature of the Bell—incomprehensibly, a figure and the Bell itself. Gigantic, grave, and darkly watchful of him, as he stood rooted to the ground.

"Mysterious and awful figures! Resting on nothing; poised in the night air of the tower, with their draped and hooded heads merged in the dim roof; motion-less and shadowy. Shadowy and dark, although he saw them by some light belonging to themselves—none else was there—each with its muffled hand upon its goblin mouth." 3

Margaret, infant. "Who can tell how spare, how sickly, and how poor an infant! Who can tell how dear!" 4

Medical man. " . . . a gentleman in black, who, with his wristbands tucked up, and his hat cocked loungingly on one side, and his hands in his pockets, sat down astride on the table-beer barrel . . . [he] appeared to be some authorised medical attendant upon the poor . . . not otherwise hard-hearted or indifferent to such scenes [he] laid his hand upon the heart that beat no more, and listened for the breath, and said, 'His pain is over. It's better as it is!'

Red-faced gentleman. " . . . a full-sized, sleek, well-conditioned gentle-man, in a blue coat with bright buttons, and a white cravat. This gentleman had a very red face, as if an undue proportion of the blood in his body were squeezed up into his head; which perhaps accounted for his having also the ap-pearance of being rather cold about the heart." 1

Spirit, of the Chimes. "'The Spirit . . . is your companion,' said the [**Phantom**]. "Go! It stands behind you!'

"**Trotty** turned, and saw—the child! The child **Will Fern** had carried in the street . . . . " 2

Spirits. " . . . vast multitudes of phantoms . . . .'They take such shapes and occupations as the hopes and thoughts of mortals, and the recollections they have stored up, give them [said the **Spirit** of the Chimes].'" 3

𝕬 𝕹𝖊𝖜 𝖄𝖊𝖆𝖗'𝖘 𝖂𝖎𝖘𝖍

"Had **Trotty** dreamed? Or, are his joys and sorrows, and the actors in them, but a dream; himself a dream; the teller of this tale a dreamer, waking but now? If it be so, O listener, dear to him in all his visions, try to bear in mind the stern realities from which these shadows come; and in your sphere— none is too wide and none too limited for such an end—endeavour to correct, improve, and soften them. So may the New Year be a happy one to you, happy to many more whose happiness depends on you! So may each year be happier than the last, and not the meanest of our brethren or sisterhood debarred their rightful share in what our Great Creator formed them to enjoy." 4

Spear-carriers

Lady Bowley: stately and greatly younger than her husband	quarter 2
Deedles son: ran wild and drew bills on his father without authority	3
Kidney pieman, at the corner	2
Man, bearing a stone pitcher of flip	4
Officer, public: appointed to administer charity	4
Joseph Strutt[H], author of a definitive compendium on costumes	1
Mrs Veck: she got up linen and died at Meg's birth	1

NOTE (Sir Peter Laurie):

Alderman Cute was a real person: magistrate Sir Peter Laurie, whose conservative views and evident mean-spiritedness CD particularly detested. In his preface to the Cheap Edition (1850) of OT, CD calls Laurie "a gentleman of infallible authority, of great innate modesty, and of a most sweet humanity" and notes his comment that the noisome London slum Jacob's Island, where **Bill Sikes** met his end, did not exist: it was, after all, described in a work of fiction. [As given by Kathleen Tillotson, ed., in the Clarendon edition of OT:]

"Reflecting upon this logic, and its universal application; remembering that when FIELDING described Newgate, the prison immediately ceased to exist; than when SMOLLETT took Roderick Random to Bath, that city instantly sank into the earth; that when SCOTT exercised his genius on Whitefriars, it incontinently glided into the Thames; that an ancient place called Windsor was entirely destroyed in the reign of Queen Elizabeth by two Merry Wives of that town, acting under the direction of a person called SHAKESPEARE; and that Mr POPE, after having at a great expense completed his grotto at Twickenham, incautiously reduced it to ashes by writing a poem about it;—I say, when I came to consider these things, I was inclined to make this preface a vehicle of my humble tribute of admiration to SIR PETER LAURIE. But, I am restrained by a very painful consideration—by no less a consideration than the impossibility of his existence. For SIR PETER LAURIE having been himself described in a book (as I understand he was, one Christmas time, for his conduct on the seat of justice), it is but too clear that there CAN be no such man!"

The Cricket on the Hearth

Frontispiece by Daniel Maclise

Definitive U..S. data not available; *Le Grillon du Foyer* was in France by 1854

The Cricket on the Hearth

A FAIRY TALE OF HOME

PRÉCIS

Dot Peerybingle puts the kettle on. The clock strikes six. The kettle begins to sing. The **Cricket** chimes in. Dot collects her baby boy from nurse **Tilly Slowboy**, and carrier **John Peerybingle** arrives home for supper. He has a cake for the wedding of old **Tackleton** the toy-maker and pretty young **May Fielding**. Dot is shocked at the news. He also has a deaf old gentleman in his cart, found beside the road. **Caleb Plummer** appears to collect a parcel, and then Tackleton comes in, to announce his wedding and seek moral support from John, as another older husband. Dot suddenly breaks out in hysterics, and John soothes her. The stranger asks to rent a bed for the night, and Dot immediately agrees. She fills John's pipe. He smokes while the Cricket sings. 1

Caleb and his blind daughter **Bertha** live in a shabby little house and make toys and dolls' houses for the Tackleton firm. Loving her, Caleb has deceived her, telling her of the richness of her surroundings, and the charm of hard, surly, grinding Tackleton, whom she regards as her Guardian Angel. He visits to announce his wedding plans. He invites himself, with May and her mother, for later when Dot comes for her weekly picnic. Bertha is stunned and mute.

John and Dot get in their cart and jog along. They speak of the mysterious old man. At the Plummers' Dot is surprisingly tactless about old husbands and lost lovers. She bungles John's pipe. He goes off on his job. Bertha is distraught: her beloved is marrying another. Caleb realizes his deception has resulted in heartbreak. John returns with the old man. Tackleton takes John outside and shows him Dot with the stranger, false white hair off, his arm around her waist. John is thunderstruck. On the way home, he does not sit with Dot but walks beside the horse. 2

John sits heart-broken by the fire. He broods and thinks of murder. Dot first wonders at his mood, then divines the reason and leaves him, weeping. John is about to beat his gun on the stranger's door, when the Cricket begins to chirp and then appears to John in Fairy shape. The Fairy—many fairies— show him Dot in many aspects, and John passes a long night in deep reflection.

In the morning, John tells Tackleton he was wrong to marry Dot, so much younger than he. He will release her. Tackleton is discomfited. Dot overhears. Tackleton leaves, and so does John, to return for talk later. Caleb and Bertha arrive, and Caleb confesses to Bertha that he has deceived her for years. With Dot's good offices, father and daughter embrace.

The stranger rushes in, revealed as Caleb's lost son **Edward**, and John walks in on the scene. Edward explains: when he left for South America he was in love with May. Returning, he heard of the planned marriage and went undercover to learn how May really felt. He realizes **Mrs Fielding** overpersuaded her. Dot: "Tackleton may die a bachelor." John and Dot rapturously reconnect. Tackleton arrives and sees May's wedding ring. He accepts the situation and leaves, sending back the cake, and toys for the baby. He returns himself, enlightened and softened, and is heartily welcomed at the wedding party. 3

CONTENTS

Illustrations

CHARACTERS

Boxer: excitable, redoubtable dog	SR
CRICKET (the Spirit of the Hearth): an important Voice	TR
Fairies, assisting the Cricket	O
Fielding, May: beautiful and engaged	O
Mrs: very genteel and patronising indeed	SR
Man, who delivered a wedding cake	O
Mother, of Dot: she never stood on anything but her feet	O
Old Dot: Dot's father; a good-natured kind of man	O
Old Gentleman (Edward Plummer): well-defined features for age	P
Peerybingle, boy baby: a major project to take anywhere	SR
Dot (Mary): agreeable dumpling shape	P
John: much taller and much older than Dot	P
Plummer, Bertha: blind, well-protected and busy	P
Caleb: meagre man, protective father	P
Edward: he dropped out of nowhere	O
Professional assistants: called in from somewhere	O
Slowboy, Tilly: inclined to acquire notches in her legs	SR
Tackleton: antagonistic personality: surly, sordid, grinding	P

Title Role

The Cricket. " . . . the Cricket DID chime in! with a Chirrup, Chirrup, Chirrup of such magnitude, by way of chorus; with a voice so astoundingly disproportionate to its size, as compared with the kettle; (size! you couldn't see it!) that if it had then and there burst itself like an overcharged gun, if it had fallen a victim on the spot, and chirruped its little body into fifty pieces, it would have seemed a natural and inevitable consequence . . . .

"The kettle . . . persevered with undiminished ardour; but the Cricket took first fiddle and kept it. Good Heaven, how it chirped! Its shrill, sharp, piercing voice resounded through the house, and seemed to twinkle in the outer darkness like a star. There was an indescribable little trill and tremble in it, at its loudest, which suggested its being carried off its legs, and made to leap again, by its own intense enthusiasm. Yet they went very well together, the Cricket and the kettle. The burden of the song was still the same; and louder, louder, louder still, they sang it in their emulation." 1

—*the audience:* "'Heyday!' said **John**, in his slow way. 'It's merrier than ever, to-night, I think.'

"'And it's sure to bring us good fortune, John! It always has done so. To have a Cricket on the Hearth, is the luckiest thing in all the world!'" 1

—*on fairy duty:* " . . . as the Cricket chirped; that Genius of his Hearth and Home (for such the Cricket was) came out, in fairy shape, into the room, and summoned many forms of Home about him. **Dot**s of all ages, and all sizes, filled the chamber. Dots who were merry children, running on before him gathering flowers in the fields; coy Dots, half shrinking from, half yielding to, the pleading of his own rough image; newly-married Dots, alighting at the door, and taking wondering possession of the household keys; motherly little Dots, attended by fictitious **Slowboy**s, bearing babies to be christened; matronly Dots, still young and blooming, watching Dots of daughters, as they danced at rustic balls; fat Dots, encircled and beset by troops of rosy grand-children; withered Dots, who leaned on sticks, and tottered as they crept along. Old carriers, too, appeared, with blind old **Boxer**s lying at their feet; and newer carts with younger drivers ('Peerybingle Brothers' on the tilt); and sick old carriers, tended by the gentlest hands; and graves of dead and gone old carriers, green in the churchyard . . . [his] heart grew light and happy, and he thanked his Household Gods with all his might . . . . " I

—*plain talk:* "'Upon your own hearth—'

"'The hearth she has blighted,' interposed the carrier.

"'The hearth she has—how often!—blessed and brightened,' said the Cricket: 'the hearth which, but for her, were only a few stones and bricks and rusty bars, but which has been, through her, the Altar of your Home; on which you have nightly sacrificed some petty passion, selfishness, or care, and offered up the homage of a tranquil mind, a trusting nature, and an overflowing heart; so that the smoke from this poor chimney has gone upward with a better fragrance than the richest incense that is burnt before the richest shrines in all the gaudy temples of this world!—Upon your own hearth; in its quiet sanctuary; surrounded by its gentle influences and associations; hear her! Hear me! Hear everything that speaks the language of your hearth and home!'

"'And pleads for her?' inquired the carrier.

"'All things that speak the language of your hearth and home, *must* plead for her!' returned the Cricket. 'For they speak the truth.'" 3

Other Principals

Old man. "The Stranger, who had long white hair, good features, singularly bold and well defined for an old man, and dark, bright, penetrating eyes, looked round with a smile, and saluted the carrier's wife by gravely inclining his head.

"His garb was very quaint and odd—a long, long way behind the time. Its hue was brown, all over. In his hand he held a great brown club or walking-stick; and striking this upon the floor, it fell asunder, and became a chair. On which he sat down, quite composedly.

"'There!' said the carrier, turning to his wife. 'That's the way I found him, sitting by the roadside! Upright as a milestone. And almost as deaf.'" 1 *See* **John Peerybingle**—*thunderstruck, and* **Edward Plummer** O

Dot (Mary) Peerybingle. " . . . fair she was, and young, though something of what is called the dumpling shape; but I don't myself object to that . . . . [she] looked out the window, where she saw nothing, owing to the darkness, but her own face imaged in the glass. And my opinion is (and so would yours have been) that she might have looked a long way, and seen nothing half so agreeable." 1

—*and the Spirit of the Hearth:* "'The first time I heard its cheerful little note, **John**, was on that night when you brought me home . . . .

"Its chirp was such a welcome to me! It seemed so full of promise and encouragement. It seemed to say, you would be kind and gentle with me, and would not expect (I had a fear of that, John, then) to find an old head on the shoulders of your foolish little wife . . . .

"' . . . . This has been a happy home, John; and I love the Cricket for its sake!'

"'Why, so do I then,' said the carrier. 'So do I, Dot.'

"'I love it for the many times I have heard it, and the many thoughts its harmless music has given me. Sometimes, in the twilight, when I have felt a little solitary and downhearted, John—before baby was here to keep me company and make the house gay—when I have thought how lonely you would be if I should die; how lonely I should be if I could know that you had lost me, dear; its Chirp, Chirp, Chirp upon the hearth, has seemed to tell me of another little voice, so sweet, so very dear to me, before whose coming sound my trouble vanished like a dream.

"'And when I used to fear . . . that ours might prove to be an ill-assorted marriage, I being such a child, and you more like my guardian than my husband; and that you might not, however hard you tried, be able to learn to love me, as you hoped and prayed you might; its Chirp, Chirp, Chirp has cheered me up again, and filled me with new trust and confidence. I was thinking of these things to-night, dear, when I sat expecting you; and I love the Cricket for their sake!'" ¶I

—a specialty: "She was, out and out, the very best filler of a pipe, I should say, in the four quarters of the globe. To see her put that chubby little finger in the bowl, and then blow down the pipe to clear the tube, and, when she had done so, affect to think that there was really something in the tube, and blow a dozen times, and hold it to her eye like a telescope, with a most provoking twist in her capital little face, as she looked down it, was quite a brilliant thing. As to the tobacco, she was perfect mistress of the subject; and her lighting of the pipe, with a wisp of paper, when the carrier had it in his mouth—going so very near his nose, and yet not scorching it—was Art, high Art." 1

—self-restraint, and a test: "She had been above-stairs with the baby, getting it to bed. As he sat brooding on the hearth, she came close beside him, without his knowledge—in the turning of the rack of his great misery, he lost all other sounds—and put her little stool at his feet. He only knew it, when he felt her hand upon his own, and saw her looking up into his face.

"With wonder? No. It was his first impression, and he was fain to look at her again, to set it right. No, not with wonder. With an eager and inquiring look; but not with wonder. At first it was alarmed and serious; then, it changed into a strange, wild, dreadful smile of recognition of his thoughts; then, there was nothing but her clasped hands on her brow, and her bent head, and falling hair.

" . . . she rose and left him, sobbing as she went . . . . " 3

—speaking out: "'No, don't love me for another minute or two, if you please, **John**! What I want most to tell you, I have kept to the last. My dear, good, generous John, when we were talking the other night about the **Cricket**, I had it on my lips to say, that at first I did not love you quite so dearly as I do now; that when I first came home here, I was half afraid I mightn't learn to love you every bit as well as I hoped and prayed I might—being so very young, John!

"'But, dear John, every day and hour I loved you more and more. And if I could have loved you better than I do, the noble words I heard you say this morning, would have made me. But I can't. All the affection that I had (it was a great deal, John) I gave you, as you well deserve, long, long ago, and I have no more left to give. Now, my dear husband, take me to your heart again! That's my home, John; and never, never think of sending me to any other!'" *And see* **The Cricket**—*on fairy duty*

John Peerybingle. " . . . a sturdy figure of a man, much taller and much older than [**Dot**], who had to stoop a long way down to kiss her. But she was worth the trouble. Six foot six, with the lumbago, might have done it." 1

"He was often near to something or other very clever, by his own account: this lumbering, slow, honest John; this John so heavy, but so light of spirit; so rough upon the surface, but so gentle at the core; so dull without, so quick within; so stolid, but so good! Oh Mother Nature, give thy children the true poetry of heart that hid itself in this poor Carrier's breast—he was but a Carrier by the way—and we can bear to have them talking prose, and leading lives of prose; and bear to bless thee for their company!" 1

—*with his family:* "It was pleasant to see **Dot**, with her little figure, and her **baby** in her arms: a very doll of a baby: glancing with a coquettish thoughtfulness at the fire, and inclining her delicate little head just enough on one side to let it rest in an odd, half-natural, half-affected, wholly nestling and agreeable manner, on the great rugged figure of the carrier. It was pleasant to see him, with his tender awkwardness, endeavouring to adapt his rude support to her slight need, and make his burly middle-age a leaning-staff not inappropriate to her blooming youth . . . . Nor was it less agreeable to observe how John the carrier . . . checked his hand when on the point of touching the infant, as if he thought he might crack it; and bending down, surveyed it from a safe distance, with a kind of puzzled pride, such as an amiable mastiff might be supposed to show, if he found himself, one day, the father of a young canary." 1

—*thunderstruck:* "Oh Shadow on the Hearth! Oh truthful **Cricket**! Oh per-fidious Wife!

"He saw her, with the **old man**—old no longer, but erect and gallant—bearing in his hand the false white hair that had won his way into their desolate and miserable home. He saw her listening to him, as he bent his head to whisper in her ear; and suffering him to clasp her round the waist, as they moved slowly down the dim wooden gallery towards the door by which they had entered it. He saw them stop, and saw her turn—to have the face, the face he loved so, so presented to his view!—and saw her, with her own hands, adjust the lie upon his head, laughing as she did it, at his unsuspicious nature!

"He clenched his strong right hand at first, as if it would have beaten down a lion. But opening it immediately again, he spread it out before the eyes of **Tackleton** (for he was tender of her, even then), and so, as they passed out, fell down upon a desk, and was as weak as any infant." 2

—*his heart:* "It was a heart so full of love for her; so bound up and held together by innumerable threads of winning remembrance, spun from the daily working of her many qualities of endearment; it was a heart in which she had enshrined herself so gently and so closely; a heart so single and so earnest in its truth, so strong in right, so weak in wrong; that it could cherish neither passion nor revenge at first, and had only room to hold the broken image of its idol." 3

—*at the sound of a Voice:* "No sound he could have heard, no human voice, not even hers, could so have moved and softened him. The artless words in which she had told him of her love for this same **Cricket**, were once more freshly spoken; her trembling, earnest manner at the moment, was again before him; her pleasant voice—O what a voice it was, for making household music at the fireside of an honest man!—thrilled through and through his better nature, and awoke it into life and action.

"He recoiled from the door, like a man walking in his sleep, awakened from a frightful dream; and put the gun aside. Clasping his hands before his face, he then sat down again beside the fire, and found relief in tears." 3

—*the morning after:* "' . . . I knew how much I loved her, and how happy I should be,' pursued the carrier. 'But I had not—I feel it now—sufficiently considered her.'

"'To be sure,' said **Tackleton**. 'Giddiness, frivolity, fickleness, love of admiration! Not considered! All left out of sight! Hah!'

"'You had best not interrupt me,' said the carrier, with some sternness, 'till you understand me; and you're wide of doing so. If, yesterday, I'd have struck that man down at a blow, who dared to breathe a word against her, to-day I'd set my foot upon his face, if he was my brother!'" 3

—*a conclusion:* "'I sat upon that hearth, last night, all night,' exclaimed the carrier. 'On the spot where she has often sat beside me, with her sweet face looking into mine. I called up her whole life, day by day. I had her dear self, in its every passage, in review before me. And upon my soul she is innocent, if there is One to judge the innocent and guilty!'

"Staunch Cricket on the Hearth! Loyal household Fairies!

"'Passion and distrust have left me! . . . and nothing but my grief remains. In an unhappy moment some old lover, better suited to her tastes and years than I; forsaken, perhaps for me, against her will; returned. In an unhappy moment, taken by surprise, and wanting time to think of what she did, she made herself a party to his treachery, by concealing it. Last night she saw him, in the interview we witnessed. It was wrong. But otherwise than this she is innocent if there is truth on earth!'" 3

Bertha Plummer. "The Blind Girl as busy as a doll's dressmaker . . . never knew that ceilings were discoloured, walls blotched and bare of plaster here and there, high crevices unstopped and widening every day, beams mouldering and tending downward . . . that iron was rusting, wood rotting, paper peeling off. . . that sorrow and faintheartedness were in the house; that **Caleb**'s scanty hairs were turning greyer and more grey, before her sightless face. The Blind Girl never knew they had a master, cold, exacting, and uninterested . . . but lived in the belief of an eccentric humourist who loved to have his jest with them, and who, while he was the Guardian Angel of their lives, disdained to hear one word of thankfulness." 2

—*on her blindness:* "'I have sometimes wished that I could see you, or could see him [**Tackleton**]—only once, dear father, only for one little minute— that I might know what it is I treasure up . . . . That I might be sure and have it right! And sometimes (but then I was a child) I have wept in my prayers at night, to think that when your images ascended from my heart to Heaven, they might not be the true resemblances of yourselves. But I have never had these feelings long. They have passed away and left me tranquil and contented.'" 2

—*her heart:* "'Every blessing on your head! Light upon your happy course! Not the less, my dear **May**;' and she drew towards her, in a closer grasp; 'not the less, my bird, because, to-day, the knowledge that you are to be His wife has wrung my heart almost to breaking! Father, May, **Mary**! oh forgive me that it is so, for the sake of all he has done to relieve the weariness of my dark life . . . .'" 2

—*disabused:* "'The marriage that takes place to-day,' said **Caleb**, 'is with a stern, sordid, grinding man. A hard master to you and me, my dear, for many years. Ugly in his looks, and in his nature. Cold and callous always. Unlike what I have painted him to you in everything, my child . . . .

"'Oh why,' cried the Blind Girl, tortured, as it seemed, almost beyond endurance, 'why did you ever do this? Why did you ever fill my heart so full, and then come in like Death, and tear away the objects of my love? O Heaven, how blind I am! How helpless and alone!'" 3

Caleb Plummer. " . . . a little, meagre, thoughtful, dingy-faced man, who seemed to have made himself a great-coat from the sack-cloth covering of some old box; for when he turned to shut the door, and keep the weather out, he disclosed upon the back of that garment, the inscription G & T in large black capitals. Also the word GLASS in bold characters." 1

—*his home:* ". . . Caleb Plummer and his Blind Daughter lived all alone by themselves, in a little cracked nutshell of a wooden house, which was, in truth, no better than a pimple on the prominent red-brick nose of **Gruff** and **Tackleton** . . . [or] a barnacle to a ship's keel, or a snail to a door, or a little bunch of toadstools to the stem of a tree." 2

"I have said that Caleb and his poor Blind Daughter lived here. I should have said that Caleb lived here, and his poor Blind Daughter somewhere else— in an enchanted home of Caleb's furnishing, where scarcity and shabbiness were not, and trouble never entered. Caleb was no sorcerer, but in the only magic art that still remains to us, the magic of devoted, deathless love, Nature had been the mistress of his study; and from her teaching all the wonder came." 2

—*at work:* " . . . Caleb painting and glazing the four-pair front of a desirable family mansion.

"The care imprinted in the lines of Caleb's face, and his absorbed and dreamy manner, which would have sat well on some alchemist or abstruse student, were at first sight an odd contrast to his occupation, and the trivialities about him. " 2

—*deception, and its cost:* "How different the picture in [**Bertha**'s] mind, from Caleb, as he sat observing her! She had spoken of his free step. She was right in that. For years and years he had never once crossed that threshold at his own slow pace, but with a footfall counterfeited for her ear; and never had he, when his heart was heaviest, forgotten the light tread that was to render hers so cheerful and courageous!

"Heaven knows! But I think Caleb's vague bewilderment of manner may have half originated in his having confused himself about himself, and everything around him, for the love of his Blind Daughter. How could the little man be otherwise than bewildered, after labouring for so many years to destroy his own identity, and that of all the objects that had any bearing on it!" 2

—*described:* "'I see him now, despondent and bowed down, and striving against nothing. But, **Bertha**, I have seen him many times before, and striving hard in many ways for one great sacred object. And I honour his grey head, and bless him!'" 3

Tackleton. " . . . the toy-merchant was a man whose vocation had been quite misunderstood by his Parents and Guardians. If they had made him a Money Lender, or a sharp Attorney, or a Sheriff's Officer, or a Broker, he might have sown his discontented oats in his youth, and, after having had the full run of himself in ill-natured transactions, might have turned out amiable, at last, for the sake of a little freshness and novelty.

"But, cramped and chafing in the peaceable pursuit of toymaking, he was a domestic ogre, who had been living on children all his life, and was their implacable enemy. He despised all toys; wouldn't have bought one for the world; delighted, in his malice, to insinuate grim expressions into the faces of brown-paper farmers who drove pigs to market, bellmen who advertised lost lawyers' consciences, movable old ladies who darned stockings or carved pies; and other like samples of his stock in trade.

"In appalling masks; hideous, hairy, red-eyed Jacks in Boxes; Vampire Kites; demoniacal Tumblers who wouldn't lie down, and were perpetually flying forward, to stare infants out of countenance; his soul perfectly revelled. They were his only relief and safety-valve. He was great in such inventions. Anything suggestive of a pony-nightmare was delicious to him. He had even lost money (and he took to that toy very kindly) by getting up goblin slides for magic-lanterns whereon the Powers of Darkness were depicted as a sort of supernatural shell-fish, with human faces.

"In intensifying the portraiture of giants, he had sunk quite a little capital; and, though no painter himself, he could indicate, for the instruction of his artists, with a piece of chalk, a certain furtive leer for the countenances of those monsters, which was safe to destroy the peace of mind of any young gentleman between the ages of six and eleven, for the whole Christmas or Midsummer Vacation . . . .

"He . . . stood in the carrier's kitchen, with a twist in his dry face, and a screw in his body, and his hat jerked over the bridge of his nose, and his hands tucked down into the bottoms of his pockets, and his whole sarcastic ill-conditioned self peering out of one little corner of one little eye, like the concentrated essence of any number of ravens." ¶I

—*an admirer:* "'Always merry and light-hearted with us!' cried the smiling **Bertha**.

"'O, you're there, are you?' answered Tackleton. 'Poor idiot!'

"He really did believe she was an idiot; and he founded the belief, I can't say whether consciously or not, upon her being fond of him." 2 *But see* **Bertha—** *disabused*

—*at ease:* "Gruff and Tackleton was also there, doing the agreeable, with the evident sensation of being as perfectly at home, and as unquestionably in his own element, as a fresh young salmon on the top of the Great Pyramid . . . . Tackleton couldn't get on at all; and the more cheerful his intended bride became in **Dot**'s society, the less he liked it, though he had brought them together for that purpose. For he was a regular dog in the manger, was Tackleton; and when they laughed and he couldn't, he took it into his head, immediately, that they must be laughing at him." 2

—*at last:* "'**John Peerybingle**! I'm sour by disposition; but I can't help being sweetened, more or less, by coming face to face with such a man as you. **Caleb**! . . . I blush to think how easily I might have bound you and your daughter to me, and what a miserable idiot I was, when I took her for one! Friends, one and all, my house is very lonely to-night. I have not so much as a Cricket on my Hearth. I have scared them all away. Be gracious to me; let me join this happy party!'

"He was at home in five minutes. You never saw such a fellow. What *had* he been doing with himself all his life, never to have known, before, his great capacity of being jovial!" 3

Supporting Roles

Boxer. "Everybody knew him, all along the road—especially the fowls and pigs, who when they saw him approaching, with his body all on one side, and his ears pricked up inquisitively, and that knob of a tail making the most of itself in the air, immediately withdrew into remote back settlements, without waiting for the honour of a nearer acquaintance. He had business everywhere; going down all the turnings, looking into all the wells, bolting in and out of all the cottages, dashing into the midst of all the Dame-Schools, fluttering all the pigeons, magnifying the tails of all the cats, and trotting into the public houses like a regular customer." 2

—with the Blind Girl: "Boxer, by the way, made certain delicate distinctions of his own, in his communication with **Bertha**, which persuade me fully that he knew her to be blind. He never sought to attract her attention by looking at her, as he often did with other people, but touched her invariably. What experience he could ever have had of blind people or blind dogs, I don't know. He had never lived with a blind master; nor had Mr Boxer the elder, nor Mrs Boxer, nor any of his respectable family on either side, ever been visited with blindness, that I am aware of. He may have found it out for himself, perhaps, but he had got hold of it somehow; and therefore he had hold of Bertha too, by the skirt, and kept hold, until **Mrs Peerybingle** and the **baby**, and **Miss Slowboy**, and the basket, were all got safely within doors." 2

Mrs Fielding. " . . . a little querulous chip of an old lady with a peevish face, who, in right of having preserved a waist like a bed-post, was supposed to be a most transcendent figure; and who, in consequence of having once been better off, or of labouring under an impression than she might have been . . . was very genteel and patronising indeed . . . . For the better gracing of this place at the high festival, the majestic old soul had adorned herself with a cap, calculated to inspire the thoughtless with sentiments of awe. She also wore her gloves. But let us be genteel, or die!" 2

—her views: " . . . she delivered it . . . that those marriages in which there was least of what was romantically and sillily called love, were always the happiest; and that she anticipated the greatest possible amount of bliss—not rapturous bliss; but the solid, steady-going article—from the approaching nuptials." 2

Baby Peerybingle. " . . . a live baby there was in [**Dot**'s] arms; and a pretty tolerable amount of pride she seemed to have in it . . . . " 1

—going out: " . . . to get the baby under weigh took time. Not that there was much of the baby, speaking of it as a thing of weight and measure, but there was a vast deal to do about and about it, and it all had to be done by easy stages. For instance, when the baby was got, by hook and by crook, to a certain point of dressing, and you might have rationally supposed that another touch or two would finish him off, and turn him out a tip-top baby challenging the world, he was unexpectedly extinguished in a flannel cap, and hustled off to bed; where he simmered (so to speak) between two blankets for the best part

of an hour. From this state of inaction he was then recalled, shining very much and roaring violently, to partake of—well? I would rather say, if you'll permit me to speak generally—of a slight repast. After which, he went to sleep again . . . the baby, being all alive again was invested . . . with a cream-coloured mantle for its body, and a sort of nankeen raised-pie for its head; and so in course of time they all three got down to the door . . . . " 2

Tilly Slowboy. "She was of a spare and straight shape, this young lady, insomuch that her garments appeared to be in constant danger of sliding off those sharp pegs, her shoulders, on which they were loosely hung. Her costume was remarkable for the partial development, on all possible occasions, of some flannel vestment of a singular structure; also for affording glimpses, in the region of the back, of a corset, or pair of stays, in colour a dead-green.

"Being always in a state of gaping admiration at everything, and absorbed, besides, in the perpetual contemplation of her mistress's perfections and the baby's, Miss Slowboy, in her little errors of judgment, may be said to have done equal honour to her head and to her heart; and though these did less honour to the baby's head, which they were the occasional means of bringing into contact with deal doors, dressers, stair-rails, bed-posts, and other foreign substances, still they were the honest results of Tilly Slowboy's constant astonishment at finding herself so kindly treated, and installed in such a comfortable home." 1

—*dressing:* " . . . [she] insinuated herself into a spencer of a fashion so surprising and ingenious, that it had no connection with herself, or anything else in the universe, but was a shrunken, dog's-eared, independent fact, pursuing its lonely course without the least regard to anybody." 1

—*her nether limbs:* "If I might be allowed to mention a young lady's legs, on any terms, I would observe of Miss Slowboy's that there was a fatality about them which rendered them singularly liable to be grazed; and that she never effected the smallest ascent or descent, without recording the circumstance upon them with a notch, as Robinson Crusoe marked the days upon his wooden calendar." 2

—*in the way:* " . . . everybody tumbled over Tilly Slowboy and the **baby**, everywhere. Tilly never came out in such force before. Her ubiquity was the theme of general admiration. She was a stumbling-block in the passage at five-and-twenty minutes past two; a man-trap in the kitchen at half-past two precisely; and a pitfall in the garret at five-and-twenty minutes to three. The baby's head was, as it were, a test and touchstone for every description of matter—animal, vegetable, and mineral. Nothing was in use that day that didn't come, at some time or other, into close acquaintance with it." 3

Others

Fairies. "They never showed [**Dot**], otherwise than beautiful and bright, for they were Household Spirits to whom falsehood is annihilation . . . . " 3

May Fielding. "'Father. . . tell me something about May. She is very fair?'

"'She is indeed,' said **Caleb**. And she was indeed . . . .

"'Her hair is dark,' said **Bertha**, pensively, 'darker than mine. Her voice is sweet and musical, I know. I have often loved to hear it. Her shape——'

"'There's not a doll's in all the room to equal it,' said Caleb. 'And her eyes!— —'" 2

"'Mr **Tackleton**'s compliments, and as he hasn't got no use for the cake himself, p'raps you'll eat it.'" 3

Old Dot and Mrs Dot. "At last they came: a chubby little couple, jogging along in a snug and comfortable little way that quite belonged to the Dot family; and Dot and her mother, side by side, were wonderful to see. They were so like each other.

"Then, Dot's mother had to renew her acquaintance with **May**'s mother; and May's mother always stood on her gentility; and Dot's mother never stood on anything but her active little feet. And old Dot—so to call Dot's father, I forgot it wasn't his right name, but never mind—took liberties, and shook hands at first sight, and seemed to think a cap but so much starch and muslin . . . and, in **Mrs Fielding**'s summing up, was a good-natured kind of man—but coarse, my dear." 3

Edward Plummer. " . . . the sunburnt sailor-fellow, with his dark streaming hair . . . . " 3 *And see* **Old man**

Porter. "There was a tap at the door; and a man came staggering in, without saying with your leave, or by your leave, with something heavy on his head. Setting this down in the middle of the table, symmetrically in the centre of the nuts and apples, he said:

Professional assistants. " . . . hastily called in from somewhere in the neighbourhood, as on a point of life and death, ran against each other in all the doorways and round all the corners . . . . " 3

Spear-carriers

Boy, who cares for the Peerybingle horse	chirp 1
Deputy carrier, unsatisfactory to Boxer	3
Gruff: original partner in a toy manufacturer; spirit of the firm?	1

1845-46 partially in *The Daily News*   1 vol 1846 B&E **PI**
    American publication 1846 by Wiley & Putnam, New York

Pictures from Italy

CD's trip through France to Italy and his year based in Genoa with his family, from July 1844 until July 1845. He touches on Chalons, Lyons, Avignon, and Marseilles en route, and excurses to Nice. He visits and describes towns in the North. He wrote C and returned home at Christmas to read it, and that trip is sketched briefly. Venice as in a dream, then Naples and Pompeii, and a climb of Vesuvius; Florence on the return trip. The book's delights, not surprisingly, are CD's depictions of working people. CD's own family is briefly characterized.

> *"The greater part of the descriptions were written on the spot, and sent home, from time to time. . . they were at least penned in the fulness of the subject, and with the liveliest impressions of novelty and freshness."* 1

No Jesuit in Italy, to CD, peregrinated otherwise than stealthily. Clarkson Stanfield, who illustrated four of the Christmas Book's, withdrew from the commission to do *Pictures* because he perceived an anti-Catholic bias in the text. CD dealt aggressively (not convincingly) with the point (*and see* HW/CB):

> *"I hope I am not likely to be misunderstood by Professors of the Roman Catholic faith, on account of anything [herein]. I have done my best, in one of my former productions*, to do justice to them; and I trust, in this, they will do justice to me. When I mention any exhibition that impressed me as absurd or disagreeable, I do not seek to connect it, or recognise it as necessarily connected with, any essentials of their creed."* 1 [*BR? It is a tangential and inexact support for his case.]

CD did not number the sections of this work. EID numbering follows:

[The Pictures] are, of course,
very vivacious, but there is no
great need to insist on them, considered as Italian sketches; there is no
need whatever to worry about them as
a phase of the mind of Dickens when he
travelled out of England. He never travelled out of England. There is no trace in all
these amusing pages that he really felt
the great foreign things which lie in wait
for us in the south of Europe, the Latin
civilization, the Catholic Church, the
art of the centre, the endless end of
Rome. His travels are not travels
in Italy, but travels in
Dickensland."
GCICD 155

CONTENTS

France

PERSONS MENTIONED

Chevalier. " . . . a silly, old, meek-faced, garlic-eating, immeasurably polite Chevalier, with a dirty scrap of red ribbon hanging at his button-hole, as if he had tied it there to remind himself of something . . . ." 3

Concierge (the **Goblin**) at Avignon. "A little, old, swarthy woman, with a pair of flashing black eyes—proof that the world hadn't conjured down the devil within her, though it had had between sixty and seventy years to do it in . . . with some large keys in her hands . . . such a fierce, little, rapid, sparkling, energetic she-devil I never beheld. She was alight and flaming, all the time. Her action was violent in the extreme. She never spoke, without stopping expressly for the purpose. She stamped her feet, clutched us by the arms, flung herself into attitudes, hammered against the walls with her keys, for mere emphasis: now whispered as if the Inquisition were there still: now shrieked as if she were on the rack herself; and had a mysterious, hag-like way with her forefinger, when approaching the remains of some new horror—looking back and walking stealthily, and making horrible grimaces—that might alone have qualified her to walk up and down a sick man's counterpane, to the exclusion of all other figures, through a whole fever." 3

Courier [**Louis Roche**]. " . . . the radiant embodiment of good humour who sat beside me in the person of a French Courier—best of servants and most beaming of men! . . he looked a great deal more patriarchal than I, who, in the shadow of his portly presence, dwindled down to no account at all." 2

—*arriving*: "He keeps his hand upon the carriage-door, and asks some other question to enhance the expectation. He carries a green leathern purse outside his coat, suspended by a belt. The idlers look at it; one touches it. It is full of five-franc pieces. Murmurs of admiration are heard among the boys.

The **landlord** falls upon the Courier's neck, and folds him to his breast. He is so much fatter than he was, he says! He looks so rosy and so well!" 2

"The brave Courier, in particular, is everywhere: looking after the beds, having wine poured down his throat by his dear brother the landlord, and picking up green cucumbers—always cucumbers; Heaven knows where he gets them—with which he walks about, one in each hand, like truncheons." 2

—*departing:* "What has he got in his hand now? More cucumbers? No. A long strip of paper. It's the bill.

"The brave Courier has two belts on, this morning: one supporting the purse: another, a mighty good sort of leathern bottle, filled to the throat with the best light Bordeaux wine in the house. He never pays the bill till this bottle is full. Then he disputes it.

"He disputes it now, violently. He is still the landlord's brother, but by another father or mother. He is not so nearly related to him as he was last night . . . . The landlord goes into a little counting-house. The brave Courier follows, forces the bill and a pen into his hand, and talks more rapidly than ever. The landlord takes the pen. The Courier smiles. The landlord makes an alteration. The Courier cuts a joke . . . . The brave Courier traverses all round the carriage once, looks at the drag, inspects the wheels, jumps up, gives the word, and away we go!" 2

Dog. " . . . a very self-possessed dog, who had marked out for himself a little course or platform for exercise, beginning at the altar-rails and ending at the door, up and down which constitutional walk he trotted, during the service, as methodically and calmly, as any old gentleman out of doors." 3

Frenchman. " . . . the loquacious Frenchman . . . gradually patronised the **Friar** very much, and seemed to commiserate him as one who might have been born a Frenchman himself, but for an unfortunate destiny. Although his patronage was such as a mouse might bestow upon a lion, he had a vast opinion of its condescension; and in the warmth of that sentiment, occasionally rose on tiptoe, to slap the Friar on the back." 5

—*at a procession in Nice:* " . . . he squeezed himself into a front place, elaborately renovated; threw back his little coat, to show a broad-barred velvet waistcoat, sprinkled all over with stars; then adjusted himself and his cane so as utterly to bewilder and transfix the **Friar** . . . . " 5

"I observed the little Frenchman chuckle over the idea that when the Friar saw him in the broad-barred waistcoat, he would mentally exclaim, 'Is that my Patron! *That* distinguished man!' and would be covered with confusion. Ah! never was the Frenchman so deceived . . . . The Frenchman, quite humbled, took off his hat at last, but the Friar still passed on, with the same imperturbable serenity; and the broad-barred waistcoat, fading into the crowd, was seen no more." 5

Friar. " . . . a sturdy Cappuccino Friar, who had taken everybody's fancy mightily, and was one of the best friars in the world, I verily believe.

"He had a free, open countenance; and a rich brown, flowing beard; and was a remarkably handsome man, of about fifty . . . saying that, friar as he was, he would engage to take up the two strongest men on board, one after the other, with his teeth, and carry them along the deck. Nobody gave him the opportunity, but I dare say he could have done it; for he was a gallant, noble figure of a man, even in the Cappuccino dress, which is the ugliest and most ungainly that can well be." 5

" . . . it being then too late for Mass: the Friar went to work bravely: eating prodigiously of the cold meat and bread, drinking deep draughts of the wine, smoking cigars, taking snuff, sustaining an uninterrupted conversation with all hands, and occasionally running to the boat's side and hailing somebody on shore with the intelligence that we *must* be got out of this quarantine somehow or other, as he had to take part in a great religious procession in the afternoon." 5

—*at a procession in Nice:* "As our friend the Cappuccino advanced, with folded arms, he looked straight into the visage of the little **Frenchman**, with a bland, serene, composed abstraction, not to be described. There was not the faintest trace of recognition or amusement on his features; not the smallest consciousness of bread and meat, wine, snuff, or cigars . . . . He walked in great state; being one of the Superiors of the Order: and looked his part to admiration. There never was anything so perfect of its kind as the contemplative way in which he allowed his placid gaze to rest on us, his late companions, as if he had never seen us in his life and didn't see us then." 5

Hairdresser, at Marseilles. " . . . a hairdresser's shop opposite, exhibiting in one of its windows two full-length waxen ladies, twirling round and round: which so enchanted the hairdresser himself, that he and his family sat in armchairs, and in cool undresses, on the pavement outside, enjoying the gratification of the passers-by, with lazy dignity. The family had retired to rest when we went to bed, at midnight; but the hairdresser (a corpulent man, in drab slippers) was still sitting there, with his legs stretched out before him, and evidently couldn't bear to have the shutters put up." 4

Landlord. "The landlord of the Hotel de l'Écu d'Or dotes to that extent upon the **Courier**, that he can hardly wait for his coming down from the box, but embraces his very legs and boot-heels as he descends." 2

—*altering the bill:* "The landlord is affectionate, but not weakly so. He bears it like a man. He shakes hands with his brave brother [the **Courier**]; but he don't hug him. Still, he loves his brother; for he knows that he will be returning that way, one of these fine days, with another family, and he foresees that his heart will yearn towards him again." 2

Postillion, "who has a very long whip, and drives his team, something like the Courier of Saint Petersburg in the circle at Astley's or Franconi's: only he sits his own horse instead of standing on him. The immense jack-boots worn by these postillions, are sometimes a century or two old; and are so ludicrously disproportionate to the wearer's foot, that the spur, which is put where his own heel comes, is generally halfway up the legs of the boots.

"The man often comes out of the stable-yard, with his whip in his hand and his shoes on, and brings out, in both hands, one boot at a time, which he plants on the ground by the side of his horse, with great gravity, until everything is ready. When it is . . . he gets into the boots, shoes and all, or is hoisted into them by a couple of friends; adjusts the rope harness, embossed by the labours of innumerable pigeons in the stables; makes all the horses kick and plunge; cracks his whip like a madman; shouts 'En route—Hi!' and away we go. He is sure to have a contest with his horse before we have gone very far; and then he calls him a Thief, and a Brigand, and a Pig, and what not; and beats him about the head as if he were made of wood." ¶2

Sacristan. " . . . very solemn and grand [the cathedral] is, in the dim light: so dim at last, that the polite, old, lantern-jawed Sacristan has a feeble little bit of candle in his hand, to grope among the tombs with—and looks among the grim columns, very like a lost ghost who is searching for his own." 2

Vetturino. "The half-French, half-Italian Vetturino, who undertook, with his little rattling carriage and pair, to convey us [from Nice to Genoa] in three days, was a careless, good-looking fellow, whose light-heartedness and singing propensities knew no bounds as long as we went on smoothly. So long, he had a word and a smile, and a flick of his whip, for all the peasant girls, and odds and ends of the Sonnambula for all the echoes. So long, he went jingling through every little village, with bells on his horses and rings in his ears: a very meteor of gallantry and cheerfulness.

"But, it was highly characteristic to see him under a slight reverse of circumstances . . . . His hands were twined in his hair immediately, as if a combination of all the direst accidents in life had suddenly fallen on his devoted head. He swore in French, prayed in Italian, and went up and down, beating his feet on the ground in a very ecstasy of despair." ¶5

Card-players, hairy company; cards like them are limp and dirty	9
Chambermaid, at the Hotel de l'Écu d'Or, Chalons	2
Curé, shovel hat, black gown; book in one hand, umbrella in the other	2
Dickens, Catherine; the lady of the family: sweet lady! beautiful lady!	2
Charles Culliford Boz, aged seven: Ah, what a beautiful little boy!	2
Francis Jeffrey, a few months old: Angelic baby! All rapture expended!	2
Kate Macready, five; out of the coach at the Hotel de l'Écu d'Or	2
Mary (Mamie), six: Oh, but this is an enchanting child!	2
Walter Landor, three: Oh, the sweet boy! Oh, the tender little family!	2
Guest, at l'Ecu d'O; glazed cap, red beard like a bosom friend	2
Georgina Hogarth, at l'Écu d'Or: Great Heaven, Ma'amselle is charming!	2
Landlady, at l'Écu d'Or; yielding to the finest impulse of our common nature	2
Nurses, two; they tumble out of the coach	2
Porter, who persisted in asking questions; delicious purchases in his basket	3
Scavengers: extraordinary adventurers in heaps of rags, raking snowy streets	9
Servants, at l'Écu d'Or; supper in open air; thin wine, very merry	2
Soldier, small: all the little men in France are soldiers, big ones postillions	2
Woman, at Avignon; sober (she must have a congenial life, with the Goblin)	4

Genoa and the North of Italy; and Switzerland

PERSONS MENTIONED

Antonio. " . . . three cows . . . are presided over, and slept with, by an old man named Antonio, and his **son**; two burnt-sienna natives with naked legs and feet, who wear, each, a shirt, a pair of trousers, and a red sash, with a relic, or some sacred charm like the bonbon of a twelfth-cake, hanging round the neck. The old man is very anxious to convert me to the Catholic faith, and exhorts me frequently. We sit upon a stone by the door, sometimes in the evening, like Robinson Crusoe and Friday reversed; and he generally relates, towards my conversion, an abridgment of the History of Saint Peter—chiefly, I believe, from the unspeakable delight he has in his imitation of the cock." 5

Baby. " . . . an unfortunate baby, tightly swathed up, arms and legs and all, in an enormous quantity of wrapper, so that it is unable to move a toe or finger . . . I had no more idea, until the ceremony was all over, that it was a baptism, or that the curious little stiff instrument, that was passed from one to another, in the course of the ceremony, by the handle—like a short poker— was a child, than I had that it was my own christening. I borrowed the child afterwards, for a minute or two (it was lying across the font then), and found it very red in the face but perfectly quiet, and not to bent on any terms. The number of cripples in the streets, soon ceased to surprise me." 5

Beggars, at Parma. " . . . such crowds of phantom-looking men and women, leading other men and women with twisted limbs or chattering jaws, or paralytic gestures, or idiotic heads, or some other sad infirmity, came hobbling out to beg . . . . " 6

Capuchin monks. "Having been duly astonished, here, by the sight of a few Cappuccini monks, who were watching the fair-weighing of some wood upon the wharf . . . ." 4

"Perhaps the Cappuccini, though not a learned body, are, as an order, the best friends of the people. They seem to mingle with them more immediately, as their counsellors and comforters; and to go among them more, when they are sick; and to pry less than some other orders, into the secrets of families, for the purpose of establishing a baleful ascendency over their weaker members; and to be influenced by a less fierce desire to make converts, and once made, to let them go to ruin, soul and body." 5

Cicerone, at Bologna, "who was excessively anxious for the honour of the place, and most solicitous to divert my attention from the bad monuments: whereas he was never tired of extolling the good ones. Seeing this little man (a good-humoured little man he was, who seemed to have nothing in his face but shining teeth and eyes) looking wistfully at a certain plot of grass, I asked him who was buried there. 'The poor people, Signore,' he said, with a shrug and a smile, and stopping to look back at me—for he always went on a little before, and took off his hat to introduce every new monument. ' . . . . There are five'— holding up all the fingers of his right hand to express the number, which an Italian peasant will always do, if it be within the compass of his ten fingers— 'there are five of my little children buried there, Signore; just there; a little to the right. Well! Thanks to God! It's very cheerful. How green it is, how cool it is! It's quite a meadow!'

"He looked me very hard in the face, and seeing I was sorry for him, took a pinch of snuff (every Cicerone takes snuff), and made a little bow; partly in deprecation of his having alluded to such a subject, and partly in memory of the children and of his favourite saint. It was as unaffected and as perfectly natural a little bow, as ever man made. Immediately afterwards, he took his hat off altogether, and begged to introduce me to the next monument; and his eyes and his teeth shone brighter than before." 6

Cicerone, at Mantua. " . . . an intensely shabby little man looked in, to inquire if the gentleman would have a Cicerone to show the town. His face was so very wistful and anxious, in the half-opened doorway, and there was so much poverty expressed in his faded suit and little pinched hat, and in the threadbare worsted glove with which he held it—not expressed the less, because these were evidently his genteel clothes, hastily slipped on—that I would as soon have trodden on him as dismissed him." 9

" . . . he stood, beaming by himself in a corner, making a feint of brushing my hat with his arm. If his fee had been as many napoleons as it was francs, there could not have shot over the twilight of his shabbiness such a gleam of sun, as lighted up the whole man, now that he was hired." 9

Conductor. " . . . the organ played away, lustily, and a full band did the like; while a conductor, in a little gallery opposite to the band, hammered away on the desk before him, with a scroll; and a tenor, without any voice, sang. The band played one way, the organ played another, the singer went a third, and the unfortunate conductor banged and banged, and flourished his scroll on some principle of his own: apparently well satisfied with the whole performance." 5

Courier (the **Brave**). "Before I can sit down in my own chamber [at an inn in Stradella] and think it of the dampest, the door opens, and the Brave comes moving in, in the middle of such a quantity of fuel that he looks like Birnam Wood taking a winter walk. He kindles this heap in a twinkling, and produces a jorum of hot brandy and water; for that bottle of his keeps company with the seasons, and now holds nothing but the purest *eau de vie*. When he has accomplished this feat, he retires for the night; and I hear him, for an hour afterwards, and indeed until I fall asleep, making jokes in some outhouse (apparently under the pillow), where he is smoking cigars with a party of confidential friends. He never was in the house in his life before; but he knows everybody everywhere, before he has been anywhere five minutes; and is certain to have attracted to himself in the meantime, the enthusiastic devotion of the whole establishment.

"This is at twelve o'clock at night. At four o'clock next morning, he is up again, fresher than a new-blown rose; making blazing fires without the least authority from the landlord; producing mugs of scalding coffee when nobody else can get anything but cold water; and going out into the dark streets, and roaring for fresh milk, on the chance of somebody with a cow getting up to supply it." 6

—*dealing with Customs:* "The brave Courier and the soldiery had first quarrelled, for half an hour or more, over our eternal passport. But this was a daily relaxation with the Brave, who was always stricken deaf when shabby functionaries in uniform came, as they constantly did come, plunging out of wooden boxes to look at it—or in other words to beg—and who, stone deaf to my entreaties that the man might have a trifle given him, and we resume our journey in peace, was wont to sit reviling the functionary in broken English: while the unfortunate man's face was a portrait of mental agony framed in the coach window, from his perfect ignorance of what was being said to his disparagement." 7

Jesuit. " . . . we were packed up . . . in company with a very old **priest**; a young Jesuit, his companion—who carried their breviaries and other books, and who, in the exertion of getting into the coach, had made a gash of pink leg between his black stocking and his black knee-shorts, that reminded one of Hamlet in Ophelia's closet, only it was visible on both legs ...."6

Jews, in Mantua. " . . . there were some business-dealings going on, and some profits realising; for there were arcades full of Jews, where those extraordinary people were sitting outside their shops, contemplating their stores of stuffs, and woollens, and bright handkerchiefs, and trinkets: and looking, in all respects, as wary and business-like, as their brethren in Houndsditch, London." 9

Ladies, at Modena. " . . . six or eight Roman chariots: each with a beautiful lady in extremely short petticoats, and unnaturally pink tights, erect within: shedding beaming looks upon the crowd, in which there was a latent expression of discomposure and anxiety, for which I couldn't account, until, as the open back of each chariot presented itself, I saw the immense difficulty with which the pink legs maintained their perpendicular, over the uneven pavement of the town: which gave me quite a new idea of the ancient Romans and Britons." 6

Landlord. " . . . Bozzolo . . . now one of the most deserted and poverty-stricken of towns: where the landlord of the miserable inn (God bless him! it was his weekly custom) was distributing infinitesimal coins among a clamorous herd of women and children, whose rags were fluttering in the wind and rain outside his door, where they were gathered to receive his charity." 9

Man, legless. " . . . on a little go-cart, but who has such a fresh-coloured, lively face, and such a respectable, well-conditioned body, that he looks as if he had sunk into the ground up to his middle, or had come, but partially, up a flight of cellar-steps to speak to somebody." 5

Men of Albaro. "The men, in red caps, and with loose coats hanging on their shoulders (they never put them on), were playing bowls, and buying sweetmeats, immediately outside the church. When half-a-dozen of them finished a game, they came into the aisle, crossed themselves with the holy water, knelt on one knee for an instant, and walked off again to play another game at bowls. They are remarkably expert at this diversion, and will play in the stony lanes and streets, and on the most uneven and disastrous ground for such a purpose, with as much nicety as on a billiard-table." 5

Monk, in a dream. " . . . at midnight, the confessor came—a monk brown-robed, and hooded—ghastly in the day, and free bright air, but in the mid-night of that murky prison, Hope's extinguisher, and Murder's herald." 8

Official. "There was such a very smart official in attendance at the Bologna Cemetery . . . that when the little **Cicerone** suggested to me, in a whisper, that there would be no offence in presenting this officer, in return for some slight extra service, with a couple of pauls (about tenpence, English money), I looked incredulously at his cocked hat, wash-leather gloves, well-made uniform, and dazzling buttons . . . . For in splendour of appearance, he was at least equal to the Deputy Usher of the Black Rod . . . . He took it in excellent part, however, when I made bold to give it him, and pulled off his cocked hat with a flourish that would have been a bargain at double the money." 7

Old man. "There was a little fiery-eyed old man with a crooked shoulder, in the cathedral, who took it very ill that I made no effort to see the bucket (kept in an old tower) which the people of Modena took away from the people of Bologna in the fourteenth century . . . . " 6

Old women. " . . . the withered old women, with their wiry grey hair twisted up into a knot on the top of the head, like a pad to carry loads on, are so intensely ugly, both along the Rivera, and in Genoa, too, that, seen straggling about in dim doorways with their spindles, or crooning together in by-corners, they are like a population of Witches—except that they certainly are not to be suspected of brooms or any other instrument of cleanliness." 5

Peasant women, around Genoa. "The Peasant Women, with naked feet and legs, are so constantly washing clothes, in the public tanks, and in every stream and ditch, that one cannot help wondering, in the midst of all this dirt, who wears them when they are clean. The custom is to lay the wet linen which is being operated upon, on a smooth stone, and hammer away at it, with a flat wooden mallet. This they do, as furiously as if they were revenging themselves on dress in general for being connected with the Fall of Mankind." 5

Samuel Pepys "once heard a clergyman assert in his sermon, in illustration of his respect for the Priestly office, that if he could meet a Priest and angel together, he would salute the Priest first." 5

[Francesco] Petrarch, "who, when **[Boccaccio]** wrote to him in great tribulation, that he had been visited and admonished for his writings by a Carthusian Friar who claimed to be a messenger immediately commissioned by Heaven for that purpose, replied, that for his own part, he would take the liberty of testing the reality of the commission by personal observation of the Messenger's face, eyes, forehead, behaviour, and discourse." 5

Physicians. "Most of the apothecaries' shops are great lounging-places. Here, grave men with sticks, sit down in the shade for hours together, passing a meagre Genoa paper from hand to hand, and talking, drowsily and sparingly, about the News. Two or three of these are poor physicians, ready to proclaim themselves on an emergency, and tear off with any messenger who may arrive. You may know them by the way in which they stretch their necks to listen, when you enter; and by the sigh with which they fall back again into their dull corners, on finding that you only want medicine." 5

Postillion, out of Ferrara. "There was a postillion, in the course of this day's journey, as wild and savagely good-looking a vagabond as you would desire to see. He was a tall, stout-made, dark-complexioned fellow, with a profusion of shaggy black hair hanging all over his face, and great black whiskers stretching down his throat.

"His dress was a torn suit of rifle green, garnished here and there with red; a steeple-crowned hat, innocent of nap, with a broken and bedraggled feather stuck in the band; and a flaming red neckerchief hanging on his shoulders. He was not in the saddle, but reposed, quite at his ease, on a sort of low foot-board in front of the post-chaise, down amongst the horses' tails—convenient for having his brains kicked out, at any moment.

"To this Brigand, the brave **Courier**, when we were at a reasonable trot, happened to suggest the practicability of going faster. He received the proposal with a perfect yell of derision; brandished his whip about his head (such a whip! it was more like a home-made bow); flung up his heels, much higher than the horses'; and disappeared, in a paroxysm, somewhere in the neighbourhood of the axletree.

"I fully expected to see him lying in the road, a hundred yards behind, but up came the steeple-crowned hat again, next minute, and he was seen reposing, as on a sofa, entertaining himself with the idea, and crying, 'Haha! what next! Oh the devil! Faster too! Shoo-hoo-o-o!' (This last ejaculation, an inexpressibly defiant hoot.)." ¶7

Postillion, at Piacenza. "[This] concentrated essence of all the shabbiness of Italy, pauses for a moment in his animated conversation, to touch his hat to a blunt-nosed little Virgin, hardly less shabby than himself . . . . " 6

Rowers, in a dream. " . . . the rowers, with a low melodious cry of warning, sent [the boat] skimming on without a pause. Sometimes, the rowers of another black boat like our own, echoed the cry, and slackening their speed (as I thought we did ours) would come flitting past us like a dark shadow." 8

Travellers. "As we went sledging on, there came out of the [Simplon] Hospice . . . a group of Peasant travellers, with staves and knapsacks, who had rested there last night: attended by a **Monk** or two, their hospitable entertainers, trudging slowly forward with them, for company's sake." 9

Very old man, in Verona. " . . . there was a collection . . . of Greek, Roman, and Etruscan remains, presided over by an ancient man who might have been an Etruscan relic himself; for he was not strong enough to open the iron gate, when he had unlocked it, and had neither voice enough to be audible when he described the curiosities, nor sight enough to see them: he was so very old." 9

Waiter, at an inn in Bologna, "of one idea in connexion with the English; and the subject of this harmless monomania, was Lord Byron . . . . At first, I took it for granted, in my innocence, that he had been one of the Beeron servants; but no, he said, no, he was in the habit of speaking about my Lord, to English gentlemen; that was all. He knew all about him, he said. In proof of it, he connected him with every possible topic, from the Monte Pulciano wine at dinner (which was grown on an estate he had owned), to the big bed itself, which was the very model of his. When I left the inn, he coupled with his final bow in the yard, a parting assurance that the road by which I was going, had been Milor Beeron's favourite ride . . . . " 7

To Rome; including Pisa and Siena

PERSONS MENTIONED

The following entries are quoted from chapter 11 unless otherwise indicated

Artists, "in inconceivable hats of the middle-ages, and beards (thank Heaven!) of no age at all, flashed picturesque scowls about them from their stations in the throng. One gentleman (connected with the fine arts, I presume) went up and down in a pair of Hessian-boots, with a red beard hanging down to his breast, and his long and bright red hair, plaited into two tails, one on either side of his head, which fell over his shoulders in front of him, very nearly to his waist, and were carefully entwined and braided!"

Beggars. "If Pisa be the seventh wonder of the world in right of its Tower, it may claim to be, at least, the second or third in right of its beggars. They waylay the unhappy visitor at every turn, escort him to every door he enters at, and lie in wait for him, with strong reinforcements, at every door by which they know he must come out. The grating of the portal on its hinges is the signal for a general shout, and the moment he appears, he is hemmed in, and fallen on, by heaps of rags and personal distortions. The beggars seem to embody all the trade and enterprise of Pisa. Nothing else is stirring, but warm air." 10

Boys, at the Holy Staircase. "A whole school of boys, twenty at least, were about half-way up—evidently enjoying it very much. They were all wedged together, pretty closely; but the rest of the company gave the boys as wide a berth as possible, in consequence of their betraying some recklessness in the management of their boots."

Boys, at St Peter's. " . . . there are certain schools and seminaries, priestly and otherwise, that come in, twenty or thirty strong. These boys always kneel down in single file, one behind the other, with a tall grim master in a black gown, bringing up the rear: like a pack of cards arranged to be tumbled down at a touch, with a disproportionately large Knave of clubs at the end. When they have had a minute or so at the chief altar, they scramble up, and filing off to the chapel of the Madonna, or the sacrament, flop down again in the same order; so that if anybody *did* stumble against the master, a general and sudden overthrow of the whole line must inevitably ensue."

Carnival participants. " . . . I was fortunate enough to observe one gentleman attired as a **Greek warrior**, catch a light-whiskered **brigand** on the nose (he was in the very act of tossing up a bouquet to a **young lady** in a first-floor window) with a precision that was much applauded by the bystanders. As this victorious Greek was exchanging a facetious remark with a stout **gentleman** in a doorway—one-half black and one-half white, as if he had been peeled up the middle—who had offered him his congratulations on this achievement, he received an orange from a house-top, full on his left ear, and was much surprised, not to say discomfited. Especially, as he was standing up at the time; and in consequence of the carriage moving on suddenly, at the same moment, staggered ignominiously, and buried himself among his flowers."

" . . . in every nook and corner, from the pavement to the chimney-tops, where **women**'s eyes could glisten, there they danced, and laughed, and sparkled, like the light in water. Every sort of bewitching madness of dress was there. Little preposterous scarlet jackets; quaint old stomachers, more wicked than the smartest bodices; Polish pelisses, strained and tight as ripe gooseberries; tiny Greek caps, all awry, and clinging to the dark hair, Heaven knows how; every wild, quaint, bold, shy, pettish, madcap fancy had its illustration in a dress; and every fancy was as dead forgotten by its owner, in the tumult of merriment, as if the three old aqueducts that still remain entire had brought Lethe into Rome, upon their sturdy arches, that morning."

Cicerone. "There was a professional Cicerone always attached to the party . . . and if he so much as looked at **Mrs Davis**, she invariably cut him short by saying, 'There, God bless the man, don't worrit me! I don't understand a word you say, and shouldn't if you was to talk till you was black in the face!'"

The **Davises**. " . . . a company of English Tourists, with whom I had an ardent, but ungratified longing, to establish a speaking acquaintance. They were one Mr Davis, and a small circle of friends. It was impossible not to know Mrs Davis's name, from her being always in great request among her party, and her party being everywhere."

" . . . I hardly ever observed Mrs Davis to be silent for a moment . . . . I don't think she ever saw anything, or ever looked at anything; and she had always lost something out of a straw hand-basket, and was trying to find it, with all her might and main, among an immense quantity of English halfpence, which lay, like sands upon the sea-shore, at the bottom of it."

"Mr Davis always had a snuff-coloured great-coat on, and carried a great green umbrella in his hand, and had a slow curiosity constantly devouring him, which prompted him to do extraordinary things, such as taking the covers off urns in tombs, and looking in at the ashes as if they were pickles—and tracing out inscriptions with the ferrule of his umbrella, and saying, with intense thoughtfulness, 'Here's a B you see, and there's a R, and this is the way we goes on in; is it?' His antiquarian habits occasioned his being frequently in the rear of the rest; and one of the agonies of Mrs Davis, and the party in general, was an ever-present fear that Davis would be lost. This caused them to scream for him, in the strangest places, and at the most improper seasons . . . he came slowly emerging out of some sepulchre or other, like a peaceful Ghoul, saying 'Here I am!' . . . . "

Ecclesiastics, at St Peter's. "Upon the green carpet itself, and gathered round the altar, was a perfect army of cardinals and priests, in red, gold, purple, violet, white, and fine linen. Stragglers from these, went to and fro among the crowd, conversing two and two, or giving and receiving introductions, and exchanging salutations; other functionaries in black gowns, and other functionaries in court-dresses, were similarly engaged."

Englishman, at the foot-washing ceremony. " . . . one Englishman seemed to have embarked the whole energy of his nature in the determination to discover whether there was any mustard. 'By Jupiter there's vinegar!' I heard him say to his friend, after he had stood on tiptoe an immense time, and had been crushed and beaten on all sides. 'And there's oil! I saw them distinctly, in cruets! Can any gentleman, in front there, see mustard on the table? Sir, will you oblige me? *Do* you see a Mustard-Pot?'"

Fishermen, at Camoglia. " . . . on the parapet of the rude pier, a few amphibious-looking fellows lie asleep, with their legs dangling over the wall, as though earth or water were all one to them, and if they slipped in, they would float away, dozing comfortably among the fishes . . . . " 10

Friars, at St Peter's. "Dotted here and there, were little knots of friars (Francescani, or Cappuccini, in their coarse brown dresses and peaked hoods) making a strange contrast to the gaudy ecclesiastics of higher degree, and having their humility gratified to the utmost, by being shouldered about, and elbowed right and left, on all sides. Some of these had muddy sandals and umbrellas, and stained garments: having trudged in from the country. The faces of the greater part were as coarse and heavy as their dress; their dogged, monotonous stare at all the glory and splendour, having something in it, half miserable, and half ridiculous."

Kneeling **gentleman**. " . . . a sedate gentleman with a very thick walking-staff, arose from his devotions to belabour his dog, who was growling at another dog: and whose yelps and howls resounded through the church, as his master quietly relapsed into his former train of meditation—keeping his eye upon the dog, at the same time, nevertheless."

Guards. "The gentlemen of the Pope's guard, in red coats, leather breeches, and jack-boots . . . with drawn swords that were very flashy in every sense . . . . the Pope's Swiss guard, who wear a quaint striped surcoat, and striped tight legs, and carry halberds like those which are usually shouldered by those theatrical supernumeraries, who never *can* get off the stage fast enough. . . . "

Ladies, at the feet-washing ceremony. "The ladies were particularly ferocious, in their struggles for places. One lady of my acquaintance was seized round the waist, in the ladies' box, by a strong matron, and hoisted out of her place; and there was another lady (in a back row in the same box) who improved her position by sticking a large pin into the ladies before her."

Man, with a ladder, "lighting a great quantity of candles; but at each and every opening, there was a terrific rush made at this ladder and this man . . . . The man was never brought down, however, nor the ladder; for it performed the strangest antics in the world among the crowd—where it was carried by the man, when the candles were all lighted . . . . "

Thirteen **men**, at the feet-washing ceremony, "representing the twelve apostles, and Judas Iscariot . . . sitting 'all of a row,' on a very high bench, and looking particularly uncomfortable . . . . They are robed in white; and on their heads they wear a stiff white cap, like a large English porter-pot, without a handle. Each carries in his hand, a nosegay, of the size of a fine cauliflower; and two of them, on this occasion, wore spectacles; a droll appendage to the costume. There was a great eye to character. St. John was represented by a good-looking young man. St Peter, by a grave-looking old gentleman, with a flowing brown beard; and Judas Iscariot by such an enormous hypocrite (I could not make out, though, whether the expression of his face was real or assumed) that if he had acted the part to the death and had gone away and hanged himself, he would have left nothing to be desired."

"The manner in which Judas grew more white-livered over his victuals, and languished, with his head on one side, as if he had no appetite, defies all description."

"Peter was a good, sound, old man, and went in, as the saying is, 'to win;' eating everything that was given him (he got the best: being first in the row) and saying nothing to anybody."

Murderer. "He was newly married, and gave some of [the **Countess's**] apparel to his **wife**: saying that he had bought it at a fair."

" . . . he appeared on the platform, bare-footed; his hands bound; and with the collar and neck of his shirt cut away, almost to the shoulder. A young man—six-and-twenty—vigorously made, and well-shaped. Face pale; small dark moustache; and dark brown hair."

Old man, at St Peter's. "There was a great pile of candles lying down on the floor near me, which a very old man in a rusty black grown with an open-work tippet, like a summer ornament for a fireplace in tissue-paper, made himself very busy in dispensing to all the ecclesiastics: one a-piece."

Ox-driver, at Carrara. "When we stood aside, to see one of these cars drawn by only a pair of oxen (for it had but one small block of marble on it), coming down, I hailed, in my heart, the man who sat upon the heavy yoke, to keep it on the neck of the poor beasts—and who faced backwards: not before him—as the very Devil of true despotism. He had a great rod in his hand, with an iron point; and when they could plough and force their way through the loose bed of the torrent no longer, and came to a stop, he poked it into their bodies, beat it on their heads, screwed it round and round in their nostrils, got them on a yard or two, in the madness of intense pain . . . and when their writhing and smarting, and the weight behind them, bore them plunging down the precipice in a cloud of scattered water, whirled his rod above his head, and gave a great whoop and hallo, as if he had achieved something, and had no idea that they might shake him off, and blindly mash his brains upon the road, in the noontide of his triumph." 10

Penitents, on the Holy Staircase. "This man touched every stair with his forehead, and kissed it; that man scratched his head all the way . . . most of the penitents came down, very sprightly and fresh, as having done a real good substantial deed which it would take a good deal of sin to counterbalance . . . . "

Pope. "I must say, that I never saw anything, out of November, so like the popular English commemoration of the fifth of that month [Guy Fawkes Day]. A bundle of matches and a lantern, would have made it perfect. Nor did the Pope, himself, at all mar the resemblance, though he has a pleasant and venerable face; for as this part of the ceremony [he is carried in his chair about the church] makes him giddy and sick, he shuts his eyes when it is performed: and having his eyes shut and a great mitre on his head, and his head itself wagging to and fro as they shook him in carrying, he looked as if his mask were going to tumble off."

Priests. " . . . a great many priests, walking two and two, and carrying—the good-looking priests at least—their lighted tapers, so as to throw the light with a good effect upon their faces: for the room was darkened. Those who were not handsome, or who had not long beards, carried *their* tapers anyhow, and abandoned themselves to spiritual contemplation."

Shepherd, on the Campagna. " . . . a villainous-looking shepherd: with matted hair all over his face, and himself wrapped to the chin in a frowzy brown mantle, tending his sheep." 10

Singers, at St Peter's. "The singers were in a crib of wirework (like a large meat-safe or bird-cage) in one corner; and sang most atrociously."

Worshippers, at St Peter's. " . . . some few steady persons in black cassocks, who had knelt down with their faces to the wall, and were poring over their missals, became, unintentionally, a sort of humane man-traps, and with their own devout legs, tripped up other people's by the dozen."

Aurelius, Marcus; emperor and philosopher
Bernini, Gianlorenzo; painter and sculptor
Boy, a dirty ragamuffin, who had walked in from the street
Brigand, in Carnival
Canova, Antonio; sculptor
Catholic tourists, two or three gentleman and ladies (not Italians)
Cato, Marcius Porcius the Elder; ancient Roman statesman
Choristers
Cicero, Marcus Tullius; ancient Roman statesman and orator
Cicerone, a guide to English tourists; Mrs Davis always cut him short
Cigar-merchant, with an earthen pot of charcoal ashes in one hand
Coachman; stops abruptly and uncovers; a van comes by preceded by a cross
Correggio, Antonio Allegri da; painter
Countess, Bavarian; waylaid by a murder on a pilgrimage to Rome on foot
Dolci, Carlo; painter
Domenichino (Zampieri)
Dragoons
Executioner
Foot-soldiers; two or three hundred, under arms, standing at ease in clusters
Friar, gaunt Franciscan, with a wild bright eye; guide in the Catacombs
Gentleman, Catholic; near relation of a priest
-stout; participating in the Carnival
Greek warrior, costumed for the Carnival
Guido; sculptor
Harris, a bookseller   10
Iscariot, Judas; represented in the feet-washing ceremony
Jesuits, at St Peter's; stealthy; creeping in and out
Ladies at St Peter's, in a large box on either side of the altar; black dress and veils
Lady, praying in church; got up to give her business card as music teacher
-on Holy Staircase; demure, looking back to assure her legs properly disposed
Man, bearing a large cross before a procession
-on the Holy Staircase; with an umbrella, hoisting himself from stair to stair
Monk, hollow-cheeked, lighting candles
-putting clerical robes over his coarse brown habit

Murillo, Bartolome Esteban; Spanish painter
Music teacher, praying in church; got up to give her business card
Officer, corpulent, in a cocked hat
-*pl* walking up and down in twos and threes, chatting and smoking cigars
Old gentleman, in a watch-box; rattled a tin canister to remind he took money
Pastry-merchant; divided attention between scaffold and his customers
Pompey, Gnaeus; ancient Roman general
Priest, warning against the Bambino relic into a sick woman's chamber
-chaunting as he goes
Raphael (Rafaello Sanzio); painter
Rembrandt (Harmenszoon van Rijn); Dutch painter
Romans; fierce-looking, of the lowest class; blue cloaks, russet cloaks, rags
Rosa, Salvator; painter
Simond; travel writer   10
Spagnoletto; painter
Titian (Tiziano Veceli); Venetian painter
Torch-bearer
Trajan, Roman emperor
Vandyke, Anthony (or **Van Dyck**); Flemish painter
Vetturino [driver for hire], good-tempered; with four horses; hired for the trip to Rome   10
Waitress; like a dramatic brigand's wife, with the same headdress   10
Wife, of murderer
Wiseman, Nicholas Cardinal; published four lectures on Holy Week ceremonies   1
Women, Carnival participants
Young lady, participant in the Carnival

Diorama

PERSONS MENTIONED

The following entries are quoted from chapter 12 unless otherwise indicated

Boy, "who is to draw the numbers [for the Naples lottery] . . . becomes the prominent feature of the proceedings. He is already dressed for his part, in a tight brown Holland coat, with only one (the left) sleeve to it, which leaves his right arm bared to the shoulder, ready for plunging down into the mysterious chest."

Capo Lazzarone, for the lottery. " . . . a kind of tribune of the people, appointed on their behalf to see that all is fairly conducted . . . . A ragged swarthy fellow he is: with long matted hair hanging down all over his face: and covered, from head to foot, with most unquestionably genuine dirt."

"The only new incident in the proceedings, is the gradually deepening intensity of the change in the Capo Lazzarone, who has, evidently, speculated to the very utmost extent of his means; and who, when he sees the last number, and finds that it is not one of his, clasps his hands, and raises his eyes to the ceiling before proclaiming it, as though remonstrating, in a secret agony, with his patron saint, for having committed so gross a breach of confidence. I hope the Capo Lazzarone may not desert him for some other member of the Calendar, but he seems to threaten it."

Galley-slave, "in chains, who wants a letter written to a friend. He approaches a clerkly-looking man, sitting under the corner arch, and makes his bargain. He has obtained permission of the **sentinel** who guards him: who stands near, leaning against the wall and cracking nuts. The galley-slave dictates in the ear of the **letter-writer**, what he desires to say; and as he can't read writing, looks intently in his face, to read there whether he sets down faithfully what he is told.

"After a time, the galley-slave becomes discursive—incoherent. The secretary pauses and rubs his chin. The galley-slave is voluble and energetic. The secretary, at length, catches the idea, and with the air of a man who knows how to word it, sets it down; stopping, now and then, to glance back at his text admiringly. The galley-slave is silent. The soldier stoically cracks his nuts.

"Is there anything more to say? inquires the letter-writer. No more. Then listen, friend of mine. He reads it through. The galley-slave is quite enchanted. It is folded, and addressed, and given to him, and he pays the fee. The secretary falls back indolently in his chair, and takes a book. The galley-slave gathers up an empty sack. The sentinel throws away a handful of nut-shells, shoulders his musket, and away they go together." ¶

Gentleman. " . . . the third [litter], to a rather heavy gentleman from Naples, whose hospitality and good-nature have attached him to the expedition, and determined him to assist in doing the honours of the mountain [Vesuvius]. The rather heavy gentleman is carried by fifteen men . . . . "

Grand Duke of Florence "has a worthier secret passage through the streets, in his black robe and hood, as a member of the Compagnia della Misericordia, which brotherhood includes all ranks of men . . . . Those who are on duty for the time, are all called together, on a moment's notice, by the tolling of the great bell of the Tower; and it is said that the Grand Duke has been seen, at this sound, to rise from his seat at table, and quietly withdraw to attend the summons."

Jailer, in Florence. "'They are merry enough, Signor,' says the Jailer. 'They are all blood-stained here,' he adds, indicating, with his hand, three-fourths of the whole building."

Old man. "Before the hour is out, an old man, eighty years of age, quarrelling over a bargain with a young girl of seventeen, stabs her dead, in the market-place full of bright flowers; and is brought in prisoner, to swell the number."

Old men. "The old, old men who live in hovels at the entrance of these ancient catacombs [at Naples], and who, in their age and infirmity, seem waiting here, to be buried themselves, are members of a curious body, called the Royal Hospital, who are the official attendants at funerals. Two of these old spectres totter away, with lighted tapers, to show the caverns of death—as unconcerned as if they were immortal."

People, of Fondi. "A hollow-cheeked and scowling people they are! All **beggars**; but that's nothing. Look at them as they gather round. Some, are too indolent to come downstairs, or are too wisely mistrustful of the stairs, perhaps, to venture: so stretch out their lean hands from upper windows, and howl; others, come flocking about us, fighting and jostling one another, and demanding, incessantly, charity for the love of God, charity for the love of the Blessed Virgin, charity for the love of all the Saints.

A group of miserable **children**, almost naked, screaming forth the same petition, discover that they can see themselves reflected in the varnish of the carriage, and begin to dance and make grimaces, that they may have the pleasure of seeing their antics repeated in this mirror.

"A crippled **idiot**, in the act of striking one of them who drowns his clamorous demand for charity, observes his angry counterpart in the panel, stops short, and thrusting out his tongue, begins to wag his head and chatter.

"The shrill cry raised at this, awakens half-a-dozen wild creatures wrapped in frowzy brown cloaks, who are lying on the church-steps with pots and pans for sale. These, scrambling up, approach, and beg defiantly. 'I am hungry. Give me something. Listen to me, Signor. I am hungry!'

"Then, a ghastly **old woman**, fearful of being too late, comes hobbling down the street, stretching out one hand, and scratching herself all the way with the other, and screaming, long before she can be heard, 'Charity, charity! I'll go and pray for you directly, beautiful lady, if you'll give me charity!'

"Lastly, the members of a brotherhood for burying the dead: hideously masked, and attired in shabby black robes, white at the skirts, with the splashes of many muddy winters: escorted by a dirty **priest**, and a congenial **cross-bearer**: come hurrying past. Surrounded by this motley concourse, we move out of Fondi: bad bright eyes glaring at us, out of the darkness of every crazy tenement, like glistening fragments of its filth and putrefaction." ¶

Mr Pickle of Portici. " . . . the head-guide looks oddly about him when one of the company—not an Italian, though an habitué of the mountain for many years: whom we will call, for our present purpose, Mr Pickle of Portici—suggests that, as it is freezing hard, and the usual footing of ashes is covered by the snow and ice, it will surely be difficult to descend."

" . . . [he] stumbles, falls, disengages himself, with quick presence of mind, from those about him, plunges away head foremost, and rolls, over and over, down the whole surface of the cone!

"Sickening as it is to look, and be so powerless to help him, I see him there, in the moonlight—I have had such a dream often—skimming over the white ice, like a cannon-ball."

Raven, at Monte Cassino, "croaking in answer to the bell, and uttering, at intervals, the purest Tuscan. How like a Jesuit he looks! There never was a sly and stealthy fellow so at home as is this raven, standing now at the refectory door, with his head on one side, and pretending to glance another way, while he is scrutinizing the visitors keenly, and listening with fixed attention. What a dull-headed monk the **porter** becomes in comparison!

"'He speaks like us!' says the porter: 'quite as plainly.' Quite as plainly, Porter. Nothing could be more expressive than his reception of the peasants who are entering the gate with baskets and burdens. There is a roll in his eye, and a chuckle in his throat, which should qualify him to be chosen Superior of an Order of Ravens. He knows all about it. 'It's all right,' he says. 'We know what we know. Come along, good people. Glad to see you!'"

Under-guides, "all scuffling and screaming at once, are preparing half-a-dozen saddled ponies, three litters, and some stout staves, for the journey [up Mount Vesuvius]. Every one of the thirty, quarrels with the other twenty-nine, and frightens the six ponies . . . . Eight go forward with the litters that are to be used by-and-by; and the remaining two-and-twenty beg."

" . . . there is a cry from behind; and a man who has carried a light basket of spare cloaks on his head, comes rolling past, at the same frightful speed [as **Pickle**], closely followed by a boy."

Woman, at an inn near Valmontone. "There is a flaring country lamp on the table; and, hovering about it, scratching her thick black hair continually, a yellow dwarf of a woman, who stands on tiptoe to arrange the hatchet knives, and takes a flying leap to look into the water-jug . . . the yellow dwarf sets on the table a good flask of excellent wine, holding a quart at least; and produces, among half-a-dozen other dishes, two-thirds of a roasted kid, smoking hot. She is as good-humoured, too, as dirty, which is saying a great deal. So here's long life to her, in the flask of wine, and prosperity to the establishment."

Women, near Valmontone. "The women wear a bright red bodice laced before and behind, a white skirt, and the Neapolitan head-dress of square folds of linen, primitively meant to carry loads on."

Beggars, of Fondi
Boys, dirty, little; following a priest and carrying his vestments
Children, of Fondi
Cross-bearer
Catherine Dickens, assigned a litter
Driver, sinking in his saddle, casting his eyes up to heaven: a horse lost a shoe
Farrier
Frenchman, lying on some straw in a stable with a broken limb, suffering greatly
Herdsmen, loitering on the banks of the stream beside the road
Georgina Hogarth, assigned a litter
Horseman, carrying a long gun cross-wise on the saddle, with fierce dogs
Idiot, at Fondi
Judge, in the Naples lottery; little old man, dreaded as possessing the Evil Eye
-the last to take his place at the horse-shoe table
Lazzaroni, in Naples; ragged, asleep in doorways, archways and kennels
Letter-writer, providing services to the galley-slave
Old woman, at Fondi
Peasants, driving wine carts, reclining beneath canopies of sheep-skin
Porter, at Monte Cassino
President of the Court of Justice
Priest, at Fondi
-officiating; advances gravely to his place, followed by dirty little boy
Signor Salvatore, the recognised head-guide with the gold band round his cap
Sentinel, watching the galley-slave
Soldiers, as dirty and rapacious as the dogs

The Battle of Life
Frontispiece by Daniel Maclise

CB 4 December 1846 by B&E   **BL**
Definitive U.S. data not available; *La Bataille de la Vie* was in France by 1854

𝕿𝖍𝖊 𝕭𝖆𝖙𝖙𝖑𝖊 𝖔𝖋 𝕷𝖎𝖋𝖊

A LOVE STORY

PRÉCIS

Grace and **Marion Jeddler** dance in an orchard on an old battlefield near their father's house. **Alfred Heathfield** has hired the wandering harp and fiddle to celebrate Marion's birthday. **Snitchey** and **Craggs**, lawyers, arrive for breakfast, followed by Alfred, whose birthday it also is. They argue over Life— a farce, **Doctor Jeddler** thinks; or a serious battle. Dour, dried-up **Benjamin Britain** and awkward **Clemency Newcome** serve. Alfred is engaged to Marion. He will study medicine abroad for three years. He leaves Marion in Grace's care. Marion is stoic, but breaks into tears at last. 1

Three years later, Snitchey and Craggs's client, **Michael Warden**, who has spent himself into a corner and must leave the country, states he is in love with Marion, by whom he was nursed after a fall from a horse. The lawyers assure him she is engaged, but he feels he can persuade her to marry and go with him. He believes she dreads Alfred's return. He leaves. The lawyers agree they cannot interfere.

In the Doctor's study, Marion breaks down reading aloud about Home. She reads a letter from Alfred. He will be back in one month. In the kitchen, a transformed, jollier Britain hears a noise in the garden and goes to look. Marion appears and warns off Warden, outside in the dark, saying she will speak with him in a moment. Britain retires. Clemency standing by, Marion speaks long to Warden, then returns and goes to bed. The month passes. The Doctor prepares a welcome-home party. Snitchey is delayed by a final conference with Warden. Alfred arrives. As he walks through the orchard, he hears Grace scream and sees the Doctor with a letter from Marion: she has left without explanation. Alfred is frozen in shock. 2

Six years later, a village inn By Benjamin Britain called The Nutmeg Grater depends primarily on its practical landlady Clemency, whom the Doctor had turned out for complicity in Marion's disappearance (though he quickly forgave her). A strange man appears and asks for ale. He hears the Doctor has forgiven Marion. Grace has happily married Heathfield. Clemency recognizes Warden, and then Snitchey arrives to meet him. The lawyer says he knows

Warden lost Marion and that her father knew it almost from the first. Craggs has died, and Snitchey is bereft.

Grace and Alfred sit in the garden. He is a country doctor. Marion has often written, and Grace now confesses that Marion had begged her to return Alfred's affection, if transferred to her. Marion has promised that Grace would learn the truth about her today. The messenger is at the gate—it is Marion. She says she loved Alfred but she realized Grace did also, and so she resolved to get out of the way. Warden had written her, offering his hand; to convince Grace that there was no chance of her marrying Alfred, she timed her departure with Warden's, having his promise of secrecy. But she is still a maid and has lived all the while with her Aunt Martha. The sisters blissfully reunite. Michael apologizes and makes to depart, but he will stay because Marion will marry him.

CONTENTS

CHARACTERS

Britain, Benjamin: dour butler (Little Britain)	P	694
Mrs Clemency (formerly Newcome): the pillar of the Inn	P	698
Craggs: partner of Snitchey	SR	700
Mrs: on principle suspicious of Snitchey	O	701
Heathfield, Alfred: evidently a lovable young man; a good doctor	P	695
Mrs Grace (formerly Jeddler): "Alfred's Wife" as a child	P	696
Jeddler, Anthony: philosophical doctor	P	696
Grace: home-adorning, retiring and quiet elder daughter	P	696
Marion: younger, more beautiful, but weaker—perhaps	P	697
Martha: spinster sister of the doctor	O	702
Newcome, Clemency (Clementina): awkward but practical	P	698
Snitchey: a "tender-hearted attorney" and partner of Craggs	P	700
Mrs: on principle suspicious of Craggs	O	701
Warden, Michael: close to ruin, he leaves town and improves	SR	701

Principals

Benjamin Britain. "A small man, with an uncommonly sour and discontented face . . . . "

—on duty: " . . . the melancholy Britain, at another and a smaller board, acted as Grand Carver of a round of beef and a ham.

"'Meat?' said Britain, approaching Mr **Snitchey**, with the carving knife and fork in his hands, and throwing the question at him like a missile." 1

—his laugh: "Britain, who had been paying the profoundest and most melancholy attention to each speaker in his turn, seemed suddenly to decide in favour of the same preference, if a deep sepulchral sound that escaped him might be construed into a demonstration of risibility. His face, however, was so perfectly unaffected by it, both before and afterwards, that although one or two of the breakfast party looked round as being startled by a mysterious noise, nobody connected the offender with it." 1

—apathy: " 'I don't know anything,' said Britain, with a leaden eye and an immovable visage. 'I don't care for anything. I don't make out anything. I don't believe anything. And I don't want anything.'

" . . . serving as a sort of man Miles to the Doctor's Friar Bacon, and listening day after day to innumerable orations addressed by the Doctor to various people, all tending to show that his very existence was at best a mistake and an absurdity, this unfortunate servitor had fallen, by degrees, into such an abyss of confused and contradictory suggestions from within and without, that Truth at the bottom of her well, was on the level surface as compared with Britain in the depths of his mystification." 1

—a legal witness: "How he laboured under an apprehension not uncommon to persons in his degree, to whom the use of pen and ink is an event, that he couldn't append his name to a document, not of his own writing, without committing himself in some shadowy manner, or somehow signing away vague and enormous sums of money; and how he approached the deeds under protest, and

by dint of the **Doctor**'s coercion, and insisted on pausing to look at them before writing (the cramped hand, to say nothing of the phraseology, being so much Chinese to him), and also on turning them round to see whether there was anything fraudulent underneath; and how, having signed his name, he became desolate as one who had parted with his property and rights; I want the time to tell. Also, how the blue bag containing his signature, afterwards had a mysterious interest for him, and he couldn't leave it . . . . " 1

—*nine years later:* "On the door-step appeared a proper figure of a landlord, too; for, although he was a short man, he was round and broad, and stood with his hands in his pockets, and his legs just wide enough apart to express a mind at rest upon the subject of the cellar, and an easy confidence—too calm and virtuous to become a swagger—in the general resources of the inn." 3

And see **Clemency Newcome**—*the truth of the matter*

Alfred Heathfield. " . . . the active figure of a handsome young man, dressed for a journey . . . entered the orchard at a brisk pace, and with an air of gaiety and hope that accorded well with the morning . . . . " 1

—*a keynote:* "'. . . there are quiet victories and struggles, great sacrifices of self, and noble acts of heroism, in [the Battle of Life]—even in many of its apparent lightnesses and contradictions—not the less difficult to achieve, because they have no earthly chronicle or audience—done every day in nooks and corners, and in little households, and in men's and women's hearts—any one of which might reconcile the sternest man to such a world, and fill him with belief and hope in it, though two-fourths of its people were at war, and another fourth at law . . . .'" 1

—*deserted by his love:* "He started up, as if to follow in pursuit; but, when they gave way to let him pass, looked wildly round upon them, staggered back, and sunk down in his former attitude, clasping one of **Grace**'s cold hands in his own . . . .

"The snow fell fast and thick. He looked up for a moment in the air, and thought that those white ashes strewn upon his hopes and misery, were suited to them well. He looked round on the whitening ground, and thought how **Marion**'s footprints would be hushed and covered up, as soon as made, and even that remembrance of her blotted out. But he never felt the weather and he never stirred." 2

—*established:* "He had not become a great man; he had not grown rich; he had not forgotten the scenes and friends of his youth; he had not fulfilled any one of the Doctor's old predictions. But in his useful, patient, unknown visiting of poor men's homes; and in his watching of sick beds; and in his daily knowledge of the gentleness and goodness flowering the by-paths of this world, not to be trodden down beneath the heavy foot of poverty, but springing up, elastic, in its track, and making its way beautiful, he had better learned and proved, in each succeeding year, the truth of his old faith. The manner of his life, though quiet and remote, had shown him how often men still entertained angels, unawares, as in the olden time; and how the most unlikely forms—even some that were mean and ugly to the view, and poorly clad—became irradiated by the couch of sorrow, want, and pain, and changed to ministering spirits with a glory round their heads.

"He lived to better purpose on the altered battle-ground, perhaps, than if he had contended restlessly in more ambitious lists; and he was happy with his wife, dear **Grace**." 3

Doctor Anthony Jeddler. " . . . the Doctor had a streaked face like a win-ter-pippin, with here and there a dimple to express the peckings of the birds, and a very little pigtail behind that stood for the stalk." 1

—on life: "Doctor Jeddler was, as I have said, a great philosopher, and the heart and mystery of his philosophy was to look upon the world as a gigantic practical joke; as something too absurd to be considered seriously, by any ra-tional man." 1

"A kind and generous man by nature, he had stumbled, by chance, over that common Philosopher's stone (much more easily discovered than the object of the alchemists' researches), which sometimes trips up kind and generous men, and has the fatal property of turning gold to dross and every precious thing to poor account." 1

—his thinking revised: "'It's a world full of hearts,' said the Doctor, hugging his younger daughter, and bending across her to hug **Grace**—for he couldn't separate the sisters; 'and a serious world, with all its folly—even with mine, which was enough to have swamped the whole globe; and it is a world on which the sun never rises, but it looks upon a thousand bloodless battles that are some set-off against the miseries and wickedness of Battle-Fields; and it is a world we need be careful how we libel, Heaven forgive us, for it is a world of sa-cred mysteries, and its Creator only knows what lies beneath the surface of His lightest image!'" 3

Grace Jeddler. " . . . the home-adorning, self-denying qualities of Grace, and her sweet temper, so gentle and retiring, yet including so much constancy and bravery of spirit, seemed all expressed to [Doctor **Jeddler**] in the contrast between her quiet household figure and that of his younger and more beautiful child [**Marion**]. . . . " 1

"'Ah, Grace! If I had your well-governed heart, and tranquil mind, how bravely I would leave this place to-day! [said **Alfred**].'" 1

—and her sister: "It was agreeable to see the graceful figures of the bloom-ing sisters, twined together, lingering among the trees, conversing thus, with earnestness opposed to lightness, yet, with love responding tenderly to love. And it was very curious indeed to see the younger sister's eyes suffused with tears, and something fervently and deeply felt, breaking through the wilfulness of what she said, and striving with it painfully.

"The difference between them, in respect of age, could not exceed four years at most; but Grace, as often happens in such cases, when no mother watches over both (the Doctor's wife was dead), seemed, in her gentle care of her young sister, and in the steadiness of her devotion to her, older than she was; and more removed, in course of nature, from all competition with her, or participation, otherwise than through her sympathy and true affection, in her wayward fancies, than their ages seemed to warrant." 1

—on hearing her sister's lover would return: " . . . her own face glowed with hope and joy.

"And with a something else; a something shining more and more through all the rest of its expression; for which I have no name. It was not exultation, tri-umph, proud enthusiasm. They are not so calmly shown. It was not love and gratitude alone, though love and gratitude were part of it. It emanated from no sordid thought, for sordid thoughts do not light up the brow, and hover on the lips, and move the spirit like a fluttered light, until the sympathetic figure trembles." 2

—*a child:* " 'She was a staid little woman, was Grace, and a wise house-keeper, and a busy, quiet, pleasant body; bearing with our humours and anticipating our wishes, and always ready to forget her own, even in those times. I never knew you positive or obstinate, Grace, my darling, even then, on any subject but one.'

"'I am afraid I have changed sadly for the worse, since,' laughed Grace, still busy at her work. 'What was that one, father?'

"'**Alfred**, of course,' said the Doctor. 'Nothing would serve you but you must be called Alfred's wife; so we called you Alfred's wife;' and you liked it better, I believe (odd as it seems now), than being called a Duchess, if we could have made you one.'" 2

—*as a wife:* " . . . a lady sat in the familiar place, from whose heart [her sister] had never passed away; in whose true memory she lived, unchanging, youthful, radiant with all promise and all hope; in whose affection—and it was a mother's now, there was a cherished little daughter playing by her side—she had no rival, no successor; upon whose gentle lips her name was trembling then." 3

Marion Jeddler. "'Dear **Grace**! a moment! Marion—so young and beautiful, so winning and so much admired, dear to my heart as nothing else in life is—remember! I leave Marion to you! [said **Alfred**].'" 1

—*three years later:* "They were very beautiful to look upon. Two better faces for a fireside, never made a fireside bright and sacred. Something of the difference between them had been softened down in three years' time; and enthroned upon the clear brow of the younger sister, looking through her eyes, and thrilling in her voice, was the same earnest nature that her own motherless youth had ripened in the elder sister long ago. But she still appeared at once the lovelier and weaker of the two; still seemed to rest her head upon her sister's breast, and put her trust in her, and look into her eyes for counsel and reliance. Those loving eyes, so calm, serene, and cheerful, as of old." 2

—*her Battle:* "'When this was my dear home, **Grace**, as it will be now again, I loved [**Alfred**] from my soul. I loved him most devotedly. I would have died for him, though I was so young. I never slighted his affection in my secret breast for one brief instant. It was far beyond all price to me. Although it is so long ago, and past, and gone, and everything is wholly changed, I could not bear to think that you, who love so well, should think I did not truly love him once ....'

"'But he had gained, unconsciously,' said Marion, with a gentle smile, 'another heart, before I knew that I had one to give him. That heart—yours, my sister!—was so yielded up, in all its other tenderness, to me; was so devoted, and so noble, that it plucked its love away, and kept its secret from all eyes but mine . . . and was content to sacrifice itself to me.

"'But I knew something of its depths. I knew the struggle it had made. I knew its high, inestimable worth to him, and his appreciation of it, let him love me as he would. I knew the debt I owed it. I had its great example every day before me.

"'What you had done for me, I knew that I could do, Grace, if I would, for you. I never laid my head down on my pillow, but I prayed with tears to do it. I never laid my head down on my pillow, but I thought of Alfred's own words on the day of his departure, and how truly he had said (for I knew that, knowing you) that there were victories gained every day, in struggling hearts, to which these fields of battle were nothing.

"'Thinking more and more upon the great endurance cheerfully sustained, and never known or cared for, that there must be, every day and hour, in that great strife of which he spoke, my trial seemed to grow light and easy. And He who knows our hearts, my dearest, at this moment, and who knows there is no drop of bitterness or grief—of anything but unmixed happiness—in mine, enabled me to make the resolution that I never would be Alfred's wife. That he should be my brother, and your husband, if the course I took could bring that happy end to Pass; but that I never would (Grace, I then loved him dearly, dearly!) be his wife!'

"'O Marion! O Marion!'

"'I had tried to seem indifferent to him;' and she pressed her sister's face against her own; 'but that was hard, and you were always his true advocate. I had tried to tell you of my resolution, but you would never hear me; you would never understand me. The time was drawing near for his return. I felt that I must act, before the daily intercourse between us was renewed I knew that one great pang, undergone at that time, would save a lengthened agony to all of us. I knew that if I went away then, that end must follow which *has* followed, and which has made us both so happy.'" ¶3

Clemency Newcome. "She was about thirty years old, and had a sufficiently plump and cheerful face, though it was twisted up into an odd expression of tightness that made it comical. But the extraordinary homeliness of her gait and manner would have superseded any face in the world.

"To say that she had two left legs, and somebody else's arms, and that all four limbs seemed to be out of joint, and to start from perfectly wrong places when they were set in motion, is to offer the mildest outline of the reality. To say that she was perfectly content and satisfied with these arrangements, and regarded them as being no business of hers, and that she took her arms and legs as they came, and allowed them to dispose of themselves just as it happened, is to render faint justice to her equanimity.

"Her dress was a prodigious pair of self-willed shoes, that never wanted to go where her feet went; blue stockings; a printed gown of many colours, and the most hideous pattern procurable for money; and a white apron. She always wore short sleeves, and always had, by some accident, grazed elbows, in which she took so lively an interest, that she was continually trying to turn them round and get impossible views of them.

"In general, a little cap placed somewhere on her head; though it was rarely to be met with in the place usually occupied in other subjects, by that article of dress; but from head to foot she was scrupulously clean, and maintained a kind of dislocated tidiness. Indeed, her laudable anxiety to be tidy and compact in her own conscience as well as in the public eye, gave rise to one of her most startling evolutions, which was to grasp herself sometimes by a sort of wooden handle (part of her clothing, and familiarly called a busk), and wrestle as it were with her garments, until they fell into a symmetrical arrangement." ¶1

—*her reading:* "'I only reads a thimble.'

"'Read a thimble!' echoed **Snitchey**. 'What are you talking about, young woman?'

"Clemency nodded. 'And a nutmeg-grater.'" 1

"How Clemency . . . held one pocket open, and looked down into its yawning depths for the thimble which wasn't there—and how she then held an opposite pocket open, and seeming to descry it, like a pearl of great price, at the bottom, cleared away such intervening obstacles as a handkerchief, an end of wax candle, a flushed apple, an orange, a lucky penny, a cramp bone, a padlock, a pair of scissors in a sheath more expressively describable as promising young shears, a handful or so of loose beads, several balls of cotton, a needle-case, a cabinet collection of curl-papers, and a biscuit, all of which articles she entrusted individually and separately to Britain to hold—is of no consequence.

"Nor how, in her determination to grasp this pocket by the throat and keep it prisoner (for it had a tendency to swing, and twist itself round the nearest corner), she assumed and calmly maintained, an attitude apparently inconsistent with the human anatomy and laws of gravity. It is enough that at last she triumphantly produced the thimble on her finger, and rattled the nutmeg-grater: the literature of both those trinkets being obviously in course of wearing out and wasting away, through excessive friction.

"'That's the thimble, is it, young woman?' said Mr Snitchey, diverting himself at her expense. 'And what does the thimble say?'

"'It says,' replied Clemency, reading slowly round as if it were a tower, 'For-get and For-give.'

" . . . 'And the nutmeg-grater?' inquired the head of the Firm.

"'The grater says,' returned Clemency, 'Do as you—would—be—done by.'"
1

—*a legal witness:* " . . . how Clemency Newcome, in an ecstasy of laughter at the idea of her own importance, and dignity, brooded over the whole table with her two elbows, like a spread eagle, and reposed her head upon her left arm as a preliminary to the formation of certain cabalistic characters, which required a deal of ink, and imaginary counterparts whereof she executed at the same time with her tongue. Also, how, having once tasted ink, she became thirsty in that regard, as tame tigers are said to be after tasting another sort of fluid, and wanted to sign everything, and put her name in all kinds of places."
1

—*her elbows:* "'Oh, bless you, nothing an't the matter with me,' returned Clemency—and truly too, to judge from her well-soaped face, in which there gleamed as usual the very soul of good-humour, which, ungainly as she was, made her quite engaging. Abrasions on the elbows are not generally understood, it is true, to range with that class of personal charms called beauty-spots. But it is better, going through the world, to have the arms chafed in that narrow passage, than the temper: and Clemency's was sound and whole as any beauty's in the land." 2

—*married and content:* " . . . a plump figure of a matronly woman, with her bare arms folded across a basket which she carried on her knee, several other baskets and parcels lying crowded around her, and a certain bright good nature in her face and contented awkwardness in her manner, as she jogged to and fro with the motion of her carriage, which smacked of old times, even in the distance. Upon her nearer approach, this relish of bygone days was not diminished; and when the cart stopped at the Nutmeg-Grater door, a pair of shoes, alighting from it, slipped nimbly through Mr **Britain**'s open arms, and came down with a substantial weight upon the pathway, which shoes could hardly have belonged to any one but Clemency Newcome.

"In fact they did belong to her, and she stood in them, and a rosy comfortable-looking soul she was: with as much soap on her glossy face as in times of yore, but with whole elbows now, that had grown quite dimpled in her improved condition." 3

Jonathan Snitchey. "'Ladies!' said Mr Snitchey, 'for Self and **Craggs**,' who bowed, 'good morning! Miss,' to **Marion**, 'I kiss your hand.' Which he did. 'And I wish you'—which he might or might not, for he didn't look, at first sight, like a gentleman troubled with many warm outpourings of soul, in behalf of other people, 'a hundred happy returns of this auspicious day.'" 1

—*on the law:* "'. . . in [the world's] having gone to law, and in its legal system altogether, I do observe a serious side—now, really, a something tangible, and with a purpose and intention in it . . . that commands respect. Life a farce, Dr **Jeddler**? With law in it?. . . .

"'Granted, if your please, that war is foolish,' said Snitchey. 'There we agree. For example. Here's a smiling country,' pointing it out with his fork, 'once overrun by soldiers—trespassers every man of 'em—and laid waste by fire and sword. He, he he! The idea of any man exposing himself, voluntarily, to fire and sword! Stupid, wasteful, positively ridiculous; you laugh at your fellow-creatures, you know, when you think of it!

"'But take this smiling country as it stands. Think of the laws appertaining to real property; to the bequest and devise of real property; to the mortgage and redemption of real property; to leasehold, freehold, and copyhold estate; think,' said Mr Snitchey, with such great emotion that he actually smacked his lips, 'of the complicated laws relating to title and proof of title, with all the contradictory precedents and numerous acts of parliament connected with them; think of the infinite number of ingenious and interminable chancery suits, to which this pleasant prospect may give rise; and acknowledge, Dr Jeddler, that there is a green spot in the scheme about us!" ¶1

—*bereaved:* "'Mr **Craggs**, sir,' said Snitchey, shutting his eyes tight for an instant, and opening them again, 'was struck off the roll of life too soon' . . . . "

"'Mr Craggs, sir,' observed Snitchey, 'didn't find life, I regret to say, as easy to have and to hold as his theory made it out, or he would have been among us now. It's a great loss to me. He was my right arm, my right leg, my right ear, my right eye, was Mr Craggs. I am paralytic without him. He bequeathed his share of the business to Mrs Craggs, her executors, administrators, and assigns. His name remains in the Firm to this hour. I try, in a childish sort of a way, to make believe, sometimes, he's alive. You may observe that I speak for Self and Craggs—deceased, sir—deceased,' said the tender-hearted attorney, waving his pocket-handkerchief." 3

Supporting Roles

Craggs. "Craggs, who seemed to be represented by **Snitchey**, and to be conscious of little or no separate existence or personal individuality, offered a remark of his own in this place. It involved the only idea of which he did not stand seized and possessed in equal moieties with Snitchey; but he had some partners in it among the wise men of the world.

"'It's made a great deal too easy,' said Mr Craggs.

"'Law is?' asked the Doctor.

"'Yes,' said Mr Craggs, 'everything is. Everything appears to me to be made too easy, now-a-days. It's the vice of these times. If the world is a joke (I am not prepared to say it isn't), it ought to be made a difficult joke to crack. It ought to be as hard a struggle, sir, as possible. That's the intention. But it's being made far too easy. We are oiling the gates of life. They ought to be rusty.

We shall have them beginning to turn, soon, with a smooth sound. Whereas they ought to grate upon their hinges, sir.'

"Mr Craggs seemed positively to grate upon his own hinges, as he delivered this opinion; to which he communicated immense effect—being a cold, hard, dry man, dressed grey and white, like a flint; with small twinkles in his eyes, as if something struck sparks out of them." 1

Michael Warden. " . . . a man of thirty, or about that time of life, negligently dressed, and somewhat haggard in the face, but well-made, well-attired, and well-looking, who sat in the arm-chair of state, with one hand in his breast, and the other in his dishevelled hair, pondering moodily." 2

"'Ruined at thirty!' said the client. 'Humph!'

"'Not ruined, Mr Warden,' returned **Snitchey**. 'Not so bad as that. You have done a good deal towards it, I must say, but you are not ruined. A little nursing—'

"'A little Devil,' said the client." 2

—*a rival:* "' . . . she may be tired of his idea. . . and not indisposed to exchange it for the newer one of another lover, who presents himself (or is presented by his horse) under romantic circumstances; has the not unfavourable reputation—with a country girl—of having lived thoughtlessly and gaily, without doing much harm to anybody; and who, for his youth and figure, and so forth—this may seem foppish again, but upon my soul I don't mean it in that light—might perhaps pass muster in a crowd with Mr **Alfred** himself.'

"There was no gainsaying the last clause, certainly; and **Mr Snitchey**, glancing at him, thought so. There was something naturally graceful and pleasant in the very carelessness of his air. It seemed to suggest, of his comely face and well-knit figure, that they might be greatly better if he chose: and that, once roused and made earnest (but he never had been earnest yet), he could be full of fire and purpose." 2

Others

Mrs Craggs and **Mrs Snitchey**. "**Snitchey** and **Craggs** had each, in private life as in professional existence, a partner of his own. Snitchey and Craggs were the best friends in the world and had a real confidence in one another; but Mrs Snitchey, by a dispensation not uncommon in the affairs of life, was on principle suspicious of Mr Craggs; and Mrs Craggs was on principle suspicious of Mr Snitchey. 'Your Snitcheys indeed,' the latter lady would observe, sometimes, to Mr Craggs; using that imaginative plural as if in disparagement of an objectionable pair of pantaloons, or other articles not possessed of a singular number; 'I don't see what you want with your Snitcheys, for my part. You trust a great deal too much to your Snitcheys, *I* think, and I hope you may never find my words come true.'

"While Mrs Snitchey would observe to Mr Snitchey, of Craggs, 'that if ever he was led away by man he was led away by that man, and that if she read a double purpose in a mortal eye, she read that purpose in Craggs's eye. Notwithstanding this, however, they were all very good friends in general: and Mrs Snitchey and Mrs Craggs maintained a close bond of alliance against 'the office,' which they both considered the Blue chamber, and common enemy, full of dangerous (because unknown) machinations." ¶2

" . . . perhaps the ladies had instituted, and taken upon themselves, these two shares in the business, rather than be left out of it altogether. But certain it is, that each wife went as gravely and steadily to work in her vocation as her husband did in his, and would have considered it almost impossible for the Firm to maintain a successful and respectable existence, without her laudable exertions." 2

Martha Jeddler. "'. . . my good spinster, sister, Martha Jeddler; who had what she calls her domestic trials ages ago, and has led a sympathising life with all sorts of people ever since . . . .'" 1

"'This is a weary day for me,' said good Aunt Martha, smiling through her tears, as she embraced her nieces; 'for I lose my dear companion in making you all happy; and what can you give me, in return for my Marion?'" 3

"'I think it might be a good speculation if I were to set my cap at **Michael Warden**, who, I hear, is come home much the better for his absence in all respects. But as I knew him when he was a boy, and I was not a very young woman then, perhaps he mightn't respond.'" 3

Spear-carriers

Apple-pickers, on ladders: raised applause for the music	part 1
Betsey: two Master Britains under the supervision of one Betsey	3
Boy, driving a chaise-cart	3
Clem Britain, sleeping like a picture	3
Two Britain boys	3
Fiddler, wandering: sent by Alfred to play for the Jeddler girls	1
Harpist, wandering: sent by Alfred to play for the Jeddler girls	1
Harry, who takes care of the horse at The Nutmeg Grater	3
Little Marion Heathfield	3
Little Britain: a name for Benjamin to distinguish him from Great	1
Porter, bearing Alfred's packages and baskets	1
Servant, of Warden's, sent to Snitchey	3

Mrs Gamp and the Strollers

(complete; side-captions added)

   In 1847, CD and others gave a series of amateur theatrical benefit performances. CD began writing a history of the trip, intended to supplement its
earnings, with **Mrs Gamp** as narrator. The work was not completed and never
published, but the following extracts were included in Forster's life of CD. They
are much the longest and among the most delightful of Mrs Gamp's **Harris**
apostrophes and include some characteristic CD spoofs of himself and his
friends. The text below is from HMCD, vol 28.

PERSONS MENTIONED

Fictional	*Occupation*
Mrs Caudle	housewife*
Mrs Colliber	baker's wife**
Mrs Sairey Gamp	midwife in MC
Mrs Harris	unseen interlocutor in MC
Sweedlepipe	barber, bird fancier MC
Nonfictional	
George Cruikshank	illustrator
Augustus Egg	illustrator
John Forster	critic, biographer
Leigh Hunt	author, editor
Douglas Jerrold	author
John Leech	illustrator
Mark Lemon	editor of Punch
George Henry Lewes	author
John Poole	author
Frank Stone	illustrator
William Wilson	theatrical hairdresser

   **Mrs Caudle's Curtain Lectures*, by Jerrold. 1846
   **spelling presumbly reflects Mrs Gamp's pronunciation: original—?

A Professional Risk

"Which **Mrs Harris**'s own words to me, was these: '**Sairey Gamp**,' she says, 'why not go to Margate? Srimps,' says that dear creetur, 'is to your liking, Sairey; why not go to Margate for a week, bring your constitootion up with srimps, and come back to them loving 'arts as knows and wallies of you, blooming? Sairey,' Mrs Harris says, 'you are but poorly. Don't denige it, Mrs Gamp, for books is in your looks. You must have rest. Your mind,' she says, 'is too strong for you; it gets you down and treads upon you, Sairey. It is useless to disguige the fact—the blade is a wearing out the sheets.'

"'Mrs Harris,' I says to her, 'I could not undertake to say, and I will not deceive you ma'am, that I am the woman I could wish to be. The time of worrit as I had with **Mrs Colliber**, the baker's lady, which was so bad in her mind with her first, that she would not so much as look at bottled stout, and kept to gruel through the month, has agued me, Mrs Harris. But ma'am,' I says to her, 'talk not of Margate, for if I do go anywheres, it is elsewheres and not there.'

"'Sairey,' says Mrs Harris, solemn, 'whence this mystery? If I have ever deceived the hardest-working, soberest, and best of women, which her name is well beknown is S. Gamp Midwife Kingsgate Street High Holborn, mention it. If not,' says Mrs Harris, with the tears a standing in her eyes, 'reweal your intentions.'

"'Yes, Mrs Harris, ' I says, 'I will. Well I knows you, Mrs Harris; well you knows me; well we both knows wot the characters of one another is. Mrs Harris then,' I says, 'I *have* heerd as there *is* a expedition going down to Manjestir and Liverpool, a play-acting. If I goes anywheres for change, it is along with that.'

"Mrs Harris clasps her hands, and drops into a chair, as if her time was come—which I know'd it couldn't be, by rights, for six weeks odd. 'And have I lived to hear,' she says, 'of Sairey Gamp, as always kept hersef respectable, in company with play-actors!' 'Mrs Harris,' I says to her, 'be not alarmed—not reg'lar play-actors—hammertoors.' 'Thank Evans!' says Mrs Harris, and bustiges into a flood of tears.

"When the sweet creetur had compoged hersef (which a sip of brandy and water warm, and sugared pleasant, with a little nutmeg did it), I proceeds in these words. 'Mrs Harris, I am told as these hammertoors are litter'ry and artistickle.' 'Sairey,' says that best of wimmin, with a shiver and a slight relasp, 'go on, it might be worse.' 'I likewise hears,' I says to her, 'that they're a goin' play-acting, for the benefit of two litter'ry men; one [**Leigh Hunt**] as has had his wrongs a long time ago, and has got his rights at last, and one [**John Poole**] as has made a many people merry in his time, but is very dull and sick and lonely his own sef, indeed.' 'Sairey,' says Mrs Harris, 'you're an Inglish woman, and that's no business of your'n.'

"'No, Mrs Harris,' I says, 'that's very true; I hope I knows my dooty and my country. But,' I says, 'I am informed as there is Ladies in this party, and that half a dozen of 'em, if not more, is in various stages of a interesting state. Mrs Harris, you and me well knows what Ingeins often does. If I accompanies this expedition, unbeknown and second cladge, may I not combine my calling with change of air, and prove a service to my feller creeturs?'

"'Sairey,' was Mrs Harris's reply, 'you was born to be a blessing to your sex, and bring 'em through it. Good go with you! But keep your distance till called in, Lord bless you, Mrs Gamp; for people is known by the company they keeps, and litterary and artistickle society might be the ruin of you before you was aware, with your best customers, both sick and monthly, if they took a pride in themselves.'" ¶

Befriended by a Wig-maker

"The number of the cab had a seven in it I think, and a ought I know—and if this should meet his eye (which it was a black 'un, new done, that he saw with; the other was tied up), I give him warning that he'd better take that um-bereller and patten to the Hackney-coach Office before he repents it. He was a young man in a weskit with sleeves to it and strings behind, and needn't flatter himsef with a suppogition of escape, as I gave this description of him to the Police the moment I found he had drove off with my property; and if he thinks there ain't laws enough he's much mistook—I tell him that.

"I do assure you, Mrs Harris, when I stood in the railways office that morning with my bundle on my arm and one patten in my hand, you might have knocked me down with a feather, far less porkmangers which was a lumping against me, continual and sewere all round. I was drove about like a brute animal and almost worritted into fits, when a gentleman with a large shirt-collar and a hook nose, and a eye like one of Mr **Sweedlepipes**'s hawks, and long locks of hair, and whiskers that I wouldn't have no lady as I was en-gaged to meet suddenly a turning round a corner, for any sum of money you could offer me, says, laughing, 'Halloa, Mrs Gamp, what are *you* up to!'

"I didn't know him from a man (except by his clothes); but I says faintly, 'If you're a Christian man, show me where to get a second-cladge ticket for Manjester, and have me put in a carriage, or I shall drop!' Which he kindly did, in a cheerful kind of a way, skipping about in the strangest manner as ever I see, making all kinds of actions, and looking and vinking at me from under the brim of his hat (which was a good deal turned up), to that extent, that I should have thought he meant something but for being so flurried as not to have no thoughts at all until I was put in a carriage along with a individgle—the politest as ever I see—in a shepherd's plaid suit with a long gold watch-guard hanging round his neck, and his hand a trembling through nervousness worse than a aspian leaf.

"'I'm wery 'appy, ma'am,' he says—the politest vice as ever I heerd!—'to go down with a lady belonging to our party.'

"'Our party, sir!' I says.

"'Yes, ma'am,' he says, 'I'm Mr **Wilson**. I'm going down with the wigs.'

"Mrs Harris, wen he said he was a going down with the wigs, such was my state of confugion and worrit that I thought he must be connected with the Government in some ways or another, but directly moment he explains himsef, for he says:—

"'There's not a theatre in London worth mentioning that I don't attend punctually. There's five and twenty wigs in these boxes, ma'am,' he says, a pinting towards a heap of luggage, 'as was worn at the Queen's Fancy Ball. There's a black wig, ma'am,' he says, 'as was worn by [**David**] **Garrick**; there's a red one, ma'am,' he says, 'as was worn by [**Edmund**] **Kean**; there's a brown one, ma'am,' he says, 'as was worn by [**Charles**] **Kemble**; there's a yellow one, ma'am,' he says, 'as was made for [**T. P.**] **Cooke**; there's a gray one, ma'am,' he says, as I measured Mr [**Charles**] **Young** for, mysef; and there's a white one, ma'am, that Mr [**William Charles**] **Macready** went mad in. There's a flaxen one as was got up express for **Jenny Lind** the night she came out at the Italian Opera. It was very much applauded was that wig, ma'am, through the evening. It had a great reception. The audience broke out, the moment they see it.'

"'Are you in Mr Sweedlepipes's line, sir?' I says.

"'Which is that, ma'am?' he says—the softest and genteelest vice I ever heerd, I do declare, Mrs Harris!

"'Hair-dressing,' I says.

"'Yes, ma'am,' he replies, 'I have that honor. Do you see this, ma'am?' he says, holding up his right hand.

"'I never see such a trembling,' I says to him. And I never did!

"'All along of Her Majesty's Costume Ball, ma'am,' he says. 'The excitement did it. Two hundred and fifty-seven ladies of the first rank and fashion had their heads got up on that occasion by this hand, and my t'other one. I was at it eight and forty hours on my feet, ma'am, without rest. It was a Powder ball, ma'am. We have a Powder piece at Liverpool. Have I not the pleasure,' he says, looking at me curious, 'of addressing Mrs Gamp?'

"'Gamp I am, sir,' I replies. 'Both by name and natur'.'

"'Would you like to see your beeograffer's moustache and wiskers, ma'am?' he says. 'I've got 'em in this box.'

"'Drat my beeograffer, sir,' I says; 'he has given me no region to wish to know anythink about him.'

"'Oh, Mrs Gamp, I ask your parden'—I never see such a polite man, Mrs Harris! 'P'raps,' he says, 'if you're not of the party, you don't know who it was that assisted you into this carriage!'

"'No, sir,' I says, 'I don't, indeed.'

"'Why, ma'am' he says a wisperin', 'that was George, ma'am.'

"'What George, sir? I don't know no George,' says I.

"'The great **George**, ma'am,' says he. 'The Crookshanks [**Cruikshank**].'

"'If you'll believe me, Mrs Harris, I turns my head, and see the wery man a making picturs of me on his thumb nail, at the winder! while another of 'em—a tall, slim, melancolly gent [**John Leech**], with dark hair and a bage vice—looks over his shoulder, with his head o'one side as if he understood the subject, and cooly says, '*I*'ve draw'd her several times—in Punch, he says too! The owdacious wretch!

"'Which I never touches, Mr Wilson,' I remarks out loud—I couldn't have helped it, Mrs Harris, if you had took my life for it—'which I never touches, Mr Wilson, on account of the lemon!' [***Mark Lemon**, a passionate amateur actor, was on the tour.*]

"'Hush!' says Mr Wilson. 'There he is!'

"'I only see a fat gentleman with curly black hair and a merry face, a standing on the platform rubbing his two hands over one another, as if he was washing of 'em, and shaking his head and shoulders wery much; and I was a wondering wot Mr Wilson meant, wen he says, 'There's Dougladge [**Douglas Jerrold**], Mrs Gamp!' he says. 'There's him as wrote the life of Mrs **Caudle**.'

"'Mrs Harris, wen I see that little willain bodily before me, it give me such a turn that I was all in a tremble. If I hadn't lost my umbereller in the cab, I must have done him a injury with it! Oh the bragian little traitor! right among the ladies, Mrs Harris; looking his wickedest and deceit-fullest of eyes while he was a talking to 'em; laughing at his own jokes as loud as you please; holding his hat in one hand to cool his'sef, and tossing back his iron-gray mop of a head of hair with the other, as if it was so much shavings—there, Mrs Harris, I see him, getting encouragement from the pretty delooded creeturs, which never know'd that sweet saint, Mrs C., as I did, and being treated with as much confidence as if he'd never wiolated none of the domestic ties, and never showed up nothing!

"Oh the aggrawation of that Dougladge! Mrs Harris, if I hadn't apologized to Mr Wilson, and put a little bottle to my lips which was in my pocket for the journey, and which it is very rare indeed I have about me, I could not have abared the sight of him—there, Mrs Harris! I could not!—I must have tore him, or have give way and fainted.

"While the bell was a ringing, and the luggage of the hammertoors in great confugion—all a litter'ry indeed—was handled up, Mr Wilson demeens his-sef politer than ever. 'That,' he says, 'Mrs Gamp,' a pinting to a officer-looking gentleman [**George Henry Lewes**], that a lady with a little basket was a taking care on, is another of our party. 'He's a author too—continivally going up the wallye of the Muses, Mrs Gamp.

"There,' he says, alluding to a fine looking, portly gentleman, with a face like a amiable full moon, and a short mild gent, with a pleasant smile, 'is two more of our artists [**Frank Stone** and **Augustus Egg**], Mrs G., well beknowed at the Royal Academy, as sure as stones is stones, and eggs is eggs. This resolute gent,' he says, 'a coming along here as is aperrently going to take the railways by storm—him with the tight legs, and his weskit very much buttoned, and his mouth very much shut, and his coat a flying open, and his heels a giving it to the platform, is a cricket and beeograffer [**John Forster**], and our principal tragegian.'

"'But who,' says I, when the bell had left off, and the train had begun to move, 'who, Mr Wilson, is the wild gent in the prespiration, that's been a tearing up and down all this time with a great box of papers under his arm, a talking to everybody wery indistinct, and exciting of himself dreadful?' 'Why?' says Mr Wilson, with a smile. 'Because, sir,' I says, 'he's being left behind.' 'Good God!' cries Mr Wilson, turning pale and putting out his head, 'it's *your* beeograffer—the Manager—and he has got the money, Mrs Gamp!'

"Hous'ever, some one chucked him into the train and we went off. At the first shreek of the whistle, Mrs Harris, I turned white, for I had took notice of some of them dear creeturs as was the cause of my being in company, and I know'd the danger that—but Mr Wilson, which is a married man, puts his hand on mine, and says, 'Mrs Gamp, calm yourself; it's only the Ingein.'" ¶xv-xix

Mrs Annie Leech went into labour at the railway station and was not able to board. Helen Lemon and Catherine Dickens, both pregnant, did accompany their husbands on the tour.

Title page for *Dombey and Son*. Clockwise from top: Fanny Dombey, little Paul, Florence kneeling, Dr Peps looking on; Polly Toodle, Flo, Paul and Susan Nipper; Edith and Flo; Carker, Edith, Bagstock, Mr Dombey (Flo at his feet, Edith fleeing behind him); Mrs Pipchin getting her hereafter deserts; Susan watching Bagstock going under, Biler Toodle crawling away; water nymphs bearing up the deserving Toots; Walter surviving the wreck of the *Son and Heir,* reuniting with Flo as Captain Cuttle (hook on the wrong arm) dances with delight; Mr Dombey going under, but will be rescued by Flo and her child; Avenging Angel presiding as Carker is run down; Paul learning about money from his father; Feeder instructing Paul; Cornelia Blimber and her father with a luckless pupil; Paul's death bed, with his father, Flo and Polly Toodle; the angels bearing Paul to reunion with his mother. All surround Paul, pensive, with his arm around his beloved sister's neck.

N 7 Oct 1846-April 1848 monthly by B&E   l vol 1848 **DS**
U.S. publication 1846-48 in 17 parts by Wiley & Putnam, 2 parts by John Wiley

Dealings with the Firm of
Dombey and Son:

Wholesale, Retail and For Exportation

"Mr Dombey undergoes no violent change, either in this book, or in real life. A sense of his injustice is within him, all along. The more he represses it, the more unjust he necessarily is. Internal shame and external circumstances may bring the contest to a close in a week, or a day; but, it has been a contest for years, and is only fought out after a long balance of victory." —*Preface*

"This marks his final resolution to be a novelist and nothing else, to be a serious constructor of fiction in the serious sense. Before *Dombey and Son* even his pathos had been really frivolous. After *Dombey and Son* even his absurdity was intentional and grave." —*GKC p 118*

"He wishes to have as little as possible in the novel that does not really assist it as a novel. Previously he had asked with the assistance of what incidents could his hero wander farther and farther from the pathway. Now he has really begun to ask with the assistance of what incidents his hero can get nearer and near to the goal."
—*GKC 120-1*

PRÉCIS

Paul Dombey acquires a son and loses his wife. Daughter **Florence**, whom he ignores, is six. **Polly Toodle**, called **Richards**, is chosen by his sister **Mrs Chick**, aided by her friend **Lucretia Tox**, to nurse little **Paul**. 1-3

Walter Gay becomes a clerk with Dombey and Son. He celebrates with his uncle, **Solomon Gills**, who sells nautical instruments, and their friend, retired **Captain Cuttle**. 4

Little **Paul** is christened. Mr Dombey observes the occasion by presenting the susceptible Miss Tox with a bracelet and informing Richards that he has placed her son **Rob** in a charity school. Richards violates a strict rule and visits Rob, accompanied by Florence and nurse **Susan Nipper**. Florence is separated and lost. Her clothes are stolen by "Good **Mrs Brown**," but Walter meets her and takes her home. Richards is discharged. 5-6

Miss Tox, attentive to young Paul, neglects blue-faced **Major Bagstock**, her neighbour, whose pride is stung. He scrapes acquaintance with Mr Dombey. Frail little Paul is ordered to the sea-side, and he and Florence attend school with **Mrs Pipchin** at Brighton. 7-8

Gills has financial trouble, and Captain Cuttle, **Mrs MacStinger**'s cowed tenant, advises Walter to seek Mr Dombey's aid, which is provided at little Paul's behest. 9-10

Solemn, old-fashioned little Paul is transferred to **Dr Blimber**'s school, where **Alfred Feeder** force-feeds and the amiable, addled **Mr Toots** is head boy. Florence's love sustains Paul on the weekends. 11-12

Walter, having inadvertently incurred Dombey displeasure, is to be sent overseas. The manager, the smiling and conniving **James Carker**, announces the move. He hates his older brother, **John**, who has never risen from clerk because of a youthful peculation. 13

Paul begins to fail seriously. Florence attends the term-end party. Walter knows his going abroad is not an advancement. He consults Captain Cuttle but is called to little Paul's bedside. Paul dies, with his thoughts and love concentrated on Florence and What the Waves are saying. 14-16

Captain Cuttle calls on James Carker, who lets him infer Walter's transfer is a promotion. Paul's death embitters Dombey against Florence, the survivor. Florence. Gills, Cuttle and Florence give Walter a send-off. 17-19

Dombey and Bagstock sojourn at Leamington. They meet **Mrs Skewton** and her daughter, the widow **Edith Granger**. Carker hires Rob Toodle, the "**Biler**," to work at the Gills shop and spy. 20-22

The lonely Florence visits Sol Gills. They call on Cuttle, who takes them to his friend and oracle, **Jack Bunsby**. All worry at having no news from Walter. Bunsby is delphic. 22-3

Lady Skettles entertains Florence, who meets James Carker there. Gills disappears, leaving a packet to be opened in a year. Cuttle tiptoes away from the MacStinger clan and moves in to take charge of the shop. 24-5

Carker wants to widen Dombey's estrangement from Florence. He has an odd encounter with Edith, now to become Mrs Dombey. 26-7

Mr Toots regularly calls on Florence at the Skettles'. Home again, she meets Edith and is surprised to learn of the marriage plans. These blight Miss Tox's hopes—to Mrs Chick's indignation. 28-9

Edith and Florence become close, but Edith feels degraded: she knows she is selling herself and that Carker realizes it. 30-1

Walter's ship has sunk. Toots informs Cuttle. 32

At Carker's house there is a portrait resembling Edith. **Harriet Carker**, kind sister who has chosen to live with her disgraced brother John, gives alms to a woman wayfarer **Alice Marwood**, home from prison. Alice's reunion with her mother is spoiled when she learns the aid she received came from a Carker. She returns to Harriet and without explanation casts the money down. 33-4

Mr Dombey and his new wife do not get along. Dombey cannot bend her. Carker foments discord. Miss Tox faints on learning her idol has remarried. Louisa indignantly drops her. She cultivates the Toodle family. 35-38

A year having passed, Cuttle opens the packet Gills left. The MacStinger clan find him out. Bunsby pacifies Mrs MacStinger and escorts her out. 39

Dombey strains increase, Edith's opposition goading Mr Dombey. He tries to use her affection for Florence as a lever, but without success. The breaking-point nears. 40

Florence goes with Edith and her mother to Brighton, where Mr Toots proposes. He is gently refused. Dombey commissions Carker to inform Edith of his commands. He falls from his horse and is laid up for a while. Florence suspects she is somehow the cause of her parents' estrangement. 41-3

Susan Nipper confronts Dombey on Florence's behalf and is discharged. Carker transmits Dombey's instruction to Edith to distance herself from Florence. 44-5

Rob, who now works for Carker, is under some threat from Good Mrs Brown. She and her daughter, Alice Marwood, hate Carker intensely. 46

Dombey strains reach the snapping point. Edith flees in the night with Carker and, beside himself, Dombey blames Florence and strikes her down. She flees and finds refuge with Captain Cuttle. Within days Walter Gay returns from shipwreck. Florence and Walter are in love. 47-50

Dombey discovers Edith's and Carker's whereabouts by watching Mrs Brown extort their destination's name, Dijon, from Rob. Regretful, Alice tries to warn Carker through Harriet. In Dijon, Edith spurns Carker. She has used him only to goad Dombey. She staves off his advances, knife in hand and vanishes through a back door as Dombey arrives in front. Demoralized, Carker flees back to England and seeks a remote railroad inn. Walking by the tracks, he sees Dombey, recoils onto the line and is killed by a train. 51-5

Susan Nipper joins Florence, and Sol Gills reappears. He had written the Captain at his old address. Walter and Florence marry, amid rejoicings. 56-7

Dombey and Son fails, brought down by Dombey's distracted refusal to trim sails. Dombey pays off all debts, impoverishing himself. He is covertly provided for by Harriet and John Carker, heirs to James Carker. Mrs Brown reveals Edith's cousinship with Alice. Eyes open at last, Dombey embraces his daughter's love. 58-9

Matrimonial: Toots marries Susan. Mrs MacStinger processes the cowed Bunsby, to the altar. Feeder and **Cornelia** Blimber are united. 60

Florence is brought to Edith's bedside and learns her essential truth. A loyal Dombey employee, **Morfin**, and Harriet Carker are one. Gills, fortunate in investments, is partners with Captain Cuttle. Dombey is at peace with Florence, Walter and their children. 61-2

CONTENTS

Illustrations by *Hablôt K Browne*

CHARACTERS

The Dombeys

—**Fanny**. "A transient flush of faint surprise overspread the sick lady's face as she raised her eyes towards [her husband]. . . . **[Dombey]** had been married . . . as some said, to a lady with no heart to give him; whose happiness was in the past, and who was content to bind her broken spirit to the dutiful and meek endurance of the present." 1

—*her death:* "'Mama!' said **[Florence]**.

"The little voice, familiar and dearly loved, awakened some show of consciousness, even at that ebb. For a moment, the closed eyelids trembled, and the nostril quivered, and the faintest shadow of a smile was seen.

"'Mama!' cried the child sobbing aloud. 'Oh dear mama! oh dear mama!'

"The doctor gently brushed the scattered ringlets of the child, aside from the face and mouth of the mother. Alas how calm they lay there; how little breath there was to stir them!

"Thus, clinging fast to that slight spar within her arms, the mother drifted out upon the dark and unknown sea that rolls round all the world." 1

—**Florence**. "[Her parents] had been married ten years, and . . . had had no issue.

"—To speak of; none worth mentioning. There had been a girl some six years before . . . . But what was a girl to Dombey and Son! In the capital of the house's name and dignity, such a child was merely a piece of base coin that couldn't be invested—a bad Boy—nothing more." 1

"The child, in her grief and neglect, was so gentle, so quiet, and uncomplaining; was possessed of so much affection that no one seemed to care to have, and so much sorrowful intelligence that no one seemed to mind or think about the wounding of: that **Polly**'s heart was sore . . . . " 3 *And see* **Paul Dombey**, father—*and his daughter*

—*and her father:* "Had he looked with greater interest and with a father's eye, he might have read in her keen glance the impulses and fears that made her waver; the passionate desire to run clinging to him, crying, as she hid her face in his embrace, 'Oh father, try to love me! there's no one else!' the dread of a repulse; the fear of being too bold, and of offending him; the pitiable need in which she stood of some assurance and encouragement; and how her overcharged young heart was wandering to find some natural resting-place, for its sorrow and affection." 3 *And see* **Lucretia Tox**—*her heart*

"When no one in the house was stirring, and the lights were all extinguished, she would softly leave her own room, and with noiseless feet descend the staircase, and approach her father's door. Against it, scarcely breathing, she would rest her face and head, and press her lips, in the yearning of her love. She crouched upon the cold stone floor outside it, every night, to listen even for his breath; and in her one absorbing wish to be allowed to show him some affection, to be a consolation to him, to win him over to the endurance of some tenderness from her, his solitary child, she would have knelt down at his feet, if she had dared, in humble supplication." 18

"If anything had frightened her, it was the face he turned upon her. The glowing love within the breast of his young daughter froze before it, and she stood and looked at him as if stricken into stone.

"There was not one touch of tenderness or pity in it. There was not one gleam of interest, parental recognition, or relenting in it. There was a change in it, but not of that kind. The old indifference and cold constraint had given place to something: what, she never thought and did not dare to think, and yet she felt it in its force, and knew it well without a name: that as it looked upon her, seemed to cast a shadow on her head.

"Did he see before him the successful rival of his son, in health and life? Did he look upon his own successful rival in that son's affection? Did a mad jealousy and withered pride, poison sweet remembrances that should have endeared and made her precious to him? Could it be possible that it was gall to him to look upon her in her beauty and her promise: thinking of his infant boy!

"Florence had no such thoughts. But love is quick to know when it is spurned and hopeless: and hope died out of hers, as she stood looking in her father's face." 18

—*grieving for her brother:* "And was there no one nearer and dearer than **Susan**, to uphold the striving heart in its anguish? Was there no other neck to clasp; no other face to turn to? no one else to say a soothing word to such deep sorrow? Was Florence so alone in the bleak world that nothing else remained to her? Nothing. Stricken motherless and brotherless at once—for in the loss of little Paul, that first and greatest loss fell heavily upon her—this was the only help she had. Oh, who can tell how much she needed help at first! . . .

"But it is not in the nature of pure love to burn so fiercely and unkindly long. The flame that in its grosser composition has the taint of earth, may prey upon the breast that gives it shelter; but the sacred fire from heaven is as gentle in the heart, as when it rested on the heads of the assembled twelve, and showed each man his brother, brightened and unhurt. The image conjured up, there soon returned the placid face, the softened voice, the loving looks, the quiet trustfulness and peace; and Florence, though she wept still, wept more tranquilly, and courted the remembrance." 18 *And see* **What the Waves were always saying**—*his sister; and* —*brother and sister together*

—*her goal:* "Her father did not know . . . how much she loved him. She was very young, and had no mother, and had never learned, by some fault or misfortune, how to express to him that she loved him. She would be patient, and

and would try to gain that art in time, and win him to a better knowledge of his only child.

"This became the purpose of her life. The morning sun shone down upon the faded house, and found the resolution bright and fresh within the bosom of its solitary mistress. Through all the duties of the day, it animated her; for Florence hoped that the more she knew, and the more accomplished she became the more glad he would be when he came to know and like her. Sometimes she wondered, with a swelling heart and rising tear, whether she was proficient enough in anything to surprise him when they should become companions. Sometimes she tried to think if there were any kind of knowledge that would bespeak his interest more readily than another. Always: at her books, her music, and her work: in her morning walks, and in her nightly prayers: she had her engrossing aim in view. Strange study for a child, to learn the road to a hard parent's heart!" 23

—*her moment of truth:* "'**Kate**, said the lady . . . 'I will tell you the whole truth about Florence as I have heard it, and believe it to be. Tell no one else, my dear, because it may be little known here, and your doing so would give her pain . . . . I fear then, Kate, that Florence's father cares little for her, very seldom sees her, never was kind to her in her life, and now quite shuns her and avoids her. She would love him dearly if he would suffer her, but he will not—though for no fault of hers, and she is greatly to be loved and pitied by all gentle hearts . . . your misfortune is a lighter one than Florence's; for not an orphan in the wide world can be so deserted as the child who is an outcast from a living parent's love.'

"The flowers were scattered on the ground like dust; the empty hands were spread upon the face; and orphaned Florence, shrinking down upon the ground, wept long and bitterly.

" . . . . He did not know how much she loved him. However long the time in coming, and however slow the interval, she must try to bring that knowledge to her father's heart one day or other. Meantime she must be careful in no thoughtless word, or look, or burst of feeling awakened by any chance circumstance, to complain against him, or to give occasion for these whispers to his prejudice.

" . . . . What she had overheard was a reason, not for soothing herself, but for saving him; and Florence did it, in pursuance of the study of her heart." 24

—*torn:* "It had been hard—how hard may none but Florence ever know!—to have the natural affection of a true and earnest nature turned to agony; and slight, or stern repulse, substituted for the tenderest protection and the dearest care. It had been hard to feel in her deep heart what she felt, and never know the happiness of one touch of response. But it was much more hard to be compelled to doubt either her father or **Edith**, so affectionate and dear to her, and to think of her love for each of them, by turns, with fear, distrust, and wonder.

"Yet Florence now began to do so; and the doing of it was a task imposed upon her by the very purity of her soul, as one she could not fly from. She saw her father cold and obdurate to Edith, as to her; hard, inflexible, unyielding. Could it be, she asked herself with starting tears, that her own dear mother had been made unhappy by such treatment, and had pined away and died?

"Then she would think how proud and stately Edith was to every one but her, with what disdain she treated him, how distantly she kept apart from him, and what she had said on the night when she came home; and quickly it would

come on Florence, almost as a crime, that she loved one who was set in opposition to her father, and that her father knowing of it, must think of her in his
solitary room as the unnatural child who added this wrong to the old fault, so
much wept for, of never having won his fatherly affection from her birth.

"The next kind word from Edith, the next kind glance, would shake these
thoughts again, and make them seem like black ingratitude; for who but she
had cheered the drooping heart of Florence, so lonely and so hurt, and been its
best of comforters! Thus, with her gentle nature yearning to them both, feeling
the misery of both, and whispering doubts of her own duty to both, Florence in
her wider and expanded love, and by the side of Edith, endured more than when
she had hoarded up her undivided secret in the mournful house, and her beautiful mama had never dawned upon it." ¶43

—*a last sight:* "What was Florence's affright and wonder when, at sight of
her, with her tearful face, and outstretched arms, Edith recoiled and shrieked!

"'Don't come near me!' she cried. 'Keep away! Let me go by!'

"'Mama!' said Florence.

"'Don't call me by that name! Don't speak to me! Don't look at me!—
Florence!' shrinking back, as Florence moved a step towards her, 'don't touch
me!'

"As Florence stood transfixed before the haggard face and staring eyes, she
noted, as in a dream, that Edith spread her hands over them, and shuddering
through all her form, and crouching down against the wall, crawled by her like
some lower animal, sprang up, and fled away.

"Florence dropped upon the stairs in a swoon . . . . " 47

—*a fatherly encounter:* "Yielding at once to the impulse of her affection,
timid at all other times, but bold in its truth to him in his adversity, and undaunted by past repulse, Florence, dressed as she was, hurried downstairs. As
she set her light foot in the hall, he came out of his room. She hastened towards him unchecked, with her arms stretched out, and crying 'Oh dear, dear
papa!' as if she would have clasped him round the neck.

"And so she would have done. But in his frenzy, he lifted up his cruel arm,
and struck her, crosswise, with that heaviness, that she tottered on the marble
floor; and as he dealt the blow, he told her what **Edith** was, and bade her follow
her, since they had always been in league.

"She did not sink down at his feet; she did not shut out the sight of him with
her trembling hands; she did not weep; she did not utter one word of reproach.
But she looked at him, and a cry of desolation issued from her heart. For as
she looked, she saw him murdering that fond idea to which she had held in spite
of him. She saw his cruelty, neglect, and hatred dominant above it, and
stamping it down. She saw she had no father upon earth, and ran out, orphaned, from his house." 47

—**Paul**, father, "about eight-and-forty years of age . . . rather bald, rather
red, and though a handsome well-made man, too stern and pompous in
appearance, to be prepossessing . . . . On the brow of Dombey, Time and his
brother Care had set some marks, as on a tree that was to come down in good
time—remorseless twins they are for striding through their human forests,
notching as they go . . . . " 1 " . . . one of those close-shaved close-cut moneyed
gentlemen who are glossy and crisp like new bank-notes, and who seem to be
artificially braced and tightened as by the stimulating action of golden shower-
baths." 2

—and the firm: "The earth was made for Dombey and Son to trade in, and the sun and moon were made to give them light. Rivers and seas were formed to float their ships; rainbows gave them promise of fair weather; winds blew for or against their enterprises; stars and planets circled in their orbits, to preserve inviolate a system of which they were the centre. Common abbreviations took new meanings in his eyes, and had sole reference to them: A. D. had no concern with anno Domini, but stood for anno Dombey—and Son." 1

—on news of his wife's danger: " . . . he certainly had a sense within him, that if his wife should sicken and decay, he would be very sorry, and that he would find a something gone from among his plate and furniture, and other household possessions, which was well worth the having, and could not be lost without sincere regret. Though it would be a cool, business-like, gentlemanly, self-possessed regret, no doubt." 1

—and his daughter: "The last time he had seen his slighted child, there had been that in the sad embrace between her and her dying mother, which was at once a revelation and a reproach to him. Let him be absorbed as he would in the Son on whom he built such high hopes, he could not forget that closing scene. He could not forget that he had had no part in it. That, at the bottom of its clear depths of tenderness and truth, lay those two figures clasped in each other's arms, while he stood on the bank above them, looking down a mere spectator—not a sharer with them—quite shut out.

"Unable to exclude these things from his remembrance, or to keep his mind free from such imperfect shapes of the meaning with which they were fraught, as were able to make themselves visible to him through the mist of his pride, his previous feelings of indifference towards little Florence changed into an uneasiness of an extraordinary kind. He almost felt as if she watched and distrusted him. As if she held the clue to something secret in his breast, of the nature of which he was hardly informed himself. As if she had an innate knowledge of one jarring and discordant string within him, and her very breath could sound it.

"His feeling about the child had been negative from her birth. He had never conceived an aversion to her: it had not been worth his while or in his humour. She had never been a positively disagreeable object to him. But now he was ill at ease about her. She troubled his peace. He would have preferred to put her idea aside altogether, if he had known how. Perhaps—who shall decide on such mysteries!—he was afraid that he might come to hate her." 3 *And see* **Statuary**

—and his son. "'So that **Paul**'s infancy and childhood pass away well, and I see him becoming qualified without waste of time for the career on which he is destined to enter, I am satisfied. He will make what powerful friends he pleases in after-life, when he is actively maintaining—and extending, if that is possible—the dignity and credit of the firm. Until then, I am enough for him, perhaps, and all in all. I have no wish that people should step in between us ....'

"In the course of these remarks, delivered with great majesty and grandeur, Mr Dombey had truly revealed the secret feelings of his breast. An indescribable distrust of anybody stepping in between himself and his son; a haughty dread of having any rival or partner in the boy's respect and deference; a sharp misgiving, recently acquired, that he was not infallible in his power of bending and binding human wills; as sharp a jealousy of any second check or cross; these were, at that time, the master keys of his soul. In all his life, he had never made a friend. His cold and distant nature had neither sought one, nor found one. And now when that nature concentrated its whole force so strongly on a partial scheme of parental interest and ambition, it seemed as if its icy current, instead of being released by this influence, and running clear and free, had thawed for but an instant to admit its burden, and then frozen with it into one unyielding block." 5

"He had settled, within himself, that the child must necessarily pass through a certain routine of minor maladies, and that the sooner he did so the better. If he could have bought him off, or provided a substitute, as in the case of an unlucky drawing for the militia, he would have been glad to do so on liberal terms. But as this was not feasible, he merely wondered, in his haughty manner, now and then, what Nature meant by it; and comforted himself with the reflection that there was another milestone passed upon the road, and that the great end of the journey lay so much the nearer. For the feeling uppermost in his mind, now and constantly intensifying, and increasing in it as Paul grew older, was impatience. Impatience for the time to come, when his visions of their united consequence and grandeur would be triumphantly realized.

"Some philosophers tell us that selfishness is at the root of our best loves and affections. Mr Dombey's young child was, from the beginning, so distinctly important to him as a part of his own greatness, or (which is the same thing) of the greatness of Dombey and Son, that there is no doubt his parental affection might have been easily traced, like many a goodly superstructure of fair fame, to a very low foundation. But he loved his son with all the love he had. If there were a warm place in his frosty heart, his son occupied it; if its very hard surface could receive the impression of any image, the image of that son was there; though not so much as an infant, or as a boy, but as a grown man—the 'Son' of the firm. Therefore he was impatient to advance into the future, and to hurry over the intervening passages of his history. Therefore he had little or no anxiety about them, in spite of his love; feeling as if the boy had a charmed life, and *must* become the man with whom he held such constant communication in his thoughts, and for whom he planned and projected, as for an existing reality, every day." 8

—*saying goodbye:* "The limp and careless little hand that Mr Dombey took in his, was singularly out of keeping with the wistful face. But he had no part in its sorrowful expression. It was not addressed to him. No, no. To **Florence**—all to Florence.

"If Mr Dombey in his insolence of wealth, had ever made an enemy, hard to appease and cruelly vindictive in his hate, even such an enemy might have received the pang that wrung his proud heart then, as compensation for his injury.

"He bent down over his boy, and kissed him. If his sight were dimmed as he did so, by something that for a moment blurred the little face, and made it indistinct to him, his mental vision may have been, for that short time, the clearer perhaps." 11

"Oh! could he but have seen, or seen as others did, the slight spare boy above, watching the waves and clouds at twilight, with his earnest eyes, and breasting the window of his solitary cage when birds flew by, as if he would have emulated them, and soared away!" 12

See **What the Waves were always saying**—*his father*

—*and his brother-in-law:* "[**Chick**] gave Mr **Dombey** his hand, as if he feared it might electrify him. Mr Dombey took it as if it were a fish, or seaweed, or some such clammy substance, and immediately returned it to him with exalted politeness." 5

—haunted: "There was a face—he had looked upon it, on the previous night, and it on him with eyes that read his soul, though they were dim with tears, and hidden soon behind two quivering hands—that often had attended him in fancy, on this ride. He had seen it, with the expression of last night, timidly pleading to him. It was not reproachful, but there was something of doubt, almost of hopeful incredulity in it, which, as he once more saw that fade away into a desolate certainty of his dislike, was like reproach. It was a trouble to him to think of this face of **Florence**.

"Because he felt any new compunction towards it? No. Because the feeling it awakened in him—of which he had had some old foreshadowing in older times—was full-formed now, and spoke out plainly, moving him too much, and threatening to grow too strong for his composure. Because the face was abroad, in the expression of defeat and persecution that seemed to encircle him like the air. Because it barbed the arrow of that cruel and remorseless enemy on which his thoughts so ran, and put into its grasp a double-handed sword. Because he knew full well, in his own breast, as he stood there, tinging the scene of transition before him with the morbid colours of his own mind, and making it a ruin and a picture of decay, instead of hopeful change, and promise of better things, that life had quite as much to do with his complainings as death. One child was gone, and one child left. Why was the object of his hope removed instead of her?

"The sweet, calm, gentle presence in his fancy, moved him to no reflection but that. She had been unwelcome to him from the first; she was an aggravation of his bitterness now. If his son had been his only child, and the same blow had fallen on him, it would have been heavy to bear; but infinitely lighter than now, when it might have fallen on her (whom he could have lost, or he believed it, without a pang), and had not. Her loving and innocent face rising before him, had no softening or winning influence. He rejected the angel, and took up with the tormenting spirit crouching in his bosom. Her patience, goodness, youth, devotion, love, were as so many atoms in the ashes upon which he set his heel. He saw her image in the blight and blackness all around him, not irradiating but deepening the gloom. More than once upon this journey, and now again as he stood pondering at this journey's end, tracing figures in the dust with his stick, the thought came into his mind, what was there he could interpose between himself and it?" 20

—decked for nuptials: "Gorgeous are Mr Dombey's new blue coat, fawn-coloured pantaloons, and lilac waistcoat; and a whisper goes about the house, that Mr Dombey's hair is curled." 31

—observing his daughter: "And what were his thoughts meanwhile? With what emotions did he prolong the attentive gaze covertly directed on his unknown daughter? Was there reproach to him in the quiet figure and the mild eyes? Had he begun to feel her disregarded claims, and did they touch him home at last, and waken him to some sense of his cruel injustice?

"There are yielding moments in the lives of the sternest and harshest men, though such men often keep their secret well. The sight of her in her beauty, almost changed into a woman without his knowledge, may have struck out some such moments even in his life of pride.

"Some passing thought that he had had a happy home within his reach—had had a household spirit bending at his feet—had overlooked it in his stiff-necked sullen arrogance, and wandered away and lost himself, may have engendered them. Some simple eloquence distinctly heard, though only uttered in her eyes, unconscious that he read them, as 'By the death-beds I have tended, by the childhood I have suffered, by our meeting in this dreary house at midnight, by the cry wrung from me in the anguish of my heart, oh, father, turn to me and seek a refuge in my love before it is too late?' may have arrested them.

"Meaner and lower thoughts, as that his dead boy was now superseded by new ties, and he could forgive the having been supplanted in his affection, may have occasioned them. The mere association of her as an ornament, with all the ornament and pomp about him, may have been sufficient. But as he looked, he softened to her, more and more. As he looked, she became blended with the child he had loved, and he could hardly separate the two. As he looked, he saw her for an instant by a clearer and a brighter light, not bending over that child's pillow as his rival—monstrous thought—but as the spirit of his home, and in the action tending himself no less, as he sat once more with his bowed-down head upon his hand at the foot of the little bed.

"He felt inclined to speak to her, and call her to him. The words '**Florence**, come here!' were rising to his lips—but slowly and with difficulty, they were so very strange—when they were checked and stifled by a footstep on the stair." ¶35

—*his pride and his wife:* "It was not in the nature of things that a man of Mr Dombey's mood, opposed to such a spirit as he had raised against himself, should be softened in the imperious asperity of his temper; or that the cold hard armour of pride in which he lived encased, should be made more flexible by constant collision with haughty scorn and defiance . . . .

"Towards his first wife, Mr Dombey, in his cold and lofty arrogance, had borne himself like the removed being he almost conceived himself to be. He had been 'Mr Dombey' with her when she first saw him, and he was 'Mr Dombey' when she died.

"He had asserted his greatness during their whole married life, and she had meekly recognised it. He had kept his distant seat of state on the top of his throne, and she her humble station on its lowest step; and much good it had done him, so to live in solitary bondage to his one idea!

"He had imagined that the proud character of his second wife would have been added to his own—would have merged into it, and exalted his greatness. He had pictured himself haughtier than ever, with Edith's haughtiness subservient to his. He had never entertained the possibility of its arraying itself against him.

"And now, when he found it rising in his path at every step and turn of his daily life, fixing its cold, defiant, and contemptuous face upon him, this pride of his, instead of withering, or hanging down its head beneath the shock, put forth new shoots, became more concentrated and intense, more gloomy, sullen, irksome, and unyielding, than it had ever been before." ¶40

"Let us be just to him: In the monstrous delusion of his life, swelling with every grain of sand that shifted in its glass, he urged her on, he little thought to what, or considered how; but still his feeling towards her, such as it was, remained as at first. She had the grand demerit of unaccountably putting herself in opposition to the recognition of his vast importance, and to the acknowledgement of her complete submission to it, and so far it was necessary to correct and reduce her; but otherwise he still considered her, in his cold way, a lady capable of doing honour, if she would, to his choice and name, and of reflecting credit on his proprietorship." 47

—*a message from his wife:* "He read that she was gone. He read that he was dishonoured. He read that she had fled, upon her shameful wedding-day, with the man whom he had chosen for her humiliation; and he tore out of the room, and out of the house, with a frantic idea of finding her yet, at the place to which she had been taken, and beating all trace of beauty out of the triumphant face with his bare hand." 47

—*avenging:* "Prying and tormenting as the world was, it did Mr Dombey the service of nerving him to pursuit and revenge. It roused his passion, stung his pride, twisted the one idea of his life into a new shape, and made some gratification of his wrath, the object into which his whole intellectual existence resolved itself. All the stubbornness and implacability of his nature, all its hard impenetrable quality, all its gloom and moroseness, all its exaggerated sense of personal importance, all its jealous disposition to resent the least flaw in the ample recognition of his importance by others, set this way like many streams united into one, and bore him on upon their tide. The most impetuously passionate and violently impulsive of mankind would have been a milder enemy to encounter than the sullen Mr Dombey wrought to this. A wild beast would have been easier turned or soothed than the grave gentleman without a wrinkle in his starched cravat." 53 *And see* **James Carker**—*dawn and death*

—*the other side of pride:* "'The extent of Mr Dombey's resources is not accurately within my knowledge [said Mr **Morfin**]; but though they are doubtless very large, his obligations are enormous. He is a gentleman of high honour and integrity. Any man in his position could, and many a man in his position would, have saved himself, by making terms which would have very slightly, almost insensibly, increased the losses of those who had had dealings with him, and left him a remnant to live upon. But he is resolved on payment to the last farthing of his means. His own words are, that they will clear, or nearly clear, the house, and that no one can lose much. Ah, Miss **Harriet** [**Carker**], it would do us no harm to remember oftener than we do, that vices are sometimes only virtues carried to excess! His pride shows well in this.'" 58

And see **Purgatory, Hell** —**and Redemption**; *and* **Florence Gay**

—**Paul**, son. " . . . in spite of his early promise, all [the] vigilance and care [of **Mrs Chick** and **Miss Tox**] could not make little Paul a thriving boy. Naturally delicate, perhaps, he pined and wasted after the dismissal of his nurse, and, for a long time, seemed but to wait his opportunity of gliding through their hands, and seeking his lost mother. This dangerous ground in his steeple-chase towards manhood passed, he still found it very rough riding, and was grievously beset by all the obstacles in his course." 8

—*signs:* "Thus Paul grew to be nearly five years old. He was a pretty little fellow; though there was something wan and wistful in his small face, that gave occasion to many significant shakes of **Mrs Wickam**'s head, and many long-drawn inspirations of Mrs Wickam's breath. His temper gave abundant promise of being imperious in after-life; and he had as hopeful an apprehension of his own importance, and the rightful subservience of all other things and persons to it, as heart could desire.

"He was childish and sportive enough at times, and not of a sullen disposition; but he had a strange, old-fashioned, thoughtful way, at other times, of sitting brooding in his miniature arm-chair, when he looked (and talked) like one of those terrible little beings in the fairy tales, who, at a hundred and fifty or two hundred years of age, fantastically represent the children for whom they have been substituted . . . at no time did he fall into it so surely, as when, his little chair being carried down into his father's room, he sat there with him after dinner, by the fire.

"They were the strangest pair at such a time that ever firelight shone upon. **Mr Dombey** so erect and solemn, gazing at the blaze; his little image, with an old, old face, peering into the red perspective with the fixed and rapt attention of a sage. Mr Dombey entertaining complicated worldly schemes and plans; the little image entertaining Heaven knows what wild fancies, half-formed thoughts, and wandering speculations. Mr Dombey stiff with starch and arrogance; the little image by inheritance, and in unconscious imitation. The two so very much alike, and yet so monstrously contrasted." ¶8

—*being left at school:* " . . . **Mrs Pipchin** . . . was crowded out of the study before she could clutch **Florence**. To which happy accident Paul stood afterwards indebted for the dear remembrance, that Florence ran back to throw her arms round his neck, and that hers was the last face in the doorway: turned towards him with a smile of encouragement, the brighter for the tears through which it beamed.

"It made his childish bosom heave and swell when it was gone; and sent the globes, the books, blind Homer and Minerva, swimming round the room. But they stopped, all of a sudden; and then he heard the loud clock in the hall still gravely inquiring 'how, is, my, lit, tle, friend? how, is, my, lit, tle, friend?' as it had done before.

"He sat, with folded hands, upon his pedestal, silently listening. But he might have answered 'weary, weary! very lonely, very sad!' And there, with an aching void in his young heart, and all outside so cold, and bare, and strange, Paul sat as if he had taken life unfurnished, and the upholsterer were never coming." 11

—*and his sister:* "His quick transition to a state of unbounded pleasure, as he stood at his window, kissing and clapping his hands: and the way in which the light retreated from his features as she passed out of his view, and left a patient melancholy on the little face: were too remarkable wholly to escape even **Toots**'s notice." 12

—*his need for affection:* "[Paul] had secretly become more and more solicitous from day to day, as the time of his departure drew more near, that all the [**Blimber**] house should like him. From some hidden reason, very imperfectly understood by himself—if understood at all—he felt a gradually increasing impulse of affection, towards almost everything and everybody in the place.

"He could not bear to think that they would be quite indifferent to him when he was gone. He wanted them to remember him kindly; and he had made it his business even to conciliate a great hoarse shaggy dog, chained up at the back of the house, who had previously been the terror of his life: that even he might miss him when he was no longer there . . . .

" . . . over and above the getting through his tasks, he had long had another purpose always present to him, and to which he still held fast. It was, to be a gentle, useful, quiet little fellow, always striving to secure the love and attachment of the rest; and though he was yet often to be seen at his old post on the stairs, or watching the waves and clouds from his solitary window, he was oftener found, too, among the other boys, modestly rendering them some little voluntary service. Thus it came to pass, that even among those rigid and absorbed young anchorites, who mortified themselves beneath the roof of Doctor Blimber, Paul was an object of general interest; a fragile little plaything that they all liked, and that no one would have thought of treating roughly. But he could not change his nature, or rewrite the analysis; and so they all agreed that Dombey was old-fashioned." ¶14

—his musing: " . . . all that the child observed, and felt, and thought, that night—the present and the absent; what was then and what had been—were blended like the colours in the rainbow, or in the plumage of rich birds when the sun is shining on them, or in the softening sky when the same sun is setting. The many things he had had to think of lately, passed before him in the music; not as claiming his attention over again, or as likely evermore to occupy it, but as peacefully disposed of and gone.

"A solitary window, gazed through years ago, looked out upon an ocean, miles and miles away; upon its waters, fancies, busy with him only yesterday, were hushed and lulled to rest like broken waves. The same mysterious murmur he had wondered at, when lying on his couch upon the beach, he thought he still heard sounding through his sister's song, and through the hum of voices, and the tread of feet, and having some part in the faces flitting by, and even in the heavy gentleness of Mr **Toots**, who frequently came up to shake him by the hand. Through the universal kindness he still thought he heard it, speaking to him; and even his old-fashioned reputation seemed to be allied to it, he knew not how. Thus little Paul sat musing, listening, looking on, and dreaming; and was very happy." 14 *And see* **What the Waves were always saying**

Other Principals

Major **Joe Bagstock**, "a wooden-featured, blue-faced major, with his eyes starting out of his head . . . . Although Major Bagstock had arrived at what is called in polite literature, the grand meridian of life, and was proceeding on his journey down-hill with hardly any throat, and a very rigid pair of jaw-bones, and long-flapped elephantine ears, and his eyes and complexion in the state of artificial excitement already mentioned, he was mightily proud of awakening an interest in **Miss Tox**, and tickled his vanity with the fiction that she was a splendid woman, who had her eye on him. This he had several times hinted at the club: in connexion with little jocularities, of which old Joe Bagstock, old Joey Bagstock, old J. Bagstock, old Josh Bagstock, or so forth, was the perpetual theme: it being, as it were, the major's stronghold and donjon-keep of light humour, to be on the most familiar terms with his own name.

"' . . . he's hard-hearted, sir, is Joe—he's tough, sir, tough, and de-vilish sly!' After such a declaration wheezing sounds would be heard; and the major's blue would deepen into purple, while his eyes strained and started convulsively.

"Notwithstanding his very liberal laudation of himself, however, the major was selfish. It may be doubted whether there ever was a more entirely selfish person at heart; or at stomach is perhaps a better expression, seeing that he was more decidedly endowed with that latter organ than with the former. He had no idea of being overlooked or slighted by anybody; least of all, had he the remotest comprehension of being overlooked and slighted by Miss Tox." 7

". . . the major, with his complexion like a Stilton cheese, and his eyes like a prawn's, went roving about . . . . " 10

—his diet: " . . . 'here is a devilled grill, a savoury pie, a dish of kidneys, and so forth. Pray sit down. Old Joe can give you nothing but camp fare, you see' . . . the major always took the best possible care of himself, and indeed ate rather more of rich meats than was good for him, insomuch that his imperial complexion was mainly referred by the faculty to that circumstance." 20

"During the first course or two, the major was usually grave; for the **Native**, in obedience to general orders, secretly issued, collected every sauce and cruet round him, and gave him a great deal to do, in taking out the stoppers, and mixing up the contents in his plate. Besides which, the Native had private zests and flavours on a side-table, with which the major daily scorched himself; to say nothing of strange machines out of which he spirited unknown liquids into the major's drink." 26

—*preparing to travel:* "The major being by this time in a state of repletion, with essence of savoury pie oozing out at the corners of his eyes, and devilled grill and kidneys tightening his cravat: and the time moreover approaching for the departure of the railway train to Birmingham, by which they were to leave town: the **Native** got him into his greatcoat with immense difficulty, and buttoned him up until his face looked staring and gasping, over the top of that garment, as if he were in a barrel.

"The Native then handed him separately, and with a decent interval between each supply, his wash-leather gloves, his thick stick, and his hat; which latter article the major wore with a rakish air on one side of his head, by way of toning down his remarkable visage. The Native had previously packed, in all possible and impossible parts of **Mr Dombey**'s chariot, which was in waiting, an unusual quantity of carpet-bags and small portmanteaus, no less apoplectic in appearance than the major himself: and having filled his own pockets with Seltzer water, East India sherry, sandwiches, shawls, telescopes, maps, and newspapers, any or all of which light baggage the major might require at any instant of the journey, he announced that everything was ready." ¶20

"In Bagstock Dickens has blasted for ever that type which pretends to be sincere by the simple operation of being explosively obvious. He tells about a quarter of the truth, and then poses as truthful because a quarter of the truth is much simpler than the whole of it.... A man is not any the less a toad-eater because he eats his toads with a huge appetite and gobbles them up, as Bagstock did his breakfast, with the eyes starting out of his purple face. He flatters brutally. He cringes with a swagger. And men of the world like Dombey are always taken in by him, because men of the world are probably the simplest of all the children of Adam." GKC 122-3

James Carker, the Manager. "Mr Carker, as Grand Vizier, inhabited the room that was nearest to the Sultan . . . . [He] was a gentleman thirty-eight or forty years old, of a florid complexion, and with two unbroken rows of glistening teeth, whose regularity and whiteness were quite distressing. It was impossible to escape the observation of them, for he showed them whenever he spoke; and bore so wide a smile upon his countenance (a smile, however, very rarely, indeed, extending beyond his mouth), that there was something in it like the snarl of a cat.

"He affected a stiff white cravat, after the example of his principal, and was always closely buttoned up and tightly dressed. His manner towards **Mr Dombey** was deeply conceived and perfectly expressed. He was familiar with him, in the very extremity of his sense of the distance between them. 'Mr Dombey, to a man in your position from a man in mine, there is no show of subservience compatible with the transaction of business between us, that I should think sufficient. I frankly tell you, sir, I give it up altogether. I feel that I could not satisfy my own mind; and Heaven knows, Mr Dombey, you can afford to dispense with the endeavour.' If he had carried these words about with him, printed on a placard, and had constantly offered it to Mr Dombey's perusal on the breast of his coat, he could not have been more explicit than he was." ¶13

" . . . . The stiffness and nicety of Mr Carker's dress, and a certain arrogance of manner, either natural to him or imitated from a pattern not far off, gave great additional effect to his humility. He seemed a man who would contend against the power that vanquished him, if he could, but who was utterly borne down by the greatness and superiority of Mr Dombey." 13

—*attentive:* " . . . looking down upon the captain with an eye in every tooth and gum." 17

—*his smile:* "A cat, or a monkey, or a hyena, or a death's-head, could not have shown the captain more teeth at one time, than Mr Carker showed him at this period of their interview." 17

—*feline:* "In whose sly look and watchful manner; in whose false mouth, stretched but not laughing; in whose spotless cravat and very whiskers; even in whose silent passing of his soft hand over his white linen and his smooth face; there was something desperately cat-like." 17

—*a cat at business:* ". . . feline from sole to crown was Mr Carker the manager, as he basked in the strip of summer-light and warmth that shone upon his table and the ground as if they were a crooked dial-plate, and himself the only figure on it. With hair and whiskers deficient in colour at all times, but feebler than common in the rich sunshine, and more like the coat of a sandy tortoise-shell cat; with long nails, nicely pared and sharpened; with a natural antipathy to any speck of dirt, which made him pause sometimes and watch the falling motes of dust, and rub them off his smooth white hand or glossy linen: Mr Carker the manager, sly of manner, sharp of tooth, soft of foot, watchful of eye, oily of tongue, cruel of heart, nice of habit, sat with a dainty steadfastness and patience at his work, as if he were waiting at a mouse's hole." 21

—*machinations:* "'Has he taken money? Is it that?'

"'Yes.'

"'He has not.'

"'I thank Heaven!' said **Harriet**. 'For the sake of **John**.'

"'That he has abused his trust in many ways,' said Mr **Morfin**; 'that he has oftener dealt and speculated to advantage for himself, than for the House he represented; that he has led the House on, to prodigious ventures, often resulting in enormous losses; that he has always pampered the vanity and ambition of his employer, when it was his duty to have held them in check, and shown, as it was in his power to do, to what they tended here or there; will not, perhaps, surprise you now. Undertakings have been entered on, to swell the reputation of the house for vast resources, and to exhibit it in magnificent contrast to other merchants' houses, of which it requires a steady head to contemplate the possibly—a few disastrous changes of affairs might render them the probably—ruinous consequences. In the midst of the many transactions of the House, in most parts of the world: a great labyrinth of which only he has held the clue: he has had the opportunity, and he seems to have used it, of keeping the various results afloat, when ascertained, and substituting estimates and generalities for facts.'" ¶53

—*callousness:* "' . . . my mother [said **Alice Marwood**] . . . sent to him in my name , told the true story of my case, and humbly prayed and petitioned for a small last gift—for not so many pounds as I have fingers on this hand. Who was it, do you think, who snapped his fingers at me in my misery, lying, as he believed, at his feet, and left me without even this poor sign of remembrance; well satisfied that I should be sent abroad, beyond the reach of further trouble to him, and should die, and rot there? Who was this, do you think?'" 53

—*disabused and undone:* "In the fever of his mortification and unavailing rage, the panic that had seized upon him mastered him completely. It rose to such a height that he would have blindly encountered almost any risk, rather than meet the man of whom, two hours ago, he had been utterly regardless. His fierce arrival, which he had never expected; the sound of his voice; their having been so near a meeting, face to face, he would have braved out this, after the first momentary shock of alarm, and would have put as bold a front upon his guilt as any villain. But the springing of his mine upon himself, seemed to have rent and shivered all his hardihood and self-reliance. Spurned like any reptile; entrapped and mocked; turned upon, and trodden down by the proud woman whose mind he had slowly poisoned, as he thought, until she had sunk into the mere creature of his pleasure; undeceived in his deceit, and with his fox's hide stripped off, he sneaked away, abashed, degraded, and afraid." 55

—*distracted:* "He could not think to any purpose. He could not separate one subject of reflection from another, sufficiently to dwell upon it, by itself, for a minute at a time. The crash of his project for the gaining of a voluptuous compensation for past restraint; the overthrow of his treachery to one who had been true and generous to him, but whose least proud word and look he had treasured up, at interest, for years . . . these were the themes uppermost in his mind. A lurking rage against the woman who had so entrapped him and avenged herself was always there; crude and misshapen schemes of retaliation upon her, floated in his brain; but nothing was distinct. A hurry and contradiction pervaded all his thoughts. Even while he was so busy with this fevered, ineffectual thinking, his one constant idea was, that he would postpone reflection until some indefinite time . . . . To have his confidence in his own knavery so shattered at a blow—to be within his own knowledge such a miserable tool—

was like being paralysed. With an impotent ferocity he raged at **Edith**, and hated **Mr Dombey** and hated himself, but still he fled, and could do nothing else." 55

Captain Edward (Ned) Cuttle. " . . . a gentleman in a wide suit of blue, with a hook instead of a hand attached to his right wrist; very bushy black eyebrows; and a thick stick in his left hand, covered all over (like his nose) with knobs. He wore a loose black silk handkerchief round his neck, and such a very large coarse shirt collar, that it looked like a small sail . . . having taken off his rough outer coat, and hung up, on a particular peg behind the door, such a hard glazed hat as a sympathetic person's head might ache at the sight of, and which left a red rim round his own forehead as if he had been wearing a tight basin . . . . He was usually addressed as Captain, this visitor; and had been a pilot, or a skipper, or a privateers-man, or all three perhaps; and was a very salt-looking man indeed." 4

—*no longer perplexed:* " . . . his visage cleared like a doubtful morning when it gives place to a bright noon. His eyebrows, which had been in the highest degree portentous, smoothed their rugged bristling aspect, and became serene; his eyes, which had been nearly closed in the severity of his mental exercise, opened freely; a smile which had been at first but three specks—one at the right-hand corner of his mouth, and one at the corner of each eye—gradually overspread his whole face, and rippling up into his forehead, lifted the glazed hat: as if that too had been aground with Captain Cuttle, and were now, like him, happily afloat again." 15

—*his hat:* " . . . the glazed hat, which he jammed between his knees (without injury to its shape, for nothing human could bend it) . . . . " 17

—*his foot in it:* "'There's a son gone; pretty little creetur. Ain't there?'

"Yes, there's a son gone,' said the acquiescent **Carker**.

"'Pass the word, and there's another ready for you,' quoth the captain. 'Nevy of a scientific uncle! Nevy of **Sol Gills**! **Wal'r**! Wal'r, as is already in your business! And'—said the captain, rising gradually to a quotation he was preparing for a final burst, 'who—comes from Sol Gills's daily, *to* your business, and your buzzums.'

"The captain's complacency as he gently jogged Mr Carker with his elbow, on concluding each of the foregoing short sentences, could be surpassed by nothing but the exultation with which he fell back and eyed him when he had finished this brilliant display of eloquence and sagacity; his great blue waistcoat heaving with the throes of such a masterpiece, and his nose in a state of violent inflammation from the same cause." 17

—*his handshake:* " . . . the captain once again extended his enormous hand (not unlike an old block in colour), and gave [**Carker**] a grip that left upon his smoother flesh a proof impression of the chinks and crevices with which the captain's palm was liberally tattooed." 17

—*Beauty and the Captain:* "Unlike as they were externally—and there could scarcely be a more decided contrast than between **Florence** in her delicate youth and beauty, and Captain Cuttle with his knobby face, his great broad weather-beaten person, and his gruff voice—in simple innocence of the world's ways and the world's perplexities and dangers, they were nearly on a level.

"No child could have surpassed Captain Cuttle in inexperience of everything but wind and weather; in simplicity, credulity, and generous trustfulness. Faith, hope, and charity, shared his whole nature among them. An odd sort of romance, perfectly unimaginative, yet perfectly unreal, and subject to no considerations of worldly prudence or practicability, was the only partner they had in his character.

"As the captain sat and smoked, and looked at Florence, God knows what impossible pictures, in which she was the principal figure, presented themselves to his mind. Equally vague and uncertain, though not so sanguine, were her own thoughts of the life before her; and even as her tears made prismatic colours in the light she gazed at, so, through her new and heavy grief, she already saw a rainbow faintly shining in the far-off sky. A wandering princess and a good monster in a story-book might have sat by the fireside, and talked as Captain Cuttle and poor Florence thought—and not have looked very much unlike them." ¶49

Walter Gay, "a boy of fourteen who looked quite enough like a midshipman, to carry out the prevailing [nautical] idea . . . . A cheerful-looking, merry boy, fresh with running home in the rain; fair-faced, bright-eyed, and curly-haired." 4 "That spice of romance and love of the marvellous, of which there was a pretty strong infusion in the nature of young Walter Gay . . . a frank, free-spirited, open-hearted boy . . . ." 9

—*doubted:* "When **Mr Dombey** had looked at him, and told him he was young, and that his uncle's circumstances were not good, there had been an expression of disdain in his face; a contemptuous and disparaging assumption that he would be quite content to live idly on a reduced old man, which stung the boy's generous soul. Determined to assure Mr Dombey, in so far as it was possible to give him the assurance without expressing it in words, that indeed he mistook his nature, Walter had been anxious to show even more cheerfulness and activity after the West Indian interview than he had shown before: if that were possible, in one of his quick and zealous disposition. He was too young and inexperienced to think, that possibly this very quality in him was not agreeable to Mr Dombey . . . . " 15

—*not doubted:* "' . . . and if you'll be a brother to me, Walter, now that he is gone and I have none on earth, I'll be your sister all my life, and think of you like one wherever we may be! This is what I wished to say, dear Walter, but I cannot say it as I would, because my heart is full.'

"And in its fulness and its sweet simplicity, [**Florence**] held out both her hands to him. Walter taking them, stooped down and touched the tearful face that neither shrunk nor turned away, nor reddened as he did so, but looked up at him with confidence and truth. In that one moment, every shadow of doubt or agitation passed away from Walter's soul. It seemed to him that he responded to her innocent appeal, beside the dead child's bed: and, in the solemn presence he had seen there, pledged himself to cherish and protect her very image, in his banishment, with brotherly regard; to garner up her simple faith, inviolate; and hold himself degraded if he breathed upon it any thought that was not in her own breast when she gave it to him." 19

—*loved and missed:* "'No, Heart's-delight,' said **Captain Cuttle**, 'I am not afeard. Wal'r is a lad as'll go through a deal o' hard weather. Wal'r is a lad as'll bring as much success to that 'ere brig as a lad is capable on. Wal'r,' said the Captain, his eyes glistening with the praise of his young friend, and his hook raised to announce a beautiful quotation, 'is what you may call a out'ard and visible sign of an in'ard and spirited grasp, and when found make a note of.'" 23

—*a story is told:* "'Aboard o' that there unfort'nate wessel,' said the captain, rising from his chair, and clenching his hand with prodigious energy and exultation, 'was a lad, a gallant lad—as I've heerd tell—that had loved, when he was a boy, to read and talk about brave actions in shipwrecks—I've heerd him! I've heerd him!—and he remembered of 'em in his hour of need; for when the stoutest hearts and oldest hands was hove down, he was firm and cheery. It warn't the want of objects to like and love ashore that gave him courage, it was his nat'ral mind. I've seen it in his face, when he was no more than a child—aye, many a time!—and when I thought it nothing but his good looks, bless him!

"' . . . . That there lad . . . arter working with the best, and standing by the faint-hearted, and never making no complaint nor sign of fear, and keeping up a spirit in all hands that made 'em honour him as if he'd been a admiral—that lad, along with the second-mate and one seaman, was left, of all the beatin' hearts that went aboard that ship, the only living creeturs—lashed to a fragment of the wreck, and driftin' on the stormy sea.'" 49

Edith Granger. "Walking by the side of [**Mrs Skewton**'s] chair, and carrying her gossamer parasol with a proud and weary air, as if so great an effort must be soon abandoned and the parasol dropped, sauntered a much younger lady, very handsome, very haughty, very wilful, who tossed her head and drooped her eyelids, as though, if there were anything in all the world worth looking into, save a mirror, it certainly was not the earth or sky." 21

"Edith, so beautiful and stately, but so cold and so repelling . . . . The quiet scorn that sat upon her handsome face—a scorn that evidently lighted on herself, no less than [her mother and the major]—was so intense and deep, that her mother's simper, for the instant, though of a hardy constitution, drooped before it." 25

—*observed:* "[The figure] was that of a lady, elegantly dressed and very handsome, whose dark proud eyes were fixed upon the ground, and in whom some passion or struggle was raging. For as she sat looking down, she held a corner of her under lip within her mouth, her bosom heaved, her nostril quivered, her head trembled, indignant tears were on her cheek, and her foot was set upon the moss as though she would have crushed it into nothing. and yet almost the self-same glance that showed him this, showed him the self-same lady rising with a scornful air of weariness and lassitude, and turning away with nothing expressed in face or figure but careless beauty and imperious disdain." 27

—*with her husband-to-be:* "They were not interchanging a word or a look. Standing together, arm in arm, they had the appearance of being more divided than if seas had rolled between them. There was a difference even in the pride of the two, that removed them farther from each other, than if one had been the proudest and the other the humblest specimen of humanity in all creation. He, self-important, unbending, formal, austere. She, lovely and graceful in an uncommon degree, but totally regardless of herself and him and everything around, and spurning her own attractions with her haughty brow and lip, as if they were a badge or livery she hated." 27

—*truth to parent:* "'A child! . . . when was I a child? What childhood did you ever leave to me? I was a woman—artful, designing, mercenary, laying snares for men—before I knew myself, or you, or even understood the base and wretched aim of every new display I learnt. You gave birth to a woman. Look upon her. She is in her pride to-night . . . .

"There is no slave in a market; there is no horse in a fair: so shown and offered and examined and paraded, mother, as I have been, for ten shameful years,' cried Edith, with a burning brow . . . . 'Is it not so? Have I been made the bye-word of all kinds of men? Have fools, have profligates, have boys, have dotards, dangled after me, and one by one rejected me, and fallen off, because you were too plain with all your cunning: yes, and too true, with all those false pretences: until we have almost come to be notorious? The licence of look and touch,' she said, with flashing eyes, 'have I submitted to it, in half the places of resort upon the map of England. Have I been hawked and vended here and there, until the last grain of self-respect is dead within me, and I loathe myself? Has *this* been my late childhood? I had none before. Do not tell me that I had, to-night, of all nights in my life!'

"' . . . my education was completed long ago. I am too old now, and have fallen too low, by degrees, to take a new course, and to stop yours, and to help myself. The germ of all that purifies a woman's breast, and makes it true and good, has never stirred in mine, and I have nothing else to sustain me when I despise myself.'" 27

—*the other side:* "Was this the woman whom **Florence**—an innocent girl, strong only in her earnestness and simple truth—could so impress and quell, that by her side she was another creature, with her tempest of passion hushed, and her very pride itself subdued? Was this the woman who now sat beside her in a carriage, with her arms entwined, and who, while she courted and entreated her to love and trust her, drew her fair head to nestle on her breast, and would have laid down life to shield it from wrong or harm?" 30

—admiring her new home: "An expression of scorn was habitual to the proud face, and seemed inseparable from it; but the contempt with which it received any appeal to admiration, respect, or consideration on the ground of his riches, no matter how slight or ordinary in itself, was a new and different expression, unequalled in intensity by any other of which it was capable.

"Whether **Mr Dombey**, wrapped in his own greatness, was at all aware of this, or no, there had not been wanting opportunities already for his complete enlightenment; and at that moment it might have been effected by the one glance of the dark eye that lighted on him, after it had rapidly and scornfully surveyed the theme of his self-glorification. He might have read in that one glance that nothing that his wealth could do, though it were increased ten thousand fold, could win him for its own sake, one look of softened recognition from the defiant woman, linked to him, but arrayed with her whole soul against him.

"He might have read in that one glance that even for its sordid and mercenary influence upon herself, she spurned it, while she claimed its utmost power
as her right, her bargain—as the base and worthless recompense for which she
had become his wife. He might have read in it that, ever baring her own head
for the lightning of her own contempt and pride to strike, the most innocent allusion to the power of his riches degraded her anew, sunk her deeper in her own
respect, and made the blight and waste within her more complete." ¶35

—*wiser:* "'When he loves his **Florence** most, he will hate me least. When
he is most proud and happy in her and her children, he will be most repentant
of his own part in the dark vision of our married life. At that time, I will be repentant too—let him know it then—and think that when I thought so much of
all the causes that had made me what I was, I needed to have allowed more for
the causes that had made him what he was. I will try, then, to forgive him his
share of blame. Let him try to forgive me mine!'" 61

Mrs Skewton. " . . . a wheeled chair, in which a lady was seated, indolently
steering her carriage by a kind of rudder in front, while it was propelled by some
unseen power in the rear. Although the lady was not young, she was very
blooming in the face—quite rosy—and her dress and attitude were perfectly juvenile." 21

"The discrepancy between Mrs Skewton's fresh enthusiasm of words, and
forlornly faded manner, was hardly less observable than that between her age,
which was about seventy, and her dress, which would have been youthful for
twenty-seven. Her attitude in the wheeled chair (which she never varied) was
one in which she had been taken in a barouche, some fifty years before, by a
then fashionable artist who had appended to his published sketch the name of
Cleopatra: in consequence of a discovery made by the critics of the time, that it
bore an exact resemblance to that princess as she reclined on board her galley.
Mrs Skewton was a beauty then, and bucks threw wine-glasses over their
heads by dozens in her honour. The beauty and the barouche had both passed
away, but she still preserved the attitude, and for this reason expressly, maintained the wheeled chair and the butting page: there being nothing whatever,
except the attitude, to prevent her from walking." 21

—*Mediævalist:* "'Oh!' cried Mrs Skewton, with a faded little scream of rapture, 'the [Warwick] castle is charming!—associations of the Middle Ages—and
all that—which is so truly exquisite. Don't you doat upon the Middle Ages, Mr
Carker? . . . such charming times!' cried Cleopatra. 'So full of faith! So vigorous and forcible! So picturesque! So perfectly removed from commonplace!
Oh dear! If they would only leave us a little more of the poetry of existence in
these terrible days! . . . We are dreadfully real, Mr Carker,' said Mrs Skewton;
'are we not?' . . .

"'Those darling bygone times . . . with their delicious fortresses, and their
dear old dungeons, and their delightful places of torture, and their romantic ven-
geances, and their picturesque assaults and sieges, and everything that makes
life truly charming! How dreadfully we have degenerated!' . . .

"'We have no faith left, positively,' said Mrs Skewton . . . . 'We have no faith
in the dear old barons, who were the most delightful creatures—or in the dear
old priests, who were the most warlike of men—or even in the days of that inestimable Queen Bess, upon the wall there, which were so extremely golden.
Dear creature! She was all Heart! And that charming father of hers! I hope
you doat on Harry the Eighth!'

"'I admire him very much,' said **Carker**.

"'So bluff!' cried Mrs Skewton, 'wasn't he? So burly. So truly English. Such a picture, too, he makes, with his dear little peepy eyes, and his benevolent chin!'" 27

—*to bed:* " . . . Mrs Skewton's **maid** appeared, according to custom, to prepare her gradually for night. At night, she should have been a skeleton, with dart and hour-glass, rather than a woman, this attendant; for her touch was as the touch of death. The painted object shrivelled underneath her hand; the form collapsed, the hair dropped off, the arched dark eye-brows changed to scanty tufts of grey; the pale lips shrunk, the skin became cadaverous and loose; an old, worn, yellow, nodding woman, with red eyes, alone remained in Cleopatra's place, huddled up, like a slovenly bundle, in a greasy flannel gown." 27

—*stricken:* "Cleopatra was arrayed in full dress, with the diamonds, short sleeves, rouge, curls, teeth, and other juvenility all complete; but Paralysis was not to be deceived, had known her for the object of its errand, and had struck her at her glass, where she lay like a horrible doll that had tumbled down." 37

P. Toots. " . . . one young gentleman, with a swollen nose and an excessively large head (the oldest of the ten who had 'gone through' everything), suddenly left off blowing one day, and remained in the **[Blimber]** establishment a mere stalk. And people did say that the doctor had rather overdone it with young Toots, and that when he began to have whiskers he left off having brains.

"There young Toots was, at any rate; possessed of the gruffest of voices and the shrillest of minds; sticking ornamental pins into his shirt, and keeping a ring in his waistcoat pocket to put on his little finger by stealth, when the pupils went out walking; constantly falling in love by sight with nurserymaids, who had no idea of his existence; and looking at the gas-lighted world over the little iron bars in the left-hand corner window of the front three pairs of stairs, after bed-time, like a greatly over-grown cherub who had sat up aloft much too long." 11

—*dressed up:* " . . . Mr Toots appeared to be involved in a good deal of uncertainty whether, on the whole, it was judicious to button the bottom button of his waistcoat, and whether, on a calm revision of all the circumstances, it was best to wear his wristbands turned up or turned down. Observing that Mr **Feeder**'s were turned up, Mr Toots turned his up; but the wristbands of the next arrival being turned down, Mr Toots turned his down. The differences in point of waistcoat buttoning, not only at the bottom, but at the top too, became so numerous and complicated as the arrivals thickened, that Mr Toots was continually fingering that article of dress, as if he were performing on some instrument; and appeared to find the incessant execution it demanded, quite bewildering." 14

—*paying a call:* "'How d'ye do, **Miss Dombey**?' said Mr Toots. 'I'm very well, I thank you; how are you?'

"Mr Toots—than whom there were few better fellows in the world, though there may have been one or two brighter spirits—had laboriously invented this long burst of discourse with the view of relieving the feelings both of Florence and himself. But finding that he had run though his property, as it were, in an injudicious manner, by squandering the whole before taking a chair, or before Florence had uttered a word, or before he had well got in at the door, he deemed it advisable to begin again.

"'How d'ye do, Miss Dombey?' said Mr Toots. 'I'm very well, I thank you; how are you?'" 18

(no, that's not Florence)

—*rejected:* "'You have been so good to me,' says **Florence**, 'I am so grateful to you, I have such reason to like you for being a kind friend to me, and I do like you so much;' and here the ingenuous face smiles upon him with the pleasantest look of honesty in the world; 'that I am sure you are only going to say good-bye!' . . . .

"'Good-bye, Miss Dombey!' stammers Mr Toots. 'I hope you won't think anything about it. It's—it's of no consequence, thank you. It's not of the least consequence in the world.'

"Poor Mr Toots goes home to his hotel in a state of desperation, locks himself into his bedroom, flings himself upon his bed, and lies there for a long time; as if it were of the greatest consequence, nevertheless." 61

—*as seen by an admirer:* "' . . . he may not be a Solomon,' pursued the **Nipper**, with her usual volubility, 'nor do I say he is but this I do say a less selfish human creature human nature never knew!'" 56

" . . . the admirable study of Toots, who may be considered as being in some ways the masterpiece of Dickens. Nowhere else did Dickens express with such astonishing insight and truth his main contention, which is that to be good and idiotic is not a poor fate, but, on the contrary, an experience of primeval innocence, which wonders at all things." GKC 126-7

Lucretia Tox. "The lady . . . was a long lean figure, wearing such a faded air that she seemed not to have been made in what linen-drapers call 'fast colours' originally, and to have, by little and little, washed out. But for this she might have been described as the very pink of general propitiation and politeness. From a long habit of listening admirably to everything that was said in her presence, and looking at the speakers as if she were mentally engaged in taking off impressions of their images upon her soul, never to part with the same but with life, her head had quite settled on one side. Her hands had contracted a spasmodic habit of raising themselves of their own accord as in involuntary admiration. Her eyes were liable to a similar affection. She had the softest voice that ever was heard; and her nose, stupendously aquiline, had a little knob in the very centre or key-stone of the bridge, whence it tended downwards towards her face, as in an invincible determination never to turn up at anything.

"Miss Tox's dress, though perfectly genteel and good, had a certain character of angularity and scantiness. She was accustomed to wear odd weedy little flowers in her bonnets and caps. Strange grasses were sometimes perceived in her hair; and it was observed . . . of all her collars, frills, tuckers, wristbands, and other gossamer articles—indeed of everything she wore which had two ends to it intended to unite—that the two ends were never on good terms, and wouldn't quite meet without a struggle.

"She had furry articles for winter wear, as tippets, boas, and muffs, which stood up on end in a rampant manner, and were not at all sleek. She was much given to the carrying about of small bags with snaps to them, that went off like little pistols when they were shut up; and when full-dressed, she wore round her neck the barrenest of lockets, representing a fishy old eye, with no approach to speculation in it. These and other appearances of a similar nature, had served to propagate the opinion, that Miss Tox was a lady of what is called a limited independence, which she turned to the best account. Possibly her mincing gait encouraged the belief, and suggested that her clipping a step of ordinary compass into two or three, originated in her habit of making the most of everything." 1

—*her canary:* " . . . a very high-shouldered canary, stricken in years, and much rumpled, but a piercing singer, as Princess's Place well knew . . . . " 29

—*straightforward:* " . . . if she were a fawner and toad-eater, [she] was at least an honest and a constant one . . . . " 29

—*resilient:* "Miss Tox . . . was not of an age or of a disposition long to abandon herself to unavailing regrets. Only two notes of the harpsichord were dumb from disuse when the Bird Waltz again warbled and trilled in the crooked drawing-room: only one slip of geranium fell a victim to imperfect nursing, before she was gardening at her green baskets again, regularly every morning; the powdered-headed ancestor had not been under a cloud for more than six weeks, when Miss Tox breathed on his benignant visage, and polished him up with a piece of wash-leather." 38

—hurt: "Still, Miss Tox was lonely, and at a loss. Her attachments, however ludicrously shown, were real and strong; and she was, as she expressed it, 'deeply hurt by the unmerited contumely she had met with from **Louisa.**' But there was no such thing as anger in Miss Tox's composition. If she had ambled on through life, in her soft-spoken way, without any opinions, she had, at least, got so far without any harsh passions. The mere sight of Louisa **Chick** . . . so over-powered her milky nature, that she was fain to seek immediate refuge in a pastry-cook's, and there . . . relieve her feelings by weeping plentifully." 38

—heart: "Miss Tox's sympathy is such that she can scarcely speak. She is no chicken, but she has not grown tough with age and celibacy. Her heart is very tender, her compassion very genuine, her homage very real. Beneath the locket with the fishy eye in it, Miss Tox bears better qualities than many a less whimsical outside; such qualities as will outlive, by many courses of the sun, the best outsides and brightest husks that fall in the harvest of the great reaper." 59

Supporting Roles

Doctor Blimber. "The doctor was a portly gentleman in a suit of black, with strings at his knees, and stockings below them. He had a bald head, highly polished; a deep voice, and a chin so very double, that it was a wonder how he ever managed to shave into the creases. He had likewise a pair of little eyes that were always half shut up, and a mouth that was always half expanded into a grin, as if he had, that moment, posed a boy, and were waiting to convict him from his own lips. Insomuch, that when the doctor put his right hand into the breast of his coat, and with his other hand behind him, and a scarcely perceptible wag of his head, made the commonest observation to a nervous stranger, it was like a sentiment from the sphynx, and settled his business." 11

—his school: "Whenever a young gentleman was taken in hand by Doctor Blimber, he might consider himself sure of a pretty tight squeeze. The doctor only undertook the charge of ten young gentlemen, but he had, always ready, a supply of learning for a hundred, on the lowest estimate; and it was at once the business and delight of his life to gorge the unhappy ten with it.

"In fact, Doctor Blimber's establishment was a great hot-house, in which there was a forcing apparatus incessantly at work. All the boys blew before their time. Mental green-peas were produced at Christmas, and intellectual asparagus all the year round. Mathematical gooseberries (very sour ones too) were common at untimely seasons, and from mere sprouts of bushes, under Doctor Blimber's cultivation. Every description of Greek and Latin vegetable was got off the driest twigs of boys, under the frostiest circumstances. Nature was of no consequence at all. No matter what a young gentleman was intended to bear, Doctor Blimber made him bear to pattern, somehow or other.

"This was all very pleasant and ingenious, but the system of forcing was attended with its usual disadvantages. There was not the right taste about the premature productions, and they didn't keep well." 11 *And see* **P. Toots**.

—his students: " . . . there was no sound through all the house but the ticking of a great clock in the hall, which made itself audible in the very garrets: and sometimes a dull crying of young gentlemen at their lessons, like the murmurings of an assemblage of melancholy pigeons.

" . . . . The young gentlemen were prematurely full of carking anxieties. They knew no rest from the pursuit of stony-hearted verbs, savage noun-substantives, inflexible syntactic passages, and ghosts of exercises that appeared to them in their dreams. Under the forcing system, a young gentleman usually took leave of his spirits in three weeks. He had all the cares of the world on his head in three months. He conceived bitter sentiments against his parents or guardians in four; he was an old misanthrope, in five; envied **Curtius** that blessed refuge in the earth, in six; and at the end of the first twelvemonth had arrived at the conclusion, from which he never afterwards departed, that all the fancies of the poets, and lessons of the sages, were a mere collection of words and grammar, and had no other meaning in the world.

"But he went on blow, blow, blowing, in the doctor's hot-house, all the time; and the doctor's glory and reputation were great, when he took his wintry growth home to his relations and friends." 11

—reading: " . . . the doctor, leaning back in his chair, with his hand in his breast as usual, held a book from him at arm's length, and read. There was something very awful in this manner of reading. It was such a determined, unimpassioned, inflexible, cold-blooded way of going to work. It left the doctor's countenance exposed to view; and when the doctor smiled auspiciously at his author, or knit his brows, or shook his head and made wry faces at him, as much as to say, 'Don't tell me, sir; I know better,' it was terrific." 11

Captain Jack Bunsby.—*at home:* "Immediately there appeared, coming slowly up above the bulk-head of the cabin, another bulk-head—human, and very large—with one stationary eye in the mahogany face, and one revolving one, on the principle of some lighthouses. This head was decorated with shaggy hair, like oakum, which had no governing inclination towards the north, east, west, or south, but inclined to all four quarters of the compass, and to every point upon it. The head was followed by a perfect desert of chin, and by a shirt-collar and neckerchief, and by a dreadnought pilot-coat, and by a pair of dreadnought pilot-trousers, whereof the waistband was so very broad and high, that it became a succedaneum for a waistcoat: being ornamented near the wearer's breast-bone with some massive wooden buttons, like backgammon men. As the lower portions of these pantaloons became revealed, Bunsby stood confessed; his hands in their pockets, which were of vast size; and his gaze directed, not to **Captain Cuttle** or the ladies, but the mast-head.

"The profound appearance of this philosopher, who was bulky and strong, and on whose extremely red face an expression of taciturnity sat enthroned, not inconsistent with his character, in which that quality was proudly conspicuous, almost daunted Captain Cuttle, though on familiar terms with him. Whispering to **Florence** that Bunsby had never in his life expressed surprise, and was considered not to know what it meant, the captain watched him as he eyed his mast-head, and afterwards swept the horizon; and when the revolving eye seemed to be coming round in his direction, said:

"'Bunsby, my lad, how fares it?'

"A deep, gruff, husky utterance, which seemed to have no connexion with Bunsby, and certainly had not the least effect upon his face, replied, 'Aye, aye, shipmet, how goes it?' At the same time Bunsby's right hand and arm, emerging from a pocket, shook the captain's, and went back again." 23

—*giving an opinion:* "'If so be . . . as [**Walter**]'s dead, my opinion is he won't come back no more. If so be as he's alive, my opinion is he will. Do I say he will? No. Why not? Because the bearings of this obserwation lays in the application on it.'

"'Bunsby!' said **Captain Cuttle**, who would seem to have estimated the value of his distinguished friend's opinions in proportion to the immensity of the difficulty he experienced in making anything out of them; 'Bunsby,' said the captain, quite confounded by admiration, 'you carry a weight of mind easy, as would swamp one of my tonnage soon.'" 39

—*his calming influence:* "'Aye, aye, aye,' said Bunsby, in a soothing tone. 'Awast, my lass, awast!'

"'And who may YOU be, if you please!' retorted **Mrs MacStinger**, with chaste loftiness. 'Did you ever lodge at Number Nine, Brig Place, sir? My memory may be bad, but not with me, I think. There was a **Mrs Jollson** lived at Number Nine before me, and perhaps you're mistaking me for her. That is my only ways of accounting for your familiarity, sir.'

"'Come, come, my lass, awast, awast!' said Bunsby.

"Captain **Cuttle** could hardly believe it, even of this great man, though he saw it done with his waking eyes; but Bunsby, advancing boldly, put his shaggy blue arm round Mrs MacStinger, and so softened her by his magic way of doing it, and by these few words—he said no more—that she melted into tears, after looking upon him for a few moments, and observed that a child might conquer her now, she was so low in her courage." 39

—*in custody:* "'Jack Bunsby,' whispered the captain, 'do you do this here, o' your own free will?"

"Mr Bunsby answered 'No.'

"'Why do you do it, then, my lad?' inquired the captain, not unnaturally.

"Bunsby, still looking, and always looking with an immovable countenance, at the opposite side of the world, made no reply.

"'Why not sheer off?' said the captain.

"'Eh?' whispered Bunsby, with a momentary gleam of hope.

"'Sheer off,' said the captain.

"'Where's the good?' retorted the forlorn sage. 'She'd capter me agen.'

"'Try!' replied the captain. 'Cheer up! Come! Now's your time. Sheer off, Jack Bunsby!' . . . .

"'Come!' said the captain, nudging him with his elbow, 'now's your time! Sheer off! I'll cover your retreat. The time's a flying. Bunsby! It's for liberty. Will you once?'

"Bunsby was immovable.

"'Bunsby!' whispered the captain, 'will you twice?'

"Bunsby wouldn't twice.

"'Bunsby!' urged the captain, 'it's for liberty; will you three times? Now or never!'

"Bunsby didn't then and didn't ever; for **Mrs MacStinger** immediately afterwards married him." 60

Harriet Carker. "This slight, small, patient figure, neatly dressed in homely stuffs, and indicating nothing but the dull, household virtues, that have so little in common with the received idea of heroism and greatness, unless, indeed, any ray of them should shine through the lives of the great ones of the earth, when it becomes a constellation and is tracked in Heaven straightway—this slight, small, patient figure, leaning on the man still young but worn and grey, is she, his sister, who, of all the world, went over to him in his shame and put her hand in his, and with a sweet composure and determination, led him hopefully upon his barren way." 33

—*briefly misunderstood:* "'And **Mr Dombey**, is he personally ruined?'

"'Ruined.'

"'Will he have no private fortune left? Nothing?'

"A certain eagerness in her voice, and something that was almost joyful in her look, seemed to surprise [**Morfin**] more and more; to disappoint him too, and jar discordantly against his own emotions . . . .

" . . . . "Mr Dombey, whom [**John Carker**] served so many years—you know upon what terms—reduced, as you describe; and we quite rich?'

"Good, true face, as that face of hers was, and pleasant as it had been to him, Mr Morfin, the hazel-eyed bachelor, since the first time he had ever looked upon it, it pleased him less at that moment, lighted with a ray of exultation, than it had ever pleased him before." 58 *But see* **Morfin** 0 —*relieved*

Louisa Dombey Chick. " . . . a lady rather past the middle age than otherwise, but dressed in a very juvenile manner, particularly as to the tightness of her bodice, who, running up to him with a kind of screw in her face and carriage, expressive of suppressed emotion, flung her arms round [her brother's] neck, and said in a choking voice,

"'My dear **Paul**! He's quite a Dombey!'" 1

—*her philosophy:* "' . . . if any misanthrope were to put, in my presence, the question "Why were we born?" I should reply, "To make an effort.'" 18

—*dismissive:* "'There is a point,' said Mrs Chick, rising, not as if she were going to stop at the floor, but as if she were about to soar up, high, into her native skies, 'beyond which endurance becomes ridiculous, if not culpable . . . . **Lucretia** [**Tox**], I have been mistaken in you. It is better for us both that this subject should end here. I wish you well, and I shall ever wish you well. But, as an individual who desires to be true to herself in her own poor position, whatever that position may be, or may not be—and as the sister of my brother— and as the sister-in-law of my brother's wife—and as a connexion by marriage of my brother's wife's mother—may I be permitted to add, as a Dombey?—I can wish you nothing else but good morning.'

"These words, delivered with cutting suavity, tempered and chastened by a lofty air of moral rectitude, carried the speaker to the door. There she inclined her head in a ghostly and statue-like manner, and so withdrew to her carriage, to seek comfort and consolation in the arms of Mr **Chick** her lord." 29

Lord Feenix. "Cousin Feenix was a man about town, forty years ago; but he is still so juvenile in figure and in manner, and so well got up, that strangers are amazed when they discover latent wrinkles in his lordship's face, and crows' feet in his eyes; and first observe him, not exactly certain when he walks across a room, of going quite straight to where he wants to go." 31

—*giving the bride away:* "Cousin Feenix, meaning to go in a straight line, but turning off sideways by reason of his wilful legs, gives the wrong woman to be married to this man, at first—to wit, a **bridesmaid** of some condition, distantly connected with the family, and ten years **Mrs Skewton**'s junior—but **Mrs Miff**, interposing her mortified bonnet, dexterously turns him back, and runs him, as on castors, full at the 'good lady;' whom Cousin Feenex giveth to be married to this man accordingly." 31 *And see* **Jack Adams** O

—*self-appraising:* "'The only description of society I have kept, has been my own; and it certainly is anything but flattering to a man's good opinion of his own resources, to know that, in point of fact, he has the capacity of boring himself to a perfectly unlimited extent.'

—*his manner*, "which was always a gentleman's, in spite of the harmless little eccentricities that attached to it . . . . " 61

Solomon Gills. " . . . Solomon Gills himself (more generally called old Sol) was far from having a maritime appearance. To say nothing of his Welsh wig, which was as plain and stubborn a Welsh wig as ever was worn, and in which he looked like anything but a rover, he was a slow, quiet-spoken, thoughtful old fellow, with eyes as red as if they had been small suns looking at you through a fog; and a newly-awakened manner, such as he might have acquired by having stared for three or four days successively through every optical instrument in his shop, and suddenly came back to the world again, to find it green.

"The only change ever known in his outward man, was from a complete suit of coffee-colour cut very square, and ornamented with glaring buttons, to the same suit of coffee-colour minus the inexpressibles, which were then of a pale nankeen. He wore a very precise shirt-frill, and carried a pair of first-rate spectacles on his forehead, and a tremendous chronometer in his fob, rather than doubt which precious possession, he would have believed in a conspiracy against it on the part of all the clocks and watches in the City, and even of the very Sun itself.

"Such as he was, such he had been in the shop and parlour behind the little **midshipman**, for years upon years; going regularly aloft to bed every night in a howling garret remote from the lodgers, where, when gentlemen of England who lived below at ease had little or no idea of the state of the weather, it often blew great guns." ¶4

Mrs MacStinger, landlady to Captain **Cuttle**. " . . . a widow lady, with her sleeves rolled up to her shoulders, and her arms frothy with soap-suds and smoking with hot water . . . . " 9

—*cleaning house:* "On these occasions, Mrs MacStinger was knocked up by the policeman at a quarter before three in the morning, and rarely succumbed before twelve o'clock next night. The chief object of this institution appeared to be, that Mrs MacStinger should move all the furniture into the back garden at early dawn, walk about the house in pattens all day, and move the furniture back again after dark. These ceremonies greatly fluttered those doves the young **MacStingers**, who were not only unable at such times to find any resting-place for the soles of their feet, but generally came in for a good deal of pecking from the maternal bird during the progress of the solemnities." 23

—*on her tenant:* "'I said it wasn't Cap'en **Cuttle**'s house—and it ain't his house—and forbid it, that it ever should be his house—for Cap'en Cuttle don't know how to keep a house—and don't deserve to have a house—it's my house—and when I let the upper floor to Cap'en Cuttle, oh I do a thankless thing, and cast pearls before swine!'

"Mrs MacStinger pitched her voice for the upper windows in offering these remarks, and cracked off each clause sharply by itself as if from a rifle possessing an infinity of barrels. After the last shot, the captain's voice was heard to say, in feeble remonstrance from his own room, 'Steady below!'" 23

—*collecting same:* "'Oh, Cap'en **Cuttle**, Cap'en Cuttle!' said Mrs MacStinger, making her chin rigid, and shaking it in unison with what, but for the weakness of her sex, might be described as her fist. 'Oh, Cap'en Cuttle, Cap'en Cuttle, do you dare to look me in the face, and not be struck down in the herth!'

"The captain, who looked anything but daring, feebly muttered 'Stand by!'

"'Oh I was a weak and trusting fool when I took you under *my* roof, Cap'en Cuttle, I was!' cried Mrs MacStinger. 'To think of the benefits I've showered on that man, and the way in which I brought my children up to love and *h*onour him as if he was a father to 'em, when there an't a 'ouse- keeper, no nor a lodger in our street, don't know that I lost money by that man, and by his guzzlings and his muzzlings'—Mrs MacStinger used the last word for the joint sake of alliteration and aggravation, rather than for the expression of any idea—'and when they cried out one and all, shame upon him for putting upon an industrious woman, up early and late for the good of her young family, and keeping her poor place so clean that a individual might have ate his dinner, yes, and his tea too, if he was so disposed, off any one of the floors or stairs, in spite of all his guzzlings *and* his muzzlings, such was the care and pains bestowed upon him!'"

"'And he runs awa-a-a-y!' cried Mrs MacStinger, with a lengthening out of the last syllable that made the unfortunate captain regard himself as the meanest of men; 'and keeps away a twelve-month! From a woman! Sitch is his conscience! He hasn't the courage to meet her hi-i-i-igh;' long syllable again; 'but steals away, like a felion . . . .

"'A pretty sort of a man is Cap'en Cuttle,' said Mrs MacStinger, with a sharp stress on the first syllable of the captain's name, 'to take on for—and to lose sleep for—and to faint along of—and to think dead forsooth—and to go up and down the blessed town like a madwoman, asking questions after! Oh, a pretty sort of a man! Ha ha ha ha! He's worth all that trouble and distress of mind, and much more. *That's* nothing, bless you! Ha ha ha ha! Cap'en Cuttle,' said Mrs MacStinger, with severe reaction in her voice and manner, 'I wish to know if you're a-coming home?'

"The frightened captain looked into his hat, as if he saw nothing for it but to put it on, and give himself up." 39

Alice Marwood. "A solitary woman of some thirty years of age; tall; well-formed; handsome; miserably dressed; the soil of many country roads in varied weather—dust, chalk, clay, gravel—clotted on her grey cloak by the streaming wet; no bonnet on her head, nothing to defend her rich black hair from the rain, but a torn handkerchief; with the fluttering ends of which, and with her hair, the wind blinded her so that she often stopped to push them back, and look upon the way she was going.

"She was in the act of doing so, when **Harriet** observed her. As her hands, parting on her sunburnt forehead, swept across her face, and threw aside the hindrances that encroached upon it, there was a reckless and regardless beauty in it: a dauntless and depraved indifference to more than weather: a carelessness of what was cast upon her bare head from Heaven or earth: that, coupled with her misery and loneliness, touched the heart of her fellow-woman. She thought of . . . the many gifts of the Creator flung to the winds like the wild hair; of all the beautiful ruin upon which the storm was beating and the night was coming." 33

—*early fate:* "'There was a child called Alice Marwood,' said the daughter, with a laugh, and looking down at herself in terrible derision of herself, 'born, among poverty and neglect, and nursed in it. Nobody taught her, nobody stepped forward to help her, nobody cared for her.'

"'Nobody!' echoed the mother, pointing to herself, and striking her breast.

"'The only care she knew,' returned the daughter, 'was to be beaten, and stinted, and abused sometimes; and she might have done better without that. She lived in homes like this [bare flat], and in the streets, with a crowd of little wretches like herself; and yet she brought good looks out of this childhood. So much the worse for her. She had better have been hunted and worried to death for ugliness.'" 34

—*returned home:* "As she subsided into silence, and her face which had been harshly agitated, quieted down; while her dark eyes, fixed upon the fire, exchanged the reckless light that had animated them, for one that was softened by something like sorrow; there shone through all her way-worn misery and fatigue, a ray of the departed radiance of the fallen angel." 34

Mrs Marwood ("**Good Mrs Brown**"). "She was a very ugly old woman, with red rims round her eyes, and a mouth that mumbled and chattered of itself when she was not speaking. She was miserably dressed, and carried some skins over her arm. She seemed to have followed **Florence** some little way at all events, for she had lost her breath; and this made her uglier still, as she stood trying to regain it: working her shrivelled yellow face and throat into all sorts of contortions." 6

—*plying a trade:* "Munching like that sailor's wife of yore, who had chestnuts in her lap, and scowling like the witch who asked for some in vain,* the old woman picked [**Carker**'s] shilling up, and going backwards, like a crab, or like a heap of crabs: for her alternately expanding and contracting hands might have represented two of that species, and her creeping face, some half-a-dozen more: crouched on the veinous root of an old tree, pulled out a short black pipe from within the crown of her bonnet, lighted it with a match, and smoked in silence, looking fixedly at her questioner." 27 [*Macbeth* I iii]

—*intimidating:* " . . . finding it uncomfortable to encounter the yellow face with its grotesque action, and the ferret eyes with their keen old wintry gaze, so close to his own, [**Biler Toodle**] looked down uneasily . . . . " 52

—at her daughter's bedside: "Her laugh, as she retreated, was worse than her cry; worse than the burst of imbecile lamentation in which it ended; worse than the doting air with which she sat down in her old seat, and stared out at the darkness." 58

Susan Nipper. "'Oh well, Miss **Floy**! And won't your pa be angry neither!' cried a quick voice at the door, proceeding from a short, brown, womanly girl of fourteen, with a little snub nose, and black eyes like jet beads. 'When it was 'tickerlerly given out that you wasn't to go and worrit the wet nurse' . . . [the] young Spitfire, whose real name was Susan Nipper, detached the child from her new friend by a wrench—as if she were a tooth. But she seemed to do it, more in the excessively sharp exercise of her official functions, than with any deliberate unkindness." 3

"Susan seemed to be in the main a good-natured little body, although a disciple of that school of trainers of the young idea which holds that childhood, like money, must be shaken and rattled and jostled about a good deal of keep it bright. For, being thus appealed to with some endearing gestures and caresses, she folded her small arms and shook her head, and conveyed a relenting expression into her very-wide-open black eyes." 3

—at Brighton: " . . . Miss Nipper, now a smart young woman, had come down. To many a single combat with **Mrs Pipchin**, did Miss Nipper gallantly devote herself; and if ever Mrs Pipchin in all her life had found her match, she had found it now. Miss Nipper threw away the scabbard the first morning she arose in Mrs Pipchin's house. She asked and gave no quarter. She said it must be war, and war it was; and Mrs Pipchin lived from that time in the midst of surprises, harassings, and defiances, and skirmishing attacks that came bouncing in upon her from the passage, even in unguarded moments of chops, and carried desolation to her very toast." 12

—delighted: "'And is my darling,' pursued Susan, with another close embrace and burst of tears, 'really really going to be married!'

"The mixture of compassion, pleasure, tenderness, protection, and regret with which the Nipper constantly recurred to this subject, and at every such recurrence, raised her head to look in the young face and kiss it, and then laid her head again upon her mistress's shoulder, caressing her and sobbing, was as womanly and good a thing, in its way, as ever was seen in the world." 56

Mrs Pipchin. "'Mrs Pipchin, my dear Paul,' returned his sister, 'is an elderly lady . . . who has for some time devoted all the energies of her mind, with the greatest success, to the study and treatment of infancy, and who has been extremely well connected.'" 8

"The celebrated Mrs Pipchin was a marvellous ill-favoured, ill-conditioned old lady, of a stooping figure, with a mottled face, like bad marble, a hook nose, and a hard grey eye, that looked as if it might have been hammered at on an anvil without sustaining any injury. Forty years at least had elapsed since the Peruvian mines had been the death of Mr **Pipchin**; but his relict still wore black bombazeen, of such a lustreless, deep, dead, sombre shade, that gas itself couldn't light her up after dark, and her presence was a quencher to any number of candles. She was generally spoken of as 'a great manager' of children; and the secret of her management was, to give them everything that they didn't like, and nothing that they did—which was found to sweeten their dispositions very much. She was such a bitter old lady, that one was tempted to believe there had been some mistake in the application of the Peruvian machinery, and that all her waters of gladness and milk of human kindness, had been pumped out dry, instead of the mines." 8

—*exit:* "Mrs Pipchin . . . has her chair (late a favourite chair of Mr **Dombey**'s and the dead bargain of the sale) ready near the street door; and is only waiting for a fly-van, going to-night to Brighton on private service, which is to call for her, by private contract, and convey her home.

"Presently it comes. Mrs Pipchin's wardrobe being handed in and stowed away, Mrs Pipchin's chair is next handed in, and placed in a convenient corner among certain trusses of hay; it being the intention of the amiable woman to occupy the chair during her journey. Mrs Pipchin herself is next handed in, and grimly takes her seat. There is a snaky gleam in her hard grey eye, as of anticipated rounds of buttered toast, relays of hot chops, worryings and quellings of young children, sharp snappings at poor **Berry**, and all the other delights of her ogress's castle. Mrs Pipchin almost laughs as the fly-van drives off, and she composes her black bombazeen skirts, and settles herself among the cushions of her easy chair." ¶59

Sir Barnet Skettles, "who was in the House of Commons, and of whom Mr **Feeder** had said that when he *did* catch the Speaker's eye (which he had been expected to do for three or four years), it was anticipated that he would rather touch up the Radicals." 14

"Sir Barnet Skettles expressed his personal consequence chiefly through an antique gold snuff-box, and a ponderous silk pocket-handkerchief, which he had an imposing manner of drawing out of his pocket like a banner, and using with both hands at once. Sir Barnet's object in life was constantly to extend the range of his acquaintance. Like a heavy body dropped into water—not to disparage so worthy a gentleman by the comparison—it was in the nature of things that Sir Barnet must spread an ever-widening circle about him, until there was no room left. Or, like a sound in air, the vibration of which, according to the speculation of an ingenious modern philosopher, may go on travelling for ever through the interminable fields of space, nothing but coming to the end of his moral tether could stop Sir Barnet Skettles in his voyage of discovery through the social system." 24

Polly Toodle (Mrs Richards on duty). " . . . a plump rosy-cheeked wholesome apple-faced young woman, with an infant in her arms . . . . " 2

"Notwithstanding Mr **Toodle**'s great reliance on Polly, she was perhaps in point of artificial accomplishments very little his superior. But she was a good plain sample of a nature that is ever, in the mass, better, truer, higher, nobler, quicker to feel, and much more constant to retain, all tenderness and pity, self-denial and devotion, than the nature of men." 3

And see **What the Waves were always saying**—*the nurse*

Robin (Biler) Toodle. " . . . another plump and also apple-faced boy who walked by himself . . . . 'The fine little boy with the blister on his nose is the eldest. The blister, I believe' said **Miss Tox**, looking round upon the family, 'is not constitutional, but accidental?'

"The apple-faced man was understood to growl, 'Flat iron.'" 2

—*nickname explained:* " . . . the eldest (known in the family by the name of Biler, in remembrance of the steam engine) beat a demoniacal tattoo with his boots, expressive of grief. . . . " 2

—*in charity school uniform:* " . . . poor Biler's life had been, since yester-day morning, rendered weary by the costume of the Charitable Grinders. The youth of the streets could not endure it. No young vagabond could be brought to bear its contemplation for a moment, without throwing himself upon the un-offending wearer, and doing him a mischief. His social existence had been more like that of an early Christian, than an innocent child of the nineteenth century. He had been stoned in the streets. He had been overthrown into gutters; bespattered with mud; violently flattened against posts. Entire strangers to his person had lifted his yellow cap off his head and cast it to the winds. His legs had not only undergone verbal criticisms and revilings, but had been handled and pinched." 6

—*job-hunting:* "Mr **Perch** then ushered into the presence [of the manager] a strong-built lad of fifteen, with a round red face, a round sleek head, round black eyes, round limbs, and round body, who, to carry out the general rotundity of his appearance, had a round hat in his hand, without a particle of brim to it . . . his head presenting the appearance (which it always did) of having been newly drawn out of a bucket of cold water . . . . " 22

—*typically aggrieved:* "'Oh, it's very hard upon a cove, captain,' cried the tender Rob, injured and indignant in a moment, 'that he can't give lawful warn-

ing, without being frowned at in that way, and called a deserter. You haven't
any right to call a poor cove names, captain. It ain' t because I'm a servant
and you're a master, that you're to go and libel me. What wrong have I done?
Come, captain, let me know what my crime is, will you?'

"The stricken grinder wept, and put his coat-cuff in his eye." 39

Others

Jack Adams. "'Jack—little Jack— man with a cast in his eye, and slight
impediment in his speech—man who sat for somebody's borough. We used to
call him in my parliamentary time W. P. Adams, in consequence of his being
Warming Pan for a young fellow who was in his minority.'" 36

—*a bloomer:* "'So my friend was invited down to this marriage in Anyshire
. . . Jack goes. Now, this marriage was, in point of fact, the marriage of an uncommonly fine girl with a man for whom she didn't care a button, but whom
she accepted on account of his property, which was immense. When Jack returned to town, after the nuptials, a man he knew, meeting him in the lobby of
the House of Commons, says, "Well, Jack, how are the ill-matched couple?"
"Ill-matched," says Jack. "not at all. It's a perfectly fair and equal transaction. *She* is regularly bought, and you may take your oath *he* is as regularly
sold!"'"

"In his full enjoyment of this culminating point of his story, the shudder,
which had gone all round the table like an electric spark, struck Cousin
Feenix, and he stopped. Not a smile occasioned by the only general topic of
conversation broached that day, appeared on any face." 36

Amelia. "[Paul] saw a pretty young woman in leather gloves, cleaning a
stove. The young woman seemed surprised at his appearance, and asked him
where his mother was. When Paul told her she was dead, she took her gloves
off, and did what he wanted; and furthermore rubbed his hands to warm them;
and gave him a kiss; and told him whenever he wanted anything of that sort—
meaning in the dressing way—to ask for 'Melia; which Paul, thanking her very
much, said he certainly would." 12

Anne—*her master married:* "All the housemaid hopes is, happiness for
'em—but marriage is a lottery, and the more she thinks about it, the more she
feels the independence and the safety of a single life." 35

—*but:* "Mr **Towlinson** . . adjourning in quest of the housemaid, and
presently returning with that young lady on his arm, informs the kitchen that
foreigners is only his fun, and that him and Anne have now resolved to take one
another for better for worse, and to settle in Oxford Market in the general
greengrocery and herb and leech line, where your kind favours is particular requested." 59 *And see* **Towlinson**

Apothecary. "There was a certain calm apothecary, who attended at the
establishment when any of the young gentlemen were ill . . . . [Paul] was very
chatty with the apothecary, and they parted excellent friends. Lying down
again with his eyes shut, he heard the apothecary say, out of the room and
quite a long way off—or he dreamed it—that there was a want of vital power
. . . and great constitutional weakness." 14

Aunt, of **Kate**. " . . . a grey-haired lady, who spoke much to **Florence**, and
who greatly liked (but that they all did) to hear her sing of an evening, and
would always sit near her at that time, with motherly interest." 24 *See*
Florence Dombey—*her moment of truth*

Bank director. " ... reputed to be able to buy up anything—human nature generally, if he should take it in his head to influence the money market in
that direction—but who was a wonderfully modest-spoken man, almost boast-
fully so, and mentioned his 'little place' at Kingston-upon-Thames, and its just
being barely equal to giving **Dombey** a bed and chop, if he would come and visit
it .... Carrying out his character, this gentleman was very plainly dressed, in
a wisp of cambric for a neckcloth, big shoes, a coat that was too loose for him,
and a pair of trousers that were too spare; and mention being made of the
Opera by **Mrs Skewton**, he said he very seldom went there, for he couldn't afford it. It seemed greatly to delight and exhilarate him to say so: and he
beamed on his audience afterwards, with his hands in his pockets, and excessive satisfaction twinkling in his eyes." 36

Baps, a dancing master. "Mr Baps was a very grave gentleman, with a
slow and measured manner of speaking; and before he had stood under the
lamp five minutes, he began to talk to **Toots** (who had been silently comparing
pumps with him) about what you were to do with your raw materials when
they came into your ports in return for your drain of gold. Mr Toots, to whom
the question seemed perplexing, suggested 'Cook 'em.' But Mr Baps did not appear to think that would do." 14

Mrs Baps, "to whom **Mrs Blimber** was extremely kind and condescending
... (who, being quite deserted, was pretending to look over the music-book of
the gentleman who played the harp) .... " 14

Beadle. " ... the beadle of that quarter, a man of an ambitious character,
who had expected to have the distinction of being present at the breaking open
of the door, and of giving evidence in full uniform before the coroner, went so far
as to say to an opposite neighbour, that the chap in the glazed hat had better
not try it on there—without more particularly mentioning what—and further,
that he, the beadle, would keep his eye upon him." 50

Berinthia (Berry). "**Mrs Pipchin**'s middle-aged niece, her good-natured
and devoted slave, but possessing a gaunt and iron-bound aspect, and much
afflicted with boils on her nose .... " 8

"Poor Berry ... drudged and slaved away as usual; perfectly convinced that
Mrs Pipchin was one of the most meritorious persons in the world, and making
every day innumerable sacrifices of herself upon the altar of that noble old
woman. But all these immolations of Berry were somehow carried to the credit
of Mrs Pipchin by Mrs Pipchin's friends and admirers; and were made to har-
monise with, and carry out, that melancholy fact of the deceased Mr Pipchin
having broken his heart in the Peruvian mines." 11 *And see* **Grocer**

Betsey Jane, child of **Mrs Wickam**'s uncle. "'Betsey Jane,' said Mrs
Wickam, 'was as sweet a child as I could wish to see. I couldn't wish to see a
sweeter. Everything that a child could have in the way of illnesses, Betsey
Jane had come through. The cramps was as common to her,' said Mrs
Wickam, 'as biles is to yourself, **Miss Berry**.'"

"'She took fancies to people; whimsical fancies, some of them; others, affections that one might expect to see—only stronger than common. They all
died.'" 8

Master **Bitherstone**. "Master Bitherstone read aloud to the rest a pedi-
gree from Genesis (judiciously selected by **Mrs Pipchin**), getting over the
names with the ease and clearness of a person tumbling up the treadmill. That
done, **Miss Pankey** was borne away to be shampoo'd; and Master Bitherstone

to have something else done to him with salt water, from which he always returned very blue and dejected." 8

—at a new school: "[He] shows in collars and a neckcloth, and wears a watch. But Bitherstone, born beneath some Bengal star of ill-omen, is extremely inky; and his Lexicon has got so dropsical from constant reference, that it won't shut, and yawns as if it really could not bear to be so bothered. So does Bitherstone its master, forced at **Doctor Blimber**'s highest pressure; but in the yawn of Bitherstone there is malice and snarl, and he has been heard to say that he wishes he could catch 'old Blimber' in India. He'd precious soon find himself carried up the country by a few of his (Bitherstone's) Coolies, and handed over to the Thugs; he can tell him that." 41

Cornelia Blimber. " . . . although a slim and graceful maid, did no soft violence to the gravity of the house. There was no light nonsense about Miss Blimber. She kept her hair short and crisp, and wore spectacles. She was dry and sandy with working in the graves of deceased languages. None of your live languages for Miss Blimber. They must be dead—stone dead—and then Miss Blimber dug them up like a ghoul." 11

" . . . her spectacles, by reason of the glistening of the glasses, made her so mysterious, that [**Paul**] didn't know where she was looking, and was not indeed quite sure that she had any eyes at all behind them." 12

"Miss Blimber presented exactly the appearance she had presented yesterday, except that she wore a shawl. Her little light curls were as crisp as ever, and she had already her spectacles on, which made Paul wonder whether she went to bed in them. She had a cool little sitting-room of her own up there, with some books in it, and no fire. But Miss Blimber was never cold, and never sleepy." 12

Mrs Blimber. "[She] was not learned herself, but she pretended to be, and that did quite as well . . . a lady of great suavity, and a wiry figure, and who wore a cap composed of sky-blue materials . . . . " 11

—meeting a new pupil: " . . . she turned to admire his classical and intellectual lineaments, and turning again to **Mr Dombey**, said, with a sigh, that she envied his dear son.

"'Like a bee, sir,' said Mrs Blimber, with uplifted eyes, 'about to plunge into a garden of the choicest flowers, and sip the sweets for the first time. Virgil, Horace, Ovid, Terence, Plautus, Cicero. What a world of honey have we here. It may appear remarkable, Mr Dombey, in one who is a wife—the wife of such a husband . . . . But really . . . I think if I could have known Cicero, and been his friend, and talked with him in his retirement at Tusculum (beautiful Tusculum!) I could have died contented.'" 11

Blockitt. "'I needn't beg you,' [**Mr Dombey**] added . . . 'to take particular care of this young gentleman, Mrs—'

"'Blockitt, sir?' suggested the nurse, a simpering piece of faded gentility, who did not presume to state her name as a fact, but merely offered it as a mild suggestion." 1

Mrs Bokum. " . . . she was the widow of a Mr Bokum, who had held an employment in the Custom House . . . the dearest friend of **Mrs MacStinger**, whom she considered a pattern for her sex; that she had often heard of the captain, and now hoped he had repented of his past life; that she trusted Mr **Bunsby** knew what a blessing he had gained, but that she feared men seldom did know what such blessings were . . . Mrs Bokum kept her eyes steadily on the bridegroom, and . . . whenever they came near a court or other narrow turning which appeared favourable for flight, she was on the alert to cut him off if he attempted escape." 60

Briggs.—*his father:* "He never would leave him alone. So numerous and severe were the mental trials of that unfortunate youth in vacation time, that the friends of the family (then resident near Bayswater, London) seldom approached the ornamental piece of water in Kensington Gardens, without a vague expectation of seeing Master Briggs's hat floating on the surface, and an unfinished exercise lying on the bank." 14

—*graduated:* "[**Tozer**'s] triumph . . . caused the father and mother of Mr Briggs (whose learning, like ill-arranged luggage, was so tightly packed that he couldn't get at anything he wanted) to hide their diminished heads. The fruit laboriously gathered from the tree of knowledge by this latter young gentleman, in fact, had been subjected to so much pressure, that it had become a kind of intellectual Norfolk Biffin, and had nothing of its original form or flavour remaining." 60

Brogley, sworn broker and appraiser. "Mr Brogley himself was a moist-eyed, pink-complexioned, crisp-haired man, of a bulky figure and an easy temper—for that class of **Caius Marius** who sits upon the ruins of other people's Carthages, can keep up his spirits well enough." 9

Broker's men. "After a few days, strange people begin to call at the house, and to make appointments with one another in the dining-room, as if they lived there. Especially, there is a gentleman, of a Mosaic Arabian cast of countenance, with a very massive watch-guard, who whistles in the drawing-room, and, while he is waiting for the other gentleman, who always has pen and ink in his pocket, asks Mr **Towlinson** (by the easy name of 'Old Cock') , if he happens to know what the figure of them crimson and gold hangings might have been, when new bought.

"The callers and appointments in the dining-room become more numerous every day, and every gentleman seems to have pen and ink in his pocket, and to have some occasion to use it. At last it is said that there is going to be a sale; and then more people arrive, with pen and ink in their pockets, commanding a detachment of men with carpet caps, who immediately begin to pull up the carpets, and knock the furniture about, and to print off thousands of impressions of their shoes upon the hall and stair-case." ¶59

Butler, at **Doctor Blimber**'s. "In particular, there was a butler in a blue coat and bright buttons, who gave quite a winey flavour to the table beer; he poured it out so superbly." 11

John Carker, the clerk. "He was not old, but his hair was white; his body was bent, or bowed as if by the weight of some great trouble: and there were deep lines in his worn and melancholy face. The fire of his eyes, the expression of his features, the very voice in which he spoke, were all subdued and quenched, as if the spirit within him lay in ashes. He was respectably, though very plainly dressed, in black; but his clothes, moulded to the general character of his figure, seemed to shrink and abase themselves upon him, and to join in the sorrowful solicitation which the whole man from head to foot expressed, to be left unnoticed, and alone in his humility." 6

—*conscience cleared:* "'The favour [**Harriet** said] . . . [is] you will never speak of it to John, whose chief happiness in this act of restitution is to do it secretly, unknown, and unapproved of: that only a very small part of the inerhitance may be reserved to us, until **Mr Dombey** shall have possessed the interest of the rest for the remainder of his life . . . . '" 58

John Chick, "who was a stout bald gentleman, with a very large face, and his hands continually in his pockets, and who had a tendency in his nature to whistle and hum tunes . . . . " 2

—*dealing with his spouse:* "Mr Chick, finding that his destiny was, for the time, against him, said no more, and walked off. But it was not always thus with Mr Chick. He was often in the ascendant himself, and at those times punished Louisa roundly. In their matrimonial bickerings they were, upon the whole, a well-matched, fairly-balanced, give-and-take couple. It would have been, generally speaking, very difficult to have betted on the winner. Often when Mr Chick seemed beaten, he would suddenly make a start, turn the tables, clatter them about the ears of Mrs Chick, and carry all before him. Being liable himself to similar unlooked-for checks from Mrs Chick, their little contests usually possessed a character of uncertainty that was very animating." 2

Children. "Now the rosy children living opposite to **Mr Dombey**'s house, peep from their nursery windows down into the street . . . . " 18

—the youngest: " . . . and the youngest of the rosy children at the high window opposite, needs no restraining hand to check her in her glee, when, pointing [at **Paul**'s coffin] with her dimpled finger, she looks into her nurse's face, and asks 'What's that?'" 18

—observed: "Why did the dark eyes turn so often . . . to where the rosy children lived? They were not immediately suggestive of her loss; for they were all girls: four little sisters. But they were motherless like her—and had a **father**.

"It was easy to know when he had gone out and was expected home, for the elder child was always dressed and waiting for him at the drawing-room window, or in the balcony; and when he appeared, her expectant face lighted up with joy, while the others at the high window, and always on the watch too, clapped their hands, and drummed them on the sill, and called to him . . . . Florence would sometimes look no more at this, and bursting into tears would hide behind the curtain as if she were frightened, or would hurry from the window. Yet she could not help returning; and her work would soon fall unheeded from her hands again." 18

Clark. " . . . a little wooden house on wheels, outside of which, looking at the neighbouring masts and boats, a stout man stood whistling, with his pen behind his ear, and his hands in his pockets, as if his day's work were nearly done." 6

Clerks. "The clerks within were not a whit behind-hand in their demonstrations of respect. A solemn hush prevailed, as **Mr Dombey** passed through the outer office." 13

Clock repairman. " . . . there was something the matter with the great clock; and a workman on a pair of steps had taken its face off, and was poking instruments into the works by the light of a candle! This was a great event for **Paul** . . . . " 14

Cook, for **Mr Dombey**. "Mr **Towlinson** proposes with a sigh, 'Amendment to us all!' for which, as cook says with another sigh, 'There's room enough, God knows.'" 18

—the house refurbished: "Cook is high spirits, and says give *her* a place where there's plenty of company (as she'll bet you sixpence there will be now), for she is of a lively disposition, and she always was from a child, and she don't mind who knows it . . . . " 35

Cook, for **Mr Toots**. "'My cook's a most respectable woman—one of the most motherly people I ever saw—and she'll be delighted to make you [**Susan Nipper**] comfortable. Her son,' said Mr Toots, as an additional recommendation, 'was educated in the Blue-coat School, and blown up in a powder-mill.'" 43

Mary Daws. " . . . a young kitchen-maid of inferior rank—in black stockings—who, having sat with her mouth open for a long time, unexpectedly discharges from it words to this effect, 'Suppose the wages shouldn't be paid!' The company sit for a moment speechless; but **cook** recovering first, turns upon the young woman, and requests to know how she dares insult the family, whose bread she eats, by such a dishonest supposition, and whether she thinks that anybody, with a scrap of honour left, could deprive poor servants of their pittance? 'Because if *that* is your religious feelings, Mary Daws,' says cook warmly, 'I don't know where you mean to go to.'" 59

Diogenes. "'Ask them to take care of Diogenes, if you please [said **Paul**].'

"Diogenes was the dog: who had never in his life received a friend into his confidence, before Paul." 14

—*delivered:* " . . . though Diogenes was as ridiculous a dog as one would meet with on a summer's day; a blundering, ill-favoured, clumsy, bullet-headed dog, continually acting on a wrong idea that there was an enemy in the neighbourhood, whom it was meritorious to bark at; and though he was far from good-tempered, and certainly was not clever, and had hair all over his eyes, and a comic nose, and an inconsistent tail, and a gruff voice; he was dearer to **Florence**, in virtue of that parting remembrance of him, and that request that he might be taken care of, than the most valuable and beautiful of his kind." 18

Director. " . . . an East India director, of immense wealth, in a waistcoat apparently constructed in serviceable deal by some plain carpenter, but really engendered in the tailor's art, and composed of the material called nankeen, arrived and was received by **Mr Dombey** alone." 36

Feeder. "As to Mr Feeder, B. A., **Doctor Blimber**'s assistant, he was a kind of human barrel-organ, with a little list of tunes at which he was continually working, over and over again, without any variation. He might have been fitted up with a change of barrels, perhaps, in early life, if his destiny had been favourable; but it had not been; and he had only one, with which, in a monotonous round, it was his occupation to bewilder the young ideas of Doctor Blimber's young gentlemen." 11

"Mr Feeder . . . was in the habit of shaving his head for coolness, and had nothing but little bristles on it . . . . " 12

—*teaching:* "Mr Feeder, B. A. . . . had his Virgil stop on, and was slowly grinding that tune to four young gentlemen. Of the remaining four, two, who grasped their foreheads convulsively, were engaged in solving mathematical problems; one with his face like a dirty window, from much crying, was endeavouring to flounder through a hopeless number of lines before dinner; and one [**Briggs**] sat looking at his task in stony stupefaction and despair—which it seemed had been his condition ever since breakfast time." 12

Flower-seller. " . . . a man with bulgy legs, and rough voice, and a heavy basket on his head that crushed his hat into a mere black muffin, came crying flowers down Princess's Place, making his timid little roots of daisies shudder in the vibration of every yell he gave, as though he had been an ogre, hawking little children . . . . " 29

Flowers.—*her mistress's daughter married:* "The maid [to **Mrs Skewton**] who ought to be a skeleton, but is in truth a buxom damsel, is . . . in a most amiable state: considering her quarterly stipend much safer than heretofore, and foreseeing a great improvement in her board and lodging." 35

Footman, at **Doctor Blimber's.** "He was a weak-eyed young man, with the first faint streaks or early dawn of a grin on his countenance. It was mere imbecility; but **Mrs Pipchin** took it into her head that it was impudence, and made a snap at him directly . . . leaving the young man, who was all meekness and incapacity, affected even to tears by the incident." 11

Footmen. "One of the very tall young men already smells of sherry, and his eyes have a tendency to become fixed in his head, and to stare at objects without seeing them. The very tall young man is conscious of this failing in himself; and informs his comrade that it's his 'exciseman'. The very tall young man would say excitement, but his speech is hazy." 31

—*later:* "The very tall young man who suffered from excitement early, is better; but a vague sentiment of repentance has seized upon him, and he hates the other very tall young man, and wrests dishes from him by violence, and takes a grim delight in disobliging the company." 31

—*still later:* "The very tall young man has recovered his spirits, and again alludes to the exciseman. His comrade's eye begins to emulate his own, and he, too, stares at objects without taking cognizance thereof." 31

—*much later:* "The very tall young man whose excitement came on so soon, appears to have his head glued to the table in the pantry, and cannot be detached from it." 31

Game Chicken. " . . . Mr **Toots** devoted himself to the cultivation of those gentle arts which refine and humanise existence, his chief instructor in which was an interesting character called the Game Chicken, who was always to be heard of at the bar of the Black Badger, wore a shaggy white great-coat in the warmest weather, and knocked Mr Toots about the head three times a week, for the small consideration of ten and six per visit." 22 [*There was a pugilist who fought in the early 1800's under this sobriquet.*]

—defeated but dreaming: " . . . Susan set out for the coach-office in another cabriolet, with Mr **Toots** inside, as before, and the Chicken on the box, who, whatever distinction he conferred on the little party by the moral weight and heroism of his character, was scarcely ornamental to it, physically speaking, on account of his plasters; which were numerous. But the Chicken had registered a vow, in secret, that he would never leave Mr Toots (who was secretly pining to get rid of him), for any less consideration than the good-will and fixtures of a public-house; and being ambitious to go into that line, and drink himself to death as soon as possible, he felt it his cue to make his company unacceptable." 44

Florence Gay. "But no one, except **Florence**, knows the measure of the white-haired gentleman's affection for the girl. That story never goes about. The child herself almost wonders at a certain secrecy he keeps in it. He hoards her in his heart. He cannot bear to see a cloud upon her face. He cannot bear to see her sit apart. He fancies that she feels a slight, when there is none. He steals away to look at her, in her sleep. It pleases him to have her come, and wake him in the morning. He is fondest of her and most loving to her, when there is no creature by. The child says then, sometimes:

"'Dear grandpapa, why do you cry when you kiss me?'

"He only answers, 'Little Florence! Little Florence!' and smooths away the curls that shade her earnest eyes." 62

Paul Gay. "'You will come home with me, papa, and see my baby. A boy, papa. His name is Paul.'" 59

Glubb. "Consistent with his odd tastes, [**Paul**] set aside a ruddy-faced **lad** who was proposed as the drawer of [his] carriage, and selected, instead, his grandfather—a weazen, old, crab-faced man, in a suit of battered oilskin, who had got tough and stringy from long pickling in salt water, and who smelt like a weedy sea-beach when the tide is out." 8

"'He's a very nice old man, ma'am,' [Paul] said. 'He used to draw my couch. . . . And though old Glubb don't know why the sea should make me think of my mama that's dead, or what it is that it is always saying—always saying! he knows a great deal about it. And I wish . . . that you'd let old Glubb come here to see me, for I know him very well, and he knows me.'" 12

Grocer. " . . . there was an honest grocer and general dealer in the retail line of business, between whom and **Mrs Pipchin** there was a small memorandum book, with a greasy red cover, perpetually in question, and concerning which divers secret councils and conferences were continually being held between the parties to the register, on the mat in the passage, and with closed doors in the parlour . . . . This grocer being a bachelor, and not a man who looked upon the surface for beauty, had once made honourable offers for the hand of **Berry**, which Mrs Pipchin had, with contumely and scorn, rejected . . . poor Berry . . . cried for six weeks (being soundly rated by her good aunt all the time), and lapsed into a state of hopeless spinsterhood." 11

Guests, at the **Dombeys'**: " . . . a young lady of sixty-five, remarkably coolly dressed as to her back and shoulders, who spoke with an engaging lisp, and whose eyelids wouldn't keep up well, without a great deal of trouble on her part, and whose manners had that indefinable charm which so frequently attaches to the giddiness of youth." 36

—" . . . an old lady like a crimson velvet pincushion stuffed with bank notes, who might have been the identical old lady of Threadneedle Street, she was so rich, and looked so unaccommodating. . . . " 36

—" . . . a gloomy black velvet hat surmounting a bony and speechless female with a fan . . . . " 36

—". . . friends of **Mrs Skewton**, with the same bright bloom on their complexions, and very precious necklaces on very withered necks." 36

Hairdresser. "There was a grand array of white waistcoats and cravats in the young gentlemen's bedrooms as evening approached; and such a smell of singed hair, that **Doctor Blimber** sent up the **footman** with his compliments, and wished to know if the house was on fire. But it was only the hairdresser curling the young gentlemen, and over-heating his tongs in the ardour of business." 14

Reverend **Melchisedech Howler**, "who, having been one day discharged from the West India Docks on a false suspicion (got up expressly against him by the general enemy) of screwing gimlets into puncheons, and applying his lips to the orifice, had announced the destruction of the world for that day two years, at ten in the morning, and opened a front parlour for the reception of ladies and gentlemen of the Ranting persuasion, upon whom, on the first occasion of their assemblage, the admonitions of the Reverend Melchisedech had produced so powerful an effect, that, in their rapturous performance of a sacred jig, which closed the service, the whole flock broke through into a kitchen below, and disabled a mangle belonging to one of the fold." 15

Jemima, **Polly**'s sister. " . . . a younger woman not so plump [as Polly], but apple-faced also, who led a plump and apple-faced child in each hand . . . . " 2

John. "There was one man whom [**Florence**] several times observed at work very early, and often with a girl [**Martha**] of about her own age seated near him. He was a very poor man, who seemed to have no regular employment . . . . " 24

Johnson, a student at **Doctor Blimber**'s. "At the mention of this terrible people [the Romans], their implacable enemies, every young gentleman fastened his gaze upon the doctor, with an assumption of the deepest interest. One of the number who happened to be drinking, and who caught the doctor's eye glaring at him through the side of his tumbler, left off so hastily that he was convulsed for some moments, and in the sequel ruined Doctor Blimber's point." 12

Juggler. "The juggler who was going to twirl the basin, puts his loose coat on again over his fine dress . . . . " 18

Juggler's wife. " . . . his trudging wife, one-sided with her heavy baby in her arms, loiters to see the company come out . . . [and] is less alert than usual with the money-box, for a child's burial has set her thinking that perhaps the baby underneath her shabby shawl may not grow up to be a man, and wear a sky-blue fillet round his head, and salmon-coloured worsted drawers, and tumble in the mud." 18

Kate. "There came among the other visitors, soon after **Florence**, one beautiful girl, three or four years younger than she who was an orphan child, and who was accompanied by her **aunt** . . . . " 24 *See* **Florence Dombey**—*her moment of truth*

MacStinger children. "These innocent MacStingers were so many daggers to the captain's breast, when they appeared in a swarm, and tore at him with the confiding trustfulness he so little deserved. The eye of **Alexander MacStinger**, who had been his favourite, was insupportable to the captain; the voice of **Juliana MacStinger**, who was the picture of her mother, made a coward of him.

"Captain Cuttle kept up appearances, nevertheless, tolerably well, and for an hour or two was very hardly used and roughly handled by the young MacStingers: who in their childish frolics, did a little damage also to the glazed hat, by sitting in it, two at a time, as in a nest, and drumming on the inside of the crown with their shoes." 25

—**Alexander**. "[His mother] was in the act of conveying Alexander . . . aged two years and three months, along the passage for forcible deposition in a sitting posture on the street pavement; Alexander being black in the face with holding his breath after punishment, and a cool paving-stone being usually found to act as a powerful restorative in such cases." 23

—*his mother retrieves a tenant:* "'Why, if that baby of mine,' said Mrs MacStinger, with sudden rapidity, 'was to offer to go and steal away, I'd do my duty as a mother by him, till he was covered with wales!'

"The young Alexander, interpreting this into a positive promise, to be shortly redeemed, tumbled over with fear and grief, and lay upon the floor, exhibiting the soles of his shoes and making such a deafening outcry, that Mrs MacStinger found it necessary to take him up in her arms, where she quieted him, ever and anon, as he broke out again, by a shake that seemed enough to loosen his teeth." 39

—**Charles**. " . . . the sweet child's brother, Charles MacStinger, popularly known about the scenes of his youthful sports, as **Chowley** . . . . " 39

—**Juliana**.—*at a wedding:* "One of the most frightful circumstances of the ceremony to the captain, was the deadly interest exhibited therein by Juliana MacStinger; and the fatal concentration of her faculties, with which that promising child, already the image of her parent, observed the whole proceedings. The captain saw in this a succession of man-traps stretching out infinitely; a series of ages of oppression and coercion, through which the seafaring line was doomed . . . . Another year or two, the captain thought, and to lodge where that child was, would be destruction." 60

Martha. "The girl made an impatient gesture with her cowering shoulders, and turned her head another way. Ugly, misshapen, peevish, ill-conditioned, ragged, dirty—but beloved! Oh, yes! **Florence** had seen her father 's look towards her, and she knew whose look it had no likeness to." 24

Mrs Miff. "A vinegary face has Mrs Miff, and a mortified bonnet, and eke a thirsty soul for sixpences and shillings. Beckoning to stray people to come into pews, has given Mrs Miff an air of mystery; and there is reservation in the eye of Mrs Miff, as always knowing of a softer seat, but having her suspicions of the fee. There is no such fact as Mr **Miff**, nor has there been, these twenty years, and Mrs Miff would rather not allude to him. He held some bad opinions, it would seem, about free seats; and though Mrs Miff hopes he may be gone upwards, she couldn't positively undertake to say so." 31

" . . . whose cough is drier than the hay in any hassock in her charge . . . . She is such a spare, straight, dry old lady—such a pew of a woman—that you should find as many individual sympathies in a chip." 57

Mild man. "When all the rest were got in and were seated, one of these mild men still appeared, in smiling confusion, totally destitute and unprovided for, and escorted by the **butler**, made the complete circuit of the table twice before his chair could be found, which it finally was . . . after which the mild man never held up his head again." 36

Morfin. "The gentleman last mentioned was a cheerful-looking, hazel-eyed elderly bachelor: gravely attired, as to his upper man, in black; and as to his legs, in pepper-and-salt colour. His dark hair was just touched here and there was specks of grey, as though the tread of Time had splashed it; and his whiskers were already white.

"He had a mighty respect for Mr **Dombey**, and rendered him due homage; but as he was of a genial temper himself, and never wholly at his ease in that stately presence, he was disquieted by no jealousy of the many conferences enjoyed by Mr **Carker**, and felt a secret satisfaction in having duties to discharge, which rarely exposed him to be singled out for such distinction.

"He was a great musical amateur in his way—after business; and had a paternal affection for his violoncello, which was once in every week transported from Islington, his place of abode, to a certain club-room hard by the bank, where quartettes of the most tormenting and excruciating nature were executed every Wednesday evening by a private party." 13

" . . . a gentleman, a very little past his prime of life perhaps, but of a healthy florid hue, an upright presence, and a bright clear aspect, that was gracious and good-humoured. His eyebrows were still black, and so was much of his hair; the sprinkling of grey observable among the latter, graced the former very much, and showed his broad frank brow and honest eyes to great advantage." ¶33

—*relieved:* "[**Harriet**] raised her eyes again; and the light of exultation in her face began to appear beautiful, in the observant eyes that watched her ....

"'My dear Harriet,' said Mr Morfin, after a silence, "I was not prepared for this. Do I understand you that you wish to make your own part in the inheritance available for your good purpose [to support **Mr Dombey**], as well as **John**'s?' . . .

"'Harriet,' he said . . . . I have every right to bend my head before what you confide to me . . . I am your faithful steward; and I would rather be so, and your chosen friend, than I would be anybody in the world, except yourself.'" 58

Musicians. "The men who play the bells have got scent of the marriage; and the marrow-bones and cleavers too; and a brass band too. The first, are practising in a back settlement near Battlebridge; the second, put themselves in communication, through their chief, with Mr **Towlinson**, to whom they offer terms to be bought off; and the third in the person of an artful trombone, lurks and dodges round the corner, waiting for some traitor tradesman to reveal the place and hour of breakfast, for a bribe." 31

Native, servant to **Major Bagstock**, who "was made so rabid by the gout, with which he happened to be then laid up, that he threw a footstool at the dark servant . . . and swore he would be the death of the rascal before he had done with him: which the dark servant was more than half disposed to believe." 10

—*his attire:* " . . . who wore a pair of ear-rings in his dark-brown ears, and on whom his European clothes sat with an outlandish impossibility of adjustment—being, of their own accord, and without any reference to the tailor's art, long where they ought to be short, short where they ought to be long, tight where they ought to be loose, and loose where they ought to be tight—and to which he imparted a new grace, whenever the major attacked him, by shrinking into them like a shrivelled nut, or a cold monkey . . . . " 20

Neighbour's viewpoint. "' . . . you've favoured and humoured [**Martha**], **John**, till she's got to be a burden to herself, and everybody else.'" 24

Miss Pankey. " . . . Miss Pankey (a mild little blue-eyed morsel of a child, who was shampoo'd every morning, and seemed in danger of being rubbed away, altogether) was led in from captivity by the ogress herself, and instructed that nobody who sniffed before visitors ever went to Heaven . . . . At last it was the children's bedtime, and after prayers they went to bed. As little Miss Pankey was afraid of sleeping alone in the dark, Mrs Pipchin always made a point of driving her upstairs herself, like a sheep; and it was cheerful to hear Miss Pankey moaning long afterwards, in the least eligible chamber, and Mrs Pipchin now and then going in to shake her." 8

Doctor Parker Peps, "one of the court physicians, and a man of immense reputation for assisting at the increase of great families, was walking up and down the drawing-room with his hands behind him, to the unspeakable admiration of the family surgeon [Mr **Pilkins**], who had regularly puffed the case for the last six weeks, among all his patients, friends, and acquaintances, as one to which he was in hourly expectation day and night of being summoned, in conjunction with Doctor Parker Peps.

"'Well, sir,' said Doctor Parker Peps in a round, deep, sonorous voice, muffled for the occasion, like the knocker; 'do you find that your dear lady is at all roused by your visit?'" 1

Perch. "When Perch, the messenger, whose place was on a little bracket, like a timepiece, saw **Mr Dombey** come in—or rather when he felt that he was coming, for he had usually an instinctive sense of his approach—he hurried into Mr Dombey's room, stirred the fire, quarried fresh coals from the bowels of the coal-box, hung the newspaper to air upon the fender, put the chair ready, and the screen in its place, and was round upon his heel on the instant of Mr Dombey's entrance, to take his great-coat and hat, and hang them up. Then Perch took the newspaper, and gave it a turn or two in his hands before the fire, and laid it, deferentially, at Mr Dombey's elbow. And so little objection had Perch to doing deferential in the last degree, that if he might have laid himself at Mr Dombey's feet, or might have called him by some such title as used to be bestowed upon the Caliph **Haroun Alraschid**, he would have been all the better pleased.

"As this honour would have been an innovation and an experiment, Perch was fain to content himself by expressing as well as he could, in his manner, You are the light of my Eyes. You are the Breath of my Soul. You are the commander of the Faithful Perch! With this imperfect happiness to cheer him, he would shut the door softly, walk away on tiptoe, and leave his great chief ...." 13

" ... Mr Perch the messenger knocked softly at the door, and coming in on tiptoe, bending his body at every step as if it were the delight of his life to bow, laid some papers on the table.

"'Would you please to be engaged, sir?' asked Mr Perch, rubbing his hands, and deferentially putting his head on one side, like a man who felt he had no business to hold it up in such a presence, and would keep it as much out of the way as possible." 22

Mrs Perch "is in the kitchen taking tea; and has made the tour of the [**Dombey**] establishment, and priced the silks and damasks by the yard, and exhausted every interjection in the dictionary and out of it expressive of admiration and wonder .... [She] has the happy social faculty of always wondering when other people wonder, without being at all particular what she wonders at." 35

Pilkins. "'Mr Pilkins here, who from his position of medical adviser in this family—no one better qualified to fill that position, I am sure.'

"'Oh!' murmured the family practitioner. "'Praise from Sir **Hubert Stanley**!'"" 1

Reporters. "'One of the Sunday ones [said **Perch**], in a blue cloak and a white hat, that had previously offered for to bribe me—need I say with what success?—was dodging about our court last night as late as twenty minutes after eight o'clock. I see him myself, with his eye at the counting-house keyhole, which being patent is impervious. Another one ... with milintary frogs, is in the parlour of the King's Arms all the blessed day. I happened, last week, to let a little obserwation fall there, and next morning, which was Sunday, I see it worked up in print, in a most surprising manner.'" 52

Ship's cook. "And the Son and Heir was in a pretty state of confusion, with sails lying all bedraggled on the wet decks, loose ropes tripping people up, men in red shirts running barefoot to and fro, casks blockading every foot of space, and, in the thickest of the fray, a black cook in a black caboose up to his eyes in vegetables and blinded with smoke." 19

Short gentleman. "The other lady, too, as well as her husband, the short gentleman with the tall hat, were plainly on guard, according to a preconcerted plan; and the wretched [**Bunsby**] was so secured . . . that any effort at self-preservation by flight was rendered futile." 60

Lady Skettles "took a panoramic survey of [the **Blimber** study] through her glass, and said to Sir **Barnet Skettles**, with a nod of approval, 'Very good.'" 14

Master **Barnet Skettles**, "who was revenging himself for the studies to come, on the plum-cake . . . ." 14

Skipper. "The last line [of a sailors' song] reaching the quick ears of an ardent skipper not quite sober, who lodged opposite, and who instantly sprung out of bed, threw up his window, and joined in, across the street, at the top of his voice, produced a fine effect. When it was impossible to sustain the concluding note any longer, the skipper bellowed forth a terrific 'ahoy!' intended in part as a friendly greeting, and in part to show that he was not at all breathed. That done, he shut down his window, and went to bed again." 15

Slipper and dogs' collar man, "who considered himself a public character, and whose portrait was screwed on to an artist's door in Cheapside—threw up his forefinger to the brim of his hat as Mr **Dombey** went by."13

Sownds, the beadle, at **Paul**'s christening: "Arriving at the church steps, they were received by a portentous beadle . . . .

"Before he turned again to lead the way, he gave Mr **Dombey** a bow and a half smile of recognition, importing that he (the beadle) remembered to have had the pleasure of attending on him when he buried his wife, and hoped he had enjoyed himself since." 5

—*before a wedding:* " . . . sitting in the sun upon the church steps . . . (and seldom does anything else, except, in cold weather, sitting by the fire) . . . asks if **Mrs Miff** has heard it said, that the lady is uncommon handsome? . . . though orthodox and corpulent, [he] is still an admirer of female beauty, [and] observes, with unction, yes, he hears she is a spanker—an expression that seems somewhat forcible to Mrs Miff, or would, from any lips but those of Mr Sownds the Beadle." 21

Statuary. "The man bows, glancing at the paper . . . .'I think there's a mistake.'

"'Where?'

"The statuary gives [Mr **Dombey**] back the paper, and points out, with his pocket rule, the words, 'beloved and only child.'

"'It should be "son," I think, sir?'

"'You are right. Of course. Make the correction.'" 18

Ticket-porter, "if he were not absent on a job, always ran officiously before to open **Mr Dombey**'s office door as wide as possible, and hold it open, with his hat off, while he entered." 13

Toodles

—**baby**, "who was making convulsive efforts with his arms and legs to launch himself on **Biler**, through the ambient air . . . . " 22

—**boy**. " . . . another plump and apple-faced boy, whom [**Toodle**] stood down on the floor, and admonished, in a husky whisper, to 'kitch hold of his brother **Johnny**.'" 2

—**boy**. " . . . the smallest boy but one divining [his mother's] intent, immediately began swarming upstairs after her—if that word of doubtful etymology be admissible—on his arms and legs . . . . " 2

"The ill-starred youngest Toodle but one, who would appear, from the frequency of his domestic troubles, to have been born under an unlucky planet, was prevented from performing his part in this general salutation [to **Miss Tox**] by having fixed the sou-wester hat (with which he had been previously trifling) deep on his head, hind side before, and being unable to get it off again; which accident presenting to his terrified imagination a dismal picture of his passing the rest of his days in darkness, and in hopeless seclusion from his friends and family, caused him to struggle with great violence, and to utter suffocating cries. Being released, his face was discovered to be very hot, and red, and damp; and Miss Tox took him on her lap, much exhausted." 38

—**Johnny**. " . . . a plump and apple-faced child . . . . " 2

—Mr. " . . . a plump and apple-faced man . . . . 'Stoker,' said the man. 'Steam ingine . . . . The ashes sometimes gets in here;' touching his chest: 'and makes a man speak gruff, as at the present time. But it *is* ashes, mum, not crustiness.' . . . "He was a strong, loose, round-shouldered, shuffling, shaggy fellow, on whom his clothes sat negligently: with a good deal of hair and whisker, deepened in its natural tint, perhaps by smoke and coal-dust: hard knotty hands: and a square forehead, as coarse in grain as the bark of an oak." 2

—on the railroad: "He was dressed in a canvas suit abundantly besmeared with coal-dust and oil, and had cinders in his whiskers, and a smell of half-slaked ashes all over him. He was not a bad-looking fellow, nor even what could be fairly called a dirty-looking fellow, in spite of this; and, in short, he was Mr Toodle, professionally clothed.

"'I shall have the honour of stokin' of you down, sir'. . . . " 19

"Mr Toodle had only three stages of existence. He was either taking refreshment in the bosom [of his family], or he was tearing through the country at from twenty-five to fifty miles an hour, or he was sleeping after his fatigues. He was always in a whirlwind or a calm, and a peaceable, contented, easy-going man Mr Toodle was in either state, who seemed to have made over all his own inheritance of fuming and fretting to the engines with which he was connected, which panted, and gasped, and chafed, and wore themselves out, in a most unsparing manner, while Mr Toodle led a mild and equable life." 38

And see **Polly Toodle** SR and **Robin (Biler) Toodle** SR

Tom Towlinson, footman. "In the evening also, Mr Towlinson goes out to take the air, accompanied by the housemaid, who has not yet tried her mourning bonnet. They are very tender to each other at dusky street-corners, and Towlinson has visions of leading an altered and blameless existence as a serious greengrocer in Oxford Market." 18 *And see* **Anne**

Tozer, a student at **Doctor Blimber**'s. "'You sleep in my room, don't you?' asked a solemn young gentleman, whose shirt-collar curled up the lobes of his ears." 12

—a relative: " . . . a dreadful **uncle**, who not only volunteered examinations of him, in the holidays, on abstruse points, but twisted innocent events and things, and wrenched them to the same fell purpose. So that if this uncle took him to the play, or, on a similar pretence of kindness, carried him to see a giant, or a dwarf, or a conjuror, or anything, Tozer knew he had read up some classical allusion to the subject beforehand, and was thrown into a state of mortal apprehension: not foreseeing where he might break out, or what authority he might not quote against him." 14

—graduated: "Mr Tozer, now a young man of lofty stature, in Wellington boots, was so extremely full of antiquity as to be nearly on a par with a genuine ancient Roman in his knowledge of English: a triumph that affected his good parents with the tenderest emotions . . . . " 60

Upholsterer. "The upholsterer's foreman, who has left his hat, with a pocket-handkerchief in it, both smelling strongly of varnish, under a chair in the hall, lurks about the house, gazing upwards at the cornices, and downward at the carpets, and occasionally, in a silent transport of enjoyment, taking a rule out of his pocket, and skirmishingly measuring expensive objects, with unutterable feelings." 35

Waiter. " . . . a dark, bilious subject, in a jacket, close shaved, and with a black head of hair close cropped . . . . " 54

Waiter in Dijon. " . . . a bald man, with a large beard from a neighbouring restaurant: 'with despair! Monsieur had said that supper was to be ready at that hour: also that he had forewarned made of the commands he had given, in his letter.'" 54

Waterman. " . . . they were boarded by various excited watermen, and among others by a dirty cyclops of the captain's acquaintance, who, with his one eye, had made the captain out some mile and a half off, and had been exchanging unintelligible roars with him ever since. Becoming the lawful prize of this personage, who was frightfully hoarse and constitutionally in want of shaving, they were all three put aboard the Son and Heir." 19

Mrs Wickam. "Mrs Wickam was a waiter's wife—which would seem equivalent to being any other man's widow—whose application for an engagement in Mr **Dombey**'s service had been favourably considered, on account of the apparent impossibility of her having any followers, or any one to follow; and who, from within a day or two of **Paul**'s sharp weaning, had been engaged as his nurse.

"Mrs Wickam was a meek woman, of a fair complexion, with her eyebrows always elevated, and her head always drooping; who was always ready to pity herself, or to be pitied, or to pity anybody else; and who had a surprising natural gift of viewing all subjects in an utterly forlorn and pitiable light, and bringing dreadful precedents to bear upon them, and deriving the greatest consolation from the exercise of that talent." ¶8

—*as a nurse:* "The excellent and thoughtful old system, hallowed by long prescription, which has usually picked out from the rest of mankind the most dreary and uncomfortable people that could possibly be laid hold of, to act as instructors of youth, finger-posts to the virtues, matrons, monitors, attendants on sick beds, and the like, had established Mrs Wickam in very good business as a nurse, and had led to her serious qualities being particularly commended by an admiring and numerous connexion." 58

Withers, a page. "And now, [**Mrs Skewton**'s] chair having stopped, the motive power became visible in the shape of a flushed page pushing behind, who seemed to have in part outgrown and in part out-pushed his strength, for when he stood upright he was tall, and wan, and thin, and his plight appeared the more forlorn from his having injured the shape of his hat, by butting at the carriage with his head to urge it forward, as is sometimes done by elephants in Oriental countries." 21

Youth, white-haired. " . . . **Susan** was not easily baffled . . . and having entrapped a white-haired youth, in a black calico apron, from a library where she was known, to accompany her in her quest [for books, with which **Florence** planned to tutor **Paul**], she led him such a life in going up and down, that he exerted himself to the utmost, if it were only to get rid of her; and finally enabled her to return home in triumph." 12

Walk-ons

Attorney's clerk. " . . . an over-aged and over-worked and under-paid attorney's clerk, 'making a search,' was running his forefinger down the parchment pages of an immense register (one of a long series of similar volumes) gorged with burials." 5

Beadle. "There is a dusty old beadle . . . who has something to do with a Worshipful Company who have got a hall in the next yard, with a stained-glass window in it that no mortal ever saw." 57

Bell-ringer. " . . . a shabby little old man in the porch behind the screen, who was ringing the [disappointed bell high up in the tower], like the bull in Cock Robin, with his foot in a stirrup." 56

Bill Bitherstone of Bengal, "who had written to ask [**Major Bagstock**], if he ever went [to Brighton], to bestow a call upon his only son." 10

Two **bridesmaids**. "Mr **Toots** escorted the fair bride [**Miss Blimber**], around whose lambent spectacles two gauzy little bridesmaids fluttered like moths." 60

Conversation Brown. "' . . . four-bottle man at the Treasury Board, with whom the father of my friend **Gay** was probably acquainted, for it was before my friend Gay's time . . . .'" 61

Butler (retired). "At [the] other private house in Princess's Place, tenanted by a retired butler who had married a **housekeeper**, apartments were let furnished, to a single gentleman [**Major Bagstock**]." 7

Butler. " . . . a silver-headed butler (who was charged extra on that account, as having the appearance of an ancient family retainer) . . . . " 30

Clerk. "Presently the clerk (the only cheerful-looking object there, and *he* was an undertaker) came up with a jug of warm water, and said something, as he poured it into the font, about taking the chill off . . . . " 5

Clerk "There is a dusty old clerk, who keeps a sort of evaporated news shop underneath an archway opposite, behind a perfect fortification of posts." 57

Clerk, at a dinner. " . . . one gentleman who has been in the [**Dombey**] office three years, under continual notice to quit on account of lapses in his arithmetic, appears in a perfectly new light, suddenly bursting out with a thrilling speech, in which he says, May their respected chief never again know the desolation which has fallen on his hearth! and says a great variety of things, beginning with 'May he never again,' which are received with thunders of applause." 51

Coachman, "who said he had been at home and in bed since ten o'clock. He had driven his mistress to her old house in Brook Street, where she had been met by Mr **Carker**——" 47

Curate. "Then the clergyman, an amiable and mild-looking young curate, but obviously afraid of the baby, appeared like the principal character in a ghost-story, 'a tall figure all in white;' at sight of whom **Paul** rent the air with his cries, and never left off again till he was taken out black in the face." 5

Damsel. "During **Florence**'s slumber in the morning, [**Captain Cuttle**] had engaged the daughter of an **elderly lady**, who usually sat under a blue umbrella in Leadenhall Market, selling poultry, to come and put her room in order, and render her any little services she required; and this damsel now appearing, Florence found everything about her as convenient and orderly, if not as handsome, as in the terrible dream she had once called Home." 49

Foreigner. "Mr **Towlinson** . . . being rendered something gloomy by the engagement of a foreigner with whiskers (Mr Towlinson is whiskerless himself), who has been hired to accompany the happy pair to Paris, and who is busy packing the new chariot." 31

Gentleman, rich. "A yellow-faced old gentleman from India, is going to take unto himself a young wife this morning, and six carriages full of company are expected, and **Mrs Miff** has been informed that the yellow-faced old gentleman could pave the road to church with diamonds and hardly miss them." 57

Guardian, of **Toots**. "'I have never had anybody belonging to me but my guardian, and him . . . I have always considered as a Pirate and a Corsair.'" 60

Harpist. " . . . in the course of his perambulations, **Paul** made acquaintance with various strange benches and candlesticks, and met a harp in a green greatcoat standing on the landing outside the drawing-room door." 14

Idlers. "The idlers and vagabonds had been particularly interested in the Captain's fate; constantly grovelling in the mud to apply their eyes to the cellar-grating, under the shop-window, and delighting their imaginations with the fancy that they could see a piece of his coat as he hung in a corner; though this settlement of him was stoutly disputed by an opposite faction, who were of opinion that he lay murdered with a hammer, on the stairs." 50

Jackson. "' . . . who kept the boxing-rooms in Bond Street—a man of very superior qualifications, with whose reputation my friend **Gay** is no doubt acquainted . . . .'" 61

Tom Johnson, at **Mrs Skewton**'s funeral. "'Man with cork leg from White's.'" 41

Two **juniors**, in the **Dombey** counting house, "who, quarrelling about the probable amount of Mr **Carker**'s late receipts per annum, defy each other with decanters, and are taken out greatly excited." 51

Man, in a carpet cap. "The housemaid . . . relates . . . that a strange man, in a carpet cap, offered this very morning to kiss her on the stairs." 59

Midshipman. " . . . one of . . . the woodenest . . . which thrust itself out above the pavement, right leg foremost, with a suavity the least endurable, and had the shoe buckles and flapped waistcoat the least reconcilable to human reason, and bore at its right eye the most offensively disproportionate piece of machinery . . . ." 4

Midshipmen, of wood." . . . little timber midshipmen in obsolete naval uniforms, eternally employed outside the shop doors of nautical instrument-makers in taking observations of the hackney coaches . . . ." 4

Nurse. "' . . . the nurse before Mrs Richards *did* make unpleasant remarks when I was in company , and hint at little Pitchers, but that could only be attributed, poor thing,' observed **Susan [Nipper]**, with composed forbearance, 'to habits of intoxication, for which she was required to leave, and did.'" 28

Postillion. " . . . with a loud shouting and lashing, a shadowy postillion muffled to the eyes, checked his four struggling horses at [**Carker**'s] side." 55

Relative, of **Mrs Skewton**, "who did not object to lending [his house] in the handsomest manner, for nuptial purposes, as the loan implied his final release and acquittance from all further loans and gifts to Mrs Skewton and her daughter." 30

Tommy Screwzer. "' . . . a man of an extremely bilious habit, with whom my friend **Gay** is probably acquainted . . . . '" 61

Skewton brothers. " . . . Mrs [**Edith**] Dombey's father and his brother were the gayest gentlemen and the best-liked that came a visiting from London—they have long been dead, though! . . . The brother, who was my **Ally**'s father, longest of the two." 58

Surgeons, attending **Dombey**. " . . . who seemed to come by some mysterious instinct, as vultures are said to gather about a camel who dies in the desert." 42

Tox. "**Miss Tox** sat down upon the window-seat, and thought of her good papa deceased—Mr Tox, of the Customs Department of the public service; and of her childhood, passed at a seaport, among a considerable quantity of cold tar, and some rusticity." 29

Mrs Tox. " . . . Miss Tox thought likewise of her good mama deceased . . . of her virtues and her rheumatism." 29

Tradesman, "resident in the parish of Mary-le-bone, who lent out all sorts of articles to the nobility and gentry, from a service of plate to an army of footmen . . . . " 30

Young man. " . . . a modest young man, with a fresh-coloured face, at the next table [to **Major Bagstock**] (who would give a handsome sum to be able to rise and go away but cannot do it) . . . . " 31

What the Waves were always saying

Chapter XVI is given here complete. This and **Nell Trent's** offstage demise are the most famous deaths in Dickens. We have added side captions.

"There's no writing against such power as this. One has no chance . . . . It is unsurpassed. It is stupendous." —William Makepeace Thackeray

"Paul had never risen from his little bed. He lay there, listening to the noises in the street, quite tranquilly; not caring much how the time went, but watching it and watching everything about him with observing eyes.

Dusk. "When the sunbeams struck into his room through the rustling blinds, and quivered on the opposite wall like golden water, he knew that evening was coming on, and that the sky was red and beautiful. As the reflection died away, and a gloom went creeping up the wall, he watched it deepen, deepen, deepen, into night. Then he thought how the long streets were dotted with lamps, and how the peaceful stars were shining overhead.

The River in the Night. "His fancy had a strange tendency to wander to the river, which he knew was flowing through the great city; and now he thought how black it was, and how deep it would look, reflecting the hosts of stars—and more than all, how steadily it rolled away to meet the sea.

"As it grew later in the night, and footsteps in the street became so rare that he could hear them coming, count them as they passed, and lose them in the hollow distance, he would lie and watch the many-coloured ring about the candle, and wait patiently for day. His only trouble was, the swift and rapid river. He felt forced, sometimes, to try to stop it—to stem it with his childish hands—or choke its way with sand—and when he saw it coming on, resistless, he cried out! But a word from **Florence**, who was always at his side, restored him to himself; and leaning his poor head upon her breast, he told Floy of his dream, and smiled.

The River in the Day. "When day began to dawn again, he watched for the sun; and when its cheerful light began to sparkle in the room, he pictured to himself—pictured! he saw—the high church towers rising up into the morning sky, the town reviving, waking, starting into life once more, the river glistening as it rolled (but rolling fast as ever), and the country bright with dew. Familiar sounds and cries came by degrees into the street below; the servants in the house were roused and busy; faces looked in at the door, and voices asked his attendants softly how he was. Paul always answered for himself, 'I am better. I am a great deal better, thank you! Tell papa so!'

"By little and little, he got tired of the bustle of the day, the noise of carriages and carts, and people passing and repassing; and would fall asleep, or be troubled with a restless and uneasy sense again—the child could hardly tell whether this were in his sleeping or his waking moments—of that rushing river. 'Why, will it never stop, Floy?' he would sometimes ask her. 'It is bearing me away, I think!'

His Sister. "But Floy could always soothe and reassure him; and it was his daily delight to make her lay her head down on his pillow, and take some rest.

"'You are always watching me, Floy. Let me watch *you*, now!' They would prop him up with cushions in a corner of his bed, and there he would recline the while she lay beside him: bending forward oftentimes to kiss her, and whispering to those who were near that she was tired, and how she had sat up so many nights beside him.

"Thus, the flush of the day, in its heat and light, would gradually decline; and again the golden water would be dancing on the wall.

The Doctors. "He was visited by as many as three grave doctors—they used to assemble down-stairs, and come up together—and the room was so quiet, and Paul was so observant of them (though he never asked of anybody what they said), that he even knew the difference in the sound of their watches. But his interest centered in Sir **Parker Peps**, who always took his seat on the side of the bed. For Paul had heard them say long ago, that that gentleman had been with his mama when she clasped Florence in her arms, and died. And he could not forget it, now. He liked him for it. He was not afraid.

His Father. "The people round him changed as unaccountably as on that first night at **Doctor Blimber**'s—except Florence; Florence never changed— and what had been Sir Parker Peps, was now his father, sitting with his head upon his hand. Old **Mrs Pipchin** dozing in an easy chair, often changed to **Miss Tox**, or his aunt; and Paul was quite content to shut his eyes again, and see what happened next without emotion. But this figure with its head upon its hand returned so often, and remained so long, and sat so still and solemn, never speaking, never being spoken to, and rarely lifting up its face, that Paul began to wonder languidly, if it were real; and in the night-time saw it sitting there, with fear.

"'Floy!' he said. 'What *is* that?'

"'Where, dearest?'

"'There! at the bottom of the bed.'

"'There's nothing there, except papa!'

"The figure lifted up its head, and rose, and coming to the bedside, said: 'My own boy! Don't you know me?'

"Paul looked it in the face, and thought, was this his father? But the face so altered to his thinking, thrilled while he gazed, as if it were in pain; and before he could reach out both his hands to take it between them, and draw it towards him, the figure turned away quickly from the little bed, and went out at the door.

"Paul looked at Florence with a fluttering heart, but he knew what she was going to say, and stopped her with his face against her lips. The next time he observed the figure sitting at the bottom of the bed, he called to it.

"'Don't be so sorry for me, dear papa! Indeed I am quite happy!'

"His father coming and bending down to him—which he did quickly, and without first pausing by the bedside—Paul held him round the neck, and repeated those words to him several times, and very earnestly; and Paul never saw him in his room again at any time, whether it were day or night, but he called out, 'Don't be so sorry for me! Indeed I am quite happy!' This was the beginning of his always saying in the morning that he was a great deal better, and that they were to tell his father so.

A Blur of Time. "How many times the golden water danced upon the wall; how many nights the dark, dark river rolled towards the sea in spite of him; Paul never counted, never sought to know. If their kindness, or his sense of it, could have increased, they were more kind, and he more grateful every day; but whether they were many days or few, appeared of little moment now, to the gentle boy.

His Mother. "One night he had been thinking of his mother, and her picture in the drawing-room down-stairs, and thought she must have loved sweet Florence better than his father did, to have held her in her arms when she felt that she was dying—for even he, her brother, who had such dear love for her, could have no greater wish than that. The train of thought suggested to him to inquire if he had ever seen his mother; for he could not remember whether they had told him, yes or no, the river running very fast, and confusing his mind.

"'Floy, did I ever see mama?'

"'No, darling, why?'

His Nurse. "'Did I ever see any kind face, like mama's, looking at me when I was a baby, Floy?'

"He asked, incredulously, as if he had some vision of a face before him.

"'Oh yes, dear!'

"'Whose, Floy?'

"'Your old nurse's. Often.'

"'And where is my old nurse?' said Paul. 'Is she dead too? Floy, are we *all* dead, except you?'

"There was a hurry in the room, for an instant—longer, perhaps; but it seemed no more—then all was still again; and Florence, with her face quite colourless, but smiling, held his head upon her arm. Her arm trembled very much.

"'Show me that old nurse, Floy, if you please!'

"'She is not here, darling. She shall come to-morrow.'

"'Thank you, Floy!'

"Paul closed his eyes with those words, and fell asleep. When he awoke, the sun was high, and the broad day was clear and warm. He lay a little, looking at the windows, which were open, and the curtains rustling in the air, and waving to and fro: then he said, 'Floy, is it to-morrow? Is she come?'

"Some one seemed to go in quest of her. Perhaps it was **Susan**. Paul thought he heard her telling him when he had closed his eyes again, that she would soon be back; but he did not open them to see. She kept her word—perhaps she had never been away—but the next thing that happened was a noise of footsteps on the stairs, and then Paul woke—woke mind and body—and sat upright in his bed. He saw them now about him. There was no grey mist before them, as there had been sometimes in the night. He knew them every one, and called them by their names.

"'And who is this? Is this my old nurse?' said the child, regarding with a radiant smile, a figure coming in.

"Yes, yes. No other stranger would have shed those tears at sight of him, and called him her dear boy, her pretty boy, her own poor blighted child. No other woman would have stooped down by his bed, and taken up his wasted hand, and put it to her lips and breast, as one who had some right to fondle it. No other woman would have so forgotten everybody there but him and Floy, and been so full of tenderness and pity.

"'Floy! this is a kind good face!' said Paul. 'I am glad to see it again. Don't go away, old nurse! Stay here.'

A Friend. "His senses were all quickened, and he heard a name he knew.

"'Who was that, who said "**Walter**"?' he asked, looking round. 'Some one said Walter. Is he here? I should like to see him very much.'

"Nobody replied directly; but his father soon said to Susan, 'Call him back, then: let him come up!' After a short pause of expectation, during which he looked with smiling interest and wonder, on his nurse, and saw that she had not forgotten Floy, Walter was brought into the room. His open face and manner, and his cheerful eyes, had always made him a favourite with Paul; and when Paul saw him, he stretched out his hand, and said 'Good-bye!'

"'Good-bye, my child!' said Mrs Pipchin, hurrying to his bed's head. 'Not good-bye?'

"For an instant, Paul looked at her with the wistful face with which he had so often gazed upon her in his corner by the fire. 'Ah yes,' he said placidly, 'good-bye! Walter dear, good-bye!'—turning his head to where he stood, and putting out his hand again. 'Where is papa?'

"He felt his father's breath upon his cheek, before the words had parted from his lips.

"'Remember Walter, dear papa,' he whispered, looking in his face. 'Remember Walter. I was fond of Walter!' The feeble hand waved in the air, as if it cried 'good-bye!' to Walter once again.

Brother and Sister Together. "'Now lay me down,' he said, 'and, Floy, come close to me, and let me see you!'

"Sister and brother wound their arms around each other, and the golden light came streaming in, and fell upon them, locked together.

"'How fast the river runs, between its green banks and the rushes, Floy! But it's very near the sea. I hear the waves! They always said so!'

"Presently he told her that the motion of the boat upon the stream was lulling him to rest. How green the banks were now, how bright the flowers growing on them, and how tall the rushes! Now the boat was out at sea, but gliding smoothly on. And now there was a shore before him. Who stood on the bank!—

"He put his hands together, as he had been used to do at his prayers. He did not remove his arms to do it; but they saw him fold them so, behind her neck.

"'Mama is like you, Floy. I know her by the face! But tell them that the print upon the stairs at school is not divine enough. The light about the head is shining on me as I go!'

Certain Old Fashions. "The golden ripple on the wall came back again, and nothing else stirred in the room. The old, old fashion! The fashion that came in with our first garments, and will last unchanged until our race has run its course, and the wide firmament is rolled up like a scroll. The old, old fashion—Death!

"Oh thank GOD, all who see it, for that older fashion yet, of Immortality! And look upon us, angels of young children, with regards not quite estranged, when the swift river bears us to the ocean!"

Purgatory, Hell—and Redemption

Here, in our judgement, is CD's central myth and preoccupation. Its happy outcome probably is his best effort—other than CC—at overcoming, through an Author's imaginative edict, the avoidable, but not avoided, waste, loss and pain of Life. The passage reminds us too of CD's life-long battle for the restoration of Woman's role in partnership with Man.

Purgatory. "And the ruined man. How does he pass the hours, alone?

"'Let him remember it in that room, years to come!' He did remember it. It was heavy on his mind now; heavier than all the rest.

"'Let him remember it in that room, years to come! The rain that falls upon the roof, the wind that mourns outside the door, may have foreknowledge in their melancholy sound. Let him remember it in that room, years to come!'

"He did remember it. In the miserable night he thought of it; in the dreary day, the wretched dawn, the ghostly, memory-haunted twilight. He did remember it. In agony, in sorrow, in remorse, in despair! 'Papa! papa! Speak to me, dear papa!' He heard the words again, and saw the face. He saw it fall upon the trembling hands, and heard the one prolonged low cry go upward.

"He was fallen, never to be raised up any more. For the night of his worldly ruin there was no to-morrow's sun; for the stain of his domestic shame there was no purification; nothing, thank Heaven, could bring his dead child back to life. But that which he might have made so different in all the Past—which might have made the Past itself so different, though this he hardly thought of now—that which was his own work, that which he could so easily have wrought into a blessing, and had set himself so steadily for years to form into a curse: that was the sharp grief of his soul.

"Oh! He did remember it! The rain that fell upon the roof, the wind that mourned outside the door that night, had had foreknowledge in their melancholy sound. He knew, now, what he had done. He knew, now, that he had called down that upon his head, which bowed it lower than the heaviest stroke of fortune. He knew, now, what it was to be rejected and deserted; now, when every loving blossom he had withered in his innocent daughter's heart was snowing down in ashes on him.

"He thought of her, as she had been that night when he and his bride came home. He thought of her as she had been, in all the home-events of the abandoned house. He thought, now, that of all around him, she alone had never changed. His boy had faded into dust, his proud wife had sunk into a polluted creature, his flatterer and friend had been transformed into the worst of villains, his riches had melted away, the very walls that sheltered him looked on him as a stranger; she alone had turned the same mild gentle look upon him always. Yes, to the latest and the last. She had never changed to him—nor had he ever changed to her—and she was lost.

"As, one by one, they fell away before his mind—his baby-hope, his wife, his friend, his fortune—oh how the mist, through which he had seen her, cleared, and showed him her true self! Oh, how much better than this that he had loved her as he had his boy, and lost her as he had his boy, and laid them in their early grave together!

"In his pride—for he was proud yet—he let the world go from him freely. As it fell away, he shook it off. Whether he imagined its face as expressing pity for him, or indifference to him, he shunned it alike. It was in the same degree to be avoided, in either aspect. He had no idea of any one companion in his misery, but the one he had driven away. What he would have said to her, or what consolation submitted to receive from her, he never pictured to himself. But he always knew she would have been true to him, if he had suffered her. He always knew she would have loved him better now, than at any other time: he was as certain that it was in her nature, as he was that there was a sky above him; and he sat thinking so, in his loneliness, from hour to hour. Day after day uttered this speech; night after night showed him this knowledge.

"It began, beyond all doubt (however slow it advanced for some time), in the receipt of her young husband's letter, and the certainty that she was gone. And yet—so proud he was in his ruin, or so reminiscent of her, only as something that might have been his, but was lost beyond redemption—that if he could have heard her voice in an adjoining room, he would not have gone to her. If he could have seen her in the street, and she had done no more than look at him as she had been used to look, he would have passed on with his old cold unforgiving face, and not addressed her, or relaxed it, though his heart should have broken soon afterwards. However turbulent his thoughts, or harsh his anger had been, at first, concerning her marriage, or her husband, that was all past now. He chiefly thought of what might have been, and what was not. What was, was all summed up in this: that she was lost, and he bowed down with sorrow and remorse.

"And now he felt that he had had two children born to him in that house, and that between him and the bare wide empty walls there was a tie, mournful, but hard to rend asunder, connected with a double childhood, and a double loss. He had thought to leave the house—knowing he must go, not knowing whither—upon the evening of the day on which this feeling first struck root in his breast; but he resolved to stay another night, and in the night to ramble through the rooms once more.

"He came out of his solitude when it was the dead of night, and with a candle in his hand went softly up the stairs. Of all the footmarks there, making them as common as the common street, there was not one, he thought, but had seemed at the time to set itself upon his brain while he had kept close, listening. He looked at their number, and their hurry, and contention—foot treading foot out, and upward track and downward jostling one another—and thought, with absolute dread and wonder, how much he must have suffered during that trial, and what a changed man he had cause to be. He thought, besides, oh was there, somewhere in the world, a light footstep that might have worn out in a moment half those marks!—and bent his head, and wept as he went up.

"He almost saw it, going on before. He stopped, looking up towards the skylight; and a figure, childish itself, but carrying a child, and singing as it went, seemed to be there again. Anon, it was the same figure, alone, stopping for an instant, with suspended breath; the bright hair clustering loosely round its tearful face; and looking back at him.

"He wandered through the rooms: lately so luxurious; now so bare and dismal and so changed, apparently, even in their shape and size. The press of footsteps was as thick here; and the same consideration of the suffering he had had, perplexed and terrified him. He began to fear that all this intricacy in his brain would drive him mad; and that his thoughts already lost coherence as the footprints did, and were pieced on to one another, with the same trackless involutions, and varieties of indistinct shapes.

"He did not so much as know in which of these rooms she had lived, when she was alone. He was glad to leave them, and go wandering higher up. Abundance of associations were here, connected with his false wife, his false friend and servant, his false grounds of pride; but he put them all by now, and only recalled miserably, weakly, fondly, his two children.

"Everywhere, the footsteps! They had had no respect for the old room high up, where the little bed had been; he could hardly find a clear space there, to throw himself down, on the floor, against the wall, poor broken man, and let his tears flow as they would. He had shed so many tears here, long ago, that he was less ashamed of his weakness in this place than in any other—perhaps, with that consciousness, had made excuses to himself for coming here. Here, with stooping shoulders, and his chin dropped on his breast, he had come. Here, thrown upon the bare boards, in the dead of night, he wept, alone—a proud man, even then; who, if a kind hand could have been stretched out, or a kind face could have looked in, would have risen up, and turned away, and gone down to his cell.

"When the day broke he was shut up in his rooms again. He had meant to go away to-day, but clung to this tie in the house as the last and only thing left to him. He would go to-morrow. To-morrow came. He would go to-morrow. Every night, within the knowledge of no human creature, he came forth, and wandered through the despoiled house like a ghost. Many a morning when the day broke, his altered face, drooping behind the closed blind in his window, imperfectly transparent to the light as yet, pondered on the loss of his two children. It was one child no more. He reunited them in his thoughts, and they were never asunder. Oh, that he could have united them in his past love, and in death, and that one had not been so much worse than dead!

"Strong mental agitation and disturbance was no novelty to him, even before his late sufferings. It never is, to obstinate and sullen natures; for they struggle hard to be such. Ground, long undermined, will often fall down in a moment; what was undermined here in so many ways, weakened, and crumbled, little by little, more and more, as the hand moved on the dial.

Hell. "At last he began to think he need not go at all. He might yet give up what his creditors had spared him (that they had not spared him more, was his own act), and only sever the tie between him and the ruined house, by severing that other link——

"It was then that his footfall was audible in the late house-keeper's room, as he walked to and fro; but not audible in its true meaning, or it would have had an appalling sound.

"The world was very busy and restless about him. He became aware of that again. It was whispering and babbling. It was never quiet. This, and the intricacy and complication of the footsteps, harassed him to death. Objects began to take a bleared and russet colour in his eyes. Dombey and Son was no more—his children no more. This must be thought of, well, tomorrow.

"He thought of it to-morrow; and sitting thinking in his chair, saw in the glass, from time to time, this picture:

"A spectral, haggard, wasted likeness of himself, brooded and brooded over the empty fireplace. Now it lifted up its head, examining the lines and hollows in its face; now hung it down again, and brooded afresh. Now it rose and walked about; now passed into the next room, and came back with something from the dressing-table in its breast. Now, it was looking at the bottom of the door, and thinking.

—Hush! what?

"It was thinking that if blood were to trickle that way, and to leak out into the hall, it must be a long time going so far. It would move so stealthily and slowly, creeping on, with here a lazy little pool, and there a start, and then another little pool, that a desperately wounded man could only be discovered through its means, either dead or dying. When it had thought of this a long while, it got up again, and walked to and fro with its hand in its breast. He glanced at it occasionally, very curious to watch its motions, and he marked how wicked and murderous that hand looked.

"Now it was thinking again! What was it thinking?

"Whether they would tread in the blood when it crept so far, and carry it about the house among those many prints of feet, or even out into the street.

"It sat down, with its eyes upon the empty fireplace, and as it lost itself in thought there shone into the room a gleam of light; a ray of sun. It was quite unmindful, and sat thinking. Suddenly it rose, with a terrible face, and that guilty hand grasping what was in its breast. Then it was arrested by a cry—a wild, loud, piercing, loving, rapturous cry—and he only saw his own reflection in the glass, and at his knees, his daughter!

Redemption. "Yes. His daughter! Look at her! Look here! Down upon the ground, clinging to him, calling to him, folding her hands, praying to him.

"'Papa! Dearest papa! Pardon me, forgive me! I have come back to ask forgiveness on my knees. I never can be happy more, without it!'

"Unchanged still. Of all the world, unchanged. Raising the same face to his, as on that miserable night. Asking *his* forgiveness!

"'Dear papa, oh don't look strangely on me! I never meant to leave you. I never thought of it, before or afterwards. I was frightened when I went away, and could not think. Papa, dear, I am changed. I am penitent. I know my fault. I know my duty better now, Papa, don't cast me off, or I shall die!'

"He tottered to his chair. He felt her draw his arms about her neck; he felt her put her own round his; he felt her kisses on his face; he felt her wet cheek laid against his own; he felt—oh, how deeply!—all that he had done." ...

"As she clung close to him, in another burst of tears, he kissed her on her lips, and, lifting up his eyes, said, 'Oh my God, forgive me, for I need it very much!'" ...

"'And so Dombey and Son, as I observed upon a certain sad occasion,' said **Miss Tox**, winding up a host of recollections, 'is indeed a daughter ... after all.'"
59

CB 5 December 1848 by B&E
Definitive data on first U.S. publication not available

The Haunted Man

and

The Ghost's Bargain

A FANCY FOR CHRISTMAS TIME

PRÉCIS

The Gift Bestowed: **Redlaw**, teacher of chemistry, is brooding in his library *cum* laboratory. His servant, talkative **William Swidger**, brings the dinner-tray, and then William's wife **Milly** arrives with the fowl. His father, old **Philip**, brings holly. They tell of the ill student in nearby chambers, who wants to remain hidden and unaided by Redlaw. When they leave, Redlaw's **Ghost** manifests and reviews the story of Redlaw's betrayal by a trusted friend. The Ghost offers the gift of obliterated memory of the sorrow and the wrong. Redlaw agrees, and the Ghost then tells him that everyone he contacts will receive it too, and disappears. A tattered, derelict, literally feral, **Child** appears, looking for Milly. Redlaw shows him the way and sits down to eat alone. 1

The Gift Diffused: **Adolphus (Dolf) Tetterby**, news-seller, is sitting with a large brood of active children, of whom **Johnny**, the oldest, is walking **Sally**, a large and demanding baby, the only female of her generation. **Sophia Tetterby** arrives from the market, with Master **Adolphus**, who has been hawking newspapers. Redlaw enters, looking for the student. He borrows a light, touching Dolf as he does so. Both Dolf and Sophia speak coldly and roughly to their children as he leaves. Redlaw's cold mood unnerves the ill student, who confesses his true name is **Longford**. Redlaw speaks rudely and tosses him a purse. The young man declines it. Redlaw approaches and touches him.

They hear Milly outside the door. To avoid harm to her, Redlaw hides in the next room. Milly enters to find Denham petulant and ungrateful. She gently withdraws. The student charges Redlaw with infecting him. Redlaw casts him off and rushes out. He collects the Child and gives him money, directing him to guide him to miserable or wicked people. He observes he has no effect on the Child. At a filthy tenement, Redlaw speaks to a battered woman on the stairs and then encounters, first a wreck of a man who knows him and shrinks away, and then Philip and William, at the deathbed of wastrel **George Swidger**. He is called to the bedside and observes the penitent suddenly defiant, the old man rejecting of his son, William coldly uninterested. Redlaw flees with the Child to his lodgings. He refuses to admit Milly, who calls out that her family is all changed and that a desperate man, the student's father, is suicidal. Redlaw begs the Ghost to take back the dreadful Gift. 2

The Gift Reversed: In his workroom, Redlaw hears music and is moved—and grateful for the emotion. He sees the Ghost, with the shadow of Milly. The Ghost directs Redlaw to seek her out in the morning. He points to the Child as an example of what happens when the memory of sorrow and pain is absent.

At dawn, the Tetterbys are sadly disaffected from each other. Milly's appearance wakes them as though from a bad dream. She tells of a visit from Redlaw and a healing trip to see George. The student appears and begs forgiveness for his ingratitude. A young lady has come—his beloved, worried about him. Redlaw is subdued, his memory impaired. William and Philip are overjoyed at seeing Milly. She brings Redlaw the wreck he had seen at the tenement. It is Longford, his faithless friend. Redlaw stares at him unknowingly. Milly mediates, and Redlaw forgives, not knowing for what. Longford speaks handsomely and leaves. Milly recalls her dead child as a spirit always with her, and Redlaw's memory returns. The student and his lady appear, and Redlaw embraces them as his children. He vows to teach and reclaim the Child and holds a mammoth Christmas dinner for all the Swidgers and Tetterbys—and the Child, not fully domesticated but no longer feral, is there. 3

*"Some people have said since, that he only thought what has been herein set down; others, that he read it in the fire, one winter night about the twilight time; others, that the **Ghost** was but the representation of his own gloomy thoughts, and **Milly** the embodiment of his better wisdom. I say nothing."* 3

CONTENTS

CHARACTERS

Child, tattered and derelict; a symbol of the Soul's obliteration	P	786
Denham, Edmund (Longford); a poor student incognito	SR	789
Ghost, or Phantom, of Redlaw: makes a gift	P	786
Longford, Redlaw's dearest friend, who betrayed him and his sister	O	792
Phantom, or Ghost, of Redlaw	P	786
Redlaw, a man with a past, and Haunted	P	787
Miss;a deeply loving sister, now dead: jilted by Longford	O	792
Swidger, Charley, junior; nephew of Milly	O	792
family: cousins, uncles, aunts; Tumblers all	O	792
George; eldest son of Philip, fallen into vice	O	792
Milly (Mrs William; sometimes "Mouse" or Swidge)	P	788
Philip; eighty-seven years old; father of William	SR	789
William; Milly's fresh-coloured, busy, talkative husband	P	788
Tetterby, Adolphus (Dolf); has a small shop	SR	789
Adolphus (the younger); varied pronunciation of "Paper!!!"	SR	790
Children; large number of small fry (seven sons, all told)	SR	791
Johnny; biggest there but little	SR	790
Sally; a very Moloch of a baby	SR	790
Sophia; magnificent and imposing wife and mother: once wooed by four	SR	791
Woman, sitting on the stairs; a ruined Temple of God	O	792
Young lady, very like the miniature precious to Denham	O	792

Principals

The Child. "' . . . a creature more like a young wild beast than a young child, shivering upon a door-step . . . . A bundle of tatters, held together by a hand, in size and form almost an infant's, but, in its greedy, desperate little clutch, a bad old man's. A face rounded and smoothed by some half-dozen years, but pinched and twisted by the experiences of a life. Bright eyes, but not youthful. Naked feet, beautiful in their childish delicacy—ugly in the blood and dirt that cracked upon them. A baby-savage, a young monster, a child who had never been a child, a creature who might live to take the outward form of man, but who, within, would live and perish a mere beast.

"Used, already, to be worried and hunted like a beast, the boy crouched down as he was looked at, and looked back again, and interposed his arm to ward off the expected blow.

"'I'll bite,' he said, 'if you hit me!'" 1

"'This,' said the **Phantom**, pointing to the boy, 'is the last, completest illustration of a human creature, utterly bereft of such remembrances as you [**Redlaw**] have yielded up. No softening memory of sorrow, wrong, or trouble enters here, because this wretched mortal from his birth has been abandoned to a worse condition than the beasts, and has, within his knowledge, no one contrast, no humanising touch, to make a grain of such a memory spring up in his hardened breast. All within this desolate creature is barren wilderness." 3

—*at the grand celebration:* "It was sad to see the child who had no name or lineage, watching the other children as they played, not knowing how to talk with them, or sport with them, and more strange to the ways of childhood than a rough dog . . . . But he kept by **Milly**, and began to love her . . . and when they saw him peeping at them from behind her chair, they were pleased that he was so close to it." 3

Ghost, or **Phantom**, of **Redlaw**. "Ghastly and cold, colourless in its leaden face and hands, but with his features, and his bright eyes, and his grizzled hair, and dressed in the gloomy shadow of his dress, it came into his terrible appearance of existence, motionless, without a sound. As *he* leaned his arm upon the elbow of his chair, ruminating before the fire, *it* leaned upon the chairback, close above him, with its appalling copy of his face looking where his face looked, and bearing the expression his face bore." 1

—*the Gift:* "'. . . take this with you, man whom I here renounce! The gift that I have given [loss of memory of sorrow, wrong and trouble], you shall give again, go where you will. Without recovering yourself the power that you have yielded up, you shall henceforth destroy its like in all whom you approach. Your wisdom has discovered that the memory of sorrow, wrong, and trouble is the lot of all mankind, and that mankind would be the happier, in its other memories, without it. Go! Be its benefactor! Freed from such remembrance, from this hour, carry involuntarily the blessing of such freedom with you. Its diffusion is inseparable and inalienable from you. Go! Be happy in the good you have won, and in the good you do!'" 1

Redlaw. "Who could have seen his hollow cheek, his sunken brilliant eye; his black attired figure, indefinably grim, although well-knit and well-proportioned; his grizzled hair hanging, like tangled sea-weed about his face—as if he had been, through his whole life, a lonely mark for the chafing and beating of the great deep of humanity—but might have said he looked like a haunted man?

"Who could have observed his manner, taciturn, thoughtful, gloomy, shadowed by habitual reserve, retiring always and jocund never, with a distraught air of reverting to a bygone place and time, or of listening to some old echoes in his mind, but might have said it was the manner of a haunted man?

"Who could have heard his voice, slow-speaking, deep, and grave, with a natural fulness and melody in it which he seemed to set himself against and stop, but might have said it was the voice of a haunted man?" 1

—*parenting:* "'A stranger came into my father's place when I was but a child, and I was easily an alien from my mother's heart. My parents, at the best, were of that sort whose care soon ends, and whose duty is soon done; who cast their offspring loose, early, as birds do theirs; and, if they do well, claim the merit; and, if ill, the pity.'" 1

—*responding to an offer:* "' . . . I have never been a hater of my kind—never morose, indifferent, or hard, to anything around me. If, living here alone, I have made too much of all that was and might have been, and too little of what is, the evil, I believe, has fallen on me, and not on others. But, if there were poison in my body, should I not, possessed of antidotes and knowledge how to use them, use them? If there be poison in my mind, and through this fearful shadow I can cast it out, shall I not cast it out? . . . *I would forget it if I could!* . . . My memory is as the memory of other men, but other men have not this choice. Yes, I close the bargain. Yes! I WILL forget my sorrow, wrong, and trouble!'" 1

—*after the Gift:* " . . . there was a cold, monotonous apathy, which rendered him more like a marble image on the tomb of the man who had started from his dinner yesterday at the first mention of [**Denham**'s] case, than the breathing man himself . . ." 2

—*the lesson learned:* "'Phantoms! Punishers of impious thoughts! . . let the glimmering of contrition that I know is there, shine up, and show my misery! In the material world, as I have long taught, nothing can be spared; no step or atom in the wondrous structure could be lost, without a blank being made in the great universe. I know, now, that it is the same with good and evil, happiness and sorrow, in the memories of men.'" 2

"The abiding change that had come upon him . . . was, that now he truly felt how much he had lost, and could compassionate his own condition, and contrast it, clearly, with the natural state of those who were around him. In this, an interest in those who were around him was revived, and a meek, submissive sense of his calamity was bred, resembling that which sometimes obtains in age, when its mental powers are weakened, without insensibility or sullenness being added to the list of its infirmities." 3

Milly and **William Swidger**. "Mrs William, like Mr William, was a simple, innocent-looking person, in whose smooth cheeks the cheerful red of her husband's official waistcoat was very pleasantly repeated. But whereas Mr William's light hair stood on end all over his head, and seemed to draw his eyes up with it in an excess of bustling readiness for anything, the dark brown hair of Mrs William was carefully smoothed down, and waved away under a trim tidy cap, in the most exact and quiet manner imaginable.

"Whereas Mr William's very trousers hitched themselves up at the ankles, as if it were not in their iron-grey nature to rest without looking about them, Mrs William's neatly-flowered skirts—red and white, like her own pretty face—were as composed and orderly, as if the very wind that blew so hard out of doors could not disturb one of their folds.

"Whereas his coat had something of a fly-away and half-off appearance about the collar and breast, her little bodice was so placid and neat, that there should have been protection for her in it, had she needed any, with the roughest people. Who could have had the heart to make so calm a bosom swell with grief, or throb with fear, or flutter with a thought of shame! To whom would its repose and peace have not appealed against disturbance, like the innocent slumber of a child!" ¶1

—*a foreshadowing:* "'. . . I have read in your face [she said to the student], as plain as if it was a book, that but for some trouble and sorrow we should never know half the good there is about us.'" 2

—*received:* " '. . . as she came in, they kissed her, and kissed one another, and kissed the baby, and kissed their father and mother, and then ran back and flocked and danced about her, trooping on with her in triumph.

". . . . She came among them like the spirit of all goodness, affection, gentle consideration, love, and domesticity." 3

—*the definitive lesson:* "'May I tell you why it seems to me a good thing for us to remember wrong that has been done us? . . . That we may forgive it.'" 3

Supporting Roles

Edmund (Longford) Denham. "'It's a sick young gentleman, sir—and very poor, I am afraid—who is too ill to go home this holiday-time, and lives, unknown to any one, in but a common kind of lodging for a gentleman, down in Jerusalem Buildings.'" 1

"'I am the child of a marriage that has not proved itself a well-assorted or a happy one. From infancy, I have heard you spoken of with honour and respect. . . . At last, a poor student myself, from whom could I learn but you?' . . .

"**[Redlaw]** tossed his purse upon the table . . . the student took it up, and held it out to him.

"'Take it back, sir,' he said proudly, though not angrily. 'I wish you could take from me, with it, the remembrance of your words and offer.'" 2

Philip Swidger. "'Why there's my father, sir, superannuated keeper and custodian of this Institution, eighty-seven year old.'. . . a venerable old man with long grey hair." 1

—*his lesson:* "'It's a heavy sorrow to think of that time, but it does me good, **George**. Oh, think of it too, think of it too, and your heart will be softened more and more! . . . . There is hope . . . for all who are softened and penitent. There is hope for all such.'" 2

Tetterbys

—**Adolphus**. "A small man sat in a small parlour, partitioned off from a small shop by a small screen, pasted all over with small scraps of newspapers." 2

—*disciplinarian:* "Tetterby . . . having the presence of a young family impressed upon his mind in a manner too clamorous to be disregarded . . . laid down his paper, wheeled, in his distraction, a few times round the parlour, like an undecided carrier-pigeon, made an ineffectual rush at one or two flying little figures in bedgowns that skimmed past him, and then, bearing suddenly down upon the only unoffending member of the family, boxed the ears of [**Johnny**], little Moloch's nurse . . . .

"Softening more and more, as his own tender feelings and those of his injured son were worked on, Mr Tetterby concluded by embracing him, and immediately breaking away to catch one of the real delinquents. A reasonably good

start occurring, he succeeded, after a short but smart run, and some rather severe cross-country work under and over the bedsteads, and in and out among the intricacies of the chairs, in capturing his infant, whom he condignly punished, and bore to bed.

"This example had a powerful, and apparently, mesmeric influence on him of the boots, who instantly fell into a deep sleep, though he had been, but a moment before, broad awake, and in the highest possible feather. Nor was it lost upon the two young architects, who retired to bed, in an adjoining closet, with great privacy and speed. The comrade of the Intercepted One also shrinking into his nest with similar discretion, Mr Tetterby, when he paused for breath, found himself unexpectedly in a scene of peace.

"'My little woman herself,' said Mr Tetterby, wiping his flushed face, 'could hardly have done it better! I only wish my little woman had had it to do, I do indeed! . . .

"'Let anybody, I don't care who it is, get out of bed again,' said [he], as a general proclamation, delivered in a very soft-hearted manner, 'and astonishment will be the portion of that respected contemporary!'" ¶2

—Master **Adolphus** "unwound his torso out of a prismatic comforter, apparently interminable . . . [he was] employed . . . to vend newspapers at a railway station, where his chubby little person, like a shabbily disguised Cupid, and his shrill little voice (he was not much more than ten years old), were as well known as the hoarse panting of the locomotives, running in and out.

"His juvenility might have been at some loss for a harmless outlet, in his early application to traffic, but for a fortunate discovery he made of a means of entertaining himself, and of dividing the long day into stages of interest, without neglecting business. This ingenious invention, remarkable, like many great discoveries, for its simplicity, consisted in varying the first vowel in the word 'paper,' and substituting, in its stead, at different periods of the day, all the other vowels in grammatical succession. Thus, before daylight in the winter time, he went to and fro, in his little oilskin cap and cape, and his big comforter, piercing the heavy air with his cry of 'Morn-ing Pa-per!' which, about an hour before noon, changed to 'Morn-ing Pep-per!' which, at about two, changed to 'Morn-ing Pip-per!' which, in a couple of hours, changed to 'Morn-ing Pop-per!' and so declined with the sun into 'Eve-ning Pup-per!' to the great relief and comfort of this young gentleman's spirits." 2

—**Johnny**. " . . . another little boy—the biggest there, but still little—was tottering to and fro, bent on one side, and considèrably affected in his knees by the weight of a large baby, which he was supposed, by a fiction that obtains sometimes in sanguine families, to be hushing to sleep." 2

—**Sally**. " . . . oh! the inexhaustible regions of contemplation and watchfulness into which this baby's eyes were then only beginning to compose themselves to stare, over his unconscious shoulder!

"It was a very Moloch of a baby, on whose insatiate altar the whole existence of this particular young brother was offered up a daily sacrifice. Its personality may be said to have consisted in its never being quiet, in any one place, for five consecutive minutes, and never going to sleep when required.

"'Tetterby's baby' was as well known in the neighbourhood as the postman or the pot-boy. It roved from door-step to door-step, in the arms of little Johnny Tetterby, and lagged heavily at the rear of troops of juveniles who followed the Tumblers or the Monkey, and came up, all on one side, a little too late for everything that was attractive, from Monday morning until Saturday night.

"Wherever childhood congregated to play, there was little Moloch making Johnny fag and toil. Wherever Johnny desired to stay, little Moloch became fractious, and would not remain. Whenever Johnny wanted to go out, Moloch was asleep, and must be watched. Whenever Johnny wanted to stay at home, Moloch was awake, and must be taken out.

"Yet Johnny was verily persuaded that it was a faultless baby, without its peer in the realm of England; and was quite content to catch meek glimpses of things in general from behind its skirts, or over its limp flapping bonnet, and to go staggering about with it like a very little porter with a very large parcel, which was not directed to anybody, and could never be delivered anywhere." ¶2

—**Sons**. "In company with the small man, was almost any amount of small children you may please to name—at least, it seemed so; they made, in that very limited sphere of action, such an imposing effect, in point of numbers.

"Of these small fry, two had, by some strong machinery, been got into bed in a corner, where they might have reposed snugly enough in the sleep of innocence, but for a constitutional propensity to keep awake, and also to scuffle in and out of bed. The immediate occasion of these predatory dashes at the waking world, was the construction of an oyster-shell wall in a corner, by two other youths of tender age; on which fortification the two in bed made harassing descents (like those accursed Picts and Scots who beleaguer the historical studies of most young Britons), and then withdrew to their own territory.

"In addition to the stir attendant on these inroads, and the retorts of the invaded, who pursued hotly, and made lunges at the bed-clothes, under which the marauders took refuge, another little boy, in another little bed, contributed his mite of confusion to the family stock, by casting his boots upon the waters; in other words, by launching these and several small objects inoffensive in themselves, though of a hard substance considered as missiles, at the disturbers of his repose—who were not slow to return these compliments." 2

—**Sophia**. "The process of induction, by which Mr **Tetterby** had come to the conclusion that his wife was a little woman, was his own secret. She would have made two editions of himself, very easily. Considered as an individual, she was rather remarkable for being robust and portly; but considered with reference to her husband, her dimensions became magnificent. Nor did they assume a less imposing proportion, when studied with reference to the size of her seven sons, who were but diminutive." 2

—*out of sorts:* "Mrs Tetterby . . . laid the cloth, but rather as if she were punishing the table than preparing the family supper; hitting it unnecessarily hard with the knives and forks, slapping it with the plates, dinting it with the salt-cellar, and coming heavily down upon it with the loaf." 2

—*in better sorts:* "'I felt as if there was a rush of recollection on me, all at once, that softened my hard heart, and filled it up till it was bursting. All our struggles for a livelihood, all our cares and wants since we have been married, all the times of sickness, all the hours of watching, we have ever had, by one another, or by the children, seemed to speak to me, and say that they had made us one, and that I never might have been, or could have been, or would have been, any other than the wife and mother I am. Then, the cheap enjoyments that I could have trodden on so cruelly, got to be so precious to me—oh, so priceless, and dear!—that I couldn't bear to think how much I had wronged them . . . .

"The good woman, quite carried away by her honest tenderness and remorse, was weeping with all her heart . . . ." 2

Others

Longford, "about his own age; and although [**Redlaw**] knew no such hopeless decay and broken man as he appeared to be, there was something in the turn of his figure, as he stood with his back towards him 2

"'I am too decayed a wretch to make professions; I recollect my own career too well, to array any such before you. But from the day on which I made my first step downward, in dealing falsely by you, I have gone down with a certain, steady, doomed progression.'" 3

Miss Redlaw, sister. "'Such glimpses of the light of home as I had ever known, had streamed from her. How young she was, how fair, how loving! . . . Better had she loved [**Longford**] less—less secretly, less dearly, from the shallower depths of a more divided heart!'" 1

Swidgers. "'Then you come to all my brothers and their families . . . man and woman, boy and girl. Why, what with cousins, uncles, aunts, and relationships of this, that, and t'other degree, and what-not degree, and marriages, and lyings-in, the Swidgers—Tumblers—might take hold of hands, and make a ring round England!'" 1

—**George**. "'. . . my son George (our eldest, who was her pride more than all the rest!) is fallen very low. . . .'" 1

". . . a man, who should have been in the vigour of his life, but on whom it was not likely the sun would ever shine again. The vices of his forty or fifty years' career had so branded him, that, in comparison with their effects upon his face, the heavy hand of time upon the old man's face who watched him had been merciful and beautifying." 2

—**Charley**, junior. "'**Mrs William** may be taken off her balance by Water; as at Battersea, when rowed into the piers by her young nephew, Charley Swidger junior, aged twelve, which had no idea of boats whatever.'" 1

Woman, "sitting on the stairs, either asleep or forlorn . . . Looking up, she showed . . . quite a young face, but one whose bloom and promise were all swept away, as if the haggard winter should unnaturally kill the spring . . . . [Redlaw] looked upon the ruined Temple of God, so lately made, so soon disfigured . . . . "2

Young lady. "'The young lady (she is very like the miniature, Mr **Edmund**, but she is prettier) was too unhappy to rest without satisfying her doubts, and came up, last night . . . .'

"Then the student entered, leading by the hand a lovely girl, who was afraid to come." 3

Associated Newspapers Ltd 1934 **LL**

"The Life of Our Lord"

CD began this paraphrase of the New Testament at Villa Rosemont, Lausanne, in the summer of 1846 and completed it three years later. He did not have publication in mind: he wrote it out for his children and intended to and did read it to them. On his death, the manuscript came to Georgina Hogarth, his sister-in-law and stalwart housekeeper and factotum, and on her death to CD's son Henry, who gave the work its title. A majority of his family being in favour, it was published after Henry's death. Unlike CHE, in LL CD's language and imagination are held in rigid check. His Biblical knowledge is impressive but not impeccable; his conviction of the importance of what he is writing is obvious and moving.

"My dear children, I am very anxious that you should know something about the History of Jesus Christ. For everybody ought to know about Him. No one ever lived, who was so good, so kind, so gentle, and so sorry for all people who did wrong, or were in any way ill or miserable, as he was. And as he is now in Heaven, where we hope to go, and all to meet each other after we are dead, and there be happy always together, you never can think what a good place Heaven is without knowing who he was and what he did." 1

BIBLICAL FIGURES MENTIONED

(Bible citations are for material covered in LL only. ¶ indicates an entry below.)

	LL chapter	Bible refs
Abraham, holding beggar Lazarus in his bosom	7 ¶	Luke 16:22ff
Adultress, a woman who had done wrong	6	John 8:3ff
Ananias, a liar struck down dead before Peter	11	Acts 5:1ff
Andrew, a fisherman and disciple	3, 5	Matt 4:18, Mark 1:16ff
Angel, appearing to the shepherds	1	Luke 2:9ff
Angel, at the sepulchre	11 ¶	Matt 28:2ff
Angels, two; inside the tomb	11	Luke 24:4ff John 20:12ff
Apostles, disciples	3	Luke 6:13ff
Barabbas, whose release the People demanded	10	Matt 27:16, 20ff, Mark 15:7ff
		Luke 23:18ff John 18:40
Bartholomew, a disciple	3	Matt 10:3
Caesar [Augustus]	7 ¶	Matt 22:17ff, Mark 12:14ff
		Luke 20:22ff
Caiaphas, the High Priest	10	Matt 26:3, 57 John 18:14ff,
Centurion	3	Matt 8:5ff Luke 7:2ff
Child, stood by Jesus in the midst of the disciples	6	Matt 18:1ff, Mark 9:36ff
		Luke 9:47ff
Cleopas, a follower of Jesus, on the road to Emmaus	11	Luke 24:18ff
Cleophas [Clopas], brother-in-law of mother Mary	11	John 19:25
David, who had been a great king	8	Mark 11:10
Daughter of a magistrate [Jairus], healed by Jesus	3	Mark 5:39ff Luke 8:42, 49ff
Disciple, unidentified, known to Caiaphas [John?]	10	John 18:15
Disciples	3 ¶	Mark 3:14ff
Dives, rich man saw Lazarus in Abraham's bosom	7	Luke 16:19ff
Elder son, brother of the Prodigal	7 ¶	Luke 15:25ff
Elizabeth, John the Baptist's mother; Mary's cousin	2	Luke 1:5ff
Farmer, who hired vineyard workers through the day	6	Matt 20:1ff
Father, of the prodigal and another son	7 ¶	Luke 15:11ff
Father, of a distracted son healed by Jesus	6	Matt 17:15ff, Mark 9:17ff
		Luke 9: 38ff
Guard, of men and officers: at Gethsemane	9 ¶	Matt, 26:47 Mark 14:43ff
Guard, at the tomb of Jesus	11	Matt 27:64ff, 28:4, 11ff
Herod, King	1 ¶	Matt 2:3ff Mark 6:14ff
Herod the younger; tetrarch	4	Matt 14:1ff
Herodias	4 ¶	Matt 14:3ff Mark 17ff
Invalid at Bethesda, healed by Jesus	5 ¶	John 5:5ff
Jairus: *see* Magistrate		
James [Mark, Luke say Levi], disciple son of Alphaeus	3	Matt 10:3 Mark 2:14 Luke 5:27
James, the son of Zebedee, a fisherman and disciple	3, 6	Matt 4:21 Mark 1:19 Luke 5:10
Jesus Christ	1-11 ¶	Matt, Mark, Luke, John passim
John the Baptist, son of Elizabeth	2 ¶	Matt 3:1ff, Mark 1:5ff
		Luke 3:2ff John 1:15ff
John, fisherman disciple, son of Zebedee	3, 6, 9, 11 ¶	Matt 4:21 Mark 1:19 Luke 5:10
Joseph of Arimathea	11	Matt 27:57ff, Mark 15:43ff
Joseph, father of Jesus	1	Luke 2:4
Judas Iscariot	3, 8, 9, 10 ¶	Matt 10:4, 26:14ff, 25, 47ff
		Matt 27:3ff, Mark 14:10-11
		Luke 22:3ff John 12:4ff
Labbæus [Thaddeus], disciple		
[in Matthew he is Lebbæus, in Luke: Judas]	3	Matt 10:3
Lawyer, with a question about his neighbour	7	Luke 10:25ff
Lazarus, a beggar (*see* CC, page 515)	7	Luke 16:20ff
Lazarus, brother of Mary Magdalene and Martha;		
raised from dead	8	John 11:1ff
Leper healed by Jesus	3 ¶	Matt 8:2ff Mark 1:40ff
		Luke 5:12ff
Levite, who passed the wounded traveller by	7	Luke 10:32

Abraham. " . . . [he] had been a very good man who lived many years before that time [of the deaths of **Lazarus** and **Dives**—so-named in the Vulgate], and was then in Heaven." 7

Angel. "While [the baby Jesus] was asleep, some Shepherds who were watching Sheep in the Fields, saw an Angel from God, all light and beautiful, come moving over the grass towards Them. At first they were afraid and fell down and hid their faces. But it said 'There is a child born to-day in the City of Bethlehem near here, who will grow up to be so good that God will love him as his own son; and he will teach men to love one another, and not to quarrel and hurt one another; and his name will be Jesus Christ; and people will put that name in their prayers, because they will know God loves it, and will know that they should love it too.'" 1

Angel. "As [the two **Marys**] were saying to each other, 'How shall we roll away the stone?' the earth trembled and shook, and an angel, descending from Heaven, rolled it back, and then sat resting on it. His countenance was like lightning, and his garments were white as snow; and at sight of him, the men of the guard fainted away with fear, as if they were dead." 11

Caesar. "The Emperor of that country, who was called Cæsar, having commanded tribute-money to be regularly paid to him by the people, and being cruel against any one who disputed his right to it . . . . " 7

Centurion. "There was a Centurion too, or officer over the Soldiers, who came to [**Jesus**], and said, 'Lord! My servant lies at home in my house, very ill.'—Jesus Christ made answer, 'I will come and cure him.' But the Centurion said 'Lord! I am not worthy that Thou shoulds't come to my house. Say the word only, and I know he will be cured.'" 3

Disciples. "That there might be some good men to go about with Him, teaching the people, Jesus Christ chose Twelve poor men to be his companions. These twelve are called *The apostles* or *Disciples*, and he chose them from among Poor Men, in order that the Poor might know—always after that; in all years to come—that Heaven was made for them as well as for the rich . . . . " 3

Elder son. ""Father," said the elder brother, "you do not treat me justly, to shew so much joy for my younger brother's return. For these many years I have remained with you constantly, and have been true to you, yet you have never made a feast for me. But when my younger brother returns, who has been prodigal, and riotous, and spent his money in many bad ways, you are full of delight, and the whole house makes merry!"" 7

Father. "When [the **Prodigal Son**] was yet a great way off, his father saw him, and knew him in the midst of all his rags and misery, and ran towards him, and wept, and fell upon his neck, and kissed him. And he told his servants to clothe this poor repentant Son in the best robes, and to make a great feast to celebrate his return." 7

Guard. " . . . a strong guard of men and officers, which had been sent by the chief Priests and Pharisees. It being dark, they carried lanterns and torches. They were armed with swords and staves too; for they did not know but that the people would rise and defend Jesus Christ; and this had made them afraid to seize him Him boldly in the day, when he sat teaching the people." 9

Herod [the elder] "was jealous, for he was a wicked man. But he pretended not to be, and said to the wise men, 'Whereabouts is this child?' . . . [He] ordered [the wise men], if they found the child, to come back to him . . .

they did not go back to King Herod; for they thought he was jealous, though he had not said so. . . .

"But when this cruel Herod found that the wise men did not come back to him, and that he could not, therefore, find out where this child, **Jesus Christ**, lived, he called his soldiers and captains to him, and told them to go and Kill all the children in his dominions that were not more than two years old . . . [Jesus] had escaped safely into Egypt. And he lived there, with his father and mother, until Bad King Herod died." 1

Herodias. "While **Herod** [the younger] was in this angry humour with **John** [**the Baptist**], his birthday came; and his daughter [*sic.*], **Herodias**,* who was a fine dancer, danced before him, to please him. She pleased him so much that he swore an oath he would give her whatever she would ask him for. 'Then', said she, 'father, give me the head of John the Baptist in a charger.' For she hated John, and was a wicked, cruel woman." 4 [*Herodias, Herod's wife, tells her daughter, the dancer, not named in the Bible story though we know her as **Salome** (which means "very shady"), what to ask for in reward.]

Invalid, at Bethesda. "Among these poor persons, was one man who had been ill, thirty eight years; and he told **Jesus Christ** . . . that he never could be dipped in the pool, because he was so weak and ill that he could not move to get there. Our Saviour said to him, 'take up thy bed and go away.' And he went away, quite well." 5

John the Baptist. "And people being wicked, and violent, and killing each other, and not minding their duty towards God, John (to teach them better) went about the country, preaching to them, and entreating them to be better men and women. And because he loved them more than himself, and didn't mind himself when he was doing them good, he was poorly dressed in the skin of a camel, and ate little but some insects called locusts, which he found as he travelled: and wild honey, which the bees left in the Hollow Trees." 2

John, a disciple. "None were there, to take pity on Him, but one disciple and four women . . . . The disciple was he whom Jesus loved—John, who had leaned upon his breast and asked Him which was the Betrayer. When Jesus saw them standing at the foot of the Cross, He said to His mother that John would be her son, to comfort her when He was dead; and from that hour John was as a son to her, and loved her." 11

Judas Iscariot, "one of the Disciples, pretended to be angry at [**Mary**'s anointing **Jesus**' feet with spikenard] and said that the ointment might have been sold for Three Hundred Pence, and the money given to the poor. But he only said so, in reality, because he carried the Purse, and was (unknown to the rest, at that time) a Thief, and wished to get all the money he could. He now began to plot for betraying Christ into the hands of the chief Priests." 8

"When Judas Iscariot saw that His Master was indeed condemned, he was so full of horror for what he had done, that he took the Thirty Pieces of Silver back to the chief Priests, and said 'I have betrayed innocent blood! I cannot keep it!' with those words, he threw the money down upon the floor, and rushing away, wild with despair, hanged himself. The rope, being weak, broke with the weight of his body, and it fell down on the ground, after Death, all bruised and burst—a dreadful sight to see!" 10

Leper. " . . . there came to [**Jesus**] a man with a dreadful disease called the leprosy. It was common in those times, and those who were ill with it, were called lepers. This Leper fell at the feet of Jesus Christ, and said 'Lord! If thou wilt, thou cans't make me well!'" 3

Madman. " . . . they had to pass a wild and lonely burying-ground that was outside the City . . . . In this place there was a dreadful madman who lived among the tombs, and houled [*sic*] all day and night, so that it made travellers afraid, to hear him. They had tried to chain him, but he broke his chains, he was so strong; and he would throw himself on the sharp stones, and cut himself in the most dreadful manner: crying and houling all the while. When this wretched man saw **Jesus Christ** a long way off, he cried out 'It is the son of God! Oh son of God, do not torment me!' Jesus, coming near him, perceived that he was torn by an Evil Spirit, and cast the madness out of him . . . . " 4

Magistrate. "But of all the people who came to him, none were so full of grief and distress, as one man who was a Ruler or Magistrate over many people, and he wrung his hands, and cried, and said 'Oh Lord, my daughter—my beautiful, good, innocent little girl, is dead. Oh come to her, come to her, and lay Thy blessed hand upon her, and I know she will revive, and come to life again, and make me and her mother happy.'" 3

Mary Magdalene. "And while our Saviour sat eating at the table, there crept into the room a woman of that city who had led a bad and sinful life, and was ashamed that the Son of God should see her; and yet she trusted so much to his goodness, and his compassion for all who, having done wrong were truly sorry for it in their hearts, that, by little and little, she went behind the seat on which he sat, and dropped down at his feet, and wetted them with her sorrowful tears; then she kissed them and dried them on her long hair, and rubbed them with some sweet-smelling ointment she had brought with her in a box." 5

Mother, at Nain. " . . . near the Gate of the city, He met a funeral. It was the funeral of a young man, who was carried on what is called a Bier, which was open, as the custom was in that country . . . . His poor mother followed the bier, and wept very much, for she had no other child." 4

Pharisees. "They were very proud, and believed that no people were good but themselves; and they were all afraid of Jesus Christ, because he taught the people better. *So were the Jews, in general.** Most of the Inhabitants of that country, were Jews." 4 [*Emphasis added. CD alludes only once, and then by quoting a figure in the story, to the fact that Jesus was a Jew. *See* **Pilate**]

"Now the Pharisees received these lessons from our Saviour, scornfully; for they were rich, and covetous, and thought themselves superior to all mankind." 7

Pontius Pilate. "Pilate (who was not a Jew) said to Him 'your own nation, the Jews, and your own Priests have delivered you to me. What have you done?' Finding that He had done no harm, Pilate went out and told the Jews so. . . . As **Herod** had the right to punish people who offended against the law in Galilee, Pilate said, 'I find no wrong in him. Let him be taken before Herod!'" 10

Samaritan. "'But a certain Samaritan who came travelling along that road, no sooner saw [the wounded **traveller**] than he had compassion on him, and dressed his wounds with oil and wine, and set him on the beast he rode himself, and took him to an Inn, and next morning took out of his pocket Two pence and gave them to the **Landlord**, saying "take care of him and whatever you may spend beyond this, in doing so, I will repay you when I come here again."'" 7

Saul, "who had held the clothes of some barbarous persons who pelted one of the Christians named **Stephen**, to death with stones, was always active in doing them harm. But God turned Saul's heart afterwards; for as he was travelling to Damascus to find out some Christians who were there, and drag them to prison, there shone about him a great light from Heaven; a voice cried, 'Saul, Saul, why persecutest thou me!' and he was struck down from his horse, by an invisible hand, in sight of all the guards and soldiers who were riding with him. When they raised him, they found that he was blind . . . . After which, he became a Christian, and preached, and taught, and believed, with the apostles, and did great service." 11

Scholars. "They found [**Jesus**], sitting in the Temple, talking about the goodness of God, and how we should all pray to him, with some learned men who were called Doctors. They were not what you understand by the word 'doctors' now; they did not attend sick people; they were scholars and clever men." 2

Simon Peter. "Late in the night, when the wind was against [the disciples] and the waves were running high, they saw Him coming walking towards them on the water, as if it were dry land. When they saw this, they were terrified, and cried out, but Jesus said, 'It is I. Be not afraid!' Peter taking courage, said, 'Lord, if it be thou, tell me to come to thee upon the water.' Jesus Christ said, 'Come!' Peter then walked towards Him, but seeing the angry waves, and hearing the wind roar, he was frightened and began to sink, and would have done so, but that Jesus took him by the hand, and led him into the boat." 5

Soldiers, at Golgotha. "Meantime, a guard of four soldiers, sitting on the ground, divided His clothes (which they had taken off) into four parcels for themselves, and cast lots for His coat, and sat there, gambling and talking, while He suffered. They offered him vinegar to drink, mixed with gall; and wine, mixed with myrrh; but he took none." 11

Thieves, at Golgotha. "One of the thieves too, railed at him, in his torture, and said, 'If Thou be Christ, save thyself, and us.' But the other Thief, who was penitent, said 'Lord! Remember me when Thou comest into Thy Kingdom!' And Jesus answered, 'To-day, thou shalt be with me in Paradise.' 11

* * * * *

"Remember!—It is christianity TO DO GOOD always—even to those who do evil to us. It is christianity to love our neighbour as ourself, and to do to all men as we would have them Do to us. It is christianity to be gentle, merciful, and forgiving, and to keep those qualities quiet in our own hearts, and never make a boast of them, or of our prayers or of our love of God, but always to shew that we love Him by humbly trying to do right in everything. If we do this, and remember the life and lessons of Our Lord Jesus Christ, and try to act up to them, we may confidently hope that God will forgive us our sins and mistakes, and enable us to live and die in Peace." 11

Miscellaneous Pieces

Part Two, 1847-1849

CONTENTS

PERSONS MENTIONED

MP October 1847   leaflet **FW**

An Appeal to Fallen Women

CD wrote the leaflet for prison governor **George Laval Chesterton** to read to inmates at Coldbath Fields prison, exhorting them to consider coming to live in Urania Cottage, a Home for "fallen women," instead of returning to the streets. CD enclosed it in a letter to **Angela Burdett Coutts**, his friend and the heiress who funded and worked on many social projects, often with his advice.

Companions. "You know what the streets are; you know how cruel the companions that you find there, are; you know the vices practised there, and to what wretched consequences they bring you, even while you are young."

Lady [Angelina Georgina Burdett Coutts]. "There is a lady in this town, who, from the windows of her house, has seen such as you going past at night, and has felt her heart bleed at the sight. She is what is called a great lady; but she has looked after you with compassion, as being of her own sex and nature; and the thought of such fallen women has troubled her in her bed. She has resolved to open, at her own expense, a place of refuge very near London, for a small number of females, who, without such help, are lost for ever: and to make it A HOME for them."

Very young woman. " . . . I address [this letter] to a woman—a very young woman still—who was born to be happy, and has lived miserably; who has no prospect before her but sorrow, or behind her but a wasted youth; who, if she has ever been a mother, has felt shame, instead of pride, in her own unhappy child."

MP November 13, 17 1849 (PE 644, 651)　　　　　London *Times* **PE**

Public Executions

Two Letters to the Editor: The debasement of humankind, gathered in mob to watch one of its own swing by the neck until dead, was a torment to CD. He campaigned to eliminate such public displays, and before his death they had ceased: executions were removed inside prison walls.

Calcraft, "the hangman . . . should be restrained in his unseemly briskness, in his jokes, his oaths, and his brandy." 2

Crowd. " . . . a sight so inconceivably awful as the wickedness and levity of the immense crowd collected at that execution this morning [November 13, 1849] could be imagined by no man, and could be presented in no heathen land under the sun. The horrors of the gibbet and of the crime which brought the wretched murderers to it faded in my mind before the atrocious bearing, looks, and language of the assembled spectators.

"When I came upon the scene at midnight, the *shrillness* of the cries and howls that were raised from time to time, denoting that they came from a concourse of boys and girls already assembled in the best places, made my blood run cold. As the night went on, screeching, and laughing and yelling in strong chorus of parodies on Negro melodies, with substitutions of '**Mrs Manning**' for 'Susannah,' and the like, were added to these.

"When the day dawned, thieves, low prostitutes, ruffians and vagabonds of every kind, flocked on to the ground, with every variety of offensive and foul behaviour. Fightings, faintings, whistlings, imitations of Punch, brutal jokes, tumultuous demonstrations of indecent delight when swooning women were dragged out of the crowd by the police with their dresses disordered, gave a new zest to the general entertainment. When the sun rose brightly—as it did—it gilded thousands upon thousands of upturned faces, so inexpressibly odious in their brutal mirth or callousness, that a man had cause to feel ashamed of the shape he wore, and to shrink from himself, as fashioned in the image of the Devil." ¶1

Sir G. Grey. " . . . an intimation given by Sir G. Grey in the last session of Parliament, that the government might be induced to give its support to a measure making the infliction of capital punishment a private solemnity within the prison walls . . . . " 1

Rush. "From the moment of a murderer's being sentenced to death, I would dismiss him to the dread obscurity to which the wisest **judge** upon the bench consiged the murderer Rush." 2

Woman. " . . . the ferocious woman who was charged on the same day with threatening to murder another in the midst of the multitude, proclaiming that she had a knife about her, and would have her heart's blood, and be hanged on the same gibbet with her namesake, **Mrs Manning**, whose death she had come to see . . . . " 2

Chaplain, of the prison, to be present at private executions	2
Fielding, Henry: quoted on the desirability of private executions	2
Governor of the jail, to be present at private executions	2
Inspectors of prisons, two: to be present at private executions	2
Sheriff, of the county or city: to be present at private executions	2
Surgeon, of the prison, to be present at private executions	2
Ned Ward, London spy; regularly visited Bridewell to watch whippings	2

MP December 3, 1849 (PE V 665, 708)   **CC**

Elegy Written in a Country Churchyard

After a weekend at Rockingham Castle (model for Chesney Wold BH) which included performing scenes from Sheridan's *A School for Scandal* with his friend Mary Boyle, CD sent her a parody, which included:

> *"The small dog **Spitz** has given a shrill bark,*
> *And gone off with her tail uprais'd in air;*
> *I don't know where she's gone, it is so dark,*
> *And (what is more) I don't think that I care . . . .*

> *"From them no more does **Lady Teazle** win*
> *Applause, fit tribute to her graces quaint:*
> *For them no more **Sir Peter** daubs his skin*
> *And looks out from a mist of flour and paint."*

Autobiographical Fragments

Beginning probably in the spring of 1847, CD experimented with writing an autobiography, partly as a psychological exercise. He did not develop anything he thought would be publishable—at least not in his lifetime—but in January 1849 he gave what he had done to his friend and (as CD hoped and expected) first biographer, John Forster, who included the material in his *Life of Charles Dickens* (1872). The stirrings engendered by the exercise found their fictional transmutation in DC and later works.

The writings are given here as JF has passed them on to us, but rearranged in the EID format. Chapter citations are to JF. Some of the DC entry in the next volume (and vastly more of the novel itself) shows how literally CD mined what he wrote in AF to tell the story of another little boy.

CONTENTS

PERSONS MENTIONED

Principals

Elizabeth Dickens.—*educationist entrepreneur:* "I left, at a great many other doors, a great many circulars calling attention to the merits of the establishment [in which Mrs Dickens proposed to educate young ladies]. Yet nobody ever came to school, nor do I recollect that anybody ever proposed to come, or that the least preparation was made to received anybody. But I know that we got on very badly with the **butcher** and **baker**; that very often we had not too much for dinner; and that at last my **father** was arrested." 1

—*and children:* "My mother and my brothers and sisters (excepting **Fanny** in the royal academy of music) were still encamped, with a young **servant-girl** from Chatham-workhouse, in the two parlours in the emptied house in Gower-street north." 2

—*a son fed:* "It was a long way to go and return within the dinner-hour, and, usually, I either carried my dinner with me, or went and bought it at some neighbouring shop. In the latter case, it was commonly a saveloy and a penny loaf; sometimes, a fourpenny plate of beef from a [**pastry**] **cook**'s shop; sometimes, a plate of bread and cheese, and a glass of beer, from a miserable old public-house over the way: the Swan, if I remember right, or the Swan and something else that I have forgotten." 2

"My own exclusive breakfast [in lodgings], of a penny cottage loaf and a pennyworth of milk, I provided for myself. I kept another small loaf, and a quarter of a pound of cheese, on a particular shelf of a particular cupboard; to make my supper on when I came back at night. They made a hole in the six or seven shllings, I know well; and I was out at the blacking-warehouse all day, and had to support myself upon that money all the week." 2

—*a son back on her hands:* "My mother set herself to accommodate the quarrel [between **John Dickens** and **James Lamert**], and did so next day. She brought home a request for me to return next morning, and a high character of me, which I am very sure I deserved. My father said, I should go back no more, and should go to school [*see* **Jones** O]. I do not write resentfully or angrily: for I know how all these things have worked together to make me what I am: but I NEVER AFTERWARDS FORGOT, I NEVER SHALL FORGET, I NEVER CAN FORGET, THAT MY MOTHER WAS WARM FOR MY BEING SENT BACK." 2 [*Editor's* *emphasis: from this incident, many believe, the great dynamic of CD's creativity and his self-orphaning was engendered. See* **Aunt** of **Kate** DS]

John Dickens. "I know my father to be as kindhearted and generous a man as ever lived in the world. Everything that I can remember of his conduct to his wife, or children, or friends, in sickness or affliction, is beyond all praise. By me, as a sick child, he has watched night and day, unweariedly and patiently, many nights and days. He never undertook any business, charge or trust, that he did not zealously, conscientiously, punctually, honourably discharge. His industry has always been untiring. He was proud of me, in his way, and had a great admiration of the comic singing."1

—his son's education: "But, in the case of his temper, and the straitness of his means, he appeared to have utterly lost at this time the idea of educating me at all, and to have utterly put from him the notion that I had any claim upon him, in that regard, whatever. So I degenerated into cleaning his boots of a morning, and my own; and making myself useful in the work of the little house; and looking after my younger brothers and sisters (we were now six in all); and going on such poor errands as arose out of our poor way of living." 1

—debtor: "My father was waiting for me in the lodge, and we went up to his room (on the top story but one), and cried very much. And he told me, I remember, to take warning by the Marshalsea, and to observe that if a man had twenty pounds a-year, and spent nineteen pounds nineteen shillings and sixpence, he would be happy; but that a shilling spent the other way would make him wretched. I see the fire we sat before, now; with two bricks inside the rusted grate, one on each side, to prevent its burning too many coals. Some other debtor shared the room with him, who came in by-and-by; and as the dinner was a joint-stock repast, I was sent up to 'Captain Porter' in the room overhead, with Mr Dickens's compliments, and I was his son, and could he, Captain P, lend me a knife and fork?" 1 *See* **Debtors** SR and **Mr Micawber** DC

—a son neglected: "It is wonderful to me how I could have been so easily cast away at such an age. It is wonderful to me, that, even after my descent into the poor little drudge I had been since we came to London, no one had compassion enough on me—a child of singular abilities, quick, eager, delicate, and soon hurt, bodily or mentally—to suggest that something might have been spared, as certainly it might have been, to place me at any common school. Our friends, I take it, were tired out. No one made any sign." 2

"I know I do not exaggerate, unconsciously and unintentionally, the scantiness of my resources and the difficulties of my life. I know that if a shilling or so were given me by any one, I spent it in a dinner or a tea. I know that I worked, from morning to night, with common men and boys, a shabby child. I know that I tried, but ineffectually, not to anticipate my money, and to make it last the week through; by putting it away in a drawer I had in the counting-house, wrapped into six little parcels, each parcel containing the same amount, and labelled with a different day.

"I know that I have lounged about the streets, insufficiently and unsatisfactorily fed. I know that, but for the mercy of God, I might easily have been, for any care that was taken of me, a little robber or a little vagabond." ¶2

—a son employed: "My father and **mother** were quite satisfied. They could hardly have been more so, if I had been twenty years of age, distinguished at a grammar-school, and going to Cambridge.

"The blacking warehouse was the last house on the left-hand side of the way, at old Hungerford-stairs. It was a crazy, tumble-down old house, abutting of course on the river, and literally overrun with rats. Its wainscotted rooms, and its rotten floors and staircase, and the old grey rats swarming down in the cellars, and the sound of their squeaking and scuffling coming up the stairs at all times, and the dirt and decay of the place, rise up visibly before me, as if I were there again.

"The counting-house was on the first floor, looking over the coal-barges and the river. There was a recess in it, in which I was to sit and work. My work was to cover the pots of paste-blacking; first with a piece of oil-paper, and then with a piece of blue paper; to tie them round with a string; and then to clip the paper close and neat, all round, until it looked as smart as a pot of ointment from an apoethecary's shop. When a certain number of grosses of pots had attained this pitch of perfection, I was to paste on each a printed label; and then go on again with more pots." ¶2

—*a son lodged elsewhere:* "I suppose my lodging was paid for, by my father. I certainly did not pay it myself; and I certainly had no other assistance whatever (the making of my clothes, I think, excepted), from Monday morning until Saturday night. No advice, no counsel, no encouragement, no consolation, no support, from any one that I can call to mind, so help me God." 2

—*a son protests:* "My rescue from this kind of existence I considered quite hopeless, and abandoned as such, altogether; though I am solemnly convinced that I never, for one hour, was reconciled to it, or was otherwise than miserably unhappy. I felt keenly, however, the being so cut off from my parents, my brothers, and sisters; and, when my day's work was done, going home to such a miserable blank; and *that,* I thought, might be corrected.

"One Sunday night I remonstrated with my father on this head, so pathetically and with so many tears, that his kind nature gave way. He began to think that it was not quite right. I do believe he had never thought so before, or thought about it. It was the first remonstrance I had ever made about my lot, and perhaps it opened up a little more than I intended. A back-attic was found for me at the house of an insolvent-court **agent**, who lived in Lant-street in the borough, where **Bob Sawyer** lodged many years afterwards. A bed and bedding were sent over for me, and made up on the floor. The little window had a pleasant prospect of a timber-yard; and when I took possession of my new abode, I thought it was a Paradise." ¶2

—*his pride of authorship:* " . . . my poor father meanwhile listening [to **Captain Porter** reading the debtors' petition] with a little of an author's vanity, and contemplating (not severely) the spikes on the opposite wall." 2 *See* **Wilkins Micawber** DC.

—*aroused at last:* "I am not sure that it was before this time [**Fanny**'s prize ceremony], or after it, that the blacking warehouse was removed to Chandos-street, Covent-garden. It is no matter. Next to the shop at the corner of Bedford-street in Chandos-street, are two rather old-fashioned houses and shops adjoining one another. They were one then, or thrown into one, for the blacking business; and had been a butter shop. Opposite to them was, and is, a public-house, where I got my ale, under these new circumstances. The stones in the street may be smoothed by my small feet going across to it at dinner-time, and back again.

"The establishment was larger now, and we had one or two new **boys. Bob Fagin** and I had attained to great dexterity in tying up the pots. I forget how many we could do, in five minutes. We worked, for the light's sake, near the second window as you come from Bedford-street; and we were so brisk at it, that the people ued to stop and look in. Sometimes there would be quite a little crowd there. I saw my father coming in at the door one day when we were very busy, and I wondered how he could bear it.

"Now, I generally had my dinner in the warehouse. Sometimes I brought it from home, so I was better off. I see myself coming across Russell-square from Somers-town, one morning, with some cold hotch-potch in a small basin tied up in a handkerchief. I had the same wanderings about the streets as I used to have, and was just as solitary and self-dependent as before; but I had not the same difficulty in merely living. I never however heard a word of being taken away, or of being otherwise than quite provided for.

"At last, one day, my father, and the relative so often mentioned [**James Lamert**], quarrelled; quarrelled by letter, for I took the letter from my father to him which caused the explosion, but quarrelled very fiercely. It was about me. It may have had some backward reference, in part, for anything I know, to my employment at the window." 2

—*complicit amnesia:* "From that hour [when CD came home and his **mother** failed in her attempt to have him go back] until this at which I write, no word of that part of my childhood which I have now gladly brought to a close, has passed my lips to any human being. I have no idea how long it lasted; whether for a year, or much more, or less. From that hour, until this, my father and my mother have been stricken dumb upon it. I have never heard the least allusion to it, however far off and remote, from either of them. I have never, until I now impart it to this paper, in any burst of confidence with any one, my own wife not excepted, raised the curtain I then dropped, thank God.

"Until old Hungerford-market was pulled down, until old Hungerford-stairs were destroyed, and the very nature of the ground changed, I never had the courage to go back to the place where my servitude began. I never saw it. I could not endure to go near it. For many years, when I came near to **Robert Warren**'s in the Strand, I crossed over to the opposite side of the way, to avoid a certain smell of the cement they put upon the blacking-corks, which reminded me of what I was once. It was a very long time before I liked to go up Chandos-street. My old way home by the borough made me cry, after my eldest child could speak.

In my walks at night I have walked there often, since then, and by degrees I have come to write this. It does not seem a tithe of what I might have written, or of what I meant to write." 2

Supporting Roles

Bookseller. "The keeper of this bookstall, who lived in a little house behind it, used to get tipsy every night, and to be violently scolded by his wife every morning. More than once, when I went there early, I had audience of him in a turn-up bedstead, with a cut in his forehead or a black eye, bearing witness to his excesses over night (I am afraid he was quarrelsome in his drink); and he, with a shaking hand, endeavouring to find the needful shillings in one or other of the pockets of his clothes, which lay upon the floor, while his **wife**, with a baby in her arms and her shoes down at heel, never left off rating him. Sometimes he had lost his money, and then he would ask me to call again; but his wife had always got some (had taken his, I dare say, while he was drunk), and secretly completed the bargain on the stairs, as we went down together." 1

Debtors at the Marshalsea. "I mention the circumstance because it illustrates, to me, my early interest in observing people. When I went to the

Marshalsea of a night, I was always delighted to hear from my **mother** what she knew about the histories of the different debtors in the prison; and when I heard of this approaching [petition-signing] ceremony, I was so anxious to see them all come in, one after another (though I knew the greater part of them already, to speak to, and they me), that I got leave of absence on purpose, and established myself in a corner, near the petition. It was stretched out, I recollect, on a great ironing-board, under the window, which in another part of the room made a bedstead at night.

"The internal regulations of the place, for cleanliness and order, and for the government of a common room in the ale-house; where hot water and some means of cooking, and a good fire, were provided for all who paid a very small subscription; were excellently administered by a governing committee of debtors, of which my **father** was chairman for the time being. As many of the principal officers of this body as could be got into the small room without filling it up, supported him, in front of the petition . . . . " ¶2 *See* **Wilkins Micawber** DC

"Whatever was comical in this scene, and whatever was pathetic, I sincerely believe I perceived in my corner, whether I demonstrated or not, quite as well as I should perceive it now. I made out my own little character and story for every man who put his name to the sheet of paper. I might be able to do that now, more truly: not more earnestly, or with a closer interest.

"Their different peculiarities of dress, of face, of gait, of manner, were written indelibly upon my memory. I would rather have seen it than the best play ever played; and I thought about it afterwards, over the pots of paste-blacking, often and often. When I looked, with my mind's eye, into the Fleet-prison during **Mr Pickwick**'s incarceration, I wonder whether half-a-dozen men were wanting from the Marshalsea crowd that came filing in again, to the sound of **Captain Porter**'s voice!" ¶2

Fanny Dickens. "Sundays, Fanny and I passed in the prison. I was at the [music] academy in Tenderden-street, Hanover-square, at nine o'clock in the morning, to fetch her; and we walked back there together, at night." *And see* **Elizabeth Dickens** P

—*given a prize before her family:* "I could not bear to think of myself—beyond the reach of all such honourable emulation and success. The tears ran down my face. I felt as if my heart were rent. I prayed, when I went to bed that night, to be lifted out of the humiliation and neglect in which I was. I never had suffered so much before. There was no envy in this." 2

Bob Fagin. "Two or three other boys were kept on similar duty down stairs on similar wages. One of them came up, in a ragged apron and a paper cap, on the first Monday morning, to show me the trick of using the string and tying the knot. His name was Bob Fagin; and I took the liberty of using his name, long afterwards, in *Oliver Twist* . . . . It was not long, before Bob Fagin and I, and another boy whose name was **Paul Green**, but who was currently believed to have been christened **Poll** (a belief which I transferred, long afterwards again, to Mr **Sweedlepipe**, in *Martin Chuzzlewit*), worked generally, side by side. Bob Fagin was an orphan, and lived with his brother-in-law, a waterman." 1

"Bob Fagin was very good to me on the occasion of a bad attack of my old disorder. I suffered such excruciating pain that time, that they made a temporary bed of straw in my old recess in the counting-house, and I rolled about on the floor, and Bob filled empty blacking-bottles with hot water, and applied relays of them to my side, half the day. I got better, and quite easy towards evening; but Bob (who was much bigger and older than I) did not like the idea of my going home alone, and took me under his protection. I was too proud to let him know about the prison; and after making several efforts to get rid of him, to all of which Bob Fagin in his goodness was deaf, shook hands with him on the steps of a house near Southward-bridge on the Surrey side, making believe that I lived there. As a finishing piece of reality in case of his looking back, I knocked at the door, I recollect, and asked, when the woman opened it, if that was Mr Robert Fagin's house." 2

And see **Warehouse boys**

James Lamert. "[The blacking business's] chief manager, James Lamert, the relative who had lived with us in Bayham-street, seeing how I was employed from day to day, and knowing what our domestic circumstances then were, proposed that I should go into the blacking warehouse, to be as useful as I could, at a salary, I think, of six shillings a week. I am not clear whether it was six or seven. I am inclined to believe, from my uncertainty on this head, that it was six at first, and seven afterwards. At any rate the offer was accepted very willingly by my father and mother, and on a Monday morning I went down to the blacking warehouse to begin my business life." 2

—well-meaning: "Our relative had kindly arranged to teach me something in the dinner-hour; from twelve to one, I think it was; every day. But an arrangement so incompatible with counting-house business soon died away, from no fault of his or mine; and for the same reason, my small work-table, and my grosses of pots, my papers, string, scizzors [*sic*.], paste-pot, and labels, by little and little, vanished out of the recess in the counting-house, and kept company with the other small work-tables, grosses of pots, papers, string, scizzors, and paste-pots, downstairs." 2

"But I held some station at the blacking warehouse too. Besides that my relative at the counting-house did what a man so occupied, and dealing with a thing so anomalous, could, to treat me as one upon a different footing from the rest, I never said, to man or boy, how it was that I came to be there, or gave the least indication of being sorry that I was there." 2

—insulted: "All I am certain of is, that, soon after I had given him the letter [from **John Dickens**], my cousin (he was a sort of cousin, by marriage) told me he was very much insulted about me; and that it was impossible to keep me, after that. I cried very much, partly because it was so sudden, and partly because in his anger he was violent about my father, though gentle to me." 2

Old lady. "The key of the [Gower-street] house was sent back to the landlord, who was very glad to get it; and I (small **Cain** that I was, except that I had never done harm to any one) was handed over as a lodger to a reduced old lady [**Mrs Roylance**], long known to our family, in Little-college-street, Camden-town, who took children in to board, and had once done so at Brighton; and who, with a few alterations and embellishments, unconsciously began to sit for **Mrs Pipchin** in *Dombey* when she took in me.

"She had a little brother and sister under care then; somebody's natural **children**, who were very irregularly paid for; and a widow's little **son**. The two boys and I slept in the same room." 2

Captain Porter "lent the knife and fork, with his compliments in return. There was a very dirty **lady** in his little room; and two wan **girls**, his daughters, with shock heads of hair. I thought I should not have liked to borrow Captain Porter's comb. The Captain himself was in the last extremity of shabbiness;

and if I could draw at all, I would draw an accurate portrait of the old, old, brown great-coat he wore, with no other coat below it. His whiskers were large. I saw his bed rolled up in a corner; and what plates, and dishes, and pots he had, on a shelf; and I knew (God knows how) that the two girls with the shock heads were Captain Porter's natural children, and that the dirty lady was not married to Captain P. My timid wondering station on his threshold, was not occupied more than a couple of minutes, I dare say; but I came down again to the room below with all this as surely in my knowledge, as the knife and fork, were in my hand." 1

—the sound of his own voice: " . . . my old friend Captain Porter (who had washed himself, to do honour to so solemn an occasion) stationed himself close to [the petition], to read it to all who were unacquainted with its contents. The door was then thrown open, and they began to come in, in a long file; several waiting on the landing outside, while one entered, affixed his signature, and went out.

"To everybody in succession, Captain Porter, said 'Would you like to hear it read?' If he weakly showed the least disposition to hear it, Captain Porter, in a loud sonorous voice, gave him every word of it. I remember a certain luscious roll he gave to such words as 'Majesty—gracious Majesty—your gracious Majesty's unfortunate subjects—your Majesty's well-known munificence,'—as if the words were something real in his mouth, and delicious to taste . . . . " ¶2

Warehouse boys.—*not ideal colleagues:* "No words can express the secret agony of my soul as I sunk into this companionship; compared these every day associates with those of my happier childhood; and felt my early hopes of growing up to be a learned and distinguished man, crushed in my breast. The deep remembrance of the sense I had of being utterly neglected and hopeless; of the shame I felt in my position; of the misery it was to my young heart to believe that, day by day, what I had learned, and thought, and delighted in, and raised my fancy and my emulation up by, was passing away from me, never to be brought back any more; cannot be written. My whole nature was so penetrated with the grief and humiliation of such considerations, that even now, famous and caressed and happy, I often forget in my dreams that I have a dear wife and children; even that I am a man; and wander desolately back to that time of my life." 2

—and the newcomer: "That I suffered in secret, and that I suffered exquisitely, no one ever knew but I. How much I suffered, it is, as I have said already, utterly beyond my power to tell. No man's imagination can overtep the reality. But I kept my own counsel, and I did my work. I knew from the first, that if I could not do my work as well as any of the rest, I could not hold myself above slight and contempt.

"I soon became at least as expeditious and as skilful with my hands, as either of the other boys. Though perfectly familiar with them, my conduct and manners were different enough from theirs to place a space between us. They, and the men, always spoke of me as 'the young gentleman' . . . . **Poll Green** uprose once, and rebelled against the 'young gentleman' usage; but **Bob Fagin** settled him speedily." ¶2

Others

Appraiser. "It was necessary, as a matter of form, that the clothes I wore should be seen by the official appraiser. I had a half-holiday to enable me to call upon him, at his own time, at a house somewhere beyond the Obelisk. I recollect his coming out to look at me with his mouth full, and a strong smell of beer upon him, and saying good-naturedly that 'that would do,' and 'it was all right.' Certainly the hardest creditor would not have been disposed (even if he had been legally entitled) to avail himself of my poor white hat, little jacket, or corduroy trowsers. But I had a fat old silver watch in my pocket, which had been given me by my **grandmother** before the blacking days, and I had entertained my doubts as I went along whether that valuable possession might not bring me over the twenty pounds [the limit allowed]. So I was greatly relieved, and made him a bow of acknowledgment as I went out." 2

Coffee-shop keepers. "We had half-an-hour, I think, for tea. When I had money enough, I used to go to a coffee-shop, and have half-a-pint of coffee, and a slice of bread and butter. When I had no money, I took a turn in Covent-garden market, and stared at the pine-apples. The coffee-shops to which I most resorted were, one in Maiden-lane; one in a court (non-existent now) close to Hungerford-market; and one in St. Martin's-lane, of which I only recollect that it stood near the church, and that in the door there was an oval glass-plate, with COFFEE-ROOM painted on it, addressed towards the street. If I ever find myself in a very different kind of coffee-room now, but where there is such an inscription on glass, and read it backward on the wrong side MOOR-EEFFOC (as I often used to do then, in a dismal reverie), a shock goes through my blood." 2

Confectioners. "I was so young and childish, and so little qualified—how could I be otherwise?—to undertake the whole charge of my own existence, that, in going to Hungerford-stairs of a morning, I could not resist the stale pastry put out at half-price on trays at the confectioners' doors in Tottenham-court-road; and I often spent on that, the money I should have kept for my dinner. Then I went without my dinner, or bought a roll, or a slice of pudding." 2

Paul Green. "Poll Green's father had the additional distinction of being a fireman, and was employed at Drury-lane theatre; where another relation of Poll's, I think his little sister, did imps in the pantomimes." 2 *See* **Warehouse boys**

Jones. "There was a school in the Hampstead-road kept by Mr Jones, a Welshman, to which my **father** dispatched me to ask for a card of terms. The boys were at dinner, and Mr Jones was carving for them with a pair of holland sleeves on, when I acquitted myself of this commission. He came out, and gave me what I wanted; and hoped I should become a pupil. I did. At seven o'clock one morning, very soon afterwards, I went as day scholar to Mr Jones's establishment, which was in Mornington-place, and had its school-room sliced away by the Birmingham-railway, when that change came about. The school-room however was not threatened by directors or civil engineers then, and there was a board over the door graced with the words WELLINGTON HOUSE ACADEMY." 3

Landlord and **wife**. "I was such a little fellow, with my poor white hat, little jacket, and corduroy trowsers, that frequently, when I went into the bar of a strange public-house for a glass of ale or porter to wash down the saveloy and the loaf I had eaten in the street, they didn't like to give it me.

"I remember, one evening (I had been somewhere for my **father**, and was going back to the borough over Westminster-bridge), that I went into a public-house in Parliament-street, which is still there though altered, at the corner of the short street leading into Cannon-row, and said to the landlord behind the bar, 'What is your very best—the VERY best—ale, a glass?' For, the occasion was a festive one, for some reason: I forget why. It may have been my birthday, or somebody else's.

"'Two-pence,' says he. 'Then,' says I, 'just draw me a glass of that, if you please, with a good head to it.' The landlord looked at me, in return, over the bar, from head to foot, with a strange smile on his face; and instead of drawing the beer, looked round the screen and said something to his wife, who came out from behind it, with her work in her hand, and joined him in surveying me.

"Here we stand, all three, before me now, in my study in Devonshire-terrace. The landlord, in his shirt sleeves, leaning against the bar window-frame; his wife, looking over the little half-door; and I, in some confusion, looking up at them from outside the partition. They asked me a good many questions, as what my name was, how old I was, where I lived, how I was employed, &c. &c. To all of which, that I might commit nobody, I invented appropriate answers.

"They served me with the ale, though I suspect it was not the strongest on the premises; and the landlord's wife, opening the little half-door and bending down, gave me a kiss that was half-admiring and half-compassionate, but all womanly and good, I am sure." ¶2 *See* page 909 in Volume II

Pudding-shop keepers. —*their product:* "There were two pudding shops between which I was divided, according to my finances. One was in a court close to St Martin's-church (at the back of the church) which is now removed altogether. The pudding at that shop was made with currants, and was rather a special pudding, but was dear: two penn'orth not being larger than a penn'orth of more ordinary pudding. A good shop for the latter was in the Strand, somewhere near where the Lowther-arcade is now. It was a stout, hale pudding, heavy and flabby; with great raisins in it, stuck in whole, at great distances apart. It came up hot, at about noon every day; and many and many a day did I dine off it." 2

Thomas and **Harry**. "A certain man (a soldier once) named Thomas, who was the foreman, and another named Harry, who was the carman and wore a red jacket, used to call me 'Charles' sometimes, in speaking to me; but I think it was mostly when we were very confidential, and when I had made some efforts to entertain them over our work with the results of some of the old readings, which were fast perishing out of my mind." 2

—*CD dismissed:* "Thomas, the old soldier, comforted me, and said he was sure it was for the best. With a relief so strange that it was like oppression, I went home." 2

Warren brothers. "This [commercial] speculation [of **George Lamert**] was a rivalry of 'Warren's Blacking, 30, Strand,'—at that time very famous. One **Jonathan** Warren (the famous one was **Robert**), living at 30, Hungerford-stairs, or market, Strand (for I forget which it was called then), claimed to have been the original inventor or proprietor of the blacking recipe, and to have been deposed and ill-used by his renowned relation. At last he put himself in the way of selling his recipe, and his name, and his 30, Hungerford-stairs, Strand (30, Strand, very large, and the intermediate direction very small), for an annuity; and he set forth by his agents that a little capital would make a great business of it." 2

Walk-ons

George Lamert. "The man of some property was found in George Lamert, the cousin and brother-in-law of **James** [Lamert]. He bought this right and title [in **Jonathan Warren**'s shoe blacking business], and went into the blacking business and the blacking premises.

"—In an evil hour for me, as I often bitterly thought." 2

Shopkeepers. "My usual way home was over Blackfriars-bridge, and down that turning in the Blackfriars-road which has Rowland Hill's chapel on one side, and the likeness of a golden dog licking a golden pot over a shop door on the other. There are a good many little low-browed old shops in that street, of a wretched kind; and some are unchanged now." 2

—*hatters:* "There were two or three hat-manufactories there, then (I think they are there still); and among the things which, encountered anywhere, or under any circumstances, will instantly recall that time, is the smell of hat-making." 2

—*shoe store:* "I looked into one a few weeks ago, where I used to buy boot-laces on Saturday nights, and saw the corner where I once sat down on a stool to have a pair of ready-made half-boots fitted on." 2

—*show-van:* I have been seduced more than once, in that street on a Saturday night, by a show-van at a corner; and have gone in, with a very motley assemblage, to see the Fat-pig, the Wild-indian, and the Little-lady." 2

Waiters. "Once, I remember tucking my own bread (which I had brought from home in the morning) under my arm, wrapped up in a piece of paper like a book, and going into the best dining-room in **Johnson**'s alamode beef-house in Claro court, Drury-lane, and magnificently ordering a small plate of alamode beef to eat with it. What the waiter thought of such a strange little apparition, coming in all alone, I don't know; but I can see him now, staring at me as I ate my dinner, and bringing up the other waiter to look. I gave him a halfpenny, and I wish, now, that he hadn't taken it." 2

Spear-carriers

Agent, in the insolvent-court; CD's new landlord	2
Baker, with whom the indigent Dickenses did not get along	1
Bookseller's wife, down at heel	1
Butcher, with whom the indigent Dickenses did not get along	1
Children, unparented: lodged with an old lady	2
Grandmother Dickens, who had given little CD a silver watch	2
Johnson: gave his name to a beef-house	2
Landlord, of house in Gower-street: very glad to get his key back	2
Pastrycook	2
Servant-girl, raised in a workhouse	2
Son, of a widow; lodged with an old lady	2

Indexes of Characters and Persons in Volume I

All those given entries and/or illustrations in Volume I are shown below. For others, refer to the work for chapter citations, or look at the Indexes in Volume III. Illustration pages are in italics. There are six Indexes: Characters with Surnames (below); Characters without Surnames (page 823) Characters Identified by Sobriquet or Nickname (824); Historical Figures (824); Others' Fictional, and Allegorical, Biblical and Mythological Figures (827); and Generic Figures (827).

Characters with Surnames

Characters without Surnames

Agnes, lady's maid SB/BH 92
Alice, bowyer's only daughter MH/F 422
Alice, Sister of York NN 374
Alick, damp, earthy child SB/R 37
Alphonse, page NN 359
Amelia, daughter SB/TR 102
Amelia, servant DS 754
Anne, housemaid YC/Y, O 296, 307
Anne, maidservant DS 754
Antonio PI 675
Augustus, vivisected dog B/M1 269

Barbara, maidservant OCS 445, *440*
  mother 458
Barney, waiter and thief OT 253
Belinda, scented correspondent MHC 419
Bella, prisoner SB/PV 83
Belle, who loved Ebenezer CC 624
  daughter CC 627
  husband CC 627
Ben, postoffice guard OT 259
Benjamin, lanky apprentice BR 498
Benjamin, lawyer's boy PP 201
'Berry' (Berinthia) DS 755
Bet (or Betsy), prostitute OT 253
Betsey Jane, Wickam relation DS 755
Betsy, dirty little maidservant PP 218
Bill, a coach guard MC 598
Bill, a gravedigger OT 259
Boxer, a dog CH 666
Bull's-Eye, a dog OT 248

Caroline, a debtor's wife CC 626
Charles, who is cool YC/I 302
Charlotte, contradictory YC/C 300
Charlotte, a servant OT 249, *242*
Cicero, American servant MC 589

David, butler NN 361
Davy, gravedigger OCS 455
Dick, a blackbird NN 370
Dick, coach guard NN 361
Dick, a hostler MC 610
Dick, pale and thin OT 255
Diogenes, a dog DS 759, *741, 760*
Edward, contradictory YC/C 300
Emily, a prisoner; depraved SB/PV 83
Emma, astrologer's daughter L 467
Emma, servant PP 219

Fred, a nephew CC 625
  wife CC 629

Galileo Isaac Newton Flamstead L 467
George, a bachelor NN 362
George, elder brother SB/A 39

George, caravan driver OCS 455
George, an insolvent coachman PP 204
George, uncle SB/CD 69
Grip, a raven BR 493, *477*
Hannah, dirty servant-girl NN 363
Harry, debtor SB/WT 123
Harry, dying boy OCS 456
Harry, antic salesman OT 257
Henry, cousin PP 222
Hugh, unfathered rioter BR 482, *483*
  mother, a gipsy; hanged BR 493
Ikey, spunging house denizen SB/WT 123
Isaac, shabby man PP 219

Jack, alderman MHC 421
Jack, prisoner SB/HP 73
Jane, daughter SB/TR 102
Jane, Pecksniffian servant MC 611
Jane, pillar of Bellamy's SB/P 52
Jem, spunging house employee SB/WT 123
Jemima, sister of Polly Toodle DS 764, *769*
Jemmy, "Dismal" PP 206
Jerry, with a dog act OCS 452
Joe, fence CC 626
Joe, hotel waiter OT 260
John, actor PP 221
  wife PP 221
John, indigent father DS 764
John, amorous footman YC/Y 297
John, temporary footman SB/HS 107
John, waiter at St James's Arms P/SG 228

Kate, child DS 764
  her aunt DS 754
Kate, cousin PP 222
Kate, despairing wife SB/WT 123

Louisa, indifferent and cool YC/I 302
Lucy, childhood sweetheart YC/O 308

Margaret, aunt SB/CD 70
Margaret, sickly infant C 652
Martha, housemaid SB/WT 123
Martha, pauper OT 258
Martha, ugly and loved DS 765
Mary, maidservant PP 195, *193*
Mary, servant of all work STH 1 157
Mary, of Seven Dials 29
Nancy, murdered OT 246, *246, 247*
Neddy, turnkey PP 220
Nicholas, pillary of Bellamy's SB/P 53

Peter, Lord; intended spouse SB/WD 116
  ditto P/SG 227
'Phib' (Phoebe), servant NN 365

Richard, suitor C 651, *649, 651*
Rose, beloved SB/BV 108
Rose, cousin P/VC 229
Sally, pauper OT 258
Sally, teased by Uncle Bill SB/LR 36
Sam, cabman PP 211
Sophia, affluent daughter MC 607
Thomas, waiter SB/WD 116
Tom, clerk NN 367
Tom, coachman SB/HC 33
Tom, manservant at the Wardles' PP 215

Tom, omnibus conductor SB/BC 127
Tom, surgeon's boy SB/BV 108
Tom, unfortunate oarsman SB/R 38
Tom, waiter at St James's Arms P/SG 228
Tommy, a waterman PP 221
Whisker, pony OCS 461
Will, waiter at St James's Arms P/SG 228
William, attired for recreation STH 1 158
William, tenant SB/NN 16
William, waiter at Saracen's Head NN 373
Willy, who died OCS 461

Characters Identified by Sobriquet or Nickname

African Swallower NN 359
Artful Dodger OT 243, *247, 249*
Bachelor, The OCS 445
Black Lion, a landlord BR 500
Boz B/M1 270
Brass and Copper family MC 598
The Brave (courier Roche) PI 671, 676
The Captain, inebriated SB/P 52
Carter the Lion King E/TE2 386
Chair/Man PP 222
Edener MC 590
-pl settlers MC 590
Fitz, a professional singer SB/PD 56
Game Chicken DS 761, *762*
Genius of Despair and Suicide NN 374
Gimlet-eyed Tommy B/M2 271
Goblin of Avignon PI/F 671
Good Mrs Brown DS 749
Honest Tom, M. P. SB/P 52
Keeper, of a lion B/L 276
Ladyship, Her; parader SB/FM 58

Lion, literary B/L 276
Lord, My; parader SB/FM 58
Lummy Ned MC 605
Man in the Monument MC 604
Marchioness, the OCS 448, *449*
Native, the DS 766, *736*
Old Dot and Mrs Dot CH 668
Pickle of Portici PI 689
Mrs Richards: *see* Polly Toodle
Scientific gentleman PP 211
Shepherd, the PP 212
Shiny William PP 220
Single Gentleman OCS 442
Slammons (Smike) NN 332
Somebody, Madame; fireworks SB/VG 46
Strange Gentleman, the P/SG 227
Stranger, the BR 485
Sweet William; cards trickster OCS 453
Waistcoat, intruding flirt SB/EE 72
Whiskers, intruding flirt SB/EE 72
Youngest Gentleman (Moddle) MC 583, *584*

Historical Figures

Adams, John Couch E/PS 398
Adelaide, Queen E/CC 409
Agnew, Sir Andrew STH 2 159
Akerman, Newgate Prison governor BR 505
Alderson, Baron E/JP, /C 399, 409
Allen, Captain William E/NE 396
Anderson, actor MC/MC 142 E/MB 390
Andrews, an orphan E/VD 403
Apperley, Charles E/S 381
Attah of Iddah E/NE 396
[Augustus] Caesar LL 762
Austin, Henry EC/DH 405, /SC 407

Ballantynes E/SP 384
  James, father E/SP 384
  James, son E/SP 384
  John, son E/SP 384

Banvard, panoramicist E/AP 398
Barnum, Phineas T. MP/TH 637
Barristers, young MC/MN 153
Beggs, pamphleteer E/DA 407
Bentham, Jeremy E/CP 404
Bishop, John SB/VN 64
Blackmore, daredevil showman SB/VG 45
Bladud, Prince PP 224
Blues (Tory sympathizers) MC/EE 138
Boys, hissing Sir Henry Smyth 138
Braham, John MC/W 150
Bridgman, Laura AN 528
Brown, King and Gibson B/P 275
Buckstone, John MC/BF, /DS 136, 147
Buller, civil engineer EC/SC 407
Burritt, Elihu E/DA 408

Others' Fictional, and
Allegorical, Biblical and Mythological Figures

Generic Figures

Subject-matter Index to the
Non-fiction Pieces in Volume I

See also Generic Figures Index in Volume III. Works covered in this Index: *Sketches by Boz* (except *Tales* and other fiction lacking reportorial elements warranting reflection here), contributions to *The Morning Chronicle* and to *The Examiner,* and *Miscellaneous Pieces.*

About the Editor

Until 1988, GEORGE NEWLIN had spent his professional career combining activities in law and finance with volunteer service in the arts and serious avocational musical performance. At that time, he withdrew from most of his activities in venture capital and assets management and began developing his concept for a new kind of literary anthology, beginning with the works of Charles Dickens. He continues his *pro bono* services in the music field.

ISBN 0-313-29581-6

EAN

9 780313 295812

90000>